CATECHISM OF THE CATHOLIC CHURCH

Full Text and
Theological Commentary

Direction and Coordination
of the Theological Commentary by
RINO FISICHELLA

On the cover:

Official emblem of the *Catechism of the Catholic Church*, featuring a detail of a Christian sepulchral stone of the catacombs of Domitilla (Rome), which dates back to end of the third century.

Editorial coordination:

Enrico Maria Beraudo
Giuseppe Occhipinti
Riccardo Piacci

27 26 25 24 23 2 3 4 5 6 7 8 9

ISBN: 978-1-68192-274-4 (Inventory No. T1961)
eISBN: 978-1-68192-275-1
LCCN: 2018958067

Cover design: Tyler Ottinger
Interior design: Composure Graphics

PRINTED IN THE UNITED STATES OF AMERICA

TABLE OF CONTENTS

THEOLOGICAL AND PASTORAL COMMENTARY

INTRODUCTORY QUESTIONS

PART ONE: THE PROFESSION OF FAITH

SECTION ONE: "I BELIEVE"—"WE BELIEVE"

SECTION TWO: THE PROFESSION OF THE CHRISTIAN FAITH

ABBREVIATIONS

The following are abbreviations cited in the text:

AA	*Apostolicam actuositatem*
AAS	*Acta Apostolicae Sedis*
AF	J. B. Lightfoot, ed., *The Apostolic Fathers* (New York: Macmillan, 1889–1890)
AG	*Ad gentes*
Ben	*de Benedictionibus*
CA	*Centesimus annus*
Catech. R.	*Catechismus Romanus*
CCEO	Corpus Canonum Ecclesiarum Orientalium
CCL	Corpus Christianorum, Series Latina (Turnhout, 1953–)
CD	*Christus Dominus*
CDF	Congregation for the Doctrine of the Faith
CELAM	Consejo Episcopal Latinoamericano
CIC	Codex Iuris Canonici
CL	*Christifideles laici*
COD	*Conciliorum oecumenicorum decreta*
CPG	*Solemn Profession of Faith:* Credo of the People of God
CSEL	Corpus Scriptorum Ecclesiasticorum Latinorum (Vienna, 1866–)
CT	*Catechesi tradendae*
DeV	*Dominum et Vivificantem*
DH	*Dignitatis humanae*
DM	*Dives in misericordia*
DS	*Denzinger-Schönmetzer, Enchiridion Symbolorum, definitionum et declarationum de rebus fidei et morum* (1965)
DV	*Dei Verbum*
EN	*Evangelii nuntiandi*
EP	Eucharistic Prayer
FC	*Familiaris consortio*
GCD	*General Catechetical Directory*
GE	*Gravissimum educationis*
GILH	General Introduction to LH
GIRM	General Instruction to RomM
GS	*Gaudium et spes*
HV	*Humanae vitae*
ICEL	International Commission on English in the Liturgy
IM	*Inter mirifica*
LE	*Laborem exercens*
LG	*Lumen gentium*
LH	*Liturgy of the Hours*
LXX	Septuagint
MC	*Marialis cultus*
MD	*Mulieris dignitatem*
MF	*Mysterium fidei*

MM	*Mater et magistra*
NA	*Nostra aetate*
NCCB	*National Conference of Catholic Bishops (U.S.A.)*
ND	*Neuner-Dupuis, The Christian Faith in the Doctrinal Documents of the Catholic Church*
OBA	*Ordo baptismi adultorum*
OC	*Ordo confirmationis*
OCF	*Order of Christian Funerals*
OCM	*Ordo celebrandi Matrimonium*
OCV	*Ordo consecrationis virginum*
OE	*Orientalium ecclesiarum*
OP	*Ordo paenitentiae*
OR	*Office of Readings*
OT	*Optatam totius*
PC	*Perfectae caritatis*
PG	*J. P. Migne, ed., Patrologia Graeca (Paris, 1857–1866)*
PL	*J. P. Migne, ed., Patrologia Latina (Paris: 1841–1855)*
PLS	*J. P. Migne, ed., Patrologia Latina Supplement*
PO	*Presbyterorum ordinis*
PP	*Populorum progressio*
PT	*Pacem in terris*
RBC	*Rite of Baptism of Children*
RCIA	*Rite of christian initiation of adults*
RH	*Redemptor hominis*
RomM	*Roman Missal*
RMat	*Redemptoris Mater*
RMiss	*Redemptoris Missio*
RP	*Reconciliatio et paenitentia*
SC	*Sacrosanctum concilium*
SCG	Summa Contra Gentiles
SCh	Sources Chrétiennes (Paris: 1942–)
SRS	*Sollicitudo rei socialis*
STh	Summa Theologiae
UR	*Unitatis redintegratio*

The following abbreviations are used for the books of the Bible cited in the text:

Gen	Genesis
Ex	Exodus
Lev	Leviticus
Num	Numbers
Deut	Deuteronomy
Josh	Joshua
Judg	Judges
1 Sam	1 Samuel
2 Sam	2 Samuel
1 Kings	1 Kings
2 Kings	2 Kings
1 Chr	1 Chronicles
2 Chr	2 Chronicles
Ezra	Ezra
Neh	Nehemiah
Tob	Tobit
Jdt	Judith
Esth	Esther
2 Macc	2 Maccabees
Job	Job
Ps	Psalms
Prov	Proverbs

Eccl	Ecclesiastes	*Rom*	Romans
Song	Song of Songs	*1 Cor*	1 Corinthians
Wis	Wisdom	*2 Cor*	2 Corinthians
Sir	Sirach	*Gal*	Galatians
Isa	Isaiah	*Eph*	Ephesians
Jer	Jeremiah	*Phil*	Philippians
Lam	Lamentations	*Col*	Colossians
Bar	Baruch	*1 Thess*	1 Thessalonians
Ezek	Ezekiel	*2 Thess*	2 Thessalonians
Dan	Daniel	*1 Tim*	1 Timothy
Hos	Hosea	*2 Tim*	2 Timothy
Joel	Joel	*Titus*	Titus
Am	Amos	*Philem*	Philemon
Jon	Jonah	*Heb*	Hebrews
Mic	Micah	*Jas*	James
Zeph	Zephaniah	*1 Pet*	1 Peter
Zech	Zechariah	*2 Pet*	2 Peter
Mal	Malachi	*1 Jn*	1 John
Mt	Matthew	*2 Jn*	2 John
Mk	Mark	*3 Jn*	3 John
Lk	Luke	*Jude*	Jude
Jn	John	*Rev*	Revelation
Acts	Acts of the Apostles		

Apostolic Letter
LAETAMUR MAGNOPERE
In which the Latin typical edition of the CATECHISM OF THE CATHOLIC CHURCH is approved and promulgated

JOHN PAUL, BISHOP
Servant of the servants of God
for everlasting memory

To my Venerable Brother Cardinals, Patriarchs, Archbishops, Bishops, Priests, Deacons and to other members of the People of God.

It is a cause for great joy that the latin typical edition of the *Catechism of the Catholic Church* is being published. It is approved and promulgated by me in this Apostolic Letter and thus becomes the definitive text of the aforementioned Catechism. This is occurring about five years after the Apostolic Constitution *Fidei Depositum* of October 11, 1992, which, on the 30th anniversary of the opening of the Second Vatican Council, accompanied the publication of the first, French-language text of the *Catechism*.

We have all been able to note with pleasure the broad positive reception and wide dissemination of the *Catechism* in these years, especially in the particular Churches, which have had it translated into their respective languages, thus making it as accessible as possible to the various linguistic communities of the world. This fact confirms how fitting was the request submitted to me in 1985 by the Extraordinary Assembly of the Synod of Bishops that a catechism or compendium of all Catholic doctrine regarding faith and morals be composed.

Drawn up by the special Commission of Cardinals and Bishops established in 1986, the *Catechism* was approved and promulgated by me in the aforementioned Apostolic Constitution, which today retains all its validity and timeliness, and finds its definitive achievement in this Latin typical edition.

This edition was prepared by an Interdicasterial Commission which I appointed for this purpose in 1993. Presided over by Cardinal Joseph Ratzinger, this Commission worked diligently to fulfill the mandate it received. It devoted particular attention to a study of the many suggested changes to the contents of the text, which in these years had come from around the world and from various parts of the ecclesial community.

In this regard one can certainly understand that such a remarkable number of suggested improvements shows the extraordinary interest that the *Catechism* has raised throughout the world, even among non-Christians, and confirms its purpose of being presented as a full, complete exposition of Catholic doctrine, enabling everyone to know what the Church professes, celebrates, lives, and prays in her daily life. At the same time it draws attention to the eager desire of all to make their contribution so that the Christian faith, whose essential and necessary elements are summarized in the *Catechism*, can be presented to the people of our day in the most suitable way possible. Furthermore, this collaboration of the various members of the Church will once again achieve what I wrote in the Apostolic Constitution *Fidei Depositum*: "The harmony of so many voices truly expresses what could be called the 'symphony' of the faith" (no. 2).

For these reasons too, the Commission seriously considered the suggestions offered, carefully examined them at various levels and submitted its conclusions for my approval. These conclusions, insofar as they allow for a better expression of the *Catechism*'s contents regarding the deposit of the Catholic faith, or enable certain truths of this faith to be formulated in a way more suited to the requirements of contemporary catechetical instruction, have been approved by me and thus have been incorporated into this Latin typical edition. Therefore it faithfully repeats the doctrinal content which I officially presented to the Church and to the world in December 1992.

With today's promulgation of the Latin typical edition, therefore, the task of composing the *Catechism*, begun in 1986, is brought to a close and the desire of the aforementioned Extraordinary Synod of Bishops is happily fulfilled. The Church now has at her disposal this new, authoritative exposition of the one and perennial apostolic faith, and it will serve as a "valid and legitimate instrument for ecclesial communion" and as a "sure norm for teaching the faith," as well as a "sure and authentic reference text" for preparing local catechisms (cf. Apostolic Constitution *Fidei Depositum*, no. 4).

Catechesis will find in this genuine, systematic presentation of the faith and of Catholic doctrine a totally reliable way to present, with renewed fervor, each and every part of the Christian message to the people of our time. This text will provide every catechist with sound help for communicating the one, perennial deposit of faith within the local Church, while seeking, with the help of the Holy Spirit, to link the wondrous unity of the Christian mystery with the varied needs and conditions of those to whom this message is addressed. All catechetical activity will be able to experience a new, widespread impetus among the People of God, if it can properly use and appreciate this post-conciliar *Catechism*.

All this seems even more important today with the approach of the third millennium. For an extraordinary commitment to evangelization is urgently needed so that everyone can know and receive the Gospel message and thus grow "to the measure of the stature of the fullness of Christ" (*Eph* 4:13).

I therefore strongly urge my Venerable Brothers in the Episcopate, for whom the *Catechism* is primarily intended, to take the excellent opportunity afforded by the promulgation of this Latin edition to intensify their efforts to disseminate the text more widely and to ensure that it is well received as an outstanding gift for the communities entrusted to them, which will thus be able to rediscover the inexhaustible riches of the faith.

Through the harmonious and complementary efforts of all the ranks of the People of God, may this *Catechism* be known and shared by everyone, so that the unity in faith whose supreme model and origin is found in the Unity of the Trinity may be strengthened and extended to the ends of the earth.

To Mary, Mother of Christ, whose Assumption body and soul into heaven we celebrate today, I entrust these wishes so that they may be brought to fulfillment for the spiritual good of all humanity.

From Castel Gandolfo, August 15, 1997, the nineteenth year of the Pontificate.

Apostolic Letter
FIDEI DEPOSITUM
on the publication of the
CATECHISM OF THE CATHOLIC CHURCH
prepared following the second
vatican ecumenical council

JOHN PAUL, BISHOP
Servant of the servants of God
for everlasting memory

To my Venerable Brother Cardinals, Patriarchs, Archbishops, Bishops, Priests, Deacons and to other members of the People of God.

Guarding the deposit of faith is the mission which the lordentrusted to his church, and which she fulfills in every age. The Second Vatican Ecumenical Council, which was opened 30 years ago by my predecessor Pope John XXIII, of happy memory, had as its intention and purpose to highlight the Church's apostolic and pastoral mission and by making the truth of the Gospel shine forth to lead all people to seek and receive Christ's love which surpasses all knowledge (cf. *Eph* 3:19).

The principal task entrusted to the Council by Pope John XXIII was to guard and present better the precious deposit of Christian doctrine in order to make it more accessible to the Christian faithful and to all people of good will. For this reason the Council was not first of all to condemn the errors of the time, but above all to strive calmly to show the strength and beauty of the doctrine of the faith. "Illumined by the light of this Council," the Pope said, "the Church…will become greater in spiritual riches and gaining the strength of new energies therefrom, she will look to the future without fear.… Our duty is to dedicate ourselves with an earnest will and without fear to that work which our era demands of us, thus pursuing the path which the Church has followed for 20 centuries."[1]

With the help of God, the Council Fathers in four years of work were able to produce a considerable number of doctrinal statements and pastoral norms which were presented to the whole Church. There the Pastors and Christian

[1] John XXIII, Discourse at the Opening of the Second Vatican Ecumenical Council, October 11, 1962: AAS 54 (1962) pp. 788–91.

faithful find directives for that "renewal of thought, action, practices, and moral virtue, of joy and hope, which was the very purpose of the Council."[2]

After its conclusion, the Council did not cease to inspire the Church's life. In 1985 I was able to assert, "For me, then—who had the special grace of participating in it and actively collaborating in its development—Vatican II has always been, and especially during these years of my Pontificate, the constant reference point of my every pastoral action, in the conscious commitment to implement its directives concretely and faithfully at the level of each Church and the whole Church."[3]

In this spirit, on January 25, 1985, I convoked an extraordinary assembly of the Synod of Bishops for the 20th anniversary of the close of the Council. The purpose of this assembly was to celebrate the graces and spiritual fruits of Vatican II, to study its teaching in greater depth in order that all the Christian faithful might better adhere to it and to promote knowledge and application of it.

On that occasion the Synod Fathers stated: "Very many have expressed the desire that a catechism or compendium of all catholic doctrine regarding both faith and morals be composed, that it might be, as it were, a point of reference for the catechisms or compendiums that are prepared in various regions. The presentation of doctrine must be biblical and liturgical. It must be sound doctrine suited to the present life of Christians."[4] After the Synod ended, I made this desire my own, considering it as "fully responding to a real need of the universal Church and of the particular Churches."[5]

For this reason we thank the Lord wholeheartedly on this day when we can offer the entire Church this "reference text" entitled the *Catechism of the Catholic Church* for a catechesis renewed at the living sources of the faith!

Following the renewal of the Liturgy and the new codification of the canon law of the Latin Church and that of the Oriental Catholic Churches, this catechism will make a very important contribution to that work of renewing the whole life of the Church, as desired and begun by the Second Vatican Council.

1. The Process and Spirit of Drafting the Text

The *Catechism of the Catholic Church* is the result of very extensive collaboration; it was prepared over six years of intense work done in a spirit of complete openness and fervent zeal.

In 1986, I entrusted a commission of twelve Cardinals and Bishops, chaired by Cardinal Joseph Ratzinger, with the task of preparing a draft of the

[2] Paul VI, Discourse at the Closing of the Second Vatican Ecumenical Council, December 7, 1965: AAS 58 (1966) pp. 7–8. — [3] John Paul II, Discourse of January 25, 1985: *L'Osservatore Romano*, January 27, 1985. — [4] *Final Report* of the Extraordinary Synod of Bishops, December 7, 1985, *Enchiridion Vaticanum*, vol. 9, II, B, a, n. 4: p. 1758, n. 1797. — [5] John Paul II, Discourse at the Closing of the Extraordinary Synod of Bishops, December 7, 1985, n. 6: AAS 78 (1986) p. 435.

catechism requested by the Synod Fathers. An editorial committee of seven diocesan Bishops, experts in theology and catechesis, assisted the commission in its work.

The commission, charged with giving directives and with overseeing the course of the work, attentively followed all the stages in editing the nine subsequent drafts. The editorial committee, for its part, assumed responsibility for writing the text, making the emendations requested by the commission and examining the observations of numerous theologians, exegetes and catechists, and, above all, of the Bishops of the whole world, in order to produce a better text. In the committee various opinions were compared with great profit, and thus a richer text has resulted whose unity and coherence are assured.

The project was the object of extensive consultation among all Catholic Bishops, their Episcopal Conferences or Synods, and of theological and catechetical institutes. As a whole, it received a broadly favorable acceptance on the part of the Episcopate. It can be said that this *Catechism* is the result of the collaboration of the whole Episcopate of the Catholic Church, who generously accepted my invitation to share responsibility for an enterprise which directly concerns the life of the Church. This response elicits in me a deep feeling of joy, because the harmony of so many voices truly expresses what could be called the "symphony" of the faith. The achievement of this *Catechism* thus reflects the collegial nature of the Episcopate; it testifies to the Church's catholicity.

2. Arrangement of the Material

A catechism should faithfully and systematically present the teaching of Sacred Scripture, the living Tradition in the Church and the authentic Magisterium, as well as the spiritual heritage of the Fathers, Doctors, and saints of the Church, to allow for a better knowledge of the Christian mystery and for enlivening the faith of the People of God. It should take into account the doctrinal statements which down the centuries the Holy Spirit has intimated to his Church. It should also help to illumine with the light of faith the new situations and problems which had not yet emerged in the past.

This catechism will thus contain both the new and the old (cf. *Mt* 13:52), because the faith is always the same yet the source of ever new light.

To respond to this twofold demand, the *Catechism of the Catholic Church* on the one hand repeats the "old," traditional order already followed by the Catechism of St. Pius V, arranging the material in four parts: the *Creed,* the *Sacred Liturgy*, with pride of place given to the sacraments, the *Christian way of life*, explained beginning with the Ten Commandments, and finally, *Christian prayer*. At the same time, however, the contents are often presented in a "new" way in order to respond to the questions of our age.

The four parts are related one to another: the Christian mystery is the object of faith (first part); it is celebrated and communicated in liturgical actions (second part); it is present to enlighten and sustain the children of God in their actions (third part); it is the basis for our prayer, the privileged expression of which is the *Our Father*, and it represents the object of our supplication, our praise and our intercession (fourth part).

The Liturgy itself is prayer; the confession of faith finds its proper place in the celebration of worship. Grace, the fruit of the sacraments, is the irreplaceable condition for Christian living, just as participation in the Church's Liturgy requires faith. If faith is not expressed in works, it is dead (cf. *Jas* 2:14–16) and cannot bear fruit unto eternal life.

In reading the *Catechism of the Catholic Church* we can perceive the wonderful unity of the mystery of God, his saving will, as well as the central place of Jesus Christ, the only-begotten Son of God, sent by the Father, made man in the womb of the Blessed Virgin Mary by the power of the Holy Spirit, to be our Savior. Having died and risen, Christ is always present in his Church, especially in the sacraments; he is the source of our faith, the model of Christian conduct, and the Teacher of our prayer.

3. The Doctrinal Value of the Text

The *Catechism of the Catholic Church*, which I approved June 25th last and the publication of which I today order by virtue of my Apostolic Authority, is a statement of the Church's faith and of catholic doctrine, attested to or illumined by Sacred Scripture, the Apostolic Tradition, and the Church's Magisterium. I declare it to be a sure norm for teaching the faith and thus a valid and legitimate instrument for ecclesial communion. May it serve the renewal to which the Holy Spirit ceaselessly calls the Church of God, the Body of Christ, on her pilgrimage to the undiminished light of the Kingdom!

The approval and publication of the *Catechism of the Catholic Church* represent a service which the Successor of Peter wishes to offer to the Holy Catholic Church, to all the particular Churches in peace and communion with the Apostolic See: the service, that is, of supporting and confirming the faith of all the Lord Jesus' disciples (cf. *Lk* 22:32), as well as of strengthening the bonds of unity in the same apostolic faith.

Therefore, I ask all the Church's Pastors and the Christian faithful to receive this catechism in a spirit of communion and to use it assiduously in fulfilling their mission of proclaiming the faith and calling people to the Gospel life. This catechism is given to them that it may be a sure and authentic reference text for teaching catholic doctrine and particularly for preparing local catechisms. It is also offered to all the faithful who wish to deepen their knowledge of the unfathomable riches of salvation (cf. *Eph* 3:8). It is meant to support ecumenical efforts that are moved by the holy desire for the unity of all Christians, showing carefully the content and wondrous harmony of the catholic faith. The *Catechism of the Catholic Church*, lastly, is offered to every individual who asks us to give an account of the hope that is in us (cf. *1 Pet* 3:15) and who wants to know what the Catholic Church believes.

This catechism is not intended to replace the local catechisms duly approved by the ecclesiastical authorities, the diocesan Bishops and the Episcopal Conferences, especially if they have been approved by the Apostolic See. It is meant to encourage and assist in the writing of new local catechisms, which take into account various situations and cultures, while carefully preserving the unity of faith and fidelity to catholic doctrine.

At the conclusion of this document presenting the *Catechism of the Catholic Church*, I beseech the Blessed Virgin Mary, Mother of the Incarnate Word and Mother of the Church, to support with her powerful intercession the catechetical work of the entire Church on every level, at this time when she is called to a new effort of evangelization. May the light of the true faith free humanity from the ignorance and slavery of sin in order to lead it to the only freedom worthy of the name (cf. *Jn* 8:32): that of life in Jesus Christ under the guidance of the Holy Spirit, here below and in the Kingdom of heaven, in the fullness of the blessed vision of God face to face (cf. *1 Cor* 13:12; *2 Cor* 5:6–8)!

Given October 11, 1992, the thirtieth anniversary of the opening of the Second Vatican Ecumenical Council, in the fourteenth year of my Pontificate.

PROLOGUE

"FATHER,...this is eternal life, that they may know you, the only true God, and Jesus Christ whom you have sent."[1] "God our Savior desires all men to be saved and to come to the knowledge of the truth."[2] "There is no other name under heaven given among men by which we must be saved"[3] than the name of JESUS.

I. The Life of Man—To Know and Love God

1 God, infinitely perfect and blessed in himself, in a plan of sheer goodness freely created man to make him share in his own blessed life. For this reason, at every time and in every place, God draws close to man. He calls man to seek him, to know him, to love him with all his strength. He calls together all men, scattered and divided by sin, into the unity of his family, the Church. To accomplish this, when the fullness of time had come, God sent his Son as Redeemer and Savior. In his Son and through him, he invites men to become, in the Holy Spirit, his adopted children and thus heirs of his blessed life.

2 So that this call should resound throughout the world, Christ sent forth the apostles he had chosen, commissioning them to proclaim the gospel: "Go therefore and make disciples of all nations, baptizing them in the name of the Father and of the Son and of the Holy Spirit, teaching them to observe all that I have commanded you; and lo, I am with you always, to the close of the age."[4] Strengthened by this mission, the apostles "went forth and preached everywhere, while the Lord worked with them and confirmed the message by the signs that attended it."[5]

3 Those who with God's help have welcomed Christ's call and freely responded to it are urged on by love of Christ to proclaim the Good News everywhere in the world. This treasure, received from the apostles, has been faithfully guarded by their successors. All Christ's faithful are called to hand it on from generation to generation, by professing the faith, by living it in fraternal sharing, and by celebrating it in liturgy and prayer.[6]

II. Handing on the Faith: Catechesis

4 Quite early on, the name *catechesis* was given to the totality of the Church's efforts to make disciples, to help men believe that Jesus is the Son of God so that believing they might have life in his name, and to educate and instruct them in this life, thus building up the body of Christ.[7]

5 "Catechesis is an *education in the faith* of children, young people, and adults which includes especially the teaching of Christian doctrine imparted, generally speaking, in an organic and systematic way, with a view to initiating the hearers into the fullness of Christian life."[8]

[1] Jn 17:3. — [2] 1 Tim 2:3–4. — [3] Acts 4:12. — [4] Mt 28:18–20. — [5] Mk 16:20. — [6] Cf. Acts 2:42. — [7] Cf. John Paul II, apostolic exhortation, *Catechesi tradendae* 1; 2. — [8] *CT* 18.

6 While not being formally identified with them, catechesis is built on a certain number of elements of the Church's pastoral mission which have a catechetical aspect, that prepare for catechesis, or spring from it. They are: the initial proclamation of the Gospel or missionary preaching to arouse faith; examination of the reasons for belief; experience of Christian living; celebration of the sacraments; integration into the ecclesial community; and apostolic and missionary witness.[9]

7 "Catechesis is intimately bound up with the whole of the Church's life. Not only her geographical extension and numerical increase, but even more her inner growth and correspondence with God's plan depend essentially on catechesis."[10]

8 Periods of renewal in the Church are also intense moments of catechesis. In the great era of the Fathers of the Church, saintly bishops devoted an important part of their ministry to catechesis. St. Cyril of Jerusalem and St. John Chrysostom, St. Ambrose and St. Augustine, and many other Fathers wrote catechetical works that remain models for us.[11]

9 "The ministry of catechesis draws ever fresh energy from the councils. The Council of Trent is a noteworthy example of this. It gave catechesis priority in its constitutions and decrees. It lies at the origin of the *Roman Catechism*, which is also known by the name of that council and which is a work of the first rank as a summary of Christian teaching...."[12] The Council of Trent initiated a remarkable organization of the Church's catechesis. Thanks to the work of holy bishops and theologians such as St. Peter Canisius, St. Charles Borromeo, St. Turibius of Mongrovejo, or St. Robert Bellarmine, it occasioned the publication of numerous catechisms.

10 It is therefore no surprise that catechesis in the Church has again attracted attention in the wake of the Second Vatican Council, which Pope Paul VI considered the great catechism of modern times. The General Catechetical Directory (1971), the sessions of the Synod of Bishops devoted to evangelization (1974) and catechesis (1977), the apostolic exhortations *Evangelii nuntiandi* (1975) and *Catechesi tradendae* (1979) attest to this. The Extraordinary Synod of Bishops in 1985 asked "that a catechism or compendium of all Catholic doctrine regarding both faith and morals be composed."[13] The Holy Father, Pope John Paul II, made the Synod's wish his own, acknowledging that "this desire wholly corresponds to a real need of the universal Church and of the particular Churches."[14] He set in motion everything needed to carry out the Synod Fathers' wish.

III. The Aim and Intended Readership of this Catechism

11 This catechism aims at presenting an organic synthesis of the essential and fundamental contents of Catholic doctrine, as regards both faith and morals, in the light of the Second Vatican Council and

[9] *CT* 18. — [10] 10 *CT* 13. — [11] Cf. *CT* 12. — [12] *CT* 13. — [13] Extraordinary Synod of Bishops 1985, *Final Report*, II B a, 4. — [14] John Paul II, Discourse at the Closing of the Extraordinary Synod of Bishops, December 7, 1985: AAS 78 (1986).

the whole of the Church's Tradition. Its principal sources are the Sacred Scriptures, the Fathers of the Church, the liturgy, and the Church's Magisterium. It is intended to serve "as a point of reference for the catechisms or compendia that are composed in the various countries."[15]

12 This work is intended primarily for those responsible for catechesis: first of all the bishops, as teachers of the faith and pastors of the Church. It is offered to them as an instrument in fulfilling their responsibility of teaching the People of God. Through the bishops, it is addressed to redactors of catechisms, to priests, and to catechists. It will also be useful reading for all other Christian faithful.

IV. Structure of This Catechism

13 The plan of this catechism is inspired by the great tradition of catechisms which build catechesis on four pillars: the baptismal profession of faith (the *Creed*), the sacraments of faith, the life of faith (the *Commandments*), and the prayer of the believer (the *Lord's Prayer*).

Part One: The profession of faith

14 Those who belong to Christ through faith and Baptism must confess their baptismal faith before men.[16] First therefore the Catechism expounds revelation, by which God addresses and gives himself to man, and the faith by which man responds to God (*Section One*). The profession of faith summarizes the gifts that God gives man: as the Author of all that is good; as Redeemer; and as Sanctifier. It develops these in the three chapters on our baptismal faith in the one God: the almighty *Father*, the Creator; his *Son* Jesus Christ, our Lord and Savior; and the *Holy Spirit*, the Sanctifier, in the Holy Church (*Section Two*).

Part Two: The sacraments of faith

15 The second part of the Catechism explains how God's salvation, accomplished once for all through Christ Jesus and the Holy Spirit, is made present in the sacred actions of the Church's liturgy (Section One), especially in the seven sacraments (Section Two).

Part Three: The life of faith

16 The third part of the Catechism deals with the final end of man created in the image of God: beatitude, and the ways of reaching it—through right conduct freely chosen, with the help of God's law and grace (*Section One*), and through conduct that fulfills the twofold commandment of charity, specified in God's Ten Commandments (*Section Two*).

Part Four: Prayer in the life of faith

17 The last part of the Catechism deals with the meaning and importance of prayer in the life of believers (*Section One*). It concludes with a brief commentary on the seven petitions of the Lord's Prayer (*Section Two*), for indeed we find in these the sum of all the good things which we must hope for and which our heavenly Father wants to grant us.

[15] Extraordinary Synod of Bishops 1985, *Final Report* II B a, 4. — [16] Cf. *Mt* 10:32; *Rom* 10:9.

V. Practical Directions for Using This Catechism

18 This catechism is conceived as *an organic presentation* of the Catholic faith in its entirety. It should be seen therefore as a unified whole. Numerous cross-references in the margin of the text (italicized numbers referring to other paragraphs that deal with the same theme), as well as the analytical index at the end of the volume, allow the reader to view each theme in its relationship with the entirety of the faith.

19 The texts of Sacred Scripture are often not quoted word for word but are merely indicated by a reference (**cf.**). For a deeper understanding of such passages, the reader should refer to the Scriptural texts themselves. Such Biblical references are a valuable working-tool in catechesis.

20 The use of **small print** in certain passages indicates observations of an historical or apologetic nature, or supplementary doctrinal explanations.

21 The **quotations**, also in small print, from patristic, liturgical, magisterial or hagiographical sources, are intended to enrich the doctrinal presentations. These texts have often been chosen with a view to direct catechetical use.

22 At the end of each thematic unit, a series of brief texts sum up the essentials of that unit's teaching in condensed formulae. These **IN BRIEF** summaries may suggest to local catechists brief summary formulae that could be memorized.

VI. Necessary Adaptations

23 The Catechism emphasizes the exposition of doctrine. It seeks to help deepen understanding of faith. In this way it is oriented toward the maturing of that faith, its putting down roots in personal life and its shining forth in personal conduct.[17]

24 By design, this Catechism does not set out to provide the adaptation of doctrinal presentations and catechetical methods required by the differences of culture, age, spiritual maturity, and social and ecclesial condition among all those to whom it is addressed. Such indispensable adaptations are the responsibility of particular catechisms and, even more, of those who instruct the faithful:

> Whoever teaches must become "all things to all men" (*1 Cor* 9:22), to win everyone to Christ. ... Above all, teachers must not imagine that a single kind of soul has been entrusted to them, and that consequently it is lawful to teach and form equally all the faithful in true piety with one and the same method! Let them realize that some are in Christ as newborn babes, others as adolescents, and still others as adults in full command of their powers. ... Those who are called to the ministry of preaching must suit their words to the maturity and understanding of their hearers, as they hand on the teaching of the mysteries of faith and the rules of moral conduct.[18]

[17] Cf. *CT* 20–22, 25. — [18] *Roman Catechism*, Preface, 11; cf. *1 Cor* 9:22; *1 Pet* 2:2.

Above All—Charity

25 To conclude this Prologue, it is fitting to recall this pastoral principle stated by the *Roman Catechism*:

> The whole concern of doctrine and its teaching must be directed to the love that never ends. Whether something is proposed for belief, for hope or for action, the love of our Lord must always be made accessible, so that anyone can see that all the works of perfect Christian virtue spring from love and have no other objective than to arrive at love.[19]

[19] *Roman Catechism*, Preface, 10; cf. *1 Cor* 13:8.

PART ONE

THE PROFESSION OF FAITH

Section One

“I BELIEVE”—“WE BELIEVE”

26 We begin our profession of faith by saying: "I believe" or "We believe." Before expounding the Church's faith, as confessed in the Creed, celebrated in the liturgy, and lived in observance of God's commandments and in prayer, we must first ask what "to believe" means. Faith is man's response to God, who reveals himself and gives himself to man, at the same time bringing man a superabundant light as he searches for the ultimate meaning of his life. Thus we shall consider first that search (*chapter one*), then the divine Revelation by which God comes to meet man (*chapter two*), and finally the response of faith (*chapter three*).

Chapter One:
MAN'S CAPACITY FOR GOD

I. The Desire for God

27 The desire for God is written
in the human heart, because man is
created by God and for God; and
355, 170 God never ceases to draw man to
himself. Only in God will he find
1718 the truth and happiness he never
stops searching for:

> The dignity of man rests above all on the fact that he is called to communion with God. This invitation to converse with God is addressed to man as soon as he comes into being. For if man exists, it is because God has created him through love, and through love continues to hold him in existence. He cannot live fully according to truth unless he freely acknowledges that love and entrusts himself to his creator.[1]

28 In many ways, throughout his
43, 2566 tory down to the present day, men
have given expression to their quest
95–2109 for God in their religious beliefs and
behavior: in their prayers, sacrifices, rituals, meditations, and so forth. These forms of religious expression, despite the ambiguities they often bring with them, are so universal that one may well call man a *religious being*:

> From one ancestor [God] made all nations to inhabit the whole earth, and he allotted the times of their existence and the boundaries of the places where they would live, so that they would search for God and perhaps grope for him and find him—though indeed he is not far from each one of us. For "in him we live and move and have our being."[2]

29 But this "intimate and vital
bond of man to God" (GS 19,1) can
be forgotten, overlooked, or even 2123–2128
explicitly rejected by man.[3] Such
attitudes can have different causes:
revolt against evil in the world; religious ignorance or indifference;
the cares and riches of this world;
the scandal of bad example on the
part of believers; currents of thought 398
hostile to religion; finally, that attitude of sinful man which makes him hide from God out of fear and flee his call.[4]

30 "Let the hearts of those who
seek the Lord rejoice."[5] Although
man can forget God or reject him, 2567, 845
He never ceases to call every man
to seek him, so as to find life and
happiness. But this search for God 368
demands of man every effort of intellect, a sound will, "an upright heart," as well as the witness of others who teach him to seek God.

> You are great, O Lord, and greatly to be praised: great is your power and your wisdom is without measure. And man, so small a part of your creation, wants to praise you: this man, though clothed with mortality and bearing the evidence of sin and the proof that you withstand the proud. Despite everything, man, though but a small a part of your creation, wants to praise you. You

[1] Vatican Council II, *GS* 19 § 1. — [2] *Acts* 17:26–28. — [3] *GS* 19 § 1. — [4] Cf. *GS* 19–21; *Mt* 13:22; *Gen* 3:8–10; *Jon* 1:3. — [5] *Ps* 105:3.

> yourself encourage him to delight in your praise, for you have made us for yourself, and our heart is restless until it rests in you.[6]

II. Ways of Coming to Know God

31 Created in God's image and called to know and love him, the person who seeks God discovers certain ways of coming to know him. These are also called proofs for the existence of God, not in the sense of proofs in the natural sciences, but rather in the sense of "converging and convincing arguments," which allow us to attain certainty about the truth.
These "ways" of approaching God from creation have a twofold point of departure: the physical world and the human person.

32 The *world*: starting from movement, becoming, contingency, and the world's order and beauty, one
54, 337 can come to a knowledge of God as the origin and the end of the universe.

> As St. Paul says of the Gentiles: For what can be known about God is plain to them, because God has shown it to them. Ever since the creation of the world his invisible nature, namely, his eternal power and deity, has been clearly perceived in the things that have been made.[7]
> And St. Augustine issues this challenge: Question the beauty of the earth, question the beauty of the sea, question the beauty of the air distending and diffusing itself, question the beauty of the sky... question all these realities. All respond: "See, we are beautiful." Their beauty is a profession [*confessio*]. These beauties are subject to change. Who made them if not the Beautiful One [*Pulcher*] who is not subject to change?[8]

33 The *human person*: With his openness to truth and beauty, his sense of moral goodness, his freedom and the voice of his conscience, 2500, 173
with his longings for the infinite and 1776
for happiness, man questions himself about God's existence. In all this 1703
he discerns signs of his spiritual soul.
The soul, the "seed of eternity we 366
bear in ourselves, irreducible to the merely material,"[9] can have its origin only in God.

34 The world, and man, attest that they contain within themselves neither their first principle nor their final end, but rather that they participate in Being itself, which alone is without origin or end. Thus, in different ways, man can come to know that there exists a reality which is the first cause and final end of all things, a reality "that everyone calls
'God.'"[10] 199

35 Man's faculties make him capable of coming to a knowledge of the existence of a personal God. But
for man to be able to enter into real 50
intimacy with him, God willed both to reveal himself to man and to give him the grace of being able to welcome this revelation in faith. The proofs of God's existence, however,
can predispose one to faith and help 159
one to see that faith is not opposed to reason.

[6] St. Augustine, *Conf.* 1, 1, 1: PL 32, 659–661. — [7] *Rom* 1:19–20; cf. *Acts* 14:15, 17; 17:27–28; *Wis* 13:1–9. — [8] St. Augustine, *Sermo* 241, 2: PL 38, 1134. — [9] *GS* 18 § 1; cf. 14 § 2. [10] St. Thomas Aquinas, *STh* I, 2, 3.

III. The Knowledge of God According to the Church

36 "Our holy mother, the Church, holds and teaches that God, the first principle and last end of all things, can be known with certainty from the created world by the natural light of human reason."[11] Without this capacity, man would not be able
355 to welcome God's revelation. Man has this capacity because he is created "in the image of God."[12]

37 In the historical conditions in which he finds himself, however, man experiences many difficulties in
1960 coming to know God by the light of reason alone:

> Though human reason is, strictly speaking, truly capable by its own natural power and light of attaining to a true and certain knowledge of the one personal God, who watches over and controls the world by his providence, and of the natural law written in our hearts by the Creator; yet there are many obstacles which prevent reason from the effective and fruitful use of this inborn faculty. For the truths that concern the relations between God and man wholly transcend the visible order of things, and, if they are translated into human action and influence it, they call for self-surrender and abnegation. The human mind, in its turn, is hampered in the attaining of such truths, not only by the impact of the senses and the imagination, but also by disordered appetites which are the consequences of original sin. So it happens that men in such matters easily persuade themselves that what they would not like to be true is false or at least doubtful.[13]

38 This is why man stands in need of being enlightened by God's revelation, not only about those things
that exceed his understanding, but 2036
also "about those religious and moral truths which of themselves are not beyond the grasp of human reason, so that even in the present condition of the human race, they can be known by all men with ease, with firm certainty and with no admixture of error."[14]

IV. How Can We Speak about God?

39 In defending the ability of human reason to know God, the Church is expressing her confidence
in the possibility of speaking about 851
him to all men and with all men, and therefore of dialogue with other religions, with philosophy and science, as well as with unbelievers and atheists.

40 Since our knowledge of God is limited, our language about him is equally so. We can name God only by taking creatures as our starting point, and in accordance with our limited human ways of knowing and thinking.

41 All creatures bear a certain resemblance to God, most especially man, created in the image and likeness of God. The manifold perfections of creatures—their truth, their goodness, their beauty—all reflect the infinite perfection of God. Consequently we can name God by tak- 213, 299
ing his creatures' perfections as our starting point, "for from the greatness and beauty of created things

[11] Vatican Council I, *Dei Filius* 2: DS 3004; cf. 3026; Vatican Council II, *Dei Verbum* 6. — [12] Cf. *Gen* 1:27. — [13] Pius XII, *Humani Generis*, 561: DS 3875. — [14] Pius XII, *Humani Generis*, 561: DS 3876; cf. *Dei Filius* 2: DS 3005; *DV* 6; St. Thomas Aquinas, *STh* I, 1, 1.

comes a corresponding perception of their Creator."[15]

42 God transcends all creatures. We must therefore continually purify our language of everything in it
212, 300 that is limited, image-bound or im
370 perfect, if we are not to confuse our image of God—"the inexpressible, the incomprehensible, the invisible, the ungraspable"—with our human representations.[16] Our human words always fall short of the mystery of God.

43 Admittedly, in speaking about God like this, our language is using human modes of expression; nevertheless it really does attain to God himself, though unable to express him in his infinite simplicity. Likewise, we must recall that "between Creator and creature no similitude can be expressed without implying an even greater dissimilitude";[17] and that "concerning God, we cannot grasp what he is, but only what he is
206 not, and how other beings stand in relation to him."[18]

In Brief

44 *Man is by nature and vocation a religious being. Coming from God, going toward God, man lives a fully human life only if he freely lives by his bond with God.*

45 *Man is made to live in communion with God in whom he finds happiness: "When I am completely united to you, there will be no more sorrow or trials; entirely full of you, my life will be complete" (St. Augustine,* Conf. *10, 28, 39: PL 32, 795).*

46 *When he listens to the message of creation and to the voice of conscience, man can arrive at certainty about the existence of God, the cause and the end of everything.*

47 *The Church teaches that the one true God, our Creator and Lord, can be known with certainty from his works, by the natural light of human reason (cf. Vatican Council I, can. 2, § 1: DS 3026).*

48 *We really can name God, starting from the manifold perfections of his creatures, which are likenesses of the infinitely perfect God, even if our limited language cannot exhaust the mystery.*

49 *"Without the Creator, the creature vanishes" (GS 36). This is the reason why believers know that the love of Christ urges them to bring the light of the living God to those who do not know him or who reject him.*

[15] *Wis* 13:5. — [16] *Liturgy of St. John Chrysostom,* Anaphora. — [17] Lateran Council IV: DS 806. — [18] St. Thomas Aquinas, *SCG* I, 30.

Chapter Two:
GOD COMES TO MEET MAN

50 By natural reason man can know God with certainty, on the basis of his works. But there is another order of knowledge, which man
cannot possibly arrive at by his own
36 powers: the order of divine Revelation.[1] Through an utterly free deci-
1066 sion, God has revealed himself and
given himself to man. This he does by revealing the mystery, his plan of loving goodness, formed from all eternity in Christ, for the benefit of all men. God has fully revealed this plan by sending us his beloved Son, our Lord Jesus Christ, and the Holy Spirit.

Article 1:
THE REVELATION OF GOD

I. God Reveals His "Plan of Loving Goodness"

51 "It pleased God, in his goodness and wisdom, to reveal himself
and to make known the mystery of
2823 his will. His will was that men should
have access to the Father, through
Christ, the Word made flesh, in the
1996 Holy Spirit, and thus become sharers in the divine nature."[2]

52 God, who "dwells in unapproachable light," wants to communicate his own divine life to the men he freely created, in order to adopt them as his sons in his only-begotten Son.[3] By revealing himself God wishes to make them capable of responding to him, and of knowing him, and of loving him far beyond their own natural capacity.

53 The divine plan of Revelation is realized simultaneously "by deeds and words which are intrinsically bound up with each other"[4] and shed light on each other. It involves a specific divine pedagogy: God communicates himself to man gradually. He prepares him to welcome by 1953
stages the supernatural Revelation 1950
that is to culminate in the person and mission of the incarnate Word, Jesus Christ.

St. Irenaeus of Lyons repeatedly speaks of this divine pedagogy using the image of God and man becoming accustomed to one another: The Word of God dwelt in man and became the Son of man in order to accustom man to perceive God and to accustom God to dwell in man, according to the Father's pleasure.[5]

II. The Stages of Revelation

In the beginning God makes himself known

54 "God, who creates and conserves all things by his Word, provides men with constant evidence 32
of himself in created realities. And furthermore, wishing to open up the

[1] Cf. Dei Filius: DS 3015. — [2] *DV* 2; cf. *Eph* 1:9; 2:18; 2 *Pet* 1:4. — [3] *1 Tim* 6:16; cf. *Eph* 1:4–5. — [4] *DV* 2. — [5] St. Irenaeus, *Adv. haeres.* 3, 20, 2: PG 7/1, 944; cf. 3, 17, 1; 4, 12, 4; 4, 21, 3.

way to heavenly salvation, he manifested himself to our first parents from the very beginning."[6] He invited them to intimate communion
374 with himself and clothed them with resplendent grace and justice.

55 This revelation was not broken off by our first parents' sin. "After
397, 410 the fall, [God] buoyed them up with the hope of salvation, by promising redemption; and he has never ceased to show his solicitude for the human race. For he wishes to give eternal life to all those who seek salvation by patience in well-doing."[7]

> Even when he disobeyed you and lost your friendship you did not abandon him to the power of death.... Again and again you offered a covenant to
> 761 man.[8]

The Covenant with Noah

56 After the unity of the human race was shattered by sin God at once sought to save humanity part
401 by part. The covenant with Noah after the flood gives expression to the principle of the divine economy to
1219 ward the "nations," in other words, toward men grouped "in their lands, each with [its] own language, by their families, in their nations."[9]

57 This state of division into many nations is at once cosmic, social, and religious. It is intended to limit the pride of fallen humanity,[10] united only in its perverse ambition to forge its own unity as at Babel.[11] But, because of sin, both polytheism and the idolatry of the nation and of its rulers constantly threaten this provisional economy with the perversion of paganism.[12]

58 The covenant with Noah remains in force during the times of the Gentiles, until the universal proclamation of the Gospel.[13] The Bible venerates several great figures
among the Gentiles: Abel the just, 674
the king-priest Melchizedek—a figure of Christ—and the upright "Noah, Daniel, and Job."[14] Scripture thus expresses the heights of sanctity that can be reached by those who live according to the covenant of Noah, waiting for Christ to "gather
into one the children of God who 2569
are scattered abroad."[15]

God chooses Abraham

59 In order to gather together scattered humanity God calls Abram from his country, his kindred, and
his father's house,[16] and makes him 145, 2570
Abraham, that is, "the father of a multitude of nations." "In you all the nations of the earth shall be blessed."[17]

60 The people descended from Abraham would be the trustees of the promise made to the patriarchs,
the chosen people, called to prepare 760
for that day when God would gather
all his children into the unity of the 762, 781
Church.[18] They would be the root onto which the Gentiles would be grafted, once they came to believe.[19]

61 The patriarchs, prophets, and certain other Old Testament figures have been and always will be honored as saints in all the Church's liturgical traditions.

[6] *DV* 3; cf. *Jn* 1:3; *Rom* 1:19–20. — [7] *DV* 3; cf. *Gen* 3:15; *Rom* 2:6–7. — [8] *Roman Missal,* Eucharistic Prayer IV, 118. — [9] *Gen* 10:5; cf. 9:9–10, 16; 10:20–31. — [10] Cf. *Acts* 17:26–27. — [11] Cf. *Wis* 10:5; *Gen* 11:4–6. — [12] Cf. *Rom* 1:18–25. — [13] Cf. *Gen* 9:16; *Lk* 21:24; *DV* 3. — [14] Cf. *Gen* 14:18; *Heb* 7:3; *Ezek* 14:14. — [15] *Jn* 11:52. — [16] *Gen* 12:1. — [17] *Gen* 17:5; 12:3 (LXX); cf. *Gal* 3:8. — [18] Cf. *Rom* 11:28; *Jn* 11:52; 10:16. — [19] Cf. *Rom* 11:17–18, 24.

God forms his people Israel

62 After the patriarchs, God
060, 2574 formed Israel as his people by freeing them from slavery in Egypt. He
established with them the covenant
of Mount Sinai and, through Moses,
gave them his law so that they would
recognize him and serve him as the
one living and true God, the provident Father and just judge, and so
1961 that they would look for the promised Savior.[20]

204, 2801 **63** Israel is the priestly people of
God, "called by the name of the
839 Lord," and "the first to hear the
word of God,"[21] the people of "elder
brethren" in the faith of Abraham.

64 Through the prophets, God
forms his people in the hope of salvation, in the expectation of a new
and everlasting Covenant intend-
711 ed for all, to be written on their
hearts.[22] The prophets proclaim a
1965 radical redemption of the People of
God, purification from all their infidelities, a salvation which will include all the nations.[23]Above all, the
poor and humble of the Lord will
bear this hope. Such holy women
as Sarah, Rebecca, Rachel, Miriam,
489 Deborah, Hannah, Judith, and Esther kept alive the hope of Israel's
salvation. The purest figure among
them is Mary.[24]

III. Christ Jesus—"Mediator and Fullness of All Revelation"[25]

God has said everything in his Word

65 "In many and various ways
God spoke of old to our fathers by
the prophets, but in these last days
he has spoken to us by a Son."[26] 102
Christ, the Son of God made man,
is the Father's one, perfect, and unsurpassable Word. In him he has said everything; there will be no other word than this one. St. John of the Cross, among others, commented strikingly on *Hebrews* 1:1–2:

> In giving us his Son, his only Word
> (for he possesses no other), he spoke
> everything to us at once in this sole
> Word—and he has no more to say...
> because what he spoke before to the
> prophets in parts, he has now spoken
> all at once by giving us the All Who
> is His Son. Any person questioning 516
> God or desiring some vision or
> revelation would be guilty not only of
> foolish behavior but also of offending
> him, by not fixing his eyes entirely
> upon Christ and by living with the
> desire for some other novelty.[27] 2717

There will be no further Revelation

66 "The Christian economy, therefore, since it is the new and definitive Covenant, will never pass away; and no new public revelation is to be expected before the glorious manifestation of our Lord Jesus Christ."[28] Yet even if Revelation is already complete, it has not been made completely explicit; it remains for Christian faith gradually to grasp its full significance over the course
of the centuries. 94

67 Throughout the ages, there have been so-called "private" revelations, some of which have been recognized by the authority of the Church. They do not belong,

[20] Cf. *DV* 3. — [21] *Deut* 28:10; *Roman Missal,* Good Friday, General Intercession VI; see also *Ex* 19:6. — [22] Cf. *Isa* 2:2–4; *Jer* 31:31–34; *Heb* 10:16. — [23] Cf. *Ezek* 36; *Isa* 49:5–6; 53:11. — [24] Cf. *Zeph* 2:3; *Lk* 1:38. — [25] *DV* 2. — [26] *Heb* 1:1–2. — [27] St. John of the Cross, *The Ascent of Mount Carmel,* 2, 22, 3–5, in *The Collected Works,* tr. K. Kavanaugh, OCD, and O. Rodriguez, OCD (Washington DC: Institute of Carmelite Studies, 1979), 179–180: *LH,* OR Advent, wk 2, Mon. — [28] *DV* 4; cf. 1 *Tim* 6:14; *Titus* 2:13.

however, to the deposit of faith. It
84 is not their role to improve or complete Christ's definitive Revelation, but to help live more fully by it in a certain period of history. Guided by the magisterium of the Church, the *sensus fidelium* knows how to discern and welcome in these revelations whatever constitutes an authentic call of Christ or his saints to
93 the Church.

Christian faith cannot accept "revelations" that claim to surpass or correct the Revelation of which Christ is the fulfillment, as is the case in certain non-Christian religions and also in certain recent sects which base themselves on such "revelations."

In Brief

68 *By love, God has revealed himself and given himself to man. He has thus provided the definitive, superabundant answer to the questions that man asks himself about the meaning and purpose of his life.*

69 *God has revealed himself to man by gradually communicating his own mystery in deeds and in words.*

70 *Beyond the witness to himself that God gives in created things, he manifested himself to our first parents, spoke to them and, after the fall, promised them salvation (cf.* Gen *3:15) and offered them his covenant.*

71 *God made an everlasting covenant with Noah and with all living beings (cf.* Gen *9:16). It will remain in force as long as the world lasts.*

72 *God chose Abraham and made a covenant with him and his descendants. By the covenant God formed his people and revealed his law to them through Moses. Through the prophets, he prepared them to accept the salvation destined for all humanity.*

73 *God has revealed himself fully by sending his own Son, in whom he has established his covenant for ever. The Son is his Father's definitive Word; so there will be no further Revelation after him.*

Article 2: THE TRANSMISSION OF DIVINE REVELATION

74 God "desires all men to be saved and to come to the knowledge of the truth":[29] that is, of Christ Jesus.[30] Christ must be proclaimed to
851 all nations and individuals, so that this revelation may reach to the ends of the earth:

> God graciously arranged that the things he had once revealed for the salvation of all peoples should remain in their entirety, throughout the ages, and be transmitted to all generations.[31]

I. The Apostolic Tradition

75 "Christ the Lord, in whom the entire Revelation of the most high God is summed up, commanded the apostles to preach the Gospel, which had been promised beforehand by the prophets, and which he fulfilled in his own person and promulgated

[29] *1 Tim* 2:4. — [30] Cf. *Jn* 14:6. — [31] *DV* 7; cf. *2 Cor* 1:20; 3:16–4:6.

with his own lips. In preaching the Gospel, they were to communicate the gifts of God to all men. This Gospel was to be the source of all
171 saving truth and moral discipline."[32]

In the apostolic preaching...

76 In keeping with the Lord's command, the Gospel was handed on in two ways:

– *orally* "by the apostles who handed on, by the spoken word of their preaching, by the example they gave, by the institutions they established, what they themselves had received—whether from the lips of Christ, from his way of life and his works, or whether they had learned it at the prompting of the Holy Spirit";[33]

– *in writing* "by those apostles and other men associated with the apostles who, under the inspiration of the same Holy Spirit, committed the message of salvation to writing."[34]

...continued in apostolic succession

77 "In order that the full and living Gospel might always be preserved in the Church the apostles left bishops as their successors. They gave them 'their own position of
861 teaching authority.'"[35] Indeed, "the apostolic preaching, which is expressed in a special way in the inspired books, was to be preserved in a continuous line of succession until the end of time."[36]

78 This living transmission, accomplished in the Holy Spirit, is called Tradition, since it is distinct from Sacred Scripture, though closely connected to it. Through Tradition, "the Church, in her doctrine, 174
life, and worship perpetuates and
transmits to every generation all that 1124, 2651
she herself is, all that she believes."[37] "The sayings of the holy Fathers are a witness to the life-giving presence of this Tradition, showing how its riches are poured out in the practice and life of the Church, in her belief and her prayer."[38]

79 The Father's self-communication made through his Word in the Holy Spirit, remains present and active in the Church: "God, who spoke in the past, continues to converse with the Spouse of his beloved Son. And the Holy Spirit, through whom the living voice of the Gospel rings out in the Church—and through her in the world—leads believers to the full truth, and makes the Word of Christ dwell in them in all its richness."[39]

II. The Relationship between Tradition and Sacred Scripture

One common source...

80 "Sacred Tradition and Sacred Scripture, then, are bound closely together and communicate one with the other. For both of them, flowing out from the same divine well-spring, come together in some fashion to form one thing and move towards the same goal."[40] Each of them makes present and fruitful in the Church the mystery of Christ, who promised to remain with his own "always, to the close of the age."[41]

...two distinct modes of transmission

[32] *DV* 7; cf. *Mt* 28:19–20; *Mk* 16:15. — [33] *DV* 7. — [34] *DV* 7. — [35] *DV* 7 § 2; St. Irenaeus, *Adv. haeres.* 3, 3, 1: PG 7, 848; Harvey, 2, 9. — [36] *DV* 8 § 1. — [37] *DV* 8 § 1. — [38] *DV* 8 § 3. — [39] *DV* 8 § 3; cf. *Col* 3:16. — [40] *DV* 9. — [41] *Mt* 28:20.

81 “*Sacred Scripture* is the speech of God as it is put down in writing under the breath of the Holy Spirit.”[42]
113 “And [Holy] *Tradition* transmits in its entirety the Word of God which has been entrusted to the apostles by Christ the Lord and the Holy Spirit. It transmits it to the successors of the apostles so that, enlightened by the Spirit of truth, they may faithfully preserve, expound, and spread it abroad by their preaching.”[43]

82 As a result the Church, to whom the transmission and interpretation of Revelation is entrusted, “does not derive her certainty about all revealed truths from the holy Scriptures alone. Both Scripture and Tradition must be accepted and honored with equal sentiments of devotion and reverence.”[44]

Apostolic Tradition and ecclesial traditions

83 The Tradition here in question comes from the apostles and hands on what they received from Jesus' teaching and example and what they learned from the Holy Spirit. The first generation of Christians did not yet have a written New Testament, and the New Testament itself demonstrates the process of living Tradition.
1201, 2041 Tradition is to be distinguished from the various theological, disci-
2684 plinary, liturgical, or devotional traditions, born in the local churches over time. These are the particular forms, adapted to different places and times, in which the great Tradition is expressed. In the light of Tradition, these traditions can be retained, modified or even abandoned under the guidance of the Church's magisterium.

III. The Interpretation of the Heritage of Faith

The heritage of faith entrusted to the whole of the Church

84 The apostles entrusted the “Sacred deposit” of the faith (the *depositum fidei*),[45] contained in Sacred Scripture and Tradition, to the
whole of the Church. “By adhering 857, 871
to [this heritage] the entire holy people, united to its pastors, remains always faithful to the teaching of the apostles, to the brotherhood,
to the breaking of bread and the 2033
prayers. So, in maintaining, practicing, and professing the faith that has been handed on, there should be a remarkable harmony between the bishops and the faithful.”[46]

The Magisterium of the Church

85 “The task of giving an authentic interpretation of the Word of God, whether in its written form or in the form of Tradition, has been entrusted to the living, teaching office of the Church alone. Its authority in this matter is exercised
in the name of Jesus Christ.”[47] This 888–892
means that the task of interpretation
has been entrusted to the bishops in 2032–20
communion with the successor of Peter, the Bishop of Rome.

86 “Yet this Magisterium is not superior to the Word of God, but is its servant. It teaches only what has been handed on to it. At the divine

[42] *DV* 9. — [43] *DV* 9. — [44] *DV* 9. — [45] *DV* 10 § 1; cf. *1 Tim* 6:20; *2 Tim* 1:12–14 (Vulg.). — [46] *DV* 10 § 1; cf. *Acts* 2:42 (Gk.); Pius XII, apostolic constitution, *Munificentissimus Deus*, November 1, 1950: AAS 42 (1950), 756, taken along with the words of St. Cyprian, *Epist.* 66, 8: CSEL3, 2, 733: “The Church is the people united to its Priests, the flock adhering to its Shepherd.” — [47] *DV* 10 § 2.

command and with the help of the
Holy Spirit, it listens to this devot-
edly, guards it with dedication, and
688 expounds it faithfully. All that it
proposes for belief as being divinely revealed is drawn from this single
deposit of faith."[48]

1548 **87** Mindful of Christ's words to
his apostles: "He who hears you,
hears me,"[49] the faithful receive with
2037 docility the teachings and directives
that their pastors give them in different forms.

The dogmas of the faith

888–892 **88** The Church's Magisterium exercises the authority it holds from
Christ to the fullest extent when
2032–2040 it defines dogmas, that is, when it
proposes, in a form obliging the
Christian people to an irrevocable
adherence of faith, truths contained
in divine Revelation or also when it
proposes, in a definitive way, truths
having a necessary connection with
these.

89 There is an organic connection
2625 between our spiritual life and the
dogmas. Dogmas are lights along
the path of faith; they illuminate it
and make it secure. Conversely, if
our life is upright, our intellect and
heart will be open to welcome the
light shed by the dogmas of faith.[50]

90 The mutual connections between dogmas, and their coherence, can be found in the whole
of the Revelation of the mystery
114, 158 of Christ.[51] "In Catholic doctrine
234 there exists an order or 'hierarchy' of
truths, since they vary in their relation to the foundation of the Christian faith."[52]

The supernatural sense of faith

91 All the faithful share in understanding and handing on revealed truth. They have received the 737
anointing of the Holy Spirit, who
instructs them[53] and guides them
into all truth.[54]

92 "The whole body of the faithful...cannot err in matters of belief.
This characteristic is shown in the
supernatural appreciation of faith 785
(*sensus fidei*) on the part of the whole
people, when, 'from the bishops to
the last of the faithful,' they manifest a universal consent in matters of
faith and morals."[55]

93 "By this appreciation of the
faith, aroused and sustained by the
Spirit of truth, the People of God,
guided by the sacred teaching authority (Magisterium),...receives... 889
the faith, once for all delivered to
the saints.... The People unfailingly adheres to this faith, penetrates it
more deeply with right judgment,
and applies it more fully in daily
life."[56]

Growth in understanding the faith

94 Thanks to the assistance of the
Holy Spirit, the understanding of
both the realities and the words of
the heritage of faith is able to grow 66
in the life of the Church:
– "through the contemplation
and study of believers who ponder 2651
these things in their hearts";[57] it is
in particular "theological research

[48] *DV* 10 § 2. — [49] *Lk* 10:16; cf. *LG* 20 — [50] Cf. *Jn* 8:31–32. — [51] Cf. Vatican Council I: DS 3016: *nexus mysteriorum*; *LG* 25. — [52] *UR* 11. — [53] Cf. *1 Jn* 2:20, 27. — [54] Cf. *Jn* 16:13. — [55] *LG* 12; cf. St. Augustine, *De praed. sanct.* 14, 27: PL 44, 980. — [56] *LG* 12; cf. *Jude* 3. — [57] *DV* 8 § 2; cf. *Lk* 2:19, 51.

[which] deepens knowledge of revealed truth."[58]

– "from the intimate sense of
2038, 2519 spiritual realities which [believers] experience,"[59] the sacred Scriptures "grow with the one who reads them."[60]

– "from the preaching of those who have received, along with their right of succession in the episcopate, the sure charism of truth."[61]

95 "It is clear therefore that, in the supremely wise arrangement of God, sacred Tradition, Sacred Scripture, and the Magisterium of the Church are so connected and associated that one of them cannot stand without the others. Working together, each in its own way, under the action of the one Holy Spirit, they all contribute effectively to the salvation of souls."[62]

In Brief

96 *What Christ entrusted to the apostles, they in turn handed on by their preaching and writing, under the inspiration of the Holy Spirit, to all generations, until Christ returns in glory.*

97 *"Sacred Tradition and Sacred Scripture make up a single sacred deposit of the Word of God"* (DV *10), in which, as in a mirror, the pilgrim Church contemplates God, the source of all her riches.*

98 *"The Church, in her doctrine, life, and worship, perpetuates and transmits to every generation all that she herself is, all that she believes"* (DV *8 §1).*

99 *Thanks to its supernatural sense of faith, the People of God as a whole never ceases to welcome, to penetrate more deeply, and to live more fully from the gift of divine Revelation.*

100 *The task of interpreting the Word of God authentically has been entrusted solely to the Magisterium of the Church, that is, to the Pope and to the bishops in communion with him.*

Article 3:
SACRED SCRIPTURE

I. Christ—The Unique Word of Sacred Scripture

101 In order to reveal himself to men, in the condescension of his goodness God speaks to them in human words: "Indeed the words of God, expressed in the words of men, are in every way like human language, just as the Word of the eternal Father, when he took on himself the flesh of human weakness, became like men."[63]

102 Through all the words of Sacred Scripture, God speaks only one
single Word, his one Utterance in 65, 2763
whom he expresses himself completely:[64]

> You recall that one and the same Word 426–429
> of God extends throughout Scripture, that it is one and the same Utterance that resounds in the mouths of all

[58] *GS* 62 § 7; cf. *GS* 44 § 2; *DV* 23, 24; *UR* 4. — [59] *DV* 8 § 2. — [60] St. Gregory the Great, *Hom. in Ez.* 1, 7, 8: PL 76, 843 D. — [61] *DV* 8 § 2. — [62] DV 10 § 3. — [63] *DV* 13. — [64] Cf. *Heb* 1:1–3.

the sacred writers, since he who was in the beginning God with God has no need of separate syllables; for he is not subject to time.[65]

103 For this reason, the Church has always venerated the Scriptures as she venerates the Lord's Body. She never ceases to present to the faith
00, 1184 ful the bread of life, taken from the
1378 one table of God's Word and Christ's
Body.[66]

104 In Sacred Scripture, the Church constantly finds her nourishment and her strength, for she welcomes it not as a human word, "but as what it really is, the word of God."[67] "In the sacred books, the Father who is in heaven comes lovingly to meet his children, and talks with them."[68]

II. Inspiration and Truth of Sacred Scripture

105 *God is the author of Sacred Scripture.* "The divinely revealed realities, which are contained and presented in the text of Sacred Scripture, have been written down under the inspiration of the Holy Spirit."[69]

"For Holy Mother Church, relying on the faith of the apostolic age, accepts as sacred and canonical the books of the Old and the New Testaments, whole and entire, with all their parts, on the grounds that, written under the inspiration of the Holy Spirit, they have God as their author and have been handed on as such to the Church herself."[70]

106 God inspired the human authors of the sacred books. "To compose the sacred books, God chose certain men who, all the while he employed them in this task, made full use of their own faculties and powers so that, though he acted in them and by them, it was as true authors that they consigned to writing whatever he wanted written, and no more."[71]

107 The inspired books teach the truth. "Since therefore all that the inspired authors or sacred writers affirm should be regarded as affirmed by the Holy Spirit, we must acknowledge that the books of Scripture firmly, faithfully, and without error
teach that truth which God, for the 702
sake of our salvation, wished to see confided to the Sacred Scriptures."[72]

108 Still, the Christian faith is not a "religion of the book." Christianity is the religion of the "Word" of God, a word which is "not a written and mute word, but the Word which is incarnate and living."[73] If the Scriptures are not to remain a dead letter, Christ, the eternal Word of the living God, must, through the Holy Spirit, "open [our] minds to understand the Scriptures."[74]

III. The Holy Spirit, Interpreter of Scripture

109 In Sacred Scripture, God speaks to man in a human way. To interpret Scripture correctly, the reader must be attentive to what the human authors truly wanted to affirm and to what God wanted to reveal to us by their words.[75]

[65] St. Augustine, *En. in Ps.* 103, 4, 1: PL 37, 1378; cf. *Ps* 104; *Jn* 1:1. — [66] Cf. *DV* 21. — [67] *1 Thess* 2:13; cf. *DV* 24. — [68] *DV* 21. — [69] *DV* 11. — [70] *DV* 11; cf. *Jn* 20:31; *2 Tim* 3:16; *2 Pet* 1:19–21; 3:15–16. — [71] *DV* 11. — [72] *DV* 11. — [73] St. Bernard, S. *missus est hom.* 4, 11: PL 183, 86. — [74] Cf. *Lk* 24:45. — [75] Cf. *DV* 12 § 1.

110 In order to discover *the sacred authors' intention*, the reader must take into account the conditions of their time and culture, the literary genres in use at that time, and the modes of feeling, speaking, and narrating then current. "For the fact is that truth is differently presented and expressed in the various types of historical writing, in prophetical and poetical texts, and in other forms of literary expression."[76]

111 But since Sacred Scripture is inspired, there is another and no less important principle of correct interpretation, without which Scripture would remain a dead letter. "Sacred Scripture must be read and interpreted in the light of the same Spirit by whom it was written."[77]
The Second Vatican Council indicates three criteria for interpreting Scripture in accordance with the Spirit who inspired it.[78]

112 1. *Be especially attentive "to the content and unity of the whole Scripture."* Different as the books which comprise it may be, Scripture
128 is a unity by reason of the unity of God's plan, of which Christ Jesus is
368 the center and heart, open since his Passover.[79]

> The phrase "heart of Christ" can refer to Sacred Scripture, which makes known his heart, closed before the Passion, as the Scripture was obscure. But the Scripture has been opened since the Passion; since those who from then on have understood it, consider and discern in what way the prophecies must be interpreted.[80]

113 2. *Read the Scripture within "the living Tradition of the whole Church."* According to a saying of the Fathers, Sacred Scripture is written principally in the Church's 81
heart rather than in documents and records, for the Church carries in her Tradition the living memorial of God's Word, and it is the Holy Spirit who gives her the spiritual interpretation of the Scripture ("according to the spiritual meaning which the Spirit grants to the Church"[81]).

114 3. *Be attentive to the analogy of faith.*[82] By "analogy of faith" we 90
mean the coherence of the truths of faith among themselves and within the whole plan of Revelation.

The senses of Scripture

115 According to an ancient tradition, one can distinguish between two *senses* of Scripture: the literal and the spiritual, the latter being subdivided into the allegorical, moral, and anagogical senses. The profound concordance of the four senses guarantees all its richness to the living reading of Scripture in the Church.

116 The *literal sense* is the meaning conveyed by the words of Scripture and discovered by exegesis, following the rules of sound interpretation: "All other senses of Sacred Scripture are based on the literal."[83] 110–114

117 The *spiritual sense*. Thanks to the unity of God's plan, not only the text of Scripture but also the realities and events about which it speaks can 1101
be signs.

[76] *DV* 12 § 2. — [77] *DV* 12 § 3. — [78] Cf. *DV* 12 § 4. — [79] Cf. *Lk* 24:25–27, 44–46. — [80] St. Thomas Aquinas, *Expos. in Ps* 21,11; cf. *Ps* 22:15. — [81] Origen, *Hom. in Lev.* 5, 5: PG 12, 454D. — [82] Cf. *Rom* 12:6. — [83] St. Thomas Aquinas, *STh* I, 1, 10, *ad* 1.

1. The *allegorical sense.* We can acquire a more profound understanding of events by recognizing their significance in Christ; thus the crossing of the Red Sea is a sign or type of Christ's victory and also of Christian Baptism.[84]

2. The *moral sense.* The events reported in Scripture ought to lead us to act justly. As St. Paul says, they were written "for our instruction."[85]

3. The *anagogical sense* (Greek: *anagoge*, "leading"). We can view realities and events in terms of their eternal significance, leading us toward our true homeland: thus the Church on earth is a sign of the heavenly Jerusalem.[86]

118 A medieval couplet summarizes the significance of the four senses:

> The Letter speaks of deeds; Allegory to faith;
> The Moral how to act; Anagogy our destiny.[87]

119 "It is the task of exegetes to work, according to these rules, toward a better understanding and explanation of the meaning of Sacred Scripture in order that their research
94 may help the Church to form a
firmer judgment. For, of course, all that has been said about the manner of interpreting Scripture is ultimately subject to the judgment of the Church which exercises the divinely conferred commission and ministry of watching over and interpreting the Word of God."[88]

> But I would not believe in the Gospel, 113
> had not the authority of the Catholic Church already moved me.[89]

IV. The Canon of Scripture

120 It was by the apostolic Tradition that the Church discerned
which writings are to be included 1117
in the list of the sacred books.[90] This complete list is called the canon of Scripture. It includes 46 books for the Old Testament (45 if we count Jeremiah and Lamentations as one) and 27 for the New.[91]

The Old Testament: Genesis, Exodus, Leviticus, Numbers, Deuteronomy, Joshua, Judges, Ruth, 1 *and* 2 Samuel, 1 *and* 2 Kings, 1 *and* 2 Chronicles, Ezra and Nehemiah, Tobit, Judith, Esther, 1 and 2 Maccabees, Job, Psalms, Proverbs, Ecclesiastes, *the* Song of Songs, *the* Wisdom of Solomon, Sirach (Ecclesiasticus), Isaiah, Jeremiah, Lamentations, Baruch, Ezekiel, Daniel, Hosea, Joel, Amos, Obadiah, Jonah, Micah, Nahum, Habakkuk, Zephaniah, Haggai, Zechariah and Malachi.

The New Testament: *the Gospels according to* Matthew, Mark, Luke *and* John, the Acts of the Apostles, the Letters of St. Paul to the Romans, 1 *and* 2 Corinthians, Galatians, Ephesians, Philippians, Colossians, 1 *and* 2 Thessalonians, 1 *and* 2 Timothy, Titus, Philemon, *the* Letter to the Hebrews, *the* Letters of James, 1 *and* 2 Peter, 1, 2, *and* 3 John, *and* Jude, *and* Revelation (the Apocalypse).

[84] Cf. *1 Cor* 10:2. — [85] *1 Cor* 10:11; cf. *Heb* 3–4:11. — [86] Cf. *Rev* 21:1–22:5. — [87] Littera gesta docet, quid credas allegoria, moralis quid agas, quo tendas anagogia. Augustine of Dacia, *Rotulus pugillaris,* I: ed. A. Walz: Angelicum 6 (1929) 256. — [88] *DV* 12 § 3. — [89] St. Augustine, *Contra epistolam Manichaei,* 5, 6: PL 42, 176. — [90] Cf. *DV* 8 § 3. — [91] Cf. DS 179; 1334–1336; 1501–1504.

The Old Testament

121 The Old Testament is an indispensable part of Sacred Scripture.
1093 Its books are divinely inspired and retain a permanent value,[92] for the Old Covenant has never been revoked.

122 Indeed, "the economy of the Old Testament was deliberately so oriented that it should prepare for and declare in prophecy the coming
702, 763 of Christ, redeemer of all men."[93] "Even though they contain matters imperfect and provisional,"[94] the books of the Old Testament bear
708 witness to the whole divine pedagogy of God's saving love: these writings "are a storehouse of sublime teaching on God and of sound wisdom on human life, as well as a wonderful treasury of prayers; in
2568 them, too, the mystery of our salvation is present in a hidden way."[95]

123 Christians venerate the Old Testament as true Word of God. The Church has always vigorously opposed the idea of rejecting the Old Testament under the pretext that the New has rendered it void (Marcionism).

The New Testament

124 "The Word of God, which is the power of God for salvation to everyone who has faith, is set forth and displays its power in a most wonderful way in the writings of the New Testament"[96] which hand on the ultimate truth of God's Revelation. Their central object is Jesus Christ, God's incarnate Son: his acts, teachings, Passion and glorification, and his Church's beginnings under the Spirit's guidance.[97]

125 The *Gospels* are the heart of all the Scriptures "because they are our principal source for the life and
teaching of the Incarnate Word, our 515
Savior."[98]

126 We can distinguish three stages in the formation of the Gospels:

1. *The life and teaching of Jesus.* The Church holds firmly that the four Gospels, "whose historicity she unhesitatingly affirms, faithfully hand on what Jesus, the Son of God, while he lived among men, really did and taught for their eternal salvation, until the day when he was taken up."[99]

2. *The oral tradition.* "For, after the 76
ascension of the Lord, the apostles handed on to their hearers what he had said and done, but with that fuller understanding which they, instructed by the glorious events of Christ and enlightened by the Spirit of truth, now enjoyed."[100]

3. *The written Gospels.* "The sacred 76
authors, in writing the four Gospels, selected certain of the many elements which had been handed on, either orally or already in written form; others they synthesized or explained with an eye to the situation of the churches, while sustaining the form of preaching, but always in such a fashion that they have told us the honest truth about Jesus."[101]

127 The fourfold Gospel holds a 1154
unique place in the Church, as is evident both in the veneration which the liturgy accords it and in the

[92] Cf. *DV* 14. — [93] *DV* 15. — [94] *DV* 15. — [95] *DV* 15. — [96] *DV* 17; cf. *Rom* 1:16. — [97] Cf. *DV* 20. — [98] *DV* 18. — [99] *DV* 19; cf. *Acts* 1:1–2. — [100] *DV* 19. — [101] *DV* 19.

surpassing attraction it has exercised on the saints at all times:

> There is no doctrine which could be better, more precious and more splendid than the text of the Gospel. Behold and retain what our Lord and Master, Christ, has taught by his words and accomplished by his deeds.[102]
>
> 2705 But above all it's the Gospels that occupy my mind when I'm at prayer; my poor soul has so many needs, and yet this is the one thing needful. I'm always finding fresh lights there, hidden and enthralling meanings.[103]

The unity of the Old and New Testaments

128 The Church, as early as apostolic times,[104] and then constantly in her Tradition, has illuminated the unity of the divine plan in the two Testaments through typology, which
1094 discerns in God's works of the Old Covenant prefigurations of what he
489 accomplished in the fullness of time in the person of his incarnate Son.

129 Christians therefore read the Old Testament in the light of Christ crucified and risen. Such typological reading discloses the inexhaustible
681 content of the Old Testament; but it must not make us forget that the Old Testament retains its own intrinsic value as Revelation reaffirmed by our Lord himself.[105] Besides, the
2055 New Testament has to be read in the light of the Old. Early Christian catechesis made constant use of the Old Testament.[106] As an old saying put it, the New Testament lies hidden in the Old and the Old Testa- 1968
ment is unveiled in the New.[107]

130 Typology indicates the dynamic movement toward the fulfillment of the divine plan when "God [will] be everything to everyone."[108] Nor do the calling of the patriarchs and the exodus from Egypt, for example, lose their own value in God's plan, from the mere fact that they were intermediate stages.

V. Sacred Scripture in the Life of the Church

131 "And such is the force and power of the Word of God that it can serve the Church as her support and vigor and the children of the Church as strength for their faith, food for the soul, and a pure and lasting font of spiritual life."[109] Hence "access to Sacred Scripture ought to be open wide to the Christian faithful."[110]

132 "Therefore, the 'study of the sacred page' should be the very soul of sacred theology. The ministry of the Word, too—pastoral preaching, catechetics, and all forms of Christian instruction, among which the 94
liturgical homily should hold pride of place—is healthily nourished and thrives in holiness through the Word of Scripture."[111]

133 The Church "forcefully and specifically exhorts all the Christian faithful...to learn 'the surpassing knowledge of Jesus Christ,' by fre- 2653
quent reading of the divine Scriptures. 'Ignorance of the Scriptures is 1792
ignorance of Christ.'"[112]

[102] St. Caesaria the Younger to St. Richildis and St. Radegunde, *SCh* 345, 480. — [103] St. Thérèse of Lisieux, *ms. autob.* A 83v. — [104] Cf. *1 Cor* 10:6, 11; *Heb* 10:1; *1 Pet* 3:21. — [105] Cf. *Mk* 12:29–31. — [106] Cf. *1 Cor* 5:6–8; 10:1–11. — [107] Cf. St. Augustine, *Quaest. in Hept.* 2, 73: PL 34, 623; cf. *DV* 16.— [108] *1 Cor* 15:28. — [109] *DV* 21. — [110] *DV* 22. — [111] *DV* 24. — [112] *DV* 25; cf. *Phil* 3:8 and St. Jerome, *Commentariorum in Isaiam libri xviii*prol.: PL 24, 17b.

In Brief

134 *All Sacred Scripture is but one book, and this one book is Christ, "because all divine Scripture speaks of Christ, and all divine Scripture is fulfilled in Christ" (Hugh of St. Victor,* De arca Noe *2, 8: PL 176, 642: cf. ibid. 2, 9: PL 176, 642–643).*

135 *"The Sacred Scriptures contain the Word of God and, because they are inspired they are truly the Word of God"* (DV *24).*

136 *God is the author of Sacred Scripture because he inspired its human authors; he acts in them and by means of them. He thus gives assurance that their writings teach without error his saving truth (cf.* DV *11).*

137 *Interpretation of the inspired Scripture must be attentive above all to what God wants to reveal through the sacred authors for our salvation. What comes from the Spirit is not fully "understood except by the Spirit's action" (cf. Origen,* Hom. *in Ex. 4, 5: PG 12, 320).*

138 *The Church accepts and venerates as inspired the 46 books of the Old Testament and the 27 books of the New.*

139 *The four Gospels occupy a central place because Christ Jesus is their center.*

140 *The unity of the two Testaments proceeds from the unity of God's plan and his Revelation. The Old Testament prepares for the New and the New Testament fulfills the Old; the two shed light on each other; both are true Word of God.*

141 *"The Church has always venerated the divine Scriptures as she venerated the Body of the Lord"* (DV *21): both nourish and govern the whole Christian life. "Your word is a lamp to my feet and a light to my path"* (Ps *119:105; cf.* Isa *50:4).*

Chapter Three:
MAN'S RESPONSE TO GOD

142 *By his Revelation,* "the invisible God, from the fullness of his love, addresses men as his friends, and moves among them, in order to invite and receive them into his own company."[1] The adequate response
1102 to this invitation is faith.

143 *By faith,* man completely submits his intellect and his will to God.[2] With his whole being man gives his assent to God the revealer. Sacred Scripture calls this human response to God, the author of revelation, "the obedience of faith."[3] 2087

Article 1:
I BELIEVE

I. The Obedience of Faith

144 To obey (from the Latin *ob-audire,* to "hear or listen to") in faith is to submit freely to the word that has been heard, because its truth is guaranteed by God, who is Truth itself. Abraham is the model of such obedience offered us by Sacred Scripture. The Virgin Mary is its most perfect embodiment.

Abraham—"father of all who believe"

145 The *Letter to the Hebrews,* in its great eulogy of the faith of Israel's ancestors, lays special emphasis on Abraham's faith: "By faith, Abraham
59, 2570 obeyed when he was called to go out to a place which he was to receive as an inheritance; and he went out, not knowing where he was to go."[4] By faith, he lived as a stranger and pilgrim in the promised land.[5] By faith, Sarah was given to conceive the son of the promise. And by faith
489 Abraham offered his only son in sacrifice.[6]

146 Abraham thus fulfills the
definition of faith in *Hebrews* 11:1: 1819
"Faith is the assurance of things hoped for, the conviction of things not seen":[7] "Abraham believed God, and it was reckoned to him as righteousness."[8] Because he was "strong in his faith," Abraham became the "father of all who believe."[9]

147 The Old Testament is rich in witnesses to this faith. The *Letter to*
the Hebrews proclaims its eulogy of 839
the exemplary faith of the ancestors who "received divine approval."[10] Yet "God had foreseen something better for us": the grace of believing in his Son Jesus, "the pioneer and perfecter of our faith."[11]

Mary—"Blessed is she who believed"

148 The Virgin Mary most perfectly embodies the obedience of faith. By faith Mary welcomes the
tidings and promise brought by the 494, 2617
angel Gabriel, believing that "with God nothing will be impossible"

[1] *DV* 2; cf. *Col* 1:15; *1 Tim* 1:17; *Ex* 33:11; *Jn* 15:14–15; *Bar* 3:38 (Vulg.). — [2] Cf. *DV* 5. — [3] Cf. *Rom* 1:5; 16:26. — [4] *Heb* 11:8; cf. *Gen* 12:1–4. — [5] Cf. *Gen* 23:4. — [6] Cf. *Heb* 11:17. — [7] *Heb* 11:1. — [8] *Rom* 4:3; cf. *Gen* 15:6. — [9] *Rom* 4:11, 18; 4:20; cf. *Gen* 15:5.— [10] *Heb* 11:2, 39. — [11] *Heb* 11:40; 12:2.

and so giving her assent: "Behold I am the handmaid of the Lord; let it be [done] to me according to
506 your word."[12] Elizabeth greeted her: "Blessed is she who believed that there would be a fulfillment of what was spoken to her from the Lord."[13] It is for this faith that all generations have called Mary blessed.[14]

149 Throughout her life and until
969 her last ordeal[15] when Jesus her son died on the cross, Mary's faith never wavered. She never ceased to believe
507, 829 in the fulfillment of God's word. And so the Church venerates in Mary the purest realization of faith.

II. "I Know Whom I Have Believed"[16]

To believe in God alone

150 Faith is first of all a personal adherence of man to God. At the same time, and inseparably, it is a *free assent to the whole truth that*
222 *God has revealed.* As personal adherence to God and assent to his truth, Christian faith differs from our faith in any human person. It is right and just to entrust oneself wholly to God and to believe absolutely what he says. It would be futile and false to place such faith in a creature.[17]

To believe in Jesus Christ, the Son of God

151 For a Christian, believing in God cannot be separated from believing in the One he sent, his "beloved Son," in whom the Father is "well pleased"; God tells us to listen to him.[18] The Lord himself said to his disciples: "Believe in God, believe also in me."[19] We can believe in Jesus Christ because he is himself God, the Word made flesh: "No one has ever seen God; the only Son, who is in the bosom of the Father, he has made him known."[20] Because
he "has seen the Father," Jesus Christ 424
is the only one who knows him and can reveal him.[21]

To believe in the Holy Spirit

152 One cannot believe in Jesus Christ without sharing in his Spirit. It is the Holy Spirit who reveals
to men who Jesus is. For "no one 243, 683
can say 'Jesus is Lord,' except by the Holy Spirit,"[22] who "searches everything, even the depths of God.... No one comprehends the thoughts of God, except the Spirit of God."[23] Only God knows God completely: we believe in the Holy Spirit because he is God.

The Church never ceases to proclaim 232
her faith in one only God: Father, Son, and Holy Spirit.

III. The Characteristics of Faith

Faith is a grace

153 When St. Peter confessed that Jesus is the Christ, the Son of the living God, Jesus declared to him that 552
this revelation did not come "from flesh and blood," but from "my Father who is in heaven."[24] *Faith is a gift of God, a supernatural virtue infused by him.* "Before this faith can be exercised, man must have the grace
of God to move and assist him; he 1814
must have the interior helps of the
Holy Spirit, who moves the heart 1996
and converts it to God, who opens

[12] *Lk* 1:37–38; cf. *Gen* 18:14. — [13] *Lk* 1:45. — [14] Cf. *Lk* 1:48. — [15] Cf. *Lk* 2:35. — [16] *2 Tim* 1:12. — [17] Cf. *Jer* 17:5–6; *Ps* 40:5; 146:3–4. — [18] *Mk* 1:11; cf. 9:7. — [19] *Jn* 14:1. — [20] *Jn* 1:18. — [21] *Jn* 6:46; cf. *Mt* 11:27 — [22] *1 Cor* 12:3. — [23] *1 Cor* 2:10–11. — [24] *Mt* 16:17; cf. *Gal* 1:15; *Mt* 11:25.

2606 the eyes of the mind and 'makes it easy for all to accept and believe the truth.'"[25]

Faith is a human act

154 Believing is possible only by grace and the interior helps of the
1749 Holy Spirit. But it is no less true that believing is an authentically human act. Trusting in God and cleaving to the truths he has revealed are contrary neither to human freedom nor to human reason. Even in human relations it is not contrary to our dignity to believe what other persons tell us about themselves and their intentions or to trust their promises (for example, when a man
2126 and a woman marry) to share a communion of life with one another. If this is so, still less is it contrary to our dignity to "yield by faith the full submission of...intellect and will to God who reveals,"[26] and to share in an interior communion with him.

155 In faith, the human intellect and will cooperate with divine grace:
2008 "Believing is an act of the intellect assenting to the divine truth by command of the will moved by God through grace."[27]

Faith and understanding

156 What moves us to believe is not the fact that revealed truths appear as true and intelligible in the light of our natural reason: we
1063 believe "because of the authority of God himself who reveals them, who can neither deceive nor be deceived."[28] So "that the submission of our faith might nevertheless be in
accordance with reason, God willed 2465
that external proofs of his Revelation should be joined to the internal helps of the Holy Spirit."[29] Thus
the miracles of Christ and the saints, 548
prophecies, the Church's growth and
holiness, and her fruitfulness and 812
stability "are the most certain signs of divine Revelation, adapted to the intelligence of all"; they are "motives of credibility" (*motiva credibilitatis*), which show that the assent of faith is "by no means a blind impulse of the mind."[30]

157 Faith is *certain*. It is more certain than all human knowledge because it is founded on the very word of God who cannot lie. To be sure, revealed truths can seem obscure to human reason and experience, but "the certainty that the divine light gives is greater than that which the light of natural reason gives."[31] "Ten thousand difficulties do not make
one doubt."[32] 2088

158 "Faith *seeks understanding*":[33] it is intrinsic to faith that a believer desires to know better the One in whom he has put his faith and to understand better what He has
revealed; a more penetrating knowl- 2705
edge will in turn call forth a greater faith, increasingly set afire by love.
The grace of faith opens "the eyes of 1827
your hearts"[34] to a lively understanding of the contents of Revelation: that is, of the totality of God's plan and the mysteries of faith, of their connection with each other and with
Christ, the center of the revealed 90

[25] *DV* 5; cf. DS 377; 3010. — [26] *Dei Filius* 3: DS 3008. — [27] St. Thomas Aquinas, *STh* II–II, 2, 9; cf. *Dei Filius* 3: DS 3010. — [28] *Dei Filius* 3: DS 3008. — [29] *Dei Filius* 3: DS 3009. — [30] *Dei Filius* 3: DS 3008–10; cf. *Mk* 16:20; *Heb* 2:4. — [31] St. Thomas Aquinas, *STh* II–II, 171, 5, obj. 3. — [32] John Henry Cardinal Newman, *Apologia pro vita sua* (London: Longman, 1878), 239. — [33] St. Anselm, *Prosl. prooem.*: PL 153, 225A. — [34] *Eph* 1:18.

mystery. "The same Holy Spirit constantly perfects faith by his gifts, so that Revelation may be more and more profoundly understood."[35] In
2518 the words of St. Augustine, "I believe, in order to understand; and I understand, the better to believe."[36]

159 *Faith and science*: "Though faith is above reason, there can never be any real discrepancy between faith and reason. Since the same God who reveals mysteries and infuses faith has bestowed the light of reason on the human mind, God
283 cannot deny himself, nor can truth ever contradict truth."[37] "Consequently, methodical research in all branches of knowledge, provided it is carried out in a truly scientific manner and does not override
2293 moral laws, can never conflict with the faith, because the things of the world and the things of faith derive from the same God. The humble and persevering investigator of the secrets of nature is being led, as it were, by the hand of God in spite of himself, for it is God, the conserver of all things, who made them what they are."[38]

The freedom of faith

160 To be human, "man's response to God by faith must be free, and… therefore nobody is to be forced to
1738, 2106 embrace the faith against his will. The act of faith is of its very nature a free act."[39] "God calls men to serve him in spirit and in truth. Consequently they are bound to him in conscience, but not coerced.… This fact received its fullest manifestation in Christ Jesus."[40] Indeed, Christ invited people to faith and conversion, but never coerced them. "For he bore witness to the truth but refused to use force to impose it on those who spoke against it. His kingdom…grows by the love with which Christ, lifted up on the cross,
draws men to himself."[41] 616

The necessity of faith

161 Believing in Jesus Christ and in the One who sent him for our salvation is necessary for obtaining that
salvation.[42] "Since 'without faith it is 432, 1257
impossible to please [God]' and to attain to the fellowship of his sons, therefore without faith no one has ever attained justification, nor will anyone obtain eternal life 'but he
who endures to the end.'"[43] 846

Perseverance in faith

162 Faith is an entirely free gift that God makes to man. We can lose this priceless gift, as St. Paul indicated to St. Timothy: "Wage the
good warfare, holding faith and a 2089
good conscience. By rejecting conscience, certain persons have made shipwreck of their faith."[44] To live, grow, and persevere in the faith until the end we must nourish it with the word of God; we must beg the Lord to increase our faith;[45] it must be
"working through charity," abound- 1037, 201
ing in hope, and rooted in the faith 2573, 284
of the Church.[46]

Faith—the beginning of eternal life

163 Faith makes us taste in advance the light of the beatific vision,

[35] *DV* 5. — [36] St. Augustine, *Sermo* 43, 7, 9: PL 38, 257–258. — [37] *Dei Filius* 4: DS 3017. — [38] *GS* 36 § 1. — [39] *DH* 10; cf. CIC, can. 748 § 2. — [40] *DH* 11. — [41] *DH* 11; cf. *Jn* 18:37; 12:32. — [42] Cf. *Mk* 16:16; *Jn* 3:36; 6:40 et al. — [43] *Dei Filius* 3: DS 3012; cf. *Mt* 10:22; 24:13 and *Heb* 11:6; Council of Trent: DS 1532. — [44] *1 Tim* 1:18–19. — [45] Cf. *Mk* 9:24; *Lk* 17:5; 22:32. — [46] *Gal* 5:6; *Rom* 15:13; cf. *Jas* 2:14–26.

the goal of our journey here below.
1088 Then we shall see God "face to face," "as he is."[47] So faith is already the beginning of eternal life:

> When we contemplate the blessings of faith even now, as if gazing at a reflection in a mirror, it is as if we already possessed the wonderful things which our faith assures us we shall one day enjoy.[48]

164 Now, however, "we walk by faith, not by sight";[49] we perceive God as "in a mirror, dimly" and only "in part."[50] Even though enlightened by him in whom it believes, faith is often lived in darkness and can be put to the test. The world
2846 we live in often seems very far from the one promised us by faith. Our experiences of evil and suffering, injustice, and death, seem to contradict the Good News; they can shake
our faith and become a temptation 309
against it. 1502, 1006

165 It is then we must turn to the *witnesses of faith*: to Abraham, who "in hope...believed against hope";[51] to the Virgin Mary, who, in "her pilgrimage of faith," walked into the "night of faith"[52] in sharing the darkness of her son's suffering and death; 2719
and to so many others: "Therefore, since we are surrounded by so great a cloud of witnesses, let us also lay aside every weight, and sin which clings so closely, and let us run with perseverance the race that is set before us, looking to Jesus the pioneer and perfecter of our faith."[53]

Article 2:
WE BELIEVE

166 Faith is a personal act—the free response of the human person to the initiative of God who reveals
875 himself. But faith is not an isolated act. No one can believe alone, just as no one can live alone. You have not given yourself faith as you have not given yourself life. The believer has received faith from others and should hand it on to others. Our love for Jesus and for our neighbor impels us to speak to others about our faith. Each believer is thus a link in the great chain of believers. I cannot believe without being carried by the faith of others, and by my faith I help support others in the faith.

167 "I believe" (*Apostles' Creed*) is the faith of the Church professed
personally by each believer, princi- 1124
pally during Baptism. "We believe" (*Niceno-Constantinopolitan Creed*) is the faith of the Church confessed by the bishops assembled in council or more generally by the liturgical assembly of believers. "I believe" is also the Church, our mother, responding to God by faith as she teaches us to say both "I believe"
and "We believe." 2040

[47] *1 Cor* 13:12; *1 Jn* 3:2. — [48] St. Basil, *De Spiritu Sancto*, 15, 36: PG 32, 132; cf. St. Thomas Aquinas, *STh* II–II, 4, 1. — [49] *2 Cor* 5:7. — [50] *1 Cor* 13:12. — [51] *Rom* 4:18. — [52] *LG* 58; John Paul II, *RMat* 18. — [53] *Heb* 12:1–2.

I. "Lord, Look upon the Faith of Your Church"

168 It is the Church that believes first, and so bears, nourishes, and sustains my faith. Everywhere, it is the Church that first confesses the Lord: "Throughout the world the holy Church acclaims you," as we sing in the hymn "*Te Deum*"; with her and in her, we are won over and brought to confess: "I believe," "We believe." It is through the Church that we receive faith and new life in Christ by Baptism. In the *Rituale Romanum*, the minister of Baptism asks the catechumen: "What do you ask of God's Church?" And the an-
1253 swer is: "Faith." "What does faith offer you?" "Eternal life."[54]

169 Salvation comes from God alone; but because we receive the life of faith through the Church, she is our mother: "We believe the Church as the mother of our new birth, and not *in* the Church as if she were the
750 author of our salvation."[55] Because
2030 she is our mother, she is also our teacher in the faith.

II. The Language of Faith

170 We do not believe in formulas, but in those realities they express, which faith allows us to touch. "The believer's act [of faith] does not terminate in the propositions, but in the realities [which they express]."[56] All the same, we do approach these
186 realities with the help of formulations of the faith which permit us to express the faith and to hand it on, to celebrate it in community, to assimilate and live on it more and more.

171 The Church, "the pillar and
bulwark of the truth," faithfully 78, 857, 84
guards "the faith which was once
for all delivered to the saints." She 185
guards the memory of Christ's words; it is she who from generation to generation hands on the apostles' confession of faith.[57] As a mother who teaches her children to speak and so to understand and communicate, the Church our Mother teaches us the language of faith in order to introduce us to the understanding and the life of faith.

III. Only One Faith

172 Through the centuries, in so many languages, cultures, peoples, and nations, the Church has constantly confessed this one faith, received from the one Lord, transmitted by one Baptism, and grounded in the conviction that all people
have only one God and Father.[58] St. 813
Irenaeus of Lyons, a witness of this faith, declared:

173 "Indeed, the Church, though scattered throughout the whole world, even to the ends of the earth, having received the faith from the apostles and their disciples...guards
[this preaching and faith] with care, 830
as dwelling in but a single house, and similarly believes as if having but one soul and a single heart, and preaches, teaches, and hands on this faith with a unanimous voice, as if possessing only one mouth."[59]

174 "For though languages differ throughout the world, the content of the Tradition is one and the same. The Churches established in Germany have no other faith or Tradi-

[54] *Roman Ritual*, Rite of baptism of adults. — [55] Faustus of Riez, *De Spiritu Sancto* 1, 2: PL 62, 11. — [56] St. Thomas Aquinas, *STh* II–II, 1, 2, ad 2. — [57] *1 Tim* 3:15; *Jude* 3. — [58] Cf. *Eph* 4:4–6. — [59] St. Irenaeus, *Adv. haeres.* 1, 10, 1–2: PG 7/1, 549–552.

78 tion, nor do those of the Iberians, nor those of the Celts, nor those of the East, of Egypt, of Libya, nor those established at the center of the world...."[60] The Church's message "is true and solid, in which one and the same way of salvation appears throughout the whole world."[61]

175 "We guard with care the faith that we have received from the Church, for without ceasing, under the action of God's Spirit, this deposit of great price, as if in an excellent vessel, is constantly being renewed and causes the very vessel that contains it to be renewed."[62]

In Brief

176 *Faith is a personal adherence of the whole man to God who reveals himself. It involves an assent of the intellect and will to the self-revelation God has made through his deeds and words.*

177 *"To believe" has thus a two-fold reference: to the person and to the truth: to the truth, by trust in the person who bears witness to it.*

178 *We must believe in no one but God: the Father, the Son, and the Holy Spirit.*

179 *Faith is a supernatural gift from God. In order to believe, man needs the interior helps of the Holy Spirit.*

180 *"Believing" is a human act, conscious and free, corresponding to the dignity of the human person.*

181 *"Believing" is an ecclesial act. The Church's faith precedes, engenders, supports, and nourishes our faith. The Church is the mother of all believers. "No one can have God as Father who does not have the Church as Mother" (St. Cyprian,* De unit. *6: PL 4, 519).*

182 *We believe all "that which is contained in the word of God, written or handed down, and which the Church proposes for belief as divinely revealed" (Paul VI,* CPG, *§ 20).*

183 *Faith is necessary for salvation. The Lord himself affirms: "He who believes and is baptized will be saved; but he who does not believe will be condemned" (*Mk *16:16).*

184 *"Faith is a foretaste of the knowledge that will make us blessed in the life to come" (St. Thomas Aquinas,* Comp. theol. *1, 2).*

[60] St. Irenaeus, *Adv. haeres.* 1, 10, 1–2: PG 7/1, 552–553. — [61] St. Irenaeus, *Adv. haeres.* 5, 20, 1: PG 7/2, 1177. — [62] St. Irenaeus, *Adv. haeres.* 3, 24, 1: PG 7/1, 966.

Section Two

THE PROFESSION OF THE CHRISTIAN FAITH

THE CREEDS

185 Whoever says "I believe" says "I pledge myself to what we believe." Communion in faith needs a com-
171, 949 mon language of faith, normative for all and uniting all in the same confession of faith.

186 From the beginning, the apostolic Church expressed and handed on her faith in brief formulae for all.[1] But already early on, the Church also wanted to gather the essential elements of its faith into organic and articulated summaries, intended especially for candidates for Baptism:

> This synthesis of faith was not made to accord with human opinions, but rather what was of the greatest importance was gathered from all the Scriptures, to present the one teaching of the faith in its entirety. And just as the mustard seed contains a great number of branches in a tiny grain, so too this summary of faith encompassed in a few words the whole knowledge of the true religion contained in the Old and New Testaments.[2]

187 Such syntheses are called "professions of faith" since they summarize the faith that Christians profess. They are called "creeds" on account of what is usually their first word in Latin: *credo* ("I believe"). They are also called "symbols of faith."

188 The Greek word *symbolon* meant half of a broken object, for example, a seal presented as a token of recognition. The broken parts were placed together to verify the bearer's identity. The symbol of faith, then, is a sign of recognition and communion between believers. *Symbolon* also means a gathering, collection, or summary. A symbol of faith is a summary of the principal truths of the faith and therefore serves as the first and fundamental point of reference for catechesis.

189 The first "profession of faith" is made during Baptism. The symbol of faith is first and foremost the 1237, 232
baptismal creed. Since Baptism is given "in the name of the Father and of the Son and of the Holy Spirit,"[3] the truths of faith professed during Baptism are articulated in terms of their reference to the three persons of the Holy Trinity.

190 And so the Creed is divided into three parts: "the first part speaks of the first divine Person and the wonderful work of creation; the next speaks of the second divine Person and the mystery of his redemption of men; the final part speaks of the third divine Person, the origin and source of our sanctification."[4] These are "the three chapters of our [baptismal] seal."[5]

191 "These three parts are distinct although connected with one another. According to a comparison often used by the Fathers, we call them *articles*. Indeed, just as in our bodily members there are certain articulations which distinguish and separate them, so too in this profession of faith, the name *articles* has justly

[1] Cf. *Rom* 10:9; *1 Cor* 15:3–5, etc. — [2] St. Cyril of Jerusalem, Catech. *illum.* 5, 12: PG 33, 521–524. — [3] *Mt* 28:19. — [4] *Roman Catechism*, I, 1, 3. — [5] St. Irenaeus, *Dem. ap.* 100: SCh 62, 170.

and rightly been given to the truths we must believe particularly and distinctly."[6] In accordance with an ancient tradition, already attested to by St. Ambrose, it is also customary to reckon the articles of the Creed as *twelve*, thus symbolizing the fullness of the apostolic faith by the number of the apostles.[7]

192 Through the centuries many professions or symbols of faith have been articulated in response to the needs of the different eras: the creeds of the different apostolic and ancient Churches,[8] e.g., the *Quicumque*, also called the Athanasian Creed;[9] the professions of faith of certain Councils, such as Toledo, Lateran, Lyons, Trent;[10] or the symbols of certain popes, e.g., the *Fides Damasi*[11] or the *Credo of the People of God* of Paul VI.[12]

193 None of the creeds from the difference stages in the Church's life can be considered superseded or irrelevant. They help us today to attain and deepen the faith of all times by means of the different summaries made of it.

Among all the creeds, two occupy a special place in the Church's life:

194 *The Apostles' Creed* is so called because it is rightly considered to be a faithful summary of the apostles' faith. It is the ancient baptismal symbol of the Church of Rome. Its great authority arises from this fact: it is "the Creed of the Roman Church, the See of Peter, the first of the apostles, to which he brought the common faith."[13]

195 T*he Niceno-Constantinopolitan or Nicene Creed* draws its great authority from the fact that it stems from the first two ecumenical Councils (in 325 and 381). It remains common to all the great Churches 242, 245,
of both East and West to this day.

196 Our presentation of the faith will follow the Apostles' Creed, which constitutes, as it were, "the oldest Roman catechism." The presentation will be completed however by constant references to the Nicene Creed which is often more explicit and more detailed.

197 As on the day of our Baptism, when our whole life was entrusted to the "standard of teaching,"[14] let us embrace the Creed of our life-giving 1064
faith. To say the Credo with faith is to enter into communion with God, Father, Son, and Holy Spirit, and also with the whole Church which transmits the faith to us and in whose midst we believe:

> This Creed is the spiritual seal, 1274
> our hearts's meditation and an ever-present guardian; it is, unquestionably, the treasure of our soul.[15]

[6] *Roman Catechism*, I, 1, 4. — [7] Cf. St. Ambrose, *Expl. symb.* 8. — [8] Cf. DS 1–64. — [9] Cf. DS 75–76. — [10] Cf. DS 525–541; 800–802; 851–861; 1862–1870. — [11] Cf. DS 71–72. — [12] Paul VI, *CPG* (1968). — [13] St. Ambrose, *Expl. symb.* 7: PL 17, 1196. — [14] *Rom* 6:17. — [15] St. Ambrose, *Expl. symb.* 1: PL 17, 1193.

Chapter One:
I BELIEVE IN GOD THE FATHER

198 Our profession of faith begins with *God*, for God is the First and the Last,[1] the beginning and the end of everything. The Credo begins with God the *Father*, for the Father is the first divine person of the Most Holy Trinity; our Creed begins with the creation of heaven and earth, for creation is the beginning and the foundation of all God's works.

Article 1:
"I BELIEVE IN GOD THE FATHER ALMIGHTY, CREATOR OF HEAVEN AND EARTH"

Paragraph 1
I Believe in God

199 "I believe in God": this first affirmation of the Apostles' Creed is also the most fundamental. The whole Creed speaks of God, and when it also speaks of man and of the world it does so in relation to God. The other articles of the Creed all depend on the first, just as the remaining Commandments make the
2083 first explicit. The other articles help us to know God better as he revealed himself progressively to men. "The faithful first profess their belief in God."[2]

I. "I Believe in One God"

200 These are the words with which the Niceno-Constantinopolitan Creed begins. The confession of God's one-
2085 ness, which has its roots in the divine revelation of the Old Covenant, is inseparable from the profession of God's existence and is equally fundamental. God is unique; there is only one God: "The Christian faith confesses that God is one in nature, substance, and essence."[3]

201 To Israel, his chosen, God revealed himself as the only One:
"Hear, O Israel: The Lord our God 2083
is one Lord; and you shall love the Lord your God with all your heart, and with all your soul, and with all your might."[4] Through the prophets, God calls Israel and all nations to turn to him, the one and only God: "Turn to me and be saved, all the ends of the earth! For I am God, and there is no other.... To me every knee shall bow, every tongue shall swear. 'Only in the Lord, it shall be said of me, are righteousness and strength.'"[5]

202 Jesus himself affirms that God is "the one Lord" whom you must love "with all your heart, and with all your soul, and with all your mind, and with all your strength."[6] At the same time Jesus gives us to understand that he himself is "the
Lord."[7] To confess that Jesus is Lord 446
is distinctive of Christian faith. This

[1] Cf. *Isa* 44:6. — [2] *Roman Catechism*, I, 2, 2. — [3] *Roman Catechism*, I, 2, 2. — [4] *Deut* 6:4–5. — [5] *Isa* 45:22–24; cf. *Phil* 2:10–11. — [6] *Mk* 12:29–30. — [7] Cf. *Mk* 12:35–37.

is not contrary to belief in the One God. Nor does believing in the Holy Spirit as "Lord and giver of life" in
152 troduce any division into the One God:

42 We firmly believe and confess without reservation that there is only one true God, eternal, infinite (immensus) and unchangeable, incomprehensible, almighty, and ineffable, the Father and the Son and the Holy Spirit; three persons indeed, but one essence, substance or nature entirely simple.[8]

II. God Reveals His Name

203 God revealed himself to his people Israel by making his name known to them. A name expresses a person's essence and identity and the meaning of this person's life.
2143 God has a name; he is not an anonymous force. To disclose one's name is to make oneself known to others; in a way it is to hand oneself over by becoming accessible, capable of being known more intimately and addressed personally.

204 God revealed himself progressively and under different names to his people, but the revelation that proved to be the fundamental one for both the Old and the New Covenants was the revelation of the
63 divine name to Moses in the theophany of the burning bush, on the threshold of the Exodus and of the covenant on Sinai.

The living God

205 God calls Moses from the midst of a bush that burns without being consumed: "I am the God of
2575 your father, the God of Abraham, the God of Isaac, and the God of Jacob."[9] God is the God of the fathers, the One who had called and guided the patriarchs in their wanderings. He is the faithful and compassionate God who remembers them and his promises; he comes to free their descendants from slavery. He is the God who, from beyond space and time, can do this and wills to do it,
the God who will put his almighty 268
power to work for this plan.

"I Am who I Am"

> Moses said to God, "If I come to the people of Israel and say to them, 'The God of your fathers has sent me to you', and they ask me, 'What is his name?' what shall I say to them?" God said to Moses, "I AM WHO I AM." And he said, "Say this to the people of Israel, 'I Am has sent me to you'… this is my name for ever, and thus I am to be remembered throughout all generations."[10]

206 In revealing his mysterious name, YHWH ("I AM HE WHO IS," "I AM WHO AM" or "I AM WHO I AM"), God says who he is and by what name he is to be called. This divine name is mysterious just as God is mystery. It is at once a name revealed and something like the refusal of a name, and hence it better expresses God as what he is—infinitely above everything that we can understand or say: he is the "hidden God," his name is ineffable, and he is the God
who makes himself close to men.[11] 43

207 By revealing his name God at the same time reveals his faithfulness which is from everlasting to everlasting, valid for the past ("I am the God of your fathers"), as for the future ("I will be with you").[12] God, who reveals his name as "I AM,"

[8] Lateran Council IV: DS 800. — [9] *Ex* 3:6. — [10] *Ex* 3:13–15. — [11] Cf. *Isa* 45:15; *Judg* 13:18. — [12] *Ex* 3:6, 12.

reveals himself as the God who is always there, present to his people in order to save them.

724 **208** Faced with God's fascinating and mysterious presence, man discovers his own insignificance. Before the burning bush, Moses takes off his sandals and veils his face in the presence of God's holiness.[13] Before the glory of the thrice-holy God, Isaiah cries out: "Woe is me! I am lost; for I am a man of unclean lips."[14] Before the divine signs wrought by Jesus, Peter exclaims: "Depart from me, for I am a sinful
448 man, O Lord."[15] But because God is holy, he can forgive the man who realizes that he is a sinner before him: "I will not execute my fierce anger… for I am God and not man, the Holy One in your midst."[16] The apostle
388 John says likewise: "We shall…reassure our hearts before him whenever our hearts condemn us; for God is greater than our hearts, and he knows everything."[17]

209 Out of respect for the holiness of God, the people of Israel do not pronounce his name. In the reading of Sacred Scripture, the revealed name (YHWH) is replaced by the divine title "LORD" (in Hebrew *Adonai*, in Greek *Kyrios*). It is under this title that the divinity of Jesus will be acclaimed: "Jesus is
446 LORD."

"A God merciful and gracious"

210 After Israel's sin, when the people had turned away from God to worship the golden calf, God hears Moses' prayer of intercession
and agrees to walk in the midst of an 2116, 2577
unfaithful people, thus demonstrating his love.[18] When Moses asks to see his glory, God responds "I will make all my goodness pass before you, and will proclaim before you my name 'the LORD' [YHWH]."[19] Then the Lord passes before Moses and proclaims, "YHWH, YHWH, a God merciful and gracious, slow to anger, and abounding in steadfast love and faithfulness"; Moses then confesses that the LORD is a forgiving God.[20]

211 The divine name, "I Am" or "He Is," expresses God's faithfulness: despite the faithlessness of men's sin and the punishment it deserves, he keeps "steadfast love for thousands."[21] By going so far as to give
up his own Son for us, God reveals 604
that he is "rich in mercy."[22] By giving his life to free us from sin, Jesus reveals that he himself bears the divine name: "When you have lifted up the Son of man, then you will realize that 'I Am.'"[23]

God alone IS

212 Over the centuries, Israel's faith was able to manifest and deepen realization of the riches contained in the revelation of the divine name. God is unique; there are no other gods besides him.[24] He transcends the world and history. He made heaven and earth: "They will
perish, but you endure; they will all 42
wear out like a garment…but you are the same, and your years have no
end."[25] In God "there is no variation 469, 2086
or shadow due to change."[26] God is "He who Is," from everlasting to ev-

[13] Cf. *Ex* 3:5–6. — [14] *Isa* 6:5. — [15] *Lk* 5:8. — [16] *Hos* 11:9. — [17] *1 Jn* 3:19–20. — [18] Cf. *Ex* 32; 33:12–17. — [19] *Ex* 33:18–19. — [20] *Ex* 34:5–6; cf. 34:9. — [21] *Ex* 34:7. — [22] *Eph* 2:4. — [23] *Jn* 8:28 (Gk.) — [24] Cf. *Isa* 44:6. — [25] *Ps* 102:26–27 — [26] *Jas* 1:17.

erlasting, and as such remains ever faithful to himself and to his promises.

213 The revelation of the ineffable
name "I Am who Am" contains then
the truth that God alone IS. The
Greek Septuagint translation of the
Hebrew Scriptures, and following it
the Church's Tradition, understood
the divine name in this sense: God
is the fullness of Being and of every
perfection, without origin and with
41 out end. All creatures receive all that
they are and have from him; but he
alone *is* his very being, and he is of
himself everything that he is.

III. God, "He Who *Is*," Is Truth and Love

214 God, "He who is," revealed
himself to Israel as the one "abounding in steadfast love and faithfulness."[27] These two terms express
summarily the riches of the divine
name. In all his works God displays
1062 not only his kindness, goodness,
grace, and steadfast love, but also his
trustworthiness, constancy, faithfulness, and truth. "I give thanks to
your name for your steadfast love
and your faithfulness."[28] He is the
Truth, for "God is light and in him
there is no darkness"; "God is love,"
as the apostle John teaches.[29]

God is truth

215 "The sum of your word is
truth; and every one of your righteous ordinances endures forever."[30]
"And now, O Lord God, you are
2465 God, and your words are true;"[31]
this is why God's promises always
1063, 156 come true.[32] God is Truth itself,
whose words cannot deceive. This is
why one can abandon oneself in full
trust to the truth and faithfulness of
his word in all things. The beginning
of sin and of man's fall was due to
a lie of the tempter who induced
doubt of God's word, kindness, and
faithfulness. 397

216 God's truth is his wisdom,
which commands the whole created
order and governs the world.[33] God,
who alone made heaven and earth, 295
can alone impart true knowledge 32
of every created thing in relation to
himself.[34]

217 God is also truthful when he
reveals himself—the teaching that
comes from God is "true instruction."[35] When he sends his Son into
the world it will be "to bear witness
to the truth":[36] "We know that the
Son of God has come and has given 851
us understanding, to know him who 2466
is true."[37]

God is love

218 In the course of its history,
Israel was able to discover that God
had only one reason to reveal himself
to them, a single motive for choosing them from among all peoples
as his special possession: his sheer
gratuitous love.[38] And thanks to the 295
prophets Israel understood that it
was again out of love that God never
stopped saving them and pardoning
their unfaithfulness and sins.[39]

219 God's love for Israel is compared to a father's love for his son. 239
His love for his people is stronger
than a mother's for her children. 796, 458
God loves his people more than a

[27] *Ex* 34:6. — [28] *Ps* 138:2; cf. *Ps* 85:11. — [29] *1 Jn* 1:5; 4:8. — [30] *Ps* 119:160. — [31] *2 Sam* 7:28. — [32] Cf. *Deut* 7:9. — [33] Cf. *Wis* 13:1–9. — [34] Cf. *Ps* 115:15; *Wis* 7:17–21. — [35] *Mal* 2:6. — [36] *Jn* 18:37. — [37] *1 Jn* 5:20; cf. *Jn* 17:3. — [38] Cf. *Deut* 4:37; 7:8; 10:15. — [39] Cf. *Isa* 43:1–7; *Hos* 2.

bridegroom his beloved; his love will be victorious over even the worst infidelities and will extend to his most precious gift: "God so loved the world that he gave his only Son."[40]

220 God's love is "everlasting":[41] "For the mountains may depart and the hills be removed, but my steadfast love shall not depart from you."[42] Through Jeremiah, God declares to his people, "I have loved you with an everlasting love; therefore I have continued my faithfulness to you."[43]

221 But St. John goes even further when he affirms that "God is
733 love":[44] God's very being is love. By sending his only Son and the Spirit
851 of Love in the fullness of time, God has revealed his innermost secret:[45]
257 God himself is an eternal exchange of love, Father, Son, and Holy Spirit, and he has destined us to share in that exchange.

IV. The Implications of Faith in One God

222 Believing in God, the only One, and loving him with all our being has enormous consequences for our whole life.

400 **223** *It means coming to know God's greatness and majesty*: "Behold, God is great, and we know him not."[46] Therefore, we must "serve God first."[47]

2637 **224** *It means living in thanksgiving*: if God is the only One, everything we are and have comes from him: "What have you that you did not receive?"[48] "What shall I render to the Lord for all his bounty to me?"[49]

225 *It means knowing the unity and true dignity of all men*: Everyone 356, 360
is made in the image and likeness of God.[50] 1700, 1934

226 *It means making good use of created things*: faith in God, the only 339, 2402
One, leads us to use everything that is not God only insofar as it brings us closer to him, and to detach ourselves from it insofar as it turns us away from him: 2415

> My Lord and my God, take from me everything that distances me from you.
> My Lord and my God, give me everything that brings me closer to you.
> My Lord and my God, detach me from myself to give my all to you.[51]

227 It means trusting God in every circumstance, even in adversity. A prayer of St. Teresa of Jesus wonderfully expresses this trust: 313, 2090

> Let nothing trouble you / Let nothing frighten you
> Everything passes / God never changes
> Patience / Obtains all
> Whoever has God / Wants for nothing 2830
> God alone is enough.[52] 1723

In Brief

228 *"Hear, O Israel, the* Lord *our God is one* Lord*…"* (Deut *6:4;* Mk *12:29). "The supreme being must be unique, without equal.… If God is*

[40] *Jn* 3:16; cf. *Hos* 11:1; *Isa* 49:14–15; 62:4–5; *Ezek* 16; *Hos* 11. — [41] *Isa* 54:8. — [42] *Isa* 54:10; cf. 54:8. — [43] *Jer* 31:3. — [44] *1 Jn* 4:8, 16. — [45] Cf. *1 Cor* 2:7–16; *Eph* 3:9–12. — [46] *Job* 36:26. — [47] St. Joan of Arc. — [48] *1 Cor* 4:7. — [49] *Ps* 116:12. — [50] *Gen* 1:26. — [51] St. Nicholas of Flüe; cf. *Mt* 5:29–30; 16:24–26 — [52] St. Teresa of Jesus, *Poesías* 30, in *The Collected Works of St. Teresa of Avila*, vol. III, tr. by K. Kavanaugh, OCD, and O. Rodriguez, OCD (Washington DC: Institute of Carmelite Studies, 1985), 386 no. 9, tr. by John Wall.

not one, he is not God" (Tertullian, Adv. Marc., *1, 3, 5: PL 2, 274).*

229 *Faith in God leads us to turn to him alone as our first origin and our ultimate goal, and neither to prefer anything to him nor to substitute anything for him.*

230 *Even when he reveals himself, God remains a mystery beyond words: "If you understood him, it would not be God" (St. Augustine,* Sermo *52, 6, 16: PL 38:360 and* Sermo *117, 3, 5: PL 38, 663).*

231 *The God of our faith has revealed himself as He who is; and he has made himself known as "abounding in steadfast love and faithfulness"* (Ex *34:6). God's very being is Truth and Love.*

Paragraph 2
The Father

I. "In the Name of the Father and of the Son and of the Holy Spirit"

232 Christians are baptized "in the name of the Father and of the Son and of the Holy Spirit."[53] Before receiving the sacrament, they re-
189, 1223 spond to a three-part question when asked to confess the Father, the Son, and the Spirit: "I do." "The faith of all Christians rests on the Trinity."[54]

233 Christians are baptized in the *name* of the Father and of the Son and of the Holy Spirit: not in their *names*,[55] for there is only one God, the almighty Father, his only Son, and the Holy Spirit: the Most Holy Trinity.

234 The mystery of the Most Holy Trinity is the central mystery of Christian faith and life. It is the mystery of God in himself. It is
therefore the source of all the other 2157
mysteries of faith, the light that enlightens them. It is the most fundamental and essential teaching in the "hierarchy of the truths of faith."[56] The whole history of salvation is
identical with the history of the way 90
and the means by which the one
true God, Father, Son, and Holy 1449
Spirit, reveals himself to men "and reconciles and unites with himself those who turn away from sin."[57]

235 This paragraph expounds briefly (I) how the mystery of the Blessed Trinity was revealed, (II) how the Church has articulated the doctrine of the faith regarding this mystery, and (III) how, by the divine missions of the Son and the Holy Spirit, God the Father fulfills the "plan of his loving goodness" of creation, redemption, and sanctification.

236 The Fathers of the Church distinguish between theology (*theo-*
logia) and economy (*oikonomia*). 1066
"Theology" refers to the mystery of God's inmost life within the Blessed Trinity and "economy" to all the works by which God reveals himself and communicates his life. Through the *oikonomia* the theologia is revealed to us; but conversely, the *theologia* illuminates the whole
oikonomia. God's works reveal who 259
he is in himself; the mystery of his inmost being enlightens our understanding of all his works. So it is, analogously, among human persons. A person discloses himself in

[53] *Mt* 28:19. — [54] St. Caesarius of Arles, *Sermo* 9, *Exp. symb.*: CCL 103, 47. — [55] Cf. Profession of faith of Pope Vigilius I (552): DS 415. — [56] *GCD* 43. — [57] *GCD* 47.

his actions, and the better we know a person, the better we understand his actions.

50 **237** The Trinity is a mystery of faith in the strict sense, one of the "mysteries that are hidden in God, which can never be known unless they are revealed by God."[58] To be sure, God has left traces of his Trinitarian being in his work of creation and in his Revelation throughout the Old Testament. But his inmost Being as Holy Trinity is a mystery that is inaccessible to reason alone or even to Israel's faith before the Incarnation of God's Son and the sending of the Holy Spirit.

II. The Revelation of God as Trinity

The Father revealed by the Son

238 Many religions invoke God as "Father." The deity is often considered the "father of gods and of men." In Israel, God is called "Father" inasmuch as he is Creator of the world.[59] Even more, God is Father because of the covenant and the gift of the law to Israel, "his first-born son."[60] God is also called the Father of the king of Israel. Most especially he is "the Father of the poor," of the orphaned
2443 and the widowed, who are under his loving protection.[61]

239 By calling God "Father," the language of faith indicates two main things: that God is the first origin of everything and transcendent authority; and that he is at the same time goodness and loving care for all his children. God's parental tenderness can also be expressed by the image of motherhood,[62] which emphasizes God's immanence, the intimacy between Creator and creature. The language of faith thus draws on the human experience of parents, who are in a way the first representatives of God for man. But this experience also tells us that human parents are fallible and can disfigure the face of fatherhood and motherhood. We ought therefore to recall that God transcends the human distinction between the sexes. He is neither man nor woman: he is God. He also transcends human fatherhood and motherhood, although 370, 2779
he is their origin and standard:[63] no one is father as God is Father.

240 Jesus revealed that God is Father in an unheard-of sense: he is Father not only in being Creator; he is eternally Father in relation to his only Son, who is eternally Son only 2780
in relation to his Father: "No one knows the Son except the Father, and no one knows the Father except 441–445
the Son and any one to whom the Son chooses to reveal him."[64]

241 For this reason the apostles confess Jesus to be the Word: "In the beginning was the Word, and the Word was with God, and the Word was God"; as "the image of the invisible God"; as the "radiance of the glory of God and the very stamp of his nature."[65]

242 Following this apostolic tradition, the Church confessed at the first ecumenical council at Nicaea (325) that the Son is "consubstantial" with the Father, that is, one only God with him.[66] The second

[58] *Dei Filius* 4: DS 3015. — [59] Cf. *Deut* 32:6; *Mal* 2:10. — [60] *Ex* 4:22. — [61] Cf. *2 Sam* 7:14; *Ps* 68:6. — [62] Cf. *Isa* 66:13; *Ps* 131:2 — [63] Cf. *Ps* 27:10; *Eph* 3:14; *Isa* 49:15. — [64] *Mt* 11:27. — [65] *Jn* 1:1; *Col* 1:15; *Heb* 1:3. — [66] The English phrases "of one being" and "one in being" translate the Greek word *homoousios,* which was rendered in Latin by *consubstantialis.*

465 ecumenical council , held at Constantinople in 381, kept this expression in its formulation of the Nicene Creed and confessed "the only-begotten Son of God, eternally begotten of the Father, light from light, true God from true God, begotten not made, consubstantial with the Father."[67]

The Father and the Son revealed by the Spirit

243 Before his Passover, Jesus announced the sending of "anoth-
683 er Paraclete" (Advocate), the Holy Spirit. At work since creation, having previously "spoken through the prophets," the Spirit will now be
2780 with and in the disciples, to teach them and guide them "into all the
687 truth."[68] The Holy Spirit is thus revealed as another divine person with Jesus and the Father.

244 The eternal origin of the Holy Spirit is revealed in his mission in time. The Spirit is sent to the apostles and to the Church both by the Father in the name of the Son, and by the Son in person, once he had returned to the Father.[69] The sending of the person of the Spirit after Jesus' glorification[70] reveals in its fullness
732 the mystery of the Holy Trinity.

152 **245** The apostolic faith concerning the Spirit was confessed by the second ecumenical council at Constantinople (381): "We believe in the Holy Spirit, the Lord and giver of life, who proceeds from the Father."[71] By this confession, the Church recognizes the Father as "the source and origin of the whole divinity."[72] But the eternal origin of the Spirit is not unconnected with the Son's origin: "The Holy Spirit, the third person of the Trinity, is God, one and equal with the Father and the Son, of the same substance and also of the same nature.... Yet he is not called the Spirit of the Father alone,...but the Spirit of both the Father and the Son."[73] The Creed of the Church from the Council of Constantinople confesses: "With the Father and the Son, he is worshipped and glorified."[74] 685

246 The Latin tradition of the Creed confesses that the Spirit "proceeds from the Father and the Son (filioque)." The Council of Florence in 1438 explains: "The Holy Spirit is eternally from Father and Son; He has his nature and subsistence at once (simul) from the Father and the Son. He proceeds eternally from both as from one principle and through one spiration.... And, since the Father has through generation given to the only-begotten Son everything that belongs to the Father, except being Father, the Son has also eternally from the Father, from whom he is eternally born, that the Holy Spirit proceeds from the Son."[75]

247 The affirmation of the filioque does not appear in the Creed confessed in 381 at Constantinople. But Pope St. Leo I, following an ancient Latin and Alexandrian tradition, had already confessed it dogmatically in 447,[76] even before

[67] Niceno-Constantinopolitan Creed; cf. DS 150. — [68] Cf. *Gen* 1:2; Nicene Creed (DS 150); *Jn* 14:17, 26; 16:13. — [69] Cf. *Jn* 14:26; 15:26; 16:14. — [70] Cf. *Jn* 7:39. — [71] Nicene Creed; cf. DS 150. — [72] Council of Toledo VI (638): DS 490. — [73] Council of Toledo XI (675): DS 527. — [74] Nicene Creed; cf. DS 150. — [75] Council of Florence (1439): DS 1300–1301. — [76] Cf. Leo I, *Quam laudabiliter* (447): DS 284.

Rome, in 451 at the Council of Chalcedon, came to recognize and receive the Symbol of 381. The use of this formula in the Creed was gradually admitted into the Latin liturgy (between the eighth and eleventh centuries). The introduction of the filioque into the Niceno-Constantinopolitan Creed by the Latin liturgy constitutes moreover, even today, a point of disagreement with the Orthodox Churches.

248 At the outset the Eastern tradition expresses the Father's character as first origin of the Spirit. By confessing the Spirit as he "who proceeds from the Father," it affirms that he comes from the Father through the Son.[77] The Western tradition expresses first the consubstantial communion between Father and Son, by saying that the Spirit proceeds from the Father and the Son (filioque). It says this, "legitimately and with good reason,"[78] for the eternal order of the divine persons in their consubstantial communion implies that the Father, as "the principle without principle,"[79] is the first origin of the Spirit, but also that as Father of the only Son, he is, with the Son, the single principle from which the Holy Spirit proceeds.[80] This legitimate complementarity, provided it does not become rigid, does not affect the identity of faith in the reality of the same mystery confessed.

III. The Holy Trinity in the Teaching of the Faith

The formation of the Trinitarian dogma

249 From the beginning, the revealed truth of the Holy Trinity has
been at the very root of the Church's
living faith, principally by means of
Baptism. It finds its expression in 683
the rule of baptismal faith, formulated in the preaching, catechesis, 189
and prayer of the Church. Such formulations are already found in the apostolic writings, such as this salutation taken up in the Eucharistic liturgy: "The grace of the Lord Jesus Christ and the love of God and the fellowship of the Holy Spirit be with you all."[81]

250 During the first centuries the Church sought to clarify its Trinitarian faith, both to deepen its own understanding of the faith and to
defend it against the errors that were 94
deforming it. This clarification was the work of the early councils, aided by the theological work of the Church Fathers and sustained by the Christian people's sense of the faith.

251 In order to articulate the dogma of the Trinity, the Church had to develop its own terminology with the help of certain notions of philosophical origin: "substance," "person" or "hypostasis," "relation," and so on. In doing this, she did not submit the faith to human wisdom, but gave a new and unprecedented meaning to these terms, which from then on would be used to signify an ineffable mystery, "infinitely beyond all that we can humanly understand."[82] 170

252 The Church uses (I) the term "substance" (rendered also at times by "essence" or "nature") to desig-

[77] *Jn* 15:26; cf. *AG* 2. — [78] Council of Florence (1439): DS 1302. — [79] Council of Florence (1442): DS 1331. — [80] Cf. Council of Lyons II (1274): DS 850. — [81] *2 Cor* 13:13; cf. *1 Cor* 12:4–6; *Eph* 4:4–6. — [82] Paul VI, *CPG* § 2.

nate the divine being in its unity, (II) the term "person" or "hypostasis" to designate the Father, Son, and Holy Spirit in the real distinction among them, and (III) the term "relation" to designate the fact that their distinction lies in the relationship of each to the others.

The dogma of the Holy Trinity

253 *The Trinity is One.* We do not confess three Gods, but one God in
2789 three persons, the "consubstantial Trinity."[83] The divine persons do not share the one divinity among themselves but each of them is God whole and entire: "The Father is that which the Son is, the Son that which the Father is, the Father and the Son that which the Holy Spirit is, i.e., by nature one God."[84] In the words of the Fourth Lateran Council (1215): "Each of the persons is that supreme reality, viz., the divine substance, es
590 sence or nature."[85]

254 *The divine persons are really distinct from one another.* "God is one but not solitary."[86] "Father," "Son," "Holy Spirit" are not simply
468, 689 names designating modalities of the divine being, for they are really distinct from one another: "He is not the Father who is the Son, nor is the Son he who is the Father, nor is the Holy Spirit he who is the Father or the Son."[87] They are distinct from one another in their relations of origin: "It is the Father who generates, the Son who is begotten, and the Holy Spirit who proceeds."[88] The divine Unity is Triune.

255 *The divine persons are relative to one another.* Because it does not divide the divine unity, the real distinction of the persons from one another resides solely in the relationships which relate them to one another: "In the relational names of the persons the Father is related to the Son, the Son to the Father, and the Holy Spirit to both. While they
are called three persons in view of 240
their relations, we believe in one nature or substance."[89] Indeed "everything (in them) is one where there is no opposition of relationship."[90] "Because of that unity the Father is wholly in the Son and wholly in the Holy Spirit; the Son is wholly in the Father and wholly in the Holy Spirit; the Holy Spirit is wholly in the Father and wholly in the Son."[91]

256 St. Gregory of Nazianzus, also called "the Theologian," entrusts this
summary of Trinitarian faith to the 236, 984
catechumens of Constantinople: 84

> Above all guard for me this great deposit of faith for which I live and fight, which I want to take with me as a companion, and which makes me bear all evils and despise all pleasures: I mean the profession of faith in the Father and the Son and the Holy Spirit. I entrust it to you today. By it I am soon going to plunge you into water and raise you up from it. I give it to you as the companion and patron of your whole life. I give you but one divinity and power, existing one in three, and containing the three in a distinct way. Divinity without disparity of substance or nature, without superior degree that raises up or inferior degree that casts down…

[83] Council of Constantinople II (553): DS 421. — [84] Council of Toledo XI (675): DS 530:26. — [85] Lateran Council IV (1215): DS 804. — [86] *Fides Damasi*: DS 71. — [87] Council of Toledo XI (675): DS 530:25. — [88] Lateran Council IV (1215): DS 804. — [89] Council of Toledo XI (675): DS 528. — [90] Council of Florence (1442): DS 1330. — [91] Council of Florence (1442): DS 1331.

> the infinite co-naturality of three infinites. Each person considered in himself is entirely God...the three considered together.... I have not even begun to think of unity when the Trinity bathes me in its splendor. I have not even begun to think of the Trinity when unity grasps me.... [92]

IV. The Divine Works and the Trinitarian Missions

257 "O blessed light, O Trinity and first Unity!"[93] God is eternal blessedness, undying life, unfading light. God is love: Father, Son, and
221 Holy Spirit. God freely wills to communicate the glory of his blessed
758 life. Such is the "plan of his loving kindness," conceived by the Father before the foundation of the world, in his beloved Son: "He destined us in love to be his sons" and "to be conformed to the image of his Son," through "the spirit of sonship."[94] This plan is a "grace [which] was given to us in Christ Jesus before the ages began," stemming immediately from Trinitarian love.[95] It unfolds in the work of creation, the whole history of salvation after the fall,
292 and the missions of the Son and the Spirit, which are continued in the
850 mission of the Church.[96]

258 The whole divine economy is the common work of the three divine persons. For as the Trinity has only one and the same nature, so too does it have only one and the same operation: "The Father, the Son, and the Holy Spirit are not three principles of creation but one princi-
686 ple."[97] However each divine person performs the common work according to his unique personal property. Thus the Church confesses, following the New Testament, "one God and Father from whom all things are, and one Lord Jesus Christ, through whom all things are, and one Holy Spirit in whom all things are."[98] It is above all the divine missions of the Son's Incarnation and the gift of the Holy Spirit that show forth the properties of the divine persons.

259 Being a work at once com- 236
mon and personal, the whole divine economy makes known both what is proper to the divine persons and their one divine nature. Hence the whole Christian life is a communion with each of the divine persons, without in any way separating them. Everyone who glorifies the Father does so through the Son in the Holy Spirit; everyone who follows Christ does so because the Father draws him and the Spirit moves him.[99]

260 The ultimate end of the whole divine economy is the entry of God's creatures into the perfect unity of the Blessed Trinity.[100] But even now
we are called to be a dwelling for the 1050, 1721
Most Holy Trinity: "If a man loves
me," says the Lord, "he will keep my 1997
word, and my Father will love him, and we will come to him, and make our home with him":[101]

> O my God, Trinity whom I adore, 2565
> help me forget myself entirely so to establish myself in you, unmovable and peaceful as if my soul were already in eternity. May nothing be able to trouble my peace or make me leave you, O my unchanging God,

[92] St. Gregory of Nazianzus, *Oratio* 40, 41: PG 36, 417. — [93] *LH*, Hymn for Evening Prayer. — [94] *Eph* 1:4–5, 9; *Rom* 8:15, 29. — [95] *2 Tim* 1:9–10. — [96] Cf. *AG* 2–9. — [97] Council of Florence (1442): DS 1331; cf. Council of Constantinople II (553): DS 421. — [98] Council of Constantinople II: DS 421. — [99] Cf. *Jn* 6:44; *Rom* 8:14. — [100] Cf. *Jn* 17:21–23. — [101] *Jn* 14:23.

but may each minute bring me more deeply into your mystery! Grant my soul peace. Make it your heaven, your beloved dwelling and the place of your rest. May I never abandon you there, but may I be there, whole and entire, completely vigilant in my faith, entirely adoring, and wholly given over to your creative action.[102]

In Brief

261 *The mystery of the Most Holy Trinity is the central mystery of the Christian faith and of Christian life. God alone can make it known to us by revealing himself as Father, Son, and Holy Spirit.*

262 *The Incarnation of God's Son reveals that God is the eternal Father and that the Son is consubstantial with the Father, which means that, in the Father and with the Father, the Son is one and the same God.*

263 *The mission of the Holy Spirit, sent by the Father in the name of the Son (*Jn *14:26) and by the Son "from the Father" (*Jn *15:26), reveals that, with them, the Spirit is one and the same God. "With the Father and the Son he is worshipped and glorified" (Nicene Creed).*

264 *"The Holy Spirit proceeds from the Father as the first principle and, by the eternal gift of this to the Son, from the communion of both the Father and the Son" (St. Augustine,* De Trin. *15, 26, 47: PL 42:1095).*

265 *By the grace of Baptism "in the name of the Father and of the Son and of the Holy Spirit," we are called to share in the life of the Blessed Trinity, here on earth in the obscurity of faith, and after death in eternal light (Cf. Paul VI, CPG § 9).*

266 *"Now this is the Catholic faith: We worship one God in the Trinity and the Trinity in unity, without either confusing the persons or dividing the substance; for the person of the Father is one, the Son's is another, the Holy Spirit's another; but the Godhead of the Father, Son, and Holy Spirit is one, their glory equal, their majesty coeternal" (Athanasian Creed; DS 75; ND 16).*

267 *Inseparable in what they are, the divine persons are also inseparable in what they do. But within the single divine operation each shows forth what is proper to him in the Trinity, especially in the divine missions of the Son's Incarnation and the gift of the Holy Spirit.*

Paragraph 3
The Almighty

268 Of all the divine attributes, only God's omnipotence is named in the Creed: to confess this power has great bearing on our lives. We believe that his might is *universal,* 222
for God who created everything also rules everything and can do everything. God's power is *loving,* for he is our Father, and *mysterious,* for only faith can discern it when it "is made perfect in weakness."[103]

"He does whatever he pleases"[104]

[102] Prayer of Blessed Elizabeth of the Trinity. — [103] Cf. *Gen* 1:1; *Jn* 1:3; *Mt* 6:9; *2 Cor* 12:9; cf. *1 Cor* 1:18. — [104] *Ps* 115:3.

269 The Holy Scriptures repeatedly confess the *universal* power of God. He is called the "Mighty One of Jacob," the "LORD of hosts," the "strong and mighty" one. If God is almighty "in heaven and on earth," it is because he made them.[105] Nothing is impossible with God, who disposes his works according to his will.[106] He is the Lord of the universe, whose order he established and which remains wholly subject to him and at his disposal. He is mas-
303 ter of history, governing hearts and events in keeping with his will: "It is always in your power to show great strength, and who can withstand the strength of your arm?"[107]

"You are merciful to all, for you can do all things"[108]

270 God is the *Father* Almighty, whose fatherhood and power shed light on one another: God reveals his fatherly omnipotence by the way he
2777 takes care of our needs; by the filial adoption that he gives us ("I will be a father to you, and you shall be my sons and daughters, says the Lord Almighty."):[109] finally by his infinite mercy, for he displays his power at
1441 its height by freely forgiving sins.

271 God's almighty power is in no way arbitrary: "In God, power, essence, will, intellect, wisdom, and justice are all identical. Nothing therefore can be in God's power which could not be in his just will or his wise intellect."[110]

The mystery of God's apparent powerlessness

272 Faith in God the Father Almighty can be put to the test by the experience of evil and suffering. God can sometimes seem to be ab-
sent and incapable of stopping evil. 309
But in the most mysterious way God the Father has revealed his almighty power in the voluntary hu-
miliation and Resurrection of his 412
Son, by which he conquered evil. Christ crucified is thus "the power of God and the wisdom of God.
For the foolishness of God is wis- 609
er than men, and the weakness of
God is stronger than men."[111] It is in 648
Christ's Resurrection and exaltation that the Father has shown forth "the immeasurable greatness of his power in us who believe."[112]

273 Only faith can embrace the mysterious ways of God's almighty power. This faith glories in its weaknesses in order to draw to itself
Christ's power.[113] The Virgin Mary 148
is the supreme model of this faith, for she believed that "nothing will be impossible with God," and was able to magnify the Lord: "For he who is mighty has done great things for me, and holy is his name."[114]

274 "Nothing is more apt to confirm our faith and hope than holding it fixed in our minds that nothing is impossible with God. Once
our reason has grasped the idea of 1814, 1817
God's almighty power, it will easily and without any hesitation admit everything that [the Creed] will afterwards propose for us to believe—even if they be great and marvellous things, far above the ordinary laws of nature."[115]

[105] *Gen* 49:24; *Isa* 1:24 etc.; *Ps* 24:8–10; 135:6. — [106] Cf. *Jer* 27:5; 32:17; *Lk* 1:37. — [107] *Wis* 11:21; cf. *Esth* 4:17b; *Prov* 21:1; *Tob* 13:2. — [108] *Wis* 11:23. — [109] *2 Cor* 6:18; cf. *Mt* 6:32. — [110] St. Thomas Aquinas, *STh* I, 25, 5, ad 1. — [111] *1 Cor* 1:24–25. — [112] *Eph* 1:19–22. — [113] Cf. *2 Cor* 12:9; *Phil* 4:13. — [114] *Lk* 1:37, 49. — [115] *Roman Catechism*, I, 2, 13.

In Brief

275 *With Job, the just man, we confess: "I know that you can do all things, and that no purpose of yours can be thwarted"* (Job *42:2).*

276 *Faithful to the witness of Scripture, the Church often addresses its prayer to the "almighty and eternal God" ("omnipotens sempiterne Deus…"), believing firmly that "nothing will be impossible with God" (*Gen *18:14;* Lk *1:37;* Mt *19:26).*

277 *God shows forth his almighty power by converting us from our sins and restoring us to his friendship by grace. "God, you show your almighty power above all in your mercy and forgiveness…" (*Roman Missal, *26th Sunday, Opening Prayer).*

278 *If we do not believe that God's love is almighty, how can we believe that the Father could create us, the Son redeem us, and the Holy Spirit sanctify us?*

Paragraph 4
The Creator

279 "In the beginning God created the heavens and the earth."[116] Holy Scripture begins with these solemn words. The profession of faith takes them up when it confesses that God the Father almighty is "Creator of heaven and earth" (*Apostles' Creed*), "of all that is, seen and unseen" (*Nicene Creed*). We shall speak first of the Creator, then of creation, and finally of the fall into sin from which Jesus Christ, the Son of God, came to raise us up again.

280 Creation is the foundation of
"all God's saving plans," the "beginning of the history of salvation"[117] 288
that culminates in Christ. Conversely, the mystery of Christ casts conclusive light on the mystery of creation and reveals the end for which 1043
"in the beginning God created the
heavens and the earth": from the beginning, God envisaged the glory of the new creation in Christ.[118]

281 And so the readings of the
Easter Vigil, the celebration of the
new creation in Christ, begin with
the creation account; likewise in
the Byzantine liturgy, the account
of creation always constitutes the 1095
first reading at the vigils of the great feasts of the Lord. According to ancient witnesses the instruction of catechumens for Baptism followed the same itinerary.[119]

I. Catechesis on Creation

282 Catechesis on creation is of major importance. It concerns the very foundations of human and Christian life: for it makes explicit the response of the Christian faith to the basic question that men of all times have asked themselves:[120] "Where do we come from?" "Where are we going?" "What is our origin?" "What is our end?" "Where does everything that exists come from and where is it going?" The two questions, the first about the origin and the second about the end, are inseparable. They are decisive for the meaning and orientation of our life and actions. 1730

283 The question about the origins of the world and of man has been the object of many scientific

[116] *Gen* 1:1. — [117] *GCD* 51. — [118] *Gen* 1:1; cf. *Rom* 8:18–23. — [119] Cf. Egeria, *Peregrinatio ad loca sancta,* 46: PLS I, 1047; St. Augustine, *De catechizandis rudibus* 3, 5: PL 40, 256. — [120] Cf. NA 2.

studies which have splendidly enriched our knowledge of the age
159 and dimensions of the cosmos, the development of life-forms and the appearance of man. These discoveries invite us to even greater admiration for the greatness of the Creator, prompting us to give him thanks for
341 all his works and for the understanding and wisdom he gives to scholars and researchers. With Solomon they can say: "It is he who gave me unerring knowledge of what exists, to know the structure of the world and the activity of the elements...for wisdom, the fashioner of all things, taught me."[121]

284 The great interest accorded to these studies is strongly stimulated by a question of another order, which goes beyond the proper domain of the natural sciences. It is not only a question of knowing when and how the universe arose physically, or when man appeared, but rather of discovering the meaning of such an origin: is the universe governed by chance, blind fate, anonymous necessity, or by a transcendent, intelligent and good Being called "God"? And if the world does come from God's wisdom and goodness, why is there evil? Where does it come from? Who is responsible for it? Is there any liberation from it?

285 Since the beginning the Christian faith has been challenged by responses to the question of origins that differ from its own. Ancient religions and cultures produced many myths concerning origins. Some philosophers have said that everything is God, that the world is God, or that the development of the world is the development of God (Pantheism). Others have said that
the world is a necessary emanation 295
arising from God and returning to him. Still others have affirmed the existence of two eternal principles, Good and Evil, Light and Darkness, locked in permanent conflict (Dualism, Manichaeism). According to some of these conceptions, the world (at least the physical world) is evil, the product of a fall, and is thus to be rejected or left behind (Gnosticism). Some admit that the world was made by God, but as by a watchmaker who, once he has made a watch, abandons it to itself (Deism). Finally, others reject any transcendent origin for the world, but see it as merely the interplay of matter that has always existed (Materialism). All these attempts bear witness
to the permanence and universality 28
of the question of origins. This inquiry is distinctively human.

286 Human intelligence is surely 32
already capable of finding a response to the question of origins. The existence of God the Creator can be known with certainty through his works, by the light of human reason,[122] even if this knowledge is often obscured and disfigured by error. This is why faith comes to confirm and enlighten reason in the correct understanding of this truth: "By
faith we understand that the world 37
was created by the word of God, so that what is seen was made out of things which do not appear."[123]

287 The truth about creation is so important for all of human life that God in his tenderness wanted to reveal to his People everything that is

[121] *Wis* 7:17–22. — [122] Cf. Vatican Council I, can. 2 § 1: DS 3026. — [123] *Heb* 11:3.

107 salutary to know on the subject. Beyond the natural knowledge that every man can have of the Creator,[124] God progressively revealed to Israel the mystery of creation. He who chose the patriarchs, who brought Israel out of Egypt, and who by choosing Israel created and formed it, this same God reveals himself as the One to whom belong all the peoples of the earth, and the whole earth itself; he is the One who alone "made heaven and earth."[125]

288 Thus the revelation of creation is inseparable from the revelation and forging of the covenant of the one God with his People.
280, 2569 Creation is revealed as the first step toward this covenant, the first and universal witness to God's all-powerful love.[126] And so, the truth of creation is also expressed with growing vigor in the message of the prophets, the prayer of the psalms and the liturgy, and in the wisdom sayings of the Chosen People.[127]

289 Among all the Scriptural texts about creation, the first three
390 chapters of Genesis occupy a unique place. From a literary standpoint these texts may have had diverse sources. The inspired authors have placed them at the beginning of Scripture to express in their solemn language the truths of creation—its origin and its end in God, its order and goodness, the vocation of man, and finally the drama of sin and the hope of salvation. Read in the light
111 of Christ, within the unity of Sacred Scripture and in the living Tradition of the Church, these texts remain the principal source for catechesis on the mysteries of the "beginning": creation, fall, and promise of salvation.

II. Creation—Work of the Holy Trinity

290 "In the beginning God created the heavens and the earth":[128] three things are affirmed in these first words of Scripture: the eternal God gave a beginning to all that exists outside of himself; he alone is Creator (the verb "create"—Hebrew *bara*—always has God for its subject). The totality of what exists (ex- 326
pressed by the formula "the heavens and the earth") depends on the One who gives it being.

291 "In the beginning was the Word…and the Word was God… all things were made through him, and without him was not anything made that was made."[129] The New 241
Testament reveals that God created everything by the eternal Word, his beloved Son. In him "all things were created, in heaven and on earth… all things were created through him 331
and for him. He is before all things, and in him all things hold together."[130] The Church's faith likewise confesses the creative action of the 703
Holy Spirit, the "giver of life," "the Creator Spirit" ("*Veni, Creator Spiritus*"), the "source of every good."[131]

292 The Old Testament suggests and the New Covenant reveals the creative action of the Son and the Spirit,[132] inseparably one with that of the Father. This creative cooperation is clearly affirmed in the

[124] Cf. *Acts* 17:24–29; *Rom* 1:19–20. — [125] Cf. *Isa* 43:1; *Ps* 115:15; 124:8; 134:3. — [126] Cf. *Gen* 15:5; *Jer* 33:19–26. — [127] Cf. *Isa* 44:24; *Ps* 104; *Prov* 8:22–31. — [128] *Gen* 1:1. — [129] *Jn* 1:1–3. — [130] *Col* 1:16–17. — [131] Cf. Nicene Creed; DS 150; Hymn "*Veni, Creator Spiritus*"; Byzantine Troparion of Pentecost vespers, "*O heavenly King, Consoler.*" — [132] Cf. *Ps* 33:6; 104:30; *Gen* 1:2–3.

Church's rule of faith: "There exists but one God…he is the Father, God, the Creator, the author, the giver of order. He made all things *by himself*, that is, by his Word and by his Wisdom," "by the Son and the Spirit"
699 who, so to speak, are "his hands."[133]
257 Creation is the common work of the Holy Trinity.

III. "The World Was Created for the Glory of God"

293 Scripture and Tradition never cease to teach and celebrate this fundamental truth: "The world
337, 344 was made for the glory of God."[134]
1361 St. Bonaventure explains that God created all things "not to increase his glory, but to show it forth and to communicate it,"[135] for God has no other reason for creating than his love and goodness: "Creatures came into existence when the key of love opened his hand."[136] The First Vatican Council explains:

> 759 This one, true God, of his own goodness and "almighty power," not for increasing his own beatitude, nor for attaining his perfection, but in order to manifest this perfection through the benefits which he bestows on creatures, with absolute freedom of counsel "and from the beginning of time, made out of nothing both orders of creatures, the spiritual and the corporeal…."[137]

294 The glory of God consists in the realization of this manifestation and communication of his goodness, for which the world was cre-
2809 ated. God made us "to be his sons through Jesus Christ, according to the purpose of his will, *to the praise of his glorious grace*,"[138] for "the glory of God is man fully alive; moreover man's life is the vision of God:
if God's revelation through creation 1722
has already obtained life for all the beings that dwell on earth, how much more will the Word's manifestation of the Father obtain life for those who see God."[139] The ultimate purpose of creation is that God
"who is the creator of all things may 1992
at last become 'all in all,' thus simultaneously assuring his own glory and our beatitude."[140]

IV. The Mystery of Creation

God creates by wisdom and love

295 We believe that God created the world according to his wisdom.[141] It is not the product of any necessity whatever, nor of blind fate or chance. We believe that it proceeds from God's free will; he wanted to make his creatures share in his being, wisdom, and goodness: "For you created all things, and by your will they existed and were
created."[142] Therefore the Psalmist 216, 1951
exclaims: "O Lord, how manifold are your works! In wisdom you have made them all"; and "The Lord is good to all, and his compassion is over all that he has made."[143]

God creates "out of nothing"

296 We believe that God needs no pre-existent thing or any help in order to create, nor is creation any sort of necessary emanation from the di

[133] St. Irenaeus, *Adv. haeres* 2, 30, 9; 4, 20, 1: PG 7/1, 822, 1032. — [134] *Dei Filius*, can. § 5: DS 3025. — [135] St. Bonaventure, *In II Sent.* I, 2, 2, 1. — [136] St. Thomas Aquinas, *Sent. 2*, Prol. — [137] *Dei Filius*, 1: DS 3002; cf. Lateran Council IV (1215): DS 800. — [138] *Eph* 1:5–6. — [139] St. Irenaeus, *Adv. haeres* 4, 20, 7: PG 7/1, 1037. — [140] *AG* 2; cf. *1 Cor* 15:28. — [141] Cf. *Wis* 9:9. — [42] *Rev* 4:11. — [143] *Ps* 104:24; 145:9.

285 vine substance.[144] God creates freely "out of nothing":[145]

> If God had drawn the world from pre-existent matter, what would be so extraordinary in that? A human artisan makes from a given material whatever he wants, while God shows his power by starting from nothing to make all he wants.[146]

297 Scripture bears witness to faith in creation "out of nothing" as a truth full of promise and hope. Thus the mother of seven sons en
338 courages them for martyrdom:

> I do not know how you came into being in my womb. It was not I who gave you life and breath, nor I who set in order the elements within each of you. Therefore the Creator of the world, who shaped the beginning of man and devised the origin of all things, will in his mercy give life and breath back to you again, since you now forget yourselves for the sake of his laws.... Look at the heaven and the earth and see everything that is in them, and recognize that God did not make them out of things that existed. Thus also mankind comes into being.[147]

298 Since God could create everything out of nothing, he can also, through the Holy Spirit, give spiritual life to sinners by creating a pure heart
1375 in them[148] and bodily life to the dead through the Resurrection. God "gives life to the dead and calls into existence
992 the things that do not exist."[149] And since God was able to make light shine in darkness by his Word, he can also give the light of faith to those who do not yet know him.[150]

God creates an ordered and good world

299 Because God creates through 339
wisdom, his creation is ordered: "You have arranged all things by measure and number and weight."[151] The universe, created in and by the eternal Word, the "image of the invisible God," is destined for and addressed to man, himself created in the "image of God" and called to a personal relationship with God.[152] Our human understanding, which shares in the
light of the divine intellect, can under- 41, 1147
stand what God tells us by means of his creation, though not without great effort and only in a spirit of humility and respect before the Creator and his work.[153] Because creation comes forth from God's goodness, it shares in that goodness—"And God saw that it was good...very good"[154]—for God willed creation as a gift addressed to man, an inheritance destined for and entrusted to him. On many occasions the
Church has had to defend the good- 358
ness of creation, including that of the 2415
physical world.[155]

God transcends creation and is present to it

300 God is infinitely greater than all his works: "You have set your glory above the heavens."[156] Indeed, God's "greatness is unsearchable."[157]
But because he is the free and sov- 42
ereign Creator, the first cause of all
that exists, God is present to his crea- 223
tures' inmost being: "In him we live

[144] Cf. *Dei Filius*, can. 2–4: DS 3022–3024. — [145] Lateran Council IV (1215): DS 800; cf. DS 3025. — [146] St. Theophilus of Antioch, *Ad Autolycum* II, 4: PG 6, 1052. — [147] *2 Macc* 7:22–23, 28. —[148] Cf. *Ps* 51:12. — [149] *Rom* 4:17. — [150] Cf. *Gen* 1:3; *2 Cor* 4:6. — [151] *Wis* 11:20. — [152] *Col* 1:15; *Gen* 1:26. — [153] Cf. *Ps* 19:2–5; *Job* 42:3. — [154] *Gen* 1:4, 10, 12, 18, 21, 31. — [155] Cf. DS 286; 455–463; 800; 1333; 3002. — [156] *Ps* 8:2; cf. *Sir* 43:28. — [157] *Ps* 145:3.

and move and have our being."[158] In the words of St. Augustine, God is "higher than my highest and more inward than my innermost self."[159]

God upholds and sustains creation

301 With creation, God does not abandon his creatures to themselves. He not only gives them being and existence, but also, and at every moment, upholds and sustains them in being, enables them to act and
1951 brings them to their final end. Recognizing this utter dependence with
396 respect to the Creator is a source of wisdom and freedom, of joy and confidence:

> For you love all things that exist, and detest none of the things that you have made; for you would not have made anything if you had hated it. How would anything have endured, if you had not willed it? Or how would anything not called forth by you have been preserved? You spare all things, for they are yours, O Lord, you who love the living.[160]

V. God Carries out His Plan: Divine Providence

302 Creation has its own goodness and proper perfection, but it did not spring forth complete from the hands of the Creator. The universe was created "in a state of journeying" (*in statu viae*) toward an ultimate perfection yet to be attained, to which God has destined it. We call "divine providence" the dispositions by which God guides his creation toward this perfection:

> By his providence God protects and governs all things which he has made, "reaching mightily from one end of the earth to the other, and ordering all things well." For "all are open and laid bare to his eyes," even those things which are yet to come into existence through the free action of creatures.[161]

303 The witness of Scripture is unanimous that the solicitude of divine providence is concrete and immediate; God cares for all, from the least things to the great events of the world and its history. The sacred books powerfully affirm God's absolute sovereignty over the course of events: "Our God is in the heavens; he does whatever he pleases."[162] 269
And so it is with Christ, "who opens and no one shall shut, who shuts and no one opens."[163] As the book of Proverbs states: "Many are the plans in the mind of a man, but it is the purpose of the Lord that will be established."[164]

304 And so we see the Holy Spirit, the principal author of Sacred Scripture, often attributing actions to God without mentioning any secondary causes. This is not a "primitive mode of speech," but a profound way of recalling God's primacy and absolute Lordship over history and the world,[165] and so of
educating his people to trust in him. 2568
The prayer of the Psalms is the great school of this trust.[166]

305 Jesus asks for childlike abandonment to the providence of our heavenly Father who takes care of his children's smallest needs: "There

[158] *Acts* 17:28. — [159] St. Augustine, *Conf.* 3, 6, 11: PL 32, 688. — [160] *Wis* 11:24–26. — [161] Vatican Council I, *Dei Filius* 1: DS 3003; cf. *Wis* 8:1; *Heb* 4:13. — [162] *Ps* 115:3. — [163] *Rev* 3:7. — [164] *Prov* 19:21. — [165] Cf. *Isa* 10:5–15; 45:5–7; *Deut* 32:39; *Sir* 11:14. — [166] Cf. *Ps* 22; 32; 35; 103; 138; et al.

2115 fore do not be anxious, saying, 'What shall we eat?' or 'What shall we drink?'.... Your heavenly Father knows that you need them all. But seek first his kingdom and his righteousness, and all these things shall be yours as well."[167]

Providence and secondary causes

306 God is the sovereign master of his plan. But to carry it out he also makes use of his creatures' cooperation. This use is not a sign
1884 of weakness, but rather a token of almighty God's greatness and goodness. For God grants his creatures not only their existence, but also the dignity of acting on their own, of being causes and principles for each
1951 other, and thus of cooperating in the accomplishment of his plan.

307 To human beings God even gives the power of freely sharing in his providence by entrusting them
106, 373 with the responsibility of "subduing" the earth and having dominion over it.[168] God thus enables men to
1954 be intelligent and free causes in order to complete the work of creation, to
2427 perfect its harmony for their own good and that of their neighbors. Though often unconscious collaborators with God's will, they can also enter deliberately into the divine plan by their actions, their prayers, and their sufferings.[169] They then
2738 fully become "God's fellow workers"
618, 1505 and co-workers for his kingdom.[170]

308 The truth that God is at work in all the actions of his creatures is inseparable from faith in God the Creator. God is the first cause who operates in and through secondary causes: "For God is at work in you, both to will and to work for his good pleasure."[171] Far from diminishing the creature's dignity, this truth enhances it. Drawn from nothingness by God's power, wisdom, and
goodness, it can do nothing if it is 970
cut off from its origin, for "without a Creator the creature vanishes."[172] Still less can a creature attain its ultimate end without the help of God's grace.[173]

Providence and the scandal of evil

309 If God the Father almighty, the Creator of the ordered and good world, cares for all his creatures, why does evil exist? To this question, as
pressing as it is unavoidable and as 164, 385
painful as it is mysterious, no quick
answer will suffice. Only Christian 2850
faith as a whole constitutes the answer to this question: the goodness of creation, the drama of sin, and the patient love of God who comes to meet man by his covenants, the redemptive Incarnation of his Son, his gift of the Spirit, his gathering of the Church, the power of the sacraments, and his call to a blessed life to which free creatures are invited to consent in advance, but from which, by a terrible mystery, they can also turn away in advance. *There is not a single aspect of the Christian message that is not in part an answer to the question of evil.*

310 But why did God not create a world so perfect that no evil could exist in it? With infinite power God could always create something better.[174] But with infinite wisdom and 412
goodness God freely willed to create

[167] *Mt* 6:31–33; cf. 10:29–31. — [168] Cf. *Gen* 1:26–28. — [169] Cf. *Col* 1:24. — [170] *1 Cor* 3:9; *1 Thess* 3:2; *Col* 4:11. — [171] *Phil* 2:13; cf. *1 Cor* 12:6. — [172] *GS* 36 § 3. — [173] Cf. *Mt* 19:26; *Jn* 15:5; 14:13. — [174] Cf. St. Thomas Aquinas, *STh* I, 25, 6.

42–1050 a world "in a state of journeying" toward its ultimate perfection. In God's plan this process of becoming involves the appearance of certain beings and the disappearance of others, the existence of the more perfect
342 alongside the less perfect, both constructive and destructive forces of nature. With physical good there exists also physical evil as long as creation has not reached perfection.[175]

311 Angels and men, as intelligent and free creatures, have to journey toward their ultimate destinies by their free choice and preferential
396 love. They can therefore go astray. Indeed, they have sinned. Thus has
1849 moral evil, incommensurably more harmful than physical evil, entered the world. God is in no way, directly or indirectly, the cause of moral evil.[176] He permits it, however, because he respects the freedom of his creatures and, mysteriously, knows how to derive good from it:

> For almighty God..., because he is supremely good, would never allow any evil whatsoever to exist in his works if he were not so all-powerful and good as to cause good to emerge from evil itself.[177]

312 In time we can discover that God in his almighty providence can bring a good from the consequences of an evil, even a moral evil, caused by his creatures: "It was not you," said Joseph to his brothers, "who sent me here, but God.... You meant evil against me; but God meant it for good, to bring it about that many people should be kept alive."[178] From 598–600
the greatest moral evil ever committed—the rejection and murder of God's only Son, caused by the sins of all men—God, by his grace that "abounded all the more,"[179] brought the greatest of goods: the glorification of Christ and our redemption. But for all that, evil never becomes 1994
a good.

313 "We know that in everything God works for good for those who love him."[180] The constant witness of the saints confirms this truth: 227

> St. Catherine of Siena said to "those who are scandalized and rebel against what happens to them": "Everything comes from love, all is ordained for the salvation of man, God does nothing without this goal in mind."[181]
> St. Thomas More, shortly before his martyrdom, consoled his daughter: "Nothing can come but that that God wills. And I make me very sure that whatsoever that be, seem it never so bad in sight, it shall indeed be the best."[182]
> Dame Julian of Norwich: "Here I was taught by the grace of God that I should steadfastly keep me in the faith...and that at the same time I should take my stand on and earnestly believe in what our Lord shewed in this time—that 'all manner [of] thing shall be well.'"[183]

314 We firmly believe that God is master of the world and of its history. But the ways of his providence are often unknown to us. Only at the end, when our partial knowledge ceases, when we see God "face

[175] Cf. St. Thomas Aquinas, *SCG* III, 71. — [176] Cf. St. Augustine, *De libero arbitrio* 1, 1, 2: PL 32, 1223; St. Thomas Aquinas, *STh* I–II, 79, 1. — [177] St. Augustine, *Enchiridion* 3, 11: PL 40, 236. — [178] *Gen* 45:8; 50:20; cf. *Tob* 2:12–18 (Vulg.). — [179] Cf. *Rom* 5:20. — [180] *Rom* 8:28. — [181] St. Catherine of Siena, *Dialogue on Providence*, ch. IV, 138. — [182] *The Correspondence of Sir Thomas More*, ed. Elizabeth F. Rogers (Princeton: Princeton University Press, 1947), letter 206, lines 661–663. — [183] Julian of Norwich, *The Revelations of Divine Love*, tr. James Walshe, SJ (London: 1961), ch. 32, 99–100.

1040 to face,"[184] will we fully know the ways by which—even through the
2550 dramas of evil and sin—God has guided his creation to that definitive sabbath rest[185] for which he created heaven and earth.

In Brief

315 *In the creation of the world and of man, God gave the first and universal witness to his almighty love and his wisdom, the first proclamation of the "plan of his loving goodness," which finds its goal in the new creation in Christ.*

316 *Though the work of creation is attributed to the Father in particular, it is equally a truth of faith that the Father, Son, and Holy Spirit together are the one, indivisible principle of creation.*

317 *God alone created the universe freely, directly, and without any help.*

318 *No creature has the infinite power necessary to "create" in the proper sense of the word, that is, to produce and give being to that which had in no way possessed it (to call into existence "out of nothing") (cf. DS 3624).*

319 *God created the world to show forth and communicate his glory. That his creatures should share in his truth, goodness, and beauty—this is the glory for which God created them.*

320 *God created the universe and keeps it in existence by his Word, the Son "upholding the universe by his word of power"* (Heb *1:3) and by his Creator Spirit, the giver of life.*

321 *Divine providence consists of the dispositions by which God guides all his creatures with wisdom and love to their ultimate end.*

322 *Christ invites us to filial trust in the providence of our heavenly Father (cf.* Mt *6:26–34), and St. Peter the apostle repeats: "Cast all your anxieties on him, for he cares about you"* (1 Pet *5:7; cf.* Ps *55:23).*

323 *Divine providence works also through the actions of creatures. To human beings God grants the ability to cooperate freely with his plans.*

324 *The fact that God permits physical and even moral evil is a mystery that God illuminates by his Son Jesus Christ who died and rose to vanquish evil. Faith gives us the certainty that God would not permit an evil if he did not cause a good to come from that very evil, by ways that we shall fully know only in eternal life.*

Paragraph 5
Heaven and Earth

325 The Apostles' Creed professes that God is "Creator of heaven and earth." The Nicene Creed makes it explicit that this profession includes "all that is, seen and unseen."

326 The Scriptural expression "heaven and earth" means all that exists, creation in its entirety. It also indicates the bond, deep within creation, that both unites heaven and 290
earth and distinguishes the one from the other: "the earth" is the world of men, while "heaven" or "the heavens" can designate both the firmament and God's own "place"—"our
Father in heaven" and consequently 1023, 279
the "heaven" too which is eschatological glory. Finally, "heaven" refers

[184] *1 Cor* 13:12. — [185] Cf. *Gen* 2:2.

to the saints and the "place" of the spiritual creatures, the angels, who surround God.[186]

327 The profession of faith of the Fourth Lateran Council (1215) affirms that God "from the beginning of time made at once (*simul*) out of
296 nothing both orders of creatures, the spiritual and the corporeal, that is, the angelic and the earthly, and then (*deinde*) the human creature, who as it were shares in both orders, being composed of spirit and body."[187]

I. The Angels

The existence of angels—a truth of faith

328 The existence of the spiritual, non-corporeal beings that Sacred Scripture usually calls "angels" is a truth of faith. The witness of Scripture is as clear as the unanimity of
150 Tradition.

Who are they?

329 St. Augustine says: "'Angel' is the name of their office, not of their nature. If you seek the name of their nature, it is 'spirit'; if you seek the name of their office, it is 'angel': from what they are, 'spirit,' from what they do, 'angel.'"[188] With their whole beings the angels are *servants* and messengers of God. Because they "always behold the face of my Father who is in heaven" they are the "mighty ones who do his word, hearkening to the voice of his word."[189]

330 As purely *spiritual* creatures angels have intelligence and will: they are personal and immortal creatures, surpassing in perfection all visible creatures, as the splendor of their glory bears witness.[190]

Christ "with all his angels"

331 Christ is the center of the 291
angelic world. They are his angels: "When the Son of man comes in his glory, and all the angels with him...."[191] They belong to him because they were created through and for him: "for in him all things were created in heaven and on earth, visible and invisible, whether thrones or dominions or principalities or authorities—all things were created *through* him and *for* him."[192] They belong to him still more because he has made them messengers of his saving plan: "Are they not all ministering spirits sent forth to serve, for the sake of those who are to obtain salvation?"[193]

332 Angels have been present since creation and throughout the history of salvation, announcing this salvation from afar or near and serving the accomplishment of the divine plan: they closed the earthly paradise; protected Lot; saved Hagar and her child; stayed Abraham's hand; communicated the law by their ministry; led the People of God; announced births and callings; and assisted the prophets, just to cite a few examples.[194] Finally, the angel Gabriel announced the birth of the Precursor and that of Jesus himself.[195]

[186] *Ps* 115:16; 19:2; *Mt* 5:16. — [187] Lateran Council IV (1215): DS 800; cf. DS 3002 and Paul VI, CPG § 8. — [188] St. Augustine, *En. in Ps.* 103, 1, 15: PL 37, 1348. — [189] *Mt* 18:10; *Ps* 103:20. — [190] Cf. Pius XII, *Humani Generis*: DS 3891; *Lk* 20:36; *Dan* 10:9–12. — [191] *Mt* 25:31. — [192] *Col* 1:16. — [193] *Heb* 1:14. — [194] Cf. *Job* 38:7 (where angels are called "sons of God"); *Gen* 3:24; 19; 21:17; 22:11; *Acts* 7:53; *Ex* 23:20–23; *Judg* 13; 6:11–24; *Isa* 6:6; *1 Kings* 19:5. — [195] Cf. *Lk* 1:11, 26.

333 From the Incarnation to the
Ascension, the life of the Word incarnate is surrounded by the adoration and service of angels. When
God "brings the firstborn into the
world, he says: 'Let all God's an-
559 gels worship him.'"[196] Their song of
praise at the birth of Christ has not
ceased resounding in the Church's
praise: "Glory to God in the highest!"[197] They protect Jesus in his
infancy, serve him in the desert,
strengthen him in his agony in the
garden, when he could have been
saved by them from the hands of
his enemies as Israel had been.[198]
Again, it is the angels who "evangelize" by proclaiming the Good News
of Christ's Incarnation and Resurrection.[199] They will be present at
Christ's return, which they will announce, to serve at his judgment.[200]

The angels in the life of the Church

334 In the meantime, the whole
1939 life of the Church benefits from the
mysterious and powerful help of angels.[201]

335 In her liturgy, the Church
joins with the angels to adore the
thrice-holy God. She invokes their
assistance (in the funeral liturgy's
1138 *In Paradisum deducant te angeli*...
["May the angels lead you into Paradise..."]). Moreover, in the "Cherubic Hymn" of the Byzantine Liturgy,
she celebrates the memory of certain
angels more particularly (St. Michael, St. Gabriel, St. Raphael, and
the guardian angels).

336 From its beginning until
death, human life is surrounded
by their watchful care and intercession.[202] "Beside each believer stands
an angel as protector and shepherd 1020
leading him to life."[203] Already here
on earth the Christian life shares by
faith in the blessed company of angels and men united in God.

II. The Visible World

337 God himself created the visible world in all its richness, diversity, and order. Scripture presents the
work of the Creator symbolically
as a succession of six days of divine 290
"work," concluded by the "rest" of
the seventh day.[204] On the subject of
creation, the sacred text teaches the
truths revealed by God for our salvation,[205] permitting us to "recognize
the inner nature, the value, and the
ordering of the whole of creation to
the praise of God."[206] 293

338 *Nothing exists that does not
owe its existence to God the Creator.*
The world began when God's word 297
drew it out of nothingness; all existent beings, all of nature, and all
human history are rooted in this
primordial event, the very genesis
by which the world was constituted
and time begun.[207]

339 *Each creature possesses its own
particular goodness and perfection.*
For each one of the works of the "six
days" it is said: "And God saw that
it was good." "By the very nature of 2501
creation, material being is endowed
with its own stability, truth, and

[196] *Heb* 1:6. — [197] *Lk* 2:14. — [198] Cf. *Mt* 1:20; 2:13, 19; 4:11; 26:53; *Mk* 1:13; *Lk* 22:43; *2 Macc* 10:29–30; 11:8. — [199] Cf. *Lk* 2:8–14; *Mk* 16:5–7. — [200] Cf. *Acts* 1:10–11; *Mt* 13:41; 24:31; *Lk* 12:8–9. — [201] Cf. *Acts* 5:18–20; 8:26–29; 10:3–8; 12:6–11; 27:23–25. — [202] Cf. *Mt* 18:10; *Lk* 16:22; *Ps* 34:7; 91:10–13; *Job* 33:23–24; *Zech* 1:12; *Tob* 12:12. — [203] St. Basil, *Adv. Eunomium* III, 1: PG 29, 656B. — [204] *Gen* 1:1–2:4. — [205] Cf. *DV* 11. — [206] *LG* 36 § 2. — [207] Cf. St. Augustine, *De Genesi adv. Man.* 1, 2, 4: PL 34, 175.

excellence, its own order and laws."[208] Each of the various creatures, willed in its own being, re-
299 flects in its own way a ray of God's infinite wisdom and goodness. Man must therefore respect the particular goodness of every creature, to
266 avoid any disordered use of things which would be in contempt of the Creator and would bring disastrous consequences for human beings and their environment.

1937 **340** God wills the *interdependence of creatures.* The sun and the moon, the cedar and the little flower, the eagle and the sparrow: the spectacle of their countless diversities and inequalities tells us that no creature is self-sufficient. Creatures exist only in dependence on each other, to complete each other, in the service of each other.

283 **341** The *beauty of the universe*: The order and harmony of the cre-
2500 ated world results from the diversity of beings and from the relationships which exist among them. Man discovers them progressively as the laws of nature. They call forth the admiration of scholars. The beauty of creation reflects the infinite beauty of the Creator and ought to inspire the respect and submission of man's intellect and will.

310 **342** The *hierarchy of creatures* is expressed by the order of the "six days," from the less perfect to the more perfect. God loves all his creatures[209] and takes care of each one, even the sparrow. Nevertheless, Jesus said: "You are of more value than many sparrows," or again: "Of how much more value is a man than a sheep!"[210]

343 *Man is the summit* of the Cre- 355
ator's work, as the inspired account expresses by clearly distinguishing the creation of man from that of the other creatures.[211]

344 *There is a solidarity among all* 293, 1939
creatures arising from the fact that all have the same Creator and are all or- 2416
dered to his glory:

> May you be praised, O Lord, in all 1218
> your creatures, especially brother sun, by whom you give us light for the day; he is beautiful, radiating great splendor, and offering us a symbol of you, the Most High....
> May you be praised, my Lord, for sister water, who is very useful and humble, precious and chaste....
> May you be praised, my Lord, for sister earth, our mother, who bears and feeds us, and produces the variety of fruits and dappled flowers and grasses....
> Praise and bless my Lord, give thanks and serve him in all humility.[212]

345 *The sabbath—the end of the work of the six days.* The sacred text says that "on the seventh day God finished his work which he had done," that the "heavens and the earth were finished," and that God 2168
"rested" on this day and sanctified and blessed it.[213] These inspired words are rich in profitable instruction:

346 In creation God laid a foundation and established laws that remain firm, on which the believer can rely with confidence, for they are the sign and pledge of the unshakeable faithfulness of God's cov- 2169
enant.[214] For his part man must remain faithful to this foundation and

[208] *GS* 36 § 1. — [209] Cf. *Ps* 145:9. — [210] *Lk* 12:6–7; *Mt* 12:12. — [211] Cf. *Gen* 1:26. — [212] St. Francis of Assisi, *Canticle of the Creatures.* — [213] *Gen* 2:1–3. — [214] Cf. *Heb* 4:3–4; *Jer* 31:35–37; 33:19–26.

respect the laws which the Creator has written into it.

347 Creation was fashioned with a view to the sabbath and therefore for the worship and adoration of God. Worship is inscribed in the order of creation.[215] As the rule of St.
1145–1152 Benedict says, nothing should take precedence over "the work of God," that is, solemn worship.[216] This indicates the right order of human concerns.

2172 **348** The sabbath is at the heart of Israel's law. To keep the commandments is to correspond to the wisdom and the will of God as expressed in his work of creation.

349 *The eighth day.* But for us a new day has dawned: the day of Christ's Resurrection. The seventh day completes the first creation.
2174 The eighth day begins the new creation. Thus, the work of creation
1046 culminates in the greater work of redemption. The first creation finds its meaning and its summit in the new creation in Christ, the splendor of which surpasses that of the first creation.[217]

In Brief

350 *Angels are spiritual creatures who glorify God without ceasing and who serve his saving plans for other creatures: "The angels work together for the benefit of us all" (St. Thomas Aquinas,* STh *I, 114, 3, ad 3).*

351 *The angels surround Christ their Lord. They serve him especially in the accomplishment of his saving mission to men.*

352 *The Church venerates the angels who help her on her earthly pilgrimage and protect every human being.*

353 *God willed the diversity of his creatures and their own particular goodness, their interdependence, and their order. He destined all material creatures for the good of the human race. Man, and through him all creation, is destined for the glory of God.*

354 *Respect for laws inscribed in creation and the relations which derive from the nature of things is a principle of wisdom and a foundation for morality.*

Paragraph 6
MAN

355 "God created man in his own image, in the image of God he created him, male and female he created them."[218] Man occupies a unique
place in creation: (I) he is "in the im- 1700, 343
age of God"; (II) in his own nature he unites the spiritual and material worlds; (III) he is created "male and female"; (IV) God established him in his friendship.

I. "In the Image of God"

356 Of all visible creatures only man is "able to know and love his creator."[219] He is "the only creature on earth that God has willed for its
own sake,"[220] and he alone is called 1703, 225
to share, by knowledge and love, in God's own life. It was for this end that he was created, and this is the
fundamental reason for his dignity: 225

> What made you establish man in
> so great a dignity? Certainly the 295
> incalculable love by which you have

[215] Cf. *Gen* 1:14. — [216] St. Benedict, *Regula* 43, 3: PL 66, 675–676. — [217] Cf. *Roman Missal,* Easter Vigil 24, prayer after the first reading. — [218] *Gen* 1:27. — [219] *GS* 12 § 3. — [220] *GS* 24 § 3.

looked on your creature in yourself! You are taken with love for her; for by love indeed you created her, by love you have given her a being capable of tasting your eternal Good.[221]

357 Being in the image of God the human individual possesses the dignity of a person, who is not just something, but someone. He is
1935 capable of self-knowledge, of self-possession and of freely giving him
1877 self and entering into communion with other persons. And he is called by grace to a covenant with his Creator, to offer him a response of faith and love that no other creature can give in his stead.

358 God created everything for man,[222] but man in turn was created to serve and love God and to offer all
299, 901 creation back to him:

What is it that is about to be created, that enjoys such honor? It is man—that great and wonderful living creature, more precious in the eyes of God than all other creatures! For him the heavens and the earth, the sea and all the rest of creation exist. God attached so much importance to his salvation that he did not spare his own Son for the sake of man. Nor does he ever cease to work, trying every possible means, until he has raised man up to himself and made him sit at his right hand.[223]

1701 **359** "In reality it is only in the mystery of the Word made flesh that the mystery of man truly becomes clear."[224]

388, 411 St. Paul tells us that the human race takes its origin from two men: Adam and Christ.... The first man, Adam, he says, became a living soul, the last Adam a life-giving spirit. The first Adam was made by the last Adam, from whom he also received his soul, to give him life.... The second Adam stamped his image on the first Adam when he created him. That is why he took on himself the role and the name of the first Adam, in order that he might not lose what he had made in his own image. The first Adam, the last Adam: the first had a beginning, the last knows no end. The last Adam is indeed the first; as he himself says: "I am the first and the last."[225]

360 Because of its common or- 225, 404, 775
igin *the human race forms a unity*,
for "from one ancestor [God] made 831, 842
all nations to inhabit the whole earth":[226]

O wondrous vision, which makes us contemplate the human race in the unity of its origin in God...in the unity of its nature, composed equally in all men of a material body and a spiritual soul; in the unity of its immediate end and its mission in the world; in the unity of its dwelling, the earth, whose benefits all men, by right of nature, may use to sustain and develop life; in the unity of its supernatural end: God himself, to whom all ought to tend; in the unity of the means for attaining this end;...in the unity of the redemption wrought by Christ for all.[227]

361 "This law of human solidarity and charity,"[228] without excluding
the rich variety of persons, cultures, 1939
and peoples, assures us that all men are truly brethren.

[221] St. Catherine of Siena, *Dialogue* 4, 13 "On Divine Providence": *LH*, Sunday, week 19, OR. — [222] Cf. *GS* 12 § 1; 24 § 3; 39 § 1. — [223] St. John Chrysostom, *In Gen. Sermo* II, 1: PG 54, 587D–588A. — [224] *GS* 22 § 1. — [225] St. Peter Chrysologus, *Sermo* 117; PL 52, 520–521. — [226] *Acts* 17:26; cf. *Tob* 8:6. — [227] Pius XII, encyclical, *Summi Pontificatus* 3; cf. *NA* 1. — [228] Pius XII, Summi Pontificatus *3*.

II. "Body and Soul but Truly One"

362 The human person, created in
the image of God, is a being at once
corporeal and spiritual. The biblical
account expresses this reality in sym-
1146, 2332 bolic language when it affirms that
"then the LORD God formed man of
dust from the ground, and breathed
into his nostrils the breath of life;
and man became a living being."[229]
Man, whole and entire, is therefore
willed by God.

363 In Sacred Scripture the term
"soul" often refers to human *life*
or the entire human *person.*[230] But
1703 "soul" also refers to the innermost
aspect of man, that which is of greatest value in him,[231] that by which he
is most especially in God's image:
"soul" signifies the *spiritual principle*
in man.

364 The human body shares in
the dignity of "the image of God": it
is a human body precisely because it
is animated by a spiritual soul, and
1004 it is the whole human person that is
intended to become, in the body of
Christ, a temple of the Spirit:[232]

> 2289 Man, though made of body and soul, is a unity. Through his very bodily condition he sums up in himself the elements of the material world. Through him they are thus brought to their highest perfection and can raise their voice in praise freely given to the Creator. For this reason man may not despise his bodily life. Rather he is obliged to regard his body as good and to hold it in honor since God has created it and will raise it up on the last day.[233]

365 The unity of soul and body is so profound that one has to consider the soul to be the "form" of the body:[234] i.e., it is because of its spiritual soul that the body made of matter becomes a living, human body; spirit and matter, in man, are not two natures united, but rather their union forms a single nature.

366 The Church teaches that every spiritual soul is created immediately by God—it is not "produced" 1005
by the parents—and also that it is
immortal: it does not perish when 997
it separates from the body at death,
and it will be reunited with the body
at the final Resurrection.[235]

367 Sometimes the soul is distinguished from the spirit: St. Paul for
instance prays that God may sanctify his people "wholly," with "spirit
and soul and body" kept sound and
blameless at the Lord's coming.[236] 2083
The Church teaches that this distinction does not introduce a duality into the soul.[237] "Spirit" signifies
that from creation man is ordered to
a supernatural end and that his soul
can gratuitously be raised beyond
all it deserves to communion with
God.[238]

368 The spiritual tradition of the 478, 582,
Church also emphasizes the heart, 1431
in the biblical sense of the depths 1764, 2517
of one's being, where the person de- 2562, 284
cides for or against God.[239]

[229] *Gen* 2:7. — [230] Cf. *Mt* 16:25–26; *Jn* 15:13; *Acts* 2:41. — [231] Cf. *Mt* 10:28; 26:38; *Jn* 12:27; *2 Macc* 6:30. — [232] Cf. *1 Cor* 6:19–20; 15:44–45. — [233] *GS* 14 § 1; cf. *Dan* 3:57–80. — [234] Cf. Council of Vienne (1312): DS 902. — [235] Cf. Pius XII, *Humani Generis*: DS 3896; Paul VI, CPG § 8; Lateran Council V (1513): DS 1440. — [236] *1 Thess* 5:23. — [237] Cf. Council of Constantinople IV (870): DS 657. — [238] Cf. Vatican Council I, *Dei Filius*: DS 3005; GS 22 § 5; *Humani generis*: DS 3891. — [239] Cf. *Jer* 31:33; *Deut* 6:5; 29:3; *Isa* 29:13; *Ezek* 36:26; *Mt* 6:21; *Lk* 8:15; *Rom* 5:5.

331, 2336 III. "Male and Female He Created Them"

Equality and difference willed by God

369 Man and woman have been created, which is to say, willed by God: on the one hand, in perfect equality as human persons; on the other, in their respective beings as man and woman. "Being man" or "being woman" is a reality which is good and willed by God: man and woman possess an inalienable dignity which comes to them immediately from God their Creator.[240] Man and woman are both with one and the same dignity "in the image of God." In their "being-man" and "being-woman," they reflect the Creator's wisdom and goodness.

370 In no way is God in man's image. He is neither man nor woman. God is pure spirit in which there is
42, 239 no place for the difference between the sexes. But the respective "perfections" of man and woman reflect something of the infinite perfection of God: those of a mother and those of a father and husband.[241]

"Each for the other"—
"A unity in two"

371 God created man and woman together and willed each for the other. The Word of God gives us to understand this through var-
1605 ious features of the sacred text. "It is not good that the man should be alone. I will make him a helper fit for him."[242] None of the animals can be man's partner.[243] The woman God "fashions" from the man's rib and brings to him elicits on the man's part a cry of wonder, an exclamation of love and communion: "This at last is bone of my bones and flesh of my flesh."[244] Man discovers woman as another "I," sharing the same humanity.

372 Man and woman were made "for each other"—not that God left them half-made and incomplete: he created them to be a communion of persons, in which each can be "helpmate" to the other, for they are equal as persons ("bone of my bones...") and complementary as masculine and feminine. In marriage God unites them in such a way that, by forming "one flesh,"[245] they can transmit human life: "Be fruitful
and multiply, and fill the earth."[246] 1652, 2366
By transmitting human life to their descendants, man and woman as spouses and parents cooperate in a unique way in the Creator's work.[247]

373 In God's plan man and woman have the vocation of "subduing" the earth[248] as stewards of God. This sovereignty is not to be an arbitrary
and destructive domination. God 307
calls man and woman, made in the
image of the Creator "who loves ev- 2415
erything that exists,"[249] to share in his providence toward other creatures; hence their responsibility for the world God has entrusted to them.

IV. Man in Paradise

374 The first man was not only created good, but was also established in friendship with his Creator and in harmony with himself and with the
creation around him, in a state that 54
would be surpassed only by the glory of the new creation in Christ.

[240] Cf. *Gen* 2:7, 22. — [241] Cf. *Isa* 49:14–15; 66:13; *Ps* 131:2–3; *Hos* 11:1–4; *Jer* 3:4–19. — [242] *Gen* 2:18. — [243] *Gen* 2:19–20. — [244] *Gen* 2:23. — [245] *Gen* 2:24. — [246] *Gen* 1:28. — [247] Cf. *GS* 50 § 1. — [248] *Gen* 1:28. — [249] *Wis* 11:24.

375 The Church, interpreting the symbolism of biblical language in an authentic way, in the light of the New Testament and Tradition, teaches that our first parents, Adam and Eve, were constituted in an orig-
1997 inal "state of holiness and justice."[250] This grace of original holiness was "to share in…divine life."[251]

376 By the radiance of this grace all dimensions of man's life were confirmed. As long as he remained in the divine intimacy, man would
1008, 1502 not have to suffer or die.[252] The inner harmony of the human person, the harmony between man and woman,[253] and finally the harmony between the first couple and all creation, comprised the state called "original justice."

2514 **377** The "mastery" over the world that God offered man from the beginning was realized above all within man himself: *mastery of self*. The first man was unimpaired and ordered in his whole being because he was free from the triple concupiscence[254] that subjugates him to the pleasures of the senses, covetousness for earthly goods, and self-assertion, contrary to the dictates of reason.

2415 **378** The sign of man's familiarity
2427 with God is that God places him in the garden.[255] There he lives "to till it and keep it." Work is not yet a burden,[256] but rather the collaboration of man and woman with God in perfecting the visible creation.

379 This entire harmony of original justice, foreseen for man in God's plan, will be lost by the sin of our first parents.

In Brief

380 *"Father,…you formed man in your own likeness and set him over the whole world to serve you, his creator, and to rule over all creatures"* (Roman Missal, *EP IV 118).*

381 *Man is predestined to reproduce the image of God's Son made man, the "image of the invisible God" (Col 1:15), so that Christ shall be the first-born of a multitude of brothers and sisters (cf.* Eph *1:3–6;* Rom *8:29).*

382 *"Man, though made of body and soul, is a unity "* (GS *14 § 1). The doctrine of the faith affirms that the spiritual and immortal soul is created immediately by God.*

383 *"God did not create man a solitary being. From the beginning, 'male and female he created them'* (Gen *1:27). This partnership of man and woman constitutes the first form of communion between persons"* (GS *12 § 4).*

384 *Revelation makes known to us the state of original holiness and justice of man and woman before sin: from their friendship with God flowed the happiness of their existence in paradise.*

Paragraph 7
THE FALL

385 God is infinitely good and all his works are good. Yet no one can escape the experience of suffering or the evils in nature which seem to be linked to the limitations proper to creatures: and above all to the question of moral evil. Where does evil

[250] Cf. Council of Trent (1546): DS 1511. — [251] Cf. *LG* 2. — [252] Cf. *Gen* 2:17; 3:16, 19. — [253] Cf. *Gen* 2:25. — [254] Cf. *1 Jn* 2:16. — [255] Cf. *Gen* 2:8. — [256] *Gen* 2:15; cf. 3:17–19.

come from? "I sought whence evil
309 comes and there was no solution,"
said St. Augustine,[257] and his own
painful quest would only be resolved
by his conversion to the living God.
For "the mystery of lawlessness"
is clarified only in the light of the
"mystery of our religion."[258] The
457 revelation of divine love in Christ
manifested at the same time the ex-
1848 tent of evil and the superabundance
of grace.[259] We must therefore ap-
539 proach the question of the origin of
evil by fixing the eyes of our faith on
him who alone is its conqueror.[260]

I. Where Sin Abounded, Grace Abounded All the More

The reality of sin

386 Sin is present in human history; any attempt to ignore it or to give this dark reality other names would be futile. To try to understand what sin is, one must first recognize *the profound relation of man to God*, for only in this relationship is the evil of sin unmasked in its true identity as
1847 humanity's rejection of God and opposition to him, even as it continues to weigh heavy on human life and history.

387 Only the light of divine Revelation clarifies the reality of sin and particularly of the sin committed at mankind's origins. Without the knowledge Revelation gives of God we cannot recognize sin clearly and
1848 are tempted to explain it as merely a developmental flaw, a psychological
1739 weakness, a mistake, or the necessary consequence of an inadequate social structure, etc. Only in the knowledge of God's plan for man can we grasp that sin is an abuse of the freedom that God gives to created persons so that they are capable of loving him and loving one another.

Original Sin—an essential truth of the faith

388 With the progress of Revelation, the reality of sin is also illuminated. Although to some extent the People of God in the Old
Testament had tried to understand 431
the pathos of the human condition
in the light of the history of the fall 208
narrated in Genesis, they could not grasp this story's ultimate meaning, which is revealed only in the light of the death and Resurrection of Jesus
Christ.[261] We must know Christ as 359
the source of grace in order to know Adam as the source of sin. The Spirit-Paraclete, sent by the risen
Christ, came to "convict the world 729
concerning sin,"[262] by revealing him who is its Redeemer.

389 The doctrine of original sin is, so to speak, the "reverse side" of the Good News that Jesus is the Savior of all men, that all need salvation,
and that salvation is offered to all 422
through Christ. The Church, which has the mind of Christ,[263] knows very well that we cannot tamper with the revelation of original sin without undermining the mystery of Christ.

How to read the account of the Fall

390 The account of the fall in *Genesis* 3 uses figurative language, but affirms a primeval event, a deed
that took place *at the beginning of the* 289
history of man.[264] Revelation gives us the certainty of faith that the whole

[257] St. Augustine, *Conf.* 7, 7, 11: PL 32, 739. — [258] *2 Thess* 2:7; *1 Tim* 3:16. — [259] Cf. *Rom* 5:20. — [260] Cf. *Lk* 11:21–22; *Jn* 16:11; *1 Jn* 3:8. — [261] Cf. 5:12–21. — [262] *Jn* 16:8. — [263] Cf. *1 Cor* 2:16. — [264] Cf. *GS* 13 § 1.

of human history is marked by the original fault freely committed by our first parents.[265]

II. The Fall of the Angels

391 Behind the disobedient choice of our first parents lurks a seductive voice, opposed to God,
2538 which makes them fall into death out of envy.[266] Scripture and the Church's Tradition see in this being a fallen angel, called "Satan" or the "devil."[267] The Church teaches that Satan was at first a good angel, made by God: "The devil and the other demons were indeed created naturally good by God, but they became evil by their own doing."[268]

392 Scripture speaks of a sin of these angels.[269] This "fall" consists in the free choice of these created spirits, who radically and irrevocably
1850 rejected God and his reign. We find a reflection of that rebellion in the tempter's words to our first parents: "You will be like God."[270] The devil "has sinned from the beginning"; he
2482 is "a liar and the father of lies."[271]

393 It is the irrevocable character of their choice, and not a defect in
1033–1037 the infinite divine mercy, that makes the angels' sin unforgivable. "There
1022 is no repentance for the angels after their fall, just as there is no repentance for men after death."[272]

394 Scripture witnesses to the disastrous influence of the one Jesus calls "a murderer from the beginning," who would even try to di-
538–540 vert Jesus from the mission received from his Father.[273] "The reason the
550 Son of God appeared was to destroy the works of the devil."[274] In its consequences the gravest of these works 2846–28
was the mendacious seduction that led man to disobey God.

395 The power of Satan is, nonetheless, not infinite. He is only a creature, powerful from the fact that he is pure spirit, but still a creature.
He cannot prevent the building 309
up of God's reign. Although Satan may act in the world out of hatred for God and his kingdom in Christ Jesus, and although his action may
cause grave injuries—of a spiritu- 1673
al nature and, indirectly, even of a
physical nature—to each man and 412
to society, the action is permitted by divine providence which with strength and gentleness guides human and cosmic history. It is a great 3850–285
mystery that providence should permit diabolical activity, but "we know that in everything God works for good with those who love him."[275]

III. Original Sin

Freedom put to the test

396 God created man in his image and established him in his friendship. A spiritual creature, man can live this friendship only in free submission to God. The prohibition against eating "of the tree of 1730
the knowledge of good and evil"
spells this out: "for in the day that 311
you eat of it, you shall die."[276] The "tree of the knowledge of good and evil"[277] symbolically evokes the insurmountable limits that man, being a creature, must freely recognize and respect with trust. Man is dependent on his Creator and subject

[265] Cf. Council of Trent: DS 1513; Pius XII: DS 3897; Paul VI: AAS 58 (1966), 654. — [266] Cf. *Gen* 3:1–5; *Wis* 2:24. — [267] Cf. *Jn* 8:44; *Rev* 12:9. — [268] Lateran Council IV (1215): DS 800. — [269] Cf. *2 Pet* 2:4. — [270] *Gen* 3:5. — [271] *1 Jn* 3:8; *Jn* 8:44. — [272] St. John Damascene, *De Fide orth.* 2, 4: PG 94, 877. — [273] *Jn* 8:44; cf. *Mt* 4:1–11. — [274] *1 Jn* 3:8. — [275] *Rom* 8:28. — [276] *Gen* 2:17. — [277] *Gen* 2:17.

to the laws of creation and to the
301 moral norms that govern the use of
freedom.

Man's first sin

707, 2541 **397** Man, tempted by the devil, let his trust in his Creator die in
1850, 215 his heart and, abusing his freedom,
disobeyed God's command. This is
what man's first sin consisted of.[278]
All subsequent sin would be disobedience toward God and lack of trust in his goodness.

398 In that sin man *preferred* himself to God and by that very act scorned him. He chose himself
over and against God, against the
2084 requirements of his creaturely status
and therefore against his own good.
Constituted in a state of holiness,
2113 man was destined to be fully "di-
vinized" by God in glory. Seduced by the devil, he wanted to "be like God," but "without God, before God, and not in accordance with God."[279]

399 Scripture portrays the tragic consequences of this first disobedience. Adam and Eve immediately lose the grace of original holiness.[280] They become afraid of the God of whom they have conceived a distorted image—that of a God jealous of his prerogatives.[281]

1607 **400** The harmony in which they
had found themselves, thanks to
original justice, is now destroyed:
2514 the control of the soul's spiritual fac-
602, 1008 ulties over the body is shattered; the
union of man and woman becomes subject to tensions, their relations henceforth marked by lust and domination.[282] Harmony with creation is broken: visible creation has become alien and hostile to man.[283] Because of man, creation is now subject "to its bondage to decay."[284] Finally, the consequence explicitly foretold for this disobedience will come true: man will "return to the ground,"[285] for out of it he was taken. *Death makes its entrance into human history.*[286]

401 After that first sin, the world is virtually inundated by sin. There is Cain's murder of his brother Abel and the universal corruption which
follows in the wake of sin. Likewise, 1865
sin frequently manifests itself in the
history of Israel, especially as infidel- 2259
ity to the God of the Covenant and
as transgression of the Law of Moses. And even after Christ's atonement, sin raises its head in countless ways among Christians.[287] Scripture and the Church's Tradition continually
recall the presence and *universality* 1739
of sin in man's history:

> What Revelation makes known to us is confirmed by our own experience. For when man looks into his own heart he finds that he is drawn toward what is wrong and sunk in many evils which cannot come from his good creator. Often refusing to acknowledge God as his source, man has also upset the relationship which should link him to his last end; and at the same time he has broken the right order that should reign within himself as well as between himself and other men and all creatures.[288]

The consequences of Adam's sin for humanity

[278] Cf. *Gen* 3:1–11; *Rom* 5:19. — [279] St. Maximus the Confessor, *Ambigua*: PG 91, 1156C; cf. Gen 3:5. — [280] Cf. *Rom* 3:23. — [281] Cf. *Gen* 3:5–10. — [282] Cf. *Gen* 3:7–16. — [283] Cf. *Gen* 3:17, 19. — [284] *Rom* 8:21. — [285] *Gen* 3:19; cf. 2:17. — [286] Cf. *Rom* 5:12. — [287] Cf. *Gen* 4:3–15; 6:5, 12; *Rom* 1:18–32; *1 Cor* 1–6; *Rev* 2–3. — [288] *GS* 13 § 1.

402 All men are implicated in Adam's sin, as St. Paul affirms: "By one man's disobedience many [that is, all men] were made sinners": "sin came into the world through one man and death through sin, and so death spread to all men because all men sinned.... "[289] The Apostle contrasts
430, 605 the universality of sin and death with the universality of salvation in Christ. "Then as one man's trespass led to condemnation for all men, so one man's act of righteousness leads to acquittal and life for all men."[290]

403 Following St. Paul, the Church has always taught that the overwhelming misery which oppresses men and their inclination
2606 toward evil and death cannot be understood apart from their connection with Adam's sin and the fact that he has transmitted to us a sin with which we are all born afflicted, a sin which is the "death of the soul."[291] Because of this certainty of faith, the Church baptizes for the re
1250 mission of sins even tiny infants who have not committed personal sin.[292]

404 How did the sin of Adam become the sin of all his descendants? The whole human race is in Adam "as one body of one man."[293] By this "unity of the human race" all men are implicated in Adam's sin, as all are im-
360 plicated in Christ's justice. Still, the transmission of original sin is a mystery that we cannot fully understand.
50 But we do know by Revelation that Adam had received original holiness and justice not for himself alone, but for all human nature. By yielding to the tempter, Adam and Eve committed a *personal sin*, but this sin affected *the human nature* that they would then transmit in a *fallen state*.[294] It is a sin which will be transmitted by propagation to all mankind, that is, by the transmission of a human nature deprived of original holiness and justice. And that is why original sin is called "sin" only in an analogical sense: it is a sin "contracted" and not "committed"—a state and not an act.

405 Although it is proper to each individual,[295] original sin does not have the character of a personal fault in any of Adam's descendants. It is a deprivation of original holiness and justice, but human nature has not been totally corrupted: it is wounded in the natural powers proper to it; subject to ignorance, suffering, and the dominion of death; and inclined to sin—an inclination to evil that is called "concupiscence." Baptism, by 2515
imparting the life of Christ's grace, erases original sin and turns a man 1264
back toward God, but the consequences for nature, weakened and inclined to evil, persist in man and summon him to spiritual battle.

406 The Church's teaching on the transmission of original sin was articulated more precisely in the fifth century, especially under the impulse of St. Augustine's reflections against Pelagianism, and in the sixteenth century, in opposition to the Protestant Reformation. Pelagius held that man could, by the natural power of free will and without the necessary help of God's grace, lead a morally good life; he thus reduced the influence of Adam's fault to bad example. The first Protestant reformers, on the contrary, taught that original sin

289 *Rom* 5:12, 19. — 290 *Rom* 5:18. — 291 Cf. Council of Trent: DS 1512. — 292 Cf. Council of Trent: DS 1514. — 293 St. Thomas Aquinas, *De Malo* 4, 1. — 294 Cf. Council of Trent: DS 1511–1512. — 295 Cf. Council of Trent: DS 1513.

has radically perverted man and destroyed his freedom; they identified the sin inherited by each man with the tendency to evil (concupiscentia), which would be insurmountable. The Church pronounced on the meaning of the data of Revelation on original sin especially at the second Council of Orange (529)[296] and at the Council of Trent (1546).[297]

A hard battle...

407 The doctrine of original sin, closely connected with that of redemption by Christ, provides lucid discernment of man's situation and
2015 activity in the world. By our first parents' sin, the devil has acquired a
2852 certain domination over man, even though man remains free. Original sin entails "captivity under the power of him who thenceforth had the power of death, that is, the devil."[298] Ignorance of the fact that man has a wounded nature inclined to evil gives rise to serious errors in the ar-
1888 eas of education, politics, social action,[299] and morals.

408 The consequences of original sin and of all men's personal sins put the world as a whole in the sinful condition aptly described in St. John's expression, "the sin of the world."[300] This expression can also refer to the negative influence exerted on people by communal situations and social structures that are
1865 the fruit of men's sins.[301]

409 This dramatic situation of "the whole world [which] is in the power of the evil one"[302] makes
2516 man's life a battle:

The whole of man's history has been the story of dour combat with the powers of evil, stretching, so our Lord tells us, from the very dawn of history until the last day. Finding himself in the midst of the battlefield man has to struggle to do what is right, and it is at great cost to himself, and aided by God's grace, that he succeeds in achieving his own inner integrity.[303]

IV. "You Did Not Abandon Him to the Power of Death"

410 After his fall, man was not abandoned by God. On the contrary, God calls him and in a mysterious way heralds the coming victory over evil and his restoration from 55, 705
his fall.[304] This passage in Genesis
is called the *Protoevangelium* ("first 1609, 2568
gospel"): the first announcement of the Messiah and Redeemer, of a
battle between the serpent and the 675
Woman, and of the final victory of a descendant of hers.

411 The Christian tradition sees in this passage an announcement of the "New Adam" who, because he "became obedient unto death, even
death on a cross," makes amends 359, 615
superabundantly for the disobedience of Adam.[305] Furthermore many Fathers and Doctors of the Church have seen the woman announced in the *Protoevangelium* as Mary, the mother of Christ, the "new Eve." Mary benefited first of all and uniquely from Christ's victory over sin: she was preserved from all stain
of original sin and by a special grace 491
of God committed no sin of any kind during her whole earthly life.[306]

[296] DS 371–372. — [297] DS 1510–1516. — [298] Council of Trent (1546): DS 1511; cf. *Heb* 2:14. — [299] Cf. John Paul II, *CA* 25. — [300] *Jn* 1:29. — [301] Cf. John Paul II, *RP* 16. — [302] *1 Jn* 5:19; cf. *1 Pet* 5:8. — [303] *GS* 37 § 2. — [304] Cf. *Gen* 3:9, 15. — [305] Cf. *1 Cor* 15:21–22, 45; *Phil* 2:8; *Rom* 5:19–20. — [306] Cf. Pius IX, *Ineffabilis Deus*: DS 2803; Council of Trent: DS 1573.

412 But *why did God not prevent the first man from sinning*? St. Leo the Great responds, "Christ's inexpressible grace gave us blessings
310, 395 better than those the demon's envy had taken away."[307] And St. Thomas Aquinas wrote, "There is nothing to prevent human nature's being raised up to something greater, even after sin; God permits evil in order to draw forth some greater good. Thus
272 St. Paul says, 'Where sin increased, grace abounded all the more'; and the Exultet sings, 'O happy fault,...
1994 which gained for us so great a Redeemer!'"[308]

In Brief

413 *"God did not make death, and he does not delight in the death of the living.... It was through the devil's envy that death entered the world"* (Wis *1:13; 2:24).*

414 *Satan or the devil and the other demons are fallen angels who have freely refused to serve God and his plan. Their choice against God is definitive. They try to associate man in their revolt against God.*

415 *"Although set by God in a state of rectitude, man, enticed by the evil one, abused his freedom at the very start of history. He lifted himself up against God and sought to attain his goal apart from him"* (GS *13 § 1).*

416 *By his sin Adam, as the first man, lost the original holiness and justice he had received from God, not only for himself but for all human beings.*

417 *Adam and Eve transmitted to their descendants human nature wounded by their own first sin and hence deprived of original holiness and justice; this deprivation is called "original sin."*

418 *As a result of original sin, human nature is weakened in its powers; subject to ignorance, suffering, and the domination of death; and inclined to sin (This inclination is called "concupiscence.").*

419 *"We therefore hold, with the Council of Trent, that original sin is transmitted with human nature, 'by propagation, not by imitation' and that it is...'proper to each'"* (Paul VI, CPG *§ 16).*

420 *The victory that Christ won over sin has given us greater blessings than those which sin had taken from us: "where sin increased, grace abounded all the more"* (Rom *5:20).*

421 *Christians believe that "the world has been established and kept in being by the Creator's love; has fallen into slavery to sin but has been set free by Christ, crucified and risen to break the power of the evil one..."* (GS *2 § 2).*

[307] St. Leo the Great, *Sermo* 73, 4: PL 54, 396. — [308] St. Thomas Aquinas, *STh* III, 1, 3, ad 3; cf. *Rom* 5:20.

Chapter Two:

I BELIEVE IN JESUS CHRIST, THE ONLY SON OF GOD

The Good News: God has sent his Son

422 "But when the time had fully come, God sent forth his Son, born of a woman, born under the law, to redeem those who were under the
389 law, so that we might receive adoption as sons."[1] This is "the gospel of Jesus Christ, the Son of God":[2] God has visited his people. He has fulfilled the promise he made to Abraham and his descendants. He acted far beyond all expectation—he has
2763 sent his own "beloved Son."[3]

423 We believe and confess that Jesus of Nazareth, born a Jew of a daughter of Israel at Bethlehem at the time of King Herod the Great and the emperor Caesar Augustus, a carpenter by trade, who died crucified in Jerusalem under the procurator Pontius Pilate during the reign of the emperor Tiberius, is the eternal Son of God made man. He "came from God,"[4] "descended from heaven,"[5] and "came in the flesh."[6] For "the Word became flesh and dwelt among us, full of grace and truth; we have beheld his glory, glory as of the only Son from the Father.... And from his fullness have we all received, grace upon grace."[7]

424 Moved by the grace of the Holy Spirit and drawn by the Father, we believe in Jesus and confess: "You are the Christ, the Son of the
683 living God."[8] On the rock of this faith confessed by St. Peter, Christ
built his Church.[9] 552

"To preach...the unsearchable riches of Christ"[10]

425 The transmission of the Christian faith consists primarily in proclaiming Jesus Christ in order to lead others to faith in him. From the beginning, the first disciples burned with the desire to proclaim Christ: "We cannot but speak of what we have seen and heard."[11] And they invite people of every era to enter into 850, 858
the joy of their communion with Christ:

> That which was from the beginning, which we have heard, which we have seen with our eyes, which we have looked upon and touched with our hands, concerning the word of life—the life was made manifest, and we saw it, and testify to it, and proclaim to you the eternal life which was with the Father and was made manifest to us—that which we have seen and heard we proclaim also to you, so that you may have fellowship with us; and our fellowship is with the Father and with his Son Jesus Christ. And we are writing this that our joy may be complete.[12]

At the heart of catechesis: Christ

426 "At the heart of catechesis we find, in essence, a Person, the Person of Jesus of Nazareth, the only Son from the Father...who suffered and

[1] *Gal* 4:4–5. — [2] *Mk* 1:1. — [3] *Mk* 1:11; cf. *Lk* 1:55, 68. — [4] *Jn* 13:3. — [5] *Jn* 3:13; 6:33. — [6] *1 Jn* 4:2. — [7] *Jn* 1:14, 16. — [8] *Mt* 16:16. — [9] Cf. *Mt* 16:18; St. Leo the Great, *Sermo* 4, 3: PL 54, 150–152; 51, 1: PL 54, 308–309; 62, 2: PL 54, 350–351; 83, 3: PL 54, 431–432. — [10] *Eph* 3:8. — [11] *Acts* 4:20. — [12] *1 Jn* 1:1–4.

1698 died for us and who now, after rising, is living with us forever."[13] To
catechize is "to reveal in the Person
of Christ the whole of God's eternal
design reaching fulfillment in that
Person. It is to seek to understand
the meaning of Christ's actions and
513 words and of the signs worked by
him."[14] Catechesis aims at putting
"people…in communion…with Jesus Christ: only he can lead us to the
love of the Father in the Spirit and
make us share in the life of the Holy
260 Trinity."[15]

427 In catechesis "Christ, the Incarnate Word and Son of God,…
is taught—everything else is taught
with reference to him—and it is
Christ alone who teaches—anyone
else teaches to the extent that he is
Christ's spokesman, enabling Christ
2145 to teach with his lips.… Every catechist should be able to apply to himself the mysterious words of Jesus:
'My teaching is not mine, but his
876 who sent me.'"[16]

428 Whoever is called "to teach Christ" must first seek "the surpassing worth of knowing Christ Jesus"; he must suffer "the loss of all things…" in order to "gain Christ and be found in him," and "to know him and the power of his resurrection, and [to] share his sufferings, becoming like him in his death, that if possible [he] may attain the resurrection from the dead."[17]

429 From this loving knowledge of Christ springs the desire to proclaim him, to "evangelize," and to lead others to the "yes" of faith in Jesus Christ. But at the same time the
need to know this faith better makes 851
itself felt. To this end, following the
order of the Creed, Jesus' principal
titles—"Christ," "Son of God," and
"Lord" (*article 2*)—will be presented. The Creed next confesses the
chief mysteries of his life—those of
his Incarnation (*article 3*), Paschal
mystery (*articles 4 and 5*), and glorification (*articles 6 and 7*).

I. Jesus

430 Jesus means in Hebrew: "God
saves." At the annunciation, the angel Gabriel gave him the name Jesus
as his proper name, which expresses
both his identity and his mission.[18] 210
Since God alone can forgive sins,
it is God who, in Jesus his eternal
Son made man, "will save his people 402
from their sins."[19] In Jesus, God recapitulates all of his history of salvation on behalf of men.

431 In the history of salvation
God was not content to deliver Israel "out of the house of bondage"[20] by
bringing them out of Egypt. He also
saves them from their sin. Because
sin is always an offense against God,
only he can forgive it.[21] For this rea- 1441, 18
son Israel, becoming more and more
aware of the universality of sin, will
no longer be able to seek salvation 388
except by invoking the name of the
Redeemer God.[22]

432 The name "Jesus" signifies
that the very name of God is present
in the person of his Son, made man
for the universal and definitive redemption from sins. It is the divine 589, 266
name that alone brings salvation,
and henceforth all can invoke his 389

[13] *CT* 5. — [14] *CT* 5. — [15] *CT* 5. — [16] *CT* 6; cf. *Jn* 7:16. — [17] *Phil* 3:8–11. — [18] Cf. *Lk* 1:31. — [19] *Mt* 1:21; cf. 2:7. — [20] *Deut* 5:6. — [21] Cf. *Ps* 51:4, 12. — [22] Cf. *Ps* 79:9.

name, for Jesus united himself to all
161 men through his Incarnation,[23] so that "there is no other name under heaven given among men by which we must be saved."[24]

433 The name of the Savior God was invoked only once in the year by the high priest in atonement for the sins of Israel, after he had sprinkled the mercy seat in the Holy of Holies with the sacrificial blood. The
615 mercy seat was the place of God's presence.[25] When St. Paul speaks of Jesus whom "God put forward as an expiation by his blood," he means that in Christ's humanity "God was in Christ reconciling the world to himself."[26]

434 Jesus' Resurrection glorifies the name of the Savior God, for from that time on it is the name of Jesus that fully manifests the su
2812 preme power of the "name which is above every name."[27] The evil spirits fear his name; in his name his disciples perform miracles, for the Father
2614 grants all they ask in this name.[28]

435 The name of Jesus is at the heart of Christian prayer. All liturgical prayers conclude with the words "through our Lord Jesus Christ." The
67–2668 *Hail Mary* reaches its high point in the words "blessed is the fruit of thy
2676 womb, Jesus." The Eastern prayer of the heart, the *Jesus Prayer*, says: "Lord Jesus Christ, Son of God, have mercy on me, a sinner." Many Christians, such as St. Joan of Arc, have died with the one word "Jesus" on their lips.

II. Christ

436 The word "Christ" comes from the Greek translation of the Hebrew *Messiah*, which means "anointed." It became the name proper to Jesus only because he accomplished 690, 695
perfectly the divine mission that "Christ" signifies. In effect, in Israel those consecrated to God for a mission that he gave were anointed in his name. This was the case for kings, for priests and, in rare instances, for prophets.[29] This had to be the case all the more so for the Messiah whom God would send to inaugurate his kingdom definitively.[30] It was necessary that the Messiah be anointed by the Spirit of the Lord at once as king and priest, and also as prophet.[31] Je- 711–716
sus fulfilled the messianic hope of Israel in his threefold office of priest, 783
prophet, and king.

437 To the shepherds, the angel announced the birth of Jesus as the Messiah promised to Israel: "To you is born this day in the city of David a Savior, who is Christ the Lord."[32] 525, 486
From the beginning he was "the one whom the Father consecrated and sent into the world," conceived as "holy" in Mary's virginal womb.[33] God called Joseph to "take Mary as your wife, for that which is conceived in her is of the Holy Spirit," so that Jesus, "who is called Christ," should be born of Joseph's spouse into the messianic lineage of David.[34]

438 Jesus' messianic consecration reveals his divine mission, "for

[23] Cf. *Jn* 3:18; *Acts* 2:21; 5:41; *3 Jn* 7; *Rom* 10:6–13. — [24] *Acts* 4:12; cf. 9:14; *Jas* 2:7. — [25] Cf. *Ex* 25:22; *Lev* 16:2,15–16; *Num* 7:89; *Sir* 50:20; *Heb* 9:5, 7. — [26] *Rom* 3:25; *2 Cor* 5:19. — [27] *Phil* 2:9–10; cf. *Jn* 12:28. — [28] Cf. *Acts* 16:16–18; 19:13–16; *Mk* 16:17: *Jn* 15:16. — [29] Cf. *Ex* 29:7; *Lev* 8:12; *1 Sam* 9:16; 10:1; 16:1,12–13; *1 Kings* 1:39; 19:16. — [30] Cf. *Ps* 2:2; *Acts* 4:26–27. — [31] Cf. *Isa* 11:2; 61:1; *Zech* 4:14; 6:13: *Lk* 4:16–21. — [32] *Lk* 2:11. — [33] *Jn* 10:36: cf. *Lk* 1:35. — [34] *Mt* 1:20; cf. *Mt* 1:16; *Rom* 1:1; *2 Tim* 2:8; *Rev* 22:16.

the name 'Christ' implies 'he who anointed,' 'he who was anointed' and 'the very anointing with which he was anointed.' The one who
727 anointed is the Father, the one who was anointed is the Son, and he was anointed with the Spirit who is the anointing."[35] His eternal messianic consecration was revealed during
535 the time of his earthly life at the moment of his baptism by John, when "God anointed Jesus of Nazareth with the Holy Spirit and with power," "that he might be revealed to Israel"[36] as its Messiah. His works and words will manifest him as "the Holy One of God."[37]

439 Many Jews and even certain Gentiles who shared their hope recognized in Jesus the fundamental attributes of the messianic "Son of
528–529 David," promised by God to Israel.[38] Jesus accepted his rightful title of
547 Messiah, though with some reserve because it was understood by some of his contemporaries in too human a sense, as essentially political.[39]

440 Jesus accepted Peter's profession of faith, which acknowledged him to be the Messiah, by announcing the imminent Passion of the Son
552 of Man.[40] He unveiled the authentic content of his messianic kingship both in the transcendent identity of the Son of Man "who came down from heaven," and in his redemptive mission as the suffering Servant: "The Son of Man came not to be served but to serve, and to give his life as a ransom for many."[41] Hence
the true meaning of his kingship is 550
revealed only when he is raised high on the cross.[42] Only after his Resurrection will Peter be able to proclaim 445
Jesus' messianic kingship to the People of God: "Let all the house of Israel therefore know assuredly that God has made him both Lord and Christ, this Jesus whom you crucified."[43]

III. The Only Son of God

441 In the Old Testament, "*son of God*" is a title given to the angels, the Chosen People, the children of Israel, and their kings.[44] It signifies an adoptive sonship that establishes a relationship of particular intimacy between God and his creature. When the promised Messiah-King is called "son of God," it does not necessarily imply that he was more than human, according to the literal meaning of these texts. Those who called Jesus "son of God," as the Messiah of Israel, perhaps meant nothing more than this.[45]

442 Such is not the case for Simon Peter when he confesses Jesus as "the Christ, the Son of the living God," for Jesus responds solemnly: "Flesh and blood has not *revealed* this to you, but *my Father* who is in
heaven."[46] Similarly Paul will write, 552
regarding his conversion on the road to Damascus, "When he who had set me apart before I was born, and had called me through his grace, was pleased to reveal his Son to me, in order that I might preach him among the Gentiles...."[47] "And in

[35] St. Irenaeus, *Adv. haeres.*, 3, 18, 3: PG 7/1, 934. — [36] *Acts* 10:38; *Jn* 1:31. — [37] *Mk* 1:24; *Jn* 6:69; *Acts* 3:14. — [38] Cf. *Mt* 2:2; 9:27; 12:23; 15:22; 20:30; 21:9, 15. — [39] Cf. *Jn* 4:25–26; 6:15;11:27; *Mt* 22:41–46; *Lk* 24:21. — [40] Cf. *Mt* 16:16–23. — [41] *Jn* 3:13: *Mt* 20:28; cf. *Jn* 6:62; *Dan* 7:13; *Isa* 53:10–12. — [42] Cf. *Jn* 19:19–22; *Lk* 23:39–43. — [43] *Acts* 2:36. — [44] Cf. *Deut* 14:1; (LXX) 32:8; *Job* 1:6; *Ex* 4:22; *Hos* 2:1; 11:1; Jer 3:19; Sir 36:11; Wis 18:13; 2 Sam 7:14; Ps 82:6. — [45] Cf. *1 Chr* 17:13; *Ps* 2:7; *Mt* 27:54; *Lk* 23:47. — [46] *Mt* 16:16–17. — [47] *Gal* 1:15–16.

the synagogues immediately [Paul] proclaimed Jesus, saying, 'He is the Son of God.'"[48] From the beginning
424 this acknowledgment of Christ's divine sonship will be the center of the apostolic faith, first professed by Peter as the Church's foundation.[49]

443 Peter could recognize the transcendent character of the Messiah's divine sonship because Jesus had clearly allowed it to be so understood. To his accusers' question before the Sanhedrin, "Are you the Son of God, then?" Jesus answered, "You say that I am."[50] Well before this, Jesus referred to himself as "the Son" who knows the Father, as distinct from the "servants" God had earlier sent to his people; he is superior even to the angels.[51] He distinguished his sonship from that of his disciples by never saying "our Father," except to command them: "You, then, pray like this: 'Our Father,'" and he em-
2786 phasized this distinction, saying "my Father and your Father."[52]

444 The Gospels report that at two solemn moments, the Baptism and the Transfiguration of Christ, the voice of the Father designates Jesus
536, 554 his "beloved Son."[53] Jesus calls himself the "only Son of God," and by this title affirms his eternal preexistence.[54] He asks for faith in "the name of the only Son of God."[55] In the centurion's exclamation before the crucified Christ, "Truly this man was the Son of God,"[56] that Christian confession is already heard. Only in the Paschal mystery can the believer give the title "Son of God" its full meaning.

445 After his Resurrection, Jesus' divine sonship becomes manifest in the power of his glorified humanity. He was "designated Son of God in power according to the Spirit of ho- 653
liness by his Resurrection from the dead."[57] The apostles can confess: "We have beheld his glory, glory as of the only Son from the Father, full of grace and truth."[58]

IV. Lord

446 In the Greek translation of 209
the Old Testament, the ineffable Hebrew name YHWH, by which God revealed himself to Moses,[59] is rendered as *Kyrios*, "Lord." From then on, "*Lord*" becomes the more usual name by which to indicate the divinity of Israel's God. The New Testament uses this full sense of the title "Lord" both for the Father and—what is new—for Jesus, who is thereby recognized as God Himself.[60]

447 Jesus ascribes this title to himself in a veiled way when he disputes with the Pharisees about the meaning of *Psalm* 110, but also in an explicit way when he addresses his apostles.[61] Throughout his public life, he demonstrated his divine 548
sovereignty by works of power over nature, illnesses, demons, death, and sin.

448 Very often in the Gospels people address Jesus as "Lord." This title testifies to the respect and trust of those who approach him for help and healing.[62] At the prompting of
the Holy Spirit, "Lord" expresses the 208, 683

[48] *Acts* 9:20. — [49] Cf. *1 Thess* 1:10; *Jn* 20:31; *Mt* 16:18 — [50] *Lk* 22:70; cf. *Mt* 26:64; *Mk* 14:61–62. — [51] Cf. *Mt* 11:27; 21:34–38; 24:36. — [52] *Mt* 5:48; 6:8–9; 7:21; *Lk* 11:13; *Jn* 20:17. — [53] Cf. *Mt* 3:17; cf. *Mt* 17:5. — [54] *Jn* 3:16; cf. 10:36. — [55] *Jn* 3:18. — [56] *Mk* 15:39. — [57] *Rom* 1:3; cf. *Acts* 13:33. — [58] *Jn* 1:14. — [59] Cf. *Ex* 3:14. — [60] Cf. *1 Cor* 2:8. — [61] Cf. *Mt* 22:41–46; cf. *Acts* 2:34–36; *Heb* 1:13; *Jn* 13:13. — [62] Cf. *Mt* 8:2; 14:30; 15:22; et al.

recognition of the divine mystery of Jesus.[63] In the encounter with the risen Jesus, this title becomes adoration: "My Lord and my God!" It thus takes on a connotation of love and affection that remains proper to the Christian tradition: "It is the
641 Lord!"[64]

449 By attributing to Jesus the divine title "Lord," the first confessions of the Church's faith affirm from the beginning that the power, honor, and glory due to God the Father are due also to Jesus, because "he was in
461 the form of God,"[65] and the Father manifested the sovereignty of Jesus
653 by raising him from the dead and exalting him into his glory.[66]

450 From the beginning of Christian history, the assertion of Christ's lordship over the world and over history has implicitly recognized
668–672 that man should not submit his personal freedom in an absolute manner to any earthly power, but only to God the Father and the Lord Jesus
2242 Christ: Caesar is not "the Lord."[67] "The Church…believes that the key, the center, and the purpose of the whole of man's history is to be found in its Lord and Master."[68]

451 Christian prayer is characterized by the title "Lord," wheth-
2664–2665 er in the invitation to prayer ("The Lord be with you."), its conclusion
2817 ("through Christ our Lord"), or the exclamation full of trust and hope: *Maran atha* ("Our Lord, come!"), or *Marana tha* ("Come, Lord!")—"Amen. Come, Lord Jesus!"[69]

In Brief

452 *The name Jesus means "God saves." The child born of the Virgin Mary is called Jesus, "for he will save his people from their sins" (*Mt *1:21): "there is no other name under heaven given among men by which we must be saved" (*Acts *4:12).*

453 *The title "Christ" means "Anointed One" (Messiah). Jesus is the Christ, for "God anointed Jesus of Nazareth with the Holy Spirit and with power" (*Acts *10:38). He was the one "who is to come" (*Lk *7:19), the object of "the hope of Israel" (*Acts *28:20).*

454 *The title "Son of God" signifies the unique and eternal relationship of Jesus Christ to God his Father: he is the only Son of the Father (cf.* Jn *1:14,18; 3:16,18); he is God himself (cf.* Jn *1:1). To be a Christian, one must believe that Jesus Christ is the Son of God (cf.* Acts *8:37;* 1 Jn *2:23).*

455 *The title "Lord" indicates divine sovereignty. To confess or invoke Jesus as Lord is to believe in his divinity. "No one can say 'Jesus is Lord' except by the Holy Spirit" (*1 Cor *12:3).*

[63] Cf. *Lk* 1:43; 2:11. — [64] *Jn* 20:28; *Jn* 21:7. — [65] Cf. *Acts* 2:34–36; *Rom* 9:5; *Titus* 2:13; *Rev* 5:13; *Phil* 2:6. — [66] Cf. *Rom* 10:9; *1 Cor* 12:3; *Phil* 2:9–11. — [67] Cf. *Rev* 11:15; *Mk* 12:17; *Acts* 5:29. — [68] *GS* 10 § 3; cf. 45 § 2. — [69] *1 Cor* 16:22; *Rev* 22:20.

Article 3: "HE WAS CONCEIVED BY THE POWER OF THE HOLY SPIRIT, AND WAS BORN OF THE VIRGIN MARY"

Paragraph 1
The Son of God Became Man

I. Why Did the Word Become Flesh?

456 With the Nicene Creed, we answer by confessing: "For us men and for our salvation he came down from heaven; by the power of the Holy Spirit, he became incarnate of the Virgin Mary, and was made man."

457 The Word became flesh for us *in order to save us by reconciling us with God*, who "loved us and sent his Son to be the expiation for our
607 sins": "the Father has sent his Son as the Savior of the world," and "he was revealed to take away sins":[70]

> 385 Sick, our nature demanded to be healed; fallen, to be raised up; dead, to rise again. We had lost the possession of the good; it was necessary for it to be given back to us. Closed in the darkness, it was necessary to bring us the light; captives, we awaited a Savior; prisoners, help; slaves, a liberator. Are these things minor or insignificant? Did they not move God to descend to human nature and visit it, since humanity was in so miserable and unhappy a state?[71]

458 The Word became flesh *so that thus we might know God's love*: "In this the love of God was made manifest among us, that God sent
219 his only Son into the world, so that we might live through him."[72] "For God so loved the world that he gave his only Son, that whoever believes in him should not perish but have eternal life."[73]

459 The Word became flesh *to be our model of holiness*: "Take my yoke upon you, and learn from me." "I
am the way, and the truth, and the 520
life; no one comes to the Father, but
by me."[74] On the mountain of the 823, 2012
Transfiguration, the Father commands: "Listen to him!"[75] Jesus is the model for the Beatitudes and the norm of the new law: "Love one
another as I have loved you."[76] This 1717, 1965
love implies an effective offering of oneself, after his example.[77]

460 The Word became flesh to make us "*partakers of the divine nature*":[78] "For this is why the Word became man, and the Son of God
became the Son of man: so that 1265, 1391
man, by entering into communion with the Word and thus receiving divine sonship, might become a son
of God."[79] "For the Son of God be- 1988
came man so that we might become God."[80] "The only-begotten Son of God, wanting to make us sharers in his divinity, assumed our nature, so that he, made man, might make men gods."[81]

II. The Incarnation

461 Taking up St. John's expression, "The Word became flesh,"[82]
the Church calls "Incarnation" the 653, 661

[70] *1 Jn* 4:10; 4:14; 3:5. — [71] St. Gregory of Nyssa, *Orat. catech.* 15: PG 45, 48B. — [72] *1 Jn* 4:9. — [73] *Jn* 3:16. — [74] *Mt* 11:29; *Jn* 14:6. — [75] *Mk* 9:7; cf. *Deut* 6:4–5. — [76] *Jn* 15:12. — [77] Cf. *Mk* 8:34. — [78] *2 Pet* 1:4. — [79] St. Irenaeus, *Adv. haeres.* 3, 19, 1: PG 7/1, 939. — [80] St. Athanasius, *De inc.*, 54, 3: PG 25, 192B. — [81] St. Thomas Aquinas, *Opusc.* 57: 1–4. — [82] *Jn* 1:14.

fact that the Son of God assumed
449 a human nature in order to accomplish our salvation in it. In a hymn cited by St. Paul, the Church sings the mystery of the Incarnation:

> Have this mind among yourselves, which is yours in Christ Jesus, who, though he was in the form of God, did not count equality with God a thing to be grasped, but emptied himself, taking the form of a servant, being born in the likeness of men. And being found in human form he humbled himself and became obedient unto death, even death on a cross.[83]

462 *The Letter to the Hebrews* refers to the same mystery:

> Consequently, when Christ came into the world, he said, "Sacrifices and offerings you have not desired, but a body have you prepared for me; in burnt offerings and sin offerings you have taken no pleasure. Then I said, 'Lo, I have come to do your will, O God.'"[84]

463 Belief in the true Incarnation of the Son of God is the distinctive sign of Christian faith: "By this you know the Spirit of God: every spir
90 it which confesses that Jesus Christ has come in the flesh is of God."[85] Such is the joyous conviction of the Church from her beginning whenever she sings "the mystery of our religion": "He was manifested in the flesh."[86]

III. True God and True Man

464 The unique and altogether singular event of the Incarnation of the Son of God does not mean that Jesus Christ is part God and part man, nor does it imply that he is the result of a confused mixture of the divine and the human. He became truly man while remaining truly God. Jesus Christ is true God and true man. During the first centuries,
the Church had to defend and clari- 88
fy this truth of faith against the heresies that falsified it.

465 The first heresies denied not so much Christ's divinity as his true humanity (Gnostic Docetism). From apostolic times the Christian faith has insisted on the true incarnation of God's Son "come in the flesh."[87] But already in the third century, the Church in a council at Antioch had to affirm against Paul of Samosata that Jesus Christ is Son of God by nature and not by adoption. The first ecumenical council of Nicaea in 325 confessed in its Creed that the Son of God is "begotten, not made, of the same substance (*homoousios*) as the Father," and condemned Arius, who had affirmed that the Son 495
of God "came to be from things that were not" and that he was "from another substance" than that of the Father.[88]

466 The Nestorian heresy regarded Christ as a human person joined to the divine person of God's Son. Opposing this heresy, St. Cyril of Alexandria and the third ecumenical council at Ephesus in 431 confessed "that the Word, uniting to himself in his person the flesh animated by a rational soul, became man."[89] Christ's humanity has no other subject than the divine person of the Son of God, who assumed it and made it his

[83] *Phil* 2:5–8; cf. *LH*, Saturday, Canticle at Evening Prayer. — [84] *Heb* 10:5–7, citing *Ps* 40:6–8 ([7–9] LXX). — [85] *1 Jn* 4:2. — [86] *1 Tim* 3:16. — [87] Cf. *1 Jn* 4:2–3; *2 Jn* 7. — [88] Council of Nicaea I (325): DS 130, 126. — [89] Council of Ephesus (431): DS 250.

own, from his conception. For this reason the Council of Ephesus proclaimed in 431 that Mary truly became the Mother of God by the human conception of the Son of God in her womb: "Mother of God, not that the nature of the Word or his divinity received the beginning of its existence from the holy Virgin, but that, since the holy body, animated by a rational soul, which the Word of God united to himself according to the hypostasis, was born from her, the Word is said to be born according to the flesh."[90]

467 The Monophysites affirmed that the human nature had ceased to exist as such in Christ when the divine person of God's Son assumed it. Faced with this heresy, the fourth ecumenical council, at Chalcedon in 451, confessed:

> Following the holy Fathers, we unanimously teach and confess one and the same Son, our Lord Jesus Christ: the same perfect in divinity and perfect in humanity, the same truly God and truly man, composed of rational soul and body; consubstantial with the Father as to his divinity and consubstantial with us as to his humanity; "like us in all things but sin." He was begotten from the Father before all ages as to his divinity and in these last days, for us and for our salvation, was born as to his humanity of the virgin Mary, the Mother of God.[91]
>
> We confess that one and the same Christ, Lord, and only-begotten Son, is to be acknowledged in two natures without confusion, change, division, or separation. The distinction between the natures was never abolished by their union, but rather the character proper to each of the two natures was preserved as they came together in one person (*prosopon*) and one hypostasis.[92]

468 After the Council of Chalcedon, some made of Christ's human nature a kind of personal subject. Against them, the fifth ecumenical council at Constantinople in 553 confessed that "there is but one *hypostasis* [or person], which is our Lord Jesus Christ, one of the Trinity."[93] Thus everything in Christ's human nature is to be attributed to his
divine person as its proper subject, 254
not only his miracles but also his sufferings and even his death: "He who was crucified in the flesh, our Lord
Jesus Christ, is true God, Lord of 616
glory, and *one of the Holy Trinity*."[94]

469 The Church thus confesses that Jesus is inseparably true God
and true man. He is truly the Son 212
of God who, without ceasing to be God and Lord, became a man and our brother:

> "What he was, he remained and what he was not, he assumed," sings the Roman Liturgy.[95] And the liturgy of St. John Chrysostom proclaims and sings: "O only-begotten Son and Word of God, immortal being, you who deigned for our salvation to become incarnate of the holy Mother of God and ever-virgin Mary, you who without change became man and were crucified, O Christ our God, you who by your death have crushed death, you who are one of the Holy Trinity, glorified with the Father and the Holy Spirit, save us!"[96]

[90] Council of Ephesus: DS 251. — [91] Council of Chalcedon (451): DS 301; cf. *Heb* 4:15. — [92] Council of Chalcedon: DS 302. — [93] Council of Constantinople II (553): DS 424. — [94] Council of Constantinople II (553): DS 432; cf. DS 424; Council of Ephesus, DS 255. — [95] *LH*, January 1, Antiphon for Morning Prayer; cf. St. Leo the Great, *Sermo in nat. Dom.* 1, 2; PL 54, 191–192. — [96] Liturgy of St. John Chrysostom, Troparion "*O monogenes*."

IV. How Is the Son of God Man?

470 Because "human nature was assumed, not absorbed,"[97] in the mysterious union of the Incarnation, the Church was led over the course of centuries to confess the full reality of Christ's human soul, with its operations of intellect and will, and of his human body. In parallel fashion, she had to recall on each occasion that Christ's human nature belongs, as his own, to the divine person of the Son of God, who assumed it. Everything that Christ is and does in
516 this nature derives from "one of the Trinity." The Son of God therefore communicates to his humanity his own personal mode of existence in
626 the Trinity. In his soul as in his body, Christ thus expresses humanly the divine ways of the Trinity:[98]

2599 The Son of God...worked with human hands; he thought with a human mind. He acted with a human will, and with a human heart he loved. Born of the Virgin Mary, he has truly been made one of us, like to us in all things except sin.[99]

Christ's soul and his human knowledge

471 Apollinarius of Laodicaea asserted that in Christ the divine Word had replaced the soul or spirit. Against this error the Church confessed that the eternal Son also
363 assumed a rational, human soul.[100]

472 This human soul that the Son of God assumed is endowed with a true human knowledge. As such, this knowledge could not in itself be unlimited: it was exercised in the historical conditions of his existence in space and time. This is why the Son of God could, when he became man, "increase in wisdom and in stature, and in favor with God and man,"[101] and would even have to inquire for himself about what one in the human condition can learn only from experience.[102] This corresponded to the reality of his voluntary emptying of himself, taking "the form of a slave."[103]

473 But at the same time, this truly human knowledge of God's Son expressed the divine life of his person.[104] "The human nature of God's Son, *not by itself but by its union with the Word*, knew and showed forth in itself everything that pertains to God."[105] Such is first of all the case
with the intimate and immediate 240
knowledge that the Son of God made man has of his Father.[106] The Son in his human knowledge also showed the divine penetration he had into the secret thoughts of human hearts.[107]

474 By its union to the divine wisdom in the person of the Word incarnate, Christ enjoyed in his human knowledge the fullness of understanding of the eternal plans he had come to reveal.[108] What he admitted to not knowing in this area, he elsewhere declared himself not sent to reveal.[109]

Christ's human will

475 Similarly, at the sixth ecumenical council, Constantinople III in 681, the Church confessed

[97] *GS* 22 § 2. — [98] Cf. *Jn* 14:9–10. — [99] *GS* 22 § 2. — [100] Cf. Damasus I: DS 149. — [101] *Lk* 2:52. — [102] Cf. *Mk* 6:38; 8:27; *Jn* 11:34; etc. — [103] *Phil* 2:7. — [104] Cf. St. Gregory the Great, *"Sicut aqua" ad Eulogium, Epist. Lib.* 10, 39: PL 77, 1097A ff.; DS 475. — [105] St. Maximus the Confessor, *Qu. et dub.* 66: PG 90, 840A. — [106] Cf. *Mk* 14:36; *Mt* 11:27; *Jn* 1:18; 8:55; etc. — [107] Cf. *Mk* 2:8; *Jn* 2:25; 6:61; etc. — [108] Cf. *Mk* 8:31; 9:31; 10:33–34; 14:18–20, 26–30. — [109] Cf. *Mk* 13:32; *Acts* 1:7.

that Christ possesses two wills and
two natural operations, divine and
human. They are not opposed to
each other, but cooperate in such a
2008 way that the Word made flesh willed
2824 humanly in obedience to his Father
all that he had decided divinely with
the Father and the Holy Spirit for
our salvation.[110] Christ's human will "does not resist or oppose but rather submits to his divine and almighty will."[111]

Christ's true body

476 Since the Word became flesh
in assuming a true humanity, Christ's
159–1162 body was finite.[112] Therefore the human face of Jesus can be portrayed;
29–2132 at the seventh ecumenical council
(Nicaea II in 787) the Church recognized its representation in holy images to be legitimate.[113]

477 At the same time the Church has always acknowledged that in the body of Jesus "we see our God made visible and so are caught up in love of the God we cannot see."[114] The individual characteristics of Christ's body express the divine person of God's Son. He has made the features of his human body his own, to the point that they can be venerated when portrayed in a holy image, for the believer "who venerates the icon is venerating in it the person of the one depicted."[115]

The heart of the Incarnate Word

478 Jesus knew and loved us each and all during his life, his agony,
and his Passion and gave himself
up for...loved me and gave himself 487
for me."[116] He has loved us all with
a human heart. For this reason, the
Sacred Heart of Jesus, pierced by our 368
sins and for our salvation,[117] "is quite 2669
rightly considered the chief sign and
symbol of that...love with which 766
the divine Redeemer continually loves the eternal Father and all human beings" without exception.[118]

In Brief

479 *At the time appointed by God, the only Son of the Father, the eternal Word, that is, the Word and substantial Image of the Father, became incarnate; without losing his divine nature he has assumed human nature.*

480 *Jesus Christ is true God and true man, in the unity of his divine person; for this reason he is the one and only mediator between God and men.*

481 *Jesus Christ possesses two natures, one divine and the other human, not confused, but united in the one person of God's Son.*

482 *Christ, being true God and true man, has a human intellect and will, perfectly attuned and subject to his divine intellect and divine will, which he has in common with the Father and the Holy Spirit.*

483 *The Incarnation is therefore the mystery of the wonderful union of the divine and human natures in the one person of the Word.*

[110] Cf. Council of Constantinople III (681): DS 556–559. — [111] Council of Constantinople III: DS 556. — [112] Cf. Council of the Lateran (649): DS 504. — [113] Cf. *Gal* 3:1; cf. Council of Nicaea II (787): DS 600–603. — [114] *Roman Missal,* Preface of Christmas I. — [115] Council of Nicaea II: DS 601. — [116] *Gal* 2:20. — [117] Cf. *Jn* 19:34. — [118] Pius XII, encyclical, *Haurietis aquas* (1956): DS 3924; cf. DS 3812.

Paragraph 2
"CONCEIVED BY THE POWER OF THE HOLY SPIRIT AND BORN OF THE VIRGIN MARY"

I. Conceived by the Power of the Holy Spirit...

484 The Annunciation to Mary inaugurates "the fullness of time,"[119] the time of the fulfillment of God's promises and preparations. Mary was invited to conceive him in whom the "whole fullness of deity"
461 would dwell "bodily."[120] The divine response to her question, "How can this be, since I know not man?" was given by the power of the Spirit:
721 "The Holy Spirit will come upon you."[121]

485 The mission of the Holy Spirit is always conjoined and ordered to that of the Son.[122] The Holy Spirit, "the Lord, the giver of Life," is sent
689, 723 to sanctify the womb of the Virgin Mary and divinely fecundate it, causing her to conceive the eternal Son of the Father in a humanity drawn from her own.

486 The Father's only Son, conceived as man in the womb of the Virgin Mary, is "Christ," that is to say, anointed by the Holy Spirit,
437 from the beginning of his human existence, though the manifestation of this fact takes place only progressively: to the shepherds, to the magi, to John the Baptist, to the disciples.[123] Thus the whole life of Jesus Christ will make manifest "how God anointed Jesus of Nazareth with the Holy Spirit and with power."[124]

II. ...Born of the Virgin Mary

487 What the Catholic faith be- 963
lieves about Mary is based on what it believes about Christ, and what it teaches about Mary illumines in turn its faith in Christ.

Mary's predestination

488 "God sent forth his Son," but to prepare a body for him,[125] he wanted the free cooperation of a creature. For this, from all eternity God chose for the mother of his Son a daughter of Israel, a young Jewish woman of Nazareth in Galilee, "a virgin betrothed to a man whose name was Joseph, of the house of David; and the virgin's name was Mary":[126]

> The Father of mercies willed that the Incarnation should be preceded by assent on the part of the predestined mother, so that just as a woman had a share in the coming of death, so also should a woman contribute to the coming of life.[127]

489 Throughout the Old Covenant the mission of many holy women *prepared* for that of Mary. At the very beginning there was Eve; despite her disobedience, she receives 722
the promise of a posterity that will
be victorious over the evil one, as 410
well as the promise that she will be
the mother of all the living.[128] By 145
virtue of this promise, Sarah conceives a son in spite of her old age.[129] Against all human expectation God chooses those who were considered powerless and weak to show forth his faithfulness to his promises: Hannah, the mother of Samuel;

[119] *Gal* 4:4. — [120] *Col* 2:9. — [121] *Lk* 1:34–35 (Gk.). — [122] Cf. *Jn* 16:14–15. — [123] Cf. *Mt* 1:20; 2:1–12; *Lk* 1:35; 2:8–20; *Jn* 1:31–34; 2:11. — [124] *Acts* 10:38. — [125] *Gal* 4:4; *Heb* 10:5. — [126] *Lk* 1:26–27. — [127] *LG* 56; cf. *LG* 61. — [128] Cf. *Gen* 3:15, 20. — [129] Cf. *Gen* 18:10–14; 21:1–2.

Deborah; Ruth; Judith and Esther;
64 and many other women.[130] Mary "stands out among the poor and humble of the Lord, who confidently hope for and receive salvation from him. After a long period of waiting the times are fulfilled in her, the exalted Daughter of Sion, and the new plan of salvation is established."[131]

The Immaculate Conception

490 To become the mother of the Savior, Mary "was enriched by God with gifts appropriate to such a role."[132] The angel Gabriel at the moment of the annunciation salutes her as "full of grace."[133] In fact, in
676, 2853 order for Mary to be able to give the free assent of her faith to the announcement of her vocation, it was necessary that she be wholly borne
2001 by God's grace.

491 Through the centuries the Church has become ever more aware that Mary, "full of grace" through God,[134] was redeemed from the
411 moment of her conception. That is what the dogma of the Immaculate Conception confesses, as Pope Pius IX proclaimed in 1854:

> The most Blessed Virgin Mary was, from the first moment of her conception, by a singular grace and privilege of almighty God and by virtue of the merits of Jesus Christ, Savior of the human race, preserved immune from all stain of original sin.[135]

492 The "splendor of an entirely unique holiness" by which Mary is "enriched from the first instant of her conception" comes wholly from Christ: she is "redeemed, in a more exalted fashion, by reason of the merits of her Son."[136] The Father blessed 2011
Mary more than any other created
person "in Christ with every spiri- 1077
tual blessing in the heavenly places" and chose her "in Christ before the foundation of the world, to be holy and blameless before him in love."[137]

493 The Fathers of the Eastern tradition call the Mother of God "the All-Holy" (*Panagia*) and celebrate her as "free from any stain of sin, as though fashioned by the Holy Spirit and formed as a new creature."[138] By the grace of God Mary remained free of every personal sin her whole life long.

"Let it be done to me according to your word..."

494 At the announcement that she would give birth to "the Son of the Most High" without knowing man, by the power of the Holy Spirit, Mary responded with the obedi- 2617
ence of faith, certain that "with God
nothing will be impossible": "Be- 148
hold, I am the handmaid of the Lord; let it be [done] to me according to your word."[139] Thus, giving her consent to God's word, Mary becomes the mother of Jesus. Espousing the divine will for salvation wholeheartedly, without a single sin to restrain her, she gave herself entirely to the
person and to the work of her Son; 968
she did so in order to serve the mystery of redemption with him and dependent on him, by God's grace:[140]

> As St. Irenaeus says, "Being obedient she became the cause of salvation for herself and for the whole human

[130] Cf. *1 Cor* 1:17; *1 Sam* 1. — [131] *LG* 55. — [132] *LG* 56. — [133] *Lk* 1:28. — [134] *Lk* 1:28. — [135] Pius IX, *Ineffabilis Deus*, 1854: DS 2803. — [136] *LG* 53, 56. — [137] Cf. *Eph* 1:3–4. — [138] *LG* 56. — [139] *Lk* 1:28–38; cf. *Rom* 1:5. — [140] Cf. *LG* 56.

race."[141] Hence not a few of the early Fathers gladly assert...: "The knot of Eve's disobedience was untied by Mary's obedience: what the virgin Eve bound through her disbelief, Mary loosened by her faith."[142] Comparing her with Eve, they call Mary "the Mother of the living" and frequently claim: "Death through
726 Eve, life through Mary."[143]

Mary's divine motherhood

495 Called in the Gospels "the mother of Jesus," Mary is acclaimed by Elizabeth, at the prompting of the Spirit and even before the birth of her son, as "the mother of my Lord."[144] In fact, the One whom she conceived as man by the Holy Spirit, who truly became her Son according to the flesh, was none other than the Father's eternal Son, the second person of the Holy Trinity. Hence the Church confesses that Mary is truly
466, 2677 "Mother of God" (*Theotokos*).[145]

Mary's virginity

496 From the first formulations of her faith, the Church has confessed that Jesus was conceived solely by the power of the Holy Spirit in the womb of the Virgin Mary, affirming also the corporeal aspect of this event: Jesus was conceived "by the Holy Spirit without human seed."[146] The Fathers see in the virginal conception the sign that it truly was the Son of God who came in a humanity like our own. Thus St. Ignatius of Antioch at the beginning of the second century says:

> You are firmly convinced about our Lord, who is truly of the race of David according to the flesh, Son of God according to the will and power of God, truly born of a virgin,...he was truly nailed to a tree for us in his flesh under Pontius Pilate...he truly suffered, as he is also truly risen.[147]

497 The gospel accounts understand the virginal conception of Jesus as a divine work that surpasses all human understanding and possibility:[148] "That which is conceived in her is of the Holy Spirit," said the angel to Joseph about Mary his fiancée.[149] The Church sees here the fulfillment of the divine promise given through the prophet Isaiah: "Behold, a virgin shall conceive and bear a son."[150]

498 People are sometimes troubled by the silence of St. Mark's Gospel and the New Testament Epistles about Jesus' virginal conception. Some might wonder if we were merely dealing with legends or theological constructs not claiming to be history. To this we must respond: Faith in the virginal conception of Jesus met with the lively opposition, mockery, or incomprehension of non-believers, Jews and pagans alike;[151] so it could hardly have been motivated by pagan mythology or by some adaptation to the ideas of the age. The meaning of this event is accessible only to faith,

[141] St. Irenaeus, *Adv. haeres.* 3, 22, 4: PG 7/1, 959A. — [142] St. Irenaeus, *Adv. haeres.* 3, 22, 4: PG 7/1, 959A. — [143] *LG* 56; Epiphanius, *Haer.* 78, 18: PG 42, 728CD–729AB; St. Jerome, *Ep.* 22, 21: PL 22, 408. — [144] *Lk* 1:43; *Jn* 2:1; 19:25; cf. *Mt* 13:55; et al. — [145] Council of Ephesus (431): DS 251. — [146] Council of the Lateran (649): DS 503; cf. DS 10–64. — [147] St. Ignatius of Antioch, *Ad Smyrn.* 1–2: Apostolic Fathers, ed. J. B. Lightfoot (London: Macmillan, 1889) II/2, 289–293; SCh 10, 154–156; cf. *Rom* 1:3; *Jn* 1:13. — [148] Cf. *Mt* 1:18–25; *Lk* 1:26–38. — [149] *Mt* 1:20. — [150] *Isa* 7:14 in the LXX, quoted in *Mt* 1:23 (Gk.). — [151] Cf. St. Justin, *Dial.*, 99, 7: PG 6, 708–709; Origen, *Contra Celsum* 1, 32, 69: PG 11, 720–721; *et al.*

which understands in it the "con
90 nection of these mysteries with one
another"[152] in the totality of Christ's
mysteries, from his Incarnation to
his Passover. St. Ignatius of Antioch
already bears witness to this connection: "Mary's virginity and giving
birth, and even the Lord's death escaped the notice of the prince of this
2717 world: these three mysteries worthy
of proclamation were accomplished
in God's silence."[153]

Mary—"ever-virgin"

499 The deepening of faith in the virginal motherhood led the Church to confess Mary's real and perpetual virginity even in the act of giving birth to the Son of God made man.[154] In fact, Christ's birth "did not diminish his mother's virginal integrity but sanctified it."[155] And so the liturgy of the Church celebrates Mary as *Aeiparthenos*, the "Ever-virgin."[156]

500 Against this doctrine the objection is sometimes raised that the Bible mentions brothers and sisters of Jesus.[157] The Church has always understood these passages as not referring to other children of the Virgin Mary. In fact James and Joseph, "brothers of Jesus," are the sons of another Mary, a disciple of Christ, whom St. Matthew significantly calls "the other Mary."[158] They are close relations of Jesus, according to an Old Testament expression.[159]

501 Jesus is Mary's only son, but
her spiritual motherhood extends
to all men whom indeed he came to
save: "The Son whom she brought
forth is he whom God placed as the 969
first-born among many brethren,
that is, the faithful in whose genera- 970
tion and formulation she cooperates
with a mother's love."[160]

Mary's virginal motherhood in God's plan

502 The eyes of faith can discover
in the context of the whole of Revelation the mysterious reasons why
God in his saving plan wanted his
Son to be born of a virgin. These 90
reasons touch both on the person of
Christ and his redemptive mission,
and on the welcome Mary gave that
mission on behalf of all men.

503 Mary's virginity manifests
God's absolute initiative in the Incarnation. Jesus has only God as
Father. "He was never estranged
from the Father because of the human nature which he assumed.... 422
He is naturally Son of the Father as
to his divinity and naturally son of
his mother as to his humanity, but
properly Son of the Father in both
natures."[161]

504 Jesus is conceived by the
Holy Spirit in the Virgin Mary's
womb because he is the New Adam,
who inaugurates the new creation:
"The first man was from the earth,
a man of dust; the second man is 359
from heaven."[162] From his conception, Christ's humanity is filled
with the Holy Spirit, for God "gives
him the Spirit without measure."[163]
From "his fullness" as the head of
redeemed humanity "we have all received, grace upon grace."[164]

[152] *Dei Filius* 4: DS 3016. — [153] St. Ignatius of Antioch, *Ad Eph.* 19, 1: AF II/2, 76–80; SCh 10, 88; cf. *1 Cor* 2:8. — [154] Cf. DS 291; 294; 427; 442; 503; 571; 1880. — [155] *LG* 57. — [156] Cf. *LG* 52. — [157] Cf. *Mk* 3:31–35; 6:3; *1 Cor* 9:5; *Gal* 1:19. — [158] *Mt* 13:55; 28:1; cf. *Mt* 27:56. — [159] Cf. *Gen* 13:8; 14:16; 29:15; etc. — [160] *LG* 63; cf. *Jn* 19:26–27; *Rom* 8:29; *Rev* 12:17. — [161] Council of Friuli (796): DS 619; cf. *Lk* 2:48–49. — [162] *1 Cor* 15:45, 47. — [163] *Jn* 3:34. — [164] *Jn* 1:16; cf. *Col* 1:18.

505 By his virginal conception, Jesus, the New Adam, ushers in *the new birth* of children adopted in the Holy Spirit through faith. "How can
1265 this be?"[165] Participation in the divine life arises "not of blood nor of the will of the flesh nor of the will of man, but of God."[166] The acceptance of this life is virginal because it is entirely the Spirit's gift to man. The spousal character of the human vocation in relation to God[167] is fulfilled perfectly in Mary's virginal motherhood.

506 Mary is a virgin because her virginity is *the sign of her faith*
148 "unadulterated by any doubt," and of her undivided gift of herself to God's will.[168] It is her faith that en-
1814 ables her to become the mother of the Savior: "Mary is more blessed because she embraces faith in Christ than because she conceives the flesh of Christ."[169]

507 At once virgin and mother, Mary is the symbol and the most perfect realization of the Church: "the Church indeed…by receiving the word of God in faith becomes
967 herself a mother. By preaching and Baptism she brings forth sons, who are conceived by the Holy Spirit and born of God, to a new and immortal life. She herself is a virgin, who keeps in its entirety and purity the
149 faith she pledged to her spouse."[170]

In Brief

508 *From among the descendants of Eve, God chose the Virgin Mary to be the mother of his Son. "Full of grace," Mary is "the most excellent fruit of redemption" (SC 103): from the first instant of her conception, she was totally preserved from the stain of original sin and she remained pure from all personal sin throughout her life.*

509 *Mary is truly "Mother of God" since she is the mother of the eternal Son of God made man, who is God himself.*

510 *Mary "remained a virgin in conceiving her Son, a virgin in giving birth to him, a virgin in carrying him, a virgin in nursing him at her breast, always a virgin" (St. Augustine,* Serm. *186, 1: PL 38, 999): with her whole being she is "the handmaid of the Lord" (Lk 1:38).*

511 *The Virgin Mary "cooperated through free faith and obedience in human salvation" (* LG *56). She uttered her yes "in the name of all human nature" (St. Thomas Aquinas, STh III, 30, 1). By her obedience she became the new Eve, mother of the living.*

Paragraph 3
The Mysteries of Christ's Life

512 Concerning Christ's life the Creed speaks only about the mysteries of the Incarnation (conception and birth) and Paschal mystery (passion, crucifixion, death, burial, descent into hell, resurrection, and ascension). It says nothing explicitly about the mysteries of Jesus' hidden or public life, but the articles of faith concerning his Incarnation and
Passover do shed light on the *whole* 1163
of his earthly life. "All that Jesus did and taught, from the beginning until the day when he was taken up to

[165] *Lk* 1:34; cf. *Jn* 3:9. — [166] *Jn* 1:13. — [167] Cf. *2 Cor* 11:2. — [168] *LG* 63; cf. *1 Cor* 7:34–35. — [169] St. Augustine, *De virg.*, 3: PL 40, 398. — [170] *LG* 64; cf. 63.

heaven,"[171] is to be seen in the light of the mysteries of Christmas and Easter.

513 According to circumstances catechesis will make use of all the richness of the mysteries of Jesus. Here it is enough merely to indicate
246, 561 some elements common to all the mysteries of Christ's life (I), in order then to sketch the principal mysteries of Jesus' hidden (II) and public (III) life.

I. Christ's Whole Life Is Mystery

514 Many things about Jesus of interest to human curiosity do not figure in the Gospels. Almost nothing is said about his hidden life at Nazareth, and even a great part of his public life is not recounted.[172] What is written in the Gospels was set down there "so that you may believe that Jesus is the Christ, the Son of God, and that believing you may have life in his name."[173]

515 The Gospels were written by men who were among the first to have the faith[174] and wanted to share it with others. Having known
126 in faith who Jesus is, they could see and make others see the traces of his mystery in all his earthly life. From the swaddling clothes of his birth to the vinegar of his Passion and the shroud of his Resurrection, everything in Jesus' life was a sign of his mystery.[175] His deeds, miracles, and words all revealed that "in him the whole fullness of deity dwells bodily."[176] His humanity appeared as
609, 774 "sacrament," that is, the sign and instrument, of his divinity and of the salvation he brings: what was visible 477
in his earthly life leads to the invisible mystery of his divine sonship and redemptive mission.

Characteristics common to Jesus' mysteries

516 Christ's whole earthly life—his words and deeds, his silences and sufferings, indeed his manner of being and speaking—is *Revelation* of the Father. Jesus can say: "Whoev- 65
er has seen me has seen the Father," and the Father can say: "This is my Son, my Chosen; listen to him!"[177] Because our Lord became man in order to do his Father's will, even the least characteristics of his mysteries manifest "God's love...among 2708
us."[178]

517 Christ's whole life is a mystery of *redemption*. Redemption comes to us above all through the blood 606
of his cross,[179] but this mystery is at work throughout Christ's entire life: 1115

– already in his Incarnation through which by becoming poor he enriches us with his poverty;[180]
– in his hidden life which by his submission atones for our disobedience;[181]
– in his word which purifies its hearers;[182]
– in his healings and exorcisms by which "he took our infirmities and bore our diseases";[183]
– and in his Resurrection by which he justifies us.[184]

518 Christ's whole life is a mystery of recapitulation. All Jesus did, said, and suffered had for its aim

[171] *Acts* 1:1–2. — [172] Cf. *Jn* 20:30. — [173] *Jn* 20:31. — [174] Cf. *Mk* 1:1; *Jn* 21:24. — [175] Cf. *Lk* 2:7; *Mt* 27:48; *Jn* 20:7. — [176] *Col* 2:9. — [177] *Jn* 14:9; *Lk* 9:35; cf. *Mt* 17:5; *Mk* 9:7 ("my beloved Son"). — [178] *1 Jn* 4:9. — [179] Cf. *Eph* 1:7; *Col* 1:13–14; *1 Pet* 1:18–19. — [180] Cf. *2 Cor* 8:9. — [181] Cf. *Lk* 2:51. — [182] Cf. *Jn* 15:3. — [183] *Mt* 8:17; cf. *Isa* 53:4. — [184] Cf. *Rom* 4:25.

restoring fallen man to his original vocation:

> When Christ became incarnate and was made man, he recapitulated in himself the long history of mankind and procured for us a 'short cut' to salvation, so that what we had lost in Adam, that is, being in the image and likeness of God, we might recover in Christ Jesus.[185] For this reason Christ experienced all the stages of life, thereby giving communion with God
> 668, 2748 to all men.[186]

Our communion in the mysteries of Jesus

519 All Christ's riches "are for every individual and are everybody's property."[187] Christ did not live his life for himself but *for us*, from his
793 Incarnation "for us men and for our salvation" to his death "for our sins"
602 and Resurrection "for our justification."[188] He is still "our advocate with the Father," who "always lives to make intercession" for us.[189] He remains ever "in the presence of God on our behalf, bringing before
1085 him all that he lived and suffered for us."[190]

520 In all of his life Jesus presents himself as *our model*. He is "the perfect man,"[191] who invites us to become his disciples and follow him.
459, 359 In humbling himself, he has given us an example to imitate, through
2607 his prayer he draws us to pray, and by his poverty he calls us to accept freely the privation and persecutions that may come our way.[192]

2715 **521** Christ enables us *to live in him* all that he himself lived, and *he lives it in us*. "By his Incarnation, he, the Son of God, has in a certain way united himself with each man."[193] 1391
We are called only to become one with him, for he enables us as the members of his Body to share in what he lived for us in his flesh as our model:

> We must continue to accomplish in ourselves the stages of Jesus' life and his mysteries and often to beg him to perfect and realize them in us and in his whole Church.... For it is the plan of the Son of God to make us and the whole Church partake in his mysteries and to extend them to and continue them in us and in his whole Church. This is his plan for fulfilling his mysteries in us.[194]

II. The Mysteries of Jesus' Infancy and Hidden Life

The preparations

522 The coming of God's Son to earth is an event of such immensity that God willed to prepare for it over centuries. He makes everything converge on Christ: all the rituals 711, 762
and sacrifices, figures and symbols of the "First Covenant."[195] He announces him through the mouths of the prophets who succeeded one another in Israel. Moreover, he awakens in the hearts of the pagans a dim expectation of this coming.

523 *St. John the Baptist* is the Lord's immediate precursor or forerunner, sent to prepare his way.[196] "Prophet of the Most High," John surpasses all the prophets, of whom 717–720
he is the last.[197] He inaugurates the Gospel, already from his mother's

[185] St. Irenaeus, *Adv. haeres.* 3, 18, 1: PG 7/1, 932. — [186] St. Irenaeus, *Adv. haeres.* 3, 18, 7: PG 7/1, 937; cf. 2, 22, 4. — [187] John Paul II, *RH* 11. — [188] *1 Cor* 15:3; *Rom* 4:25. — [189] 1 *Jn* 2:1; *Heb* 7:25. — [190] *Heb* 9:24. — [191] *GS* 38; cf. *Rom* 15:5; *Phil* 2:5. — [192] Cf. *Jn* 13:15; *Lk* 11:1; *Mt* 5:11–12. — [193] *GS* 22 § 2. — [194] St. John Eudes, *LH*, Week 33, Friday, OR. — [195] *Heb* 9:15. — [196] Cf. *Acts* 13:24; *Mt* 3:3. — [197] *Lk* 1:76; cf. 7:26; *Mt* 11:13.

womb welcomes the coming of Christ, and rejoices in being "the friend of the bridegroom," whom he points out as "the Lamb of God, who takes away the sin of the world."[198] Going before Jesus "in the spirit and power of Elijah," John bears witness to Christ in his preaching, by his Baptism of conversion, and through his martyrdom.[199]

524 When the Church celebrates
the liturgy of Advent each year, she
makes present this ancient expectancy of the Messiah, for by sharing in
1171 the long preparation for the Savior's
first coming, the faithful renew their
ardent desire for his second coming.[200] By celebrating the precursor's
birth and martyrdom, the Church
unites herself to his desire: "He must
increase, but I must decrease."[201]

The Christmas mystery

525 Jesus was born in a humble
stable, into a poor family.[202] Simple
shepherds were the first witnesses
to this event. In this poverty heav-
437 en's glory was made manifest.[203] The
Church never tires of singing the
2443 glory of this night:

> The Virgin today brings into the world the Eternal
> And the earth offers a cave to the Inaccessible.
> The angels and shepherds praise him
> And the magi advance with the star,
> For you are born for us,
> Little Child, God eternal![204]

526 To become a child in relation to God is the condition for entering the kingdom.[205] For this, we must humble ourselves and become little. Even more: to become "children of God" we must be "born from above" or "born of God."[206] Only when Christ is formed in us will the mystery of Christmas be fulfilled in us.[207] Christmas is the mystery of this "marvelous exchange":

> O marvelous exchange! Man's 460
> Creator has become man, born of the
> Virgin. We have been made sharers in
> the divinity of Christ who humbled
> himself to share our humanity.[208]

The mysteries of Jesus' infancy

527 Jesus' *circumcision*, on the
eighth day after his birth,[209] is the
sign of his incorporation into Abraham's descendants, into the people of
the covenant. It is the sign of his submission to the Law[210] and his depu-
tation to Israel's worship, in which he 580
will participate throughout his life.
This sign prefigures that "circumci- 1214
sion of Christ" which is Baptism.[211]

528 The *Epiphany* is the manifestation of Jesus as Messiah of Israel, Son of God and Savior of the
world. The great feast of Epiphany
celebrates the adoration of Jesus by 439
the wise men (*magi*) from the East,
together with his baptism in the Jordan and the wedding feast at Cana
in Galilee.[212] In the magi, representatives of the neighboring pagan
religions, the Gospel sees the first-
fruits of the nations, who welcome
the good news of salvation through
the Incarnation. The magi's coming
to Jerusalem in order to pay homage
to the king of the Jews shows that

[198] *Jn* 1:29; cf. *Acts* 1:22; *Lk* 1:41; 16:16; *Jn* 3:29. — [199] *Lk* 1:17; cf. *Mk* 6:17–29. — [200] Cf. *Rev* 22:17. — [201] *Jn* 3:30. — [202] Cf. *Lk* 2:6–7. — [203] Cf. *Lk* 2:8–20. — [204] *Kontakion* of Romanos the Melodist. — [205] Cf. *Mt* 18:3–4. — [206] *Jn* 3:7; 1:13; 1:12; cf. *Mt* 23:12. — [207] Cf. *Gal* 4:19. — [208] *LH*, Antiphon I of Evening Prayer for January 1st. — [209] Cf. *Lk* 2:21. — [210] Cf. *Gal* 4:4. — [211] Cf. *Col* 2:11–13. — [212] *Mt* 2:1; cf. *LH*, Epiphany, Evening Prayer II, Antiphon at the Canticle of Mary.

they seek in Israel, in the messianic light of the star of David, the one who will be king of the nations.[213] Their coming means that pagans can discover Jesus and worship him as Son of God and Savior of the world only by turning toward the Jews and receiving from them the messianic promise as contained in the Old
711–716 Testament.[214] The Epiphany shows that "the full number of the nations"
122 now takes its "place in the family of the patriarchs," and acquires *Israelitica dignitas*[215] (are made "worthy of the heritage of Israel").

529 The *presentation of Jesus in the temple* shows him to be the firstborn Son who belongs to the Lord.[216] With Simeon and Anna, all Israel
583 awaits its *encounter* with the Savior—the name given to this event in
439 the Byzantine tradition. Jesus is recognized as the long-expected Messiah, the "light to the nations" and the "glory of Israel," but also "a sign that is spoken against." The sword of sorrow predicted for Mary announc-
614 es Christ's perfect and unique oblation on the cross that will impart the salvation God had "prepared in the presence of all peoples."

530 The *flight into Egypt* and the massacre of the innocents[217] make manifest the opposition of darkness to the light: "He came to his own home, and his own people received him not."[218] Christ's whole life was
574 lived under the sign of persecution. His own share it with him.[219] Jesus' departure from Egypt recalls the exodus and presents him as the definitive liberator of God's people.[220]

The mysteries of Jesus' hidden life

531 During the greater part of his life Jesus shared the condition of the vast majority of human beings: a daily life spent without evident greatness, a life of manual labor. His religious life was that of a Jew obedient to the law of God,[221] a life in the 2427
community. From this whole period it is revealed to us that Jesus was "obedient" to his parents and that he "increased in wisdom and in stature, and in favor with God and man."[222]

532 Jesus' obedience to his mother and legal father fulfills the fourth commandment perfectly and was the temporal image of his filial obedience to his Father in heaven. The 2214–22
everyday obedience of Jesus to Joseph and Mary both announced and anticipated the obedience of Holy Thursday: "Not my will...."[223] The
obedience of Christ in the daily rou- 612
tine of his hidden life was already inaugurating his work of restoring what the disobedience of Adam had destroyed.[224]

533 The hidden life at Nazareth allows everyone to enter into fellowship with Jesus by the most ordinary events of daily life:

> The home of Nazareth is the school where we begin to understand the life of Jesus—the school of the Gospel. First, then, a lesson of silence. May
> esteem for *silence*, that admirable and 2712
> indispensable condition of mind, revive in us... A lesson on *family life*. May Nazareth teach us what family life is, its communion of love, its austere and simple beauty, and its sacred and inviolable character...

[213] Cf. *Mt* 2:2; *Num* 24:17–19; *Rev* 22:16. — [214] Cf. *Jn* 4:22; *Mt* 2:4–6. — [215] St. Leo the Great, *Sermo 3 in epiphania Domini* 1–3,5: PL 54, 242; *LH*, Epiphany, OR; *Roman Missal*, Easter Vigil 26, Prayer after the third reading. — [216] *Lk* 2:22–39; *Ex* 13:2, 12–13. — [217] Cf. *Mt* 2:13–18. — [218] *Jn* 1:11. — [219] Cf. *Jn* 15:20. — [220] Cf. *Mt* 2:15; *Hos* 11:1. — [221] Cf. *Gal* 4:4. — [222] *Lk* 2:51–52. — [223] *Lk* 22:42. — [224] Cf. *Rom* 5:19.

2204 A lesson of *work*. Nazareth, home of the "Carpenter's Son," in you I would choose to understand and proclaim the severe and redeeming law of human work.... To conclude, I want to greet all the workers of the world, holding up to them their great
2427 pattern, their brother who is God.[225]

534 The *finding of Jesus in the temple* is the only event that breaks the silence of the Gospels about the hidden years of Jesus.[226] Here Jesus lets
583 us catch a glimpse of the mystery of his total consecration to a mission that flows from his divine sonship:
2599 "Did you not know that I must be about my Father's work?"[227] Mary and Joseph did not understand these words, but they accepted them in faith. Mary "kept all these things
964 in her heart" during the years Jesus remained hidden in the silence of an ordinary life.

III. The Mysteries of Jesus' Public Life

The baptism of Jesus

535 Jesus' public life begins with his baptism by John in the Jordan.[228] John preaches "a baptism of repentance for the forgiveness of sins."[229]
719–720 A crowd of sinners[230]—tax collectors and soldiers, Pharisees and Sadducees, and prostitutes—come to be baptized by him. "Then Jesus appears." The Baptist hesitates, but Jesus insists and receives baptism. Then the Holy Spirit, in the form of a dove, comes upon Jesus and a
701 voice from heaven proclaims, "This is my beloved Son."[231] This is the manifestation ("Epiphany") of Jesus 438
as Messiah of Israel and Son of God.

536 The baptism of Jesus is on his part the acceptance and inauguration of his mission as God's suffering Servant. He allows himself to be numbered among sinners; he is already 606
"the Lamb of God, who takes away the sin of the world."[232] Already he is anticipating the "baptism" of his bloody death.[233] Already he is coming to "fulfill all righteousness," that 1224
is, he is submitting himself entirely to his Father's will: out of love he consents to this baptism of death for the remission of our sins.[234] The Father's voice responds to the Son's acceptance, proclaiming his entire delight in his Son.[235] The Spirit whom Jesus 444
possessed in fullness from his conception comes to "rest on him."[236] Jesus will be the source of the Spirit for all mankind. At his baptism "the heavens were opened"[237]—the heavens that Adam's sin had closed—and the 727
waters were sanctified by the descent of Jesus and the Spirit, a prelude to 739
the new creation.

537 Through Baptism the Christian is sacramentally assimilated to Jesus, who in his own baptism an- 1262
ticipates his death and resurrection. The Christian must enter into this mystery of humble self-abasement and repentance, go down into the water with Jesus in order to rise with him, be reborn of water and the Spirit so as to become the Father's beloved son in the Son and "walk in newness of life":[238]

> Let us be buried with Christ by 628
> Baptism to rise with him; let us go

[225] Paul VI at Nazareth, January 5, 1964: *LH*, Feast of the Holy Family, OR. — [226] Cf. *Lk* 2:41–52. — [227] *Lk* 2:49 alt. — [228] Cf. *Lk* 3:23; *Acts* 1:22. — [229] *Lk* 3:3. — [230] Cf. *Lk* 3:10–14; *Mt* 3:7; 21:32. — [231] *Mt* 3:13–17. — [232] *Jn* 1:29; cf. *Isa* 53:12. — [233] Cf. *Mk* 10:38; *Lk* 12:50. — [234] *Mt* 3:15; cf. 26:39. — [235] Cf. *Lk* 3:22; *Isa* 42:1. — [236] *Jn* 1:32–33; cf. *Isa* 11:2. — [237] *Mt* 3:16. — [238] *Rom* 6:4.

down with him to be raised with him; and let us rise with him to be glorified with him.[239]

Everything that happened to Christ lets us know that, after the bath of water, the Holy Spirit swoops down upon us from high heaven and that, adopted by the Father's voice, we become sons of God.[240]

Jesus' temptations

538 The Gospels speak of a time of solitude for Jesus in the desert immediately after his baptism by John. Driven by the Spirit into the desert, Jesus remains there for forty days without eating; he lives among wild beasts, and angels minister to him.[241] At the end of this time Satan tempts him three times, seeking to compromise his filial attitude toward God.
394 Jesus rebuffs these attacks, which re-
518 capitulate the temptations of Adam in Paradise and of Israel in the desert, and the devil leaves him "until an opportune time."[242]

397 **539** The evangelists indicate the salvific meaning of this mysterious event: Jesus is the new Adam who remained faithful just where the first Adam had given in to temptation. Jesus fulfills Israel's vocation perfectly: in contrast to those who had once provoked God during forty years in the desert, Christ reveals himself as
385 God's Servant, totally obedient to the divine will. In this, Jesus is the devil's conqueror: he "binds the strong man" to take back his plunder.[243] Jesus' victory over the tempter in the desert anticipates victory at
609 the Passion, the supreme act of obedience of his filial love for the Father.

540 Jesus' temptation reveals the way in which the Son of God is
Messiah, contrary to the way Satan 2119
proposes to him and the way men
wish to attribute to him.[244] This is 519–2849
why Christ vanquished the Tempter for us: "For we have not a high priest who is unable to sympathize with our weaknesses, but one who in every respect has been tested as we are, yet without sinning."[245] By the solemn forty days of Lent the Church unites herself each year to
the mystery of Jesus in the desert. 1438

"The Kingdom of God is at hand"

541 "Now after John was arrested, Jesus came into Galilee, preaching the gospel of God, and saying: 'The time is fulfilled, and the kingdom of God is at hand: repent, and believe
in the gospel.'"[246] "To carry out the 2816
will of the Father Christ inaugurated the kingdom of heaven on earth."[247]
Now the Father's will is "to raise 763
up men to share in his own divine 669, 768
life."[248] He does this by gathering men around his Son Jesus Christ.
This gathering is the Church, "on 865
earth the seed and beginning of that kingdom."[249]

542 Christ stands at the heart of this gathering of men into the "family of God." By his word, through signs that manifest the reign of God,
and by sending out his disciples, Je- 2233
sus calls all people to come together around him. But above all in the great Paschal mystery—his death on the cross and his Resurrection—he would accomplish the coming of his kingdom. "And I, when I am lifted up from the earth, will draw all

[239] St. Gregory of Nazianzus, *Oratio.* 40, 9: PG 36, 369. — [240] St. Hilary of Poitiers, *In Matth.* 2, 5: PL 9, 927. — [241] Cf. *Mk* 1:12–13. — [242] *Lk* 4:13. — [243] Cf. *Ps* 95:10; *Mk* 3:27. — [244] Cf. *Mt* 16:21–23. — [245] *Heb* 4:15. — [246] *Mk* 1:14–15. — [247] *LG* 3. — [248] *LG* 2. — [249] *LG* 5.

men to myself." Into this union with
789 Christ all men are called.[250]

The proclamation of the Kingdom of God

543 Everyone is called to enter the kingdom. First announced to the children of Israel, this messianic kingdom is intended to accept men of all nations.[251] To enter it, one
764 must first accept Jesus' word:

> The word of the Lord is compared to a seed which is sown in a field; those who hear it with faith and are numbered among the little flock of Christ have truly received the kingdom. Then, by its own power, the seed sprouts and grows until the harvest.[252]

544 The kingdom belongs to *the poor and lowly*, which means those who have accepted it with humble hearts. Jesus is sent to "preach good
709 news to the poor";[253] he declares them blessed, for "theirs is the kingdom
2443 of heaven."[254] To them—the "little ones"—the Father is pleased to reveal
2546 what remains hidden from the wise and the learned.[255] Jesus shares the life of the poor, from the cradle to the cross; he experiences hunger, thirst, and privation.[256] Jesus identifies himself with the poor of every kind and makes active love toward them the condition for entering his kingdom.[257]

545 Jesus invites *sinners* to the table of the kingdom: "I came not to call the righteous, but sinners."[258] He invites them to that conversion
1443 without which one cannot enter the kingdom, but shows them in word
and deed his Father's boundless 588, 1846
mercy for them and the vast "joy
in heaven over one sinner who re- 1439
pents."[259] The supreme proof of his love will be the sacrifice of his own life "for the forgiveness of sins."[260]

546 Jesus' invitation to enter his kingdom comes in the form of *parables*, a characteristic feature of his 2613
teaching.[261] Through his parables he invites people to the feast of the kingdom, but he also asks for a radical choice: to gain the kingdom, one 542
must give everything.[262] Words are not enough; deeds are required.[263] The parables are like mirrors for man: will he be hard soil or good earth for the word?[264] What use has he made of the talents he has received?[265] Jesus and the presence of the kingdom in this world are secretly at the heart of the parables. One must enter the kingdom, that is, become a disciple of Christ, in order to "know the secrets of the kingdom of heaven."[266] For those who stay "outside," everything remains enigmatic.[267]

The signs of the Kingdom of God

547 Jesus accompanies his words with many "mighty works and wonders and signs," which manifest that 670, 439
the kingdom is present in him and attest that he was the promised Messiah.[268]

548 The signs worked by Jesus attest that the Father has sent him. They invite belief in him.[269] To those who turn to him in faith, he

[250] *Jn* 12:32; cf. *LG* 3. — [251] Cf. *Mt* 8:11; 10:5–7; 28:19. — [252] *LG* 5; cf. *Mk* 4:14, 26–29; *Lk* 12:32. — [253] *Lk* 4:18; cf. 7:22. — [254] *Mt* 5:3. — [255] Cf. *Mt* 11:25. — [256] Cf. *Mt* 21:18; *Mk* 2:23–26; *Jn* 4:6–7; 19:28; *Lk* 9:58. — [257] Cf. *Mt* 25:31–46. — [258] *Mk* 2:17; cf. *1 Tim* 1:15. — [259] *Lk* 15:7; cf. 7:11–32. — [260] *Mt* 26:28. — [261] Cf. *Mk* 4:33–34. — [262] Cf. *Mt* 13:44–45; 22:1–14. — [263] Cf. *Mt* 21:28–32. — [264] Cf. *Mt* 13:3–9. — [265] Cf. *Mt* 25:14–30. — [266] *Mt* 13:11. — [267] *Mk* 4:11; cf. *Mt* 13:10–15. — [268] *Acts* 2:22; cf. *Lk* 7:18–23. — [269] Cf. *Jn* 5:36; 10:25, 38.

156, 2616 grants what they ask.[270] So miracles strengthen faith in the One who does his Father's works; they bear witness that he is the Son of God.[271] But his miracles can also be occasions for "offense";[272] they are not
574 intended to satisfy people's curiosity or desire for magic. Despite his
447 evident miracles some people reject Jesus; he is even accused of acting by the power of demons.[273]

549 By freeing some individuals from the earthly evils of hunger, injustice, illness, and death,[274] Jesus performed messianic signs. Never-
1503 theless he did not come to abolish all evils here below,[275] but to free men
440 from the gravest slavery, sin, which thwarts them in their vocation as God's sons and causes all forms of human bondage.[276]

550 The coming of God's kingdom means the defeat of Satan's: "If it is by the Spirit of God that I cast out demons, then the kingdom of God has come upon you."[277] Je-
394 sus' exorcisms free some individuals from the domination of demons.
1673 They anticipate Jesus' great victory over "the ruler of this world."[278] The
440, 2816 kingdom of God will be definitively established through Christ's cross: "God reigned from the wood."[279]

"The keys of the kingdom"

551 From the beginning of his public life Jesus chose certain men, twelve in number, to be with him and to participate in his mission.[280]
858 He gives the Twelve a share in his authority and "sent them out to preach the kingdom of God and to heal."[281] 765
They remain associated for ever with Christ's kingdom, for through them he directs the Church:

> As my Father appointed a kingdom for me, so do I appoint for you that you may eat and drink at my table in my kingdom, and sit on thrones judging the twelve tribes of Israel.[282]

552 Simon Peter holds the first place in the college of the Twelve;[283] Jesus entrusted a unique mission to him. Through a revelation from the Father, Peter had confessed: "You 880
are the Christ, the Son of the living God." Our Lord then declared 153, 442
to him: "You are Peter, and on this rock I will build my Church, and the gates of Hades will not prevail against it."[284] Christ, the "living stone,"[285] thus assures his Church, built on Peter, of victory over the powers of death. Because of the faith he confessed Peter will remain the unshakeable rock of the Church. His mission will be to keep this faith from every lapse and to strengthen 424
his brothers in it.[286]

553 Jesus entrusted a specific authority to Peter: "I will give you the keys of the kingdom of heaven, and whatever you bind on earth shall be bound in heaven, and whatever 881
you loose on earth shall be loosed in heaven."[287] The "power of the keys" designates authority to govern the house of God, which is the Church. Jesus, the Good Shepherd, confirmed this mandate after his Resurrection: "Feed my sheep."[288]
The power to "bind and loose" con- 1445

[270] Cf. *Mk* 5:25–34; 10:52; etc. — [271] Cf. *Jn* 10:31–38. — [272] *Mt* 11:6. — [273] Cf. *Jn* 11:47–48; *Mk* 3:22. — [274] Cf. *Jn* 6:5–15; *Lk* 19:8; *Mt* 11:5. — [275] Cf. *Lk* 12:13–14; *Jn* 18:36. — [276] Cf. *Jn* 8:34–36. — [277] *Mt* 12:26, 28. — [278] *Jn* 12:31; cf. *Lk* 8:26–39. — [279] *LH*, Lent, Holy Week, Evening Prayer, *Hymn Vexilla Regis: "Regnavit a ligno Deus."* — [280] Cf. *Mk* 3:13–19. — [281] *Lk* 9:2. — [282] *Lk* 22:29–30. — [283] Cf. *Mk* 3:16; 9:2; *Lk* 24:34; *1 Cor* 15:5. — [284] *Mt* 16:18. — [285] *1 Pet* 2:4. — [286] Cf. *Lk* 22:32. — [287] *Mt* 16:19. — [288] *Jn* 21:15–17; cf. 10:11.

notes the authority to absolve sins, to pronounce doctrinal judgments, and to make disciplinary decisions in the Church. Jesus entrusted this authority to the Church through the ministry of the apostles[289] and
641, 881 in particular through the ministry of Peter, the only one to whom he specifically entrusted the keys of the kingdom.

A foretaste of the Kingdom: the Transfiguration

554 From the day Peter confessed that Jesus is the Christ, the Son of the living God, the Master "began to show his disciples that he must go to Jerusalem and suffer many things...and be killed, and on the third day be raised."[290] Peter scorns this prediction, nor do the others understand it any better than he.[291] In this context the mysterious episode of Jesus' Transfiguration takes place on a high mountain,[292] before three witnesses chosen by himself: Peter, James, and John. Jesus' face
697, 2600 and clothes become dazzling with light, and Moses and Elijah appear, speaking "of his departure, which he was to accomplish at Jerusalem."[293] A cloud covers him and a voice from
440 heaven says: "This is my Son, my Chosen; listen to him!"[294]

555 For a moment Jesus discloses his divine glory, confirming Peter's confession. He also reveals that he will have to go by the way of the cross at Jerusalem in order to "enter into his glory."[295] Moses and Elijah
2576, 2583 had seen God's glory on the Mountain; the Law and the Prophets had announced the Messiah's sufferings.[296] Christ's Passion is the will of the Father: the Son acts as God's servant;[297] the cloud indicates the pres- 257
ence of the Holy Spirit. "The whole Trinity appeared: the Father in the voice; the Son in the man; the Spirit in the shining cloud."[298]

> You were transfigured on the mountain, and your disciples, as much as they were capable of it, beheld your glory, O Christ our God, so that when they should see you crucified they would understand that your Passion was voluntary, and proclaim to the world that you truly are the splendor of the Father.[299]

556 On the threshold of the public life: the baptism; on the threshold of the Passover: the Transfiguration. Jesus' baptism proclaimed "the mystery of the first regeneration," namely, our Baptism; the Transfiguration "is the sacrament of the second regeneration": our own Resurrection.[300] From now on we share in the Lord's Resurrection through the Spirit who acts in the sacraments of the Body of Christ. The
Transfiguration gives us a foretaste 1003
of Christ's glorious coming, when he "will change our lowly body to be like his glorious body."[301] But it also recalls that "it is through many persecutions that we must enter the kingdom of God":[302]

> Peter did not yet understand this when he wanted to remain with Christ on the mountain. It has been reserved for you, Peter, but for after death. For now, Jesus says: "Go down to toil on earth, to serve on earth, to

289 Cf. *Mt* 18:18. — 290 *Mt* 16:21. — 291 Cf. *Mt* 16:22–23; *Mt* 17:23; *Lk* 9:45. — 292 Cf. *Mt* 17:1–8 and parallels; *2 Pet* 1:16–18. — 293 *Lk* 9:31. — 294 *Lk* 9:35. — 295 *Lk* 24:26. — 296 Cf. *Lk* 24:27. — 297 Cf. *Isa* 42:1. — 298 Thomas Aquinas, *STh* III, 45, 4, *ad* 2. — 299 Byzantine Liturgy, Feast of the Transfiguration, *Kontakion*. — 300 St. Thomas Aquinas, *STh* III, 45, 4, *ad* 2. — 301 *Phil* 3:21. — 302 *Acts* 14:22.

be scorned and crucified on earth. Life goes down to be killed; Bread goes down to suffer hunger; the Way goes down to be exhausted on his journey; the Spring goes down to suffer thirst; and you refuse to suffer?"[303]

Jesus' ascent to Jerusalem

557 "When the days drew near for him to be taken up [Jesus] set his face to go to Jerusalem."[304] By this decision he indicated that he was going up to Jerusalem prepared to die there. Three times he had announced his Passion and Resurrection; now, heading toward Jerusalem, Jesus says: "It cannot be that a prophet should perish away from Jerusalem."[305]

558 Jesus recalls the martyrdom of the prophets who had been put to death in Jerusalem. Nevertheless he persists in calling Jerusalem to gather around him: "How often would I have gathered your children together as a hen gathers her brood under her wings, and you would not!"[306] When Jerusalem comes into view he weeps over her and expresses once again his heart's desire: "Would that even today you knew the things that make for peace! But now they are hid from your eyes."[307]

Jesus' messianic entrance into Jerusalem

559 How will Jerusalem welcome her Messiah? Although Jesus had always refused popular attempts to make him king, he chooses the time and prepares the details for his messianic entry into the city of "his father David."[308] Acclaimed as son of David, as the one who brings salvation (*Hosanna* means "Save!" or "Give salvation!"), the "King of glory" enters his City "riding on an ass."[309] Jesus conquers the Daughter of Zion, a figure of his Church, neither by ruse nor by violence, but by the humility that bears witness to the truth.[310] And so the subjects of his kingdom on that day are children and God's poor, who acclaim him as had the angels when they announced him to the shepherds.[311] Their acclamation, "Blessed be
he who comes in the name of the 333
LORD,"[312] is taken up by the Church
in the "*Sanctus*" of the Eucharistic 1352
liturgy that introduces the memorial of the Lord's Passover.

560 *Jesus' entry into Jerusalem* manifested the coming of the kingdom that the King-Messiah was going to accomplish by the Passover of his Death and Resurrection. It is
with the celebration of that entry on 550, 2816
Palm Sunday that the Church's liturgy solemnly opens Holy Week.

In Brief

561 *"The whole of Christ's life was a continual teaching: his silences, his miracles, his gestures, his prayer, his love for people, his special affection for the little and the poor, his acceptance of the total sacrifice on the Cross for the redemption of the world, and his Resurrection are the actualization of his word and the fulfillment of Revelation" (John Paul II,* CT *9).*

[303] St. Augustine, *Sermo* 78, 6: PL 38, 492–493; cf. *Lk* 9:33. — [304] *Lk* 9:51; cf. *Jn* 13:1. — [305] *Lk* 13:33; cf. *Mk* 8:31–33; 9:31–32; 10:32–34. — [306] *Mt* 23:37. — [307] *Lk* 19:41–42. — [308] *Lk* 1:32; cf. *Mt* 21:1–11; *Jn* 6:15. — [309] *Ps* 24:7–10; *Zech* 9:9. — [310] Cf. *Jn* 18:37. — [311] Cf. *Mt* 21:15–16; cf. *Ps* 8:3; *Lk* 19:38; 2:14. — [312] Cf. *Ps* 118:26.

562 *Christ's disciples are to conform themselves to him until he is formed in them (cf.* Gal *4:19). "For this reason we, who have been made like to him, who have died with him and risen with him, are taken up into the mysteries of his life, until we reign together with him" (*LG *7 § 4).*

563 *No one, whether shepherd or wise man, can approach God here below except by kneeling before the manger at Bethlehem and adoring him hidden in the weakness of a new-born child.*

564 *By his obedience to Mary and Joseph, as well as by his humble work during the long years in Nazareth, Jesus gives us the example of holiness in the daily life of family and work.*

565 *From the beginning of his public life, at his baptism, Jesus is the "Servant," wholly consecrated to the redemptive work that he will accomplish by the "baptism" of his Passion.*

566 *The temptation in the desert shows Jesus, the humble Messiah, who triumphs over Satan by his total adherence to the plan of salvation willed by the Father.*

567 *The Kingdom of heaven was inaugurated on earth by Christ. "This kingdom shone out before men in the word, in the works, and in the presence of Christ" (*LG *5). The Church is the seed and beginning of this kingdom. Her keys are entrusted to Peter.*

568 *Christ's Transfiguration aims at strengthening the apostles' faith in anticipation of his Passion: the ascent onto the "high mountain" prepares for the ascent to Calvary. Christ, Head of the Church, manifests what his Body contains and radiates in the sacraments: "the hope of glory" (*Col *1:27; cf. St. Leo the Great,* Sermo *51, 3: PL 54, 310c).*

569 *Jesus went up to Jerusalem voluntarily, knowing well that there he would die a violent death because of the opposition of sinners (cf.* Heb *12:3).*

570 *Jesus' entry into Jerusalem manifests the coming of the kingdom that the Messiah-King, welcomed into his city by children and the humble of heart, is going to accomplish by the Passover of his Death and Resurrection.*

Article 4:
"JESUS CHRIST SUFFERED UNDER PONTIUS PILATE, WAS CRUCIFIED, DIED, AND WAS BURIED"

571 The Paschal mystery of Christ's cross and Resurrection stands at the center of the Good News that the apostles, and the Church following
1067 them, are to proclaim to the world. God's saving plan was accomplished "once for all"[313] by the redemptive death of his Son Jesus Christ.

572 The Church remains faithful to the interpretation of "all the Scriptures" that Jesus gave both before and after his Passover: "Was it
not necessary that the Christ should 599
suffer these things and enter into his glory?"[314] Jesus' sufferings took their historical, concrete form from

[313] *Heb* 9:26. — [314] *Lk* 24:26–27, 44–45.

the fact that he was "rejected by the elders and the chief priests and the scribes," who handed "him to the Gentiles to be mocked and scourged and crucified."[315]

573 Faith can therefore try to examine the circumstances of Jesus' death, faithfully handed on by the Gospels[316] and illuminated by other historical sources, the better to understand the meaning of the Re-
158 demption.

Paragraph 1
Jesus and Israel

574 From the beginning of Jesus' public ministry, certain Pharisees and partisans of Herod together with priests and scribes agreed together
530 to destroy him.[317] Because of certain of his acts—expelling demons, forgiving sins, healing on the sabbath day, his novel interpretation of the precepts of the Law regarding purity, and his familiarity with tax collectors and public sinners[318]—some ill-intentioned persons suspected Jesus of demonic possession.[319] He is accused
591 of blasphemy and false prophecy, religious crimes which the Law punished with death by stoning.[320]

575 Many of Jesus' deeds and words constituted a "sign of contradiction,"[321] but more so for the religious authorities in Jerusalem, whom the Gospel according to John often calls simply "the Jews,"[322] than for the ordinary People of God.[323] To be sure, Christ's relations with the Pharisees were not exclusively polemical. Some Pharisees warned him of the danger he was courting;[324] Jesus praises some of them, like the scribe of Mark 12:34, and dines several times at their homes.[325] Jesus endorses some of the teachings imparted by this religious elite of God's people: the resurrection of the dead,[326] certain forms of piety (almsgiving, fasting, and prayer),[327] the custom of addressing God as Father, and the centrality of the command- 993
ment to love God and neighbor.[328]

576 In the eyes of many in Israel, Jesus seems to be acting against essential institutions of the Chosen People:

– submission to the whole of the Law in its written commandments and, for the Pharisees, in the interpretation of oral tradition;

– the centrality of the Temple at Jerusalem as the holy place where God's presence dwells in a special way;

– faith in the one God whose glory no man can share.

I. Jesus and the Law

577 At the beginning of the Sermon on the Mount Jesus issued a
solemn warning in which he pre- 1965
sented God's law, given on Sinai during the first covenant, in light of the grace of the New Covenant:

> Do not think that I have come to abolish the law or the prophets: I have come not to abolish but to fulfill.
> For truly I tell you, until heaven and 1967
> earth pass away, not one letter, not one stroke of a letter, will pass from the law, until all is accomplished.

[315] *Mk* 8:31; *Mt* 20:19. — [316] Cf. *DV* 19. — [317] Cf. *Mk* 3:6; 14:1. — [318] Cf. *Mt* 12:24: *Mk* 2:7, 14–17; 3:1–6; 7:14–23. — [319] Cf. *Mk* 3:22; *Jn* 8:48; 10:20. — [320] Cf. *Mk* 2:7; *Jn* 5:18; *Jn* 7:12; 7:52; 8:59; 10:31, 33. — [321] *Lk* 2:34. — [322] Cf. *Jn* 1:19; 2:18; 5:10; 7:13; 9:22; 18:12; 19:38; 20:19. — [323] *Jn* 7:48–49. — [324] Cf. *Lk* 13:31. — [325] Cf. *Lk* 7:36; 14:1. — [326] Cf. *Mt* 22:23–34; *Lk* 20:39. — [327] Cf. *Mt* 6:18. — [328] *Mk* 12:28–34.

> Therefore, whoever breaks one of the least of these commandments, and teaches others to do the same, will be called least in the kingdom of heaven; but whoever does them and teaches them will be called great in the kingdom of heaven.[329]

578 Jesus, Israel's Messiah and therefore the greatest in the kingdom of heaven, was to fulfill the Law by keeping it in its all-embracing
1953 detail—according to his own words, down to "the least of these commandments."[330] He is in fact the only one who could keep it perfectly.[331] On their own admission the Jews were never able to observe the Law in its entirety without violating the least of its precepts.[332] This is why every year on the Day of Atonement the children of Israel ask God's forgiveness for their transgressions of the Law. The Law indeed makes up one inseparable whole, and St. James recalls, "Whoever keeps the whole law but fails in one point has become guilty of all of it."[333]

579 This principle of integral observance of the Law not only in letter but in spirit was dear to the Pharisees. By giving Israel this principle they had led many Jews of Jesus' time to an extreme religious zeal.[334] This zeal, were it not to lapse into "hypocritical" casuistry,[335] could only prepare the People for the unprecedented intervention of God through the perfect fulfillment of the Law by the only Righteous One in place of all sinners.[336]

580 The perfect fulfillment of the Law could be the work of none but the divine legislator, born subject to the Law in the person of the Son.[337]
In Jesus, the Law no longer appears 527
engraved on tables of stone but "upon the heart" of the Servant who becomes "a covenant to the people," because he will "faithfully bring forth justice."[338] Jesus fulfills the Law to the point of taking upon himself "the curse of the Law" incurred by those who do not "abide by the things written in the book of the Law, and do them," for his death took place to redeem them "from the transgressions under the first covenant."[339]

581 The Jewish people and their spiritual leaders viewed Jesus as a rabbi.[340] He often argued within the framework of rabbinical interpretation of the Law.[341] Yet Jesus could not help but offend the teachers of the Law, for he was not content to propose his interpretation alongside theirs but taught the people "as one
who had authority, and not as their 2054
scribes."[342] In Jesus, the same Word of God, that had resounded on Mount Sinai to give the written Law to Moses, made itself heard anew on the Mount of the Beatitudes.[343] Jesus did not abolish the Law but fulfilled it by giving its ultimate interpretation in a divine way: "You have heard that it was said to the men of old.... But I say to you...."[344] With this same divine authority, he disavowed certain human traditions of the Pharisees that were "making void the word of God."[345]

[329] *Mt* 5:17–19. — [330] *Mt* 5:19. — [331] Cf. *Jn* 8:46. — [332] Cf. *Jn* 7:19; *Acts* 13:38–41; 15:10. — [333] *Jas* 2:10; cf. *Gal* 3:10; 5:3. — [334] Cf. *Rom* 10:2. — [335] Cf. *Mt* 15:3–7, *Lk* 11:39–54. — [336] Cf. *Isa* 53:11; *Heb* 9:15. — [337] Cf. *Gal* 4:4. — [338] *Jer* 31:33; *Isa* 42:3, 6. — [339] *Gal* 3:13; 3:10; *Heb* 9:15. — [340] Cf. *Jn* 11:28; 3:2; *Mt* 22:23–24, 34–36. — [341] Cf. *Mt* 12:5; 9:12; *Mk* 2:23–27; *Lk* 6:6–9; *Jn* 7:22–23. — [342] *Mt* 7:28–29. — [343] Cf. *Mt* 5:1. — [344] *Mt* 5:33–34. — [345] *Mk* 7:13; cf. 3:8.

582 Going even further, Jesus perfects the dietary law, so important in Jewish daily life, by revealing its pedagogical meaning through a divine interpretation: "Whatever goes into a man from outside cannot defile him;...(Thus he declared all foods clean.). What comes out of a man is what defiles a man. For from within, out of the heart of man, come evil thoughts...."[346] In presenting with divine authority the definitive interpretation of the Law, Jesus found
368 himself confronted by certain teachers of the Law who did not accept his interpretation of the Law, guar-
548 anteed though it was by the divine signs that accompanied it.[347] This was the case especially with the sabbath laws, for he recalls often with rabbinical arguments, that the sab-
2173 bath rest is not violated by serving God and neighbor,[348] which his own healings did.

II. Jesus and the Temple

583 Like the prophets before him Jesus expressed the deepest respect for the Temple in Jerusalem. It was in the Temple that Joseph and Mary
529 presented him forty days after his birth.[349] At the age of twelve he de-
534 cided to remain in the Temple to remind his parents that he must be about his Father's business.[350] He went there each year during his hidden life at least for Passover.[351] His public ministry itself was patterned by his pilgrimages to Jerusalem for the great Jewish feasts.[352]

584 Jesus went up to the Temple as the privileged place of encounter with God. For him, the Temple was the dwelling of his Father, a house of
prayer, and he was angered that its 2599
outer court had become a place of commerce.[353] He drove merchants out of it because of jealous love for his Father: "You shall not make my Father's house a house of trade. His disciples remembered that it was written, 'Zeal for your house will consume me.'"[354] After his Resurrection his apostles retained their reverence for the Temple.[355]

585 On the threshold of his Passion Jesus announced the coming destruction of this splendid building, of which there would not remain "one stone upon another."[356] By doing so, he announced a sign of the last days, which were to begin with his own Passover.[357] But this prophecy would be distorted in its telling by false witnesses during his interrogation at the high priest's house and would be thrown back at him as an insult when he was nailed to the cross.[358]

586 Far from having been hostile to the Temple, where he gave the essential part of his teaching, Jesus was willing to pay the temple-tax, associating with him Peter, whom he had just made the foundation of his future Church.[359] He even identified himself with the Temple by presenting himself as God's definitive dwelling-place among men.[360]
Therefore his being put to bodily 797
death[361] presaged the destruction of the Temple, which would manifest the dawning of a new age in the his-

[346] *Mk* 7:18– 21; cf. *Gal* 3:24. — [347] Cf. *Jn* 5:36; 10:25, 37–38; 12:37. — [348] Cf. *Num* 28:9; *Mt* 12:5; *Mk* 2:25–27; *Lk* 13:15–16; 14:3–4; *Jn* 7:22–24. — [349] *Lk* 2:22–39. — [350] Cf. *Lk* 2:46–49. — [351] Cf. *Lk* 2:41. — [352] Cf. *Jn* 2:13–14; 5:1, 14; 7:1, 10, 14; 8:2; 10:22–23. — [353] Cf. *Mt* 21:13 — [354] *Jn* 2:16–17; cf. *Ps* 69:10. — [355] Cf. *Acts* 2:46; 3:1; 5:20, 21; etc. — [356] Cf. *Mt* 24:1–2. — [357] Cf. *Mt* 24:3; *Lk* 13:35. — [358] Cf. *Mk* 14:57–58: *Mt* 27:39–40. — [360] Cf. *Jn* 2:21; *Mt* 12:6. — [361] Cf. *Jn* 2:18–22.

tory of salvation: "The hour is coming when neither on this mountain nor in Jerusalem will you worship
1179 the Father."[362]

III. Jesus and Israel's Faith in the One God and Savior

587 If the Law and the Jerusalem Temple could be occasions of opposition to Jesus by Israel's religious authorities, his role in the redemption of sins, the divine work par excellence, was the true stumbling-block for them.[363]

588 Jesus scandalized the Pharisees by eating with tax collectors and sinners as familiarly as with themselves.[364] Against those among them "who trusted in themselves that they were righteous and despised others,"
545 Jesus affirmed: "I have not come to call the righteous, but sinners to repentance."[365] He went further by proclaiming before the Pharisees that, since sin is universal, those who pretend not to need salvation are blind to themselves.[366]

589 Jesus gave scandal above all when he identified his merciful conduct toward sinners with God's own attitude toward them.[367] He went so far as to hint that by sharing the table of sinners he was admitting them to the messianic banquet.[368] But it was most especially by forgiving sins that Jesus placed the religious authorities of Israel on the horns of a dilemma. Were they not entitled to demand in consternation, "Who can forgive sins but God alone?"[369] By forgiving
31, 1441 sins Jesus either is blaspheming as a man who made himself God's equal
or is speaking the truth, and his per- 432
son really does make present and reveal God's name.[370]

590 Only the divine identity of Jesus' person can justify so absolute a claim as "He who is not with me is against me"; and his saying that there was in him "something greater than Jonah,...greater than Solomon,"something "greater than the Temple"; his reminder that David had called the Messiah his Lord,[371] and his affirmations, "Before Abraham was, I AM"; and even "I and
the Father are one."[372] 253

591 Jesus asked the religious authorities of Jerusalem to believe in him because of the Father's works which he accomplished.[373] But such an act of faith must go through a mysterious death to self, for a new
"birth from above" under the in- 526
fluence of divine grace.[374] Such a demand for conversion in the face of so surprising a fulfillment of the promises[375] allows one to understand the Sanhedrin's tragic misunderstanding of Jesus: they judged that he deserved the death sentence as a blasphemer.[376] The members of the Sanhedrin were thus acting at the same time out of "ignorance"
and the "hardness" of their "unbe- 574
lief."[377]

In Brief

592 *Jesus did not abolish the Law of Sinai, but rather fulfilled it (cf.* Mt *5:17–19) with such perfection (cf.* Jn

[362] *Jn* 4:21; cf. *Jn* 4:23–24; *Mt* 27:51; *Heb* 9:11; *Rev* 21:22. — [363] Cf. *Lk* 2:34; 20:17–18; *Ps* 118:22. — [364] Cf. *Lk* 5:30; 7:36; 11:37; 14:1. — [365] *Lk* 18:9; 5:32; cf. *Jn* 7:49; 9:34. — [366] Cf. *Jn* 8:33–36; 9:40–41. — [367] Cf. *Mt* 9:13; *Hos* 6:6. — [368] Cf. *Lk* 15:1–2, 22–32. — [369] *Mk* 2:7. — [370] Cf. *Jn* 5:18;10:33;17:6, 26. — [371] Cf. *Mt* 12:6, 30, 36, 37, 41–42. — [372] *Jn* 8:58; 10:30. — [373] *Jn* 10:36–38. — [374] Cf. *Jn* 3:7; 6:44. — [375] Cf. *Isa* 53:1. — [376] Cf. *Mk* 3:6; *Mt* 26:64–66. — [377] Cf. *Lk* 23:34; *Acts* 3:17–18; *Mk* 3:5; *Rom* 11:25, 20.

8:46) that he revealed its ultimate meaning (cf. Mt *5:33) and redeemed the transgressions against it (cf.* Heb *9:15).*

593 *Jesus venerated the Temple by going up to it for the Jewish feasts of pilgrimage, and with a jealous love he loved this dwelling of God among men. The Temple prefigures his own mystery. When he announces its destruction, it is as a manifestation of his own execution and of the entry into a new age in the history of salvation, when his Body would be the definitive Temple.*

594 *Jesus performed acts, such as pardoning sins, that manifested him to be the Savior God himself (cf.* Jn *5:16–18). Certain Jews, who did not recognize God made man (cf.* Jn *1:14), saw in him only a man who made himself God (*Jn *10:33), and judged him as a blasphemer.*

Paragraph 2
Jesus Died Crucified

I. The Trial of Jesus

Divisions among the Jewish authorities concerning Jesus

595 Among the religious authorities of Jerusalem, not only were the Pharisee Nicodemus and the prominent Joseph of Arimathea both secret disciples of Jesus, but there was also long-standing dissension about him, so much so that St. John says of these authorities on the very eve of Christ's Passion, "many…believed in him," though very imperfectly.[378] This is not surprising, if one recalls that on the day after Pentecost "a great many of the priests were obedient to the faith" and "some believers…belonged to the party of the Pharisees," to the point that St. James could tell St. Paul, "How many thousands there are among the Jews of those who have believed; and they are all zealous for the Law."[379]

596 The religious authorities in Jerusalem were not unanimous about what stance to take toward Jesus.[380] The Pharisees threatened to excommunicate his followers.[381] To those who feared that "everyone will believe in him, and the Romans will come and destroy both our holy place and our nation," the high priest Caiaphas replied by prophesying: "It is expedient for you that
one man should die for the people, 1753
and that the whole nation should not perish."[382] The Sanhedrin, having declared Jesus deserving of death as a blasphemer but having lost the right to put anyone to death, hands him over to the Romans, accusing him of political revolt, a charge that puts him in the same category as Barabbas who had been accused of sedition.[383] The high priests also threatened Pilate politically so that he would condemn Jesus to death.[384]

Jews are not collectively responsible for Jesus' death

597 The historical complexity of Jesus' trial is apparent in the Gospel accounts. The personal sin of the participants (Judas, the Sanhedrin, Pilate) is known to God alone. Hence we cannot lay responsibility for the trial on the Jews in Jerusalem as a whole, despite the outcry of a manipulated crowd and the global reproaches contained in the apostles'

[378] *Jn* 12:42; cf. 7:50; 9:16–17; 10:19–21; 19:38–39. — [379] *Acts* 6:7; 15:5; 21:20. — [380] Cf. *Jn* 9:16; *Jn* 10:19. — [381] Cf. *Jn* 9:22. — [382] *Jn* 11:48–50. — [383] Cf. *Mt* 26:66; *Jn* 18:31; *Lk* 23:2, 19. — [384] Cf. *Jn* 19:12, 15, 21.

calls to conversion after Pentecost.[385]
1735 Jesus himself, in forgiving them on the cross, and Peter in following suit, both accept "the ignorance" of the Jews of Jerusalem and even of their leaders.[386] Still less can we extend responsibility to other Jews of different times and places, based merely on the crowd's cry: "His blood be on us and on our children!" a formula for ratifying a judicial sentence.[387] As the Church declared at the Second Vatican Council:

> ...[N]either all Jews indiscriminately at that time, nor Jews today, can be charged with the crimes committed during his Passion.... [T]he Jews
> 839 should not be spoken of as rejected or accursed as if this followed from holy Scripture.[388]

All sinners were the authors of Christ's Passion

598 In her Magisterial teaching of the faith and in the witness of her saints, the Church has never forgotten that "sinners were the authors and the ministers of all the sufferings that the divine Redeemer endured."[389] Taking into account the fact that our sins affect Christ himself,[390] the Church does not hesitate to impute to Christians the gravest responsibility for the torments inflicted upon Jesus, a responsibility with which they have all too often burdened the Jews alone:

> 1851 We must regard as guilty all those who continue to relapse into their sins. Since our sins made the Lord Christ suffer the torment of the cross, those who plunge themselves into disorders and crimes crucify the Son of God anew in their hearts (for he is in them) and hold him up to contempt. And it can be seen that our crime in this case is greater in us than in the Jews. As for them, according to the witness of the Apostle, "None of the rulers of this age understood this; for if they had, they would not have crucified the Lord of glory." We, however, profess to know him. And when we deny him by our deeds, we in some way seem to lay violent hands on him.[391]
>
> Nor did demons crucify him; it is you who have crucified him and crucify him still, when you delight in your vices and sins.[392]

II. Christ's Redemptive Death in God's Plan of Salvation

"Jesus handed over according to the definite plan of God"

599 Jesus' violent death was not the result of chance in an unfortunate coincidence of circumstances, but is part of the mystery of God's
plan, as St. Peter explains to the Jews 517
of Jerusalem in his first sermon on Pentecost: "This Jesus [was] delivered up according to the definite plan and foreknowledge of God."[393] This Biblical language does not mean that those who handed him over were merely passive players in a scenario written in advance by God.[394]

600 To God, all moments of time are present in their immediacy. When therefore he establishes his eternal plan of "predestination," he includes in it each person's free

[385] Cf. *Mk* 15:11; *Acts* 2:23, 36; 3:13–14; 4:10; 5:30; 7:52; 10:39; 13:27–28; *1 Thess* 2:14–15. — [386] Cf. *Lk* 23:34; *Acts* 3:17. — [387] *Mt* 27:25; cf. *Acts* 5:28; 18:6. — [388] *NA* 4. — [389] *Roman Catechism* I, 5, 11; cf. *Heb* 12:3. — [390] Cf. *Mt* 25:45; *Acts* 9:4–5. — [391] *Roman Catechism* I, 5, 11; cf. *Heb* 6:6; *1 Cor* 2:8. — [392] St. Francis of Assisi, *Admonitio* 5, 3. — [393] *Acts* 2:23. — [394] Cf. *Acts* 3:13.

response to his grace: "In this city, in
fact, both Herod and Pontius Pilate,
with the Gentiles and the peoples
of Israel, gathered together against
your holy servant Jesus, whom you
anointed, to do whatever your hand
and your plan had predestined to
take place."[395] For the sake of accomplishing his plan of salvation,
312 God permitted the acts that flowed
from their blindness.[396]

"He died for our sins in accordance with the Scriptures"

601 The Scriptures had foretold
this divine plan of salvation through
the putting to death of "the righteous one, my Servant" as a mystery
of universal redemption, that is, as
the ransom that would free men
from the slavery of sin.[397] Citing a
confession of faith that he himself
had "received," St. Paul professes
that "Christ died for our sins in accordance with the scriptures."[398] In
652 particular Jesus' redemptive death
fulfills Isaiah's prophecy of the suffering Servant.[399] Indeed Jesus himself explained the meaning of his
life and death in the light of God's
713 suffering Servant.[400] After his Resurrection he gave this interpretation of
the Scriptures to the disciples at Emmaus, and then to the apostles.[401]

"For our sake God made him to be sin"

602 Consequently, St. Peter can
formulate the apostolic faith in the
divine plan of salvation in this way:
"You were ransomed from the futile
ways inherited from your fathers...
with the precious blood of Christ,
like that of a lamb without blemish
or spot. He was destined before the
foundation of the world but was
made manifest at the end of the
times for your sake."[402] Man's sins,
following on original sin, are pun-
ishable by death.[403] By sending his 400
own Son in the form of a slave, in
the form of a fallen humanity, on ac- 519
count of sin, God "made him to be
sin who knew no sin, so that in him
we might become the righteousness
of God."[404]

603 Jesus did not experience
reprobation as if he himself had
sinned.[405] But in the redeeming love
that always united him to the Father, he assumed us in the state of
our waywardness of sin, to the point
that he could say in our name from
the cross: "My God, my God, why
have you forsaken me?"[406] Having
thus established him in solidarity
with us sinners, God "did not spare 2572
his own Son but gave him up for us
all," so that we might be "reconciled
to God by the death of his Son."[407]

God takes the initiative of universal redeeming love

604 By giving up his own Son
for our sins, God manifests that his
plan for us is one of benevolent love,
prior to any merit on our part: "In
this is love, not that we loved God 211, 20
but that he loved us and sent his Son
to be the expiation for our sins."[408] 1825
God "shows his love for us in that
while we were yet sinners Christ
died for us."[409]

[395] *Acts* 4:27–28; cf. *Ps* 2:1–2. — [396] Cf. *Mt* 26:54; *Jn* 18:36; 19:11; *Acts* 3:17–18. — [397] *Isa* 53:11; cf. 53:12; *Jn* 8:34–36; *Acts* 3:14. — [398] *1 Cor* 15:3; cf. also *Acts* 3:18; 7:52; 13:29; 26:22–23. — [399] Cf. *Isa* 53:7–8 and *Acts* 8:32–35. — [400] Cf. *Mt* 20:28. — [401] Cf. *Lk* 24:25–27, 44–45. — [402] *1 Pet* 1:18–20. — [403] Cf. *Rom* 5:12; *1 Cor* 15:56. — [404] *2 Cor* 5:21; cf. *Phil* 2:7; *Rom* 8:3. — [405] Cf. *Jn* 8:46. — [406] *Mk* 15:34; *Ps* 22:2; cf. *Jn* 8:29. — [407] *Rom* 8:32, 5:10. — [408] *1 Jn* 4:10; 4:19. — [409] *Rom* 5:8.

605 At the end of the parable of
the lost sheep Jesus recalled that
God's love excludes no one: "So it is
not the will of your Father who is in
heaven that one of these little ones
should perish."[410] He affirms that
he came "to give his life as a ransom
for many"; this last term is not restrictive, but contrasts the whole of
humanity with the unique person
402 of the redeemer who hands himself over to save us.[411] The Church,
following the apostles, teaches that
Christ died for all men without
exception: "There is not, never has
been, and never will be a single human being for whom Christ did not
34, 2793 suffer."[412]

III. Christ Offered Himself to His Father for Our Sins

Christ's whole life is an offering to the Father

606 The Son of God, who came
down "from heaven, not to do [his]
own will, but the will of him who
sent [him],"[413] said on coming into
517 the world, "Lo, I have come to do
your will, O God." "And by that will
we have been sanctified through the
offering of the body of Jesus Christ
once for all."[414] From the first moment of his Incarnation the Son
embraces the Father's plan of divine
salvation in his redemptive mission:
"My food is to do the will of him
who sent me, and to accomplish his
work."[415] The sacrifice of Jesus "for
536 the sins of the whole world"[416] expresses his loving communion with
the Father. "The Father loves me,
because I lay down my life," said the
Lord, "[for] I do as the Father has
commanded me, so that the world
may know that I love the Father."[417]

607 The desire to embrace his
Father's plan of redeeming love inspired Jesus' whole life,[418] for his
redemptive passion was the very reason for his Incarnation. And so he
asked, "And what shall I say? 'Father, 457
save me from this hour'? No, for this
purpose I have come to this hour."[419]
And again, "Shall I not drink the
cup which the Father has given
me?"[420] From the cross, just before
"It is finished," he said, "I thirst."[421]

"The Lamb who takes away the sin of the world"

608 After agreeing to baptize him
along with the sinners, John the
Baptist looked at Jesus and pointed
him out as the "Lamb of God, who
takes away the sin of the world."[422] 523
By doing so, he reveals that Jesus is at
the same time the suffering Servant
who silently allows himself to be led
to the slaughter and who bears the
sin of the multitudes, and also the
Paschal Lamb, the symbol of Israel's 517
redemption at the first Passover.[423]
Christ's whole life expresses his mission: "to serve and to give his life as
a ransom for many."[424]

Jesus freely embraced the Father's redeeming love

609 By embracing in his human heart the Father's love for men, Jesus "loved them to the end," for "greater love has no man than this, that a man

[410] *Mt* 18:14. — [411] *Mt* 20:28; cf. *Rom* 5:18–19. — [412] Council of Quiercy (853): DS 624; cf. *2 Cor* 5:15; *1 Jn* 2:2. — [413] *Jn* 6:38. — [414] *Heb* 10:5–10. — [415] *Jn* 4:34. — [416] *1 Jn* 2:2. — [417] *Jn* 10:17; 14:31. — [418] Cf. *Lk* 12:50; 22:15; *Mt* 16:21–23. — [419] *Jn* 12:27. — [420] *Jn* 18:11. — [421] *Jn* 19:30; 19:28. — [422] *Jn* 1:29; cf. *Lk* 3:21; *Mt* 3:14–15; *Jn* 1:36. — [423] *Isa* 53:7, 12; cf. *Jer* 11:19; *Ex* 12:3–14; *Jn* 19:36; *1 Cor* 5:7. — [424] *Mk* 10:45.

lay down his life for his friends."[425]
In suffering and death his humanity
478 became the free and perfect instru-
515 ment of his divine love which desires
the salvation of men.[426] Indeed, out
272, 539 of love for his Father and for men,
whom the Father wants to save, Jesus freely accepted his Passion and death: "No one takes [my life] from me, but I lay it down of my own accord."[427] Hence the sovereign freedom of God's Son as he went out to his death.[428]

At the Last Supper Jesus anticipated the free offering of his life

610 Jesus gave the supreme expression of his free offering of himself at the meal shared with the twelve Apostles "on the night he
766 was betrayed."[429] On the eve of his
Passion, while still free, Jesus trans
1337 formed this Last Supper with the
apostles into the memorial of his voluntary offering to the Father for the salvation of men: "This is my body which is given for you." "This is my blood of the covenant, which is poured out for many for the forgiveness of sins."[430]

611 The Eucharist that Christ institutes at that moment will be the memorial of his sacrifice.[431] Jesus includes the apostles in his own offering and bids them perpetuate it.[432]
1364 By doing so, the Lord institutes his
1341, 1566 apostles as priests of the New Cove-
nant: "For their sakes I sanctify myself, so that they also may be sanctified in truth."[433]

The agony at Gethsemani

612 The cup of the New Covenant, which Jesus anticipated when he offered himself at the Last Supper, is afterwards accepted by him from his Father's hands in his agony in the garden at Gethsemani,[434] making himself "obedient unto death." 532, 2600
Jesus prays: "My Father, if it be possible, let this cup pass from me.... [435] Thus he expresses the horror that death represented for his human nature. Like ours, his human nature is destined for eternal life; but unlike ours, it is perfectly exempt from sin, the cause of death.[436] Above all, his human nature has been assumed by the divine person of the "Author of life," the "Living One."[437] By accepting in his human will that the Father's will be done, he accepts his death as redemptive, for "he himself bore our sins in his body on the
tree."[438] 1009

Christ's death is the unique and definitive sacrifice

613 Christ's death is both the Paschal sacrifice that accomplishes the definitive redemption of men, through "the Lamb of God, who
takes away the sin of the world,"[439] 1366
and the *sacrifice of the New Cove-*
nant, which restores man to com- 2009
munion with God by reconciling him to God through the "blood of the covenant, which was poured out for many for the forgiveness of sins."[440]

[425] *Jn* 13:1;15:13. — [426] Cf. *Heb* 2:10, 17–18; 4:15; 5:7–9. — [427] *Jn* 10:18. — [428] Cf. *Jn* 18:4–6; *Mt* 26:53. — [429] *Roman Missal,* EP 111; cf. *Mt* 26:20; *1 Cor* 11:23. — [430] *Lk* 22:19; *Mt* 26:28; cf. *1 Cor* 5:7. — [431] *1 Cor* 11:25. — [432] Cf. *Lk* 22:19. — [433] *Jn* 17:19; cf. Council of Trent: DS 1752; 1764. — [434] Cf. *Mt* 26:42; *Lk* 22:20. — [435] *Phil* 2:8; *Mt* 26:39; cf. *Heb* 5:7–8. — [436] Cf. *Rom* 5:12; *Heb* 4:15. — [437] Cf. *Acts* 3:15; *Rev* 1:17; *Jn* 1:4; 5:26. — [438] *1 Pet* 2:24; cf. *Mt* 26:42. — [439] *Jn* 1:29; cf. 8:34–36; *1 Cor* 5:7; *1 Pet* 1:19. — [440] *Mt* 26:28; cf. *Ex* 24:8; *Lev* 16:15–16; *1 Cor* 11:25.

614 This sacrifice of Christ is
529, 1330 unique; it completes and surpasses
all other sacrifices.[441] First, it is a gift
2100 from God the Father himself, for
the Father handed his Son over to
sinners in order to reconcile us with
himself. At the same time it is the offering of the Son of God made man,
who in freedom and love offered his
life to his Father through the Holy
Spirit in reparation for our disobedience.[442]

Jesus substitutes his obedience for our disobedience

615 "For as by one man's disobedience many were made sinners, so
by one man's obedience many will
be made righteous."[443] By his obedi-
1850 ence unto death, Jesus accomplished
the substitution of the suffering Servant, who "makes himself an *offering
for sin*," when "he bore the sin of
433 many," and who "shall make many
to be accounted righteous," for "he
411 shall bear their iniquities."[444] Jesus
atoned for our faults and made satisfaction for our sins to the Father.[445]

Jesus consummates his sacrifice on the Cross

616 It is love "to the end"[446] that
confers on Christ's sacrifice its value as redemption and reparation,
as atonement and satisfaction. He
knew and loved us all when he offered his life.[447] Now "the love of
478 Christ controls us, because we are
convinced that one has died for all;
therefore all have died."[448] No man,
not even the holiest, was ever able to
take on himself the sins of all men
and offer himself as a sacrifice for all.
The existence in Christ of the divine
person of the Son, who at once surpasses and embraces all human per- 468
sons and constitutes himself as the
Head of all mankind, makes possi- 519
ble his redemptive sacrifice *for all*.

617 The Council of Trent emphasizes the unique character of Christ's
sacrifice as "the source of eternal salvation"[449] and teaches that "his most
holy Passion on the wood of the 1992
cross merited justification for us."[450]
And the Church venerates his cross 1235
as it sings: "Hail, O Cross, our only
hope."[451]

Our participation in Christ's sacrifice

618 The cross is the unique sacrifice
of Christ, the "one mediator between
God and men."[452] But because in his
incarnate divine person he has in some
way united himself to every man, "the
possibility of being made partners, in
a way known to God, in the paschal
mystery" is offered to all men.[453] He 1368, 1460
calls his disciples to "take up [their]
cross and follow [him],"[454] for "Christ 307, 2100
also suffered for [us], leaving [us] an
example so that [we] should follow
in his steps."[455] In fact Jesus desires to
associate with his redeeming sacrifice
those who were to be its first benefi- 964
ciaries.[456] This is achieved supremely
in the case of his mother, who was
associated more intimately than any
other person in the mystery of his redemptive suffering.[457]

> Apart from the cross there is no other ladder by which we may get to heaven.[458]

[441] Cf. *Heb* 10:10. — [442] Cf. *Jn* 10:17–18; 15:13; *Heb* 9:14; *1 Jn* 4:10. — [443] *Rom* 5:19. — [444] *Isa* 53:10–12. — [445] Cf. Council of Trent (1547): DS 1529. — [446] *Jn* 13:1. — [447] Cf. *Gal* 2:20; *Eph* 5:2, 25. — [448] *2 Cor* 5:14. — [449] *Heb* 5:9. — [450] Council of Trent: DS 1529. — [451] *LH*, Lent, Holy Week, Evening Prayer, Hymn *Vexilla regis*. — [452] *1 Tim* 2:5. — [453] *GS* 22 § 5; cf. § 2. — [454] *Mt* 16:24. — [455] *1 Pet* 2:21. — [456] Cf. *Mk* 10:39; *Jn* 21:18–19; *Col* 1:24. — [457] Cf. *Lk* 2:35. — [458] St. Rose of Lima, cf. P. Hansen, *Vita mirabilis* (Louvain, 1668).

In Brief

619 *"Christ died for our sins in accordance with the scriptures" (*1 Cor *15:3).*

620 *Our salvation flows from God's initiative of love for us, because "he loved us and sent his Son to be the expiation for our sins" (*1 Jn *4:10). "God was in Christ reconciling the world to himself" (*2 Cor *5:19).*

621 *Jesus freely offered himself for our salvation. Beforehand, during the Last Supper, he both symbolized this offering and made it really present: "This is my body which is given for you" (*Lk *22:19).*

622 *The redemption won by Christ consists in this, that he came "to give his life as a ransom for many" (*Mt *20:28), that is, he "loved [his own] to the end" (*Jn *13:1), so that they might be "ransomed from the futile ways inherited from [their] fathers"(*1 Pet *1:18).*

623 *By his loving obedience to the Father, "unto death, even death on a cross" (*Phil *2:8), Jesus fulfills the atoning mission (cf.* Isa *53:10) of the suffering Servant, who will "make many righteous; and he shall bear their iniquities" (*Isa *53:11; cf.* Rom *5:19).*

Paragraph 3
Jesus Christ Was Buried

624 "By the grace of God" Jesus tasted death "for every one."[459] In his plan of salvation, God ordained that his Son should not only "die for our sins"[460] but should also "taste death,"
1005, 362 experience the condition of death, the separation of his soul from his body, between the time he expired on the cross and the time he was raised from the dead. The state of the dead Christ is the mystery of the tomb and the descent into hell. It is the mystery of Holy Saturday, when Christ, lying in the tomb,[461] reveals God's great sabbath rest[462] after the fulfillment[463] of man's salvation, 349
which brings peace to the whole universe.[464]

Christ in the tomb in his body

625 Christ's stay in the tomb constitutes the real link between his passible state before Easter and his glorious and risen state today. The same person of the "Living One" can say, "I died, and behold I am alive for evermore":[465]

> God [the Son] did not impede death from separating his soul from his body according to the necessary order of nature, but has reunited them to one another in the Resurrection, *so that he himself might be, in his person, the meeting point for death and life*, by arresting in himself the decomposition of nature produced by death and so becoming the source of reunion for the separated parts.[466]

626 Since the "Author of life" who was killed[467] is the same "living one [who has] risen,"[468] the divine per- 470, 650
son of the Son of God necessarily continued to possess his human soul and body, separated from each other by death:

> By the fact that at Christ's death his soul was separated from his flesh, his one person is not itself divided into two persons; for the human body and soul of Christ have existed in the same way from the beginning of his

[459] *Heb* 2:9. — [460] *1 Cor* 15:3. — [461] Cf. *Jn* 19:42. — [462] Cf. *Heb* 4:7–9. — [463] Cf. *Jn* 19:30. — [464] Cf. *Col* 1:18–20. — [465] *Rev* 1:18. — [466] St. Gregory of Nyssa, *Orat. catech.*, 16: PG 45, 52D. — [467] *Acts* 3:15. — [468] *Lk* 24:5–6.

earthly existence, in the divine person of the Word; and in death, although separated from each other, both remained with one and the same person of the Word.[469]

"You will not let your Holy One see corruption"

627 Christ's death was a real death in that it put an end to his earthly human existence. But because of the union which the person of the Son
1009 retained with his body, his was not a mortal corpse like others, for "it
1683 was not possible for death to hold him"[470] and therefore "divine power preserved Christ's body from corruption."[471] Both of these statements can be said of Christ: "He was cut off out of the land of the living,"[472] and "My flesh will dwell in hope. For you will not abandon my soul to Hades, nor let your Holy One see corruption."[473] Jesus' Resurrection "on the third day" was the sign of this also, because bodily decay was held to begin on the fourth day after death.[474]

"Buried with Christ..."

628 Baptism, the original and full sign of which is immersion, efficaciously signifies the descent into the tomb by the Christian who dies to
sin with Christ in order to live a new 537
life. "We were buried therefore with
him by baptism into death, so that 1214
as Christ was raised from the dead by the glory of the Father, we too might walk in newness of life."[475]

In Brief

629 *To the benefit of every man, Jesus Christ tasted death (cf.* Heb *2:9). It is truly the Son of God made man who died and was buried.*

630 *During Christ's period in the tomb, his divine person continued to assume both his soul and his body, although they were separated from each other by death. For this reason the dead Christ's body "saw no corruption"* (Acts *13:37).*

Article 5:
"HE DESCENDED INTO HELL; ON THE THIRD DAY HE ROSE AGAIN"

631 Jesus "descended into the lower parts of the earth. He who descended is he who also ascended far above all the heavens."[476] The Apostles' Creed confesses in the same article Christ's descent into hell and his Resurrection from the dead on the third day, because in his Passover it was precisely out of the depths of death that he made life spring forth:

> Christ, that Morning Star, who came back from the dead, and shed his peaceful light on all mankind, your Son who lives and reigns for ever and ever. Amen.[477]

[469] St. John Damascene, *De fide orth.*, 3, 27: PG 94, 1098A. — [470] *Acts* 2:24. — [471] St. Thomas Aquinas, *STh* III, 51, 3. — [472] *Isa* 53:8. — [473] *Acts* 2:26–27; cf. *Ps* 16:9–10. — [474] Cf. *1 Cor* 15:4; *Lk* 24:46; *Mt* 12:40; *Jon* 2:1; *Hos* 6:2; cf. *Jn* 11:39. — [475] *Rom* 6:4; cf. *Col* 2:12; *Eph* 5:26. — [476] *Eph* 4:9–10 — [477] *Roman Missal*, Easter Vigil 18, *Exsultet*.

Paragraph 1
Christ Descended into Hell

632 The frequent New Testament affirmations that Jesus was "raised from the dead" presuppose that the crucified one sojourned in the realm of the dead prior to his resurrection.[478] This was the first meaning given in the apostolic preaching to Christ's descent into hell: that Jesus, like all men, experienced death and in his soul joined the others in the realm of the dead. But he descended there as Savior, proclaiming the Good News to the spirits imprisoned there.[479]

633 Scripture calls the abode of the dead, to which the dead Christ went down, "hell"—*Sheol* in Hebrew or *Hades* in Greek—because those who are there are deprived of the vision of God.[480] Such is the case for all the dead, whether evil or righteous, while they await the redeemer: which does not mean that their lot is identical, as Jesus shows through the parable of the poor man Lazarus who was received into "Abraham's bosom":[481] "It is precisely these holy souls, who awaited their Savior in Abraham's bosom, whom Christ the Lord delivered when he descended into hell."[482]
1033 Jesus did not descend into hell to deliver the damned, nor to destroy the hell of damnation, but to free the just who had gone before him.[483]

634 "The gospel was preached even to the dead."[484] The descent into hell brings the Gospel message of salvation to complete fulfillment. This is the last phase of Jesus' messianic mission, a phase which is condensed in time but vast in its real significance: the spread of Christ's redemptive work to all men of all times and all places, for all who are saved have been made sharers in the redemption. 605

635 Christ went down into the depths of death so that "the dead will hear the voice of the Son of God, and those who hear will live."[485] Jesus, "the Author of life," by dying destroyed "him who has the power of death, that is, the devil, and [delivered] all those who through fear of death were subject to lifelong bondage."[486] Henceforth the risen Christ holds "the keys of Death and Hades," so that "at the name of Jesus every knee should bow, in heaven and on earth and under the earth."[487]

> Today a great silence reigns on earth, a great silence and a great stillness. A great silence because the King is asleep. The earth trembled and is still because God has fallen asleep in the flesh and he has raised up all who have slept ever since the world began.... He has gone to search for Adam, our first father, as for a lost sheep. Greatly desiring to visit those who live in darkness and in the shadow of death, he has gone to free from sorrow Adam in his bonds and Eve, captive with him—He who is both their God and the son of Eve.... "I am your God, who for your sake have become your son.... I order you, O sleeper, to awake. I did not create you to be a prisoner in hell. Rise from the dead, for I am the life of the dead."[488]

[478] *Acts* 3:15; *Rom* 8:11; *1 Cor* 15:20; cf. *Heb* 13:20. — [479] Cf. *1 Pet* 3:18–19. — [480] Cf. *Phil* 2:10; *Acts* 2:24; *Rev* 1:18; *Eph* 4:9; *Pss* 6:6; 88:11–13. — [481] Cf. *Ps* 89:49; *1 Sam* 28:19; *Ezek* 32:17–32; *Lk* 16:22–26. — [482] *Roman Catechism* I, 6, 3. — [483] Cf. Council of Rome (745): DS 587; Benedict XII, *Cum dudum* (1341): DS. 1011; Clement VI, *Super quibusdam* (1351): DS 1077; Council of Toledo IV (625): DS 485; *Mt* 27:52–53. — [484] *1 Pet* 4:6. — [485] *Jn* 5:25; cf. *Mt* 12:40; *Rom* 10:7; *Eph* 4:9. — [486] *Heb* 2:14–15; cf. *Acts* 3:15. — [487] *Rev* 1:18; *Phil* 2:10. — [488] Ancient Homily for Holy Saturday: PG 43, 440A, 452C: *LH*, Holy Saturday, OR.

In Brief

636 *By the expression "He descended into hell," the Apostles' Creed confesses that Jesus did really die and through his death for us conquered death and the devil "who has the power of death" (*Heb *2:14).*

637 *In his human soul united to his divine person, the dead Christ went down to the realm of the dead. He opened heaven's gates for the just who had gone before him.*

Paragraph 2
On the Third Day He Rose from the Dead

638 "We bring you the good
news that what God promised to
the fathers, this day he has fulfilled
to us their children by raising Jesus."[489] The Resurrection of Jesus is
the crowning truth of our faith in
90 Christ, a faith believed and lived as
the central truth by the first Chris-
651 tian community; handed on as fundamental by Tradition; established
991 by the documents of the New Testament; and preached as an essential
part of the Paschal mystery along
with the cross:

> Christ is risen from the dead!
> Dying, he conquered death;
> To the dead, he has given life.[490]

I. The Historical and Transcendent Event

639 The mystery of Christ's resurrection is a real event, with manifestations that were historically verified, as the New Testament bears witness. In about *A.D.* 56, St. Paul could already write to the Corinthians: "I delivered to you as of first importance what I also received, that Christ died for our sins in accordance with the scriptures, and that he was buried, that he was raised on the third day in accordance with the scriptures, and that he appeared to Cephas, then to the Twelve..."[491] Apostle speaks here of the living tradition of the Resurrection which he had learned after his conversion at the gates of Damascus.[492]

The empty tomb

640 "Why do you seek the living among the dead? He is not here, but has risen."[493] The first element we encounter in the framework of the Easter events is the empty tomb. In itself it is not a direct proof of Resurrection; the absence of Christ's body from the tomb could be explained otherwise.[494] Nonetheless the empty tomb was still an essential sign for all. Its discovery by the disciples was the first step toward recognizing the very fact of the Resurrection. This was the case, first with the holy women, and then with Peter.[495] The disciple "whom Jesus loved" affirmed that when he entered the empty tomb and discovered "the linen cloths lying there," "he saw and believed."[496] This suggests that he realized from the empty tomb's condition that the absence of Jesus' body could not have been of human doing and that Jesus had not simply returned to earthly life as had been
the case with Lazarus.[497] 999

The appearances of the Risen One

[489] *Acts* 13:32–33. — [490] Byzantine Liturgy, Troparion of Easter. — [491] *1 Cor* 15:3–4. — [492] Cf. *Acts* 9:3–18. — [493] *Lk* 24:5–6. — [494] Cf. *Jn* 20:13; *Mt* 28:11–15. — [495] Cf. *Lk* 24:3, 12, 22–23. — [496] *Jn* 20:2, 6, 8. — [497] Cf. *Jn* 11:44; 20:5–7.

641 Mary Magdalene and the holy women who came to finish anointing the body of Jesus, which had been buried in haste because the Sabbath began on the evening of Good Friday, were the first to encounter the Risen One.[498] Thus the women were the first messengers of Christ's Resurrection for the apostles themselves.[499] They were the next to whom Jesus appears: first Peter, then the Twelve. Peter had been called to
553 strengthen the faith of his brothers,[500] and so sees the Risen One before them; it is on the basis of his testimony that the community ex
448 claims: "The Lord has risen indeed, and has appeared to Simon!"[501]

642 Everything that happened during those Paschal days involves each of the apostles—and Peter in particular—in the building of the new era begun on Easter morning. As witnesses of the Risen One, they
659, 881 remain the foundation stones of his Church. The faith of the first community of believers is based on the witness of concrete men known to the Christians and for the most part still living among them. Peter and the Twelve are the primary "witnesses to his Resurrection," but they
860 are not the only ones—Paul speaks clearly of more than five hundred persons to whom Jesus appeared on a single occasion and also of James and of all the apostles.[502]

643 Given all these testimonies, Christ's Resurrection cannot be interpreted as something outside the physical order, and it is impossible not to acknowledge it as an historical fact. It is clear from the facts that the disciples' faith was drastically put to the test by their master's Passion and death on the cross, which he had foretold.[503] The shock provoked by the Passion was so great that at least some of the disciples did not at once believe in the news of the Resurrection. Far from showing us a community seized by a mystical exaltation, the Gospels present us with disciples demoralized ("looking sad"[504]) and frightened. For they had not believed the holy women returning from the tomb and had regarded their words as an "idle tale."[505] When Jesus reveals himself to the Eleven on Easter evening, "he upbraided them for their unbelief and hardness of heart, because they had not believed those who saw him after he had risen."[506]

644 Even when faced with the reality of the risen Jesus the disciples are still doubtful, so impossible did the thing seem: they thought they were seeing a ghost. "In their joy they were still disbelieving and still wondering."[507] Thomas will also experience the test of doubt and St. Matthew relates that during the risen Lord's last appearance in Galilee "some doubted."[508] Therefore the hypothesis that the Resurrection was produced by the apostles' faith (or credulity) will not hold up. On the contrary their faith in the Resurrection was born, under the action of divine grace, from their direct experience of the reality of the risen Jesus.

The condition of Christ's risen humanity

[498] *Mk* 16:1; *Lk* 24:1; *Jn* 19:31, 42. — [499] Cf. *Lk* 24:9–10; *Mt* 28:9–10; *Jn* 20:11–18. — [500] Cf. *1 Cor* 15:5; *Lk* 22:31–32. — [501] *Lk* 24:34, 36. — [502] *1 Cor* 15:4–8; cf. *Acts* 1:22. — [503] Cf. *Lk* 22:31–32. — [504] *Lk* 24:17; cf. *Jn* 20:19. — [505] *Lk* 24:11; cf. *Mk* 16:11, 13. — [506] *Mk* 16:14. — [507] *Lk* 24:38–41. — [508] Cf. *Jn* 20:24–27; *Mt* 28:17.

645 By means of touch and the
sharing of a meal, the risen Jesus establishes direct contact with his disciples. He invites them in this way
to recognize that he is not a ghost
and above all to verify that the risen
999 body in which he appears to them
is the same body that had been tor-
tured and crucified, for it still bears
the traces of his passion.[509] Yet at the
same time this authentic, real body
possesses the new properties of a
glorious body: not limited by space
and time but able to be present how
and when he wills; for Christ's humanity can no longer be confined to
earth and belongs henceforth only to
the Father's divine realm.[510] For this
reason too the risen Jesus enjoys the
sovereign freedom of appearing as he
wishes: in the guise of a gardener or in
other forms familiar to his disciples,
precisely to awaken their faith.[511]

646 Christ's Resurrection was not
a return to earthly life, as was the
case with the raisings from the dead
that he had performed before Easter:
Jairus' daughter, the young man of
Naim, Lazarus. These actions were
miraculous events, but the persons
miraculously raised returned by Je-
934 sus' power to ordinary earthly life. At
some particular moment they would
549 die again. Christ's Resurrection is essentially different. In his risen body
he passes from the state of death to
another life beyond time and space.
At Jesus' Resurrection his body is
filled with the power of the Holy
Spirit: he shares the divine life in his
glorious state, so that St. Paul can say
that Christ is "the man of heaven."[512]

The Resurrection as transcendent event

647 O truly blessed Night, sings
the Exsultet of the Easter Vigil, which
alone deserved to know the time and
the hour when Christ rose from the
realm of the dead![513] But no one was
an eyewitness to Christ's Resurrection
and no evangelist describes it. No one
can say how it came about physical- 1000
ly. Still less was its innermost essence,
his passing over to another life, perceptible to the senses. Although the
Resurrection was an historical event
that could be verified by the sign of
the empty tomb and by the reality of
the apostles' encounters with the risen
Christ, still it remains at the very heart
of the mystery of faith as something
that transcends and surpasses history.
This is why the risen Christ does not
reveal himself to the world, but to his
disciples, "to those who came up with
him from Galilee to Jerusalem, who
are now his witnesses to the people."[514]

II. The Resurrection—A Work of the Holy Trinity

648 Christ's Resurrection is an
object of faith in that it is a transcendent intervention of God himself in creation and history. In it the
three divine persons act together as 258, 989
one, and manifest their own proper
characteristics. The Father's power
"raised up" Christ his Son and by
doing so perfectly introduced his 663
Son's humanity, including his body,
into the Trinity. Jesus is conclusive- 445
ly revealed as "Son of God in power
according to the Spirit of holiness by 272
his Resurrection from the dead."[515]
St. Paul insists on the manifestation

[509] Cf. *Lk* 24:30, 39–40, 41–43; *Jn* 20:20, 27; 21:9, 13–15. — [510] Cf. *Mt* 28:9, 16–17; *Lk* 24:15, 36; *Jn* 20:14, 17, 19, 26; 21:4. — [511] Cf. *Mk* 16:12; *Jn* 20:14–16; 21:4, 7. — [512] Cf. *1 Cor* 15:35–50. — [513] *"O vere beata nox, quae sola meruit scire tempus et horam, in qua Christus ab inferis resurrexit!"* — [514] *Acts* 13:31; cf. *Jn* 14:22. — [515] *Rom* 1:3–4; cf. *Acts* 2:24.

of God's power[516] through the working of the Spirit who gave life to Jesus' dead humanity and called it to the glorious state of Lordship.

649 As for the Son, he effects his own Resurrection by virtue of his divine power. Jesus announces that the Son of man will have to suffer much, die, and then rise.[517] Elsewhere he affirms explicitly: "I lay down my life, that I may take it again.... I have power to lay it down, and I have power to take it again."[518] "We believe that Jesus died and rose again."[519]

626 **650** The Fathers contemplate the Resurrection from the perspective of
1005 the divine person of Christ who remained united to his soul and body, even when these were separated from each other by death: "By the unity of the divine nature, which remains present in each of the two components of man, these are reunited. For as death is produced by the separation of the human components, so Resurrection is achieved by the union of the two."[520]

III. The Meaning and Saving Significance of the Resurrection

651 "If Christ has not been raised, then our preaching is in vain and your faith is in vain."[521] The Resurrection above all constitutes the confirmation of all Christ's works and teachings. All truths, even those
129 most inaccessible to human reason, find their justification if Christ by
274 his Resurrection has given the definitive proof of his divine authority, which he had promised.

652 Christ's Resurrection is the fulfillment of the promises both of the Old Testament and of Jesus him- 994, 601
self during his earthly life.[522] The phrase "in accordance with the Scriptures"[523] indicates that Christ's Resurrection fulfilled these predictions.

653 The truth of Jesus' divinity is 445
confirmed by his Resurrection. He had said: "When you have lifted up the Son of man, then you will know that I am he."[524] The Resurrection of the crucified one shows that he was truly "I Am," the Son of God and God himself. So St. Paul could declare to the Jews: "What God promised to the fathers, this he has fulfilled to us their children by raising Jesus; as also it is written in the second psalm, 'You are my Son, today I have begotten you.'"[525] Christ's Resurrection is closely linked to the Incarnation of God's Son and is its fulfillment in accordance with God's eternal plan. 461, 422

654 The Paschal mystery has two aspects: by his death, Christ liberates us from sin; by his Resurrection, he opens for us the way to a new life. This new life is above all justification that reinstates us in God's grace, "so that as Christ was raised from the 1987
dead by the glory of the Father, we too might walk in newness of life."[526] Justification consists in both victory over the death caused by sin and a new participation in grace.[527] It brings about filial adoption so that men become Christ's brethren, as Je- 1996
sus himself called his disciples after his Resurrection: "Go and tell my brethren."[528] We are brethren not

[516] Cf. *Rom* 6:4; *2 Cor* 13:4; *Phil* 3:10; *Eph* 1:19–22; *Heb* 7:16. — [517] Cf. *Mk* 8:31; 9:9–31; 10:34. — [518] *Jn* 10:17–18. — [519] *1 Thess* 4:14. — [520] St. Gregory of Nyssa, *In Christi res. orat.* 1: PG 46:617B; cf. also DS 325; 359; 369. — [521] *1 Cor* 15:14. — [522] Cf. *Mt* 28:6; *Mk* 16:7; *Lk* 24:6–7, 26–27, 44–48. — [523] Cf. *1 Cor* 15:3–4; cf. the Nicene Creed. — [524] *Jn* 8:28. — [525] *Acts* 13:32–34; cf. *Ps* 2:7. — [526] *Rom* 6:4; cf. 4:25. — [527] Cf. *Eph* 2:4–5; *1 Pet* 1:3. — [528] *Mt* 28:10; *Jn* 20:17.

by nature, but by the gift of grace, because that adoptive filiation gains us a real share in the life of the only Son, which was fully revealed in his Resurrection.

655 Finally, Christ's Resurrection—and the risen Christ himself—is the principle and source of our future resurrection: "Christ has been raised from the dead, the
989 first fruits of those who have fallen asleep.... For as in Adam all die, so also in Christ shall all be made alive."[529] The risen Christ lives in the hearts of his faithful while they await that fulfillment. In Christ, Christians "have tasted...the powers of the age to come"[530] and their lives are swept
1002 up by Christ into the heart of divine life, so that they may "live no longer for themselves but for him who for their sake died and was raised."[531]

In Brief

656 *Faith in the Resurrection has as its object an event which is historically attested to by the disciples, who really encountered the Risen One. At the same time, this event is mysteriously transcendent insofar as it is the entry of Christ's humanity into the glory of God.*

657 *The empty tomb and the linen cloths lying there signify in themselves that by God's power Christ's body had escaped the bonds of death and corruption. They prepared the disciples to encounter the Risen Lord.*

658 *Christ, "the first-born from the dead"* (Col *1:18), is the principle of our own resurrection, even now by the justification of our souls (cf.* Rom *6:4), and one day by the new life he will impart to our bodies (cf.* Rom *8:11).*

Article 6: "HE ASCENDED INTO HEAVEN AND IS SEATED AT THE RIGHT HAND OF THE FATHER"

659 "So then the Lord Jesus, after he had spoken to them, was taken up into heaven, and sat down at the right hand of God."[532] Christ's body was glorified at the moment of his Resurrection, as proved by the new
645 and supernatural properties it subsequently and permanently enjoys.[533] But during the forty days when he eats and drinks familiarly with his disciples and teaches them about the kingdom, his glory remains veiled under the appearance of ordinary humanity.[534] Jesus' final apparition ends with the irreversible entry of
his humanity into divine glory, sym- 66
bolized by the cloud and by heaven,
where he is seated from that time 697
forward at God's right hand.[535] Only
in a wholly exceptional and unique 642
way would Jesus show himself to Paul "as to one untimely born," in a last apparition that established him as an apostle.[536]

660 The veiled character of the glory of the Risen One during this time is intimated in his mysterious words to Mary Magdalene: "I have

[529] *1 Cor* 15:20–22. — [530] *Heb* 6:5. — [531] *2 Cor* 5:15; cf. *Col* 3:1–3. — [532] *Mk* 16:19. — [533] Cf. *Lk* 24:31; *Jn* 20:19, 26. — [534] Cf. *Acts* 1:3; 10:41; *Mk* 16:12; *Lk* 24:15; *Jn* 20:14–15; 21:4. — [535] Cf. *Acts* 1:9; 2:33; 7:56; *Lk* 9:34–35; 24:51; *Ex* 13:22; *Mk* 16:19; *Ps* 110:1. — [536] *1 Cor* 15:8; cf. 9:1; *Gal* 1:16.

not yet ascended to the Father; but go to my brethren and say to them, I am ascending to my Father and your Father, to my God and your God."[537] This indicates a difference in manifestation between the glory of the risen Christ and that of the Christ exalted to the Father's right hand, a transition marked by the historical and transcendent event of the Ascension.

661 This final stage stays closely linked to the first, that is, to his descent from heaven in the Incarnation. Only the one who "came from
461 the Father" can return to the Father: Christ Jesus.[538] "No one has ascended into heaven but he who descended from heaven, the Son of man."[539] Left to its own natural powers humanity does not have access to the "Father's house," to God's life and
792 happiness.[540] Only Christ can open to man such access that we, his members, might have confidence that we too shall go where he, our Head and our Source, has preceded us.[541]

662 "And I, when I am lifted up from the earth, will draw all men to myself."[542] The lifting up of Jesus on the cross signifies and announces his lifting up by his Ascension into heaven, and indeed begins it. Jesus
1545 Christ, the one priest of the new and eternal Covenant, "entered, not into a sanctuary made by human hands...but into heaven itself, now to appear in the presence of God on our behalf."[543] There Christ permanently exercises his priesthood, for he "always lives to make intercession" for "those who draw near to God through him."[544] As "high priest of the good things to come" he is the center and the principal
actor of the liturgy that honors the 1137
Father in heaven.[545]

663 Henceforth Christ is *seated at the right hand of the Father*: "By 'the Father's right hand' we understand the glory and honor of divinity, where he who exists as Son of God before all ages, indeed as God, of one being with the Father, is seated bodily after he became incarnate
and his flesh was glorified."[546] 648

664 Being seated at the Father's right hand signifies the inauguration of the Messiah's kingdom, the fulfillment of the prophet Daniel's
vision concerning the Son of man: 541
"To him was given dominion and glory and kingdom, that all peoples, nations, and languages should serve him; his dominion is an everlasting dominion, which shall not pass away, and his kingdom one that shall not be destroyed."[547] After this event the apostles became witnesses of the "kingdom [that] will have no end."[548]

In Brief

665 *Christ's ascension marks the definitive entrance of Jesus' humanity into God's heavenly domain, whence he will come again (cf.* Acts *1:11); this humanity in the meantime hides him from the eyes of men (cf.* Col *3:3).*

[537] *Jn* 20:17. — [538] Cf. *Jn* 16:28. — [539] *Jn* 3:13; cf. *Eph* 4:8–10. — [540] *Jn* 14:2. — [541] *Roman Missal*, Preface of the Ascension: *"sed ut illuc confideremus, sua membra, nos subsequi quo ipse, caput nostrum principiumque, praecessit."* — [542] *Jn* 12:32. — [543] *Heb* 9:24. — [544] *Heb* 7:25. — [545] *Heb* 9:11; cf. *Rev* 4:6–11. — [546] St. John Damascene, *De fide orth.*, 4, 2: PG 94, 1104C. — [547] *Dan* 7:14. — [548] Nicene Creed.

666 *Jesus Christ, the head of the Church, precedes us into the Father's glorious kingdom so that we, the members of his Body, may live in the hope of one day being with him for ever.*

667 *Jesus Christ, having entered the sanctuary of heaven once and for all, intercedes constantly for us as the mediator who assures us of the permanent outpouring of the Holy Spirit.*

Article 7: "FROM THENCE HE WILL COME AGAIN TO JUDGE THE LIVING AND THE DEAD"

I. He Will Come Again in Glory

Christ already reigns through the Church...

668 "Christ died and lived again,
that he might be Lord both of the
dead and of the living."[549] Christ's
Ascension into heaven signifies his
participation, in his humanity, in
God's power and authority. Jesus
450 Christ is Lord: he possesses all power in heaven and on earth. He is
"far above all rule and authority and
power and dominion," for the Father
"has put all things under his feet."[550]
Christ is Lord of the cosmos and of
history. In him human history and
518 indeed all creation are "set forth"
and transcendently fulfilled.[551]

669 As Lord, Christ is also head
of the Church, which is his Body.[552]
Taken up to heaven and glorified after he had thus fully accomplished
92, 1088 his mission, Christ dwells on earth
in his Church. The redemption is the
source of the authority that Christ,
by virtue of the Holy Spirit, exercis-
541 es over the Church. "The kingdom
of Christ [is] already present in mystery," "on earth, the seed and the beginning of the kingdom."[553]

670 Since the Ascension God's
plan has entered into its fulfillment.
We are already at "the last hour."[554]
"Already the final age of the world
is with us, and the renewal of the 1042
world is irrevocably under way; it
is even now anticipated in a certain
real way, for the Church on earth
is endowed already with a sanctity
that is real but imperfect."[555] Christ's
kingdom already manifests its pres- 825
ence through the miraculous signs
that attend its proclamation by the 547
Church.[556]

...until all things are subjected to him

671 Though already present in his
Church, Christ's reign is nevertheless
yet to be fulfilled "with power and
great glory" by the king's return to
earth.[557] This reign is still under attack by the evil powers, even though
they have been defeated definitively
by Christ's Passover.[558] Until everything is subject to him, "until there
be realized new heavens and a new 1043
earth in which justice dwells, the pilgrim Church, in her sacraments and 769, 773
institutions, which belong to this
present age, carries the mark of this
world which will pass, and she herself
takes her place among the creatures

[549] *Rom* 14:9 — [550] *Eph* 1:20–22. — [551] *Eph* 1:10; cf. *Eph* 4:10; *1 Cor* 15:24, 27–28. — [552] Cf. *Eph* 1:22. — [553] *LG* 3; 5; cf. *Eph* 4:11–13. — [554] *1 Jn* 2:18; cf. *1 Pet* 4:7. — [555] *LG* 48 § 3; cf. *1 Cor* 10:11. — [556] Cf. *Mk* 16:17–18, 20. — [557] *Lk* 21:27; cf. *Mt* 25:31. — [558] Cf. *2 Thess* 2:7.

which groan and travail yet and await the revelation of the sons of God."[559]
1043, 2046 That is why Christians pray, above all in the Eucharist, to hasten Christ's re
2817 turn by saying to him:[560] Marana tha! "Our Lord, come!"[561]

672 Before his Ascension Christ affirmed that the hour had not yet come for the glorious establishment of the messianic kingdom awaited by Israel[562] which, according to the prophets, was to bring all men the definitive order of justice, love, and peace.[563] According to the Lord, the present time is the time of the Spirit and of witness, but also a time still
732 marked by "distress" and the trial of evil which does not spare the
2612 Church[564] and ushers in the struggles of the last days. It is a time of waiting and watching.[565]

The glorious advent of Christ, the hope of Israel

673 Since the Ascension Christ's coming in glory has been imminent,[566] even though "it is not for you to know times or seasons which the
1040, 1048 Father has fixed by his own authority."[567] This eschatological coming could be accomplished at any moment, even if both it and the final trial that will precede it are "delayed."[568]

674 The glorious Messiah's coming is suspended at every moment of history until his recognition by "all Israel," for "a hardening has come upon part of Israel" in their "unbelief" toward Jesus.[569] St. Peter says to the Jews of Jerusalem after Pentecost: "Repent therefore, and turn again, that your sins may be blotted out, that times of refreshing may come from the presence of the Lord, and that he may send the Christ appointed for you, Jesus, whom heaven must receive until the time for establishing all that God spoke by the mouth of his holy prophets from of old."[570] St. Paul echoes him: "For if their rejection means the reconciliation of the world, what will their
acceptance mean but life from the 840
dead?"[571] The "full inclusion" of the Jews in the Messiah's salvation, in the wake of "the full number of the Gentiles,"[572] will enable the People
of God to achieve "the measure of 58
the stature of the fullness of Christ," in which "God may be all in all."[573]

The Church's ultimate trial

675 Before Christ's second coming the Church must pass through a final trial that will shake the faith of many believers.[574] The persecution
that accompanies her pilgrimage on 769
earth[575] will unveil the "mystery of iniquity" in the form of a religious deception offering men an apparent solution to their problems at the price of apostasy from the truth. The supreme religious deception is that of the Antichrist, a pseudo-messianism by which man glorifies himself in place of God and of his Messiah come in the flesh.[576]

676 The Antichrist's deception already begins to take shape in the

[559] *LG* 48 § 3; cf. *2 Pet* 3:13; *Rom* 8:19–22; *1 Cor* 15:28. — [560] Cf. *1 Cor* 11:26; *2 Pet* 3:11–12. — [561] *1 Cor* 16:22; *Rev* 22:17, 20. — [562] Cf. *Acts* 1:6–7. — [563] Cf. *Isa* 11:1–9. — [564] Cf. *Acts* 1:8; *1 Cor* 7:26; *Eph* 5:16; *1 Pet* 4:17 — [565] Cf. *Mt* 25:1, 13; *Mk* 13:33–37; *1 Jn* 2:18; 4:3; *1 Tim* 4:1. — [566] Cf. *Rev* 22:20. — [567] *Acts* 1:7; cf. *Mk* 13:32. — [568] Cf. *Mt* 24:44; *1 Thess* 5:2; *2 Thess* 2:3–12. — [569] *Rom* 11:20–26; cf. *Mt* 23:39. — [570] *Acts* 3:19–21. — [571] *Rom* 11:15. — [572] *Rom* 11:12, 25; cf. *Lk* 21:24. — [573] *Eph* 4:13; *1 Cor* 15:28. — [574] Cf. *Lk* 18:8; *Mt* 24:12. — [575] Cf. *Lk* 21:12; *Jn* 15:19–20. — [576] Cf. *2 Thess* 2:4–12; *1 Thess* 5:2–3; *2 Jn* 7; *1 Jn* 2:18, 22.

world every time the claim is made to realize within history that messianic hope which can only be realized beyond history through the eschatological judgment. The Church has rejected even modified forms of this falsification of the kingdom to come under the name of millenarianism,[577] especially the "intrinsically
2425 perverse" political form of a secular messianism.[578]

677 The Church will enter the glory of the kingdom only through this final Passover, when she will follow her Lord in his death and Resurrec-
1340 tion.[579] The kingdom will be fulfilled, then, not by a historic triumph of the Church through a progressive ascendancy, but only by God's victory over the final unleashing of evil, which
2853 will cause his Bride to come down from heaven.[580] God's triumph over the revolt of evil will take the form of the Last Judgment after the final cosmic upheaval of this passing world.[581]

1038–1041 II. To Judge the Living and the Dead

678 Following in the steps of the prophets and John the Baptist, Jesus
1470 announced the judgment of the Last Day in his preaching.[582] Then will the conduct of each one and the secrets of hearts be brought to light.[583] Then will the culpable unbelief that counted the offer of God's grace as nothing be condemned.[584] Our attitude about our neighbor will disclose acceptance or refusal of grace and divine love.[585] On the last day Jesus will say: "Truly I say to you, as you did it to one of the least of these my brethren, you did it to me."[586]

679 Christ is Lord of eternal life. Full right to pass definitive judgment on the works and hearts of men belongs to him as redeemer of the world. He "acquired" this right by his cross. The Father has given "all
judgment to the Son."[587] Yet the Son 1021
did not come to judge, but to save and to give the life he has in himself.[588] By rejecting grace in this life, one already judges oneself, receives according to one's works, and can even condemn oneself for all eternity by rejecting the Spirit of love.[589]

In Brief

680 *Christ the Lord already reigns through the Church, but all the things of this world are not yet subjected to him. The triumph of Christ's kingdom will not come about without one last assault by the powers of evil.*

681 *On Judgment Day at the end of the world, Christ will come in glory to achieve the definitive triumph of good over evil which, like the wheat and the tares, have grown up together in the course of history.*

682 *When he comes at the end of time to judge the living and the dead, the glorious Christ will reveal the secret disposition of hearts and will render to each man according to his works and according to his acceptance or refusal of grace.*

[577] Cf. DS 3839. — [578] Pius XI, *Divini Redemptoris*, condemning the "false mysticism" of this "counterfeit of the redemption of the lowly"; cf. *GS* 20–21. — [579] Cf. *Rev* 19:1–9. — [580] Cf. *Rev* 13:8; 20:7–10; 21:2–4. — [581] Cf. *Rev* 20:12; *2 Pet* 3:12–13. — [582] Cf. *Dan* 7:10; *Joel* 3–4; *Mal* 3:19; *Mt* 3:7–12. — [583] Cf. *Mk* 12:38–40; *Lk* 12:1–3; *Jn* 3:20–21; *Rom* 2:16; *1 Cor* 4:5. — [584] Cf. *Mt* 11:20–24; 12:41–42. — [585] *Mt* 5:22; 7:1–5. — [586] *Mt* 25:40. — [587] *Jn* 5:22; cf. 5:27; *Mt* 25:31; *Acts* 10:42; 17:31; *2 Tim* 4:1. — [588] Cf. *Jn* 3:17; 5:26. — [589] Cf. *Jn* 3:18; 12:48; *Mt* 12:32; *1 Cor* 3:12–15; *Heb* 6:4–6; 10:26–31.

Chapter Three:
I BELIEVE IN THE HOLY SPIRIT

683 "No one can say 'Jesus is Lord' except by the Holy Spirit."[1] "God has sent the Spirit of his Son into our hearts, crying, '*Abba!* Father!'"[2]
424, 2670 This knowledge of faith is possible only in the Holy Spirit: to be in
152 touch with Christ, we must first have been touched by the Holy Spirit. He comes to meet us and kindles faith in us. By virtue of our Baptism, the first sacrament of the faith, the Holy Spirit in the Church communicates to us, intimately and personally, the life that originates in the Father and is offered to us in the Son.

> 249 Baptism gives us the grace of new birth in God the Father, through his Son, in the Holy Spirit. For those who bear God's Spirit are led to the Word, that is, to the Son, and the Son presents them to the Father, and the Father confers incorruptibility on them. And it is impossible to see God's Son without the Spirit, and no one can approach the Father without the Son, for the knowledge of the Father is the Son, and the knowledge of God's Son is obtained through the Holy Spirit.[3]

684 Through his grace, the Holy Spirit is the first to awaken faith in us and to communicate to us the new life, which is to "know the Father and the one whom he has sent, Jesus Christ."[4] But the Spirit is the last of the persons of the Holy Trinity to be revealed. St. Gregory of Nazianzus, the Theologian, explains this progression in terms of the ped
236 agogy of divine "condescension":

> The Old Testament proclaimed the Father clearly, but the Son more obscurely. The New Testament revealed the Son and gave us a glimpse of the divinity of the Spirit. Now the Spirit dwells among us and grants us a clearer vision of himself. It was not prudent, when the divinity of the Father had not yet been confessed, to proclaim the Son openly and, when the divinity of the Son was not yet admitted, to add the Holy Spirit as an extra burden, to speak somewhat daringly.... By advancing and progressing "from glory to glory," the light of the Trinity will shine in ever more brilliant rays.[5]

685 To believe in the Holy Spirit is to profess that the Holy Spirit is one of the persons of the Holy Trinity, consubstantial with the Father and the Son: "with the Father and the Son he is worshipped and glorified."[6] For this reason, the divine mystery of the Holy Spirit was already treated in the context of Trinitarian "theology." Here, however, we
have to do with the Holy Spirit only 236
in the divine "economy."

686 The Holy Spirit is at work with the Father and the Son from the beginning to the completion of the plan for our salvation. But in these
"end times," ushered in by the Son's 258
redeeming Incarnation, the Spirit is revealed and given, recognized and welcomed as a person. Now can this divine plan, accomplished in Christ, the firstborn and head of the new creation, be embodied in mankind by the outpouring of the Spirit: as

[1] *1 Cor* 12:3. —[2] *Gal* 4:6. [3] St. Irenζus, *Dem. ap.* 7: SCh 62, 41–42. — [4] *Jn* 17:3. — [5] St. Gregory of Nazianzus, *Oratio theol.*, 5, 26 (= *Oratio* 31, 26): PG 36, 161–163. — [6] Nicene Creed; see above, par. 465.

the Church, the communion of saints, the forgiveness of sins, the resurrection of the body, and the life everlasting.

Article 8:
"I BELIEVE IN THE HOLY SPIRIT"

687 "No one comprehends the thoughts of God except the Spirit of God."[7] Now God's Spirit, who reveals God, makes known to us Christ, his Word, his living Utter-
243 ance, but the Spirit does not speak of himself. The Spirit who "has spoken through the prophets" makes us hear the Father's Word, but we do not hear the Spirit himself. We know him only in the movement by which he reveals the Word to us and disposes us to welcome him in faith. The Spirit of truth who "unveils" Christ to us "will not speak on his own."[8] Such properly divine self-effacement explains why "the world cannot receive [him], because it neither sees him nor knows him," while those who believe in Christ know the Spirit because he dwells with them.[9]

688 The Church, a communion living in the faith of the apostles which she transmits, is the place where we know the Holy Spirit:

– in the Scriptures he inspired;
– in the Tradition, to which the Church Fathers are always timely witnesses;
– in the Church's Magisterium, which he assists;
– in the sacramental liturgy, through its words and symbols, in which the Holy Spirit puts us into communion with Christ;
– in prayer, wherein he intercedes for us;
– in the charisms and ministries by which the Church is built up;
– in the signs of apostolic and missionary life;
– in the witness of saints through whom he manifests his holiness and continues the work of salvation.

I. The Joint Mission of the Son and the Spirit

689 The One whom the Father has sent into our hearts, the Spirit of his Son, is truly God.[10] Consubstantial with the Father and the Son,
the Spirit is inseparable from them, 245
in both the inner life of the Trinity and his gift of love for the world. In adoring the Holy Trinity, life-giving, consubstantial, and indivisible, the Church's faith also professes the distinction of persons. When the Father sends his Word, he always
sends his Breath. In their joint mis- 254
sion, the Son and the Holy Spirit are
distinct but inseparable. To be sure, 485
it is Christ who is seen, the visible image of the invisible God, but it is the Spirit who reveals him.

690 Jesus is Christ, "anointed," because the Spirit is his anointing, and everything that occurs from the Incarnation on derives from this
fullness.[11] When Christ is finally 436
glorified,[12] he can in turn send the

[7] *1 Cor* 2:11. — [8] *Jn* 16:13. — [9] *Jn* 14:17. — [10] Cf. *Gal* 4:6. — [11] Cf. *Jn* 3:34. — [12] *Jn* 7:39.

Spirit from his place with the Father to those who believe in him: he communicates to them his glory,[13] that is, the Holy Spirit who glorifies him.[14] From that time on, this joint mission will be manifested in the children adopted by the Father in the Body of his Son: the mission
788 of the Spirit of adoption is to unite them to Christ and make them live in him:

> The notion of anointing suggests... that there is no distance between the Son and the Spirit. Indeed, just as between the surface of the body and the anointing with oil neither reason nor sensation recognizes any intermediary, so the contact of the Son with the Spirit is immediate, so that anyone who would make contact with the Son by faith must first encounter the oil by contact. In fact
> 448 there is no part that is not covered by the Holy Spirit. That is why the confession of the Son's Lordship is made in the Holy Spirit by those who receive him, the Spirit coming from all sides to those who approach the Son in faith.[15]

II. The Name, Titles, and Symbols of the Holy Spirit

The proper name of the Holy Spirit

691 "Holy Spirit" is the proper name of the one whom we adore and glorify with the Father and the Son. The Church has received this name from the Lord and professes it in the Baptism of her new children.[16]

> The term "Spirit" translates the Hebrew word *ruah*, which, in its primary sense, means breath, air, wind. Jesus indeed uses the sensory image of the wind to suggest to Nicodemus the transcendent newness of him who is personally God's breath, the divine Spirit.[17] On the other hand, "Spirit" and "Holy" are divine attributes common to the three divine persons. By joining the two terms, Scripture, liturgy, and theological language designate the inexpressible person of the Holy Spirit, without any possible equivocation with other uses of the terms "spirit" and "holy."

Titles of the Holy Spirit

692 When he proclaims and promises the coming of the Holy Spirit, Jesus calls him the "Paraclete," literally, "he who is called to one's side," *ad-vocatus*.[18] "Paraclete"
is commonly translated by "consol- 1433
er," and Jesus is the first consoler.[19] The Lord also called the Holy Spirit "the Spirit of truth."[20]

693 Besides the proper name of "Holy Spirit," which is most frequently used in the *Acts of the Apostles* and in the Epistles, we also find in St. Paul the titles: the Spirit of the promise,[21] the Spirit of adoption,[22] the Spirit of Christ,[23] the Spirit of the Lord,[24] and the Spirit of God [25]—and, in St. Peter, the Spirit of glory.[26]

Symbols of the Holy Spirit

694 *Water*. The symbolism of water signifies the Holy Spirit's action in Baptism, since after the invocation of the Holy Spirit it becomes the efficacious sacramental sign of
new birth: just as the gestation of 1218
our first birth took place in water, so

[13] Cf. *Jn* 17:22. — [14] Cf. *Jn* 16:14. — [15] St. Gregory of Nyssa, *De Spiritu Sancto*, 16: PG 45, 1321A–B. — [16] Cf. *Mt* 28:19. — [17] *Jn* 3:5–8. — [18] *Jn* 14:16, 26; 15:26; 16:7. — [19] Cf. *1 Jn* 2:1. — [20] *Jn* 16:13. — [21] Cf. *Gal* 3:14; *Eph* 1:13. — [22] *Rom* 8:15; *Gal* 4:6. — [23] *Rom* 8:9. — [24] *2 Cor* 3:17. — [25] *Rom* 8:9, 14; 15:19; *1 Cor* 6:11; 7:40. — [26] *1 Pet* 4:14.

the water of Baptism truly signifies that our birth into the divine life is given to us in the Holy Spirit. As "by one Spirit we were all baptized," so we are also "made to drink of one Spirit."[27] Thus the Spirit is also personally the living water welling up from Christ crucified[28] as its source
2652 and welling up in us to eternal life.[29]

695 *Anointing*. The symbolism of anointing with oil also signifies the Holy Spirit,[30] to the point of becoming a synonym for the Holy Spirit. In Christian initiation, anointing
1293 is the sacramental sign of Confirmation, called "chrismation" in the Churches of the East. Its full force can be grasped only in relation to the primary anointing accomplished by the Holy Spirit, that of Jesus. Christ (in Hebrew "*messiah*") means the one "anointed" by God's
436 Spirit. There were several anointed ones of the Lord in the Old Covenant, pre-eminently King David.[31] But Jesus is God's Anointed in a unique way: the humanity the Son assumed was entirely anointed by the Holy Spirit. The Holy Spirit established him as "Christ."[32] The Virgin Mary conceived Christ by the Holy Spirit who, through the angel, proclaimed him the Christ at his birth, and prompted Simeon to come to the temple to see the
1504 Christ of the Lord.[33] The Spirit filled Christ and the power of the Spirit went out from him in his acts of healing and of saving.[34] Finally, it was the Spirit who raised Jesus from the dead.[35] Now, fully established as "Christ" in his humanity victorious over death, Jesus pours out the Holy Spirit abundantly until "the saints" constitute—in their union with the humanity of the Son of God—that perfect man "to the measure of the stature of the fullness of Christ":[36] "the whole Christ," in St. Augustine's expression. 794

696 *Fire*. While water signifies birth and the fruitfulness of life given in the Holy Spirit, fire symbolizes the transforming energy of the Holy Spirit's actions. The prayer of
the prophet Elijah, who "arose like 1127
fire" and whose "word burned like a torch," brought down fire from heaven on the sacrifice on Mount
Carmel.[37] This event was a "figure" 2586
of the fire of the Holy Spirit, who transforms what he touches. John the Baptist, who goes "before [the
Lord] in the spirit and power of 718
Elijah," proclaims Christ as the one who "will baptize you with the Holy Spirit and with fire."[38] Jesus will say of the Spirit: "I came to cast fire upon the earth; and would that it were already kindled!"[39] In the form of tongues "as of fire," the Holy Spirit rests on the disciples on the morning of Pentecost and fills them with himself.[40] The spiritual tradition has retained this symbolism of fire as one of the most expressive images of the Holy Spirit's actions.[41] "Do not quench the Spirit."[42]

697 *Cloud and light*. These two images occur together in the manifestations of the Holy Spirit. In the

[27] *1 Cor* 12:13. — [28] *Jn* 19:34; *1 Jn* 5:8. — [29] Cf. *Jn* 4:10–14; 7:38; *Ex* 17:1–6; *Isa* 55:1; *Zech* 14:8; *1 Cor* 10:4; *Rev* 21:6; 22:17. — [30] Cf. *1 Jn* 2:20:27; *2 Cor* 1:21. — [31] Cf. *Ex* 30:22–32; *1 Sam* 16:13. — [32] Cf. *Lk* 4:18–19; *Isa* 61:1. — [33] Cf. *Lk* 2:11, 26–27. — [34] Cf. *Lk* 4:1; 6:19; 8:46. — [35] Cf. *Rom* 1:4; 8:11. — [36] *Eph* 4:13; cf. *Acts* 2:36. — [37] *Sir* 48:1; cf. *1 Kings* 18:38–39. — [38] *Lk* 1:17; 3:16. — [39] *Lk* 12:49. — [40] *Acts* 2:3–4. — [41] Cf. St. John of the Cross, *The Living Flame of Love*, in *The Collected Works of St. John of the Cross*, tr. K. Kavanaugh, OCD, and O. Rodriguez, OCD (Washington DC: Institute of Carmelite Studies, 1979), 577 ff. — [42] *1 Thess* 5:19.

theophanies of the Old Testament, the cloud, now obscure, now luminous, reveals the living and saving God, while veiling the transcendence of his glory—with Moses on Mount Sinai,[43] at the tent of meeting,[44] and during the wandering in the desert,[45] and with Solomon at the dedication of the Temple.[46] In the Holy Spirit, Christ fulfills these figures. The Spirit comes upon the Virgin Mary and "overshadows" her,
484 so that she might conceive and give
birth to Jesus.[47] On the mountain
554 of Transfiguration, the Spirit in the
"cloud came and overshadowed" Jesus, Moses and Elijah, Peter, James and John, and "a voice came out of the cloud, saying, 'This is my Son, my Chosen; listen to him!'"[48] Finally, the cloud took Jesus out of the sight of the disciples on the day of his ascension and will reveal him as Son of man in glory on the day of
659 his final coming.[49]

698 *The seal* is a symbol close to that of anointing. "The Father has set his seal" on Christ and also seals us in him.[50] Because this seal indicates the indelible effect of the anointing
295–1296 with the Holy Spirit in the sacraments of Baptism, Confirmation, and Holy Orders, the image of the seal (*sphragis*) has been used in some
1121 theological traditions to express the
indelible "character" imprinted by these three unrepeatable sacraments.

699 The hand. Jesus heals the sick
292 and blesses little children by laying
hands on them.[51] In his name the apostles will do the same.[52] Even 1288
more pointedly, it is by the Apostles'
imposition of hands that the Holy 1300, 1573
Spirit is given.[53] The *Letter to the Hebrews* lists the imposition of hands 1668
among the "fundamental elements" of its teaching.[54] The Church has kept this sign of the all-powerful outpouring of the Holy Spirit in its sacramental epicleses.

700 *The finger.* "It is by the finger of God that [Jesus] cast out demons."[55] If God's law was written on tablets of stone "by the finger of God," then the "letter from Christ"
entrusted to the care of the apostles, 2056
is written "with the Spirit of the living God, not on tablets of stone, but on tablets of human hearts."[56] The hymn *Veni Creator Spiritus* invokes the Holy Spirit as the "*finger of the Father's right hand.*"[57]

701 *The dove.* At the end of the flood, whose symbolism refers to Baptism, a dove released by Noah returns with a fresh olive-tree branch in its beak as a sign that the
earth was again habitable.[58] When 1219
Christ comes up from the water of
his baptism, the Holy Spirit, in the 535
form of a dove, comes down upon him and remains with him.[59] The Spirit comes down and remains in the purified hearts of the baptized. In certain churches, the Eucharist is reserved in a metal receptacle in the form of a dove (*columbarium*) suspended above the altar. Christian iconography traditionally uses a dove to suggest the Spirit.

[43] Cf. *Ex* 24:15–18. — [44] Cf. *Ex* 33:9–10. — [45] Cf. *Ex* 40:36–38; *1 Cor* 10:1–2. — [46] Cf. *1 Kings* 8:10–12. — [47] *Lk* 1:35. — [48] *Lk* 9:34–35. — [49] Cf. *Acts* 1:9; cf. *Lk* 21:27. — [50] *Jn* 6:27; cf. *2 Cor* 1:22; *Eph* 1:13; 4:30. — [51] Cf. *Mk* 6:5; 8:23; 10:16. — [52] Cf. *Mk* 16:18; *Acts* 5:12; 14:3. — [53] Cf. *Acts* 8:17–19; 13:3; 19:6. — [54] Cf. *Heb* 6:2. — [55] *Lk* 11:20. — [56] *Ex* 31:18; *2 Cor* 3:3. — [57] LH, Easter Season after Ascension, Hymn at Vespers: *digitus paternae dexterae.* — [58] Cf. *Gen* 8:8–12. — [59] Cf. *Mt* 3:16 and parallels.

III. God's Spirit and Word in the Time of the Promises

702 From the beginning until "the fullness of time,"[60] the joint mission of the Father's Word and Spirit remains *hidden*, but it is at work. God's Spirit
122 prepares for the time of the Messiah. Neither is fully revealed but both are already promised, to be watched for and welcomed at their manifestation. So, for this reason, when the Church reads the Old Testament, she searches there for what the Spirit, "who has
107 spoken through the prophets," wants to tell us about Christ.[61]

243 By "prophets" the faith of the Church here understands all whom the Holy Spirit inspired in living proclamation and in the composition of the sacred books, both of the Old and the New Testaments. Jewish tradition distinguishes first the Law (the five first books or Pentateuch), then the Prophets (our historical and prophetic books) and finally the Writings (especially the wisdom literature, in particular the Psalms).[62]

In creation

292 **703** The Word of God and his Breath are at the origin of the being and life of every creature:[63]

> It belongs to the Holy Spirit to rule, sanctify, and animate creation, for he is God, consubstantial with the Father and the Son.... Power over life pertains to the Spirit, for being God
> 291 he preserves creation in the Father through the Son.[64]

704 "God fashioned man with his own hands [that is, the Son and the Holy Spirit] and impressed his own form on the flesh he had fashioned, in such a way that even what was visible might bear the divine form."[65] 356

The Spirit of the promise

705 Disfigured by sin and death, man remains "in the image of God," 410
in the image of the Son, but is deprived "of the glory of God,"[66] of his "likeness." The promise made to 2809
Abraham inaugurates the economy of salvation, at the culmination of which the Son himself will assume that "image"[67] and restore it in the Father's "likeness" by giving it again its Glory, the Spirit who is "the giver of life."

706 Against all human hope, God promises descendants to Abraham, as the fruit of faith and of the power of the Holy Spirit.[68] In Abraham's progeny all the nations of the earth 60
will be blessed. This progeny will be Christ himself,[69] in whom the outpouring of the Holy Spirit will "gather into one the children of God who are scattered abroad."[70] God commits himself by his own solemn oath to giving his beloved Son and "the promised Holy Spirit...[who is] the guarantee of our inheritance until we acquire possession of it."[71]

In Theophanies and the Law

707 Theophanies (manifestations of God) light up the way of the promise, from the patriarchs to Moses and from Joshua to the visions

[60] *Gal* 4:4. —[61] Cf. *2 Cor* 3:14; *Jn* 5:39, 46. — [62] Cf. *Lk* 24:44. — [63] Cf. *Pss* 33:6; 104:30; *Gen* 1:2; 2:7; *Eccl* 3:20–21; *Ezek* 37:10. — [64] Byzantine liturgy, Sundays of the second mode, *Troparion* of Morning Prayer. — [65] St. Irenæus, *Dem ap.* 11: *SCh* 62, 48–49. — [66] *Rom* 3:23. — [67] Cf. *Jn* 1:14; *Phil* 2:7. — [68] Cf. *Gen* 18:1–15; *Lk* 1:26–38; 54–55; *Jn* 1:12–13; *Rom* 4:16–21. — [69] Cf. *Gen* 12:3; *Gal* 3:16. — [70] Cf. *Jn* 11:52. — [71] *Eph* 1:13–14; cf. *Gen* 22:17–19; *Lk* 1:73; *Jn* 3:16; *Rom* 8:32; *Gal* 3:14.

that inaugurated the missions of the great prophets. Christian tradition has always recognized that God's Word allowed himself to be seen and heard in these theophanies, in which the cloud of the Holy Spirit both revealed him and concealed him in its shadow.

708 This divine pedagogy appears especially in the gift of the Law.[72]
God gave the Law as a "pedagogue"
to lead his people towards Christ.[73]
961–1964 But the Law's powerlessness to save
122 man deprived of the divine "likeness," along with the growing awareness of sin that it imparts,[74] enkin-
2585 dles a desire for the Holy Spirit. The
lamentations of the Psalms bear witness to this.

In the Kingdom and the Exile

709 The Law, the sign of God's
promise and covenant, ought to
2579 have governed the hearts and institutions of that people to whom
544 Abraham's faith gave birth. "If you
will obey my voice and keep my covenant,...you shall be to me a king-
dom of priests and a holy nation."[75] But after David, Israel gave in to the temptation of becoming a kingdom like other nations. The Kingdom, however, the object of the promise made to David,[76] would be the work of the Holy Spirit; it would belong to the poor according to the Spirit.

710 The forgetting of the Law and the infidelity to the covenant end in death: it is the Exile, apparently the failure of the promises, which is in fact the mysterious fidelity of the Savior God and the beginning of a promised restoration, but according to the Spirit. The People of God had to suffer this purification.[77] In God's plan, the Exile already stands in the shadow of the Cross, and the Remnant of the poor that returns from the Exile is one of the most transparent prefigurations of the Church.

Expectation of the Messiah and his Spirit

711 "Behold, I am doing a new
thing."[78] Two prophetic lines were
to develop, one leading to the ex- 64
pectation of the Messiah, the other
pointing to the announcement of 522
a new Spirit. They converge in the
small Remnant, the people of the poor, who await in hope the "consolation of Israel" and "the redemption of Jerusalem."[79]

We have seen earlier how Jesus fulfills the prophecies concerning himself. We limit ourselves here to those in which the relationship of the Messiah and his Spirit appears more clearly.

712 The characteristics of the
awaited *Messiah* begin to appear in
the "Book of Emmanuel" ("Isaiah
said this when he saw his glory,"[80] 439
speaking of Christ), especially in the
first two verses of *Isaiah* 11:

> There shall come forth a shoot
> from the stump of Jesse,
> and a branch shall grow
> out of his roots.
> And the Spirit of the Lord
> shall rest upon him,
> the spirit of wisdom
> and understanding,
> the spirit of counsel and might,
> the spirit of knowledge and the fear
> of the Lord.[81]

[72] Cf. *Ex* 19–20; *Deut* 1–11; 29–30. — [73] *Gal* 3:24. — [74] Cf. *Rom* 3:20. — [75] *Ex* 19:5–6; Cf. *1 Pet* 2:9. — [76] Cf. *2 Sam* 7; Ps 89; *Lk* 1:32–33. — [77] Cf. *Lk* 24:26. — [78] *Isa* 43:19. — [79] Cf. *Zeph* 2:3; *Lk* 2:25, 38. — [80] *Jn* 12:41; cf. *Isa* 6–12. — [81] *Isa* 11:1–2.

713 The Messiah's characteristics are revealed above all in the "Ser-
601 vant songs."[82] These songs proclaim the meaning of Jesus' Passion and show how he will pour out the Holy Spirit to give life to the many: not as an outsider, but by embracing our "form as slave."[83] Taking our death upon himself, he can communicate to us his own Spirit of life.

714 This is why Christ inaugurates the proclamation of the Good News by making his own the following passage from Isaiah:[84]

> The Spirit of the LORD God
> is upon me,
> because the LORD has anointed me
> to bring good tidings to the afflicted;
> he has sent me to bind up the
> broken hearted,
> to proclaim liberty to the captives,
> and the opening of the prison
> to those who are bound;
> to proclaim the year
> of the LORD's favor.

715 The prophetic texts that directly concern the sending of the Holy Spirit are oracles by which God speaks to the heart of his people in the language of the promise, with the accents of "love and fidelity."[85]
214 St. Peter will proclaim their fulfillment on the morning of Pentecost.[86] According to these promises, at the "end time" the Lord's Spirit will renew the hearts of men, engraving a new law in them. He will gather and reconcile the scattered and divided
1965 peoples; he will transform the first creation, and God will dwell there with men in peace.

716 The People of the "poor"[87]—those who, humble and meek, rely solely on their God's mysterious plans, who await the justice, not of men but of the Messiah—are in the end the great achievement of the Holy Spirit's hidden mission during the time of the promises that prepare for Christ's coming. It is this quality of heart, purified and enlightened by the Spirit, which is expressed in the Psalms. In these poor, the Spirit
is making ready "a people prepared 368
for the Lord."[88]

IV. The Spirit of Christ in the Fullness of Time

John, precursor, prophet, and baptist

717 "There was a man sent from God, whose name was John."[89] John was "filled with the Holy Spirit even from his mother's womb"[90]
by Christ himself, whom the Virgin 523
Mary had just conceived by the Holy Spirit. Mary's visitation to Elizabeth thus became a visit from God to his people.[91]

718 John is "Elijah [who] must come."[92] The fire of the Spirit dwells in him and makes him the forerunner of the coming Lord. In John, the
precursor, the Holy Spirit completes 696
the work of "[making] ready a people prepared for the Lord."[93]

719 John the Baptist is "more than a prophet."[94] In him, the Holy Spirit concludes his speaking through the prophets. John completes the cycle of prophets begun by Elijah.[95] He proclaims the imminence of the consolation of Israel; he is the "voice"

[82] Cf. *Isa* 42:1–9; cf. *Mt* 12:18–21; *Jn* 1:32–34; then cf. *Isa* 49:1–6; cf. *Mt* 3:17; *Lk* 2:32; finally cf. *Isa* 50:4–10 and *Isa* 52:13–53:12. — [83] *Phil* 2:7. — [84] *Isa* 61:1–2; cf. *Lk* 4:18–19. — [85] Cf. *Ezek* 11:19; 36:25–28; 37:1–14; *Jer* 31:31–34; and cf. *Joel* 3:1–5. — [86] Cf. *Acts* 2:17–21. — [87] Cf. *Zeph* 2:3; *Pss* 22:27; 34:3; *Isa* 49:13; 61:1; etc. — [88] *Lk* 1:17. — [89] *Jn* 1:6. — [90] *Lk* 1:15, 41. — [91] Cf. *Lk* 1:68. — [92] *Mt* 17:10–13; cf. *Lk* 1:78. — [93] *Lk* 1:17. — [94] *Lk* 7:26. — [95] Cf. *Mt* 11:13–14.

of the Consoler who is coming.[96] As the Spirit of truth will also do, John "came to bear witness to the light."[97]
2684 In John's sight, the Spirit thus brings to completion the careful search of the prophets and fulfills the longing of the angels.[98] "He on whom you see the Spirit descend and remain, this is he who baptizes with the Holy Spirit. And I have seen and have borne witness that this is the Son of God....
536 Behold, the Lamb of God."[99]

720 Finally, with John the Baptist, the Holy Spirit begins the res-
535 toration to man of "the divine likeness," prefiguring what he would achieve with and in Christ. John's baptism was for repentance; baptism in water and the Spirit will be a new birth.[100]

"Rejoice, you who are full of grace"

721 Mary, the all-holy ever-virgin Mother of God, is the masterwork of the mission of the Son and the Spirit in the fullness of time. For the first time in the plan of salvation and because his Spirit had prepared her,
484 the Father found the *dwelling place* where his Son and his Spirit could dwell among men. In this sense the Church's Tradition has often read the most beautiful texts on wisdom in relation to Mary.[101] Mary is acclaimed and represented in the liturgy as the "Seat of Wisdom."

In her, the "wonders of God" that the Spirit was to fulfill in Christ and the Church began to be manifested:

722 The Holy Spirit *prepared*
489 Mary by his grace. It was fitting that the mother of him in whom "the whole fullness of deity dwells bodily"[102] should herself be "full of grace." She was, by sheer grace, conceived without sin as the most humble of creatures, the most capable of welcoming the inexpressible gift of the Almighty. It was quite correct for the angel Gabriel to greet her as the "Daughter of Zion": "Rejoice."[103] It is the thanksgiving of the 2676
whole People of God, and thus of the Church, which Mary in her canticle[104] lifts up to the Father in the Holy Spirit while carrying within her the eternal Son.

723 In Mary, the Holy Spirit *fulfills* the plan of the Father's loving goodness. Through the Holy Spirit, the Virgin conceives and gives birth to the Son of God. By the Holy Spir- 485
it's power and her faith, her virginity became uniquely fruitful.[105] 506

724 In Mary, the Holy Spirit *manifests* the Son of the Father, now become the Son of the Virgin. She is the burning bush of the definitive theophany. Filled with the Holy 963
Spirit she makes the Word visible in the humility of his flesh. It is to the poor and the first representatives of the gentiles that she makes him known.[106]

725 Finally, through Mary, the Holy Spirit begins to bring men, the objects of God's merciful love,[107] *into communion* with Christ. And the humble are always the first to accept him: shepherds, magi, Simeon 208, 2619
and Anna, the bride and groom at Cana, and the first disciples.

[96] *Jn* 1:23; cf. *Isa* 40:1–3. — [97] *Jn* 1:7; cf. *Jn* 15:26; 5:35. — [98] Cf. *1 Pet* 1:10–12. — [99] *Jn* 1:33–36. — [100] Cf. *Jn* 3:5. — [101] Cf. *Prov* 8:1–9:6; *Sir* 24. — [102] *Col* 2:9. — [103] Cf. *Zeph* 3:14; *Zech* 2:14. — [104] Cf. *Lk* 1:46–55. — [105] Cf. *Lk* 1:26–38; *Rom* 4:18–21; *Gal* 4:26–28. — [106] Cf. *Lk* 1:15–19; *Mt* 2:11. — [107] Cf. *Lk* 2:14.

726 At the end of this mission of the Spirit, Mary became the Woman, the new Eve ("mother of the living"), the mother of the "whole Christ."[108]
494, 2618 As such, she was present with the Twelve, who "with one accord devoted themselves to prayer,"[109] at the dawn of the "end time" which the Spirit was to inaugurate on the morning of Pentecost with the manifestation of the Church.

Christ Jesus

727 The entire mission of the Son and the Holy Spirit, in the fullness
438, 695 of time, is contained in this: that the Son is the one anointed by the Fa-
536 ther's Spirit since his Incarnation—Jesus is the Christ, the Messiah.

Everything in the second chapter of the Creed is to be read in this light. Christ's whole work is in fact a joint mission of the Son and the Holy Spirit. Here, we shall mention only what has to do with Jesus' promise of the Holy Spirit and the gift of him by the glorified Lord.

728 Jesus does not reveal the Holy Spirit fully, until he himself has been glorified through his Death and Resurrection. Nevertheless, little by little he alludes to him even in his teaching of the multitudes, as when he reveals that his own flesh will be food for the life of the world.[110] He also alludes to the Spirit in speaking to Nicodemus,[111] to the Samaritan woman,[112] and to those who take part in the feast of Tabernacles.[113] To his disciples he speaks openly of the Spirit in connection with prayer[114] and with
2615 the witness they will have to bear.[115]

729 Only when the hour has arrived for his glorification does Jesus *promise* the coming of the Holy Spirit, since his Death and Resurrection will fulfill the promise made to the fathers.[116] The Spirit of truth, the other Paraclete, will be given by the Father in answer to Jesus' prayer; he will be sent by the Father in Jesus' name; and Jesus will send him from the Father's side, since he comes from the Father. The Holy Spirit will come and we shall know him; he will be with us for ever; he will remain with us. The Spirit will teach us everything, remind us of all that Christ said to us and bear witness to him. The Holy Spirit will lead us into all truth and will glorify Christ. He will prove the world wrong about
sin, righteousness, and judgment. 388, 1433

730 At last Jesus' hour arrives:[117] he commends his spirit into the Father's hands[118] at the very moment when by his death he conquers death, so that, "raised from the dead by the glory of the Father,"[119] he might immediately give the Holy Spirit by "breathing" on his disciples.[120] From this hour onward, the mission of Christ and the Spirit becomes the mission of the Church: "As the Father has sent me,
even so I send you."[121] 850

V. The Spirit and the Church in the Last Days

Pentecost

731 On the day of Pentecost when the seven weeks of Easter had come to an end, Christ's Passover is fulfilled in the outpouring of the
Holy Spirit, manifested, given, and 2623, 767

[108] Cf. *Jn* 19:25–27. — [109] *Acts* 1:14. — [110] Cf. *Jn* 6:27, 51, 62–63. — [111] Cf. *Jn* 3:5–8. — [112] Cf. *Jn* 4:10, 14, 23–24. — [113] Cf. *Jn* 7:37–39.— [114] Cf. *Lk* 11:13. — [115] Cf. *Mt* 10:19–20. — [116] Cf. *Jn* 14:16–17, 26; 15:26; 16:7–15; 17:26. — [117] Cf. *Jn* 13:1; 17:1. — [118] Cf. *Lk* 23:46; *Jn* 19:30. — [119] *Rom* 6:4. — [120] Cf. *Jn* 20:22. — [121] *Jn* 20:21; cf. *Mt* 28:19; *Lk* 24:47–48; *Acts* 1:8.

communicated as a divine person: of his fullness, Christ, the Lord, pours
1302 out the Spirit in abundance.[122]

732 On that day, the Holy Trinity is fully revealed. Since that day, the Kingdom announced by Christ has been open to those who believe in him: in the humility of the flesh
244 and in faith, they already share in the communion of the Holy Trinity. By his coming, which never ceases,
672 the Holy Spirit causes the world to enter into the "last days," the time of the Church, the Kingdom already inherited though not yet consummated.

> We have seen the true Light, we have received the heavenly Spirit, we have found the true faith: we adore the indivisible Trinity, who has saved us.[123]

The Holy Spirit—God's gift

733 "God is Love"[124] and love is his first gift, containing all others.
218 "God's love has been poured into our hearts through the Holy Spirit who has been given to us."[125]

734 Because we are dead or at least wounded through sin, the first effect
1987 of the gift of love is the forgiveness of our sins. The communion of the Holy Spirit[126] in the Church restores to the baptized the divine likeness lost through sin.

735 He, then, gives us the "pledge" or "first fruits" of our inheritance:
1822 the very life of the Holy Trinity, which is to love as "God [has] loved us."[127] This love (the "charity" of *1 Cor* 13) is the source of the new life in Christ, made possible because we have received "power" from the Holy Spirit.[128]

736 By this power of the Spirit, God's children can bear much
fruit. He who has grafted us onto 1832
the true vine will make us bear "the fruit of the Spirit:...love, joy, peace, patience, kindness, goodness, faithfulness, gentleness, self-control."[129] "We live by the Spirit"; the more we renounce ourselves, the more we "walk by the Spirit."[130]

> Through the Holy Spirit we are restored to paradise, led back to the Kingdom of heaven, and adopted as children, given confidence to call God "Father" and to share in Christ's grace, called children of light and given a share in eternal glory.[131]

The Holy Spirit and the Church

737 The mission of Christ and the Holy Spirit is brought to completion in the Church, which is the Body of Christ and the Temple of
the Holy Spirit. This joint mission 787–798
henceforth brings Christ's faithful to share in his communion with the Father in the Holy Spirit. The Spirit
prepares men and goes out to them 1093–1109
with his grace, in order to draw them to Christ. The Spirit *manifests* the risen Lord to them, recalls his word to them and opens their minds to the understanding of his Death and Resurrection. He *makes present* the mystery of Christ, supremely in the Eucharist, in order to reconcile them, to *bring them into communion* with God, that they may "bear much fruit."[132]

[122] Cf. *Acts* 2:33–36. — [123] Byzantine liturgy, Pentecost, Vespers, *Troparion*, repeated after communion. — [124] *1 Jn* 4:8, 16. — [125] *Rom* 5:5. — [126] *2 Cor* 13:14. — [127] *1 Jn* 4:11–12; cf. *Rom* 8:23; *2 Cor* 1:21. — [128] *Acts* 1:8; cf. *1 Cor* 13. — [129] *Gal* 5:22–23. — [130] *Gal* 5:25; cf. *Mt* 16:24–26. — [131] St. Basil, *De Spiritu Sancto*, 15, 36: PG 32, 132. — [132] Jn 15:8, 16.

738 Thus the Church's mission is not an addition to that of Christ and the Holy Spirit, but is its sacrament: in her whole being and in all
850, 777 her members, the Church is sent to announce, bear witness, make present, and spread the mystery of the communion of the Holy Trinity (the topic of the next article):

> All of us who have received one and the same Spirit, that is, the Holy Spirit, are in a sense blended together with one another and with God. For if Christ, together with the Father's and his own Spirit, comes to dwell in each of us, though we are many, still the Spirit is one and undivided. He binds together the spirits of each and every one of us,...and makes all appear as one in him. For just as the power of Christ's sacred flesh unites those in whom it dwells into one body, I think that in the same way the one and undivided Spirit of God, who dwells in all, leads all into spiritual unity.[133]

739 Because the Holy Spirit is the anointing of Christ, it is Christ who, as the head of the Body, pours out the Spirit among his members to
1076 nourish, heal, and organize them in their mutual functions, to give them life, send them to bear witness, and associate them to his self-offering to the Father and to his intercession for the whole world. Through the Church's sacraments, Christ communicates his Holy and sanctifying Spirit to the members of his Body. (This will be the topic of Part Two of the Catechism.)

740 These "mighty works of God," offered to believers in the sacraments of the Church, bear their fruit in the new life in Christ, according to the Spirit. (This will be the topic of Part Three.)

741 "The Spirit helps us in our weakness; for we do not know how to pray as we ought, but the Spirit himself intercedes with sighs too deep for words."[134] The Holy Spirit, the artisan of God's works, is the master of prayer. (This will be the topic of Part Four.)

In Brief

742 *"Because you are sons, God has sent the Spirit of his Son into our hearts, crying, 'Abba! Father!'"* (Gal *4:6).*

743 *From the beginning to the end of time, whenever God sends his Son, he always sends his Spirit: their mission is conjoined and inseparable.*

744 *In the fullness of time the Holy Spirit completes in Mary all the preparations for Christ's coming among the People of God. By the action of the Holy Spirit in her, the Father gives the world Emmanuel, "God-with-us"* (Mt *1:23).*

745 *The Son of God was consecrated as Christ (Messiah) by the anointing of the Holy Spirit at his Incarnation (cf.* Ps *2:6–7).*

746 *By his Death and his Resurrection, Jesus is constituted in glory as Lord and Christ (cf.* Acts *2:36). From his fullness, he poured out the Holy Spirit on the apostles and the Church.*

747 *The Holy Spirit, whom Christ the head pours out on his members, builds, animates, and sanctifies the Church. She is the sacrament of the Holy Trinity's communion with men.*

[133] St. Cyril of Alexandria, *In Jo. ev.*, 11, 11: PG 74, 561. — [134] *Rom* 8:26.

Article 9:
"I BELIEVE IN THE HOLY CATHOLIC CHURCH"

748 "Christ is the light of humanity; and it is, accordingly, the heart-felt desire of this sacred Council, being gathered together in the Holy Spirit, that, by proclaiming his Gospel to every creature, it may bring to all men that light of Christ which shines out visibly from the Church."[135] These words open the Second Vatican Council's *Dogmatic Constitution on the Church*. By choosing this starting point, the Council demonstrates that the article of faith about the Church depends entirely on the articles concerning Christ Jesus. The Church has no other light than Christ's; according to a favorite image of the Church Fathers, the Church is like the moon, all its light reflected from the sun.

749 The article concerning the Church also depends entirely on the article about the Holy Spirit, which immediately precedes it. "Indeed, having shown that the Spirit is the source and giver of all holiness, we now confess that it is he who has endowed the Church with holiness."[136] The Church is, in a phrase used by the Fathers, the place "where the Spirit flourishes."[137]

750 To believe that the Church is "holy" and "catholic," and that she is "one" and "apostolic" (as the Nicene Creed adds), is inseparable from
811 belief in God, the Father, the Son, and the Holy Spirit. In the Apostles' Creed we profess "one Holy Church" (*Credo...Ecclesiam*), and not to believe in the Church, so as not to confuse God with his works and to
attribute clearly to God's goodness 169
all the gifts he has bestowed on his Church.[138]

Paragraph 1
The Church in God's Plan

I. Names and Images of the Church

751 The word "Church" (Latin *ecclesia*, from the Greek *ek-kalein*, to "call out of") means a convocation or an assembly. It designates the assemblies of the people, usually for a religious purpose.[139] *Ekklesia* is used frequently in the Greek Old Testament for the assembly of the Chosen People before God, above all for their assembly on Mount Sinai where Israel received the Law and was established by God as his holy people.[140] By calling itself "Church," the first community of Christian believers recognized itself as heir to that assembly. In the Church, God is "calling together" his people from all the ends of the earth. The equivalent Greek term *Kyriak*, from which the English word *Church* and the German *Kirche* are derived, means "what belongs to the Lord."

752 In Christian usage, the word "church" designates the liturgical assembly,[141] but also the local community[142] or the whole universal
community of believers.[143] These 1140, 832
three meanings are inseparable. "The
Church" is the People that God gath- 830
ers in the whole world. She exists in

[135] *LG* 1; cf. *Mk* 16:15. — [136] *Roman Catechism* I, 10, 1. — [137] St. Hippolytus, *Trad. Ap.* 35: *SCh* 11, 118. — [138] *Roman Catechism* I, 10, 22. — [139] Cf. *Acts* 19:39. — [140] Cf. *Ex* 19. — [141] Cf. *1 Cor* 11:18; 14:19, 28, 34, 35. — [142] Cf. *1 Cor* 1:2; 16:1. — [143] Cf. *1 Cor* 15:9; *Gal* 1:13; *Phil* 3:6.

local communities and is made real as a liturgical, above all a Eucharistic, assembly. She draws her life from the word and the Body of Christ and so herself becomes Christ's Body.

Symbols of the Church

753 In Scripture, we find a host
of interrelated images and figures
through which Revelation speaks
of the inexhaustible mystery of the
Church. The images taken from
the Old Testament are variations
on a profound theme: the People
of God. In the New Testament, all
781, 789 these images find a new center because Christ has become the head
of this people, which henceforth is
his Body.[144] Around this center are
grouped images taken "from the life
of the shepherd or from cultivation
of the land, from the art of building
or from family life and marriage."[145]

857 **754** "The Church is, accordingly, a sheepfold, the sole and necessary gateway to which is Christ. It is also the flock of which God himself foretold that he would be the shepherd, and whose sheep, even though governed by human shepherds, are unfailingly nourished and led by Christ himself, the Good Shepherd and Prince of Shepherds, who gave his life for his sheep.[146]

755 "The Church is a cultivated
field, the tillage of God. On that land
the ancient olive tree grows whose
holy roots were the prophets and in
which the reconciliation of Jews and
Gentiles has been brought about and
will be brought about again. That
land, like a choice vineyard, has been
planted by the heavenly cultivator.
Yet the true vine is Christ who gives
life and fruitfulness to the branches, that is, to us, who through the
Church remain in Christ, without
whom we can do nothing.[147] 795

756 "Often, too, the Church is
called the building of God. The Lord
compared himself to the stone which
the builders rejected, but which was
made into the corner-stone. On this
foundation the Church is built by 797
the apostles and from it the Church
receives solidity and unity. This edifice has many names to describe it:
the house of God in which his family dwells; the household of God in
the Spirit; the dwelling-place of God 857
among men; and, especially, the holy
temple. This temple, symbolized in
places of worship built out of stone,
is praised by the Fathers and, not
without reason, is compared in the
liturgy to the Holy City, the New Je- 1045
rusalem. As living stones we here on
earth are built into it. It is this holy
city that is seen by John as it comes
down out of heaven from God when
the world is made anew, prepared like
a bride adorned for her husband.[148]

757 "The Church, further, which is
called 'that Jerusalem which is above'
and 'our mother', is described as the
spotless spouse of the spotless lamb. 507, 796
It is she whom Christ 'loved and for
whom he delivered himself up that
he might sanctify her.' It is she whom 1616
he unites to himself by an unbreakable alliance, and whom he constantly 'nourishes and cherishes.'"[149]

[144] Cf. *Eph* 1:22; *Col* 1:18; *LG* 9. — [145] *LG* 6. — [146] *LG* 6; cf. *Jn* 10:1–10; *Isa* 40:11; *Ezek* 34:11–31; *Jn* 10:11; *1 Pet* 5:4; *Jn* 10:11–16. — [147] *LG* 6; cf. *1 Cor* 3:9; *Rom* 11:13–26; *Mt* 21:33–43 and parallels; *Isa* 5:1–7; Jn 15:1–5 — [148] *LG* 6; cf. *1 Cor* 3:9; *Mt* 21:42 and parallels; *Acts* 4:11; *1 Pet* 2:7; *Ps* 118:22; *1 Cor*3:11; *1 Tim* 3:15; *Eph* 2:19–22; *Rev* 21:3; *1 Pet* 2:5; *Rev* 21:1–2. — [149] *LG* 6; cf. *Gal* 4:26; *Rev* 12:17; 19:7; 21:2, 9; 22:17; *Eph* 5:25–26, 29.

II. The Church's Origin, Foundation, and Mission

758 We begin our investigation of
257 the Church's mystery by meditating on her origin in the Holy Trinity's plan and her progressive realization in history.

A plan born in the Father's heart

759 "The eternal Father, in accordance with the utterly gratuitous and mysterious design of his wisdom and goodness, created the whole universe
293 and chose to raise up men to share in his own divine life,"[150] to which he calls all men in his Son. "The Father… determined to call together in a holy Church those who should believe
1655 in Christ."[151] This "family of God" is gradually formed and takes shape during the stages of human history, in keeping with the Father's plan. In fact, "already present in figure at the beginning of the world, this Church was prepared in marvellous fashion in the history of the people of Israel and the old Alliance. Established in this last age of the world and made manifest in the outpouring of the Spirit, it will be brought to glorious completion at the end of time."[152]

The Church—foreshadowed from the world's beginning

760 Christians of the first centuries said, "The world was created for the sake of the Church."[153] God created the world for the sake of communion with his divine life, a communion brought about by the
294 "convocation" of men in Christ, and this "convocation" is the Church. The Church is the goal of all things,[154] and God permitted such painful upheavals as the angels' fall and man's sin only as occasions and
means for displaying all the power 309
of his arm and the whole measure of the love he wanted to give the world:

> Just as God's will is creation and is called "the world," so his intention is the salvation of men, and it is called "the Church."[155]

The Church—prepared for in the Old Covenant

761 The gathering together of the People of God began at the moment when sin destroyed the communion of men with God, and that of men among themselves. The gathering together of the Church is, as
it were, God's reaction to the chaos 55
provoked by sin. This reunification is achieved secretly in the heart of all peoples: "In every nation anyone who fears him and does what is right is acceptable" to God.[156]

762 The remote *preparation* for this gathering together of the People of God begins when he calls Abraham and promises that he will become the
father of a great people.[157] Its imme- 122, 522
diate preparation begins with Israel's
election as the People of God. By this 60
election, Israel is to be the sign of the future gathering of all nations.[158] But the prophets accuse Israel of breaking the covenant and behaving like a
prostitute. They announce a new and 64
eternal covenant. "Christ instituted this New Covenant."[159]

[150] *LG* 2. — [151] *LG* 2. — [152] *LG* 2. — [153] *Pastor Hermæ*, Vision 2, 4, 1: PG 2, 899; cf. Aristides, *Apol.* 16, 6; St. Justin, *Apol.* 2, 7: PG 6, 456; Tertullian, *Apol.* 31, 3; 32, 1: *PL* 1, 508–509. — [154] Cf. St. Epiphanius, *Panarion* 1, 1, 5: PG 41, 181C. — [155] Clement of Alex., *Pæd.* 1, 6, 27: PG 8, 281. — [156] *Acts* 10:35; cf. *LG* 9; 13; 16. — [157] Cf. *Gen* 12:2; 15:5–6. — [158] Cf. *Ex* 19:5–6; *Deut* 7:6; *Isa* 2:2–5; *Mic* 4:1–4. — [159] *LG* 9; cf. *Hos* 1; *Isa* 1:2–4; *Jer* 2; 31:31–34; *Isa* 55:3.

The Church—instituted by Christ Jesus

763 It was the Son's task to accomplish the Father's plan of salvation in the fullness of time. Its accomplishment was the reason for his being sent.[160] "The Lord Jesus inaugurated his Church by preaching
541 the Good News, that is, the coming of the Reign of God, promised over the ages in the scriptures."[161] To fulfill the Father's will, Christ ushered in the Kingdom of heaven on earth. The Church "is the Reign of Christ already present in mystery."[162]

764 "This Kingdom shines out before men in the word, in the works and in the presence of Christ."[163] To welcome Jesus' word is to welcome
543 "the Kingdom itself."[164] The seed and beginning of the Kingdom are the "little flock" of those whom Jesus came to gather around him, the flock whose shepherd he is.[165] They form Jesus' true family.[166] To those
1691 whom he thus gathered around him, he taught a new "way of acting" and
2558 a prayer of their own.[167]

765 The Lord Jesus endowed his community with a structure that will remain until the Kingdom is fully achieved. Before all else there is the choice of the Twelve with Peter as their head.[168] Representing the
610 twelve tribes of Israel, they are the foundation stones of the new Jeru-
551 salem.[169] The Twelve and the other disciples share in Christ's mission and his power, but also in his lot.[170] By all his actions, Christ prepares and builds his Church.

766 The Church is born primarily of Christ's total self-giving for our salvation, anticipated in the institution of the Eucharist and fulfilled
on the cross. "The origin and growth 813, 860
of the Church are symbolized by
the blood and water which flowed 1340
from the open side of the crucified
Jesus."[171] "For it was from the side 617
of Christ as he slept the sleep of
death upon the cross that there came 478
forth the 'wondrous sacrament of the whole Church.'"[172] As Eve was formed from the sleeping Adam's side, so the Church was born from the pierced heart of Christ hanging dead on the cross.[173]

The Church—revealed by the Holy Spirit

767 "When the work which the Father gave the Son to do on earth was accomplished, the Holy Spirit was sent on the day of Pentecost
in order that he might continually 731
sanctify the Church."[174] Then "the Church was openly displayed to the crowds and the spread of the Gospel among the nations, through preaching, was begun."[175] As the "convocation" of all men for salvation,
the Church in her very nature is 849
missionary, sent by Christ to all the nations to make disciples of them.[176]

768 So that she can fulfill her mission, the Holy Spirit "bestows upon [the Church] varied hierarchic and charismatic gifts, and in this way directs her."[177] "Henceforward the Church, endowed with the gifts of her founder and faithfully observing his precepts of charity, humility and

[160] Cf. *LG* 3; 1 3. — [161] *LG* 5. — [162] *LG* 3. — [163] *LG* 5. —[164] *LG* 5. — [165] *Lk* 12:32; cf. *Mt* 10:16; 26:31; *Jn* 10:1–21. — [166] Cf. *Mt* 12:49. — [167] Cf. *Mt* 5–6. — [168] Cf. *Mk* 3:14–15. — [169] Cf. *Mt* 19:28; *Lk* 22:30; *Rev* 21:12–14. — [170] Cf. *Mk* 6:7; *Lk* 10:1–2; *Mt* 10:25; *Jn* 15:20. — [171] *LG* 3; cf. *Jn* 19:34. — [172] *SC* 5. — [173] Cf. St. Ambrose, *In Luc.* 2, 85–89: PL 15, 1666–1668. — [174] *LG* 4; cf. *Jn* 17:4. — [175] *AG* 4. — [176] Cf. *Mt* 28:19–20; *AG* 2; 5–6. — [177] *LG* 4.

self-denial, receives the mission of proclaiming and establishing among all peoples the Kingdom of Christ and of God, and she is on earth
541 the seed and the beginning of that kingdom."[178]

The Church—perfected in glory

769 "The Church...will receive its perfection only in the glory of heaven,"[179] at the time of Christ's glorious return. Until that day, "the
671, 2818 Church progresses on her pilgrimage amidst this world's persecutions and God's consolations."[180] Here below she knows that she is in exile far from the Lord, and longs for the full coming of the Kingdom, when
675 she will "be united in glory with her king."[181] The Church, and through her the world, will not be perfected in glory without great trials. Only then will "all the just from the time of Adam, 'from Abel, the just one, to the last of the elect,'... be gathered
1045 together in the universal Church in the Father's presence."[182]

III. The Mystery of the Church

770 The Church is in history, but at the same time she transcends it. It is only "with the eyes of faith"[183] that one can see her in her visible reality
812 and at the same time in her spiritual reality as bearer of divine life.

The Church—both visible and spiritual

827 **771** "The one mediator, Christ, established and ever sustains here on earth his holy Church, the community of faith, hope, and charity, as a visible organization through which he communicates truth and grace to all men."[184] The Church is at the same time:

– a "society structured with 1880
hierarchical organs and the mystical body of Christ;

– the visible society and the 954
spiritual community;

– the earthly Church and the Church endowed with heavenly riches."[185]

These dimensions together constitute "one complex reality which comes together from a human and a divine element":[186]

> The Church is essentially both human and divine, visible but endowed with invisible realities, zealous in action and dedicated to contemplation, present in the world, but as a pilgrim, so constituted that in her the human is directed toward and subordinated to the divine, the visible to the invisible, action to contemplation, and this present world to that city yet to come, the object of our quest.[187]
>
> O humility! O sublimity! Both tabernacle of cedar and sanctuary of God; earthly dwelling and celestial palace; house of clay and royal hall; body of death and temple of light; and at last both object of scorn to the proud and bride of Christ! She is black but beautiful, O daughters of Jerusalem, for even if the labor and pain of her long exile may have discolored her, yet heaven's beauty has adorned her.[188]

The Church—mystery of man's union with God

772 It is in the Church that Christ 518
fulfills and reveals his own mystery
as the purpose of God's plan: "to 796

[178] *LG* 5. — [179] *LG* 48. — [180] St. Augustine, *De civ. Dei*, 18, 51: PL 41, 614; cf. *LG* 8. — [181] *LG* 5; cf. 6; *2 Cor* 5:6. — [182] *LG* 2. — [183] *Roman Catechism* I, 10, 20. — [184] *LG* 8 § 1. — [185] *LG* 8. — [186] *LG* 8. — [187] *SC* 2; cf. *Heb* 13:14. — [188] St. Bernard of Clairvaux, *In Cant. Sermo* 27:14: PL 183:920D.

unite all things in him."[189] St. Paul calls the nuptial union of Christ and the Church "a great mystery." Because she is united to Christ as to her bridegroom, she becomes a mystery in her turn.[190] Contemplating this mystery in her, Paul exclaims: "Christ in you, the hope of glory."[191]

773 In the Church this communion of men with God, in the "love [that] never ends," is the purpose which governs everything in her that is a sacramental means, tied to this passing world.[192] "[The Church's] structure is totally ordered to the holiness of Christ's members. And ho-
671 liness is measured according to the 'great mystery' in which the Bride responds with the gift of love to the gift of the Bridegroom."[193] Mary
972 goes before us all in the holiness that is the Church's mystery as "the bride without spot or wrinkle."[194] This is why the "Marian" dimension of the Church precedes the "Petrine."[195]

The universal Sacrament of Salvation

774 The Greek word *mysterion* was translated into Latin by two terms: *mysterium* and *sacramentum*. In later usage the term *sacramentum* emphasizes the visible sign of the hidden
1075 reality of salvation which was indicated by the term *mysterium*. In this sense, Christ himself is the mystery of salvation: "For there is no other mystery of God, except Christ."[196] The saving work of his holy and sanctifying humanity is the sacrament of salvation, which is revealed and active in the Church's sacraments (which the Eastern Churches also call "the holy mysteries"). The 515
seven sacraments are the signs and instruments by which the Holy 2014
Spirit spreads the grace of Christ the head throughout the Church which 1116
is his Body. The Church, then, both contains and communicates the invisible grace she signifies. It is in this analogical sense, that the Church is called a "sacrament."

775 "The Church, in Christ, is like a sacrament—a sign and instrument, that is, of communion with God and of unity among all men."[197] The Church's first purpose is to be the sacrament of the *inner union of men with God*. Because men's communion with one another is rooted in that union with God, the Church is also the sacrament of the *unity of the human race*. In her, this unity is already begun, since she gathers men "from every nation, from all 360
tribes and peoples and tongues";[198] at the same time, the Church is the "sign and instrument" of the full realization of the unity yet to come.

776 As sacrament, the Church is Christ's instrument. "She is taken up by him also as the instrument for the salvation of all," "the universal sacrament of salvation," by which Christ 1088
is "at once manifesting and actualizing the mystery of God's love for men."[199] The Church "is the visible plan of God's love for humanity," because God desires "that the whole human race may become one People of God, form one Body of Christ, and be built up into one temple of the Holy Spirit."[200]

[189] *Eph* 1:10. — [190] *Eph* 5:32; 3:9–11; 5:25–27. — [191] *Col* 1:27. — [192] *1 Cor* 13:8; cf. *LG* 48. — [193] John Paul II, *MD* 27. — [194] *Eph* 5:27. — [195] Cf. John Paul II, *MD* 27. — [196] St. Augustine, *Ep.* 187, 11, 34: PL 33, 846. — [197] *LG* 1. — [198] *Rev* 7:9. — [199] *LG* 9 § 2, 48 § 2; *GS* 45 § 1. — [200] Paul VI, June 22, 1973; AG 7 § 2; cf. *LG* 17.

In Brief

777 *The word "Church" means "convocation." It designates the assembly of those whom God's Word "convokes," i.e., gathers together to form the People of God, and who themselves, nourished with the Body of Christ, become the Body of Christ.*

778 *The Church is both the means and the goal of God's plan: prefigured in creation, prepared for in the Old Covenant, founded by the words and actions of Jesus Christ, fulfilled by his redeeming cross and his Resurrection, the Church has been manifested as the mystery of salvation by the outpouring of the Holy Spirit. She will be perfected in the glory of heaven as the assembly of all the redeemed of the earth (cf.* Rev *14:4).*

779 *The Church is both visible and spiritual, a hierarchical society and the Mystical Body of Christ. She is one, yet formed of two components, human and divine. That is her mystery, which only faith can accept.*

780 *The Church in this world is the sacrament of salvation, the sign and the instrument of the communion of God and men.*

Paragraph 2

THE CHURCH—PEOPLE OF GOD, BODY OF CHRIST, TEMPLE OF THE HOLY SPIRIT

I. The Church—People of God

781 "At all times and in every race, anyone who fears God and does what is right has been acceptable to him. He has, however, willed to make men holy and save them, not as individuals without any bond or link between them, but rather to make them into a people who might acknowledge him and serve him in holiness. He therefore chose the Israelite race to be his own people and established a covenant with it. He gradually instructed this people.... All these things, however, happened as a preparation for and figure of that new and perfect covenant which was to be ratified in Christ... the New Covenant in his blood; he called together a race made up of Jews and Gentiles which would be one, not according to the flesh, but in the Spirit."[201]

Characteristics of the People of God

782 The People of God is marked by characteristics that clearly distinguish it from all other religious, ethnic, political, or cultural groups found in history: 871

– It is the People *of God*: God is not the property of any one people. But he acquired a people for himself from those who previously were not a people: "a chosen race, a royal priesthood, a haoly nation."[202] 2787

– One becomes a *member* of this people not by a physical birth, but by being "born anew," a birth "of water and the Spirit,"[203] that is, by faith in Christ, and Baptism. 1267

– This People has for its Head Jesus the Christ (the anointed, the Messiah). Because the same anointing, the Holy Spirit, flows from the head into the body, this is "the messianic people." 695

– "The *status* of this people is that of the dignity and freedom of the sons of God, in whose hearts the Holy Spirit dwells as in a temple." 1741

[201] *LG* 9; cf. *Acts* 10:35; *1 Cor* 11:25. — [202] *1 Pet* 2:9. — [203] *Jn* 3:3–5.

1972 – "Its *law* is the new commandment to love as Christ loved us."[204] This is the "new" law of the Holy Spirit.[205]

849 – Its *mission* is to be salt of the earth and light of the world.[206] This people is "a most sure seed of unity, hope, and salvation for the whole human race."

769 – Its destiny, finally, "is the Kingdom of God which has been begun by God himself on earth and which must be further extended until it has been brought to perfection by him at the end of time."[207]

A priestly, prophetic, and royal people

783 Jesus Christ is the one whom the Father anointed with the Holy Spirit and established as priest,
436 prophet, and king. The whole People of God participates in these
873 three offices of Christ and bears the responsibilities for mission and service that flow from them.[208]

784 On entering the People of God through faith and Baptism, one receives a share in this people's unique, *priestly* vocation: "Christ the
1268 Lord, high priest taken from among men, has made this new people 'a kingdom of priests to God, his Father.' The baptized, by regeneration
1546 and the anointing of the Holy Spirit, are *consecrated* to be a spiritual house and a holy priesthood."[209]

785 "The holy People of God shares also in Christ's *prophetic* office," above all in the supernatural sense of faith that belongs to
92 the whole People, lay and clergy, when it "unfailingly adheres to this faith...once for all delivered to the saints,"[210] and when it deepens its understanding and becomes Christ's witness in the midst of this world.

786 Finally, the People of God shares in the *royal* office of Christ. He exercises his kingship by drawing all men to himself through his death and Resurrection.[211] Christ, King and Lord of the universe, made himself the servant of all, for he came "not to be served but to serve, and to give his life as a ransom for many."[212] For the Christian, "to reign is to serve him," particularly when serving "the poor and the suffering, in whom the Church recognizes the image of
her poor and suffering founder."[213] 2449
The People of God fulfills its royal dignity by a life in keeping with its
vocation to serve with Christ. 2443

> The sign of the cross makes kings of all those reborn in Christ and the anointing of the Holy Spirit consecrates them as priests, so that, apart from the particular service of our ministry, all spiritual and rational Christians are recognized as members of this royal race and sharers in Christ's priestly office. What, indeed, is as royal for a soul as to govern the body in obedience to God? And what is as priestly as to dedicate a pure conscience to the Lord and to offer the spotless offerings of devotion on the altar of the heart?[214]

II. The Church—Body of Christ

The Church is communion with Jesus

787 From the beginning, Jesus associated his disciples with his own life, revealed the mystery of the Kingdom to them, and gave them a share in his mission, joy, and suf-

[204] Cf. *Jn* 13:34. — [205] *Rom* 8:2; *Gal* 5:25. — [206] Cf. *Mt* 5:13–16. — [207] *LG* 9 § 2. — [208] Cf. John Paul II, *RH* 18–21. — [209] *LG* 10; cf. *Heb* 5:1–5; *Rev* 1:6. — [210] *LG* 12; cf. *Jude* 3. — [211] Cf. *Jn* 12:32. — [212] *Mt* 20:28. — [213] *LG* 8; cf. 36. — [214] St. Leo the Great, *Sermo* 4, 1: PL 54, 149.

ferings.[215] Jesus spoke of a still more intimate communion between him and those who would follow him: "Abide in me, and I in you.... I am the vine, you are the branches."[216]
755 And he proclaimed a mysterious and real communion between his own body and ours: "He who eats my flesh and drinks my blood abides in me, and I in him."[217]

788 When his visible presence was taken from them, Jesus did not leave his disciples orphans. He promised to remain with them until the end of time; he sent them his Spirit.[218] As a result communion with Jesus has
690 become, in a way, more intense: "By communicating his Spirit, Christ mystically constitutes as his body those brothers of his who are called together from every nation."[219]

789 The comparison of the Church with the body casts light on the intimate bond between Christ and his Church. Not only is she gathered *around him*; she is united
521 *in him*, in his body. Three aspects of the Church as the Body of Christ are to be more specifically noted: the unity of all her members with each other as a result of their union with Christ; Christ as head of the Body; and the Church as bride of Christ.

"One Body"

790 Believers who respond to God's word and become members of Christ's Body, become intimately united with him: "In that body
947 the life of Christ is communicated to those who believe, and who, through the sacraments, are united in a hidden and real way to Christ in his Passion and glorification."[220] This is especially true of Baptism, which unites us to Christ's death 1227
and Resurrection, and the Eucharist, by which "really sharing in the body 1329
of the Lord,...we are taken up into communion with him and with one another."[221]

791 The body's unity does not do away with the diversity of its members: "In the building up of Christ's Body there is engaged a diversity of members and functions. There is 814
only one Spirit who, according to his own richness and the needs of the 1937
ministries, gives his different gifts for the welfare of the Church."[222] The unity of the Mystical Body produces and stimulates charity among the faithful: "From this it follows that if one member suffers anything, all the members suffer with him, and if one member is honored, all the members together rejoice."[223] Finally, the unity of the Mystical Body triumphs over all human divisions: "For as many of you as were baptized into Christ have put on Christ. There is neither Jew nor Greek, there is neither slave nor free, there is neither male nor female; for you are all one in Christ Jesus."[224]

"Christ is the Head of this Body"

792 Christ "is the head of the 669
body, the Church."[225] He is the principle of creation and redemption. Raised to the Father's glory, "in 1119
everything he [is] preeminent,"[226] especially in the Church, through whom he extends his reign over all things.

[215] *Mk* 1:16–20; 3:13–19; *Mt* 13:10–17; *Lk* 10:17–20; 22:28–30. — [216] *Jn* 15:4–5. — [217] *Jn* 6:56. — [218] Cf. *Jn* 14:18; 20:22; *Mt* 28:20; *Acts* 2:33. — [219] *LG* 7. — [220] *LG* 7. — [221] *LG* 7; cf. *Rom* 6:4–5; *1 Cor* 12:13. — [222] *LG* 7 § 3. — [223] *LG* 7 § 3; cf. *1 Cor* 12:26. — [224] *Gal* 3:27–28. — [225] *Col* 1:18. — [226] *Col* 1:18.

661 **793** *Christ unites us with his Passover*: all his members must strive
519 to resemble him, "until Christ be formed" in them.[227] "For this reason we…are taken up into the mysteries of his life,…associated with his sufferings as the body with its head, suffering with him, that with him we may be glorified."[228]

794 *Christ provides for our growth*: to make us grow toward him, our head,[229] he provides in his Body, the Church, the gifts and assistance by
872 which we help one another along the way of salvation.

795 Christ and his Church thus together make up the "whole Christ" (*Christus totus*). The Church is one with Christ. The saints are acutely
695 aware of this unity:

> Let us rejoice then and give thanks that we have become not only Christians, but Christ himself. Do you understand and grasp, brethren, God's grace toward us? Marvel and rejoice: we have become Christ. For if he is the head, we are the members; he and we together are the whole man.… The fullness of Christ then is the head and the members. But what does "head and members" mean? Christ and the Church.[230]
>
> Our redeemer has shown himself to be one person with the holy Church whom he has taken to himself.[231]
>
> 1474 Head and members form as it were one and the same mystical person.[232]
>
> A reply of St. Joan of Arc to her judges sums up the faith of the holy doctors and the good sense of the believer: "About Jesus Christ and the Church, I simply know they're just one thing, and we shouldn't complicate the matter."[233]

The Church is the Bride of Christ

796 The unity of Christ and the Church, head and members of one Body, also implies the distinction of the two within a personal relationship. This aspect is often expressed by the image of bridegroom and
bride. The theme of Christ as Bride- 757
groom of the Church was prepared for by the prophets and announced by John the Baptist.[234] The Lord
referred to himself as the "bride- 219
groom."[235] The Apostle speaks of the whole Church and of each of the faithful, members of his Body, as a bride "betrothed" to Christ the
Lord so as to become but one spirit 772
with him.[236] The Church is the spotless bride of the spotless Lamb.[237]
"Christ loved the Church and gave 1602
himself up for her, that he might sanctify her."[238] He has joined her
with himself in an everlasting cov- 1616
enant and never stops caring for her as for his own body:[239]

> This is the whole Christ, head and body, one formed from many… whether the head or members speak, it is Christ who speaks. He speaks in his role as the head (*ex persona capitis*) and in his role as body (*ex persona corporis*). What does this mean? "The two will become one flesh. This is a great mystery, and I am applying it to Christ and the Church."[240] And the Lord himself says in the Gospel: "So they are no longer two, but one flesh."[241] They are, in fact, two different persons, yet they are one in the conjugal union,…*as head, he calls himself the bridegroom, as body, he calls himself "bride."*[242]

[227] *Gal* 4:19. — [228] *LG* 7 § 4; cf. *Phil* 3:21; *Rom* 8:17. — [229] Cf. *Col* 2:19; *Eph* 4:11–16. — [230] St. Augustine, *In Jo. ev.* 21, 8: PL 35, 1568. — [231] Pope St. Gregory the Great, *Moralia in Job, prǽf.*, 14: PL 75, 525A. — [232] St. Thomas Aquinas, *STh* III, 48, 2. — [233] Acts of the Trial of Joan of Arc. — [234] *Jn* 3:29. — [235] *Mk* 2:19. — [236] Cf. *Mt* 22:1–14; 25:1–13; *1 Cor* 6:15–17; *2 Cor* 11:2. — [237] Cf. *Rev* 22:17; *Eph* 1:4, 5:27. — [238] *Eph* 5:25–26. — [239] Cf. *Eph* 5:29. — [240] *Eph* 5:31–32. — [241] *Mt* 19:6. — [242] St. Augustine, *En. in Ps.* 74:4: PL 36, 948–949.

III. The Church Is the Temple of the Holy Spirit

797 "What the soul is to the
human body, the Holy Spirit is to
the Body of Christ, which is the
Church."[243] "To this Spirit of Christ,
813 as an invisible principle, is to be ascribed the fact that all the parts of
the body are joined one with the
other and with their exalted head;
for the whole Spirit of Christ is in
the head, the whole Spirit is in the
body, and the whole Spirit is in each
of the members."[244] The Holy Spirit makes the Church "the temple of
586 the living God":[245]

> Indeed, it is to the Church herself that the "Gift of God" has been entrusted.... In it is in her that communion with Christ has been deposited, that is to say: the Holy Spirit, the pledge of incorruptibility, the strengthening of our faith and the ladder of our ascent to God.... For where the Church is, there also is God's Spirit; where God's Spirit is, there is the Church and every grace.[246]

798 The Holy Spirit is "the principle of every vital and truly saving action in each part of the Body."[247] He
works in many ways to build up the
737 whole Body in charity:[248] by God's
Word "which is able to build you
up";[249] by Baptism, through which
he forms Christ's Body;[250] by the
1091–1109 sacraments, which give growth and
healing to Christ's members; by "the
grace of the apostles, which holds
first place among his gifts";[251] by the
virtues, which make us act according
to what is good; finally, by the many
special graces (called "charisms"), by
which he makes the faithful "fit and
ready to undertake various tasks and
offices for the renewal and building 791
up of the Church."[252]

Charisms

799 Whether extraordinary or
simple and humble, charisms are
graces of the Holy Spirit which
directly or indirectly benefit the
Church, ordered as they are to her
building up, to the good of men, 951, 2003
and to the needs of the world.

800 Charisms are to be accepted with gratitude by the person who receives them and by all members of the Church as well. They are a wonderfully rich grace for the apostolic vitality and for the holiness of the entire Body of Christ, provided they really are genuine gifts of the Holy Spirit and are used in full conformity with authentic promptings of this same Spirit, that is, in keeping with charity, the true measure of all charisms.[253]

801 It is in this sense that discernment of charisms is always necessary.
No charism is exempt from being referred and submitted to the Church's
shepherds. "Their office [is] not in- 894
deed to extinguish the Spirit, but to
test all things and hold fast to what
is good,"[254] so that all the diverse
and complementary charisms work
together "for the common good."[255] 1905

[243] St. Augustine, *Sermo* 267, 4: PL 38, 1231D. — [244] Pius XII, encyclical, *Mystici Corporis*: DS 3808. — [245] *2 Cor* 6:16; cf. *1 Cor* 3:16–17; *Eph* 2:21. — [246] St. Irenaeus, *Adv. haeres.* 3, 24, 1: PG 7/1, 966. — [247] Pius XII, encyclical, *Mystici Corporis*: DS 3808. — [248] Cf. *Eph* 4:16. — [249] *Acts* 20:32. — [250] Cf. *1 Cor* 12:13. — [251] *LG* 7 § 2. — [252] *LG* 12 § 2; cf. AA 3. — [253] Cf. *1 Cor* 13. — [254] *LG* 12; cf. 30; *1 Thess* 5:12, 19–21; John Paul II, *Christifideles Laici*, 24. — [255] *1 Cor* 12:7.

In Brief

802 *Christ Jesus "gave himself for us to redeem us from all iniquity and to purify for himself a people of his own"* (Titus *2:14).*

803 *"You are a chosen race, a royal priesthood, a holy nation, God's own people"* (1 Pet *2:9).*

804 *One enters into the People of God by faith and Baptism. "All men are called to belong to the new People of God"* (LG *13), so that, in Christ, "men may form one family and one People of God"* (AG *1).*

805 *The Church is the Body of Christ. Through the Spirit and his action in the sacraments, above all the Eucharist, Christ, who once was dead and is now risen, establishes the community of believers as his own Body.*

806 *In the unity of this Body, there is a diversity of members and functions. All members are linked to one another, especially to those who are suffering, to the poor and persecuted.*

807 *The Church is this Body of which Christ is the head: she lives from him, in him, and for him; he lives with her and in her.*

808 *The Church is the Bride of Christ: he loved her and handed himself over for her. He has purified her by his blood and made her the fruitful mother of all God's children.*

809 *The Church is the Temple of the Holy Spirit. The Spirit is the soul, as it were, of the Mystical Body, the source of its life, of its unity in diversity, and of the riches of its gifts and charisms.*

810 *"Hence the universal Church is seen to be 'a people brought into unity from the unity of the Father, the Son, and the Holy Spirit'"* (LG *4 citing St. Cyprian,* De Dom. orat. *23:* PL *4, 553).*

Paragraph 3
The Church Is One, Holy, Catholic, and Apostolic

811 "This is the sole Church of Christ, which in the Creed we profess to be one, holy, catholic and apostolic."[256] These four characteristics, inseparably linked with each 750
other,[257] indicate essential features of the Church and her mission. The Church does not possess them of herself; it is Christ who, through the 832, 865
Holy Spirit, makes his Church one, holy, catholic, and apostolic, and it is he who calls her to realize each of these qualities.

812 Only faith can recognize that the Church possesses these properties from her divine source. But their historical manifestations are signs that also speak clearly to hu- 156, 770
man reason. As the First Vatican Council noted, the "Church herself, with her marvellous propagation, eminent holiness, and inexhaustible fruitfulness in everything good, her catholic unity and invincible stability, is a great and perpetual motive of credibility and an irrefutable witness of her divine mission."[258]

I. The Church Is One

"The sacred mystery of the Church's unity" (UR 2)

813 *The Church is one because of her source*: "the highest exemplar and source of this mystery is the unity, in

[256] *LG* 8. — [257] Cf. DS 2888. — [258] Vatican Council I, *Dei Filius* 3: DS 3013.

the Trinity of Persons, of one God,
172 the Father and the Son in the Holy Spirit."[259] The Church is one *because*
766 *of her founder*: for "the Word made flesh, the prince of peace, reconciled all men to God by the cross,...restoring the unity of all in one people
797 and one body."[260] The Church is one *because of her "soul"*: "It is the Holy Spirit, dwelling in those who believe and pervading and ruling over the entire Church, who brings about that wonderful communion of the faithful and joins them together so intimately in Christ that he is the principle of the Church's unity."[261] Unity is of the essence of the Church:

> What an astonishing mystery! There is one Father of the universe, one Logos of the universe, and also one Holy Spirit, everywhere one and the same; there is also one virgin become mother, and I should like to call her "Church."[262]

814 From the beginning, this one Church has been marked by a great diversity which comes from both the variety of God's gifts and the diversi-
791, 873 ty of those who receive them. Within the unity of the People of God, a multiplicity of peoples and cultures is gathered together. Among the Church's members, there are different
1202 gifts, offices, conditions, and ways of life. "Holding a rightful place in the communion of the Church there are also particular Churches that retain their own traditions."[263] The great richness of such diversity is not op
832 posed to the Church's unity. Yet sin and the burden of its consequences constantly threaten the gift of unity. And so the Apostle has to exhort Christians to "maintain the unity of the Spirit in the bond of peace."[264]

815 What are these bonds of 1827
unity? Above all, charity "binds everything together in perfect harmo- 830, 837
ny."[265] But the unity of the pilgrim Church is also assured by visible 173
bonds of communion:

– profession of one faith received from the Apostles;
– common celebration of divine worship, especially of the sacraments;
– apostolic succession through the sacrament of Holy Orders, maintaining the fraternal concord of God's family.[266]

816 "The sole Church of Christ [is that] which our Savior, after his Resurrection, entrusted to Peter's pastoral care, commissioning him and the other apostles to extend and rule it.... This Church, constituted and organized as a society in the present world, subsists in (*subsistit in*) the Catholic Church, which is governed by the successor of Peter and by the bishops in communion with him."[267]

> The Second Vatican Council's *Decree* 830
> *on Ecumenism* explains: "For it is through Christ's Catholic Church alone, which is the universal help toward salvation, that the fullness of the means of salvation can be obtained. It was to the apostolic college alone, of which Peter is the head, that we believe that our Lord entrusted all the blessings of the New Covenant, in order to establish on earth the one Body of Christ into which all those should be fully incorporated who belong in any way to the People of God."[268]

259 *UR* 2 § 5. — 260 *GS* 78 § 3. — 261 *UR* 2 § 2. — 262 St. Clement of Alexandria, *Paed.* 1, 6, 42: PG 8, 300. — 263 *LG* 13 § 2. — 264 *Eph* 4:3. — 265 *Col* 3:14. — 266 Cf. *UR* 2; *LG* 14; CIC, can. 205. — 267 *LG* 8 § 2. — 268 *UR* 3 § 5.

Wounds to unity

817 In fact, "in this one and only Church of God from its very beginnings there arose certain rifts, which the Apostle strongly censures as damnable. But in subsequent centuries much more serious dissensions appeared and large communities became separated from full communion with the Catholic Church—for which, often enough, men of both sides were to blame."[269] The ruptures that wound the unity of Christ's Body—here we must distinguish heresy, apostasy, and schism[270]—do
2089 not occur without human sin:

> Where there are sins, there are also divisions, schisms, heresies, and disputes. Where there is virtue, however, there also are harmony and unity, from which arise the one heart and one soul of all believers.[271]

818 "However, one cannot charge with the sin of the separation those who at present are born into these communities [that resulted from such separation] and in them are brought up in the faith of Christ, and the Catholic Church accepts them with respect and affection as brothers.... All who have been justified by faith in Baptism are incor-
1271 porated into Christ; they therefore have a right to be called Christians, and with good reason are accepted as brothers in the Lord by the children of the Catholic Church."[272]

819 "Furthermore, many elements of sanctification and of truth"[273] are found outside the visible confines of the Catholic Church: "the written Word of God; the life of grace; faith, hope, and charity, with the other interior gifts of the Holy Spirit, as well as visible elements."[274] Christ's Spirit uses these Churches and ecclesial communities as means of salvation, whose power derives from the fullness of grace and truth that Christ has entrusted to the Catholic Church. All these blessings come from Christ and lead to him,[275] and are in themselves calls to "Catholic unity."[276]

Toward unity

820 "Christ bestowed unity on his Church from the beginning. This unity, we believe, subsists in the Catholic Church as something she can never lose, and we hope that it will continue to increase until the end of time."[277] Christ always gives his Church the gift of unity, but the Church must always pray and work to maintain, reinforce, and perfect the unity that Christ wills for her. This is why Jesus himself prayed at
the hour of his Passion, and does 2748
not cease praying to his Father, for the unity of his disciples: "That they may all be one. As you, Father, are in me and I am in you, may they also be one in us,...so that the world may know that you have sent me."[278] The desire to recover the unity of all Christians is a gift of Christ and a call of the Holy Spirit.[279]

821 Certain things are required in order to respond adequately to this call:

– a permanent *renewal* of the Church in greater fidelity to her vocation; such renewal is the driving-force of the movement toward unity;[280]

[269] *UR* 3 § 1. — [270] Cf. CIC, can. 751. — [271] Origen, *Hom. in Ezech.* 9, 1: PG 13, 732. — [272] *UR* 3 § 1. — [273] *LG* 8 § 2. — [274] *UR* 3 § 2; cf. *LG* 15. — [275] Cf. *UR* 3. — [276] Cf. *LG* 8. — [277] *UR* 4 § 3. — [278] *Jn* 17:21; cf. *Heb* 7:25. — [279] Cf. *UR* 1. — [280] Cf. *UR* 6.

827 – *conversion of heart* as the faithful "try to live holier lives according to the Gospel";[281] for it is the unfaithfulness of the members to Christ's gift which causes divisions;
2791 – *prayer in common*, because "change of heart and holiness of life, along with public and private prayer for the unity of Christians, should be regarded as the soul of the whole ecumenical movement, and merits the name 'spiritual ecumenism;'"[282]
– *fraternal knowledge of each other*;[283]
– *ecumenical formation* of the faithful and especially of priests;[284]
– *dialogue* among theologians and meetings among Christians of the different churches and communities;[285]

– *collaboration* among Christians in various areas of service to mankind.[286] "Human service" is the idiomatic phrase.

822 Concern for achieving unity "involves the whole Church, faithful and clergy alike."[287] But we must realize "that this holy objective—the reconciliation of all Christians in the unity of the one and only Church of Christ—transcends human powers and gifts." That is why we place all our hope "in the prayer of Christ for the Church, in the love of the Father for us, and in the power of the Holy Spirit."[288]

II. The Church Is Holy

823 "The Church...is held, as a matter of faith, to be unfailingly holy. This is because Christ, the Son of God, who with the Father and the
459 Spirit is hailed as 'alone holy,' loved the Church as his Bride, giving him-
self up for her so as to sanctify her; 796
he joined her to himself as his body and endowed her with the gift of the Holy Spirit for the glory of God."[289] The Church, then, is "the holy People of God,"[290] and her members are 946
called "saints."[291]

824 United with Christ, the Church is sanctified by him; through him and with him she becomes sanctifying. "All the activities of the Church are directed, as toward their end, to the sanctification of men in Christ and the glorification of God."[292] It is in the Church that "the fullness of the means of salvation"[293] has been deposited. It is
in her that "by the grace of God we 816
acquire holiness."[294]

825 "The Church on earth is endowed already with a sanctity that is real though imperfect."[295] In her members perfect holiness is something yet to be acquired: "Strength- 670
ened by so many and such great means of salvation, all the faithful, whatever their condition or state—
though each in his own way—are 2013
called by the Lord to that perfection of sanctity by which the Father himself is perfect."[296]

826 Charity is the soul of the 1827, 2658
holiness to which all are called: it "governs, shapes, and perfects all the means of sanctification."[297]

> If the Church was a body composed of different members, it couldn't lack the noblest of all; *it must have a Heart, and a Heart BURNING WITH LOVE*. And I realized that *this love alone* was the true motive force which enabled the other members
> of the Church to act; if it ceased 864

[281] *UR* 7 § 3. — [282] *UR* 8 § 1. — [283] Cf. *UR* 9. — [284] Cf. *UR* 10. — [285] Cf. *UR* 4; 9; 11. — [286] Cf. *UR* 12. — [287] *UR* 5. — [288] *UR* 24 § 2. — [289] *LG* 39; cf. *Eph* 5:25–26. — [290] *LG* 12. — [291] *Acts* 9:13; *1 Cor* 6:1; 16:1. — [292] *SC* 10. — [293] *UR* 3 § 5. — [294] *LG* 48. — [295] *LG* 48 § 3. — [296] *LG* 11 § 3. — [297] *LG* 42.

to function, the Apostles would forget to preach the gospel, the Martyrs would refuse to shed their blood. LOVE, IN FACT, IS THE VOCATION WHICH INCLUDES ALL OTHERS; IT'S A UNIVERSE OF ITS OWN, COMPRISING ALL TIME AND SPACE—IT'S ETERNAL![298]

827 "Christ, 'holy, innocent, and undefiled,' knew nothing of sin, but came only to expiate the sins of the people. The Church, howev-
1425–1429 er, clasping sinners to her bosom, at once holy and always in need of
821 purification, follows constantly the path of penance and renewal."[299] All members of the Church, including her ministers, must acknowledge that they are sinners.[300] In everyone, the weeds of sin will still be mixed with the good wheat of the Gospel until the end of time.[301] Hence the Church gathers sinners already caught up in Christ's salvation but still on the way to holiness:

> The Church is therefore holy, though having sinners in her midst, because she herself has no other life but the life of grace. If they live her life, her members are sanctified; if they move away from her life, they fall into sins and disorders that prevent the radiation of her sanctity. This is why she suffers and does penance for those offenses, of which she has the power to free her children through the blood of Christ and the gift of the Holy Spirit.[302]

828 By *canonizing* some of the faithful, i.e., by solemnly proclaiming that they practiced heroic virtue and lived in fidelity to God's grace,
the Church recognizes the power 1173
of the Spirit of holiness within her and sustains the hope of believers by proposing the saints to them as models and intercessors.[303] "The saints have always been the source and origin of renewal in the most
difficult moments in the Church's 2045
history."[304] Indeed, "holiness is the hidden source and infallible measure of her apostolic activity and missionary zeal."[305]

829 "But while in the most Blessed Virgin the Church has already
reached that perfection whereby she 1172
exists without spot or wrinkle, the
faithful still strive to conquer sin 972
and increase in holiness. And so they turn their eyes to Mary":[306] in her, the Church is already the "all-holy."

III. The Church Is Catholic

What does "catholic" mean?

830 The word "catholic" means "universal," in the sense of "according to the totality" or "in keeping with the whole." The Church is catholic in a double sense:

First, the Church is catholic because Christ is present in her. "Where
there is Christ Jesus, there is the 795
Catholic Church."[307] In her subsists
the fullness of Christ's body united 815–816
with its head; this implies that she receives from him "the fullness of the means of salvation"[308] which he has willed: correct and complete confession of faith, full sacramental life,

[298] St. Thérèse of Lisieux, *Autobiography of a Saint*, tr. Ronald Knox (London: Harvill, 1958) 235. — [299] *LG* 8 § 3; cf. *UR* 3; 6; *Heb* 2:17; 7:26; *2 Cor* 5:21. — [300] Cf. *1 Jn* 1:8–10. — [301] Cf. *Mt* 13:24–30. — [302] Paul VI, *CPG* § 19. — [303] Cf. *LG* 40; 48–51. — [304] John Paul II, *CL* 16, 3. — [305] *CL* 17, 3. — [306] *LG* 65; cf. *Eph* 5:26–27. — [307] St. Ignatius of Antioch, *Ad Smyrn.* 8, 2: *Apostolic Fathers*, II/2, 311. — [308] *UR* 3; *AG* 6; *Eph* 1:22–23.

and ordained ministry in apostolic succession. The Church was, in this fundamental sense, catholic on the day of Pentecost[309] and will always be so until the day of the Parousia.

831 Secondly, the Church is catholic because she has been sent out by
849 Christ on a mission to the whole of the human race:[310]

> All men are called to belong to the new People of God. This People, therefore, while remaining one and only one, is to be spread throughout the whole world and to all ages in order that the design of God's will may be fulfilled: he made human
> 360 nature one in the beginning and has decreed that all his children who were scattered should be finally gathered together as one.... The character of universality which adorns the People of God is a gift from the Lord himself whereby the Catholic Church
> 518 ceaselessly and efficaciously seeks for the return of all humanity and all its goods, under Christ the Head in the unity of his Spirit.[311]

Each particular Church is "catholic"

814 **832** "The Church of Christ is really present in all legitimately or-
811 ganized local groups of the faithful, which, in so far as they are united to their pastors, are also quite appropriately called Churches in the New Testament.... In them the faithful are gathered together through the preaching of the Gospel of Christ, and the mystery of the Lord's Supper is celebrated.... In these communities, though they may often be small and poor, or existing in the diaspora, Christ is present, through whose power and influence the One, Holy, Catholic, and Apostolic Church is constituted."[312]

833 The phrase "particular church," which is first of all the diocese (or eparchy), refers to a community of the Christian faithful in communion of faith and sacraments with their bishop ordained in apostolic succession.[313] These particular 886
Churches "are constituted after the model of the universal Church; it is in these and formed out of them that the one and unique Catholic Church exists."[314]

834 Particular Churches are fully catholic through their communion with one of them, the Church of Rome "which presides in charity."[315]
"For with this church, by reason of 882, 1369
its pre-eminence, the whole Church, that is the faithful everywhere, must necessarily be in accord."[316] Indeed, "from the incarnate Word's descent to us, all Christian churches everywhere have held and hold the great Church that is here [at Rome] to be their only basis and foundation since, according to the Savior's promise, the gates of hell have never prevailed against her."[317]

835 "Let us be very careful not to conceive of the universal Church as the simple sum, or...the more or less anomalous federation of essentially different particular churches. In the mind of the Lord the Church is universal by vocation and mission, but when she puts down her roots in a variety of cultural, social, and human terrains, she takes on different external expressions and appear-

309 Cf. *AG* 4. — 310 Cf. *Mt* 28:19. — 311 *LG* 13 §§ 1–2; cf. *Jn* 11:52. — 312 *LG* 26. — 313 Cf. *CD* 11; CIC, cann. 368–369; CCEO, cann. 177, 1; 178; 311, 1; 312. — 314 *LG* 23. — 315 St. Ignatius of Antioch, *Ad Rom.* 1, 1: *Apostolic Fathers*, II/2, 192; cf. *LG* 13. — 316 St. Irenaeus, *Adv. haeres.* 3, 3, 2: PG 7/1, 849; cf. Vatican Council I: DS 3057. — 317 St. Maximus the Confessor, *Opuscula theo.*: PG 91:137–140.

ances in each part of the world."[318] The rich variety of ecclesiastical disciplines, liturgical rites, and theological and spiritual heritages proper to the local churches "unified in a common effort, shows all the more
1202 resplendently the catholicity of the undivided Church."[319]

Who belongs to the Catholic Church?

836 "All men are called to this catholic unity of the People of God.... And to it, in different ways, belong or are ordered: the Catho-
831 lic faithful, others who believe in Christ, and finally all mankind, called by God's grace to salvation."[320]

837 "Fully incorporated into the society of the Church are those who, possessing the Spirit of Christ, accept all the means of salvation given
771 to the Church together with her entire organization, and who—by the
815 bonds constituted by the profession of faith, the sacraments, ecclesiastical government, and communion—are joined in the visible structure of the Church of Christ, who rules her through the Supreme Pontiff and the bishops. Even though incorporated into the Church, one who does not however persevere in char-
882 ity is not saved. He remains indeed in the bosom of the Church, but 'in body' not 'in heart.'"[321]

838 "The Church knows that she is joined in many ways to the baptized who are honored by the name of Christian, but do not profess the
818 Catholic faith in its entirety or have not preserved unity or communion under the successor of Peter."[322] Those "who believe in Christ and have been properly baptized are put in a certain, although imperfect, communion with the Catho- 1271
lic Church."[323] *With the Orthodox Churches*, this communion is so profound "that it lacks little to attain the fullness that would permit a common celebration of the Lord's Eucharist."[324] 1399

The Church and non-Christians

839 "Those who have not yet received the Gospel are related to the People of God in various ways."[325]

The relationship of the Church with the Jewish People. When she delves into her own mystery, the Church, the People of God in the New Covenant, discovers her link with the Jewish People,[326] "the first to hear the Word of God."[327] The Jewish 63
faith, unlike other non-Christian religions, is already a response to 147
God's revelation in the Old Covenant. To the Jews "belong the sonship, the glory, the covenants, the giving of the law, the worship, and the promises; to them belong the patriarchs, and of their race, according to the flesh, is the Christ";[328] "for the gifts and the call of God are irrevocable."[329]

840 And when one considers the future, God's People of the Old Covenant and the new People of God tend towards similar goals: expectation of the coming (or the re- 674
turn) of the Messiah. But one awaits the return of the Messiah who died and rose from the dead and is recognized as Lord and Son of God; the other awaits the coming of a Messiah, whose features remain hidden

[318] Paul VI, *EN* 62. — [319] *LG* 23. — [320] *LG* 13. — [321] *LG* 14. — [322] *LG* 15. — [323] *UR* 3. — [324] Paul VI, Discourse, December 14, 1975; cf. *UR* 13–18. — [325] *LG* 16. — [326] Cf. *NA* 4. — [327] *Roman Missal*, Good Friday 13: General Intercessions, VI. — [328] *Rom* 9:4–5. — [329] *Rom* 11:29.

till the end of time; and the latter waiting is accompanied by the dra-
597 ma of not knowing or of misunderstanding Christ Jesus.

841 *The Church's relationship with the Muslims.* "The plan of salvation also includes those who acknowledge the Creator, in the first place amongst whom are the Muslims; these profess to hold the faith of Abraham, and together with us they adore the one, merciful God, mankind's judge on the last day."[330]

842 *The Church's bond with non-Christian religions* is in the first place the common origin and end of
360 the human race:

> All nations form but one community. This is so because all stem from the one stock which God created to people the entire earth, and also because all share a common destiny, namely God. His providence, evident goodness, and saving designs extend to all against the day when the elect are gathered together in the holy city....[331]

843 The Catholic Church recognizes in other religions that search, among shadows and images, for the God who is unknown yet near since
28 he gives life and breath and all things and wants all men to be saved. Thus,
856 the Church considers all goodness and truth found in these religions as "a preparation for the Gospel and given by him who enlightens all men that they may at length have life."[332]

844 In their religious behavior, however, men also display the limits and errors that disfigure the image
29 of God in them:

> Very often, deceived by the Evil One, men have become vain in their reasonings, and have exchanged the truth of God for a lie, and served the creature rather than the Creator. Or else, living and dying in this world without God, they are exposed to ultimate despair.[333]

845 To reunite all his children, scattered and led astray by sin, the Father willed to call the whole of humanity together into his Son's
Church. The Church is the place 30
where humanity must rediscover its
unity and salvation. The Church is 953
"the world reconciled." She is that bark which "in the full sail of the Lord's cross, by the breath of the Holy Spirit, navigates safely in this world." According to another image dear to the Church Fathers, she 1219
is prefigured by Noah's ark, which alone saves from the flood.[334]

"Outside the Church there is no salvation"

846 How are we to understand this affirmation, often repeated by the Church Fathers?[335] Re-formulated positively, it means that all salvation comes from Christ the Head through the Church which is his Body:

> Basing itself on Scripture and Tradition, the Council teaches that the Church, a pilgrim now on earth, is necessary for salvation: the one Christ is the mediator and the way of salvation; he is present to us in his body which is the Church. He himself explicitly asserted the necessity of faith and Baptism, and
> thereby affirmed at the same time the 161, 1257

330 *LG* 16; cf. NA 3. — 331 *NA* 1. — 332 *LG* 16; cf. *NA* 2; *EN* 53. — 333 *LG* 16; cf. *Rom* 1:21, 25. — 334 St. Augustine, *Serm.* 96, 7, 9: PL 38, 588; St. Ambrose, *De virg.* 18, 118: PL 16, 297B; cf. already *1 Pet* 3:20–21. — 335 Cf. Cyprian, *Ep.* 73.21: PL 3, 1169; *De unit.*: PL 4, 509–536.

> necessity of the Church which men enter through Baptism as through a door. Hence they could not be saved who, knowing that the Catholic Church was founded as necessary by God through Christ, would refuse either to enter it or to remain in it.[336]

847 This affirmation is not aimed at those who, through no fault of their own, do not know Christ and his Church:

> Those who, through no fault of their own, do not know the Gospel of Christ or his Church, but who nevertheless seek God with a sincere heart, and, moved by grace, try in their actions to do his will as they know it through the dictates of their conscience—those too may achieve eternal salvation.[337]

848 "Although in ways known to himself God can lead those who, through no fault of their own, are ignorant of the Gospel, to that faith
1260 without which it is impossible to please him, the Church still has the obligation and also the sacred right to evangelize all men."[338]

Mission—a requirement of the Church's catholicity

849 *The missionary mandate.* "Having been divinely sent to the nations that she might be 'the universal sacrament of salvation,' the Church, in obedience to the com-
738, 767 mand of her founder and because it is demanded by her own essential universality, strives to preach the Gospel to all men":[339] "Go therefore and make disciples of all nations, baptizing them in the name of the Father and of the Son and of the Holy Spirit, teaching them to observe all that I have commanded you; and Lo, I am with you always, until the close of the age."[340]

850 *The origin and purpose of mission.* The Lord's missionary mandate is ultimately grounded in the eternal love of the Most Holy Trinity: "The Church on earth is by her nature 257
missionary since, according to the plan of the Father, she has as her origin the mission of the Son and the 730
Holy Spirit."[341] The ultimate purpose of mission is none other than to make men share in the communion between the Father and the Son in their Spirit of love.[342]

851 *Missionary motivation.* It is from God's love for all men that the Church in every age receives both the obligation and the vigor of her missionary dynamism, "for the love of Christ urges us on."[343] Indeed, God "desires all men to be saved 221, 429
and to come to the knowledge of the truth";[344] that is, God wills the 74, 217
salvation of everyone through the knowledge of the truth. Salvation is 2104
found in the truth. Those who obey the prompting of the Spirit of truth are already on the way of salvation. But the Church, to whom this truth has been entrusted, must go out to meet their desire, so as to bring them the truth. Because she believes 890
in God's universal plan of salvation, the Church must be missionary.

852 *Missionary paths.* The Holy Spirit is the protagonist, "the principal agent of the whole of the 2044
Church's mission."[345] It is he who

336 *LG* 14; cf. *Mk* 16:16; *Jn* 3:5. — 337 *LG* 16; cf. *DS* 3866–3872. — 338 *AG* 7; cf. *Heb* 11:6; *1 Cor* 9:16. — 339 *AG* 1; cf. *Mt* 16:15. — 340 *Mt* 28:19–20. — 341 *AG* 2. — 342 Cf. John Paul II, *RMiss* 23. — 343 *2 Cor* 5:14 ; cf. *AA* 6; *RMiss* 11. — 344 *1 Tim* 2:4. — 345 John Paul II, *RMiss* 21.

2473 leads the Church on her missionary paths. "This mission continues and, in the course of history, unfolds the mission of Christ, who was sent to evangelize the poor; so the Church, urged on by the Spirit of Christ, must walk the road Christ himself walked, a way of poverty and obedience, of service and self-sacrifice even to death, a death from which he emerged victorious by his resurrection."[346] So it is that "the blood of martyrs is the seed of Christians."[347]

853 On her pilgrimage, the Church has also experienced the "discrepancy existing between the message she proclaims and the human weakness of those to whom the Gospel has been entrusted."[348] Only by taking the "way of penance and renewal," the "narrow way of the cross," can the People of God extend
1428 Christ's reign.[349] For "just as Christ carried out the work of redemption in poverty and oppression, so the Church is called to follow the same
2443 path if she is to communicate the fruits of salvation to men."[350]

854 By her very mission, "the Church...travels the same journey as all humanity and shares the same earthly lot with the world: she is to be a leaven and, as it were, the soul of human society in its renewal by Christ and transformation into the family of God."[351] Missionary endeavor requires *patience*. It begins with the proclamation of the Gospel to peoples and groups who do not
2105 yet believe in Christ,[352] continues with the establishment of Christian communities that are "a sign of God's presence in the world,"[353] and leads to the foundation of local churches.[354] It must involve a pro-
cess of inculturation if the Gospel 1204
is to take flesh in each people's culture.[355] There will be times of defeat. "With regard to individuals, groups, and peoples it is only by degrees that [the Church] touches and penetrates them, and so receives them into a fullness which is Catholic."[356]

855 The Church's mission stimulates efforts *towards Christian unity*.[357] Indeed, "divisions among Christians prevent the Church from realizing in practice the fullness of
catholicity proper to her in those 821
of her sons who, though joined to her by Baptism, are yet separated from full communion with her. Furthermore, the Church herself finds it more difficult to express in actual life her full catholicity in all its aspects."[358]

856 The missionary task implies a *respectful dialogue* with those who do not yet accept the Gospel.[359] Believers can profit from this dialogue by learning to appreciate better
"those elements of truth and grace 839
which are found among peoples, and which are, as it were, a secret presence of God."[360] They proclaim the Good News to those who do not know it, in order to consolidate, complete, and raise up the truth and the goodness that God has distributed among men and nations, and 843
to purify them from error and evil "for the glory of God, the confusion of the demon, and the happiness of man."[361]

[346] *AG* 5. — [347] Tertullian, *Apol.* 50, 13: PL 1, 603. — [348] *GS* 43 § 6. — [349] *LG* 8 § 3; 15; *AG* 1 § 3; cf. *RMiss* 12–20. — [350] *LG* 8 § 3. — [351] *GS* 40 § 2. — [352] Cf. *RMiss* 42–47. — [353] *AG* 15 § 1. — [354] Cf. *RMiss* 48–49. — [355] Cf. *RMiss* 52–54. — [356] *AG* 6 § 2. — [357] Cf. *RMiss* 50. — [358] *UR* 4 § 8. — [359] Cf. *RMiss* 55. — [360] *AG* 9. — [361] *AG* 9.

IV. The Church Is Apostolic

75 **857** The Church is apostolic because she is founded on the apostles, in three ways:

– she was and remains built on "the foundation of the Apostles,"[362] the witnesses chosen and sent on mission by Christ himself;[363]
171 – with the help of the Spirit dwelling in her, the Church keeps and hands on the teaching,[364] the "good deposit," the salutary words she has heard from the apostles;[365]
– she continues to be taught, sanctified, and guided by the apostles until Christ's return, through their successors in pastoral office: the college of bishops, "assisted by
880 priests, in union with the successor of Peter, the Church's supreme
1575 pastor":[366]

> You are the eternal Shepherd who never leaves his flock untended. Through the apostles you watch over us and protect us always. You made them shepherds of the flock to share in the work of your Son....[367]

The Apostles' mission

858 Jesus is the Father's Emissary. From the beginning of his ministry, he "called to him those whom he desired;.... And he appointed
551 twelve, whom also he named apostles, to be with him, and to be sent out to preach."[368] From then on, they would also be his "emissaries" (Greek *apostoloi*). In them, Christ continues his own mission: "As the Father has sent me, even so I send you."[369] The apostles' ministry is the
425, 1086 continuation of his mission; Jesus said to the Twelve: "he who receives you receives me."[370]

859 Jesus unites them to the mission he received from the Father. As "the Son can do nothing of his own accord," but receives everything from the Father who sent him, so those whom Jesus sends can do nothing apart from him,[371] from whom they received both the mandate for their mission and the power to carry it out. Christ's apostles knew that they were called by God as "ministers of a new covenant," "servants of God,"
"ambassadors for Christ," "servants 876
of Christ and stewards of the mysteries of God."[372]

860 In the office of the apostles there is one aspect that cannot be transmitted: to be the chosen witnesses of the Lord's Resurrection and so the foundation stones of the Church. But their office also has a permanent aspect. Christ promised to remain with them always. The
divine mission entrusted by Jesus to 642
them "will continue to the end of time, since the Gospel they handed on is the lasting source of all life for
the Church. Therefore,...the apostles 765
took care to appoint successors."[373] 1087

The bishops—successors of the apostles

861 "In order that the mission entrusted to them might be continued after their death, [the apostles] consigned, by will and testament,
as it were, to their immediate col- 77
laborators the duty of completing and consolidating the work they had begun, urging them to tend to the whole flock, in which the Holy

[362] *Eph* 2:20; *Rev* 21:14. — [363] Cf. *Mt* 28:16–20; *Acts* 1:8; *1 Cor* 9:1; 15:7–8; *Gal* 1:1; etc. — [364] Cf. *Acts* 2:42. — [365] Cf. *2 Tim* 1:13–14. — [366] *AG* 5. — [367] *Roman Missal,* Preface of the Apostles I. — [368] *Mk* 3:13–14. — [369] *Jn* 20:21; cf. 13:20; 17:18. — [370] *Mt* 10:40; cf. *Lk* 10:16. — [371] *Jn* 5:19, 30; cf. *Jn* 15:5. — [372] *2 Cor* 3:6; 6:4; 5:20; *1 Cor* 4:1. — [373] *LG* 20; cf. *Mt* 28:20.

Spirit had appointed them to shepherd the Church of God. They accordingly designated such men and
1087 then made the ruling that likewise on their death other proven men should take over their ministry."[374]

862 "Just as the office which the Lord confided to Peter alone, as first of the apostles, destined to be transmitted to his successors, is a
880 permanent one, so also endures the office, which the apostles received, of shepherding the Church, a charge destined to be exercised without
1556 interruption by the sacred order of bishops."[375] Hence the Church teaches that "the bishops have by divine institution taken the place of the apostles as pastors of the Church, in such wise that whoever listens to them is listening to Christ and whoever despises them despises Christ and him who sent Christ."[376]

The apostolate

863 The whole Church is apostolic, in that she remains, through the successors of St. Peter and the other apostles, in communion of faith and
900 life with her origin: and in that she is "sent out" into the whole world. All members of the Church share in this mission, though in various ways. "The Christian vocation is, of its na-
2472 ture, a vocation to the apostolate as well." Indeed, we call an apostolate "every activity of the Mystical Body" that aims "to spread the Kingdom of Christ over all the earth."[377]

864 "Christ, sent by the Father, is the source of the Church's whole apostolate"; thus the fruitfulness of apostolate for ordained ministers as well as for lay people clearly depends 828
on their vital union with Christ.[378] In keeping with their vocations, the demands of the times and the various gifts of the Holy Spirit, the apostolate assumes the most varied forms. But charity, drawn from the 824
Eucharist above all, is always "as it were, the soul of the whole aposto- 1324
late."[379]

865 The Church is ultimately *one, holy, catholic, and apostolic* in her deepest and ultimate identity, because it is in her that "the Kingdom of heaven," the "Reign of God,"[380] 811, 541
already exists and will be fulfilled at the end of time. The kingdom has come in the person of Christ and grows mysteriously in the hearts of those incorporated into him, until its full eschatological manifestation. Then all those he has redeemed and made "holy and blameless before him in love,"[381] will be gathered together as the one People of God, the "Bride of the Lamb,"[382] "the holy city Jerusalem coming down out of heaven from God, having the glory of God."[383] For "the wall of the city had twelve foundations, and on them the twelve names of the *twelve apostles of the Lamb*."[384]

In Brief

866 *The Church is one: she acknowledges one Lord, confesses one faith, is born of one Baptism, forms only one Body, is given life by the one Spirit, for the sake of one hope (cf.* Eph *4:3–5), at whose fulfillment all divisions will be overcome.*

[374] *LG* 20; cf. *Acts* 20:28; St. Clement of Rome, *Ad Cor.* 42, 44: PG 1, 291–300. — [375] *LG* 20 § 2. — [376] *LG* 20 § 2. — [377] *AA* 2. — [378] *AA* 4; cf. *Jn* 15:5. — [379] *AA* 3. — [380] *Rev* 19:6. — [381] *Eph* 1:4. — [382] *Rev* 21:9. — [383] *Rev* 21:10–11. — [384] *Rev* 21:14.

867 *The Church is holy: the Most Holy God is her author; Christ, her bridegroom, gave himself up to make her holy; the Spirit of holiness gives her life. Since she still includes sinners, she is "the sinless one made up of sinners." Her holiness shines in the saints; in Mary she is already all-holy.*

868 *The Church is catholic: she proclaims the fullness of the faith. She bears in herself and administers the totality of the means of salvation. She is sent out to all peoples. She speaks to all men. She encompasses all times. She is "missionary of her very nature"* (AG *2).*

869 *The Church is apostolic. She is built on a lasting foundation: "the twelve apostles of the Lamb"* (Rev *21:14). She is indestructible (cf.* Mt *16:18). She is upheld infallibly in the truth: Christ governs her through Peter and the other apostles, who are present in their successors, the Pope and the college of bishops.*

870 *"The sole Church of Christ which in the Creed we profess to be one, holy, catholic, and apostolic,…subsists in the Catholic Church, which is governed by the successor of Peter and by the bishops in communion with him. Nevertheless, many elements of sanctification and of truth are found outside its visible confines"* (LG *8).*

Paragraph 4
Christ's Faithful—Hierarchy, Laity, Consecrated Life

871 "The Christian faithful are those who, inasmuch as they have been incorporated in Christ through Baptism, have been constituted as
the people of God; for this reason, 1268–126
since they have become sharers in
Christ's priestly, prophetic, and royal
office in their own manner, they are
called to exercise the mission which 782–786
God has entrusted to the Church to
fulfill in the world, in accord with
the condition proper to each one."[385]

872 "In virtue of their rebirth in
Christ there exists among all the
Christian faithful a true equality
with regard to dignity and the activity whereby all cooperate in the 1934
building up of the Body of Christ in
accord with each one's own condi- 794
tion and function."[386]

873 The very differences which
the Lord has willed to put between
the members of his body serve
its unity and mission. For "in the
Church there is diversity of ministry 814, 1937
but unity of mission. To the apostles
and their successors Christ has entrusted the office of teaching, sanctifying, and governing in his name and by his power. But the laity are made to share in the priestly, prophetical, and kingly office of Christ; they have therefore, in the Church and in the world, their own assignment in the mission of the whole People of God."[387] Finally, "from both groups [hierarchy and laity] there exist Christian faithful who are consecrated to God in their own special manner and serve the salvific mission of the Church through the profession of the evangelical counsels."[388]

I. The Hierarchical Constitution of the Church

Why the ecclesial ministry?

[385] CIC, can. 204 § 1; cf. *LG* 31. — [386] CIC, can. 208; cf. *LG* 32. — [387] *AA* 2. — [388] CIC, can. 207 § 2.

874 Christ is himself the source of ministry in the Church. He instituted the Church. He gave her
1544 authority and mission, orientation and goal:

> In order to shepherd the People of God and to increase its numbers without cease, Christ the Lord set up in his Church a variety of offices which aim at the good of the whole body. The holders of office, who are invested with a sacred power, are, in fact, dedicated to promoting the interests of their brethren, so that all who belong to the People of God... may attain to salvation.[389]

875 "How are they to believe in him of whom they have never heard? And how are they to hear without a preacher? And how can men
166 preach unless they are sent?"[390] No one—no individual and no community—can proclaim the Gospel to himself: "Faith comes from what is heard."[391] No one can give himself the mandate and the mission to proclaim the Gospel. The one sent by the Lord does not speak and act on his own authority, but by virtue of Christ's authority; not as a member of the community, but speaking to it in the name of Christ. No one can bestow grace on himself; it must be given and offered. This fact presupposes ministers of grace, authorized and empowered by Christ. From him, bishops and priests receive the mission and faculty ("the sacred
1548 power") to act *in persona Christi Ca-*
1536 *pitis*; deacons receive the strength to serve the people of God in the *diaconia* of liturgy, word, and charity, in communion with the bishop and his presbyterate. The ministry in which Christ's emissaries do and give by God's grace what they cannot do and give by their own powers, is called a "sacrament" by the Church's tradition. Indeed, the ministry of the Church is conferred by a special sacrament.

876 Intrinsically linked to the sacramental nature of ecclesial ministry is *its character as service*. Entirely dependent on Christ who gives mission and authority, ministers are tru- 1551
ly "slaves of Christ,"[392] in the image of him who freely took "the form of a slave" for us.[393] Because the word and grace of which they are minis-
ters are not their own, but are giv- 427
en to them by Christ for the sake of others, they must freely become the slaves of all.[394]

877 Likewise, it belongs to the sacramental nature of ecclesial ministry that it have a *collegial character*. In fact, from the beginning of his
ministry, the Lord Jesus instituted 1559
the Twelve as "the seeds of the new Israel and the beginning of the sacred hierarchy."[395] Chosen together, they were also sent out together, and their fraternal unity would be at the service of the fraternal communion of all the faithful: they would reflect and witness to the communion of the divine persons.[396] For this reason every bishop exercises his ministry from within the episcopal college, in communion with the bishop of Rome, the successor of St. Peter and head of the college. So also priests exercise their ministry from within the *presbyterium* of the diocese, under the direction of their bishop.

[389] *LG* 18. — [390] *Rom* 10:14–15. — [391] *Rom* 10:17. — [392] Cf. *Rom* 1:1. — [393] *Phil* 2:7. — [394] Cf. *1 Cor* 9:19. — [395] *AG* 5. — [396] Cf. *Jn* 17:21–23.

878 Finally, it belongs to the sacramental nature of ecclesial ministry that it have a *personal character.* Although Christ's ministers act in communion with one another, they also always act in a personal way. Each one is called personally: "You, follow me"[397] in order to be a personal witness within the common mission, to bear personal responsibility before him who gives the mission, acting "in his person" and for
1484 other persons: "I baptize you in the name of the Father and of the Son and of the Holy Spirit..."; "I absolve you...."

879 Sacramental ministry in the Church, then, is a service exercised in the name of Christ. It has a personal character and a collegial form. This is evidenced by the bonds between the episcopal college and its head, the successor of St. Peter, and in the relationship between the bishop's pastoral responsibility for his particular church and the common solicitude of the episcopal college for the universal Church.

The episcopal college and its head, the Pope

880 When Christ instituted the Twelve, "he constituted [them] in the form of a college or permanent assembly, at the head of which he
552, 862 placed Peter, chosen from among them."[398] Just as "by the Lord's institution, St. Peter and the rest of the apostles constitute a single apostolic college, so in like fashion the Roman Pontiff, Peter's successor, and the bishops, the successors of the apostles, are related with and united to one another."[399]

881 The Lord made Simon alone, whom he named Peter, the "rock" of his Church. He gave him the keys of his Church and instituted him
shepherd of the whole flock.[400] "The 553
office of binding and loosing which was given to Peter was also assigned to the college of apostles united to its head."[401] This pastoral office of
Peter and the other apostles belongs 642
to the Church's very foundation and is continued by the bishops under the primacy of the Pope.

882 The *Pope,* Bishop of Rome and Peter's successor, "is the perpetual and visible source and foundation of the unity both of the bishops
and of the whole company of the 834, 1369
faithful."[402] "For the Roman Pontiff, by reason of his office as Vicar 837
of Christ, and as pastor of the entire Church has full, supreme, and universal power over the whole Church, a power which he can always exercise unhindered."[403]

883 "The *college or body of bishops* has no authority unless united with the Roman Pontiff, Peter's successor, as its head." As such, this college has "supreme and full authority over the universal Church; but this power cannot be exercised without the agreement of the Roman Pontiff."[404]

884 "The college of bishops exercises power over the universal Church in a solemn manner in an ecumenical council."[405] But "there never is an ecumenical council which is not confirmed or at least recognized as such by Peter's successor."[406]

397 *Jn* 21:22; Cf. *Mt* 4:19. 21; *Jn* 1:4. — 398 *LG* 19; cf. *Lk* 6:13; *Jn* 21:15–17. — 399 *LG* 22; cf. CIC, can. 330. — 400 Cf. *Mt* 16:18–19; *Jn* 21:15–17. — 401 *LG* 22 § 2. — 402 *LG* 23. — 403 *LG* 22; cf. *CD* 2, 9. — 404 *LG* 22; cf. CIC, can. 336. — 405 CIC, can. 337 § 1. — 406 *LG* 22.

885 "This college, in so far as it is composed of many members, is the expression of the variety and universality of the People of God; and of the unity of the flock of Christ, in so far as it is assembled under one head."[407]

886 "The individual *bishops* are the visible source and foundation of unity in their own particular Churches."[408] As such, they "exercise
1560, 833 their pastoral office over the portion of the People of God assigned to them,"[409] assisted by priests and deacons. But, as a member of the episcopal college, each bishop shares in the concern for all the Churches.[410] The bishops exercise this care first "by ruling well their own Churches as portions of the universal Church," and so contributing "to the welfare of the whole Mystical Body, which, from another point of view, is a corporate body of Churches."[411] They extend it especially to the poor,[412] to those persecuted for the faith, as well
2448 as to missionaries who are working throughout the world.

887 Neighboring particular Churches who share the same culture form ecclesiastical provinces or larger groupings called patriarchates or regions.[413] The bishops of these groupings can meet in synods or provincial councils. "In a like fashion, the episcopal conferences at the present time are in a position to contribute in many and fruitful ways to the concrete realization of the collegiate spirit."[414]

5–87,
032–2040 *The teaching office*

888 Bishops, with priests as co-workers, have as their first task "to preach the Gospel of God to all men," in keeping with the Lord's
command.[415] They are "heralds of 2068
faith, who draw new disciples to Christ; they are authentic teachers" of the apostolic faith "endowed with the authority of Christ."[416]

889 In order to preserve the Church in the purity of the faith handed on by the apostles, Christ who is the Truth willed to confer on
her a share in his own infallibility. 92
By a "supernatural sense of faith" the People of God, under the guidance of the Church's living Magisterium, "unfailingly adheres to this faith."[417]

890 The mission of the Magisterium is linked to the definitive nature of the covenant established by God with his people in Christ. It is this Magisterium's task to preserve God's people from deviations and defec-
tions and to guarantee them the ob- 851
jective possibility of professing the true faith without error. Thus, the pastoral duty of the Magisterium is aimed at seeing to it that the People of God abides in the truth that liberates. To fulfill this service, Christ endowed the Church's shepherds with the charism of infallibility in matters
of faith and morals. The exercise of 1785
this charism takes several forms:

891 "The Roman Pontiff, head of the college of bishops, enjoys this infallibility in virtue of his office, when, as supreme pastor and teacher of all the faithful—who confirms his brethren in the faith—he proclaims by a definitive act a doctrine pertaining to faith or morals.... The

[407] *LG* 22. — [408] *LG* 23. — [409] *LG* 23. — [410] Cf. *CD* 3. — [411] *LG* 23. — [412] Cf. *Gal* 2:10. — [413] Cf. *Apostolic Constitutions* 34. — [414] *LG* 23 § 3. — [415] *PO* 4; cf. *Mk* 16:15. — [416] *LG* 25. — [417] *LG* 12; cf. *DV* 10.

infallibility promised to the Church is also present in the body of bishops when, together with Peter's successor, they exercise the supreme Magisterium," above all in an Ecumenical Council.[418] When the Church through its supreme Magisterium proposes a doctrine "for belief as being divinely revealed,"[419] and as the teaching of Christ, the definitions "must be adhered to with the obedience of faith."[420] This infallibility extends as far as the deposit of divine Revelation itself.[421]

892 Divine assistance is also given to the successors of the apostles, teaching in communion with the successor of Peter, and, in a particular way, to the bishop of Rome, pastor of the whole Church, when, without arriving at an infallible definition and without pronouncing in a "definitive manner," they propose in the exercise of the ordinary Magisterium a teaching that leads to better understanding of Revelation in matters of faith and morals. To this ordinary teaching the faithful "are to adhere to it with religious assent"[422] which, though distinct from the assent of faith, is nonetheless an extension of it.

The sanctifying office

893 The bishop is "the steward of the grace of the supreme priesthood,"[423] especially in the Eucharist which he offers personally or
1561 whose offering he assures through
the priests, his co-workers. The Eucharist is the center of the life of the particular Church. The bishop and priests sanctify the Church by their prayer and work, by their ministry of the word and of the sacraments. They sanctify her by their example, "not as domineering over those in your charge but being examples to the flock."[424] Thus, "together with the flock entrusted to them, they may attain to eternal life."[425]

The governing office

894 "The bishops, as vicars and legates of Christ, govern the particular Churches assigned to them by their counsels, exhortations, and example, but over and above that also by the authority and sacred power"
which indeed they ought to exercise 801
so as to edify, in the spirit of service which is that of their Master.[426]

895 "The power which they exercise personally in the name of Christ, is proper, ordinary, and immediate, although its exercise is ultimately controlled by the supreme 1558
authority of the Church."[427] But the bishops should not be thought of as vicars of the Pope. His ordinary and immediate authority over the whole Church does not annul, but on the contrary confirms and defends that of the bishops. Their authority must be exercised in communion with the whole Church under the guidance of the Pope.

896 The Good Shepherd ought to be the model and "form" of the bishop's pastoral office. Conscious of his own weaknesses, "the bishop...can have compassion for those who are ignorant and erring. He should not
refuse to listen to his subjects whose 1550
welfare he promotes as of his very own children....The faithful...should be closely attached to the bishop as the

[418] *LG* 25; cf. Vatican Council I: DS 3074. — [419] *DV* 10 § 2. — [420] *LG* 25 § 2. — [421] Cf. *LG* 25. — [422] *LG* 25. — [423] *LG* 26. — [424] *1 Pet* 5:3. — [425] *LG* 26 § 3. — [426] *LG* 27; cf. *Lk* 22:26–27. — [427] *LG* 27. — [428] *LG* 27 § 2.

Church is to Jesus Christ, and as Jesus Christ is to the Father":[428]

> Let all follow the bishop, as Jesus Christ follows his Father, and the college of presbyters as the apostles; respect the deacons as you do God's law. Let no one do anything concerning the Church in separation from the bishop.[429]

II. The Lay Faithful

897 "The term 'laity' is here understood to mean all the faithful except those in Holy Orders and those who belong to a religious state approved
873 by the Church. That is, the faithful, who by Baptism are incorporated into Christ and integrated into the People of God, are made sharers in their particular way in the priestly, prophetic, and kingly office of Christ, and have their own part to play in the mission of the whole Christian people in the Church and in the world."[430]

The vocation of lay people

898 "By reason of their special vocation it belongs to the laity to seek the kingdom of God by engaging in temporal affairs and directing
2105 them according to God's will.... It pertains to them in a special way so to illuminate and order all temporal things with which they are closely associated that these may always be effected and grow according to Christ and may be to the glory of the Creator and Redeemer."[431]

899 The initiative of lay Christians is necessary especially when the matter involves discovering or inventing the means for permeating social, po-
2442 litical, and economic realities with the demands of Christian doctrine and life. This initiative is a normal element of the life of the Church:

> Lay believers are in the front line of Church life; for them the Church is the animating principle of human society. Therefore, they in particular ought to have an ever-clearer consciousness not only of belonging to the Church, but of being the Church, that is to say, the community of the faithful on earth under the leadership of the Pope, the common Head, and of the bishops in communion with him. They are the Church.[432]

900 Since, like all the faithful, lay Christians are entrusted by God with the apostolate by virtue of their Baptism and Confirmation, they have
the right and duty, individually or 863
grouped in associations, to work so that the divine message of salvation may be known and accepted by all men throughout the earth. This duty is the more pressing when it is only through them that men can hear the Gospel and know Christ. Their activity in ecclesial communities is so necessary that, for the most part, the apostolate of the pastors cannot be fully effective without it.[433]

The participation of lay people in Christ's priestly office

901 "Hence the laity, dedicated as they are to Christ and anointed by the Holy Spirit, are marvelously called and prepared so that
even richer fruits of the Spirit may 784, 1268
be produced in them. For all their works, prayers, and apostolic undertakings, family and married life, daily work, relaxation of mind and body, if they are accomplished in the

[429] St. Ignatius of Antioch, *Ad Smyrn.* 8, 1: *Apostolic Fathers*, II/2, 309. — [430] *LG* 31. — [431] *LG* 31 § 2. — [432] Pius XII, Discourse, February 20, 1946: AAS 38 (1946) 149; quoted by John Paul II, *CL* 9. — [433] Cf. *LG* 33.

Spirit—indeed even the hardships of life if patiently born—all these become spiritual sacrifices acceptable to God through Jesus Christ. In the celebration of the Eucharist these may most fittingly be offered to the Father along with the body of the Lord. And so, worshipping everywhere by their holy actions, the
358 laity consecrate the world itself to God, everywhere offering worship by the holiness of their lives."[434]

902 In a very special way, parents share in the office of sanctifying "by leading a conjugal life in the Christian spirit and by seeing to the Christian education of their children."[435]

903 Lay people who possess the required qualities can be admitted permanently to the ministries of lector and acolyte.[436] "When the necessity of the Church warrants it
1143 and when ministers are lacking, lay persons, even if they are not lectors or acolytes, can also supply for certain of their offices, namely, to exercise the ministry of the word, to preside over liturgical prayers, to confer Baptism, and to distribute Holy Communion in accord with the prescriptions of law."[437]

Participation in Christ's prophetic office

904 "Christ…fulfills this prophetic office, not only by the hierarchy…
785 but also by the laity. He accordingly both establishes them as witnesses
92 and provides them with the sense of the faith [*sensus fidei*] and the grace of the word"[438]

> To teach in order to lead others to faith is the task of every preacher and of each believer.[439]

905 Lay people also fulfill their 2044
prophetic mission by evangelization, "that is, the proclamation of Christ by word and the testimony of life." For lay people, "this evangelization…acquires a specific property and peculiar efficacy because it is accomplished in the ordinary circumstances of the world."[440]

> This witness of life, however, is not the sole element in the apostolate; the true apostle is on the lookout for occasions of announcing Christ by word, either to unbelievers…or to the faithful.[441] 2472

906 Lay people who are capable 2495
and trained may also collaborate in catechetical formation, in teaching the sacred sciences, and in use of the communications media.[442]

907 "In accord with the knowledge, competence, and preeminence which they possess, [lay people] have the right and even at times a duty to manifest to the sacred pastors their opinion on matters which pertain to the good of the Church, and they have a right to make their opinion known to the other Christian faithful, with due regard to the integrity of faith and morals and reverence toward their pastors, and with consideration for the common good and the dignity of persons."[443]

Participation in Christ's kingly office

908 By his obedience unto death,[444] Christ communicated to his disciples the gift of royal freedom, so that they might "by the self-abnegation of a holy life, overcome the 786
reign of sin in themselves":[445]

[434] *LG* 34; cf. *LG* 10; *1 Pet* 2:5. — [435] CIC, can. 835 § 4. — [436] Cf. CIC, can. 230 § 1. — [437] CIC, can. 230 § 3. — [438] *LG* 35. — [439] St. Thomas Aquinas, *STh*. III, 71, 4 ad 3. — [440] *LG* 35 § 1, § 2. — [441] *AA* 6 § 3; cf. *AG* 15. — [442] Cf. CIC, cann. 229; 774; 776; 780; 823 § 1. — [443] CIC, can. 212 § 3. — [444] Cf. *Phil* 2:8–9. — [445] *LG* 36.

> That man is rightly called a king who makes his own body an obedient subject and, by governing himself with suitable rigor, refuses to let his passions breed rebellion in his soul, for he exercises a kind of royal power over himself. And because he knows how to rule his own person as king, so too does he sit as its judge. He will not let himself be imprisoned by sin, or thrown headlong into wickedness.[446]

909 "Moreover, by uniting their forces let the laity so remedy the institutions and conditions of the world when the latter are an in-
1887 ducement to sin, that these may be conformed to the norms of justice, favoring rather than hindering the practice of virtue. By so doing they will impregnate culture and human works with a moral value."[447]

910 "The laity can also feel called, or be in fact called, to cooperate with their pastors in the service of the ecclesial community, for the sake
799 of its growth and life. This can be done through the exercise of different kinds of ministries according to the grace and charisms which the Lord has been pleased to bestow on them."[448]

911 In the Church, "lay members of the Christian faithful can cooperate in the exercise of this power [of governance] in accord with the norm of law."[449] And so the Church provides for their presence at particular councils, diocesan synods, pastoral councils; the exercise of the pastoral care of a parish, collaboration in finance committees, and participation in ecclesiastical tribunals, etc.[450]

912 The faithful should "distinguish carefully between the rights and the duties which they have as belonging to the Church and those which fall to them as members of 2245
the human society. They will strive to unite the two harmoniously, remembering that in every temporal affair they are to be guided by a Christian conscience, since no human activity, even of the temporal order, can be withdrawn from God's dominion."[451]

913 "Thus, every person, through these gifts given to him, is at once the witness and the living instrument of the mission of the Church itself 'according to the measure of Christ's bestowal.'"[452]

III. The Consecrated Life

914 "The state of life which is constituted by the profession of the evangelical counsels, while not entering into the hierarchical structure of the Church, belongs undeniably 2103
to her life and holiness."[453]

Evangelical counsels, consecrated life

915 Christ proposes the evangelical counsels, in their great variety, to every disciple. The perfection of charity, to which all the faithful are called, entails for those who freely 1973–1974
follow the call to consecrated life the obligation of practicing chastity in celibacy for the sake of the Kingdom, poverty and obedience. It is the *profession* of these counsels, within a permanent state of life recognized by the Church, that characterizes the life consecrated to God.[454]

[446] St. Ambrose, *Psal.* 118:14:30: PL 15:1476. — [447] *LG* 36 § 3. — [448] Paul VI, *EN* 73. — [449] CIC, can. 129 § 2. — [450] Cf. CIC, cann. 443 § 4; 463 §§ 1 and 2; 492 § 1; 511; 517 § 2; 536; 1421 § 2. — [451] *LG* 36 § 4. — [452] *LG* 33 § 2; cf. *Eph* 4:7. — [453] *LG* 44 § 4. — [454] Cf. *LG* 42–43; *PC* 1.

916 The state of consecrated life is thus one way of experiencing a "more intimate" consecration, rooted in Baptism and dedicated totally
2687 to God.[455] In the consecrated life, Christ's faithful, moved by the Holy Spirit, propose to follow Christ more nearly, to give themselves to God who is loved above all and, pursuing the perfection of charity in
933 the service of the Kingdom, to signify and proclaim in the Church the glory of the world to come.[456]

One great tree, with many branches

917 "From the God-given seed of the counsels a wonderful and wide-spreading tree has grown up in the field of the Lord, branching out
2684 into various forms of the religious life lived in solitude or in community. Different religious families have come into existence in which spiritual resources are multiplied for the progress in holiness of their members and for the good of the entire Body of Christ."[457]

918 From the very beginning of the Church there were men and women who set out to follow Christ with greater liberty, and to imitate him more closely, by practicing the evangelical counsels. They led lives dedicated to God, each in his own way. Many of them, under the inspiration of the Holy Spirit, became hermits or founded religious families. These the Church, by virtue of her authority, gladly accepted and approved.[458]

919 Bishops will always strive to discern new gifts of consecrated life granted to the Church by the Holy Spirit; the approval of new forms of consecrated life is reserved to the Apostolic See.[459]

The eremitic life

920 Without always professing the three evangelical counsels publicly, hermits "devote their life to the praise of God and salvation of the world through a stricter separation from the world, the silence of solitude and assiduous prayer and penance."[460]

921 They manifest to everyone the interior aspect of the mystery of the Church, that is, personal intimacy with Christ. Hidden from the
eyes of men, the life of the hermit 2719
is a silent preaching of the Lord, to whom he has surrendered his life simply because he is everything to
him. Here is a particular call to find 2015
in the desert, in the thick of spiritual battle, the glory of the Crucified One.

Consecrated virgins and widows

922 From apostolic times Christian virgins[461] and widows,[462] called by the Lord to cling only to him with greater freedom of heart, body,
and spirit, have decided with the 1618–1620
Church's approval to live in the respective states of virginity or perpetual chastity "for the sake of the Kingdom of heaven."[463]

923 "Virgins who, committed to the holy plan of following Christ more closely, are consecrated to God by the diocesan bishop according to
the approved liturgical rite, are be- 1537
trothed mystically to Christ, the Son of God, and are dedicated to the ser-

[455] Cf. *PC* 5. — [456] Cf. CIC, can. 573. — [457] *LG* 43. — [458] *PC* 1. — [459] Cf. CIC, can. 605. — [460] CIC, can. 603 § 1. — [461] Cf. *1 Cor* 7:34–36. — [462] Cf. John Paul II, *Vita consecrata* 7. — [463] *Mt* 19:12.

vice of the Church."[464] By this solemn
1672 rite (*Consecratio Virginum*), the virgin is "constituted...a sacred person, a transcendent sign of the Church's love for Christ, and an eschatological image of this heavenly Bride of Christ and of the life to come."[465]

924 "As with other forms of consecrated life," the order of virgins establishes the woman living in the world (or the nun) in prayer, penance, service of her brethren, and apostolic activity, according to the state of life and spiritual gifts given to her.[466] Consecrated virgins can form themselves into associations to observe their commitment more faithfully.[467]

Religious life

925 Religious life was born in the East during the first centuries of Christianity. Lived within institutes canonically erected by the Church, it is distinguished from other forms of consecrated life by its liturgical char-
1672 acter, public profession of the evangelical counsels, fraternal life led in common, and witness given to the union of Christ with the Church.[468]

926 Religious life derives from the mystery of the Church. It is a gift she has received from her Lord, a gift she offers as a stable way of life to the faithful called by God to profess the counsels. Thus, the Church can both show forth Christ and acknowledge herself to be the Savior's
796 bride. Religious life in its various forms is called to signify the very charity of God in the language of our time.

927 All religious, whether exempt or not, take their place among the collaborators of the diocesan bishop in his pastoral duty.[469] From the outset of the work of evangelization, the missionary "planting" and expansion of the Church require the 854
presence of the religious life in all its forms.[470] "History witnesses to the outstanding service rendered by religious families in the propagation of the faith and in the formation of new Churches: from the ancient monastic institutions to the medieval orders, all the way to the more recent congregations."[471]

Secular institutes

928 "A secular institute is an institute of consecrated life in which the Christian faithful living in the world strive for the perfection of charity and work for the sanctification of the world especially from within."[472]

929 By a "life perfectly and entirely consecrated to [such] sanctification," the members of these institutes share in the Church's task of evangelization, "in the world and from within the world," where their presence acts as "leaven in the 901
world."[473] "Their witness of a Christian life" aims "to order temporal things according to God and inform the world with the power of the gospel." They commit themselves to the evangelical counsels by sacred bonds and observe among themselves the communion and fellowship appropriate to their "particular secular way of life."[474]

[464] CIC, can. 604 § 1. — [465] *Ordo Consecrationis Virginum, Praenotanda* 1. — [466] Cf. CIC, can. 604 § 1; OCV *Praenotanda* 2. — [467] Cf. CIC, can. 604 § 2. — [468] Cf. CIC, cann. 607; 573; UR 15. — [469] Cf. *CD* 33–35; CIC, can. 591. — [470] Cf. *AG* 18; 40. — [471] John Paul II, *RMiss* 69. — [472] CIC, can. 710. — [473] Pius XII, *Provida Mater*; cf. *PC* 11. — [474] Cf. CIC, can. 713 § 2.

Societies of apostolic life

930 Alongside the different forms of consecrated life are "societies of apostolic life whose members without religious vows pursue the particular apostolic purpose of their society, and lead a life as brothers or sisters in common according to a particular manner of life, strive for the perfection of charity through the observance of the constitutions. Among these there are societies in which the members embrace the evangelical counsels" according to their constitutions.[475]

Consecration and mission: proclaiming the King who is coming

931 Already dedicated to him through Baptism, the person who surrenders himself to the God he loves above all else thereby consecrates himself more intimately to God's service and to the good of the Church. By this state of life consecrated to God, the Church manifests Christ and shows us how the Holy Spirit acts so wonderfully in her. And so the first mission of those who profess the evangelical counsels is to live out their consecration. Moreover, "since members of institutes of consecrated life dedicate themselves through their consecration to the service of the Church they are obliged in a special manner to engage in missionary work, in accord with the character of the institute."[476]

932 In the Church, which is like the sacrament—the sign and instrument—of God's own life, the consecrated life is seen as a special sign of
775 the mystery of redemption. To follow and imitate Christ more nearly and to manifest more clearly his self-emptying is to be more deeply present to one's contemporaries, in the heart of Christ. For those who are on this "narrower" path encourage their brethren by their example, and bear striking witness "that the world cannot be transfigured and offered to God without the spirit of the Beatitudes."[477]

933 Whether their witness is public, as in the religious state, or less public, or even secret, Christ's coming remains for all those consecrated both the origin and rising sun of
their life: 672

> For the People of God has here no 769
> lasting city,...[and this state] reveals more clearly to all believers the heavenly goods which are already present in this age, witnessing to the new and eternal life which we have acquired through the redemptive work of Christ and preluding our future resurrection and the glory of the heavenly kingdom.[478]

In Brief

934 *"Among the Christian faithful by divine institution there exist in the Church sacred ministers, who are also called clerics in law, and other Christian faithful who are also called laity." In both groups there are those Christian faithful who, professing the evangelical counsels, are consecrated to God and so serve the Church's saving mission (cf. CIC, can. 207 § 1, 2).*

935 *To proclaim the faith and to plant his reign, Christ sends his apostles and their successors. He gives them a share in his own mission. From him they receive the power to act in his person.*

[475] Cf. CIC, can. 731 §§ 1 and 2. — [476] CIC, can. 783; cf. *RM* 69. — [477] *LG* 31 § 2. — [478] *LG* 44 § 3.

936 *The Lord made St. Peter the visible foundation of his Church. He entrusted the keys of the Church to him. The bishop of the Church of Rome, successor to St. Peter, is "head of the college of bishops, the Vicar of Christ and Pastor of the universal Church on earth" (CIC, can. 331).*

937 *The Pope enjoys, by divine institution, "supreme, full, immediate, and universal power in the care of souls" (*CD *2).*

938 *The Bishops, established by the Holy Spirit, succeed the apostles. They are "the visible source and foundation of unity in their own particular Churches" (*LG *23).*

939 *Helped by the priests, their co-workers, and by the deacons, the bishops have the duty of authentically teaching the faith, celebrating divine worship, above all the Eucharist, and guiding their Churches as true pastors. Their responsibility also includes concern for all the Churches, with and under the Pope.*

940 *"The characteristic of the lay state being a life led in the midst of the world and of secular affairs, lay people are called by God to make of their apostolate, through the vigor of their Christian spirit, a leaven in the world" (*AA *2 § 2).*

941 *Lay people share in Christ's priesthood: ever more united with him, they exhibit the grace of Baptism and Confirmation in all dimensions of their personal, family, social, and ecclesial lives, and so fulfill the call to holiness addressed to all the baptized.*

942 *By virtue of their prophetic mission, lay people "are called...to be witnesses to Christ in all circumstances and at the very heart of the community of mankind" (*GS *43 § 4).*

943 *By virtue of their kingly mission, lay people have the power to uproot the rule of sin within themselves and in the world, by their self-denial and holiness of life (cf.* LG *36).*

944 *The life consecrated to God is characterized by the public profession of the evangelical counsels of poverty, chastity, and obedience, in a stable state of life recognized by the Church.*

945 *Already destined for him through Baptism, the person who surrenders himself to the God he loves above all else thereby consecrates himself more intimately to God's service and to the good of the whole Church.*

Paragraph 5
THE COMMUNION OF SAINTS 1474–1477

946 After confessing "the holy catholic Church," the Apostles' Creed adds "the communion of saints." In a certain sense this article
is a further explanation of the pre- 823
ceding: "What is the Church if not the assembly of all the saints?"[479] The communion of saints is the Church.

947 "Since all the faithful form one body, the good of each is communicated to the others.... We must therefore believe that there exists a communion of goods in the Church. But the most important member is
Christ, since he is the head.... There- 790
fore, the riches of Christ are communicated to all the members, through the sacraments."[480] "As this Church is governed by one and the same Spirit, all the goods she has received necessarily become a common fund."[481]

[479] Nicetas, *Expl. symb.* 10: PL 52:871B. — [480] St. Thomas Aquinas, *Symb.*, 10. — [481] *Roman Catechism* I, 10, 24.

948 The term "communion of saints" therefore has two closely linked meanings: communion "in
1331 holy things (*sancta*)" and "among holy persons (*sancti*)."

Sancta sanctis! ("God's holy gifts for God's holy people") is proclaimed by the celebrant in most Eastern liturgies during the elevation of the holy Gifts before the distribution of communion. The faithful (*sancti*) are fed by Christ's holy body and blood (sancta) to grow in the communion of the Holy Spirit (koinonia) and to communicate it to the world.

I. Communion in Spiritual Goods

949 In the primitive community of Jerusalem, the disciples "devoted themselves to the apostles' teaching and fellowship, to the breaking of the bread and the prayers."[482]

185 *Communion in the faith.* The faith of the faithful is the faith of the Church, received from the apostles. Faith is a treasure of life which is enriched by being shared.

950 *Communion of the sacraments.* "The fruit of all the sacraments be
1130 longs to all the faithful. All the sacraments are sacred links uniting the faithful with one another and binding them to Jesus Christ, and above all Baptism, the gate by which we enter into the Church. The communion of saints must be understood as the communion of the sacraments.... The name 'communion' can be applied to all of them, for
1331 they unite us to God.... But this name is better suited to the Eucharist than to any other, because it is primarily the Eucharist that brings this communion about."[483]

951 *Communion of charisms.* Within the communion of the Church, the Holy Spirit "distributes special graces among the faithful of every rank" for the building up of 799
the Church.[484] Now, "to each is given the manifestation of the Spirit for the common good."[485]

952 *"They had everything in common."*[486] "Everything the true Christian has is to be regarded as a good possessed in common with everyone else. All Christians should be ready 2402
and eager to come to the help of the needy...and of their neighbors in want."[487] A Christian is a steward of the Lord's goods.[488]

953 *Communion in charity.* In the sanctorum communio, "None of us lives to himself, and none of us dies 1827
to himself."[489] "If one member suffers, all suffer together; if one member is honored, all rejoice together. Now you are the body of Christ and individually members of it."[490]
"Charity does not insist on its own 2011
way."[491] In this solidarity with all men, living or dead, which is founded on the communion of saints, the least of our acts done in charity re- 845, 146
dounds to the profit of all. Every sin harms this communion.

II. The Communion of the Church of Heaven and Earth

954 *The three states of the Church.* "When the Lord comes in glory, and all his angels with him, death will be no more and all things will be subject to him. But at the present time 771
some of his disciples are pilgrims on

[482] *Acts* 2:42. — [483] *Roman Catechism* I, 10, 24. — [484] *LG* 12 § 2. — [485] *1 Cor* 12:7. — [486] *Acts* 4:32. — [487] *Roman Catechism* I, 10, 27. — [488] Cf. *Lk* 16:1, 3. — [489] *Rom* 14:7. — [490] *1 Cor* 12:26–27. — [491] *1 Cor* 13:5; cf. 10:24.

1031 earth. Others have died and are being purified, while still others are in
1023 glory, contemplating 'in full light, God himself triune and one, exactly as he is'":[492]

> All of us, however, in varying degrees and in different ways share in the same charity towards God and our neighbours, and we all sing the one hymn of glory to our God. All, indeed, who are of Christ and who have his Spirit form one Church and in Christ cleave together.[493]

955 "So it is that the union of the wayfarers with the brethren who sleep in the peace of Christ is in no way interrupted, but on the contrary, according to the constant faith of the Church, this union is reinforced by an exchange of spiritual goods."[494]

956 *The intercession of the saints.* "Being more closely united to Christ, those who dwell in heaven fix the whole Church more firmly
1370 in holiness.... [T]hey do not cease to intercede with the Father for us,
2683 as they proffer the merits which they acquired on earth through the one mediator between God and men, Christ Jesus.... So by their fraternal concern is our weakness greatly helped."[495]

> Do not weep, for I shall be more useful to you after my death and I shall help you then more effectively than during my life.[496]
> I want to spend my heaven in doing good on earth.[497]

957 *Communion with the saints.* "It is not merely by the title of example that we cherish the memory of those in heaven; we seek, rather, that by this
devotion to the exercise of fraternal 672
charity the union of the whole Church in the Spirit may be strengthened. Exactly as Christian communion among our fellow pilgrims brings us closer to Christ, so our communion with the saints joins us to Christ, from whom as from its fountain and head issues all grace, and the life of the People of God itself"[498]:

> We worship Christ as God's Son; we love the martyrs as the Lord's disciples and imitators, and rightly so because of their matchless devotion towards their king and master. May we also be their companions and fellow disciples![499]

958 *Communion with the dead.* "In full consciousness of this communion of the whole Mystical Body 1371
of Jesus Christ, the Church in its pilgrim members, from the very earliest days of the Christian religion, 1032, 1689
has honored with great respect the memory of the dead; and 'because it is a holy and a wholesome thought to pray for the dead that they may be loosed from their sins' she offers her suffrages for them."[500] Our prayer for them is capable not only of helping them, but also of making their intercession for us effective.

959 In the one family of God. "For if we continue to love one another and to join in praising the Most Holy Trinity—all of us who are sons of God and form one family
in Christ—we will be faithful to the 1027
deepest vocation of the Church."[501]

[492] *LG* 49; cf. *Mt* 25:31; *1 Cor* 15:26–27; Council of Florence (1439): DS 1305. — [493] *LG* 49; cf. *Eph* 4:16. — [494] *LG* 49. — [495] *LG* 49; cf. *1 Tim* 2:5. — [496] St. Dominic, dying, to his brothers. — [497] St. Thérèse of Lisieux, *The Final Conversations*, tr. John Clarke (Washington: ICS, 1977), 102. — [498] *LG* 50; cf. *Eph* 4:1–6. — [499] *Martyrium Polycarpi*, 17: *Apostolic Fathers* II/3, 396. — [500] *LG* 50; cf. *2 Macc* 12:45. — [501] *LG* 51; cf. *Heb* 3:6.

In Brief

960 *The Church is a "communion of saints": this expression refers first to the "holy things" (sancta), above all the Eucharist, by which "the unity of believers, who form one body in Christ, is both represented and brought about" (*LG *3).*

961 *The term "communion of saints" refers also to the communion of "holy persons" (*sancti*) in Christ who "died for all," so that what each one does or suffers in and for Christ bears fruit for all.*

962 *"We believe in the communion of all the faithful of Christ, those who are pilgrims on earth, the dead who are being purified, and the blessed in heaven, all together forming one Church; and we believe that in this communion, the merciful love of God and his saints is always [attentive] to our prayers" (Paul VI,* CPG *§ 30).*

Paragraph 6

MARY—MOTHER OF CHRIST, MOTHER OF THE CHURCH

963 Since the Virgin Mary's role in the mystery of Christ and the Spirit has been treated, it is fitting now to consider her place in the mystery of
484–507, the Church. "The Virgin Mary…is
721–726 acknowledged and honored as being truly the Mother of God and of the redeemer.… She is 'clearly the mother of the members of Christ'… since she has by her charity joined in bringing about the birth of believers in the Church, who are members of its head."[502] "Mary, Mother of Christ, Mother of the Church."[503]

I. Mary's Motherhood with Regard to the Church

Wholly united with her Son…

964 Mary's role in the Church is inseparable from her union with Christ and flows directly from it. "This union of the mother with the Son in the work of salvation is made manifest from the time of Christ's virginal conception up to his death";[504] it is made manifest above all at the hour of his Passion:

> Thus the Blessed Virgin advanced in 534
> her pilgrimage of faith, and faithfully persevered in her union with her Son unto the cross. There she stood, in keeping with the divine plan, enduring with her only begotten Son the intensity of his suffering, joining herself with his sacrifice in her mother's heart, and lovingly consenting to the immolation of this
> victim, born of her: to be given, by 618
> the same Christ Jesus dying on the cross, as a mother to his disciple, with these words: "Woman, behold your son."[505]

965 After her Son's Ascension, Mary "aided the beginnings of the Church by her prayers."[506] In her association with the apostles and several women, "we also see Mary by her prayers imploring the gift of the Spirit, who had already overshadowed her in the Annunciation."[507]

…also in her Assumption

966 "Finally the Immaculate Virgin, preserved free from all stain of original sin, when the course of her earthly life was finished, was tak-
en up body and soul into heavenly 491
glory, and exalted by the Lord as

[502] *LG* 53; cf. St. Augustine, *De virg.* 6: PL 40, 399. — [503] Paul VI, Discourse, November 21, 1964. — [504] *LG* 57. — [505] *LG* 58; cf. *Jn* 19:26–27. — [506] *LG* 69. — [507] *LG* 59.

Queen over all things, so that she might be the more fully conformed to her Son, the Lord of lords and conqueror of sin and death."[508] The Assumption of the Blessed Virgin is a singular participation in her Son's Resurrection and an anticipation of the resurrection of other Christians:

> In giving birth you kept your virginity; in your Dormition you did not leave the world, O Mother of God, but were joined to the source of Life. You conceived the living God and, by your prayers, will deliver our souls from death.[509]

...she is our Mother in the order of grace

967 By her complete adherence to the Father's will, to his Son's redemptive work, and to every prompting of the Holy Spirit, the Virgin Mary
2679 is the Church's model of faith and charity. Thus she is a "preeminent and...wholly unique member of the Church"; indeed, she is the "exem-
507 plary realization" (*typus*)[510] of the Church.

968 Her role in relation to the Church and to all humanity goes still further. "In a wholly singular way she cooperated by her obedi-
494 ence, faith, hope, and burning charity in the Savior's work of restoring supernatural life to souls. For this reason she is a mother to us in the order of grace."[511]

969 "This motherhood of Mary in the order of grace continues unin-
149, 501 terruptedly from the consent which she loyally gave at the Annunciation and which she sustained without wavering beneath the cross, until the eternal fulfilment of all the elect. Taken up to heaven she did not lay aside this saving office but by her manifold intercession continues to
bring us the gifts of eternal salva- 1370
tion.... Therefore the Blessed Virgin is invoked in the Church under the titles of Advocate, Helper, Benefactress, and Mediatrix."[512]

970 "Mary's function as mother of men in no way obscures or diminishes this unique mediation of Christ, but rather shows its power. But the
Blessed Virgin's salutary influence on 2008
men...flows forth from the superabundance of the merits of Christ, rests on his mediation, depends entirely on it, and draws all its power from it."[513] "No creature could ever be counted along with the Incarnate
Word and Redeemer; but just as the 1545
priesthood of Christ is shared in various ways both by his ministers and the faithful, and as the one goodness of God is radiated in different ways among his creatures, so also the unique mediation of the Redeemer does not exclude but rather gives rise to a manifold cooperation which is
but a sharing in this one source."[514] 308

II. Devotion to the Blessed Virgin 2673–2679

971 *"All generations will call me blessed"*: "The Church's devotion to the Blessed Virgin is intrinsic to Christian worship."[515] The Church
rightly honors "the Blessed Virgin 1172
with special devotion. From the most ancient times the Blessed Virgin has been honored with the title of 'Mother of God,' to whose pro-

[508] *LG* 59; cf. Pius XII, *Munificentissimus Deus* (1950): DS 3903; cf. *Rev* 19:16. — [509] Byzantine Liturgy, *Troparion*, Feast of the Dormition, August 15th. — [510] *LG* 53; 63. — [511] *LG* 61. — [512] *LG* 62. — [513] *LG* 60. — [514] *LG* 62. — [515] *Lk* 1:48; Paul VI, *MC* 56.

tection the faithful fly in all their dangers and needs.... This very special devotion...differs essentially from the adoration which is given to the incarnate Word and equally
2678 to the Father and the Holy Spirit, and greatly fosters this adoration."[516] The liturgical feasts dedicated to the Mother of God and Marian prayer, such as the rosary, an "epitome of the whole Gospel," express this devotion to the Virgin Mary.[517]

III. Mary—Eschatological Icon of the Church

972 After speaking of the Church, her origin, mission, and destiny, we can find no better way to conclude than by looking to Mary. In her we contemplate what the Church already is in her mystery on her own
773 "pilgrimage of faith," and what she will be in the homeland at the end of her journey. There, "in the glory of the Most Holy and Undivided Trinity," "in the communion of all the saints,"[518] the Church is awaited
829 by the one she venerates as Mother of her Lord and as her own mother.

2853 In the meantime the Mother of Jesus, in the glory which she possesses in body and soul in heaven, is the image and beginning of the Church as it is to be perfected in the world to come. Likewise she shines forth on earth, until the day of the Lord shall come, a sign of certain hope and comfort to the pilgrim People of God.[519]

In Brief

973 *By pronouncing her "fiat" at the Annunciation and giving her consent to the Incarnation, Mary was already collaborating with the whole work her Son was to accomplish. She is mother wherever he is Savior and head of the Mystical Body.*

974 *The Most Blessed Virgin Mary, when the course of her earthly life was completed, was taken up body and soul into the glory of heaven, where she already shares in the glory of her Son's Resurrection, anticipating the resurrection of all members of his Body.*

975 *"We believe that the Holy Mother of God, the new Eve, Mother of the Church, continues in heaven to exercise her maternal role on behalf of the members of Christ" (Paul VI, CPG § 15).*

Article 10: "I BELIEVE IN THE FORGIVENESS OF SINS"

976 The Apostle's Creed associates faith in the forgiveness of sins not only with faith in the Holy Spirit, but also with faith in the Church and in the communion of saints. It was when he gave the Holy Spirit to his apostles that the risen Christ conferred on them his own divine power to forgive sins: "Receive the Holy Spirit. If you forgive the sins of any, they are forgiven; if you retain the sins of any, they are retained."[520]

(Part Two of the catechism will deal explicitly with the forgiveness of sins through Baptism, the sacrament of Penance, and the other sacraments,

[516] *LG* 66. — [517] Cf. Paul VI, *MC* 42; SC 103. — [518] *LG* 69. — [519] *LG* 68; cf. *2 Pet* 3:10. — [520] *Jn* 20:22–23.

especially the Eucharist. Here it will suffice to suggest some basic facts briefly.)

1263 I. One Baptism for the Forgiveness of Sins

977 Our Lord tied the forgiveness of sins to faith and Baptism: "Go into all the world and preach the gospel to the whole creation. He who believes and is baptized will be saved."[521] Baptism is the first and chief sacrament of forgiveness of sins because it unites us with Christ, who died for our sins and rose for our justification, so that "we too might walk in newness of life."[522]

978 "When we made our first profession of faith while receiving the holy Baptism that cleansed us, the forgiveness we received then was so full and complete that there remained in us absolutely nothing left to efface, neither original sin nor offenses committed by our own will, nor was there left any penalty to suffer in order to expiate them.... Yet the grace of Baptism delivers no one from all the weakness of nature. On the contrary, we must still combat the movements
1264 of concupiscence that never cease leading us into evil."[523]

979 In this battle against our inclination towards evil, who could be brave and watchful enough to escape every wound of sin? "If the Church has the power to forgive sins, then Baptism cannot be her only means of using the keys of the Kingdom of heaven received from Jesus Christ.
1446 The Church must be able to forgive all penitents their offenses, even if they should sin until the last moment of their lives."[524]

980 It is through the sacrament of Penance that the baptized can be reconciled with God and with the Church: 1422–1484

> Penance has rightly been called by the holy Fathers "a laborious kind of baptism." This sacrament of Penance is necessary for salvation for those who have fallen after Baptism, just as Baptism is necessary for salvation for those who have not yet been reborn.[525]

II. The Power of the Keys

981 After his Resurrection, Christ sent his apostles "so that repentance and forgiveness of sins should be preached in his name to all nations."[526] The apostles and their successors carry out this "ministry of reconciliation," not only by announcing to men God's forgiveness merited for us by Christ, and calling them to conversion and faith; but also by communicating to them the forgiveness of sins in Baptism,
and reconciling them with God and 1444
with the Church through the power of the keys, received from Christ:[527]

> [The Church] has received the keys 553
> of the Kingdom of heaven so that, in her, sins may be forgiven through Christ's blood and the Holy Spirit's action. In this Church, the soul dead through sin comes back to life in order to live with Christ, whose grace has saved us.[528]

982 There is no offense, however serious, that the Church cannot forgive. "There is no one, however

[521] *Mk* 16:15–16. — [522] *Rom* 6:4; cf. 4:25. — [523] *Roman Catechism* I, 11, 3. — [524] *Roman Catechism* I, 11, 4. — [525] Council of Trent (1551): DS 1672; cf. St. Gregory of Nazianzus, *Oratio* 39, 17: PG 36, 356. — [526] *Lk* 24:47. — [527] *2 Cor* 5:18. — [528] St. Augustine, *Sermo* 214, 11: PL 38, 1071–1072.

wicked and guilty, who may not con
1463 fidently hope for forgiveness, provided his repentance is honest."[529] Christ
605 who died for all men desires that in
his Church the gates of forgiveness should always be open to anyone who turns away from sin.[530]

983 Catechesis strives to awaken and nourish in the faithful faith in
1442 the incomparable greatness of the
risen Christ's gift to his Church: the mission and the power to forgive sins through the ministry of the apostles and their successors:

> 1465 The Lord wills that his disciples possess a tremendous power: that his lowly servants accomplish in his name all that he did when he was on earth.[531]
>
> Priests have received from God a power that he has given neither to angels nor to archangels.... God above confirms what priests do here below.[532]
>
> Were there no forgiveness of sins in the Church, there would be no hope of life to come or eternal liberation. Let us thank God who has given his Church such a gift.[533]

In Brief

984 *The Creed links "the forgiveness of sins" with its profession of faith in the Holy Spirit, for the risen Christ entrusted to the apostles the power to forgive sins when he gave them the Holy Spirit.*

985 *Baptism is the first and chief sacrament of the forgiveness of sins: it unites us to Christ, who died and rose, and gives us the Holy Spirit.*

986 *By Christ's will, the Church possesses the power to forgive the sins of the baptized and exercises it through bishops and priests normally in the sacrament of Penance.*

987 *"In the forgiveness of sins, both priests and sacraments are instruments which our Lord Jesus Christ, the only author and liberal giver of salvation, wills to use in order to efface our sins and give us the grace of justification" (*Roman Catechism, *I, 11, 6).*

Article 11:
"I BELIEVE IN THERESURRECTION OF THE BODY"

988 The Christian Creed—the profession of our faith in God, the Father, the Son, and the Holy Spirit, and in God's creative, saving, and sanctifying action—culminates in the proclamation of the resurrection of the dead on the last day and in life everlasting.

989 We firmly believe, and hence we hope that, just as Christ is truly risen from the dead and lives for
ever, so after death the righteous will
live for ever with the risen Christ 655
and he will raise them up on the
last day.[534] Our resurrection, like his 648
own, will be the work of the Most
Holy Trinity:

[529] *Roman Catechism* I, 11, 5. — [530] Cf. *Mt* 18:21–22. — [531] Cf. St. Ambrose, *De poenit.* I, 15: PL 16, 490. — [532] St. John Chrysostom, *De sac.* 3, 5: PG 48, 643. — [533] St. Augustine, *Sermo* 213, 8: PL 38, 1064. — [534] Cf. *Jn* 6:39–40

> If the Spirit of him who raised Jesus from the dead dwells in you, he who raised Christ Jesus from the dead will give life to your mortal bodies also through his Spirit who dwells in you.[535]

990 The term "flesh" refers to man in his state of weakness and mortality.[536] The "resurrection of the flesh" (the literal formulation of the Apostles' Creed) means not only that the immortal soul will live on after death, but that even our "mortal
364 body" will come to life again.[537]

991 Belief in the resurrection of the dead has been an essential ele-
638 ment of the Christian faith from its beginnings. "The confidence of Christians is the resurrection of the dead; believing this we live."[538]

> How can some of you say that there is no resurrection of the dead? But if there is no resurrection of the dead, then Christ has not been raised; if Christ has not been raised, then our preaching is in vain and your faith is in vain.... But in fact Christ has been raised from the dead, the first fruits of those who have fallen asleep.[539]

I. Christ's Resurrection and Ours

The progressive revelation of the Resurrection

992 God revealed the resurrection of the dead to his people progressively. Hope in the bodily resurrection of the dead established itself as a consequence intrinsic to faith in God as creator of the whole man, soul and body. The creator of heaven and earth is also the one who faithfully maintains his covenant with Abraham and his posterity. It
was in this double perspective that 297
faith in the resurrection came to be expressed. In their trials, the Maccabean martyrs confessed:

> The King of the universe will raise us up to an everlasting renewal of life, because we have died for his laws.[540] One cannot but choose to die at the hands of men and to cherish the hope that God gives of being raised again by him.[541]

993 The Pharisees and many of the Lord's contemporaries hoped for the resurrection. Jesus teaches it firmly. To the Sadducees who deny it
he answers, "Is not this why you are 575
wrong, that you know neither the scriptures nor the power of God?"[542] Faith in the resurrection rests on faith in God who "is not God of the
dead, but of the living."[543] 205

994 But there is more. Jesus links faith in the resurrection to his own person: "I am the Resurrection and the life."[544] It is Jesus himself who on the last day will raise up those who have believed in him, who have eaten his body and drunk his blood.[545] Already now in this present life he gives a sign and pledge of this by restoring some of the dead to life,[546] 646
announcing thereby his own Resurrection, though it was to be of another order. He speaks of this unique event as the "sign of Jonah,"[547] the sign of the temple: he announces that he will be put to death but rise thereafter on the third day.[548]

[535] *Rom* 8:11; cf. *1 Thess* 4:14; *1 Cor* 6:14; *2 Cor* 4:14; *Phil* 3:10–11. — [536] Cf. *Gen* 6:3; *Ps* 56:5; *Isa* 40:6. — [537] *Rom* 8:11. — [538] Tertullian, *De res.* 1, 1: PL 2, 841. — [539] *1 Cor* 15:12–14. — [540] *2 Macc* 7:9. — [541] *2 Macc* 7:14; cf. 7:29; *Dan* 12:1–13. — [542] *Mk* 12:24; cf. *Jn* 11:24; *Acts* 23:6. — [543] *Mk* 12:27. — [544] *Jn* 11:25. — [545] Cf. *Jn* 5:24–25; 6:40, 54. — [546] Cf. *Mk* 5:21–42; *Lk* 7:11–17; *Jn* 11. — [547] *Mt* 12:39. — [548] Cf. *Mk* 10:34; *Jn* 2:19–22.

860 **995** To be a witness to Christ is to
be a "witness to his Resurrection," to
655 "[have eaten and drunk] with him
after he rose from the dead."[549] Encounters with the risen Christ characterize the Christian hope of resurrection. We shall rise like Christ, with him, and through him.

996 From the beginning, Christian faith in the resurrection has met with incomprehension and opposition.[550] "On no point does
643 the Christian faith encounter more
opposition than on the resurrection of the body."[551] It is very commonly accepted that the life of the human person continues in a spiritual fashion after death. But how can we believe that this body, so clearly mortal, could rise to everlasting life?

How do the dead rise?

997 *What is "rising"?* In death, the separation of the soul from the body, the human body decays and the soul goes to meet God, while awaiting
366 its reunion with its glorified body.
God, in his almighty power, will definitively grant incorruptible life to our bodies by reuniting them with our souls, through the power of Jesus' Resurrection.

998 *Who will rise?* All the dead will rise, "those who have done good, to the resurrection of life, and those who have done evil, to the res-
1038 urrection of judgment."[552]

999 *How?* Christ is raised with his own body: "See my hands and my feet, that it is I myself";[553] but he did not return to an earthly life. So,
in him, "all of them will rise again
with their own bodies which they
now bear," but Christ "will change 640
our lowly body to be like his glorious body," into a "spiritual body":[554] 645

> But someone will ask, "How are the dead raised? With what kind of body do they come?" You foolish man! What you sow does not come to life unless it dies. And what you sow is not the body which is to be, but a bare kernel.... What is sown is perishable, what is raised is imperishable.... The dead will be raised imperishable.... For this perishable nature must put on the imperishable, and this mortal nature must put on immortality.[555]

1000 This "how" exceeds our imagination and understanding; it is accessible only to faith. Yet our participation in the Eucharist already gives us a foretaste of Christ's transfiguration of our bodies: 647

> Just as bread that comes from the 1405
> earth, after God's blessing has been invoked upon it, is no longer ordinary bread, but Eucharist, formed of two things, the one earthly and the other heavenly: so too our bodies, which partake of the Eucharist, are no longer corruptible, but possess the hope of resurrection.[556]

1001 *When?* Definitively "at the 1038
last day," "at the end of the world."[557]
Indeed, the resurrection of the dead 673
is closely associated with Christ's Parousia:

> For the Lord himself will descend from heaven, with a cry of command, with the archangel's call, and with the sound of the trumpet of God. And the dead in Christ will rise first.[558]

[549] *Acts* 1:22; 10:41; cf. 4:33. — [550] Cf. *Acts* 17:32; *1 Cor* 15:12–13. — [551] St. Augustine, *En. in Ps.* 88, 5: PL 37, 1134. — [552] *Jn* 5:29; cf. *Dan* 12:2. — [553] *Lk* 24:39. — [554] Lateran Council IV (1215): DS 801; *Phil* 3:21; *1 Cor* 15:44. — [555] *1 Cor* 15:35–37, 42, 52, 53. — [556] St. Irenaeus, *Adv. haeres.* 4, 18, 4–5: PG 7/1, 1028–1029. — [557] *Jn* 6:39–40, 44, 54; 11:24; *LG* 48 § 3. — [558] *1 Thess* 4:16.

Risen with Christ

1002 Christ will raise us up "on the last day"; but it is also true that, in a certain way, we have already risen with Christ. For, by virtue of the
655 Holy Spirit, Christian life is already
now on earth a participation in the death and Resurrection of Christ:

> And you were buried with him in Baptism, in which you were also raised with him through faith in the working of God, who raised him from the dead.... If then you have been raised with Christ, seek the things that are above, where Christ is, seated at the right hand of God.[559]

1003 United with Christ by Baptism, believers already truly participate in the heavenly life of the risen Christ, but this life remains "hidden
1227 with Christ in God."[560] The Father
has already "raised us up with him,
2796 and made us sit with him in the
heavenly places in Christ Jesus."[561] Nourished with his body in the Eucharist, we already belong to the Body of Christ. When we rise on the last day we "also will appear with him in glory."[562]

1004 In expectation of that day, the believer's body and soul already participate in the dignity of belonging to Christ. This dignity entails
364 the demand that he should treat
with respect his own body, but also
1397 the body of every other person, especially the suffering:

> The body [is meant] for the Lord, and the Lord for the body. And God raised the Lord and will also raise us up by his power. Do you not know that your bodies are members of Christ?... You are not your own;... So glorify God in your body.[563]

II. Dying in Christ Jesus

1005 To rise with Christ, we must die with Christ: we must "be away from the body and at home with the Lord."[564] In that "departure" which is death the soul is separated from the body.[565] It will be reunited with the body on the day of resurrection
of the dead.[566] 650

Death

1006 "It is in regard to death that man's condition is most shrouded in doubt."[567] In a sense bodily death is natural, but for faith it is in fact "the wages of sin."[568] For those who die in Christ's grace it is a participation in the death of the Lord, so that they can also share his Resurrection.[569]

1007 *Death is the end of earthly life.* Our lives are measured by time, in the course of which we change, grow old and, as with all living beings on earth, death seems like the normal end of life. That aspect of death lends urgency to our lives: remembering our mortality helps us realize that we have only a limited time in which to bring our lives to fulfillment:

> Remember also your Creator in the days of your youth,...before the dust returns to the earth as it was, and the spirit returns to God who gave it.[570]

1008 *Death is a consequence of sin.* The Church's Magisterium, as authentic interpreter of the affirmations of Scripture and Tradition,

[559] *Col* 2:12; 3:1. — [560] *Col* 3:3; cf. *Phil* 3:20. — [561] *Eph* 2:6. — [562] *Col* 3:4. — [563] *1 Cor* 6:13–15, 19–20. — [564] *2 Cor* 5:8. — [565] Cf. *Phil* 1:23. — [566] Cf. Paul VI, *CPG* § 28. — [567] *GS* 18. — [568] *Rom* 6:23; cf. *Gen* 2:17. — [569] Cf. *Rom* 6:3–9; *Phil* 3:10–11. — [570] *Eccl* 12:1, 7.

teaches that death entered the world on account of man's sin.[571] Even
401 though man's nature is mortal, God had destined him not to die. Death was therefore contrary to the plans of God the Creator and entered the world as a consequence of sin.[572] "Bodily death, from which man
376 would have been immune had he not sinned" is thus "the last enemy" of man left to be conquered.[573]

1009 *Death is transformed by Christ.* Jesus, the Son of God, also himself suffered the death that is part of the human condition. Yet,
612 despite his anguish as he faced death, he accepted it in an act of complete and free submission to his Father's will.[574] The obedience of Jesus has transformed the curse of death into a blessing.[575]

1681–1690 *The meaning of Christian death*

1010 Because of Christ, Christian death has a positive meaning: "For to me to live is Christ, and to die is gain."[576] "The saying is sure: if we have died with him, we will also live with him."[577] What is essentially new about Christian death is this: through Baptism, the Christian has already "died with Christ" sacramentally, in
1220 order to live a new life; and if we die in Christ's grace, physical death completes this "dying with Christ" and so completes our incorporation into him in his redeeming act:

> It is better for me to die in (eis) Christ Jesus than to reign over the ends of the earth. Him it is I seek—who died for us. Him it is I desire—who rose for us. I am on the point of giving birth.... Let me receive pure light; when I shall have arrived there, then shall I be a man.[578]

1011 In death, God calls man to himself. Therefore the Christian can experience a desire for death like St. Paul's: "My desire is to depart and be with Christ."[579] He can transform his own death into an act of obedience and love towards the Father, after the example of Christ:[580] 1025

> My earthly desire has been crucified;...there is living water in me, water that murmurs and says within me: Come to the Father.[581]

> I want to see God and, in order to see him, I must die.[582]

> I am not dying; I am entering life.[583]

1012 The Christian vision of death receives privileged expression in the liturgy of the Church:[584]

> Lord, for your faithful people life is changed, not ended. When the body of our earthly dwelling lies in death we gain an everlasting dwelling place in heaven.[585]

1013 Death is the end of man's earthly pilgrimage, of the time of grace and mercy which God offers him so as to work out his earthly life in keeping with the divine plan, and to decide his ultimate destiny. When "the single course of our earthly life" is completed,[586] we shall not return

[571] Cf. *Gen* 2:17; 3:3; 3:19; *Wis* 1:13; *Rom* 5:12; 6:23; *DS* 1511. — [572] Cf. *Wis* 2:23–24. — [573] *GS* 18 § 2; cf. *1 Cor* 15:26. — [574] Cf. *Mk* 14:33–34; *Heb* 5:7–8. — [575] Cf. *Rom* 5:19–21. — [576] *Phil* 1:21. — [577] *2 Tim* 2:11. — [578] St. Ignatius of Antioch, *Ad Rom.*, 6, 1–2: *Apostolic Fathers*, II/2, 217–220. — [579] *Phil* 1:23. — [580] Cf. *Lk* 23:46. — [581] St. Ignatius of Antioch, *Ad Rom.*, 6, 1– 2: *Apostolic Fathers*, II/2, 223–224. — [582] St. Teresa of Avila, *Life*, chap. 1. — [583] St. Thérèse of Lisieux, *The Last Conversations.* — [584] Cf. 1 *Thess* 4:13–14. — [585] *Roman Missal*, Preface of Christian Death I. — [586] *LG* 48 § 3.

to other earthly lives: "It is appointed for men to die once."[587] There is no "reincarnation" after death.

1014 The Church encourages us to prepare ourselves for the hour of our death. In the ancient litany of the saints, for instance, she has us pray: "From a sudden and unforeseen death, deliver us, O Lord";[588] to ask the Mother of God to intercede for us "at the hour of our death" in the *Hail Mary*; and to entrust ourselves to St. Joseph, the patron of a
676–2677 happy death.

> Every action of yours, every thought, should be those of one who expects to die before the day is out. Death would have no great terrors for you if you had a quiet conscience.... Then why not keep clear of sin instead of running away from death? If you aren't fit to face death today, it's very unlikely you will be tomorrow....[589]

> Praised are you, my Lord, for our sister bodily Death,
> from whom no living man can escape.
> Woe on those who will die in mortal sin!
> Blessed are they who will be found in your most holy will,
> for the second death will not harm them.[590]

In Brief

1015 *"The flesh is the hinge of salvation" (Tertullian,* De res. *8, 2: PL 2, 852). We believe in God who is creator of the flesh; we believe in the Word made flesh in order to redeem the flesh; we believe in the resurrection of the flesh, the fulfillment of both the creation and the redemption of the flesh.*

1016 *By death the soul is separated from the body, but in the resurrection God will give incorruptible life to our body, transformed by reunion with our soul. Just as Christ is risen and lives for ever, so all of us will rise at the last day.*

1017 *"We believe in the true resurrection of this flesh that we now possess" (Council of Lyons II: DS 854). We sow a corruptible body in the tomb, but he raises up an incorruptible body, a "spiritual body" (cf.* 1 Cor *15:42–44).*

1018 *As a consequence of original sin, man must suffer "bodily death, from which man would have been immune had he not sinned"* (GS *§ 18).*

1019 *Jesus, the Son of God, freely suffered death for us in complete and free submission to the will of God, his Father. By his death he has conquered death, and so opened the possibility of salvation to all men.*

Article 12:
"I BELIEVE IN LIFE EVERLASTING"

523–1525 **1020** The Christian who unites his own death to that of Jesus views it as a step towards him and an entrance into everlasting life. When the Church for the last time speaks Christ's words of pardon and absolution over the dying Christian, seals him for the last time with a strengthening anointing, and gives him Christ in viaticum as nourishment for the journey, she speaks with gentle assurance:

[587] *Heb* 9:27. — [588] *Roman Missal,* Litany of the Saints. — [589] *The Imitation of Christ,* 1, 23, 1. — [590] St. Francis of Assisi, *Canticle of the Creatures.*

Go forth, Christian soul, from this world in the name of God the almighty Father, who created you, in the name of Jesus Christ, the Son of the living God, who suffered for you, in the name of the Holy Spirit, who was poured out upon you. Go forth, faithful Christian!

May you live in peace this day, may your home be with God in Zion, with Mary, the virgin Mother of God, with Joseph, and all the angels and saints....

2677, 336 May you return to [your Creator] who formed you from the dust of the earth. May holy Mary, the angels, and all the saints come to meet you as you go forth from this life.... May you see your Redeemer face to face....[591]

I. The Particular Judgment

1021 Death puts an end to human life as the time open to either accepting or rejecting the divine grace manifested in Christ.[592] The New Testament speaks of judgment primarily in its aspect of the final encounter with Christ in his second coming, but also repeatedly affirms that each will be rewarded immediately after death in
379 accordance with his works and faith. The parable of the poor man Lazarus and the words of Christ on the cross to the good thief, as well as other New Testament texts speak of a final destiny of the soul—a destiny which can be different for some and for others.[593]

1022 Each man receives his eternal retribution in his immortal soul
393 at the very moment of his death, in a particular judgment that refers his life to Christ: either entrance into the blessedness of heaven—through a purification[594] or immediately,[595]—or immediate and everlasting damnation.[596]

At the evening of life, we shall be judged on our love.[597] 1470

II. Heaven

1023 Those who die in God's grace and friendship and are perfectly purified live for ever with Christ.
They are like God for ever, for they 954
"see him as he is," face to face:[598]

By virtue of our apostolic authority, we define the following: According to the general disposition of God, the souls of all the saints...and other faithful who died after receiving Christ's holy Baptism (provided they were not in need of purification when they died,...or, if they then did need or will need some purification, when they have been purified after death,...) already before they take up their bodies again and before the general judgment—and this since the Ascension of our Lord and Savior Jesus Christ into heaven—have been, are and will be in heaven, in the heavenly Kingdom and celestial paradise with Christ, joined to the company of the holy angels. Since the Passion and death of our Lord Jesus Christ, these souls have seen and do see the divine essence with an intuitive vision, and even face to face, without the mediation of any creature.[599]

1024 This perfect life with the Most Holy Trinity—this communion

[591] *OCF*, Prayer of Commendation. — [592] Cf. *2 Tim* 1:9–10. — [593] Cf. *Lk* 16:22; 23:43; *Mt* 16:26; *2 Cor* 5:8; *Phil* 1:23; *Heb* 9:27; 12:23. — [594] Cf. Council of Lyons II (1274): DS 857–858; Council of Florence (1439): DS 1304–1306; Council of Trent (1563): DS 1820. — [595] Cf. Benedict XII, *Benedictus Deus* (1336): DS 1000–1001; John XXII, *Ne super his* (1334): DS 990. — [596] Cf. Benedict XII, *Benedictus Deus* (1336): DS 1002. — [597] St. John of the Cross, *Dichos* 64. — [598] *1 Jn* 3:2; cf. *1 Cor* 13:12; *Rev* 22:4. — [599] Benedict XII, *Benedictus Deus* (1336): DS 1000; cf. *LG* 49.

of life and love with the Trinity, with the Virgin Mary, the angels and all the
260, 326 blessed—is called "heaven." Heaven is the ultimate end and fulfillment of the
794, 1718 deepest human longings, the state of supreme, definitive happiness.

1025 To live in heaven is "to be with Christ." The elect live "in Christ,"[600] but they retain, or rather
1011 find, their true identity, their own name.[601]

> For life is to be with Christ; where Christ is, there is life, there is the kingdom.[602]

1026 By his death and Resurrection, Jesus Christ has "opened" heaven to us. The life of the blessed consists in the full and perfect possession of the fruits of the redemption accomplished by Christ. He makes partners in his heavenly glorification those who have believed
793 in him and remained faithful to his will. Heaven is the blessed community of all who are perfectly incorporated into Christ.

1027 This mystery of blessed communion with God and all who are in Christ is beyond all understanding and description. Scripture speaks of
59, 1720 it in images: life, light, peace, wedding feast, wine of the kingdom, the Father's house, the heavenly Jerusalem, paradise: "no eye has seen, nor ear heard, nor the heart of man conceived, what God has prepared for those who love him."[603]

1028 Because of his transcendence, God cannot be seen as he is, unless he
himself opens up his mystery to man's 1722
immediate contemplation and gives
him the capacity for it. The Church 163
calls this contemplation of God in his heavenly glory "the beatific vision":

> How great will your glory and happiness be, to be allowed to see God, to be honored with sharing the joy of salvation and eternal light with Christ your Lord and God,... to delight in the joy of immortality in the Kingdom of heaven with the righteous and God's friends.[604]

1029 In the glory of heaven the 956
blessed continue joyfully to fulfill
God's will in relation to other men 668
and to all creation. Already they reign with Christ; with him "they shall reign for ever and ever."[605]

III. The Final Purification, or Purgatory

1030 All who die in God's grace and friendship, but still imperfectly purified, are indeed assured of their eternal salvation; but after death they undergo purification, so as to achieve the holiness necessary to enter the joy of heaven.

1031 The Church gives the name
Purgatory to this final purification
of the elect, which is entirely dif- 954, 1472
ferent from the punishment of the damned.[606] The Church formulated her doctrine of faith on Purgatory especially at the Councils of Florence and Trent. The tradition of the Church, by reference to certain texts of Scripture, speaks of a cleansing fire:[607]

[600] *Phil* 1:23; cf. *Jn* 14:3; *1 Thess* 4:17. — [601] Cf. *Rev* 2:17. — [602] St. Ambrose, *In Luc.*, 10, 121: PL 15, 1834A. — [603] *1 Cor* 2:9. — [604] St. Cyprian, *Ep.* 58, 10, 1: CSEL 3/2, 665. — [605] *Rev* 22:5; cf. *Mt* 25:21, 23. — [606] Cf. Council of Florence (1439): DS 1304; Council of Trent (1563): DS 1820; (1547): 1580; see also Benedict XII, *Benedictus Deus* (1336): DS 1000. — [607] Cf. *1 Cor* 3:15; *1 Pet* 1:7.

> As for certain lesser faults, we must believe that, before the Final Judgment, there is a purifying fire. He who is truth says that whoever utters blasphemy against the Holy Spirit will be pardoned neither in this age nor in the age to come. From this sentence we understand that certain offenses can be forgiven in this age, but certain others in the age to come.[608]

1032 This teaching is also based on the practice of prayer for the dead,
958 already mentioned in Sacred Scripture: "Therefore [Judas Maccabeus] made atonement for the dead, that they might be delivered from their
1371 sin."[609] From the beginning the Church has honored the memory of the dead and offered prayers in suffrage for them, above all the Eucha-
1479 ristic sacrifice, so that, thus purified, they may attain the beatific vision of God.[610] The Church also commends almsgiving, indulgences, and works of penance undertaken on behalf of the dead:

> Let us help and commemorate them. If Job's sons were purified by their father's sacrifice, why would we doubt that our offerings for the dead bring them some consolation? Let us not hesitate to help those who have died and to offer our prayers for them.[611]

IV. Hell

1033 We cannot be united with God unless we freely choose to love him. But we cannot love God if we sin gravely against him, against our neighbor or against ourselves: "He who does not love remains in death. Anyone who hates his brother is a murderer, and you know that no murderer has eternal life abiding in him."[612] Our Lord warns us
that we shall be separated from him 1861
if we fail to meet the serious needs
of the poor and the little ones who 393
are his brethren.[613] To die in mortal
sin without repenting and accepting 633
God's merciful love means remaining separated from him for ever by our own free choice. This state of definitive self-exclusion from communion with God and the blessed is called "hell."

1034 Jesus often speaks of "Gehenna," of "the unquenchable fire" reserved for those who to the end of their lives refuse to believe and be converted, where both soul and body can be lost.[614] Jesus solemnly proclaims that he "will send his angels, and they will gather...all evil doers, and throw them into the furnace of fire,"[615] and that he will pronounce the condemnation: "Depart from me, you cursed, into the eternal fire!"[616]

1035 The teaching of the Church affirms the existence of hell and its eternity. Immediately after death the souls of those who die in a state of mortal sin descend into hell, where they suffer the punishments of hell, "eternal fire."[617] The chief punishment of hell is eternal separation
from God, in whom alone man can 393
possess the life and happiness for which he was created and for which he longs.

[608] St. Gregory the Great, *Dial.* 4, 39: PL 77, 396; cf. *Mt* 12:31. — [609] *2 Macc* 12:46. — [610] Cf. Council of Lyons II (1274): DS 856. — [611] St. John Chrysostom, *Hom. in 1 Cor.* 41, 5: PG 61, 361; cf. *Job* 1:5. — [612] *1 Jn* 3:14–15. — [613] Cf. *Mt* 25:31–46. — [614] Cf. *Mt* 5:22, 29; 10:28; 13:42, 50; *Mk* 9:43–48. — [615] *Mt* 13:41–42. — [616] *Mt* 25:41. — [617] Cf. DS 76; 409; 411; 801; 858; 1002; 1351; 1575; Paul VI, *CPG* § 12

1036 The affirmations of Sacred Scripture and the teachings of the Church on the subject of hell are a *call to the responsibility* incumbent
1734 upon man to make use of his freedom in view of his eternal destiny.
1428 They are at the same time an urgent *call to conversion*: "Enter by the narrow gate; for the gate is wide and the way is easy, that leads to destruction, and those who enter by it are many. For the gate is narrow and the way is hard, that leads to life, and those who find it are few."[618]

> Since we know neither the day nor the hour, we should follow the advice of the Lord and watch constantly so that, when the single course of our earthly life is completed, we may merit to enter with him into the marriage feast and be numbered among the blessed, and not, like the wicked and slothful servants, be ordered to depart into the eternal fire, into the outer darkness where "men will weep and gnash their teeth."[619]

1037 God predestines no one to go to hell;[620] for this, a willful turn-
162 ing away from God (a mortal sin) is necessary, and persistence in it until
1014, 1821 the end. In the Eucharistic liturgy and in the daily prayers of her faithful, the Church implores the mercy of God, who does not want "any to perish, but all to come to repentance":[621]

> Father, accept this offering from your whole family. Grant us your peace in this life, save us from final damnation, and count us among those you have chosen.[622]

V. The Last Judgment 678–679

1038 The resurrection of all the dead, "of both the just and the unjust,"[623] will precede the Last Judgment. This will be "the hour when 1001, 998
all who are in the tombs will hear [the Son of man's] voice and come forth, those who have done good, to the resurrection of life, and those who have done evil, to the resurrection of judgment."[624] Then Christ will come "in his glory, and all the angels with him.... Before him will be gathered all the nations, and he will separate them one from another as a shepherd separates the sheep from the goats, and he will place the sheep at his right hand, but the goats at the left.... And they will go away into eternal punishment, but the righteous into eternal life."[625]

1039 In the presence of Christ, who is Truth itself, the truth of each man's relationship with God will be laid bare.[626] The Last Judgment will reveal even to its furthest consequences the good each person
has done or failed to do during his 678
earthly life:

> All that the wicked do is recorded, and they do not know. When "our God comes, he does not keep silence."...he will turn towards those at his left hand:..."I placed my poor little ones on earth for you. I as their head was seated in heaven at the right hand of my Father—but on earth my members were suffering, my members on earth were in need. If you gave anything to my members, what you gave would reach their Head. Would that you had known that my little

[618] *Mt* 7:13–14. — [619] *LG* 48 § 3; *Mt* 22:13; cf. *Heb* 9:27; *Mt* 25:13, 26, 30, 31–46. — [620] Cf. Council of Orange II (529): DS 397; Council of Trent (1547): 1567. — [621] 1 *Pet* 3:9. — [622] *Roman Missal*, EP I (Roman Canon) 88. — [623] *Acts* 24:15. — [624] *Jn* 5:28–29. — [625] *Mt* 25:31, 32, 46. — [626] Cf. *Jn* 12:49.

ones were in need when I placed them on earth for you and appointed them your stewards to bring your good works into my treasury. But you have placed nothing in their hands; therefore you have found nothing in my presence."[627]

1040 The Last Judgment will come when Christ returns in glory. Only the Father knows the day and the hour; only he determines the moment of its coming. Then
637 through his Son Jesus Christ he will pronounce the final word on all history. We shall know the ultimate meaning of the whole work of creation and of the entire economy of salvation and understand the marvellous ways by which his
314 Providence led everything towards its final end. The Last Judgment will reveal that God's justice triumphs over all the injustices committed by his creatures and that God's love is stronger than death.[628]

1041 The message of the Last Judgment calls men to conversion while God is still giving them "the acceptable time,...the day of salva-
1432 tion."[629] It inspires a holy fear of God and commits them to the justice of the Kingdom of God. It proclaims the "blessed hope" of the Lord's return, when he will come "to be glorified in his saints, and to be marvelled at in all who have believed."[630]

2854 VI. The Hope of the New Heaven and the New Earth

1042 At the end of time, the Kingdom of God will come in its fullness. After the universal judgment, the righteous will reign for
ever with Christ, glorified in body 769
and soul. The universe itself will be
renewed: 670

> The Church...will receive her perfection only in the glory of heaven, when will come the time of the renewal of all things. At that
> time, together with the human race, 310
> the universe itself, which is so closely related to man and which attains its destiny through him, will be perfectly re-established in Christ.[631]

1043 Sacred Scripture calls this mysterious renewal, which will transform humanity and the world, "new heavens and a new earth."[632] It
will be the definitive realization of 671
God's plan to bring under a single
head "all things in [Christ], things in 280, 518
heaven and things on earth.[633]

1044 In this new universe, the heavenly Jerusalem, God will have his dwelling among men.[634] "He will wipe away every tear from their eyes, and death shall be no more, neither shall there be mourning nor crying nor pain any more, for the former things have passed away."[635]

1045 *For man*, this consummation will be the final realization of the unity of the human race, which God willed from creation and of which
the pilgrim Church has been "in the 775
nature of sacrament."[636] Those who are united with Christ will form the community of the redeemed, "the
holy city" of God, "the Bride, the 1404
wife of the Lamb."[637] She will not be wounded any longer by sin, stains, self-love, that destroy or wound the earthly community.[638] The beatific

[627] St. Augustine, *Sermo* 18, 4: PL 38, 130–131; cf. *Ps* 50:3. — [628] Cf. *Song* 8:6. — [629] *2 Cor* 6:2. — [630] *Titus* 2:13; *2 Thess* 1:10. — [631] *LG* 48; cf. *Acts* 3:21; *Eph* 1:10; *Col* 1:20; *2 Pet* 3:10–13. — [632] *2 Pet* 3:13; cf. *Rev* 21:1. — [633] *Eph* 1:10. — [634] Cf. *Rev* 21:5. — [635] *Rev* 21:4. — [636] Cf. *LG* 1. — [637] *Rev* 21:2, 9. — [638] Cf. *Rev* 21:27.

vision, in which God opens himself in an inexhaustible way to the elect, will be the ever-flowing well-spring of happiness, peace, and mutual communion.

1046 *For the cosmos,* Revelation affirms the profound common destiny of the material world and man:

349 For the creation waits with eager longing for the revealing of the sons of God…in hope because the creation itself will be set free from its bondage to decay.… We know that the whole creation has been groaning in travail together until now; and not only the creation, but we ourselves, who have the first fruits of the Spirit, groan inwardly as we wait for adoption as sons, the redemption of our bodies.[639]

1047 The visible universe, then, is itself destined to be transformed, "so that the world itself, restored to its original state, facing no further obstacles, should be at the service of the just," sharing their glorification in the risen Jesus Christ.[640]

1048 "We know neither the moment of the consummation of the earth and of man, nor the way in which the universe will be transformed. The form of this world,
673 distorted by sin, is passing away, and we are taught that God is preparing a new dwelling and a new earth in which righteousness dwells, in which happiness will fill and surpass all the desires of peace arising in the hearts of men."[641]

1049 "Far from diminishing our concern to develop this earth, the expectancy of a new earth should spur us on, for it is here that the body of a new human family grows, foreshadowing in some way the age which is to come. That is why, although we must be careful to distinguish earthly progress clearly from the increase of the kingdom of
Christ, such progress is of vital con- 2820
cern to the kingdom of God, insofar as it can contribute to the better ordering of human society."[642]

1050 "When we have spread on earth the fruits of our nature and our enterprise…according to the command of the Lord and in his
Spirit, we will find them once again, 1709
cleansed this time from the stain of sin, illuminated and transfigured, when Christ presents to his Father an eternal and universal king- 260
dom."[643] God will then be "all in all" in eternal life:[644]

True and subsistent life consists in this: the Father, through the Son and in the Holy Spirit, pouring out his heavenly gifts on all things without exception. Thanks to his mercy, we too, men that we are, have received the inalienable promise of eternal life.[645]

In Brief

1051 *Every man receives his eternal recompense in his immortal soul from the moment of his death in a particular judgment by Christ, the judge of the living and the dead.*

1052 *"We believe that the souls of all who die in Christ's grace…are the People of God beyond death. On the day of resurrection, death will be definitively conquered, when these souls will be reunited with their bodies" (Paul VI,* CPG *§ 28).*

[639] *Rom* 8:19–23. — [640] St. Irenaeus, *Adv. haeres.* 5, 32, 1: PG 7/2, 210. — [641] *GS* 39 § 1. — [642] *GS* 39 § 2. — [643] *GS* 39 § 3. — [644] 1 *Cor* 5:28. — [645] St. Cyril of Jerusalem, *Catech. illum.* 18, 29: PG 33, 1049.

1053 *"We believe that the multitude of those gathered around Jesus and Mary in Paradise forms the Church of heaven, where in eternal blessedness they see God as he is and where they are also, to various degrees, associated with the holy angels in the divine governance exercised by Christ in glory, by interceding for us and helping our weakness by their fraternal concern" (Paul VI,* CPG *§ 29).*

1054 *Those who die in God's grace and friendship imperfectly purified, although they are assured of their eternal salvation, undergo a purification after death, so as to achieve the holiness necessary to enter the joy of God.*

1055 *By virtue of the "communion of saints," the Church commends the dead to God's mercy and offers her prayers, especially the holy sacrifice of the Eucharist, on their behalf.*

1056 *Following the example of Christ, the Church warns the faithful of the "sad and lamentable reality of eternal death" (*GCD *69), also called "hell."*

1057 *Hell's principal punishment consists of eternal separation from God in whom alone man can have the life and happiness for which he was created and for which he longs.*

1058 *The Church prays that no one should be lost: "Lord, let me never be parted from you." If it is true that no one can save himself, it is also true that God "desires all men to be saved" (*1 Tim *2:4), and that for him "all things are possible" (*Mt *19:26).*

1059 *"The holy Roman Church firmly believes and confesses that on the Day of Judgment all men will appear in their own bodies before Christ's tribunal to render an account of their own deeds" (Council of Lyons II [1274]: DS 859; cf. DS 1549).*

1060 *At the end of time, the Kingdom of God will come in its fullness. Then the just will reign with Christ for ever, glorified in body and soul, and the material universe itself will be transformed. God will then be "all in all" (*1 Cor *15:28), in eternal life.*

"Amen"

1061 The Creed, like the last book of the Bible,[646] ends with the Hebrew word amen. This word frequently concludes prayers in the New Testament. The Church like
2856 wise ends her prayers with "Amen."

1062 In Hebrew, amen comes from the same root as the word "believe." This root expresses solidity, trustworthiness, faithfulness. And
214 so we can understand why "Amen" may express both God's faithfulness towards us and our trust in him.

1063 In the book of the prophet Isaiah, we find the expression "God of truth" (literally "God of the Amen"), that is, the God who is faithful to his promises: "He who
blesses himself in the land shall 215
bless himself by the God of truth [amen]."[647] Our Lord often used the
word "Amen," sometimes repeat- 156
ed,[648] to emphasize the trustworthiness of his teaching, his authority founded on God's truth.

[646] Cf. *Rev* 22:21. — [647] *Isa* 65:16. — [648] Cf. *Mt* 6:2, 5, 16; *Jn* 5:19.

1064 Thus the Creed's final "Amen" repeats and confirms its first words: "I believe." To believe is to say "Amen" to God's words, prom-
197, 2101 ises and commandments; to entrust oneself completely to him who is the "Amen" of infinite love and perfect faithfulness. The Christian's everyday life will then be the "Amen" to the "I believe" of our baptismal profession of faith:

> May your Creed be for you as a mirror. Look at yourself in it, to see if you believe everything you say you believe. And rejoice in your faith each day.[649]

1065 Jesus Christ himself is the "Amen."[650] He is the definitive "Amen" of the Father's love for us. He takes up and completes our "Amen" to the Father: "For all the promises of God find their Yes in him. That is why we utter the Amen through him, to the glory of God":[651]

> Through him, with him, in him,
> in the unity of the Holy Spirit,
> all glory and honor is yours,
> almighty Father,
> God, for ever and ever.
> **AMEN.**

[649] St. Augustine, *Sermo* 58, 11, 13: PL 38, 399. — [650] *Rev* 3:14. — [651] *2 Cor* 1:20.

PART TWO

THE CELEBRATION OF THE CHRISTIAN MYSTERY

Why the liturgy?

1066 In the Symbol of the faith the Church confesses the mystery of the Holy Trinity and of the plan of God's "good pleasure" for all creation: the Father accomplishes the
50 "mystery of his will" by giving his beloved Son and his Holy Spirit for the salvation of the world and for the glory of his name.[1] Such is the mystery of Christ, revealed and fulfilled in history according to the wisely ordered plan that St. Paul
236 calls the "plan of the mystery"[2] and the patristic tradition will call the "economy of the Word incarnate" or the "economy of salvation."

1067 "The wonderful works of God among the people of the Old Testament were but a prelude to the work of Christ the Lord in redeeming mankind and giving perfect glory to God. He accomplished this work principally by the Paschal mystery of his blessed Passion, Resurrection from the dead, and glorious Ascension, whereby 'dying he destroyed our death, rising he restored our life.' For it was from the side of Christ as he slept the sleep of death upon the cross that there came forth 'the wondrous sacrament of the whole Church.'"[3] For this reason, the Church celebrates in the liturgy above all the Paschal mystery by which Christ accomplished the
571 work of our salvation.

1068 It is this mystery of Christ that the Church proclaims and celebrates in her liturgy so that the faithful may live from it and bear witness to it in the world:

> For it is in the liturgy, especially in the divine sacrifice of the Eucharist, that "the work of our redemption is accomplished," and it is through the liturgy especially that the faithful are enabled to express in their lives and manifest to others the mystery of Christ and the real nature of the true Church.[4]

What does the word liturgy mean?

1069 The word "liturgy" originally meant a "public work" or a "service in the name of/on behalf of the people." In Christian tradition it means the participation of the People of God in "the work of God."[5] Through the liturgy Christ, our redeemer and high priest, continues the work of our redemption in, with, and through his Church.

1070 In the New Testament the word "liturgy" refers not only to the celebration of divine worship but also to the proclamation of the Gospel and to active charity.[6] In all of these situations it is a question of the service of God and neighbor. In a liturgical celebration the Church is servant in the image of her Lord, the one "*leitourgos*";[7] she shares
in Christ's priesthood (worship), 783
which is both prophetic (proclamation) and kingly (service of charity):

> The liturgy then is rightly seen as an exercise of the priestly office of Jesus Christ. It involves the presentation of man's sanctification under the guise of signs perceptible by the senses and its accomplishment in ways appropriate to each of these signs. In it full public worship is performed by the Mystical Body of Jesus Christ, that is, by the Head and his

[1] *Eph* 1:9. — [2] *Eph* 3:9; cf. 3:4. — [3] *SC* 5 § 2; cf. St. Augustine, *En. in Ps.* 138, 2: PL 37, 1784–1785. — [4] *SC* 2. — [5] Cf. *Jn* 17:4. — [6] Cf. *Lk* 1:23; *Acts* 13:2; *Rom* 15:16, 27; 2 *Cor* 9:12; *Phil* 2:14–17, 25, 30. — [7] Cf. *Heb* 8:2, 6.

members. From this it follows that every liturgical celebration, because it is an action of Christ the priest and of his Body which is the Church, is a sacred action surpassing all others. No other action of the Church can equal its efficacy by the same title and to the same degree.[8]

Liturgy as source of life

1071 As the work of Christ liturgy is also an action of his *Church*. It makes the Church present and manifests her as the visible sign of the communion in Christ between God and men. It engages the faithful in the new life of the community and involves the "conscious, active, and
1692 fruitful participation" of everyone.[9]

1072 "The sacred liturgy does not exhaust the entire activity of the Church":[10] it must be preceded by evangelization, faith, and conversion. It can then produce its fruits in the lives of the faithful: new life in the Spirit, involvement in the mission of the Church, and service to her unity.

Prayer and liturgy

1073 The liturgy is also a participation in Christ's own prayer addressed to the Father in the Holy Spirit. In the liturgy, all Christian prayer finds its source and goal. Through the liturgy the inner man is rooted and grounded in "the great love with which [the Father] loved us" in his beloved Son.[11] It is the same "marvelous work of God" that is lived and internalized by all
prayer, "at all times in the Spirit."[12] 2558

Catechesis and liturgy

1074 "The liturgy is the summit toward which the activity of the Church is directed; it is also the font from which all her power flows."[13] It is therefore the privileged place for catechizing the People of God. "Catechesis is intrinsically linked with the whole of liturgical and sacramental activity, for it is in the sacraments, especially in the Eucharist, that Christ Jesus works in fullness for the transformation of men."[14]

1075 Liturgical catechesis aims to 426
initiate people into the mystery of Christ (It is "mystagogy.") by proceeding from the visible to the invisible, from the sign to the thing signified, from the "sacraments" to the
"mysteries." Such catechesis is to be 774
presented by local and regional catechisms. This Catechism, which aims to serve the whole Church in all the diversity of her rites and cultures,[15] will present what is fundamental and common to the whole Church in the liturgy as mystery and as celebration (*Section One*), and then the seven sacraments and the sacramentals (*Section Two*).

[8] *SC* 7 § 2–3. — [9] *SC* 11. — [10] *SC* 9. — [11] *Eph* 2:4; 3:16–17. — [12] *Eph* 6:18. — [13] *SC* 10. — [14] John Paul II, *CT* 23. — [15] Cf. *SC* 3–4.

Section One

THE SACRAMENTAL ECONOMY

1076 The Church was made manifest to the world on the day of Pentecost by the outpouring of the Holy Spirit.[1] The gift of the Spirit ushers in a new era in the "dispensation of the mystery"—the age of the Church, during which Christ manifests, makes present, and
739 communicates his work of salvation through the liturgy of his Church, "until he comes."[2] In this age of the Church Christ now lives and acts in and with his Church, in a new way appropriate to this new age. He acts through the sacraments in what the common Tradition of the East and the West calls "the sacramental economy"; this is the communication (or "dispensation") of the fruits of Christ's Paschal mystery in the celebration of the Church's "sacramental" liturgy. It is therefore important first to explain this "sacramental dispensation" (*chapter one*). The nature and essential features of liturgical celebration will then appear more clearly (*chapter two*).

[1] Cf. *SC* 6; *LG* 2. — [2] *1 Cor* 11:26.

Chapter One:

THE PASCHAL MYSTERY IN THE AGE OF THE CHURCH

Article 1:

THE LITURGY—WORK OF THE HOLY TRINITY

I. The Father—Source and Goal of the Liturgy

1077 "Blessed be the God and Father of our Lord Jesus Christ, who has blessed us in Christ with every spiritual blessing in the heav-
492 enly places, even as he chose us in him before the foundation of the world, that we should be holy and blameless before him. He destined us before him in love to be his sons through Jesus Christ, according to the purpose of his will, to the praise of his glorious grace which he freely bestowed on us in the Beloved."[3]

2626 **1078** Blessing is a divine and life-giving action, the source of which is the Father; his blessing is both word and gift.[4] When applied to man, the word "blessing" means adoration and surrender to his Creator in thanksgiving.

1079 From the beginning until the end of time the whole of God's work is a *blessing*. From the liturgical poem of the first creation to the canticles of the heavenly Jerusalem, the inspired authors proclaim the plan of salvation as one vast divine blessing.

1080 From the very beginning God blessed all living beings, especially man and woman. The covenant with Noah and with all living things renewed this blessing of fruitfulness despite man's sin which had brought a curse on the ground. But with Abraham, the divine blessing entered into human history which was moving toward death, to redirect it toward life, toward its source. By the faith of "the father of all believers," who embraced the blessing, the history of salvation is inaugurated.

1081 The divine blessings were made manifest in astonishing and saving events: the birth of Isaac, the escape from Egypt (Passover and Exodus), the gift of the promised land, the election of David, the presence of God in the Temple, the purifying exile, and return of a "small remnant." The Law, the Prophets, and the Psalms, interwoven in the liturgy of the Chosen People, recall these divine blessings and at the same time respond to them with blessings of praise and thanksgiving.

1082 In the Church's liturgy the divine blessing is fully revealed and communicated. The Father is acknowledged and adored as the source and the end of all the blessings of creation and salvation. In his Word who became incarnate, died, and rose for us, he fills us with his blessings. Through his Word, he pours into our hearts the Gift that contains all gifts, the Holy Spirit.

[3] *Eph* 1:3–6. — [4] *eu-logia, bene-dictio.*

2627 **1083** The dual dimension of the Christian liturgy as a response of faith and love to the spiritual blessings the Father bestows on us is thus evident. On the one hand, the Church, united with her Lord and "in the Holy Spirit,"[5] blesses the Father "for his inexpressible gift"[6] in her adoration, praise, and thanksgiving. On the other hand, until the consummation of God's plan, the Church never ceases to present to the Father the offering
1360 of his own gifts and to beg him to send the Holy Spirit upon that offering, upon herself, upon the faithful, and upon the whole world, so that through communion in the death and resurrection of Christ the Priest, and by the power of the Spirit, these divine blessings will bring forth the fruits of life "to the praise of his glorious grace."[7]

II. Christ's Work in the Liturgy

Christ glorified...

662 **1084** "Seated at the right hand of the Father" and pouring out the Holy Spirit on his Body which is the Church, Christ now acts through the sacraments he instituted to communicate his grace. The sacraments
1127 are perceptible signs (words and actions) accessible to our human nature. By the action of Christ and the power of the Holy Spirit they make present efficaciously the grace that they signify.

1085 In the liturgy of the Church, it is principally his own Paschal mystery that Christ signifies and makes present. During his earthly life Jesus announced his Paschal mystery by his teaching and anticipated it by his actions. When his Hour comes, he lives out the unique event of history which does not pass away: Jesus dies, is buried, rises from the dead, and is seated at the right hand of the Father "once for all."[8] His Paschal mystery is a real event that occurred in our history, but it is unique: all other historical events happen once, and then they pass away, swallowed up in the past. The Paschal mystery of Christ, by contrast, cannot remain only in the past, because by
his death he destroyed death, and all 519
that Christ is—all that he did and suffered for all men—participates in the divine eternity, and so transcends all times while being made
present in them all. The event of the 1165
Cross and Resurrection *abides* and draws everything toward life.

...from the time of the Church of the Apostles...

1086 "Accordingly, just as Christ 858
was sent by the Father so also he sent the apostles, filled with the Holy Spirit. This he did so that they might preach the Gospel to every creature and proclaim that the Son of God by his death and resurrection had freed us from the power of Satan and from death and brought us into the Kingdom of his Father. But he also willed that the work of salvation which they preached should be set in train through the sacrifice and sacraments, around which the entire liturgical life revolves."[9]

1087 Thus the risen Christ, by giving the Holy Spirit to the apostles, entrusted to them his power of sanctifying:[10] they became sacramental signs of Christ. By the power of

[5] *Lk* 10:21. — [6] *2 Cor* 9:15. — [7] *Eph* 1:6. — [8] *Rom* 6:10; Heb 7:27; 9:12; cf. *Jn* 13:1; 17:1. — [9] *SC* 6. — [10] Cf. *Jn* 20:21-23.

the same Holy Spirit they entrusted
861 this power to their successors. This "apostolic succession" structures the whole liturgical life of the Church and is itself sacramental, handed on
1536 by the sacrament of Holy Orders.

...is present in the earthly liturgy...

1088 "To accomplish so great a work"—the dispensation or communication of his work of salvation—"Christ is always present in his Church, especially in her litur-
776 gical celebrations. He is present in the Sacrifice of the Mass not only in
669 the person of his minister, 'the same now offering, through the ministry of priests, who formerly offered himself on the cross,' but especially in the Eucharistic species. By his power he is present in the sacraments
1373 so that when anybody baptizes, it is really Christ himself who baptizes. He is present in his word since it is he himself who speaks when the holy Scriptures are read in the Church. Lastly, he is present when the Church prays and sings, for he has promised 'where two or three are gathered together in my name there am I in the midst of them.'"[11]

1089 "Christ, indeed, always associates the Church with himself in this great work in which God is perfectly glorified and men are sanctified. The Church is his beloved
796 Bride who calls to her Lord and through him offers worship to the eternal Father."[12]

...which participates in the liturgy of heaven

7–1139 **1090** "In the earthly liturgy we share in a foretaste of that heavenly liturgy which is celebrated in the Holy City of Jerusalem toward which we journey as pilgrims, where Christ is sitting at the right hand of God, Minister of the sanctuary and of the true tabernacle. With all the warriors of the heavenly army we sing a hymn of glory to the Lord; venerating the memory of the saints, we hope for some part and fellowship with them; we eagerly await the Savior, our Lord Jesus Christ, until he, our life, shall appear and we too will appear with him in glory."[13]

III. The Holy Spirit and the Church in the Liturgy

1091 In the liturgy the Holy Spirit is teacher of the faith of the People of God and artisan of "God's masterpieces," the sacraments of the New
Covenant. The desire and work of 798
the Spirit in the heart of the Church is that we may live from the life of the risen Christ. When the Spirit encounters in us the response of faith which he has aroused in us, he brings about genuine cooperation. Through it, the liturgy becomes the common work of the Holy Spirit and the Church.

1092 In this sacramental dispensation of Christ's mystery the Holy Spirit acts in the same way as at other times in the economy of salvation:
he prepares the Church to encounter 737
her Lord; he recalls and makes Christ manifest to the faith of the assembly. By his transforming power, he makes the mystery of Christ present here and now. Finally the Spirit of communion unites the Church to the life and mission of Christ.

[11] *SC* 7; *Mt* 18:20. — [12] *SC* 7. — [13] *SC* 8; cf. *LG* 50.

The Holy Spirit prepares for the reception of Christ

1093 In the sacramental economy the Holy Spirit fulfills what was prefigured in the Old Covenant. Since Christ's Church was "prepared in
762 marvellous fashion in the history of the people of Israel and in the Old Covenant,"[14] the Church's liturgy has retained certain elements of the worship of the Old Covenant as integral and irreplaceable, adopting them as her own:

121 – notably, reading the Old Testament;

2585 – praying the Psalms;

1081 – above all, recalling the saving events and significant realities which have found their fulfillment in the mystery of Christ (promise and covenant, Exodus and Passover, kingdom and temple, exile and return).

128–130 **1094** It is on this harmony of the two Testaments that the Paschal catechesis of the Lord is built,[15] and then, that of the Apostles and the Fathers of the Church. This catechesis unveils what lay hidden under the letter of the Old Testament: the mystery of Christ. It is called "typological" because it reveals the newness of Christ on the basis of the "figures" (types) which announce him in the deeds, words, and symbols of the first covenant. By this re-reading in the Spirit of Truth, starting from Christ, the figures are unveiled.[16] Thus the flood and Noah's ark prefigured salvation by Baptism,[17] as did the cloud and the crossing of the Red Sea. Water from the rock was the figure of the spiritual gifts of Christ, and manna in the desert prefigured the Eucharist, "the true bread from heaven."[18]

1095 For this reason the Church, especially during Advent and Lent and above all at the Easter Vigil, rereads and re-lives the great events of
salvation history in the "today" of 281
her liturgy. But this also demands that catechesis help the faithful to open themselves to this spiritual understanding of the economy of sal- 117
vation as the Church's liturgy reveals it and enables us to live it.

1096 *Jewish liturgy and Christian liturgy.* A better knowledge of the Jewish people's faith and religious life as professed and lived even now can help our better understanding of certain aspects of Christian liturgy. For both Jews and Christians Sacred Scripture is an essential part of their respective liturgies: in the proclamation of the Word of God, the response to this word, prayer of praise and intercession for the living and the dead, invocation of God's mercy. In its characteristic structure the Liturgy of the Word originates in Jewish prayer. The Liturgy of the Hours and other liturgical texts
and formularies, as well as those of 1174
our most venerable prayers, including the Lord's Prayer, have parallels in Jewish prayer. The Eucharistic Prayers also draw their inspiration from the Jewish tradition. The relationship between Jewish liturgy 1352
and Christian liturgy, but also their differences in content, are particularly evident in the great feasts of the liturgical year, such as Passover. Christians and Jews both celebrate the Passover. For Jews, it is the

[14] *LG* 2. — [15] Cf. *DV* 14–16; *Lk* 24:13–49. — [16] Cf. *2 Cor* 3:14–16. — [17] Cf. *1 Pet* 3:21. — [18] *Jn* 6:32; cf. *1 Cor* 10:1–6.

840 Passover of history, tending toward the future; for Christians, it is the Passover fulfilled in the death and Resurrection of Christ, though always in expectation of its definitive consummation.

1097 In the *liturgy of the New Covenant* every liturgical action, especially the celebration of the Eucharist and the sacraments, is an encounter between Christ and the Church. The liturgical assembly derives its unity from the "communion of the Holy Spirit" who gathers the children of God into the one Body of Christ. This assembly transcends racial, cultural, social—indeed, all human affinities.

1098 The assembly should *prepare* itself to encounter its Lord and to become "a people well disposed." The preparation of hearts is the joint work of the Holy Spirit and the assembly, especially of its ministers. The grace of the Holy Spirit seeks to awaken faith, conversion of heart,
1430 and adherence to the Father's will. These dispositions are the precondition both for the reception of other graces conferred in the celebration itself and the fruits of new life which the celebration is intended to produce afterward.

The Holy Spirit recalls the mystery of Christ

1099 The Spirit and the Church cooperate to manifest Christ and his work of salvation in the liturgy. Primarily in the Eucharist, and by analogy in the other sacraments, the liturgy is the memorial of the mys-
91 tery of salvation. The Holy Spirit is the Church's living memory.[19]

1100 *The Word of God.* The Holy 1134
Spirit first recalls the meaning of the salvation event to the liturgical assembly by giving life to the Word of God, which is proclaimed so that it may be received and lived:

> In the celebration of the liturgy, Sacred 103, 131
> Scripture is extremely important. From it come the lessons that are read and explained in the homily and the psalms that are sung. It is from the Scriptures that the prayers, collects, and hymns draw their inspiration and their force, and that actions and signs derive their meaning.[20]

1101 The Holy Spirit gives a spir- 117
itual understanding of the Word of God to those who read or hear it, according to the dispositions of their hearts. By means of the words, actions, and symbols that form the structure of a celebration, the Spirit puts both the faithful and the ministers into a living relationship with Christ, the Word and Image of the Father, so that they can live out the meaning of what they hear, contemplate, and do in the celebration.

1102 "By the saving word of God, faith…is nourished in the hearts of believers. By this faith then the congregation of the faithful begins and grows."[21] The proclamation does not stop with a teaching; it elicits the *response of faith* as consent and commitment, directed at the covenant
between God and his people. Once 143
again it is the Holy Spirit who gives the grace of faith, strengthens it and makes it grow in the community. The liturgical assembly is first of all a communion in faith.

1103 *Anamnesis.* The liturgical 1362
celebration always refers to God's

[19] Cf. *Jn* 14:26. — [20] *SC* 24. — [21] *PO* 4.

saving interventions in history. "The economy of Revelation is realized by deeds and words which are intrinsically bound up with each other.... [T]he words for their part proclaim the works and bring to light the mystery they contain."[22] In the Liturgy of the Word the Holy Spirit "recalls" to the assembly all that Christ has done for us. In keeping with the nature of liturgical actions and the ritual traditions of the churches, the celebration "makes a remembrance" of the marvelous works of God in an anamnesis which may be more or less developed. The Holy Spirit who thus awakens the memory of the Church then inspires thanksgiving and praise (*doxology*).

The Holy Spirit makes present the mystery of Christ

1104 Christian liturgy not only recalls the events that saved us but actualizes them, makes them present. The Paschal mystery of Christ
1085 is celebrated, not repeated. It is the celebrations that are repeated, and in each celebration there is an outpouring of the Holy Spirit that makes the unique mystery present.

1105 The *Epiclesis* ("invocation upon") is the intercession in which the priest begs the Father to send the Holy Spirit, the Sanctifier, so that the
1153 offerings may become the body and blood of Christ and that the faithful, by receiving them, may themselves become a living offering to God.[23]

1106 Together with the anamnesis, the epiclesis is at the heart of each sacramental celebration, most especially of the Eucharist:

> You ask how the bread becomes the 1375
> Body of Christ, and the wine... the Blood of Christ. I shall tell you: the Holy Spirit comes upon them and accomplishes what surpasses every word and thought.... Let it be enough for you to understand that it is by the Holy Spirit, just as it was of the Holy Virgin and by the Holy Spirit that the Lord, through and in himself, took flesh.[24]

1107 The Holy Spirit's transforming power in the liturgy hastens the coming of the kingdom and the consummation of the mystery of salvation. While we wait in hope he causes us really to anticipate the fullness of communion with the Holy 2816
Trinity. Sent by the Father who hears the epiclesis of the Church, the Spirit gives life to those who accept him and is, even now, the "guarantee" of their inheritance.[25]

The communion of the Holy Spirit

1108 In every liturgical action the Holy Spirit is sent in order to bring us into communion with Christ and so to form his Body. The Holy Spirit is like the sap of the Father's vine 788
which bears fruit on its branches.[26]
The most intimate cooperation of 1091
the Holy Spirit and the Church is achieved in the liturgy. The Spirit, who is the Spirit of communion, abides indefectibly in the Church. For this reason the Church is the
great sacrament of divine commu- 775
nion which gathers God's scattered children together. Communion with the Holy Trinity and fraternal communion are inseparably the fruit of the Spirit in the liturgy.[27]

[22] *DV* 2. — [23] Cf. *Rom* 12:1. — [24] St. John Damascene, *De fide orth.* 4, 13: PG 94, 1145A. — [25] *Eph* 1:14; *2 Cor* 1:22. — [26] Cf. *Jn* 15:1–17; *Gal* 5:22. — [27] Cf. 1 *Jn* 1:3–7.

1109 The epiclesis is also a prayer for the full effect of the assembly's communion with the mystery of Christ. "The grace of the Lord Jesus Christ and the love of God and the fellowship of the Holy Spirit"[28] have to remain with us always and bear fruit beyond the Eucharistic celebration. The Church therefore asks the Father to send the Holy Spirit to make the lives of the faithful a living sacrifice to
1368 God by their spiritual transformation into the image of Christ, by concern for the Church's unity, and by taking part in her mission through the witness and service of charity.

In Brief

1110 *In the liturgy of the Church, God the Father is blessed and adored as the source of all the blessings of creation and salvation with which he has blessed us in his Son, in order to give us the Spirit of filial adoption.*

1111 *Christ's work in the liturgy is sacramental: because his mystery of salvation is made present there by the power of his Holy Spirit; because his Body, which is the Church, is like a sacrament (sign and instrument) in which the Holy Spirit dispenses the mystery of salvation; and because through her liturgical actions the pilgrim Church already participates, as by a foretaste, in the heavenly liturgy.*

1112 *The mission of the Holy Spirit in the liturgy of the Church is to prepare the assembly to encounter Christ; to recall and manifest Christ to the faith of the assembly; to make the saving work of Christ present and active by his transforming power; and to make the gift of communion bear fruit in the Church.*

Article 2: THE PASCHAL MYSTERY IN THE CHURCH'S SACRAMENTS

1210 **1113** The whole liturgical life of the Church revolves around the Eucharistic sacrifice and the sacraments.[29] There are seven sacraments in the Church: Baptism, Confirmation or Chrismation, Eucharist, Penance, Anointing of the Sick, Holy Orders, and Matrimony.[30] This article will discuss what is common to the Church's seven sacraments from a doctrinal point of view. What is common to them in terms of their celebration will be presented in the second chapter, and what is distinctive about each will be the topic of the *Section Two*.

I. The Sacraments of Christ

1114 "Adhering to the teaching of the Holy Scriptures, to the apostolic traditions, and to the consensus... of the Fathers," we profess that "the sacraments of the new law were... all instituted by Jesus Christ our Lord."[31]

1115 Jesus' words and actions during his hidden life and public ministry were already salvific, for they anticipated the power of his Paschal mystery. They announced and prepared what he was going

[28] *2 Cor* 13:13. — [29] Cf. *SC* 6. — [30] Cf. Council of Lyons II (1274) DS 860; Council of Florence (1439): DS 1310; Council of Trent (1547): DS 1601. — [31] Council of Trent (1547): DS 1600-1601.

512–560 to give the Church when all was accomplished. The mysteries of Christ's life are the foundations of what he would henceforth dispense in the sacraments, through the ministers of his Church, for "what was visible in our Savior has passed over into his mysteries."[32]

1116 Sacraments are "powers
1504 that comes forth" from the Body of Christ,[33] which is ever-living and
774 life-giving. They are actions of the Holy Spirit at work in his Body, the Church. They are "the masterworks of God" in the new and everlasting covenant.

II. The Sacraments of the Church

120 **1117** As she has done for the canon of Sacred Scripture and for the doctrine of the faith, the Church, by the power of the Spirit who guides her "into all truth," has gradually recognized this treasure received from Christ and, as the faithful steward of God's mysteries, has determined its "dispensation."[34] Thus the Church has discerned over the centuries that among liturgical celebrations there are seven that are, in the strict sense of the term, sacraments instituted by the Lord.

1118 The sacraments are "of the Church" in the double sense that they are "by her" and "for her." They are "by the Church," for she is the sacrament of Christ's action at work in her through the mission
1396 of the Holy Spirit. They are "for the Church" in the sense that "the sacraments make the Church,"[35] since they manifest and communicate to men, above all in the Eucharist, the mystery of communion with the God who is love, One in three persons.

1119 Forming "as it were, one 792
mystical person" with Christ the head, the Church acts in the sacraments as "an organically structured priestly community."[36] Through Baptism and Confirmation the priestly people is enabled to celebrate the liturgy, while those of the faithful "who have received Holy Orders, are appointed to nourish the Church with the word and grace of God in the name of Christ."[37]

1120 The ordained ministry or 1547
ministerial priesthood is at the service of the baptismal priesthood.[38] The ordained priesthood guarantees that it really is Christ who acts in the sacraments through the Holy Spirit for the Church. The saving mission entrusted by the Father to his incarnate Son was committed to the apostles and through them to their successors: they receive the Spirit of Jesus to act in his name and in his person.[39] The ordained minister is the sacramental bond that ties the liturgical action to what the apostles said and did and, through them, to the words and actions of Christ, the source and foundation of the sacraments.

1121 The three sacraments of Baptism, Confirmation, and Holy Orders confer, in addition to grace, a sacramental *character* or "seal" by
which the Christian shares in Christ's 1272, 1
priesthood and is made a member of
the Church according to different 1582

[32] St. Leo the Great, *Sermo*. 74, 2: PL 54, 398. — [33] Cf. *Lk* 5:17; 6:19; 8:46. — [34] *Jn* 16:13; cf. *Mt* 13:52; *1 Cor* 4:1. — [35] St. Augustine, *De civ. Dei*, 22, 17: PL 41, 779; cf. St. Thomas Aquinas, *STh* III, 64, 2 *ad* 3. — [36] *LG* 11; cf. Pius XII, *Mystici Corporis* (1943). — [37] *LG* 11 § 2. — [38] Cf. *LG* 10 § 2. — [39] Cf. *Jn* 20:21–23; *Lk* 24:47; *Mt* 28:18–20.

states and functions. This configuration to Christ and to the Church, brought about by the Spirit, is indelible;[40] it remains for ever in the Christian as a positive disposition for grace, a promise and guarantee of divine protection, and as a vocation to divine worship and to the service of the Church. Therefore these sacraments can never be repeated.

III. The Sacraments of Faith

1122 Christ sent his apostles so that "repentance and forgiveness of sins should be preached in his name to all nations."[41] "Go therefore and make disciples of all nations, baptizing them in the name of the Father and of the Son and of the Holy Spirit."[42] The mission to baptize, and so the sacramental mission, is implied in the mission to evangelize, because
849 the sacrament is prepared for *by the word of God and by the faith* which is
1236 assent to this word:

> The People of God is formed into one in the first place by the Word of the living God.... The preaching of the Word is required for the sacramental ministry itself, since the sacraments are sacraments of faith, drawing their origin and nourishment from the Word.[43]

1123 "The purpose of the sacraments is to sanctify men, to build up the Body of Christ and, finally, to give worship to God. Because they are signs they also instruct. They not only presuppose faith, but by words and
1154 objects they also nourish, strengthen, and express it. That is why they are called 'sacraments *of faith*.'"[44]

1124 The Church's faith precedes the faith of the believer who 166
is invited to adhere to it. When the Church celebrates the sacraments, she confesses the faith received from the apostles—whence the ancient saying: *lex orandi, lex credendi* (or: 1327
legem credendi lex statuat supplicandi, according to Prosper of Aquitaine [5th cent.]).[45] The law of prayer is the law of faith: the Church believes 78
as she prays. Liturgy is a constitutive element of the holy and living Tradition.[46]

1125 For this reason no sacramen- 1205
tal rite may be modified or manipulated at the will of the minister or the community. Even the supreme authority in the Church may not change the liturgy arbitrarily, but only in the obedience of faith and with religious respect for the mystery of the liturgy.

1126 Likewise, since the sacraments express and develop the communion of faith in the Church, the *lex orandi* is one of the essential criteria of the dialogue that seeks to 815
restore the unity of Christians.[47]

IV. The Sacraments of Salvation

1127 Celebrated worthily in faith, the sacraments confer the grace that they signify.[48] They are *efficacious* because in them Christ himself is at work: it is he who baptizes, he who acts in his sacraments 1084
in order to communicate the grace that each sacrament signifies. The Father always hears the prayer of his Son's Church which, in the epiclesis of each sacrament, expresses her 1105
faith in the power of the Spirit. As fire transforms into itself everything 696

[40] Cf. Council of Trent (1547): DS 1609. — [41] *Lk* 24:47. — [42] *Mt* 28:19. — [43] *PO* 4 §§ 1, 2. — [44] *SC* 59. — [45] *Ep.* 8. — [46] Cf. *DV* 8. — [47] Cf. *UR* 2; 15. — [48] Cf. Council of Trent (1547): DS 1605; DS 1606.

it touches, so the Holy Spirit transforms into the divine life whatever is subjected to his power.

1128 This is the meaning of the Church's affirmation[49] that the sacraments act *ex opere operato* (literally: "by the very fact of the action's being performed"), i.e., by virtue of the saving work of Christ, accomplished once for all. It follows that "the sacrament is not wrought by the righteousness of either the celebrant or the recipient, but by the
1584 power of God."[50] From the moment that a sacrament is celebrated in accordance with the intention of the Church, the power of Christ and his Spirit acts in and through it, independently of the personal holiness of the minister. Nevertheless, the fruits of the sacraments also depend on the disposition of the one who receives them.

1257 **1129** The Church affirms that for believers the sacraments of the New
2003 Covenant are *necessary for salvation.*[51] "Sacramental grace" is the grace of the Holy Spirit, given by Christ and proper to each sacrament. The Spirit heals and transforms those who receive him by conforming them
460 to the Son of God. The fruit of the sacramental life is that the Spirit of adoption makes the faithful partakers in the divine nature[52] by uniting them in a living union with the only Son, the Savior.

V. The Sacraments of Eternal Life

1130 The Church celebrates the mystery of her Lord "until he comes," when God will be "everything to everyone."[53] Since the apostolic age the liturgy has been drawn toward its goal by the Spirit's groaning in the Church: *Marana tha!*[54] The liturgy thus shares in Jesus' desire: "I have earnestly desired to eat this Passover with you…until it is ful- 2817
filled in the kingdom of God."[55] In the sacraments of Christ the Church already receives the guarantee of her inheritance and even now shares in everlasting life, while "awaiting our blessed hope, the appearing of the glory of our great God and Savior Christ Jesus."[56] The "Spirit and the Bride say, 'Come…Come, Lord Jesus!'"[57] 950

St. Thomas sums up the various aspects of sacramental signs: "Therefore a sacrament is a sign that commemorates what precedes it—Christ's Passion; demonstrates what is accomplished in us through Christ's Passion—grace; and prefigures what that Passion pledges to us—future glory."[58]

In Brief

1131 *The sacraments are efficacious signs of grace, instituted by Christ and entrusted to the Church, by which divine life is dispensed to us. The visible rites by which the sacraments are celebrated signify and make present the graces proper to each sacrament. They bear fruit in those who receive them with the required dispositions.*

1132 *The Church celebrates the sacraments as a priestly community structured by the baptismal priesthood and the priesthood of ordained ministers.*

[49] Cf. Council of Trent (1547): DS 1608. — [50] Thomas Aquinas, *STh* III, 68, 8. — [51] Cf. Council of Trent (1547): DS 1604. — [52] Cf. *2 Pet* 1:4. — [53] *1 Cor* 11:26; 15:28. — [54] *1 Cor* 16:22. — [55] *Lk* 22:15. — [56] *Titus* 2:13. — [57] *Rev* 22:17, 20. — [58] St. Thomas Aquinas, *STh* III, 60, 3.

1133 *The Holy Spirit prepares the faithful for the sacraments by the Word of God and the faith which welcomes that word in well-disposed hearts. Thus the sacraments strengthen faith and express it.*

1134 *The fruit of sacramental life is both personal and ecclesial. For every one of the faithful on the one hand, this fruit is life for God in Christ Jesus; for the Church, on the other, it is an increase in charity and in her mission of witness.*

Chapter Two:

THE SACRAMENTAL CELEBRATION OF THE PASCHAL MYSTERY

1135 The catechesis of the liturgy entails first of all an understanding of the sacramental economy (*chapter one*). In this light, the innovation of its *celebration* is revealed. This chapter will therefore treat of the celebration of the sacraments of the Church. It will consider that which, through the diversity of liturgical traditions, is common to the celebration of the seven sacraments. What is proper to each will be treated later. This fundamental catechesis on the sacramental celebrations responds to the first questions posed by the faithful regarding this subject:

- Who celebrates the liturgy?
- How is the liturgy celebrated?
- When is the liturgy celebrated?
- Where is the liturgy celebrated?

Article 1: CELEBRATING THE CHURCH'S LITURGY

I. Who Celebrates?

795 **1136** Liturgy is an "action" of the *whole Christ* (*Christus totus*). Those who even now celebrate it without
1090 signs are already in the heavenly liturgy, where celebration is wholly communion and feast.

2642 *The celebrants of the heavenly liturgy*

1137 The book of Revelation of St. John, read in the Church's liturgy, first reveals to us, "A throne stood in heaven, with one seated on the throne": "the Lord God."[1] It then shows the Lamb, "standing, as though it had been slain": Christ crucified and risen, the one high priest of the true sanctuary, the same one "who offers and is offered, who
662 gives and is given."[2] Finally it presents "the river of the water of life… flowing from the throne of God and of the Lamb," one of most beautiful symbols of the Holy Spirit.[3]

1138 "Recapitulated in Christ," these are the ones who take part in the service of the praise of God and the fulfillment of his plan: the
heavenly powers, all creation (the 335
four living beings), the servants of the Old and New Covenants (the twenty-four elders), the new People of God (the one hundred and forty-four thousand),[4] especially the martyrs "slain for the word of God," and the all-holy Mother of God (the
Woman), the Bride of the Lamb,[5] 1370
and finally "a great multitude which no one could number, from every nation, from all tribes, and peoples and tongues."[6]

[1] *Rev* 4:2, 8; *Isa* 6:1; cf. *Ezek* 1:26–28. — [2] *Rev* 5:6; *Liturgy of St. John Chrysostom*, Anaphora; cf. *Jn* 1:29; *Heb* 4:14–15; 10:19–2. — [3] *Rev* 22:1; cf. 21:6; *Jn* 4:10–14. — [4] Cf. *Rev* 4–5; 7:1–8; 14:1; *Isa* 6:2–3. — [5] *Rev* 6:9–11; *Rev* 21:9; cf. 12. — [6] *Rev* 7:9.

1139 It is in this eternal liturgy that the Spirit and the Church enable us to participate whenever we celebrate the mystery of salvation in the sacraments.

The celebrants of the sacramental liturgy

752, 1348 **1140** It is the whole *community*, the Body of Christ united with its Head, that celebrates. "Liturgical services are not private functions but are celebrations of the Church which is 'the sacrament of unity,' namely, the holy people united and organized under the authority of the bishops. Therefore, liturgical services pertain to the whole Body of the Church. They manifest it, and have effects upon it. But they touch individual members of the Church in different ways, depending on their orders, their role in the liturgical services, and their actual participation in them."[7] For this reason, "rites which are meant to be celebrated in common, with the faithful
1372 present and actively participating, should as far as possible be celebrated in that way rather than by an individual and quasi-privately."[8]

1141 The celebrating assembly is the community of the baptized who, "by regeneration and the anointing of the Holy Spirit, are consecrated to be a spiritual house and a holy priesthood, that through
1120 all the works of Christian men they may offer spiritual sacrifices."[9] This "common priesthood" is that of Christ the sole priest, in which all his members participate:[10]

> Mother Church earnestly desires that all the faithful should be led to that full, conscious, and active participation in liturgical celebrations which is demanded by the very nature of the liturgy, and to which the Christian people, "a chosen race, a royal priesthood, a holy nation, a redeemed people," have a right
> and an obligation by reason of their 1268
> Baptism.[11]

1142 But "the members do not all have the same function."[12] Certain members are called by God, in and through the Church, to a special service of the community. These servants are chosen and consecrated by the sacrament of Holy Orders, by which the Holy Spirit enables them to act in the person of Christ the head, for the service of all the members of the Church.[13] The ordained minister is, as it were, an "icon" of
Christ the priest. Since it is in the 1549
Eucharist that the sacrament of the Church is made fully visible, it is in his presiding at the Eucharist that the bishop's ministry is most evident, as well as, in communion with 1561
him, the ministry of priests and deacons.

1143 For the purpose of assisting the work of the common priesthood of the faithful, other *particular ministries* also exist, not consecrated by
the sacrament of Holy Orders; their 903
functions are determined by the bishops, in accord with liturgical traditions and pastoral needs. "Servers, readers, commentators, and members of the choir also exercise a
genuine liturgical function."[14] 1672

1144 In the celebration of the sacraments it is thus the whole assembly that is *leitourgos*, each according

[7] *SC* 26. — [8] *SC* 27. — [9] *LG* 10; cf. *1 Pet* 2:4–5. — [10] Cf. *LG* 10; 34; PO 2. — [11] *SC* 14; cf. *1 Pet* 2:9; 2:4–5. — [12] *Rom* 12:4. — [13] Cf. *PO* 2; 15. — [14] *SC* 29.

to his function, but in the "unity of the Spirit" who acts in all. "In liturgical celebrations each person, minister or layman, who has an office to perform, should carry out *all* and *only* those parts which pertain to his office by the nature of the rite and the norms of the liturgy."[15]

II. How Is the Liturgy Celebrated?

333–1340 *Signs and symbols*

53 **1145** A sacramental celebration is woven from signs and symbols. In keeping with the divine pedagogy of salvation, their meaning is rooted in the work of creation and in human culture, specified by the events of the Old Covenant and fully revealed in the person and work of Christ.

1146 *Signs of the human world.* In human life, signs and symbols occupy an important place. As a being at once body and spirit, man express-
62, 2702 es and perceives spiritual realities through physical signs and symbols. As a social being, man needs signs and symbols to communicate with others, through language, gestures, and actions. The same holds true for
1879 his relationship with God.

299 **1147** God speaks to man through the visible creation. The material cosmos is so presented to man's intelligence that he can read there traces of its Creator.[16] Light and darkness, wind and fire, water and earth, the tree and its fruit speak of God and symbolize both his greatness and his nearness.

1148 Inasmuch as they are creatures, these perceptible realities can become means of expressing the action of God who sanctifies men, and the action of men who offer worship to God. The same is true of signs and symbols taken from the social life of man: washing and anointing, breaking bread and sharing the cup can express the sanctifying presence of God and man's gratitude toward his Creator.

1149 The great religions of man- 843
kind witness, often impressively, to this cosmic and symbolic meaning of religious rites. The liturgy of the Church presupposes, integrates and sanctifies elements from creation and human culture, conferring on them the dignity of signs of grace, of the new creation in Jesus Christ.

1150 *Signs of the covenant.* The 1334
Chosen People received from God distinctive signs and symbols that marked its liturgical life. These are no longer solely celebrations of cosmic cycles and social gestures, but signs of the covenant, symbols of God's mighty deeds for his people. Among these liturgical signs from the Old Covenant are circumcision, anointing and consecration of kings and priests, laying on of hands, sacrifices, and above all the Passover. The Church sees in these signs a prefiguring of the sacraments of the New Covenant.

1151 *Signs taken up by Christ.* In 1335
his preaching the Lord Jesus often makes use of the signs of creation to make known the mysteries of the Kingdom of God.[17] He performs healings and illustrates his preaching with physical signs or symbolic gestures.[18] He gives new meaning to the deeds and signs of the Old Covenant, above all to the Exodus and

[15] *SC* 28. — [16] Cf. *Wis* 13:1; *Rom* 1:19 f.; *Acts* 14:17. — [17] Cf. *Lk* 8:10. — [18] Cf. *Jn* 9:6; *Mk* 7:33 ff.; 8:22 ff.

the Passover,[19] for he himself is the meaning of all these signs.

1152 *Sacramental signs.* Since Pentecost, it is through the sacramental signs of his Church that the Holy Spirit carries on the work of sanctification. The sacraments of the Church do not abolish but purify and integrate all the richness of the signs and symbols of the cosmos and of social life. Further, they fulfill the types and figures of the Old Covenant, signify and make actively present the salvation wrought by Christ, and prefigure and anticipate the glory of heaven.

Words and actions

1153 A sacramental celebration is a meeting of God's children with their Father, in Christ and the Holy Spirit; this meeting takes the form
53 of a dialogue, through actions and words. Admittedly, the symbolic actions are already a language, but the Word of God and the response of faith have to accompany and give life to them, so that the seed of the Kingdom can bear its fruit in good soil. The liturgical actions signify what the Word of God expresses: both his free initiative and his people's response of faith.

1100 **1154** The *liturgy of the Word* is an integral part of sacramental celebrations. To nourish the faith of believers, the signs which accompany the Word of God should be emphasized: the book of the Word (a lectionary
103 or a book of the Gospels), its veneration (procession, incense, candles), the place of its proclamation (lectern or ambo), its audible and intelligible reading, the minister's homily which extends its proclamation, and the responses of the assembly (acclamations, meditation psalms, litanies, and profession of faith).

1155 The liturgical word and action are inseparable both insofar as
they are signs and instruction and 1127
insofar as they accomplish what they signify. When the Holy Spirit awakens faith, he not only gives an understanding of the Word of God, but through the sacraments also makes present the "wonders" of God which it proclaims. The Spirit makes present and communicates the Father's work, fulfilled by the beloved Son.

Singing and music

1156 "The musical tradition of the universal Church is a treasure of inestimable value, greater even than that of any other art. The main reason for this pre-eminence is that, as a combination of sacred music and words, it forms a necessary or integral part of solemn liturgy."[20] The composition and singing of inspired psalms, often accompanied by musical instruments, were already closely linked to the liturgical celebrations of the Old Covenant. The Church continues and develops this tradition: "Address...one another in psalms and hymns and spiritual songs, singing and making melody to the Lord with all your heart." "He who sings prays twice."[21]

1157 Song and music fulfill their function as signs in a manner all the more significant when they are "more closely connected...with the liturgical action,"[22] according to

[19] Cf. *Lk* 9:31; 22:7–20. — [20] *SC* 112. — [21] *Eph* 5:19; St. Augustine, *En. in Ps.* 72, 1: PL 36, 914; cf. *Col* 3:16. — [22] *SC* 112 § 3.

three principal criteria: beauty expressive of prayer, the unanimous participation of the assembly at the designated moments, and the sol-
2502 emn character of the celebration. In this way they participate in the purpose of the liturgical words and actions: the glory of God and the sanctification of the faithful:[23]

> How I wept, deeply moved by your hymns, songs, and the voices that echoed through your Church! What emotion I experienced in them! Those sounds flowed into my ears, distilling the truth in my heart. A feeling of devotion surged within me, and tears streamed down my face—tears that did me good.[24]

1158 The harmony of signs (song, music, words, and actions) is all the more expressive and fruitful when
1201 expressed in the *cultural richness* of the People of God who celebrate.[25] Hence "religious singing by the
1674 faithful is to be intelligently fostered so that in devotions and sacred exercises as well as in liturgical services," in conformity with the Church's norms, "the voices of the faithful may be heard." But "the texts intended to be sung must always be in conformity with Catholic doctrine. Indeed they should be drawn chiefly from the Sacred Scripture and from liturgical sources."[26]

6–477
29–2132 *Holy images*

1159 The sacred image, the liturgical icon, principally represents *Christ.* It cannot represent the invisible and incomprehensible God, but the incarnation of the Son of God has ushered in a new "economy" of images:

> Previously God, who has neither a body nor a face, absolutely could not be represented by an image. But now that he has made himself visible in the flesh and has lived with men, I can make an image of what I have seen of God...and contemplate the glory of the Lord, his face unveiled.[27]

1160 Christian iconography expresses in images the same Gospel message that Scripture communicates by words. Image and word illuminate each other:

> We declare that we preserve intact all the written and unwritten traditions of the Church which have been entrusted to us. One of these traditions consists in the production of representational artwork, which accords with the history of the preaching of the Gospel. For it confirms that the incarnation of the Word of God was real and not imaginary, and to our benefit as well, for realities that illustrate each other undoubtedly reflect each other's meaning.[28]

1161 All the signs in the liturgical celebrations are related to Christ: as are sacred images of the holy Mother of God and of the saints as well. They truly signify Christ, who is glorified in them. They make manifest the "cloud of witnesses"[29] who continue to participate in the salvation of the world and to whom we are united, above all in sacramental celebrations. Through their icons, it is man "in the image of God," finally transfigured "into his likeness,"[30] who is revealed to our faith. So too are the angels, who also are recapitulated in Christ:

[23] Cf. *SC* 112. — [24] St. Augustine, *Conf.* 9, 6, 14: PL 32, 769–770. — [25] Cf. *SC* 119. — [26] *SC* 118; 121. — [27] St. John Damascene, *De imag.* 1, 16: PG 96:1245–1248. — [28] Council of Nicaea II (787): *COD* 111. — [29] *Heb* 12:1. — [30] Cf. *Rom* 8:29; *1 Jn* 3:2.

> Following the divinely inspired teaching of our holy Fathers and the tradition of the Catholic Church (for we know that this tradition comes from the Holy Spirit who dwells in her) we rightly define with full certainty and correctness that, like the figure of the precious and life-giving cross, venerable and holy images of our Lord and God and Savior, Jesus Christ, our inviolate Lady, the holy Mother of God, and the venerated angels, all the saints and the just, whether painted or made of mosaic or another suitable material, are to be exhibited in the holy churches of God, on sacred vessels and vestments, walls and panels, in houses and on streets.[31]

2502 **1162** "The beauty of the images moves me to contemplation, as a meadow delights the eyes and subtly infuses the soul with the glory of God."[32] Similarly, the contemplation of sacred icons, united with meditation on the Word of God and the singing of liturgical hymns, enters into the harmony of the signs of celebration so that the mystery celebrated is imprinted in the heart's memory and is then expressed in the new life of the faithful.

III. When Is the Liturgy Celebrated?

Liturgical seasons

1163 "Holy Mother Church believes that she should celebrate the saving work of her divine Spouse in a sacred commemoration on certain days throughout the course of the year. Once each week, on the day which she has called the Lord's Day, she keeps the memory of the Lord's resurrection. She also celebrates it once every year, together with his blessed Passion, at Easter, that most solemn of all feasts. In the course of the year, moreover, she unfolds the
whole mystery of Christ.... Thus re- 512
calling the mysteries of the redemption, she opens up to the faithful the riches of her Lord's powers and merits, so that these are in some way made present in every age; the faithful lay hold of them and are filled with saving grace."[33]

1164 From the time of the Mosaic law, the People of God have observed fixed feasts, beginning with Passover, to commemorate the astonishing actions of the Savior God, to give him thanks for them, to perpetuate their remembrance, and to teach new generations to conform their conduct to them. In the age of the Church, between the Passover of Christ already accomplished once for all, and its consummation in the kingdom of God, the liturgy celebrated on fixed days bears the imprint of the newness of the mystery of Christ.

1165 When the Church cele- 2659–28
brates the mystery of Christ, there is a word that marks her prayer: "Today!"—a word echoing the prayer her Lord taught her and the call of the Holy Spirit.[34] This "today" of the living God which man is called to enter is "the hour" of Jesus' Passover,
which reaches across and underlies 1085
all history:

> Life extends over all beings and fills them with unlimited light; the Orient of orients pervades the universe, and he who was "before the daystar" and before the heavenly bodies, immortal

[31] Council of Nicaea II: DS 600. — [32] St. John Damascene, *De imag.* 1, 27: PG 94, 1268A, B. — [33] SC 102. — [34] Cf. *Mt* 6:11; *Heb* 3:7–4:11; *Ps* 95:7.

> and vast, the great Christ, shines over all beings more brightly than the sun. Therefore a day of long, eternal light is ushered in for us who believe in him, a day which is never blotted out: the mystical Passover.[35]

2174–2188 *The Lord's day*

1166 "By a tradition handed down from the apostles which took its origin from the very day of Christ's Resurrection, the Church celebrates the Paschal mystery every seventh day, which day is appropriately called the
1343 Lord's Day or Sunday."[36] The day of Christ's Resurrection is both the first day of the week, the memorial of the first day of creation, and the "eighth day," on which Christ after his "rest" on the great sabbath inaugurates the "day that the Lord has made," the "day that knows no evening."[37] The Lord's Supper is its center, for there the whole community of the faithful encounters the risen Lord who invites them to his banquet:[38]

> The Lord's day, the day of Resurrection, the day of Christians, is our day. It is called the Lord's day because on it the Lord rose victorious to the Father. If pagans call it the "day of the sun," we willingly agree, for today the light of the world is raised, today is revealed the sun of justice with healing in his rays.[39]

1167 Sunday is the pre-eminent day for the liturgical assembly, when the faithful gather "to listen to the word of God and take part in the Eucharist, thus calling to mind the Passion, Resurrection, and glory of the Lord Jesus, and giving thanks to God who 'has begotten them again, by the resurrection of Jesus Christ from the dead' unto a living hope":[40]

> When we ponder, O Christ, the marvels accomplished on this day, the Sunday of your holy resurrection, we say: "Blessed is Sunday, for on it began creation...the world's salvation...the renewal of the human race.... On Sunday heaven and earth rejoiced and the whole universe was filled with light. Blessed is Sunday, for on it were opened the gates of paradise so that Adam and all the exiles might enter it without fear.[41]

The liturgical year

1168 Beginning with the Easter Triduum as its source of light, the new age of the Resurrection fills the whole liturgical year with its brilliance. Gradually, on either side of 2698
this source, the year is transfigured by the liturgy. It really is a "year of the Lord's favor."[42] The economy of salvation is at work within the framework of time, but since its fulfillment in the Passover of Jesus and the outpouring of the Holy Spirit, the culmination of history is anticipated "as a foretaste," and the kingdom of God enters into our time.

1169 Therefore *Easter* is not simply one feast among others, but the "Feast of feasts," the "Solemnity of solemnities," just as the Eucharist is
the "Sacrament of sacraments" (the 1330
Great Sacrament). St. Athanasius calls Easter "the Great Sunday"[43] and the Eastern Churches call Holy Week "the Great Week." The mystery of the Resurrection, in which
Christ crushed death, permeates 560
with its powerful energy our old

[35] St. Hippolytus, *De pasch.* 1–2: SCh 27, 117. — [36] *SC* 106. — [37] Byzantine liturgy. — [38] Cf. *Jn* 21:12; *Lk* 24:30. — [39] St. Jerome, *Pasch.*: CCL 78, 550. — [40] *SC* 106. — [41] Fanqîth, *The Syriac Office of Antioch,* vol. VI, first part of Summer, 193 B. — [42] *Lk* 4:19. — [43] St. Athanasius (*ad* 329) *ep. fest.* 1: PG 24, 1366.

time, until all is subjected to him.

1170 At the Council of Nicaea in 325, all the Churches agreed that Easter, the Christian Passover, should be celebrated on the Sunday following the first full moon (14 Nisan) after the vernal equinox. Because of different methods of calculating the 14th day of the month of Nisan, the date of Easter in the Western and Eastern Churches is not always the same. For this reason, the Churches are currently seeking an agreement in order once again to celebrate the day of the Lord's Resurrection on a common date.

1171 In the liturgical year the various aspects of the one Paschal mystery unfold. This is also the case with the cycle of feasts surrounding the mystery of the incarnation (Annunciation, Christmas, Epiphany). They
524 commemorate the beginning of our salvation and communicate to us the first fruits of the Paschal mystery.

The sanctoral in the liturgical year

1172 "In celebrating this annual cycle of the mysteries of Christ, Holy Church honors the Blessed Mary, Mother of God, with a special love.
971 She is inseparably linked with the saving work of her Son. In her the
2030 Church admires and exalts the most excellent fruit of redemption and joyfully contemplates, as in a faultless image, that which she herself desires and hopes wholly to be."[44]

957 **1173** When the Church keeps the memorials of martyrs and other saints during the annual cycle, she proclaims the Paschal mystery in those "who have suffered and have been glorified with Christ. She proposes them to the faithful as examples who draw all men to the Father through Christ, and through their merits she begs for God's favors."[45]

The Liturgy of the Hours

1174 The mystery of Christ, his Incarnation and Passover, which we celebrate in the Eucharist especially at the Sunday assembly, permeates and transfigures the time of each day, through the celebration of the Liturgy of the Hours, "the divine office."[46] This celebration, faithful to
the apostolic exhortations to "pray 2698
constantly," is "so devised that the whole course of the day and night is made holy by the praise of God."[47] In this "public prayer of the Church,"[48] the faithful (clergy, religious, and lay people) exercise the royal priesthood of the baptized. Celebrated in "the form approved" by the Church, the Liturgy of the Hours "is truly the voice of the Bride herself addressed to her Bridegroom. It is the very prayer which Christ himself together with his Body addresses to the Father."[49]

1175 The Liturgy of the Hours is intended to become the prayer of the whole People of God. In it Christ himself "continues his priestly work through his Church."[50] His members participate according to their own place in the Church and the circumstances of their lives: priests devoted to the pastoral ministry, because they are called to remain diligent in prayer and the service of the word; religious, by the charism of their consecrated lives; all the faithful as much as possible:

[44] *SC* 103. — [45] *SC* 104; cf. *SC* 108, 111. — [46] Cf. *SC*, ch. IV, 83–101. — [47] *SC* 84; *1 Thess* 5:17; *Eph* 6:18. — [48] *SC* 98. — [49] *SC* 84. — [50] *SC* 83.

"Pastors of souls should see to it that the principal hours, especially Vespers, are celebrated in common in church on Sundays and on the more solemn feasts. The laity, too, are encouraged to recite the divine office, either with the priests, or among themselves, or even individually."[51]

1176 The celebration of the Liturgy of the Hours demands not only harmonizing the voice with the
2700 praying heart, but also a deeper "understanding of the liturgy and of the Bible, especially of the Psalms."[52]

1177 The hymns and litanies of the Liturgy of the Hours integrate the prayer of the psalms into the age of the Church, expressing the
2586 symbolism of the time of day, the liturgical season, or the feast being celebrated. Moreover, the reading from the Word of God at each Hour (with the subsequent responses or *troparia*) and readings from the Fathers and spiritual masters at certain Hours, reveal more deeply the meaning of the mystery being celebrated, assist in understanding the psalms, and prepare for silent prayer. The *lectio divina*, where the Word of God is so read and meditated that it becomes prayer, is thus rooted in the liturgical celebration.

1178 The Liturgy of the Hours, which is like an extension of the Eucharistic celebration, does not exclude but rather in a complementary way calls forth the various devotions of the People of God, especially ad-
1378 oration and worship of the Blessed Sacrament.

IV. Where Is the Liturgy Celebrated?

1179 The worship "in Spirit and in truth"[53] of the New Covenant is not tied exclusively to any one place. The whole earth is sacred and entrusted to the children of men. What matters above all is that, when the faithful assemble in the same place, they are the "living stones," gathered to be "built into a spiritual house."[54]
For the Body of the risen Christ is 586
the spiritual temple from which the source of living water springs forth: incorporated into Christ by the Holy Spirit, "we are the temple of the living God."[55]

1180 When the exercise of re- 2106
ligious liberty is not thwarted,[56] Christians construct buildings for divine worship. These visible churches are not simply gathering places but signify and make visible the Church living in this place, the dwelling of God with men reconciled and united in Christ.

1181 A church, "a house of prayer 2691
in which the Eucharist is celebrated and reserved, where the faithful assemble, and where is worshipped the presence of the Son of God our Savior, offered for us on the sacrificial altar for the help and consolation of the faithful—this house ought to be in good taste and a worthy place for prayer and sacred ceremonial."[57] In this "house of God" the truth and the harmony of the signs that make it up should show Christ to be present and active in this place.[58]

1182 The *altar* of the New Cov- 617, 1383
enant is the Lord's Cross,[59] from which the sacraments of the Paschal

[51] *SC* 100; cf. 86; 96; 98; *PO* 5. — [52] *SC* 90. — [53] *Jn* 4:24. — [54] *1 Pet* 2:4–5. — [55] *2 Cor* 6:16. — [56] Cf. *DH* 4. — [57] *PO* 5; cf. *SC* 122–127. — [58] Cf. *SC* 7. — [59] Cf. *Heb* 13:10.

mystery flow. On the altar, which is the center of the church, the sacrifice of the Cross is made present under sacramental signs. The altar is also the table of the Lord, to which the People of God are invited.[60] In certain Eastern liturgies, the altar is also the symbol of the tomb (Christ truly died and is truly risen).

1379 **1183** The *tabernacle* is to be situated "in churches in a most worthy
2120 place with the greatest honor."[61] The dignity, placing, and security of the Eucharistic tabernacle should foster adoration before the Lord really present in the Blessed Sacrament of the altar.[62]

1241 The *sacred chrism (myron)*, used in anointings as the sacramental sign of the seal of the gift of the Holy Spirit, is traditionally reserved and venerated in a secure place in the sanctuary. The oil of catechumens and the oil of the sick may also be placed there.

1348 **1184** The *chair* of the bishop (*cathedra*) or that of the priest "should express his office of presiding over the assembly and of directing prayer."[63]

103 The *lectern (ambo)*: "The dignity of the Word of God requires the church to have a suitable place for announcing his message so that the attention of the people may be easily directed to that place during the liturgy of the Word."[64]

1185 The gathering of the People of God begins with Baptism; a church must have a place for the celebration of *Baptism* (baptistry) and for fostering remembrance of the baptismal promises (holy water font).

The renewal of the baptismal life requires *penance*. A church, then, must lend itself to the expression of repentance and the reception of forgiveness, which requires an appropriate place to receive penitents.

A church must also be a space that 2717
invites us to the recollection and silent prayer that extend and internalize the great prayer of the Eucharist.

1186 Finally, the church has an eschatological significance. To enter into the house of God, we must cross a *threshold*, which symbolizes passing
from the world wounded by sin to 1130
the world of the new Life to which all men are called. The visible church is a symbol of the Father's house toward which the People of God is journeying and where the Father "will wipe every tear from their eyes."[65] Also for this reason, the Church is the house of *all* God's children, open and welcoming.

In Brief

1187 *The liturgy is the work of the whole Christ, head and body. Our high priest celebrates it unceasingly in the heavenly liturgy, with the holy Mother of God, the apostles, all the saints, and the multitude of those who have already entered the kingdom.*

1188 *In a liturgical celebration, the whole assembly is* leitourgos, *each member according to his own function. The baptismal priesthood is that of the whole Body of Christ. But some of the faithful are ordained through the sacrament of Holy Orders to represent Christ as head of the Body.*

1189 *The liturgical celebration involves signs and symbols relating to cre-*

[60] Cf. GIRM 259. — 61. Paul VI, *Mysterium Fidei:* AAS (1965) 771. — [62] Cf. *SC* 128. — [63] GIRM 271. — [64] GIRM 272. — [65] *Rev* 21:4.

ation (candles, water, fire), human life (washing, anointing, breaking bread), and the history of salvation (the rites of the Passover). Integrated into the world of faith and taken up by the power of the Holy Spirit, these cosmic elements, human rituals, and gestures of remembrance of God become bearers of the saving and sanctifying action of Christ.

1190 *The Liturgy of the Word is an integral part of the celebration. The meaning of the celebration is expressed by the Word of God which is proclaimed and by the response of faith to it.*

1191 *Song and music are closely connected with the liturgical action. The criteria for their proper use are the beauty expressive of prayer, the unanimous participation of the assembly, and the sacred character of the celebration.*

1192 *Sacred images in our churches and homes are intended to awaken and nourish our faith in the mystery of Christ. Through the icon of Christ and his works of salvation, it is he whom we adore. Through sacred images of the holy Mother of God, of the angels and of the saints, we venerate the persons represented.*

1193 *Sunday, the "Lord's Day," is the principal day for the celebration of the Eucharist because it is the day of the Resurrection. It is the pre-eminent day of the liturgical assembly, the day of the Christian family, and the day of joy and rest from work. Sunday is "the foundation and kernel of the whole liturgical year"* (SC *106).*

1194 *The Church, "in the course of the year,…unfolds the whole mystery of Christ from his Incarnation and Nativity through his Ascension, to Pentecost and the expectation of the blessed hope of the coming of the Lord"* (SC *102 § 2).*

1195 *By keeping the memorials of the saints—first of all the holy Mother of God, then the apostles, the martyrs, and other saints—on fixed days of the liturgical year, the Church on earth shows that she is united with the liturgy of heaven. She gives glory to Christ for having accomplished his salvation in his glorified members; their example encourages her on her way to the Father.*

1196 *The faithful who celebrate the Liturgy of the Hours are united to Christ our high priest, by the prayer of the Psalms, meditation on the Word of God, and canticles and blessings, in order to be joined with his unceasing and universal prayer that gives glory to the Father and implores the gift of the Holy Spirit on the whole world.*

1197 *Christ is the true temple of God, "the place where his glory dwells"; by the grace of God, Christians also become temples of the Holy Spirit, living stones out of which the Church is built.*

1198 *In its earthly state the Church needs places where the community can gather together. Our visible churches, holy places, are images of the holy city, the heavenly Jerusalem, toward which we are making our way on pilgrimage.*

1199 *It is in these churches that the Church celebrates public worship to the glory of the Holy Trinity, hears the word of God and sings his praise, lifts up her prayer, and offers the sacrifice of Christ sacramentally present in the midst of the assembly. These churches are also places of recollection and personal prayer.*

Article 2: LITURGICAL DIVERSITY AND THE UNITY OF THE MYSTERY

Liturgical traditions and the catholicity of the Church

1200 From the first community of Jerusalem until the parousia, it is the same Paschal mystery that the Churches of God, faithful to the apostolic faith, celebrate in every place. The mystery celebrated in the liturgy is one, but the forms of its
2625 celebration are diverse.

1201 The mystery of Christ is so unfathomably rich that it cannot be exhausted by its expression in any single liturgical tradition. The his-
2663 tory of the blossoming and development of these rites witnesses to a remarkable complementarity. When the Churches lived their respective liturgical traditions in the communion of the faith and the sacraments
1558 of the faith, they enriched one another and grew in fidelity to Tradition and to the common mission of the whole Church.[66]

814 **1202** The diverse liturgical traditions have arisen by very reason of the Church's mission. Churches of the same geographical and cultural area came to celebrate the mystery of Christ through particular expres-
1674 sions characterized by the culture: in the tradition of the "deposit of faith,"[67] in liturgical symbolism, in the organization of fraternal communion, in the theological understanding of the mysteries, and in various forms of holiness. Through the liturgical life of a local church, Christ, the light and salvation of all peoples, is made manifest to the particular people and culture to which that Church is sent and in which she is rooted. The Church is catholic, capable of integrating into her 835
unity, while purifying them, all the authentic riches of cultures.[68] 1937

1203 The liturgical traditions or rites presently in use in the Church are the Latin (principally the Roman rite, but also the rites of certain local churches, such as the Ambrosian rite, or those of certain religious orders) and the Byzantine, Alexandrian or Coptic, Syriac, Armenian, Maronite, and Chaldean rites. In "faithful obedience to tradition, the sacred Council declares that Holy Mother Church holds all lawfully recognized rites to be of equal right and dignity, and that she wishes to preserve them in the future and to foster them in every way."[69]

Liturgy and culture

1204 The celebration of the lit- 2684
urgy, therefore, should correspond to the genius and culture of the different peoples.[70] In order that the mystery of Christ be "made known to all the nations...to bring about the obedience of faith,"[71] it must be proclaimed, celebrated, and lived in all cultures in such a way that they themselves are not abolished by it, but redeemed and fulfilled:[72] It is 854, 1232
with and through their own human culture, assumed and transfig- 2527
ured by Christ, that the multitude of God's children has access to the Father, in order to glorify him in the one Spirit.

[66] Cf. Paul VI, *EN* 63–64. — [67] *2 Tim* 1:14 (Vulg.). — [68] Cf. *LG* 23; *UR* 4. — [69] *SC* 4. — [70] Cf. *SC* 37–40. — [71] *Rom* 16:26. — [72] Cf. *CT* 53.

1125 **1205** "In the liturgy, above all that of the sacraments, there is an *immutable part*, a part that is divinely instituted and of which the Church is the guardian, and parts that can be changed, which the Church has the power and on occasion also the duty to adapt to the cultures of recently evangelized peoples."[73]

1206 "Liturgical diversity can be a source of enrichment, but it can also provoke tensions, mutual misunderstandings, and even schisms. In this matter it is clear that diversity must not damage unity. It must express only fidelity to the common faith, to the sacramental signs that the Church has received from Christ, and to hierarchical communion. Cultural adaptation also requires a conversion of heart and even, where necessary, a breaking with ancestral customs incompatible with the Catholic faith."[74]

In Brief

1207 *It is fitting that liturgical celebration tends to express itself in the culture of the people where the Church finds herself, though without being submissive to it. Moreover, the liturgy itself generates cultures and shapes them.*

1208 *The diverse liturgical traditions or rites, legitimately recognized, manifest the catholicity of the Church, because they signify and communicate the same mystery of Christ.*

1209 *The criterion that assures unity amid the diversity of liturgical traditions is fidelity to apostolic Tradition, i.e., the communion in the faith and the sacraments received from the apostles, a communion that is both signified and guaranteed by apostolic succession.*

[73] John Paul II, *Vicesimus quintus annus*, 16; cf. *SC* 21. — [74] John Paul II, *Vicesimus quintus annus*, 16.

Section Two

THE SEVEN SACRAMENTS OF THE CHURCH

1113 **1210** Christ instituted the sacraments of the new law. There are seven: Baptism, Confirmation (or Chrismation), the Eucharist, Penance, the Anointing of the Sick, Holy Orders, and Matrimony. The seven sacraments touch all the stages and all the important moments of Christian life:[1] they give birth and increase, healing and mission to the Christian's life of faith. There is thus a certain resemblance between the stages of natural life and the stages of the spiritual life.

1211 Following this analogy, the *first chapter* will expound the three sacraments of Christian initiation; the *second*, the sacraments of healing; and the *third*, the sacraments at the service of communion and the mission of the faithful. This order, while not the only one possible, does allow one to see that the sacraments form an organic whole in which each particular sacrament has its own vital place. In this organic whole, the Eucharist occupies a unique place as the "Sacrament of sacraments": "all
the other sacraments are ordered to 1374
it as to their end."[2]

[1] Cf. St. Thomas Aquinas, *STh* III, 65, 1. — [2] St. Thomas Aquinas, *STh* III, 65, 3.

Chapter One: THE SACRAMENTS OF CHRISTIAN INITIATION

1212 The sacraments of Christian initiation—Baptism, Confirmation, and the Eucharist—lay the *foundations* of every Christian life. "The sharing in the divine nature given to men through the grace of Christ bears a certain likeness to the origin, development, and nourishing of natural life. The faithful are born anew by Baptism, strengthened by the sacrament of Confirmation, and receive in the Eucharist the food of eternal life. By means of these sacraments of Christian initiation, they thus receive in increasing measure the treasures of the divine life and advance toward the perfection of charity."[3]

Article 1: THE SACRAMENT OF BAPTISM

1213 Holy Baptism is the basis of the whole Christian life, the gateway to life in the Spirit (*vitae spiritualis ianua*),[4] and the door which gives access to the other sacraments. Through Baptism we are freed from sin and reborn as sons of God; we become members of Christ, are incorporated into the Church and made sharers in her mission: "Baptism is the sacrament of regeneration through water and in the word."[5]

I. What Is This Sacrament Called?

1214 This sacrament is called *Baptism*, after the central rite by which it is carried out: to baptize (Greek *baptizein*) means to "plunge" or "immerse"; the "plunge" into the water symbolizes the catechumen's burial
into Christ's death, from which he 628
rises up by resurrection with him, as "a new creature."[6]

1215 This sacrament is also called "*the washing of regeneration and renewal by the Holy Spirit,*" for it signifies and actually brings about the
birth of water and the Spirit without 1257
which no one "can enter the kingdom of God."[7]

1216 "This bath is called *enlightenment,* because those who receive this [catechetical] instruction are enlightened in their understanding. . . ."[8] Having received in Baptism the Word, "the true light that enlightens every man," the person baptized has been "enlightened," he becomes a
"son of light," indeed, he becomes 1243
"light" himself:[9]

[3] Paul VI, apostolic constitution, *Divinae consortium naturae*: AAS 63 (1971) 657; cf. RCIA Introduction 1–2. — [4] Cf. Council of Florence: DS 1314: *vitae spiritualis ianua.* —[5] *Roman Catechism* II, 2, 5; cf. Council of Florence: DS 1314; CIC, cann. 204 § 1; 849; CCEO, can. 675 § 1. — [6] *2 Cor* 5:17; *Gal* 6:15; cf. *Rom* 6:3–4; *Col* 2:12. — [7] *Titus* 3:5; *Jn* 3:5. — [8] St. Justin, *Apol.* 1, 61, 12: PG 6, 421. — [9] *Jn* 1:9; 1 *Thess* 5:5; *Heb* 10:32; *Eph* 5:8.

> Baptism is God's most beautiful and magnificent gift.... We call it gift, grace, anointing, enlightenment, garment of immortality, bath of rebirth, seal, and most precious gift. It is called gift because it is conferred on those who bring nothing of their own; grace since it is given even to the guilty; Baptism because sin is buried in the water; anointing for it is priestly and royal as are those who are anointed; enlightenment because it radiates light; clothing since it veils our shame; bath because it washes; and seal as it is our guard and the sign of God's Lordship.[10]

II. Baptism in the Economy of Salvation

Prefigurations of Baptism in the Old Covenant

1217 In the liturgy of the Easter Vigil, during the *blessing of the baptismal water*, the Church solemnly commemorates the great events in salvation history that already prefigured the mystery of Baptism:

> Father, you give us grace through sacramental signs, which tell us of the wonders of your unseen power. In Baptism we use your gift of water, which you have made a rich symbol of the grace you give us in this sacrament.[11]

344 **1218** Since the beginning of the world, water, so humble and won-
694 derful a creature, has been the source of life and fruitfulness. Sacred Scripture sees it as "overshadowed" by the Spirit of God:[12]

> At the very dawn of creation your Spirit breathed on the waters, making them the wellspring of all holiness.[13]

1219 The Church has seen in No- 701, 845
ah's ark a prefiguring of salvation by Baptism, for by it "a few, that is, eight persons, were saved through water":[14]

> The waters of the great flood you made a sign of the waters of Baptism, that make an end of sin and a new beginning of goodness.[15]

1220 If water springing up from the earth symbolizes life, the water of the sea is a symbol of death and so can represent the mystery of the
cross. By this symbolism Baptism 1010
signifies communion with Christ's death.

1221 But above all, the crossing of the Red Sea, literally the liberation of Israel from the slavery of Egypt, announces the liberation wrought by Baptism:

> You freed the children of Abraham from the slavery of Pharaoh, bringing them dry-shod through the waters of the Red Sea, to be an image of the people set free in Baptism.[16]

1222 Finally, Baptism is prefigured in the crossing of the Jordan River by which the People of God received the gift of the land promised to Abraham's descendants, an image of eternal life. The promise of this blessed inheritance is fulfilled in the New Covenant.

[10] St. Gregory of Nazianzus, *Oratio* 40, 3–4: PG 36, 361C. — [11] *Roman Missal*, Easter Vigil 42: Blessing of Water. — [12] Cf. *Gen* 1:2. — [13] *Roman Missal*, Easter Vigil 42: Blessing of Water. — [14] *1 Pet* 3:20. — [15] *Roman Missal*, Easter Vigil 42: Blessing of Water. — [16] *Roman Missal*, Easter Vigil 42: Blessing of Water: "Abrahae filios per mare Rubrum sicco vestigio transire fecisti, ut plebs, a Pharaonis servitute liberata, populum baptizatorum præfiguraret."

Christ's Baptism

1223 All the Old Covenant prefigurations find their fulfillment in Christ Jesus. He begins his public life after having himself baptized by St. John the Baptist in the Jordan.[17] After his resurrection Christ gives this mission to his apostles: "Go therefore and make disciples of all nations, baptizing them in the name
232 of the Father and of the Son and of the Holy Spirit, teaching them to observe all that I have commanded you."[18]

536 **1224** Our Lord voluntarily submitted himself to the baptism of St. John, intended for sinners, in order to "fulfill all righteousness."[19] Jesus' gesture is a manifestation of his self-emptying.[20] The Spirit who had hovered over the waters of the first creation descended then on the Christ as a prelude of the new creation, and the Father revealed Jesus as his "beloved Son."[21]

1225 In his Passover Christ opened to all men the fountain of Baptism. He had already spoken of his Passion, which he was about to suffer in Jerusalem, as a "Baptism" with which he had to be baptized.[22]
766 The blood and water that flowed from the pierced side of the crucified Jesus are types of Baptism and the Eucharist, the sacraments of new life.[23] From then on, it is possible "to be born of water and the Spirit"[24] in order to enter the Kingdom of God.

> See where you are baptized, see where Baptism comes from, if not from the cross of Christ, from his death. There is the whole mystery: he died for you. In him you are redeemed, in him you are saved.[25]

Baptism in the Church

1226 From the very day of Pentecost the Church has celebrated and administered holy Baptism. Indeed St. Peter declares to the crowd astounded by his preaching: "Repent, and be baptized every one of you in
the name of Jesus Christ for the for- 849
giveness of your sins; and you shall receive the gift of the Holy Spirit."[26] The apostles and their collaborators offer Baptism to anyone who believed in Jesus: Jews, the God-fearing, pagans.[27] Always, Baptism is seen as connected with faith: "Believe in the Lord Jesus, and you will be saved, you and your household," St. Paul declared to his jailer in Philippi. And the narrative continues, the jailer "was baptized at once, with all his family."[28]

1227 According to the Apostle Paul, the believer enters through Baptism into communion with
Christ's death, is buried with him, 790
and rises with him:

> Do you not know that all of us who have been baptized into Christ Jesus were baptized into his death? We were buried therefore with him by baptism into death, so that as Christ was raised from the dead by the glory of the Father, we too might walk in newness of life.[29]

The baptized have "put on Christ."[30] Through the Holy Spirit, Baptism is a bath that purifies, justifies, and sanctifies.[31]

[17] Cf. *Mt* 3:13. — [18] *Mt* 28:19–20; cf. *Mk* 16:15–16. — [19] *Mt* 3:15. — [20] Cf. *Phil* 2:7. — [21] *Mt* 3:16–17. — [22] *Mk* 10:38; cf. *Lk* 12:50. — [23] Cf. *Jn* 19:34; 1 *Jn* 5:6–8. — [24] Cf. *Jn* 3:5. — [25] St. Ambrose, *De sacr.* 2, 2, 6: PL 16, 444; cf. *Jn* 3:5. — [26] *Acts* 2:38. — [27] Cf. *Acts* 2:41; 8:12–13; 10:48; 16:15. — [28] *Acts* 16:31–33. — [29] *Rom* 6:3–4; cf. *Col* 2:12. — [30] *Gal* 3:27. — [31] Cf. *1 Cor* 6:11; 12:13.

1228 Hence Baptism is a bath of water in which the "imperishable seed" of the Word of God produces its life-giving effect.[32] St. Augustine says of Baptism: "The word is brought to the material element, and it becomes a sacrament."[33]

III. How Is the Sacrament of Baptism Celebrated?

Christian Initiation

1229 From the time of the apostles, becoming a Christian has been accomplished by a journey and initiation in several stages. This journey can be covered rapidly or slowly, but certain essential elements will always have to be present: proclamation of the Word, acceptance of the Gospel entailing conversion, profession of faith, Baptism itself, the outpouring of the Holy Spirit, and admission to Eucharistic communion.

1230 This initiation has varied greatly through the centuries according to circumstances. In the first centuries of the Church, Christian initiation saw considerable development. A long period of catechumenate included a series of preparatory
1248 rites, which were liturgical landmarks along the path of catechumenal preparation and culminated in the celebration of the sacraments of Christian initiation.

1231 Where infant Baptism has become the form in which this sacrament is usually celebrated, it has become a single act encapsulating the preparatory stages of Christian initiation in a very abridged way. By its very nature infant Baptism requires a *post-baptismal catechumenate.* Not only is there a need for instruction after Baptism, but also for the necessary flowering of baptismal grace in personal growth. The *cate-* 13
chism has its proper place here.

1232 The second Vatican Council restored for the Latin Church "the catechumenate for adults, comprising several distinct steps."[34] The rites for these stages are to be found in the *Rite of Christian Initiation of Adults (RCIA).*[35] The Council also gives permission that: "In mission countries, in addition to what is furnished by the Christian tradition, those elements of initiation rites
may be admitted which are already 1204
in use among some peoples insofar as they can be adapted to the Christian ritual."[36]

1233 Today in all the rites, Latin and Eastern, the Christian initiation of adults begins with their entry into the catechumenate and reaches its culmination in a single celebration of the three sacraments of initiation: Baptism, Confirmation, and the Eucharist.[37] In the Eastern rites the Christian initiation of infants also begins with Baptism followed immediately by Confirmation and the Eucharist, while in the Roman rite it is followed by years of catechesis before being completed later by Confirmation and the Eucharist, the summit of their Christian initiation.[38]

The mystagogy of the celebration

1234 The meaning and grace of the sacrament of Baptism are clearly seen in the rites of its celebration. By following the gestures and words

[32] *1 Pet* 1:23; cf. *Eph* 5:26. — [33] St. Augustine, *In Jo. ev.* 80, 3: PL 35, 1840. — [34] *SC* 64. — [35] Cf. RCIA (1972). — [36] *SC* 65; cf. *SC* 37–40. — [37] Cf. AG 14; CIC, cann. 851; 865; 866. — [38] Cf. CIC, cann. 851, 2°; 868.

of this celebration with attentive participation, the faithful are initiated into the riches this sacrament signifies and actually brings about in each newly baptized person.

617 **1235** *The sign of the cross*, on the threshold of the celebration, marks with the imprint of Christ the one who is going to belong to him and
2157 signifies the grace of the redemption Christ won for us by his cross.

1236 The proclamation of the Word of God enlightens the candidates and the assembly with the revealed truth and elicits the response
1112 of faith, which is inseparable from Baptism. Indeed Baptism is "the sacrament of faith" in a particular way, since it is the sacramental entry into the life of faith.

1237 Since Baptism signifies liberation from sin and from its instigator the devil, one or more *exorcisms* are pronounced over the candidate. The celebrant then anoints him with the oil of catechumens, or lays his
1673 hands on him, and he explicitly renounces Satan. Thus prepared, he
189 is able to confess the faith of the Church, to which he will be "entrusted" by Baptism.[39]

1217 **1238** The *baptismal water* is consecrated by a prayer of epiclesis (either at this moment or at the Easter Vigil). The Church asks God that through his Son the power of the Holy Spirit may be sent upon the water, so that those who will be baptized in it may be "born of water and the Spirit."[40]

1214 **1239** The *essential rite* of the sacrament follows: *Baptism* properly speaking. It signifies and actually brings about death to sin and entry into the life of the Most Holy Trinity through configuration to the Paschal mystery of Christ. Baptism is performed in the most expressive way by triple immersion in the baptismal water. However, from ancient times it has also been able to be conferred by pouring the water three times over the candidate's head.

1240 In the Latin Church this triple infusion is accompanied by the minister's words: "N., I baptize you in the name of the Father, and of the Son, and of the Holy Spirit." In the Eastern liturgies the catechumen turns toward the East and the priest says: "The servant of God, N., is baptized in the name of the Father, and of the Son, and of the Holy Spirit." At the invocation of each person of the Most Holy Trinity, the priest immerses the candidate in the water and raises him up again.

1241 The *anointing with sacred* 1294, 1574
chrism, perfumed oil consecrated by the bishop, signifies the gift of the Holy Spirit to the newly baptized, who has become a Christian, that is, one "anointed" by the Holy Spirit, incorporated into Christ who is
anointed priest, prophet, and king.[41] 783

1242 In the liturgy of the Eastern Churches, the post-baptismal anointing is the sacrament of Chrismation (Confirmation). In the Roman liturgy the post-baptismal anointing announces a second anointing with sacred chrism to be conferred later by the bishop—Confirmation, which will as it were
"confirm" and complete the baptis- 1291
mal anointing.

[39] Cf. *Rom* 6:17. — [40] *Jn* 3:5. — [41] Cf. RBC 62.

1243 The white garment symbolizes that the person baptized has "put on Christ,"[42] has risen with Christ. The candle, lit from the Easter candle, signifies that Christ has enlightened the neophyte. In him the bap-
1216 tized are "the light of the world."[43]

The newly baptized is now, in the only Son, a child of God entitled
2769 to say the prayer of the children of God: "Our Father."

1244 *First Holy Communion.* Having become a child of God clothed with the wedding garment, the neophyte is admitted "to the marriage supper of the Lamb"[44] and receives the food of the new life, the body and blood of Christ. The Eastern Churches maintain a lively awareness of the unity of Christian initiation by giving Holy Communion to all the newly baptized and confirmed, even little children, re-
1292 calling the Lord's words: "Let the children come to me, do not hinder them."[45] The Latin Church, which reserves admission to Holy Communion to those who have attained the age of reason, expresses the orientation of Baptism to the Eucharist by having the newly baptized child brought to the altar for the praying of the Our Father.

1245 The *solemn blessing* concludes the celebration of Baptism. At the Baptism of newborns the blessing of the mother occupies a special place.

IV. Who Can Receive Baptism?

1246 "Every person not yet baptized and only such a person is able to be baptized."[46]

The Baptism of adults

1247 Since the beginning of the Church, adult Baptism is the common practice where the proclamation of the Gospel is still new. The catechumenate (preparation for Baptism) therefore occupies an important place. This initiation into Christian faith and life should dispose the catechumen to receive the gift of God in Baptism, Confirmation, and the Eucharist.

1248 The catechumenate, or for- 1230
mation of catechumens, aims at bringing their conversion and faith to maturity, in response to the divine initiative and in union with an ecclesial community. The catechumenate is to be "a formation in the whole Christian life...during which the disciples will be joined to Christ their teacher. The catechumens should be properly initiated into the mystery of salvation and the practice of the evangelical virtues, and they should be introduced into the life of faith, liturgy, and charity of the People of God by successive sacred rites."[47]

1249 Catechumens "are already 1259
joined to the Church, they are already of the household of Christ, and are quite frequently already living a life of faith, hope, and charity."[48] "With love and solicitude mother Church already embraces them as her own."[49]

The Baptism of infants

1250 Born with a fallen human 403
nature and tainted by original sin, children also have need of the new birth in Baptism to be freed from

[42] *Gal* 3:27. — [43] *Mt* 5:14; cf. *Phil* 2:15. — [44] *Rev* 19:9. — [45] *Mk* 10:14. — [46] CIC, can. 864; cf. CCEO, can. 679. — [47] *AG* 14; cf. RCIA 19; 98. — [48] *AG* 14 § 5. — [49] *LG* 14 § 3; cf. CIC, cann. 206; 788 § 3.

the power of darkness and brought into the realm of the freedom of the children of God, to which all men are called.[50] The sheer gratuitousness
1996 of the grace of salvation is particularly manifest in infant Baptism. The Church and the parents would deny a child the priceless grace of becoming a child of God were they not to confer Baptism shortly after birth.[51]

1251 Christian parents will recognize that this practice also accords with their role as nurturers of the life that God has entrusted to them.[52]

1252 The practice of infant Baptism is an immemorial tradition of the Church. There is explicit testimony to this practice from the second century on, and it is quite possible that, from the beginning of the apostolic preaching, when whole "households" received baptism, infants may also have been baptized.[53]

Faith and Baptism

1123 **1253** Baptism is the sacrament of faith.[54] But faith needs the community of believers. It is only within the faith of the Church that each of the faithful can believe. The faith required for Baptism is not a perfect and mature faith, but a beginning that is called to develop. The
168 catechumen or the godparent is asked: "What do you ask of God's Church?" The response is: "Faith!"

1254 For all the baptized, children or adults, faith must grow *after* Baptism. For this reason the Church celebrates each year at the Easter Vigil the renewal of baptismal promises. Preparation for Baptism leads only to the threshold of new life. Baptism is the source of that new life in 2101
Christ from which the entire Christian life springs forth.

1255 For the grace of Baptism to unfold, the parents' help is important. So too is the role of the *godfather and godmother*, who must be firm believers, able and ready to help the newly baptized—child or adult—on 1311
the road of Christian life.[55] Their task is a truly ecclesial function (*officium*).[56] The whole ecclesial community bears some responsibility for the development and safeguarding of the grace given at Baptism.

V. Who Can Baptize?

1256 The ordinary ministers of Baptism are the bishop and priest and, in the Latin Church, also the 1239–1240
deacon.[57] In case of necessity, anyone, even a non-baptized person, with the required intention, can baptize,[58] by using the Trinitarian baptismal formula. The intention required is to will to do what the Church does when she baptizes. The Church finds the reason for this pos- 1752
sibility in the universal saving will of God and the necessity of Baptism for salvation.[59]

VI. The Necessity of Baptism

1257 The Lord himself affirms 1129
that Baptism is necessary for salvation.[60] He also commands his disciples to proclaim the Gospel to all nations and to baptize them.[61] Baptism is necessary for salvation for

[50] Cf. Council of Trent (1546): DS 1514; cf. *Col* 1:12–14. — [51] Cf. CIC, can. 867; CCEO, cann. 681; 686, 1. — [52] Cf. *LG* 11; 41; *GS* 48; CIC, can. 868. — [53] Cf. *Acts* 16:15, 33; 18:8; *1 Cor* 1:16; CDF, instruction, *Pastoralis actio:* AAS 72 (1980) 1137–1156. — [54] Cf. *Mk* 16:16. — [55] Cf. CIC, cann. 872–874. — [56] Cf. *SC* 67. — [57] Cf. CIC, can. 861 § 1; CCEO, can. 677 § 1. — [58] CIC, can. 861 § 2. — [59] Cf. *1 Tim* 2:4. — [60] Cf. *Jn* 3:5. — [61] Cf. *Mt* 28:19–20; cf. Council of Trent (1547) DS 1618; *LG* 14; *AG* 5.

those to whom the Gospel has been proclaimed and who have had the
161, 846 possibility of asking for this sacrament.[62] The Church does not know of any means other than Baptism that assures entry into eternal beatitude; this is why she takes care not to neglect the mission she has received from the Lord to see that all who can be baptized are "reborn of water and the Spirit." *God has bound salvation to the sacrament of Baptism, but he himself is not bound by his sacraments.*

1258 The Church has always held the firm conviction that those who suffer death for the sake of the faith without having received Baptism are baptized by their death for and with Christ. This *Baptism of blood*, like
2473 the *desire for Baptism*, brings about the fruits of Baptism without being a sacrament.

1249 **1259** For *catechumens* who die before their Baptism, their explicit desire to receive it, together with repentance for their sins, and charity, assures them the salvation that they were not able to receive through the sacrament.

1260 "Since Christ died for all, and since all men are in fact called to one and the same destiny, which is divine, we must hold that the Holy Spirit offers to all the possibility of being made partakers, in a
848 way known to God, of the Paschal mystery."[63] Every man who is ignorant of the Gospel of Christ and of his Church, but seeks the truth and does the will of God in accordance with his understanding of it, can be saved. It may be supposed that such persons would have desired Baptism explicitly if they had known its necessity.

1261 As regards *children who have* 1257
died without Baptism, the Church can only entrust them to the mercy of God, as she does in her funeral rites for them. Indeed, the great mercy of God who desires that all men should be saved, and Jesus' tenderness toward children which caused him to say: "Let the children come to me, do not hinder them,"[64] allow us to hope that there is a way of salvation for children who have died without Baptism. All the more urgent is the Church's call not to
prevent little children coming to 1250
Christ through the gift of holy Baptism.

VII. The Grace of Baptism

1262 The different effects of Bap- 1234
tism are signified by the perceptible elements of the sacramental rite. Immersion in water symbolizes not only death and purification, but also regeneration and renewal. Thus the two principal effects are purification from sins and new birth in the Holy Spirit.[65]

For the forgiveness of sins...

1263 By Baptism *all sins* are for- 977
given, original sin and all personal
sins, as well as all punishment for 1425
sin.[66] In those who have been reborn nothing remains that would impede their entry into the Kingdom of God, neither Adam's sin, nor personal sin, nor the consequences of sin, the gravest of which is separation from God.

[62] Cf. *Mk* 16:16. — [63] *GS* 22 § 5; cf. *LG* 16; *AG* 7. — [64] *Mk* 10:14; cf. *1 Tim* 2:4. — [65] Cf. *Acts* 2:38; *Jn* 3:5. — [66] Cf. Council of Florence (1439): DS 1316.

1264 Yet certain temporal consequences of sin remain in the baptized, such as suffering, illness, death, and such frailties inherent in life as weaknesses of character, and so on, as well as an inclination to sin
975, 2514 that Tradition calls *concupiscence*, or metaphorically, "the tinder for sin"
1426 (*fomes peccati*); since concupiscence "is left for us to wrestle with, it cannot harm those who do not consent but manfully resist it by the grace of Jesus Christ."[67] Indeed, "an athlete
405 is not crowned unless he competes according to the rules."[68]

"A new creature"

505 **1265** Baptism not only purifies from all sins, but also makes the neo-
460 phyte "a new creature," an adopted son of God, who has become a "partaker of the divine nature,"[69] member of Christ and co-heir with him,[70] and a temple of the Holy Spirit.[71]

1266 The Most Holy Trinity gives the baptized sanctifying grace, the grace of *justification:*

1992 – enabling them to believe in God, to hope in him, and to love him through the theological virtues;

1812 – giving them the power to live and act under the prompting of the Holy Spirit through the gifts of the Holy Spirit;

1831 – allowing them to grow in goodness through the moral virtues.

1810 Thus the whole organism of the Christian's supernatural life has its roots in Baptism.

Incorporated into the Church, the Body of Christ

1267 Baptism makes us members 782
of the Body of Christ: "Therefore... we are members one of another."[72] Baptism incorporates us *into the Church*. From the baptismal fonts is born the one People of God of the New Covenant, which transcends all the natural or human limits of nations, cultures, races, and sexes: "For by one Spirit we were all baptized into one body."[73]

1268 The baptized have become "living stones" to be "built into a spiritual house, to be a holy priesthood."[74] By Baptism they share in the priesthood of Christ, in his prophetic and royal mission. They are
"a chosen race, a royal priesthood, 1141
a holy nation, God's own people, that [they] may declare the wonderful deeds of him who called [them] out of darkness into his marvelous light."[75] *Baptism gives a share in the*
common priesthood of all believers. 784

1269 Having become a member of the Church, the person baptized belongs no longer to himself, but to him who died and rose for us.[76] From now on, he is called to be subject to others, to serve them in the communion of the Church, and to "obey and submit" to the Church's leaders,[77] holding 871
them in respect and affection.[78] Just as Baptism is the source of responsibilities and duties, the baptized person also enjoys rights within the Church: to receive the sacraments, to be nourished with the Word of God and to be sustained by the other spiritual helps of the Church.[79]

[67] Council of Trent (1546): DS 1515. — [68] *2 Tim* 2:5. — [69] *2 Cor* 5:17; *2 Pet* 1:4; cf. *Gal* 4:5–7. — [70] Cf. *1 Cor* 6:15; 12:27; *Rom* 8:17. — [71] Cf. *1 Cor* 6:19. — [72] *Eph* 4:25. — [73] *1 Cor* 12:13. — [74] *1 Pet* 2:5. — [75] *1 Pet* 2:9. — [76] Cf. *1 Cor* 6:19; *2 Cor* 5:15. — [77] *Heb* 13:17. — [78] Cf. *Eph* 5:21; *1 Cor* 16:15–16; *1 Thess* 5:12–13; *Jn* 13:12–15. — [79] Cf. *LG* 37; CIC, cann. 208–223; CCEO, can. 675:2.

1270 "Reborn as sons of God, [the baptized] must profess before men the faith they have received from God through the Church" and participate in the apostolic and missionary activity of the People of God.[80]

The sacramental bond of the unity of Christians

1271 Baptism constitutes the foundation of communion among all Christians, including those who are not yet in full communion with the Catholic Church: "For men who believe in Christ and have been properly baptized are put in some, though imperfect, communion with the Catholic Church. Justified by faith in Baptism, [they] are incorporated into Christ; they therefore have a right to be called Christians, and with good reason are accepted as brothers by the children of the Catholic Church."[81] "Baptism therefore constitutes *the sacramental bond of unity* existing among all who through it are reborn."[82]

An indelible spiritual mark...

1272 Incorporated into Christ by Baptism, the person baptized is configured to Christ. Baptism seals the Christian with the indelible spiritual mark (*character*) of his belonging to Christ. No sin can erase this mark, even if sin prevents Baptism from bearing the fruits of salvation.[83] Given once for all, Baptism cannot be repeated.

1273 Incorporated into the Church by Baptism, the faithful have received the sacramental character that consecrates them for Christian religious worship.[84] The baptismal seal enables and commits Christians to serve God by a vital participation in the holy liturgy of the Church and to exercise their baptismal priesthood by the witness of holy lives and practical charity.[85]

1274 The Holy Spirit has marked us with the *seal of the Lord* ("*Dominicus character*") "for the day of redemption."[86] "Baptism indeed is the seal of eternal life."[87] The faithful Christian who has "kept the seal" until the end, remaining faithful to the demands of his Baptism, will be able to depart this life "marked with the sign
of faith,"[88] with his baptismal faith, 197
in expectation of the blessed vision of
God—the consummation of faith— 2016
and in the hope of resurrection.

In Brief

1275 *Christian initiation is accomplished by three sacraments together: Baptism which is the beginning of new life; Confirmation which is its strengthening; and the Eucharist which nourishes the disciple with Christ's Body and Blood for his transformation in Christ.*

1276 *"Go therefore and make disciples of all nations, baptizing them in the name of the Father and of the Son and of the Holy Spirit, teaching them to observe all that I have commanded you" (*Mt *28:19–20).*

1277 *Baptism is birth into the new life in Christ. In accordance with the Lord's will, it is necessary for salvation, as is the Church herself, which we enter by Baptism.*

[80] *LG* 11; cf. *LG* 17; *AG* 7; 23. — [81] *UR* 3. — [82] *UR* 22 § 2. — [83] Cf. *Rom* 8:29; Council of Trent (1547): DS 1609–1619. — [84] Cf. *LG* 11. — [85] Cf. *LG* 10. — [86] St. Augustine, *Ep.* 98, 5: PL 33, 362; *Eph* 4:30; cf. 1:13–14; *2 Cor* 1:21–22. — [87] St. Irenaeus, *Dem ap.* 3: SCh 62, 32. — [88] *Roman Missal*, EP I (Roman Canon) 97.

1278 *The essential rite of Baptism consists in immersing the candidate in water or pouring water on his head, while pronouncing the invocation of the Most Holy Trinity: the Father, the Son, and the Holy Spirit.*

1279 *The fruit of Baptism, or baptismal grace, is a rich reality that includes forgiveness of original sin and all personal sins, birth into the new life by which man becomes an adoptive son of the Father, a member of Christ and a temple of the Holy Spirit. By this very fact the person baptized is incorporated into the Church, the Body of Christ, and made a sharer in the priesthood of Christ.*

1280 *Baptism imprints on the soul an indelible spiritual sign, the character, which consecrates the baptized person for Christian worship. Because of the character Baptism cannot be repeated (cf. DS 1609 and DS 1624).*

1281 *Those who die for the faith, those who are catechumens, and all those who, without knowing of the Church but acting under the inspiration of grace, seek God sincerely and strive to fulfill his will, can be saved even if they have not been baptized (cf.* LG *16).*

1282 *Since the earliest times, Baptism has been administered to children, for it is a grace and a gift of God that does not presuppose any human merit; children are baptized in the faith of the Church. Entry into Christian life gives access to true freedom.*

1283 *With respect to children who have died without Baptism, the liturgy of the Church invites us to trust in God's mercy and to pray for their salvation.*

1284 *In case of necessity, any person can baptize provided that he have the intention of doing that which the Church does and provided that he pours water on the candidate's head while saying: "I baptize you in the name of the Father, and of the Son, and of the Holy Spirit."*

Article 2: THE SACRAMENT OF CONFIRMATION

1285 Baptism, the Eucharist, and the sacrament of Confirmation together constitute the "sacraments of Christian initiation," whose unity must be safeguarded. It must be explained to the faithful that the reception of the sacrament of Confirmation is necessary for the completion of baptismal grace.[89] For "by the sacrament of Confirmation, [the baptized] are more perfectly bound to the Church and are enriched with a special strength of the Holy Spirit. Hence they are, as true witnesses of Christ, more strictly obliged to spread and defend the faith by word and deed."[90]

I. Confirmation in the Economy of Salvation

1286 In the Old Testament the prophets announced that the Spirit of the Lord would rest on the hoped-for Messiah for his saving 702–716

[89] Cf. *Roman Ritual,* Rite of Confirmation (OC), Introduction 1. — [90] *LG* 11; cf. *OC,* Introduction 2.

mission.[91] The descent of the Holy Spirit on Jesus at his baptism by John was the sign that this was he who was to come, the Messiah, the Son of God.[92] He was conceived of the Holy Spirit; his whole life and his whole mission are carried out in total communion with the Holy Spirit whom the Father gives him "without measure."[93]

1287 This fullness of the Spirit was not to remain uniquely the Messiah's, but was to be communicated to *the whole messianic people*.[94]
739 On several occasions Christ promised this outpouring of the Spirit,[95] a promise which he fulfilled first on Easter Sunday and then more strikingly at Pentecost.[96] Filled with the Holy Spirit the apostles began to proclaim "the mighty works of God," and Peter declared this outpouring of the Spirit to be the sign of the messianic age.[97] Those who believed in the apostolic preaching and were baptized received the gift of the Holy Spirit in their turn.[98]

1288 "From that time on the apostles, in fulfillment of Christ's will, imparted to the newly baptized by the laying on of hands the gift of the Spirit that completes the grace of Baptism. For this reason in the *Letter to*
699 *the Hebrews* the doctrine concerning Baptism and the laying on of hands is listed among the first elements of Christian instruction. The imposition of hands is rightly recognized by the Catholic tradition as the origin of the sacrament of Confirmation, which in a certain way perpetuates the grace of Pentecost in the Church."[99]

1289 Very early, the better to signify the gift of the Holy Spirit, an anointing with perfumed oil 695
(*chrism*) was added to the laying on of hands. This anointing highlights the name "Christian," which means "anointed" and derives from that of Christ himself whom God "anointed with the Holy Spirit."[100] This rite of 436
anointing has continued ever since, in both East and West. For this reason the Eastern Churches call this sacrament *Chrismation*, anointing with chrism, or *myron* which means 1297
"chrism." In the West, the term *Confirmation* suggests that this sacrament both confirms baptism and strengthens baptismal grace.

Two traditions: East and West

1290 In the first centuries Confirmation generally comprised one single celebration with Baptism, forming with it a "double sacrament," according to the expression of St. Cyprian. Among other reasons, the multiplication of infant baptisms all through the year, the increase of rural parishes, and the growth of dioceses often prevented the bishop from being present at all baptismal celebrations. In the West the desire to reserve the completion of Baptism to the bishop caused the temporal separation of the two sacraments. The East has kept them united, so that Confirmation is conferred by the priest who baptizes. 1233
But he can do so only with the "myron" consecrated by a bishop.[101]

1291 A custom of the Roman 1242
Church facilitated the development

[91] Cf. *Isa* 11:2; 61:1; *Lk* 4:16–22. — [92] Cf. *Mt* 3:13-17; *Jn* 1:33–34. — [93] *Jn* 3:34. — [94] Cf. *Ezek* 36:25–27; *Joel* 3:1–2. — [95] Cf. *Lk* 12:12; *Jn* 3:5–8; 7:37–39; 16:7–15; *Acts* 1:8. — [96] Cf. *Jn* 20:22; *Acts* 2:1–4. — [97] *Acts* 2:11; cf. 2:17–18. — [98] Cf. *Acts* 2:38. — [99] Paul VI, *Divinae consortium naturae*, 659; cf. *Acts* 8:15–17; 19:5–6; *Heb* 6:2.— [100] *Acts* 10:38. — [101] Cf. CCEO, can. 695 § 1; 696 § 1.

of the Western practice: a double anointing with sacred chrism after Baptism. The first anointing of the neophyte on coming out of the baptismal bath was performed by the priest; it was completed by a second anointing on the forehead of the newly baptized by the bishop.[102] The first anointing with sacred chrism, by the priest, has remained attached to the baptismal rite; it signifies the participation of the one baptized in the prophetic, priestly, and kingly offices of Christ. If Baptism is conferred on an adult, there is only one post-baptismal anointing, that of Confirmation.

1244 **1292** The practice of the Eastern Churches gives greater emphasis to the unity of Christian initiation. That of the Latin Church more clearly expresses the communion of the new Christian with the bishop as guarantor and servant of the unity, catholicity and apostolicity of his Church, and hence the connection with the apostolic origins of Christ's Church.

II. The Signs and the Rite of Confirmation

1293 In treating the rite of Confirmation, it is fitting to consider the sign of *anointing* and what it signifies and imprints: a spiritual *seal*.

695 Anointing, in Biblical and other ancient symbolism, is rich in meaning: oil is a sign of abundance and joy;[103] it cleanses (anointing before and after a bath) and limbers (the anointing of athletes and wrestlers); oil is a sign of healing, since it is soothing to bruises and wounds;[104] and it makes radiant with beauty, health, and strength.

1294 Anointing with oil has all 1152
these meanings in the sacramental life. The pre-baptismal anointing with the oil of catechumens signifies cleansing and strengthening; the anointing of the sick expresses healing and comfort. The post-baptismal anointing with sacred chrism in Confirmation and ordination is the sign of consecration. By Confirmation Christians, that is, those who are anointed, share more completely in the mission of Jesus Christ and the fullness of the Holy Spirit with which he is filled, so that their lives may give off "the aroma of Christ."[105]

1295 By this anointing the confir- 698
mand receives the "mark," the *seal* of the Holy Spirit. A seal is a symbol of a person, a sign of personal authority, or ownership of an object.[106] Hence soldiers were marked with their leader's seal and slaves with their master's. A seal authenticates a juridical act or document and occasionally makes it secret.[107]

1296 Christ himself declared that he was marked with his Father's seal.[108] Christians are also marked with a seal: "It is God who establishes us with you in Christ and has
commissioned us; he has put his seal 121
on us and given us his Spirit in our hearts as a guarantee."[109] This seal of the Holy Spirit marks our total belonging to Christ, our enrollment in his service for ever, as well as the promise of divine protection in the great eschatological trial.[110]

The celebration of Confirmation

1297 *The consecration of the sacred* 1183
chrism is an important action that

[102] Cf. St. Hippolytus, *Trad. Ap.* 21: SCh 11, 80–95. — [103] *Deut* 11:14; *Pss* 23:5; 104:15. — [104] Cf. *Isa* 1:6; *Lk* 10:34. — [105] *2 Cor* 2:15. — [106] Cf. *Gen* 38:18; 41:42; *Deut* 32:34; *CT* 8:6. — [107] Cf. *1 Kings* 21:8; *Jer* 32:10; *Isa* 29:11. — [108] Cf. *Jn* 6:27. — [109] *2 Cor* 1:21–22; cf. *Eph* 1:13; 4, 30. — [110] Cf. *Rev* 7:2–3; 9:4; *Ezek* 9:4–6.

precedes the celebration of Confirmation, but is in a certain way a part of it. It is the bishop who, in the course of the Chrism Mass of Holy Thursday, consecrates the sacred chrism for his whole diocese. In some
1241 Eastern Churches this consecration is even reserved to the patriarch:

> The liturgy of Antioch expresses the epiclesis for the consecration of the sacred chrism (myron) in this way: "[Father…send your Holy Spirit] on us and on this oil which is before us and consecrate it, so that it may be for all who are anointed and marked with it holy myron, priestly myron, royal myron, anointing with gladness, clothing with light, a cloak of salvation, a spiritual gift, the sanctification of souls and bodies, imperishable happiness, the indelible seal, a buckler of faith, and a fearsome helmet against all the works of the adversary."

1298 When Confirmation is celebrated separately from Baptism, as is the case in the Roman Rite, the Liturgy of Confirmation begins with the renewal of baptismal promises and the profession of faith by the confirmands. This clearly shows that Confirmation follows Baptism.[111] When adults are baptized, they immediately receive Confirmation and participate in the Eucharist.[112]

1299 In the Roman Rite the bishop extends his hands over the whole group of the confirmands. Since the time of the apostles this gesture has signified the gift of the Spirit. The bishop invokes the outpouring of the Spirit in these words:

> All-powerful God, Father of our Lord Jesus Christ, by water and the Holy Spirit you freed your sons and daughters from sin and gave them new life.Send your Holy Spirit upon them to be their helper and guide.Give them the spirit of wisdom and understanding, the spirit of right judgment and courage, the spirit of knowledge and reverence. Fill them with the spirit of wonder and awe in your presence. We ask this through
> Christ our Lord.[113] 1831

1300 The *essential rite* of the sacrament follows. In the Latin rite, "the sacrament of Confirmation is conferred through the anointing with chrism on the forehead, which is done by the laying on of the hand,
and through the words: *'Accipe signac-* 699
ulum doni Spiritus Sancti' [Be sealed with the Gift of the Holy Spirit.]."[114] In the Eastern Churches of Byzantine rite, after a prayer of epiclesis, the more significant parts of the body are anointed with myron: forehead, eyes, nose, ears, lips, chest, back, hands, and feet. Each anointing is accompanied by the formula Σφραγίς δωρεᾶς Πνεύματος Ἁγίου (*Signaculum doni Spiritus Sancti*): "the seal of the gift of the Holy Spirit."[115]

1301 The sign of peace that concludes the rite of the sacrament signifies and demonstrates ecclesial communion with the bishop and with all the faithful.[116]

III. The Effects of Confirmation

1302 It is evident from its celebration that the effect of the sacrament of Confirmation is the special outpouring of the Holy Spirit as once granted
to the apostles on the day of Pentecost. 731

[111] Cf. *SC* 71. — [112] Cf. CIC, can. 866. — [113] OC 25. — [114] Paul VI, apostolic constitution, *Divinae consortium naturae*, 663. — [115] *Rituale per le Chiese orientali di rito bizantino in lingua greca,* Pars Prima (Libreria Editrice Vaticana, 1954), 36. — [116] Cf. St. Hippolytus, *Trad. Ap.* 21: SCh 11, 80–95.

262–1274 **1303** From this fact, Confirmation brings an increase and deepening of baptismal grace:

– it roots us more deeply in the divine filiation which makes us cry, "Abba! Father!";[117]

– it unites us more firmly to Christ;

– it increases the gifts of the Holy Spirit in us;

– it renders our bond with the Church more perfect;[118]

– it gives us a special strength of the Holy Spirit to spread and defend
2044 the faith by word and action as true witnesses of Christ, to confess the name of Christ boldly, and never to be ashamed of the Cross:[119]

> Recall then that you have received the spiritual seal, the spirit of wisdom and understanding, the spirit of right judgment and courage, the spirit of knowledge and reverence, the spirit of holy fear in God's presence. Guard what you have received. God the Father has marked you with his sign; Christ the Lord has confirmed you and has placed his pledge, the Spirit, in your hearts.[120]

1121 **1304** Like Baptism which it completes, Confirmation is given only once, for it too imprints on the soul an *indelible spiritual mark*, the "character," which is the sign that Jesus Christ has marked a Christian with the seal of his Spirit by clothing him with power from on high so that he may be his witness.[121]

1268 **1305** This "character" perfects the common priesthood of the faithful, received in Baptism, and "the confirmed person receives the power to profess faith in Christ publicly and as it were officially (*quasi ex officio*)."[122]

IV. Who Can Receive This Sacrament?

1306 Every baptized person not yet confirmed can and should receive the sacrament of Confirmation.[123] Since Baptism, Confirmation, and Eucharist form a unity, it 1212
follows that "the faithful are obliged to receive this sacrament at the appropriate time,"[124] for without Confirmation and Eucharist, Baptism is certainly valid and efficacious, but Christian initiation remains incomplete.

1307 For centuries, Latin custom has indicated "the age of discretion" as the reference point for receiving Confirmation. But in danger of death children should be confirmed even if they have not yet attained the age of discretion.[125]

1308 Although Confirmation is sometimes called the "sacrament of Christian maturity," we must not confuse adult faith with the adult age of natural growth, nor forget that the
baptismal grace is a grace of free, un- 1250
merited election and does not need "ratification" to become effective. St. Thomas reminds us of this:

> Age of body does not determine age of soul. Even in childhood man can attain spiritual maturity: as the book of Wisdom says: "For old age is not honored for length of time, or measured by number of years." Many children, through the strength of the Holy Spirit they have received, have bravely fought for Christ even to the shedding of their blood.[126]

[117] *Rom* 8:15. — [118] Cf. *LG* 11. — [119] Cf. Council of Florence (1439): DS 1319; *LG* 11; 12. — [120] St. Ambrose, *De myst.* 7, 42: PL 16, 402–403. — [121] Cf. Council of Trent (1547): DS 1609; *Lk* 24:48–49. — [122] St. Thomas Aquinas, *STh* III, 72, 5, *ad* 2. — [123] 2Cf. CIC, can. 889 § 1. — [124] CIC can. 890. — [125] Cf. CIC, cann. 891; 883, 3°. — [126] St. Thomas Aquinas, *STh* III, 72, 8, *ad* 2; cf. *Wis* 4:8.

1309 *Preparation* for Confirmation should aim at leading the Christian toward a more intimate union with Christ and a more lively familiarity with the Holy Spirit—his actions, his gifts, and his biddings—in order to be more capable of assuming the apostolic responsibilities of Christian life. To this end catechesis for Confirmation should strive to awaken a sense of belonging to the Church of Jesus Christ, the universal Church as well as the parish community. The latter bears special responsibility for the preparation of confirmands.[127]

1310 To receive Confirmation one must be in a state of grace. One should receive the sacrament of Penance in order to be cleansed for the
2670 gift of the Holy Spirit. More intense prayer should prepare one to receive the strength and graces of the Holy Spirit with docility and readiness to act.[128]

1311 Candidates for Confirmation, as for Baptism, fittingly seek the spiritual help of a *sponsor*. To emphasize the unity of the two sac
1255 raments, it is appropriate that this be one of the baptismal godparents.[129]

V. The Minister of Confirmation

1312 The *original minister* of Confirmation is the bishop.[130]

1233 In the East, ordinarily the priest who baptizes also immediately confers Confirmation in one and the same celebration. But he does so with sacred chrism consecrated by the patriarch or the bishop, thus expressing the apostolic unity of the Church whose bonds are strengthened by the sacrament of Confirmation. In the Latin Church, the same discipline applies to the Baptism of adults or to the reception into full communion with the Church of a person baptized in another Christian community that does not have valid Confirmation.[131]

1313 *In the Latin Rite*, the or- 1290
dinary minister of Confirmation is the bishop.[132] If the need arises, the bishop may grant the faculty of administering Confirmation[133] to priests, although it is fitting that he confer it himself, mindful that the celebration of Confirmation has been temporally separated from Baptism for this reason. Bishops are the successors of the apostles. They have received the fullness of the sacrament of Holy Orders. The administration of this sacrament by them demonstrates clearly that its effect is to unite those who receive it more closely to the Church, to her apostolic origins, and to her mission of 1285
bearing witness to Christ.

1314 If a Christian is in danger of 1307
death, any priest can give him Confirmation.[134] Indeed the Church desires that none of her children, even the youngest, should depart this world without having been perfected by the Holy Spirit with the gift of Christ's fullness.

In Brief

1315 *"Now when the apostles at Jerusalem heard that Samaria had received the word of God, they sent to*

[127] Cf. *OC* Introduction 3. — [128] Cf. *Acts* 1:14. — [129] Cf. *OC* Introduction 5; 6; CIC, can. 893 §§ 1–2. — [130] Cf. *LG* 26. — [131] Cf. CIC, can. 883 § 2. — [132] Cf. CIC, can. 882. — [133] Cf. CIC, can. 884 § 2. — [134] Cf. CIC, can. 883 § 3.

them Peter and John, who came down and prayed for them that they might receive the Holy Spirit; for it had not yet fallen on any of them, but they had only been baptized in the name of the Lord Jesus. Then they laid their hands on them and they received the Holy Spirit" (Acts *8:14–17).*

1316 *Confirmation perfects Baptismal grace; it is the sacrament which gives the Holy Spirit in order to root us more deeply in the divine filiation, incorporate us more firmly into Christ, strengthen our bond with the Church, associate us more closely with her mission, and help us bear witness to the Christian faith in words accompanied by deeds.*

1317 *Confirmation, like Baptism, imprints a spiritual mark or indelible character on the Christian's soul; for this reason one can receive this sacrament only once in one's life.*

1318 *In the East this sacrament is administered immediately after Baptism and is followed by participation in the Eucharist; this tradition highlights the unity of the three sacraments of Christian initiation. In the Latin Church this sacrament is administered when the age of reason has been reached, and its celebration is ordinarily reserved to the bishop, thus signifying that this sacrament strengthens the ecclesial bond.*

1319 *A candidate for Confirmation who has attained the age of reason must profess the faith, be in the state of grace, have the intention of receiving the sacrament, and be prepared to assume the role of disciple and witness to Christ, both within the ecclesial community and in temporal affairs.*

1320 *The essential rite of Confirmation is anointing the forehead of the baptized with sacred chrism (in the East other sense-organs as well), together with the laying on of the minister's hand and the words:* "Accipe signaculum doni Spiritus Sancti" *(Be sealed with the Gift of the Holy Spirit.) in the Roman rite, or:* Signaculum doni Spiritus Sancti *(the seal of the gift of the Holy Spirit) in the Byzantine rite.*

1321 *When Confirmation is celebrated separately from Baptism, its connection with Baptism is expressed, among other ways, by the renewal of baptismal promises. The celebration of Confirmation during the Eucharist helps underline the unity of the sacraments of Christian initiation.*

Article 3: THE SACRAMENT OF THE EUCHARIST

1212 **1322** The holy Eucharist completes Christian initiation. Those who have been raised to the dignity of the royal priesthood by Baptism and configured more deeply to Christ by Confirmation participate with the whole community in the Lord's own sacrifice by means of the Eucharist.

1323 "At the Last Supper, on the night he was betrayed, our Savior instituted the Eucharistic sacrifice of his Body and Blood. This he did in order to perpetuate the sacrifice of the cross throughout the ages until he should come again, and so to entrust to his beloved Spouse, the Church, a me-

morial of his death and resurrection: a sacrament of love, a sign of unity, a bond of charity, a Paschal banquet 'in
1402 which Christ is consumed, the mind is filled with grace, and a pledge of future glory is given to us.'"[135]

I. The Eucharist—Source and Summit of Ecclesial Life

864 **1324** The Eucharist is "the source and summit of the Christian life."[136] "The other sacraments, and indeed all ecclesiastical ministries and works of the apostolate, are bound up with the Eucharist and are oriented toward it. For in the blessed Eucharist is contained the whole spiritual good of the Church, namely Christ himself, our Pasch."[137]

1325 "The Eucharist is the efficacious sign and sublime cause of that communion in the divine life and that unity of the People of God by which the Church is kept in being.
775 It is the culmination both of God's action sanctifying the world in Christ and of the worship men offer to Christ and through him to the Father in the Holy Spirit."[138]

1090 **1326** Finally, by the Eucharistic celebration we already unite ourselves with the heavenly liturgy and anticipate eternal life, when God will be all in all.[139]

1327 In brief, the Eucharist is the sum and summary of our faith: "Our
1124 way of thinking is attuned to the Eucharist, and the Eucharist in turn confirms our way of thinking."[140]

II. What Is This Sacrament Called?

1328 The inexhaustible richness of this sacrament is expressed in the different names we give it. Each name evokes certain aspects of it. It is called:

Eucharist, because it is an action 2637
of thanksgiving to God. The Greek
words *eucharistein*[141] and *eulogein*[142] 1082
recall the Jewish blessings that proclaim—especially during a meal— 1359
God's works: creation, redemption, and sanctification.

1329 The Lord's Supper, because of 1382
its connection with the supper which the Lord took with his disciples on the eve of his Passion and because it anticipates the wedding feast of the Lamb in the heavenly Jerusalem.[143]

The *Breaking of Bread*, because Jesus used this rite, part of a Jewish meal, when as master of the table he blessed and distributed the bread,[144] above all at the Last Supper.[145] It is by this action that his disciples will recognize him after his Resurrection,[146] and it is this expression that the first Christians will use to designate their
Eucharistic assemblies;[147] by doing 790
so they signified that all who eat the one broken bread, Christ, enter into communion with him and form but one body in him.[148]

The *Eucharistic assembly* (*synaxis*), 1348
because the Eucharist is celebrated amid the assembly of the faithful, the visible expression of the Church.[149]

[135] *SC* 47. — [136] *LG* 11. — [137] *PO* 5. — [138] Congregation of Rites, instruction, *Eucharisticum mysterium*, 6. — [139] *1 Cor* 15:28. — [140] St. Irenaeus, *Adv. haeres.* 4, 18, 5: PG 7/1, 1028. — [141] Cf. *Lk* 22:19; *1 Cor* 11:24. — [142] Cf. *Mt* 26:26; *Mk* 14:22. [143] Cf. *1 Cor* 11:20; *Rev* 19:9. — [144] Cf. *Mt* 14:19; 15:36; *Mk* 8:6, 19. — [145] Cf. *Mt* 26:26; *1 Cor* 11:24. — [146] Cf. *Lk* 24:13–35. — [147] Cf. *Acts* 2:42, 46; 20:7, 11. — [148] Cf. *1 Cor* 10:16–17. — [149] Cf. *1 Cor* 11:17–34.

1341 **1330** The *memorial* of the Lord's Passion and Resurrection.

The *Holy Sacrifice*, because it makes present the one sacrifice of Christ the Savior and includes the Church's offering. The terms *holy sacrifice of the Mass, "sacrifice of praise," spiritual sacrifice, pure and holy sacrifice* are
614, 2643 also used,[150] since it completes and surpasses all the sacrifices of the Old Covenant.

The *Holy and Divine Liturgy*, because the Church's whole liturgy finds its center and most intense expression in the celebration of this sacrament; in the same sense we also call its celebration the *Sacred Mys-*
1169 *teries*. We speak of the *Most Blessed Sacrament* because it is the Sacrament of sacraments. The Eucharistic species reserved in the tabernacle are designated by this same name.

950 **1331** *Holy Communion*, because by this sacrament we unite ourselves to Christ, who makes us sharers in his Body and Blood to form a single body.[151] We also call it: *the holy things (ta hagia; sancta)*[152]—the first
948 meaning of the phrase "communion of saints" in the Apostles' Creed—
1405 *the bread of angels, bread from heaven, medicine of immortality*,[153] *viaticum*....

1332 *Holy Mass (Missa)*, because the liturgy in which the mystery of salvation is accomplished concludes with the sending forth (*missio*) of the faithful, so that they may fulfill
849 God's will in their daily lives.

III. The Eucharist in the Economy of Salvation

The signs of bread and wine

1333 At the heart of the Eucharistic celebration are the bread and 1350
wine that, by the words of Christ and the invocation of the Holy Spirit, become Christ's Body and Blood. Faithful to the Lord's command the Church continues to do, in his memory and until his glorious return, what he did on the eve of his Passion: "He took bread...." "He took the cup filled with wine...." The signs of bread and wine become, in a way surpassing understanding, the Body and Blood of Christ; they continue also to signify the goodness of creation. Thus in the Offertory we give thanks to the Creator for bread and
wine,[154] fruit of the "work of human 1147
hands," but above all as "fruit of the earth" and "of the vine"—gifts of the
Creator. The Church sees in the ges- 1148
ture of the king-priest Melchizedek, who "brought out bread and wine," a prefiguring of her own offering.[155]

1334 In the Old Covenant bread 1150
and wine were offered in sacrifice among the first fruits of the earth as a sign of grateful acknowledgment to the Creator. But they also received a
new significance in the context of the 1363
Exodus: the unleavened bread that Israel eats every year at Passover commemorates the haste of the departure that liberated them from Egypt; the remembrance of the manna in the desert will always recall to Israel that

[150] *Heb* 13:15; cf. *1 Pet* 2:5; Ps 116:13, 17; *Mal* 1:11. — [151] Cf. *1 Cor* 10:16–17. — [152] *Apostolic Constitutions* 8, 13, 12: PG 1, 1108; *Didache* 9, 5; 10:6: SCh248, 176–178. — [153] St. Ignatius of Antioch, *Ad Eph.* 20, 2: SCh 10, 76. — [154] Cf. *Ps* 104:13–15. — [155] *Gen* 14:18; cf. *Roman Missal*, EP I (Roman Canon) 95.

it lives by the bread of the Word of God;[156] their daily bread is the fruit of the promised land, the pledge of God's faithfulness to his promises. The "cup of blessing"[157] at the end of the Jewish Passover meal adds to the festive joy of wine an eschatological dimension: the messianic expectation of the rebuilding of Jerusalem. When Jesus instituted the Eucharist, he gave a new and definitive meaning to the blessing of the bread and the cup.

1151 **1335** The miracles of the multiplication of the loaves, when the Lord says the blessing, breaks and distributes the loaves through his disciples to feed the multitude, prefigure the superabundance of this unique bread of his Eucharist.[158] The sign of water turned into wine at Cana already announces the Hour of Jesus' glorification. It makes manifest the fulfillment of the wedding feast in the Father's kingdom, where the faithful will drink the new wine that has become the Blood of Christ.[159]

1336 The first announcement of the Eucharist divided the disciples, just as the announcement of the Passion scandalized them: "This is a hard saying; who can listen to it?"[160] The Eucharist and the Cross are stumbling blocks. It is the same mystery and it never ceases to be an occasion of division. "Will you also go away?":[161] the Lord's question echoes through the ages, as a loving invitation to discover that only he has "the words of eternal life"[162] *and that to receive in faith the gift of his Eucharist is*
1327 *to receive the Lord himself.*

The institution of the Eucharist

1337 The Lord, having loved those 610
who were his own, loved them to the end. Knowing that the hour had come to leave this world and return to the Father, in the course of a meal he washed their feet and gave them the commandment of love.[163] In order to leave them a pledge of this love, in order never to depart from his own and to make them sharers in his Passover, he instituted the Eucharist as the memorial of his death and Resurrection, and commanded his apostles to celebrate it until his return; "thereby he constituted them
priests of the New Testament."[164] 611

1338 The three synoptic Gospels and St. Paul have handed on to us the account of the institution of the Eucharist; St. John, for his part, reports the words of Jesus in the synagogue of Capernaum that prepare for the institution of the Eucharist: Christ calls himself the bread of life, come down from heaven.[165]

1339 Jesus chose the time of 1169
Passover to fulfill what he had announced at Capernaum: giving his disciples his Body and his Blood:

> Then came the day of Unleavened Bread, on which the passover lamb had to be sacrificed. So Jesus sent Peter and John, saying, "Go and prepare the passover meal for us, that we may eat it...." They went...and prepared the passover. And when the hour came, he sat at table, and the apostles with him. And he said to them, "I have earnestly desired to eat this passover with you before I suffer; for I tell you I shall not eat it again

[156] Cf. *Deut* 8:3. — [157] *1 Cor* 10:16. — [158] Cf. *Mt* 14:13–21; 15:32–39. — [159] Cf. *Jn* 2:11; *Mk* 14:25. — [160] *Jn* 6:60. — [161] *Jn* 6:67. — [162] *Jn* 6:68. — [163] Cf. *Jn* 13:1–17; 34–35. — [164] Council of Trent (1562): DS 1740. — [165] Cf. *Jn* 6.

> until it is fulfilled in the kingdom of God.".... And he took bread, and when he had given thanks he broke it and gave it to them, saying, "This is my body which is given for you. Do this in remembrance of me." And likewise the cup after supper, saying, "This cup which is poured out for you is the New Covenant in my blood."[166]

1340 By celebrating the Last Supper with his apostles in the course of the Passover meal, Jesus gave the Jewish Passover its definitive meaning.
1151 Jesus' passing over to his father by his death and Resurrection, the new Passover, is anticipated in the Supper and celebrated in the Eucharist, which fulfills the Jewish Passover and anticipates the final Passover of the
677 Church in the glory of the kingdom.

"Do this in memory of me"

611 **1341** The command of Jesus to repeat his actions and words "until he comes" does not only ask us to remember Jesus and what he did. It is directed at the liturgical celebration, by the apostles and their successors,
1363 of the *memorial* of Christ, of his life, of his death, of his Resurrection, and of his intercession in the presence of the Father.[167]

2624 **1342** From the beginning the Church has been faithful to the Lord's command. Of the Church of Jerusalem it is written:

> They devoted themselves to the apostles' teaching and fellowship, to the breaking of bread and the prayers. ... Day by day, attending the temple together and breaking bread in their homes, they partook of food with glad and generous hearts.[168]

1343 It was above all on "the first 1166, 2177
day of the week," Sunday, the day of Jesus' resurrection, that the Christians met "to break bread."[169] From that time on down to our own day the celebration of the Eucharist has been continued so that today we encounter it everywhere in the Church with the same fundamental structure. It remains the center of the Church's life.

1344 Thus from celebration to 1404
celebration, as they proclaim the Paschal mystery of Jesus "until he comes," the pilgrim People of God advances, "following the narrow way of the cross,"[170] toward the heavenly banquet, when all the elect will be seated at the table of the kingdom.

IV. The Liturgical Celebration of the Eucharist

The Mass of all ages

1345 As early as the second century we have the witness of St. Justin Martyr for the basic lines of the order of the Eucharistic celebration. They have stayed the same until our own day for all the great liturgical families. St. Justin wrote to the pagan emperor Antoninus Pius (138–161) around the year 155, explaining what Christians did:

> On the day we call the day of the sun, all who dwell in the city or country gather in the same place.
> The memoirs of the apostles and the writings of the prophets are read, as much as time permits.
> When the reader has finished, he who presides over those gathered admonishes and challenges them to imitate these beautiful things.

[166] *Lk* 22:7–20; cf. *Mt* 26:17–29; *Mk* 14:12-25; *1 Cor* 11:23–26. — [167] Cf. *1 Cor* 11:26. — [168] *Acts* 2:42, 46. — [169] *Acts* 20:7. — [170] AG 1; cf. *1 Cor* 11:26.

> Then we all rise together and offer prayers* for ourselves…and for all others, wherever they may be, so that we may be found righteous by our life and actions, and faithful to the commandments, so as to obtain eternal salvation.
> When the prayers are concluded we exchange the kiss.
> Then someone brings bread and a cup of water and wine mixed together to him who presides over the brethren.
> He takes them and offers praise and glory to the Father of the universe, through the name of the Son and of the Holy Spirit and for a considerable time he gives thanks (in Greek: eucharistian) that we have been judged worthy of these gifts.
> When he has concluded the prayers and thanksgivings, all present give voice to an acclamation by saying: 'Amen.'
> When he who presides has given thanks and the people have responded, those whom we call deacons give to those present the "eucharisted" bread, wine and water and take them to those who are absent.[171]

1346 The liturgy of the Eucharist unfolds according to a fundamental structure which has been preserved throughout the centuries down to our own day. It displays two great parts that form a fundamental unity:

– the gathering, the liturgy of the Word, with readings, homily, and general intercessions;

– the liturgy of the Eucharist, with the presentation of the bread and wine, the consecratory thanksgiving, and communion.

The liturgy of the Word and liturgy of the Eucharist together form "one single act of worship";[172] the Eucharistic table set for us is the table both of the Word of God and of the Body 103
of the Lord.[173]

1347 Is this not the same movement as the Paschal meal of the risen Jesus with his disciples? Walking with them he explained the Scriptures to them; sitting with them at table "he took bread, blessed and broke it, and gave it to them."[174]

The movement of the celebration

1348 *All gather together.* Christians come together in one place for the Eucharistic assembly. At its head is Christ himself, the principal agent
of the Eucharist. He is high priest 1140
of the New Covenant; it is he himself who presides invisibly over every Eucharistic celebration. It is in representing him that the bishop or priest
acting *in the person of Christ the head* 1548
(in persona Christi capitis) presides over the assembly, speaks after the readings, receives the offerings, and says the Eucharistic Prayer. *All* have their own active parts to play in the celebration, each in his own way: readers, those who bring up the offerings, those who give communion, and the whole people whose "Amen" manifests their participation.

1349 The *Liturgy of the Word* in- 1184
cludes "the writings of the prophets," that is, the Old Testament, and "the memoirs of the apostles" (their letters and the Gospels). After the homily, which is an exhortation to accept this Word as what it truly is, the Word of God,[175] and to put it into practice, come the intercessions for all men, according to the

[171] St. Justin, *Apol.* 1, 65–67: PG 6, 428–429; the text before the asterisk (*) is from chap. 67. — [172] *SC* 56. — [173] Cf. *DV* 21. — [174] Cf. *Lk* 24:13–35. — [175] Cf. 1 *Thess* 2:13.

Apostle's words: "I urge that supplications, prayers, intercessions, and thanksgivings be made for all men, for kings, and all who are in high positions."[176]

1350 *The presentation of the offerings* (the Offertory). Then, sometimes in procession, the bread and wine are brought to the altar; they will be offered by the priest in the name of Christ in the Eucharistic sacrifice in which they will become his body and blood. It is the very action of Christ at the Last Supper—"taking the bread and a cup." "The Church alone offers this pure oblation to the Creator, when she
1359 offers what comes forth from his creation with thanksgiving."[177] The presentation of the offerings at the altar takes up the gesture of Melchizedek and commits the Creator's gifts into the hands of Christ who, in his sacrifice, brings to perfection all human
614 attempts to offer sacrifices.

1351 From the very beginning Christians have brought, along with the bread and wine for the Eucharist, gifts to share with those in need. This custom of the *collection*,
1397 ever appropriate, is inspired by the example of Christ who became poor
2186 to make us rich:[178]

> Those who are well off, and who are also willing, give as each chooses. What is gathered is given to him who presides to assist orphans and widows, those whom illness or any other cause has deprived of resources, prisoners, immigrants and, in a word, all who are in need.[179]

1352 The *anaphora*: with the Eucharistic Prayer—the prayer of thanksgiving and consecration—we come to the heart and summit of the celebration:

In the *preface*, the Church gives thanks 559
to the Father, through Christ, in the Holy Spirit, for all his works: creation, redemption, and sanctification. The whole community thus joins in the unending praise that the Church in heaven, the angels and all the saints, sing to the thrice-holy God.

1353 In the *epiclesis*, the Church 1105
asks the Father to send his Holy Spirit (or the power of his blessing[180]) on the bread and wine, so that by his power they may become the body and blood of Jesus Christ and so that those who take part in the Eucharist may be one body and one spirit (some liturgical traditions put the epiclesis after the anamnesis).

In the *institution narrative*, the pow- 1375
er of the words and the action of Christ, and the power of the Holy Spirit, make sacramentally present under the species of bread and wine Christ's body and blood, his sacrifice offered on the cross once for all.

1354 In the *anamnesis* that fol- 1103
lows, the Church calls to mind the Passion, resurrection, and glorious return of Christ Jesus; she presents to the Father the offering of his Son which reconciles us with him.

In the *intercessions*, the Church indicates that the Eucharist is celebrated in communion with the whole 954
Church in heaven and on earth, the

[176] *1 Tim* 2:1–2. — [177] St. Irenaeus, *Adv. haeres.* 4, 18, 4: PG 7/1, 1027; cf. *Mal* 1:11. — [178] Cf. *1 Cor* 16:1; *2 Cor* 8:9. — [179] St. Justin, *Apol.* 1, 67: PG 6, 429. — [180] Cf. *Roman Missal*, EP I (Roman Canon) 90.

living and the dead, and in communion with the pastors of the Church, the Pope, the diocesan bishop, his presbyterium and his deacons, and all the bishops of the whole world together with their Churches.

1382 **1355** In the communion, preceded by the Lord's prayer and the breaking of the bread, the faithful receive "the bread of heaven" and "the cup of salvation," the body and blood of Christ who offered himself "for the life of the world":[181]

1327 Because this bread and wine have been made Eucharist ("eucharisted," according to an ancient expression), "we call this food *Eucharist*, and no one may take part in it unless he believes that what we teach is true, has received baptism for the forgiveness of sins and new birth, and lives in keeping with what Christ taught."[182]

V. The Sacramental Sacrifice: Thanksgiving, Memorial, Presence

1356 If from the beginning Christians have celebrated the Eucharist and in a form whose substance has not changed despite the great diversity of times and liturgies, it is because we know ourselves to be bound by the command the Lord gave on the eve of his Passion: "Do this in remembrance of me."[183]

1357 We carry out this command of the Lord by celebrating the *memorial of his sacrifice*. In so doing, *we offer to the Father* what he has himself given us: the gifts of his creation, bread and wine which, by the power of the Holy Spirit and by the words of Christ, have become the body and blood of Christ. Christ is thus really and mysteriously made present.

1358 We must therefore consider the Eucharist as:

– thanksgiving and praise to the *Father*;
– the sacrificial memorial of *Christ* and his Body;
– the presence of Christ by the power of his word and of his *Spirit*.

Thanksgiving and praise to the Father

1359 The Eucharist, the sacrament of our salvation accomplished by Christ on the cross, is also a sacrifice of praise in thanksgiving for the 293
work of creation. In the Eucharistic sacrifice the whole of creation loved by God is presented to the Father through the death and the Resurrection of Christ. Through Christ the Church can offer the sacrifice of praise in thanksgiving for all that God has made good, beautiful, and just in creation and in humanity.

1360 The Eucharist is a sacrifice of 1083
thanksgiving to the Father, a blessing by which the Church expresses her gratitude to God for all his benefits, for all that he has accomplished through creation, redemption, and sanctification. Eucharist means first of all "thanksgiving."

1361 The Eucharist is also the sacrifice of praise by which the Church sings the glory of God in the name of all creation. This sacrifice of praise is possible only through Christ: he 294
unites the faithful to his person, to his praise, and to his intercession, so that the sacrifice of praise to the Father is offered through Christ and with him, to be accepted in him.

[181] *Jn* 6:51. — [182] St. Justin, *Apol.* 1, 66, 1–2: PG 6, 428. — [183] *1 Cor* 11:24–25.

The sacrificial memorial of Christ and of his Body, the Church

1362 The Eucharist is the memorial of Christ's Passover, the making present and the sacramental offering of his unique sacrifice, in the liturgy of the Church which is his Body. In all the Eucharistic Prayers we find after the words of institution a prayer
1103 called the *anamnesis* or memorial.

1099 **1363** In the sense of Sacred Scripture the *memorial* is not merely the recollection of past events but the proclamation of the mighty works wrought by God for men.[184] In the liturgical celebration of these events, they become in a certain way present and real. This is how Israel understands its liberation from Egypt: every time Passover is celebrated, the Exodus events are made present to the memory of believers so that they may conform their lives to them.

1364 In the New Testament, the memorial takes on new meaning. When the Church celebrates the Eucharist, she commemorates Christ's Passover, and it is made present: the
611 sacrifice Christ offered once for all
on the cross remains ever present.[185]
1085 "As often as the sacrifice of the Cross by which 'Christ our Pasch has been sacrificed' is celebrated on the altar, the work of our redemption is carried out."[186]

2100 **1365** Because it is the memorial of Christ's Passover, the Eucharist is also a sacrifice. The sacrificial character of the Eucharist is manifested in the very words of institution: "This is my body which is given for you" and "This cup which is poured out for you is the New Covenant in my blood."[187] In the Eucharist Christ gives us the very body which he gave up for us on the cross, the very blood which he "poured out for
many for the forgiveness of sins."[188] 1846

1366 The Eucharist is thus a sac- 613
rifice because it *re-presents* (makes present) the sacrifice of the cross, because it is its *memorial* and because it *applies* its fruit:

> [Christ], our Lord and God, was once and for all to offer himself to God the Father by his death on the altar of the cross, to accomplish there an everlasting redemption. But because his priesthood was not to end with his death, at the Last Supper "on the night when he was betrayed," [he wanted] to leave to his beloved spouse the Church a visible sacrifice (as the nature of man demands) by which the bloody sacrifice which he was to accomplish once for all on the cross would be re-presented, its memory perpetuated until the end of the world, and its salutary power be applied to the forgiveness of the sins we daily commit.[189]

1367 The sacrifice of Christ and 1545
the sacrifice of the Eucharist are *one single sacrifice*: "The victim is one and the same: the same now offers through the ministry of priests, who then offered himself on the cross; only the manner of offering is different." "And since in this divine sacrifice which is celebrated in the Mass, the same Christ who offered himself once in a bloody manner on the altar of the cross is contained and offered in an unbloody manner...this sacrifice is truly propitiatory."[190]

[184] Cf. *Ex* 13:3. — [185] Cf. *Heb* 7:25–27. — [186] *LG* 3; cf. *1 Cor* 5:7. — [187] *Lk* 22:19–20. — [188] *Mt* 26:28. — [189] Council of Trent (1562): DS 1740; cf. *1 Cor* 11:23; *Heb* 7:24, 27. — [190] Council of Trent (1562): *Doctrina de ss. Missae sacrificio*, c. 2: DS 1743; cf. *Heb* 9:14, 27.

1368 *The Eucharist is also the sacrifice of the Church.* The Church which is the Body of Christ participates in the offering of her Head. With him, she herself is offered whole and entire. She unites herself to his intercession with the Father for all men. In the Eucharist the sacrifice of Christ becomes also the sacrifice of the members of his Body. The lives of
618 the faithful, their praise, sufferings, prayer, and work, are united with
2031 those of Christ and with his total offering, and so acquire a new value.
1109 Christ's sacrifice present on the altar makes it possible for all generations of Christians to be united with his offering.

In the catacombs the Church is often represented as a woman in prayer, arms outstretched in the praying position. Like Christ who stretched out his arms on the cross, through him, with him, and in him, she offers herself and intercedes for all men.

1369 *The whole Church is united with the offering and intercession of Christ.* Since he has the ministry of Peter in the Church, the Pope is associated with every celebration of
834, 882 the Eucharist, wherein he is named as the sign and servant of the unity of the universal Church. The *bishop* of the place is always responsible for the Eucharist, even when a *priest*
1561, 1566 presides; the bishop's name is mentioned to signify his presidency over the particular Church, in the midst of his presbyterium and with the assistance of *deacons.* The community intercedes also for all ministers who, for it and with it, offer the Eucharistic sacrifice:

> Let only that Eucharist be regarded as legitimate, which is celebrated under [the presidency of] the bishop or him to whom he has entrusted it.[191]
> Through the ministry of priests the spiritual sacrifice of the faithful is completed in union with the sacrifice of Christ the only Mediator, which in the Eucharist is offered through the priests' hands in the name of the whole Church in an unbloody and sacramental manner until the Lord himself comes.[192]

1370 To the offering of Christ are united not only the members still here on earth, but also those already in *the glory of heaven.* In communion with and commemorating 956
the Blessed Virgin Mary and all the saints, the Church offers the Eucha- 969
ristic sacrifice. In the Eucharist the Church is as it were at the foot of the cross with Mary, united with the offering and intercession of Christ.

1371 The Eucharistic sacrifice is 958, 1689
also offered for the *faithful departed* who "have died in Christ but are not 1032
yet wholly purified,"[193] so that they may be able to enter into the light and peace of Christ:

> Put this body anywhere! Don't trouble yourselves about it! I simply ask you to remember me at the Lord's altar wherever you are.[194]
> Then, we pray [in the anaphora] for the holy fathers and bishops who have fallen asleep, and in general for all who have fallen asleep before us, in the belief that it is a great benefit to the souls on whose behalf the supplication is offered, while the holy and tremendous Victim is present.... By offering to God our supplications for those who have fallen asleep, if

[191] St. Ignatius of Antioch, *Ad Smyrn.* 8:1; SCh 10, 138. — [192] *PO* 2 § 4. — [193] Council of Trent (1562): DS 1743. — [194] St. Monica, before her death, to her sons, St. Augustine and his brother; *Conf.* 9, 11, 27: PL 32, 775.

> they have sinned, we...offer Christ sacrificed for the sins of all, and so render favorable, for them and for us, the God who loves man.[195]

1372 St. Augustine admirably summed up this doctrine that moves us to an ever more complete participation in our Redeemer's sacrifice
1140 which we celebrate in the Eucharist:

> This wholly redeemed city, the assembly and society of the saints, is offered to God as a universal sacrifice by the high priest who in the form of a slave went so far as to offer himself for us in his Passion, to make us the Body of so great a head.... Such is the sacrifice of Christians: "we who are many are one Body in Christ." The Church continues to reproduce this sacrifice in the sacrament of the altar so well-known to believers wherein it is evident to them that in what she offers she herself is offered.[196]

The presence of Christ by the power of his word and the Holy Spirit

1373 "Christ Jesus, who died, yes, who was raised from the dead, who is at the right hand of God, who indeed intercedes for us," is present in many ways to his Church:[197] in his word, in his Church's prayer, "where two or three are gathered in my name,"[198] in the poor, the sick, and the imprisoned,[199] in the sacraments of which he is the author, in the sacrifice of the Mass, and in the person of the minis-
1088 ter. But "he is present...most *especially in the Eucharistic species.*"[200]

1374 The mode of Christ's presence under the Eucharistic species is unique. It raises the Eucharist above all the sacraments as "the perfection
of the spiritual life and the end to 1211
which all the sacraments tend."[201] In the most blessed sacrament of the Eucharist "the body and blood, together with the soul and divinity, of our Lord Jesus Christ and, therefore, *the whole Christ is truly, really, and substantially contained.*"[202] "This presence is called 'real'—by which is not intended to exclude the other types of presence as if they could not be 'real' too, but because it is presence in the fullest sense: that is to say, it is a *substantial* presence by which Christ, God and man, makes himself wholly and entirely present."[203]

1375 It is by the conversion of the bread and wine into Christ's body
and blood that Christ becomes pres- 1105
ent in this sacrament. The Church Fathers strongly affirmed the faith of the Church in the efficacy of the Word of Christ and of the action of the Holy Spirit to bring about this conversion. Thus St. John Chrysostom declares:

> It is not man that causes the things offered to become the Body and Blood of Christ, but he who was crucified for us, Christ himself. The priest, in the role of Christ, pronounces these
> words, but their power and grace are 1128
> God's. This is my body, he says. This word transforms the things offered.[204]

And St. Ambrose says about this conversion:

> Be convinced that this is not what nature has formed, but what the blessing has consecrated. The power of the blessing prevails over that of nature, because by the blessing

[195] St. Cyril of Jerusalem, *Catech. myst.* 5, 9. 10: PG 33, 1116–1117. — [196] St. Augustine, *De civ. Dei,* 10, 6: PL 41, 283; cf. *Rom* 12:5. — [197] *Rom* 8:34; cf. *LG* 48. — [198] *Mt* 18:20. — [199] Cf. *Mt* 25:31–46. — [200] *SC* 7. — [201] St. Thomas Aquinas, *STh* III, 73, 3c. — [202] Council of Trent (1551): DS 1651. — [203] Paul VI, *MF* 39. — [204] St. John Chrysostom, *prod. Jud.* 1:6: PG 49, 380.

nature itself is changed.... Could not Christ's word, which can make from
298 nothing what did not exist, change existing things into what they were not before? It is no less a feat to give things their original nature than to change their nature.[205]

1376 The Council of Trent summarizes the Catholic faith by declaring: "Because Christ our Redeemer said that it was truly his body that he was offering under the species of bread, it has always been the conviction of the Church of God, and this holy Council now declares again, that by the consecration of the bread and wine there takes place a change of the whole substance of the bread into the substance of the body of Christ our Lord and of the whole substance of the wine into the substance of his blood. This change the holy Catholic Church has fittingly and properly called transubstantiation."[206]

1377 The Eucharistic presence of Christ begins at the moment of the consecration and endures as long as the Eucharistic species subsist. Christ is present whole and entire in each of the species and whole and entire in each of their parts, in such a way that the breaking of the bread does not divide Christ.[207]

1178 **1378** *Worship of the Eucharist.* In the liturgy of the Mass we express our faith in the real presence of Christ under the species of bread and wine by, among other ways, genuflecting or bowing deeply as a sign of adoration of the Lord. "The Catholic
103 Church has always offered and still
offers to the sacrament of the Eucharist the cult of adoration, not only 2628
during Mass, but also outside of it, reserving the consecrated hosts with the utmost care, exposing them to the solemn veneration of the faithful, and carrying them in procession."[208]

1379 The tabernacle was first in- 1183
tended for the reservation of the Eucharist in a worthy place so that it could be brought to the sick and those absent, outside of Mass. As faith in the real presence of Christ in his Eucharist deepened, the Church became conscious of the meaning of silent adoration of the Lord present under the Eucharistic species. It is for this reason that the tabernacle should be located in an especially worthy place in the church and should be constructed in such a way that it emphasizes and manifests the truth of the real presence of Christ 2691
in the Blessed Sacrament.

1380 It is highly fitting that Christ should have wanted to remain present to his Church in this unique way. Since Christ was about to take his departure from his own in his visible form, he wanted to give us his sacramental presence; since he was about to offer himself on the cross to save us, he wanted us to have 669
the memorial of the love with which he loved us "to the end,"[209] even to the giving of his life. In his Eucharistic presence he remains mysteriously in our midst as the one who loved us and gave himself up for us,[210] and he 478
remains under signs that express and communicate this love:

The Church and the world have a great need for Eucharistic worship.

[205] St. Ambrose, *De myst.* 9, 50; 52: PL 16, 405–407. — [206] Council of Trent (1551): DS 1642; cf. *Mt* 26:26 ff.; *Mk* 14:22 ff.; *Lk* 22:19 ff.; *1 Cor* 11:24 ff. — [207] Cf. Council of Trent: DS 1641. — [208] Paul VI, *MF* 56. — [209] *Jn* 13:1. — [210] Cf. *Gal* 2:20

> Jesus awaits us in this sacrament of love. Let us not refuse the time
> 2715 to go to meet him in adoration, in contemplation full of faith, and open to making amends for the serious offenses and crimes of the world. Let our adoration never cease.[211]

1381 "That in this sacrament are the true Body of Christ and his true Blood is something that 'cannot be apprehended by the senses,' says St.
156 Thomas, 'but *only by faith*, which relies on divine authority.' For this rea-
215 son, in a commentary on *Luke* 22:19 ('This is my body which is given for you.'), St. Cyril says: 'Do not doubt whether this is true, but rather receive the words of the Savior in faith, for since he is the truth, he cannot lie.'"[212]

> Godhead here in hiding,
> whom I do adore
> Masked by these bare shadows,
> shape and nothing more,
> See, Lord, at thy service low
> lies here a heart
> Lost, all lost in wonder at
> the God thou art.Seeing, touching,
> tasting are
>
> in thee deceived;
> How says trusty hearing?
> that shall be believed;
> What God's Son has told me,
> take for truth I do;
> Truth himself speaks truly or
> there's nothing true.[213]

VI. The Paschal Banquet

1382 The Mass is at the same time, and inseparably, the sacrificial memorial in which the sacrifice of the cross is perpetuated and the sacred banquet of communion with the Lord's body and blood. But the celebration of the Eucharistic sacrifice is wholly directed toward the intimate union of the faithful with Christ through communion. To receive communion is to receive Christ himself who has
offered himself for us. 950

1383 The *altar*, around which 1182
the Church is gathered in the celebration of the Eucharist, represents the two aspects of the same mystery: the altar of the sacrifice and the table of the Lord. This is all the more so since the Christian altar is the symbol of Christ himself, present in the midst of the assembly of his faithful, both as the victim offered for our reconciliation and as food from heaven who is giving himself to us. "For what is the altar of Christ if not the image of the Body of Christ?"[214] asks St. Ambrose. He says elsewhere, "The altar represents the body [of Christ] and the Body of Christ is on the altar."[215] The liturgy expresses this unity of sacrifice and communion in many prayers. Thus the Roman Church prays in its anaphora:

> We entreat you, almighty God, that by the hands of your holy Angel this offering may be borne to your altar in heaven in the sight of your divine majesty, so that as we receive in communion at this altar the most holy Body and Blood of your Son, we may be filled with every heavenly blessing and grace.[216]

[211] John Paul II, *Dominicae cenae*, 3. — [212] St. Thomas Aquinas, *STh* III, 75, 1; cf. Paul VI, *MF* 18; St. Cyril of Alexandria, *In Luc.* 22, 19: PG 72, 912; cf. Paul VI, *MF* 18. — [213] St. Thomas Aquinas (attr.), *Adoro te devote*; tr. Gerard Manley Hopkins. — [214] St. Ambrose, *De Sacr.* 5, 2, 7: PL 16, 447C. — [215] St. Ambrose, *De Sacr.* 4, 2, 7: PL 16, 437D. — [216] *Roman Missal*, EP I (Roman Canon) 96: Supplices te rogamus, omnipotens Deus: iube hæc perferri per manus sancti Angeli tui in sublime altare tuum, in conspectu divinae maiestatis tuae: ut, quotquot ex hac altaris participatione sacrosanctum Filii Corpus et Sanguinem sumpserimus, omni benedictione cælesti et gratia repleamur.

"Take this and eat it, all of you": communion

2835 **1384** The Lord addresses an invitation to us, urging us to receive him in the sacrament of the Eucharist: "Truly, I say to you, unless you eat the flesh of the Son of man and drink his blood, you have no life in you."[217]

1385 To respond to this invitation we must *prepare ourselves* for so great and so holy a moment. St. Paul urges us to examine our conscience: "Whoever, therefore, eats the bread or drinks the cup of the Lord in an unworthy manner will be guilty of profaning the body and blood of the Lord. Let a man examine himself, and so eat of the bread and drink of the cup. For any one who eats and drinks without discerning the body eats and drinks judgment upon himself."[218] Anyone
1457 conscious of a grave sin must receive the sacrament of Reconciliation before coming to communion.

1386 Before so great a sacrament, the faithful can only echo humbly and with ardent faith the words of the Centurion: "*Domine, non sum dignus ut intres sub tectum meum, sed tantum dic verbo, et sanabitur anima mea*" ("Lord, I am not worthy that you should enter under my roof, but only say the word and my soul will be healed.").[219] And in the Divine Liturgy of St. John Chrysostom the faithful pray in the same spirit:

732 O Son of God, bring me into communion today with your mystical supper. I shall not tell your enemies the secret, nor kiss you with Judas' kiss. But like the good thief I cry, "Jesus, remember me when you come into your kingdom."

1387 To prepare for worthy reception of this sacrament, the faithful should observe the fast required in their Church.[220] Bodily demeanor
(gestures, clothing) ought to convey 2043
the respect, solemnity, and joy of this moment when Christ becomes our guest.

1388 It is in keeping with the very meaning of the Eucharist that the faithful, if they have the required dispositions,[221] *receive communion when* they participate in the Mass.[222] As the Second Vatican Council says: "That more perfect form of participation in the Mass whereby the faithful, after the priest's communion, receive the Lord's Body from the same sacrifice, is warmly recommended."[223]

1389 The Church obliges the 2042
faithful to take part in the Divine Liturgy on Sundays and feast days and, prepared by the sacrament of Reconciliation, to receive the Eucharist at least once a year, if possible during the Easter season.[224] But the Church strongly encourages the faithful to receive the holy Eucharist on Sundays
and feast days, or more often still, 2837
even daily.

1390 Since Christ is sacramentally present under each of the species, communion under the species of bread alone makes it possible to receive all the fruit of Eucharistic grace. For pastoral reasons this manner of receiving communion

[217] *Jn* 6:53. — [218] *1 Cor* 11:27–29. — [219] *Roman Missal*, response to the invitation to communion; cf. *Mt* 8:8. — [220] Cf. CIC, can. 919. — [221] Cf. CIC, can. 916. — [222] Cf. CIC, can. 917; The *faithful may receive the Holy Eucharist only a second time on the same day* [Cf. Pontificia Commissio Codici Iuris Canonici Authentice Intrepretando, *Responsa ad proposita dubia*, 1: AAS 76 (1984) 746]. — [223] *SC* 55. — [224] Cf. *OE* 15; CIC, can. 920.

has been legitimately established as the most common form in the Latin rite. But "the sign of communion is more complete when given under both kinds, since in that form the sign of the Eucharistic meal appears more clearly."[225] This is the usual form of receiving communion in the Eastern rites.

The fruits of Holy Communion

1391 *Holy Communion augments our union with Christ.* The principal fruit of receiving the Eucharist in Holy Communion is an intimate
460 union with Christ Jesus. Indeed, the Lord said: "He who eats my flesh and drinks my blood abides in me, and I in him."[226] Life in Christ has its foundation in the Eucharistic banquet: "As the living Father sent me, and I live because of the Father,
521 so he who eats me will live because of me."[227]

> On the feasts of the Lord, when the faithful receive the Body of the Son, they proclaim to one another the Good News that the first fruits of life have been given, as when the angel said to Mary Magdalene, "Christ is risen!" Now too are life and resurrection conferred on whoever receives Christ.[228]

1212 **1392** What material food produces in our bodily life, Holy Communion wonderfully achieves in our spiritual life. Communion with the flesh of the risen Christ, a flesh "given life and giving life through the Holy Spirit,"[229] preserves, increases, and renews the life of grace received at Baptism. This growth in Christian life needs the nourishment of Eucharistic Communion, the bread for our pilgrimage until the moment of death, when it will be given to us
as viaticum. 1524

1393 *Holy Communion separates us from sin.* The body of Christ we receive in Holy Communion is "given up for us," and the blood we drink "shed for the many for the forgiveness of sins." For this reason the
Eucharist cannot unite us to Christ 613
without at the same time cleansing us from past sins and preserving us from future sins:

> For as often as we eat this bread and drink the cup, we proclaim the death of the Lord. If we proclaim the Lord's death, we proclaim the forgiveness of sins. If, as often as his blood is poured out, it is poured for the forgiveness of sins, I should always receive it, so that it may always forgive my sins. Because I always sin, I should always have a remedy.[230]

1394 As bodily nourishment restores lost strength, so the Eucharist strengthens our charity, which tends to be weakened in daily life; and
this living charity *wipes away venial* 1863
sins.[231] By giving himself to us Christ
revives our love and enables us to 1436
break our disordered attachments to creatures and root ourselves in him:

> Since Christ died for us out of love, when we celebrate the memorial of his death at the moment of sacrifice we ask that love may be granted to us by the coming of the Holy Spirit. We humbly pray that in the strength of this love by which Christ willed to die for us, we, by receiving the gift of the Holy Spirit, may be able to consider the world as crucified for

225 GIRM 240. — 226 *Jn* 6:56. — 227 *Jn* 6:57. — 228 Fanqîth, Syriac Office of Antioch, Vol. I, Commun., 237 a–b. — 229 *PO* 5. — 230 St. Ambrose, *De Sacr.* 4, 6, 28: PL 16, 446; cf. *1 Cor* 11:26. — 231 Cf. Council of Trent (1551): DS 1638.

> us, and to be ourselves as crucified to the world.... Having received the gift of love, let us die to sin and live for God.[232]

1395 By the same charity that it enkindles in us, the Eucharist *preserves us from future mortal sins.* The more we share the life of Christ and
1855 progress in his friendship, the more difficult it is to break away from him by mortal sin. The Eucharist is not ordered to the forgiveness of mortal sins—that is proper to the sacrament of Reconciliation. The
1446 Eucharist is properly the sacrament of those who are in full communion with the Church.

1118 **1396** *The unity of the Mystical Body: the Eucharist makes the Church.* Those who receive the Eucharist are united more closely to Christ. Through it Christ unites them to all the faithful in one body—the Church. Communion renews, strengthens, and deepens this incorporation into the Church, already achieved by Baptism. In Baptism we have been called to form but one body.[233] The Eucharist fulfills this call: "The cup of
1267 blessing which we bless, is it not a participation in the blood of Christ? The bread which we break, is it not a participation in the body of Christ? Because there is one bread, we who are many are one body, for we all par-
790 take of the one bread:"[234]

> If you are the body and members of Christ, then it is your sacrament
> 1064 that is placed on the table of the Lord; it is your sacrament that you receive. To that which you are you respond "Amen" ("yes, it is true!") and by responding to it you assent to it. For you hear the words, "the Body of Christ" and respond "Amen." Be then a member of the Body of Christ that your Amen may be true.[235]

1397 *The Eucharist commits us to the poor.* To receive in truth the
Body and Blood of Christ given up 2449
for us, we must recognize Christ in the poorest, his brethren:

> You have tasted the Blood of the Lord, yet you do not recognize your brother,.... You dishonor this table when you do not judge worthy of sharing your food someone judged worthy to take part in this meal.... God freed you from all your sins and invited you here, but you have not become more merciful.[236]

1398 *The Eucharist and the unity of Christians.* Before the greatness of this mystery St. Augustine exclaims, "*O sacrament of devotion! O sign of unity! O bond of charity!*"[237] The
more painful the experience of the 817
divisions in the Church which break the common participation in the table of the Lord, the more urgent are our prayers to the Lord that the time of complete unity among all who believe in him may return.

1399 The Eastern churches that 838
are not in full communion with the Catholic Church celebrate the Eucharist with great love. "These Churches, although separated from us, yet possess true sacraments, above all—by apostolic succession—the priesthood and the Eucharist, whereby they are still joined to us in closest intimacy." A certain

[232] St. Fulgentius of Ruspe, *Contra Fab.* 28, 16–19: CCL 19A, 813–814. — [233] Cf. *1 Cor* 12:13. — [234] *1 Cor* 10:16–17. — [235] St. Augustine, *Sermo* 272: PL 38, 1247. — [236] St. John Chrysostom, *Hom. in 1 Cor.* 27, 4: PG 61, 229–230; cf. Mt 25:40. — [237] St. Augustine, *In Jo. ev.* 26, 13: PL 35, 1613; cf. *SC* 47.

communion in *sacris*, and so in the Eucharist, "given suitable circumstances and the approval of Church authority, is not merely possible but is encouraged."[238]

1400 Ecclesial communities derived from the Reformation and separated from the Catholic Church, "have not preserved the proper reality of the Eucharistic mystery in its fullness, especially because of the absence of the sacrament of Holy Orders."[239] It is for this reason that, for the Catholic Church, Eucharistic
1536 intercommunion with these communities is not possible. However these ecclesial communities, "when they commemorate the Lord's death and resurrection in the Holy Supper...profess that it signifies life in communion with Christ and await his coming in glory."[240]

1483 **1401** When, in the Ordinary's judgment, a grave necessity arises, Catholic ministers may give the sacraments of Eucharist, Penance, and Anointing of the Sick to other Christians not in full communion with the Catholic Church, who ask for them of their own will, provided they give evidence of holding the
1385 Catholic faith regarding these sacraments and possess the required dispositions.[241]

VII. The Eucharist—"Pledge of the Glory to Come"

1402 In an ancient prayer the Church acclaims the mystery of the Eucharist: "O sacred banquet in which Christ is received as food, the
memory of his Passion is renewed, 1323
the soul is filled with grace and a pledge of the life to come is given to us." If the Eucharist is the memorial of the Passover of the Lord Jesus, if by our communion at the altar we are filled "with every heavenly blessing and grace,"[242] then the Eucharist
is also an anticipation of the heav- 1130
enly glory.

1403 At the Last Supper the Lord himself directed his disciples' attention toward the fulfillment of the Passover in the kingdom of God: "I tell you I shall not drink again of this fruit of the vine until that day when I drink it new with you in my Father's kingdom."[243] Whenever the Church celebrates the Eucharist she remembers this promise and turns her gaze "to him who is to come." In her prayer she calls for his coming: "*Marana tha!*" "Come, Lord Je- 671
sus!"[244] "May your grace come and this world pass away!"[245]

1404 The Church knows that the Lord comes even now in his Eucharist and that he is there in our midst. However, his presence is veiled. Therefore we celebrate the Eucharist "awaiting the blessed hope and the coming of our Savior, Jesus Christ,"[246] asking "to share in
your glory when every tear will be 1041
wiped away. On that day we shall see
you, our God, as you are. We shall 1028
become like you and praise you for ever through Christ our Lord."[247]

1405 There is no surer pledge 1042
or clearer sign of this great hope in the new heavens and new earth

[238] *UR* 15 § 2; cf. CIC, can. 844 § 3. — [239] *UR* 22 § 3. — [240] *UR* 22 § 3. — [241] Cf. CIC, can. 844 § 4. — [242] *Roman Missal,* EP I (Roman Canon) 96: *Supplices te rogamus.* — [243] *Mt* 26:29; cf. *Lk* 22:18; *Mk* 14:25. — [244] *Rev* 1:4; 22:20; *1 Cor* 16:22. — [245] *Didache* 10, 6: SCh 248, 180. — [246] *Roman Missal* 126, embolism after the Our Father: *expectantes beatam spem et adventum Salvatoris nostri Jesu Christi;* cf. *Titus* 2:13. — [247] EP III 116: prayer for the dead.

"in which righteousness dwells,"[248] than the Eucharist. Every time this mystery is celebrated, "the work of our redemption is carried on" and we "break the one bread that provides the medicine of immortality, the antidote for death, and the food
1000 that makes us live for ever in Jesus Christ."[249]

In Brief

1406 *Jesus said: "I am the living bread that came down from heaven; if any one eats of this bread, he will live for ever;...he who eats my flesh and drinks my blood has eternal life and...abides in me, and I in him"* (Jn *6:51, 54, 56).*

1407 *The Eucharist is the heart and the summit of the Church's life, for in it Christ associates his Church and all her members with his sacrifice of praise and thanksgiving offered once for all on the cross to his Father; by this sacrifice he pours out the graces of salvation on his Body which is the Church.*

1408 *The Eucharistic celebration always includes: the proclamation of the Word of God; thanksgiving to God the Father for all his benefits, above all the gift of his Son; the consecration of bread and wine; and participation in the liturgical banquet by receiving the Lord's body and blood. These elements constitute one single act of worship.*

1409 *The Eucharist is the memorial of Christ's Passover, that is, of the work of salvation accomplished by the life, death, and resurrection of Christ, a work made present by the liturgical action.*

1410 *It is Christ himself, the eternal high priest of the New Covenant who, acting through the ministry of the priests, offers the Eucharistic sacrifice. And it is the same Christ, really present under the species of bread and wine, who is the offering of the Eucharistic sacrifice.*

1411 *Only validly ordained priests can preside at the Eucharist and consecrate the bread and the wine so that they become the Body and Blood of the Lord.*

1412 *The essential signs of the Eucharistic sacrament are wheat bread and grape wine, on which the blessing of the Holy Spirit is invoked and the priest pronounces the words of consecration spoken by Jesus during the Last Supper: "This is my body which will be given up for you.... This is the cup of my blood...."*

1413 *By the consecration the transubstantiation of the bread and wine into the Body and Blood of Christ is brought about. Under the consecrated species of bread and wine Christ himself, living and glorious, is present in a true, real, and substantial manner: his Body and his Blood, with his soul and his divinity (cf. Council of Trent: DS 1640; 1651).*

1414 *As sacrifice, the Eucharist is also offered in reparation for the sins of the living and the dead and to obtain spiritual or temporal benefits from God.*

1415 *Anyone who desires to receive Christ in Eucharistic communion must be in the state of grace. Anyone aware of having sinned mortally must not receive communion without having received absolution in the sacrament of penance.*

[248] *2 Pet* 3:13. — [249] *LG* 3; St. Ignatius of Antioch, *Ad Eph.* 20, 2: SCh 10, 76.

1416 *Communion with the Body and Blood of Christ increases the communicant's union with the Lord, forgives his venial sins, and preserves him from grave sins. Since receiving this sacrament strengthens the bonds of charity between the communicant and Christ, it also reinforces the unity of the Church as the Mystical Body of Christ.*

1417 *The Church warmly recommends that the faithful receive Holy Communion when they participate in the celebration of the Eucharist; she obliges them to do so at least once a year.*

1418 *Because Christ himself is present in the sacrament of the altar, he is to be honored with the worship of adoration. "To visit the Blessed Sacrament is...a proof of gratitude, an expression of love, and a duty of adoration toward Christ our Lord" (Paul VI,* MF *66).*

1419 *Having passed from this world to the Father, Christ gives us in the Eucharist the pledge of glory with him. Participation in the Holy Sacrifice identifies us with his Heart, sustains our strength along the pilgrimage of this life, makes us long for eternal life, and unites us even now to the Church in heaven, the Blessed Virgin Mary, and all the saints.*

Chapter Two:
THE SACRAMENTS OF HEALING

1420 Through the sacraments of Christian initiation, man receives the new life of Christ. Now we carry this life "in earthen vessels," and it remains "hidden with Christ in God."[1] We are still in our "earthly tent," subject to suffering, illness, and death.[2] This new life as a child of God can be weakened and even lost by sin.

1421 The Lord Jesus Christ, physician of our souls and bodies, who forgave the sins of the paralytic and restored him to bodily health,[3] has willed that his Church continue, in the power of the Holy Spirit, his work of healing and salvation, even among her own members. This is the purpose of the two sacraments of healing: the sacrament of Penance and the sacrament of Anointing of the Sick.

Article 4:
THE SACRAMENT OF PENANCE AND RECONCILIATION

980 **1422** "Those who approach the sacrament of Penance obtain pardon from God's mercy for the offense committed against him, and are, at the same time, reconciled with the Church which they have wounded by their sins and which by charity, by example, and by prayer labors for their conversion."[4]

I. What Is This Sacrament Called?

1989 **1423** It is called the *sacrament of conversion* because it makes sacramentally present Jesus' call to conversion, the first step in returning to the Father[5] from whom one has strayed by sin.

1440 It is called the *sacrament of Penance*, since it consecrates the Christian sinner's personal and ecclesial steps of conversion, penance, and satisfaction.

1424 It is called the *sacrament of confession*, since the disclosure or confession of sins to a priest is an essential element of this sacrament. In a profound sense it is also a "confession"—acknowledgment and praise—of the holiness of God and of his mercy toward sinful man. 1456

It is called the *sacrament of forgiveness*, since by the priest's sacramental absolution God grants the penitent "pardon and peace."[6] 1442

It is called the *sacrament of Reconciliation*, because it imparts to the sinner the love of God who reconciles: "Be reconciled to God."[7] He who lives by God's merciful love is ready to respond to the Lord's call: "Go; first be reconciled to your brother."[8]

[1] *2 Cor* 4:7; *Col* 3:3. — [2] *2 Cor* 5:1. — [3] Cf. *Mk* 2:1–12. — [4] *LG* 11 § 2. — [5] Cf. *Mk* 1:15; *Lk* 15:18. — [6] OP 46: formula of absolution. — [7] *2 Cor* 5:20. — [8] *Mt* 5:24.

II. Why a Sacrament of Reconciliation after Baptism?

1263 **1425** "You were washed, you were sanctified, you were justified in the name of the Lord Jesus Christ and in the Spirit of our God."[9] One must appreciate the magnitude of the gift God has given us in the sacraments of Christian initiation in order to grasp the degree to which sin is excluded for him who has "put on Christ."[10] But the apostle John also says: "If we say we have no sin, we deceive ourselves, and the truth is not in us."[11] And the Lord himself taught us to pray: "Forgive us our
2838 trespasses,"[12] linking our forgiveness of one another's offenses to the forgiveness of our sins that God will grant us.

1426 *Conversion* to Christ, the new birth of Baptism, the gift of the Holy Spirit and the Body and Blood of Christ received as food have made us "holy and without blemish," just as the Church herself, the Bride of Christ, is "holy and without blemish."[13] Nevertheless the new life received in Christian initiation has not abolished the frailty and weakness of human nature, nor the inclination to sin that tradition calls
405, 978 *concupiscence*, which remains in the baptized such that with the help of
1264 the grace of Christ they may prove themselves in the struggle of Christian life.[14] This is the struggle of conversion directed toward holiness and eternal life to which the Lord never ceases to call us.[15]

III. The Conversion of the Baptized

1427 Jesus calls to conversion. 541
This call is an essential part of the proclamation of the kingdom: "The time is fulfilled, and the kingdom of God is at hand; repent, and believe in the gospel."[16] In the Church's preaching this call is addressed first to those who do not yet know Christ and his Gospel. Also, Baptism is the principal place for the first and fundamental conversion. It is by faith in the Gospel and by Baptism[17] that one renounces evil and gains salva- 1226
tion, that is, the forgiveness of all sins and the gift of new life.

1428 Christ's call to conversion continues to resound in the lives of Christians. This *second conversion* is an uninterrupted task for the whole Church who, "clasping sinners to 1036
her bosom, [is] at once holy and always in need of purification, [and] follows constantly the path of penance and renewal."[18] This endeavor 853
of conversion is not just a human work. It is the movement of a "contrite heart," drawn and moved by grace to respond to the merciful love 1996
of God who loved us first.[19]

1429 St. Peter's conversion after he had denied his master three times bears witness to this. Jesus' look of infinite mercy drew tears of repentance from Peter and, after the Lord's resurrection, a threefold affirmation of love for him.[20] The second conversion also has a *communitarian* dimension, as is clear in the Lord's call to a whole Church: "Repent!"[21]

[9] *1 Cor* 6:11. — [10] *Gal* 3:27. — [11] *1 Jn* 1:8. — [12] Cf. *Lk* 11:4; *Mt* 6:12. — [13] *Eph* 1:4; 5:27. — [14] Cf. Council of Trent (1546): DS 1515. — [15] Cf. Council of Trent (1547): DS 1545; *LG* 40. — [16] *Mk* 1:15. — [17] Cf. *Acts* 2:38. — [18] *LG* 8 § 3. — [19] *Ps* 51:17; cf. *Jn* 6:44; 12:32; 1 *Jn* 4:10. — [20] Cf. *Lk* 22:61; *Jn* 21:15–17. — [21] *Rev* 2:5, 16.

St. Ambrose says of the two conversions that, in the Church, "there are water and tears: the water of Baptism and the tears of repentance."[22]

IV. Interior Penance

1430 Jesus' call to conversion and penance, like that of the prophets before him, does not aim first at outward works, "sackcloth and ashes," fasting and mortification, but at the *conversion of the heart, interior conversion.* Without this, such penances remain sterile and false; however, in-
1098 terior conversion urges expression in visible signs, gestures and works of penance.[23]

1431 Interior repentance is a radical reorientation of our whole life, a return, a conversion to God with all our heart, an end of sin, a turning away from evil, with repug-
1451 nance toward the evil actions we have committed. At the same time it entails the desire and resolution to change one's life, with hope in God's mercy and trust in the help of his grace. This conversion of heart is accompanied by a salutary pain and sadness which the Fathers called *animi cruciatus* (affliction of spirit)
368 and *compunctio cordis* (repentance of heart).[24]

1432 The human heart is heavy and hardened. God must give man a new heart.[25] Conversion is first of all a work of the grace of God who
1989 makes our hearts return to him: "Restore us to thyself, O Lord, that we may be restored!"[26] God gives us the strength to begin anew. It is in discovering the greatness of God's love that our heart is shaken by the horror and weight of sin and begins to fear offending God by sin and being separated from him. The human heart is converted by looking upon him whom our sins have pierced:[27]

> Let us fix our eyes on Christ's blood and understand how precious it is to his Father, for, poured out for our salvation, it has brought to the whole world the grace of repentance.[28]

1433 Since Easter, the Holy Spirit 729
has proved "the world wrong about sin,"[29] i.e., proved that the world has not believed in him whom the Father has sent. But this same Spirit who brings sin to light is also
the Consoler who gives the human 692, 1848
heart grace for repentance and conversion.[30]

V. The Many Forms of Penance in Christian Life

1434 The interior penance of the 1969
Christian can be expressed in many and various ways. Scripture and the Fathers insist above all on three forms, *fasting, prayer,* and *almsgiving,*[31] which express conversion in relation to oneself, to God, and to others. Alongside the radical purification brought about by Baptism or martyrdom they cite as means of obtaining forgiveness of sins: efforts at reconciliation with one's neighbor, tears of repentance, concern for the salvation of one's neighbor, the intercession of the saints, and the practice of charity "which covers a multitude of sins."[32]

[22] St. Ambrose, ep. 41, 12: PL 16, 1116. — [23] Cf. *Joel* 2:12-13; *Isa* 1:16-17; *Mt* 6:1–6; 16-18. — [24] Cf. Council of Trent (1551): DS 1676–1678; 1705; cf. *Roman Catechism,* II, V, 4. — [25] Cf. *Ezek* 36:26–27. — [26] *Lam* 5:21. — [27] Cf. *Jn* 19:37; *Zech* 12:10. — [28] St. Clement of Rome, Ad Cor. 7, 4: PG 1, 224. — [29] Cf. *Jn* 16:8–9. — [30] Cf. *Jn* 15:26; *Acts* 2:36–38; John Paul II, DeV 27–48. — [31] Cf. *Tob* 12:8; *Mt* 6:1–18. — [32] *1 Pet* 4:8; cf. *Jas* 5:20.

1435 Conversion is accomplished in daily life by gestures of reconciliation, concern for the poor, the exercise and defense of justice and right,[33] by the admission of faults to one's brethren, fraternal correction, revision of life, examination of conscience, spiritual direction, acceptance of suffering, endurance of persecution for the sake of righteousness. Taking up one's cross each day and following Jesus is the surest way of penance.[34]

1436 *Eucharist and Penance.* Daily conversion and penance find their source and nourishment in the Eucharist, for in it is made present the sacrifice of Christ which has reconciled us with God. Through the Eucharist those who live from the life of Christ are fed and strengthened. "It is a remedy to free us from our
1394 daily faults and to preserve us from mortal sins."[35]

1437 Reading Sacred Scripture, praying the Liturgy of the Hours and the Our Father—every sincere act of worship or devotion revives the spirit of conversion and repentance within us and contributes to the forgiveness of our sins.

540 **1438** *The seasons and days of penance* in the course of the liturgical year (Lent, and each Friday in memory of the death of the Lord) are intense moments of the Church's penitential practice.[36] These times are particularly appropriate for spiritual exercises, penitential liturgies, pilgrimages as signs of penance, voluntary self-denial such as fasting and almsgiving, and fraternal sharing
2043 (charitable and missionary works).

1439 *The process of conversion and repentance* was described by Jesus in the parable of the prodigal son, the center of which is the merciful father:[37] the fascination of illusory
freedom, the abandonment of the 545
father's house; the extreme misery in which the son finds himself after squandering his fortune; his deep humiliation at finding himself obliged to feed swine, and still worse, at wanting to feed on the husks the pigs ate; his reflection on all he has lost; his repentance and decision to declare himself guilty before his father; the journey back; the father's generous welcome; the father's joy—all these are characteristic of the process of conversion. The beautiful robe, the ring, and the festive banquet are symbols of that new life—pure, worthy, and joyful—of anyone who returns to God and to the bosom of his family, which is the Church. Only the heart of Christ who knows the depths of his Father's love could reveal to us the abyss of his mercy in so simple and beautiful a way.

VI. The Sacrament of Penance and Reconciliation

1440 Sin is before all else an of- 1850
fense against God, a rupture of communion with him. At the same time it damages communion with the Church. For this reason conversion entails both God's forgiveness and reconciliation with the Church, which are expressed and accomplished liturgically by the sacrament of Penance and Reconciliation.[38]

[33] Cf. *Am* 5:24; *Isa* 1:17. — [34] Cf. *Lk* 9:23. — [35] Council of Trent (1551): DS 1638. — [36] 36 Cf. SC 109–110; CIC, cann. 1249–1253; CCEO, cann. 880–883. — [37] Cf. *Lk* 15:11–24. — [38] Cf. *LG* 11.

Only God forgives sin

270, 431 **1441** Only God forgives sins.[39] Since he is the Son of God, Jesus says of himself, "The Son of man has authority on earth to forgive sins"
589 and exercises this divine power: "Your sins are forgiven."[40] Further, by virtue of his divine authority he gives this power to men to exercise in his name.[41]

1442 Christ has willed that in her prayer and life and action his whole Church should be the sign and instrument of the forgiveness and reconciliation that he acquired for us at the price of his blood. But he entrusted the exercise of the power of absolution to the apostolic ministry
983 which he charged with the "ministry of reconciliation."[42] The apostle is sent out "on behalf of Christ" with "God making his appeal" through him and pleading: "Be reconciled to God."[43]

Reconciliation with the Church

1443 During his public life Jesus not only forgave sins, but also made plain the effect of this forgiveness: he reintegrated forgiven sinners into the community of the People of God from which sin had alienated
545 or even excluded them. A remarkable sign of this is the fact that Jesus receives sinners at his table, a gesture that expresses in an astonishing way both God's forgiveness and the return to the bosom of the People of God.[44]

981 **1444** In imparting to his apostles his own power to forgive sins the Lord also gives them the authority to reconcile sinners with the Church. This ecclesial dimension of their task is expressed most notably in Christ's solemn words to Simon Peter: "I will give you the keys of the kingdom of heaven, and whatever you bind on earth shall be bound in heaven, and whatever you loose on earth shall be loosed in heaven."[45] "The office of binding and loosing which was given to Peter was also assigned to the college of the apostles united to its head."[46]

1445 The words bind and loose 553
mean: whomever you exclude from your communion, will be excluded from communion with God; whomever you receive anew into your communion, God will welcome back into his. *Reconciliation with the Church is inseparable from reconciliation with God.*

The sacrament of forgiveness

1446 Christ instituted the sacra- 979
ment of Penance for all sinful members of his Church: above all for those who, since Baptism, have fall-
en into grave sin, and have thus lost 1856
their baptismal grace and wounded ecclesial communion. It is to them that the sacrament of Penance offers a new possibility to convert and to recover the grace of justification.
The Fathers of the Church present 1990
this sacrament as "the second plank [of salvation] after the shipwreck which is the loss of grace."[47]

1447 Over the centuries the concrete form in which the Church has exercised this power received from the Lord has varied considerably. During the first centuries the

[39] Cf. *Mk* 2:7. — [40] *Mk* 2:5, 10; *Lk* 7:48. — [41] Cf. *Jn* 20:21–23. — [42] *2 Cor* 5:18. — [43] *2 Cor* 5:20. — [44] Cf. *Lk* 15; 19:9. — [45] *Mt* 16:19; cf. *Mt* 18:18; 28:16–20. — [46] *LG* 22 § 2. — [47] Tertullian, De Pænit. 4, 2: PL 1, 1343; cf. Council of Trent (1547): DS 1542.

reconciliation of Christians who had committed particularly grave sins after their Baptism (for example, idolatry, murder, or adultery) was tied to a very rigorous discipline, according to which penitents had to do public penance for their sins, often for years, before receiving reconciliation. To this "order of penitents" (which concerned only certain grave sins), one was only rarely admitted and in certain regions only once in a lifetime. During the seventh century Irish missionaries, inspired by the Eastern monastic tradition, took to continental Europe the "private" practice of penance, which does not require public and prolonged completion of penitential works before reconciliation with the Church. From that time on, the sacrament has been performed in secret between penitent and priest. This new practice envisioned the possibility of repetition and so opened the way to a regular frequenting of this sacrament. It allowed the forgiveness of grave sins and venial sins to be integrated into one sacramental celebration. In its main lines this is the form of penance that the Church has practiced down to our day.

1448 Beneath the changes in discipline and celebration that this sacrament has undergone over the centuries, the same *fundamental structure* is to be discerned. It comprises two equally essential elements: on the one hand, the acts of the man who undergoes conversion through the action of the Holy Spirit: namely, contrition, confession, and satisfaction; on the other, God's action through the intervention of the Church. The Church, who through the bishop and his priests forgives sins in the name of Jesus Christ and determines the manner of satisfaction, also prays for the sinner and does penance with him. Thus the sinner is healed and re-established in ecclesial communion.

1449 The formula of absolution 1481
used in the Latin Church expresses the essential elements of this sacrament: the Father of mercies is the source of all forgiveness. He effects the reconciliation of sinners through
the Passover of his Son and the gift 234
of his Spirit, through the prayer and ministry of the Church:

> God, the Father of mercies, through the death and the resurrection of his Son has reconciled the world to himself and sent the Holy Spirit among us for the forgiveness of sins; through the ministry of the Church may God give you pardon and peace, and I absolve you from your sins in the name of the Father, and of the Son, and of the Holy Spirit.[48]

VII. The Acts of the Penitent

1450 "Penance requires...the sinner to endure all things willingly, be contrite of heart, confess with the lips, and practice complete humility and fruitful satisfaction."[49]

Contrition

1451 Among the penitent's acts contrition occupies first place. Contrition is "sorrow of the soul and detestation for the sin committed,
together with the resolution not to 431
sin again."[50]

[48] OP 46: formula of absolution. — [49] Roman Catechism II, V, 21; cf. Council of Trent (1551): DS 1673. — [50] Council of Trent (1551): DS 1676.

1822 **1452** When it arises from a love by which God is loved above all else, contrition is called "perfect" (contrition of charity). Such contrition remits venial sins; it also obtains forgiveness of mortal sins if it includes the firm resolution to have recourse to sacramental confession as soon as possible.[51]

1453 The contrition called "imperfect" (or "attrition") is also a gift of God, a prompting of the Holy Spirit. It is born of the consideration of sin's ugliness or the fear of eternal damnation and the other penalties threatening the sinner (contrition of fear). Such a stirring of conscience can initiate an interior process which, under the prompting of grace, will be brought to completion by sacramental absolution. By itself however, imperfect contrition cannot obtain the forgiveness of grave sins, but it disposes one to obtain forgiveness in the sacrament of Penance.[52]

1454 The reception of this sacrament ought to be prepared for by an examination of conscience made in the light of the Word of God. The passages best suited to this can be found in the Ten Commandments, the moral catechesis of the Gospels and the apostolic Letters, such as the Sermon on the Mount and the apostolic teachings.[53]

The confession of sins

1424 **1455** The confession (or disclosure) of sins, even from a simply human point of view, frees us and facilitates our reconciliation with others. Through such an admission man looks squarely at the sins he is guilty
of, takes responsibility for them, 1734
and thereby opens himself again to God and to the communion of the Church in order to make a new future possible.

1456 Confession to a priest is an essential part of the sacrament of Penance: "All mortal sins of which penitents after a diligent self-examination are conscious must be 1855
recounted by them in confession, even if they are most secret and have been committed against the last two precepts of the Decalogue; for these sins sometimes wound the soul more grievously and are more dangerous than those which are committed openly."[54]

> When Christ's faithful strive to confess all the sins that they can remember, they undoubtedly place all of them before the divine mercy for
> pardon. But those who fail to do so 1505
> and knowingly withhold some, place nothing before the divine goodness for remission through the mediation of the priest, "for if the sick person is too ashamed to show his wound to the doctor, the medicine cannot heal what it does not know."[55]

1457 According to the Church's 2042
command, "after having attained the age of discretion, each of the faithful is bound by an obligation faithfully to confess serious sins at least once a year."[56] Anyone who is aware of having committed a mortal sin must not receive Holy Communion, even if he experiences deep contrition, without having first received 1385

[51] Cf. Council of Trent (1551): DS 1677. — [52] Cf. Council of Trent (1551): DS 1678; 1705. — [53] Cf. *Mt* 5–7; Rom 12–15; 1 Cor 12–13; *Gal* 5; *Eph* 4–6; etc. — [54] Council of Trent (1551): DS 1680 (ND 1626); cf. Ex 20:17; Mt 5:28. — [55] Council of Trent (1551): DS 1680 (ND 1626); cf. St. Jerome, In Eccl. 10, 11: PL 23:1096. — [56] Cf. CIC, can. 989; Council of Trent (1551): DS 1683; DS 1708.

sacramental absolution, unless he has a grave reason for receiving Communion and there is no possibility of going to confession.[57] Children must go to the sacrament of Penance before receiving Holy Communion for the first time.[58]

1458 Without being strictly necessary, confession of everyday faults (venial sins) is nevertheless strongly recommended by the Church.[59] Indeed the regular confession of our venial sins helps us form our con
1783 science, fight against evil tendencies, let ourselves be healed by Christ and progress in the life of the Spirit. By receiving more frequently through this sacrament the gift of the Father's mercy, we are spurred to be merciful as he is merciful:[60]

> Whoever confesses his sins...is already working with God. God indicts your sins; if you also indict them, you are joined with God. Man and sinner are, so to speak, two realities: when you hear "man"—this is what God has made; when you hear "sinner"—this is what man himself has made. Destroy what you have made, so that God may save what he has made.... When you begin to abhor what you have made, it is then that your good works are beginning, since you are accusing yourself of your evil works. The beginning of good works is the
> 2468 confession of evil works. You do the truth and come to the light.[61]

Satisfaction

1459 Many sins wrong our neighbor. One must do what is possible in order to repair the harm (e.g., return stolen goods, restore the reputation
of someone slandered, pay compen- 2412
sation for injuries). Simple justice requires as much. But sin also injures 2487
and weakens the sinner himself, as well as his relationships with God and neighbor. Absolution takes away sin, but it does not remedy all the disorders sin has caused.[62] Raised up from sin, the sinner must still recover his full spiritual health by doing something more to make amends for the sin: he must "make satisfaction for"
or "expiate" his sins. This satisfaction 1473
is also called "penance."

1460 *The penance* the confessor imposes must take into account the penitent's personal situation and must seek his spiritual good. It must correspond as far as possible with the gravity and nature of the sins
committed. It can consist of prayer, 2447
an offering, works of mercy, service of neighbor, voluntary self-denial, sacrifices, and above all the patient acceptance of the cross we must bear. Such penances help configure
us to Christ, who alone expiated our 618
sins once for all. They allow us to become co-heirs with the risen Christ, "provided we suffer with him."[63]

> The satisfaction that we make for our sins, however, is not so much ours as though it were not done through Jesus Christ. We who can do nothing ourselves, as if just by ourselves, can do all things with the cooperation of "him who strengthens" us. Thus man has nothing of which to boast, but all our boasting is in Christ...in whom
> we make satisfaction by bringing 2011
> forth "fruits that befit repentance."

[57] Cf. Council of Trent (1551): DS 1647; 1661; CIC, can. 916; CCEO, can. 711. — [58] Cf. CIC, can. 914. — [59] Cf. Council of Trent: DS 1680; CIC, can. 988 § 2. — [60] Cf. *Lk* 6:36. — [61] St. Augustine, In Jo. ev. 12, 13: PL 35, 1491. — [62] Cf. Council of Trent (1551): DS 1712. — [63] *Rom* 8:17; *Rom* 3:25; *1 Jn* 2:1–2; cf. Council of Trent (1551): DS 1690.

These fruits have their efficacy from him, by him they are offered to the Father, and through him they are accepted by the Father.[64]

VIII. The Minister of This Sacrament

981 **1461** Since Christ entrusted to his apostles the ministry of reconciliation,[65] bishops who are their successors, and priests, the bishops' collaborators, continue to exercise this ministry. Indeed bishops and priests, by virtue of the sacrament of Holy Orders, have the power to forgive all sins "in the name of the Father, and of the Son, and of the Holy Spirit."

1462 Forgiveness of sins brings reconciliation with God, but also with the Church. Since ancient times the bishop, visible head of a
886 particular Church, has thus rightfully been considered to be the one who principally has the power and ministry of reconciliation: he is the
1567 moderator of the penitential discipline.[66] Priests, his collaborators, exercise it to the extent that they have received the commission either from their bishop (or religious superior) or the Pope, according to the law of the Church.[67]

1463 Certain particularly grave sins incur excommunication, the most severe ecclesiastical penalty, which impedes the reception of the sacraments and the exercise of certain ecclesiastical acts, and for which absolution consequently cannot be granted, according to canon law, except by the Pope, the bishop of the place or priests authorized by them.[68] In danger of death any priest, even if deprived of faculties for hearing confessions, can absolve from every
sin and excommunication.[69] 982

1464 Priests must encourage the faithful to come to the sacrament of Penance and must make themselves available to celebrate this sacrament each time Christians reasonably ask for it.[70]

1465 When he celebrates the sacrament of Penance, the priest is fulfilling the ministry of the Good Shepherd who seeks the lost sheep,
of the Good Samaritan who binds 983
up wounds, of the Father who awaits the prodigal son and welcomes him on his return, and of the just and impartial judge whose judgment is both just and merciful. The priest is the sign and the instrument of God's merciful love for the sinner.

1466 The confessor is not the 1551
master of God's forgiveness, but its servant. The minister of this sacrament should unite himself to the intention and charity of Christ.[71] He should have a proven knowledge
of Christian behavior, experience of 2690
human affairs, respect and sensitivity toward the one who has fallen; he must love the truth, be faithful to the Magisterium of the Church, and lead the penitent with patience toward healing and full maturity. He must pray and do penance for his penitent, entrusting him to the Lord's mercy.

[64] Council of Trent (1551): DS 1691; cf. *Phil* 4:13; *1 Cor* 1:31; *2 Cor* 10:17; *Gal* 6:14; *Lk* 3:8. — [65] Cf. *Jn* 20:23; *2 Cor* 5:18. — [66] Cf. *LG* 26 § 3. — [67] Cf. CIC, cann. 844; 967–969; 972; CCEO, can. 722 §§ 3–4. — [68] Cf. CIC, cann. 1331; 1354–1357; CCEO, can. 1431; 1434; 1420. — [69] Cf. CIC, can. 976; CCEO, can. 725. — [70] Cf. CIC, can. 986; CCEO, can. 735; PO 13. — [71] Cf. PO 13.

1467 Given the delicacy and greatness of this ministry and the respect due to persons, the Church declares that every priest who hears confessions is bound under very severe penalties to keep absolute secrecy regarding the sins that his penitents have confessed to him. He can
2490 make no use of knowledge that confession gives him about penitents' lives.[72] This secret, which admits of no exceptions, is called the "sacramental seal," because what the penitent has made known to the priest remains "sealed" by the sacrament.

IX. The Effects of This Sacrament

1468 "The whole power of the sacrament of Penance consists in restoring us to God's grace and joining us with him in an intimate friendship."[73] Reconciliation with God is thus the purpose and effect of this sacrament. For those who receive the sacrament of Penance with contrite heart and religious disposition, reconciliation "is usually followed by peace and serenity of conscience with strong spiritual consolation."[74] In-
2305 deed the sacrament of Reconciliation with God brings about a true "spiritual resurrection," restoration of the dignity and blessings of the life of the children of God, of which the most precious is friendship with God.[75]

953 **1469** This sacrament *reconciles us with the Church.* Sin damages or even breaks fraternal communion. The sacrament of Penance repairs or restores it. In this sense it does not simply heal the one restored to ecclesial communion, but has also a revitalizing effect on the life of the Church which suffered from the sin of one of her members.[76] Re-established or strengthened in the communion of saints, the sinner is made stronger by the exchange of spiritual goods among all the living members of the Body of Christ, whether still on pilgrimage or already in the heavenly homeland:[77] 949

> It must be recalled that…this reconciliation with God leads, as it were, to other reconciliations, which repair the other breaches caused by sin. The forgiven penitent is reconciled with himself in his inmost being, where he regains his innermost truth. He is reconciled with his brethren whom he has in some way offended and wounded. He is reconciled with the Church. He is reconciled with all creation.[78]

1470 In this sacrament, the sinner, placing himself before the merciful judgment of God, *anticipates* in a certain way the judgment to which
he will be subjected at the end of 678, 1039
his earthly life. For it is now, in this life, that we are offered the choice between life and death, and it is only by the road of conversion that we can enter the Kingdom, from which one is excluded by grave sin.[79] In converting to Christ through penance and faith, the sinner passes from death to life and "does not come into judgment."[80]

X. Indulgences

1471 The doctrine and practice of indulgences in the Church are closely linked to the effects of the sacrament of Penance.

[72] Cf. CIC, can. 1388 § 1; CCEO, can. 1456. — [73] *Roman Catechism,* II, V, 18. — [74] Council of Trent (1551): DS 1674. — [75] Cf. *Lk* 15:32. — [76] Cf. *1 Cor* 12:26. — [77] Cf. *LG* 48–50. — [78] John Paul II, RP 31, 5. — [79] Cf. *1 Cor* 5:11; *Gal* 5:19–21; *Rev* 22:15. — [80] *Jn* 5:24.

What is an indulgence?

"An indulgence is a remission before God of the temporal punishment due to sins whose guilt has already been forgiven, which the faithful Christian who is duly disposed gains under certain prescribed conditions through the action of the Church which, as the minister of redemption, dispenses and applies with authority the treasury of the satisfactions of Christ and the saints."[81]

"An indulgence is partial or plenary according as it removes either part or all of the temporal punishment due to sin."[82] The faithful can gain indulgences for themselves or apply them to the dead.[83]

The punishments of sin

1472 To understand this doctrine and practice of the Church, it is necessary to understand that sin has *a double consequence.* Grave sin deprives us of communion with God
1861 and therefore makes us incapable of eternal life, the privation of which is called the "eternal punishment" of sin. On the other hand every sin, even venial, entails an unhealthy attachment to creatures, which must be purified either here on earth, or after death in the state called Purgatory. This purification frees one from what is called the "temporal punishment"
1031 of sin. These two punishments must not be conceived of as a kind of vengeance inflicted by God from without, but as following from the very nature of sin. A conversion which proceeds from a fervent charity can attain the complete purification of the sinner in such a way that no punishment would remain.[84]

1473 The forgiveness of sin and restoration of communion with God entail the remission of the eternal punishment of sin, but temporal punishment of sin remains. While patiently bearing sufferings and trials of all kinds and, when the day comes, serenely facing death, the Christian must strive to accept this temporal punishment of sin as a grace. He should strive by works of mercy and charity, as well as by
prayer and the various practices of 2447
penance, to put off completely the "old man" and to put on the "new man."[85]

In the Communion of Saints

1474 The Christian who seeks to 946–959
purify himself of his sin and to become holy with the help of God's grace is not alone. "The life of each of God's children is joined in Christ and through Christ in a wonderful way to the life of all the other Christian brethren in the supernatural unity of the Mystical Body of Christ, as in a
single mystical person."[86] 795

1475 In the communion of saints, "a perennial link of charity exists between the faithful who have already reached their heavenly home, those who are expiating their sins in purgatory and those who are still pilgrims on earth. Between them there is, too, an abundant exchange of all good things."[87] In this wonderful exchange, the holiness of one profits others, well beyond the harm that the sin of one could cause others.

[81] Paul VI, apostolic constitution, *Indulgentiarum doctrina,* Norm 1. — [82] *Indulgentiarum doctrina,* Norm 2; cf. Norm 3. — [83] CIC, can. 994. — [84] Cf. Council of Trent (1551): DS 1712–1713; (1563): 1820. — [85] *Eph* 4:22, 24. — [86] *Indulgentiarum doctrina,* 5. — [87] *Indulgentiarum doctrina,* 5.

Thus recourse to the communion of saints lets the contrite sinner be more promptly and efficaciously purified of the punishments for sin.

1476 We also call these spiritual goods of the communion of saints the *Church's treasury*, which is "not the sum total of the material goods which have accumulated during the course of the centuries. On the contrary the 'treasury of the Church' is the infinite value, which can never
617 be exhausted, which Christ's merits have before God. They were offered so that the whole of mankind could be set free from sin and attain communion with the Father. In Christ, the Redeemer himself, the satisfactions and merits of his Redemption exist and find their efficacy."[88]

969 **1477** "This treasury includes as well the prayers and good works of the Blessed Virgin Mary. They are truly immense, unfathomable, and even pristine in their value before God. In the treasury, too, are the prayers and good works of all the saints, all those who have followed in the footsteps of Christ the Lord and by his grace have made their lives holy and carried out the mission the Father entrusted to them. In this way they attained their own salvation and at the same time cooperated in saving their brothers in the unity of the Mystical Body."[89]

Obtaining indulgence from God through the Church

981 **1478** An indulgence is obtained through the Church who, by virtue of the power of binding and loosing granted her by Christ Jesus, intervenes in favor of individual Christians and opens for them the treasury of the merits of Christ and the saints to obtain from the Father of mercies the remission of the temporal punishments due for their sins. Thus the Church does not want simply to come to the aid of these Christians, but also to spur them to works of devotion, penance, and charity.[90]

1479 Since the faithful departed 1032
now being purified are also members of the same communion of saints, one way we can help them is to obtain indulgences for them, so that the temporal punishments due for their sins may be remitted.

XI. The Celebration of the Sacrament of Penance

1480 Like all the sacraments, Penance is a liturgical action. The elements of the celebration are ordinarily these: a greeting and blessing from the priest, reading the word of God to illuminate the conscience and elicit contrition, and an exhortation to repentance; the confession, which acknowledges sins and makes them known to the priest; the imposition and acceptance of a penance; the priest's absolution; a prayer of thanksgiving and praise and dismissal with the blessing of the priest.

1481 The Byzantine Liturgy rec- 1449
ognizes several formulas of absolution, in the form of invocation, which admirably express the mystery of forgiveness: "May the same God, who through the Prophet Nathan forgave David when he confessed his sins, who forgave Peter when he wept bitterly, the prostitute when she washed his feet with her

[88] *Indulgentiarum doctrina*, 5. — [89] *Indulgentiarum doctrina*, 5. — [90] Cf. *Indulgentiarum doctrina*, 5.

tears, the publican, and the prodigal son, through me, a sinner, forgive you both in this life and in the next and enable you to appear before his awe-inspiring tribunal without condemnation, he who is blessed for ever and ever. Amen."

1482 The sacrament of Penance can also take place in the framework of a *communal celebration* in which we prepare ourselves together for confession and give thanks together for the forgiveness received. Here, the personal confession of sins and individual absolution are inserted into a liturgy of the word of God with readings and a homily, an examination of conscience conducted in common, a communal request for forgiveness, the Our Father and a thanksgiving in common. This communal celebration expresses more clearly the ecclesial character of penance. However, regardless of its manner of celebration the sacrament of Penance is always, by its very nature, a liturgical action, and
1140 therefore an ecclesial and public action.[91]

1401 **1483** In case of grave necessity recourse may be had to a *communal celebration of reconciliation with general confession and general absolution.* Grave necessity of this sort can arise when there is imminent danger of death without sufficient time for the priest or priests to hear each penitent's confession. Grave necessity can also exist when, given the number of penitents, there are not enough confessors to hear individual confessions properly in a reasonable time, so that the penitents through no fault of their own would be deprived of sacramental grace or Holy Communion for a long time. In this case, for the absolution to be valid the faithful must have the intention of individually confessing their grave sins in the time required.[92] The diocesan bishop is the judge of whether or not the conditions required for general absolution exist.[93] A large gathering of the faithful on the occasion of major feasts or pilgrimages does not constitute a case of grave necessity.[94]

1484 "Individual, integral confession and absolution remain the only ordinary way for the faithful to reconcile themselves with God and the Church, unless physical or moral impossibility excuses from this kind of confession."[95] There are profound reasons for this. Christ is at work in each of the sacraments. He personally addresses every sinner: "My son, 878
your sins are forgiven."[96] He is the physician tending each one of the sick who need him to cure them.[97] He raises them up and reintegrates them into fraternal communion. Personal confession is thus the form most expressive of reconciliation with God and with the Church.

In Brief

1485 *"On the evening of that day, the first day of the week," Jesus showed himself to his apostles. "He breathed on them, and said to them: 'Receive the Holy Spirit. If you forgive the sins of any, they are forgiven; if you retain the sins of any, they are retained'"* (Jn *20:19, 22–23).*

[91] Cf. SC 26–27. — [92] Cf. CIC, can. 962 § 1. — [93] Cf. CIC, can. 961 § 2. — [94] Cf. CIC, can. 961 § 1. — [95] OP 31. — [96] *Mk* 2:5. — [97] Cf. *Mk* 2:17.

1486 *The forgiveness of sins committed after Baptism is conferred by a particular sacrament called the sacrament of conversion, confession, penance, or reconciliation.*

1487 *The sinner wounds God's honor and love, his own human dignity as a man called to be a son of God, and the spiritual well-being of the Church, of which each Christian ought to be a living stone.*

1488 *To the eyes of faith no evil is graver than sin and nothing has worse consequences for sinners themselves, for the Church, and for the whole world.*

1489 *To return to communion with God after having lost it through sin is a process born of the grace of God who is rich in mercy and solicitous for the salvation of men. One must ask for this precious gift for oneself and for others.*

1490 *The movement of return to God, called conversion and repentance, entails sorrow for and abhorrence of sins committed, and the firm purpose of sinning no more in the future. Conversion touches the past and the future and is nourished by hope in God's mercy.*

1491 *The sacrament of Penance is a whole consisting in three actions of the penitent and the priest's absolution. The penitent's acts are repentance, confession or disclosure of sins to the priest, and the intention to make reparation and do works of reparation.*

1492 *Repentance (also called contrition) must be inspired by motives that arise from faith. If repentance arises from love of charity for God, it is called "perfect" contrition; if it is founded on other motives, it is called "imperfect."*

1493 *One who desires to obtain reconciliation with God and with the Church, must confess to a priest all the unconfessed grave sins he remembers after having carefully examined his conscience. The confession of venial faults, without being necessary in itself, is nevertheless strongly recommended by the Church.*

1494 *The confessor proposes the performance of certain acts of "satisfaction" or "penance" to be performed by the penitent in order to repair the harm caused by sin and to re-establish habits befitting a disciple of Christ.*

1495 *Only priests who have received the faculty of absolving from the authority of the Church can forgive sins in the name of Christ.*

1496 *The spiritual effects of the sacrament of Penance are:*
– *reconciliation with God by which the penitent recovers grace;*
– *reconciliation with the Church;*
– *remission of the eternal punishment incurred by mortal sins;*
– *remission, at least in part, of temporal punishments resulting from sin;*
– *peace and serenity of conscience, and spiritual consolation;*
– *an increase of spiritual strength for the Christian battle.*

1497 *Individual and integral confession of grave sins followed by absolution remains the only ordinary means of reconciliation with God and with the Church.*

1498 *Through indulgences the faithful can obtain the remission of temporal punishment resulting from sin for themselves and also for the souls in Purgatory.*

Article 5: THE ANOINTING OF THE SICK

1499 "By the sacred anointing of the sick and the prayer of the priests the whole Church commends those who are ill to the suffering and glorified Lord, that he may raise them up and save them. And indeed she exhorts them to contribute to the good of the People of God by freely uniting themselves to the Passion and death of Christ."[98]

I. Its Foundations in the Economy of Salvation

Illness in human life

1500 Illness and suffering have always been among the gravest problems confronted in human life. In illness, man experiences his powerlessness, his limitations, and his finitude. Every illness can make us
1006 glimpse death.

1501 Illness can lead to anguish, self-absorption, sometimes even despair and revolt against God. It can also make a person more mature, helping him discern in his life what is not essential so that he can turn toward that which is. Very often illness provokes a search for God and a return to him.

The sick person before God

1502 The man of the Old Testament lives his sickness in the presence of God. It is before God that he laments his illness, and it is of God, Master of life and death, that he implores healing.[99] Illness becomes a way to conversion; God's forgiveness initiates the healing.[100] It is the experience of Israel that illness is mysteriously linked to sin and evil, and
that faithfulness to God according 164
to his law restores life: "For I am the
Lord, your healer."[101] The prophet 376
intuits that suffering can also have a redemptive meaning for the sins of others.[102] Finally Isaiah announces that God will usher in a time for Zion when he will pardon every offense and heal every illness.[103]

Christ the physician

1503 Christ's compassion toward 549
the sick and his many healings of every kind of infirmity are a resplendent sign that "God has visited his people"[104] and that the Kingdom of God is close at hand. Jesus has the power not only to heal, but also to forgive sins;[105] he has come to heal the whole man, soul and body; he is the physician the sick have need
of.[106] His compassion toward all 1421
who suffer goes so far that he identifies himself with them: "I was sick and you visited me."[107] His preferential love for the sick has not ceased through the centuries to draw the very special attention of Christians
toward all those who suffer in body 2288
and soul. It is the source of tireless efforts to comfort them.

1504 Often Jesus asks the sick to believe.[108] He makes use of signs to heal: spittle and the laying on of hands,[109] mud and washing.[110] The

[98] *LG* 11; cf. *Jas* 5:14–16; *Rom* 8:17; *Col* 1:24; *2 Tim* 2:11–12; *1 Pet* 4:13. — [99] Cf. *Pss* 6:3; 38; *Isa* 38. — [100] Cf. *Pss* 32:5; 38:5; 39:9, 12; 107:20; cf. *Mk* 2:5–12. — [101] *Ex* 15:26. — [102] Cf. *Isa* 53:11. — [103] Cf. *Isa* 33:24. — [104] *Lk* 7:16; cf. *Mt* 4:24. — [105] Cf. *Mk* 2:5–12. — [106] Cf. *Mk* 2:17. — [107] *Mt* 25:36. — [108] Cf. *Mk* 5:34, 36; 9:23. — [109] Cf. *Mk* 7:32–36; 8:22–25. — [110] Cf. *Jn* 9:6–7.

sick try to touch him, "for power came forth from him and healed
695 them all."[111] And so in the sacraments Christ continues to "touch"
1116 us in order to heal us.

1505 Moved by so much suffering Christ not only allows himself to be touched by the sick, but he makes their miseries his own: "He took our infirmities and bore our diseases."[112] But he did not heal all the sick. His healings were signs of the coming of the Kingdom of God. They announced a more radical healing: the
440 victory over sin and death through his Passover. On the cross Christ took upon himself the whole weight of evil and took away the "sin of the world,"[113] of which illness is only a consequence. By his passion and death on the cross Christ has given a new meaning to suffering: it can henceforth configure us to him and
307 unite us with his redemptive Passion.

"Heal the sick…"

1506 Christ invites his disciples to follow him by taking up their cross in their turn.[114] By following him they acquire a new outlook on illness and the sick. Jesus associates them with his own life of poverty and service. He makes them share in his ministry of compassion and heal-
859 ing: "So they went out and preached that men should repent. And they cast out many demons, and anointed with oil many that were sick and healed them."[115]

1507 The risen Lord renews this mission ("In my name … they will lay their hands on the sick, and they will recover."[116]) and confirms it through the signs that the Church performs by invoking his name.[117] These signs demonstrate in a special way that Jesus is truly "God who saves."[118] 430

1508 The Holy Spirit gives to 798
some a special charism of healing[119] so as to make manifest the power of the grace of the risen Lord. But even the most intense prayers do not always obtain the healing of all illnesses. Thus St. Paul must learn from the Lord that "my grace is sufficient for
you, for my power is made perfect 618
in weakness," and that the sufferings to be endured can mean that "in my flesh I complete what is lacking in Christ's afflictions for the sake of his Body, that is, the Church."[120]

1509 "Heal the sick!"[121] The Church has received this charge from the Lord and strives to carry it out by taking care of the sick as well as by accompanying them with her prayer of intercession. She believes in the life-giving presence of Christ, the physician of souls and bodies. This presence is particularly active through the sacraments, and in an altogether special way through the Eucharist, the bread that gives eternal life and that St. Paul suggests is 1405
connected with bodily health.[122]

1510 However, the apostolic Church has its own rite for the sick, attested to by St. James: "Is any among you sick? Let him call for the elders [presbyters] of the Church and let them pray over him, anointing him with oil in the name of the Lord; and the prayer of faith will save the sick man, and the Lord will raise him up; and if he has committed sins, he

[111] *Lk* 6:19; cf. *Mk* 1:41; 3:10; 6:56. — [112] *Mt* 8:17; cf. *Isa* 53:4. — [113] *Jn* 1:29; cf. *Isa* 53:4–6. — [114] Cf. *Mt* 10:38. — [115] *Mk* 6:12–13. — [116] *Mk* 16:17–18. — [117] Cf. *Acts* 9:34; 14:3. — [118] Cf. *Mt* 1:21; *Acts* 4:12. — [119] Cf. *1 Cor* 12:9, 28, 30. — [120] *2 Cor* 12:9; *Col* 1:24. — [121] *Mt* 10:8. — [122] Cf. *Jn* 6:54, 58; *1 Cor* 11:30.

will be forgiven."[123] Tradition has rec
1117 ognized in this rite one of the seven sacraments.[124]

A sacrament of the sick

1511 The Church believes and confesses that among the seven sacraments there is one especially intended to strengthen those who are being tried by illness, the Anointing of the Sick:

> This sacred anointing of the sick was instituted by Christ our Lord as a true and proper sacrament of the New Testament. It is alluded to indeed by Mark, but is recommended to the faithful and promulgated by James the apostle and brother of the Lord.[125]

1512 From ancient times in the liturgical traditions of both East and West, we have testimonies to the practice of anointings of the sick with blessed oil. Over the centuries the Anointing of the Sick was conferred more and more exclusively on those at the point of death. Because of this it received the name "Extreme Unction." Notwithstanding this evolution the liturgy has never failed to beg the Lord that the sick person may recover his health if it would be conducive to his salvation.[126]

1513 The Apostolic Constitution *Sacram unctionem infirmorum*,[127] following upon the Second Vatican Council,[128] established that henceforth, in the Roman Rite, the following be observed:

> The sacrament of Anointing of the Sick is given to those who are seriously ill by anointing them on the forehead and hands with duly blessed oil—pressed from olives or from other plants—saying, only once: "Through this holy anointing may the Lord in his love and mercy help you with the grace of the Holy Spirit. May the Lord who frees you from sin save you and raise you up."[129]

II. Who Receives and Who Administers This Sacrament?

In case of grave illness...

1514 The Anointing of the Sick "is not a sacrament for those only who are at the point of death. Hence, as soon as anyone of the faithful begins to be in danger of death from sickness or old age, the fitting time for him to receive this sacrament has certainly already arrived."[130]

1515 If a sick person who received this anointing recovers his health, he can in the case of another grave illness receive this sacrament again. If during the same illness the person's condition becomes more serious, the sacrament may be repeated. It is fitting to receive the Anointing of the Sick just prior to a serious operation. The same holds for the elderly whose frailty becomes more pronounced.

"...let him call for the presbyters of the Church"

1516 Only priests (bishops and presbyters) are ministers of the

[123] *Jas* 5:14–15. — [124] Cf. Council of Constantinople II (553): DS 216; Council of Florence (1439): 1324–1325; Council of Trent (1551) 1695–1696; 1716–1717. — [125] Council of Trent (1551): DS 1695; cf. *Mk* 6:13; *Jas* 5:14-15. — [126] Cf. Council of Trent (1551): DS 1696. — [127] Paul VI, apostolic constitution, *Sacram unctionem infirmorum*, November 30, 1972. — [128] Cf. SC 73. — [129] Cf. CIC, can. 847 § 1. — [130] SC 73; cf. CIC, cann. 1004 § 1; 1005; 1007; CCEO, can. 738.

Anointing of the Sick.[131] It is the duty of pastors to instruct the faithful on the benefits of this sacrament. The faithful should encourage the sick to call for a priest to receive this sacrament. The sick should prepare themselves to receive it with good dispositions, assisted by their pastor and the whole ecclesial community, which is invited to surround the sick in a special way through their prayers and fraternal attention.

III. How Is This Sacrament Celebrated?

1140 **1517** Like all the sacraments the Anointing of the Sick is a liturgical and communal celebration,[132] whether it takes place in the family home, a hospital or church, for a single sick person or a whole group of sick persons. It is very fitting to celebrate it within the Eucharist, the memorial of the Lord's Passover. If circumstances suggest it, the celebration of the sacrament can be preceded by the sacrament of Penance and followed by the sacrament of the Eucharist. As the sacrament of Christ's Passover the Eucharist should always be the last sacrament of the earthly journey, the "viati-
1524 cum" for "passing over" to eternal life.

1518 Word and sacrament form an indivisible whole. The Liturgy of the Word, preceded by an act of repentance, opens the celebration. The words of Christ, the witness of the apostles, awaken the faith of the sick person and of the community to ask the Lord for the strength of his Spirit.

1519 The celebration of the sacrament includes the following principal elements: the "priests of the Church"[133]—in silence—lay hands on the sick; they pray over them in the faith of the Church[134]—this is the epiclesis proper to this sacrament; they then anoint them with oil blessed, if possible, by the bishop.

These liturgical actions indicate what grace this sacrament confers upon the sick.

IV. The Effects of the Celebration of This Sacrament

1520 *A particular gift of the Holy* 733
Spirit. The first grace of this sacrament is one of strengthening, peace and courage to overcome the difficulties that go with the condition of serious illness or the frailty of old age. This grace is a gift of the Holy Spirit, who renews trust and faith in God and strengthens against the temptations of the evil one, the temptation to discouragement and anguish in the face of death.[135] This assistance from the Lord by the power of his Spirit is meant to lead the sick person to healing of the soul, but also of the body if such is God's will.[136] Furthermore, "if he has committed sins, he will be forgiven."[137]

1521 *Union with the passion of Christ.* By the grace of this sacrament the sick person receives the strength and the gift of uniting himself more closely to Christ's Passion: in a certain way he is consecrated to bear
fruit by configuration to the Savior's 1535
redemptive Passion. Suffering, a consequence of original sin, acquires a new meaning; it becomes a participation in the saving work of Jesus. 1499

[131] Cf. Council of Trent (1551): DS 1697; 1719; CIC, can. 1003; CCEO, can. 739 § 1. — [132] Cf. *SC* 27. — [133] *Jas* 5:14. — [134] Cf. *Jas* 5:15. — [135] Cf. *Heb* 2:15. — [136] Cf. Council of Florence (1439): DS 1325. — [137] *Jas* 5:15; cf. Council of Trent (1551): DS 1717.

1522 An *ecclesial grace.* The sick who receive this sacrament, "by freely uniting themselves to the passion and death of Christ," "contribute to the good of the People of God."[138] By celebrating this sacrament the Church, in the communion of saints, intercedes for the benefit of
953 the sick person, and he, for his part, though the grace of this sacrament, contributes to the sanctification of the Church and to the good of all men for whom the Church suffers and offers herself through Christ to God the Father.

1020 **1523** A *preparation for the final journey.* If the sacrament of anointing of the sick is given to all who suffer from serious illness and infirmity, even more rightly is it given to those at the point of departing this life; so it is also called *sacramentum exeuntium* (the sacrament of those departing).[139] The Anointing of the Sick completes our conformity to the death and Resurrection of Christ, just as Baptism began it. It completes the holy anointings that mark the whole Christian life: that of Baptism which sealed the new life in us, and that of Confirmation which strengthened us
1294 for the combat of this life. This last anointing fortifies the end of our
1020 earthly life like a solid rampart for the final struggles before entering the Father's house.[140]

V. Viaticum, The Last Sacrament of the Christian

1392 **1524** In addition to the Anointing of the Sick, the Church offers those who are about to leave this life the Eucharist as viaticum. Communion in the body and blood of Christ, received at this moment of "passing over" to the Father, has a particular significance and importance. It is the seed of eternal life and the power of resurrection, according to the words of the Lord: "He who eats my flesh and drinks my blood has eternal life, and I will raise him up at the last day."[141] The sacrament of Christ once dead and now risen, the Eucharist is here the sacrament of passing over from death to life, from this world to the Father.[142]

1525 Thus, just as the sacraments 1680
of Baptism, Confirmation, and the Eucharist form a unity called "the sacraments of Christian initiation," so too it can be said that Penance, the Anointing of the Sick and the Eucharist as viaticum constitute at the end of Christian life "the sacraments that prepare for our heavenly homeland" or the sacraments that
complete the earthly pilgrimage. 2299

In Brief

1526 *"Is any among you sick? Let him call for the presbyters of the Church, and let them pray over him, anointing him with oil in the name of the Lord; and the prayer of faith will save the sick man, and the Lord will raise him up; and if he has committed sins, he will be forgiven"* (Jas *5:14-15).*

1527 *The sacrament of Anointing of the Sick has as its purpose the conferral of a special grace on the Christian experiencing the difficulties inherent in the condition of grave illness or old age.*

[138] *LG* 11 § 2. — [139] Council of Trent (1551): DS 1698. — [140] Council of Trent (1551): DS 1694. — [141] *Jn* 6:54. — [142] Cf. *Jn* 13:1.

1528 *The proper time for receiving this holy anointing has certainly arrived when the believer begins to be in danger of death because of illness or old age.*

1529 *Each time a Christian falls seriously ill, he may receive the Anointing of the Sick, and also when, after he has received it, the illness worsens.*

1530 *Only priests (presbyters and bishops) can give the sacrament of the Anointing of the Sick, using oil blessed by the bishop, or if necessary by the celebrating presbyter himself.*

1531 *The celebration of the Anointing of the Sick consists essentially in the anointing of the forehead and hands of the sick person (in the Roman Rite) or of other parts of the body (in the Eastern rite), the anointing being accompanied by the liturgical prayer of the celebrant asking for the special grace of this sacrament.*

1532 *The special grace of the sacrament of the Anointing of the Sick has as its effects:*

– the uniting of the sick person to the passion of Christ, for his own good and that of the whole Church;
– the strengthening, peace, and courage to endure in a Christian manner the sufferings of illness or old age;
– the forgiveness of sins, if the sick person was not able to obtain it through the sacrament of Penance;
– the restoration of health, if it is conducive to the salvation of his soul;
– the preparation for passing over to eternal life.

Chapter Three:

THE SACRAMENTS AT THE SERVICE OF COMMUNION

1212 **1533** Baptism, Confirmation, and Eucharist are sacraments of Christian initiation. They ground the common vocation of all Christ's disciples, a vocation to holiness and to the mission of evangelizing the world. They confer the graces needed for the life according to the Spirit during this life as pilgrims on the march towards the homeland.

1534 Two other sacraments, Holy Orders and Matrimony, are directed towards the salvation of others; if they contribute as well to personal salvation, it is through service to others that they do so. They confer a particular mission in the Church and serve to build up the People of God.

1535 Through these sacraments 784
those already *consecrated* by Baptism and Confirmation[1] for the common priesthood of all the faithful can receive particular *consecrations*. Those who receive the sacrament of Holy Orders are *consecrated* in Christ's name "to feed the Church by the word and grace of God."[2] On their part, "Christian spouses are fortified and, as it were, *consecrated* for the duties and dignity of their state by a special sacrament."[3]

Article 6:
THE SACRAMENT OF HOLY ORDERS

1536 Holy Orders is the sacrament through which the mission entrusted by Christ to his apostles continues to be exercised in the Church
860 until the end of time: thus it is the sacrament of apostolic ministry. It includes three degrees: episcopate, presbyterate, and diaconate.

(On the institution and mission of the apostolic ministry by Christ, see above, no. 874 ff. Here only the sacramental means by which this ministry is handed on will be treated.)

I. Why Is This Sacrament Called "Orders"?

1537 The word *order* in Roman antiquity designated an established
civil body, especially a governing 922
body. *Ordinatio* means incorporation into an *ordo*. In the Church there are established bodies which Tradition, not without a basis in Sacred Scripture,[4] has since ancient times called *taxeis* (Greek) or *ordines*. And so the liturgy speaks of the ordo episcoporum, the *ordo presbyterorum*, the *ordo*

[1] Cf. *LG* 10. — [2] *LG* 11 § 2. — [3] *GS* 48 § 2. — [4] Cf. *Heb* 5:6; 7:11; *Ps* 110:4.

923, 1631 *diaconorum*. Other groups also receive this name of *ordo*: catechumens, virgins, spouses, widows,....

1538 Integration into one of these bodies in the Church was accomplished by a rite called *ordinatio*, a religious and liturgical act which was a consecration, a blessing or a sacrament. Today the word "*ordination*" is reserved for the sacramental act which integrates a man into the order of bishops, presbyters, or deacons, and goes beyond a simple *election*, *designation*, *delegation*, or *institution* by the community, for it confers a gift of the Holy Spirit that permits the exercise of a "sacred power" (*sacra potestas*)[5] which can come only from Christ himself through his Church. Ordination is also
875 called *consecratio*, for it is a setting apart and an investiture by Christ himself for his Church. The *laying*
699 *on of hands* by the bishop, with the consecratory prayer, constitutes the visible sign of this ordination.

II. The Sacrament of Holy Orders in the Economy of Salvation

The priesthood of the Old Covenant

1539 The chosen people was constituted by God as "a kingdom of priests and a holy nation."[6] But within the people of Israel, God chose one of the twelve tribes, that of Levi, and set it apart for liturgical service; God himself is its inheritance.[7] A special rite consecrated the beginnings of the priesthood of the Old Covenant. The priests are "appointed to act on behalf of men in relation to God, to offer gifts and sacrifices for sins."[8]

1540 Instituted to proclaim the 2099
Word of God and to restore communion with God by sacrifices and prayer,[9] this priesthood nevertheless remains powerless to bring about salvation, needing to repeat its sacrifices ceaselessly and being unable to achieve a definitive sanctification, which only the sacrifice of Christ would accomplish.[10]

1541 The liturgy of the Church, however, sees in the priesthood of Aaron and the service of the Levites, as in the institution of the seventy elders,[11] a prefiguring of the ordained ministry of the New Covenant. Thus in the Latin Rite the Church prays in the consecratory preface of the ordination of bishops:

> God the Father of our Lord Jesus Christ,...by your gracious word you have established the plan of your Church. From the beginning, you chose the descendants of Abraham to be your holy nation. You established rulers and priests, and did not leave your sanctuary without ministers to serve you....[12]

1542 At the ordination of priests, the Church prays:

> Lord, holy Father,...when you had appointed high priests to rule your people, you chose other men next to them in rank and dignity to be with them and to help them in their task....you extended the spirit of Moses to seventy wise men....You shared among the sons of Aaron the fullness of their father's power.[13]

[5] Cf. *LG* 10. — [6] *Ex* 19:6; cf. *Isa* 61:6. — [7] Cf. *Num* 1:48–53; *Josh* 13:33. — [8] *Heb* 5:1; cf. *Ex* 29:1–30; *Lev* 8. — [9] Cf. *Mal* 2:7–9. — [10] Cf. *Heb* 5:3; 7:27;10:1–4. — [11] Cf. *Num* 11:24–25. — [12] *Roman Pontifical*, Ordination of Bishops 26, Prayer of Consecration. — *Roman Pontifical*, Ordination of Priests 22, Prayer of Consecration.

1543 In the consecratory prayer for ordination of deacons, the Church confesses:

> Almighty God..., You make the Church, Christ's body, grow to its full stature as a new and greater temple. You enrich it with every kind of grace and perfect it with a diversity of members to serve the whole body in a wonderful pattern of unity. You established a threefold ministry of worship and service, for the glory of your name. As ministers of your tabernacle you chose the sons of Levi and gave them your blessing as their everlasting inheritance.[14]

The one priesthood of Christ

1544 Everything that the priesthood of the Old Covenant prefigured finds its fulfillment in Christ Jesus, the "one mediator between God and men."[15] The Christian tradition considers Melchizedek,
874 "priest of God Most High," as a prefiguration of the priesthood of Christ, the unique "high priest after the order of Melchizedek";[16] "holy, blameless, unstained,"[17] "by a single offering he has perfected for all time those who are sanctified,"[18] that is, by the unique sacrifice of the cross.

1367 **1545** The redemptive sacrifice of Christ is unique, accomplished once for all; yet it is made present in the Eucharistic sacrifice of the Church. The same is true of the one priesthood of Christ; it is made present
662 through the ministerial priesthood without diminishing the uniqueness of Christ's priesthood: "Only Christ is the true priest, the others being only his ministers."[19]

Two participations in the one priesthood of Christ

1546 Christ, high priest and unique mediator, has made of the Church "a kingdom, priests for his God and Father."[20] The whole community of believers is, as such, priestly. The faithful exercise their baptismal priesthood through their participation, each according to his
own vocation, in Christ's mission as 1268
priest, prophet, and king. Through the sacraments of Baptism and Confirmation the faithful are "consecrated to be...a holy priesthood."[21]

1547 The ministerial or hierar- 1142
chical priesthood of bishops and priests, and the common priesthood of all the faithful participate, "each in its own proper way, in the one priesthood of Christ." While being "ordered one to another," they differ essentially.[22] In what sense? While the common priesthood of the faithful is exercised by the unfolding of baptismal grace—a life of faith, hope, and charity, a life according to the Spirit—, the ministerial priesthood is at the service of the common priesthood. It is directed at the unfolding of the baptismal
grace of all Christians. The ministe- 1120
rial priesthood is a *means* by which Christ unceasingly builds up and leads his Church. For this reason it is transmitted by its own sacrament, the sacrament of Holy Orders.

In the person of Christ the Head...

1548 In the ecclesial service of the 875
ordained minister, it is Christ himself who is present to his Church as

[14] *Roman Pontifical*, Ordination of Deacons 21, Prayer of Consecration. — [15] *1 Tim* 2:5. — [16] *Heb* 5:10; cf. 6:20; *Gen* 14:18. — [17] *Heb* 7:26. — [18] *Heb* 10:14. — [19] St. Thomas Aquinas, *Hebr.* 8, 4. — [20] *Rev* 1:6; cf. *Rev* 5:9–10; *1 Pet* 2:5, 9. — [21] *LG* 10 §1. — [22] *LG* 10 § 2.

792 Head of his Body, Shepherd of his flock, high priest of the redemptive sacrifice, Teacher of Truth. This is what the Church means by saying that the priest, by virtue of the sacrament of Holy Orders, acts *in persona Christi Capitis*:[23]

> It is the same priest, Christ Jesus, whose sacred person his minister truly represents. Now the minister, by reason of the sacerdotal consecration which he has received, is truly made like to the high priest and possesses the authority to act in the power and place of the person of Christ himself (virtute ac persona ipsius Christi).[24]

> Christ is the source of all priesthood: the priest of the old law was a figure of Christ, and the priest of the new law acts in the person of Christ.[25]

1549 Through the ordained ministry, especially that of bishops and priests, the presence of Christ as head of the Church is made visible in the midst of the community of believers.[26] In the beautiful expres-
1142 sion of St. Ignatius of Antioch, the bishop is *typos tou Patros*: he is like the living image of God the Father.[27]

1550 This presence of Christ in the minister is not to be understood as if the latter were preserved from all human weaknesses, the spirit of domination, error, even sin. The
896 power of the Holy Spirit does not guarantee all acts of ministers in the same way. While this guarantee extends to the sacraments, so that even the minister's sin cannot impede the
1128 fruit of grace, in many other acts the minister leaves human traces that are not always signs of fidelity 1584
to the Gospel and consequently can harm the apostolic fruitfulness of the Church.

1551 This priesthood is ministerial. "That office...which the Lord committed to the pastors of his people, is in the strict sense of the term a *service*."[28] It is entirely related to 876
Christ and to men. It depends entirely on Christ and on his unique priesthood; it has been instituted for the good of men and the communion of the Church. The sacrament of Holy Orders communicates a "sacred power" which is none other than that of Christ. The exercise 1538
of this authority must therefore be measured against the model of 608
Christ, who by love made himself the least and the servant of all.[29] "The Lord said clearly that concern for his flock was proof of love for him."[30]

... "in the name of the whole Church"

1552 The ministerial priesthood has the task not only of representing Christ—Head of the Church—before the assembly of the faithful, but also of acting in the name of the whole Church when presenting to God the prayer of the Church, and above all when offering the Eucharistic sacrifice.[31]

1553 "In the name of the *whole* Church" does not mean that priests are the delegates of the community. The prayer and offering of the Church are inseparable from the prayer and offering of Christ, her head; it is always the case that

[23] Cf. *LG* 10; 28; *SC* 33; *CD* 11; *PO* 2; 6. — [24] Pius XII, encyclical, *Mediator Dei* : AAS, 39 (1947) 548. — [25] St. Thomas Aquinas, *STh* III, 22, 4c. — [26] Cf. *LG* 21. — [27] St. Ignatius of Antioch, *Ad Trall.* 3,1: SCh. 10, 96; cf. *Ad Magn.* 6,1: SCh 10, 82–84. — [28] *LG* 24. — [29] Cf. *Mk* 10:43–45; *Pet* 15:3. — [30] St. John Chrysostom, *De sac.* 2, 4: PG 48, 636; cf. *Jn* 21:15–17. — [31] Cf. *SC* 33N; *LG* 10.

Christ worships in and through his Church. The whole Church, the Body of Christ, prays and offers herself "through him, with him, in him," in the unity of the Holy Spirit, to God the Father. The whole
795 Body, *caput et membra*, prays and offers itself, and therefore those who in the Body are especially his ministers are called ministers not only of Christ, but also of the Church. It is because the ministerial priesthood represents Christ that it can represent the Church.

III. The Three Degrees of the Sacrament of Holy Orders

1554 "The divinely instituted ecclesiastical ministry is exercised in different degrees by those who even from ancient times have been called
1536 bishops, priests, and deacons."[32] Catholic doctrine, expressed in the liturgy, the Magisterium, and the constant practice of the Church, recognizes that there are two degrees of ministerial participation in the priesthood of Christ: the episcopacy and the presbyterate. The diaconate is intended to help and serve them. For this reason the term *sacerdos* in current usage denotes bishops and priests but not deacons. Yet Catholic doctrine teaches that the degrees of priestly participation (episcopate and presbyterate) and the degree of service (diaconate) are all three conferred by a sacramental act
1538 called "ordination," that is, by the sacrament of Holy Orders:

> Let everyone revere the deacons as Jesus Christ, the bishop as the image of the Father, and the presbyters as the senate of God and the assembly of the apostles. For without them one cannot speak of the Church.[33]

Episcopal ordination—fullness of the sacrament of Holy Orders

1555 "Amongst those various offices which have been exercised in the Church from the earliest times the chief place, according to the witness of tradition, is held by the function of those who, through their appointment to the dignity and responsibility of bishop, and in virtue consequently of the unbroken succession going back to the beginning, are regarded as transmitters of 861
the apostolic line."[34]

1556 To fulfil their exalted mission, "the apostles were endowed by Christ with a special outpouring of the Holy Spirit coming upon them, and by the imposition of hands they 862
passed on to their auxiliaries the gift of the Spirit, which is transmitted down to our day through episcopal consecration."[35]

1557 The Second Vatican Council "teaches…that *the fullness of the sacrament of Holy Orders* is conferred by episcopal consecration, that fullness namely which, both in the liturgical tradition of the Church and the language of the Fathers of the Church, is called the high priesthood, the acme (*summa*) of the sacred ministry."[36]

1558 "Episcopal consecration con- 895
fers, together with the office of sanctifying, also the offices of teaching and ruling.… In fact…by the imposition of hands and through the words of the 1121
consecration, the grace of the Holy Spirit is given, and a sacred character is impressed in such wise that bish-

[32] *LG* 28. — [33] St. Ignatius of Antioch, *Ad Trall.* 3,1: Sch 10, 96. — [34] *LG* 20. — [35] *LG* 21; cf. *Acts* 1:8; 2:4; *Jn* 20:22–23; *1 Tim* 4:14; *2 Tim* 1:6–7. — [36] *LG* 21 § 2.

ops, in an eminent and visible manner, take the place of Christ himself, teacher, shepherd, and priest, and act as his representative (*in Eius persona agant*)."[37] "By virtue, therefore, of the Holy Spirit who has been given to them, bishops have been constituted true and authentic teachers of the faith and have been made pontiffs and pastors."[38]

1559 "One is constituted a member of the episcopal body in virtue of the sacramental consecration and by the hierarchical communion with the head and members of the college."[39] The character and *collegial nature* of the episcopal order are evidenced among other ways by
877 the Church's ancient practice which calls for several bishops to participate in the consecration of a new bishop.[40] In our day, the lawful ordination of a bishop requires a special intervention of the Bishop of Rome, because he is the supreme visible
882 bond of the communion of the particular Churches in the one Church and the guarantor of their freedom.

833 **1560** As Christ's vicar, each bishop has the pastoral care of the particular Church entrusted to him, but at the same time he bears collegially with all his brothers in the episcopacy the *solicitude for all the*
886 *Churches*: "Though each bishop is the lawful pastor only of the portion of the flock entrusted to his care, as a legitimate successor of the apostles he is, by divine institution and precept, responsible with the other bishops for the apostolic mission of the Church."[41]

1561 The above considerations 1369
explain why the Eucharist celebrated by the bishop has a quite special significance as an expression of the Church gathered around the altar, with the one who represents Christ, the Good Shepherd and Head of his Church, presiding.[42]

The ordination of priests—co-workers of the bishops

1562 "Christ, whom the Father hallowed and sent into the world, has, through his apostles, made their successors, the bishops namely, sharers in his consecration and mission; and these, in their turn, duly entrusted in varying degrees various members of the Church with the office of their ministry."[43] "The function of the bishops' ministry was handed over in a subordinate degree to priests so that they might be appointed in the order of the priesthood and be *co-workers of the episcopal order* for the proper fulfillment of the apostolic mission that had been entrusted to it by Christ."[44]

1563 "Because it is joined with the episcopal order the office of priests shares in the authority by which Christ himself builds up and sanctifies and rules his Body. Hence the priesthood of priests, while presupposing the sacraments of initiation, is nevertheless conferred by its own particular sacrament. Through that sacrament priests by the anointing of the Holy Spirit are signed with a special character and so are configured to Christ the priest in such a 1121
way that they are able to act in the person of Christ the head."[45]

[37] *LG* 21. — [38] *CD* 2 § 2. — [39] *LG* 22. — [40] Cf. *LG* 22. — [41] Pius XII, *Fidei donum*: AAS 49 (1957) 237; cf. *LG* 23; *CD* 4; 36; 37; *AG* 5; 6; 38. — [42] Cf. *SC* 41; *LG* 26. — [43] *LG* 28; *Jn* 10:36. — [44] *PO* 2 § 2.

1564 "Whilst not having the supreme degree of the pontifical office, and notwithstanding the fact that they depend on the bishops in the exercise of their own proper power, the priests are for all that associated with them by reason of their sacerdotal dignity; and in virtue of the sacrament of Holy Orders, after the image of Christ, the supreme and eternal priest, they are consecrated in order to preach the Gospel and shepherd the faithful as well as to celebrate divine worship *as true*
611 *priests of the New Testament.*"[46]

1565 Through the sacrament of Holy Orders priests share in the universal dimensions of the mission that Christ entrusted to the apostles. The
849 spiritual gift they have received in ordination prepares them, not for a limited and restricted mission, "but for the fullest, in fact the universal mission of salvation 'to the end of the earth,'"[47] "prepared in spirit to preach the Gospel everywhere."[48]

1369 **1566** "It is in the Eucharistic cult or in the *Eucharistic assembly* of the faithful (*synaxis*) that they exercise in a supreme degree their sacred office; there, acting in the person of Christ and proclaiming his mystery, they unite the votive offerings of the faithful to the sacrifice of Christ their head, and in the sacrifice of the Mass they make present again and apply, until the coming of the Lord, the unique sacrifice of the New Testament, that namely of Christ offering himself once for all a spotless
611 victim to the Father."[49] From this unique sacrifice their whole priestly ministry draws its strength.[50]

1567 "The priests, prudent coop- 1462
erators of the episcopal college and its support and instrument, called to the service of the People of God, constitute, together with their bishop, a unique sacerdotal college (*presbyterium*) dedicated, it is true, to a variety of distinct duties. In each local assembly of the faithful they represent, in a certain sense, the bishop,
with whom they are associated in 2179
all trust and generosity; in part they take upon themselves his duties and solicitude and in their daily toils discharge them."[51] Priests can exercise their ministry only in dependence on the bishop and in communion with him. The promise of obedience they make to the bishop at the moment of ordination and the kiss of peace from him at the end of the ordination liturgy mean that the bishop considers them his co-workers, his sons, his brothers and his friends, and that they in return owe him love and obedience.

1568 "All priests, who are consti- 1537
tuted in the order of priesthood by the sacrament of Order, are bound together by an intimate sacramental brotherhood, but in a special way they form one priestly body in the diocese to which they are attached under their own bishop...."[52] The unity of the presbyterium finds liturgical expression in the custom of the presbyters' imposing hands, after the bishop, during the rite of ordination.

The ordination of deacons— "in order to serve"

1569 "At a lower level of the hierarchy are to be found deacons, who

[45] *PO* 2. — [46] *LG* 28; cf. *Heb* 5:1–10; 7:24; 9:11–28; Innocent I, *Epist. ad Decentium*: PL 20, 554 A; St. Gregory of Nazianzus, *Oratio* 2, 22: PG 35, 432B. — [47] *PO* 10; *OT* 20; cf. *Acts* 1:8. — [48] *OT* 20. — [49] *LG* 28; cf. *Cor* 11:26. — [50] Cf. *PO* 2. — [51] *LG* 28 § 2. — [52] *PO* 8.

receive the imposition of hands 'not unto the priesthood, but unto the ministry.'"[53] At an ordination to the diaconate only the bishop lays hands on the candidate, thus signifying the deacon's special attachment to the bishop in the tasks of his "diakonia."[54]

1570 Deacons share in Christ's mission and grace in a special
1121 way.[55] The sacrament of Holy Orders marks them with an *imprint* ("character") which cannot be removed and which configures them to Christ, who made himself the "deacon" or servant of all.[56] Among other tasks, it is the task of deacons to assist the bishop and priests in the celebration of the divine mysteries, above all the Eucharist, in the distribution of Holy Communion, in assisting at and blessing marriages, in the proclamation of the Gospel and preaching, in presiding over funerals, and in dedicating themselves to the various ministries of charity.[57]

1571 Since the Second Vatican Council the Latin Church has restored the diaconate "as a proper and permanent rank of the hierarchy,"[58] while the Churches of the East had always maintained it. This *permanent diaconate*, which can be conferred on married men, constitutes an important enrichment for the Church's mission. Indeed it
1579 is appropriate and useful that men who carry out a truly diaconal ministry in the Church, whether in its liturgical and pastoral life or whether in its social and charitable works, should "be strengthened by the imposition of hands which has come down from the apostles. They would be more closely bound to the altar and their ministry would be made more fruitful through the sacramental grace of the diaconate."[59]

IV. The Celebration of This Sacrament

1572 Given the importance that the ordination of a bishop, a priest, or a deacon has for the life of the particular Church, its celebration calls for as many of the faithful as possible to take part. It should take place preferably on Sunday, in the cathedral, with solemnity appropriate to the occasion. All three ordinations, of the bishop, of the priest, and of the deacon, follow the same movement. Their proper place is within the Eucharistic liturgy.

1573 The *essential rite* of the sacrament of Holy Orders for all three degrees consists in the bishop's imposition of hands on the head of the ordinand and in the bishop's specific
consecratory prayer asking God for 699
the outpouring of the Holy Spirit 1585
and his gifts proper to the ministry to which the candidate is being ordained.[60]

1574 As in all the sacraments additional rites surround the celebration. Varying greatly among the different liturgical traditions, these rites have in common the expression of the multiple aspects of sacramental grace. Thus in the Latin Church, the initial rites—presentation and election of the ordinand, instruction by the bishop, examination of the candidate, litany of the saints—attest that the choice of the candidate

[53] *LG* 29; cf. *CD* 15. — [54] Cf. St. Hippolytus, *Trad. ap.* 8: SCh 11, 58–62. — [55] Cf. *LG* 41; *AA* 16. — [56] Cf. *Mk* 10:45; *Lk* 22:27; St. Polycarp, *Ad Phil.* 5, 2: SCh 10, 182. — [57] Cf. *LG* 29; SC 35 § 4; *AG* 16. — [58] *LG* 29 § 2. — [59] *AG* 16 § 6. — [60] Cf. Pius XII, apostolic constitution, *Sacramentum Ordinis*: DS 3858.

is made in keeping with the practice of the Church and prepare for the solemn act of consecration, after which several rites symbolically express and complete the mystery accomplished: for bishop and priest, an anointing with holy chrism, a sign of the special anointing of the
1294 Holy Spirit who makes their ministry fruitful; giving the book of the Gospels, the ring, the miter, and the crosier to the bishop as the sign of his apostolic mission to proclaim the Word of God, of his fidelity to the Church, the bride of Christ, and his office as shepherd of the Lord's
796 flock; presentation to the priest of the paten and chalice, "the offering of the holy people" which he is called to present to God; giving the book of the Gospels to the deacon who has just received the mission to proclaim the Gospel of Christ.

V. Who Can Confer This Sacrament?

1575 Christ himself chose the apostles and gave them a share in his mission and authority. Raised to the Father's right hand, he has not forsaken his flock but he keeps it under his constant protection through the apostles, and guides it still through
857 these same pastors who continue his work today.[61] Thus, it is Christ whose gift it is that some be apostles, others pastors. He continues to act through the bishops.[62]

1536 **1576** Since the sacrament of Holy Orders is the sacrament of the apostolic ministry, it is for the bishops as the successors of the apostles to hand on the "gift of the Spirit,"[63] the "apostolic line."[64] Validly ordained bishops, i.e., those who are in the line of apostolic succession, validly confer the three degrees of the sacrament of Holy Orders.[65]

VI. Who Can Receive This Sacrament?

1577 "Only a baptized man (*vir*) validly receives sacred ordination."[66] The Lord Jesus chose men (*ver*) to form the college of the twelve apostles, and the apostles did the same 551
when they chose collaborators to succeed them in their ministry.[67] The 861
college of bishops, with whom the priests are united in the priesthood, makes the college of the twelve an ever-present and ever-active reality 862
until Christ's return. The Church recognizes herself to be bound by this choice made by the Lord himself. For this reason the ordination of women is not possible.[68]

1578 No one has a *right* to receive the sacrament of Holy Orders. Indeed no one claims this office for himself; he is called to it by God.[69] Anyone who thinks he recognizes the 2121
signs of God's call to the ordained ministry must humbly submit his desire to the authority of the Church, who has the responsibility and right to call someone to receive orders. Like every grace this sacrament can be *received* only as an unmerited gift.

1579 All the ordained ministers of the Latin Church, with the exception of permanent deacons, are normally

[61] Cf. *Roman Missal*, Preface of the Apostles I. — [62] Cf. *LG* 21; *Eph* 4:11. — [63] *LG* 21 § 2. — [64] *LG* 20. — [65] Cf. DS 794 and Cf. DS 802; CIC, can.1012; CCEO, can. 744; 747. — [66] CIC, can.1024. — [67] Cf. *Mk* 3:14–19; *Lk* 6:12–16; *1 Tim* 3:1–13; *2 Tim* 1:6; *Titus* 1:5–9; St. Clement of Rome, *Ad Cor.* 42, 4; 44, 3: PG 1, 292–293; 300. — [68] Cf. John Paul II, *MD* 26–27; CDF, declaration, *Inter insigniores*: AAS 69 (1977) 98–116. — [69] Cf. *Heb* 5:4.

chosen from among men of faith who live a celibate life and who intend to remain *celibate* "for the sake of the
1618 kingdom of heaven."[70] Called to consecrate themselves with undivided heart to the Lord and to "the affairs of the Lord,"[71] they give themselves entirely to God and to men. Celibacy is a sign of this new life to the service of which the Church's minister is consecrated; accepted with a joyous heart celibacy radiantly proclaims the
2233 Reign of God.[72]

1580 In the Eastern Churches a different discipline has been in force for many centuries: while bishops are chosen solely from among celibates, married men can be ordained as deacons and priests. This practice has long been considered legitimate; these priests exercise a fruitful ministry within their communities.[73] Moreover, priestly celibacy is held in great honor in the Eastern Churches and many priests have freely chosen it for the sake of the Kingdom of God. In the East as in the West a man who has already received the sacrament of Holy Orders can no longer marry.

VII. The Effects of the Sacrament of Holy Orders

The indelible character

1581 This sacrament configures the recipient to Christ by a special grace of the Holy Spirit, so that he may serve as Christ's instrument for
1548 his Church. By ordination one is enabled to act as a representative of Christ, Head of the Church, in his triple office of priest, prophet, and king.

1582 As in the case of Baptism and Confirmation this share in 1121
Christ's office is granted once for all. The sacrament of Holy Orders, like the other two, confers *an indelible spiritual character* and cannot be repeated or conferred temporarily.[74]

1583 It is true that someone validly ordained can, for grave reasons, be discharged from the obligations and functions linked to ordination, or can be forbidden to exercise them; but he cannot become a layman again in the strict sense,[75] because the character imprinted by ordination is for ever.

The vocation and mission received on the day of his ordination mark him permanently.

1584 Since it is ultimately Christ 1128
who acts and effects salvation through the ordained minister, the unworthiness of the latter does not prevent Christ from acting.[76] St. Augustine states this forcefully:

> As for the proud minister, he is to be ranked with the devil. Christ's gift is not thereby profaned: what flows through him keeps its purity, and what passes through him remains 1550
> clear and reaches the fertile earth.... The spiritual power of the sacrament is indeed comparable to light: those to be enlightened receive it in its purity, and if it should pass through defiled beings, it is not itself defiled.[77]

The grace of the Holy Spirit

1585 The grace of the Holy Spirit proper to this sacrament is configuration to Christ as Priest, Teacher, and Pastor, of whom the ordained is made a minister.

[70] *Mt* 19:12. — [71] *1 Cor* 7:32. — [72] *PO* 16. — [73] Cf. *PO* 16. — [74] Cf. Council of Trent: DS 1767; *LG* 21; 28; 29; *PO* 2. — [75] Cf. CIC, cann. 290–293;1336 §1 3°, 5°;1338 § 2; Council of Trent: DS 1774. — [76] Cf. Council of Trent: DS 1612; DS 1154. — [77] St. Augustine, *In Jo. ev.* 5, 15: PL 35, 1422.

1586 For the bishop, this is first of all a grace of strength ("the governing spirit": Prayer of Episcopal Consecration in the Latin rite):[78] the grace to guide and defend his Church with strength and prudence
2448 as a father and pastor, with gratuitous love for all and a preferential love for the poor, the sick, and the needy. This grace impels him to proclaim the Gospel to all, to be the model for his flock, to go before it on the way of sanctification by identifying himself in the Eucharist with Christ the priest and victim, not fearing to give his life for his sheep:

1558 Father, you know all hearts. You have chosen your servant for the office of bishop. May he be a shepherd to your holy flock, and a high priest blameless in your sight, ministering to you night and day; may he always gain the blessing of your favor and offer the gifts of your holy Church. Through the Spirit who gives the grace of high priesthood grant him the power to forgive sins as you have commanded, to assign ministries as you have decreed, and to loose from every bond by the authority which you gave to your apostles. May he be pleasing to you by his gentleness and purity of heart, presenting a fragrant offering to you, through Jesus Christ, your Son. . . .[79]

1564 **1587** The spiritual gift conferred by presbyteral ordination is expressed by this prayer of the Byzantine Rite. The bishop, while laying on his hand, says among other things:

Lord, fill with the gift of the Holy Spirit him whom you have deigned to raise to the rank of the priesthood, that he may be worthy to stand without reproach before your altar, to proclaim the Gospel of your kingdom, to fulfill the ministry of your word of truth, to offer you spiritual gifts and sacrifices, to renew your people by the bath of rebirth; so that he may go out to meet our great God and Savior Jesus Christ, your only Son, on the day of his second coming, and may receive from your vast goodness the recompense for a faithful administration of his order.[80]

1588 With regard to deacons, 1569
"strengthened by sacramental grace they are dedicated to the People of God, in conjunction with the bishop and his body of priests, in the service (*diakonia*) of the liturgy, of the Gospel, and of works of charity."[81]

1589 Before the grandeur of the priestly grace and office, the holy doctors felt an urgent call to conversion in order to conform their whole lives to him whose sacrament had made them ministers. Thus St. Gregory of Nazianzus, as a very young priest, exclaimed:

We must begin by purifying ourselves before purifying others; we must be instructed to be able to instruct, become light to illuminate, draw close to God to bring him close to others, be sanctified to sanctify, lead by the hand and counsel prudently. I know whose ministers we are, where we find ourselves and to where we strive. I know God's greatness and man's weakness, but also his potential. [Who then is the priest? He is] the defender of truth, who stands with angels, gives glory with archangels, causes sacrifices to rise to the altar on high, shares Christ's

[78] Cf. *Roman Pontifical*, Ordination of Bishops 26, Prayer of Consecration; cf. CD 113;16. — [79] *Roman Pontifical*, Ordination of Bishops 26, Prayer of Consecration; cf. St. Hippolytus, *Trad. ap.* 3: SCh11, 44–46. — [80] Byzantine Liturgy, *Euchologion*. — [81] *LG* 29.

priesthood, refashions creation, restores it in God's image, recreates
460 it for the world on high and, even greater, is divinized and divinizes.[82]
And the holy Curé of Ars: "The priest continues the work of redemption on earth.... If we really understood the priest on earth, we would die not of
1551 fright but of love.... The Priesthood is the love of the heart of Jesus."[83]

In Brief

1590 *St. Paul said to his disciple Timothy: "I remind you to rekindle the gift of God that is within you through the laying on of my hands" (*2 Tim *1:6), and "If any one aspires to the office of bishop, he desires a noble task." (*1 Tim *3:1) To Titus he said: "This is why I left you in Crete, that you amend what was defective, and appoint presbyters in every town, as I directed you" (*Titus *1:5).*

1591 *The whole Church is a priestly people. Through Baptism all the faithful share in the priesthood of Christ. This participation is called the "common priesthood of the faithful." Based on this common priesthood and ordered to its service, there exists another participation in the mission of Christ: the ministry conferred by the sacrament of Holy Orders, where the task is to serve in the name and in the person of Christ the Head in the midst of the community.*

1592 *The ministerial priesthood differs in essence from the common priesthood of the faithful because it confers a sacred power for the service of the faithful. The ordained ministers exercise their service for the People of God by teaching (*munus docendi*), divine worship (*munus liturgicum*) and pastoral governance (*munus regendi*).*

1593 *Since the beginning, the ordained ministry has been conferred and exercised in three degrees: that of bishops, that of presbyters, and that of deacons. The ministries conferred by ordination are irreplaceable for the organic structure of the Church: without the bishop, presbyters, and deacons, one cannot speak of the Church (cf. St. Ignatius of Antioch,* Ad Trall. *3,1).*

1594 *The bishop receives the fullness of the sacrament of Holy Orders, which integrates him into the episcopal college and makes him the visible head of the particular Church entrusted to him. As successors of the apostles and members of the college, the bishops share in the apostolic responsibility and mission of the whole Church under the authority of the Pope, successor of St. Peter.*

1595 *Priests are united with the bishops in sacerdotal dignity and at the same time depend on them in the exercise of their pastoral functions; they are called to be the bishops' prudent co-workers. They form around their bishop the presbyterium which bears responsibility with him for the particular Church. They receive from the bishop the charge of a parish community or a determinate ecclesial office.*

1596 *Deacons are ministers ordained for tasks of service of the Church; they do not receive the ministerial priesthood, but ordination confers on them important functions in*

[82] St. Gregory of Nazianzus, *Oratio* 2, 71, 74, 73: PG 35, 480–481. — [83] St. John Vianney, quoted in B. Nodet, *Jean-Marie Vianney, Curé d'Ars*, 100.

the ministry of the word, divine worship, pastoral governance, and the service of charity, tasks which they must carry out under the pastoral authority of their bishop.

1597 *The sacrament of Holy Orders is conferred by the laying on of hands followed by a solemn prayer of consecration asking God to grant the ordinand the graces of the Holy Spirit required for his ministry. Ordination imprints an indelible sacramental character.*

1598 *The Church confers the sacrament of Holy Orders only on baptized men (*viri*), whose suitability for the exercise of the ministry has been duly recognized. Church authority alone has the responsibility and right to call someone to receive the sacrament of Holy Orders.*

1599 *In the Latin Church the sacrament of Holy Orders for the presbyterate is normally conferred only on candidates who are ready to embrace celibacy freely and who publicly manifest their intention of staying celibate for the love of God's kingdom and the service of men.*

1600 *It is bishops who confer the sacrament of Holy Orders in the three degrees.*

Article 7: THE SACRAMENT OF MATRIMONY

1601 "The matrimonial covenant, by which a man and a woman establish between themselves a partnership of the whole of life, is by its nature ordered toward the good of the spouses and the procreation and education of offspring; this covenant between baptized persons has been raised by Christ the Lord to the dignity of a sacrament."[84]

I. Marriage in God's Plan

369 **1602** Sacred Scripture begins with the creation of man and woman in
796 the image and likeness of God and concludes with a vision of "the wedding-feast of the Lamb."[85] Scripture speaks throughout of marriage and its "mystery," its institution and the meaning God has given it, its origin and its end, its various realizations throughout the history of salvation, the difficulties arising from sin and its renewal "in the Lord" in the New Covenant of Christ and the Church.[86]

Marriage in the order of creation

1603 "The intimate community of life and love which constitutes the married state has been established by the Creator and endowed
by him with its own proper laws.... 371
God himself is the author of marriage."[87] The vocation to marriage is written in the very nature of man and woman as they came from the
hand of the Creator. Marriage is not 2331
a purely human institution despite the many variations it may have undergone through the centuries in different cultures, social structures, and spiritual attitudes. These differences should not cause us to forget its common and permanent

[84] CIC, can. 1055 § 1; cf. *GS* 48 § 1. — [85] *Rev* 19:7, 9; cf. *Gen* 1:26–27. — [86] *1 Cor* 7:39; cf. *Eph* 5:31-32. — [87] *GS* 48 § 1.

characteristics. Although the dignity of this institution is not transparent everywhere with the same clarity,[88] some sense of the greatness of the matrimonial union exists in
all cultures. "The well-being of the
2210 individual person and of both human and Christian society is closely bound up with the healthy state of conjugal and family life."[89]

1604 God who created man out of love also calls him to love—the fundamental and innate vocation of every human being. For man is created in the image and likeness of God who is himself love.[90] Since God created him man and woman,
their mutual love becomes an im
355 age of the absolute and unfailing
love with which God loves man. It is good, very good, in the Creator's eyes. And this love which God blesses is intended to be fruitful and to be realized in the common work of watching over creation: "And God blessed them, and God said to them: 'Be fruitful and multiply, and fill the earth and subdue it.'"[91]

372 **1605** Holy Scripture affirms that
man and woman were created for one another: "It is not good that the man should be alone."[92] The woman, "flesh of his flesh," his equal, his nearest in all things, is given to him by God as a "helpmate"; she thus represents God from whom comes our help.[93] "Therefore a man leaves his father and his mother and cleaves to his wife, and they become one flesh."[94] The Lord himself shows that this signifies an unbreakable union of their two lives by
1614 recalling what the plan of the Creator
had been "in the beginning": "So they are no longer two, but one flesh."[95]

Marriage under the regime of sin

1606 Every man experiences evil around him and within himself. This experience makes itself felt in the relationships between man and woman. Their union has always been threatened by discord, a spirit of domination, infidelity, jealousy, and conflicts that can escalate into hatred and separation. This disorder can manifest itself more or less acutely, and can be more or less overcome according to the circumstances of cultures, eras, and individuals, but it does seem to have a universal character.

1607 According to faith the disorder we notice so painfully does not stem from the nature of man and
woman, nor from the *nature* of their 1849
relations, but from sin. As a break
with God, the first sin had for its first
consequence the rupture of the orig- 400
inal communion between man and woman. Their relations were distorted by mutual recriminations;[96] their mutual attraction, the Creator's own gift, changed into a relationship of domination and lust;[97] and the beautiful vocation of man and woman to be fruitful, multiply, and subdue the earth was burdened by the pain of childbirth and the toil of work.[98]

1608 Nevertheless, the order of 55
creation persists, though seriously disturbed. To heal the wounds of sin, man and woman need the help of the grace that God in his infinite mercy never refuses them.[99] Without his help man and woman cannot achieve the union of their lives for which God created them "in the beginning."

[88] Cf. *GS* 47 § 2. — [89] *GS* 47§ 1. — [90] Cf. *Gen* 1:27; *1 Jn* 4:8, 16. — [91] *Gen* 1:28; cf. 1:31. — [92] *Gen* 2:18. — [93] Cf. *Gen* 2:18–25. — [94] *Gen* 2:24. — [95] *Mt* 19:6. — [96] Cf. *Gen* 3:12.

Marriage under the pedagogy of the law

410 **1609** In his mercy God has not forsaken sinful man. The punishments consequent upon sin, "pain in childbearing" and toil "in the sweat of your brow,"[100] also embody remedies that limit the damaging effects of sin. After the fall, marriage helps to overcome self-absorption, egoism, pursuit of one's own pleasure, and to open oneself to the other, to mutual aid and to self-giving.

1610 Moral conscience concerning the unity and indissolubility of marriage developed under the pedagogy of the old law. In the Old
1963 Testament the polygamy of patriarchs and kings is not yet explicitly
2387 rejected. Nevertheless, the law given to Moses aims at protecting the wife from arbitrary domination by the husband, even though according to the Lord's words it still carries traces of man's "hardness of heart" which was the reason Moses permitted men to divorce their wives.[101]

219 **1611** Seeing God's covenant with Israel in the image of exclusive and faithful married love, the prophets
2380 prepared the Chosen People's con
2361 science for a deepened understanding of the unity and indissolubility of marriage.[102] The books of *Ruth* and *Tobit* bear moving witness to an elevated sense of marriage and to the fidelity and tenderness of spouses. Tradition has always seen in the *Song of Solomon* a unique expression of human love, insofar as it is a reflection of God's love—a love "strong as death" that "many waters cannot quench."[103]

Marriage in the Lord

1612 The nuptial covenant between God and his people Israel had prepared the way for the new and everlasting covenant in which the Son
of God, by becoming incarnate and 521
giving his life, has united to himself in a certain way all mankind saved by him, thus preparing for "the wedding-feast of the Lamb."[104]

1613 On the threshold of his public life Jesus performs his first sign—at his mother's request—during a wedding feast.[105] The Church attaches great importance to Jesus' presence at the wedding at Cana. She sees in it the confirmation of the goodness of marriage and the proclamation that thenceforth marriage will be an efficacious sign of Christ's presence.

1614 In his preaching Jesus un- 2336
equivocally taught the original meaning of the union of man and woman as the Creator willed it from the beginning: permission given by Moses to divorce one's wife was a concession to the hardness of
hearts.[106] The matrimonial union 2382
of man and woman is indissoluble: God himself has determined it: "what therefore God has joined together, let no man put asunder."[107]

1615 This unequivocal insistence 2364
on the indissolubility of the marriage bond may have left some perplexed and could seem to be a demand impossible to realize. However, Jesus has not placed on spouses a burden

[97] Cf. *Gen* 2:22; 3:16b. — [98] Cf. *Gen* 1:28; 3:16–19. — [99] Cf. *Gen* 3:21. — [100] *Gen* 3:16,19. — [101] Cf. *Mt* 19:8; *Deut* 24:1. — [102] *Hos* 1–3; *Isa* 54; 62; *Jer* 2–3; 31; *Ezek* 16; 23; *Mal* 2:13–17. — [103] *Song* 8:6–7. — [104] *Rev* 19:7, 9; cf. *GS* 22. — [105] Cf. *Jn* 2:1–11. — [106] *Mt* 19:8. — [107] *Mt* 19:6.

impossible to bear, or too heavy—heavier than the Law of Moses.[108] By coming to restore the original order of creation disturbed by sin, he himself gives the strength and grace to live marriage in the new dimension of the Reign of God. It is by following Christ, renouncing themselves, and taking up their crosses that spouses will be able to "receive" the original meaning of marriage and live it with the help of Christ.[109] This grace of Christian marriage is a fruit of Christ's cross, the source of
1642 all Christian life.

1616 This is what the Apostle Paul makes clear when he says: "Husbands, love your wives, as Christ loved the church and gave himself up for her, that he might sanctify her," adding at once: "For this reason a man shall leave his father and mother and be joined to his wife, and the two shall become one. This is a great mystery, and I mean in reference to Christ and the Church."[110]

796 **1617** The entire Christian life bears the mark of the spousal love of Christ and the Church. Already Baptism, the entry into the People of God, is a nuptial mystery; it is so to speak the nuptial bath[111] which precedes the wedding feast, the Eucharist. Christian marriage in its turn becomes an efficacious sign, the sacrament of the covenant of Christ and the Church. Since it signifies and communicates grace, marriage between baptized persons is a true sacrament of the New Covenant.[112]

Virginity for the sake of the Kingdom

1618 Christ is the center of all 2232
Christian life. The bond with him takes precedence over all other bonds, familial or social.[113] From the very beginning of the Church there have been men and women who have renounced the great good of marriage to follow the Lamb wherever he goes, to be intent on the things of the Lord, to seek to please him, and to go out to meet
the Bridegroom who is coming.[114] 1579
Christ himself has invited certain persons to follow him in this way of life, of which he remains the model:

> "For there are eunuchs who have been so from birth, and there are eunuchs who have been made eunuchs by men, and there are eunuchs who have made themselves eunuchs for the sake of the kingdom of heaven. He who is able to receive this, let him receive it."[115]

1619 Virginity for the sake of the 922–924
kingdom of heaven is an unfolding of baptismal grace, a powerful sign of the supremacy of the bond with Christ and of the ardent expectation of his return, a sign which also recalls that marriage is a reality of this present age which is passing away.[116]

1620 Both the sacrament of Matrimony and virginity for the Kingdom of God come from the Lord himself. It is he who gives them meaning and grants them the grace which is indispensable for living them out in conformity with his will.[117] Esteem of virginity for the
sake of the kingdom[118] and the 2349
Christian understanding of mar-

[108] Cf. *Mk* 8:34; *Mt* 11:29–30. — [109] Cf. *Mt* 19:11. — [110] *Eph* 5:25–26, 31–32; cf. *Gen* 2:24. — [111] Cf. *Eph* 5:26–27. — [112] Cf. DS 1800; CIC, can. 1055 § 2. — [113] Cf. *Lk* 14:26; *Mk* 10:28–31. — [114] Cf. *Rev* 14:4; *1 Cor* 7:32; *Mt* 25:6. — [115] *Mt* 19:12. — [116] Cf. *Mk* 12:25; *1 Cor* 7:31. — [117] Cf. *Mt* 19:3–12. — [118] Cf. *LG* 42; *PC* 12; *OT* 10.

riage are inseparable, and they reinforce each other:

> Whoever denigrates marriage also diminishes the glory of virginity. Whoever praises it makes virginity more admirable and resplendent. What appears good only in comparison with evil would not be truly good. The most excellent good is something even better than what is admitted to be good.[119]

II. The Celebration of Marriage

1621 In the Latin Rite the celebration of marriage between two Catholic faithful normally takes place during Holy Mass, because of the connection of all the sacraments with the Paschal mystery of Christ.[120]
1323 In the Eucharist the memorial of the New Covenant is realized, the New Covenant in which Christ has united himself for ever to the Church, his beloved bride for whom he gave himself up.[121] It is therefore fitting that the spouses should seal their consent to give themselves to each other through the offering of their own lives by uniting it to the offering of Christ for his Church made
1368 present in the Eucharistic sacrifice, and by receiving the Eucharist so that, communicating in the same Body and the same Blood of Christ, they may form but "one body" in Christ.[122]

1622 "Inasmuch as it is a sacramental action of sanctification, the liturgical celebration of marriage... must be, per se, valid, worthy, and fruitful."[123] It is therefore appropriate for the bride and groom to prepare themselves for the celebration of their marriage by receiving the
sacrament of penance. 1422

1623 According to the Latin tradition, the spouses as ministers of Christ's grace mutually confer upon each other the sacrament of Matrimony by expressing their consent before the Church. In the traditions of the Eastern Churches, the priests (bishops or presbyters) are witnesses to the mutual consent given by the spouses,[124] but for the validity of the sacrament their blessing is also necessary.[125]

1624 The various liturgies abound in prayers of blessing and epiclesis asking God's grace and blessing on the new couple, especially the bride. In the epiclesis of this sacrament the spouses receive the Holy Spirit as the communion of love of Christ and the Church.[126] The Holy
Spirit is the seal of their covenant, 736
the ever-available source of their love and the strength to renew their fidelity.

III. Matrimonial Consent

1625 The parties to a marriage covenant are a baptized man and
woman, free to contract marriage, 1734
who freely express their consent; "to be free" means:

- not being under constraint;
- not impeded by any natural or ecclesiastical law.

1626 The Church holds the exchange of consent between the spouses to be the indispensable element 2201
that "makes the marriage."[127] If consent is lacking there is no marriage.

[119] St. John Chrysostom, *De virg.* 10, 1: PG 48, 540; cf. John Paul II, *FC* 16. — [120] Cf. *SC* 61. — [121] Cf. *LG* 6. — [122] Cf. *1 Cor* 10:17. — [123] *FC* 67. — [124] Cf. CCEO, can. 817. — [125] Cf. CCEO, can. 828. — [126] Cf. *Eph* 5:32. — [127] CIC, can. 1057 § 1.

1627 The consent consists in a "human act by which the partners mutually give themselves to each other": "I take you to be my wife"—"I take you to be my husband."[128] This consent that binds the spouses to each other finds its fulfillment in the two "becoming one flesh."[129]

1735 **1628** The consent must be an act of the will of each of the contracting parties, free of coercion or grave external fear.[130] No human power can substitute for this consent.[131] If this freedom is lacking the marriage is invalid.

1629 For this reason (or for other reasons that render the marriage null and void) the Church, after an examination of the situation by the competent ecclesiastical tribunal, can declare the nullity of a marriage, i.e., that the marriage never existed.[132] In this case the contracting parties are free to marry, provided the natural obligations of a previous union are discharged.[133]

1630 The priest (or deacon) who assists at the celebration of a marriage receives the consent of the spouses in the name of the Church and gives the blessing of the Church. The presence of the Church's minister (and also of the witnesses) visibly expresses the fact that marriage is an ecclesial reality.

1631 This is the reason why the Church normally requires that the faithful contract marriage according to the ecclesiastical form. Several reasons converge to explain this requirement:[134]

– Sacramental marriage is a liturgical act. It is therefore appropriate that it should be celebrated in the public liturgy of the Church; 1069

– Marriage introduces one into an ecclesial *order*, and creates rights and duties in the Church between the spouses and towards their children; 1537

– Since marriage is a state of life in the Church, certainty about it is necessary (hence the obligation to have witnesses);

– The public character of the consent protects the "I do" once given and helps the spouses remain faithful to it. 2365

1632 So that the "I do" of the spouses may be a free and responsible act and so that the marriage covenant may have solid and lasting human and Christian foundations, preparation for marriage is of prime importance.

The example and teaching given by parents and families remain the special form of this preparation. 2206

The role of pastors and of the Christian community as the "family of God" is indispensable for the transmission of the human and Christian values of marriage and family,[135] and much more so in our era when many young people experience broken homes which no longer sufficiently assure this initiation:

> It is imperative to give suitable and timely instruction to young people, above all in the heart of their own families, about the dignity of married love, its role and its exercise, so that, having learned the value of chastity, they will be able at a suitable age to

[128] *GS* 48 § 1; *OCM* 45; cf. CIC, can. 1057 § 2. — [129] *Gen* 2:24; cf. *Mk* 10:8; *Eph* 5:31. — [130] Cf. CIC, can. 1103. — [131] Cf. CIC, can. 1057 § 1. — [132] Cf. CIC, cann. 1095–1107. — [133] Cf. CIC, can. 1071. — [134] Cf. Council of Trent: DS 1813–1816; CIC, can. 1108. — [135] Cf. CIC, can. 1063.

engage in honorable courtship and
2350 enter upon a marriage of their own.[136]

Mixed marriages and disparity of cult

1633 In many countries the situation of a *mixed marriage* (marriage between a Catholic and a baptized non-Catholic) often arises. It requires particular attention on the part of couples and their pastors. A case of marriage with *disparity of cult* (between a Catholic and a non-baptized person) requires even greater circumspection.

1634 Difference of confession between the spouses does not constitute an insurmountable obstacle for marriage, when they succeed in placing in common what they have received from their respective communities, and learn from each other the way in which each lives in fidelity to Christ. But the difficulties of mixed marriages must not be underestimated. They arise from the fact that the separation of Christians has not yet been overcome. The spouses risk experiencing the tragedy of
817 Christian disunity even in the heart of their own home. Disparity of cult can further aggravate these difficulties. Differences about faith and the very notion of marriage, but also different religious mentalities, can become sources of tension in marriage, especially as regards the education of children. The temptation to religious indifference can then arise.

1635 According to the law in force in the Latin Church, a mixed marriage needs for liceity the *express permission* of ecclesiastical authority.[137] In case of disparity of cult an *express dispensation* from this impediment is required for the validity of the marriage.[138] This permission or dispensation presupposes that both parties know and do not exclude the essential ends and properties of marriage; and furthermore that the Catholic party confirms the obligations, which have been made known to the non-Catholic party, of preserving his or her own faith and ensuring the baptism and education of the children in the Catholic Church.[139]

1636 Through ecumenical di- 821
alogue Christian communities in many regions have been able to put into effect a *common pastoral practice for mixed marriages.* Its task is to help such couples live out their particular situation in the light of faith, overcome the tensions between the couple's obligations to each other and towards their ecclesial communities, and encourage the flowering of what is common to them in faith and respect for what separates them.

1637 In marriages with disparity of cult the Catholic spouse has a particular task: "For the unbelieving husband is consecrated through his wife, and the unbelieving wife is consecrated through her husband."[140] It is a great joy for the Christian spouse and for the Church if this "consecration" should lead to the free conversion of the other spouse to the Christian faith.[141] Sincere married love, the humble and patient practice of the family virtues, and perseverance in prayer can prepare the non-believing spouse to accept the grace of conversion.

[136] *GS* 49 § 3. – [137] Cf. CIC, can. 1124. — [138] Cf. CIC, can. 1086. — [139] Cf. CIC, can. 1125. — [140] *1 Cor* 7:14.

IV. The Effects of the Sacrament of Matrimony

1638 "From a valid marriage arises a *bond* between the spouses which by its very nature is perpetual and exclusive; furthermore, in a Christian marriage the spouses are strengthened and, as it were, consecrated for the duties and the dignity of their state *by a special sacrament.*"[142]

The marriage bond

1639 The consent by which the spouses mutually give and receive one another is sealed by God himself.[143] From their covenant arises "an institution, confirmed by the divine law,...even in the eyes of society."[144] The covenant between the spouses is integrated into God's covenant with man: "Authentic married love is caught up into divine love."[145]

1640 Thus *the marriage bond* has been established by God himself in such a way that a marriage concluded and consummated between baptized persons can never be dissolved. This bond, which results from the free human act of the spouses and their consummation of the marriage, is a reality, henceforth irrevocable, and gives rise to a covenant guaranteed by
2365 God's fidelity. The Church does not have the power to contravene this disposition of divine wisdom.[146]

The grace of the sacrament of Matrimony

1641 "By reason of their state in life and of their order, [Christian spouses] have their own special gifts in the People of God."[147] This grace proper to the sacrament of Matrimony is intended to perfect the couple's love and to strengthen their indissoluble unity. By this grace they "help one another to attain holiness in their married life and in welcoming and educating their children."[148]

1642 *Christ is the source of this* 1615
grace. "Just as of old God encountered his people with a covenant of
love and fidelity, so our Savior, the 796
spouse of the Church, now encounters Christian spouses through the sacrament of Matrimony."[149] Christ dwells with them, gives them the strength to take up their crosses and so follow him, to rise again after they have fallen, to forgive one another, to bear one another's burdens, to "be subject to one another out of reverence for Christ,"[150] and to love one another with supernatural, tender, and fruitful love. In the joys of their love and family life he gives them here on earth a foretaste of the wedding feast of the Lamb:

> How can I ever express the happiness of a marriage joined by the Church, strengthened by an offering, sealed by a blessing, announced by angels, and ratified by the Father?... How wonderful the bond between two believers, now one in hope, one in desire, one in discipline, one in the same service! They are both children of one Father and servants of the same Master, undivided in spirit and flesh, truly two in one flesh. Where the flesh is one, one also is the spirit.[151]

[141] *1 Cor* 7:16. — [142] Cf. CIC, can. 1134. — [143] Cf. *Mk* 10:9. — [144] *GS* 48 § 1. — [145] *GS* 48 § 2. — [146] Cf. CIC, can. 1141. — [147] *LG* 11 § 2. — [148] *LG* 11 § 2; cf. *LG* 41. — [149] *GS* 48 § 2. — [150] *Eph* 5:21; cf. *Gal* 6:2. — [151] Tertullian, *Ad uxorem.* 2, 8, 6–7: PL 1, 1412–1413; cf. FC 13.

V. The Goods and Requirements of Conjugal Love

2361 **1643** "Conjugal love involves a totality, in which all the elements of the person enter—appeal of the body and instinct, power of feeling and affectivity, aspiration of the spirit and of will. It aims at a deeply personal unity, a unity that, beyond union in one flesh, leads to forming one heart and soul; it demands indissolubility and *faithfulness* in definitive mutual giving; and it is open to *fertility*. In a word it is a question of the normal characteristics of all natural conjugal love, but with a new significance which not only purifies and strengthens them, but raises them to the extent of making them the expression of specifically Christian values."[152]

The unity and indissolubility of marriage

1644 The love of the spouses requires, of its very nature, the unity and indissolubility of the spouses' community of persons, which embraces their entire life: "so they are no longer two, but one flesh."[153] They "are called to grow continually in their communion through day-to-day fidelity to their marriage promise of total mutual self-giving."[154] This human communion is confirmed, purified, and completed by communion in Jesus Christ, given through the sacrament of Matrimony. It is deepened by lives of the common faith and by the Eucharist received together.

1645 "The unity of marriage, distinctly recognized by our Lord, is made clear in the equal personal dignity which must be accorded to man and wife in mutual and unreserved 369
affection."[155] *Polygamy* is contrary to conjugal love which is undivided and exclusive.[156]

The fidelity of conjugal love 2364–2365

1646 By its very nature conjugal love requires the inviolable fidelity of the spouses. This is the consequence of the gift of themselves which they make to each other. Love seeks to be definitive; it cannot be an arrangement "until further notice." The "intimate union of marriage, as a mutual giving of two persons, and the good of the children, demand total fidelity from the spouses and require an unbreakable union between them."[157]

1647 The deepest reason is found in the fidelity of God to his covenant, in that of Christ to his Church. Through the sacrament of Matrimony the spouses are enabled to represent this fidelity and witness to it. Through the sacrament, the indissolubility of marriage receives a new and deeper meaning.

1648 It can seem difficult, even impossible, to bind oneself for life to another human being. This makes it all the more important to proclaim the Good News that God loves us with a definitive and irrevocable love, that married couples share in this love, that it supports and sustains them, and that by their own faithfulness they can be witnesses to God's faithful love. Spouses who with God's grace give this witness, often in very difficult conditions, deserve the gratitude and support of the ecclesial community.[158]

[152] *FC* 13. — [153] *Mt* 19:6; cf. *Gen* 2:24. — [154] *FC* 19. — [155] *GS* 49 § 2. — [156] Cf. *FC* 19. — [157] *GS* 48 § 1. — [158] Cf. *FC* 20.

1649 Yet there are some situations in which living together becomes practically impossible for a variety of reasons. In such cases the Church
2383 permits the physical *separation* of the couple and their living apart. The spouses do not cease to be husband and wife before God and so are not free to contract a new union. In this difficult situation, the best solution would be, if possible, reconciliation. The Christian community is called to help these persons live out their situation in a Christian manner and in fidelity to their marriage bond which remains indissoluble.[159]

2384 **1650** Today there are numerous Catholics in many countries who have recourse to civil *divorce* and contract new civil unions. In fidelity to the words of Jesus Christ—"Whoever divorces his wife and marries another, commits adultery against her; and if she divorces her husband and marries another, she commits adultery"[160]—the Church maintains that a new union cannot be recognized as valid, if the first marriage was. If the divorced are remarried civilly, they find themselves in a situation that objectively contravenes God's law. Consequently, they cannot receive Eucharistic communion as long as this situation persists. For the same reason, they cannot exercise certain ecclesial responsibilities. Reconciliation through the sacrament of Penance can be granted only to those who have repented for having violated the sign of the covenant and of fidelity to Christ, and who are committed to living in complete continence.

1651 Toward Christians who live in this situation, and who often keep the faith and desire to bring up their children in a Christian manner, priests and the whole community must manifest an attentive solicitude, so that they do not consider themselves separated from the Church, in whose life they can and must participate as baptized persons:

> They should be encouraged to listen to the Word of God, to attend the Sacrifice of the Mass, to persevere in prayer, to contribute to works of charity and to community efforts for justice, to bring up their children in the Christian faith, to cultivate the spirit and practice of penance and thus implore, day by day, God's grace.[161]

The openness to fertility 2366–2367

1652 "By its very nature the institution of marriage and married love is ordered to the procreation and education of the offspring and it is in them that it finds its crowning glory."[162]

> Children are the supreme gift of 372
> marriage and contribute greatly to the good of the parents themselves. God himself said: "It is not good that man should be alone," and "from the beginning [he] made them male and female"; wishing to associate them in a special way in his own creative work, God blessed man and woman with the words: "Be fruitful and multiply." Hence, true married love and the whole structure of family life which results from it, without diminishment of the other ends of marriage, are directed to disposing the spouses to cooperate valiantly with the love of the Creator and Savior, who through them will increase and enrich his family from day to day.[163]

[159] Cf. *FC* 83; CIC, cann. 1151–1155. — [160] *Mk* 10:11–12. — [161] *FC* 84. — [162] *GS* 48 § 1; 50. — [163] *GS* 50 § 1; cf. *Gen* 2:18; *Mt* 19:4; *Gen* 1:28.

1653 The fruitfulness of conjugal love extends to the fruits of the moral, spiritual, and supernatural life that parents hand on to their children by education. Parents are the principal and first educators of their children.[164] In this sense the fundamental task of marriage and family
2231 is to be at the service of life.[165]

1654 Spouses to whom God has not granted children can nevertheless have a conjugal life full of meaning, in both human and Christian terms. Their marriage can radiate a fruitfulness of charity, of hospitality, and of sacrifice.

VI. The Domestic Church

1655 Christ chose to be born and grow up in the bosom of the holy
759 family of Joseph and Mary. The Church is nothing other than "the family of God." From the beginning, the core of the Church was often constituted by those who had become believers "together with all [their] household."[166] When they were converted, they desired that "their whole household" should also be saved.[167] These families who became believers were islands of Christian life in an unbelieving world.

1656 In our own time, in a world often alien and even hostile to faith, believing families are of primary importance as centers of living, radiant faith. For this reason the Second Vatican Council, using an ancient expression, calls the family the *Ecclesia domestica*.[168] It is in the bosom
2204 of the family that parents are "by word and example...the first heralds of the faith with regard to their children. They should encourage them in the vocation which is proper to each child, fostering with special care any religious vocation."[169]

1657 It is here that the father of the family, the mother, children, and all members of the family exercise the *priesthood of the baptized* in a privileged way "by the reception of the sacraments, prayer and 1268
thanksgiving, the witness of a holy life, and self-denial and active charity."[170] Thus the home is the first 2214–2231
school of Christian life and "a school for human enrichment."[171] Here one learns endurance and the joy of work, fraternal love, generous—even repeated—forgiveness, and above all divine worship in prayer and the offering of one's life. 2685

1658 We must also remember the great number of *single persons* who, because of the particular circumstances in which they have to live—often not of their choosing—are especially close to Jesus' heart and therefore deserve the special affection and active solicitude of the Church, especially of pastors. Many remain *without a human family*, often due to conditions of poverty. Some live their situation in the spirit of the Beatitudes, serving God and neighbor in exemplary fashion. The doors of homes, the "domestic churches," and of the great family which is the Church must be open to all of them. "No one is without a family in this world: the Church is a home and 2231
family for everyone, especially those who 'labor and are heavy laden.'"[172] 2233

[164] Cf. *GE* 3. — [165] Cf. *FC* 28. — [166] Cf. *Acts* 18:8. — [167] Cf. *Acts* 16:31; *Acts* 11:14. — [168] *LG* 11; cf. *FC* 21. — [169] *LG* 11. — [170] *LG* 10. — [171] *GS* 52 § 1. — [172] *FC* 85; cf. *Mt* 11:28.

In Brief

1659 *St. Paul said: "Husbands, love your wives, as Christ loved the Church.... This is a great mystery, and I mean in reference to Christ and the Church" (*Eph *5:25, 32).*

1660 *The marriage covenant, by which a man and a woman form with each other an intimate communion of life and love, has been founded and endowed with its own special laws by the Creator. By its very nature it is ordered to the good of the couple, as well as to the generation and education of children. Christ the Lord raised marriage between the baptized to the dignity of a sacrament (cf. CIC, can. 1055 § 1; cf.* GS *48 § 1).*

1661 *The sacrament of Matrimony signifies the union of Christ and the Church. It gives spouses the grace to love each other with the love with which Christ has loved his Church; the grace of the sacrament thus perfects the human love of the spouses, strengthens their indissoluble unity, and sanctifies them on the way to eternal life (cf. Council of Trent: DS 1799).*

1662 *Marriage is based on the consent of the contracting parties, that is, on their will to give themselves, each to the other, mutually and definitively, in order to live a covenant of faithful and fruitful love.*

1663 *Since marriage establishes the couple in a public state of life in the Church, it is fitting that its celebration be public, in the framework of a liturgical celebration, before the priest (or a witness authorized by the Church), the witnesses, and the assembly of the faithful.*

1664 *Unity, indissolubility, and openness to fertility are essential to marriage. Polygamy is incompatible with the unity of marriage; divorce separates what God has joined together; the refusal of fertility turns married life away from its "supreme gift," the child (*GS *50 §1).*

1665 *The remarriage of persons divorced from a living, lawful spouse contravenes the plan and law of God as taught by Christ. They are not separated from the Church, but they cannot receive Eucharistic communion. They will lead Christian lives especially by educating their children in the faith.*

1666 *The Christian home is the place where children receive the first proclamation of the faith. For this reason the family home is rightly called "the domestic church," a community of grace and prayer, a school of human virtues and of Christian charity.*

Chapter Four:
OTHER LITURGICAL CELEBRATION

Article 1:
SACRAMENTALS

1667 "Holy Mother Church has, moreover, instituted sacramentals. These are sacred signs which bear a resemblance to the sacraments. They signify effects, particularly of a spiritual nature, which are obtained through the intercession of the Church. By them men are disposed to receive the chief effect of the sacraments, and various occasions in life are rendered holy."[173]

The characteristics of sacramentals

1668 Sacramentals are instituted for the sanctification of certain ministries of the Church, certain states of life, a great variety of circumstances in Christian life, and the use of many things helpful to man. In accordance with bishops' pastoral decisions, they can also respond to the needs, culture, and special history of the Christian people of a particular region or time. They always include a prayer, often accompanied by a specific sign, such as the laying on of hands, the sign of the cross, or
99, 2157 the sprinkling of holy water (which recalls Baptism).

784 **1669** Sacramentals derive from the baptismal priesthood: every bap-
2626 tized person is called to be a "blessing," and to bless.[174] Hence lay people may preside at certain blessings; the more a blessing concerns ecclesial and sacramental life, the more is its administration reserved to the ordained ministry (bishops, priests, or deacons).[175]

1670 Sacramentals do not confer 1128
the grace of the Holy Spirit in the way that the sacraments do, but by the Church's prayer, they prepare us to receive grace and dispose us to cooperate with it. "For well-disposed members of the faithful, the liturgy 2001
of the sacraments and sacramentals sanctifies almost every event of their lives with the divine grace which flows from the Paschal mystery of the Passion, Death, and Resurrection of Christ. From this source all sacraments and sacramentals draw their power. There is scarcely any proper use of material things which cannot be thus directed toward the sanctification of men and the praise of God."[176]

Various forms of sacramentals

1671 Among sacramentals *bless-* 1078
ings (of persons, meals, objects, and places) come first. Every blessing praises God and prays for his gifts. In Christ, Christians are blessed by God the Father "with every spiritual blessing."[177] This is why the Church imparts blessings by invoking the name of Jesus, usually while making the holy sign of the cross of Christ.

[173] *SC* 60; cf. CIC, can. 1166; CCEO, can. 867. — [174] Cf. *Gen* 12:2; *Lk* 6:28; Rom 12:14; *1 Pet* 3:9. — [175] Cf. *SC* 79; CIC, can. 1168; *De Ben* 16, 18. — [176] *SC* 61. — [177] *Eph* 1:3.

1672 Certain blessings have a lasting importance because they *consecrate* persons to God, or reserve objects and places for liturgical use. Among those blessings which are intended for persons—not to be confused with sacramental ordination—are the blessing of the abbot or abbess of a monastery, the consecration of virgins and widows, the rite of religious profession and
923, 925 the blessing of certain ministries of the Church (readers, acolytes, catechists, etc.). The dedication or
903 blessing of a church or an altar, the blessing of holy oils, vessels, and vestments, bells, etc., can be mentioned as examples of blessings that concern objects.

1673 When the Church asks publicly and authoritatively in the name of Jesus Christ that a person or object be protected against the power
395 of the Evil One and withdrawn from his dominion, it is called *exorcism*. Jesus performed exorcisms and from him the Church has received the power and office of exorcizing.[178] In
550 a simple form, exorcism is performed at the celebration of Baptism. The
1237 solemn exorcism, called "a major exorcism," can be performed only by a priest and with the permission of the bishop. The priest must proceed with prudence, strictly observing the rules established by the Church. Exorcism is directed at the expulsion of demons or to the liberation from demonic possession through the spiritual authority which Jesus entrusted to his Church. Illness, especially psychological illness, is a very different matter; treating this is the concern of medical science. Therefore, before an exorcism is performed, it is important to ascertain that one is dealing with the presence of the Evil One, and not an illness.[179]

Popular piety

1674 Besides sacramental liturgy and sacramentals, catechesis must take into account the forms of piety 2688
and popular devotions among the faithful. The religious sense of the Christian people has always found expression in various forms of piety surrounding the Church's sacramental life, such as the veneration of relics, visits to sanctuaries, pilgrimages, processions, the stations of the cross, religious dances, the rosary, 2669, 267
medals,[180] etc.

1675 These expressions of piety extend the liturgical life of the Church, but do not replace it. They "should be so drawn up that they harmonize with the liturgical seasons, accord with the sacred liturgy, are in some way derived from it and lead the people to it, since in fact the liturgy by its very nature is far superior to any of them."[181]

1676 Pastoral discernment is needed to sustain and support popular piety and, if necessary, to purify and correct the religious sense which underlies these devotions so that the faithful may advance in knowledge of the mystery of Christ.[182] Their exercise is subject to the care and 426
judgment of the bishops and to the general norms of the Church.

At its core the piety of the people is a storehouse of values that offers answers of Christian wisdom to the great questions of life. The Catho-

[178] Cf. *Mk* 1:25–26; 3:15; 6:7, 13; 16:17. — [179] Cf. CIC, can. 1172. — [180] Cf. Council of Nicæa II: DS 601; 603; Council of Trent: DS 1822. — [181] *SC* 13 § 3. — [182] Cf. John Paul II, CT 54.

lic wisdom of the people is capable of fashioning a vital synthesis.... It creatively combines the divine and the human, Christ and Mary, spirit and body, communion and institution, person and community, faith and homeland, intelligence and emotion. This wisdom is a Christian humanism that radically affirms the dignity of every person as a child of God, establishes a basic fraternity, teaches people to encounter nature and understand work, provides reasons for joy and humor even in the midst of a very hard life. For the people this wisdom is also a principle of discernment and an evangelical instinct through which they spontaneously sense when the Gospel is served in the Church and when it is emptied of its content and stifled by other interests.[183]

In Brief

1677 *Sacramentals are sacred signs instituted by the Church. They prepare men to receive the fruit of the sacraments and sanctify different circumstances of life.*

1678 *Among the sacramentals blessings occupy an important place. They include both praise of God for his works and gifts, and the Church's intercession for men that they may be able to use God's gifts according to the spirit of the Gospel.*

1679 *In addition to the liturgy, Christian life is nourished by various forms of popular piety, rooted in the different cultures. While carefully clarifying them in the light of faith, the Church fosters the forms of popular piety that express an evangelical instinct and a human wisdom and that enrich Christian life.*

Article 2: CHRISTIAN FUNERALS

1525 **1680** All the sacraments, and principally those of Christian initiation, have as their goal the last Passover of the child of God which, through death, leads him into the life of the Kingdom. Then what he confessed in faith and hope will be fulfilled: "I look for the resurrection of the dead, and the life of the world to come."[184]

I. The Christian's Last Passover

0–1014 **1681** The Christian meaning of death is revealed in the light of the *Paschal mystery* of the death and resurrection of Christ in whom resides our only hope. The Christian who dies in Christ Jesus is "away from the body and at home with the Lord."[185]

1682 For the Christian the day of death inaugurates, *at the end of his sacramental life*, the fulfillment of his new birth begun at Baptism, the definitive "conformity" to "the image of the Son" conferred by the anointing of the Holy Spirit, and participation in the feast of the Kingdom which was anticipated in the Eucharist—even if final purifications are still necessary for him in order to be clothed with the nuptial garment.

[183] CELAM, Third General Conference (Puebla, 1979), Final Document, § 448 (tr. NCCB, 1979); cf. Paul VI, *EN* 48. — [184] Niceno-Constantinopolitan Creed. — [185] *2 Cor* 5:8.

1683 The Church who, as Mother, has borne the Christian sacramentally in her womb during his earthly pilgrimage, accompanies
1020 him at his journey's end, in order to surrender him "into the Father's hands." She offers to the Father, in Christ, the child of his grace, and she commits to the earth, in hope, the seed of the body that will rise
627 in glory.[186] This offering is fully celebrated in the Eucharistic sacrifice; the blessings before and after Mass are sacramentals.

II. The Celebration of Funerals

1684 The Christian funeral is a liturgical celebration of the Church. The ministry of the Church in this instance aims at expressing efficacious communion with *the deceased*, at the participation in that communion of *the community* gathered for the funeral, and at the proclamation of eternal life to the community.

1685 The different funeral rites express the *Paschal character* of Christian death and are in keeping with the situations and traditions of each region, even as to the color of the liturgical vestments worn.[187]

1686 The *Order of Christian Funerals (Ordo exsequiarum)* of the Roman liturgy gives three types of funeral celebrations, corresponding to the three places in which they are conducted (the home, the church, and the cemetery), and according to the importance attached to them by the family, local customs, the culture, and popular piety. This order of celebration is common to all the liturgical traditions and comprises four principal elements:

1687 T*he greeting of the community.* A greeting of faith begins the celebration. Relatives and friends of the deceased are welcomed with a word of "consolation" (in the New Testament sense of the Holy Spirit's power in hope).[188] The community assembling in prayer also awaits the "words of eternal life." The death of a member of the community (or the anniversary of a death, or the seventh or thirtieth day after death) is an event that should lead beyond the perspectives of "this world" and should draw the faithful into the true perspective of faith in the risen Christ.

1688 The liturgy of the Word during funerals demands very careful preparation because the assembly present for the funeral may include some faithful who rarely attend the liturgy, and friends of the deceased who are not Christians. The homily in particular must "avoid the literary genre of funeral eulogy"[189] and illumine the mystery of Christian death in the light of the risen Christ.

1689 *The Eucharistic Sacrifice.* 1371
When the celebration takes place in church, the Eucharist is the heart of the Paschal reality of Christian death.[190] In the Eucharist, the Church expresses her efficacious communion with the departed: offering to the Father in the Holy Spirit the sacrifice of the death and resurrection of Christ, she asks to purify his child of his sins and their consequences, and to admit him to the Paschal fullness of the table of the Kingdom.[191] It is by the Eucharist thus celebrated that the community of the faithful, especial-

[186] *1 Cor* 15:42–44. — [187] Cf. *SC* 81. — [188] Cf. *1 Thess* 4:18. — [189] *OCF* 41. — [190] Cf. *OCF* 1. — [191] Cf. *OCF* 57.

ly the family of the deceased, learn to live in communion with the one
958 who "has fallen asleep in the Lord," by communicating in the Body of Christ of which he is a living member and, then, by praying for him and with him.

1690 A *farewell* to the deceased is his final "commendation to God" by the Church. It is "the last farewell by which the Christian community
2300 greets one of its members before his body is brought to its tomb."[192] The Byzantine tradition expresses this by the kiss of farewell to the deceased:

> By this final greeting "we sing for his departure from this life and separation from us, but also because there is a communion and a reunion. For even dead, we are not at all separated from one another, because we all run the same course and we will find one another again in the same place. We shall never be separated, for we live for Christ, and now we are united with Christ as we go toward him... we shall all be together in Christ."[193]

[192] *OCF* 10. — [193] St. Simeon of Thessalonica, *De ordine sepulturæ.* 336: PG 155, 684.

PART THREE

LIFE IN CHRIST

1691 "Christian, recognize your dignity and, now that you share in God's own nature, do not return to your former base condition by sinning. Remember who is your head and of whose body you are a mem-
790 ber. Never forget that you have been rescued from the power of darkness and brought into the light of the Kingdom of God."[1]

1692 The Symbol of the faith confesses the greatness of God's gifts to man in his work of creation, and even more in redemption and sanctification. What faith confesses, the sacraments communicate: by the sacraments of rebirth, Christians have become "children of God,"[2] "partakers of the divine nature."[3] Coming to see in the faith their new dignity, Christians are called to lead henceforth a life "worthy of the gospel of Christ."[4] They are made capable of doing so by the grace of Christ and the gifts of his Spirit, which they receive through the sacraments and through prayer.

1693 Christ Jesus always did what was pleasing to the *Father*,[5] and always lived in perfect communion with him. Likewise Christ's disciples are invited to live in the sight of the Father "who sees in secret,"[6] in order to become "perfect as your heavenly Father is perfect."[7]

1694 Incorporated into *Christ* by 1267
Baptism, Christians are "dead to sin and alive to God in Christ Jesus" and so participate in the life of the Risen Lord.[8] Following Christ and united with him,[9] Christians can strive to be "imitators of God as beloved children, and walk in love"[10] by conforming their thoughts, words and actions to the "mind...which is yours in Christ Jesus,"[11] and by following his example.[12]

1695 "Justified in the name of the Lord Jesus Christ and in the Spirit of our God,"[13] "sanctified...[and] called to be saints,"[14] Christians have become the temple of the *Holy Spirit*.[15] This "Spirit of the Son" teaches them to pray to the Father[16] and, having become their life, prompts them to act so as to bear "the fruit of the Spirit"[17] by charity in action. Healing the wounds of sin, the *Holy Spirit* renews us interiorly through a spiritual transformation.[18] He enlightens and strengthens us to live as "children of light" through "all that is good and right and true."[19]

1696 The way of Christ "leads to life"; a contrary way "leads to destruction."[20] The Gospel parable of the *two ways* remains ever present
in the catechesis of the Church; 1970
it shows the importance of moral decisions for our salvation: "There are two ways, the one of life, the other of death; but between the two, there is a great difference."[21]

[1] St. Leo the Great, *Sermo 21 in nat. Dom.*, 3: PL 54, 192C. — [2] *Jn* 1:12; 1 *Jn* 3:1. [3] *2 Pet* 1:4. — [4] *Phil* 1:27. — [5] Cf. *Jn* 8:29. — [6] *Mt* 6:6. — [7] *Mt* 5:48. — [8] *Rom* 6:11 and cf. 6:5; cf. *Col* 2:12. — [9] Cf. *Jn* 15:5. — [10] *Eph* 5:1–2. — [11] *Phil* 2:5. — [12] Cf. *Jn* 13:12–16. — [13] *1 Cor* 6:11. — [14] *1 Cor* 1:2. — [15] Cf. *1 Cor* 6:19. — [16] Cf. *Gal* 4:6. — [17] *Gal* 5:22, 25. — [18] Cf. *Eph* 4:23. — [19] *Eph* 5:8, 9. — [20] *Mt* 7:13; cf. *Deut* 30:15–20. — [21] *Didache* 1, 1: SCh 248, 140.

1697 *Catechesis* has to reveal in all clarity the joy and the demands of the way of Christ.[22] Catechesis for the "newness of life"[23] in him should be:

737 *ff.* – *a catechesis of the Holy Spirit,* the interior Master of life according to Christ, a gentle guest and friend who inspires, guides, corrects, and strengthens this life;

1988 *ff.* – *a catechesis of grace,* for it is by grace that we are saved and again it is by grace that our works can bear fruit for eternal life;

1716 *ff.* – *a catechesis of the beatitudes,* for the way of Christ is summed up in the beatitudes, the only path that leads to the eternal beatitude for which the human heart longs;

1846 *ff.* – *a catechesis of sin and forgiveness,* for unless man acknowledges that he is a sinner he cannot know the truth about himself, which is a condition for acting justly; and without the offer of forgiveness he would not be able to bear this truth;

1803 *ff.* – *a catechesis of the human virtues* which causes one to grasp the beauty and attraction of right dispositions towards goodness;

1812 *ff.* – *a catechesis of the Christian virtues* of faith, hope, and charity, generously inspired by the example of the saints;

– *a catechesis of the twofold commandment of charity* set forth in the Decalogue; 2067 *ff.*

– *an ecclesial catechesis,* for it is through the manifold exchanges of "spiritual goods" in the "communion of saints" that Christian life can grow, develop, and be communicated. 946 *ff.*

1698 The first and last point of reference of this catechesis will always be Jesus Christ himself, who is "the way, and the truth, and the life."[24] It is by looking to him in faith that Christ's faithful can hope that he himself fulfills his promises in them, and that, by loving him with the same love with which he has loved them, they may perform works in keeping with their dignity: 426

> I ask you to consider that our Lord Jesus Christ is your true head, and that you are one of his members. He belongs to you as the head belongs to its members; all that is his is yours: his spirit, his heart, his body and soul, and all his faculties. You must make use of all these as of your own, to serve, praise, love, and glorify God. You belong to him, as members belong to their head. And so he longs for you to use all that is in you, as if it were his own, for the service and glory of the Father.[25]
>
> For to me, to live is Christ.[26]

[22] Cf. John Paul II, *CT* 29. — [23] *Rom* 6:4. — [24] *Jn* 14:6. — [25] St. John Eudes, *Tract. de admirabili corde Jesu,* 1, 5. — [26] *Phil* 1:21.

Section One

MAN'S VOCATION: LIFE IN THE SPIRIT

1699 Life in the Holy Spirit fulfills the vocation of man (*chapter one*). This life is made up of divine charity and human solidarity (*chapter two*). It is graciously offered as salvation (*chapter three*).

Chapter One:

THE DIGNITY OF THE HUMAN PERSON

356 **1700** The dignity of the human person is rooted in his creation in the image and likeness of God (*article 1*); it is fulfilled in his vocation to divine beatitude (*article 2*). It is essential to a human being freely to direct himself to this fulfillment (*article 3*). By his deliberate actions (*article 4*), the human person does, or does not, conform to the good promised by God and attested by moral conscience (*article 5*). Human beings make their own contribution to their interior growth; they make their whole sentient and spiritual lives into means of this growth (*article 6*). With the help of grace they grow in virtue (*article 7*), avoid sin, and if they sin they entrust themselves as did the prodigal son[1] to the 1439
mercy of our Father in heaven (*article 8*). In this way they attain to the perfection of charity.

Article 1:

MAN: THE IMAGE OF GOD

359 **1701** "Christ,...in the very revelation of the mystery of the Father and of his love, makes man fully manifest to himself and brings to light his exalted vocation."[2] It is in Christ, "the image of the invisible God,"[3] that man has been created "in the image and likeness"of the Creator. It is in Christ, Redeemer and Savior, that the divine image, disfigured in man by the first sin, has been restored to its original beauty and ennobled by the grace of God.[4]

1878 **1702** The divine image is present in every man. It shines forth in the communion of persons, in the likeness of the unity of the divine persons among themselves (cf. *chapter two*).

363 **1703** Endowed with "a spiritual and immortal" soul,[5] the human person is "the only creature on earth that God has willed for its own sake."[6] From his conception, he is
destined for eternal beatitude. 2258

1704 The human person participates in the light and power of the divine Spirit. By his reason, he is capable of understanding the order of
things established by the Creator. By 339
free will, he is capable of directing himself toward his true good. He finds his perfection "in seeking and
loving what is true and good."[7] 30

1705 By virtue of his soul and his spiritual powers of intellect and will, man is endowed with freedom, an
"outstanding manifestation of the 1730
divine image."[8]

1706 By his reason, man recognizes the voice of God which urges him "to do what is good and avoid

[1] *Lk* 15:11–32. — [2] *GS* 22. — [3] *Col* 1:15; cf. *2 Cor* 4:4. — [4] Cf. *GS* 22. — [5] *GS* 14 § 2. — [6] *GS* 24 § 3. — [7] *GS* 15 § 2. — [8] *GS* 17. — [9] *GS* 16.

what is evil."[9] Everyone is obliged to follow this law, which makes itself heard in conscience and is fulfilled
1776 in the love of God and of neighbor. Living a moral life bears witness to the dignity of the person.

1707 "Man, enticed by the Evil One, abused his freedom at the very beginning of history."[10] He succumbed to temptation and did what
397 was evil. He still desires the good, but his nature bears the wound of original sin. He is now inclined to evil and subject to error:

> Man is divided in himself. As a result, the whole life of men, both individual and social, shows itself to be a struggle, and a dramatic one, between good and evil, between light and darkness.[11]

617 **1708** By his Passion, Christ delivered us from Satan and from sin. He merited for us the new life in the Holy Spirit. His grace restores what sin had damaged in us.

1265 **1709** He who believes in Christ becomes a son of God. This filial adoption transforms him by giving him the ability to follow the example of Christ. It makes him capable of acting rightly and doing good. In union with his Savior, the disciple attains the perfection of charity which is holiness. Having matured in grace, the moral life blossoms into
eternal life in the glory of heaven. 1050

In Brief

1710 *"Christ...makes man fully manifest to man himself and brings to light his exalted vocation"* (GS *22 § 1).*

1711 *Endowed with a spiritual soul, with intellect and with free will, the human person is from his very conception ordered to God and destined for eternal beatitude. He pursues his perfection in "seeking and loving what is true and good"* (GS *15 § 2).*

1712 *In man, true freedom is an "outstanding manifestation of the divine image"* (GS *17).*

1713 *Man is obliged to follow the moral law, which urges him "to do what is good and avoid what is evil"* (*cf.* GS *16). This law makes itself heard in his conscience.*

1714 *Man, having been wounded in his nature by original sin, is subject to error and inclined to evil in exercising his freedom.*

1715 *He who believes in Christ has new life in the Holy Spirit. The moral life, increased and brought to maturity in grace, is to reach its fulfillment in the glory of heaven.*

Article 2: OUR VOCATION TO BEATITUDE

I. The Beatitudes

1716 The Beatitudes are at the heart of Jesus' preaching. They take up the promises made to the chosen people since Abraham. The Beatitudes fulfill the promises by ordering them no longer merely to the

[10] *GS* 13 § 1. — [11] *GS* 13 § 2.

possession of a territory, but to the Kingdom of heaven:

2546 Blessed are the poor in spirit, for theirs is the kingdom of heaven.
Blessed are those who mourn, for they shall be comforted.
Blessed are the meek, for they shall inherit the earth.
Blessed are those who hunger and thirst for righteousness, for they shall be satisfied.
Blessed are the merciful, for they shall obtain mercy.
Blessed are the pure in heart, for they shall see God.
Blessed are the peacemakers, for they shall be called sons of God.
Blessed are those who are persecuted for righteousness' sake, for theirs is the kingdom of heaven.
Blessed are you when men revile you and persecute you and utter all kinds of evil against you falsely on my account. Rejoice and be glad, for your reward is great in heaven.[12]

459 **1717** The Beatitudes depict the countenance of Jesus Christ and portray his charity. They express the vocation of the faithful associated with the glory of his Passion and Resurrection; they shed light on the actions and attitudes characteristic of the Christian life; they are the paradoxical promises that sustain hope in the midst of tribu-
1820 lations; they proclaim the blessings and rewards already secured, however dimly, for Christ's disciples; they have begun in the lives of the Virgin Mary and all the saints.

II. The Desire for Happiness

1718 The Beatitudes respond to the natural desire for happiness. This desire is of divine origin: God
has placed it in the human heart in 27, 1024
order to draw man to the One who alone can fulfill it:

> We all want to live happily; in the whole human race there is no one who does not assent to this proposition, even before it is fully articulated.[13]
> How is it, then, that I seek you, Lord? 2541
> Since in seeking you, my God, I seek a happy life, let me seek you so that my soul may live, for my body draws life from my soul and my soul draws life from you.[14]
> God alone satisfies.[15]

1719 The Beatitudes reveal the 1950
goal of human existence, the ultimate end of human acts: God calls us to his own beatitude. This vocation is addressed to each individual personally, but also to the Church as a whole, the new people made up of those who have accepted the promise and live from it in faith.

III. Christian Beatitude

1720 The New Testament uses 1027
several expressions to characterize the beatitude to which God calls man:

– the coming of the Kingdom of God;[16]
– the vision of God: "Blessed are the pure in heart, for they shall see God";[17]
– entering into the joy of the Lord;[18]
– entering into God's rest:[19] There we shall rest and see, we shall see and love, we shall love and praise. Behold what will be at the end without end. For what other end do we have, if not to reach the kingdom which has no end?[20]

[12] *Mt* 5:3–12. — [13] St. Augustine, *De moribus eccl.* 1, 3, 4: PL 32, 1312. — [14] St. Augustine, *Conf.* 10, 20: PL 32, 791. — [15] St. Thomas Aquinas, *Expos. in symb. apost.* I. — [16] Cf. *Mt* 4:17. — [17] *Mt* 5:8; cf. *1 Jn* 2; *1 Cor* 13:12. — [18] *Mt* 25:21–23. — [19] Cf. *Heb* 4:7–11. — [20] St. Augustine, *De civ. Dei* 22, 30, 5: PL 41, 804.

1721 God put us in the world to know, to love, and to serve him, and so to come to paradise. Beatitude makes us "partakers of the divine nature" and of eternal life.[21] With beatitude, man enters into the glory of Christ[22] and
260 into the joy of the Trinitarian life.

1722 Such beatitude surpasses the understanding and powers of man. It comes from an entirely free gift of God: whence it is called supernatu-
1028 ral, as is the grace that disposes man to enter into the divine joy.

> "Blessed are the pure in heart, for they shall see God." It is true, because of the greatness and inexpressible glory of God, that "man shall not see me and live," for the Father cannot be grasped. But because of God's love and goodness toward us, and because he can do all things, he goes so far as to grant those who love him the privilege of seeing him.... For "what
> 294 is impossible for men is possible for God."[23]

1723 The beatitude we are promised confronts us with decisive moral choices. It invites us to purify our hearts of bad instincts and to
2519 seek the love of God above all else. It teaches us that true happiness is not found in riches or well-being, in human fame or power, or in any human achievement—however beneficial it may be—such as science, technology, and art, or indeed in any creature, but in God alone, the
227 source of every good and of all love:

> All bow down before wealth. Wealth is that to which the multitude of men pay an instinctive homage. They measure happiness by wealth; and by wealth they measure respectability.... It is a homage resulting from a profound faith...that with wealth he may do all things. Wealth is one idol of the day and notoriety is a second.... Notoriety, or the making of a noise in the world—it may be called "newspaper fame"—has come to be considered a great good in itself, and a ground of veneration.[24]

1724 The Decalogue, the Sermon on the Mount, and the apostolic catechesis describe for us the paths that lead to the Kingdom of heaven. Sustained by the grace of the Holy Spirit, we tread them, step by step, by everyday acts. By the working of the Word of Christ, we slowly bear fruit in the Church to the glory of God.[25]

In Brief

1725 *The Beatitudes take up and fulfill God's promises from Abraham by ordering them to the Kingdom of heaven. They respond to the desire for happiness that God has placed in the human heart.*

1726 *The Beatitudes teach us the final end to which God calls us: the Kingdom, the vision of God, participation in the divine nature, eternal life, filiation, rest in God.*

1727 *The beatitude of eternal life is a gratuitous gift of God. It is supernatural, as is the grace that leads us there.*

1728 *The Beatitudes confront us with decisive choices concerning earthly goods; they purify our hearts in order to teach us to love God above all things.*

[21] *2 Pet* 1:4; cf. *Jn* 17:3. — [22] Cf. *Rom* 8:18. — [23] St. Irenaeus, *Adv. haeres.* 4, 20, 5: PG 7/1, 1034–1035. — [24] John Henry Cardinal Newman, "Saintliness the Standard of Christian Principle," in *Discourses to Mixed Congregations* (London: Longmans, Green and Co., 1906) V, 89–90. — [25] Cf. the parable of the sower: *Mt* 13:3–23.

1729 *The beatitude of heaven sets the standards for discernment in the use of earthly goods in keeping with the law of God.*

Article 3:
MAN'S FREEDOM

1730 God created man a rational being, conferring on him the dignity of a person who can initiate and control his own actions. "God willed that man should be 'left in the hand of his own counsel,' so that he might of his own accord seek his Creator and freely attain his full and blessed
30 perfection by cleaving to him."[26]

> Man is rational and therefore like God; he is created with free will and is master over his acts.[27]

I. Freedom and Responsibility

1731 Freedom is the power, rooted in reason and will, to act or not to act, to do this or that, and so to perform deliberate actions on one's own responsibility. By free will one shapes one's own life. Human freedom is a force for growth and maturity in truth and goodness; it attains
1721 its perfection when directed toward God, our beatitude.

1732 As long as freedom has not bound itself definitively to its ultimate good which is God, there is
396 the possibility of *choosing between*
1849 *good and evil*, and thus of growing in perfection or of failing and sinning. This freedom characterizes properly human acts. It is the basis of praise
2006 or blame, merit or reproach.

1803 **1733** The more one does what is good, the freer one becomes. There is no true freedom except in the service of what is good and just. The choice to disobey and do evil is an abuse of freedom and leads to "the slavery of sin."[28]

1734 Freedom makes man re- 1036
sponsible for his acts to the extent that they are voluntary. Progress in
virtue, knowledge of the good, and 1804
ascesis enhance the mastery of the will over its acts.

1735 Imputability and responsibility for an action can be diminished or even nullified by ignorance, inadvertence, duress, fear, habit, inordinate attachments, and other
psychological or social factors. 597

1736 Every act directly willed is 2568
imputable to its author:

> Thus the Lord asked Eve after the sin in the garden: "What is this that you have done?"[29] He asked Cain the same question.[30] The prophet Nathan questioned David in the same way after he committed adultery with the wife of Uriah and had him murdered.[31]
> An action can be indirectly voluntary when it results from negligence regarding something one should have known or done: for example, an accident arising from ignorance of traffic laws.

1737 An effect can be tolerated 2263
without being willed by its agent;

[26] *GS* 17; *Sir* 15:14. — [27] St. Irenaeus, *Adv. haeres.* 4, 4, 3: PG 7/1, 983. — [28] Cf. *Rom* 6:17. — [29] *Gen* 3:13. — [30] Cf. *Gen* 4:10. — [31] Cf. *2 Sam* 12:7–15.

for instance, a mother's exhaustion from tending her sick child. A bad effect is not imputable if it was not willed either as an end or as a means of an action, e.g., a death a person incurs in aiding someone in danger. For a bad effect to be imputable it must be foreseeable and the agent must have the possibility of avoiding it, as in the case of manslaughter caused by a drunken driver.

1738 Freedom is exercised in relationships between human beings. Every human person, created in the image of God, has the natural right to be recognized as a free and responsible being. All owe to each other this duty of respect. The *right to the exercise of freedom*, especially in moral and religious matters, is an inalienable requirement of the dig-
2106 nity of the human person. This right must be recognized and protected by civil authority within the lim-
2109 its of the common good and public order.[32]

II. Human Freedom in the Economy of Salvation

387 **1739** *Freedom and sin.* Man's freedom is limited and fallible. In fact, man failed. He freely sinned. By refusing God's plan of love, he deceived himself and became a slave to sin. This first alienation engendered a multitude of others. From
401 its outset, human history attests the wretchedness and oppression born of the human heart in consequence of the abuse of freedom.

2108 **1740** *Threats to freedom.* The exercise of freedom does not imply a right to say or do everything. It is false to maintain that man, "the subject of this freedom," is "an individual who is fully self-sufficient and whose finality is the satisfaction of his own interests in the enjoyment of earthly goods."[33] Moreover, the economic, social, political, and cultural conditions that are needed for a just exercise of freedom are too often disregarded or violated. Such situations of blindness and injustice
injure the moral life and involve the 1887
strong as well as the weak in the temptation to sin against charity. By deviating from the moral law man violates his own freedom, becomes imprisoned within himself, disrupts neighborly fellowship, and rebels against divine truth.

1741 Liberation and salvation. By his glorious Cross Christ has won salvation for all men. He redeemed them from the sin that held them in bondage. "For freedom Christ has set us free."[34] In him we have communion with the "truth that
makes us free."[35] The Holy Spirit has 782
been given to us and, as the Apostle teaches, "Where the Spirit of the Lord is, there is freedom."[36] Already we glory in the "liberty of the children of God."[37]

1742 *Freedom and grace.* The grace of Christ is not in the slightest way a rival of our freedom when this freedom accords with the sense of the
true and the good that God has put 2002
in the human heart. On the contrary, as Christian experience attests especially in prayer, the more docile we are to the promptings of grace, the more we grow in inner freedom and confidence during trials, such
as those we face in the pressures and 1784

[32] Cf. *DH* 2 § 7. — [33] CDF, instruction, *Libertatis conscientia* 13. — [34] *Gal* 5:1. — [35] Cf. *Jn* 8:32. — [36] *2 Cor* 17. — [37] *Rom* 8:21.

constraints of the outer world. By the working of grace the Holy Spirit educates us in spiritual freedom in order to make us free collaborators in his work in the Church and in the world:

> Almighty and merciful God, in your goodness take away from us all that is harmful, so that, made ready both in mind and body, we may freely accomplish your will.[38]

In Brief

1743 *"God willed that man should be left in the hand of his own counsel (cf.* Sir *15:14), so that he might of his own accord seek his creator and freely attain his full and blessed perfection by cleaving to him"* (GS *17 § 1).*

1744 *Freedom is the power to act or not to act, and so to perform deliberate acts of one's own. Freedom attains perfection in its acts when directed toward God, the sovereign Good.*

1745 *Freedom characterizes properly human acts. It makes the human being responsible for acts of which he is the voluntary agent. His deliberate acts properly belong to him.*

1746 *The imputability or responsibility for an action can be diminished or nullified by ignorance, duress, fear, and other psychological or social factors.*

1747 *The right to the exercise of freedom, especially in religious and moral matters, is an inalienable requirement of the dignity of man. But the exercise of freedom does not entail the putative right to say or do anything.*

1748 *"For freedom Christ has set us free"* (Gal *5:1).*

Article 4: THE MORALITY OF HUMAN ACTS

1749 Freedom makes man a moral subject. When he acts deliberately, man is, so to speak, the *father of his acts*. Human acts, that is, acts that
1732 are freely chosen in consequence of a judgment of conscience, can be morally evaluated. They are either good or evil.

I. The Sources of Morality

1750 The morality of human acts depends on:

– the object chosen;
– the end in view or the intention;
– the circumstances of the action.

The object, the intention, and the circumstances make up the "sources," or constitutive elements, of the morality of human acts.

1751 The *object* chosen is a good toward which the will deliberately directs itself. It is the matter of a human act. The object chosen morally specifies the act of the will, insofar as reason recognizes and judges it to be or not to be in conformity with the true good. Objective norms of morality express the rational order of good and evil, attested to by conscience. 1794

[38] *Roman Missal,* 32nd Sunday, Opening Prayer: *Omnipotens et misericors Deus, universa nobis adversantia propitiatus exclude, ut, mente et corpore pariter expediti, quæ tua sunt liberis mentibus exsequamur.*

1752 In contrast to the object, the *intention* resides in the acting subject. Because it lies at the voluntary source of an action and determines it by its end, intention is an element essential to the moral evaluation of an action. The end is the first goal of the intention and indicates the
2520 purpose pursued in the action. The intention is a movement of the will toward the end: it is concerned with the goal of the activity. It aims at the good anticipated from the action undertaken. Intention is not limited to directing individual actions, but can guide several actions toward one and the same purpose; it can orient one's whole life toward its ultimate end. For example, a service done
1731 with the end of helping one's neighbor can at the same time be inspired by the love of God as the ultimate end of all our actions. One and the same action can also be inspired by several intentions, such as performing a service in order to obtain a favor or to boast about it.

1753 A good intention (for example, that of helping one's neighbor) does not make behavior that is intrinsically disordered, such as lying and calumny, good or just. The end does not justify the means. Thus
2479 the condemnation of an innocent person cannot be justified as a legitimate means of saving the nation. On the other hand, an added bad
596 intention (such as vainglory) makes an act evil that, in and of itself, can be good (such as almsgiving).[39]

1754 The *circumstances*, including the consequences, are secondary elements of a moral act. They contribute to increasing or diminishing the moral goodness or evil of human acts (for example, the amount of a theft). They can also diminish or increase the agent's responsibility (such as acting out of a fear of death). Circumstances of themselves
cannot change the moral quality of 1735
acts themselves; they can make neither good nor right an action that is in itself evil.

II. Good Acts and Evil Acts

1755 A *morally good* act requires the goodness of the object, of the end, and of the circumstances together. An evil end corrupts the action, even if the object is good in itself (such as praying and fasting "in order to be seen by men").

The *object of the choice* can by itself vitiate an act in its entirety. There are some concrete acts—such as fornication—that it is always wrong to choose, because choosing them entails a disorder of the will, that is, a moral evil.

1756 It is therefore an error to judge the morality of human acts by considering only the intention that inspires them or the circumstances (environment, social pressure, duress or emergency, etc.) which supply their context. There are acts which, in and of themselves, independently of circumstances and intentions, are always gravely illicit by reason of their object; such as blasphemy and perjury, murder and adultery. One
may not do evil so that good may 1789
result from it.

[39] Cf. *Mt* 6:2–4.

In Brief

1757 *The object, the intention, and the circumstances make up the three "sources" of the morality of human acts.*

1758 *The object chosen morally specifies the act of willing accordingly as reason recognizes and judges it good or evil.*

1759 *"An evil action cannot be justified by reference to a good intention" (cf. St. Thomas Aquinas, Dec.* praec. *6). The end does not justify the means.*

1760 *A morally good act requires the goodness of its object, of its end, and of its circumstances together.*

1761 *There are concrete acts that it is always wrong to choose, because their choice entails a disorder of the will, i.e., a moral evil. One may not do evil so that good may result from it.*

Article 5:
THE MORALITY OF THE PASSIONS

1762 The human person is ordered to beatitude by his deliberate acts: the passions or feelings he experiences can dispose him to it and contribute to it.

I. Passions

1763 The term "passions" belongs to the Christian patrimony. Feelings or passions are emotions or movements of the sensitive appetite that incline us to act or not to act in regard to something felt or imagined to be good or evil.

1764 The passions are natural components of the human psyche; they form the passageway and ensure the connection between the life of the senses and the life of the mind. Our Lord called man's heart
368 the source from which the passions spring.[40]

1765 There are many passions. The most fundamental passion is love, aroused by the attraction of the good. Love causes a desire for the absent good and the hope of obtaining it; this movement finds completion in the pleasure and joy of the good possessed. The apprehension of evil causes hatred, aversion, and fear of the impending evil; this movement ends in sadness at some present evil, or in the anger that resists it.

1766 "To love is to will the good of another."[41] All other affections have their source in this first movement of the human heart toward the
good. Only the good can be loved.[42] 1704
Passions "are evil if love is evil and good if it is good."[43]

II. Passions and Moral Life

1767 In themselves passions are neither good nor evil. They are morally qualified only to the extent that they effectively engage reason and
will. Passions are said to be volun- 1860
tary, "either because they are commanded by the will or because the will does not place obstacles in their way."[44] It belongs to the perfection

[40] Cf. *Mk* 7:21. — [41] St. Thomas Aquinas, *STh* I–II, 26, 4, *corp. art.* — [42] Cf. St. Augustine, *De Trin.*, 8, 3, 4: PL 42, 949–950. — [43] St. Augustine, *De civ. Dei* 14, 7, 2: PL 41, 410. — [44] St. Thomas Aquinas, *STh* I–II, 24, 1 *corp.* art.

of the moral or human good that the passions be governed by reason.[45]

1768 Strong feelings are not decisive for the morality or the holiness of persons; they are simply the inexhaustible reservoir of images and affections in which the moral life is expressed. Passions are morally good when they contribute to a good action, evil in the opposite case. The upright will orders the movements of the senses it appropriates to the good and to beatitude; an evil will succumbs to disordered passions and exacerbates them. Emotions and feelings can be taken up into
1803, 1865 the *virtues* or perverted by the vices.

1769 In the Christian life, the Holy Spirit himself accomplishes his work by mobilizing the whole being, with all its sorrows, fears and sadness, as is visible in the Lord's agony and passion. In Christ human feelings are able to reach their consummation in charity and divine beatitude.

1770 Moral perfection consists in man's being moved to the good not by his will alone, but also by his sensitive appetite, as in the words of the
psalm: "My heart and flesh sing for 30
joy to the living God."[46]

In Brief

1771 *The term "passions" refers to the affections or the feelings. By his emotions man intuits the good and suspects evil.*

1772 *The principal passions are love and hatred, desire and fear, joy, sadness, and anger.*

1773 *In the passions, as movements of the sensitive appetite, there is neither moral good nor evil. But insofar as they engage reason and will, there is moral good or evil in them.*

1774 *Emotions and feelings can be taken up in the virtues or perverted by the vices.*

1775 *The perfection of the moral good consists in man's being moved to the good not only by his will but also by his "heart."*

Article 6: MORAL CONSCIENCE

1776 "Deep within his conscience man discovers a law which he has not laid upon himself but which he must obey. Its voice, ever calling him
1954 to love and to do what is good and to avoid evil, sounds in his heart at the right moment.... For man has in his heart a law inscribed by God... His conscience is man's most secret core and his sanctuary. There he is alone with God whose voice echoes in his depths."[47]

I. The Judgment of Conscience

1777 Moral conscience,[48] present at the heart of the person, enjoins him at the appropriate moment to do good and to avoid evil. It also judges particular choices, approving those that are good and denouncing

[45] Cf. St. Thomas Aquinas, *STh* I–II, 24, 3. — [46] *Ps* 84:2. — [47] *GS* 16. — [48] Cf. *Rom* 2:14–16.

those that are evil.[49] It bears witness to the authority of truth in reference to the supreme Good to which the human person is drawn, and it wel
1766 comes the commandments. When he listens to his conscience, the pru-
2071 dent man can hear God speaking.

1778 Conscience is a judgment of reason whereby the human person recognizes the moral quality of a concrete act that he is going to per
1749 form, is in the process of performing, or has already completed. In all he says and does, man is obliged to follow faithfully what he knows to be just and right. It is by the judgment of his conscience that man perceives and recognizes the prescriptions of the divine law:

> Conscience is a law of the mind; yet [Christians] would not grant that it is nothing more; I mean that it was not a dictate, nor conveyed the notion of responsibility, of duty, of a threat and a promise.... [Conscience] is a messenger of him, who, both in nature and in grace, speaks to us behind a veil, and teaches and rules us by his representatives. Conscience is the aboriginal Vicar of Christ.[50]

1779 It is important for every person to be sufficiently present to himself in order to hear and follow the voice of his conscience. This
1886 requirement of *interiority* is all the more necessary as life often distracts us from any reflection, self-examination or introspection:

> Return to your conscience, question it.... Turn inward, brethren, and in everything you do, see God as your witness.[51]

1780 The dignity of the human person implies and requires *uprightness of moral conscience.* Conscience includes the perception of the principles of morality (synderesis); their application in the given circumstances by practical discernment of reasons and goods; and finally judgment about concrete acts yet to be performed or already performed. The truth about the moral good, stated in the law of reason, is recognized practically and concretely by the *prudent judgment* of conscience. We call that man prudent
who chooses in conformity with this 1806
judgment.

1781 Conscience enables one 1731
to assume *responsibility* for the acts performed. If man commits evil, the just judgment of conscience can remain within him as the witness to the universal truth of the good, at the same time as the evil of his particular choice. The verdict of the judgment of conscience remains a pledge of hope and mercy. In attesting to the fault committed, it calls to mind the forgiveness that must be asked, the good that must still be practiced, and the virtue that must be constantly cultivated with the grace of God:

> We shall...reassure our hearts before him whenever our hearts condemn us; for God is greater than our hearts, and he knows everything.[52]

1782 Man has the right to act in conscience and in freedom so as personally to make moral decisions. "He must not be forced to act contrary to his conscience. Nor must he

[49] Cf. *Rom* 1:32. — [50] John Henry Cardinal Newman, "Letter to the Duke of Norfolk," V, in *Certain Difficulties felt by Anglicans in Catholic Teaching* II (London: Longmans Green, 1885), 248. — [51] St. Augustine, *In ep Jo.* 8, 9: PL 35, 2041. — [52] 1 *Jn* 3:19–20.

be prevented from acting according to his conscience, especially in reli-
2106 gious matters."[53]

II. The Formation of Conscience

1783 Conscience must be informed and moral judgment enlightened. A well-formed conscience is upright and truthful. It formulates its judgments according to reason, in conformity with the true good willed by the wisdom of the Creator. The education of conscience is indispensable for human beings who are subjected to negative influences and tempted by sin to prefer their
2039 own judgment and to reject authoritative teachings.

1784 The education of the conscience is a lifelong task. From the earliest years, it awakens the child to the knowledge and practice of the interior law recognized by conscience. Prudent education teaches virtue; it prevents or cures fear, selfishness and pride, resentment arising from guilt, and feelings of complacency, born of human weakness and faults. The education of the conscience guarantees freedom and
1742 engenders peace of heart.

1785 In the formation of conscience the Word of God is the light for our path;[54] we must assimilate it in faith and prayer and put it into practice. We must also examine our conscience before the Lord's Cross. We are assisted by the gifts of the Holy Spirit, aided by the witness or advice of others and guided by
890 the authoritative teaching of the Church.[55]

III. To Choose in Accord with Conscience

1786 Faced with a moral choice, conscience can make either a right judgment in accordance with reason and the divine law or, on the contrary, an erroneous judgment that departs from them.

1787 Man is sometimes confronted by situations that make moral judgments less assured and decision difficult. But he must always seriously seek what is right and good and
discern the will of God expressed in 1955
divine law.

1788 To this purpose, man strives to interpret the data of experience and the signs of the times assisted by the virtue of prudence, by the advice
of competent people, and by the 1806
help of the Holy Spirit and his gifts.

1789 Some rules apply in every case:

– One may never do evil so that 1756
good may result from it;
– the Golden Rule: "Whatever 1970
you wish that men would do to you, do so to them."[56]
– charity always proceeds by 1827
way of respect for one's neighbor
and his conscience: "Thus sinning 1971
against your brethren and wounding their conscience...you sin against Christ."[57] Therefore "it is right not to...do anything that makes your brother stumble."[58]

IV. Erroneous Judgment

1790 A human being must always obey the certain judgment of his conscience. If he were deliberately

[53] *DH* 3 § 2. — [54] Cf. *Ps* 119:105. — [55] Cf. *DH* 14. — [56] *Mt* 7:12; cf. *Lk* 6:31; *Tob* 4:15. — [57] *1 Cor* 8:12. — [58] *Rom* 14:21.

to act against it, he would condemn himself. Yet it can happen that moral conscience remains in ignorance and makes erroneous judgments about acts to be performed or already committed.

1791 This ignorance can often be imputed to personal responsibility. This is the case when a man "takes little trouble to find out what is true
1704 and good, or when conscience is by degrees almost blinded through the habit of committing sin."[59] In such cases, the person is culpable for the evil he commits.

133 **1792** Ignorance of Christ and his Gospel, bad example given by others, enslavement to one's passions, assertion of a mistaken notion of autonomy of conscience, rejection of the Church's authority and her teaching, lack of conversion and of charity: these can be at the source of errors of judgment in moral conduct.

1860 **1793** If—on the contrary—the ignorance is invincible, or the moral subject is not responsible for his erroneous judgment, the evil committed by the person cannot be imputed to him. It remains no less an evil, a privation, a disorder. One must therefore work to correct the errors of moral conscience.

1794 A good and pure conscience is enlightened by true faith, for charity proceeds at the same time "from a pure heart and a good conscience and sincere faith."[60]

1751 The more a correct conscience prevails, the more do persons and groups turn aside from blind choice and try to be guided by objective standards of moral conduct.[61]

In Brief

1795 *"Conscience is man's most secret core, and his sanctuary. There he is alone with God whose voice echoes in his depths"* (GS *16).*

1796 *Conscience is a judgment of reason by which the human person recognizes the moral quality of a concrete act.*

1797 *For the man who has committed evil, the verdict of his conscience remains a pledge of conversion and of hope.*

1798 *A well-formed conscience is upright and truthful. It formulates its judgments according to reason, in conformity with the true good willed by the wisdom of the Creator. Everyone must avail himself of the means to form his conscience.*

1799 *Faced with a moral choice, conscience can make either a right judgment in accordance with reason and the divine law or, on the contrary, an erroneous judgment that departs from them.*

1800 *A human being must always obey the certain judgment of his conscience.*

1801 *Conscience can remain in ignorance or make erroneous judgments. Such ignorance and errors are not always free of guilt.*

1802 *The Word of God is a light for our path. We must assimilate it in faith and prayer and put it into practice. This is how moral conscience is formed.*

[59] *GS* 16. — [60] *1 Tim* 5; cf. 3:9; *2 Tim* 3; *1 Pet* 3:21; *Acts* 24:16. — [61] *GS* 16.

Article 7: THE VIRTUES

1803 "Whatever is true, whatever is honorable, whatever is just, whatever is pure, whatever is lovely, whatever is gracious, if there is any excellence, if there is anything worthy of praise, think about these things."[62]

1733 A virtue is an habitual and firm disposition to do the good. It allows the person not only to perform good acts, but to give the best of himself. The virtuous person tends toward the good with all his sensory and spiritu-
1768 al powers; he pursues the good and chooses it in concrete actions.

The goal of a virtuous life is to become like God.[63]

I. The Human Virtues

1804 *Human virtues* are firm attitudes, stable dispositions, habitual perfections of intellect and will that govern our actions, order our passions, and guide our conduct according to reason and faith. They
2500 make possible ease, self-mastery, and joy in leading a morally good life. The virtuous man is he who freely practices the good.

The moral virtues are acquired by human effort. They are the fruit
1827 and seed of morally good acts; they dispose all the powers of the human being for communion with divine love.

The cardinal virtues

1805 Four virtues play a pivotal role and accordingly are called "cardinal"; all the others are grouped around them. They are: prudence, justice, fortitude, and temperance. "If anyone loves righteousness, [Wisdom's] labors are virtues; for she teaches temperance and prudence, justice, and courage."[64] These virtues are praised under other names in many passages of Scripture.

1806 *Prudence* is the virtue that disposes practical reason to discern our true good in every circumstance and to choose the right means of achieving it; "the prudent man looks where he is going."[65] "Keep sane and sober for your prayers."[66] Prudence
is "right reason in action," writes St. 1788
Thomas Aquinas, following Aristotle.[67] It is not to be confused with timidity or fear, nor with duplicity or dissimulation. It is called *auriga virtutum* (the charioteer of the virtues); it guides the other virtues by setting rule and measure. It is prudence that immediately guides the judgment of
conscience. The prudent man de- 1780
termines and directs his conduct in accordance with this judgment. With the help of this virtue we apply moral principles to particular cases without error and overcome doubts about the good to achieve and the evil to avoid.

1807 *Justice* is the moral virtue that consists in the constant and firm will to give their due to God and neighbor. Justice toward God is
called the "virtue of religion." Justice 2095
toward men disposes one to respect the rights of each and to establish in human relationships the harmony that promotes equity with regard to

[62] *Phil* 4:8. — [63] St. Gregory of Nyssa, *De beatitudinibus*, 1: PG 44, 1200D. — [64] *Wis* 8:7. — [65] *Prov* 14:15. — [66] *1 Pet* 4:7. — [67] St. Thomas Aquinas, *STh* II–II, 47, 2.

persons and to the common good.
2401 The just man, often mentioned in the Sacred Scriptures, is distinguished by habitual right thinking and the uprightness of his conduct toward his neighbor. "You shall not be partial to the poor or defer to the great, but in righteousness shall you judge your neighbor."[68] "Masters, treat your slaves justly and fairly, knowing that you also have a Master in heaven."[69]

1808 *Fortitude* is the moral virtue that ensures firmness in difficulties and constancy in the pursuit of the good. It strengthens the resolve to resist temptations and to overcome obstacles in the moral life. The virtue of fortitude enables one to conquer fear, even fear of death, and
2848 to face trials and persecutions. It disposes one even to renounce and
2473 sacrifice his life in defense of a just cause. "The Lord is my strength and my song."[70] "In the world you have tribulation; but be of good cheer, I have overcome the world."[71]

1809 *Temperance* is the moral virtue that moderates the attraction of pleasures and provides balance in the use of created goods. It ensures the will's mastery over instincts and keeps desires within the limits of what is honorable. The temperate
2341 person directs the sensitive appetites toward what is good and maintains a healthy discretion: "Do not follow your inclination and strength, walking according to the desires of your heart."[72] Temperance is often praised in the Old Testament: "Do
2517 not follow your base desires, but restrain your appetites."[73] In the New Testament it is called "moderation" or "sobriety." We ought "to live sober, upright, and godly lives in this world."[74]

> To live well is nothing other than to love God with all one's heart, with all one's soul and with all one's efforts; from this it comes about that love is kept whole and uncorrupted (through temperance). No misfortune can disturb it (and this is fortitude). It obeys only [God] (and this is justice), and is careful in discerning things, so as not to be surprised by deceit or trickery (and this is prudence).[75]

The virtues and grace

1810 Human virtues acquired by education, by deliberate acts and by a perseverance ever-renewed in repeated efforts are purified and elevated by divine grace. With God's 1266
help, they forge character and give facility in the practice of the good. The virtuous man is happy to practice them.

1811 It is not easy for man, wounded by sin, to maintain moral balance. Christ's gift of salvation offers us the grace necessary to persevere in the pursuit of the virtues. Everyone should always ask for this 2015
grace of light and strength, frequent the sacraments, cooperate with the Holy Spirit, and follow his calls to love what is good and shun evil.

II. The Theological Virtues 2086–2094 2656–2658

1812 The human virtues are rooted in the theological virtues, which adapt man's faculties for participation in the divine nature:[76] for the theological virtues relate directly to God. They dispose Christians to

[68] *Lev* 19:15. — [69] *Col* 4:1. — [70] *Ps* 118:14. — [71] *Jn* 16:33. — [72] *Sir* 5:2; cf. 37:27–31. — [73] *Sir* 18:30. — [74] *Titus* 2:12. — [75] St. Augustine, *De moribus eccl.* 1, 25, 46: PL 32, 1330–1331. — [76] Cf. *2 Pet* 1:4.

live in a relationship with the Holy Trinity. They have the One and Tri-
1266 une God for their origin, motive, and object.

1813 The theological virtues are the foundation of Christian moral activity; they animate it and give it its special character. They inform and give life to all the moral virtues. They are infused by God into the souls of the faithful to make them capable of acting as his children and of meriting eternal life. They are the pledge of the presence and action of the Holy Spirit in the faculties of the human being. There are three
2008 theological virtues: faith, hope, and charity.[77]

142–175 *Faith*

1814 Faith is the theological virtue by which we believe in God and believe all that he has said and revealed to us, and that Holy Church
506 proposes for our belief, because he is truth itself. By faith "man freely commits his entire self to God."[78] For this reason the believer seeks to know and do God's will. "The righteous shall live by faith." Living faith "work[s] through charity."[79]

1815 The gift of faith remains in one who has not sinned against it.[80] But "faith apart from works is dead":[81] when it is deprived of hope and love, faith does not fully unite the believer to Christ and does not make him a living member of his Body.

2471 **1816** The disciple of Christ must not only keep the faith and live on it, but also profess it, confidently bear witness to it, and spread it: "All however must be prepared to confess Christ before men and to follow him along the way of the Cross, amidst the persecutions which the Church never lacks."82 Service of and witness to the faith are necessary for salvation: "So every one who acknowledges me before men, I also will acknowledge before my Father who is in heaven; but whoever denies me before men, I also will deny before my Father who is in heaven."[83]

Hope

1817 Hope is the theological virtue by which we desire the kingdom of heaven and eternal life as our happiness, placing our trust in
Christ's promises and relying not on 1024
our own strength, but on the help of the grace of the Holy Spirit. "Let us hold fast the confession of our hope without wavering, for he who promised is faithful."[84] "The Holy Spirit…he poured out upon us richly through Jesus Christ our Savior, so that we might be justified by his grace and become heirs in hope of eternal life."[85]

1818 The virtue of hope responds 27
to the aspiration to happiness which God has placed in the heart of every man; it takes up the hopes that inspire men's activities and purifies them so as to order them to the Kingdom of heaven; it keeps man from discouragement; it sustains him during times of abandonment; it opens up his heart in expectation of eternal beatitude. Buoyed up by hope, he is preserved from selfishness and led to the happiness that flows from charity.

[77] Cf. 1 *Cor* 13:13. — [78] *DV* 5. — [79] *Rom* 1:17; *Gal* 5:6. — [80] Cf. Council of Trent (1547): DS 1545. — [81] *Jas* 2:26. — [82] *LG* 42; cf. *DH* 14. — [83] *Mt* 10:32–33. — [84] *Heb* 10:23. — [85] *Titus* 3:6–7.

1819 Christian hope takes up and fulfills the hope of the chosen people which has its origin and model in the *hope of Abraham,* who was blessed abundantly by the promises of God fulfilled in Isaac, and who was
146 purified by the test of the sacrifice.[86]
"Hoping against hope, he believed, and thus became the father of many nations."[87]

1820 Christian hope unfolds from the beginning of Jesus' preaching in the proclamation of the beatitudes. The *beatitudes* raise our hope
1716 toward heaven as the new Promised
Land; they trace the path that leads through the trials that await the disciples of Jesus. But through the merits of Jesus Christ and of his Passion, God keeps us in the "hope that does not disappoint."[88] Hope is the "sure and steadfast anchor of the soul... that enters...where Jesus has gone as a forerunner on our behalf."[89] Hope is also a weapon that protects us in the struggle of salvation: "Let us... put on the breastplate of faith and charity, and for a helmet the hope of salvation."[90] It affords us joy even under trial: "Rejoice in your hope, be patient in tribulation."[91] Hope is expressed and nourished in prayer,
2772 especially in the Our Father, the
summary of everything that hope leads us to desire.

1821 We can therefore hope in the glory of heaven promised by God to those who love him and do his will.[92] In every circumstance, each one of us should hope, with the grace of God, to persevere "to the
end"[93] and to obtain the joy of heav- 2016
en, as God's eternal reward for the
good works accomplished with the 1037
grace of Christ. In hope, the Church prays for "all men to be saved."[94] She longs to be united with Christ, her Bridegroom, in the glory of heaven:

> Hope, O my soul, hope. You know neither the day nor the hour. Watch carefully, for everything passes quickly, even though your impatience makes doubtful what is certain, and turns a very short time into a long one. Dream that the more you struggle, the more you prove the love that you bear your God, and the more you will rejoice one day with your Beloved, in a happiness and rapture that can never end.[95]

Charity

1822 Charity is the theological 1723
virtue by which we love God above all things for his own sake, and our neighbor as ourselves for the love of God.

1823 Jesus makes charity the *new* 1970
commandment.[96] By loving his own "to the end,"[97] he makes manifest the Father's love which he receives. By loving one another, the disciples imitate the love of Jesus which they themselves receive. Whence Jesus says: "As the Father has loved me, so have I loved you; abide in my love." And again: "This is my commandment, that you love one another as I have loved you."[98]

[86] Cf. *Gen* 17:4–8; 22:1–18. — [87] *Rom* 4:18. — [88] *Rom* 5:5. — [89] *Heb* 6:19–20. — [90] *1 Thess* 5:8. — [91] *Rom* 12:12. — [92] Cf. *Rom* 8:28–30; *Mt* 7:21. — [93] *Mt* 10:22; cf. Council of Trent: DS 1541. — [94] *1 Tim* 2:4. — [95] St. Teresa of Avila, *Excl.* 15:3. — [96] Cf. *Jn* 13:34. — [97] *Jn* 13:1. — [98] *Jn* 15:9, 12.

735 **1824** Fruit of the Spirit and fullness of the Law, charity keeps the *commandments* of God and his Christ: "Abide in my love. If you keep my commandments, you will abide in my love."[99]

604 **1825** Christ died out of love for us, while we were still "enemies."[100] The Lord asks us to love as he does, even our *enemies*, to make ourselves the neighbor of those farthest away, and to love children and the poor as Christ himself.[101]

> The Apostle Paul has given an incomparable depiction of charity: "charity is patient and kind, charity is not jealous or boastful; it is not arrogant or rude. Charity does not insist on its own way; it is not irritable or resentful; it does not rejoice at wrong, but rejoices in the right. Charity bears all things, believes all things, hopes all things, endures all things."[102]

1826 "If I...have not charity," says the Apostle, "I am nothing." Whatever my privilege, service, or even virtue, "if I...have not charity, I gain nothing."[103] Charity is superior to all the virtues. It is the first of the theological virtues: "So faith, hope, charity abide, these three. But *the greatest of these is charity*."[104]

1827 The practice of all the virtues is animated and inspired by charity, which "binds everything together in perfect harmony";[105] it is the *form of the virtues*; it articulates
815 and orders them among themselves;
it is the source and the goal of their
826 Christian practice. Charity upholds and purifies our human ability to love, and raises it to the supernatural perfection of divine love.

1828 The practice of the moral life animated by charity gives to the Christian the spiritual freedom of the children of God. He no longer stands before God as a slave, in 1972
servile fear, or as a mercenary looking for wages, but as a son responding to the love of him who "first loved us":[106]

> If we turn away from evil out of fear of punishment, we are in the position of slaves. If we pursue the enticement of wages,...we resemble mercenaries. Finally if we obey for the sake of the good itself and out of love for him who commands...we are in the position of children.[107]

1829 The *fruits* of charity are joy, peace, and mercy; charity demands beneficence and fraternal correction; it is benevolence; it fosters reciprocity and remains disinterested and 2540
generous; it is friendship and communion:

> Love is itself the fulfillment of all our works. There is the goal; that is why we run: we run toward it, and once we reach it, in it we shall find rest.[108]

III. The Gifts and Fruits of the Holy Spirit

1830 The moral life of Christians is sustained by the gifts of the Holy Spirit. These are permanent dispositions which make man docile in following the promptings of the Holy Spirit.

[99] *Jn* 15:9–10; cf. *Mt* 22:40; *Rom* 13:8–10. — [100] *Rom* 5:10. — [101] Cf. *Mt* 5:44; *Lk* 10:27–37; *Mk* 9:37; *Mt* 25:40, 45. — [102] *1 Cor* 13:4–7. — [103] *1 Cor* 13:1–4. — [104] *1 Cor* 13:13. — [105] *Col* 3:14. — [106] Cf. 1 *Jn* 4:19. — [107] St. Basil, *Reg. fus. tract., prol.* 3: PG 31, 896 B. — [108] St. Augustine, *In ep. Jo.* 10, 4: PL 35, 2057.

1831 The seven *gifts* of the Holy Spirit are wisdom, understanding, counsel, fortitude, knowledge, piety, and fear of the Lord. They belong in their fullness to Christ, Son of David.[109] They complete and perfect the
1266, 1299 virtues of those who receive them. They make the faithful docile in readily obeying divine inspirations.

> Let your good spirit lead me on a level path.[110]
> For all who are led by the Spirit of God are sons of God... If children, then heirs, heirs of God and fellow heirs with Christ.[111]

1832 The *fruits* of the Spirit are
736 perfections that the Holy Spirit forms in us as the first fruits of eternal glory. The tradition of the Church lists twelve of them: "charity, joy, peace, patience, kindness, goodness, generosity, gentleness, faithfulness, modesty, self-control, chastity."[112]

In Brief

1833 *Virtue is a habitual and firm disposition to do good.*

1834 *The human virtues are stable dispositions of the intellect and the will that govern our acts, order our passions, and guide our conduct in accordance with reason and faith. They can be grouped around the four cardinal virtues: prudence, justice, fortitude, and temperance.*

1835 *Prudence disposes the practical reason to discern, in every circumstance, our true good and to choose the right means for achieving it.*

1836 *Justice consists in the firm and constant will to give God and neighbor their due.*

1837 *Fortitude ensures firmness in difficulties and constancy in the pursuit of the good.*

1838 *Temperance moderates the attraction of the pleasures of the senses and provides balance in the use of created goods.*

1839 *The moral virtues grow through education, deliberate acts, and perseverance in struggle. Divine grace purifies and elevates them.*

1840 *The theological virtues dispose Christians to live in a relationship with the Holy Trinity. They have God for their origin, their motive, and their object—God known by faith, God hoped in and loved for his own sake.*

1841 *There are three theological virtues: faith, hope, and charity. They inform all the moral virtues and give life to them.*

1842 *By faith, we believe in God and believe all that he has revealed to us and that Holy Church proposes for our belief.*

1843 *By hope we desire, and with steadfast trust await from God, eternal life and the graces to merit it.*

1844 *By charity, we love God above all things and our neighbor as ourselves for love of God. Charity, the form of all the virtues, "binds everything together in perfect harmony"* (Col *3:14).*

1845 *The seven gifts of the Holy Spirit bestowed upon Christians are wisdom, understanding, counsel, fortitude, knowledge, piety, and fear of the Lord.*

[109] Cf. *Isa* 11:1–2. — [110] *Ps* 143:10. — [111] *Rom* 8:14, 17. — [112] *Gal* 5:22–23 (Vulg.).

Article 8:
SIN

I. Mercy and Sin

430 **1846** The Gospel is the revelation in Jesus Christ of God's mercy to sinners.[113] The angel announced to Joseph: "You shall call his name Jesus, for he will save his people from their sins."[114] The same is true of the
1365 Eucharist, the sacrament of redemption: "This is my blood of the covenant, which is poured out for many for the forgiveness of sins."[115]

387, 1455 **1847** "God created us without us: but he did not will to save us without us."[116] To receive his mercy, we must admit our faults. "If we say we have no sin, we deceive ourselves, and the truth is not in us. If we confess our sins, he is faithful and just, and will forgive our sins and cleanse us from all unrighteousness."[117]

1848 As St. Paul affirms, "Where sin increased, grace abounded all the more."[118] But to do its work grace must uncover sin so as to convert
385 our hearts and bestow on us "righteousness to eternal life through Jesus Christ our Lord."[119] Like a physician who probes the wound before treating it, God, by his Word and by his Spirit, casts a living light on sin:

> Conversion *requires convincing of sin*; it includes the interior judgment of conscience, and this, being a proof of the action of the Spirit of truth in man's inmost being, becomes at the same time the start of a new grant of grace and love: "Receive the Holy
> 1433 Spirit." Thus in this "convincing concerning sin" we discover a *double gift*: the gift of the truth of conscience and the gift of the certainty of redemption. The Spirit of truth is the Consoler.[120]

II. The Definition of Sin

1849 Sin is an offense against rea- 311
son, truth, and right conscience; it is failure in genuine love for God and neighbor caused by a perverse attachment to certain goods. It wounds the nature of man and injures human solidarity. It has been defined as "an utterance, a deed, or a
desire contrary to the eternal law."[121] 1952

1850 Sin is an offense against 1440
God: "Against you, you alone, have I sinned, and done that which is evil in your sight."[122] Sin sets itself against God's love for us and turns our hearts away from it. Like the
first sin, it is disobedience, a revolt 397
against God through the will to become "like gods,"[123] knowing and determining good and evil. Sin is thus "love of oneself even to contempt of God."[124] In this proud self-exaltation, sin is diametrically opposed to the obedience of Jesus,
which achieves our salvation.[125] 615

1851 It is precisely in the Passion, when the mercy of Christ is about to vanquish it, that sin most clearly manifests its violence and its many forms: unbelief, murderous hatred, shunning and mockery by the leaders and the people, Pilate's coward-

[113] Cf. *Lk* 15. — [114] *Mt* 1:21. — [115] *Mt* 26:28. — [116] St. Augustine, *Sermo* 169, 11, 13: PL 38, 923. — [117] 1 *Jn* 8–9. — [118] *Rom* 5:20. — [119] *Rom* 5:21. — [120] John Paul II, *DeV* 31 § 2. — [121] St. Augustine, Contra *Faustum* 22: PL 42, 418; St. Thomas Aquinas, *STh* I–II, 71, 6. — [122] *Ps* 51:4. — [123] *Gen* 3:5. — [124] St. Augustine, *De civ. Dei* 14, 28: PL 41, 436. — [125] Cf. *Phil* 2:6–9.

ice and the cruelty of the soldiers,
598 Judas' betrayal—so bitter to Jesus, Peter's denial and the disciples' flight. However, at the very hour of
2746, 616 darkness, the hour of the prince of this world,[126] the sacrifice of Christ secretly becomes the source from which the forgiveness of our sins will pour forth inexhaustibly.

III. The Different Kinds of Sins

1852 There are a great many kinds of sins. Scripture provides several lists of them. The *Letter to the Galatians* contrasts the works of the flesh with the fruit of the Spirit: "Now the works of the flesh are plain: fornication, impurity, licentiousness, idolatry, sorcery, enmity, strife, jealousy, anger, selfishness, dissension, factions, envy, drunkenness, carousing, and the like. I warn you, as I warned you before, that those who do such things shall not inherit the Kingdom of God."[127]

1751 **1853** Sins can be distinguished according to their objects, as can every human act; or according to the virtues they oppose, by excess or defect; or according to the commandments they violate. They can also be classed according to whether they concern God, neighbor, or oneself; they can be divided into spiritual and carnal
2067 sins, or again as sins in thought, word, deed, or omission. The root of sin is in the heart of man, in his free will, according to the teaching of the Lord: "For out of the heart come evil thoughts, murder, adultery, for-
368 nication, theft, false witness, slander. These are what defile a man."[128] But in the heart also resides charity, the source of the good and pure works, which sin wounds.

IV. The Gravity of Sin: Mortal and Venial Sin

1854 Sins are rightly evaluated according to their gravity. The distinction between mortal and venial sin, already evident in Scripture,[129] became part of the tradition of the Church. It is corroborated by human experience.

1855 *Mortal sin* destroys charity 1395
in the heart of man by a grave violation of God's law; it turns man away from God, who is his ultimate end and his beatitude, by preferring an inferior good to him.

Venial sin allows charity to subsist, even though it offends and wounds it.

1856 Mortal sin, by attacking the vital principle within us—that is, charity—necessitates a new initia- 1446
tive of God's mercy and a conversion of heart which is normally accomplished within the setting of the sacrament of reconciliation:

> When the will sets itself upon something that is of its nature incompatible with the charity that orients man toward his ultimate end, then the sin is mortal by its very object...whether it contradicts the love of God, such as blasphemy or perjury, or the love of neighbor, such as homicide or adultery.... But when the sinner's will is set upon something that of its nature involves a disorder, but is not opposed to the love of God and neighbor, such as thoughtless chatter or immoderate laughter and the like, such sins are venial.[130]

[126] Cf. *Jn* 14:30. — [127] *Gal* 5:19–21; cf. *Rom* 1:28–32; 1 *Cor* 6:9–10; *Eph* 5:3–5; *Col* 3:5–9; 1 *Tim* 1:9–10; 2 *Tim* 3:2–5. — [128] *Mt* 15:19–20. — [129] Cf. *1 Jn* 5:16–17. — [130] St. Thomas Aquinas, *STh* I–II, 88, 2, *corp. art.*

1857 For a *sin* to be *mortal*, three conditions must together be met: "Mortal sin is sin whose object is grave matter and which is also committed with full knowledge and deliberate consent."[131]

2072 **1858** *Grave matter* is specified by the Ten Commandments, corresponding to the answer of Jesus to the rich young man: "Do not kill, Do not commit adultery, Do not steal, Do not bear false witness, Do not defraud, Honor your father and your mother."[132] The gravity of sins is more or less great: murder is graver than theft. One must also take into account who is wronged: violence against parents is in itself grav-
2214 er than violence against a stranger.

1734 **1859** Mortal sin requires *full knowledge* and *complete consent.* It presupposes knowledge of the sinful character of the act, of its opposition to God's law. It also implies a consent sufficiently deliberate to be a personal choice. Feigned ignorance and hardness of heart[133] do not diminish, but rather increase, the voluntary character of a sin.

1735 **1860** *Unintentional ignorance* can diminish or even remove the imputability of a grave offense. But no one is deemed to be ignorant of the principles of the moral law, which are written in the conscience of every man. The promptings of feelings and passions can also diminish the
1767 voluntary and free character of the offense, as can external pressures or pathological disorders. Sin committed through malice, by deliberate choice of evil, is the gravest.

1742 **1861** Mortal sin is a radical possibility of human freedom, as is love itself. It results in the loss of charity and the privation of sanctifying grace, that is, of the state of grace. If it is not redeemed by repentance and God's forgiveness, it causes exclusion from Christ's kingdom and the eternal death of hell, for our freedom has the power to make choices for
ever, with no turning back. Howev- 1033
er, although we can judge that an act is in itself a grave offense, we must entrust judgment of persons to the justice and mercy of God.

1862 One commits *venial sin* when, in a less serious matter, he does not observe the standard prescribed by the moral law, or when he disobeys the moral law in a grave matter, but without full knowledge or without complete consent.

1863 Venial sin weakens charity; 1394
it manifests a disordered affection for created goods; it impedes the soul's progress in the exercise of the virtues and the practice of the moral good; it merits temporal punishment. Deliberate and unrepented venial sin disposes us little by little
to commit mortal sin. However 1472
venial sin does not break the covenant with God. With God's grace it is humanly reparable. "Venial sin does not deprive the sinner of sanctifying grace, friendship with God, charity, and consequently eternal happiness."[134]

> While he is in the flesh, man cannot help but have at least some light sins. But do not despise these sins which we call "light": if you take them for light when you weigh them, tremble when you count them. A number of light objects makes a great mass; a number of drops fills a river; a number

[131] *RP* 17 § 12. — [132] *Mk* 10:19. — [133] Cf. *Mk* 3:5–6; *Lk* 16:19–31. — [134] John Paul II, *RP* 17 § 9.

of grains makes a heap. What then is our hope? Above all, confession....[135]

1864 "Therefore I tell you, every sin and blasphemy will be forgiven men, but the blasphemy against the Spirit will not be forgiven."[136] There are no limits to the mercy of God, but anyone who deliberately refus-
2091 es to accept his mercy by repenting, rejects the forgiveness of his sins and the salvation offered by the Holy Spirit.[137] Such hardness of heart
1037 can lead to final impenitence and eternal loss.

V. The Proliferation of Sin

401 **1865** Sin creates a proclivity to sin; it engenders vice by repetition of the same acts. This results in perverse inclinations which cloud conscience and corrupt the concrete judgment of good and evil. Thus sin
1768 tends to reproduce itself and reinforce itself, but it cannot destroy the moral sense at its root.

1866 Vices can be classified according to the virtues they oppose, or also be linked to the *capital sins* which Christian experience has distinguished, following St. John Cassian and St. Gregory the Great. They are called "capital" because they engender other sins, other vices.[138] They are pride, avarice, envy, wrath,
2539 lust, gluttony, and sloth or acedia.

2268 **1867** The catechetical tradition also recalls that there are "*sins that cry to heaven*": the blood of Abel,[139] the sin of the Sodomites,[140] the cry of the people oppressed in Egypt,[141] the cry of the foreigner, the widow, and the orphan,[142] injustice to the wage earner.[143]

1868 Sin is a personal act. Moreover, we have a responsibility for the sins committed by others when *we cooperate in them*: 1736

– by participating directly and voluntarily in them;
– by ordering, advising, praising, or approving them;
– by not disclosing or not hindering them when we have an obligation to do so;
– by protecting evil-doers.

1869 Thus sin makes men accomplices of one another and causes concupiscence, violence, and injustice to reign among them. Sins give rise to social situations and institutions that are contrary to the divine goodness. "Structures of sin" are the ex- 408
pression and effect of personal sins. They lead their victims to do evil in 1887
their turn. In an analogous sense, they constitute a "social sin."[144]

In Brief

1870 *"God has consigned all men to disobedience, that he may have mercy upon all" (*Rom *11:32).*

1871 *Sin is an utterance, a deed, or a desire contrary to the eternal law (St. Augustine,* Faust *22: PL 42, 418). It is an offense against God. It rises up against God in a disobedience contrary to the obedience of Christ.*

1872 *Sin is an act contrary to reason. It wounds man's nature and injures human solidarity.*

[135] St. Augustine, *In ep. Jo.* 1, 6: PL 35, 1982. — [136] *Mt* 12:31; cf. *Mk* 3:29; *Lk* 12:10. — [137] Cf. John Paul II, *DeV* 46. — [138] Cf. St. Gregory the Great, *Moralia in Job*, 31, 45: PL 76, 621A. — [139] Cf. *Gen* 4:10. — [140] Cf. *Gen* 18:20; 19:13. — [141] Cf. *Ex* 3:7–10. — [142] Cf. *Ex* 20:20–22. — [143] Cf. *Deut* 24:14–15; *Jas* 5:4. — [144] John Paul II, *RP* 16.

1873 *The root of all sins lies in man's heart. The kinds and the gravity of sins are determined principally by their objects.*

1874 *To choose deliberately—that is, both knowing it and willing it—something gravely contrary to the divine law and to the ultimate end of man is to commit a mortal sin. This destroys in us the charity without which eternal beatitude is impossible. Unrepented, it brings eternal death.*

1875 *Venial sin constitutes a moral disorder that is reparable by charity, which it allows to subsist in us.*

1876 *The repetition of sins—even venial ones—engenders vices, among which are the capital sins.*

Chapter Two:
THE HUMAN COMMUNITY

355 **1877** The vocation of humanity is to show forth the image of God and to be transformed into the image of the Father's only Son. This vocation takes a personal form since each of us is called to enter into the divine beatitude; it also concerns the human community as a whole.

Article 1:
THE PERSON AND SOCIETY

I. The Communal Character of the Human Vocation

1878 All men are called to the same end: God himself. There is a certain resemblance between the
1702 unity of the divine persons and the fraternity that men are to establish among themselves in truth and love.[1] Love of neighbor is inseparable from love for God.

1936 **1879** The human person needs to live in society. Society is not for him an extraneous addition but a requirement of his nature. Through the exchange with others, mutual service and dialogue with his brethren, man develops his potential; he thus responds to his vocation.[2]

771 **1880** A *society* is a group of persons bound together organically by a principle of unity that goes beyond each one of them. As an assembly that is at once visible and spiritual, a society endures through time: it gathers up the past and prepares for the future. By means of society, each man is established as an "heir" and receives certain "talents" that enrich his identity and whose fruits he must develop.[3] He rightly owes loyalty to the communities of which he is part and respect to those in authority who have charge of the common good.

1881 Each community is defined by its purpose and consequently obeys specific rules; but "the *human person*...is and ought to be the principle, the subject and the end of all 1929
social institutions."[4]

1882 Certain societies, such as the family and the state, correspond more directly to the nature of man; they are necessary to him. To promote the participation of the greatest number in the life of a society, the creation of voluntary associations and institutions must be encouraged "on both national and 1913
international levels, which relate to economic and social goals, to cultural and recreational activities, to sport, to various professions, and to political affairs."[5] This "*socialization*" also expresses the natural tendency for human beings to associate with one another for the sake of attaining objectives that exceed individual capacities. It develops the qualities

[1] Cf. *GS* 24 § 3. — [2] Cf. *GS* 25 § 1. — [3] Cf. *Lk* 19:13, 15. — [4] *GS* 25 § 1. — [5] John XXIII, *MM* 60.

of the person, especially the sense of initiative and responsibility, and helps guarantee his rights.[6]

1883 Socialization also presents dangers. Excessive intervention by the state can threaten personal freedom and initiative. The teaching of the Church has elaborated the principle of *subsidiarity*, according to which "a community of a higher order should not interfere in the internal life of a community of a lower order, depriving the latter of its functions, but rather should support it in case of need and help to co-or-
2431 dinate its activity with the activities of the rest of society, always with a view to the common good."[7]

1884 God has not willed to reserve to himself all exercise of power. He entrusts to every creature the functions it is capable of perform-
307 ing, according to the capacities of its own nature. This mode of governance ought to be followed in social life. The way God acts in governing the world, which bears witness to such great regard for human freedom, should inspire the wisdom of those who govern human communi-
302 ties. They should behave as ministers of divine providence.

1885 The principle of subsidiarity is opposed to all forms of collectivism. It sets limits for state intervention. It aims at harmonizing the relationships between individuals and societies. It tends toward the establishment of true international order.

II. Conversion and Society

1886 Society is essential to the fulfillment of the human vocation. To attain this aim, respect must be accorded to the just hierarchy of values, which "subordinates physical 1779
and instinctual dimensions to interior and spiritual ones:"[8]

> Human society must primarily be considered something pertaining to the spiritual. Through it, in the bright light of truth, men should share their knowledge, be able to exercise their rights and fulfill their obligations, be inspired to seek spiritual values; mutually derive genuine pleasure from the beautiful, of whatever order
> it be; always be readily disposed to 2500
> pass on to others the best of their own cultural heritage; and eagerly strive to make their own the spiritual achievements of others. These benefits not only influence, but at the same time give aim and scope to all that has bearing on cultural expressions, economic, and social institutions, political movements and forms, laws, and all other structures by which society is outwardly established and constantly developed.[9]

1887 The inversion of means and ends,[10] which results in giving the
value of ultimate end to what is only 909
a means for attaining it, or in viewing persons as mere means to that end, engenders unjust structures which "make Christian conduct in keeping with the commandments of the divine Law-giver difficult and
almost impossible."[11] 1869

1888 It is necessary, then, to appeal 407
to the spiritual and moral capacities
of the human person and to the per- 1430
manent need for his *inner conversion*, so as to obtain social changes that will really serve him. The acknowledged priority of the conversion of

[6] Cf. *GS* 25 § 2; *CA* 12. — [7] *CA* 48 § 4; cf. Pius XI, *Quadragesimo anno* I, 184–186. — [8] *CA* 36 § 2. — [9] John XXIII, *PT* 36. — [10] Cf. *CA* 41. — [11] Pius XII, Address at Pentecost, June 1, 1941.

heart in no way eliminates but on the contrary imposes the obligation of bringing the appropriate remedies to institutions and living conditions when they are an inducement to sin, so that they conform to the norms of justice and advance the good rather than hinder it.[12]

1889 Without the help of grace, men would not know how "to discern the often narrow path between the cowardice which gives in to evil, and the violence which under the illusion of fighting evil only makes it worse."[13] This is the path of charity, that is, of the love of God and of
1825 neighbor. Charity is the greatest social commandment. It respects others and their rights. It requires the practice of justice, and it alone makes us capable of it. Charity inspires a life of self-giving: "Whoever seeks to gain his life will lose it, but whoever loses his life will preserve it."[14]

In Brief

1890 *There is a certain resemblance between the unity of the divine persons and the fraternity that men ought to establish among themselves.*

1891 *The human person needs life in society in order to develop in accordance with his nature. Certain societies, such as the family and the state, correspond more directly to the nature of man.*

1892 *"The human person... is and ought to be the principle, the subject, and the object of every social organization"* (GS 25 *§ 1).*

1893 *Widespread participation in voluntary associations and institutions is to be encouraged.*

1894 *In accordance with the principle of subsidiarity, neither the state nor any larger society should substitute itself for the initiative and responsibility of individuals and intermediary bodies.*

1895 *Society ought to promote the exercise of virtue, not obstruct it. It should be animated by a just hierarchy of values.*

1896 *Where sin has perverted the social climate, it is necessary to call for the conversion of hearts and appeal to the grace of God. Charity urges just reforms. There is no solution to the social question apart from the Gospel (cf.* CA *3, 5).*

Article 2: PARTICIPATION IN SOCIAL LIFE

I. Authority

1897 "Human society can be neither well-ordered nor prosperous unless it has some people invested with legitimate authority to preserve its in-
2234 stitutions and to devote themselves as far as is necessary to work and care for the good of all."[15]

By "authority" one means the quality by virtue of which persons or institutions make laws and give orders to men and expect obedience from them.

[12] *Jas* 1:27. — [13] Cf. *GS* 47 § 1. — [14] *GS* 52 § 2. — [15] John XXIII, *PT* 46.

1898 Every human community needs an authority to govern it.[16] The foundation of such authority lies in human nature. It is necessary for the unity of the state. Its role is to ensure as far as possible the common good of the society.

2235 **1899** The authority required by the moral order derives from God: "Let every person be subject to the governing authorities. For there is no authority except from God, and those that exist have been instituted by God. Therefore he who resists the authorities resists what God has appointed, and those who resist will incur judgment."[17]

2238 **1900** The duty of obedience requires all to give due honor to authority and to treat those who are charged to exercise it with respect, and, insofar as it is deserved, with gratitude and good-will.

2240 Pope St. Clement of Rome provides the Church's most ancient prayer for political authorities:[18] "Grant to them, Lord, health, peace, concord, and stability, so that they may exercise without offense the sovereignty that you have given them. Master, heavenly King of the ages, you give glory, honor, and power over the things of earth to the sons of men. Direct, Lord, their counsel, following what is pleasing and acceptable in your sight, so that by exercising with devotion and in peace and gentleness the power that you have given to them, they may find favor with you."[19]

1901 If authority belongs to the order established by God, "the choice of the political regime and the appointment of rulers are left to the free decision of the citizens."[20]

The diversity of political regimes is morally acceptable, provided they serve the legitimate good of the communities that adopt them. Regimes whose nature is contrary to 2242
the natural law, to the public order, and to the fundamental rights of persons cannot achieve the common good of the nations on which they have been imposed.

1902 Authority does not derive its 1930
moral legitimacy from itself. It must not behave in a despotic manner, but must act for the common good as a "moral force based on freedom and a sense of responsibility":[21]

> A human law has the character of 1951
> law to the extent that it accords with right reason, and thus derives from the eternal law. Insofar as it falls short of right reason it is said to be an unjust law, and thus has not so much the nature of law as of a kind of violence.[22]

1903 Authority is exercised legitimately only when it seeks the common good of the group concerned and if it employs morally licit means to attain it. If rulers were to enact unjust laws or take measures contrary to the moral order, such ar- 2242
rangements would not be binding in conscience. In such a case, "authority breaks down completely and results in shameful abuse."[23]

1904 "It is preferable that each power be balanced by other powers and by other spheres of responsibility which keep it within proper bounds. This is the principle of

[16] Cf. Leo XIII, *Immortale Dei; Diuturnum illud.* — [17] *Rom* 13:1–2; cf. *1 Pet* 2:13–17. — [18] Cf. as early as *1 Tim* 2:1–2. — [19] St. Clement of Rome, *Ad Cor.* 61: SCh 167, 198–200. — [20] *GS* 74 § 3. — [21] *GS* 74 § 2. — [22] St. Thomas Aquinas, STh I–II, 93, 3, *ad* 2. — [23] John XXIII, *PT* 51.

the 'rule of law,' in which the law is sovereign and not the arbitrary will of men."[24]

II. The Common Good

1905 In keeping with the social nature of man, the good of each in
801 dividual is necessarily related to the common good, which in turn can
1881 be defined only in reference to the human person:

> Do not live entirely isolated, having retreated into yourselves, as if you were already justified, but gather instead to seek the common good together.[25]

1906 By common good is to be understood "the sum total of social conditions which allow people, either as groups or as individuals, to reach their fulfillment more fully and more easily."[26] The common good concerns the life of all. It calls for prudence from each, and even more from those who exercise the office of authority. It consists of *three essential elements*:

1929 **1907** First, the common good presupposes *respect for the person* as such. In the name of the common good, public authorities are bound to respect the fundamental and inalienable rights of the human person. Society should permit each of its members to fulfill his vocation. In particular, the common good resides in the conditions for the exercise of the natural freedoms indispensable for the development of the human vocation, such as "the right to act according to a sound norm of conscience and to safeguard...privacy, and rightful freedom also in matters
of religion."[27] 2106

1908 Second, the common good requires the *social well-being* and *development* of the group itself. Development is the epitome of all social duties. Certainly, it is the proper
function of authority to arbitrate, 2441
in the name of the common good, between various particular interests; but it should make accessible to each what is needed to lead a truly human life: food, clothing, health, work, education and culture, suitable information, the right to establish a family, and so on.[28]

1909 Finally, the common good 2304
requires *peace*, that is, the stability and security of a just order. It presupposes that authority should ensure by morally acceptable means the *security* of society and its members. It
is the basis of the right to legitimate 2310
personal and collective defence.

1910 Each human community possesses a common good which permits it to be recognized as such; it is in the *political community* that its most complete realization is
found. It is the role of the state to 2244
defend and promote the common good of civil society, its citizens, and intermediate bodies.

1911 Human interdependence is increasing and gradually spreading throughout the world. The unity of the human family, embracing people who enjoy equal natural digni- 2438
ty, implies a *universal common good.* This good calls for an organization of the community of nations able to "provide for the different needs of men; this will involve the sphere of

[24] *CA* 44. — [25] *Ep. Barnabae*, 4, 10: PG 2, 734. — [26] *GS* 26 § 1; cf. *GS* 74 § 1. — [27] *GS* 26 § 2. — [28] Cf. *GS* 26 § 2.

social life to which belong questions of food, hygiene, education,…and certain situations arising here and there, as for example…alleviating the miseries of refugees dispersed throughout the world, and assisting migrants and their families."[29]

1912 The common good is always oriented towards the progress of persons: "The order of things must be subordinate to the order of persons,
1881 and not the other way around."[30]
This order is founded on truth, built up in justice, and animated by love.

III. Responsibility and Participation

1913 "Participation" is the voluntary and generous engagement of a person in social interchange. It is necessary that all participate, each according to his position and role, in promoting the common good. This obligation is inherent in the dignity of the human person.

1914 Participation is achieved first of all by taking charge of the areas for which one assumes *personal responsibility*: by the care taken for
1734 the education of his family, by conscientious work, and so forth, man participates in the good of others and of society.[31]

2239 **1915** As far as possible citizens should take an active part in *public life*. The manner of this participation may vary from one country or culture to another. "One must pay tribute to those nations whose systems permit the largest possible number of the citizens to take part in public life in a climate of genuine freedom."[32]

1916 As with any ethical obligation, the participation of all in realizing the common good calls for a continually renewed *conversion* of
the social partners. Fraud and other 1888
subterfuges, by which some people evade the constraints of the law and the prescriptions of societal obligation, must be firmly condemned because they are incompatible with the
requirements of justice. Much care 2409
should be taken to promote institutions that improve the conditions of human life.[33]

1917 It is incumbent on those who exercise authority to strengthen the values that inspire the confidence of the members of the group and encourage them to put themselves at the service of others. Participation begins with education and culture. "One is entitled to think that the future of humanity is in the hands of those who are capable of providing the generations to come with reasons for life and optimism."[34] 1818

In Brief

1918 *"There is no authority except from God, and those authorities that exist have been instituted by God"* (Rom *13:1).*

1919 *Every human community needs an authority in order to endure and develop.*

1920 *"The political community and public authority are based on human nature and therefore…belong to an order established by God"* (GS *74 § 3).*

[29] *GS* 84 § 2. — [30] *GS* 26 § 3. — [31] Cf. *CA* 43. — [32] *GS* 31 § 3. — [33] Cf. *GS* 30 § 1. — [34] *GS* 31 § 3.

1921 *Authority is exercised legitimately if it is committed to the common good of society. To attain this it must employ morally acceptable means.*

1922 *The diversity of political regimes is legitimate, provided they contribute to the good of the community.*

1923 *Political authority must be exercised within the limits of the moral order and must guarantee the conditions for the exercise of freedom.*

1924 *The common good comprises "the sum total of social conditions which allow people, either as groups or as individuals, to reach their fulfillment more fully and more easily"* (GS *26 § 1).*

1925 *The common good consists of three essential elements: respect for and promotion of the fundamental rights of the person; prosperity, or the development of the spiritual and temporal goods of society; the peace and security of the group and of its members.*

1926 *The dignity of the human person requires the pursuit of the common good. Everyone should be concerned to create and support institutions that improve the conditions of human life.*

1927 *It is the role of the state to defend and promote the common good of civil society. The common good of the whole human family calls for an organization of society on the international level.*

Article 3:
SOCIAL JUSTICE

1928 Society ensures social justice when it provides the conditions that allow associations or individuals to obtain what is their due, according to
2832 their nature and their vocation. Social justice is linked to the common good and the exercise of authority.

I. Respect for the Human Person

1881 **1929** Social justice can be obtained only in respecting the transcendent dignity of man. The person represents the ultimate end of society, which is ordered to him:

> What is at stake is the dignity of the human person, whose defense and promotion have been entrusted to us by the Creator, and to whom the men and women at every moment of history are strictly and responsibly in debt.[35]

1930 Respect for the human person entails respect for the rights that flow from his dignity as a creature. These rights are prior to society and
must be recognized by it. They are 1700
the basis of the moral legitimacy of
every authority: by flouting them, 1902
or refusing to recognize them in its positive legislation, a society undermines its own moral legitimacy.[36] If it does not respect them, authority can rely only on force or violence to obtain obedience from its subjects. It is the Church's role to remind men of good will of these rights and to distinguish them from unwarranted or false claims.

1931 Respect for the human person proceeds by way of respect for
the principle that "everyone should 2212

[35] John Paul II, *SRS* 47. — [36] Cf. John XXIII, *PT* 65.

look upon his neighbor (without any exception) as 'another self,' above all bearing in mind his life and the means necessary for living it with dignity."[37] No legislation could by itself do away with the fears, prejudices, and attitudes of pride and selfishness which obstruct the establishment of truly fraternal
1825 societies. Such behavior will cease only through the charity that finds in every man a "neighbor," a brother.

1932 The duty of making oneself a neighbor to others and actively serving them becomes even more urgent when it involves the disadvantaged, in whatever area this may be. "As you did it to one of the least of these my
2449 brethren, you did it to me."[38]

1933 This same duty extends to those who think or act differently from us. The teaching of Christ goes so far as to require the forgiveness of offenses. He extends the commandment of love, which is that of the New Law, to all enemies.[39] Liberation in the spirit of the Gospel is in
2303 compatible with hatred of one's enemy as a person, but not with hatred of the evil that he does as an enemy.

II. Equality and Differences among Men

1934 Created in the image of the one God and equally endowed with rational souls, all men have the same nature and the same origin. Redeemed by the sacrifice of Christ, all are called to participate in the same
225 divine beatitude: all therefore enjoy an equal dignity.

1935 The equality of men rests essentially on their dignity as persons and the rights that flow from it: 357

> Every form of social or cultural discrimination in fundamental personal rights on the grounds of sex, race, color, social conditions, language, or religion must be curbed and eradicated as incompatible with God's design.[40]

1936 On coming into the world, 1879
man is not equipped with everything he needs for developing his bodily and spiritual life. He needs others. Differences appear tied to age, physical abilities, intellectual or moral aptitudes, the benefits derived from social commerce, and the distribution of wealth.[41] The "talents" are not distributed equally.[42]

1937 These differences belong 340
to God's plan, who wills that each receive what he needs from others, and that those endowed with particular "talents" share the benefits 791
with those who need them. These differences encourage and often 1202
oblige persons to practice generosity, kindness, and sharing of goods; they foster the mutual enrichment of cultures:

> I distribute the virtues quite diversely; I do not give all of them to each person, but some to one, some to others.... I shall give principally charity to one; justice to another; humility to this one, a living faith to that one.... And so I have given many gifts and graces, both spiritual and temporal, with such diversity that I have not given everything to one single person, so that you may be constrained to practice charity towards one another.... I have willed that one should need another

[37] *GS* 27 § 1. — [38] *Mt* 25:40. — [39] Cf. *Mt* 5:43–44. — [40] *GS* 29 § 2. — [41] Cf. *GS* 29 § 2. — [42] Cf. *Mt* 25:14–30; *Lk* 19:11–27.

and that all should be my ministers in distributing the graces and gifts they have received from me.[43]

2437 **1938** There exist also *sinful inequalities* that affect millions of men and women. These are in open contradiction of the Gospel:

> Their equal dignity as persons demands that we strive for fairer and
> 2317 more humane conditions. Excessive economic and social disparity between individuals and peoples of the one human race is a source of scandal and militates against social justice, equity, human dignity, as well as social and international peace.[44]

III. Human Solidarity

2213 **1939** The principle of solidarity, also articulated in terms of "friendship" or "social charity," is a direct demand of human and Christian brotherhood.[45]

> An error, "today abundantly widespread, is disregard for the law of human solidarity and charity, dictated and imposed both by our common
> 360 origin and by the equality in rational nature of all men, whatever nation they belong to. This law is sealed by the sacrifice of redemption offered by Jesus Christ on the altar of the Cross to his heavenly Father, on behalf of sinful humanity."[46]

2402 **1940** Solidarity is manifested in the first place by the distribution of goods and remuneration for work. It also presupposes the effort for a more just social order where tensions are better able to be reduced and conflicts more readily settled by negotiation.

1941 Socio-economic problems 2317
can be resolved only with the help of all the forms of solidarity: solidarity of the poor among themselves, between rich and poor, of workers among themselves, between employers and employees in a business, solidarity among nations and peoples. International solidarity is a requirement of the moral order; world peace depends in part upon this.

1942 The virtue of solidarity goes beyond material goods. In spreading the spiritual goods of the faith, the Church has promoted, and often opened new paths for, the develop- 1887
ment of temporal goods as well. And so throughout the centuries has the Lord's saying been verified: "Seek first his kingdom and his righteousness, and all these things shall be yours as well":[47] 2632

> For two thousand years this sentiment has lived and endured in the soul of the Church, impelling souls then and now to the heroic charity of monastic farmers, liberators of slaves, healers of the sick, and messengers of faith, civilization, and science to all generations and all peoples for the sake of creating the social conditions capable of offering to everyone possible a life worthy of man and of a Christian.[48]

In Brief

1943 *Society ensures social justice by providing the conditions that allow associations and individuals to obtain their due.*

[43] St. Catherine of Siena, Dial. I, 7. — [44] *GS* 29 § 3. — [45] Cf. John Paul II, *SRS* 38–40; CA 10. — [46] Pius XII, *Summi pontificatus*, October 20, 1939; AAS 31 (1939) 423 ff. — [47] *Mt* 6:33. — [48] Pius XII, Discourse, June 1, 1941.

1944 *Respect for the human person considers the other "another self." It presupposes respect for the fundamental rights that flow from the dignity intrinsic of the person.*

1945 *The equality of men concerns their dignity as persons and the rights that flow from it.*

1946 *The differences among persons belong to God's plan, who wills that we should need one another. These differences should encourage charity.*

1947 *The equal dignity of human persons requires the effort to reduce excessive social and economic inequalities. It gives urgency to the elimination of sinful inequalities.*

1948 *Solidarity is an eminently Christian virtue. It practices the sharing of spiritual goods even more than material ones.*

Chapter Three:

GOD'S SALVATION: LAW AND GRACE

1949 Called to beatitude but wounded by sin, man stands in need of salvation from God. Divine help comes to him in Christ through the law that guides him and the grace that sustains him:

> Work out your own salvation with fear and trembling; for God is at work in you, both to will and to work for his good pleasure.[1]

Article 3:
THE MORAL LAW

1950 The moral law is the work of divine Wisdom. Its biblical meaning can be defined as fatherly instruction, God's pedagogy. It prescribes
53 for man the ways, the rules of conduct that lead to the promised beat-
1719 itude; it proscribes the ways of evil which turn him away from God and his love. It is at once firm in its precepts and, in its promises, worthy of love.

1951 Law is a rule of conduct enacted by competent authority for the sake of the common good. The moral law presupposes the rational order, established among creatures for their good and to serve their final end, by the power, wisdom, and goodness of the Creator. All law finds its first and ultimate truth in the eternal law. Law is declared
295 and established by reason as a participation in the providence of the
306 living God, Creator and Redeemer of all. "Such an ordinance of reason is what one calls law."[2]

> Alone among all animate beings, man can boast of having been counted worthy to receive a law from God: as an animal endowed with reason, capable of understanding and discernment, he is to govern his conduct by using his freedom and
> reason, in obedience to the One who 301
> has entrusted everything to him.[3]

1952 There are different expressions of the moral law, all of them interrelated: eternal law—the source, in God, of all law; natural law; revealed law, comprising the Old Law and the New Law, or Law of the Gospel; finally, civil and ecclesiastical laws.

1953 The moral law finds its full- 578
ness and its unity in Christ. Jesus Christ is in person the way of perfection. He is the end of the law, for only he teaches and bestows the justice of God: "For Christ is the end of the law, that every one who has faith may be justified."[4]

[1] *Phil* 2:12–13. — [2] Leo XIII, *Libertas præstantissimum*: AAS 20 (1887/88), 597; cf. St. Thomas Aquinas, *STh* I–II, 90, 1. — [3] Cf. Tertullian, *Adv. Marc*, 2, 4: PL 2, 288–289. — [4] *Rom* 10:4.

I. The Natural Moral Law

1954 Man participates in the wisdom and goodness of the Creator who gives him mastery over his acts and the ability to govern himself with a view to the true and the good. The natural law expresses the
307 original moral sense which enables man to discern by reason the good
1776 and the evil, the truth and the lie:

> The natural law is written and engraved in the soul of each and every man, because it is human reason ordaining him to do good and forbidding him to sin... But this command of human reason would not have the force of law if it were not the voice and interpreter of a higher reason to which our spirit and our freedom must be submitted.[5]

1787 **1955** The "divine and natural" law[6] shows man the way to follow so as to practice the good and attain his end. The natural law states the first and essential precepts which govern the moral life. It hinges upon the
396 desire for God and submission to him, who is the source and judge of all that is good, as well as upon the sense that the other is one's equal. Its principal precepts are expressed in the Decalogue. This law is called
2070 "natural," not in reference to the nature of irrational beings, but because reason which decrees it properly belongs to human nature:

> Where then are these rules written, if not in the book of that light we call the truth? In it is written every just law; from it the law passes into the heart of the man who does justice, not that it migrates into it, but that it places its imprint on it, like a seal on a ring that passes onto wax, without leaving the ring.[7]
> The natural law is nothing other than the light of understanding placed in us by God; through it we know what we must do and what we must avoid. God has given this light or law at the creation.[8]

1956 The natural law, present in the heart of each man and established by reason, is universal in its precepts and its authority extends to all men.
It expresses the dignity of the person 2261
and determines the basis for his fundamental rights and duties:

> For there is a true law: right reason. It is in conformity with nature, is diffused among all men, and is immutable and eternal; its orders summon to duty; its prohibitions turn away from offense.... To replace it with a contrary law is a sacrilege; failure to apply even one of its provisions is forbidden; no one can abrogate it entirely.[9]

1957 Application of the natural law varies greatly; it can demand reflection that takes account of various conditions of life according to places, times, and circumstances. Nevertheless, in the diversity of cultures, the natural law remains as a rule that binds men among themselves and imposes on them, beyond the inevitable differences, common principles.

1958 The natural law is *immutable* 2072
and permanent throughout the variations of history;[10] it subsists under the flux of ideas and customs and supports their progress. The rules that express it remain substantially valid. Even when it is rejected in its very principles, it

[5] Leo XIII, *Libertas præstantissimum*, 597. — [6] *GS* 89 § 1. — [7] St. Augustine, *De Trin.* 14, 15, 21: PL 42, 1052. — [8] St. Thomas Aquinas, Dec. *præc.* I. — [9] Cicero, *Rep.* III, 22, 33. — [10] Cf. *GS* 10.

cannot be destroyed or removed from the heart of man. It always rises again in the life of individuals and societies:

> Theft is surely punished by your law, O Lord, and by the law that is written in the human heart, the law that iniquity itself does not efface.[11]

1959 The natural law, the Creator's very good work, provides the solid foundation on which man can build the structure of moral rules to guide his choices. It also provides the indispensable moral foundation
1879 for building the human community. Finally, it provides the necessary basis for the civil law with which it is connected, whether by a reflection that draws conclusions from its principles, or by additions of a positive and juridical nature.

1960 The precepts of natural law are not perceived by everyone clearly and immediately. In the present situation sinful man needs grace and
2071 revelation so moral and religious truths may be known "by everyone
37 with facility, with firm certainty and with no admixture of error."[12] The natural law provides revealed law and grace with a foundation prepared by God and in accordance with the work of the Spirit.

II. The Old Law

62 **1961** God, our Creator and Redeemer, chose Israel for himself to be his people and revealed his Law to them, thus preparing for the coming of Christ. The Law of Moses expresses many truths naturally accessible to reason. These are stated and authenticated within the covenant of salvation.

1962 The Old Law is the first stage of revealed Law. Its moral prescriptions are summed up in the Ten Commandments. The precepts of
the Decalogue lay the foundations 2058
for the vocation of man fashioned in the image of God; they prohibit what is contrary to the love of God and neighbor and prescribe what is essential to it. The Decalogue is a light offered to the conscience of every man to make God's call and ways known to him and to protect him against evil:

> God wrote on the tables of the Law what men did not read in their hearts.[13]

1963 According to Christian tradition, the Law is holy, spiritual, and good,[14] yet still imperfect. Like a tutor[15] it shows what must be done, but
does not of itself give the strength, 1610
the grace of the Spirit, to fulfill it. Because of sin, which it cannot remove, it remains a law of bondage. According to St. Paul, its special function is to denounce and *disclose*
sin, which constitutes a "law of con- 2542
cupiscence" in the human heart.[16]
However, the Law remains the first 2515
stage on the way to the kingdom. It prepares and disposes the chosen people and each Christian for conversion and faith in the Savior God. It provides a teaching which endures for ever, like the Word of God.

1964 The Old Law is a *prepara-* 122
tion for the Gospel. "The Law is a pedagogy and a prophecy of things to come."[17] It prophesies and presages the work of liberation from sin which will be fulfilled in Christ: it

[11] St. Augustine, *Conf.* 2, 4, 9: PL 32, 678. — [12] Pius XII, *Humani generis*: DS 3876; cf. *Dei Filius* 2: DS 3005. — [13] St. Augustine, *En. in Ps.* 57, 1: PL 36, 673. — [14] Cf. *Rom* 7:12, 14, 16. — [15] Cf. *Gal* 3:24. — [16] Cf. *Rom* 7. — [17] St. Irenæus, *Adv. haeres.* 4, 15, 1: PG 7/1, 1012.

provides the New Testament with images, "types," and symbols for expressing the life according to the Spirit. Finally, the Law is completed by the teaching of the sapiential books and the prophets which set its course toward the New Covenant and the Kingdom of heaven.

> There were...under the regimen of the Old Covenant, people who possessed the charity and grace of the Holy Spirit and longed above all for the spiritual and eternal promises by which they were associated with the New Law. Conversely, there exist carnal men under the New Covenant,
> 1828 still distanced from the perfection of the New Law: the fear of punishment and certain temporal promises have been necessary, even under the New Covenant, to incite them to virtuous works. In any case, even though the Old Law prescribed charity, it did not give the Holy Spirit, through whom "God's charity has been poured into our hearts."[18]

III. The New Law or the Law of the Gospel

459 **1965** The New Law or the Law of the Gospel is the perfection here on earth of the divine law, natural and revealed. It is the work of Christ and is expressed particularly in the Sermon on the Mount. It is also the
581 work of the Holy Spirit and through him it becomes the interior law of charity: "I will establish a New Covenant with the house of Israel.... I will put my laws into their minds, and write them on their hearts, and
715 I will be their God, and they shall be my people."[19]

1966 The New Law is the *grace of* 1999
the Holy Spirit given to the faithful through faith in Christ. It works through charity; it uses the Sermon on the Mount to teach us what must be done and makes use of the sacraments to give us the grace to do it:

> If anyone should meditate with devotion and perspicacity on the sermon our Lord gave on the mount, as we read in the Gospel of Saint Matthew, he will doubtless find there...the perfect way of the Christian life....This sermon contains...all the precepts needed to shape one's life.[20]

1967 The Law of the Gospel "fulfills," refines, surpasses, and leads the Old Law to its perfection.[21] In the Beatitudes, the New Law *fulfills the*
divine promises by elevating and ori- 577
enting them toward the "kingdom of heaven." It is addressed to those open to accepting this new hope with faith—the poor, the humble, the afflicted, the pure of heart, those persecuted on account of Christ—and so marks out the surprising ways of the Kingdom.

1968 The Law of the Gospel *fulfills the commandments* of the Law. The Lord's Sermon on the Mount, far from abolishing or devaluing the moral prescriptions of the Old Law, releases their hidden potential and
has new demands arise from them: 129
it reveals their entire divine and human truth. It does not add new external precepts, but proceeds to reform the heart, the root of human acts, where man chooses between
the pure and the impure,[22] where 582
faith, hope, and charity are formed and with them the other virtues.

[18] St. Thomas Aquinas, *STh* I–II, 107, 1 ad 2; cf. *Rom* 5:5. — [19] *Heb* 8:8, 10; cf. *Jer* 31:31–34. — [20] St. Augustine, *De serm. Dom.* 1, 1: PL 34, 1229–1230. — [21] Cf. *Mt* 5:17–19. — [22] Cf. *Mt* 15:18–19.

The Gospel thus brings the Law to its fullness through imitation of the perfection of the heavenly Father, through forgiveness of enemies and prayer for persecutors, in emulation of the divine generosity.[23]

1434 **1969** The New Law *practices the acts of religion*: almsgiving, prayer and fasting, directing them to the "Father who sees in secret," in contrast with the desire to "be seen by men."[24] Its prayer is the Our Father.[25]

1970 The Law of the Gospel requires us to make the decisive choice between "the two ways" and to put into practice the words of the Lord.[26]
1696 It is summed up in the *Golden Rule*, "Whatever you wish that men would
1789 do to you, do so to them; this is the law and the prophets."[27]

1823 The entire Law of the Gospel is contained in the "*new commandment*" of Jesus, to love one another as he has loved us.[28]

1971 To the Lord's Sermon on the Mount it is fitting to add the *moral catechesis of the apostolic* teachings, such as *Romans* 12–15, *1 Corinthians* 12–13, *Colossians* 3–4, *Ephesians* 4–5, etc. This doctrine hands on the Lord's teaching with the authority of the apostles, particularly in the presentation of the virtues that flow from faith in Christ and are animated by charity, the principal gift of the Holy Spirit. "Let charity be genuine.... Love one another with brotherly affection.... Rejoice in your hope, be patient in tribulation, be constant in prayer. Contribute to the needs of the saints, practice hospitality."[29] This catechesis also teach- 1789
es us to deal with cases of conscience in the light of our relationship to Christ and to the Church.[30]

1972 The New Law is called a *law* 782
of love because it makes us act out of the love infused by the Holy Spirit, rather than from fear; a *law of grace*, because it confers the strength of grace to act, by means of faith and the sacraments; a *law of freedom*, because it sets us free from the ritual and juridical observances of the Old Law, inclines us to act spontaneously by the prompting of charity and, finally, lets us pass from the condition of a servant who "does not 1828
know what his master is doing" to that of a friend of Christ—"For all that I have heard from my Father I have made known to you"—or even to the status of son and heir.[31]

1973 Besides its precepts, the New 2053
Law also includes the *evangelical counsels*. The traditional distinction between God's commandments and the evangelical counsels is drawn in relation to charity, the perfection of
Christian life. The precepts are in- 915
tended to remove whatever is incompatible with charity. The aim of the counsels is to remove whatever might hinder the development of charity, even if it is not contrary to it.[32]

1974 The evangelical counsels manifest the living fullness of charity, which is never satisfied with not giving more. They attest its vitality and call forth our spiritual readiness. The perfection of the New Law
consists essentially in the precepts 2013
of love of God and neighbor. The

[23] Cf. *Mt* 5:44, 48. — [24] Cf. *Mt* 6:1–6; 16–18. — [25] Cf. *Mt* 6:9–13; *Lk* 11:2–4. — [26] Cf. *Mt* 7:13–14, 21–27. — [27] *Mt* 7:12; cf. *Lk* 6:31. — [28] Cf. *Jn* 15:12; 13:34. — [29] *Rom* 12:9–13. — [30] Cf. *Rom* 14; *1 Cor* 5–10. — [31] *Jn* 15:15; cf. *Jas* 1:25; 2:12; *Gal* 4:1–7. 21–31; *Rom* 8:15. — [32] Cf. St. Thomas Aquinas, *STh* II–II, 184, 3.

counsels point out the more direct ways, the readier means, and are to be practiced in keeping with the vocation of each:

> [God] does not want each person to keep all the counsels, but only those appropriate to the diversity of persons, times, opportunities, and strengths, as charity requires; for it is charity, as queen of all virtues, all commandments, all counsels, and, in short, of all laws and all Christian actions, that gives to all of them their rank, order, time, and value.[33]

In Brief

1975 *According to Scripture the Law is a fatherly instruction by God which prescribes for man the ways that lead to the promised beatitude, and proscribes the ways of evil.*

1976 *"Law is an ordinance of reason for the common good, promulgated by the one who is in charge of the community" (St. Thomas Aquinas,* STh *I–II, 90, 4).*

1977 *Christ is the end of the law (cf.* Rom *10:4); only he teaches and bestows the justice of God.*

1978 *The natural law is a participation in God's wisdom and goodness by man formed in the image of his Creator. It expresses the dignity of the human person and forms the basis of his fundamental rights and duties.*

1979 *The natural law is immutable, permanent throughout history. The rules that express it remain substantially valid. It is a necessary foundation for the erection of moral rules and civil law.*

1980 *The Old Law is the first stage of revealed law. Its moral prescriptions are summed up in the Ten Commandments.*

1981 *The Law of Moses contains many truths naturally accessible to reason. God has revealed them because men did not read them in their hearts.*

1982 *The Old Law is a preparation for the Gospel.*

1983 *The New Law is the grace of the Holy Spirit received by faith in Christ, operating through charity. It finds expression above all in the Lord's Sermon on the Mount and uses the sacraments to communicate grace to us.*

1984 *The Law of the Gospel fulfills and surpasses the Old Law and brings it to perfection: its promises, through the Beatitudes of the Kingdom of heaven; its commandments, by reforming the heart, the root of human acts.*

1985 *The New Law is a law of love, a law of grace, a law of freedom.*

1986 *Besides its precepts the New Law includes the evangelical counsels. "The Church's holiness is fostered in a special way by the manifold counsels which the Lord proposes to his disciples in the Gospel" (*LG *42 §2).*

[33] St. Francis de Sales, *Love of God* 8, 6.

Article 2: GRACE AND JUSTIFICATION

I. Justification

1987 The grace of the Holy Spirit has the power to justify us, that is, to cleanse us from our sins and to communicate to us "the righteousness of
734 God through faith in Jesus Christ" and through Baptism:[34]

> But if we have died with Christ, we believe that we shall also live with him. For we know that Christ being raised from the dead will never die again; death no longer has dominion over him. The death he died he died to sin, once for all, but the life he lives he lives to God. So you also must consider yourselves as dead to sin and alive to God in Christ Jesus.[35]

1988 Through the power of the Holy Spirit we take part in Christ's Passion by dying to sin, and in his Resurrection by being born to a new
654 life; we are members of his Body which is the Church, branches grafted onto the vine which is himself:[36]

> [God] gave himself to us through his Spirit. By the participation of the
> 460 Spirit, we become communicants in the divine nature.... For this reason, those in whom the Spirit dwells are divinized.[37]

1989 The first work of the grace of the Holy Spirit is *conversion*, effecting justification in accordance with Jesus' proclamation at the beginning of the Gospel: "Repent, for
1427 the kingdom of heaven is at hand."[38] Moved by grace, man turns toward God and away from sin, thus accepting forgiveness and righteousness from on high. "Justification is not only the remission of sins, but also the sanctification and renewal of the interior man."[39]

1990 Justification *detaches man from sin* which contradicts the love of God, and purifies his heart of sin. Justification follows upon God's merciful initiative of offering for- 1446
giveness. It reconciles man with God. It frees from the enslavement 1733
to sin, and it heals.

1991 Justification is at the same time the *acceptance of God's righteousness* through faith in Jesus Christ. Righteousness (or "justice") here means the rectitude of divine love. With justification, faith, hope, and charity are poured into our 1812
hearts, and obedience to the divine will is granted us.

1992 Justification has been *mer-* 617
ited for us by the Passion of Christ who offered himself on the cross as a living victim, holy and pleasing to God, and whose blood has become the instrument of atonement for the sins of all men. Justification is conferred in Baptism, the sacrament of faith. It conforms us to the righ- 1266
teousness of God, who makes us inwardly just by the power of his mercy. Its purpose is the glory of God and of Christ, and the gift of eternal 294
life:[40]

> But now the righteousness of God has been manifested apart from law, although the law and the prophets

[34] *Rom* 3:22; cf. 6:3–4. — [35] Rom 6:8–11. — [36] Cf. *1 Cor* 12; *Jn* 15:1–4. — [37] St. Athanasius, *Ep. Serap.* 1, 24: PG 26, 585 and 588. — [38] *Mt* 4:17. — [39] Council of Trent (1547): DS 1528. — [40] Cf. Council of Trent (1547): DS 1529.

> bear witness to it, the righteousness of God through faith in Jesus Christ for all who believe. For there is no distinction: since all have sinned and fall short of the glory of God, they are justified by his grace as a gift, through the redemption which is in Christ Jesus, whom God put forward as an expiation by his blood, to be received by faith. This was to show God's righteousness, because in his divine forbearance he had passed over former sins; it was to prove at the present time that he himself is righteous and that he justifies him who has faith in Jesus.[41]

2008 **1993** Justification establishes *co-operation between God's grace and man's freedom.* On man's part it is expressed by the assent of faith to the Word of God, which invites him to conversion, and in the cooperation of charity with the prompting of the Holy Spirit who precedes and preserves his assent:

2068 When God touches man's heart through the illumination of the Holy Spirit, man himself is not inactive while receiving that inspiration, since he could reject it; and yet, without God's grace, he cannot by his own free will move himself toward justice in God's sight.[42]

1994 Justification is the *most excellent work of God's love* made manifest in Christ Jesus and granted by the Holy Spirit. It is the opinion of St. Augustine that "the justification of the wicked is a greater work than the
312 creation of heaven and earth," because "heaven and earth will pass away but the salvation and justification of the elect...will not pass away."[43] He holds also that the justification of sinners surpasses the creation of the angels 412
in justice, in that it bears witness to a greater mercy.

1995 The Holy Spirit is the mas- 741
ter of the interior life. By giving birth to the "inner man,"[44] justification entails the *sanctification* of his whole being:

> Just as you once yielded your members to impurity and to greater and greater iniquity, so now yield your members to righteousness for sanctification.... But now that you have been set free from sin and have become slaves of God, the return you get is sanctification and its end, eternal life.[45]

II. Grace

1996 Our justification comes from the grace of God. Grace is *favor,* the *free and undeserved help* that God gives us to respond to his call to become children of God, adoptive 153
sons, partakers of the divine nature and of eternal life.[46]

1997 Grace is a *participation in* 375
the life of God. It introduces us into the intimacy of Trinitarian life: by Baptism the Christian participates 260
in the grace of Christ, the Head of his Body. As an "adopted son" he can henceforth call God "Father," in union with the only Son. He receives the life of the Spirit who breathes charity into him and who forms the Church.

1998 This vocation to eternal life 1719
is *supernatural.* It depends entirely on God's gratuitous initiative, for he alone can reveal and give himself. It surpasses the power of human intel-

[41] *Rom* 3:21–26. — [42] Council of Trent (1547): DS 1525. — [43] St. Augustine, *In Jo. ev.* 72, 3: PL 35, 1823. — [44] Cf. *Rom* 7:22; *Eph* 3:16. — [45] *Rom* 6:19, 22. — [46] Cf. *Jn* 1:12–18; 17:3; *Rom* 8:14–17; *2 Pet* 1:3–4.

lect and will, as that of every other creature.[47]

1999 The grace of Christ is the gratuitous gift that God makes to us of his own life, infused by the Holy Spirit into our soul to heal it of sin and to sanctify it. It is the sancti
1966 fying or deifying grace received in Baptism. It is in us the source of the work of sanctification:[48]

> Therefore if any one is in Christ, he is a new creation; the old has passed away, behold, the new has come. All this is from God, who through Christ reconciled us to himself.[49]

2000 Sanctifying grace is an habitual gift, a stable and supernatural disposition that perfects the soul itself to enable it to live with God, to act by his love. *Habitual grace*, the permanent disposition to live and act in keeping with God's call, is distinguished from *actual graces* which refer to God's interventions, whether at the beginning of conversion or in the course of the work of sanctification.

490 **2001** The *preparation of man* for the reception of grace is already a work of grace. This latter is needed to arouse and sustain our collaboration in justification through faith, and in sanctification through charity. God brings to completion in us what he has begun, "since he who completes his work by cooperating with our will began by working so that we might will it:"[50]

> Indeed we also work, but we are only collaborating with God who works, for his mercy has gone before us. It has gone before us so that we may be healed, and follows us so that once healed, we may be given life; it goes before us so that we may be called, and follows us so that we may be glorified; it goes before us so that we may live devoutly, and follows us so that we may always live with God: for without him we can do nothing.[51]

2002 God's free initiative demands *man's free response*, for God has created man in his image by conferring on him, along with freedom,
the power to know him and love 1742
him. The soul only enters freely into the communion of love. God immediately touches and directly moves the heart of man. He has placed in man a longing for truth and goodness that only he can satisfy. The promises of "eternal life" respond, beyond all hope, to this desire:

> If at the end of your very good works..., you rested on the seventh day, it was to foretell by the voice of your book that at the end of our works, which are indeed "very good" since you have given them to us, we shall also rest in you on the sabbath
> of eternal life.[52] 2550

2003 Grace is first and foremost 1108
the gift of the Spirit who justifies and sanctifies us. But grace also includes the gifts that the Spirit grants us to associate us with his work, to enable us to collaborate in the salvation of others and in the growth of the Body of Christ, the Church.
There are *sacramental graces*, gifts 1127
proper to the different sacraments. There are furthermore *special graces*, also called *charisms* after the Greek term used by St. Paul and meaning

[47] Cf. *1 Cor* 2:7–9. — [48] Cf. *Jn* 4:14; 7:38–39. — [49] *2 Cor* 5:17–18. — [50] St. Augustine, *De gratia et libero arbitrio*, 17: PL 44, 901. — [51] St. Augustine, *De natura et gratia*, 31: PL 44, 264. — [52] St. Augustine, *Conf.* 13, 36, 51: PL 32, 868; cf. *Gen* 1:31.

"favor," "gratuitous gift," "benefit."[53] Whatever their character—sometimes it is extraordinary, such as the gift of miracles or of tongues—charisms are oriented toward sancti-
799–801 fying grace and are intended for the common good of the Church. They are at the service of charity which builds up the Church.[54]

2004 Among the special graces ought to be mentioned the *graces of state* that accompany the exercise of the responsibilities of the Christian life and of the ministries within the Church:

> Having gifts that differ according to the grace given to us, let us use them: if prophecy, in proportion to our faith; if service, in our serving; he who teaches, in his teaching; he who exhorts, in his exhortation; he who contributes, in liberality; he who gives aid, with zeal; he who does acts of mercy, with cheerfulness.[55]

2005 Since it belongs to the supernatural order, grace *escapes our experience* and cannot be known except by faith. We cannot therefore rely on our feelings or our works to conclude that we are justified and saved.[56] However, according to the Lord's words—"Thus you will know them by their fruits"[57]—reflection on God's blessings in our life and in the lives of the saints offers us a guarantee that grace is at work in us and spurs us on to an ever greater faith and an attitude of trustful poverty.

> A pleasing illustration of this attitude is found in the reply of St. Joan of Arc to a question posed as a trap by her ecclesiastical judges: "Asked if she knew that she was in God's grace, she replied: 'If I am not, may it please God to put me in it; if I am, may it please God to keep me there.'"[58]

III. Merit

> You are glorified in the assembly of your Holy Ones, for in crowning their merits you are crowning your own gifts.[59]

2006 The term "merit" refers in 1723
general to the *recompense owed* by a community or a society for the action of one of its members, experienced either as beneficial or harmful, deserving reward or punishment.
Merit is relative to the virtue of jus- 1807
tice, in conformity with the principle of equality which governs it.

2007 With regard to God, there is no strict right to any merit on the
part of man. Between God and us 42
there is an immeasurable inequality, for we have received everything from him, our Creator.

2008 The merit of man before God in the Christian life arises from the fact that *God has freely chosen to associate man with the work of his*
grace. The fatherly action of God is 306
first on his own initiative, and then
follows man's free acting through 155
his collaboration, so that the merit
of good works is to be attributed in 970
the first place to the grace of God, then to the faithful. Man's merit, moreover, itself is due to God, for his good actions proceed in Christ, from the predispositions and assistance given by the Holy Spirit.

[53] Cf. *LG* 12. — [54] Cf. 1 *Cor* 12. — [55] *Rom* 12:6–8. — [56] Cf. Council of Trent (1547): DS 1533–1534. — [57] *Mt* 7:20. — [58] Acts of the trial of St. Joan of Arc. — [59] *Roman Missal*, Prefatio I de Sanctis; *Qui in Sanctorum concilio celebraris, et eorum coronando merita tua dona coronas*, citing the "Doctor of grace," St. Augustine, *En. in Ps.* 102, 7: PL 37, 1321–1322.

2009 Filial adoption, in making us partakers by grace in the divine nature, can bestow *true merit* on us as a result of God's gratuitous justice. This is our right by grace, the full right of love, making us "co-heirs" with Christ and worthy of obtaining "the promised inheritance of eternal life."[60] The merits of our good works are gifts of the divine goodness.[61] "Grace has gone before
604 us; now we are given what is due.... Our merits are God's gifts."[62]

1998 **2010** Since the initiative belongs to God in the order of grace, *no one can merit the initial grace* of forgiveness and justification, at the beginning of conversion. Moved by the Holy Spirit and by charity, *we can then merit* for ourselves and for others the graces needed for our sanctification, for the increase of grace and charity, and for the attainment of eternal life. Even temporal goods like health and friendship can be merited in accordance with God's wisdom. These graces and goods are the object of Christian prayer. Prayer attends to the grace we need for meritorious actions.

492 **2011** *The charity of Christ is the source in us of all our merits* before God. Grace, by uniting us to Christ in active love, ensures the supernatural quality of our acts and consequently their merit before God and before men. The saints have always had a lively awareness that their merits were pure grace.

> After earth's exile, I hope to go and enjoy you in the fatherland, but I do not want to lay up merits for heaven. I want to work for your love alone.... In the evening of this life, I shall appear before you with empty hands, for I do not ask you, Lord, to
> count my works. All our justice is 1460
> blemished in your eyes. I wish, then, to be clothed in your own justice and to receive from your love the eternal possession of yourself.[63]

IV. Christian Holiness

2012 "We know that in everything God works for good with those who love him... For those whom he foreknew he also predestined to be
conformed to the image of his Son, 459
in order that he might be the first-born among many brethren. And those whom he predestined he also called; and those whom he called he also justified; and those whom he justified he also glorified."[64]

2013 "All Christians in any state or walk of life are called to the fullness of Christian life and to the per- 915, 2545
fection of charity."[65] All are called to
holiness: "Be perfect, as your heav- 825
enly Father is perfect."[66]

> In order to reach this perfection the faithful should use the strength dealt out to them by Christ's gift, so that...doing the will of the Father in everything, they may wholeheartedly devote themselves to the glory of God and to the service of their neighbor. Thus the holiness of the People of God will grow in fruitful abundance, as is clearly shown in the history of the Church through the lives of so many saints.[67]

2014 Spiritual progress tends toward ever more intimate union with Christ. This union is called "mystical" because it participates in the

[60] Council of Trent (1547): DS 1546. — [61] Cf. Council of Trent (1547): DS 1548. — [62] St. Augustine, *Sermo* 298, 4–5: PL 38, 1367. — [63] St. Thérèse of Lisieux, "Act of Offering" in *Story of a Soul*, tr. John Clarke (Washington DC: ICS, 1981), 277. — [64] *Rom* 8:28–30. — [65] *LG* 40 § 2. — [66] *Mt* 5:48. — [67] *LG* 40 § 2.

774 mystery of Christ through the sacraments—"the holy mysteries"—and, in him, in the mystery of the Holy Trinity. God calls us all to this intimate union with him, even if the special graces or extraordinary signs of this mystical life are granted only to some for the sake of manifesting the gratuitous gift given to all.

2015 The way of perfection passes by way of the Cross. There is no holiness without renunciation and spiritual battle.[68] Spiritual progress
407, 2725 entails the ascesis and mortification that gradually lead to living in the
1438 peace and joy of the Beatitudes:

> He who climbs never stops going from beginning to beginning, through beginnings that have no end. He never stops desiring what he already knows.[69]

2016 The children of our holy mother the Church rightly hope for *the grace of final perseverance and the recompense* of God their Father for
162, 1821 the good works accomplished with his grace in communion with Jesus.[70]
1274 Keeping the same rule of life, believers share the "blessed hope" of those whom the divine mercy gathers into the "holy city, the new Jerusalem, coming down out of heaven from God, prepared as a bride adorned for her husband."[71]

In Brief

2017 *The grace of the Holy Spirit confers upon us the righteousness of God. Uniting us by faith and Baptism to the Passion and Resurrection of Christ, the Spirit makes us sharers in his life.*

2018 *Like conversion, justification has two aspects. Moved by grace, man turns toward God and away from sin, and so accepts forgiveness and righteousness from on high.*

2019 *Justification includes the remission of sins, sanctification, and the renewal of the inner man.*

2020 *Justification has been merited for us by the Passion of Christ. It is granted us through Baptism. It conforms us to the righteousness of God, who justifies us. It has for its goal the glory of God and of Christ, and the gift of eternal life. It is the most excellent work of God's mercy.*

2021 *Grace is the help God gives us to respond to our vocation of becoming his adopted sons. It introduces us into the intimacy of the Trinitarian life.*

2022 *The divine initiative in the work of grace precedes, prepares, and elicits the free response of man. Grace responds to the deepest yearnings of human freedom, calls freedom to cooperate with it, and perfects freedom.*

2023 *Sanctifying grace is the gratuitous gift of his life that God makes to us; it is infused by the Holy Spirit into the soul to heal it of sin and to sanctify it.*

2024 *Sanctifying grace makes us "pleasing to God." Charisms, special graces of the Holy Spirit, are oriented to sanctifying grace and are intended for the common good of the Church. God also acts through many actual graces, to be distinguished from habitual grace which is permanent in us.*

[68] Cf. *2 Tim* 4. — [69] St. Gregory of Nyssa, *Hom. in Cant.* 8: PG 44, 941C. — [70] Cf. Council of Trent (1547): DS 1576. — [71] *Rev* 21:2.

2025 *We can have merit in God's sight only because of God's free plan to associate man with the work of his grace. Merit is to be ascribed in the first place to the grace of God, and secondly to man's collaboration. Man's merit is due to God.*

2026 *The grace of the Holy Spirit can confer true merit on us, by virtue of our adoptive filiation, and in accordance with God's gratuitous justice. Charity is the principal source of merit in us before God.*

2027 *No one can merit the initial grace which is at the origin of conversion. Moved by the Holy Spirit, we can merit for ourselves and for others all the graces needed to attain eternal life, as well as necessary temporal goods.*

2028 *"All Christians...are called to the fullness of Christian life and to the perfection of charity" (*LG *40 § 2). "Christian perfection has but one limit, that of having none" (St. Gregory of Nyssa,* De vita Mos.*: PG 44, 300D).*

2029 *"If any man would come after me, let him deny himself and take up his cross and follow me" (*Mt *16:24).*

Article 3: THE CHURCH, MOTHER AND TEACHER

2030 It is in the Church, in communion with all the baptized, that the Christian fulfills his vocation. From the Church he receives the Word of God containing the teachings of "the law of Christ."[72] From the Church he receives the grace of the sacraments that sustains him on the "way." From the Church he learns the *example of holinessand* rec
828 ognizes its model and source in the all-holy Virgin Mary; he discerns it in the authentic witness of those who live it; he discovers it in the spiritual tradition and long history of the saints who have gone before him and whom the liturgy celebrates
1172 in the rhythms of the sanctoral cycle.

2031 *The moral life is spiritual worship.* We "present [our] bodies as a living sacrifice, holy and acceptable to God,"[73] within the Body of Christ
1368 that we form and in communion with the offering of his Eucharist. In the liturgy and the celebration of the sacraments, prayer and teaching are conjoined with the grace of Christ to enlighten and nourish Christian activity. As does the whole of the Christian life, the moral life finds its source and summit in the Eucharistic sacrifice.

I. Moral Life and the 85–87
Magisterium of the Church 888–892

2032 The Church, the "pillar and bulwark of the truth," "has received this solemn command of Christ from the apostles to announce the saving truth."[74] "To the Church belongs the right always and everywhere to announce moral principles, including those pertaining to the social order, and to make judgments 2246
on any human affairs to the extent that they are required by the fundamental rights of the human person or the salvation of souls."[75] 2420

[72] *Gal* 6:2. — [73] *Rom* 12:1. — [74] *1 Tim* 3:15; *LG* 17. — [75] CIC, can. 747 § 2.

2033 *The Magisterium of the Pastors of the Church* in moral matters is ordinarily exercised in catechesis and preaching, with the help of the works of theologians and spiritual authors. Thus from generation to generation, under the aegis and vigilance of the pastors, the "deposit" of
84 Christian moral teaching has been handed on, a deposit composed of a characteristic body of rules, commandments, and virtues proceeding from faith in Christ and animated by charity. Alongside the Creed and the Our Father, the basis for this catechesis has traditionally been the Decalogue which sets out the principles of moral life valid for all men.

2034 The Roman Pontiff and the bishops are "authentic teachers, that is, teachers endowed with the authority of Christ, who preach the faith to the people entrusted to them, the faith to be believed and put into practice."[76] The *ordinary* and universal *Magisterium* of the Pope and the bishops in communion with him teach the faithful the truth to believe, the charity to practice, the beatitude to hope for.

2035 The supreme degree of participation in the authority of Christ is ensured by the charism of *infallibility*. This infallibility extends as far as does the deposit of divine Revelation; it also extends to all those elements of doctrine, including morals, without which the saving truths of the faith cannot be preserved, explained, or observed.[77]

2036 The authority of the Magisterium extends also to the specific precepts of the *natural law*, because their observance, demanded by the
Creator, is necessary for salvation. 1960
In recalling the prescriptions of the natural law, the Magisterium of the Church exercises an essential part of its prophetic office of proclaiming to men what they truly are and reminding them of what they should be before God.[78]

2037 The law of God entrusted to the Church is taught to the faithful as the way of life and truth. The faithful therefore have the *right* to be instructed in the divine saving precepts that purify judgment and, with grace, heal wounded human reason.[79] They have the *duty* of observing the constitutions and decrees conveyed by the legitimate authority
of the Church. Even if they concern 2041
disciplinary matters, these determinations call for docility in charity.

2038 In the work of teaching and applying Christian morality, the Church needs the dedication of pastors, the knowledge of theologians, and the contribution of all Christians and men of good will. Faith
and the practice of the Gospel pro- 2442
vide each person with an experience of life "in Christ," who enlightens him and makes him able to evaluate the divine and human realities according to the Spirit of God.[80] Thus the Holy Spirit can use the humblest to enlighten the learned and those in the highest positions.

2039 Ministries should be exercised in a spirit of fraternal service and dedication to the Church, in the name of the Lord.[81] At the same time the conscience of each person should avoid confining itself to indi-

[76] *LG* 25. — [77] Cf. *LG* 25; CDF, declaration, *Mysterium Ecclesiae* 3. — [78] Cf. *DH* 14. — [79] Cf. CIC, can. 213. — [80] Cf. *1 Cor* 2:10–15.

vidualistic considerations in its moral judgments of the person's own acts. As far as possible conscience should take account of the good of all, as expressed in the moral law, natural and revealed, and consequently in the law of the Church and in the authoritative teaching of the Magisterium on moral questions. Personal conscience
1783 and reason should not be set in opposition to the moral law or the Magisterium of the Church.

2040 Thus a true *filial spirit toward the Church* can develop among Christians. It is the normal flowering of the baptismal grace which has begotten us in the womb of the Church and made us members of the Body of Christ. In her motherly care, the Church grants us the mercy of God which prevails over all our sins and is especially at work in the sacrament of reconciliation. With a mother's foresight, she also lavishes
167 on us day after day in her liturgy the nourishment of the Word and Eucharist of the Lord.

II. The Precepts of the Church

2041 The precepts of the Church are set in the context of a moral life bound to and nourished by liturgical life. The obligatory character of these positive laws decreed by the pastoral authorities is meant to guarantee to the faithful the very necessary minimum in the spirit of prayer and moral effort, in the growth in love of God and neighbor:

2042 The first precept ("You shall attend Mass on Sundays and on holy
1389 days of obligation and rest from servile labor") requires the faithful to sanctify the day commemorating
the Resurrection of the Lord as well 2180
as the principle liturgical feasts honoring the mysteries of the Lord, the Blessed Virgin Mary, and the saints; in the first place, by participating in the Eucharistic celebration, in which the Christian community is gathered, and by resting from those works and activities which could impede such a sanctification of these days.[82]

The second precept ("You shall confess your sins at least once a year.")
ensures preparation for the Eucha- 1457
rist by the reception of the sacrament of reconciliation, which continues Baptism's work of conversion and forgiveness.[83]

The third precept ("You shall re- 1389
ceive the sacrament of the Eucharist at least during the Easter season") guarantees as a minimum the reception of the Lord's Body and Blood in connection with the Paschal feasts, the origin and center of the Christian liturgy.[84]

2043 The fourth precept ("You shall observe the days of fasting and abstinence established by the Church") ensures the times of ascesis and penance which prepare us for
the liturgical feasts and help us ac- 2177
quire mastery over our instincts and freedom of heart.[85]

The fifth precept ("You shall help 1387
to provide for the needs of the
Church") means that the faithful are 1438
obliged to assist with the material needs of the Church, each according to his own ability.[86]

[81] Cf. *Rom* 12:8, 11. — [82] Cf. CIC, cann. 1246–1248; CCEO, can. 880 § 3, 881 §§ 1, 2, 4. — [83] Cf. CIC, can. 989; CCEO, can. 719. — [84] Cf. CIC, can. 920; CCEO, cann. 708; 881 § 3. — [85] Cf. CIC, cann. 1249–1251: CCEO can. 882. — [86] Cf. CIC, can. 222; CCEO, can. 25; *Furthermore, episcopal conferences can establish other ecclesiastical precepts for their own territories* (Cf. CIC, can. 455).

1351 The faithful also have the duty of providing for the material needs of the Church, each according to his abilities.[87]

III. Moral Life and Missionary Witness

2044 The fidelity of the baptized is a primordial condition for the proclamation of the Gospel and for the Church's mission in the world.
852, 905 In order that the message of salvation can show the power of its truth and radiance before men, it must be authenticated by the witness of the life of Christians. "The witness of a Christian life and good works done in a supernatural spirit have great power to draw men to the faith and to God."[88]

753 **2045** Because they are members of the Body whose Head is Christ,[89] Christians contribute to *building up the Church* by the constancy of their convictions and their moral lives. The Church increases, grows, and
828 develops through the holiness of her faithful, until "we all attain to the unity of the faith and of the knowledge of the Son of God, to mature manhood, to the measure of the stature of the fullness of Christ."[90]

2046 By living with the mind of Christ, Christians *hasten the coming of the Reign of God*, "a kingdom of justice, love, and peace."[91] They do not, for all that, abandon their
earthly tasks; faithful to their master, 671, 2819
they fulfill them with uprightness, patience, and love.

In Brief

2047 *The moral life is a spiritual worship. Christian activity finds its nourishment in the liturgy and the celebration of the sacraments.*

2048 *The precepts of the Church concern the moral and Christian life united with the liturgy and nourished by it.*

2049 *The Magisterium of the Pastors of the Church in moral matters is ordinarily exercised in catechesis and preaching, on the basis of the Decalogue which states the principles of moral life valid for every man.*

2050 *The Roman Pontiff and the bishops, as authentic teachers, preach to the People of God the faith which is to be believed and applied in moral life. It is also incumbent on them to pronounce on moral questions that fall within the natural law and reason.*

2051 *The infallibility of the Magisterium of the Pastors extends to all the elements of doctrine, including moral doctrine, without which the saving truths of the faith cannot be preserved, expounded, or observed.*

[87] Cf. CIC, can. 222. — [88] *AA* 6 § 2. — [89] Cf. *Eph* 1:22. — [90] *Eph* 4:13; cf. *LG* 39. — [91] *Roman Missal*, Preface of Christ the King.

Section Two

THE TEN COMMANDMENTS

"Teacher, what must I do...?"

2052 "Teacher, what good deed must I do, to have eternal life?" To the young man who asked this question, Jesus answers first by invoking the necessity to recognize God as the "One there is who is good," as the supreme Good and the source of all good. Then Jesus tells him: "If you would enter life, keep the commandments." And he cites for his
1858 questioner the precepts that concern love of neighbor: "You shall not kill, You shall not commit adultery, You shall not steal, You shall not bear false witness, Honor your father and mother." Finally Jesus sums up these commandments positively: "You shall love your neighbor as yourself."[1]

2053 To this first reply Jesus adds a second: "If you would be perfect, go, sell what you possess and give to the poor, and you will have treasure in heaven; and come, follow me."[2] This reply does not do away with the first: following Jesus Christ involves keeping the Commandments. The Law has not been abolished,[3] but rather man is invited to rediscover it
1968 in the person of his Master who is its perfect fulfillment. In the three synoptic Gospels, Jesus' call to the rich young man to follow him, in the obedience of a disciple and in the observance of the Commandments, is joined to the call to poverty and
1973 chastity.[4] The evangelical counsels are inseparable from the Commandments.

2054 Jesus acknowledged the Ten Commandments, but he also showed the power of the Spirit at work in their letter. He preached a
"righteousness [which] exceeds that 581
of the scribes and Pharisees"[5] as well as that of the Gentiles.[6] He unfolded all the demands of the Commandments. "You have heard that it was said to the men of old, 'You shall not kill.'... But I say to you that every one who is angry with his brother shall be liable to judgment."[7]

2055 When someone asks him, "Which commandment in the Law is the greatest?"[8] Jesus replies: "You shall love the Lord your God with all your heart, and with all your
soul, and with all your mind. This 129
is the greatest and first commandment. And a second is like it: You shall love your neighbor as yourself. On these two commandments hang all the Law and the prophets."[9] The Decalogue must be interpreted in light of this twofold yet single commandment of love, the fullness of the Law:

> The commandments: "You shall not commit adultery, You shall not kill, You shall not steal, You shall not covet," and any other commandment, are summed up in this sentence: "You shall love your neighbor as yourself." Love does no wrong to a neighbor; therefore love is the fulfilling of the law.[10]

The Decalogue in Sacred Scripture

2056 The word "Decalogue" means literally "ten words."[11] God revealed these "ten words" to his people on the holy mountain. They
were written "with the finger of 700
God,"[12] unlike the other commandments written by Moses.[13] They are 62

[1] *Mt* 19:16–19. — [2] *Mt* 19:21. — [3] Cf. *Mt* 5:17. — [4] Cf. *Mt* 19:6–12, 21, 23–29. — [5] *Mt* 5:20. — [6] Cf. *Mt* 5:46–47. — [7] *Mt* 5:21–22. — [8] *Mt* 22:36. — [9] *Mt* 22:37–40; cf. *Deut* 6:5; *Lev* 19:18. — [10] *Rom* 13:9–10. — [11] *Ex* 34:28; *Deut* 4:13; 10:4. — [12] *Ex* 31:18; *Deut* 5:22. — [13] Cf. *Deut* 31:9, 24.

pre-eminently the words of God. They are handed on to us in the books of Exodus[14] and *Deuteronomy*.[15] Beginning with the Old Testament, the sacred books refer to the "ten words,"[16] but it is in the New Covenant in Jesus Christ that their full meaning will be revealed.

2057 The Decalogue must first be understood in the context of the Exodus, God's great liberating event at the center of the Old Covenant.
2084 Whether formulated as negative commandments, prohibitions, or as positive precepts such as: "Honor your father and mother," the "ten words" point out the conditions of a life freed from the slavery of sin. The Decalogue is a path of life:

> If you love the LORD your God, by walking in his ways, and by keeping his commandments and his statutes and his ordinances, then you shall live and multiply.[17]

2170 This liberating power of the Decalogue appears, for example, in the commandment about the sabbath rest, directed also to foreigners and slaves:

> You shall remember that you were a servant in the land of Egypt, and the LORD your God brought you out thence with a mighty hand and an outstretched arm.[18]

1962 **2058** The "ten words" sum up and proclaim God's law: "These words the LORD spoke to all your assembly at the mountain out of the midst of the fire, the cloud, and the thick darkness, with a loud voice; and he added no more. And he wrote them upon two tablets of stone, and gave them to me."[19] For this reason these two tablets are called "the Testimony." In fact, they contain the terms of the covenant concluded between God and his people. These "tablets of the Testimony" were to be deposited in "the ark."[20]

2059 The "ten words" are pro- 707
nounced by God in the midst of a theophany ("The LORD spoke with you face to face at the mountain, out of the midst of the fire."[21]). They belong to God's revelation of himself and his glory. The gift of the Commandments is the gift of God
himself and his holy will. In making 2823
his will known, God reveals himself to his people.

2060 The gift of the commandments and of the Law is part of the covenant God sealed with his own. In *Exodus*, the revelation of the "ten words" is granted between the proposal of the covenant[22] and its conclusion—after the people had committed themselves to "do" all that the Lord had said, and to "obey" it.[23] The Decalogue is never handed on
without first recalling the covenant 62
("The LORD our God made a covenant with us in Horeb.").[24]

2061 The Commandments take on their full meaning within the covenant. According to Scripture, man's moral life has all its meaning in and through the covenant. The first of the "ten words" recalls that God loved his people first:

> Since there was a passing from the paradise of freedom to the slavery of this world, in punishment for sin,

[14] Cf. *Ex* 20:1–17. — [15] Cf. *Deut* 5:6–22. — [16] Cf. for example *Hos* 4:2; *Jer* 7:9; *Ezek* 18:5–9. — [17] *Deut* 30:16. — [18] *Deut* 5:15. — [19] *Deut* 5:22. — [20] *Ex* 25:16; 31:18; 32:15; 34:29; 40:1–2. — [21] *Deut* 5:4. — [22] Cf. *Ex* 19. — [23] Cf. *Ex* 24:7. — [24] *Deut* 5:2.

the first phrase of the Decalogue, the first word of God's commandments, bears on freedom: "I am the LORD your God, who brought you out of
2086 the land of Egypt, out of the house of slavery."[25]

2062 The Commandments properly so-called come in the second place: they express the implications of belonging to God through the establishment of the covenant. Moral existence is a *response* to the Lord's
142 loving initiative. It is the acknowledgement and homage given to God
2002 and a worship of thanksgiving. It is cooperation with the plan God pursues in history.

2063 The covenant and dialogue between God and man are also attested to by the fact that all the obligations are stated in the first person ("I am the Lord.") and addressed by God to another personal subject ("you"). In all God's commandments, the *singular* personal pro-
878 noun designates the recipient. God makes his will known to each person in particular, at the same time as he makes it known to the whole people:

> The Lord prescribed love towards God and taught justice towards neighbor, so that man would be neither unjust, nor unworthy of God. Thus, through the Decalogue, God prepared man to become his friend and to live in harmony with his neighbor.... The words of the Decalogue remain likewise for us Christians. Far from being abolished, they have received amplification and development from the fact of the coming of the Lord in the flesh.[26]

The Decalogue in the Church's tradition

2064 In fidelity to Scripture and in conformity with the example of Jesus, the tradition of the Church has acknowledged the primordial importance and significance of the Decalogue.

2065 Ever since St. Augustine, the Ten Commandments have occupied a predominant place in the catechesis of baptismal candidates and the faithful. In the fifteenth century, the custom arose of expressing the commandments of the Decalogue in rhymed formulae, easy to memorize and in positive form. They are still in use today. The catechisms of the Church have often expounded Christian morality by following the order of the Ten Commandments.

2066 The division and numbering of the Commandments have varied in the course of history. The present catechism follows the division of the Commandments established by St. Augustine, which has become traditional in the Catholic Church. It is also that of the Lutheran confessions. The Greek Fathers worked out a slightly different division, which is found in the Orthodox Churches and Reformed communities.

2067 The Ten Commandments state what is required in the love of God and love of neighbor. The first three concern love of God, and the other seven love of neighbor. 1853

> As charity comprises the two commandments to which the Lord related the whole Law and the prophets...so the Ten Commandments

[25] Origen, *Hom. in Ex.* 8, 1: PG 12, 350; cf. *Ex* 20:2; *Deut* 5:6. — [26] St. Irenaeus, *Adv. haeres.*, 4, 16, 3–4: PG 7/1, 1017–1018.

were themselves given on two tablets. Three were written on one tablet and seven on the other.[27]

2068 The Council of Trent teaches that the Ten Commandments are obligatory for Christians and that the justified man is still bound to
1993 keep them;[28] the Second Vatican Council confirms: "The bishops, successors of the apostles, receive from the Lord...the mission of teaching all peoples, and of preaching the Gospel to every creature, so
888 that all men may attain salvation through faith, Baptism and the observance of the Commandments."[29]

The unity of the Decalogue

2069 The Decalogue forms a coherent whole. Each "word" refers to each of the others and to all of them; they reciprocally condition one an-
2534 other. The two tablets shed light on one another; they form an organic unity. To transgress one commandment is to infringe all the others.[30] One cannot honor another person without blessing God his Creator. One cannot adore God without loving all men, his creatures. The Decalogue brings man's religious and social life into unity.

The Decalogue and the natural law

1955 **2070** The Ten Commandments belong to God's revelation. At the same time they teach us the true humanity of man. They bring to light the essential duties, and therefore, indirectly, the fundamental rights inherent in the nature of the human person. The Decalogue contains a privileged expression of the natural law:

> From the beginning, God had implanted in the heart of man the precepts of the natural law. Then he was content to remind him of them. This was the Decalogue.[31]

2071 The commandments of the Decalogue, although accessible to reason alone, have been revealed. To
attain a complete and certain under- 1960
standing of the requirements of the natural law, sinful humanity needed this revelation:

> A full explanation of the commandments of the Decalogue became necessary in the state of sin because the light of reason was obscured and the will had gone astray.[32]

We know God's commandments through the divine revelation proposed
to us in the Church, and through the 1777
voice of moral conscience.

The obligation of the Decalogue

2072 Since they express man's fundamental duties towards God and towards his neighbor, the Ten Commandments reveal, in their primordial content, grave obligations. 1858
They are fundamentally immutable,
and they oblige always and every- 1958
where. No one can dispense from them. The Ten Commandments are engraved by God in the human heart.

[27] St. Augustine, *Sermo* 33, 2, 2: PL 38, 208. — [28] Cf. DS 1569–1570. — [29] *LG* 24. — [30] Cf. *Jas* 2:10–11. — [31] St. Irenaeus, *Adv. haeres.* 4, 15, 1: PG 7/1, 1012. — [32] St. Bonaventure, *Comm. sent.* 4, 37, 1, 3.

2073 Obedience to the Commandments also implies obligations in matter which is, in itself, light. Thus abusive language is forbidden by the fifth commandment, but would be a grave offense only as a result of circumstances or the offender's intention.

"Apart from me you can do nothing"

2074 Jesus says: "I am the vine, you are the branches. He who abides in me, and I in him, he it is that bears much fruit, for apart from me you can do nothing."[33] The fruit
2732 referred to in this saying is the holiness of a life made fruitful by union with Christ. When we believe in Jesus Christ, partake of his mysteries, and keep his commandments, the Savior himself comes to love,
521 in us, his Father and his brethren, our Father and our brethren. His person becomes, through the Spirit, the living and interior rule of our activity. "This is my commandment, that you love one another as I have loved you."[34]

In Brief

2075 *"What good deed must I do, to have eternal life?"—"If you would enter into life, keep the commandments" (*Mt *19:16–17).*

2076 *By his life and by his preaching Jesus attested to the permanent validity of the Decalogue.*

2077 *The gift of the Decalogue is bestowed from within the covenant concluded by God with his people. God's commandments take on their true meaning in and through this covenant.*

2078 *In fidelity to Scripture and in conformity with Jesus' example, the tradition of the Church has always acknowledged the primordial importance and significance of the Decalogue.*

2079 *The Decalogue forms an organic unity in which each "word" or "commandment" refers to all the others taken together. To transgress one commandment is to infringe the whole Law (cf.* Jas *2:10–11).*

2080 *The Decalogue contains a privileged expression of the natural law. It is made known to us by divine revelation and by human reason.*

2081 *The Ten Commandments, in their fundamental content, state grave obligations. However, obedience to these precepts also implies obligations in matter which is, in itself, light.*

2082 *What God commands he makes possible by his grace.*

[33] *Jn* 15:5. — [34] *Jn* 15:12.

Chapter One:
"YOU SHALL LOVE YOUR GOD WITH ALL YOUR HEART, AND WITH ALL YOUR SOUL, AND WITH ALL YOUR MIND"

367 **2083** Jesus summed up man's duties toward God in this saying: "You shall love the Lord your God with all your heart, and with all your soul, and with all your mind."[1] This immediately echoes the solemn call: "Hear, O Israel: the LORD our God is one LORD."[2]

> God has loved us first. The love of 199
> the One God is recalled in the first of the "ten words." The commandments then make explicit the response of love that man is called to give to his God.

Article 1:
THE FIRST COMMANDMENT

> I am the LORD your God, who brought you out of the land of Egypt, out of the house of bondage. You shall have no other gods before me. You shall not make for yourself a graven image, or any likeness of anything that is in heaven above, or that is in the earth beneath, or that is in the water under the earth; you shall not bow down to them or serve them.[3]
>
> It is written: "You shall worship the Lord your God and him only shall you serve."[4]

I. "You Shall Worship the Lord Your God and Him Only Shall You Serve"

2084 God makes himself known by recalling his all-powerful, loving, and liberating action in the history of the one he addresses: "I brought
2057 you out of the land of Egypt, out of the house of bondage." The first word contains the first commandment of the Law: "You shall fear the LORD your God; you shall serve him.... You shall not go after other gods."[5] God's first call and just demand is that man
accept him and worship him. 398

2085 The one and true God first reveals his glory to Israel.[6] The revelation of the vocation and truth of man is linked to the revelation
of God. Man's vocation is to make 200
God manifest by acting in conformity with his creation "in the image 1701
and likeness of God":

> There will never be another God, Trypho, and there has been no other since the world began...than he who made and ordered the universe. We do not think that our God is different from yours. He is the same who brought your fathers out of

[1] *Mt* 22:37; cf. *Lk* 10:27: "... and with all your strength." — [2] *Deut* 6:4. — [3] *Ex* 20:2–5; cf. *Deut* 5:6–9. — [4] *Mt* 4:10. — [5] *Deut* 6:13–14. — [6] Cf. *Ex* 19:16–25; 24:15–18.

Egypt "by his powerful hand and his outstretched arm." We do not place our hope in some other god, for there is none, but in the same God as you do: the God of Abraham, Isaac and Jacob.[7]

2086 "The first commandment embraces faith, hope, and charity. When we say 'God' we confess a constant, unchangeable being, al-
212 ways the same, faithful and just, without any evil. It follows that we must necessarily accept his words and have complete faith in him and acknowledge his authority. He is almighty, merciful, and infinitely beneficent.... Who could not place all hope in him? Who could not love him when contemplating the treasures of goodness and love he has poured out on us? Hence the formula God employs in the Scripture at
2061 the beginning and end of his commandments: 'I am the LORD.'"[8]

1814–1816 *Faith*

2087 Our moral life has its source in faith in God who reveals his love to us. St. Paul speaks of the "obedience of faith"[9] as our first obligation.
143 He shows that "ignorance of God" is the principle and explanation of all moral deviations.[10] Our duty toward God is to believe in him and to bear witness to him.

2088 The first commandment requires us to nourish and protect our faith with prudence and vigilance, and to reject everything that is opposed to it. There are various ways of sinning against faith:

157 *Voluntary doubt* about the faith disregards or refuses to hold as true what God has revealed and the Church proposes for belief. *Involuntary doubt* refers to hesitation in believing, difficulty in overcoming objections connected with the faith, or also anxiety aroused by its obscurity. If deliberately cultivated doubt can lead to spiritual blindness.

2089 *Incredulity* is the neglect of 162
revealed truth or the willful refusal to assent to it. "*Heresy* is the obsti- 817
nate post-baptismal denial of some truth which must be believed with divine and catholic faith, or it is likewise an obstinate doubt concerning the same; *apostasy* is the total repudiation of the Christian faith; *schism* is the refusal of submission to the Roman Pontiff or of communion with the members of the Church subject to him."[11]

Hope 1817–1821

2090 When God reveals Himself and calls him, man cannot fully respond to the divine love by his own powers. He must hope that God will give him the capacity to love Him 1996
in return and to act in conformity with the commandments of charity. Hope is the confident expectation of divine blessing and the beatific vision of God; it is also the fear of offending God's love and of incurring punishment.

2091 The first commandment is also concerned with sins against hope, namely, despair and presumption:

By *despair*, man ceases to hope for his personal salvation from God, for help in attaining it or for the for- 1864
giveness of his sins. Despair is con-

[7] St. Justin, *Dial. cum Tryphone Judaeo* 11, 1: PG 6, 497. — [8] *Roman Catechism* 3, 2,4. — [9] *Rom* 1:5; 16:26. — [10] Cf. *Rom* 1:18–32. — [11] CIC, can. 751: emphasis added.

trary to God's goodness, to his justice—for the Lord is faithful to his promises—and to his mercy.

2092 There are two kinds of *presumption.* Either man presumes upon his own capacities, (hoping to be able to save himself without help
2732 from on high), or he presumes upon God's almighty power or his mercy (hoping to obtain his forgiveness without conversion and glory without merit).

1822–1829 *Charity*

2093 Faith in God's love encompasses the call and the obligation to respond with sincere love to divine charity. The first commandment enjoins us to love God above everything and all creatures for him and because of him.[12]

2094 One can sin against God's love in various ways:

– *indifference* neglects or refuses to reflect on divine charity; it fails to consider its prevenient goodness and denies its power.
– *ingratitude* fails or refuses to acknowledge divine charity and to return him love for love.
– *lukewarmness* is hesitation or negligence in responding to divine love; it can imply refusal to give oneself over to the prompting of charity.
2733 – *acedia* or spiritual sloth goes so far as to refuse the joy that comes from God and to be repelled by divine goodness.
2303 – *hatred of God* comes from pride. It is contrary to love of God, whose goodness it denies, and whom it presumes to curse as the one who forbids sins and inflicts punishments.

II. "Him Only Shall You Serve"

2095 The theological virtues of faith, hope, and charity inform and give life to the moral virtues. Thus charity leads us to render to God
what we as creatures owe him in all 1807
justice. The virtue of religion disposes us to have this attitude.

Adoration 2628

2096 Adoration is the first act of the virtue of religion. To adore God is to acknowledge him as God, as the Creator and Savior, the Lord and Master of everything that exists, as infinite and merciful Love. "You shall worship the Lord your God, and him only shall you serve," says Jesus, citing *Deuteronomy.*[13]

2097 To adore God is to acknowl- 2807
edge, in respect and absolute submission, the "nothingness of the creature" who would not exist but for God. To adore God is to praise and exalt him and to humble oneself, as Mary did in the Magnificat, confessing with gratitude that he has done great things and holy is his name.[14] The worship of the one God sets man free from turning in on himself, from the slavery of sin and the idolatry of the world.

Prayer 2558

2098 The acts of faith, hope, and charity enjoined by the first commandment are accomplished in prayer. Lifting up the mind toward God is an expression of our adoration of God: prayer of praise and thanksgiving, intercession and petition. Prayer is an indispensable condition for being able to obey

[12] Cf. *Deut* 6:4–5. — [13] *Lk* 4:8; cf. *Deut* 6:13. — [14] Cf. *Lk* 1:46-49.

God's commandments. "[We] ought
2742 always to pray and not lose heart."[15]

Sacrifice

2099 It is right to offer sacrifice to God as a sign of adoration and gratitude, supplication and communion: "Every action done so as to cling to God in communion of holiness, and
613 thus achieve blessedness, is a true sacrifice."[16]

2100 Outward sacrifice, to be genuine, must be the expression of spiritual sacrifice: "The sacrifice acceptable to God is a broken spirit...."[17]
2711 The prophets of the Old Covenant often denounced sacrifices that were not from the heart or not coupled with love of neighbor.[18] Jesus recalls the words of the prophet Hosea: "I desire mercy, and not sacrifice."[19] The only perfect sacrifice is the one that Christ offered on the cross as a
614 total offering to the Father's love and
618 for our salvation.[20] By uniting ourselves with his sacrifice we can make our lives a sacrifice to God.

Promises and vows

1237 **2101** In many circumstances, the Christian is called to make *promises* to God. Baptism and Confirmation, Matrimony and Holy Orders always entail promises. Out of personal devotion, the Christian may also promise to God this action, that prayer, this alms-giving, that
1064 pilgrimage, and so forth. Fidelity to promises made to God is a sign of the respect owed to the divine majesty and of love for a faithful God.

2102 "A *vow* is a deliberate and free promise made to God concerning a possible and better good which must be fulfilled by reason of the virtue of religion,"[21] A vow is an act of *devotion* in which the Christian dedicates himself to God or promises him some good work. By fulfilling his vows he renders to God what has been promised and consecrated to Him. The *Acts of the Apostles* shows us St. Paul concerned to fulfill the vows he had made.[22]

2103 The Church recognizes an 1973
exemplary value in the vows to practice the *evangelical counsels*:[23]

> Mother Church rejoices that she has within herself many men and women
> who pursue the Savior's self-emptying 914
> more closely and show it forth more clearly, by undertaking poverty with the freedom of the children of God, and renouncing their own will: they submit themselves to man for the sake of God, thus going beyond what is of precept in the matter of perfection, so as to conform themselves more fully to the obedient Christ.[24]

The Church can, in certain cases and for proportionate reasons, dispense from vows and promises.[25]

The social duty of religion and the right to religious freedom

2104 "All men are bound to seek 2467
the truth, especially in what concerns God and his Church, and to embrace it and hold on to it as they come to know it."[26] This duty derives from "the very dignity of the human person."[27] It does not contradict a "sincere respect" for different

[15] *Lk* 18:1. — [16] St. Augustine, *De civ. Dei* 10, 6: PL 41, 283. — [17] *Ps* 51:17. — [18] Cf. *Am* 5:21–25; *Isa* 1:10–20. — [19] *Mt* 9:13; 12:7; cf. *Hos* 6:6. — [20] Cf. *Heb* 9:13–14. — [21] CIC, can. 1191 § 1. — [22] Cf. *Acts* 18:18; 21:23–24. — [23] Cf. CIC, can. 654. — [24] *LG* 42 § 2. — [25] Cf. CIC, cann. 692; 1196–1197. — [26] *DH* 1 § 2. — [27] *DH* 2 § 1.

religions which frequently "reflect a ray of that truth which enlightens all men,"[28] nor the requirement of char-
851 ity, which urges Christians "to treat with love, prudence and patience those who are in error or ignorance with regard to the faith."[29]

2105 The duty of offering God genuine worship concerns man both individually and socially. This is "the traditional Catholic teaching on the moral duty of individuals and societies toward the true religion and the one Church of Christ."[30] By constantly evangelizing men,
854 the Church works toward enabling them "to infuse the Christian spirit into the mentality and mores, laws and structures of the communities
898 in which [they] live."[31] The social duty of Christians is to respect and awaken in each man the love of the true and the good. It requires them to make known the worship of the one true religion which subsists in the Catholic and apostolic Church.[32] Christians are called to be the light of the world. Thus, the Church shows forth the kingship of Christ over all creation and in particular over human societies.[33]

160 **2106** "Nobody may be forced to act against his convictions, nor is anyone to be restrained from acting
1782 in accordance with his conscience
1738 in religious matters in private or in public, alone or in association with others, within due limits."[34] This right is based on the very nature of the human person, whose dignity enables him freely to assent to the divine truth which transcends the temporal order. For this reason it "continues to exist even in those who do not live up to their obligation of seeking the truth and adhering to it."[35]

2107 "If because of the circumstances of a particular people special civil recognition is given to one religious community in the constitutional organization of a state, the right of all citizens and religious communities to religious freedom must be recognized and respected as well."[36]

2108 The right to religious liber- 1740
ty is neither a moral license to adhere to error, nor a supposed right to error,[37] but rather a natural right of the human person to civil liberty, i.e., immunity, within just limits, from external constraint in religious matters by political authorities. This natural right ought to be acknowledged in the juridical order of society in such a way that it constitutes a civil right.[38]

2109 The right to religious liber- 2244
ty can of itself be neither unlimited nor limited only by a "public order" conceived in a positivist or naturalist manner.[39] The "due limits" which are inherent in it must be determined for each social situation by political prudence, according to the requirements of the common good, and ratified by the civil authority in accordance with "legal principles which are in conformity with the
objective moral order."[40] 1906

[28] *NA* 2 § 2. — [29] *DH* 14 § 4. — [30] *DH* 1 § 3. — [31] *AA* 13 § 1. — [32] Cf. *DH* 1. — [33] Cf. *AA* 13; Leo XIII, *Immortale Dei* 3, 17; Pius XI, Quas primas 8, 20. — [34] *DH* 2 § 1. — [35] *DH* 2 § 2. — [36] *DH* 6 § 3. — [37] Cf. Leo XIII, *Libertas praestantissimum* 18; Pius XII, AAS 1953, 799. — [38] Cf. *DH* 2. — [39] Cf. Pius VI, *Quod aliquantum* (1791)10; Pius IX, *Quanta cura* 3. — [40] *DH* 7 § 3.

III. "You Shall Have No Other Gods Before Me"

2110 The first commandment forbids honoring gods other than the one Lord who has revealed himself to his people. It proscribes superstition and irreligion. Superstition in some sense represents a perverse excess of religion; irreligion is the vice contrary by defect to the virtue of religion.

Superstition

2111 Superstition is the deviation of religious feeling and of the practices this feeling imposes. It can even affect the worship we offer the true God, e.g., when one attributes an importance in some way magical to certain practices otherwise lawful or necessary. To attribute the efficacy of prayers or of sacramental signs to their mere external performance, apart from the interior dispositions that they demand, is to fall into superstition.[41]

Idolatry

2112 The first commandment condemns *polytheism.* It requires man neither to believe in, nor to venerate, other divinities than the one true God. Scripture constantly
210 recalls this rejection of "idols, [of]
silver and gold, the work of men's hands. They have mouths, but do not speak; eyes, but do not see." These empty idols make their worshippers empty: "Those who make them are like them; so are all who trust in them."[42] God, however, is the "living God"[43] who gives life and intervenes in history.

2113 Idolatry not only refers to false pagan worship. It remains a constant temptation to faith. Idolatry consists in divinizing what is not God. Man
commits idolatry whenever he hon- 398, 2534
ors and reveres a creature in place of God, whether this be gods or demons (for example, satanism), power, pleasure, race, ancestors, the state, money,
etc. Jesus says, "You cannot serve God 2289
and mammon."[44] Many martyrs died
for not adoring "the Beast"[45] refusing 2473
even to simulate such worship. Idolatry rejects the unique Lordship of God; it is therefore incompatible with communion with God.[46]

2114 Human life finds its unity in the adoration of the one God. The commandment to worship the Lord alone integrates man and saves him from an endless disintegration. Idolatry is a perversion of man's innate religious sense. An idolater is someone who "transfers his indestructible notion of God to anything other than God."[47]

Divination and magic

2115 God can reveal the future to his prophets or to other saints. Still, a sound Christian attitude consists in putting oneself confidently into
the hands of Providence for what- 305
ever concerns the future, and giving up all unhealthy curiosity about it. Improvidence, however, can constitute a lack of responsibility.

2116 All forms of *divination* are to be rejected: recourse to Satan or demons, conjuring up the dead or other practices falsely supposed to "unveil" the future.[48] Consulting horoscopes, astrology, palm reading,

[41] Cf. *Mt* 23:16–22. — [42] *Ps* 115:4–5, 8; cf. *Isa* 44:9–20; *Jer* 10:1–16; *Dan* 14:1–30; *Bar* 6; *Wis* 13:1–15:19. — [43] *Josh* 3:10; *Ps* 42:3; etc. — [44] *Mt* 6:24. — [45] Cf. *Rev* 13–14. — [46] Cf. *Gal* 5:20; *Eph* 5:5. — [47] Origen, *Contra Celsum* 2, 40: PG 11, 861. — [48] Cf. *Deut* 18:10; *Jer* 29:8.

interpretation of omens and lots, the phenomena of clairvoyance, and recourse to mediums all conceal a desire for power over time, history, and, in the last analysis, other human beings, as well as a wish to conciliate hidden powers. They contradict the honor, respect, and loving fear that we owe to God alone.

2117 All practices of *magic* or *sorcery*, by which one attempts to tame occult powers, so as to place them at one's service and have a supernatural power over others—even if this were for the sake of restoring their health—are gravely contrary to the virtue of religion. These practices are even more to be condemned when accompanied by the intention of harming someone, or when they have recourse to the intervention of demons. Wearing charms is also reprehensible. *Spiritism* often implies divination or magical practices; the Church for her part warns the faithful against it. Recourse to so-called traditional cures does not justify either the invocation of evil powers or the exploitation of another's credulity.

Irreligion

2118 God's first commandment condemns the main sins of irreligion: tempting God, in words or deeds, sacrilege, and simony.

2119 *Tempting God* consists in putting his goodness and almighty
394 power to the test by word or deed.
Thus Satan tried to induce Jesus to throw himself down from the Temple and, by this gesture, force God to act.[49] Jesus opposed Satan with the word of God: "You shall not put the LORD your God to the test."[50] The challenge contained in such tempting of God wounds the respect and trust we owe our Creator
and Lord. It always harbors doubt 2088
about his love, his providence, and his power.[51]

2120 *Sacrilege* consists in profaning or treating unworthily the sacraments and other liturgical actions, as well as persons, things, or places consecrated to God. Sacrilege is a grave sin especially when committed against the Eucharist, for in this sacrament the true Body of Christ is
made substantially present for us.[52] 1374

2121 *Simony* is defined as the buying or selling of spiritual things.[53] To Simon the magician, who wanted to buy the spiritual power he saw at work in the apostles, St. Peter responded: "Your silver perish with you, because you thought you could obtain God's gift with money!"[54] Peter thus held to the words of Jesus: "You received without pay, give without pay."[55] It is impossible to appropriate to oneself spiritual goods and 1578
behave toward them as their owner or master, for they have their source in God. One can receive them only from him, without payment.

2122 "The minister should ask nothing for the administration of the sacraments beyond the offerings defined by the competent authority, always being careful that the needy are not deprived of the help of the sacraments because of their poverty."[56] The competent authority determines these "offerings" in accordance with the principle that the Christian people ought to

[49] Cf. *Lk* 4:9. — [50] *Deut* 6:16. — [51] Cf. 1 *Cor* 10:9; *Ex* 17:2–7; *Ps* 95:9. — [52] Cf. CIC, cann. 1367; 1376. — [53] Cf. *Acts* 8:9–24. — [54] *Acts* 8:20. — [55] *Mt* 10:8; cf. already *Isa* 55:1. — [56] CIC, can. 848.

contribute to the support of the Church's ministers. "The laborer deserves his food."[57]

Atheism

2123 "Many...of our contemporaries either do not at all perceive, or explicitly reject, this intimate and vital bond of man to God. Atheism must therefore be regarded as
29 one of the most serious problems of our time."[58]

2124 The name "atheism" covers many very different phenomena. One common form is the practical materialism which restricts its needs and aspirations to space and time. Atheistic humanism falsely considers man to be "an end to himself, and the sole maker, with supreme control, of his own history."[59] Another form of contemporary atheism looks for the liberation of man through economic and social liberation. "It holds that religion, of its very nature, thwarts such emancipation by raising man's hopes in a future life, thus both deceiving him and discouraging him from working for a better form of life on earth."[60]

2125 Since it rejects or denies the existence of God, atheism is a sin against the virtue of religion.[61] The imputability of this offense can be
1735 significantly diminished in virtue of the intentions and the circumstances. "Believers can have more than a little to do with the rise of atheism. To the extent that they are careless about their instruction in the faith, or present its teaching falsely, or even fail in their religious, moral, or social life, they must be said to conceal rather than to reveal the true nature of God and of religion."[62]

2126 Atheism is often based on a false conception of human autonomy, exaggerated to the point of refusing any dependence on God.[63] Yet,
"to acknowledge God is in no way to 396
oppose the dignity of man, since such
dignity is grounded and brought to 154
perfection in God...."[64] "For the Church knows full well that her message is in harmony with the most secret desires of the human heart."[65]

Agnosticism

2127 Agnosticism assumes a number of forms. In certain cases the agnostic refrains from denying God; instead he postulates the existence of a transcendent being which is incapable of revealing itself, and about which nothing can be said. In other cases, the agnostic makes
no judgment about God's existence, 36
declaring it impossible to prove, or even to affirm or deny.

2128 Agnosticism can sometimes include a certain search for God, but
it can equally express indifferentism, 1036
a flight from the ultimate question of existence, and a sluggish moral conscience. Agnosticism is all too often equivalent to practical atheism.

IV. "You Shall Not Make for Yourself a Graven Image..." 115–1162

2129 The divine injunction included the prohibition of every representation of God by the hand of man. *Deuteronomy* explains: "Since you saw no form on the day that the LORD spoke to you at Horeb out of the midst of the fire, beware lest you act corruptly

[57] *Mt* 10:10; cf. *Lk* 10:7; *1 Cor* 9:5–18; *1 Tim* 5:17–18. — [58] *GS* 19 § 1. — [59] *GS* 20 § 1. — [60] *GS* 20 § 2. — [61] Cf. *Rom* 1:18. — [62] *GS* 19 § 3. — [63] Cf. *GS* 20 § 1. — [64] *GS* 21 § 3. — [65] *GS* 21 § 7.

by making a graven image for yourselves, in the form of any figure. . . ."[66]
It is the absolutely transcendent God
who revealed himself to Israel. "He is
the all," but at the same time "he is
300 greater than all his works."[67] He is "the
2500 author of beauty."[68]

2130 Nevertheless, already in the Old Testament, God ordained or permitted the making of images that pointed symbolically toward salvation by the incarnate Word: so it was with the bronze serpent, the ark of the covenant, and the cherubim.[69]

2131 Basing itself on the mystery
of the incarnate Word, the seventh
ecumenical council at Nicaea (787)
justified against the iconoclasts the
476 veneration of icons—of Christ, but
also of the Mother of God, the angels, and all the saints. By becoming
incarnate, the Son of God introduced a new "economy" of images.

2132 The Christian veneration of images is not contrary to the first commandment which proscribes idols. Indeed, "the honor rendered to an image passes to its prototype," and "whoever venerates an image venerates the person portrayed in it."[70] The honor paid to sacred images is a "respectful veneration," not the adoration due to God alone:

> Religious worship is not directed to images in themselves, considered as mere things, but under their distinctive aspect as images leading us on to God incarnate. The movement toward the image does not terminate in it as image, but tends toward that whose image it is.[71]

In Brief

2133 *"You shall love the Lord your God with all your heart, and with all your soul and with all your strength" (*Deut *6:5).*

2134 *The first commandment summons man to believe in God, to hope in him, and to love him above all else.*

2135 *"You shall worship the Lord your God" (*Mt *4:10). Adoring God, praying to him, offering him the worship that belongs to him, fulfilling the promises and vows made to him are acts of the virtue of religion which fall under obedience to the first commandment.*

2136 *The duty to offer God authentic worship concerns man both as an individual and as a social being.*

2137 *"Men of the present day want to profess their religion freely in private and in public" (*DH *15).*

2138 *Superstition is a departure from the worship that we give to the true God. It is manifested in idolatry, as well as in various forms of divination and magic.*

2139 *Tempting God in words or deeds, sacrilege, and simony are sins of irreligion forbidden by the first commandment.*

2140 *Since it rejects or denies the existence of God, atheism is a sin against the first commandment.*

2141 *The veneration of sacred images is based on the mystery of the Incarnation of the Word of God. It is not contrary to the first commandment.*

[66] *Deut* 4:15–16. — [67] *Sir* 43:27–28. — [68] *Wis* 13:3. — [69] Cf. *Num* 21:4–9; *Wis* 16:5–14; *Jn* 3:14–15; *Ex* 25:10–22; *1 Kings* 6:23–28; 7:23–26. — [70] St. Basil, *De Spiritu Sancto* 18, 45: PG 32, 149C; Council of Nicaea II: DS 601; cf. Council of Trent: DS 1821–1825; Vatican Council II: SC 126; LG 67. — [71] St. Thomas Aquinas, *STh* II–II, 81, 3 ad 3.

Article 2:
THE SECOND COMMANDMENT

> You shall not take the name of the Lord your God in vain.[72]
> You have heard that it was said to the men of old, "You shall not swear falsely...." But I say to you, Do not swear at all.[73]

2807–2815 ### I. The Name of the Lord Is Holy

2142 The second commandment *prescribes respect for the Lord's name.* Like the first commandment, it belongs to the virtue of religion and more particularly it governs our use of speech in sacred matters.

2143 Among all the words of Revelation, there is one which is unique: the revealed name of God. God confides his name to those who believe
203 in him; he reveals himself to them in his personal mystery. The gift of a name belongs to the order of trust and intimacy. "The Lord's name is holy." For this reason man must not
435 abuse it. He must keep it in mind in silent, loving adoration. He will not introduce it into his own speech except to bless, praise, and glorify it.[74]

2144 Respect for his name is an expression of the respect owed to the mystery of God himself and to the whole sacred reality it evokes. The *sense of the sacred* is part of the virtue of religion:

> Are these feelings of fear and awe Christian feelings or not?... I say this, then, which I think no one can reasonably dispute. They are the class of feelings we should have—yes, have to an intense degree—if we literally had the sight of Almighty God; therefore they are the class of feelings which we shall have, if we realize His presence. In proportion as we believe that He is present, we shall have them; and not to have them, is not to realize, not to believe that He is present.[75]

2145 The faithful should bear 2472
witness to the Lord's name by confessing the faith without giving way 427
to fear.[76] Preaching and catechizing should be permeated with adoration and respect for the name of our Lord Jesus Christ.

2146 The second commandment *forbids the abuse of God's name*, i.e., every improper use of the names of God, Jesus Christ, but also of the Virgin Mary and all the saints.

2147 *Promises* made to others in 2101
God's name engage the divine honor, fidelity, truthfulness, and authority. They must be respected in justice. To be unfaithful to them is to misuse God's name and in some way to make God out to be a liar.[77]

2148 *Blasphemy* is directly opposed to the second commandment. It consists in uttering against God—inwardly or outwardly—words of hatred, reproach, or defiance; in speaking ill of God; in failing in respect toward him in one's speech; in misusing God's name. St. James condemns those "who blaspheme that honorable name [of Jesus] by which you are called."[78] The prohibition of blasphemy extends to language against Christ's Church, the saints, and sacred things. It is also

[72] *Ex* 20:7; *Deut* 5:11. — [73] *Mt* 5:33–34. — [74] Cf. *Zech* 2:13; *Ps* 29:2; 96:2; 113:1–2. — [75] John Henry Cardinal Newman, *Parochial and Plain Sermons* V, 2 (London: Longmans, Green and Co., 1907) 21–22. — [76] Cf. *Mt* 10:32; *1 Tim* 6:12. — [77] Cf. *1 Jn* 1:10. — [78] *Jas* 2:7.

blasphemous to make use of God's name to cover up criminal practices, to reduce peoples to servitude, to torture persons or put them to death. The misuse of God's name to commit a crime can provoke others to repudiate religion.

1756 Blasphemy is contrary to the respect due God and his holy name. It is in itself a grave sin.[79]

2149 *Oaths* which misuse God's name, though without the intention of blasphemy, show lack of respect for the Lord. The second commandment also forbids *magical use* of the divine name.

> [God's] name is great when spoken with respect for the greatness of his majesty. God's name is holy when said with veneration and fear of offending him.[80]

II. Taking the Name of the Lord in Vain

2150 The second commandment *forbids false oaths*. Taking an oath or swearing is to take God as witness to what one affirms. It is to invoke the divine truthfulness as a pledge of one's own truthfulness. An oath engages the Lord's name. "You shall fear the LORD your God; you shall serve him, and swear by his name."[81]

2151 Rejection of false oaths is a duty toward God. As Creator and Lord, God is the norm of all truth. Human speech is either in accord with or in opposition to God who
215 is Truth itself. When it is truthful and legitimate, an oath highlights the relationship of human speech with God's truth. A false oath calls on God to be witness to a lie.

2152 A person commits *perjury* when he makes a promise under 2476
oath with no intention of keeping it, or when after promising on oath he does not keep it. Perjury is a grave lack of respect for the Lord of all 1756
speech. Pledging oneself by oath to commit an evil deed is contrary to the holiness of the divine name.

2153 In the Sermon on the Mount, Jesus explained the second commandment: "You have heard that it was said to the men of old, 'You shall not swear falsely, but shall perform to the Lord what you have sworn.' But I say to you, Do not swear at all.... Let what you say be simply 'Yes' or 'No'; anything more than this comes from the evil one."[82] Jesus teaches that every oath involves a reference to God and that God's presence and his truth must be honored in all speech. Discretion in calling upon God is allied with a respectful awareness of his presence, 2466
which all our assertions either witness to or mock.

2154 Following St. Paul,[83] the tradition of the Church has understood Jesus' words as not excluding oaths made for grave and right reasons (for example, in court). "An oath, that is the invocation of the divine name as a witness to truth, cannot be taken unless in truth, in judgment, and in justice."[84]

2155 The holiness of the divine name demands that we neither use it for trivial matters, nor take an oath which on the basis of the circumstances could be interpreted as

[79] Cf. CIC, can. 1369. — [80] St. Augustine, *De serm. Dom. in monte* 2, 5, 19: PL 34, 1278. — [81] *Deut* 6:13. — [82] *Mt* 5:33–34, 37; cf. *Jas* 5:12. — [83] Cf. *2 Cor* 1:23; *Gal* 1:20. — [84] CIC, can. 1199 § 1.

approval of an authority unjustly requiring it. When an oath is required by illegitimate civil authorities, it may be refused. It must be refused when it is required for purposes con-
1903 trary to the dignity of persons or to ecclesial communion.

III. The Christian Name

232 **2156** The sacrament of Baptism is conferred "in the name of the Father and of the Son and of the Holy Spirit."[85] In Baptism, the Lord's name sanctifies man, and the Christian receives his name in the Church.
1267 This can be the name of a saint, that is, of a disciple who has lived a life of exemplary fidelity to the Lord. The patron saint provides a model of charity; we are assured of his intercession. The "baptismal name" can also express a Christian mystery or Christian virtue. "Parents, sponsors, and the pastor are to see that a name is not given which is foreign to Christian sentiment."[86]

2157 The Christian begins his day, his prayers, and his activities with the Sign of the Cross: "in the name of the Father and of the Son
1235 and of the Holy Spirit. Amen." The baptized person dedicates the day to the glory of God and calls on the Savior's grace which lets him act in
1668 the Spirit as a child of the Father. The sign of the cross strengthens us in temptations and difficulties.

2158 God calls each one by name.[87] Everyone's name is sacred. The name is the icon of the person. It demands respect as a sign of the dignity of the one who bears it.

2159 The name one receives is a name for eternity. In the kingdom, the mysterious and unique character of each person marked with God's name will shine forth in splendor. "To him who conquers...I will give a white stone, with a new name written on the stone which no one knows except him who receives it."[88] "Then I looked, and Lo, on Mount Zion stood the Lamb, and with him a hundred and forty-four thousand who had his name and his Father's name written on their foreheads."[89]

In Brief

2160 *"O Lord, our Lord, how majestic is your name in all the earth" (*Ps *8:1)!*

2161 *The second commandment enjoins respect for the Lord's name. The name of the Lord is holy.*

2162 *The second commandment forbids every improper use of God's name. Blasphemy is the use of the name of God, of Jesus Christ, of the Virgin Mary, and of the saints in an offensive way.*

2163 *False oaths call on God to be witness to a lie. Perjury is a grave offence against the Lord who is always faithful to his promises.*

2164 *"Do not swear whether by the Creator, or any creature, except truthfully, of necessity, and with reverence" (St. Ignatius of Loyola,* Spiritual Exercises, *38).*

[85] *Mt* 28:19. — [86] CIC, can. 855. — [87] Cf. *Isa* 43:1; *Jn* 10:3. — [88] *Rev* 2:17. — [89] *Rev* 14:1.

2165 *In Baptism, the Christian receives his name in the Church. Parents, godparents, and the pastor are to see that he be given a Christian name. The patron saint provides a model of charity and the assurance of his prayer.*

2166 *The Christian begins his prayers and activities with the Sign of the Cross: "in the name of the Father and of the Son and of the Holy Spirit. Amen."*

2167 *God calls each one by name (cf.* Isa *43:1).*

Article 3:
THE THIRD COMMANDMENT

> Remember the sabbath day, to keep it holy. Six days you shall labor, and do all your work; but the seventh day is a sabbath to the Lord your God; in it you shall not do any work.[90]
> The sabbath was made for man, not man for the sabbath; so the Son of Man is lord even of the sabbath.[91]

346–348 ### I. The Sabbath Day

2168 The third commandment of the Decalogue recalls the holiness of the sabbath: "The seventh day is a sabbath of solemn rest, holy to the LORD."[92]

2057 **2169** In speaking of the sabbath Scripture recalls creation: "For in six days the LORD made heaven and earth, the sea, and all that is in them, and rested the seventh day; therefore the LORD blessed the sabbath day and hallowed it."[93]

2170 Scripture also reveals in the Lord's day a *memorial of Israel's liberation* from bondage in Egypt: "You shall remember that you were a servant in the land of Egypt, and the LORD your God brought you out thence with mighty hand and outstretched arm; therefore the LORD your God commanded you to keep the sabbath day."[94]

2171 God entrusted the sabbath to Israel to keep as a *sign of the irrevocable covenant.*[95] The sabbath is for the Lord, holy and set apart for the praise of God, his work of creation, and his saving actions on behalf of Israel.

2172 God's action is the model for human action. If God "rested and was refreshed" on the seventh day, man too ought to "rest" and should
let others, especially the poor, "be 2184
refreshed."[96] The sabbath brings everyday work to a halt and provides a respite. It is a day of protest against the servitude of work and the worship of money.[97]

2173 The Gospel reports many incidents when Jesus was accused of violating the sabbath law. But Jesus never fails to respect the holiness of
this day.[98] He gives this law its au- 582
thentic and authoritative interpretation: "The sabbath was made for man, not man for the sabbath."[99] With compassion, Christ declares the sabbath for doing good rather than harm, for saving life rather

[90] *Ex* 20:8–10; cf. *Deut* 5:12–15. — [91] *Mk* 2:27–28. — [92] *Ex* 31:15. — [93] *Ex* 20:11. — [94] *Deut* 5:15. — [95] Cf. *Ex* 31:16. — [96] *Ex* 31:17; cf. 23:12. — [97] Cf. *Neh* 13:15–22; *2 Chr* 36:21. — [98] Cf. *Mk* 1:21; *Jn* 9:16. — [99] *Mk* 2:27.

than killing.[100] The sabbath is the day of the Lord of mercies and a day to honor God.[101] "The Son of Man is lord even of the sabbath."[102]

II. The Lord's Day

> This is the day which the LORD has made; let us rejoice and be glad in it.[103]

The day of the Resurrection: the new creation

638 **2174** Jesus rose from the dead "on the first day of the week."[104] Because it is the "first day," the day of Christ's Resurrection recalls the first creation. Because it is the "eighth day" following the sabbath,[105] it
349 symbolizes the new creation ushered in by Christ's Resurrection. For Christians it has become the first of all days, the first of all feasts, the Lord's Day (*he kuriake hemera, dies dominica*)—Sunday:

> We all gather on the day of the sun, for it is the first day [after the Jewish sabbath, but also the first day] when God, separating matter from darkness, made the world; and on this same day Jesus Christ our Savior rose from the dead.[106]

Sunday—fulfillment of the sabbath

2175 Sunday is expressly distinguished from the sabbath which it follows chronologically every week; for Christians its ceremonial obser-
1166 vance replaces that of the sabbath. In Christ's Passover, Sunday fulfills the spiritual truth of the Jewish sabbath and announces man's eternal rest in God. For worship under the Law prepared for the mystery of Christ, and what was done there prefigured some aspects of Christ:[107]

> Those who lived according to the old order of things have come to a new hope, no longer keeping the sabbath, but the Lord's Day, in which our life is blessed by him and by his death.[108]

2176 The celebration of Sunday observes the moral commandment inscribed by nature in the human heart to render to God an outward, visible, public, and regular worship "as a sign of his universal beneficence to all."[109] Sunday worship fulfills the moral command of the Old Covenant, taking up its rhythm and spirit in the weekly celebration of the Creator and Redeemer of his people.

The Sunday Eucharist

2177 The Sunday celebration of 1167
the Lord's Day and his Eucharist is at the heart of the Church's life. "Sunday is the day on which the paschal mystery is celebrated in light of the apostolic tradition and is to be observed as the foremost holy day of obligation in the universal Church."[110]

> "Also to be observed are the day 2043
> of the Nativity of Our Lord Jesus Christ, the Epiphany, the Ascension of Christ, the feast of the Body and Blood of Christi, the feast of Mary the Mother of God, her Immaculate Conception, her Assumption, the feast of Saint Joseph, the feast of the Apostles Saints Peter and Paul, and the feast of All Saints."[111]

[100] Cf. *Mk* 3:4. — [101] Cf. *Mt* 12:5; *Jn* 7:23. — [102] *Mk* 2:28. — [103] *Ps* 118:24. — [104] Cf. *Mt* 28:1; *Mk* 16:2; *Lk* 24:1; *Jn* 20:1. — [105] Cf. *Mk* 16:1; *Mt* 28:1. — [106] St. Justin, *I Apol.* 67: PG 6, 429 and 432. — [107] Cf. *1 Cor* 10:11. — [108] St. Ignatius of Antioch, *Ad Magn.* 9, 1: SCh 10, 88. — [109] St. Thomas Aquinas, *STh* II–II, 122, 4. — [110] CIC, can. 1246 § 1. — [111] CIC, can. 1246 § 2: "The conference of bishops can abolish certain holy days of obligation or transfer them to a Sunday with prior approval of the Apostolic See."

1343 **2178** This practice of the Christian assembly dates from the beginnings of the apostolic age.[112] The *Letter to the Hebrews* reminds the faithful "not to neglect to meet together, as is the habit of some, but to encourage one another."[113]

> Tradition preserves the memory of an ever-timely exhortation: Come to Church early, approach the Lord, and confess your sins, repent in prayer.... Be present at the sacred and divine liturgy, conclude its prayer and do not leave before the dismissal.... We have often said: "This day is given to you for prayer and rest. This is the day that the Lord has made, let us rejoice and be glad in it."[114]

1567 **2179** "A *parish* is a definite community of the Christian faithful established on a stable basis within a particular church; the pastoral care of the parish is entrusted to a pastor as its own shepherd under the
2691 authority of the diocesan bishop."[115] It is the place where all the faithful can be gathered together for the Sunday celebration of the Eucharist. The parish initiates the Christian people into the ordinary expression of the li-
2226 turgical life: it gathers them together in this celebration; it teaches Christ's saving doctrine; it practices the charity of the Lord in good works and brotherly love:

> You cannot pray at home as at church, where there is a great multitude, where exclamations are cried out to God as from one great heart, and where there is something more: the union of minds, the accord of souls, the bond of charity, the prayers of the priests.[116]

The Sunday obligation

2180 The precept of the Church 2042
specifies the law of the Lord more precisely: "On Sundays and other holy days of obligation the faithful are bound to participate in the Mass."[117] "The precept of participating in the Mass is satisfied by assis- 1389
tance at a Mass which is celebrated anywhere in a Catholic rite either on the holy day or on the evening of the preceding day."[118]

2181 The Sunday Eucharist is the foundation and confirmation of all Christian practice. For this reason the faithful are obliged to participate in the Eucharist on days of obligation, unless excused for a serious reason (for example, illness, the care of infants) or dispensed by their own pastor.[119] Those who deliberately fail in this obligation commit a grave sin.

2182 Participation in the communal celebration of the Sunday Eucharist is a testimony of belonging and of being faithful to Christ
and to his Church. The faithful give 815
witness by this to their communion in faith and charity. Together they testify to God's holiness and their hope of salvation. They strengthen one another under the guidance of the Holy Spirit.

2183 "If because of lack of a sacred minister or for other grave cause participation in the celebration of the Eucharist is impossible, it is specially recommended that the faithful take part in the Liturgy of the Word if it is celebrated in the parish church or in another sacred

[112] Cf. *Acts* 2:42–46; *1 Cor* 11:17. — [113] *Heb* 10:25. — [114] *Sermo de die dominica* 2 et 6: PG 86/1, 416C and 421C. — [115] CIC, can. 515 § 1. — [116] St. John Chrysostom, *De incomprehensibili* 3, 6: PG 48, 725. — [117] CIC, can. 1247. — [118] CIC, can. 1248 § 1. — [119] Cf. CIC, can. 1245.

place according to the prescriptions of the diocesan bishop, or engage in prayer for an appropriate amount of time personally or in a family or, as occasion offers, in groups of families."[120]

A day of grace and rest from work

2184 Just as God "rested on the seventh day from all his work which
2172 he had done,"[121] human life has a rhythm of work and rest. The institution of the Lord's Day helps everyone enjoy adequate rest and leisure to cultivate their familial, cultural, social, and religious lives.[122]

2185 On Sundays and other holy days of obligation, the faithful are to refrain from engaging in work or activities that hinder the worship
2428 owed to God, the joy proper to the Lord's Day, the performance of the works of mercy, and the appropriate relaxation of mind and body.[123] Family needs or important social service can legitimately excuse from the obligation of Sunday rest. The faithful should see to it that legitimate excuses do not lead to habits prejudicial to religion, family life, and health.

> The charity of truth seeks holy leisure; the necessity of charity accepts just work.[124]

2186 Those Christians who have leisure should be mindful of their brethren who have the same needs and the same rights, yet cannot rest from work because of poverty and misery. Sunday is traditionally consecrated by Christian piety to good works and humble service of
2447 the sick, the infirm, and the elderly. Christians will also sanctify Sunday by devoting time and care to their families and relatives, often difficult to do on other days of the week. Sunday is a time for reflection, silence, cultivation of the mind, and meditation which furthers the growth of the Christian interior life.

2187 Sanctifying Sundays and holy days requires a common effort. Every Christian should avoid making unnecessary demands on others that would hinder them from observing the Lord's Day. Traditional activities (sport, restaurants, etc.), and social necessities (public services, etc.), require some people
to work on Sundays, but everyone 2289
should still take care to set aside sufficient time for leisure. With temperance and charity the faithful will see to it that they avoid the excesses and violence sometimes associated with popular leisure activities. In spite of economic constraints, public authorities should ensure citizens a time intended for rest and divine worship. Employers have a similar obligation toward their employees.

2188 In respecting religious lib- 2105
erty and the common good of all, Christians should seek recognition of Sundays and the Church's holy days as legal holidays. They have to give everyone a public example of prayer, respect, and joy and defend their traditions as a precious contribution to the spiritual life of society. If a country's legislation or other reasons require work on Sunday, the day should nevertheless be lived as the day of our deliverance which lets us share in this "festal gathering," this "assembly of the firstborn who are enrolled in heaven."[125]

[120] CIC, can. 1248 § 2. — [121] *Gen* 2:2. — [122] Cf. *GS* 67 § 3. — [123] CIC, can. 1247. — [124] St. Augustine, *De civ. Dei* 19, 19: PL 41, 647. — [125] *Heb* 12:22–23.

In Brief

2189 *"Observe the sabbath day, to keep it holy" (*Deut *5:12). "The seventh day is a sabbath of solemn rest, holy to the Lord" (*Ex *31:15).*

2190 *The sabbath, which represented the completion of the first creation, has been replaced by Sunday which recalls the new creation inaugurated by the Resurrection of Christ.*

2191 *The Church celebrates the day of Christ's Resurrection on the "eighth day," Sunday, which is rightly called the Lord's Day (cf.* SC *106).*

2192 *"Sunday…is to be observed as the foremost holy day of obligation in the universal Church" (CIC, can. 1246 § 1). "On Sundays and other holy days of obligation the faithful are bound to participate in the Mass" (CIC, can. 1247).*

2193 *"On Sundays and other holy days of obligation the faithful are bound…to abstain from those labors and business concerns which impede the worship to be rendered to God, the joy which is proper to the Lord's Day, or the proper relaxation of mind and body" (CIC, can. 1247).*

2194 *The institution of Sunday helps all "to be allowed sufficient rest and leisure to cultivate their familial, cultural, social, and religious lives" (*GS *67 § 3).*

2195 *Every Christian should avoid making unnecessary demands on others that would hinder them from observing the Lord's Day.*

Chapter Two:
"YOU SHALL LOVE YOUR NEIGHBOR AS YOURSELF"

Jesus said to his disciples: "Love one another even as I have loved you."[1]

2196 In response to the question about the first of the commandments, Jesus says: "The first is, 'Hear, O Israel: The Lord our God, the Lord is one; and you shall love the Lord your God with all your heart, and with all your soul, and with all your mind, and with all your strength.' The second is this, 'You shall love your neighbor as yourself.' There is no other commandment greater than these."[2]

The apostle St. Paul reminds us of 2822
this: "He who loves his neighbor has fulfilled the law. The commandments, '*You shall not commit adultery, You shall not kill, You shall not steal, You shall not covet,*' and any other commandment, are summed up in this sentence, 'You shall love your neighbor as yourself.' Love does no wrong to a neighbor; therefore love is the fulfilling of the law."[3]

Article 4:
THE FOURTH COMMANDMENT

Honor your father and your mother, that your days may be long in the land which the Lord your God gives you.[4]
He was obedient to them.[5]
The Lord Jesus himself recalled the force of this "commandment of God."[6] The Apostle teaches: "Children, obey your parents in the Lord, for this is right. 'Honor your father and mother,' (This is the first commandment with a promise.) 'that it may be well with you and that you may live long on the earth.'"[7]

2197 The fourth commandment opens the second table of the Decalogue. It shows us the order of charity. God has willed that, after him, we should honor our parents to whom we owe life and who have handed on to us the knowledge of God. We are obliged to honor and respect all those whom God, for our
good, has vested with his authority. 1897

2198 This commandment is expressed in positive terms of duties to be fulfilled. It introduces the subsequent commandments which are concerned with particular respect for life, marriage, earthly goods, and speech. It constitutes one of the
foundations of the social doctrine of 2419
the Church.

2199 The fourth commandment is addressed expressly to children in their relationship to their father and mother, because this relationship is the most universal. It likewise concerns the ties of kinship between members of the

[1] *Jn* 13:34. — [2] *Mk* 12:29–31; cf. *Deut* 6:4–5; *Lev* 19:18; *Mt* 22:34–40; *Lk* 10:25–28. — [3] Rom 13:8–10. — [4] *Ex* 20:12; *Deut* 5:16. — [5] *Lk* 2:51. — [6] *Mk* 7:8–13. — [7] *Eph* 6:1–3; cf. *Deut* 5:16.

extended family. It requires honor, affection, and gratitude toward elders and ancestors. Finally, it extends to the duties of pupils to teachers, employees to employers, subordinates to leaders, citizens to their country, and to those who administer or govern it.

This commandment includes and presupposes the duties of parents, instructors, teachers, leaders, magistrates, those who govern, all who exercise authority over others or over a community of persons.

2200 Observing the fourth commandment brings its reward: "Honor your father and your mother, that your days may be long in the land which the LORD your God gives you."[8] Respecting this commandment provides, along with spiritual fruits, temporal fruits of peace and
2304 prosperity. Conversely, failure to observe it brings great harm to communities and to individuals.

I. The Family in God's Plan

The nature of the family

1625 **2201** The conjugal community is established upon the consent of the spouses. Marriage and the family are ordered to the good of the spouses and to the procreation and education of children. The love of the spouses and the begetting of children create among members of the same family personal relationships and primordial responsibilities.

1882 **2202** A man and a woman united in marriage, together with their children, form a family. This institution is prior to any recognition by public authority, which has an obligation to recognize it. It should be considered the normal reference point by which the different forms of family relationship are to be evaluated.

2203 In creating man and wom- 369
an, God instituted the human family and endowed it with its fundamental constitution. Its members are persons equal in dignity. For the common good of its members and of society, the family necessarily has manifold responsibilities, rights, and duties.

The Christian family 1655–1658

2204 "The Christian family constitutes a specific revelation and realization of ecclesial communion, and for this reason it can and should
be called a *domestic church*."[9] It is a 533
community of faith, hope, and charity; it assumes singular importance in the Church, as is evident in the New Testament.[10]

2205 The Christian family is a 1702
communion of persons, a sign and image of the communion of the Father and the Son in the Holy Spirit. In the procreation and education of children it reflects the Father's work of creation. It is called to partake of the prayer and sacrifice of Christ. Daily prayer and the reading of the Word of God strengthen it in charity. The Christian family has an evangelizing and missionary task.

2206 The relationships within the family bring an affinity of feelings, affections and interests, arising above all from the members' respect for one another. The family is a *privileged community* called to achieve a "sharing of thought and common deliberation by the spouses as well as their eager cooperation as parents in the children's upbringing."[11]

[8] *Ex* 20:12; *Deut* 5:16. — [9] *FC* 21; cf. *LG* 11. — [10] Cf. *Eph* 5:21–6:4; *Col* 3:18–21; *1 Pet* 3:1–7. — [11] *GS* 52 § 1.

II. The Family and Society

1880 **2207** The family is the *original cell of social life*. It is the natural society in which husband and wife are called to give themselves in love and in the gift of life. Authority, stability, and a life of relationships within the
372 family constitute the foundations for freedom, security, and fraternity within society. The family is the
1603 community in which, from childhood, one can learn moral values, begin to honor God, and make good use of freedom. Family life is an initiation into life in society.

2208 The family should live in such a way that its members learn to care and take responsibility for the young, the old, the sick, the handicapped, and the poor. There are many families who are at times incapable of providing this help. It devolves then on other persons, other families, and, in a subsidiary way, society to provide for their needs: "Religion that is pure and undefiled before God and the Father is this: to visit orphans and widows in their affliction and to keep oneself unstained from the world."[12]

2209 The family must be helped and defended by appropriate social measures. Where families cannot fulfill their responsibilities, other social bodies have the duty of helping them and of supporting the institution of the family. Following the principle of subsidiarity, larger
1883 communities should take care not to usurp the family's prerogatives or interfere in its life.

2210 The importance of the family for the life and well-being of society[13] entails a particular responsibility for society to support and strengthen marriage and the family. Civil authority should consider it a grave duty "to acknowledge the true nature of marriage and the family, to protect and foster them, to safeguard public morality, and promote domestic prosperity."[14]

2211 The political community has a duty to honor the family, to assist it, and to ensure especially:

– the freedom to establish a family, have children, and bring them up in keeping with the family's own moral and religious convictions;
– the protection of the stability of the marriage bond and the institution of the family;
– the freedom to profess one's faith, to hand it on, and raise one's children in it, with the necessary means and institutions;
– the right to private property, to free enterprise, to obtain work and housing, and the right to emigrate;
– in keeping with the country's institutions, the right to medical care, assistance for the aged, and family benefits;
– the protection of security and health, especially with respect to dangers like drugs, pornography, alcoholism, etc.;
– the freedom to form associations with other families and so to have representation before civil authority.[15]

2212 The fourth commandment *illuminates other relationships in society*. In our brothers and sisters we see the children of our parents; in our cousins, the descendants of our ancestors; in our fellow citizens, the

[12] *Jas* 1:27. — [13] Cf. *GS* 47 § 1. — [14] *GS* 52 § 2. — [15] Cf. *FC* 46.

children of our country; in the baptized, the children of our mother the Church; in every human person, a son or daughter of the One who
225 wants to be called "our Father." In this way our relationships with our neighbors are recognized as personal in character. The neighbor is not a "unit" in the human collective;
1931 he is "someone" who by his known origins deserves particular attention and respect.

2213 Human communities are *made up of persons*. Governing them well is not limited to guaranteeing rights and fulfilling duties such as honoring contracts. Right relations between employers and employees, between those who govern and citizens, presuppose a natural good will in keeping with the dignity of human persons concerned for justice
1939 and fraternity.

III. The Duties of Family Members

The duties of children

2214 The divine fatherhood is the source of human fatherhood;[16] this is the foundation of the honor owed to parents. The respect of children, whether minors or adults, for their father and mother[17] is nourished by the natural affection born of the
1858 bond uniting them. It is required by God's commandment.[18]

2215 Respect for parents (*filial piety*) derives from *gratitude* toward those who, by the gift of life, their love and their work, have brought their children into the world and enabled them to grow in stature, wisdom, and grace. "With all your heart honor your father, and do not forget the birth pangs of your mother. Remember that through your parents you were born; what can you give back to them that equals their gift to you?"[19]

2216 Filial respect is shown by 532
true docility and *obedience*. "My son, keep your father's commandment, and forsake not your mother's teaching.... When you walk, they will lead you; when you lie down, they will watch over you; and when you awake, they will talk with you."[20] "A wise son hears his father's instruction, but a scoffer does not listen to rebuke."[21]

2217 As long as a child lives at home with his parents, the child should obey his parents in all that they ask of him when it is for his good or that of the family. "Children, obey your parents in everything, for this pleases the Lord."[22] Children should also obey the reasonable directions of their teachers and all to whom their parents have entrusted them. But if a child is convinced in conscience that it would be morally wrong to obey a particular order, he must not do so.

As they grow up, children should continue to respect their parents. They should anticipate their wishes, willingly seek their advice, and accept their just admonitions. Obedience toward parents ceases with the emancipation of the children; not so respect, which is always owed to them. This respect has its roots in the fear of God, one of the gifts of
the Holy Spirit. 1831

[16] Cf. *Eph* 3:14. — [17] Cf. *Prov* 1:8; *Tob* 4:3–4. — [18] Cf. *Ex* 20:12. — [19] *Sir* 7:27–28. — [20] *Prov* 6:20–22.
[21] *Prov* 13:1. — [22] *Col* 3:20; cf. *Eph* 6:1.

2218 The fourth commandment reminds grown children of their *responsibilities toward their parents.* As much as they can, they must give them material and moral support in old age and in times of illness, loneliness, or distress. Jesus recalls this duty of gratitude.[23]

> For the Lord honored the father above the children, and he confirmed the right of the mother over her sons. Whoever honors his father atones for sins, and whoever glorifies his mother is like one who lays up treasure. Whoever honors his father will be gladdened by his own children, and when he prays he will be heard. Whoever glorifies his father will have long life, and whoever obeys the Lord will refresh his mother.[24]
>
> O son, help your father in his old age, and do not grieve him as long as he lives; even if he is lacking in understanding, show forbearance; in all your strength do not despise him.... Whoever forsakes his father is like a blasphemer, and whoever angers his mother is cursed by the Lord.[25]

2219 Filial respect promotes harmony in all of family life; it also concerns *relationships between brothers and sisters.* Respect toward parents fills the home with light and warmth. "Grandchildren are the crown of the aged."[26] "With all humility and meekness, with patience, [support] one another in charity."[27]

2220 For Christians a special gratitude is due to those from whom they have received the gift of faith, the grace of Baptism, and life in the Church. These may include parents, grandparents, other members of the family, pastors, catechists, and other teachers or friends. "I am reminded of your sincere faith, a faith that dwelt first in your grandmother Lois and your mother Eunice and now, I am sure, dwells in you."[28]

The duties of parents

2221 The fecundity of conjugal love cannot be reduced solely to the procreation of children, but must extend to their moral education and their spiritual formation. "The *role of parents in education* is of such importance that it is almost impossible 1653
to provide an adequate substitute."[29] The right and the duty of parents to educate their children are primordial and inalienable.[30]

2222 Parents must regard their children as *children of God* and respect them as *human persons.* Showing themselves obedient to the will
of the Father in heaven, they educate 494
their children to fulfill God's law.

2223 Parents have the first responsibility for the education of their children. They bear witness to this responsibility first by *creating a home* where tenderness, forgiveness, respect, fidelity, and disinterested service are the rule. The home is well suited for *education in the virtues.* This requires an apprenticeship in self-denial, sound
judgment, and self-mastery—the pre- 1804
conditions of all true freedom. Parents should teach their children to subordinate the "material and instinctual dimensions to interior and spiritual ones."[31] Parents have a grave responsibility to give good example to their children. By knowing how to acknowledge their own failings to their

[23] Cf. *Mk* 7:10–12. — [24] *Sir* 3:2–6. — [25] *Sir* 3:12–13, 16. — [26] *Prov* 17:6. — [27] *Eph* 4:2. — [28] *2 Tim* 1:5. — [29] *GE* 3. — [30] Cf. *FC* 36. — [31] *CA* 36 § 2.

children, parents will be better able to guide and correct them:

> He who loves his son will not spare the rod.... He who disciplines his son will profit by him.[32]
> Fathers, do not provoke your children to anger, but bring them up in the discipline and instruction of the Lord.[33]

1939 **2224** The home is the natural environment for initiating a human being into solidarity and communal responsibilities. Parents should teach children to avoid the compromising and degrading influences which threaten human societies.

2225 Through the grace of the sacrament of marriage, parents receive the responsibility and privilege of *evangelizing their children*. Parents
1656 should initiate their children at an early age into the mysteries of the faith of which they are the "first heralds" for their children. They should associate them from their tenderest years with the life of the Church.[34] A wholesome family life can foster interior dispositions that are a genuine preparation for a living faith and remain a support for it throughout one's life.

2226 *Education in the faith* by the parents should begin in the child's earliest years. This already happens when family members help one another to grow in faith by the witness of a Christian life in keeping with the Gospel. Family catechesis precedes, accompanies, and enriches other forms of instruction in the faith. Parents have the mission of teaching their children to pray and
2179 to discover their vocation as children of God.[35] The parish is the Eucharistic community and the heart of the liturgical life of Christian families; it is a privileged place for the catechesis of children and parents.

2227 Children in turn contrib- 2013
ute to the *growth in holiness* of their parents.[36] Each and everyone should be generous and tireless in forgiving one another for offenses, quarrels, injustices, and neglect. Mutual affection suggests this. The charity of Christ demands it.[37]

2228 Parents' respect and affection are expressed by the care and attention they devote to bringing up their young children and *providing for their physical and spiritual needs.* As the children grow up, the same respect and devotion lead parents to educate them in the right use of their reason and freedom.

2229 As those first responsible for the education of their children, parents have the right to *choose a school for them* which corresponds to their own convictions. This right is fundamental. As far as possible parents have the duty of choosing schools that will best help them in their task as Christian educators.[38] Public authorities have the duty of guaranteeing this parental right and of ensuring the concrete conditions for its exercise.

2230 When they become adults, children have the right and duty to *choose their profession and state of life.* They should assume their new responsibilities within a trusting relationship with their parents, willingly asking and receiving their advice and counsel. Parents should be careful not to exert pressure on

[32] *Sir* 30:1–2. — [33] *Eph* 6:4. — [34] *LG* 11 § 2. — [35] Cf. *LG* 11. — [36] Cf. *GS* 48 § 4. — [37] Cf. *Mt* 18:21–22; *Lk* 17:4. — [38] Cf. *GE* 6.

their children either in the choice of
1625 a profession or in that of a spouse. This necessary restraint does not prevent them—quite the contrary—from giving their children judicious advice, particularly when they are planning to start a family.

2231 Some forgo marriage in order to care for their parents or brothers and sisters, to give themselves more completely to a profession, or to serve other honorable ends. They can contribute greatly to the good of the human family.

IV. The Family and the Kingdom

2232 Family ties are important but not absolute. Just as the child grows to maturity and human and spiritual autonomy, so his unique vocation which comes from God asserts itself more clearly and forcefully. Parents should respect this call and encourage their children to follow it. They must be convinced that the first vocation of the Christian is
1618 to *follow Jesus*: "He who loves father or mother more than me is not worthy of me; and he who loves son or daughter more than me is not worthy of me."[39]

2233 Becoming a disciple of Jesus means accepting the invitation to belong to *God's family*, to live in conformity with His way of life: "For whoever does the will of my
542 Father in heaven is my brother, and sister, and mother."[40]

Parents should welcome and respect with joy and thanksgiving the Lord's call to one of their children to follow him in virginity for the sake of the Kingdom in the consecrated life or in priestly ministry.

V. The Authorities in Civil Society

2234 God's fourth commandment also enjoins us to honor all who for our good have received authority in society from God. It clarifies the duties of those who exercise authority as well as those who ben- 1897
efit from it.

Duties of civil authorities

2235 Those who exercise authority should do so as a service. "Whoever would be great among you must be your servant."[41] The exercise of authority is measured morally in terms of its divine origin, its reasonable nature and its specific object. No one can command or establish what is contrary to the dignity of 1899
persons and the natural law.

2236 The exercise of authority is meant to give outward expression to a just hierarchy of values in order to facilitate the exercise of freedom and responsibility by all. Those in authority should practice distributive justice wisely, taking account of 2411
the needs and contribution of each, with a view to harmony and peace. They should take care that the regulations and measures they adopt are not a source of temptation by setting personal interest against that of the community.[42]

2237 *Political authorities* are obliged to respect the fundamental rights of the human person. They will dispense justice humanely by respecting the rights of everyone, especially 357
of families and the disadvantaged.

The political rights attached to citizenship can and should be granted

[39] *Mt* 10:37; cf. 16:25. — [40] *Mt* 12:49. — [41] *Mt* 20:26. — [42] Cf. *CA* 25.

according to the requirements of the common good. They cannot be suspended by public authorities without legitimate and proportionate reasons. Political rights are meant to be exercised for the common good of the nation and the human community.

The duties of citizens

2238 Those subject to authority should regard those in authority as representatives of God, who has made them stewards of his gifts:[43]
1900 "Be subject for the Lord's sake to every human institution.... Live as free men, yet without using your freedom as a pretext for evil; but live as servants of God."[44] Their loyal collaboration includes the right, and at times the duty, to voice their just criticisms of that which seems harmful to the dignity of persons and to the good of the community.

1915 **2239** It is the *duty of citizens* to contribute along with the civil authorities to the good of society in a spirit of truth, justice, solidarity, and freedom. The love and service of *one's country* follow from the duty
2310 of gratitude and belong to the order of charity. Submission to legitimate authorities and service of the common good require citizens to fulfill their roles in the life of the political community.

2240 Submission to authority and co-responsibility for the common good make it morally obligatory to pay taxes, to exercise the right to
2265 vote, and to defend one's country:

> Pay to all of them their dues, taxes to whom taxes are due, revenue to whom revenue is due, respect to whom respect is due, honor to whom honor is due.[45]
>
> [Christians] reside in their own nations, but as resident aliens. They participate in all things as citizens and endure all things as foreigners.... They obey the established laws and their way of life surpasses the laws.... So noble is the position to which God has assigned them that they are not allowed to desert it.[46]

The Apostle exhorts us to offer 1900
prayers and thanksgiving for kings and all who exercise authority, "that we may lead a quiet and peaceable life, godly and respectful in every way."[47]

2241 The more prosperous nations are obliged, to the extent they are able, to welcome the *foreigner* in search of the security and the means of livelihood which he cannot find in his country of origin. Public authorities should see to it that the natural right is respected that places a guest under the protection of those who receive him.

Political authorities, for the sake of the common good for which they are responsible, may make the exercise of the right to immigrate subject to various juridical conditions, especially with regard to the immigrants' duties toward their country of adoption. Immigrants are obliged to respect with gratitude the material and spiritual heritage of the country that receives them, to obey its laws and to assist in carrying civic burdens.

[43] Cf. *Rom* 13:1–2. — [44] *1 Pet* 2:13, 16. — [45] *Rom* 13:7. — [46] *Ad Diognetum* 5, 5 and 10; 6, 10: PG 2, 1173 and 1176. — [47] *1 Tim* 2:2.

2242 The citizen is obliged in
conscience not to follow the directives of civil authorities when they
are contrary to the demands of the
moral order, to the fundamental
1903 rights of persons or the teachings of
2313 the Gospel. *Refusing obedience* to civil authorities, when their demands
are contrary to those of an upright
conscience, finds its justification in
the distinction between serving God
and serving the political communi-
450 ty. "Render therefore to Caesar the
things that are Caesar's, and to God
the things that are God's."[48] "We
must obey God rather than men":[49]

> 1901 When citizens are under the oppression of a public authority which oversteps its competence, they should still not refuse to give or to do what is objectively demanded of them by the common good; but it is legitimate for them to defend their own rights and those of their fellow citizens against the abuse of this authority within the limits of the natural law and the Law of the Gospel.[50]

2309 **2243** Armed *resistance* to oppression by political authority is not legitimate, unless all the following conditions are met: 1) there is certain, grave, and prolonged violation of fundamental rights; 2) all other means of redress have been exhausted; 3) such resistance will not provoke worse disorders; 4) there is well-founded hope of success; and 5) it is impossible reasonably to foresee any better solution.

The political community and the Church

1910 **2244** Every institution is inspired,
at least implicitly, by a vision of man
and his destiny, from which it derives the point of reference for its
judgment, its hierarchy of values,
its line of conduct. Most societies
have formed their institutions in
the recognition of a certain preeminence of man over things. Only the
divinely revealed religion has clearly
recognized man's origin and destiny 1881
in God, the Creator and Redeemer.
The Church invites political authorities to measure their judgments and 2109
decisions against this inspired truth
about God and man:

> Societies not recognizing this vision or rejecting it in the name of their independence from God are brought to seek their criteria and goal in themselves or to borrow them from some ideology. Since they do not admit that one can defend an objective criterion of good and evil, they arrogate to themselves an explicit or implicit totalitarian power over man and his destiny, as history shows.[51]

2245 The Church, because of her
commission and competence, is not
to be confused in any way with the
political community. She is both the
sign and the safeguard of the tran- 912
scendent character of the human
person. "The Church respects and
encourages the political freedom
and responsibility of the citizen."[52]

2246 It is a part of the Church's
mission "to pass moral judgments
even in matters related to politics,
whenever the fundamental rights of
man or the salvation of souls requires 2032
it. The means, the only means, she
may use are those which are in ac- 2420
cord with the Gospel and the welfare
of all men according to the diversity
of times and circumstances."[53]

[48] *Mt* 22:21. — [49] *Acts* 5:29. — [50] *GS* 74 § 5. — [51] Cf. *CA* 45; 46. — [52] *GS* 76 § 3. — [53] *GS* 76 § 5.

In Brief

2247 *"Honor your father and your mother"* (Deut *5:16;* Mk *7:10).*

2248 *According to the fourth commandment, God has willed that, after him, we should honor our parents and those whom he has vested with authority for our good.*

2249 *The conjugal community is established upon the covenant and consent of the spouses. Marriage and family are ordered to the good of the spouses, to the procreation and the education of children.*

2250 *"The well-being of the individual person and of both human and Christian society is closely bound up with the healthy state of conjugal and family life"* (GS *47 § 1).*

2251 *Children owe their parents respect, gratitude, just obedience, and assistance. Filial respect fosters harmony in all of family life.*

2252 *Parents have the first responsibility for the education of their children in the faith, prayer, and all the virtues. They have the duty to provide as far as possible for the physical and spiritual needs of their children.*

2253 *Parents should respect and encourage their children's vocations. They should remember and teach that the first calling of the Christian is to follow Jesus.*

2254 *Public authority is obliged to respect the fundamental rights of the human person and the conditions for the exercise of his freedom.*

2255 *It is the duty of citizens to work with civil authority for building up society in a spirit of truth, justice, solidarity, and freedom.*

2256 *Citizens are obliged in conscience not to follow the directives of civil authorities when they are contrary to the demands of the moral order. "We must obey God rather than men"* (Acts *5:29).*

2257 *Every society's judgments and conduct reflect a vision of man and his destiny. Without the light the Gospel sheds on God and man, societies easily become totalitarian.*

Article 5: THE FIFTH COMMANDMENT

> You shall not kill.[54]
> You have heard that it was said to the men of old, "You shall not kill: and whoever kills shall be liable to judgment." But I say to you that every one who is angry with his brother shall be liable to judgment.[55]

356 **2258** "*Human life is sacred* because from its beginning it involves the creative action of God and it remains for ever in a special relationship with the Creator, who is its sole end. God alone is the Lord of life from its beginning until its end: no one can under any circumstance claim for himself the right directly to destroy an innocent human being."[56]

[54] *Ex* 20:13; cf. *Deut* 5:17. — [55] *Mt* 5:21–22. — [56] CDF, instruction, *Donum vitae*, intro. 5.

I. Respect for Human Life

The witness of sacred history

401 **2259** In the account of Abel's murder by his brother Cain,[57] Scripture reveals the presence of anger and envy in man, consequences of original sin, from the beginning of human history. Man has become the enemy of his fellow man. God declares the wickedness of this fratricide: "What have you done? The voice of your brother's blood is crying to me from the ground. And now you are cursed from the ground, which has opened its mouth to receive your brother's blood from your hand."[58]

2260 The covenant between God and mankind is interwoven with reminders of God's gift of human life and man's murderous violence:

> For your lifeblood I will surely require a reckoning.... Whoever sheds the blood of man, by man shall his blood be shed; for God made man in his own image.[59]

The Old Testament always considered blood a sacred sign of life.[60] This teaching remains necessary for all time.

2261 Scripture specifies the prohibition contained in the fifth commandment: "Do not slay the innocent and the righteous."[61] The deliberate murder of an innocent person is gravely contrary to the
1756 dignity of the human being, to the golden rule, and to the holiness of
1956 the Creator. The law forbidding it is universally valid: it obliges each and everyone, always and everywhere.

2262 In the Sermon on the Mount, the Lord recalls the commandment, "You shall not kill,"[62] and adds to it the proscription of anger, hatred, and vengeance. Going further, Christ asks his disciples to turn the other cheek, to love their enemies.[63] He did not defend himself and told Peter to leave his sword
in its sheath.[64] 2844

Legitimate defense

2263 The legitimate defense of persons and societies is not an exception to the prohibition against the murder of the innocent that constitutes intentional killing. "The act of self-defense can have a double effect: the preservation of one's 1737
own life; and the killing of the aggressor.... The one is intended, the other is not."[65]

2264 Love toward oneself remains 2196
a fundamental principle of morality. Therefore it is legitimate to insist on respect for one's own right to life. Someone who defends his life is not guilty of murder even if he is forced to deal his aggressor a lethal blow:

> If a man in self-defense uses more than necessary violence, it will be unlawful: whereas if he repels force with moderation, his defense will be lawful.... Nor is it necessary for salvation that a man omit the act of moderate self-defense to avoid killing the other man, since one is bound to take more care of one's own life than of another's.[66]

2265 Legitimate defense can be not only a right but a grave duty for one who is responsible for the
lives of others. The defense of the 2240
common good requires that an

[57] Cf. *Gen* 4:8–12. — [58] *Gen* 4:10–11. — [59] *Gen* 9:5–6. — [60] Cf. *Lev* 17:14. — [61] *Ex* 23:7. — [62] *Mt* 5:21. — [63] Cf. *Mt* 5:22–39; 5:44. — [64] Cf. *Mt* 26:52. — [65] St. Thomas Aquinas, *STh* II–II, 64, 7, *corp. art.* — [66] St. Thomas Aquinas, *STh* II–II, 64, 7, *corp. art.*

unjust aggressor be rendered unable to cause harm. For this reason, those who legitimately hold authority also have the right to use arms to repel aggressors against the civil community entrusted to their responsibility.

2266 The efforts of the state to curb the spread of behavior harmful to people's rights and to the basic rules of civil society correspond to the requirement of safeguarding the common good. Legitimate public
1897–1898 authority has the right and the duty to inflict punishment proportionate to the gravity of the offense. Punishment has the primary aim of redressing the disorder introduced by the offense. When it is willingly accepted by the guilty party, it assumes
2308 the value of expiation. Punishment then, in addition to defending public order and protecting people's safety, has a medicinal purpose: as far as possible, it must contribute to the correction of the guilty party.[67]

The death penalty

2267 Recourse to the death penalty on the part of legitimate authority, following a fair trial, was long considered an appropriate response to the gravity of certain crimes and an acceptable, albeit extreme, means of safeguarding the common good.

Today, however, there is an increasing awareness that the dignity of the person is not lost even after the commission of very serious crimes. In addition, a new understanding has emerged of the significance of penal sanctions imposed by the state. Lastly, more effective systems of detention have been developed, which ensure the due protection of citizens but, at the same time, do not definitively deprive the guilty of the possibility of redemption.

Consequently, the Church teaches, in the light of the Gospel, that "the death penalty is inadmissible because it is an attack on the inviolability and dignity of the person,"[68] and she works with determination for its abolition worldwide.

Intentional homicide

2268 The fifth commandment forbids *direct and intentional killing* as gravely sinful. The murderer and those who cooperate voluntarily in murder commit a sin that cries out
to heaven for vengeance.[69] 1867

Infanticide,[70] fratricide, parricide, and the murder of a spouse are especially grave crimes by reason of the natural bonds which they break. Concern for eugenics or public health cannot justify any murder, even if commanded by public authority.

2269 The fifth commandment forbids doing anything with the intention of *indirectly* bringing about a person's death. The moral law prohibits exposing someone to mortal danger without grave reason, as well as refusing assistance to a person in danger.

The acceptance by human society of murderous famines, without efforts to remedy them, is a scandalous injustice and a grave offense. Those whose usurious and avaricious dealings lead to the hunger and death of their brethren in the human family

[67] Cf. *Lk* 23:4–43. — [68] Francis, Address to participants in the meeting promoted by the Pontifical Council for the Promotion of the New Evangelization, October 11, 2017: *L'Osservatore Romano*, October 13, 2017, 5. — [69] Cf. *Gen* 4:10. — [70] Cf. *GS* 51 § 3.

indirectly commit homicide, which is imputable to them.[71]

2290 *Unintentional* killing is not morally imputable. But one is not exonerated from grave offense if, without proportionate reasons, he has acted in a way that brings about someone's death, even without the intention to do so.

Abortion

2270 Human life must be respected and protected absolutely from the moment of conception. From the first moment of his existence,
1703 a human being must be recognized as having the rights of a person—
357 among which is the inviolable right of every innocent being to life.[72]

> Before I formed you in the womb I knew you, and before you were born I consecrated you.[73]
> My frame was not hidden from you, when I was being made in secret, intricately wrought in the depths of the earth.[74]

2271 Since the first century the Church has affirmed the moral evil of every procured abortion. This teaching has not changed and remains unchangeable. Direct abortion, that is to say, abortion willed either as an end or a means, is gravely contrary to the moral law:

> You shall not kill the embryo by abortion and shall not cause the newborn to perish.[75]
> God, the Lord of life, has entrusted to men the noble mission of safeguarding life, and men must carry it out in a manner worthy of themselves. Life must be protected with the utmost care from the moment of conception: abortion and infanticide are abominable crimes.[76]

2272 Formal cooperation in an abortion constitutes a grave offense. The Church attaches the canonical penalty of excommunication to this crime against human life. "A person who procures a completed abortion incurs excommunication *latae sententiae*,"[77] "by the very commission of the offense,"[78] and subject to the conditions provided by Canon
Law.[79] The Church does not thereby 1463
intend to restrict the scope of mercy. Rather, she makes clear the gravity of the crime committed, the irreparable harm done to the innocent who is put to death, as well as to the parents and the whole of society.

2273 The inalienable right to life 1930
of every innocent human individual is a *constitutive element of a civil society and its legislation:*

"The inalienable rights of the person must be recognized and respected by civil society and the political authority. These human rights depend neither on single individuals nor on parents; nor do they represent a concession made by society and the state; they belong to human nature and are inherent in the person by virtue of the creative act from which the person took his origin. Among such fundamental rights one should mention in this regard every human being's right to life and physical integrity from the moment of conception until death."[80]

[71] Cf. *Am* 8:4–10. — [72] Cf. CDF, *Donum vitae* I, 1. — [73] *Jer* 1:5; cf. *Job* 10:8–12; *Ps* 22:10–11. — [74] *Ps* 139:15. — [75] *Didache* 2, 2: SCh 248, 148; cf. *Ep. Barnabae* 19, 5: PG 2, 777; *Ad Diognetum* 5, 6: PG 2, 1173; Tertullian, *Apol.* 9: PL 1, 319–320. — [76] *GS* 51 § 3. — [77] CIC, can. 1398. — [78] CIC, can. 1314. — [79] Cf. CIC, cann. 1323–1324. — [80] CDF, *Donum vitae* III.

"The moment a positive law deprives a category of human beings of the protection which civil legislation ought to accord them, the state is denying the equality of all before the law. When the state does not place its power at the service of the rights of each citizen, and in particular of the more vulnerable, the very foundations of a state based on law are undermined.... As a consequence of the respect and protection which must be ensured for the unborn child from the moment of conception, the law must provide appropriate penal sanctions for every deliberate violation of the child's rights."[81]

2274 Since it must be treated from conception as a person, the embryo must be defended in its integrity, cared for, and healed, as far as possible, like any other human being.

Prenatal diagnosis is morally licit, "if it respects the life and integrity of the embryo and the human fetus and is directed toward its safeguarding or healing as an individual.... It is gravely opposed to the moral law when this is done with the thought of possibly inducing an abortion, depending upon the results: a diagnosis must not be the equivalent of a death sentence."[82]

2275 "One must hold as licit procedures carried out on the human embryo which respect the life and integrity of the embryo and do not involve disproportionate risks for it, but are directed toward its healing, the improvement of its condition of health, or its individual survival."[83]

"It is immoral to produce human embryos intended for exploitation as disposable biological material."[84]

"Certain attempts to *influence chromosomic or genetic inheritance* are not therapeutic but are aimed at producing human beings selected according to sex or other predetermined qualities. Such manipulations are contrary to the personal dignity of the human being and his integrity and identity"[85] which are unique and unrepeatable.

Euthanasia

2276 Those whose lives are di- 1503
minished or weakened deserve special respect. Sick or handicapped persons should be helped to lead lives as normal as possible.

2277 Whatever its motives and means, direct euthanasia consists in putting an end to the lives of handicapped, sick, or dying persons. It is morally unacceptable.

Thus an act or omission which, of itself or by intention, causes death in order to eliminate suffering constitutes a murder gravely contrary to the dignity of the human person and to the respect due to the living God, his Creator. The error of judgment into which one can fall in good faith does not change the nature of this murderous act, which must always be forbidden and excluded.

2278 Discontinuing medical procedures that are burdensome, dangerous, extraordinary, or disproportionate to the expected outcome can be legitimate; it is the refusal of "over-zealous" treatment. Here one does not will to cause death; one's inability to impede it is merely accepted. The decisions
should be made by the patient if he is 1007
competent and able or, if not, by those

[81] CDF, *Donum vitae* III. — [82] CDF, *Donum vitae* I, 2. — [83] CDF, *Donum vitae* I, 3. — [84] CDF, *Donum vitae* I, 5. — [85] CDF, *Donum vitae* I, 6.

legally entitled to act for the patient, whose reasonable will and legitimate interests must always be respected.

2279 Even if death is thought imminent, the ordinary care owed to a sick person cannot be legitimately interrupted. The use of painkillers to alleviate the sufferings of the dying, even at the risk of shortening their days, can be morally in conformity with human dignity if death is not willed as either an end or a means, but only foreseen and tolerated as inevitable. Palliative care is a special form of disinterested charity. As such it should be encouraged.

Suicide

2280 Everyone is responsible for his life before God who has given it to him. It is God who remains the sovereign Master of life. We are obliged
2258 to accept life gratefully and preserve it for his honor and the salvation of our souls. We are stewards, not owners, of the life God has entrusted to us. It is not ours to dispose of.

2281 Suicide contradicts the natural inclination of the human being to preserve and perpetuate his life. It is gravely contrary to the just love of self. It likewise offends love of neighbor because it unjustly breaks
2212 the ties of solidarity with family, nation, and other human societies to which we continue to have obligations. Suicide is contrary to love for the living God.

2282 If suicide is committed with the intention of setting an example, especially to the young, it also takes on the gravity of scandal. Voluntary
1735 co-operation in suicide is contrary to the moral law.

Grave psychological disturbances, anguish, or grave fear of hardship, suffering, or torture can diminish the responsibility of the one committing suicide.

2283 We should not despair of the eternal salvation of persons who have taken their own lives. By ways known to him alone, God can provide the opportunity for salutary repentance. The Church prays for persons who have taken their own lives. 1037

II. Respect for the Dignity of Persons

Respect for the souls of others: scandal

2284 Scandal is an attitude or 2847
behavior which leads another to do evil. The person who gives scandal becomes his neighbor's tempter. He damages virtue and integrity; he may even draw his brother into spiritual death. Scandal is a grave offense if by deed or omission another is deliberately led into a grave offense.

2285 Scandal takes on a particu- 1903
lar gravity by reason of the authority of those who cause it or the weakness of those who are scandalized. It prompted our Lord to utter this curse: "Whoever causes one of these little ones who believe in me to sin, it would be better for him to have a great millstone fastened round his neck and to be drowned in the depth of the sea."[86] Scandal is grave when given by those who by nature or office are obliged to teach and educate others. Jesus reproaches the scribes and Pharisees on this account: he likens them to wolves in sheep's clothing.[87]

[86] *Mt* 18:6; cf. *1 Cor* 8:10–13. — [87] Cf. *Mt* 7:15.

2286 Scandal can be provoked by laws or institutions, by fashion or opinion.

1887 Therefore, they are guilty of scandal who establish laws or social structures leading to the decline of morals and the corruption of religious practice, or to "social conditions that, intentionally or not, make Christian conduct and obedience to the Commandments difficult and practically impossible."[88] This is also true of business leaders who make rules encouraging fraud, teachers who
2498 provoke their children to anger,[89] or manipulators of public opinion who turn it away from moral values.

2287 Anyone who uses the power at his disposal in such a way that it leads others to do wrong becomes guilty of scandal and responsible for the evil that he has directly or indirectly encouraged. "Temptations to sin are sure to come; but woe to him by whom they come!"[90]

Respect for health

1503 **2288** Life and physical health are precious gifts entrusted to us by God. We must take reasonable care of them, taking into account the needs of others and the common good.

1509 *Concern for the health* of its citizens requires that society help in the attainment of living-conditions that allow them to grow and reach maturity: food and clothing, housing, health care, basic education, employment, and social assistance.

2289 If morality requires respect 364
for the life of the body, it does not make it an absolute value. It rejects a neo-pagan notion that tends to promote the *cult of the body*, to sac- 2113
rifice everything for its sake, to idolize physical perfection and success at sports. By its selective preference of the strong over the weak, such a conception can lead to the perversion of human relationships.

2290 The virtue of temperance 1809
disposes us to *avoid every kind of excess*: the abuse of food, alcohol, tobacco, or medicine. Those incur grave guilt who, by drunkenness or a love of speed, endanger their own and others' safety on the road, at sea, or in the air.

2291 The *use of drugs* inflicts very grave damage on human health and life. Their use, except on strictly therapeutic grounds, is a grave offense. Clandestine production of and trafficking in drugs are scandalous practices. They constitute direct co-operation in evil, since they encourage people to practices gravely contrary to the moral law.

Respect for the person and scientific research

2292 Scientific, medical, or psychological experiments on human individuals or groups can contribute to healing the sick and the advancement of public health.

2293 Basic scientific research, as 159
well as applied research, is a significant expression of man's dominion over creation. Science and technology are precious resources when

[88] Pius XII, *Discourse*, June 1, 1941. — [89] Cf. *Eph* 6:4; *Col* 3:21. — [90] *Lk* 17:1.

placed at the service of man and promote his integral development for the benefit of all. By themselves however they cannot disclose the meaning of existence and of human progress. Science and technology are ordered to man, from whom they take their origin and development; hence they find in the person and in his moral values both evidence
1703 of their purpose and awareness of their limits.

2294 It is an illusion to claim moral neutrality in scientific research and its applications. On the other hand, guiding principles cannot be inferred from simple technical efficiency, or from the usefulness accruing to some at the expense of others or, even worse, from prevailing ideologies. Science and technology by their very nature require unconditional respect for fundamental
2375 moral criteria. They must be at the service of the human person, of his inalienable rights, of his true and integral good, in conformity with the plan and the will of God.

2295 Research or experimentation on the human being cannot legitimate acts that are in themselves
1753 contrary to the dignity of persons and to the moral law. The subjects' potential consent does not justify such acts. Experimentation on human beings is not morally legitimate if it exposes the subject's life or physical and psychological integrity to disproportionate or avoidable risks. Experimentation on human beings does not conform to the dignity of the person if it takes place without the informed consent of the subject or those who legitimately speak for him.

2296 *Organ transplants* are in 2301
conformity with the moral law if the physical and psychological dangers and risks to the donor are proportionate to the good that is sought for the recipient. Organ donation after death is a noble and meritorious act and is to be encouraged as an expression of generous solidarity. It is not morally acceptable if the donor or his proxy has not given explicit consent. Moreover, it is not morally admissible directly to bring about the disabling mutilation or death of a human being, even in order to delay the death of other persons.

Respect for bodily integrity

2297 Kidnapping and hostage taking bring on a reign of terror; by means of threats they subject their victims to intolerable pressures. They are morally wrong. *Terrorism* threatens, wounds, and kills indiscriminately; it is gravely against justice and charity. *Torture* which uses physical or moral violence to extract confessions, punish the guilty, frighten opponents, or satisfy hatred is contrary to respect for the person and for human dignity. Except when performed for strictly therapeutic medical reasons, directly intended *amputations, mutilations*, and *sterilizations* performed on innocent persons are against the moral law.[91]

2298 In times past, cruel practices were commonly used by legitimate governments to maintain law and order, often without protest from the Pastors of the Church, who

[91] Cf. DS 3722.

themselves adopted in their own tribunals the prescriptions of Roman law concerning torture. Regrettable as these facts are, the Church always taught the duty of clemency and mercy. She forbade clerics to shed blood.
2267 In recent times it has become evident that these cruel practices were neither necessary for public order, nor in conformity with the legitimate rights of the human person. On the contrary, these practices led to ones even more degrading. It is necessary to work for their abolition. We must pray for the victims and their tormentors.

Respect for the dead

2299 The dying should be given attention and care to help them live their last moments in dignity and peace. They will be helped by the prayer of their relatives, who must see to it that the sick receive at the
1525 proper time the sacraments that prepare them to meet the living God.

1681–1690 **2300** The bodies of the dead must be treated with respect and charity, in faith and hope of the Resurrection. The burial of the dead is a corporal work of mercy;[92] it honors the children of God, who are temples of the Holy Spirit.

2301 Autopsies can be morally permitted for legal inquests or scientific research. The free gift of organs after death is legitimate and can be meritorious.

The Church permits cremation, provided that it does not demonstrate a denial of faith in the resurrection of the body.[93]

III. Safeguarding Peace

Peace

2302 By recalling the commandment, "You shall not kill,"[94] our Lord asked for peace of heart and denounced murderous anger and hatred as immoral. 1765

Anger is a desire for revenge. "To desire vengeance in order to do evil to someone who should be punished is illicit," but it is praiseworthy to impose restitution "to correct vices and maintain justice."[95] If anger reaches the point of a deliberate desire to kill or seriously wound a neighbor, it is gravely against charity; it is a mortal sin. The Lord says, "Everyone who is angry with his brother shall be liable to judgment."[96]

2303 Deliberate *hatred* is contrary 2094
to charity. Hatred of the neighbor is a sin when one deliberately wishes him evil. Hatred of the neighbor is a grave
sin when one deliberately desires him 1933
grave harm. "But I say to you, Love your enemies and pray for those who persecute you, so that you may be sons of your Father who is in heaven."[97]

2304 Respect for and development 1909
of human life require peace. Peace is not merely the absence of war, and it is not limited to maintaining a balance of powers between adversaries. Peace cannot be attained on earth without safeguarding the goods of persons, free communication among men, respect for the dignity of persons and peoples, and the assiduous practice of fraternity. Peace is "the tranquillity of order."[98]
Peace is the work of justice and the ef- 1807
fect of charity.[99]

[92] Cf. *Tob* 1:16–18. — [93] Cf. CIC, can. 1176 § 3. — [94] *Mt* 5:21. — [95] St. Thomas Aquinas, *STh* II–II, 158, 1 ad 3. — [96] *Mt* 5:22. — [97] *Mt* 5:44–45. — [98] St. Augustine, *De civ. Dei*, 19, 13, 1: PL 41, 640. — [99] *Isa* 32:17; cf. *GS* 78 §§ 1–2.

2305 Earthly peace is the image and fruit of the peace of Christ, the messianic "Prince of Peace."[100] By the blood of his Cross, "in his own person he killed the hostility,"[101]
1468 he reconciled men with God and made his Church the sacrament of the unity of the human race and of its union with God. "He is our peace."[102] He has declared: "Blessed are the peacemakers."[103]

2306 Those who renounce violence and bloodshed and, in order to safeguard human rights, make use of those means of defense avail
2267 able to the weakest, bear witness to evangelical charity, provided they do so without harming the rights and obligations of other men and societies. They bear legitimate witness to the gravity of the physical and moral risks of recourse to violence, with all its destruction and death.[104]

Avoiding war

2307 The fifth commandment forbids the intentional destruction of human life. Because of the evils and injustices that accompany all war, the Church insistently urges everyone to prayer and to action so that the divine Goodness may free us from the ancient bondage of war.[105]

2308 All citizens and all governments are obliged to work for the avoidance of war.

However, "as long as the danger of war persists and there is no international authority with the necessary competence and power, govern-
2266 ments cannot be denied the right of lawful self-defense, once all peace efforts have failed."[106]

2309 The strict conditions for 2243
legitimate defense by military force require rigorous consideration. The gravity of such a decision makes it subject to rigorous conditions of moral legitimacy. At one and the same time:

– the damage inflicted by the aggressor on the nation or community of nations must be lasting, grave, and certain;
– all other means of putting an end to it must have been shown to be impractical or ineffective;
– there must be serious prospects of success;
– the use of arms must not produce evils and disorders graver than the evil to be eliminated. The power of modern means of destruction weighs very heavily in evaluating this condition.

These are the traditional elements enumerated in what is called the "just war" doctrine.

The evaluation of these conditions for moral legitimacy belongs to the
prudential judgment of those who 1897
have responsibility for the common good.

2310 Public authorities, in this case, have the right and duty to impose on citizens the *obligations necessary for national defense.*

Those who are sworn to serve their 2239
country in the armed forces are servants of the security and freedom of 1909
nations. If they carry out their duty honorably, they truly contribute to the common good of the nation and the maintenance of peace.[107]

[100] *Isa* 9:5. — [101] *Eph* 2:16 J.B.; cf. *Col* 1:20–22. — [102] *Eph* 2:14. — [103] *Mt* 5:9. — [104] Cf. *GS* 78 § 5. — [105] Cf. *GS* 81 § 4. — [106] *GS* 79 § 4. — [107] Cf. *GS* 79 § 5.

2311 Public authorities should make equitable provision for those who for reasons of conscience refuse to bear arms; these are nonetheless
1782, 1790 obliged to serve the human community in some other way.[108]

2312 The Church and human reason both assert the permanent validity of the *moral law during armed conflict.* "The mere fact that war has regrettably broken out does not mean that everything becomes licit between the warring parties."109

2313 Non-combatants, wounded soldiers, and prisoners must be respected and treated humanely.

Actions deliberately contrary to the law of nations and to its universal principles are crimes, as are the orders that command such actions. Blind obedience does not suffice to excuse those who carry them out. Thus the extermination of a people, nation, or ethnic minority must be condemned as a mortal sin. One is
2242 morally bound to resist orders that command genocide.

2314 "Every act of war directed to the indiscriminate destruction of whole cities or vast areas with their inhabitants is a crime against God and man, which merits firm and unequivocal condemnation."[110] A danger of modern warfare is that it provides the opportunity to those who possess modern scientific weapons—especially atomic, biological, or chemical weapons—to commit such crimes.

2315 The *accumulation of arms* strikes many as a paradoxically suitable way of deterring potential adversaries from war. They see it as the most effective means of ensuring peace among nations. This method of deterrence gives rise to strong moral reservations. The *arms race* does not ensure peace. Far from eliminating the causes of war, it risks aggravating them. Spending enormous sums to produce ever new types of weapons impedes efforts to aid needy populations;[111] it thwarts the development of peoples. *Over-armament* multiplies reasons for conflict and increases the danger of escalation.

2316 *The production and the sale of* 1906
arms affect the common good of nations and of the international community. Hence public authorities have the right and duty to regulate them. The short-term pursuit of private or collective interests cannot legitimate undertakings that promote violence and conflict among nations and compromise the international juridical order.

2317 Injustice, excessive eco- 1938
nomic or social inequalities, envy,
distrust, and pride raging among 2538
men and nations constantly threat-
en peace and cause wars. Everything 1941
done to overcome these disorders contributes to building up peace and avoiding war:

> Insofar as men are sinners, the threat of war hangs over them and will so continue until Christ comes again; but insofar as they can vanquish sin by coming together in charity, violence itself will be vanquished and these words will be fulfilled: "they shall beat their swords into plowshares, and their spears into pruning hooks; nation shall not lift up sword against nation, neither shall they learn war any more."[112]

[108] Cf. *GS* 79 § 3. — [109] *GS* 79 § 4. — [110] *GS* 80 § 3. — [111] Cf. Paul VI, *PP* 53. — [112] *GS* 78 § 6; cf. *Isa* 2:4.

In Brief

2318 *"In [God's] hand is the life of every living thing and the breath of all mankind" (*Job *12:10).*

2319 *Every human life, from the moment of conception until death, is sacred because the human person has been willed for its own sake in the image and likeness of the living and holy God.*

2320 *The murder of a human being is gravely contrary to the dignity of the person and the holiness of the Creator.*

2321 *The prohibition of murder does not abrogate the right to render an unjust aggressor unable to inflict harm. Legitimate defense is a grave duty for whoever is responsible for the lives of others or the common good.*

2322 *From its conception, the child has the right to life. Direct abortion, that is, abortion willed as an end or as a means, is a "criminal" practice (*GS *27 § 3), gravely contrary to the moral law. The Church imposes the canonical penalty of excommunication for this crime against human life.*

2323 *Because it should be treated as a person from conception, the embryo must be defended in its integrity, cared for, and healed like every other human being.*

2324 *Intentional euthanasia, whatever its forms or motives, is murder. It is gravely contrary to the dignity of the human person and to the respect due to the living God, his Creator.*

2325 *Suicide is seriously contrary to justice, hope, and charity. It is forbidden by the fifth commandment.*

2326 *Scandal is a grave offense when by deed or omission it deliberately leads others to sin gravely.*

2327 *Because of the evils and injustices that all war brings with it, we must do everything reasonably possible to avoid it. The Church prays: "From famine, pestilence, and war, O Lord, deliver us."*

2328 *The Church and human reason assert the permanent validity of the moral law during armed conflicts. Practices deliberately contrary to the law of nations and to its universal principles are crimes.*

2329 *"The arms race is one of the greatest curses on the human race and the harm it inflicts on the poor is more than can be endured" (*GS *81 § 3).*

2330 *"Blessed are the peacemakers, for they shall be called sons of God" (*Mt *5:9).*

Article 6:
THE SIXTH COMMANDMENT

> You shall not commit adultery.[113]
> You have heard that it was said, "You shall not commit adultery." But I say to you that every one who looks at a woman lustfully has already committed adultery with her in his heart.[114]

369–373 ### I. "Male and Female He Created Them..."

2331 "God is love and in himself he lives a mystery of personal loving communion. Creating the human race in his own image..., God inscribed in the humanity of man and woman the vocation, and thus the capacity and responsibility, *of love* and communion."[115]

1604 "God created man in his own image...male and female he created them";[116] He blessed them and said, "Be fruitful and multiply";[117] "When God created man, he made him in the likeness of God. Male and female he created them, and he blessed them and named them Man when they were created."[118]

2332 *Sexuality* affects all aspects of the human person in the unity of his body and soul. It especially concerns affectivity, the capacity to
362 love and to procreate, and in a more general way the aptitude for forming bonds of communion with others.

2333 Everyone, man and woman, should acknowledge and accept his sexual *identity*. Physical, moral, and spiritual *difference* and *complementarity* are oriented toward the goods of marriage and the flourishing of family life. The harmony of the couple and of society depends in part on
the way in which the complemen- 1603
tarity, needs, and mutual support between the sexes are lived out.

2334 "In creating men 'male and female,' God gives man and woman
an equal personal dignity."[119] "Man is 357
a person, man and woman equally so, since both were created in the image and likeness of the personal God."[120]

2335 Each of the two sexes is an image of the power and tenderness of God, with equal dignity though in a different way. The *union of man and woman* in marriage is a way of imitating in the flesh the Creator's generosity and fecundity: "Therefore a man leaves his father and
his mother and cleaves to his wife, 2205
and they become one flesh."[121] All human generations proceed from this union.[122]

2336 Jesus came to restore creation to the purity of its origins. In 1614
the Sermon on the Mount, he interprets God's plan strictly: "You have heard that it was said, 'You shall not commit adultery.' But I say to you that every one who looks at a woman lustfully has already committed adultery with her in his heart."[123] What God has joined together, let not man put asunder.[124]

The tradition of the Church has understood the sixth commandment as encompassing the whole of human sexuality.

[113] *Ex* 20:14; *Deut* 5:18. — [114] *Mt* 5:27–28. — [115] *FC* 11. — [116] *Gen* 1:27. — [117] *Gen* 1:28. — 118 *Gen* 5:1–2. — [119] *FC* 22; cf. *GS* 49 § 2. — [120] *MD* 6. — [121] *Gen* 2:24. — [122] Cf. *Gen* 4:1–2, 25–26; 5:1. — [123] *Mt* 5:27–28. — [124] Cf. *Mt* 19:6.

II. The Vocation to Chastity

2349, 2520 **2337** Chastity means the successful integration of sexuality within the person and thus the inner unity of man in his bodily and spiritual being. Sexuality, in which man's belonging to the bodily and biological world is expressed, becomes personal and truly human when it is integrated into the relationship of one person to another, in the complete and lifelong mutual gift of a man and a woman.

The virtue of chastity therefore involves the integrity of the person and the integrality of the gift.

The integrity of the person

2338 The chaste person maintains the integrity of the powers of life and love placed in him. This integrity ensures the unity of the person; it is opposed to any behavior that would impair it. It tolerates neither a double life nor duplicity in speech.[125]

2339 Chastity includes an *apprenticeship in self-mastery* which is a training in human freedom. The alternative is clear: either man governs his passions and finds peace, or he lets himself be dominated by them and becomes unhappy.[126] "Man's dignity therefore requires him to act out of conscious and free choice, as moved and drawn in a personal way from within, and not by blind impulses in himself or by mere external constraint. Man gains such dignity when, ridding himself of all slavery to the passions, he presses forward
1767 to his goal by freely choosing what is good and, by his diligence and skill, effectively secures for himself the means suited to this end."[127]

2340 Whoever wants to remain faithful to his baptismal promises and resist temptations will want to adopt the *means* for doing so: self-knowledge, practice of an ascesis adapted to the situations that confront him, obedience to God's commandments, exercise of the moral virtues, and fidelity to prayer. "Indeed it is through chastity that we are gathered together and led back to the unity from which we were fragmented into multiplicity."[128]

2341 The virtue of chastity comes under the cardinal virtue of *temperance*, which seeks to permeate the passions and appetites of the senses with reason.

2342 Self-mastery is a *long and exacting work*. One can never consider it acquired once and for all. It presupposes renewed effort at all
stages of life.[129] The effort required 409
can be more intense in certain periods, such as when the personality is being formed during childhood and adolescence.

2343 Chastity has *laws of growth* which progress through stages marked by imperfection and too often by sin. "Man...day by day
builds himself up through his many 2223
free decisions; and so he knows, loves, and accomplishes moral good by stages of growth."[130]

2344 Chastity represents an emi- 2525
nently personal task; it also involves a *cultural effort*, for there is "an interdependence between personal betterment and the improvement

[125] Cf. *Mt* 5:37. — [126] Cf. *Sir* 1:22. — [127] *GS* 17. — [128] St. Augustine, *Conf.* 10, 29, 40: PL 32, 796. — [129] Cf. *Titus* 2:1–6. — [130] *FC* 34.

of society."[131] Chastity presupposes respect for the rights of the person, in particular the right to receive information and an education that respect the moral and spiritual dimensions of human life.

1810 **2345** Chastity is a moral virtue. It is also a gift from God, a *grace*, a fruit of spiritual effort.[132] The Holy Spirit enables one whom the water of Baptism has regenerated to imitate the purity of Christ.[133]

The integrality of the gift of self

1827 **2346** Charity is the *form* of all the virtues. Under its influence, chastity appears as a school of the gift of the person. Self-mastery is ordered to the gift of self. Chastity leads him who practices it to become a witness
210 to his neighbor of God's fidelity and loving kindness.

374 **2347** The virtue of chastity blossoms in *friendship*. It shows the disciple how to follow and imitate him who has chosen us as his friends,[134] who has given himself totally to us and allows us to participate in his divine estate. Chastity is a promise of immortality.

Chastity is expressed notably in *friendship with one's neighbor*. Whether it develops between persons of the same or opposite sex, friendship represents a great good for all. It leads to spiritual communion.

The various forms of chastity

2348 All the baptized are called to chastity. The Christian has "put on Christ,"[135] the model for all chastity. All Christ's faithful are called to lead a chaste life in keeping with their particular states of life. At the moment of his Baptism, the Christian is pledged to lead his affective life in chastity.

2349 "People should cultivate [chastity] in the way that is suited to their state of life. Some profess virginity or consecrated celibacy which enables them to give themselves to God alone with an undivided heart in a remarkable manner. Others live in the way prescribed for all by the moral law, whether they are married or single."[136] Married people are called to live conjugal chastity; others practice chastity in continence: 1620

> There are three forms of the virtue of chastity: the first is that of spouses, the second that of widows, and the third that of virgins. We do not praise any one of them to the exclusion of the others.... This is what makes for the richness of the discipline of the Church.[137]

2350 Those who are *engaged to marry* are called to live chastity in continence. They should see in this time of testing a discovery of mutual respect, an apprenticeship in fidelity, and the hope of receiving one another from God. They should reserve for marriage the expressions of affection that belong to married love. They will help each other grow in chastity. 1632

Offenses against chastity

2351 *Lust* is disordered desire for or inordinate enjoyment of sexual pleasure. Sexual pleasure is morally disordered when sought for itself, isolated from its procreative and unitive purposes. 2528

[131] *GS* 25 § 1. — [132] Cf. *Gal* 5:22. — [133] Cf. *1 Jn* 3:3. — [134] Cf. *Jn* 15:15. — [135] *Gal* 3:27. — [136] CDF, *Persona humana* 11. — [137] St. Ambrose, *De viduis* 4, 23: PL 16, 255A.

2352 By *masturbation* is to be understood the deliberate stimulation of the genital organs in order to derive sexual pleasure. "Both the Magisterium of the Church, in the course of a constant tradition, and the moral sense of the faithful have been in no doubt and have firmly maintained that masturbation is an intrinsically and gravely disordered action."[138] "The deliberate use of the sexual faculty, for whatever reason, outside of marriage is essentially contrary to its purpose." For here sexual pleasure is sought outside of "the sexual relationship which is demanded by the moral order and in which the total meaning of mutual self-giving and human procreation in the context of true love is achieved."[139]

To form an equitable judgment about the subjects' moral responsibility and to guide pastoral action, one must take into account the affective immaturity, force of acquired habit, conditions of anxiety, or other psychological or social factors that can lessen, if not even reduce to a
1735 minimum, moral culpability.

2353 *Fornication* is carnal union between an unmarried man and an unmarried woman. It is gravely contrary to the dignity of persons and of human sexuality which is naturally ordered to the good of spouses and the generation and education of children. Moreover, it is a grave scandal when there is corruption of the young.

2523 **2354** *Pornography* consists in removing real or simulated sexual acts from the intimacy of the partners, in order to display them deliberately to third parties. It offends against chastity because it perverts the conjugal act, the intimate giving of spouses to each other. It does grave injury to the dignity of its participants (actors, vendors, the public), since each one becomes an object of base pleasure and illicit profit for others. It immerses all who are involved in the illusion of a fantasy world. It is a grave offense. Civil authorities should prevent the production and distribution of pornographic materials.

2355 *Prostitution* does injury to the dignity of the person who engages in it, reducing the person to an instrument of sexual pleasure. The one who pays sins gravely against himself: he violates the chastity to which his Baptism pledged him and defiles his body, the temple of the Holy Spirit.[140] Prostitution is a social scourge. It usually involves women, but also men, children, and adolescents (The latter two cases involve the added sin of scandal.). While it is always gravely sinful to engage in prostitution, the imputability of the offense can be attenuated by destitution, blackmail, or social pressure. 1735

2356 *Rape* is the forcible violation of the sexual intimacy of another person. It does injury to justice and charity. Rape deeply wounds the respect, freedom, and physical and moral integrity to which every person has a right. It causes grave damage that can mark the victim for life.
It is always an intrinsically evil act. 2297
Graver still is the rape of children 1756
committed by parents (incest) or
those responsible for the education 2388
of the children entrusted to them.

[138] CDF, *Persona humana* 9. — [139] CDF, *Persona humana* 9. — [140] Cf. *1 Cor* 6:15–20.

Chastity and homosexuality

2357 Homosexuality refers to relations between men or between women who experience an exclusive or predominant sexual attraction toward persons of the same sex. It has taken a great variety of forms through the centuries and in different cultures. Its psychological genesis remains largely unexplained. Basing itself on Sacred Scripture, which presents homosexual acts as acts of grave depravity,[141] tradition has always declared that "homosexual acts are intrinsically disordered."[142] They are contrary to the natural law. They close the sexual act to the gift of life. They do not proceed from a genuine affective and sexual complementari-
2333 ty. Under no circumstances can they be approved.

2358 The number of men and women who have deep-seated homosexual tendencies is not negligible. This inclination, which is objectively disordered, constitutes for most of them a trial. They must be accepted with respect, compassion, and sensitivity. Every sign of unjust discrimination in their regard should be avoided. These persons are called to fulfill God's will in their lives and, if they are Christians, to unite to the sacrifice of the Lord's Cross the difficulties they may encounter from their condition.

2347 **2359** Homosexual persons are called to chastity. By the virtues of self-mastery that teach them inner freedom, at times by the support of disinterested friendship, by prayer and sacramental grace, they can and should gradually and resolutely approach Christian perfection.

III. The Love of Husband and Wife

2360 Sexuality is ordered to the conjugal love of man and woman. In marriage the physical intimacy of the spouses becomes a sign and pledge
of spiritual communion. Marriage 1601
bonds between baptized persons are sanctified by the sacrament.

2361 "Sexuality, by means of which man and woman give themselves to one another through the acts which are proper and exclusive
to spouses, is not something simply 1643
biological, but concerns the innermost being of the human person as 2332
such. It is realized in a truly human way only if it is an integral part of the love by which a man and woman commit themselves totally to one another until death."[143]

> Tobias got out of bed and said to 1611
> Sarah, "Sister, get up, and let us pray and implore our Lord that he grant us mercy and safety." So she got up, and they began to pray and implore that they might be kept safe. Tobias began by saying, "Blessed are you, O God of our fathers.... You made Adam, and for him you made his wife Eve as a helper and support. From the two of them the race of mankind has sprung. You said, 'It is not good that the man should be alone; let us make a helper for him like himself.' I now am taking this kinswoman of mine, not because of lust, but with sincerity. Grant that she and I may find mercy and that we may grow old together." And they both said, "Amen, Amen." Then they went to sleep for the night.[144]

[141] Cf. *Gen* 19:1–29; *Rom* 1:24–27; *1 Cor* 6:10; *1 Tim* 1:10. — [142] CDF, *Persona humana* 8. — [143] *FC* 11. — [144] *Tob* 8:4–9.

2362 "The acts in marriage by which the intimate and chaste union of the spouses takes place are noble and honorable; the truly human performance of these acts fosters the self-giving they signify and enriches the spouses in joy and gratitude."[145] Sexuality is a source of joy and pleasure:

> The Creator himself...established that in the [generative] function, spouses should experience pleasure and enjoyment of body and spirit. Therefore, the spouses do nothing evil in seeking this pleasure and enjoyment. They accept what the Creator has intended for them. At the same time, spouses should know how to keep themselves within the limits of just moderation.[146]

2363 The spouses' union achieves the twofold end of marriage: the good of the spouses themselves and the transmission of life. These two meanings or values of marriage cannot be separated without altering the couple's spiritual life and compromising the goods of marriage and the future of the family.

The conjugal love of man and woman thus stands under the twofold obligation of fidelity and fecundity.

46–1648 *Conjugal fidelity*

2364 The married couple forms "the intimate partnership of life and love established by the Creator and governed by his laws; it is rooted in the conjugal covenant, that is, in their irrevocable personal consent."[147] Both give themselves definitively and totally to one another. They are no longer two; from now on they form one flesh. The covenant they freely contracted imposes on the spouses the obligation to preserve it as unique and indissoluble.[148] "What therefore God has joined together, let not man put asunder."[149]

2365 Fidelity expresses constancy in keeping one's given word. God is faithful. The Sacrament of Matrimony enables man and woman
to enter into Christ's fidelity for his 1640
Church. Through conjugal chastity, they bear witness to this mystery before the world.

> St. John Chrysostom suggests that young husbands should say to their wives: I have taken you in my arms, and I love you, and I prefer you to my life itself. For the present life is nothing, and my most ardent dream is to spend it with you in such a way that we may be assured of not being separated in the life reserved for us.... I place your love above all things, and nothing would be more bitter or painful to me than to be of a different mind than you.[150]

The fecundity of marriage 1652–1653

2366 Fecundity is a gift, an *end of marriage*, for conjugal love naturally tends to be fruitful. A child does not come from outside as something added on to the mutual love of the spouses, but springs from the very heart of that mutual giving, as its fruit and fulfillment. So the Church, which is "on the side of life,"[151] teaches that "it is necessary that each and every marriage act remain ordered *per se* to the procreation of human life."[152] "This particular doctrine,

[145] *GS* 49 § 2. — [146] Pius XII, *Discourse*, October 29, 1951. — [147] *GS* 48 § 1. — [148] Cf. CIC, can. 1056. — [149] *Mk* 10:9; cf. *Mt* 19:1–12; *1 Cor* 7:10–11. — [150] St. John Chrysostom, *Hom. in Eph.* 20, 8: PG 62, 146–147. — [151] *FC* 30. — [152] *HV* 11. — [152] *HV* 11.

expounded on numerous occasions by the Magisterium, is based on the inseparable connection, established by God, which man on his own initiative may not break, between the unitive significance and the procreative significance which are both inherent to the marriage act."[153]

2205 **2367** Called to give life, spouses share in the creative power and fatherhood of God.[154] "Married couples should regard it as their proper mission to transmit human life and to educate their children; they should realize that they are thereby cooperating with the love of God the Creator and are, in a certain sense, its interpreters. They will fulfill this duty with a sense of human and Christian responsibility."[155]

2368 A particular aspect of this responsibility concerns the *regulation of procreation.* For just reasons, spouses may wish to space the births of their children. It is their duty to make certain that their desire is not motivated by selfishness but is in conformity with the generosity appropriate to responsible parenthood. Moreover, they should conform their behavior to the objective criteria of morality:

> When it is a question of harmonizing married love with the responsible transmission of life, the morality of the behavior does not depend on sincere intention and evaluation of motives alone; but it must be determined by objective criteria, criteria drawn from the nature of the person and his acts, criteria that respect the total meaning of mutual self-giving and human procreation in the context of true love; this is possible only if the virtue of married chastity is practiced with sincerity of heart.[156]

2369 "By safeguarding both these essential aspects, the unitive and the procreative, the conjugal act preserves in its fullness the sense of true mutual love and its orientation toward man's exalted vocation to parenthood."[157]

2370 Periodic continence, that is, the methods of birth regulation based on self-observation and the use of infertile periods, is in conformity with the objective criteria of morality.[158] These methods respect the bodies of the spouses, encourage tenderness between them, and favor the education of an authentic freedom. In contrast, "every action which, whether in anticipation of the conjugal act, or in its accomplishment, or in the development of its natural consequences, proposes, whether as an end or as a means, to render procreation impossible" is intrinsically evil:[159]

> Thus the innate language that expresses the total reciprocal self-giving of husband and wife is overlaid, through contraception, by an objectively contradictory language, namely, that of not giving oneself totally to the other. This leads not only to a positive refusal to be open to life but also to a falsification of the inner truth of conjugal love, which is called upon to give itself in personal totality.... The difference, both anthropological and moral, between contraception and recourse to the rhythm of the cycle... involves in the final analysis two

[153] *HV* 12; cf. Pius XI, encyclical, *Casti connubii.* — [154] Cf. *Eph* 3:14; *Mt* 23:9. — [155] *GS* 50 § 2. — [156] *GS* 51 § 3. — [157] Cf. *HV* 12. — [158] *HV* 16. — [159] *HV* 14.

irreconcilable concepts of the human person and of human sexuality.[160]

2371 "Let all be convinced that human life and the duty of transmitting it are not limited by the horizons of this life only: their true evaluation and full significance can be understood only in reference to
1703 *man's eternal destiny.*"[161]

2372 The state has a responsibility for its citizens' well-being. In this capacity it is legitimate for it to intervene to orient the demography of the population. This can be done by means of objective and respectful information, but certainly not by authoritarian, coercive measures. The state may not legitimately usurp the initiative of spouses, who have the primary responsibility for the
2209 procreation and education of their children.[162] In this area, it is not authorized to employ means contrary to the moral law.

The gift of a child

2373 Sacred Scripture and the Church's traditional practice see in *large families* a sign of God's blessing and the parents' generosity.[163]

1654 **2374** Couples who discover that they are sterile suffer greatly. "What will you give me," asks Abraham of God, "for I continue childless?"[164] And Rachel cries to her husband Jacob, "Give me children, or I shall die!"[165]

2293 **2375** Research aimed at reducing human sterility is to be encouraged, on condition that it is placed "at the service of the human person, of his inalienable rights, and his true and integral good according to the design and will of God."[166]

2376 Techniques that entail the dissociation of husband and wife, by the intrusion of a person other than the couple (donation of sperm or ovum, surrogate uterus), are gravely immoral. These techniques (heterologous artificial insemination and fertilization) infringe the child's right to be born of a father and mother known to him and bound to each other by marriage. They betray the spouses' "right to become a father and a mother only through each other."[167]

2377 Techniques involving only the married couple (homologous artificial insemination and fertilization) are perhaps less reprehensible, yet remain morally unacceptable. They dissociate the sexual act from the procreative act. The act which brings the child into existence is no longer an act by which two persons give themselves to one another, but one that "entrusts the life and identity of the embryo into the power of doctors and biologists and establishes the domination of technology over the origin and destiny of the human person. Such a relationship of domination is in itself contrary to the dignity and equality that must be common to parents and children."[168] "Under the moral aspe ct procreation is deprived of its proper perfection when it is not willed as the fruit of the conjugal act, that is to say, of the specific act of the spouses' union.... Only respect for the link between the meanings of the conjugal act and respect for the

[160] *FC* 32. — [161] *GS* 51 § 4. — [162] Cf. *HV* 23; *PP* 37. — [163] Cf. *GS* 50 § 2. — [164] *Gen* 15:2. — [165] *Gen* 30:1. — [166] CDF, *Donum vitae intro.*, 2. — [167] CDF, *Donum vitae* II, 1. — [168] CDF, *Donum vitae II*, 5.

unity of the human being make possible procreation in conformity with the dignity of the person."[169]

2378 A child is not something *owed* to one, but is a *gift*. The "supreme gift of marriage" is a human person. A child may not be considered a piece of property, an idea to which an alleged "right to a child" would lead. In this area, only the child possesses genuine rights: the right "to be the fruit of the specific act of the conjugal love of his parents," and "the right to be respected as a person from the moment of his conception."[170]

2379 The Gospel shows that physical sterility is not an absolute evil. Spouses who still suffer from infertility after exhausting legitimate medical procedures should unite themselves with the Lord's Cross, the source of all spiritual fecundity. They can give expression to their generosity by adopting abandoned children or performing demanding services for others.

IV. Offenses Against the Dignity of Marriage

Adultery

2380 *Adultery* refers to marital infidelity. When two partners, of whom at least one is married to another party, have sexual relations—even transient ones—they commit adultery. Christ condemns even adultery of mere desire.[171] The sixth commandment and the New Testament forbid adultery absolutely.[172] The prophets denounce the gravity of adultery; they see it as an image
of the sin of idolatry.[173] 1611

2381 Adultery is an injustice. He who commits adultery fails in his commitment. He does injury to the sign of the covenant which the marriage bond is, transgresses the rights 1640
of the other spouse, and undermines the institution of marriage by breaking the contract on which it is based. He compromises the good of human generation and the welfare of children who need their parents' stable union.

Divorce

2382 The Lord Jesus insisted on the original intention of the Creator
who willed that marriage be indis- 2382
soluble.[174] He abrogates the accommodations that had slipped into the old Law.[175]

Between the baptized, "a ratified and consummated marriage cannot be dissolved by any human power or for any reason other than death."[176]

2383 The *separation* of spous- 1649
es while maintaining the marriage bond can be legitimate in certain cases provided for by canon law.[177]

If civil divorce remains the only possible way of ensuring certain legal rights, the care of the children, or the protection of inheritance, it can be tolerated and does not constitute a moral offense.

2384 *Divorce* is a grave offense 1650
against the natural law. It claims to break the contract, to which the spouses freely consented, to live with each other till death. Divorce does

[169] CDF, *Donum vitae* II, 4. — [170] CDF, *Donum vitae* II, 8. — [171] Cf. *Mt* 5:27–28. — [172] Cf. *Mt* 5:32; 19:6; *Mk* 10:11; *1 Cor* 6:9–10. — [173] Cf. *Hos* 2:7; *Jer* 5:7; 13:27. — [174] Cf. *Mt* 5:31–32; 19:3–9; *Mk* 10:9; *Lk* 16:18; *1 Cor* 7:10–11. — [175] Cf. *Mt* 19:7–9. — [176] CIC, can. 1141. — [177] Cf. CIC, cann. 1151–1155.

injury to the covenant of salvation, of which sacramental marriage is the sign. Contracting a new union, even if it is recognized by civil law, adds to the gravity of the rupture: the remarried spouse is then in a situation of public and permanent adultery:

> If a husband, separated from his wife, approaches another woman, he is an adulterer because he makes that woman commit adultery; and the woman who lives with him is an adulteress, because she has drawn another's husband to herself.[178]

2385 Divorce is immoral also because it introduces disorder into the family and into society. This disorder brings grave harm to the deserted spouse, to children traumatized by the separation of their parents and often torn between them, and because of its contagious effect which makes it truly a plague on society.

2386 It can happen that one of the spouses is the innocent victim of a divorce decreed by civil law; this spouse therefore has not contravened the moral law. There is a considerable difference between a spouse who has sincerely tried to be faithful to the sacrament of marriage and is unjustly abandoned, and one who
1640 through his own grave fault destroys a canonically valid marriage.[179]

Other offenses against the dignity of marriage

2387 The predicament of a man who, desiring to convert to the Gospel, is obliged to repudiate one or more wives with whom he has shared years of conjugal life, is understandable. However *polygamy* is not in accord with the moral law. 1610
"[Conjugal] communion is radically contradicted by polygamy; this, in fact, directly negates the plan of God which was revealed from the beginning, because it is contrary to the equal personal dignity of men and women who in matrimony give themselves with a love that is total and therefore unique and exclusive."[180] The Christian who has previously lived in polygamy has a grave duty in justice to honor the obligations contracted in regard to his former wives and his children.

2388 Incest designates intimate 2356
relations between relatives or in-laws within a degree that prohibits marriage between them.[181] St. Paul stigmatizes this especially grave offense: "It is actually reported that there is immorality among you... for a man is living with his father's wife.... In the name of the Lord Jesus...you are to deliver this man to Satan for the destruction of the flesh...."[182] Incest
corrupts family relationships and 2207
marks a regression toward animality.

2389 Connected to incest is any sexual abuse perpetrated by adults on children or adolescents entrusted to their care. The offense is compounded by the scandalous harm done to the physical and moral integrity of the young, who will re- 2285
main scarred by it all their lives; and the violation of responsibility for their upbringing.

[178] St. Basil, *Moralia* 73, 1: PG 31, 849–852. — [179] Cf. *FC* 84. — [180] *FC* 19; cf. *GS* 47 § 2. — [181] Cf. *Lev* 18:7–20. — [182] *1 Cor* 5:1, 4–5.

2390 In a so-called *free union*, a man and a woman refuse to give juridical and public form to a liaison
1631 involving sexual intimacy.

The expression "free union" is fallacious: what can "union" mean when the partners make no commitment to one another, each exhibiting a lack of trust in the other, in himself, or in the future?

The expression covers a number of different situations: concubinage, rejection of marriage as such, or inability to make long-term commitments.[183] All these situations offend against the dignity of marriage; they destroy the very idea of the family; they weaken the sense of fidelity.
2353 They are contrary to the moral law. The sexual act must take place exclusively within marriage. Outside of marriage it always constitutes a grave sin and excludes one from sac-
1385 ramental communion.

2391 Some today claim a "*right to a trial marriage*" where there is an intention of getting married later. However firm the purpose of those who engage in premature sexual relations may be, "the fact is that such liaisons can scarcely ensure mutual sincerity and fidelity in a relationship between a man and a woman, nor, especially, can they protect it from inconstancy of desires or whim."[184] Carnal union is morally legitimate only when a definitive community of life between a man and woman has been established. Human love
2364 does not tolerate "trial marriages." It demands a total and definitive gift of persons to one another.[185]

In Brief

2392 *"Love is the fundamental and innate vocation of every human being" (*FC *11).*

2393 *By creating the human being man and woman, God gives personal dignity equally to the one and the other. Each of them, man and woman, should acknowledge and accept his sexual identity.*

2394 *Christ is the model of chastity. Every baptized person is called to lead a chaste life, each according to his particular state of life.*

2395 *Chastity means the integration of sexuality within the person. It includes an apprenticeship in self-mastery.*

2396 *Among the sins gravely contrary to chastity are masturbation, fornication, pornography, and homosexual practices.*

2397 *The covenant which spouses have freely entered into entails faithful love. It imposes on them the obligation to keep their marriage indissoluble.*

2398 *Fecundity is a good, a gift and an end of marriage. By giving life, spouses participate in God's fatherhood.*

2399 *The regulation of births represents one of the aspects of responsible fatherhood and motherhood. Legitimate intentions on the part of the spouses do not justify recourse to morally unacceptable means (for example, direct sterilization or contraception).*

2400 *Adultery, divorce, polygamy, and free union are grave offenses against the dignity of marriage.*

[183] Cf. *FC* 81. — [184] CDF, *Persona humana* 7. — [185] Cf. *FC* 80.

Article 7: THE SEVENTH COMMANDMENT

You shall not steal.[186]

2401 The seventh commandment forbids unjustly taking or keeping the goods of one's neighbor and wronging him in any way with re
1807 spect to his goods. It commands justice and charity in the care of earthly goods and the fruits of men's labor. For the sake of the common good, it requires respect for the universal destination of goods and respect for the right to private property. Christian life strives to order this
952 world's goods to God and to fraternal charity.

I. The Universal Destination and the Private Ownership of Goods

2402 In the beginning God entrusted the earth and its resources to the common stewardship of mankind to take care of them, mas-
226 ter them by labor, and enjoy their fruits.[187] The goods of creation are destined for the whole human race. However, the earth is divided up among men to assure the security of their lives, endangered by poverty and threatened by violence. The appropriation of property is legitimate for guaranteeing the freedom and dignity of persons and for helping each of them to meet his basic needs and the needs of those in his charge. It should allow for a natural solidar-
1939 ity to develop between men.

2403 The *right to private property*, acquired or received in a just way, does not do away with the original gift of the earth to the whole of mankind. The *universal destination of goods* remains primordial, even if the promotion of the common good requires respect for the right to private property and its exercise.

2404 "In his use of things man should regard the external goods he legitimately owns not merely as exclusive to himself but common to others also, in the sense that they can benefit others as well as himself."[188] The ownership of any property makes its holder a steward of Providence, with the task of making it 307
fruitful and communicating its benefits to others, first of all his family.

2405 Goods of production—material or immaterial—such as land, factories, practical or artistic skills, oblige their possessors to employ them in ways that will benefit the greatest number. Those who hold goods for use and consumption should use them with moderation, reserving the better part for guests, for the sick and the poor.

2406 *Political authority* has the 1903
right and duty to regulate the legitimate exercise of the right to ownership for the sake of the common good.[189]

II. Respect for Persons and Their Goods

2407 In economic matters, respect for human dignity requires the practice of the virtue of *temperance*, so as to moderate attachment to this world's goods; the practice of
the virtue of *justice*, to preserve our 1809

[186] *Ex* 20:15; *Deut* 5:19; *Mt* 19:18. — [187] Cf. *Gen* 1:26–29. — [188] *GS* 69 § 1. — [189] Cf. *GS* 71 § 4; *SRS* 42; *CA* 40; 48.

1807 neighbor's rights and render him what is his due; and the practice of
1939 *solidarity*, in accordance with the golden rule and in keeping with the generosity of the Lord, who "though he was rich, yet for your sake...became poor so that by his poverty, you might become rich."[190]

Respect for the goods of others

2408 The seventh commandment forbids *theft*, that is, usurping another's property against the reasonable will of the owner. There is no theft if consent can be presumed or if refusal is contrary to reason and the universal destination of goods. This is the case in obvious and urgent necessity when the only way to provide for immediate, essential needs (food, shelter, clothing...) is to put at one's disposal and use the property of others.[191]

2409 Even if it does not contradict the provisions of civil law, any form of unjustly taking and keeping the property of others is against the seventh commandment: thus, deliberate retention of goods lent or of
1867 objects lost; business fraud; paying unjust wages; forcing up prices by taking advantage of the ignorance or hardship of another.[192]

The following are also morally illicit: speculation in which one contrives to manipulate the price of goods artificially in order to gain an advantage to the detriment of others; corruption in which one influences the judgment of those who must make decisions according to law; appropriation and use for private purposes of the common goods of an enterprise; work poorly done; tax evasion; forgery of checks and invoices; excessive expenses and waste. Willfully damaging private or public property is contrary to the moral law and requires reparation.

2410 *Promises* must be kept and 2101
contracts strictly observed to the extent that the commitments made in them are morally just. A significant part of economic and social life depends on the honoring of contracts between physical or moral persons—commercial contracts of purchase or sale, rental or labor contracts. All contracts must be agreed to and executed in good faith.

2411 Contracts are subject to 1807
commutative justice which regulates exchanges between persons and between institutions in accordance with a strict respect for their rights. Commutative justice obliges strictly; it requires safeguarding property rights, paying debts, and fulfilling obligations freely contracted. Without commutative justice, no other form of justice is possible.

One distinguishes *commutative* justice from *legal* justice which concerns what the citizen owes in fairness to the community, and from *distributive* justice which regulates what the community owes its citizens in proportion to their contributions and needs.

2412 In virtue of commutative 1459
justice, *reparation for injustice* committed requires the restitution of stolen goods to their owner:

Jesus blesses Zacchaeus for his pledge: "If I have defrauded anyone of anything, I restore it fourfold."[193] Those who, directly or indirectly,

[190] *2 Cor* 8:9. — [191] Cf. *GS* 69 § 1. — [192] Cf. *Deut* 25:13–16; 24:14–15; *Jas* 5:4; *Am* 8:4–6. — [193] *Lk* 19:8.

have taken possession of the goods of another, are obliged to make restitution of them, or to return the equivalent in kind or in money, if the goods have disappeared, as well
2487 as the profit or advantages their owner would have legitimately obtained from them. Likewise, all who in some manner have taken part in a theft or who have knowingly benefited from it—for example, those who ordered it, assisted in it, or received the stolen goods—are obliged to make restitution in proportion to their responsibility and to their share of what was stolen.

2413 *Games of chance* (card games, etc.) or *wagers* are not in themselves contrary to justice. They become morally unacceptable when they deprive someone of what is necessary to provide for his needs and those of others. The passion for gambling risks becoming an enslavement. Unfair wagers and cheating at games constitute grave matter, unless the damage inflicted is so slight that the one who suffers it cannot reasonably consider it significant.

2297 **2414** The seventh commandment forbids acts or enterprises that for any reason—selfish or ideological, commercial, or totalitarian—lead to the *enslavement of human beings*, to their being bought, sold and exchanged like merchandise, in disregard for their personal dignity. It is a sin against the dignity of persons and their fundamental rights to reduce them by violence to their productive value or to a source of profit. St. Paul directed a Christian master to treat his Christian slave "no longer as a slave but more than a slave, as a beloved brother,...both in the flesh and in the Lord."[194]

Respect for the integrity of creation

2415 The seventh commandment 226, 358
enjoins respect for the integrity of creation. Animals, like plants and inanimate beings, are by nature destined for the common good of past, present, and future humanity.[195] Use of the mineral, vegetable, and animal resources of the universe cannot be divorced from respect for moral imperatives. Man's dominion over
inanimate and other living beings 373
granted by the Creator is not absolute; it is limited by concern for the quality of life of his neighbor, including generations to come; it
requires a religious respect for the 378
integrity of creation.[196]

2416 *Animals* are God's creatures. He surrounds them with his providential care. By their mere existence they bless him and give him glory.[197] Thus men owe them kindness. We should recall the gentleness with
which saints like St. Francis of Assisi 344
or St. Philip Neri treated animals.

2417 God entrusted animals to the stewardship of those whom he created in his own image.[198] Hence it is legitimate to use animals for food and clothing. They may be domesticated to help man in his work and leisure. Medical and scientific experimentation on animals is a morally acceptable practice if it remains within reasonable limits and contributes to caring for or saving
human lives. 2234

[194] *Philem* 16. — [195] Cf. *Gen* 1:28–31. — [196] Cf. *CA* 37–38. — [197] Cf. *Mt* 6:26; *Dan* 3:79–81. — [198] Cf. *Gen* 2:19–20; 9:1–4.

2418 It is contrary to human dignity to cause animals to suffer or die needlessly. It is likewise unworthy to spend money on them that should
2446 as a priority go to the relief of human misery. One can love animals; one should not direct to them the affection due only to persons.

III. The Social Doctrine of the Church

1960 **2419** "Christian revelation…promotes deeper understanding of the
359 laws of social living."[199] The Church receives from the Gospel the full revelation of the truth about man. When she fulfills her mission of proclaiming the Gospel, she bears witness to man, in the name of Christ, to his dignity and his vocation to the communion of persons. She teaches him the demands of justice and peace in conformity with divine wisdom.

2032 **2420** The Church makes a moral judgment about economic and social matters, "when the fundamental rights of the person or the salvation of souls requires it."[200] In the moral order she bears a mission distinct from that of political authorities: the Church is concerned with the temporal aspects of the common good because they are ordered to the sov-
2246 ereign Good, our ultimate end. She strives to inspire right attitudes with respect to earthly goods and in socio-economic relationships.

2421 The social doctrine of the Church developed in the nineteenth century when the Gospel encountered modern industrial society with its new structures for the production of consumer goods, its new concept of society, the state and authority, and its new forms of labor and ownership. The development of the doctrine of the Church on economic and social matters attests the permanent value of the Church's teaching at the same time as it attests the true meaning of her Tradition, always living and active.[201]

2422 The Church's social teaching comprises a body of doctrine, which is articulated as the Church interprets events in the course of history, with the assistance of the Holy Spirit, in the light of the whole of what has been revealed by Jesus Christ.[202] This teaching can be more easily accepted by men of good will, the
more the faithful let themselves be 2044
guided by it.

2423 The Church's social teaching proposes principles for reflection; it provides criteria for judgment; it gives guidelines for action:

Any system in which social relationships are determined entirely by economic factors is contrary to the nature of the human person and his acts.[203]

2424 A theory that makes profit the exclusive norm and ultimate end of economic activity is morally unacceptable. The disordered desire for
money cannot but produce perverse 2317
effects. It is one of the causes of the many conflicts which disturb the social order.[204]

A system that "subordinates the basic rights of individuals and of groups to the collective organization of production" is contrary to human dignity.[205] Every practice that reduces persons to

[199] *GS* 23 § 1. — [200] *GS* 76 § 5. — [201] Cf. *CA* 3. — [202] Cf. *SRS* 1; 41. — [203] Cf. *CA* 24. — [204] *GS* 65 § 2. — [205] *Mt* 6:24; *Lk* 16:13.

nothing more than a means of profit enslaves man, leads to idolizing money, and contributes to the spread of atheism. "You cannot serve God and mammon."[206]

2425 The Church has rejected the totalitarian and atheistic ideologies associated in modern times with "communism" or "socialism." She has likewise refused to accept, in the
676 practice of "capitalism," individualism and the absolute primacy of the law of the marketplace over human labor.[207] Regulating the economy solely by centralized planning perverts the basis of social bonds; regulating it solely by the law of the marketplace fails social justice, for "there are many human needs which cannot be satisfied by the market."[208] Reasonable regulation of the marketplace and economic initiatives, in keeping with a just hierarchy of values and a view to the common
1886 good, is to be commended.

IV. Economic Activity and Social Justice

2426 The development of economic activity and growth in production are meant to provide for the needs of human beings. Economic life is not meant solely to multiply goods produced and increase profit or power; it is ordered first of all to the service of persons, of the whole man, and of the entire human community. Economic activity, conducted according to its own proper methods, is to be exercised within the limits of the moral order, in keeping with social justice so as to
1928 correspond to God's plan for man.[209]

2427 *Human work* proceeds di- 307
rectly from persons created in the image of God and called to prolong the work of creation by subduing the earth, both with and for one an- 378
other.[210] Hence work is a duty: "If any one will not work, let him not eat."[211] Work honors the Creator's gifts and the talents received from him. It can also be redemptive. By enduring the hardship of work[212] in 531
union with Jesus, the carpenter of Nazareth and the one crucified on Calvary, man collaborates in a certain fashion with the Son of God in his redemptive work. He shows himself to be a disciple of Christ by carrying the cross, daily, in the work he is called to accomplish.[213] Work can be a means of sanctification and a way of animating earthly realities with the Spirit of Christ.

2428 In work, the person exercis- 2834
es and fulfills in part the potential inscribed in his nature. The primordial value of labor stems from man himself, its author and its benefi- 2185
ciary. Work is for man, not man for work.[214]

Everyone should be able to draw from work the means of providing for his life and that of his family, and of serving the human community.

2429 Everyone has the *right of economic initiative*; everyone should make legitimate use of his talents to contribute to the abundance that will benefit all and to harvest the just fruits of his labor. He should seek to observe regulations issued by legitimate authority for the sake of the common good.[215]

[206] Cf. *CA* 10; 13; 44. — [207] *CA* 34. — [208] Cf. *GS* 64. — [209] Cf. *Gen* 1:28; *GS* 34; *CA* 31. — [210] *2 Thess* 3:10; cf. *1 Thess* 4:11. — [211] Cf. *Gen* 3:14–19. — [212] Cf. *LE* 27. — [213] Cf. *LE* 6. — [214] Cf. *CA* 32; 34. — [215] Cf. *LE* 11.

2430 *Economic life* brings into play different interests, often opposed to one another. This explains why the conflicts that characterize it arise.[216] Efforts should be made to reduce these conflicts by negotiation that respects the rights and duties of each social partner: those responsible for business enterprises, representatives of wage-earners (for example, trade unions), and public authorities when appropriate.

2431 The *responsibility of the state.* "Economic activity, especially the activity of a market economy, cannot be conducted in an institutional, juridical, or political vacuum. On the contrary, it presupposes sure guarantees of individual freedom and private property, as well as a stable currency and efficient public
1908 services. Hence the principal task of the state is to guarantee this security, so that those who work and produce can enjoy the fruits of their labors and thus feel encouraged to work efficiently and honestly.... Another task of the state is that of overseeing and directing the exercise of human rights in the economic sector. However, primary responsibility in
1883 this area belongs not to the state but to individuals and to the various groups and associations which make up society."[217]

2432 Those *responsible for business enterprises* are responsible to society for the economic and ecological effects of their operations.[218] They
2415 have an obligation to consider the good of persons and not only the increase of profits. Profits are necessary, however. They make possible the investments that ensure the future of a business and they guarantee employment.

2433 *Access to employment* and to professions must be open to all without unjust discrimination: men and women, healthy and disabled, natives and immigrants.[219] For its part society should, according to circumstances, help citizens find work and employment.[220]

2434 A just wage is the legitimate 1867
fruit of work. To refuse or withhold it can be a grave injustice.[221] In determining fair pay both the needs and the contributions of each person must be taken into account. "Remuneration for work should guarantee man the opportunity to provide a dignified livelihood for himself and his family on the material, social, cultural, and spiritual level, taking into account the role and the productivity of each, the state of the business, and the common good."[222] Agreement between the parties is not sufficient to justify morally the amount to be received in wages.

2435 Recourse to a *strike* is morally legitimate when it cannot be avoided, or at least when it is necessary to obtain a proportionate benefit. It becomes morally unacceptable when accompanied by violence, or when objectives are included that are not directly linked to working conditions or are contrary to the common good.

2436 It is unjust not to pay the social security *contributions* required by legitimate authority.

[216] *CA* 48. — [217] Cf. *CA* 37. — [218] Cf. *LE* 19; 22–23. — [219] Cf. *CA* 48. — [220] Cf. *Lev* 19:13; *Deut* 24:14–15; *Jas* 5:4. — [221] *GS* 67 § 2. — [222] Cf. *LE* 18.

Unemployment almost always wounds its victim's dignity and threatens the equilibrium of his life. Besides the harm done to him personally, it entails many risks for his family.[223]

V. Justice and Solidarity among Nations

1938 **2437** On the international level, inequality of resources and economic capability is such that it creates a real "gap" between nations.[224] On the one side there are those nations possessing and developing the means of growth and, on the other, those accumulating debts.

2438 Various causes of a religious, political, economic, and financial nature today give "the social question a worldwide dimension."[225]
1911 There must be solidarity among nations which are already politically interdependent. It is even more essential when it is a question of dismantling the "perverse mechanisms" that impede the development of the less advanced countries.[226] In place of abusive if not usurious financial systems, iniquitous commercial relations among nations, and the arms race, there must be substituted a common effort to mobilize resources toward objectives of moral, cultural, and economic development,
2315 "redefining the priorities and hierarchies of values."[227]

2439 *Rich nations* have a grave moral responsibility toward those which are unable to ensure the means of their development by themselves or have been prevented from doing so by tragic historical events. It is a duty in solidarity and charity; it is also an obligation in justice if the prosperity of the rich nations has come from resources that have not been paid for fairly.

2440 *Direct aid* is an appropriate response to immediate, extraordinary needs caused by natural catastrophes, epidemics, and the like. But it does not suffice to repair the grave damage resulting from destitution or to provide a lasting solution to a country's needs. It is also necessary to *reform* international economic and financial *institutions* so that they will better promote equitable relationships with less advanced countries.[228] The efforts of poor countries working for growth and liberation must be supported.[229] This doctrine must be applied especially in the area of agricultural labor. Peasants, especially in the Third World, form the overwhelming majority of the poor.

2441 An increased sense of God 1908
and increased self-awareness are fundamental to any *full development of human society*. This development multiplies material goods and puts them at the service of the person and his freedom. It reduces dire poverty and economic exploitation. It makes for growth in respect for cultural identities and openness to the transcendent.[230]

2442 It is not the role of the Pastors of the Church to intervene directly in the political structuring and organization of social life. This task is part of the vocation of the *lay faithful*, acting on their own initiative with their fellow citizens. 899

[223] Cf. *SRS* 14. — [224] *SRS* 9. — [225] Cf. *SRS* 17; 45. — [226] *CA* 28; cf. 35. — [227] Cf. *SRS* 16. — [228] Cf. *SRS* 16. — [229] Cf. *CA* 26. — [230] Cf. *SRS* 32; *CA* 51.

Social action can assume various concrete forms. It should always have the common good in view and be in conformity with the message of the Gospel and the teaching of the Church. It is the role of the laity "to animate temporal realities with Christian commitment, by which they show that they are witnesses and agents of peace and justice."[231]

2544–2547 **VI. Love for the Poor**

2443 God blesses those who come to the aid of the poor and rebukes those who turn away from them: "Give to him who begs from you, do not refuse him who would borrow from you"; "you received without pay, give without pay."[232] It is by what they have done for the poor
786, 525 that Jesus Christ will recognize his chosen ones.[233] When "the poor have
544, 853 the good news preached to them," it is the sign of Christ's presence.[234]

2444 "The Church's love for the poor...is a part of her constant tradition." This love is inspired by the Gospel of the Beatitudes, of the pov-
1716 erty of Jesus, and of his concern for the poor.[235] Love for the poor is even one of the motives for the duty of working so as to "be able to give to those in need."[236] It extends not only to material poverty but also to the many forms of cultural and religious poverty.[237]

2536 **2445** Love for the poor is incompatible with immoderate love of riches or their selfish use:

> 2547 Come now, you rich, weep and howl for the miseries that are coming upon you. Your riches have rotted and your garments are moth-eaten. Your gold and silver have rusted, and their rust will be evidence against you and will eat your flesh like fire. You have laid up treasure for the last days. Behold, the wages of the laborers who mowed your fields, which you kept back by fraud, cry out; and the cries of the harvesters have reached the ears of the Lord of hosts. You have lived on the earth in luxury and in pleasure; you have fattened your hearts in a day of slaughter. You have condemned, you have killed the righteous man; he does not resist you.[238]

2446 St. John Chrysostom vigorously recalls this: "Not to enable the poor to share in our goods is to steal from them and deprive them of life. The goods we possess are not ours, but theirs."[239] "The demands of justice must be satisfied first of all; that 2402
which is already due in justice is not to be offered as a gift of charity":[240]

> When we attend to the needs of those in want, we give them what is theirs, not ours. More than performing works of mercy, we are paying a debt of justice.[241]

2447 *The works of mercy* are char- 1460
itable actions by which we come to the aid of our neighbor in his spiritual and bodily necessities.[242] Instructing, advising, consoling, comforting are spiritual works of mercy, as are forgiving and bearing wrongs patiently. The corporal works of mercy consist especially in feeding the hungry, sheltering the home-
less, clothing the naked, visiting 1038
the sick and imprisoned, and bury-
ing the dead.[243] Among all these, 1969

[231] *SRS* 47 § 6; cf. 42. — [232] *Mt* 5:42; 10:8. — [233] Cf. *Mt* 25:31–36. — [234] *Mt* 11:5; cf. *Lk* 4:18. — [235] *CA* 57; cf. *Lk* 6:20–22, *Mt* 8:20; *Mk* 12:41–44. — [236] *Eph* 4:28. — [237] Cf. *CA* 57. — [238] *Jas* 5:1–6. — [239] St. John Chrysostom, *Hom. in Lazaro* 2, 5: PG 48, 992. — [240] *AA* 8 § 5. — [241] St. Gregory the Great, *Regula Pastoralis.* 3, 21: PL 77, 87. — [242] Cf. *Isa* 58:6–7; *Heb* 13:3. — [243] Cf. *Mt* 25:31–46.

giving alms to the poor is one of the chief witnesses to fraternal charity: it is also a work of justice pleasing to God:[244]

> He who has two coats, let him share with him who has none; and he who has food must do likewise.[245] But give for alms those things which are within; and behold, everything is clean for you.[246] If a brother or sister is ill-clad and in lack of daily food, and one of you says to them, "Go in peace, be warmed and filled," without
> 1004 giving them the things needed for the body, what does it profit?[247]

2448 "In its various forms—material deprivation, unjust oppression, physical and psychological
386 illness and death—*human misery* is the obvious sign of the inherited condition of frailty and need for salvation in which man finds himself as a consequence of original sin. This misery elicited the compassion of Christ the Savior, who willingly took it upon himself and identified himself with the least of his brethren. Hence, those who are oppressed by poverty are the object of a *prefer-*
1586 *ential love* on the part of the Church which, since her origin and in spite of the failings of many of her members, has not ceased to work for their relief, defense, and liberation through numerous works of charity which remain indispensable always and everywhere."[248]

2449 Beginning with the Old Testament, all kinds of juridical measures (the jubilee year of forgiveness of debts, prohibition of loans at interest and the keeping of collateral, the obligation to tithe, the daily payment of the day-laborer, the right to glean vines and fields) answer the exhortation of *Deuteronomy*: "For the poor will never cease out of the land; therefore I command you, 'You shall open wide your hand to your brother, to the needy and to the poor in the land.'"[249] Jesus makes these words his own: "The poor you always have with you, but you do not always have me."[250] In so doing he does not soften the vehemence of former oracles against "buying the poor for silver and the needy for a pair of sandals...," but invites us to
recognize his own presence in the 1397
poor who are his brethren:[251]

> When her mother reproached her for caring for the poor and the sick at home, St. Rose of Lima said to her: "When we serve the poor and the sick, we serve Jesus. We must not fail to help our neighbors, because in
> them we serve Jesus.[252] 786

In Brief

2450 *"You shall not steal" (*Ex *20:15;* Deut *5:19). "Neither thieves, nor the greedy..., nor robbers will inherit the kingdom of God" (*1 Cor *6:10).*

2451 *The seventh commandment enjoins the practice of justice and charity in the administration of earthly goods and the fruits of men's labor.*

2452 *The goods of creation are destined for the entire human race. The right to private property does not abolish the universal destination of goods.*

[244] Cf. *Tob* 4:5–11; *Sir* 17:22; *Mt* 6:2–4. — [245] *Lk* 3:11. — [246] *Lk* 11:41. — [247] *Jas* 2:15–16; cf. *1 Jn* 3:17. — [248] CDF, instruction, *Libertatis conscientia,* 68. — [249] *Deut* 15:11. — [250] *Jn* 12:8. — [251] *Am* 8:6; cf. *Mt* 25:40. — [252] P. Hansen, *Vita mirabilis* (Louvain, 1668).

2453 *The seventh commandment forbids theft. Theft is the usurpation of another's goods against the reasonable will of the owner.*

2454 *Every manner of taking and using another's property unjustly is contrary to the seventh commandment. The injustice committed requires reparation. Commutative justice requires the restitution of stolen goods.*

2455 *The moral law forbids acts which, for commercial or totalitarian purposes, lead to the enslavement of human beings, or to their being bought, sold or exchanged like merchandise.*

2456 *The dominion granted by the Creator over the mineral, vegetable, and animal resources of the universe cannot be separated from respect for moral obligations, including those toward generations to come.*

2457 *Animals are entrusted to man's stewardship; he must show them kindness. They may be used to serve the just satisfaction of man's needs.*

2458 *The Church makes a judgment about economic and social matters when the fundamental rights of the person or the salvation of souls requires it. She is concerned with the temporal common good of men because they are ordered to the sovereign Good, their ultimate end.*

2459 *Man is himself the author, center, and goal of all economic and social life. The decisive point of the social question is that goods created by God for everyone should in fact reach everyone in accordance with justice and with the help of charity.*

2460 *The primordial value of labor stems from man himself, its author and beneficiary. By means of his labor man participates in the work of creation. Work united to Christ can be redemptive.*

2461 *True development concerns the whole man. It is concerned with increasing each person's ability to respond to his vocation and hence to God's call (cf.* CA *29).*

2462 *Giving alms to the poor is a witness to fraternal charity: it is also a work of justice pleasing to God.*

2463 *How can we not recognize Lazarus, the hungry beggar in the parable (cf.* Lk *17:19–31), in the multitude of human beings without bread, a roof or a place to stay? How can we fail to hear Jesus: "As you did it not to one of the least of these, you did it not to me" (*Mt *25:45)?*

Article 8:
THE EIGHTH COMMANDMENT

You shall not bear false witness against your neighbor.[253]
It was said to the men of old, "You shall not swear falsely, but shall perform to the Lord what you have sworn."[254]

2464 The eighth commandment forbids misrepresenting the truth in our relations with others. This moral prescription flows from the vocation of the holy people to bear witness

[253] *Ex* 20:16; cf. *Deut* 5:20. — [254] *Mt* 5:33.

to their God who is the truth and wills the truth. Offenses against the truth express by word or deed a refusal to commit oneself to moral uprightness: they are fundamental infidelities to God and, in this sense, they undermine the foundations of the covenant.

I. Living in the Truth

215 **2465** The Old Testament attests that *God is the source of all truth*. His Word is truth. His Law is truth. His "faithfulness endures to all generations."[255] Since God is "true," the members of his people are called to live in the truth.[256]

2466 In Jesus Christ, the whole of God's truth has been made manifest. "Full of grace and truth," he came as the "light of the world," he *is the Truth*.[257] "Whoever believes in me may not remain in darkness."[258] The disciple of Jesus continues in his word so as to know "the truth [that] will make you free" and that sanctifies.[259] To follow Jesus is to live in "the Spirit of truth," whom the Father sends in his name and who
2153 leads "into all the truth."[260] To his disciples Jesus teaches the unconditional love of truth: "Let what you say be simply 'Yes or No.'"[261]

2467 Man tends by nature toward the truth. He is obliged to honor and bear witness to it: "It is in accordance with their dignity that all
2104 men, because they are persons...are both impelled by their nature and bound by a moral obligation to seek the truth, especially religious truth. They are also bound to adhere to the truth once they come to know it and direct their whole lives in accordance with the demands of truth."[262]

2468 Truth as uprightness in human action and speech is called *truthfulness*, sincerity, or candor. Truth or truthfulness is the virtue
which consists in showing oneself 1458
true in deeds and truthful in words, and in guarding against duplicity, dissimulation, and hypocrisy.

2469 "Men could not live with one another if there were not mutual confidence that they were being truthful to one another."[263] The virtue of truth gives another his just
due. Truthfulness keeps to the just 1807
mean between what ought to be expressed and what ought to be kept secret: it entails honesty and discretion. In justice, "as a matter of honor, one man owes it to another to manifest the truth."[264]

2470 The disciple of Christ consents to "live in the truth," that is, in the simplicity of a life in conformity with the Lord's example, abiding in his truth. "If we say we have fellowship with him while we walk in darkness, we lie and do not live according to the truth."[265]

II. To Bear Witness to the Truth

2471 Before Pilate, Christ proclaims that he "has come into the world, to bear witness to the truth."[266] The Christian is not to "be
ashamed then of testifying to our 1816
Lord."[267] In situations that require witness to the faith, the Christian must profess it without equivocation, after the example of St. Paul

[255] *Ps* 119:90; cf. Prov 8:7; *2 Sam* 7:28; *Ps* 119:142; *Lk* 1:50. — [256] *Rom* 3:4; cf. *Ps* 119:30. — [257] *Jn* 1:14; 8:12; cf. 14:6. — [258] *Jn* 12:46. — [259] *Jn* 8:32; cf. 17:17. — [260] *Jn* 16:13. — [261] *Mt* 5:37. — [262] *DH* 2 § 2. — [263] St. Thomas Aquinas, *STh* II–II, 109, 3 *ad* 1. — [264] St. Thomas Aquinas, *STh* II–II, 109, 3, *corp. art*. — [265] *1 Jn* 1:6. — [266] *Jn* 18:37. — [267] *2 Tim* 1:8.

before his judges. We must keep "a clear conscience toward God and toward men."[268]

2472 The duty of Christians to take part in the life of the Church impels them to act as *witnesses of the Gospel* and of the obligations that
863, 905 flow from it. This witness is a transmission of the faith in words and deeds. Witness is an act of justice that establishes the truth or makes it known.[269]

1807 All Christians by the example of their lives and the witness of their word, wherever they live, have an obligation to manifest the new man which they have put on in Baptism and to reveal the power of the Holy Spirit by whom they were strengthened at Confirmation.[270]

852 **2473** *Martyrdom* is the supreme witness given to the truth of the faith: it means bearing witness even unto death. The martyr bears witness to Christ who died and rose, to whom he is united by charity. He bears witness to the truth of the
1808 faith and of Christian doctrine. He endures death through an act of fortitude. "Let me become the food of the beasts, through whom it will be
1258 given me to reach God."[271]

2474 The Church has painstakingly collected the records of those who persevered to the end in witnessing to their faith. These are the acts of the Martyrs. They form the archives of truth written in letters of blood:

Neither the pleasures of the world 1011
nor the kingdoms of this age will be of any use to me. It is better for me to die [in order to unite myself] to Christ Jesus than to reign over the ends of the earth. I seek him who died for us; I desire him who rose for us. My birth is approaching....[272]
I bless you for having judged me worthy from this day and this hour to be counted among your martyrs.... You have kept your promise, God of faithfulness and truth. For this reason and for everything, I praise you, I bless you, I glorify you through the eternal and heavenly High Priest, Jesus Christ, your beloved Son. Through him, who is with you and the Holy Spirit, may glory be given to you, now and in the ages to come. Amen.[273]

III. Offenses Against Truth

2475 Christ's disciples have "put on the new man, created after the likeness of God in true righteousness and holiness."[274] By "putting away falsehood," they are to "put away all malice and all guile and insincerity and envy and all slander."[275]

2476 *False witness and perjury.* 2152
When it is made publicly, a statement contrary to the truth takes on a particular gravity. In court it becomes false witness.[276] When it is under oath, it is perjury. Acts such as these contribute to condemnation of the innocent, exoneration of the guilty, or the increased punishment of the accused.[277] They gravely compromise the exercise of justice and the fairness of judicial decisions.

[268] *Acts* 24:16. — [269] *Mt* 18:16. — [270] *AG* 11. — [271] St. Ignatius of Antioch, *Ad Rom.* 4, 1: SCh 10, 110. — [272] St. Ignatius of Antioch, *Ad Rom.* 6, 1–2: SCh 10, 114. — [273] *Martyrium Polycarpi* 14, 2–3: PG 5, 1040; SCh 10, 228. — [274] *Eph* 4:24. — [275] *Eph* 4:25; *1 Pet* 2:1. — [276] Cf. *Prov* 19:9. — [277] Cf. *Prov* 18:5.

2477 Respect for the reputation of persons forbids every attitude and word likely to cause them unjust injury.[278] He becomes guilty:

– of *rash judgment* who, even tacitly, assumes as true, without sufficient foundation, the moral fault of a neighbor;
– of *detraction* who, without objectively valid reason, discloses another's faults and failings to persons who did not know them;[279]
– of *calumny* who, by remarks contrary to the truth, harms the reputation of others and gives occasion for false judgments concerning them.

2478 To avoid rash judgment, everyone should be careful to interpret insofar as possible his neighbor's thoughts, words, and deeds in a favorable way:

> Every good Christian ought to be more ready to give a favorable interpretation to another's statement than to condemn it. But if he cannot do so, let him ask how the other understands it. And if the latter understands it badly, let the former correct him with love. If that does not suffice, let the Christian try all suitable ways to bring the other to a correct interpretation so that he may be saved.[280]

2479 Detraction and calumny destroy the *reputation and honor of one's neighbor*. Honor is the social witness given to human dignity, and everyone enjoys a natural right to the honor of his name and reputation
1753 and to respect. Thus, detraction and calumny offend against the virtues of justice and charity.

2480 Every word or attitude is forbidden which by *flattery, adulation, or complaisance* encourages and confirms another in malicious acts and perverse conduct. Adulation is a grave fault if it makes one an accomplice in another's vices or grave sins. Neither the desire to be of service nor friendship justifies duplicitous speech. Adulation is a venial sin when it only seeks to be agreeable, to avoid evil, to meet a need, or to obtain legitimate advantages.

2481 *Boasting* or bragging is an offense against truth. So is *irony* aimed at disparaging someone by maliciously caricaturing some aspect of his behavior.

2482 "A *lie* consists in speaking a falsehood with the intention of deceiving."[281] The Lord denounces lying as the work of the devil: "You are of your father the devil,...there is no truth in him. When he lies, he speaks according to his own nature, for he is a liar and the father
of lies."[282] 392

2483 Lying is the most direct offense against the truth. To lie is to speak or act against the truth in order to lead someone into error. By injuring man's relation to truth and to his neighbor, a lie offends against the fundamental relation of man and of his word to the Lord.

2484 The *gravity of a lie* is measured against the nature of the truth it deforms, the circumstances, the intentions of the one who lies, and
the harm suffered by its victims. To 1750
lie is to speak or act against the truth in order to lead someone into error.

[278] Cf. *CIC*, can. 220. — [279] Cf. *Sir* 21:28. — [280] St. Ignatius of Loyola, *Spiritual Exercises*, 22. — [281] St. Augustine, *De mendacio* 4, 5: PL 40, 491. — [282] *Jn* 8:44.

2485 By its very nature, lying is
1756 to be condemned. It is a profanation of speech, whereas the purpose of speech is to communicate known truth to others. The deliberate intention of leading a neighbor into error by saying things contrary to the truth constitutes a failure in justice and charity. The culpability is greater when the intention of deceiving entails the risk of deadly consequences for those who are led astray.

2486 Since it violates the virtue of truthfulness, a lie does real violence to another. It affects his ability to know, which is a condition of every judgment and decision. It contains the seed of discord and all conse-
1607 quent evils. Lying is destructive of society; it undermines trust among men and tears apart the fabric of social relationships.

1459 **2487** Every offense committed against justice and truth entails the *duty of reparation*, even if its author has been forgiven. When it is impossible publicly to make reparation for a wrong, it must be made secretly. If someone who has suffered harm cannot be directly compensated, he
2412 must be given moral satisfaction in the name of charity. This duty of reparation also concerns offenses against another's reputation. This reparation, moral and sometimes material, must be evaluated in terms of the extent of the damage inflicted. It obliges in conscience.

IV. Respect for the Truth

1740 **2488** The *right to the communication* of the truth is not unconditional. Everyone must conform his life to the Gospel precept of fraternal love. This requires us in concrete situations to judge whether or not it is appropriate to reveal the truth to someone who asks for it.

2489 Charity and respect for the truth should dictate the response to every *request for information or communication*. The good and safety of others, respect for privacy, and the common good are sufficient reasons for being silent about what ought not be known or for making use of a discreet language. The duty to avoid scandal often commands strict discretion. No one is bound to reveal 2284
the truth to someone who does not have the right to know it.[283]

2490 The *secret of the sacrament* 1467
of reconciliation is sacred, and cannot be violated under any pretext. "The sacramental seal is inviolable; therefore, it is a crime for a confessor in any way to betray a penitent by word or in any other manner or for any reason."[284]

2491 *Professional secrets*—for example, those of political office holders, soldiers, physicians, and lawyers—or confidential information given under the seal of secrecy must be kept, save in exceptional cases where keeping the secret is bound to cause very grave harm to the one who confided it, to the one who received it or to a third party, and where the very grave harm can be avoided only by divulging the truth. Even if not confided under the seal of secrecy, private information prejudicial to another is not to be divulged without a grave and proportionate reason.

[283] Cf. *Sir* 27:16; *Prov* 25:9–10. — [284] CIC, can. 983 § 1.

2522 **2492** Everyone should observe an appropriate reserve concerning persons' private lives. Those in charge of communications should maintain a fair balance between the requirements of the common good and respect for individual rights. Interference by the media in the private lives of persons engaged in political or public activity is to be condemned to the extent that it infringes upon their privacy and freedom.

V. The Use of the Social Communications Media

2493 Within modern society the communications media play a major role in information, cultural promotion, and formation. This role is increasing, as a result of technological progress, the extent and diversity of the news transmitted, and the influence exercised on public opinion.

1906 **2494** The information provided by the media is at the service of the common good.[285] Society has a right to information based on truth, freedom, justice, and solidarity:

> The proper exercise of this right demands that the content of the communication be true and—within the limits set by justice and charity—complete. Further, it should be communicated honestly and properly. This means that in the gathering and in the publication of news, the moral law and the legitimate rights and dignity of man should be upheld.[286]

906 **2495** "It is necessary that all members of society meet the demands of justice and charity in this domain. They should help, through the means of social communication, in the formation and diffusion of sound public opinion."[287] Solidarity is a consequence of genuine and right communication and the free circulation of ideas that further knowledge and respect for others.

2496 The means of social communication (especially the mass media) can give rise to a certain passivity among users, making them less than vigilant consumers of what is
said or shown. Users should practice 2525
moderation and discipline in their approach to the mass media. They will want to form enlightened and correct consciences the more easily to resist unwholesome influences.

2497 By the very nature of their profession, journalists have an obligation to serve the truth and not offend against charity in disseminating information. They should strive to respect, with equal care, the nature of the facts and the limits of critical judgment concerning individuals. They should not stoop to defamation.

2498 "*Civil authorities* have par- 2237
ticular responsibilities in this field because of the common good.... It is for the civil authority...to defend and safeguard a true and just freedom of information."[288] By promulgating laws and overseeing
their application, public authorities 2286
should ensure that "public morality and social progress are not gravely endangered" through misuse of the media.[289] Civil authorities should punish any violation of the rights of individuals to their reputation and privacy. They should give timely and reliable reports concerning the general good or respond to the well-founded concerns of the

[285] Cf. *IM* 11. — [286] *IM* 5 § 2. — [287] *IM* 8. — [288] *IM* 12. — [289] *IM* 12 § 2.

people. Nothing can justify recourse to disinformation for manipulating public opinion through the media. Interventions by public authority should avoid injuring the freedom of individuals or groups.

2499 Moral judgment must condemn the plague of totalitarian states which systematically falsify the truth, exercise political control of opinion through the media, manipulate defendants and witnesses at public trials, and imagine that they
1903 secure their tyranny by strangling and repressing everything they consider "thought crimes."

VI. Truth, Beauty, and Sacred Art

1804 **2500** The practice of goodness is accompanied by spontaneous spiritual joy and moral beauty. Likewise, truth carries with it the joy and splendor of spiritual beauty. Truth is beautiful in itself. Truth in words, the rational expression of the knowledge of created and uncreated reality, is necessary to man, who is endowed with intellect. But truth can also find other complementary forms of human expression, above all when it is a matter of evoking what is beyond words: the depths of the human heart, the exaltations of the soul, the mystery of God. Even before revealing himself to man in words of truth, God reveals himself to him through the universal language of creation, the work of
341 his Word, of his wisdom: the order and harmony of the cosmos—which both the child and the scientist discover—"from the greatness and beauty of created things comes a corresponding perception of their Creator," "for the author of beauty created them."[290] 2129

> [Wisdom] is a breath of the power of God, and a pure emanation of the glory of the Almighty; therefore nothing defiled gains entrance into her. For she is a reflection of eternal light, a spotless mirror of the working of God, and an image of his goodness.[291] For [wisdom] is more beautiful than the sun, and excels every constellation of the stars. Compared with the light she is found to be superior, for it is succeeded by the night, but against wisdom evil does not prevail.[292] I became enamored of her beauty.[293]

2501 Created "in the image of God,"[294] man also expresses the truth of his relationship with God the Creator by the beauty of his artistic works. Indeed, *art* is a distinctively human form of expression; beyond the search for the necessities of life which is common to all living creatures, art is a freely given superabundance of the human being's inner riches. Arising from talent given by the Creator and from man's own effort, art is a form of practical wisdom, uniting knowledge and skill,[295] to give form to the truth of reality in a language accessible to sight or hearing. To the extent that it is inspired by truth and love of beings, art bears a certain likeness to God's activity in what he has created. Like
any other human activity, art is not 359
an absolute end in itself, but is ordered to and ennobled by the ultimate end of man.[296]

2502 *Sacred art* is true and beau- 1156–1162
tiful when its form corresponds to its particular vocation: evoking and

290 *Wis* 13:3, 5. — 291 *Wis* 7:25–26. — 292 *Wis* 7:29–30. — 293 *Wis* 8:2. — 294 *Gen* 1:26. — 295 Cf. *Wis* 7:16–17. — 296 Cf. Pius XII, *Musicae sacrae disciplina*; Discourses of September 3 and December 25, 1950.

glorifying, in faith and adoration, the transcendent mystery of God—the surpassing invisible beauty of truth and love visible in Christ, who "reflects the glory of God and bears the very stamp of his nature," in whom "the whole fullness of deity dwells bodily."[297] This spiritual beauty of God is reflected in the most holy Virgin Mother of God, the angels, and saints. Genuine sacred art draws man to adoration, to prayer, and to the love of God, Creator and Savior, the Holy One and Sanctifier.

2503 For this reason bishops, personally or through delegates, should see to the promotion of sacred art, old and new, in all its forms and, with the same religious care, remove from the liturgy and from places of worship everything which is not in conformity with the truth of faith and the authentic beauty of sacred art.[298]

In Brief

2504 *"You shall not bear false witness against your neighbor" (*Ex *20:16). Christ's disciples have "put on the new man, created after the likeness of God in true righteousness and holiness" (*Eph *4:24).*

2505 *Truth or truthfulness is the virtue which consists in showing oneself true in deeds and truthful in words, and guarding against duplicity, dissimulation, and hypocrisy.*

2506 *The Christian is not to "be ashamed of testifying to our Lord" (*2 Tim *1:8) in deed and word. Martyrdom is the supreme witness given to the truth of the faith.*

2507 *Respect for the reputation and honor of persons forbids all detraction and calumny in word or attitude.*

2508 *Lying consists in saying what is false with the intention of deceiving one's neighbor.*

2509 *An offense committed against the truth requires reparation.*

2510 *The golden rule helps one discern, in concrete situations, whether or not it would be appropriate to reveal the truth to someone who asks for it.*

2511 *"The sacramental seal is inviolable" (CIC, can. 983 § 1). Professional secrets must be kept. Confidences prejudicial to another are not to be divulged.*

2512 *Society has a right to information based on truth, freedom, and justice. One should practice moderation and discipline in the use of the social communications media.*

2513 *The fine arts, but above all sacred art, "of their nature are directed toward expressing in some way the infinite beauty of God in works made by human hands. Their dedication to the increase of God's praise and of his glory is more complete, the more exclusively they are devoted to turning men's minds devoutly toward God" (SC 122).*

[297] *Heb* 1:3; *Col* 2:9. — [298] Cf. *SC* 122–127.

Article 9:
THE NINTH COMMANDMENT

> You shall not covet your neighbor's house; you shall not covet your neighbor's wife, or his manservant, or his maidservant, or his ox, or his ass, or anything that is your neighbor's.[299]
> Every one who looks at a woman lustfully has already committed adultery with her in his heart.[300]

377, 400 **2514** St. John distinguishes three kinds of covetousness or concupiscence: lust of the flesh, lust of the eyes, and pride of life.[301] In the Catholic catechetical tradition, the ninth commandment forbids carnal concupiscence; the tenth forbids coveting another's goods.

405 **2515** Etymologically, "concupiscence" can refer to any intense form of human desire. Christian theology has given it a particular meaning: the movement of the sensitive appetite contrary to the operation of the human reason. The apostle St. Paul identifies it with the rebellion of the "flesh" against the "spirit."[302] Concupiscence stems from the disobedience of the first sin. It unsettles man's moral faculties and, without being in itself an offense, inclines man to commit sins.[303]

362 **2516** Because man is a *composite being, spirit and body,* there already exists a certain tension in him; a certain struggle of tendencies between "spirit" and "flesh" develops. But in fact this struggle belongs to the heritage of sin. It is a consequence of sin and at the same time a confirmation of it. It is part of the daily experience
of the spiritual battle: 407

> For the Apostle it is not a matter of despising and condemning the body which with the spiritual soul constitutes man's nature and personal subjectivity. Rather, he is concerned with the morally *good* or *bad* works, or better, the permanent dispositions—virtues and vices—which are the fruit of *submission* (in the first case) or of *resistance* (in the second case) to the *saving action of the Holy Spirit.* For this reason the Apostle writes: "If we live by the Spirit, let us also walk by the Spirit."[304]

I. Purification of the Heart

2517 The heart is the seat of mor- 368
al personality: "Out of the heart come evil thoughts, murder, adultery, fornication...."[305] The struggle against carnal covetousness entails
purifying the heart and practicing 1809
temperance:

> Remain simple and innocent, and you will be like little children who do not know the evil that destroys man's life.[306]

2518 The sixth beatitude proclaims, "Blessed are the pure in heart, for they shall see God."[307] "Pure in heart" refers to those who have attuned their intellects and wills to the demands of God's holiness, chiefly in three areas: charity;[308] chastity or sexual rectitude;[309] love of truth and orthodoxy of faith.[310] There is a

[299] *Ex* 20:17. — [300] *Mt* 5:28. — [301] Cf. *1 Jn* 2:16. — [302] Cf. *Gal* 5:16, 17, 24; *Eph* 2:3. — [303] Cf. *Gen* 3:11; Council of Trent: DS 1515. — [304] John Paul II, *DeV* 55; cf. *Gal* 5:25. — [305] *Mt* 15:19. — [306] *Pastor Hermae,* Mandate 2, 1: PG 2, 916. — [307] *Mt* 5:8. — [308] Cf. *1 Tim* 4:3–9; 2 *Tim* 2:22. — [309] Cf. *1 Thess* 4:7; *Col* 3:5; *Eph* 4:19. — [310] Cf. *Titus* 1:15; *1 Tim* 1:3–4; *2 Tim* 2:23–26.

connection between purity of heart,
94 of body, and of faith:

> The faithful must believe the articles of the Creed "so that by believing they may obey God, by obeying may live well, by living well may purify their hearts, and with pure hearts may
> 158 understand what they believe."[311]

2548 **2519** The "pure in heart" are promised that they will see God face to face and be like him.[312] Purity of heart is the precondition of the vision of God. Even now it enables us to see *according to* God, to
2819 accept others as "neighbors"; it lets us perceive the human body—ours and our neighbor's—as a temple of the Holy Spirit, a manifestation of
2501 divine beauty.

II. The Battle for Purity

1264 **2520** Baptism confers on its recipient the grace of purification from all sins. But the baptized must continue to struggle against concupiscence of the flesh and disordered desires. With God's grace he will prevail

2337 – by the *virtue* and *gift of chastity*, for chastity lets us love with upright and undivided heart;
– by *purity of intention* which consists in seeking the true end of man: with simplicity of vision, the baptized person seeks to find and to fulfill God's will in everything;[313]
1752 – by *purity of vision*, external and internal; by discipline of feelings and imagination; by refusing all complicity in impure thoughts that incline us to turn aside from the path of God's commandments: "Appearance arouses yearning in fools";[314]
2846 – by *prayer*:

> I thought that continence arose from one's own powers, which I did not recognize in myself. I was foolish enough not to know...that no one can be continent unless you grant it. For you would surely have granted it if my inner groaning had reached your ears and I with firm faith had cast my cares on you.[315]

2521 Purity requires *modesty*, an integral part of temperance. Modesty protects the intimate center of the person. It means refusing to unveil what should remain hidden. It is ordered to chastity to whose sensitivity it bears witness. It guides how one looks at others and behaves toward them in conformity with the dignity of persons and their solidarity.

2522 Modesty protects the mys- 2492
tery of persons and their love. It encourages patience and moderation in loving relationships; it requires that the conditions for the definitive giving and commitment of man and woman to one another be fulfilled. Modesty is decency. It inspires one's choice of clothing. It keeps silence or reserve where there is evident risk of unhealthy curiosity. It is discreet.

2523 There is a modesty of the 2354
feelings as well as of the body. It protests, for example, against the voyeuristic explorations of the human body in certain advertisements, or against the solicitations of certain media that go too far in the exhibition of intimate things. Modesty inspires a way of life which makes it possible to resist the allurements of fashion and the pressures of prevailing ideologies.

[311] St. Augustine, *De fide et symbolo* 10, 25: PL 40, 196. — [312] Cf. *1 Cor* 13:12; *1 Jn* 3:2. — [313] Cf. *Rom* 12:2; *Col* 1:10. — [314] *Wis* 15:5. — [315] St. Augustine, *Conf.* 6, 11, 20: PL 32, 729–730.

2524 The forms taken by modesty vary from one culture to another. Everywhere, however, modesty exists as an intuition of the spiritual dignity proper to man. It is born with the awakening consciousness of being a subject. Teaching modesty to children and adolescents means awakening in them respect for the human person.

2344 **2525** Christian purity requires a *purification of the social climate.* It requires of the communications media that their presentations show concern for respect and restraint. Purity of heart brings freedom from widespread eroticism and avoids entertainment inclined to voyeurism and illusion.

1740 **2526** So-called *moral permissiveness* rests on an erroneous conception of human freedom; the necessary precondition for the development of true freedom is to let oneself be educated in the moral law. Those in charge of education can reasonably be expected to give young people instruction respectful of the truth, the qualities of the heart, and the moral and spiritual dignity of man.

1204 **2527** "The Good News of Christ continually renews the life and culture of fallen man; it combats and removes the error and evil which flow from the ever-present attraction of sin. It never ceases to purify and elevate the morality of peoples. It takes the spiritual qualities and endowments of every age and nation, and with supernatural riches it causes them to blossom, as it were, from within; it fortifies, completes, and restores them in Christ."[316]

In Brief

2528 *"Everyone who looks at a woman lustfully has already committed adultery with her in his heart"* (Mt *5:28).*

2529 *The ninth commandment warns against lust or carnal concupiscence.*

2530 *The struggle against carnal lust involves purifying the heart and practicing temperance.*

2531 *Purity of heart will enable us to see God: it enables us even now to see things according to God.*

2532 *Purification of the heart demands prayer, the practice of chastity, purity of intention and of vision.*

2533 *Purity of heart requires the modesty which is patience, decency, and discretion. Modesty protects the intimate center of the person.*

Article 10:
THE TENTH COMMANDMENT

You shall not covet...anything that is your neighbor's.... You shall not desire your neighbor's house, his field, or his manservant, or his maidservant, or his ox, or his ass, or anything that is your neighbor's.[317]
For where your treasure is, there will your heart be also.[318]

[316] *GS* 58 § 4. — [317] *Ex* 20:17; *Deut* 5:21. — [318] *Mt* 6:21.

2534 The tenth commandment unfolds and completes the ninth, which is concerned with concupiscence of the flesh. It forbids coveting the goods of another, as the root of theft, robbery, and fraud, which the seventh commandment forbids. "Lust of the eyes" leads to the violence and injustice forbidden by the fifth commandment.[319] Avarice, like fornication, originates in the idolatry prohibited by the first three prescriptions of the Law.[320] The tenth commandment concerns
2112 the intentions of the heart; with the
2069 ninth, it summarizes all the precepts of the Law.

I. The Disorder of Covetous Desires

2535 The sensitive appetite leads us to desire pleasant things we do not have, e.g., the desire to eat when we are hungry or to warm ourselves when we are cold. These desires are good in themselves; but often they
1767 exceed the limits of reason and drive us to covet unjustly what is not ours and belongs to another or is owed to him.

2536 The tenth commandment forbids *greed* and the desire to amass earthly goods without limit. It forbids *avarice* arising from a passion
2445 for riches and their attendant power. It also forbids the desire to commit injustice by harming our neighbor in his temporal goods:

> When the Law says, "You shall not covet," these words mean that we should banish our desires for whatever does not belong to us. Our thirst for another's goods is immense, infinite, never quenched. Thus it is written: "He who loves money never has money enough."[321]

2537 It is not a violation of this commandment to desire to obtain things that belong to one's neighbor, provided this is done by just means. Traditional catechesis realistically mentions "those who have a harder struggle against their criminal desires" and so who "must be urged the more to keep this commandment":

> ...merchants who desire scarcity and rising prices, who cannot bear not to be the only ones buying and selling so that they themselves can sell more dearly and buy more cheaply; those who hope that their peers will be impoverished, in order to realize a profit either by selling to them or buying from them...physicians who wish disease to spread; lawyers who are eager for many important cases and trials.[322]

2538 The tenth commandment 2317
requires that *envy* be banished from the human heart. When the prophet Nathan wanted to spur King David to repentance, he told him the story about the poor man who had only one ewe lamb that he treated like his own daughter and the rich man who, despite the great number of his flocks, envied the poor man and ended by stealing his lamb.[323] Envy can lead to the worst crimes.[324] "Through the devil's envy death entered the world":[325] 391

> We fight one another, and envy arms us against one another.... If everyone strives to unsettle the Body of Christ, where shall we end up? We are engaged in making Christ's Body a corpse.... We declare ourselves

[319] Cf. *1 Jn* 2:16; *Mic* 2:2. — [320] Cf. *Wis* 14:12. — [321] *Roman Catechism,* III, 37; cf. *Sir* 5:8. — [322] *Roman Catechism,* III, 37. — [323] Cf. *2 Sam* 12:1–4. — [324] Cf. *Gen* 4:3–7; *1 Kings* 21:1–29. — [325] *Wis* 2:24.

> members of one and the same organism, yet we devour one another like beasts.[326]

1866 **2539** Envy is a capital sin. It refers to the sadness at the sight of another's goods and the immoderate desire to acquire them for oneself, even unjustly. When it wishes grave harm to a neighbor it is a mortal sin:

> St. Augustine saw envy as "the diabolical sin."[327] "From envy are born hatred, detraction, calumny, joy caused by the misfortune of a neighbor, and displeasure caused by his prosperity."[328]

1829 **2540** Envy represents a form of sadness and therefore a refusal of charity; the baptized person should struggle against it by exercising good will. Envy often comes from pride; the baptized person should train himself to live in humility:

> Would you like to see God glorified by you? Then rejoice in your brother's progress and you will immediately give glory to God. Because his servant could conquer envy by rejoicing in the merits of others, God will be praised.[329]

II. The Desires of the Spirit

2541 The economy of law and grace turns men's hearts away from avarice and envy. It initiates them into desire for the Sovereign Good;
1718 it instructs them in the desires of
2764 the Holy Spirit who satisfies man's heart.

The God of the promises always 397
warned man against seduction by what from the beginning has seemed "good for food...a delight to the eyes...to be desired to make one wise."[330]

2542 The Law entrusted to Israel 1963
never sufficed to justify those subject to it; it even became the instrument of "lust."[331] The gap between wanting and doing points to the conflict between God's Law which is the "law of my mind," and another law "making me captive to the law of sin which dwells in my members."[332]

2543 "But now the righteousness 1992
of God has been manifested apart from law, although the law and the prophets bear witness to it, the righteousness of God through faith in Jesus Christ for all who believe."[333] Henceforth, Christ's faithful "have crucified the flesh with its passions and desires"; they are led by the Spirit and follow the desires of the Spirit.[334]

III. Poverty of Heart 2443–2449

2544 Jesus enjoins his disciples to prefer him to everything and everyone, and bids them "renounce all that [they have]" for his sake and that of the Gospel.[335] Shortly before his passion he gave them the example of the poor widow of Jerusalem who, out of her poverty, gave all that she had to live on.[336] The precept of detachment from riches is obligatory for entrance into the Kingdom
of heaven. 544

[326] St. John Chrysostom, *Hom. in 2 Cor.* 27, 3–4: PG 61, 588. — [327] Cf. St. Augustine, *De catechizandis rudibus* 4, 8: PL 40, 315–316. — [328] St. Gregory the Great, *Moralia in Job* 31, 45: PL 76, 621. — [329] St. John Chrysostom, *Hom. in Rom.* 71, 5: PG 60, 448. — [330] *Gen* 3:6. — [331] Cf. *Rom* 7:7. — [332] *Rom* 7:23; cf. 7:10. — [333] *Rom* 3:21–22. — [334] *Gal* 5:24; cf. *Rom* 8:14, 27. — [335] *Lk* 14:33; cf. *Mk* 8:35. — [336] Cf. *Lk* 21:4.

2545 All Christ's faithful are to "direct their affections rightly, lest they be hindered in their pursuit of perfect charity by the use of worldly things and by an adherence to riches which is contrary to the spirit of
2013 evangelical poverty."[337]

2546 "Blessed are the poor in spirit."[338] The Beatitudes reveal an order of happiness and grace, of beauty and peace. Jesus celebrates the joy
1716 of the poor, to whom the Kingdom already belongs:[339]

> The Word speaks of voluntary humility as "poverty in spirit"; the Apostle gives an example of God's poverty when he says: "For your sakes he became poor."[340]

2547 The Lord grieves over the rich, because they find their consolation in the abundance of goods.[341] "Let the proud seek and love earthly kingdoms, but blessed are the poor in spirit for theirs is the Kingdom of heaven."[342] Abandonment to the providence of the Father in heaven
305 frees us from anxiety about tomorrow.[343] Trust in God is a preparation for the blessedness of the poor. They shall see God.

IV. "I Want to See God"

2548 Desire for true happiness frees man from his immoderate attachment to the goods of this world so that he can find his fulfillment
2519 in the vision and beatitude of God. "The promise [of seeing God] surpasses all beatitude.... In Scripture, to see is to possess.... Whoever sees God has obtained all the goods of which he can conceive."[344]

2549 It remains for the holy people to struggle, with grace from on high, to obtain the good things God promises. In order to possess and contemplate God, Christ's faithful 2015
mortify their cravings and, with the grace of God, prevail over the seductions of pleasure and power.

2550 On this way of perfection, the Spirit and the Bride call whoever hears them[345] to perfect communion with God:

> There will true glory be, where no one will be praised by mistake or flattery; true honor will not be refused to the worthy, nor granted to the unworthy; likewise, no one unworthy will pretend to be worthy, where only those who are worthy will be admitted. There true peace will reign, where no one will experience opposition either from self or others. God himself will be virtue's reward; he gives virtue and has promised to give himself as the best and greatest reward that could exist.... "I shall be their God and they will be my people...." This is also the meaning of the Apostle's words: "So that God may be all in all." God himself will be the goal of our desires; we shall contemplate him without end, love him without surfeit, praise him without weariness. This gift, this state, this act, like eternal life itself,
> will assuredly be common to all.[346] 314

[337] *LG* 42 § 3. — [338] *Mt* 5:3. — [339] Cf. *Lk* 6:20. — [340] St. Gregory of Nyssa, De *beatitudinibus* 1: PG 44, 1200D; cf. *2 Cor* 8:9. — [341] *Lk* 6:24. — [342] St. Augustine, *De serm. Dom. in monte* 1, 1, 3: PL 34, 1232. — [343] Cf. *Mt* 6:25–34. — [344] St. Gregory of Nyssa, *De beatitudinibus* 6: PG 44, 1265A. — [345] Cf. *Rev* 22:17. — [346] St. Augustine, *De civ. Dei,* 22, 30: PL 41, 801–802; cf. *Lev* 26:12; cf. *1 Cor* 15:28.

In Brief

2551 *"Where your treasure is, there will your heart be also"* (Mt *6:21).*

2552 *The tenth commandment forbids avarice arising from a passion for riches and their attendant power.*

2553 *Envy is sadness at the sight of another's goods and the immoderate desire to have them for oneself. It is a capital sin.*

2554 *The baptized person combats envy through good-will, humility, and abandonment to the providence of God.*

2555 *Christ's faithful "have crucified the flesh with its passions and desires"* (Gal *5:24); they are led by the Spirit and follow his desires.*

2556 *Detachment from riches is necessary for entering the Kingdom of heaven. "Blessed are the poor in spirit."*

2557 *"I want to see God" expresses the true desire of man. Thirst for God is quenched by the water of eternal life (cf.* Jn *4:14).*

PART FOUR

CHRISTIAN PRAYER

Section One

PRAYER IN THE CHRISTIAN LIFE

2558 "Great is the mystery of the faith!" The Church professes this mystery in the Apostles' Creed (*Part One*) and celebrates it in the sacramental liturgy (*Part Two*), so that the life of the faithful may be conformed to Christ in the Holy Spirit to the glory of God the Father (*Part Three*). This mystery, then, requires that the faithful believe in it, that they celebrate it, and that they live from it in a vital and personal relationship with the living and true God. This relationship is prayer.

WHAT IS PRAYER?

For me, prayer is a surge of the heart; it is a simple look turned toward heaven, it is a cry of recognition and of love, embracing both trial and joy.[1]

Prayer as God's gift

2559 "Prayer is the raising of one's mind and heart to God or the requesting of good things from God."[2] But when we pray, do we speak from the height of our pride and will, or "out of the depths" of a humble and contrite heart?[3] He who humbles himself will be exalted;[4]
2613 *humility* is the foundation of prayer. Only when we humbly acknowledge
2763 that "we do not know how to pray as we ought,"[5] are we ready to receive freely the gift of prayer. "Man is a beggar before God."[6]

2560 "If you knew the gift of God!"[7] The wonder of prayer is revealed beside the well where we come seeking water: there, Christ comes to meet every human being. It is he who first seeks us and asks us for a drink. Jesus thirsts; his asking arises from the depths of God's desire for us. Whether we realize it or not, prayer is the encounter of God's thirst with ours. God thirsts that we may thirst for him.[8]

2561 "You would have asked him, and he would have given you living water."[9] Paradoxically our prayer of petition is a response to the plea of the living God: "They have forsaken me, the fountain of living waters, and hewn out cisterns for themselves, broken cisterns that can hold no water!"[10] Prayer is the response of faith to the free promise of salvation and also a response of love to the thirst of the only Son of God.[11]

Prayer as covenant

2562 Where does prayer come from? Whether prayer is expressed in words or gestures, it is the whole man who prays. But in naming the source of prayer, Scripture speaks sometimes of the soul or the spirit, but most often of the heart (more than a thousand times). According to Scripture, it is the heart that prays. If our *heart* is far from God, the words of prayer are in vain.

2563 The heart is the dwelling-place where I am, where I live; according to the Semitic or Biblical expression, the heart is the place "to which I withdraw." The heart is our hidden center, beyond the grasp of our reason and of others; only the Spirit of God can fathom the human heart and know it fully. The heart is the place of decision, deeper than our psychic drives. It is the place of truth, where we choose life or death.
It is the place of encounter, because 2699
as image of God we live in relation: 1696
it is the place of covenant.

2564 Christian prayer is a covenant relationship between God and man in Christ. It is the action of God and of man, springing forth from both the Holy Spirit and our-

[1] St. Thérèse of Lisieux, *Manuscrits autobiographiques*, C 25r. — [2] St. John Damascene, *De fide orth.* 3, 24: PG 94, 1089C. — [3] *Ps* 130:1. — [4] Cf. *Lk* 18:9–14. — [5] *Rom* 8:26. — [6] St. Augustine, *Sermo* 56, 6, 9: PL 38, 381. — [7] *Jn* 4:10. — [8] Cf. St. Augustine, *De diversis quaestionibus octoginta tribus* 64, 4: PL 40, 56. — [9] *Jn* 4:10. — [10] *Jer* 2:13. — [11] Cf. *Jn* 7:37–39; 19:28; *Isa* 12:3; 51:1; *Zech* 12:10; 13:1.

selves, wholly directed to the Father, in union with the human will of the Son of God made man.

Prayer as communion

2565 In the New Covenant, prayer is the living relationship of the children of God with their Father who is good beyond measure, with his Son Jesus Christ and with the Holy Spirit. The grace of the
260 Kingdom is "the union of the entire holy and royal Trinity...with the whole human spirit."[12] Thus, the life of prayer is the habit of being in the presence of the thrice-holy God and in communion with him. This communion of life is always possible because, through Baptism, we have already been united with Christ.[13] Prayer is Christian insofar as it is communion with Christ and extends throughout the Church, which is his Body. Its dimensions are
those of Christ's love.[14] 792

[12] St. Gregory of Nazianzus, *Oratio*, 16, 9: PG 35, 945. — [13] Cf. *Rom* 6:5. — [14] Cf. *Eph* 3:18–21.

Chapter One: THE REVELATION OF PRAYER

The Universal Call to Prayer

2566 *Man is in search of God.* In
the act of creation, God calls every
being from nothingness into existence. "Crowned with glory and
296 honor," man is, after the angels, capable of acknowledging "how majestic is the name of the Lord in all the
earth."[1] Even after losing through
his sin his likeness to God, man remains an image of his Creator, and
355 retains the desire for the one who
calls him into existence. All religions
28 bear witness to men's essential search
for God.[2]

2567 *God calls man first.* Man may
forget his Creator or hide far from his
face; he may run after idols or accuse
the deity of having abandoned him;
yet the living and true God tirelessly
calls each person to that mysterious
encounter known as prayer. In prayer, 30
the faithful God's initiative of love always comes first; our own first step is
always a response. As God gradually
reveals himself and reveals man to
himself, prayer appears as a recipro- 142
cal call, a covenant drama. Through
words and actions, this drama engages the heart. It unfolds throughout
the whole history of salvation.

Ariticle 1: IN THE OLD TESTAMENT

2568 In the Old Testament, the
revelation of prayer comes between
the fall and the restoration of man,
that is, between God's sorrowful
410 call to his first children: "Where are
you?... What is this that you have
1736 done?"[3] and the response of God's
only Son on coming into the world:
"Lo, I have come to do your will, O
God."[4] Prayer is bound up with human history, for it is the relationship
2738 with God in historical events.

Creation—source of prayer

288 **2569** *Prayer is lived in the first
place beginning with the realities of
creation.* The first nine chapters of
Genesis describe this relationship
with God as an offering of the first-
born of Abel's flock, as the invocation of the divine name at the time
of Enosh, and as "walking with
God."[5] Noah's offering is pleasing to 58
God, who blesses him and through
him all creation, because his heart
was upright and undivided; Noah,
like Enoch before him, "walks with
God."[6] This kind of prayer is lived
by many righteous people in all religions.

In his indefectible covenant with every living creature,[7] God has always
called people to prayer. But it is
above all beginning with our father 59
Abraham that prayer is revealed in
the Old Testament.

[1] *Ps* 8:5; 8:1. — [2] Cf. *Acts* 17:27. — [3] *Gen* 3:9, 13. — [4] *Heb* 10:5–7. — [5] Cf. *Gen* 4:4, 26; *Gen* 5:24. — [6] *Gen* 6:9; 8:20–9:17. — [7] *Gen* 9:8–16.

God's promise and the prayer of Faith

2570 When God calls him, Abraham goes forth "as the Lord had told him";[8] Abraham's heart is entirely submissive to the Word and so
145 he obeys. Such attentiveness of the heart, whose decisions are made according to God's will, is essential to prayer, while the words used count only in relation to it. Abraham's prayer is expressed first by deeds: a man of silence, he constructs an altar to the Lord at each stage of his journey. Only later does Abraham's first prayer in words appear: a veiled complaint reminding God of his promises which seem unfulfilled.[9] Thus one aspect of the drama of prayer appears from the beginning: the test of faith in the fidelity of God.

2571 Because Abraham believed in God and walked in his presence and in covenant with him,[10] the patriarch is ready to welcome a mysterious Guest into his tent. Abraham's remarkable hospitality at Mamre
494 foreshadows the annunciation of the true Son of the promise.[11] After that, once God had confided his plan, Abraham's heart is attuned to his Lord's compassion for men and he dares to intercede for them with
2635 bold confidence.[12]

2572 As a final stage in the purification of his faith, Abraham, "who had received the promises,"[13] is asked to sacrifice the son God had given him. Abraham's faith does not weaken ("God himself will provide the lamb for a burnt offering."), for he "considered that God was able to raise men even from the dead."[14] And so the father of believers is conformed to the likeness of the Father
who will not spare his own Son 603
but will deliver him up for us all.[15] Prayer restores man to God's likeness and enables him to share in the power of God's love that saves the multitude.[16]

2573 God renews his promise to Jacob, the ancestor of the twelve tribes of Israel.[17] Before confronting his elder brother Esau, Jacob wrestles all night with a mysterious figure who refuses to reveal his name, but who blesses him before leaving him at dawn. From this account, the spiritual tradition of the Church has retained the symbol of prayer as a
battle of faith and as the triumph of 162
perseverance.[18]

Moses and the prayer of the mediator

2574 Once the promise begins to be fulfilled (Passover, the Exodus, the gift of the Law, and the ratification of the covenant), the prayer of
Moses becomes the most striking ex- 62
ample of intercessory prayer, which will be fulfilled in "the one mediator between God and men, the man Christ Jesus."[19]

2575 Here again the initiative is 205
God's. From the midst of the burning bush he calls Moses.[20] This event will remain one of the primordial images of prayer in the spiritual tradition of Jews and Christians alike. When "the God of Abraham, of Isaac, and of Jacob" calls Moses to be his servant, it is because he is the

[8] *Gen* 12:4. — [9] Cf. *Gen* 15:2 f. — [10] Cf. *Gen* 15:6; 17:1 f. — [11] 11 Cf. *Gen* 18:1–15; Lk 1:26–38. — [12] Cf. *Gen* 18:16–33. — [13] *Heb* 11:17. — [14] *Gen* 22:8; *Heb* 11:19. — [15] *Rom* 8:32. — [16] Cf. *Rom* 8:16–21. — [17] Cf. *Gen* 28:10–22. — [18] Cf. *Gen* 32:24–30; *Lk* 18:1–8. — [19] *1 Tim* 2:5. — [20] *Ex* 3:1–10.

living God who wants men to live. God reveals himself in order to save them, though he does not do this alone or despite them: he calls Moses to be his messenger, an associate in his compassion, his work of salvation. There is something of a divine plea in this mission, and only after long debate does Moses attune his own will to that of the Savior God. But in the dialogue in which God confides in him, Moses also learns how to pray: he balks, makes excuses, above all questions: and it is in response to his question that the Lord confides his ineffable name, which will be revealed through his mighty deeds.

555 **2576** "Thus the Lord used to
speak to Moses face to face, as a man speaks to his friend."[21] Moses' prayer is characteristic of contemplative prayer by which God's servant remains faithful to his mission. Moses converses with God often and at length, climbing the mountain to hear and entreat him and coming down to the people to repeat the words of his God for their guidance. Moses "is entrusted with all my house. With him I speak face to face, clearly, not in riddles," for "Moses was very humble, more so than anyone else on the face of the earth."[22]

2577 From this intimacy with the faithful God, slow to anger and abounding in steadfast love,[23] Moses drew strength and determination for
210 his intercession. He does not pray
for himself but for the people whom God made his own. Moses already intercedes for them during the battle with the Amalekites and prays to obtain healing for Miriam.[24] But
it is chiefly after their apostasy that 2635
Moses "stands in the breach" before God in order to save the people.[25] The arguments of his prayer—for intercession is also a mysterious battle—will inspire the boldness of the great intercessors among the Jewish people and in the Church: God is love; he is therefore righteous and
faithful; he cannot contradict him- 214
self; he must remember his marvellous deeds, since his glory is at stake, and he cannot forsake this people that bears his name.

David and the prayer of the king

2578 The prayer of the People of God flourishes in the shadow of God's dwelling place, first the ark of the covenant and later the Temple. At first the leaders of the people—the shepherds and the prophets—teach them to pray. The infant Samuel must have learned from his mother Hannah how "to stand before the Lord" and from the priest Eli how to listen to his word: "Speak, Lord, for your servant is listening."[26] Later, he will also know the cost and consequence of intercession: "Moreover, as for me, far be it from me that I should sin against the Lord by ceasing to pray for you; and I will instruct you in the good and the right way."[27]

2579 David is par excellence the 709
king "after God's own heart," the shepherd who prays for his people and prays in their name. His submission to the will of God, his praise, and his repentance, will be a model for the prayer of the people. His prayer, the prayer of God's

[21] *Ex* 33:11. — [22] *Num* 12:3, 7–8. — [23] Cf. *Ex* 34:6. — [24] Cf. *Ex* 17:8–12; *Num* 12:13–14. — [25] *Ps* 106:23; cf. *Ex* 32:1–34:9. — [26] *1 Sam* 3:9–10; cf. 1:9–18 — [27] *1 Sam* 12:23.

Anointed, is a faithful adherence
436 to the divine promise and expresses a loving and joyful trust in God, the only King and Lord.[28] In the Psalms David, inspired by the Holy Spirit, is the first prophet of Jewish and Christian prayer. The prayer of Christ, the true Messiah and Son of David, will reveal and fulfill the meaning of this prayer.

583 **2580** The Temple of Jerusalem, the house of prayer that David wanted to build, will be the work of his son, Solomon. The prayer at the dedication of the Temple relies on God's promise and covenant, on the active presence of his name among his People, recalling his mighty deeds at the Exodus.[29] The king lifts his hands toward heaven and begs the Lord, on his own behalf, on behalf of the entire people, and of the generations yet to come, for the forgiveness of their sins and for their daily needs, so that the nations may know that He is the only God and that the heart of his people may belong wholly and entirely to him.

Elijah, the prophets and conversion of heart

2581 For the People of God, the Temple was to be the place of their education in prayer: pilgrimages, feasts and sacrifices, the evening offering, the incense, and the bread of the Presence ("shewbread")—all
1150 these signs of the holiness and glory of God Most High and Most Near were appeals to and ways of prayer. But ritualism often encouraged an excessively external worship. The people needed education in faith and conversion of heart; this was the mission of the prophets, both before and after the Exile.

2582 Elijah is the "father" of the prophets, "the generation of those who seek him, who seek the face of the God of Jacob."[30] Elijah's name, "The Lord is my God," foretells the people's cry in response to his prayer on Mount Carmel.[31] St. James refers to Elijah in order to encourage us to pray: "The prayer of the righteous is powerful and effective."[32]

2583 After Elijah had learned mercy during his retreat at the Wadi Cherith, he teaches the widow of Zarephath to believe in The Word of God and confirms her faith by his urgent prayer: God brings the widow's child back to life.[33]

The sacrifice on Mount Carmel is a decisive test for the faith of the People of God. In response to Elijah's plea, "Answer me, O Lord, answer
me," the Lord's fire consumes the 696
holocaust, at the time of the evening oblation. The Eastern liturgies repeat Elijah's plea in the Eucharistic *epiclesis*.

Finally, taking the desert road that leads to the place where the living and true God reveals himself to his people, Elijah, like Moses before him, hides "in a cleft of the rock" until the mysterious presence of God has passed by.[34] But only on the mountain of the Transfiguration will Moses and Elijah behold 555
the unveiled face of him whom they sought; "the light of the knowledge of the glory of God [shines] in the face of Christ," crucified and risen.[35]

[28] Cf. *2 Sam* 7:18–29. — [29] *1 Kings* 8:10–61. — [30] *Ps* 24:6. — [31] *1 Kings* 18:39. — [32] *Jas* 5:16b–18. — [33] Cf. *1 Kings* 17:7–24. — [34] Cf. *1 Kings* 19:1–14; cf. *Ex* 33:19–23. — [35] *2 Cor* 4:6; cf. *Lk* 9:30–35.

2709 **2584** In their "one to one" encounters with God, the prophets draw light and strength for their mission. Their prayer is not flight from this unfaithful world, but rather attentiveness to The Word of God. At times their prayer is an argument or a complaint, but it is always an intercession that awaits and prepares for the intervention of the Savior God, the Lord of history.[36]

The Psalms, the prayer of the assembly

2585 From the time of David to the coming of the Messiah texts appearing in these sacred books show a deepening in prayer for oneself and in prayer for others.[37] Thus
1093 the psalms were gradually collected into the five books of the Psalter (or "Praises"), the masterwork of prayer in the Old Testament.

2586 The Psalms both nourished and expressed the prayer of the People of God gathered during the great feasts at Jerusalem and each Sabbath in the synagogues. Their prayer is inseparably personal and communal; it concerns both those who are praying and all men. The Psalms arose from the communities of the Holy Land and the Diaspora, but embrace all creation. Their prayer recalls the saving events of the past, yet extends into the future, even to the end of history; it commemorates the promises God has already kept, and awaits the Messiah who will fulfill them definitively. Prayed by Christ and fulfilled in him, the Psalms remain essential to the prayer
1177 of the Church.[38]

2587 The Psalter is the book in which The Word of God becomes man's prayer. In other books of the Old Testament, "the words proclaim [God's] works and bring to light thc mystery they contain."[39] The words of the Psalmist, sung for God, both express and acclaim the Lord's saving works; the same Spirit inspires both God's work and man's response. Christ will unite the two.
In him, the psalms continue to teach 2641
us how to pray.

2588 The Psalter's many forms of prayer take shape both in the liturgy of the Temple and in the human heart. Whether hymns or prayers of lamentation or thanksgiving, whether individual or communal, whether royal chants, songs of pilgrimage or wisdom-meditations, the Psalms are a mirror of God's marvelous deeds in the history of his people, as well as reflections of the human experiences of the Psalmist. Though a given psalm may reflect an event of the past, it still possesses such direct simplicity that it can be prayed in truth by men of all times and conditions.

2589 Certain constant characteristics appear throughout the Psalms: simplicity and spontaneity of prayer; the desire for God himself through and with all that is good in his creation; the distraught situation of the believer who, in his preferential love for the Lord, is exposed to a host of enemies and temptations, but who waits upon what the faithful God will do, in the certitude of his love
and in submission to his will. The 304

[36] Cf. *Am* 7:2, 5; *Isa* 6:5, 8, 11; *Jer* 1:6; 15:15–18; 20:7–18. — [37] *Ezra* 9:6–15; *Neh* 1:4–11; *Jon* 2:3–10; *Tob* 3:11–16; *Jdt* 9:2–14. — [38] Cf. GILH, nn. 100–109. — [39] *DV* 2.

prayer of the psalms is always sustained by praise; that is why the title of this collection as handed down to us is so fitting: "The Praises." Collected for the assembly's worship, the Psalter both sounds the call to prayer and sings the response to that call: *Hallelu-Yah!* ("Alleluia"), "Praise the Lord!"

> What is more pleasing than a psalm? David expresses it well: "Praise the Lord, for a psalm is good: let there be praise of our God with gladness and grace!" Yes, a psalm is a blessing on the lips of the people, praise of God, the assembly's homage, a general acclamation, a word that speaks for all, the voice of the Church, a confession of faith in song.[40]

In Brief

2590 *"Prayer is the raising of one's mind and heart to God or the requesting of good things from God" (St. John Damascene,* De fide orth. *3, 24: PG 94, 1089C).*

2591 *God tirelessly calls each person to this mysterious encounter with Himself. Prayer unfolds throughout the whole history of salvation as a reciprocal call between God and man.*

2592 *The prayer of Abraham and Jacob is presented as a battle of faith marked by trust in God's faithfulness and by certitude in the victory promised to perseverance.*

2593 *The prayer of Moses responds to the living God's initiative for the salvation of his people. It foreshadows the prayer of intercession of the unique mediator, Christ Jesus.*

2594 *The prayer of the People of God flourished in the shadow of the dwelling place of God's presence on earth, the ark of the covenant and the Temple, under the guidance of their shepherds, especially King David, and of the prophets.*

2595 *The prophets summoned the people to conversion of heart and, while zealously seeking the face of God, like Elijah, they interceded for the people.*

2596 *The Psalms constitute the masterwork of prayer in the Old Testament. They present two inseparable qualities: the personal, and the communal. They extend to all dimensions of history, recalling God's promises already fulfilled and looking for the coming of the Messiah.*

2597 *Prayed and fulfilled in Christ, the Psalms are an essential and permanent element of the prayer of the Church. They are suitable for men of every condition and time.*

[40] St. Ambrose, *In psalmum 1 enarratio*, 1, 9: PL 14, 924; *LH*, Saturday, wk 10, OR.

Article 2:
IN THE FULLNESS OF TIME

2598 The drama of prayer is fully revealed to us in the Word who became flesh and dwells among us. To seek to understand his prayer through what his witnesses proclaim to us in the Gospel is to approach the holy Lord Jesus as Moses approached the burning bush: first to contemplate him in prayer, then to hear how he teaches us to pray, in order to know how he hears our prayer.

Jesus prays

470–473 **2599** The Son of God who became Son of the Virgin also learned to pray according to his human heart. He learns the formulas of prayer from his mother, who kept in her heart and meditated upon all the "great things" done by the Almighty.[41] He learns to pray in the words and rhythms of the prayer of his people, in the synagogue at
584 Nazareth and the Temple at Jerusalem. But his prayer springs from an otherwise secret source, as he intimates at the age of twelve: "I must be in my Father's house."[42] Here the newness of prayer in the fullness of time begins to be revealed: his *filial prayer*, which the Father awaits from
534 his children, is finally going to be lived out by the only Son in his humanity, with and for men.

2600 The Gospel according to St. Luke emphasizes the action of the Holy Spirit and the meaning of prayer in Christ's ministry. Jesus prays *before* the decisive moments of his mission: before his Father's witness to him during his baptism and 535, 554
Transfiguration, and before his own fulfillment of the Father's plan of love by his Passion.[43] He also prays before the decisive moments involv- 612
ing the mission of his apostles: at his election and call of the Twelve, before Peter's confession of him as "the Christ of God," and again that 858, 443
the faith of the chief of the Apostles may not fail when tempted.[44] Jesus' prayer before the events of salvation that the Father has asked him to fulfill is a humble and trusting commitment of his human will to the loving will of the Father.

2601 "He was praying in a certain place and when he had ceased, one of his disciples said to him, 'Lord, teach us to pray.'"[45] In seeing the Master at prayer the disciple of Christ also wants to pray. By *contemplating* and hearing the Son, the master of prayer, the children learn to pray to the Father. 2765

2602 Jesus often draws apart to pray *in solitude,* on a mountain, preferably at night.[46] *He includes all men* in his prayer, for he has taken on humanity in his incarnation, and 616
he offers them to the Father when he offers himself. Jesus, the Word who has become flesh, shares by his human prayer in all that "his brethren" experience; he sympathizes with their weaknesses in order to free them.[47] It was for this that the Father sent him. His words and works are the visible manifestation of his prayer in secret.

[41] Cf. *Lk* 1:49; 2:19; 2:51. — [42] *Lk* 2:49. — [43] Cf. *Lk* 3:21; 9:28; 22:41–44. — [44] Cf. *Lk* 6:12; 9:18–20; 22:32. — [45] *Lk* 11:1. — [46] Cf. *Mk* 1:35; 6:46; *Lk* 5:16. — [47] Cf. *Heb* 2:12, 15; 4:15.

2603 The evangelists have preserved two more explicit prayers offered by Christ during his public ministry. Each begins with thanksgiving. In the first, Jesus confess-
2673 es the Father, acknowledges, and blesses him because he has hidden the mysteries of the Kingdom from those who think themselves learned and has revealed them to infants, the poor of the Beatitudes.[48] His excla-
2546 mation, "Yes, Father!" expresses the depth of his heart, his adherence to the Father's "good pleasure," echo-
494 ing his mother's *Fiat* at the time of his conception and prefiguring what he will say to the Father in his agony. The whole prayer of Jesus is contained in this loving adherence of his human heart to the mystery of the will of the Father.[49]

2604 The second prayer, before the raising of Lazarus, is recorded by St. John.[50] Thanksgiving precedes the event: "Father, I thank you for having heard me," which implies that the Father always hears his petitions. Jesus immediately adds: "I know that you always hear me," which implies that Jesus, on his part, *constantly made such petitions*. Jesus' prayer, characterized by thanksgiving, reveals to us how to ask: *before* the gift is given, Jesus commits himself to the One who in giving gives himself. The Giver is more precious than the gift; he is the "treasure"; in him abides his Son's heart; the gift is
478 given "as well."[51]

2746 The priestly prayer of Jesus holds a unique place in the economy of salvation.[52] A meditation on it will conclude Section One. It reveals the ever present prayer of our High Priest and, at the same time, contains what he teaches us about our prayer to our Father, which will be developed in Section Two.

2605 When the hour had come for him to fulfill the Father's plan of love, Jesus allows a glimpse of the boundless depth of his filial prayer, not only before he freely delivered himself up ("*Abba*...not my will, but yours."),[53] but even in *his last words* on the Cross, where prayer and the gift of self are but one: "Father, forgive them, for they know not what they do";[54] "Truly, I say to 614
you, today you will be with me in Paradise";[55] "Woman, behold your son"—"Behold your mother";[56] "I thirst";[57] "My God, My God, why have you forsaken me?";[58] "It is finished";[59] "Father, into your hands I commit my spirit!"[60] until the "loud cry" as he expires, giving up his spirit.[61]

2606 All the troubles, for all 403
time, of humanity enslaved by sin and death, all the petitions and intercessions of salvation history are summed up in this cry of the incarnate Word. Here the Father accepts them and, beyond all hope, answers 653
them by raising his Son. Thus is fulfilled and brought to completion the drama of prayer in the economy of creation and salvation. The Psalter gives us the key to prayer in Christ. In the "today" of the Resurrection 2587
the Father says: "You are my Son, today I have begotten you. Ask of me, and I will make the nations your heritage, and the ends of the earth your possession."[62]

[48] Cf. *Mt* 11:25–27 and *Lk* 10:21–23. — [49] Cf. *Eph* 1:9. — [50] Cf. *Jn* 11:41–42. — [51] *Mt* 6:21, 33. — [52] Cf. *Jn* 17. — [53] *Lk* 22:42. — [54] *Lk* 23:34. — [55] *Lk* 23:43. — [56] *Jn* 19:26–27. — [57] *Jn* 19:28. — [58] *Mk* 15:34; cf. *Ps* 22:2. — [59] *Jn* 19:30. — [60] *Lk* 23:46. — [61] Cf. *Mk* 15:37; *Jn* 19:30b. — [62] *Ps* 2:7–8; cf. *Acts* 13:33.

The Letter to the Hebrews expresses in dramatic terms how the prayer of Jesus accomplished the victory of salvation: "In the days of his flesh, Jesus offered up prayers and supplications, with loud cries and tears, to him who was able to save him from death, and he was heard for his godly fear. Although he was a Son, he learned obedience through what he suffered, and being made perfect, he became the source of eternal salvation to all who obey him."[63]

Jesus teaches us how to pray

520 **2607** When Jesus prays he is already teaching us how to pray. His prayer to his Father is the theologal path (the path of faith, hope, and charity) of our prayer to God. But the Gospel also gives us Jesus' explicit teaching on prayer. Like a wise teacher he takes hold of us where we are and leads us progressively toward the Father. Addressing the crowds following him, Jesus builds on what they already know of prayer from the Old Covenant and opens to them the newness of the coming Kingdom. Then he reveals this newness to them in parables. Finally, he will speak openly of the Father and the Holy Spirit to his disciples who will be the teachers of prayer in his Church.

541 **2608** From the *Sermon on the Mount* onwards, Jesus insists on *conversion of heart*: reconciliation
1430 with one's brother before presenting an offering on the altar, love of enemies, and prayer for persecutors, prayer to the Father in secret, not heaping up empty phrases, prayerful forgiveness from the depths of the heart, purity of heart, and seeking the Kingdom before all else.[64] This filial conversion is entirely directed to the Father.

2609 Once committed to conver- 153
sion, the heart learns to pray in *faith*.
Faith is a filial adherence to God be- 1814
yond what we feel and understand. It is possible because the beloved Son gives us access to the Father. He can ask us to "seek" and to "knock," since he himself is the door and the way.[65]

2610 Just as Jesus prays to the Father and gives thanks before receiving his gifts, so he teaches us *filial boldness*: "Whatever you ask in prayer, believe that you receive it, and you will."[66] Such is the power of prayer and of faith that does not doubt: "all things are possible to him who believes."[67] Jesus is as saddened by the "lack of faith" of his own
neighbors and the "little faith" of his 165
own disciples[68] as he is struck with admiration at the great faith of the Roman centurion and the Canaanite woman.[69]

2611 The prayer of faith consists not only in saying "Lord, Lord," but
in disposing the heart to do the will 2827
of the Father.[70] Jesus calls his disciples to bring into their prayer this concern for cooperating with the divine plan.[71]

2612 In Jesus "the Kingdom of God is at hand."[72] He calls his hearers to conversion and faith, but also to watchfulness. In prayer the disciple keeps watch, attentive to Him 672
Who Is and Him Who Comes, in memory of his first coming in the

[63] *Heb* 5:7–9. — [64] Cf. *Mt* 5:23–24, 44–45; 6:7, 14–15, 21, 25, 33. — [65] Cf. *Mt* 7:7–11, 13–14. — [66] *Mk* 11:24. — [67] *Mk* 9:23; cf. *Mt* 21:22. — [68] Cf. *Mk* 6:6; *Mt* 8:26. — [69] Cf. *Mt* 8:10; 15:28. — [70] Cf. *Mt* 7:21. — [71] Cf. *Mt* 9:38; *Lk* 10:2; *Jn* 4:34. — [72] *Mk* 1:15.

lowliness of the flesh, and in the hope of his second coming in glory.[73] In communion with their Mas-
2725 ter, the disciples' prayer is a battle; only by keeping watch in prayer can one avoid falling into temptation.[74]

546 **2613** Three principal *parables* on prayer are transmitted to us by St. Luke:

– The first, "the importunate friend,"[75] invites us to urgent prayer: "Knock, and it will be opened to you." To the one who prays like this, the heavenly Father will "give whatever he needs," and above all the Holy Spirit who contains all gifts.

– The second, "the importunate widow,"[76] is centered on one of the qualities of prayer: it is necessary to pray always without ceasing and with the *patience* of faith. "And yet, when the Son of Man comes, will he find faith on earth?"

2559 – The third parable, "the Pharisee and the tax collector,"[77] concerns the *humility* of the heart that prays. "God, be merciful to me a sinner!" The Church continues to make this prayer its own: *Kyrie eleison!*

2614 When Jesus openly entrusts to his disciples the mystery of prayer to the Father, he reveals to them what their prayer and ours must be, once he has returned to the Father in his glorified humanity. What is new
434 is to "ask *in his name*."[78] Faith in the Son introduces the disciples into the knowledge of the Father, because Jesus is "the way, and the truth, and the life."[79] Faith bears its fruit in love: it means keeping the word and the commandments of Jesus, it means abiding with him in the Father who, in him, so loves us that he abides with us. In this new covenant the certitude that our petitions will be heard is founded on the prayer of Jesus.[80]

2615 Even more, what the Father 728
gives us when our prayer is united with that of Jesus is "another Counselor, to be with you for ever, even the Spirit of truth."[81] This new dimension of prayer and of its circumstances is displayed throughout the farewell discourse.[82] In the Holy Spirit, Christian prayer is a communion of love with the Father, not only through Christ but also *in him*: "Hitherto you have asked nothing in my name; ask, and you will receive, that your joy may be full."[83]

Jesus hears our prayer

2616 Prayer to *Jesus* is answered by him already during his ministry, through signs that anticipate the power of his death and Resurrection: Jesus hears the prayer of faith, expressed in words (the lep- 548
er, Jairus, the Canaanite woman, the good thief)[84] or in silence (the bearers of the paralytic, the woman with a hemorrhage who touches his clothes, the tears and ointment of the sinful woman).[85] The urgent request of the blind men, "Have mercy on us, Son of David" or "Jesus, Son of David, have mercy on me!" has been renewed in the traditional prayer to Jesus known as the Jesus Prayer: "Lord Jesus Christ, Son of God, have mercy on me, a sinner!"[86]

[73] Cf. *Mk* 13; *Lk* 21:34–36. — [74] Cf. *Lk* 22:40, 46. — [75] Cf. *Lk* 11:5–13. — [76] Cf. *Lk* 18:1–8. — [77] Cf. *Lk* 18:9–14. — [78] *Jn* 14:13. — [79] *Jn* 14:6. — [80] Cf. *Jn* 14:13–14. — [81] *Jn* 14:16–17. — [82] Cf. *Jn* 14:23–26; 15:7, 16; 16:13–15; 16:23–27. — [83] *Jn* 16:24. — [84] Cf. *Mk* 1:40–41; 5:36; 7:29; cf. Lk 23:39–43. — [85] Cf. *Mk* 2:5; 5:28; Lk 7:37–38. — [86] *Mt* 9:27; *Mk* 10:48.

2667 Healing infirmities or forgiving sins, Jesus always responds to a prayer offered in faith: "Your faith has made you well; go in peace."

St. Augustine wonderfully summarizes the three dimensions of Jesus' prayer: "He prays for us as our priest, prays in us as our Head, and is prayed to by us as our God. Therefore let us acknowledge our voice in him and his in us."[87]

The prayer of the Virgin Mary

148 **2617** Mary's prayer is revealed to us at the dawning of the fullness of time. Before the incarnation of the Son of God, and before the outpouring of the Holy Spirit, her prayer cooperates in a unique way with the Father's plan of loving kindness: at the Annunciation, for
494 Christ's conception; at Pentecost, for the formation of the Church, his Body.[88] In the faith of his humble handmaid, the Gift of God found the acceptance he had awaited from the beginning of time. She whom
490 the Almighty made "full of grace" responds by offering her whole being: "Behold I am the handmaid of the Lord; let it be [done] to me according to your word." "*Fiat*": this is Christian prayer: to be wholly God's, because he is wholly ours.

2674 **2618** The Gospel reveals to us how Mary prays and intercedes in faith. At Cana,[89] the mother of Jesus asks her son for the needs of a wedding feast; this is the sign of another feast—that of the wedding of the Lamb where he gives his body and blood at the request of the Church, his Bride. It is at the hour of the New Covenant, at the foot of the cross,[90] that Mary is heard as the Woman, the new Eve, the true "Mother of all 726
the living."

2619 That is why the Canticle of Mary,[91] the *Magnificat* (Latin) or *Megalynei* (Byzantine) is the song both of the Mother of God and of the Church; the song of the Daughter of Zion and of the new People of God; the song of thanksgiving for the fullness of graces poured out in the economy of salvation and the 724
song of the "poor" whose hope is met by the fulfillment of the promises made to our ancestors, "to Abraham and to his posterity for ever."

In Brief

2620 *Jesus' filial prayer is the perfect model of prayer in the New Testament. Often done in solitude and in secret, the prayer of Jesus involves a loving adherence to the will of the Father even to the Cross and an absolute confidence in being heard.*

2621 *In his teaching, Jesus teaches his disciples to pray with a purified heart, with lively and persevering faith, with filial boldness. He calls them to vigilance and invites them to present their petitions to God in his name. Jesus Christ himself answers prayers addressed to him.*

2622 *The prayers of the Virgin Mary, in her Fiat and Magnificat, are characterized by the generous offering of her whole being in faith.*

[87] St. Augustine, *En. in Ps.* 85, 1: PL 37, 1081; cf. GILH 7. — [88] Cf. *Lk* 1:38; *Acts* 1:14. — [89] Cf. *Jn* 2:1–12. — [90] Cf. *Jn* 19:25–27. — [91] Cf. *Lk* 1:46–55.

Article 3:
IN THE AGE OF THE CHURCH

731 **2623** On the day of Pentecost, the Spirit of the Promise was poured out on the disciples, gathered "together in one place."[92] While awaiting the Spirit, "all these with one accord devoted themselves to prayer."[93] The Spirit who teaches the Church and recalls for her everything that Jesus said[94] was also to form her in the life of prayer.

1342 **2624** In the first community of Jerusalem, believers "devoted themselves to the apostles' teaching and fellowship, to the breaking of bread, and the prayers."[95] This sequence is characteristic of the Church's prayer: founded on the apostolic faith; authenticated by charity; nourished in the Eucharist.

2625 In the first place these are prayers that the faithful hear and read in the Scriptures, but also that they make their own—especially those of the Psalms, in view of their fulfillment in Christ.[96] The Holy
1092 Spirit, who thus keeps the memory of Christ alive in his Church at prayer, also leads her toward the fullness of truth and inspires new formulations expressing the unfathomable mystery of Christ at work in his Church's life, sacraments, and mission. These formulations are developed in the great liturgical and spiritual traditions. The *forms of*
1200 *prayer* revealed in the apostolic and canonical Scriptures remain normative for Christian prayer.

I. Blessing and Adoration

2626 *Blessing* expresses the basic 1078
movement of Christian prayer: it is an encounter between God and man. In blessing, God's gift and man's acceptance of it are united in dialogue with each other. The prayer of blessing is man's response to God's gifts: because God blesses, the human heart can in return bless the One who is the source of every blessing.

2627 Two fundamental forms 1083
express this movement: our prayer *ascends* in the Holy Spirit through Christ to the Father—we bless him for having blessed us;[97] it implores the grace of the Holy Spirit that *descends* through Christ from the Father—he blesses us.[98]

2628 *Adoration* is the first attitude 2096–209
of man acknowledging that he is a creature before his Creator. It exalts the greatness of the Lord who made us[99] and the almighty power of the Savior who sets us free from evil. Adoration is homage of the spirit to the "King of Glory,"[100] respectful silence in the presence of the "ever greater" God.[101] Adoration of the thrice-holy and sovereign God of love blends
with humility and gives assurance to 2559
our supplications.

II. Prayer of Petition

2629 The vocabulary of supplication in the New Testament is rich in shades of meaning: ask, be-

[92] *Acts* 2:1. — [93] *Acts* 1:14. — [94] Cf. *Jn* 14:26. — [95] *Acts* 2:42. — [96] Cf. *Lk* 24:27, 44. — [97] Cf. *Eph* 1:3–14; *2 Cor* 1:3–7; *1 Pet* 1:3–9. — [98] Cf. *2 Cor* 13:14; *Rom* 15:5–6, 13; *Eph* 6:23–24. — [99] Cf. *Ps* 95:1–6. — [100] *Ps* 24, 9–10. — [101] Cf. St. Augustine, *En. in Ps.* 62, 16: PL 36, 757–758.

seech, plead, invoke, entreat, cry out, even "struggle in prayer."[102] Its most usual form, because the most spontaneous, is petition: by prayer of petition we express awareness of our relationship with God. We are creatures who are not our own be-
396 ginning, not the masters of adversity, not our own last end. We are sinners who as Christians know that we have turned away from our Father. Our petition is already a turning back to him.

2630 The New Testament contains scarcely any prayers of lamentation, so frequent in the Old Testament. In the risen Christ the Church's petition is buoyed by hope,
2090 even if we still wait in a state of expectation and must be converted anew every day. Christian petition, what St. Paul calls "groaning," arises from another depth, that of creation "in labor pains" and that of ourselves "as we wait for the redemption of our bodies. For in this hope we were saved."[103] In the end, however, "with sighs too deep for words" the Holy Spirit "helps us in our weakness; for we do not know how to pray as we ought, but the Spirit himself intercedes for us with sighs too deep for words."[104]

2838 **2631** The first movement of the prayer of petition is *asking forgiveness*, like the tax collector in the parable: "God, be merciful to me a sinner!"[105] It is a prerequisite for righteous and pure prayer. A trusting humility brings us back into the light of communion between the Father and his Son Jesus Christ and with one another, so that "we receive from him whatever we ask."[106] Asking forgiveness is the prerequisite for both the Eucharistic liturgy and personal prayer.

2632 Christian petition is cen- 2816
tered on the desire and *search for the Kingdom to come*, in keeping with the teaching of Christ.[107] There is a hierarchy in these petitions: we pray first for the Kingdom, then for what
is necessary to welcome it and coop- 1942
erate with its coming. This collaboration with the mission of Christ and the Holy Spirit, which is now that of the Church, is the object of the prayer of the apostolic community.[108] It is the prayer of Paul, the apostle par excellence, which reveals to us how the divine solicitude for all the churches ought to inspire
Christian prayer.[109] By prayer every 2854
baptized person works for the coming of the Kingdom.

2633 When we share in God's 2830
saving love, we understand that *every need* can become the object of petition. Christ, who assumed all things in order to redeem all things, is glorified by what we ask the Father in his name.[110] It is with this confidence that St. James and St. Paul exhort us to pray *at all times*.[111]

III. Prayer of Intercession

2634 Intercession is a prayer of petition which leads us to pray as Jesus did. He is the one intercessor with the Father on behalf of all men,
especially sinners.[112] He is "able for 432
all time to save those who draw near to God through him, since he al-

[102] Cf. *Rom* 15:30; *Col* 4:12. — [103] *Rom* 8:22–24. — [104] *Rom* 8:26. — [105] *Lk* 18:13. — [106] *1 Jn* 3:22; cf. 1:7–2:2. — [107] Cf. *Mt* 6:10, 33; *Lk* 11:2, 13. — [108] Cf. *Acts* 6:6; 13:3. — [109] Cf. *Rom* 10:1; *Eph* 1:16–23; *Phil* 1:9–11; *Col* 1:3–6; 4:3–4, 12. — [110] Cf. *Jn* 14:13. — [111] Cf. *Jas* 1:5–8; *Eph* 5:20; *Phil* 4:6–7; *Col* 3:16–17; *1 Thess* 5:17–18. — [112] Cf. *Rom* 8:34; *1 Jn* 2:1; *1 Tim* 2:5–8.

ways lives to make intercession for them."[113] The Holy Spirit "himself intercedes for us...and intercedes for the saints according to the will of God."[114]

2571 **2635** Since Abraham, intercession—asking on behalf of another—has been characteristic of a heart attuned to God's mercy. In the age of the Church, Christian intercession participates in Christ's, as an expression of the communion of saints. In intercession, he who prays looks "not only to his own interests, but also to the interests of others,"
2577 even to the point of praying for those who do him harm.[115]

2636 The first Christian communities lived this form of fellowship intensely.[116] Thus the Apostle Paul gives them a share in his ministry of preaching the Gospel[117] but also intercedes for them.[118] The intercession of Christians recognizes no boundaries: "for all men, for kings
1900 and all who are in high positions," for persecutors, for the salvation of
1037 those who reject the Gospel.[119]

IV. Prayer of Thanksgiving

224 **2637** Thanksgiving characterizes the prayer of the Church which, in celebrating the Eucharist, reveals and becomes more fully what she
1328 is. Indeed, in the work of salvation, Christ sets creation free from sin and death to consecrate it anew and make it return to the Father, for his glory. The thanksgiving of the mem-
2603 bers of the Body participates in that of their Head.

2638 As in the prayer of petition, every event and need can become an offering of thanksgiving. The letters of St. Paul often begin and end with thanksgiving, and the Lord Jesus is always present in it: "Give thanks in all circumstances; for this is the will of God in Christ Jesus for you"; "Continue steadfastly in prayer, being watchful in it with thanksgiving."[120]

V. Prayer of Praise

2639 Praise is the form of prayer which recognizes most immediately that God is God. It lauds God for his own sake and gives him glory, quite beyond what he does, but simply because HE IS. It shares in
the blessed happiness of the pure 213
of heart who love God in faith before seeing him in glory. By praise, the Spirit is joined to our spirits to bear witness that we are children of God,[121] testifying to the only Son in whom we are adopted and by whom we glorify the Father. Praise embraces the other forms of prayer and carries them toward him who is its source and goal: the "one God, the Father, from whom are all things and for whom we exist."[122]

2640 St. Luke in his gospel often expresses wonder and praise at the marvels of Christ and in his *Acts of the Apostles* stresses them as actions of the Holy Spirit: the community of Jerusalem, the invalid healed by Peter and John, the crowd that gives glory to God for that, and the pagans of Pisidia who "were glad and glorified the word of God."[123]

[113] *Heb* 7:25. — [114] *Rom* 8:26–27. — [115] *Phil* 2:4; cf. *Acts* 7:60; *Lk* 23:28, 34. — [116] Cf. *Acts* 12:5; 20:36; 21:5; *2 Cor* 9:14. — [117] Cf. *Eph* 6:18–20; *Col* 4:3–4; *1 Thess* 5:25. — [118] Cf. *2 Thess* 1:11; *Col* 1:3; *Phil* 1:3–4. — [119] *1 Tim* 2:1; cf. *Rom* 12:14; 10:1. — [120] *1 Thess* 5:18; *Col* 4:2. — [121] Cf. *Rom* 8:16. — [122] *1 Cor* 8:6. — [123] *Acts* 2:47; 3:9; 4:21;13:48

2641 "[Address] one another in psalms and hymns and spiritual songs, singing and making melody to the Lord with all your heart."[124] Like the inspired writers of the New Testament, the first Christian communities read the Book of Psalms in a new way, singing in it the mystery of Christ. In the newness of the
2587 Spirit, they also composed hymns and canticles in the light of the unheard-of event that God accomplished in his Son: his Incarnation, his death which conquered death, his Resurrection, and Ascension to the right hand of the Father.[125] Doxology, the praise of God, arises from this "marvelous work" of the whole economy of salvation.[126]

2642 The *Revelation* of "what must soon take place," the *Apocalypse*, is borne along by the songs of the heavenly liturgy[127] but also by
1137 the intercession of the "witnesses" (martyrs).[128] The prophets and the saints, all those who were slain on earth for their witness to Jesus, the vast throng of those who, having come through the great tribulation, have gone before us into the Kingdom, all sing the praise and glory of him who sits on the throne, and of the Lamb.[129] In communion with them, the Church on earth also sings these songs with faith in the midst of trial. By means of petition and intercession, faith hopes against all hope and gives thanks to the "Father of lights," from whom "every perfect gift" comes down.[130] Thus faith is pure praise.

2643 The Eucharist contains and expresses all forms of prayer: it is "the pure offering" of the whole Body of Christ to the glory of God's name[131] and, according to the traditions of East and West, it is *the* "sac- 1330
rifice of praise."

In Brief

2644 *The Holy Spirit who teaches the Church and recalls to her all that Jesus said also instructs her in the life of prayer, inspiring new expressions of the same basic forms of prayer: blessing, petition, intercession, thanksgiving, and praise.*

2645 *Because God blesses the human heart, it can in return bless him who is the source of every blessing.*

2646 *Forgiveness, the quest for the Kingdom, and every true need are objects of the prayer of petition.*

2647 *Prayer of intercession consists in asking on behalf of another. It knows no boundaries and extends to one's enemies.*

2648 *Every joy and suffering, every event and need can become the matter for thanksgiving which, sharing in that of Christ, should fill one's whole life: "Give thanks in all circumstances" (*1 Thess *5:18).*

2649 *Prayer of praise is entirely disinterested and rises to God, lauds him, and gives him glory for his own sake, quite beyond what he has done, but simply because HE IS.*

[124] *Eph* 5:19; *Col* 3:16. — [125] Cf. *Phil* 2:6–11; *Col* 1:15–20; *Eph* 5:14; *1 Tim* 3:16; 6:15–16; *2 Tim* 2:11–13. — [126] Cf. *Eph* 1:3–14; *Rom* 16:25–27; *Eph* 3:20–21; *Jude* 24–25. — [127] Cf. *Rev* 4:8–11; 5:9–14; 7:10–12. — [128] *Rev* 6:10. — [129] Cf. *Rev* 18:24; 19:1–8. — [130] *Jas* 1:17. — [131] Cf. *Mal* 1:11.

Chapter Two:
THE TRADITION OF PRAYER

2650 Prayer cannot be reduced to
the spontaneous outpouring of interior impulse: in order to pray, one
must have the will to pray. Nor is it
enough to know what the Scriptures
reveal about prayer: one must also
learn how to pray. Through a living transmission (Sacred Tradition)
75 within "the believing and praying
Church,"[1] the Holy Spirit teaches
the children of God how to pray.

2651 The tradition of Christian 94
prayer is one of the ways in which the tradition of faith takes shape and grows, especially through the contemplation and study of believers who treasure in their hearts the events and words of the economy of salvation, and through their profound grasp of the spiritual realities they experience.[2]

Article 1:
AT THE WELLSPRINGS OF PRAYER

694 **2652** The Holy Spirit is the *living
water* "welling up to eternal life"[3] in the heart that prays. It is he who teaches us to accept it at its source: Christ. Indeed in the Christian life there are several wellsprings where Christ awaits us to enable us to drink of the Holy Spirit.

The Word of God

133 **2653** The Church "forcefully and
specially exhorts all the Christian
faithful...to learn 'the surpassing
knowledge of Jesus Christ' (*Phil*
3:8) by frequent reading of the divine Scriptures.... Let them remember, however, that prayer should
accompany the reading of Sacred
Scripture, so that a dialogue takes
place between God and man. For
1100 'we speak to him when we pray; we
listen to him when we read the divine oracles.'"[4]

2654 The spiritual writers, *paraphrasing* Matthew 7:7, summarize in this way the dispositions of the heart nourished by the word of God in prayer: "Seek in reading and you will find in meditating; knock in mental prayer and it will be opened to you by contemplation."[5]

The Liturgy of the Church

2655 In the sacramental liturgy of 1073
the Church, the mission of Christ and
of the Holy Spirit proclaims, makes
present, and communicates the mystery of salvation, which is continued
in the heart that prays. The spiritual
writers sometimes compare the heart 368
to an altar. Prayer internalizes and
assimilates the liturgy during and
after its celebration. Even when it is
lived out "in secret,"[6] prayer is always
prayer *of the Church*; it is a communion with the Holy Trinity.[7]

[1] *DV* 8. — [2] Cf. *DV* 8. — [3] *Jn* 4:14. — [4] *DV* 25; cf. *Phil* 3:8; St. Ambrose, *De officiis ministrorum* 1, 20, 88: PL 16, 50.— [5] Guigo the Carthusian, *Scala Paradisi*: PL 40, 998. — [6] Cf. *Mt* 6:6. — [7] GILH 9.

1812–1829 *The theological virtues*

2656 One enters into prayer as one enters into liturgy: by the narrow gate of *faith*. Through the signs of his presence, it is the Face of the Lord that we seek and desire; it is his Word that we want to hear and keep.

2657 The Holy Spirit, who instructs us to celebrate the liturgy in expectation of Christ's return, teaches us to pray in *hope*. Conversely, the prayer of the Church and personal prayer nourish hope in us. The psalms especially, with their concrete and varied language, teach us to fix our hope in God: "I waited patiently for the LORD; he inclined to me and heard my cry."[8] As St. Paul prayed: "May the God of hope fill you with all joy and peace in believing, so that by the power of the Holy Spirit you may abound in hope."[9]

2658 "Hope does not disappoint us, because God's *love* has been poured into our hearts by the Holy Spirit who has been given to us."[10] Prayer, formed by the liturgical life, draws everything into the love by which we are loved in Christ and which enables us to respond to him
826 by loving as he has loved us. Love is the source of prayer; whoever draws from it reaches the summit of prayer. In the words of the Curé of Ars:

> I love you, O my God, and my only desire is to love you until the last breath of my life. I love you, O my infinitely lovable God, and I would rather die loving you, than live without loving you. I love you, Lord, and the only grace I ask is to love you eternally.... My God, if my tongue cannot say in every moment that I love you, I want my heart to repeat it to you as often as I draw breath.[11]

"Today"

2659 We learn to pray at certain 1165
moments by hearing the Word of the Lord and sharing in his Paschal mystery, but his Spirit is offered us
at all times, in the events of *each* 2837
day, to make prayer spring up from us. Jesus' teaching about praying to our Father is in the same vein as his teaching about providence:[12] time is in the Father's hands; it is in the
present that we encounter him, not 305
yesterday nor tomorrow, but today: "O that today you would hearken to his voice! Harden not your hearts."[13]

2660 Prayer in the events of each day and each moment is one of the secrets of the kingdom revealed to "little children," to the servants of
Christ, to the poor of the Beatitudes. 2546
It is right and good to pray so that
the coming of the kingdom of justice 2632
and peace may influence the march of history, but it is just as important to bring the help of prayer into humble, everyday situations; all forms of prayer can be the leaven to which the Lord compares the kingdom.[14]

In Brief

2661 *By a living transmission—Tradition—the Holy Spirit in the Church teaches the children of God to pray.*

2662 *The Word of God, the liturgy of the Church, and the virtues of faith, hope, and charity are sources of prayer.*

[8] *Ps* 40:2. — [9] *Rom* 15:13. — [10] *Rom* 5:5. — [11] St. John Vianney, *Prayer*. — [12] Cf. *Mt* 6:11, 34. — [13] *Ps* 95:7–8. — [14] Cf. *Lk* 13:20–21.

Article 2: THE WAY OF PRAYER

1201 **2663** In the living tradition of prayer, each Church proposes to its faithful, according to its historic, social, and cultural context, a language for prayer: words, melodies, gestures, iconography. The Magisterium of the Church[15] has the task of discerning the fidelity of these ways of praying to the tradition of apostolic faith; it is for pastors and catechists to explain their meaning, always in relation to Jesus Christ.

Prayer to the Father

2664 There is no other way of Christian prayer than Christ. Whether our prayer is communal or personal, vocal or interior, it has ac-
2780 cess to the Father only if we pray "in the name" of Jesus. The sacred humanity of Jesus is therefore the way by which the Holy Spirit teaches us to pray to God our Father.

Prayer to Jesus

2665 The prayer of the Church, nourished by the Word of God and the celebration of the liturgy, teaches us to pray to the Lord Jesus. Even
451 though her prayer is addressed above all to the Father, it includes in all the liturgical traditions forms of prayer addressed to Christ. Certain psalms, given their use in the Prayer of the Church, and the New Testament place on our lips and engrave in our hearts prayer to Christ in the form of invocations: Son of God, Word of God, Lord, Savior, Lamb of God, King, Beloved Son, Son of the Virgin, Good Shepherd, our Life, our Light, our Hope, our Resurrection, Friend of mankind....

2666 But the one name that contains everything is the one that the Son of God received in his in- 432
carnation: JESUS. The divine name may not be spoken by human lips, but by assuming our humanity The Word of God hands it over to us and we can invoke it: "Jesus," "YHWH saves."[16] The name "Jesus" contains all: God and man and the whole economy of creation and salvation. 435
To pray "Jesus" is to invoke him and to call him within us. His name is the only one that contains the presence it signifies. Jesus is the Risen One, and whoever invokes the name of Jesus is welcoming the Son of God who loved him and who gave himself up for him.[17]

2667 This simple invocation of faith developed in the tradition of prayer under many forms in East and West. The most usual formulation, transmitted by the spiritual writers of the Sinai, Syria, and Mt. 2616
Athos, is the invocation, "Lord Jesus Christ, Son of God, have mercy on us sinners." It combines the Christological hymn of *Philippians* 2:6–11 with the cry of the publican and the blind men begging for light.[18] By it the heart is opened to human wretchedness and the Savior's mercy.

2668 The invocation of the holy 435
name of Jesus is the simplest way of praying always. When the holy name is repeated often by a humbly attentive heart, the prayer is not

[15] Cf. *DV* 10. — [16] Cf. *Ex* 3:14; 33:19-23; *Mt* 1:21. — [17] *Rom* 10:13; *Acts* 2:21; 3:15-16; *Gal* 2:20. — [18] Cf. *Mk* 10:46-52; *Lk* 18:13.

lost by heaping up empty phrases,[19] but holds fast to the word and "brings forth fruit with patience."[20] This prayer is possible "at all times" because it is not one occupation among others but the only occupation: that of loving God, which animates and transfigures every action in Christ Jesus.

478 **2669** The prayer of the Church venerates and honors the *Heart of Jesus* just as it invokes his most holy name. It adores the incarnate Word and his Heart which, out of love for men, he allowed to be pierced by our sins. Christian prayer loves to follow the way of the cross in the Savior's steps. The stations from the Prae-
1674 torium to Golgotha and the tomb trace the way of Jesus, who by his holy Cross has redeemed the world.

"Come, Holy Spirit"

683 **2670** "No one can say 'Jesus is Lord' except by the Holy Spirit."[21] Every time we begin to pray to Jesus it is the Holy Spirit who draws us on
2001 the way of prayer by his prevenient grace. Since he teaches us to pray by recalling Christ, how could we not pray to the Spirit too? That is why the Church invites us to call upon the Holy Spirit every day, especially at the beginning and the end of ev-
1310 ery important action.

> If the Spirit should not be worshiped, how can he divinize me through Baptism? If he should be worshiped, should he not be the object of adoration?[22]

2671 The traditional form of petition to the Holy Spirit is to invoke the Father through Christ our Lord to give us the Consoler Spirit.[23] Jesus insists on this petition to be made in his name at the very moment when he promises the gift of the Spirit of Truth.[24] But the simplest and most direct prayer is also traditional, "Come, Holy Spirit," and every liturgical tradition has developed it in antiphons and hymns.

> Come, Holy Spirit, fill the hearts of your faithful and enkindle in them the fire of your love.[25]

> Heavenly King, Consoler Spirit, Spirit of Truth, present everywhere and filling all things, treasure of all good and source of all life, come dwell in us, cleanse and save us, you who are All-Good.[26]

2672 The Holy Spirit, whose 695
anointing permeates our whole being, is the interior Master of Christian prayer. He is the artisan of the living tradition of prayer. To be sure, there are as many paths of prayer as there are persons who pray, but it is the same Spirit acting in all and with all. It is in the communion of the Holy Spirit that Christian prayer is prayer in the Church.

In communion with the holy Mother of God

2673 In prayer the Holy Spirit 689
unites us to the person of the only Son, in his glorified humanity, through which and in which our filial prayer unites us in the Church with the Mother of Jesus.[27]

2674 Mary gave her consent 494
in faith at the Annunciation and

[19] Cf. *Mt* 6:7. — [20] Cf. *Lk* 8:15. — [21] *1 Cor* 12:3. — [22] St. Gregory of Nazianzus, *Oratio*, 31, 28: PG 36, 165. — [23] Cf. *Lk* 11:13. — [24] Cf. *Jn* 14:17; 15:26; 16:13. — [25] *Roman Missal*, Pentecost, Sequence. — [26] Byzantine Liturgy, Pentecost Vespers, Troparion. — [27] Cf. *Acts* 1:14.

maintained it without hesitation at the foot of the Cross. Ever since, her motherhood has extended to the brothers and sisters of her Son "who still journey on earth surrounded by dangers and difficulties."[28] Jesus, the only mediator, is the way of our prayer; Mary, his mother and ours, is wholly transparent to him: she "shows the way" (*hodigitria*), and is herself "the Sign" of the way, according to the traditional iconography of East and West.

970 **2675** Beginning with Mary's unique cooperation with the working of the Holy Spirit, the Churches developed their prayer to the holy Mother of God, centering it on the person of Christ manifested in his
512 mysteries. In countless hymns and antiphons expressing this prayer, two movements usually alternate with one another: the first "magni-
2619 fies" the Lord for the "great things" he did for his lowly servant and through her for all human beings;[29] the second entrusts the supplications and praises of the children of God to the Mother of Jesus, because she now knows the humanity which, in her, the Son of God espoused.

2676 This twofold movement of prayer to Mary has found a privileged expression in the *Ave Maria*:

722 *Hail Mary [or Rejoice, Mary]*: the greeting of the angel Gabriel opens this prayer. It is God himself who, through his angel as intermediary, greets Mary. Our prayer dares to take up this greeting to Mary with the regard God had for the lowliness of his humble servant and to exult in the joy he finds in her.[30]

Full of grace, the Lord is with thee: 490
These two phrases of the angel's greeting shed light on one another. Mary is full of grace because the Lord is with her. The grace with which she is filled is the presence of him who is the source of all grace. "Rejoice...O Daughter of Jerusalem...the Lord your God is in your midst."[31] Mary, in whom the Lord himself has just made his dwelling, is the daughter of Zion in person, the ark of the covenant, the place where the glory of the Lord dwells. She is "the dwelling of God...with men."[32] Full of grace, Mary is wholly given over to him who has come to dwell in her and whom she is about to give to the world.

Blessed art thou among women and 435
blessed is the fruit of thy womb, Jesus. After the angel's greeting, we make Elizabeth's greeting our own. "Filled with the Holy Spirit," Elizabeth is the first in the long succession of generations who have called Mary "blessed."[33] "Blessed is she who believed...."[34] Mary is "blessed among women" because she believed in the fulfillment of the Lord's
word. Abraham, because of his faith, 146
became a blessing for all the nations of the earth.[35] Mary, because of her faith, became the mother of believers, through whom all nations of the earth receive him who is God's own blessing: Jesus, the "fruit of thy womb."

2677 *Holy Mary, Mother of God*: 495
With Elizabeth we marvel, "And why is this granted me, that the mother of my Lord should come to me?"[36] Because she gives us Jesus, her son, Mary is Mother of God

[28] *LG* 62. — [29] Cf. *Lk* 1:46–55. — [30] Cf. *Lk* 1:48; *Zeph* 3:17b. — [31] *Zeph* 3:14, 17a. — [32] *Rev* 21:3. — [33] *Lk* 1:41, 48. — [34] *Lk* 1:45. — [35] Cf. *Gen* 12:3. — [36] *Lk* 1:43.

and our mother; we can entrust all our cares and petitions to her: she prays for us as she prayed for herself: "Let it be to me according to your word."[37] By entrusting ourselves to her prayer, we abandon ourselves to the will of God together with her: "Thy will be done."

Pray for us sinners, now and at the hour of our death: By asking Mary to pray for us, we acknowledge ourselves to be poor sinners and we address ourselves to the "Mother of Mercy," the All-Holy One. We give ourselves over to her now, in the Today of our lives. And our trust broadens further, already at the present moment, to surrender "the hour of our death" wholly to her care. May she be there as she was at her son's death on the cross. May she welcome us as our mother at the hour of our passing[38] to lead us to
1020 her son, Jesus, in paradise.

971, 1674 **2678** Medieval piety in the West developed the prayer of the rosary as a popular substitute for the Liturgy of the Hours. In the East, the litany called the *Akathistosand* the *Paraclesis* remained closer to the choral office in the Byzantine churches, while the Armenian, Coptic, and Syriac traditions preferred popular hymns and songs to the Mother of God. But in the *Ave Maria*, the *theotokia*, the hymns of St. Ephrem or St. Gregory of Narek, the tradition of prayer is basically the same.

2679 Mary is the perfect *Orans* 967
(pray-er), a figure of the Church. When we pray to her, we are adhering with her to the plan of the Father, who sends his Son to save all men. Like the beloved disciple we welcome Jesus' mother into our homes,[39] for she has become the mother of all the living. We can pray with and to her. The prayer of the Church is sustained by the prayer of 972
Mary and united with it in hope.[40]

In Brief

2680 *Prayer is primarily addressed to the Father; it can also be directed toward Jesus, particularly by the invocation of his holy name: "Lord Jesus Christ, Son of God, have mercy on us sinners."*

2681 *"No one can say 'Jesus is Lord', except by the Holy Spirit" (*1 Cor *12:3). The Church invites us to invoke the Holy Spirit as the interior Teacher of Christian prayer.*

2682 *Because of Mary's singular cooperation with the action of the Holy Spirit, the Church loves to pray in communion with the Virgin Mary, to magnify with her the great things the Lord has done for her, and to entrust supplications and praises to her.*

[36] *Lk* 1:43. — [37] *Lk* 1:38. — [38] Cf. *Jn* 19:27. — [39] Cf. *Jn* 19:27. — [40] Cf. *LG* 68–69.

Article 3: GUIDES FOR PRAYER

A cloud of witnesses

2683 The witnesses who have preceded us into the kingdom,[41] especially those whom the Church recognizes as saints, share in the living tradition of prayer by the example of their lives, the transmission of their writings, and their prayer today. They contemplate God, praise him and constantly care for those whom they have left on earth. When
956 they entered into the joy of their Master, they were "put in charge of many things."[42] Their intercession is their most exalted service to God's plan. We can and should ask them to intercede for us and for the whole world.

917 **2684** In the communion of saints, many and varied *spiritualities* have been developed throughout the history of the churches. The personal charism of some witnesses to God's love for men has been handed on,
919 like "the spirit" of Elijah to Elisha and John the Baptist, so that their followers may have a share in this spirit.[43] A distinct spirituality can also arise at the point of convergence of liturgical and theological currents, bearing witness to the integration of the faith into a particular
1202 human environment and its history. The different schools of Christian spirituality share in the living tradition of prayer and are essential guides for the faithful. In their rich diversity they are refractions of the one pure light of the Holy Spirit.

> The Spirit is truly the dwelling of the saints and the saints are for the Spirit a place where he dwells as in his own home, since they offer themselves as a dwelling place for God and are called his temple.[44]

Servants of prayer

2685 The *Christian family* is the 1657
first place of education in prayer. Based on the sacrament of marriage, the family is the "domestic church" where God's children learn to pray "as the Church" and to persevere in prayer. For young children in particular, daily family prayer is the first witness of the Church's living memory as awakened patiently by the Holy Spirit.

2686 *Ordained ministers* are also 1547
responsible for the formation in prayer of their brothers and sisters in Christ. Servants of the Good Shepherd, they are ordained to lead the People of God to the living waters of prayer: the Word of God, the liturgy, the theologal life (the life of faith, hope, and charity), and the Today of God in concrete situations.[45]

2687 Many *religious* have conse- 916
crated their whole lives to prayer. Hermits, monks, and nuns since the time of the desert fathers have devoted their time to praising God and interceding for his people. The consecrated life cannot be sustained or spread without prayer; it is one of the living sources of contemplation and the spiritual life of the Church.

[41] Cf. *Heb* 12:1. — [42] Cf. *Mt* 25:21. — [43] Cf. *2 Kings* 2:9; *Lk* 1:1; PC 2. — [44] St. Basil, *De Spiritu* Sancto, 26, 62: PG 32, 184. — [45] Cf. *PO* 4–6.

2688 The *catechesis* of children, young people, and adults aims at teaching them to meditate on The Word of God in personal prayer, practicing it in liturgical prayer, and internalizing it at all times in order to bear fruit in a new life. Catechesis is also a time for the discernment
1674 and education of popular piety.[46] The memorization of basic prayers offers an essential support to the life of prayer, but it is important to help learners savor their meaning.

2689 *Prayer groups*, indeed "schools of prayer," are today one of the signs and one of the driving forces of renewal of prayer in the Church, provided they drink from authentic wellsprings of Christian prayer. Concern for ecclesial communion is a sign of true prayer in the Church.

2690 The Holy Spirit gives to certain of the faithful the gifts of wisdom, faith and discernment for the sake of this common good which is prayer (*spiritual direction*). Men and women so endowed are true servants of the living tradition of prayer.

> According to St. John of the Cross, the person wishing to advance toward perfection should "take care into whose hands he entrusts himself, for as the master is, so will the disciple be, and as the father is so will be the son." And further: "In addition to being learned and discreet a director should be experienced.... If the spiritual director has no experience of the spiritual life, he will be incapable of leading into it the souls whom God is calling to it, and he will not even understand them."[47]

Places favorable for prayer

2691 The church, the house of 1181
God, is the proper place for the liturgical prayer of the parish com- 2097
munity. It is also the privileged place for adoration of the real presence 1379
of Christ in the Blessed Sacrament. The choice of a favorable place is not a matter of indifference for true prayer.

– For personal prayer, this can be a "prayer corner" with the Sacred Scriptures and icons, in order to be there, in secret, before our Father.[48] In a Christian family, this kind of little oratory fosters prayer in common.

– In regions where monasteries 1175
exist, the vocation of these communities is to further the participation of the faithful in the Liturgy of the Hours and to provide necessary solitude for more intense personal prayer.[49]

– Pilgrimages evoke our earthly 1674
journey toward heaven and are traditionally very special occasions for renewal in prayer. For pilgrims seeking living water, shrines are special places for living the forms of Christian prayer "in Church."

In Brief

2692 *In prayer, the pilgrim Church is associated with that of the saints, whose intercession she asks.*

2693 *The different schools of Christian spirituality share in the living tradition of prayer and are precious guides for the spiritual life.*

[46] Cf. *CT* 54. — [47] St. John of the Cross, *The Living Flame of Love*, stanza 3, 30, in *The Collected Works of St. John of the Cross*, eds K. Kavanaugh OCD and O. Rodriguez OCD (Washington DC: Institute of Carmelite Studies, 1979), 621. — [48] Cf. *Mt* 6:6. — [49] Cf. *PC* 7.

2694 *The Christian family is the first place for education in prayer.*

2695 *Ordained ministers, the consecrated life, catechesis, prayer groups, and "spiritual direction" ensure assistance within the Church in the practice of prayer.*

2696 *The most appropriate places for prayer are personal or family oratories, monasteries, places of pilgrimage, and above all the church, which is the proper place for liturgical prayer for the parish community and the privileged place for Eucharistic adoration.*

Chapter Three:
THE LIFE OF PRAYER

2697 Prayer is the life of the new heart. It ought to animate us at every moment. But we tend to forget him who is our life and our all. This is why the Fathers of the spiritual life in the Deuteronomic and prophetic traditions insist that prayer is a remembrance of God often awakened
1099 by the memory of the heart: "We must remember God more often than we draw breath."[1] But we cannot pray "at all times" if we do not pray at specific times, consciously willing it. These are the special times of Christian prayer, both in intensity and duration.

1168 **2698** The Tradition of the Church proposes to the faithful certain rhythms of praying intended to nourish continual prayer. Some are daily, such as morning and evening prayer, grace before and after meals,
the Liturgy of the Hours. Sundays, 1174
centered on the Eucharist, are kept
holy primarily by prayer. The cycle 2177
of the liturgical year and its great feasts are also basic rhythms of the Christian's life of prayer.

2699 The Lord leads all persons by paths and in ways pleasing to him, and each believer responds according to his heart's resolve and the personal expressions of his prayer. However, Christian Tradition has retained three major expressions of prayer: vocal, meditative, and contemplative. They have one basic trait in common: composure of heart.
This vigilance in keeping the Word 2563
and dwelling in the presence of God makes these three expressions intense times in the life of prayer.

Article 1:
EXPRESSIONS OF PRAYER

I. Vocal Prayer

1176 **2700** Through his Word, God speaks to man. By words, mental or vocal, our prayer takes flesh. Yet it is most important that the heart should be present to him to whom we are speaking in prayer: "Whether or not our prayer is heard depends not on the number of words, but on the fervor of our souls."[2]

2701 Vocal prayer is an essential element of the Christian life. To his disciples, drawn by their Master's silent prayer, Jesus teaches a vocal prayer, the Our Father. He not only prayed aloud the liturgical prayers
of the synagogue but, as the Gospels 2603
show, he raised his voice to express his personal prayer, from exultant blessing of the Father to the agony
of Gethsemani.[3] 612

2702 The need to involve the senses in interior prayer corresponds to a requirement of our human nature. We are body and spirit, and we

[1] St. Gregory of Nazianzus, *Orat. theo.*, 27, 1, 4: PG 36, 16. — [2] St. John Chrysostom, *Ecloga de oratione* 2: PG 63, 585. — [3] Cf. *Mt* 11:25–26; *Mk* 14:36.

1146 experience the need to translate our feelings externally. We must pray with our whole being to give all power possible to our supplication.

2703 This need also corresponds to a divine requirement. God seeks worshippers in Spirit and in Truth, and consequently living prayer that rises from the depths of the soul. He also wants the external expression that associates the body with interior prayer, for it renders him that
2097 perfect homage which is his due.

2704 Because it is external and so thoroughly human, vocal prayer is the form of prayer most readily accessible to groups. Even interior prayer, however, cannot neglect vocal prayer. Prayer is internalized to the extent that we become aware of him "to whom we speak."[4] Thus vocal prayer becomes an initial form of contemplative prayer.

II. Meditation

158 **2705** Meditation is above all a quest. The mind seeks to understand the why and how of the Christian life, in order to adhere and respond to what the Lord is asking. The required attentiveness is difficult to sustain. We are usually helped by books, and Christians do not want for them: the Sacred Scriptures, particularly the Gospels, holy icons, liturgical texts of the day or season,
127 writings of the spiritual fathers, works of spirituality, the great book of creation, and that of history—the page on which the "today" of God is written.

2706 To meditate on what we read helps us to make it our own by confronting it with ourselves. Here, another book is opened: the book of life. We pass from thoughts to reality. To the extent that we are humble and faithful, we discover in meditation the movements that stir the heart and we are able to discern them. It is a question of acting truthfully in order to come into the light: "Lord, what do you want me to do?"

2707 There are as many and var- 2690
ied methods of meditation as there are spiritual masters. Christians owe it to themselves to develop the desire to meditate regularly, lest they come to resemble the three first kinds of soil in the parable of the sower.[5] But a method is only a guide; the important thing is to advance, with the 2664
Holy Spirit, along the one way of prayer: Christ Jesus.

2708 Meditation engages thought, imagination, emotion, and desire. This mobilization of faculties is necessary in order to deepen our convictions of faith, prompt the conversion of our heart, and strengthen our will to follow Christ. Christian prayer tries above all to meditate on the mysteries of Christ, as in *lectio divina*
or the rosary. This form of prayerful 516
reflection is of great value, but Christian prayer should go further: to the 2678
knowledge of the love of the Lord Jesus, to union with him.

III. Contemplative Prayer

2709 What is contemplative prayer? St. Teresa answers: "Contemplative prayer [*oración mental*]

[4] St. Teresa of Jesus, *The Way of Perfection* 26, 9 in *The Collected Works of St. Teresa of Avila*, tr. K. Kavanaugh, OCD, and O. Rodriguez, OCD (Washington DC: Institute of Carmelite Studies, 1980), II, 136. — [5] Cf. *Mk* 4:4–7, 15–19.

in my opinion is nothing else than
2562–2564 a close sharing between friends; it means taking time frequently to be alone with him who we know loves us."[6] Contemplative prayer seeks him "whom my soul loves."[7] It is Jesus, and in him, the Father. We seek him, because to desire him is always the beginning of love, and we seek him in that pure faith which causes us to be born of him and to live in him. In this inner prayer we can still meditate, but our attention is fixed on the Lord himself.

2710 The choice of the *time and duration of the prayer* arises from a determined will, revealing the secrets of the heart. One does not un-
2726 dertake contemplative prayer only when one has the time: one makes time for the Lord, with the firm determination not to give up, no matter what trials and dryness one may encounter. One cannot always meditate, but one can always enter into inner prayer, independently of the conditions of health, work, or emotional state. The heart is the place of this quest and encounter, in poverty and in faith.

2711 *Entering into contemplative prayer* is like entering into the Eucharistic liturgy: we "gather up" the heart, recollect our whole being un-
1348 der the prompting of the Holy Spirit, abide in the dwelling place of the Lord which we are, awaken our faith in order to enter into the presence of him who awaits us. We let our masks fall and turn our hearts back to the Lord who loves us, so as to hand ourselves over to him as an offering
2100 to be purified and transformed.

2712 Contemplative prayer is the prayer of the child of God, of the forgiven sinner who agrees to welcome the love by which he is loved and who wants to respond to it by loving even more.[8] But he knows that the love he is returning is poured out by the Spirit in his heart, for everything is grace from God. Contemplative prayer is the poor and humble surrender to the loving will of the Father in ever deeper union with his 2822
beloved Son.

2713 Contemplative prayer is the 2559
simplest expression of the mystery of prayer. It is a *gift*, a grace; it can be accepted only in humility and poverty. Contemplative prayer is a *covenant* relationship established by God within our hearts.[9] Contemplative prayer is a *communion* in which the Holy Trinity conforms man, the image of God, "to his likeness."

2714 Contemplative prayer is also the pre-eminently *intense* time of prayer. In it the Father strengthens our inner being with power through his Spirit "that Christ may dwell in [our] hearts through faith" and we may be "grounded in love."[10]

2715 Contemplation is a *gaze* of faith, fixed on Jesus. "I look at him and he looks at me": this is what a certain peasant of Ars in the time of his holy curé used to say while praying before the tabernacle. This focus on Jesus is a renunciation of self. His gaze purifies our heart; the light of the countenance of Jesus illumines the eyes of our heart and teaches us to see everything in the light of his truth and his compassion for all

[6] St. Teresa of Jesus, *The Book of Her Life,* 8, 5 in *The Collected Works of St. Teresa of Avila,* tr. K.Kavanaugh, OCD, and O. Rodriguez, OCD (Washington DC: Institute of Carmelite Studies, 1976), I, 67. — [7] *Song* 1:7; cf. 3:1–4. — [8] Cf. *Lk* 7:36–50; 19:1–10. — [9] Cf. *Jer* 31:33. — [10] *Eph* 3:16–17.

521 men. Contemplation also turns its gaze on the mysteries of the life of Christ. Thus it learns the "interior knowledge of our Lord," the more to love him and follow him.[11]

2716 Contemplative prayer is *hearing* the Word of God. Far from being passive, such attentiveness is the obedience of faith, the uncondi-
494 tional acceptance of a servant, and the loving commitment of a child. It participates in the "Yes" of the Son become servant and the *Fiat* of God's lowly handmaid.

533 **2717** Contemplative prayer is *silence*, the "symbol of the world to come"[12] or "silent love."[13] Words in this kind of prayer are not speeches; they are like kindling that feeds the fire of love. In this silence, unbearable to the "outer" man, the Father speaks to us his incarnate Word, who suffered, died, and rose; in this silence the Spirit of adoption enables
498 us to share in the prayer of Jesus.

2718 Contemplative prayer is a union with the prayer of Christ insofar as it makes us participate in his mystery. The mystery of Christ is celebrated by the Church in the Eucharist, and the Holy Spirit makes it come alive in contemplative prayer so that our charity will manifest it in our acts.

2719 Contemplative prayer is a communion of love bearing Life for the multitude, to the extent that it consents to abide in the night of
165 faith. The Paschal night of the Resurrection passes through the night of the agony and the tomb—the three intense moments of the Hour of Jesus which his Spirit (and not "the flesh [which] is weak") brings to life in prayer. We must be willing to
"keep watch with [him] one hour."[14] 2730

In Brief

2720 *The Church invites the faithful to regular prayer: daily prayers, the Liturgy of the Hours, Sunday Eucharist , the feasts of the liturgical year.*

2721 *The Christian tradition comprises three major expressions of the life of prayer: vocal prayer, meditation, and contemplative prayer. They have in common the recollection of the heart.*

2722 *Vocal prayer, founded on the union of body and soul in human nature, associates the body with the interior prayer of the heart, following Christ's example of praying to his Father and teaching the Our Father to his disciples.*

2723 *Meditation is a prayerful quest engaging thought, imagination, emotion, and desire. Its goal is to make our own in faith the subject considered, by confronting it with the reality of our own life.*

2724 *Contemplative prayer is the simple expression of the mystery of prayer. It is a gaze of faith fixed on Jesus, an attentiveness to the Word of God, a silent love. It achieves real union with the prayer of Christ to the extent that it makes us share in his mystery.*

[11] Cf. St. Ignatius of Loyola, *Spiritual Exercises*, 104. — [12] Cf. St. Isaac of Nineveh, *Tract. myst.* 66. — [13] St. John of the Cross, *Maxims and Counsels*, 53 in *The Collected Works of St. John of the Cross*, tr. K. Kavanaugh, OCD, and O. Rodriguez, OCD (Washington DC: Institute of Carmelite Studies, 1979), 678. — [14] Cf. *Mt* 26:40.

Article 2:
THE BATTLE OF PRAYER

2725 Prayer is both a gift of grace and a determined response on our part. It always presupposes effort. The great figures of prayer of the Old Covenant before Christ, as well as the Mother of God, the saints, and he himself, all teach us this: prayer is a battle. Against whom? Against
2612 ourselves and against the wiles of the tempter who does all he can to turn
409 man away from prayer, away from union with God. We pray as we live, because we live as we pray. If we do not want to act habitually according to the Spirit of Christ, neither can we pray habitually in his name. The "spiritual battle" of the Christian's
2015 new life is inseparable from the battle of prayer.

I. Objections to Prayer

2726 In the battle of prayer, we must face in ourselves and around us *erroneous notions of prayer*. Some people view prayer as a simple psychological activity, others as an effort of concentration to reach a mental void. Still others reduce prayer to ritual words and postures. Many Christians unconsciously regard prayer as an occupation that is incompatible with all the other things they have to do: they "don't have
2710 the time." Those who seek God by prayer are quickly discouraged because they do not know that prayer comes also from the Holy Spirit and not from themselves alone.

2727 We must also face the fact that certain attitudes deriving from the *mentality* of "this present world" can penetrate our lives if we are not vigilant. For example, some would have it that only that is true which can be verified by reason and science; 37
yet prayer is a mystery that overflows both our conscious and unconscious lives. Others overly prize production and profit; thus prayer, being unproductive, is useless. Still others exalt sensuality and comfort as the criteria of the true, the good, and the beautiful; whereas prayer, the "love of beauty" (*philokalia*), is caught up in the glory of the living and true God. Finally, some see prayer as a 2500
flight from the world in reaction against activism; but in fact, Christian prayer is neither an escape from reality nor a divorce from life.

2728 Finally, our battle has to confront what we experience as *failure in prayer*: discouragement during periods of dryness; sadness that, because we have "great possessions,"[15] we have not given all to the Lord; disappointment over not being heard according to our own will; wounded pride, stiffened by the indignity that is ours as sinners; our resistance to the idea that prayer is a free and unmerited gift; and so forth. The conclusion is always the same: what good does it do to pray? To overcome these obstacles, we must battle to gain humility, trust, and perseverance.

II. Humble Vigilance of Heart

Facing difficulties in prayer

2729 The habitual difficulty in prayer is *distraction*. It can affect words and their meaning in vocal

[15] Cf. *Mk* 10:22.

prayer; it can concern, more profoundly, him to whom we are praying, in vocal prayer (liturgical or
personal), meditation, and contemplative prayer. To set about hunting
down distractions would be to fall
into their trap, when all that is necessary is to turn back to our heart:
for a distraction reveals to us what
2711 we are attached to, and this humble
awareness before the Lord should
awaken our preferential love for him
and lead us resolutely to offer him
our heart to be purified. Therein lies
the battle, the choice of which master to serve.[16]

2730 In positive terms, the battle
against the possessive and dominating self requires *vigilance*, sobriety
of heart. When Jesus insists on vigilance, he always relates it to himself,
to his coming on the last day and
2659 every day: *today*. The bridegroom
comes in the middle of the night;
the light that must not be extin-
guished is that of faith: "'Come,' my
heart says, 'seek his face!'"[17]

2731 Another difficulty, especially
for those who sincerely want to pray,
is *dryness*. Dryness belongs to contemplative prayer when the heart
is separated from God, with no
taste for thoughts, memories, and
feelings, even spiritual ones. This
is the moment of sheer faith cling-
ing faithfully to Jesus in his agony
and in his tomb. "Unless a grain of
wheat falls into the earth and dies, it
remains alone; but if it dies, it bears
much fruit."[18] If dryness is due to
the lack of roots, because the word
1426 has fallen on rocky soil, the battle
requires conversion.[19]

Facing temptations in prayer

2732 The most common yet most 2609
hidden temptation is our *lack of
faith*. It expresses itself less by declared incredulity than by our actual
preferences. When we begin to pray, 2089
a thousand labors or cares thought
to be urgent vie for priority; once
again, it is the moment of truth for
the heart: what is its real love? Sometimes we turn to the Lord as a last
resort, but do we really believe he is?
Sometimes we enlist the Lord as an
ally, but our heart remains presump-
tuous. In each case, our lack of faith
reveals that we do not yet share in the
disposition of a humble heart: "Apart
from me, you can do *nothing*."[20] 2092, 207

2733 Another temptation, to 2094
which presumption opens the gate,
is *acedia*. The spiritual writers understand by this a form of depression due to lax ascetical practice,
decreasing vigilance, carelessness of
heart. "The spirit indeed is willing,
but the flesh is weak."[21] The greater
the height, the harder the fall. Painful as discouragement is, it is the reverse of presumption. The humble
are not surprised by their distress;
it leads them to trust more, to hold 2559
fast in constancy.

III. Filial Trust

2734 Filial trust is tested—it
proves itself—in tribulation.[22] The
principal difficulty concerns the
prayer of petition, for oneself or for 2629
others in intercession. Some even
stop praying because they think
their petition is not heard. Here two
questions should be asked: Why do
we think our petition has not been

[16] Cf. *Mt* 6:21, 24. — [17] *Ps* 27:8. — [18] *Jn* 12:24. — [19] Cf. *Lk* 8:6, 13. — [20] *Jn* 15:5. — [21] *Mt* 26:41. — [22] Cf. *Rom* 5:3–5.

heard? How is our prayer heard, how is it "efficacious"?

Why do we complain of not being heard?

2735 In the first place, we ought to be astonished by this fact: when we praise God or give him thanks for his benefits in general, we are not particularly concerned whether or not our prayer is acceptable to him. On the other hand, we demand to see the results of our petitions. What is the image of God that motivates our prayer: an instrument to be
2779 used? or the Father of our Lord Jesus Christ?

2559 **2736** Are we convinced that "we do not know how to pray as we ought"?[23] Are we asking God for "what is good for us"? Our Father knows what we need before we ask him,[24] but he awaits our petition
1730 because the dignity of his children lies in their freedom. We must pray, then, with his Spirit of freedom, to be able truly to know what he wants.[25]

2737 "You ask and do not receive, because you ask wrongly, to spend it on your passions."[26] If we ask with a divided heart, we are "adulterers";[27] God cannot answer us, for he desires our well-being, our life. "Or do you suppose that it is in vain that the scripture says, 'He yearns jealously over the spirit which he has made to dwell in us?'"[28] That our God is "jealous" for us is the sign of how true his love is. If we enter into the desire of his Spirit, we shall be heard.

> Do not be troubled if you do not immediately receive from God what you ask him; for he desires to do something even greater for you, while you cling to him in prayer.[29]
> God wills that our desire should be exercised in prayer, that we may be able to receive what he is prepared to give.[30]

How is our prayer efficacious?

2738 The revelation of prayer in the economy of salvation teaches us that faith rests on God's action in history. Our filial trust is enkindled
by his supreme act: the Passion and 2568
Resurrection of his Son. Christian
prayer is cooperation with his provi- 307
dence, his plan of love for men.

2739 For St. Paul, this trust is 2778
bold, founded on the prayer of the Spirit in us and on the faithful love of the Father who has given us his only Son.[31] Transformation of the praying heart is the first response to our petition.

2740 The prayer of Jesus makes Christian prayer an efficacious petition. He is its model, he prays in us and with us. Since the heart of the Son seeks only what pleases the Father, how could the prayer of the children of adoption be centered on
the gifts rather than the Giver? 2604

2741 Jesus also prays for us—in our place and on our behalf. All our petitions were gathered up, once for all, in his cry on the Cross and, in

[23] *Rom* 8:26. — [24] Cf. *Mt* 6:8. — [25] Cf. *Rom* 8:27. — [26] *Jas* 4:3; cf. the whole context: *Jas* 4:1–10; 1:5–8; 5:16. — [27] *Jas* 4:4. — [28] *Jas* 4:5. — [29] Evagrius Ponticus, *De oratione* 34: PG 79, 1173. — [30] St. Augustine, *Ep.* 130, 8, 17: PL 33, 500. — [31] Cf. *Rom* 10:12–13; 8:26–39. — [32] Cf. *Heb* 5:7; 7:25; 9:24.

his Resurrection, heard by the Father. This is why he never ceases to intercede for us with the Father.[32] If our prayer is resolutely united with that of Jesus, in trust and boldness as children, we obtain all that we ask in
2614 his name, even more than any particular thing: the Holy Spirit himself, who contains all gifts.

IV. Persevering in Love

2098 **2742** "Pray constantly...always and for everything giving thanks in the name of our Lord Jesus Christ to God the Father."[33] St. Paul adds, "Pray at all times in the Spirit, with all prayer and supplication. To that end keep alert with all perseverance making supplication for all the saints."[34] For "we have not been commanded to work, to keep watch and to fast constantly, but it has been laid down that we are to pray without ceasing."[35] This tireless fervor can come only from love. Against our dullness and laziness, the battle of prayer is that of humble, trusting, and persevering *love.* This love opens our hearts to three
162 enlightening and life-giving facts of faith about prayer.

2743 *It is always possible to pray*: The time of the Christian is that of the risen Christ who is with us always, no matter what tempests may arise.[36] Our time is in the hands of God:

> It is possible to offer fervent prayer even while walking in public or strolling alone, or seated in your shop,...while buying or selling,...or even while cooking.[37]

2744 *Prayer is a vital necessity.* Proof from the contrary is no less convincing: if we do not allow the Spirit to lead us, we fall back into the slavery of sin.[38] How can the Holy Spirit be our life if our heart is far from him?

> Nothing is equal to prayer; for what is impossible it makes possible, what is difficult, easy.... For it is impossible, utterly impossible, for the man who prays eagerly and invokes God ceaselessly ever to sin.[39]
> Those who pray are certainly saved; those who do not pray are certainly damned.[40]

2745 Prayer and *Christian life* are *inseparable*, for they concern the same love and the same renunciation, proceeding from love; the same filial and loving conformity with the Father's plan of love; the same transforming union in the Holy Spirit who conforms us more and more to Christ Jesus; the same love for all men, the love with which Jesus has loved us. "Whatever you ask the Fa- 2660
ther in my name, he [will] give it to you. This I command you, to love one another."[41]

> He "prays without ceasing" who unites prayer to works and good works to prayer. Only in this way can we consider as realizable the principle of praying without ceasing.[42]

[33] *1 Thess* 5:17; *Eph* 5:20. — [34] *Eph* 6:18. — [35] Evagrius Ponticus, *Pract.* 49: PG 40, 1245C. — [36] Cf. *Mt* 28:20; *Lk* 8:24. — [37] St. John Chrysostom, *Ecloga de oratione* 2: PG 63, 585. — [38] Cf. *Gal* 5:16–25. — [39] St. John Chrysostom, *De Anna* 4, 5: PG 54, 666. — [40] St. Alphonsus Liguori, *Del gran mezzo della preghiera*. — [41] *Jn* 15:16–17. — [42] Origen, *De orat.* 12: PG 11, 452C.

Article 3: THE PRAYER OF THE HOUR OF JESUS

2746 When "his hour" came, Jesus prayed to the Father.[43] His prayer, the longest transmitted by the Gospel, embraces the whole economy of creation and salvation, as well as his death and Resurrection. The prayer
1085 of the Hour of Jesus always remains his own, just as his Passover "once for all" remains ever present in the liturgy of his Church.

2747 Christian Tradition rightly calls this prayer the "priestly" prayer of Jesus. It is the prayer of our high priest, inseparable from his sacrifice, from his passing over (Passover) to the Father to whom he is wholly "consecrated."[44]

518 **2748** In this Paschal and sacrificial prayer, everything is recapitulated in Christ:[45] God and the world; the Word and the flesh; eternal life and time; the love that hands itself over and the sin that betrays it; the disciples present and those who will believe in him by their word; hu-
820 miliation and glory. It is the prayer of unity.

2749 Jesus fulfilled the work of the Father completely; his prayer, like his sacrifice, extends until the end of time. The prayer of this hour fills the end-times and carries them toward their consummation. Jesus, the Son to whom the Father has given all things, has given himself wholly back to the Father, yet expresses himself with a sovereign freedom[46] by virtue of the power the Father has given him over all flesh. The Son, who made himself Servant, is Lord, the *Pantocrator.* Our high priest who prays for us is also the one who prays in us and the God who hears our prayer. 2616

2750 By entering into the holy 2815
name of the Lord Jesus we can accept, from within, the prayer he teaches us: "Our Father!" His priestly prayer fulfills, from within, the great petitions of the Lord's Prayer: concern for the Father's name;[47] passionate zeal for his kingdom (glory);[48] the accomplishment of the will of the Father, of his plan of salvation;[49] and deliverance from evil.[50]

2751 Finally, in this prayer Jesus reveals and gives to us the "knowledge," inseparably one, of the Father and of the Son,[51] which is the very mystery of the life of prayer. 240

In Brief

2752 *Prayer presupposes an effort, a fight against ourselves and the wiles of the Tempter. The battle of prayer is inseparable from the necessary "spiritual battle" to act habitually according to the Spirit of Christ: we pray as we live, because we live as we pray.*

2753 *In the battle of prayer we must confront erroneous conceptions of prayer, various currents of thought, and our own experience of failure. We must respond with humility, trust, and perseverance to these temptations which cast doubt on the usefulness or even the possibility of prayer.*

[43] Cf. *Jn* 17. — [44] Cf. *Jn* 17:11, 13, 19. — [45] Cf. *Eph* 1:10. — [46] Cf. *Jn* 17:11, 13, 19, 24. — [47] Cf. *Jn* 17:6, 11, 12, 26. — [48] Cf. *Jn* 17:1, 5, 10, 22, 23–26. — [49] Cf. *Jn* 17:2, 4, 6, 9, 11, 12, 24. — [50] Cf. *Jn* 17:15. — [51] Cf. *Jn* 17:3, 6–10, 25.

2754 *The principal difficulties in the practice of prayer are distraction and dryness. The remedy lies in faith, conversion, and vigilance of heart.*

2755 *Two frequent temptations threaten prayer: lack of faith and acedia—a form of depression stemming from lax ascetical practice that leads to discouragement.*

2756 *Filial trust is put to the test when we feel that our prayer is not always heard. The Gospel invites us to ask ourselves about the conformity of our prayer to the desire of the Spirit.*

2757 *"Pray constantly"* (1 Thess *5:17). It is always possible to pray. It is even a vital necessity. Prayer and Christian life are inseparable.*

2758 *The prayer of the hour of Jesus, rightly called the "priestly prayer"* (*cf.* Jn *17), sums up the whole economy of creation and salvation. It fulfills the great petitions of the Our Father.*

Section Two

THE LORD'S PRAYER "OUR FATHER!"

2759 Jesus "was praying at a certain place, and when he ceased, one of his disciples said to him, 'Lord, teach us to pray, as John taught his disciples.'"[1] In response to this request the Lord entrusts to his disciples and to his Church the fundamental Christian prayer. St. Luke presents a brief text of five petitions,[2] while St. Matthew gives a more developed version of seven petitions.[3] The liturgical tradition of the Church has retained St. Matthew's text:

Our Father who art in heaven,
hallowed be thy name.
Thy kingdom come.
Thy will be done on earth, as it is in heaven.
Give us this day our daily bread,
and forgive us our trespasses,
as we forgive those who trespass against us,
and lead us not into temptation,
but deliver us from evil.

2760 Very early on, liturgical usage concluded the Lord's Prayer with a doxology. In the Didache, we find, "For yours are the power and the glory for ever."[4] The *Apostolic Constitutions* add to the beginning: "the kingdom," and this is the formula retained to our day in ecumenical prayer.[5] The Byzantine tradition adds after "the glory" the words "Father, Son, and Holy Spirit." The *Roman Missal* develops the last petition in the explicit perspective of "awaiting our blessed hope" and of the Second Coming of our Lord Jesus Christ.[6] Then comes the assembly's acclamation or the repetition of the doxology from the *Apostolic Constitutions*. 2855 2854

Article 1: "THE SUMMARY OF THE WHOLE GOSPEL"

2761 The Lord's Prayer "is truly the summary of the whole gospel."[7] "Since the Lord … after handing over the practice of prayer, said elsewhere, 'Ask and you will receive,' and since everyone has petitions which are peculiar to his circumstances, the regular and appropriate prayer [the Lord's Prayer] is said first, as the foundation of further desires."[8]

I. At the Center of the Scriptures

2762 After showing how the psalms are the principal food of Christian prayer and flow together in the petitions of the Our Father, St. Augustine concludes:

> Run through all the words of the holy prayers [in Scripture], and I do not think that you will find anything in them that is not contained and included in the Lord's Prayer.[9]

2763 All the Scriptures—the Law, the Prophets, and the Psalms—are fulfilled in Christ.[10] The Gospel is this "Good News." Its first proclamation is summarized by 102

[1] *Lk* 11:1. — [2] Cf. *Lk* 11:2–4. — [3] Cf. *Mt* 6:9–13. — [4] *Didache* 8, 2: SCh 248, 174. — [5] *Apostolic Constitutions*, 7, 24, 1: PG 1, 1016. — [6] *Titus* 2:13; cf. *Roman Missal* 22, Embolism after the Lord's Prayer. — [7] Tertullian, *De orat.* 1: PL 1, 1155. — [8] Tertullian, *De orat.* 10: PL 1, 1165; cf. *Lk* 11:9. — [9] St. Augustine, *Ep.* 130, 12, 22: PL 33, 503. — [10] Cf. *Lk* 24:44.

St. Matthew in the Sermon on the Mount;[11] the prayer to our Father is at the center of this proclamation. It is in this context that each petition bequeathed to us by the Lord is illuminated:

> The Lord's Prayer is the most perfect of prayers.... In it we ask, not only
> 2541 for all the things we can rightly desire, but also in the sequence that they should be desired. This prayer not only teaches us to ask for things, but also in what order we should desire them.[12]

1965 **2764** The Sermon on the Mount is teaching for life, the Our Father is a prayer; but in both the one and the other the Spirit of the Lord gives new form to our desires, those inner movements that animate our lives. Jesus teaches us this new life by his words; he teaches us to ask for it by
1969 our prayer. The rightness of our life in him will depend on the rightness of our prayer.

II. "The Lord's Prayer"

2765 The traditional expression "the Lord's Prayer"—*oratio Dominica*—means that the prayer to our Father is taught and given to us by the Lord Jesus. The prayer that comes to us from Jesus is truly unique: it is "of the Lord." On the one hand, in the words of this prayer the only
2701 Son gives us the words the Father gave him:[13] he is the master of our prayer. On the other, as Word incarnate, he knows in his human heart the needs of his human brothers and sisters and reveals them to us: he is the model of our prayer.

2766 But Jesus does not give us a formula to repeat mechanically.[14] As in every vocal prayer, it is through the Word of God that the Holy Spirit teaches the children of God to pray to their Father. Jesus not only gives us the words of our filial prayer; at the same time he gives us the Spirit by whom these words become in us "spirit and life."[15] Even more, the proof and possibility of our filial prayer is that the Father "sent the Spirit of his Son into our hearts, crying, '*Abba!* Father!'"[16] Since our prayer sets forth our desires before God, it is again the Father, "he who searches the hearts of men," who "knows what is the mind of the Spirit, because the Spirit intercedes for the saints according to the will of God."[17] The prayer to Our Father is
inserted into the mysterious mission 690
of the Son and of the Spirit.

III. The Prayer of the Church

2767 This indivisible gift of the Lord's words and of the Holy Spirit who gives life to them in the hearts of believers has been received and lived by the Church from the beginning. The first communities prayed the Lord's Prayer three times a day,[18] in place of the "Eighteen Benedictions" customary in Jewish piety.

2768 According to the apostolic tradition, the Lord's Prayer is essentially rooted in liturgical prayer:

> [The Lord] teaches us to make prayer in common for all our brethren. For he did not say "my Father" who art in heaven, but "our" Father, offering petitions for the common Body.[19]

[11] Cf. *Mt* 5–7. — [12] St. Thomas Aquinas, *STh* II–II, 83, 9. — [13] Cf. *Jn* 17:7. — [14] Cf. *Mt* 6:7; *1 Kings* 18:26–29. — [15] *Jn* 6:63. — [16] *Gal* 4:6. — [17] *Rom* 8:27. — [18] Cf. *Didache* 8, 3: *SCh* 248, 174. — [19] St. John Chrysostom, *Hom. in Mt.* 19, 4: PG 57, 278.

In all the liturgical traditions, the Lord's Prayer is an integral part of the major hours of the Divine Office. In the three sacraments of Christian initiation its ecclesial character is especially in evidence:

2769 In *Baptism* and *Confirmation*, the handing on (*traditio*) of the Lord's Prayer signifies new birth into the divine life. Since Christian prayer
1243 is our speaking to God with the very word of God, those who are "born anew...through the living and abiding word of God"[20] learn to invoke their Father by the one Word he always hears. They can henceforth do so, for the seal of the Holy Spirit's anointing is indelibly placed on their hearts, ears, lips, indeed their whole filial being. This is why most of the patristic commentaries on the Our Father are addressed to catechumens and neophytes. When the Church prays the Lord's Prayer, it is always the people made up of the "newborn" who pray and obtain mercy.[21]

1350 **2770** In the *Eucharistic liturgy* the Lord's Prayer appears as the prayer of the whole Church and there reveals its full meaning and efficacy. Placed between the *anaphora* (the Eucharistic prayer) and the communion, the Lord's Prayer sums up on the one hand all the petitions and intercessions expressed in the movement of the *epiclesis* and, on the other, knocks at the door of the Banquet of the kingdom which sacramental communion anticipates.

2771 In the Eucharist, the Lord's Prayer also reveals the *eschatological* character of its petitions. It is the proper prayer of "the end-time," the time of salvation that began with the 1403
outpouring of the Holy Spirit and will be fulfilled with the Lord's return. The petitions addressed to our Father, as distinct from the prayers of the old covenant, rely on the mystery of salvation already accomplished, once for all, in Christ crucified and risen.

2772 From this unshakeable faith 1820
springs forth the hope that sustains each of the seven petitions, which express the groanings of the present age, this time of patience and expectation during which "it does not yet appear what we shall be."[22] The Eucharist and the Lord's Prayer look eagerly for the Lord's return, "until he comes."[23]

In Brief

2773 *In response to his disciples' request "Lord, teach us to pray"* (Lk *11:1), Jesus entrusts them with the fundamental Christian prayer, the Our Father.*

2774 *"The Lord's Prayer is truly the summary of the whole gospel,"*[24] *the "most perfect of prayers."*[25] *It is at the center of the Scriptures.*

2775 *It is called "the Lord's Prayer" because it comes to us from the Lord Jesus, the master and model of our prayer.*

2776 *The Lord's Prayer is the quintessential prayer of the Church. It is an integral part of the major hours of the Divine Office and of the sacraments of Christian initiation: Baptism, Confirmation, and Eucharist. Integrated into the Eucharist it reveals the eschatological character of its petitions, hoping for the Lord, "until he comes"* (1 Cor *11:26).*

[20] *1 Pet* 1:23. — [21] Cf. *1 Pet* 2:1–10. — [22] *1 Jn* 3:2; cf. *Col* 3:4. — [23] *1 Cor* 11:26. — [24] Tertullian, *De orat.* 1: PL 1, 1251–1255. — [25] St. Thomas Aquinas, *STh* II–II, 83, 9.

Article 2:
"OUR FATHER WHO ART IN HEAVEN"

I. "We Dare to Say"

2777 In the Roman liturgy, the Eucharistic assembly is invited to pray to our heavenly Father with filial boldness; the Eastern liturgies develop and use similar expressions: "dare in all confidence," "make us worthy of…." From the burning bush Moses heard a voice saying to him, "Do not come near; put off your shoes from your feet, for the place on which you are standing is holy ground."[26] Only Jesus could cross that threshold of the divine holiness, for "when he had made purification for sins," he brought us into the Father's presence: "Here am I, and the children God has given me."[27]

> Our awareness of our status as slaves would make us sink into the ground and our earthly condition would dissolve into dust, if the authority of our Father himself and the Spirit of his Son had not impelled us to this cry…'Abba, Father!… When would a mortal dare call God 'Father,' if man's innermost being were not animated
> 270 by power from on high?"[28]

2778 This power of the Spirit who introduces us to the Lord's Prayer is expressed in the liturgies of East and of West by the beautiful, characteristically Christian expression: *parrhesia*, straightforward simplicity,
2828 filial trust, joyous assurance, humble boldness, the certainty of being loved.[29]

II. "Father!"

2779 Before we make our own this first exclamation of the Lord's Prayer, we must humbly cleanse our hearts of certain false images drawn "from this world." *Humility* makes us recognize that "no one knows the Son except the Father, and no one knows the Father except the Son and anyone to whom the Son chooses to reveal him," that is, "to little children."[30] The *purification* of our hearts has to do with paternal or maternal images, stemming from our personal and cultural history, and influencing our relationship with God. God our Father transcends the categories of the created world. To impose our
own ideas in this area "upon him" 239
would be to fabricate idols to adore or pull down. To pray to the Father is to enter into his mystery as he is and as the Son has revealed him to us.

> The expression God the Father had never been revealed to anyone. When Moses himself asked God who he was, he heard another name. The Father's name has been revealed to us in the Son, for the name "Son" implies the new name "Father."[31]

2780 We can invoke God as "Fa- 240
ther" because *he is revealed to us* by his Son become man and because his Spirit makes him known to us. The personal relation of the Son to the Father is something that man cannot conceive of nor the angelic powers even dimly see: and yet, the

[26] *Ex* 3:5. — [27] *Heb* 1:3; 2:13. — [28] St. Peter Chrysologus, *Sermo* 71, 3: PL 52, 401CD; cf. *Gal* 4:6. — [29] Cf. *Eph* 3:12; *Heb* 3:6; 4:16; 10:19; *1 Jn* 2:28; 3:21; 5:14. — [30] *Mt* 11:25–27. — [31] Tertullian, *De orat.* 3: PL 1, 1155.

Spirit of the Son grants a participation in that very relation to us who believe that Jesus is the Christ and that we are born of God.[32]

2781 When we pray to the Father, we are in *communion with him* and with his Son, Jesus Christ.[33] Then we know and recognize him with an ever new sense of wonder. The first phrase of the Our Father is a blessing of adoration before it is a supplication. For it is the glory of God that we should recognize him as "Father," the true God. We give him thanks for having revealed his name to us, for the gift of believing in it, and for the indwelling of his Presence in us.

2782 We can adore the Father because he has caused us to be reborn to his life by *adopting* us as his children in his only Son: by Baptism,
1267 he incorporates us into the Body of his Christ; through the anointing of his Spirit who flows from the head to the members, he makes us other "Christs."

> God, indeed, who has predestined us to adoption as his sons, has conformed us to the glorious Body of Christ. So then you who have become sharers in Christ are appropriately called "Christs."[34]
> The new man, reborn and restored to his God by grace , says first of all, "Father!" because he has now begun to be a son.[35]

1701 **2783** Thus the Lord's Prayer *reveals us to ourselves* at the same time that it reveals the Father to us.[36]

> O man, you did not dare to raise your face to heaven, you lowered your eyes to the earth, and suddenly you have received the grace of Christ: all your sins have been forgiven. From being a wicked servant you have become a good son.... Then raise your eyes to the Father who has begotten you through Baptism, to the Father who has redeemed you through his Son, and say: "Our Father...." But do not claim any privilege. He is the Father in a special way only of Christ, but he is the common Father of us all, because while he has begotten only Christ, he has created us. Then also say by his grace, "Our Father," so that you may merit being his son.[37]

2784 The free gift of adoption 1428
requires on our part continual conversion and *new life*. Praying to our Father should develop in us two fundamental dispositions:

> First, *the desire to become like him*: though created in his image, we are
> restored to his likeness by grace; and 1997
> we must respond to this grace.
> We must remember...and know that when we call God "our Father" we ought to behave as sons of God.[38]
> You cannot call the God of all kindness your Father if you preserve a cruel and inhuman heart; for in this case you no longer have in you the marks of the heavenly Father's kindness.[39]
> We must contemplate the beauty of the Father without ceasing and adorn our own souls accordingly.[40]

2785 Second, a *humble and trust-* 2562
ing heart that enables us "to turn and become like children":[41] for it is to "little children" that the Father is revealed.[42]

[32] Cf. *Jn* 1:1; *1 Jn* 5:1. — [33] Cf. *1 Jn* 1:3. — [34] St. Cyril of Jerusalem, *Catech. myst.* 3, 1: PG 33, 1088A. — [35] St. Cyprian, *De Dom. orat.* 9: PL 4, 525A. — [36] Cf. *GS* 22 § 1. — [37] St. Ambrose, *De Sacr.* 5, 4, 19: PL 16:450–451. — [38] St. Cyprian, *De Dom.* orat. 11: PL 4:526B. — [39] St. John Chrysostom, *De orat Dom.* 3: PG 51, 44. — [40] St. Gregory of Nyssa, *De orat. Dom.* 2: PG 44, 1148B. — [41] *Mt* 18:3. — [42] Cf. *Mt* 11:25.

> [The prayer is accomplished] by the contemplation of God alone, and by the warmth of love, through which the soul, molded and directed to love him, speaks very familiarly to God as to its own Father with special devotion.[43]
>
> Our Father: at this name love is aroused in us...and the confidence of obtaining what we are about to ask.... What would he not give to his children who ask, since he has already granted them the gift of being his children?[44]

III. "Our" Father

443 **2786** "Our" Father refers to God. The adjective, as used by us, does not express possession, but an entirely new relationship with God.

2787 When we say "our" Father, we recognize first that all his promises of love announced by the prophets are fulfilled in the *new and*
782 *eternal covenant* in his Christ: we have become "his" people and he is henceforth "our" God. This new relationship is the purely gratuitous gift of belonging to each other: we are to respond to "grace and truth" given us in Jesus Christ with love and faithfulness.[45]

2788 Since the Lord's Prayer is that of his people in the "end-time," this "our" also expresses the certitude of our hope in God's ultimate promise: in the new Jerusalem he will say to the victor, "I will be his God and he shall be my son."[46]

2789 When we pray to "our" Father, we personally address the Father of our Lord Jesus Christ. By doing so we do not divide the Godhead, since the Father is its "source and origin," but rather confess that
the Son is eternally begotten by him 245
and the Holy Spirit proceeds from him. We are not confusing the persons, for we confess that our communion is with the Father and his Son, Jesus Christ, in their one Holy Spirit. The *Holy Trinity* is consubstantial and indivisible. When we
pray to the Father, we adore and glo- 253
rify him together with the Son and the Holy Spirit.

2790 Grammatically, "our" qualifies a reality common to more than one person. There is only one God, and he is recognized as Father by those who, through faith in his only Son, are reborn of him by water
and the Spirit.[47] The *Church* is this 787
new communion of God and men. United with the only Son, who has become "the firstborn among many brethren," she is in communion with one and the same Father in one and the same Holy Spirit.[48] In praying "our" Father, each of the baptized is praying in this communion: "The company of those who believed were of one heart and soul."[49]

2791 For this reason, in spite of 821
the divisions among Christians, this prayer to "our" Father remains our common patrimony and an urgent summons for all the baptized. In communion by faith in Christ and by Baptism, they ought to join in Jesus' prayer for the unity of his disciples.[50]

2792 Finally, if we pray the Our Father sincerely, we leave individualism behind, because the love that we receive frees us from it. The

[43] St. John Cassian, *Coll.* 9, 18: PL 49, 788C. — [44] St. Augustine, *De serm. Dom. in monte* 2, 4, 16: PL 34, 1276. — [45] *Jn* 1:17; cf. *Hos* 2:21–22; 6:1–6. — [46] *Rev* 21:7. — [47] Cf. *1 Jn* 5:1; *Jn* 3:5. — [48] *Rom* 8:29; cf. *Eph* 4:4–6. — [49] *Acts* 4:32. — [50] Cf. *UR* 8; 22.

"our" at the beginning of the Lord's Prayer, like the "us" of the last four petitions, excludes no one. If we are to say it truthfully, our divisions and oppositions have to be overcome.[51]

2793 The baptized cannot pray to "our" Father without bringing before him all those for whom he gave his beloved Son. God's love has no
604 bounds, neither should our prayer.[52]
Praying "our" Father opens to us the dimensions of his love revealed in Christ: praying with and for all who do not yet know him, so that Christ may "gather into one the children of God."[53] God's care for all men and for the whole of creation has inspired all the great practitioners of prayer; it should extend our prayer to the full breadth of love whenever we dare to say "our" Father.

IV. "Who Art in Heaven"

326 **2794** This biblical expression does not mean a place ("space"), but a way of being; it does not mean that God is distant, but majestic. Our Father is not "elsewhere": he transcends everything we can conceive of his holiness. It is precisely because he is thrice-holy that he is so close to the humble and contrite heart.

> "Our Father who art in heaven" is rightly understood to mean that God is in the hearts of the just, as in his holy temple. At the same time, it means that those who pray should desire the one they invoke to dwell in them.[54]
> "Heaven" could also be those who bear the image of the heavenly world, and in whom God dwells and tarries.[55]

2795 The symbol of the heavens refers us back to the mystery of the covenant we are living when we pray to our Father. He is in heaven, his dwelling place; the Father's house is our homeland. Sin has exiled us from the land of the covenant,[56] but conversion of heart enables us to return
to the Father, to heaven.[57] In Christ, 1024
then, heaven and earth are reconciled,[58] for the Son alone "descended from heaven" and causes us to ascend there with him, by his Cross, Resurrection, and Ascension.[59]

2796 When the Church prays "our Father who art in heaven," she is professing that we are the People of God, already seated "with him in the heavenly places in Christ Jesus" and "hidden with Christ in God;"[60]
yet at the same time, "here indeed 1003
we groan, and long to put on our heavenly dwelling."[61]

> [Christians] are in the flesh, but do not live according to the flesh. They spend their lives on earth, but are citizens of heaven.[62]

In Brief

2797 *Simple and faithful trust, humble and joyous assurance are the proper dispositions for one who prays the Our Father.*

2798 *We can invoke God as "Father" because the Son of God made man has revealed him to us. In this Son, through Baptism, we are incorporated and adopted as sons of God.*

[51] Cf. *Mt* 5:23–24; 6:14–15. — [52] Cf. *NA* 5. — [53] *Jn* 11:52. — [54] St. Augustine, *De serm. Dom. in monte* 2, 5, 18: PL 34, 1277. — [55] St. Cyril of Jerusalem, *Catech. myst.* 5:11: PG 33, 1117. — [56] Cf. *Gen* 3. — [57] *Jer* 3:19–4:1a; *Lk* 15:18, 21. — [58] Cf. *Isa* 45:8; *Ps* 85:12. — [59] *Jn* 3:13; 12:32; 14:2–3; 16:28; 20:17; *Eph* 4:9–10; *Heb* 1:3; 2:13. — [60] *Eph* 2:6; *Col* 3:3. — [61] *2 Cor* 5:2; cf. *Phil* 3:20; *Heb* 13:14. — [62] *Ad Diognetum* 5: PG 2, 1173.

2799 *The Lord's Prayer brings us into communion with the Father and with his Son, Jesus Christ. At the same time it reveals us to ourselves (cf.* GS *22 § 1).*

2800 *Praying to our Father should develop in us the will to become like him and foster in us a humble and trusting heart.*

2801 *When we say "Our" Father, we are invoking the new covenant in Jesus Christ, communion with the Holy Trinity, and the divine love which spreads through the Church to encompass the world.*

2802 *"Who art in heaven" does not refer to a place but to God's majesty and his presence in the hearts of the just. Heaven, the Father's house, is the true homeland toward which we are heading and to which, already, we belong.*

Article 3:
THE SEVEN PETITIONS

2803 After we have placed ourselves in the presence of God our Father to adore and to love and to bless him, the Spirit of adoption stirs up in our hearts seven petitions, seven blessings. The first three, more
2627 theological, draw us toward the glory
of the Father; the last four, as ways toward him, commend our wretchedness to his grace. "Deep calls to deep."[63]

2804 The first series of petitions carries us toward him, for his own sake: *thy* name, *thy* kingdom, *thy* will! It is characteristic of love to think first of the one whom we love. In none of the three petitions do we mention ourselves; the burning desire, even anguish, of the beloved Son for his Father's glory seizes us:[64] "hallowed be thy name, thy kingdom come, thy will be done...." These three supplications were already answered in the saving sacrifice of Christ, but they are henceforth directed in hope toward their final fulfillment, for God is not yet all in all.[65]

2805 The second series of petitions unfolds with the same movement as certain Eucharistic epicleses: as an offering up of our
expectations, that draws down 1105
upon itself the eyes of the Father of mercies. They go up from us and concern us from this very moment, in our present world: "give *us*...forgive *us*...lead *us* not...deliver *us*...." The fourth and fifth petitions concern our life as such—to be fed and to be healed of sin; the last two concern our battle for the victory of life—that battle of prayer.

2806 By the three first petitions, 2656–265
we are strengthened in faith, filled with hope, and set aflame by charity. Being creatures and still sinners, we have to petition for us, for that "us" bound by the world and history, which we offer to the boundless love of God. For through the name of his Christ and the reign of his Holy Spirit, our Father accomplishes his plan of salvation, for us and for the whole world.

[63] *Ps* 42:7. — [64] Cf. *Lk* 22:44; 12:50. — [65] Cf. *1 Cor* 15:28.

2142–2159 I. "Hallowed Be Thy Name"

2807 The term "to hallow" is to be understood here not primarily in its causative sense (only God hallows, makes holy), but above all in an evaluative sense: to recognize as holy, to treat in a holy way. And so, in ado-
2097 ration, this invocation is sometimes understood as praise and thanksgiving.[66] But this petition is here taught to us by Jesus as an optative: a petition, a desire, and an expectation in which God and man are involved. Beginning with this first petition to our Father, we are immersed in the innermost mystery of his Godhead and the drama of the salvation of our humanity. Asking the Father that his name be made holy draws us into his plan of loving kindness for the fullness of time, "according to his purpose which he set forth in Christ," that we might "be holy and blameless before him in love."[67]

2808 In the decisive moments of his economy God reveals his name, but he does so by accomplishing his work. This work, then, is realized for us and in us only if his name is hallowed by us and in us.

203, 432 **2809** The holiness of God is the inaccessible center of his eternal mystery. What is revealed of it in creation and history, Scripture calls
293 "glory," the radiance of his majesty.[68] In making man in his image and likeness, God "crowned him with glory and honor," but by sinning, man fell "short of the glory of God."[69] From that time on, God was to manifest
705 his holiness by revealing and giving his name, in order to restore man to the image of his Creator.[70]

2810 In the promise to Abraham and the oath that accompanied it,[71] God commits himself but without disclosing his name. He begins to reveal it to Moses and makes it known clearly before the eyes of the whole people when he saves them from the Egyptians: "he has triumphed gloriously."[72] From the covenant of Sinai onwards, this people is "his own" and it is to be a "holy (or "consecrated": the same word is used for both in Hebrew) nation,"[73] because the
name of God dwells in it. 63

2811 In spite of the holy Law 2143
that again and again their Holy God gives them—"You shall be holy, for I the LORD your God am holy"—and although the Lord shows patience for the sake of his name, the people turn away from the Holy One of Israel and profane his name among the nations.[74] For this reason the just ones of the old covenant, the poor survivors returned from exile, and the prophets burned with passion for the name.

2812 Finally, in Jesus the name of 434
the Holy God is revealed and given to us, in the flesh, as Savior, revealed by what he is, by his word, and by his sacrifice.[75] This is the heart of his priestly prayer: "Holy Father… for their sake I consecrate myself, that they also may be consecrated in truth."[76] Because he "sanctifies" his own name, Jesus reveals to us the name of the Father.[77] At the end of Christ's Passover, the Father gives him the name that is above all

[66] Cf. *Ps* 111:9; *Lk* 1:49. — [67] *Eph* 1:9, 4. — [68] Cf. *Ps* 8; *Isa* 6:3. — [69] *Ps* 8:5; *Rom* 3:23; cf. *Gen* 1:26. — [70] *Col* 3:10. — [71] Cf. *Heb* 6:13. — [72] *Ex* 15:1; cf. 3:14. — [73] Cf. *Ex* 19:5–6. — [74] *Ezek* 20:9, 14, 22, 39; cf. *Lev* 19:2. — [75] Cf. *Mt* 1:21; *Lk* 1:31; *Jn* 8:28; 17:8; 17:17–19. — [76] *Jn* 17:11, 19. — [77] Cf. *Ezek* 20:39; 36:20–21; *Jn* 17:6.

names: "Jesus Christ is Lord, to the glory of God the Father."[78]

2013 **2813** In the waters of Baptism, we have been "washed...sanctified... justified in the name of the Lord Jesus Christ and in the Spirit of our God."[79] Our Father calls us to holiness in the whole of our life, and since "he is the source of [our] life in Christ Jesus, who became for us wisdom from God, and...sanctification,"[80] both his glory and our life depend on the hallowing of his name in us and by us. Such is the urgency of our first petition.

> By whom is God hallowed, since he is the one who hallows? But since he said, "You shall be holy to me; for I the LORD am holy," we seek and ask that we who were sanctified in Baptism may persevere in what we have begun to be. And we ask this daily, for we need sanctification daily, so that we who fail daily may cleanse away our sins by being sanctified continually.... We pray that this sanctification may remain in us.[81]

2814 The sanctification of his name among the nations depends
2045 inseparably on our *life* and our *prayer*:

> We ask God to hallow his name, which by its own holiness saves and makes holy all creation.... It is this name that gives salvation to a lost world. But we ask that this name of God should be hallowed in us through our actions. For God's name is blessed when we live well, but is blasphemed when we live wickedly. As the Apostle says: "The name of God is blasphemed among the Gentiles because of you." We ask then that, just as the name of God is holy, so we may obtain his holiness in our souls.[82]
>
> When we say "hallowed be thy name," we ask that it should be hallowed in us, who are in him; but also in others whom God's grace still awaits, that we may obey the precept that obliges us to pray for everyone, even our enemies. That is why we do not say expressly "hallowed be thy name 'in us,'" for we ask that it be so in all men.[83]

2815 This petition embodies all the others. Like the six petitions that
follow, it is fulfilled by the *prayer of* 2750
Christ. Prayer to our Father is our prayer, if it is prayed *in the name of Jesus*.[84] In his priestly prayer, Jesus asks: "Holy Father, protect in your name those whom you have given me."[85]

II. "Thy Kingdom Come"

2816 In the New Testament, the 541
word *basileia* can be translated by "kingship" (abstract noun), "kingdom" (concrete noun) or "reign"
(action noun). The Kingdom of God 2632
lies ahead of us. It is brought near in the Word incarnate, it is proclaimed throughout the whole Gospel, and it has come in Christ's death and Resurrection. The Kingdom of God
has been coming since the Last Sup- 560
per and, in the Eucharist, it is in our
midst. The kingdom will come in 1107
glory when Christ hands it over to his Father:

> It may even be...that the Kingdom of God means Christ himself, whom

[78] *Phil* 2:9–11. — [79] *1 Cor* 6:11. — [80] *1 Cor* 1:30; cf. *1 Thess* 4:7. — [81] St. Cyprian, *De Dom. orat.* 12: PL 4, 527A; *Lev* 20:26. — [82] St. Peter Chrysologus, *Sermo* 71, 4: PL 52:402A; cf. *Rom* 2:24; *Ezek* 36:20–22. — [83] Tertullian, *De orat.* 3: PL 1:1157A. — [84] Cf. *Jn* 14:13; 15:16; 16:24, 26. — [85] *Jn* 17:11.

> we daily desire to come, and whose coming we wish to be manifested quickly to us. For as he is our resurrection, since in him we rise, so he can also be understood as the Kingdom of God, for in him we shall reign.[86]

451, 2632 **2817** This petition is "*Marana tha*," the cry of the Spirit and the
671 Bride: "Come, Lord Jesus."

> Even if it had not been prescribed to pray for the coming of the kingdom, we would willingly have brought forth this speech, eager to embrace our hope. In indignation the souls of the martyrs under the altar cry out to the Lord: "O Sovereign Lord, holy and true, how long before you judge and avenge our blood on those who dwell upon the earth?" For their retribution is ordained for the end of the world. Indeed, as soon as possible, Lord, may your kingdom come![87]

769 **2818** In the Lord's Prayer, "thy kingdom come" refers primarily to the final coming of the reign of God through Christ's return.[88] But, far from distracting the Church from her mission in this present world, this desire commits her to it all the more strongly. Since Pentecost, the coming of that Reign is the work of the Spirit of the Lord who "complete[s] his work on earth and brings us the fullness of grace."[89]

2046 **2819** "The kingdom of God [is] righteousness and peace and joy in the Holy Spirit."[90] The end-time in which we live is the age of the outpouring of the Spirit. Ever since
2516 Pentecost, a decisive battle has been joined between "the flesh" and the Spirit.[91]

> Only a pure soul can boldly say: 2519
> "Thy kingdom come." One who has heard Paul say, "Let not sin therefore reign in your mortal bodies," and has purified himself in action, thought, and word will say to God: "Thy kingdom come!"[92]

2820 By a discernment according to the Spirit, Christians have to distinguish between the growth of the Reign of God and the progress
of the culture and society in which 1049
they are involved. This distinction is not a separation. Man's vocation to eternal life does not suppress, but actually reinforces, his duty to put into action in this world the energies and means received from the Creator to serve justice and peace.[93]

2821 This petition is taken up 2746
and granted in the prayer of Jesus which is present and effective in the Eucharist; it bears its fruit in new life in keeping with the Beatitudes.[94]

III. "Thy Will Be Done on Earth as It Is in Heaven"

2822 Our Father "desires all men 851
to be saved and to come to the knowledge of the truth."[95] He "is forbearing toward you, not wishing that any should perish."[96] His commandment is "that you love one another; even as I have loved you, that 2196
you also love one another."[97] This commandment summarizes all the others and expresses his entire will.

[86] St. Cyprian, *De Dom. orat.* 13: PL 4, 528A. — [87] Tertullian, *De orat.* 5: PL 1, 1159A; cf. *Heb* 4:11; *Rev* 6:9; 22:20. — [88] Cf. *Titus* 2:13. — [89] *Roman Missal*, Eucharistic Prayer IV, 118. — [90] *Rom* 14:17. — [91] Cf. *Gal* 5:16–25. — [92] St. Cyril of Jerusalem, *Catech. myst.* 5, 13: PG 33, 1120A; cf. *Rom* 6:12. — [93] Cf. *GS* 22; 32; 39; 45; *EN* 31. — [94] Cf. *Jn* 17:17–20; *Mt* 5:13–16; 6:24; 7:12–13. — [95] *1 Tim* 2:3–4. — [96] *2 Pet* 3:9; cf. *Mt* 18:14. — [97] *Jn* 13:34; cf. *1 Jn* 3; 4; *Lk* 10:25–37.

59 **2823** "He has made known to us the mystery of his will, according to his good pleasure that he set forth in Christ...to gather up all things in him, things in heaven and things on earth. In Christ we have also obtained an inheritance, having been destined according to the purpose of him who accomplishes all things according to his counsel and will."[98] We ask insistently for this loving plan to be fully realized on earth as it is already in heaven.

475 **2824** In Christ, and through his human will, the will of the Father has been perfectly fulfilled once for all. Jesus said on entering into this world: "Lo, I have come to do your will, O God."[99] Only Jesus can say: "I always do what is pleasing to him."[100] In the prayer of his agony, he consents totally to this will: "not my will, but yours be done."[101]
612 For this reason Jesus "gave himself for our sins to deliver us from the present evil age, according to the will of our God and Father."[102] "And by that will we have been sanctified through the offering of the body of Jesus Christ once for all."[103]

2825 "Although he was a Son, [Jesus] learned obedience through what he suffered."[104] How much more reason have we sinful creatures to learn obedience—we who in him have become children of adoption. We ask our Father to unite our will to his Son's, in order to fulfill his
615 will, his plan of salvation for the life of the world. We are radically incapable of this, but united with Jesus and with the power of his Holy Spirit, we can surrender our will to him and decide to choose what his Son has always chosen: to do what is pleasing to the Father.[105]

> In committing ourselves to [Christ], we can become one spirit with him, and thereby accomplish his will, in such wise that it will be perfect on earth as it is in heaven.[106]
>
> Consider how [Jesus Christ] teaches us to be humble, by making us see that our virtue does not depend on our work alone but on grace from on high. He commands each of the faithful who prays to do so universally, for the whole world. For he did not say "thy will be done in me or in us," but "on earth," the whole earth, so that error may be banished from it, truth take root in it, all vice be destroyed on it, virtue flourish on it, and earth no longer differ from heaven.[107]

2826 By prayer we can discern "what is the will of God" and obtain the endurance to do it.[108] Jesus teaches us that one enters the kingdom of heaven not by speaking words, but by doing "the will of my Father in heaven."[109]

2827 "If any one is a worshiper of 2611
God and does his will, God listens to him."[110] Such is the power of the Church's prayer in the name of her Lord, above all in the Eucharist. Her prayer is also a communion of intercession with the all-holy Mother of God[111] and all the saints who have been pleasing to the Lord because they willed his will alone:

> It would not be inconsistent with the truth to understand the words,

[98] *Eph* 1:9–11. — [99] *Heb* 10:7; *Ps* 40:7. — [100] *Jn* 8:29. — [101] *Lk* 22:42; cf. *Jn* 4:34; 5:30; 6:38. — [102] *Gal* 1:4. — [103] *Heb* 10:10. — [104] *Heb* 5:8. — [105] Cf. *Jn* 8:29. — [106] Origen, *De orat.* 26: PG 11, 501B. — [107] St. John Chrysostom, *Hom. in Mt.* 19, 5: PG 57, 280. — [108] *Rom* 12:2; cf. *Eph* 5:17; cf. *Heb* 10:36. — [109] *Mt* 7:21. — [110] *Jn* 9:31; cf. *1 Jn* 5:14. — [111] Cf. *Lk* 1:38, 49.

"Thy will be done on earth as it is in heaven," to mean: "in the Church as in our Lord Jesus Christ himself";
796 or "in the Bride who has been betrothed, just as in the Bridegroom who has accomplished the will of the Father."[112]

IV. "Give Us This Day Our Daily Bread"

2778 **2828** "*Give us*": The trust of children who look to their Father for everything is beautiful. "He makes his sun rise on the evil and on the good, and sends rain on the just and on the unjust."[113] He gives to all the living "their food in due season."[114] Jesus teaches us this petition, because it glorifies our Father by acknowledging how good he is, beyond all goodness.

2829 "Give us" also expresses the covenant. We are his and he is ours, for our sake. But this "us" also recognizes him as the Father of all men and we pray to him for them all, in
1939 solidarity with their needs and sufferings.

2830 "*Our bread*": The Father who gives us life cannot but give us the nourishment life requires—all appropriate goods and blessings, both
2633 material and spiritual. In the Sermon on the Mount, Jesus insists on the filial trust that cooperates with our Father's providence.[115] He is not inviting us to idleness,[116] but wants to relieve us from nagging worry and preoccupation. Such is the filial surrender of the children of God:

To those who seek the kingdom of God and his righteousness, he has promised to give all else besides.
Since everything indeed belongs to 227
God, he who possesses God wants for nothing, if he himself is not found wanting before God.[117]

2831 But the presence of those who hunger because they lack bread opens up another profound meaning of this petition. The drama of hunger in the world calls Christians who pray sincerely to exercise responsibility toward their brethren, both in their personal behavior and in their solidarity with the human family. This petition of the Lord's Prayer cannot be isolated from the parables of the poor man Lazarus
and of the Last Judgment.[118] 1038

2832 As leaven in the dough, the newness of the kingdom should make the earth "rise" by the Spirit of Christ.[119] This must be shown by the
establishment of justice in personal 1928
and social, economic and international relations, without ever forgetting that there are no just structures without people who want to be just.

2833 "Our" bread is the "one" 2790
loaf for the "many." In the Beatitudes "poverty" is the virtue of shar- 2546
ing: it calls us to communicate and share both material and spiritual goods, not by coercion but out of love, so that the abundance of some may remedy the needs of others.[120]

2834 "Pray and work."[121] "Pray as 2428
if everything depended on God and work as if everything depended on

[112] St. Augustine, *De serm. Dom.* 2, 6, 24: PL 34, 1279. — [113] *Mt* 5:45. — [114] *Ps* 104:27. — [115] Cf. *Mt* 6:25–34. — [116] Cf. *2 Thess* 3:6–13. — [117] St. Cyprian, *De Dom. orat.* 21: PL 4, 534A. — [118] Cf. *Lk* 16:19–31; *Mt* 25:31–46. — [119] Cf. *AA* 5. — [120] Cf. *2 Cor* 8:1–15. — [121] Cf. St. Benedict, *Regula*, 20, 48.

you."[122] Even when we have done our work, the food we receive is still a gift from our Father; it is good to ask him for it and to thank him, as Christian families do when saying grace at meals.

2835 This petition, with the responsibility it involves, also applies to another hunger from which men are perishing: "Man does not live by bread alone, but...by every word that proceeds from the mouth of God,"[123] that is, by the Word he speaks and the Spirit he breathes forth. Christians must make every effort "to proclaim the good news
2443 to the poor." There is a famine on earth, "not a famine of bread, nor a thirst for water, but of hearing the words of the LORD."[124] For this reason the specifically Christian sense of this fourth petition concerns the Bread of Life: The Word of God ac-
1384 cepted in faith, the Body of Christ received in the Eucharist.[125]

1165 **2836** "*This day*" is also an expression of trust taught us by the Lord,[126] which we would never have presumed to invent. Since it refers above all to his Word and to the Body of his Son, this "today" is not only that of our mortal time, but also the "today" of God.

> If you receive the bread each day, each day is today for you. If Christ is yours today, he rises for you every day. How can this be? "You are my Son, today I have begotten you." Therefore, "today" is when Christ rises.[127]

2837 "*Daily*" (*epiousios*) occurs 2659
nowhere else in the New Testament. Taken in a temporal sense, this word is a pedagogical repetition of "this day,"[128] to confirm us in trust "without reservation." Taken in the
qualitative sense, it signifies what is 2633
necessary for life, and more broadly every good thing sufficient for subsistence.[129] Taken literally (*epi-ousios*: "super-essential"), it refers directly to the Bread of Life, the Body
of Christ, the "medicine of im- 1405
mortality," without which we have no life within us.[130] Finally in this connection, its heavenly meaning is evident: "this day" is the Day of the Lord, the day of the feast of the
kingdom, anticipated in the Eucha- 1166
rist that is already the foretaste of the kingdom to come. For this reason it is fitting for the Eucharistic liturgy
to be celebrated each day. 1389

> The Eucharist is our daily bread. The power belonging to this divine food makes it a bond of union. Its effect is then understood as unity, so that, gathered into his Body and made members of him, we may become what we receive.... This also is our daily bread: the readings you hear each day in church and the hymns you hear and sing. All these are necessities for our pilgrimage.[131]
>
> The Father in heaven urges us, as children of heaven, to ask for the bread of heaven. [Christ] himself is the bread who, sown in the Virgin, raised up in the flesh, kneaded in the Passion, baked in the oven of the tomb, reserved in churches, brought to altars, furnishes the faithful each day with food from heaven.[132]

[122] Attributed to St. Ignatius Loyola, cf. Joseph de Guibert, SJ, *The Jesuits: Their Spiritual Doctrine and Practice*, (Chicago: Loyola University Press, 1964), 148, n. 55. — [123] *Deut* 8:3; *Mt* 4:4. — [124] *Am* 8:11. — [125] Cf. *Jn* 6:26–58. — [126] Cf. *Mt* 6:34; *Ex* 16:19. — [127] St. Ambrose, *De Sacr.* 5, 4, 26: PL 16, 453A; cf. *Ps* 2:7. — [128] Cf. *Ex* 16:19–21. — [129] Cf. *1 Tim* 6:8. — [130] St. Ignatius of Antioch, *Ad Eph.* 20, 2: PG 5, 661; *Jn* 6:53–56. — [131] St. Augustine, *Sermo* 57, 7: PL 38, 389. — [132] St. Peter Chrysologus, Sermo 67: PL 52, 392; cf. Jn 6:51.

V. "And Forgive Us Our Trespasses, as We Forgive Those Who Trespass Against Us"

1425 **2838** This petition is astonishing.
If it consisted only of the first phrase,
"And forgive us our trespasses," it
might have been included, implicitly, in the first three petitions of the
Lord's Prayer, since Christ's sacrifice
1933 is "that sins may be forgiven." But,
according to the second phrase, our
petition will not be heard unless we
have first met a strict requirement.
Our petition looks to the future, but
our response must come first, for the
2631 two parts are joined by the single
word "as."

And forgive us our trespasses...

2839 With bold confidence, we
began praying to our Father. In
begging him that his name be hallowed, we were in fact asking him
that we ourselves might be always
made more holy. But though we are
1425 clothed with the baptismal garment,
we do not cease to sin, to turn away
1439 from God. Now, in this new petition, we return to him like the prodigal son and, like the tax collector,
recognize that we are sinners before
him.[133] Our petition begins with a
"confession" of our wretchedness
and his mercy. Our hope is firm because, in his Son, "we have redemption, the forgiveness of sins."[134] We
find the efficacious and undoubted
sign of his forgiveness in the sacra-
1422 ments of his Church.[135]

2840 Now—and this is daunting—this outpouring of mercy cannot penetrate our hearts as long as
we have not forgiven those who have
trespassed against us. Love, like the
Body of Christ, is indivisible; we
cannot love the God we cannot see
if we do not love the brother or sister we do see.[136] In refusing to forgive
our brothers and sisters, our hearts
are closed and their hardness makes
them impervious to the Father's merciful love; but in confessing our sins, 1864
our hearts are opened to his grace.

2841 This petition is so important that it is the only one to which the Lord returns and which he develops explicitly in the Sermon on the Mount.[137] This crucial requirement of the covenant mystery is impossible for man. But "with God all things are possible."[138]

...as we forgive those who trespass against us

2842 This "as" is not unique in Jesus' teaching: "You, therefore, must
be perfect, as your heavenly Father
is perfect"; "Be merciful, even as
your Father is merciful"; "A new
commandment I give to you, that
you love one another, even as I have
loved you, that you also love one another."[139] It is impossible to keep the
Lord's commandment by imitating
the divine model from outside; there
has to be a vital participation, coming from the depths of the heart, in 521
the holiness and the mercy and the
love of our God. Only the Spirit
by whom we live can make "ours"
the same mind that was in Christ
Jesus.[140] Then the unity of forgiveness becomes possible and we find
ourselves "forgiving one another, as
God in Christ forgave" us.[141]

[133] Cf. *Lk* 15:11–32; 18:13. — [134] *Col* 1:14; *Eph* 1:7. — [135] Cf. *Mt* 26:28; *Jn* 20:23. — [136] Cf. *1 Jn* 4:20. — [137] Cf. *Mt* 6:14–15; 5:23–24; *Mk* 11:25. — [138] *Mt* 19:26. — [139] *Mt* 5:48; *Lk* 6:36; *Jn* 13:34. — [140] Cf. *Gal* 5:25; *Phil* 2:1, 5. — [141] *Eph* 4:32.

2843 Thus the Lord's words on forgiveness, the love that loves to the end,[142] become a living reality. The parable of the merciless servant, which crowns the Lord's teaching on ecclesial communion, ends with these words: "So also my heavenly Father will do to every one of you, if you do not forgive your brother from your heart."[143] It is there, in fact, "in the depths of the heart," that everything is bound and loosed.
368 It is not in our power not to feel or to forget an offense; but the heart that offers itself to the Holy Spirit turns injury into compassion and purifies the memory in transforming the hurt into intercession.

2262 **2844** Christian prayer extends to the *forgiveness of enemies*,[144] transfiguring the disciple by configuring him to his Master. Forgiveness is a high-point of Christian prayer; only hearts attuned to God's compassion can receive the gift of prayer. Forgiveness also bears witness that, in our world, love is stronger than sin. The martyrs of yesterday and today bear this witness to Jesus. Forgiveness is the fundamental condition of the reconciliation of the children of God with their Father and of men with one another.[145]

1441 **2845** There is no limit or measure to this essentially divine forgiveness,[146] whether one speaks of "sins" as in *Luke* (11:4), or "debts" as in *Matthew* (6:12). We are always debtors: "Owe no one anything, except to love one another."[147] The communion of the Holy Trinity is the source and criterion of truth in every relationship. It is lived out in prayer, above all in the Eucharist.[148]

> God does not accept the sacrifice of a sower of disunion, but commands that he depart from the altar so that he may first be reconciled with his brother. For God can be appeased only by prayers that make peace. To God, the better offering is peace, brotherly concord, and a people made one in the unity of the Father, Son, and Holy Spirit.[149]

VI. "And Lead Us Not into Temptation"

2846 This petition goes to the root of the preceding one, for our sins result from our consenting to temptation; we therefore ask our
Father not to "lead" us into temptation. 164
It is difficult to translate the Greek verb used by a single English word: the Greek means both "do not allow us to enter into temptation" and "do not let us yield to temptation."[150] "God cannot be tempted by evil and he himself tempts no one";[151] on the contrary, he wants to set us free from evil. We ask him not to allow us to take the way that leads to sin. We are engaged in the battle
"between flesh and spirit"; this petition 2516
implores the Spirit of discernment and strength.

2847 The Holy Spirit makes us *discern* between trials, which are necessary for the growth of the inner man,[152] and temptation, which leads to sin and death.[153] We must also discern between being tempted
and consenting to temptation. Finally, 2284
discernment unmasks the lie

[142] Cf. *Jn* 13:1. — [143] Cf. *Mt* 18:23–35. — [144] Cf. *Mt* 5:43–44. — 145 Cf. *2 Cor* 5:18–21; John Paul II, *DM* 14. — [146] Cf. *Mt* 18:21–22; *Lk* 17:3–4. — [147] *Rom* 13:8. — [148] Cf. *Mt* 5:23–24; *1 Jn* 3:19–24. — [149] St. Cyprian, *De Dom. orat.* 23: PL 4, 535–536; cf. *Mt* 5:24. — [150] Cf. *Mt* 26:41. — [151] *Jas* 1:13. — [152] Cf. *Lk* 8:13–15; *Acts* 14:22; *Rom* 5:3–5; *2 Tim* 3:12. — [153] Cf. *Jas* 1:14–15.

of temptation, whose object appears to be good, a "delight to the eyes" and desirable,[154] when in reality its fruit is death.

> God does not want to impose the good, but wants free beings.... There is a certain usefulness to temptation. No one but God knows what our soul has received from him, not even we ourselves. But temptation reveals it in order to teach us to know ourselves, and in this way we discover our evil inclinations and are obliged to give thanks for the goods that temptation has revealed to us.[155]

2848 "Lead us not into temptation" implies a *decision of the heart*: "For where your treasure is, there will your heart be also.... No one can serve two masters."[156] "If we live by the Spirit, let us also walk by the Spirit."[157] In this assent to the Holy Spirit the Father gives us strength. "No testing has overtaken you that is not common to man. God is
1808 faithful, and he will not let you be tempted beyond your strength, but with the temptation will also provide the way of escape, so that you may be able to endure it."[158]

2849 Such a battle and such a victory become possible only through prayer. It is by his prayer that Jesus vanquishes the tempter, both at the outset of his public mission and in the ultimate struggle of his agony.[159] In this petition to our heavenly Father, Christ unites us to his battle
540, 612 and his agony. He urges us to *vigilance* of the heart in communion with his own. Vigilance is "custody of the heart," and Jesus prayed for us to the Father: "Keep them in your 2612
name."[160] The Holy Spirit constantly seeks to awaken us to keep watch.[161] Finally, this petition takes on all its dramatic meaning in relation to the last temptation of our earthly battle; it asks for final *perseverance*. "Lo, I am coming like a thief! Blessed is he
who is awake."[162] 162

VII. "But Deliver Us from Evil"

2850 The last petition to our Father is also included in Jesus' prayer: "I am not asking you to take them out of the world, but I ask you to protect them from the evil one."[163] It touches each of us personally, but it is always "we" who pray, in communion with the whole Church, for the deliverance of the whole human family. The Lord's Prayer continually opens us to the range of God's economy of salvation. Our interdependence in the drama of sin and death is turned into
solidarity in the Body of Christ, the 309
"communion of saints."[164]

2851 In this petition, evil is not an abstraction, but refers to a person, Satan, the Evil One, the angel who opposes God. The devil (*dia-bolos*) is
the one who "throws himself across" 391
God's plan and his work of salvation accomplished in Christ.

2852 "A murderer from the beginning,...a liar and the father of lies," Satan is "the deceiver of the whole world."[165] Through him sin and death entered the world and by his definitive defeat all creation will be "freed from the corruption of sin and death."[166] Now "we know that anyone born of God does not sin,

[154] Cf. *Gen* 3:6. — [155] Origen, *De orat.* 29: PG 11, 544CD. — [156] *Mt* 6:21, 24. — [157] *Gal* 5:25. — [158] *1 Cor* 10:13. — [159] Cf. *Mt* 4:1–11; 26:36–44. — [160] *Jn* 17:11; cf. *Mk* 13:9, 23, 33–37; 14:38; *Lk* 12:35–40. — [161] Cf. *1 Cor* 16:13; *Col* 4:2; *1 Thess* 5:6; *1 Pet* 5:8. — [162] *Rev* 16:15. — [163] *Jn* 17:15. — [164] Cf. *RP* 16. — [165] *Jn* 8:44; *Rev* 12:9. — [166] *Roman Missal*, Eucharistic Prayer IV, 125.

but He who was born of God keeps him, and the evil one does not touch him. We know that we are of God, and the whole world is in the power of the evil one."[167]

> The Lord who has taken away your sin and pardoned your faults also protects you and keeps you from the wiles of your adversary the devil, so that the enemy, who is accustomed to leading into sin, may not surprise you. One who entrusts himself to God does not dread the devil. "If God is for us, who is against us?"[168]

677 **2853** Victory over the "prince of this world"[169] was won once for all at the Hour when Jesus freely gave himself up to death to give us his life. This is the judgment of this world, and the prince of this world is "cast out."[170] "He pursued the woman"[171] but had no hold on her: the new Eve, "full of grace" of the Holy Spirit, is preserved from sin and the
972 corruption of death (the Immaculate Conception and the Assumption of the Most Holy Mother of God, Mary, ever virgin). "Then the dragon was angry with the woman, and went off to make war on the rest of her offspring."[172] Therefore the Spirit and the Church pray: "Come, Lord Jesus,"[173] since his coming will deliver us from the Evil One.

2854 When we ask to be delivered from the Evil One, we pray as well to be freed from all evils, present, past, and future, of which he is the author or instigator. In this final petition, the Church brings before the Father all the distress of the world. Along with deliverance from the evils that overwhelm humanity, she implores the precious gift of peace and the grace of perseverance in expectation of Christ's return. By praying in this 2632
way, she anticipates in humility of faith the gathering together of everyone and everything in him who has "the keys of Death and Hades," who "is and who was and who is to come, the Almighty."[174]

> Deliver us, Lord, we beseech you, from every evil and grant us peace in our day, so that aided by your mercy we might be ever free from sin and protected from all anxiety, as we await the blessed hope and the coming of our Savior, Jesus Christ.[175] 1041

Article 4:
THE FINAL DOXOLOGY

2760 **2855** The final doxology, "For the kingdom, the power and the glory are yours, now and forever," takes up again, by inclusion, the first three petitions to our Father: the glorification of his name, the coming of his reign, and the power of his saving will. But these prayers are now proclaimed as adoration and thanksgiving, as in the liturgy of heaven.[176]

[167] *1 Jn* 5:18–19. — [168] St. Ambrose, *De Sacr.* 5, 4, 30: PL 16, 454; cf. *Rom* 8:31. [169] *Jn* 14:30. — [170] *Jn* 12:31; *Rev* 12:10. — [171] *Rev* 12:13–16. — [172] *Rev* 12:17. — [173] *Rev* 22:17, 20. — [174] *Rev* 1:8, 18; cf. *Rev* 1:4; *Eph* 1:10. — [175] *Roman Missal,* Embolism after the Lord's Prayer, 126: *Libera nos, quæsumus, Domine, ab omnibus malis, da propitius pacem in diebus nostris, ut, ope misericordiæ tuæ adiuti, et a peccato simus semper liberi, et ab omni perturbatione securi: expectantes beatam spem et adventum Salvatoris nostri Iesu Christi.* — [176] Cf. *Rev* 1:6; 4:11; 5:13.

The ruler of this world has mendaciously attributed to himself the three titles of kingship, power, and glory.[177] Christ, the Lord, restores them to his Father and our Father, until he hands over the kingdom to him when the mystery of salvation will be brought to its completion and God will be all in all.[178]

1061–1065 **2856** "Then, after the prayer is over you say 'Amen,' which means 'So be it,' thus ratifying with our 'Amen' what is contained in the prayer that God has taught us."[179]

In Brief

2857 *In the Our Father, the object of the first three petitions is the glory of the Father: the sanctification of his name, the coming of the kingdom, and the fulfillment of his will. The four others present our wants to him: they ask that our lives be nourished, healed of sin, and made victorious in the struggle of good over evil.*

2858 *By asking "hallowed be thy name" we enter into God's plan, the sanctification of his name—revealed first to Moses and then in Jesus—by us and in us, in every nation and in each man.*

2859 *By the second petition, the Church looks first to Christ's return and the final coming of the Reign of God. It also prays for the growth of the Kingdom of God in the "today" of our own lives.*

2860 *In the third petition, we ask our Father to unite our will to that of his Son, so as to fulfill his plan of salvation in the life of the world.*

2861 *In the fourth petition, by saying "give us," we express in communion with our brethren our filial trust in our heavenly Father. "Our daily bread" refers to the earthly nourishment necessary to everyone for subsistence, and also to the Bread of Life: the Word of God and the Body of Christ. It is received in God's "today," as the indispensable, (super-) essential nourishment of the feast of the coming Kingdom anticipated in the Eucharist.*

2862 *The fifth petition begs God's mercy for our offences, mercy which can penetrate our hearts only if we have learned to forgive our enemies, with the example and help of Christ.*

2863 *When we say "lead us not into temptation" we are asking God not to allow us to take the path that leads to sin. This petition implores the Spirit of discernment and strength; it requests the grace of vigilance and final perseverance.*

2864 *In the last petition, "but deliver us from evil," Christians pray to God with the Church to show forth the victory, already won by Christ, over the "ruler of this world," Satan, the angel personally opposed to God and to his plan of salvation.*

2865 *By the final "Amen," we express our "fiat" concerning the seven petitions: "So be it."*

[177] Cf. *Lk* 4:5–6. — [178] *1 Cor* 15:24–28. — [179] St. Cyril of Jerusalem, *Catech. myst.* 5, 18: PG 33, 1124; cf. *Lk* 1:38.

THEOLOGICAL AND PASTORAL COMMENTARY

AUTHORS

Director and coordinator: **Rino Fisichella**

Vincenzo Battaglia
Christology, Pontifical University Antonianum, Rome

Giuseppe Biancardi
Catechetics, Salesian Pontifical University, Faculty of Theology, Torino

Enzo Bianchi
Founder, Monastic Community of Bose

Goffredo Boselli
Liturgy, monk of Bose

Pier Giordano Cabra
Former president of the Conference of Religious Orders in Italy (CISM) and in Europe (UCESM)

Anna Maria Cànopi
Abbess, "Mater Ecclesiae" Benedictine Abbey, Isola San Giulio, Orta

Martín Carbajo Núñez
Moral theology, Pontifical University Antonianum, Rome

Juan Carlos Carvajal Blanco
Theology of evangelization and catechesis, San Dámaso Ecclesiastical University, Madrid

Mauro Cozzoli
Moral theology, Pontifical Lateran University, Rome

Gaetano De Simone
Social doctrine of the Church, Pontifical Lateran University, Rome

Carmelo Dotolo
Theology of religions, Pontifical Urban University, Rome

Caroline Farey
Director of Studies, School of Annunciation, Buckfast Abbey, Devon

Rino Fisichella
President, Pontifical Council for the Promotion of the New Evangelization

Aristide Fumagalli
Moral theology, Theological Faculty of Northern Italy, Milan

José M. Galván
Moral theology, Pontifical University of the Holy Cross, Rome

Renzo Gerardi
Moral theology, Pontifical Lateran University, Rome

Philip Goyret
Ecclesiology, Pontifical University of the Holy Cross, Rome

Manuel José Jiménez R.
Pastoral theology, Center of Formation for the New Evangelization and Catechesis (CEFNEC), Bogotá

Luis F. Ladaria
Prefect, Congregation for the Doctrine of the Faith

Ramón Lucas Lucas
Philosophical anthropology and bioethics, Pontifical Gregorian University, Rome

Sabatino Majorano
Systematic moral theology, Alphonsian Academy, Rome

Raffaello Martinelli
Bishop of Frascati, former Secretary of the Commission for the preparation of the *CCC*

Giulio Maspero
Dogmatic theology, Pontifical University of the Holy Cross, Rome

Edward McNamara
Liturgy, Pontifical Athenaeum Regina Apostolorum, Rome

Cettina Militello
Ecclesiology and Mariology, Professor emeritus at the Pontifical Theological Faculty Marianum, Rome

Antonio Miralles
Sacramental theology, Professor emeritus at the Pontifical University of the Holy Cross, Rome

Joël Molinario
Practical theology, Director of the Institut Supérieur de Pastorale Catéchétique, Paris

Paul O'Callaghan
Theological anthropology, Pontifical University of the Holy Cross, Rome

Salvador Pié-Ninot
Fundamental theology, Faculty of Theology of Catalonia, Barcelona; Pontifical Gregorian University, Rome

María del Pilar Rio García
Sacramental theology, Pontifical University of the Holy Cross, Rome

Ignace de la Potterie (June 24, 1914–September 11, 2003)
Biblicist, Pontifical Biblical Institute

Ángel Rodríguez Luño
Moral theology, Pontifical University of the Holy Cross, Rome

Michael Schneider
Dogmatic theology and liturgy, Sankt Georgen Graduate School of Philosophy and Theology, Frankfurt am Main

Christoph Schönborn
Archbishop of Vienna

Ina Siviglia
Theological anthropology, Pontifical Theological Faculty of Sicily, Palermo

Réal Tremblay
Moral theology, Professor emeritus at the Alphonsian Academy, Rome

Ugo Vanni
New Testament exegesis, Professor emeritus at the Pontifical Gregorian University, Rome

Thomas Joseph White
Systematic theology, Pontifical Faculty of the Immaculate Conception, Washington, D.C.

Jared Wicks
History of theology, Jesuit School of Theology, Chicago

Regina Willi
Spiritual theology, Institute for Historical Theology, Vienna

Stefano Zamboni
Moral theology, Alphonsian Academy, Rome

Cataldo Zuccaro
Moral theology, Pontifical Urban University, Rome

ABBREVIATIONS

AA	Apostolicam actuositatem (November 18, 1965)
AG	Ad gentes (December 7, 1965)
AL	Amoris laetitia (March 19, 2016)
AS	Acta Synodalia Sacrosancti Concilii Oecumenici Vaticani II, 1970–1980
BA	Bibliothèque augustinienne, Paris: Brepols, 1933f.
CCC	Catechism of the Catholic Church (October 11, 1992)
CD	Christus Dominus (October 28, 1965)
ChL	Christifideles laici (December 30, 1988)
CIC	Codex Iuris Canonici
CT	Catechesi tradendae (October 16, 1979)
CV	Caritas in veritate (June 29, 2009)
DaS	Divino afflante Spiritu (September 30, 1943)
DB	"The Renewal of Catechesis," base document on catechesis, Italian Bishops Conference (February 2, 1970)
DCE	Deus caritas est (December 25, 2005)
DCG	General Catechetical Directory (April 11, 1971)
DeV	Dominum et vivificantem (May 18, 1986)
DGC	General Directory for Catechesis (August 15, 1997)
DF	Dei Filius (April 24, 1970)
DH	Dignitatis humanae (December 7, 1965)
DP	Dignitas personae (December 12, 2008)
DV	Dei Verbum (November 18, 1965)
EB	Enchiridion Biblicum, Bologna: EDB, 1993
EG	Evangelii gaudium (November 24, 2013)
EN	Evangelii nuntiandi (December 8, 1975)
EO	Enchiridion Oecumenicum, Bologna, EDB, 1986f.
EV	Enchiridion Vaticanum, Bologna: EDB, 1976f.
EVi	Evangelium vitae (March 25, 1995)
FC	Familiaris consortio (November 22, 1981)
FD	Fidei depositum (October 11, 1992)
FR	Fides et ratio (September 14, 1998)
GS	Gaudium et spes (December 7, 1965)
HG	Humani generis (August 12, 1950)
HV	Humanae vitae (July 25, 1968)
ID	Indulgentiarum doctrina (January 1, 1967)
LF	Lumen fidei (June 29, 2013)
LG	Lumen gentium (November 21, 1964)

LS Laudato si' (May 24, 2015)

Mansi J.D. Mansi, Sanctorum Conciliorum et Decretorum collectio nova...

MC Mystici corporis Christi (June 29, 1943)

MD Mediator Dei (November 20, 1947)

ME Mysterium Ecclesiae (July 5, 1973)

MQ Ministeria quaedam (August 15, 1972)

NA Nostra aetate (October 28, 1965)

OGMR General Instruction of the Roman Missal (January 25, 2004)

OICA Order of Christian Initiation of Adults (January 6, 1972)

OS Ordinatio sacerdotalis (May 22, 1994)

PDV Pastores dabo vobis (March 25, 1992)

PF Porta fidei (October 11, 2011)

PO Presbyterorum ordinis (December 7, 1965)

RBB Rite of Baptism of Children (May 31, 1970)

RC Rite of Confirmation (April 29, 1972)

RH Redemptor hominis (March 4, 1979)

RICA Rite of Christian Initiation of Adults (January 30, 1978); see OICA

RM Redemptoris Mater (March 25, 1987)

SA Slavorum Apostoli (June 2, 1985)

SaC Sacramentum caritatis (February 22, 2007)

SC Sacrosanctum Concilium (December 4, 1963)

SD Salvifici doloris (February 11, 1984)

SF Sensus fidei (June 10, 2014)

SRS Sollicitudo rei socialis (December 30, 1987)

UR Unitatis redintegratio (November 21, 1964)

UUS Ut unum sint (May 25, 1995)

VC Vita consecrata (March 25, 1996)

VD Verbum Domini (September 30, 2010)

VS Veritatis splendor (August 6, 1993)

INTRODUCTORY QUESTIONS

THE CATECHISM OF THE CATHOLIC CHURCH IN THE HISTORY OF CATECHISMS

A historical overview

Giuseppe Biancardi

Without a doubt, the word "catechism" deserves to be listed among the most widespread terms of the Christian lexicon, common to Catholics and Protestants. For centuries, in a single word it has named the *moment* of ecclesial catechesis, its *content*, and the *text* that, in various ways but organically, assembles that same content which every good catechist is called to communicate to those being catechized. Our attention here is centered mainly on the catechism understood as that little handbook that quickly becomes "the" instrument *par excellence* for catechesis in all the Christian communities, and therefore today can boast a history of multiple centuries, indeed varied and interesting; a history that has reached to our day, and with the relatively recent publication of the *CCC* (1992–1997) has seen one of its most notable moments.

For a better understanding of this latest authoritative *Catechism*, it can be useful now to retrace, though only in outline, the histories of the catechism books that preceded it. That is the purpose of these introductory pages.

I. The Roots of the Catechism Text in the Patristic and Medieval Eras

These "remote" roots can already be traced in the catecheses of the Fathers, which illustrate the creed, the *Our Father*, the sacraments, morality: that is, the most important core themes of future catechisms. In St. Augustine in particular, we find the justification for the linkage: creed; faith and prayer; hope, in addition to one of the first attestations of the term *catechismus*.

As for the Middle Ages, where we can identify the "proximate roots" of the helps we are concerned with, there are countless diocesan synods and provincial councils to mention that list the fundamental themes of all religious instruction, assembling them around creed, morality, sacraments, and prayer.

The same contents are repeated in the first instruments developed for pastors with the care of souls, such as the *Artes praedicandi*, which summarize themes of preaching about the *quid credendum* (creed), *quid petendum* (*Our Father* and prayer in general), *quid faciendum et vitandum* (morality), and *quid sperandum* (the Last Things). The same can be said of the very widespread *Elucidari*, which explain Christian truths, or of texts that aid the confessor in his ministry (*Summae poenitentiae*, the *Summae confessorum*, the *Confessionalia* and the *Confessiones generales*): helps that propose very detailed schemas for the examination of conscience, thereby underscoring the importance of the moral component of catechesis, which will in fact occupy the greater part of most catechetical manuals.

We find a more precise sketch of the catechism, understood in the modern sense, between the Middle Ages and the Renaissance. For example, this is the case of the celebrated *Opus tripartitum de praeceptis decalogi, de confessione et de arte moriendi* attributed to Jean Gerson (1363–1429), and of the catechetical works of Erasmus of Rotterdam (1469–1536), from whom came the *Christiani hominis institutum*, rendered in splendid Latin hendecasyllables for students in the humanistic schools.

II. The Catechism from the 1500s to the 1800s

The Affirmation of the Catechism as Text

The "birth," or rather, the affirmation, of the catechism proper should be placed in the 1500s. Above all, this is the century that saw the catechetical initiative of the Reformers, in particular of Luther (1483–1546), who in 1529 wrote both his "large" catechism and the yet more famous "small" catechism or *Enchiridion*, followed shortly by Calvin (1509–1564).

In the following decades we note the writing in the Catholic sphere of several texts destined to become "classics" and to be used for centuries across vast geographical and cultural areas. Among these we should at least mention, in chronological order, the works of St. Peter Canisius (1521–1597), author of a *Summa doctrinae christianae* (1555) for university students, which he immediately reduced to a *Catechismus minimus* (1556) and a *Parvus catechismus* (1558–1559) for the lower levels of study. Then we find the *Catechismus ad parochos*, or *Roman Catechism*, ordered by the Council of Trent and promulgated by St. Pius V in 1566: the most authoritative catechism of the whole modern and contemporary age. Furthermore, in the last decade of the century two books were written in Spain whose paternity is disputed among the two Jesuits Jerónimo de Ripalda (1563–1618) and Gaspar Astete (1573–1601). The passing of the 1500s finally saw the drafting of two other classic and enduring books under the rubric of "doctrine," in the work of St. Robert Bellarmine (1542–1621): his renowned *Dottrina cristiana breve* is from 1597, followed the next year by the *More copious declaration of Christian doctrine*.

Continuing along the same lines, there is a whole swarm of catechisms that spread not only in the long-Christian West, but also in the new worlds that were being discovered and evangelized just at the start of the modern age, from America to Asia.

The variety of texts, however, does not negate the presence of common elements and certain constants in them that can be easily traced through the whole modern era, and even to the 1800s and beyond.

Fundamental Reasons for the Origin of the Catechism

Catechisms have in common, first of all, two fundamental reasons for which they were developed.

In the 1500s, Catholics and Protestants published these instruments mainly to expound their respective doctrines against the opposing positions, and thus for a polemical and controversialist purpose. But this reason would decline gradually in the subsequent centuries, leaving more and more room for another motive, which would be continually present at the origin of every catechism, whether medieval or contemporary: to do battle against the abysmal religious ignorance that strikes Christian people at all levels, from the poorest and most outcast classes to the upper clergy. The denunciation of this deplorable situation was so strong that it became habitual, at least up to the 1700s, to compare the nominally Christian populace of Europe to infidels of the faraway Indies which, at the time, were being discovered: "Our Indies are here!" in the old continent.

From this came the unavoidable urgency to remedy a situation counted as intolerable, a cause of immorality, superstition or falling into heresy, and consequently eternal damnation. It became imperative, then, to make the content of the faith known to all, as Trent's repeated directives about preaching in general make clear, and more so about instituting parish catechesis of children, which had been unknown in the medieval era. The urgency of evangelization therefore found one of its best known and longest lasting realizations precisely in fostering a catechetical instruction that sought to be as systematic and universal as possible, supported and guided by the catechism book, understood "*quasi Christi Domini gramatica,*" that is, as a complete handbook of what a Christian is obliged to know in order to live as a Christian and obtain eternal salvation.

The Concept of the Catechism from the 1500s to the 1800s

The authors of the various catechisms also had common intentions and inspiring principles that guided their work, even if they did not always turn out in the application.

The catechism, at least according to its compilers' intentions, is in fact a "popular text," intended for simple people ignorant in matters of the faith, even if there were works for students and cultured people (such as the *Summa* of Canisius) and for pastors in the narrow sense (the *Catechismus ad parochos*).

Moreover, this instructional aid was intended to be an "exact and reliable summary of Christian doctrine." As such, the catechism would have to express only "known truths" of dogma and morality, excluding particular opinions of the various theological schools. In fact, the modern era has noted the drafting of various texts that took on the spreading of particular theological visions, so much so that quite a few of them ended up on the Index. As an example, it will suffice to mention the notable production of works inspired by Jansenism.

As to form, it should be clear, precise, easy to understand and remember, aided by its brevity, since the catechism is intended to be learned by memory. In reality we actually will have catechetical books corresponding to those objectives, but many others will turn out to be anything but clear and limited to the essentials. This happens because the editor of a catechism considers himself above all to be at the service of truths to be communicated, and as a rule, does not show himself to be particularly sensitive to concerns of the psycho-pedagogical and didactic order which we routinely consider in any form of instruction, including religious instruction.

In almost every case the catechism, be it short or long, is organized according to the didactic methodology of "question and answer," a formulation that with time becomes almost sacred and therefore untouchable. As evidence of this, we will have to wait until 1955 to find a catechism whose expression of the Magisterium, prescinding from the model of Trent, is edited in a discursive form and no longer in questions and answers; this was the year of the publication of the famous *Katholischer Katechismus der Bistümer Deutschlands* ["Catholic Catechism of the Dioceses of Germany"; English translation, *A Catholic Catechism*, Herder, 1959.]

The Structuring of Content

Basic Schemas and Their Theological Value

At first glance, catechisms can give the impression of having been edited on the basis of numerous disparate designs. In reality, that appearance only applies to the embryonic phase of their history, because at least since the 1500s the structure they follow can be traced back to two basic traditions that endure to our day.

The older schema took form from the beginnings of the 16th century and distributes the arguments clearly in *four parts* on the basis of the theological virtues, the sacraments, and the duties of Christian life. The material of religious instruction is collected within the following cores:

– the *symbol* or *creed* that illustrates *faith*;

– *commandments* that specify in detail how *charity* is lived;

– *prayer* which recalls *hope*, inasmuch as—according to the teaching of Augustine—prayer reminds man of the goods for which he can hope and whom he must ask for them;

– the sacraments.

At times this schema was completed with a "fifth part" in which space is set aside for the exposition of truths that are not essentials of the faith, and especially for a detailed listing of "the duties of Christian life." Because of this, we can consider the last portion as a simple reprise of the moral part of the catechism; this becomes understandable in light of Catholic arguments directed against the Protestant doctrine that denied the value of merit in human acts.

This "quadripartite" schema is characteristic of the "classic" formularies of the 1500s, starting with those of Luther and Calvin, and moving on to the texts of Canisius, Trent, Astete, Ripalda, and Bellarmine. We continue to find a schema in four (or five) parts in some 16th-century French texts with a historical and biblical structure; in the *Compendio* (1765) by the bishop Michele Casati (1699–1782), a distant source of the first catechism of Pius X (1905), and in many "official" catechisms of today, including the *CCC*.

The second schema came later and saw notable success in growth from the 17th to the 19th century. It can be defined as "tripartite," as it was constructed from the starting point of man's threefold duty toward God: 1) to *believe*, 2) to *observe* the commandments, and 3) to "use the means" at his disposal to enable himself to believe and observe. Starting from this logic, this schema appears analogous to the earlier one in the first two parts. The difference is found when we come to the treatment of "sacraments and prayer," precisely because they are considered *in a unitary way as means*, which the faithful must *use to obtain grace* needed for the purpose of "believing and observing" the commandments.

This model also appears periodically in the history of catechisms, as witness, for example, the exposition of Jansenist texts and the famous *Catéchisme imperial* of Napoleon (1806), and finding its greatest theological rigorization later through the 1800s, specifically in catechetical works inspired by neoscholasticism, which will significantly influence the editing of Pius X's 1912 catechism, among other things. In this text, question (and answer) number 27 nicely expresses the "logic" of the "tripartite" distribution of Christian truths: "What must I do to live according to God? To live according to God, I must *believe* the truths revealed by him and *observe his commandments*, with the help of his *grace*, which is obtained by means of the *sacraments and prayer*."

In regard to the distribution of topics in catechetical formularies, we can briefly raise two more observations.

In the first schema, the order in which the categories are placed is not casual, but obedient to a precise theological design. In Luther's choice to place the presentation of the commandments at the beginning of his catechisms (1529), followed by the exposition of the Creed, one can grasp a reflection of his vision of the human being, which he considers incapable of meritorious works and brought to salvation only by faith in divine grace. In effect, the ten commandments presented immediately at the start of the pathway of catechesis—to take up the image from the Reformer himself—show clearly to man that he is sick and can be cured (saved) only by recourse to the medicine of faith. The same can be said of Calvin's *Instruction et confession de foy* (1537); however in the *Formulaire* of 1542 he turns to put faith in the foreground, in analogy with the Catholic perspective, because the fundamental end of human life is to know and love God.

Analogous observations can be developed around the Catholic formularies. Generally, those that follow the "quadripartite" structure give priority to the treatment of faith and sacraments (liturgy), placing morals and prayer in the background. Now, texts of this type can be considered more correct from the theological point of view, because they are authentically "theocentric." Indeed they recognize in the first place the initiative of God in drawing near to man, through a history of salvation which is summarized in the Creed and actualized in liturgical-sacramental signs, while only in a second stage do they illustrate the duties of man before the divinity; that is, the observance of the law and prayer. In contrast, other catechisms, in particular those that develop the "tripartite" schema based on the religious duties of man, should be reckoned as less precise from a theological perspective, on the ground that they are too "anthropocentric," in the sense that they would put the person and what he "must do" in the foreground.

The Predominance of the Catechism Understood as a Theological Synthesis or Catechism "Text"

Another fact about the structuring of content in catechism books, made evident by historiography, is the clear predominance of texts that express the Christian message with the conceptual equipment of theological language, through all the modern era and up to the Second Vatican Council, to the extent that they could be considered little "summas" that conveyed the contents of theology manuals to the masses of the faithful in summary form. In effect, while the first embryonic catechisms were drawn up principally with moralistic intent, to help the faithful "live well and die well" (one thinks of Gerson's *Opus tripartitum*), the catechetical aids of the modern era, starting particularly from Calvin and his *Formulaire*, become progressively more dominated by the concern for catechetical communication that is precise and complete from the theological point of view.

In the history of the catechism it all too often happens that what is authoritatively defined is worn down to a theologizing or even rationalizing version of it: the formulary expresses "doctrine," doctrine rendered theologically or even philosophically, with a shift of accent that even reverberates in common speech, where "going to the catechism" becomes "going to the doctrine," that is, to a popular-level school of theology in which texts are taught by rote: texts that significantly bear titles such as "Compendium of Christian Doctrine" or simply "Christian Doctrine."

Among the causes of this phenomenon, which developed over centuries, we can list in chronological order the controversies among the various Christian confessions and the debates in systematic and moral theology within the Catholic Church herself. Later, the influence of the Enlightenment was decisive, developing in two directions. On one hand, analogously to what took place in the sphere of theology, it became the source of a catechesis with an evidently rationalist streak. On the other hand, the Age of Enlightenment reacted, in a theological and rationalistic mode, to the mythical contents of quite a few earlier catechisms, and found unacceptable certain obviously legendary, imaginary, or miraculistic elements present in texts even as authoritative as Bellarmine's and, more so, in other lesser known catechisms. The same orientation continued to grow in the 1800s, when conflict with modernity induced the Church to reaffirm her own truths by promoting the contribution of neo-scholastic and neo-Thomist reflection for this purpose and generating a catechesis that emphasizes the motive of theological integrity and systematicity, together with the rational component of the Christian proposition.

It will not be shocking that in the 19th century some emphasized the difficulty of writing a catechism, inasmuch as it would need to be a "compendium of theology" but brief and summary. Nor will anyone be surprised at the condemnation expressed by the noted neo-scholastic Jesuit Giovanni Perrone toward a catechism prepared by Bishop Guglielmo Massaja (1809–1889) for the Galla people of Ethiopia, with a notable effort at "inculturation": a condemnation motivated by the fact that the censor refused "to consider 'theology' this text stuffed with barbarisms and almost completely bereft of the 'technical terms of theology manuals.'"

One can affirm, then, that in the greater part of cases the 16th to 19th centuries left us catechetical formularies worked out with the overriding concern of expressing the content of the faith in full integrity and orthodoxy, fixed upon the technical language of theology. Texts principally focused on "fidelity to God" and much less on "fidelity to man," to take up a famous expression of the catechist Joseph Colomb (1902–1979).

In short, if we may make our own the terminology which Cardinal Joseph Ratzinger will use in the famous conference he held at Lyon and Paris in January 1983, the little book of doctrine that spread into the whole Catholic Church between the 1500s and the 1800s is the catechism "text": a theologically systematized listing of the doctrinal contents of the Catholic Christian faith, prior to any further word of explanation, adaptation, and "inculturation" toward those being catechized: certainly a necessary work, but one that should be entrusted to second-order catechisms called "commentaries."

The Scarcity of Historical-Biblical and Liturgical Catechisms

The dominance of one line of theological exposition, however, did not prevent the occasional emergence of catechisms with a more historical-biblical and also liturgical structure, catechisms that consistently tend to remain the expression of a pastoral minority or undercurrent.

The minority status of this form appears even more evident if we broaden our view to a quick comparison with Protestant practice, particularly in regard to the biblical dimension. While in the Protestant sphere there is a strong sensitivity to the link between doctrine and the history of salvation, the Catholic milieu distanced itself from the patristic concept in which catechesis is eminently a *narratio historiae salutis*; this happened because of the well known directives about biblical matters following the Council of Trent. Therefore the Bible, when it is present at all in the catechism, was limited to accompanying and supporting its doctrinal contents, with the result that it is cited sporadically, in a fragmentary way, as a collection of moralistic *exempla* and proof-texts invoked to support truths boxed in predefined schemas that are not really those of the Bible.

Yet limitations and difficulties in the use of the sacred text did not mean a total exclusion. Already in the 1500s, the hierarchical prohibitions about printing, vernacular translation, distribution and commentary on the sacred books did not completely exclude reference to the Bible in the "doctrine" books as well.

With the 17th century we observe a notable stress on attention to Scripture in the Catholic camp as well. It has been rightly said that for various reasons, "the return to the Bible is a phenomenon of great proportions in the 1600s and 1700s" (P. Braido). In this context it is possible to find several catechetical texts committed to presenting the themes of the faith in a more markedly historical-biblical mode; and the phenomenon will be repeated periodically until late in the 1900s, though remaining, as was said above, always a minority phenomenon, compared to the massive prevalence of catechisms written in a theological mode.

In the 1600s and 1700s, the most significant authors turn out to be the Frenchmen J. B. Bossuet (1627–1704), C. Fleury (1640–1723), and F. Fénelon (1651–1715). In all three, reference to the Bible is justified fundamentally on the basis of psycho-pedagogical and didactic reasons: that is, biblical narrative is valued inasmuch as the narrative makes the teaching more attractive and hence proves more effective for learning religious truths, especially for the young and the unlearned. But a theological reason is also present in them, at least at an embryonic level: the catechism has to be substantiated by historical-biblical narrative because God himself reveals himself in a *historia salutis*. The reading of these three authors, above all Fleury, even if not universally understood, will exercise a certain influence, even on more theological books: many "doctrine" books coming after them will tell a summary of sacred history, or history of religion in general, or yet again, history of the Church, as a preface, or more often, as an appendix.

In the 1700s the Bible finds a greater place in schools of the lands under the Hapsburg crown, starting in Austria. But here sacred history becomes a true discipline in itself alongside the doctrinal catechism. This was related to the need to prepare handbooks of biblical history and school Bibles, works in which Jesuits and Piarists will distinguish themselves. In that century, apart from its utilization in the school environment, the sacred text continues to be presented in a predominantly ethical and civil manner, through the influence of Enlightenment thought.

While the 1800s, on one hand, saw the Bible valued for its usefulness to apologetics and dogmatics, they also knew the call for a more biblical catechesis and catechisms, in the framework for innovation suggested by the theological school at Tübingen, as well as the *Catechismo disposto secondo l'ordine delle idee* [Catechism presented according to the order of the ideas] by Antonio Rosmini (1797–1855).

The liturgy, considered as a whole, was not given specific treatment, inasmuch as the writers of catechisms, for the most part, focused their attention on the sacraments considered individually. When the liturgy is discussed, it is spoken of simply as the collection of ecclesiastical "ceremonies." It was accorded greater attention by the "catechisms of the feasts": this refers to texts for adults, likely of French origin, that develop catechesis starting from the mysteries celebrated on the Sundays and feasts of the liturgical year, repeating the question-answer model. Bossuet and de la Salle (1651–1719) were involved in preparing catechisms of this type, producing emblematic formularies by their attention to the liturgical day.

The Catechism and Moral and Ideological Content

In addition to a theologizing and rationalizing tendency, the catechism saw another, in the area of morals, with the result that it came to emphasize the ethical content of the Christian message. And this further turn was justified by various reasons that came to impose themselves with the passage of time. They were certainly and primarily of the theological order, and easily understood when one thinks of the debates that shook modern theology from within during the modern era, the emphasis on ethics drawn from Jansenism, and the development of the catechetical schema in three parts, structured on the basis of the threefold "duty" of the human person.

But also one cannot forget the close tie that united the civil and religious powers in the modern age. Although conflictual at times, the relation between the two powers remained rooted, inducing the Church to develop a pastoral approach that was also useful to the political ideology of the *ancien régime*. Thus in the sphere of catechesis, in addition to the extreme case of catechisms written suitably for slaves, we find formularies that, for reasons of faith, justify social stratification and the corporatism of old-regime societies, considering the presence of wealth and poverty as something willed by God, inviting the poor to resign themselves to it, and signaling that stealing is a very serious sin, even if done out of necessity. By the same logic, from the presupposition that power is of divine origin, the catechism inculcates a total and undisputed obedience to the political authorities, in insistent tones.

In the light of this moral-ideological component, one can very well understand the marked interest that political powers have shown, over the course of centuries, in the books of doctrine used by their subjects. The "catechetical policy" put into action by Maria Theresa of Austria in the last decades of the 1700s can be considered an exemplary moment of this attention, and especially the promulgation of Napoleon's *Catéchisme imperial* (1806), a text in which the most important "lesson" is the seventh, *"l'irritante leçon VII"* (B. Plongeron), which—without saying so—illustrates the duties of subjects toward the emperor Bonaparte, in detail and with minute precision.

Catechism and "Inculturation"

Continuing to study the catechism books of the centuries that interest us, under the aspect of their content, we may wonder whether they contain elements that we commonly describe today as "inculturation," or in other terms, if it is possible to find "inculturated" content in them. The question obviously applies above all to catechism books that were present in territories outside Europe. Now it is evident that, lest we fall into a gross anachronism, one cannot pretend to find the full application of the principle of inculturation as it currently understood in these catechetical aids. At most we may notice some significant attempts at "adaptation" or "accommodation" of the Christian message to the local culture in them, conducted in a pastoral context where the most convenient tendency predominated: to simply translate the European texts into the native languages, an undertaking that is already objectively difficult by itself, as one can easily intuit, due to the notable difference in the cultural universes involved in that operation.

Between the 1500s and the 1800s, greater experiments of "inculturation" were also unthinkable because of a certain ambivalence shown in directives issued by Rome, particularly from the Congregation of *Propaganda Fide*. Actually that organ of the curia, erected by Gregory XV in early 1622, rightly understood at least an embryonic idea of inculturation, in various documents directed to the missionary world, as when it urged missionaries to learn the language of the natives perfectly or when it emphasized the need to respect local cultures, without wanting to submit them to Western culture. But the practice developed by that Congregation did not always turn out in harmony with the previous theoretical pronouncements. Leaving aside the decisions about the "question of rites," which were due to other curial institutions, it is noteworthy that by 1626, scarcely four years after its founding, the Congregation set up a multi-lingual printing house in Rome, where various catechisms were printed in numerous languages. Almost always, though, they were texts from Bellarmine and the *Roman Catechism*, simply "exported" to the farthest countries. And in 1632, to give another example, the Vatican Congregation, with the aim of stilling the pastoral divergences between missionaries of different religious families, imposed the adoption of Bellarmine's text on the mission of Japan: a text that spread quickly in Asia, which ended up considerably promoting a deepening of the psychological as well as social ghetto in which Christian communities on the continent came to find themselves.

In any case, we do have catechetical aids that sought to incarnate the communication of Christianity into the cultural worlds of populations outside of Europe.

The efforts completed in Latin America (Mexico) turn out particularly significant in this sense, by means of catechisms called "pictographic," because they tried to translate the complex Western-style articulation of logically formal discourse into language of a symbolic type, proper to the ideograms of Aztec culture. Equally eloquent witness of the same line of pastoral activity is the first catechetical book (and probably the first book altogether) written in Spanish in the New World. It is a text prepared at Santo Domingo by the Dominican Pedro de Córdoba (1482–1521), which reached the island in 1510, and was printed posthumously under the title *Doctrina Cristiana para instrucción e información de los Indios por manera de historia.* In this work the Christian proclamation is ordered in a historical-narrative order, as an instrument more suited to the indigenous mentality, used to organizing religious reality not on dogmatic truths but around a mythic account of the origin of the gods and the world.

Evidence of an embryonic catechetical "inculturation" is also noticeable in Asia. For India it will suffice to recall the courageous efforts of the Jesuit Roberto de Nobili (1577–1656); for China the famous efforts of the other renowned Jesuits Michele Ruggeri (1543–1607) and Matteo Ricci (1522–1610). Also important, if less known, is the analogous work developed in other areas of Asia such as Japan and Vietnam.

The "inculturation" that advanced in the modern era and reached the 1800s, however, became less daring bit by bit, as witness in the mid-19th century the aforementioned withdrawal of the catechism prepared by Massaja for the lands of Africa. As we indicated previously, the condemnation of the great missionary's formulary was basically motivated by the concept of the catechism as a theological text, a little *summa* of theology (neo-scholastic in particular). But it is probably not a stretch to think that the origin of its failure was also the tendency underway then toward the unification of catechetical formularies.

This last observation brings us to move on in our discourse, to take another aspect of the varied history of catechism books under examination: their tendency to alternate between proliferation and unification.

The Catechism Text, Between Proliferation and the Tendency to Unification

In the history of formularies written since the 16th century, a sort of pendulum swing has been quite evident, oscillating between the tendency toward an increasing variety of texts and the opposite orientation toward unification.

To be more specific: it has been observed that, when catechisms began to spread in the 1500s, some books tended to prevail over others, to the point of predominating in the field of pastoral practice, even for centuries. I am speaking of texts that have been described as "classics"; those of Canisius, which dominated in the German-speaking countries until the mid-1800s, except in Jesuit spheres; those of Bellarmine, that excelled in Italy at least until 1905, and longer among the Jesuits; those of Astete and Ripalda, very widespread in the Spanish regions of the Old and New Worlds, until Vatican II and beyond.

The multi-century predominance of these aids did not, however, impede the tendency toward a proliferation of other formularies. The phenomenon, which developed from the mid-1600s onward, presents various causes.

– One basic reason remained the enduring "finding of religious ignorance" that impelled various authors to set their hands to drafting works that were considered suitable to fill such a gap; they were also aided in this by the invention and spread of the printing press.

– In addition, for Catholics, "controversies with the world of the Reformation" had considerable weight, as did the desire of various Counter-Reformation forces (the religious orders *in primis*), to provide themselves with their own texts to present and spread Catholic orthodoxy in a controversialist and apologetical style. Hence "catechisms of controversy" were born in this context, a few of which saw notable success.

– A further reason is offered, without a doubt, by the debates and well known "controversies within the Catholic Church herself," The dialectical situation stimulated various theological schools to spread their own opinions as much as possible, including by means of the catechism, the means of promotion *par excellence*.

– Another decisive element for the multiplication of catechetical texts was the Council of Trent's choice to base the reform of the Church on the figure of the "diocesan bishop." This determination had the effect that every zealous prelate, mindful of his own *munus docendi*, once he was installed in his diocese, would be concerned about the catechesis presented there, sometimes approving his predecessor's catechism, but more often revising it and imposing a new one. This phenomenon, which gave birth to a rich series of "diocesan" catechisms, proved particularly evident in France where, especially after 1660, many diocesan formularies bore the curious but emblematic seal on their covers: P.E.S.E.D.S.D. (*Pour Être Seul Enseigné Dans Son Diocèse*) [Only to be taught in its diocese].

– With the passing of the centuries, moreover, catechesis became "specialized" on the basis of various categories of target audiences (distinguished on the basis of age or profession, for example), of various socio-cultural living environments (city or country, *petites écoles* in France and

Schools of Christian Doctrine in Italy, colleges, parishes, or confraternities), of the sacraments at which they were aimed, or particular religious events to which they were addressed (popular missions). Such a "specialization," which the noted historian of catechesis Dhôthel describes as a "push," well explains the diverse production of catechetical manuals; a production in which it is no wonder to find *ad hoc* catechisms for soldiers, starting in the 1500s; or at the start of the 1800s, the outline of a catechism developed by St. Gaspar del Bufalo for the "*fienaroli*": that is, for peasants from the Roman countryside who came into the city to sell their hay.

– Later, in the 18th century, came the ripening of the "anti-Jesuit attitude" in the Church that led to shelving the great texts of the 1500s, at least in part, nearly all of them from Jesuit authors, and replacing them with various new aids.

– Finally, not to be underestimated is the "concern of individual pastors" with responsibility for souls who considered the official texts established by the diocesan Ordinary unsuited for their faithful and felt themselves authorized to produce and print their own texts.

Starting in the 1700s, particularly, this proliferation was considered a danger that worried the Vatican authorities themselves, and yet it was not stopped, so much that nearly everywhere it reached the "monstrous Babel of catechisms" that was lamented in Austrian Lombardy at the end of the 18th century.

The contrary demand for a certain unification blossomed, supported for obvious pastoral reasons, such as concern for the orthodoxy of the contents or the demand to make catechetical teaching uniform in the dioceses which Napoleon created, reducing and merging many previous local churches.

But in chronological terms the first to impose a single catechism were the civil authorities, moved by reasons primarily of the political order: Maria Theresa of Austria, in 1777, and Napoleon, in 1806, promulgated a unified text for their respective domains, in harmony with the typical ideals of Jurisdictionalism and Gallicanism.

With the 1800s, the pastoral concerns mentioned above return to the foreground to justify the unification of catechetical formulas; in addition, account was taken of the growing migratory phenomena of increasingly imposing masses that moved with the new industrialization in search of better living conditions.

Therefore in the 19th century, a "crescendo" of calls for the unification of catechism books was noticed in many Churches, both in Europe and beyond the Old Continent, calls that were satisfied in Germany in the mid-1800s, for example, where a single formulary was reached on the basis of the catechetical work of the Jesuit Joseph Deharbe (1800–1871).

This did not lessen the contrary tendency of formularies to multiply due to the pastoral zeal of individual personalities. To cite just the best-known in this regard, it is enough to mention the catechisms developed by Rosmini, by St. John Bosco (1815–1888), by Bl. Giovanni Battista Scalabrini (1839–1905) and by the young parish priest Don Giuseppe Sarto (1835–1914) who as bishop and pope, in contrast, will be a determined promoter of unification in catechetical aids.

In any case, the ever predominant calls for unification reached the First Vatican Council, which accepted them: the Council session, though not without tensions, approved the decision to ask the Holy See to write a brief catechetical formulary in Latin, for the faithful of all the Church, on the model of Bellarmine's *Dottrina cristiana breve*. It left to the bishops the task of translating the future text into various languages and the possibility of adding to it whatever would be considered suitable for their Churches, each bearing the imprint of its own character.

The order, while approved by the Council Fathers, was not promulgated by Pius IX, probably due to the unforeseen and unexpected closure of the Council, and it remained in fact a dead letter. Hence the issue of a "universal" catechism will continue to occupy Roman authorities occasionally until Vatican II.

In the meantime, specifically in the decades immediately after Vatican I, a catechetical movement began to develop which progressively renewed catechism books and their teaching in depth, analogously to what could be seen in other spheres of the Church.

III. The Catechism Text Under the Lens of the Catechetical Movement: from "Text" Catechisms to "Commentary" Catechisms

The formulary which we were just describing suffers objectively obvious limitations, both at the level of content and of its teaching. As for content, the work is presented as a summary manual of theology, concerned only with the integrity and orthodoxy of the doctrine, without an explicit presence of its primary sources, the Bible and the liturgy. In short, it is a "text" catechism, to use Cardinal Ratzinger's expression: an aid that in fact is not concerned with making itself immediately comprehensible to the person being catechized. And as to its teaching, the memorization of its content depends on didactic methods that are also deficient, since they do not respect the psychology of human learning.

Such limitations, already criticized periodically by several authors in preceding centuries, are confronted in more systematic terms by the catechetical movement, which takes its first steps in Germany and Austria in the last decades of the 1800s. The pioneers of the movement grasped the formulary's limitations both of content and method, but due to the predominant influence of neo-scholasticism, initially could not think of directly renewing its content. They had to move only toward a methodological renewal of catechesis, yet in any case they reached their own nascent innovation at the level of content, albeit indirectly.

Methodological Renewal in the Teaching of the Doctrinal Catechism

Improvement on the methodological level occurred when the innovating movement became open to the insights of pedagogy and psychology from the late 1800s and early 1900s. At the time, pedagogy spoke of a child-centered approach, while psychology taught that human learning develops by moving from the concrete to the abstract, from the known to the unknown, by induction and through cyclic stages and the deepening of the object of knowledge, which initially is only grasped in its globality.

Based on these insights, traditional catechetical practice is outmoded, as it completely ignores them, and a new method of instruction is formulated, finding its most complete expression in the renowned "Monaco method," of five "degrees" or "formal" steps that have to be traversed in all instruction, including catechetical. These degrees are: *preparation*, which involves referring initially to what is already known, having been learned in previous lessons of catechesis, and indicating the objective that one intends to reach with the new lesson; *presentation* of truths or norms to be learned, which is carried out by means of a story in which learners can easily grasp the intended communication, by induction and by moving from concrete to abstract; *explanation*, selected by the catechist, but also with the direct and active involvement of those being catechized; *synthesis* which, at this point, explains the "doctrine" correctly learned with universal-abstract language; a*pplication to life*.

The method—which also obviously leads to changing the content of the catechism, though only indirectly—was officially approved by the German and Austrian movement in 1912 and was further supported when policies of the "pedagogical activism" movement gained critical acceptance in official terms in 1928.

The intense work of innovation that developed in Germany and Austria was a driving force in catechetical renewal in other European countries, where similar independent initiatives were already not lacking. And from Europe the methodological innovation slowly spread to the Churches beyond Europe.

Yet it goes to be said that for a long time all these innovative ideas only worked to change "private" catechetical aids, and did not leave a scratch on the "official" formularies of the various Churches.

In any case, the identity and purpose of the traditional catechism began to change: from a "text" catechism, to highlight another expression used by Cardinal Ratzinger in France, it gradually became "commentary," that is, an aid not only concerned with stating the whole doctrine in orthodox terms, but also of making this same doctrine more immediately understandable by those being taught.

Renewal of the Content of the Catechism

During the 1930s the catechetical movement took a further decisive step in the renewal of the text of the catechism, with obvious repercussions on its teaching. When the whole tormented debate around methodology had died down, it became possible to proceed to a noticeable change in the "content" of catechesis, through the recovery of the primary sources of all catechesis: the Word of God, collected in the Scripture, and the liturgy.

Requests for a more biblical catechetical presentation are naturally not new. Not wanting to go back over the French historical-biblical catechisms described above, in particular the *Catéchisme historique* by Fleury (1683), for the 1800s we can recall again the vision of catechesis as *narratio historiae salutis* brought to maturity by Rosmini, when he translated Augustine's *De catechizandis rudibus*, and the Tübingen school's contribution to the field. Later, in the first years of the 1900s, the bishops Geremia Bonomelli (1831–1914), Pierre Dadolle (1857–1911) and Maurice Landrieux (1857–1926) stood out for their critique of the doctrinal catechism and their commitment in favor of a historical-biblical catechism.

The decisive contribution to the reformulation of the catechism in a historical-biblical style came, however, from the kerygmatic theology which ripened in the Innsbruck theological school, thanks to the pivotal contribution of Jungmann (1889–1975). Reflection brought the adherents of the Austrian theological circle to clearly distinguish theology from preaching and led to the famous statement that knowing dogma is a duty, but we absolutely must proclaim the *kerygma*, drawn from the Biblical source.

As a consequence, in the field of catechesis there was a rediscovery of the importance of Scripture, which has Christ at the center, the principle giving a focus and hierarchy to all the truths of the Christian faith. In a parallel way, the other primary source of catechesis was recovered, that is, the liturgy, as the actualization of a salvation history that has its focal point in Christ.

From the mid-1930s on, when Jungmann wrote his manifesto, despite the difficulties created by the war, the proposal for a catechism renewed biblically and liturgically, and not just at the level of method, began to spread throughout the Church. The binomial "Bible and liturgy" became the *leitmotiv* that ran through catechetical reflection and animated the renewal of catechesis up to Vatican II. Yet again, as for the text of the catechism, the kerygmatic influence fell only on "private" publications. The sole but decisive and exemplary exception consists of the aforementioned *Katholischer Katechismus der Bistümer Deutschlands* [Catholic Catechism of the Dioceses of Germany]. Issued in 1955, the "green" catechism of the German bishops, totally incorporated the guidance of decades of methodological and content-oriented renewal. Every "lesson," in fact, in addition to being substantially structured according to the formal degrees of the Monaco Method, also translates the ideas of kerygmatic catechesis into practice at the level of content. Translated into at least thirty-five languages, the text has also had a pivotal influence in supporting a renewal movement in the countries where the catechetical movement had not yet been present, and likewise in the transformation of the catechism "text" into "commentary." It was such an innovation that it had the effect of blocking the work of a Vatican commission, at the time involved in a revision of the Catechism of Pius X, which we will discuss next.

The Magisterium, Amid Exhortations, Traditional Catechisms, and the Problem of the "Universal" Catechism

While the catechetical movement, starting on an ecclesial basis, imprinted decisive changes on the catechism between Vatican I and Vatican II, the Magisterium also took an interest at various times in pastoral catechesis; and it showed this interest with a variety of actions ranging from exhortation to the codification of norms, and specific attention to the text of the catechism.

However, it must be said right away that while this series of interventions insistently pushed for oversight of catechetical practice, it remained basically on the track of tradition, starting from the problem of the catechetical formulary.

At the level of the universal Church Leo XIII sought to put into effect Vatican I's decision in favor of the projected "universal" catechism. He entrusted its compilation to Bp. Scalabrini, pioneer of the Italian catechetical movement, and to a subsequent commission, but without succeeding in his aim.

Hence in regard to the local Churches in the era of Pope Pecci [Leo XIII], we can observe on one hand that the bishops continued to ask for a unification of formularies, as the first plenary council of Latin America (1899) demonstrated; on the other, they were active in publishing, sometimes with good results, as was the case for example in the USA (1885), in francophone Québec (1888–1889), in northern Italy between 1896 and the early 1900s, and in Chile in 1900.

Pius X, the "pope of the catechism," succeeded Leo XIII. Most importantly, as is well known, he dedicated to catechesis the Encyclical Letter *Acerbo nimis* (1905), which combines exhortation and canonical regulation of catechetical ministry.

In the same year, he promulgated a *Compendium of Christian Doctrine* divided in three parts, each quite extensive, whose principal source was the catechism of Casati (1765), taken in the unified text standardized in 1896 in northern Italy. The Pope was a supporter, convinced of the need for a universal formulary, but gifted with great realism and prudence, so he only imposed his text on Rome and the Roman ecclesiastical province.

This teaching aid, bearing a cleanly traditional imprint, follows the schema we have called "quadripartite," Quite soon it revealed its defects, which were announced abroad in particular by pioneers of the catechetical movement.

Its objective limitations and various difficulties in usage led Pope Sarto to promulgate a new formulary at the end of 1912: a *Catechism of Christian Doctrine*, much reduced rather than massive, and which accepted and gave an official seal to the "tripartite" schema of content. The content, therefore, continued to be presented with neo-scholastic theological language and so to encourage catechetical practice that maintained the traditional limitations on content and method. These defects once again were demonstrated by many involved in the renewal of pastoral catechesis.

This second catechism also was only imposed on Rome and the Roman ecclesiastical province, but by its authority it saw a notable distribution, as had the preceding formulary, even abroad, especially in those countries where a unified book of doctrine was desired. The *Catechism* of 1912, in particular, became "the" catechetical formulary of the Italian Church up to Vatican II.

Successive popes gave birth to a rich array of norms that intended to animate and regulate catechetical activity, expressed particularly in the 1917 *CIC* of Benedict XV; the Motu proprio *Orbem catholicum* (1923) and in *Divini illius Magistri* (1929–1930) by Pius XI, whose directions were re-presented and summarized in the Decree *Provido sane consilio* (1935) from the Congregation of the Council, delegated to govern and animate ecclesial catechesis.

Within the scope of these pages, however, it is more important to underscore that the demand for unification of formularies continued in those decades and until the eve of Vatican II, both at the local level and that of the universal Church. On the local level, the problem found gradual solutions at least in some countries, such as southern Brazil (1904), China (1934), France (1937–1947), while for other nations a unified catechism would only come in the 1950s and '60s.

At the same time a recurring activity by the Holy See appeared, which continued to look toward the drafting of a universal formulary through commissions on the subject. It will suffice to note some emblematic moments in this effort. Cardinal Pietro Gasparri, the Secretary of State of Pius XI (1852–1934), showed himself particularly committed to reach a universal formulary, desiring to show the unity of the Church around the *Codes* (western and eastern) and a unitary catechism. However, his intention clashed with the perplexity and realism of Pope Ratti [Pius XI] who asked the Holy Office for a decision on the question. That Vatican organ expressed a negative opinion on the project, provoking Gasparri's great displeasure. The Cardinal was then allowed to publish a *Catechismus catholicus*, but only under his own name; it appeared in 1930 and ended up translated into various languages, reaching countries such as Mexico and China.

Through the following period, according to the current state of the documentation, it is known that under the pontificate of Pius XII there was work on revising the 1912 formulary of Pius X, while at the beginning of the pontificate of John XXIII the work of rewriting the "Pius X" was set down in a provisionally printed text, the *Progetto di modifiche al Catechismo della dottrina cristiana di San Pio X* [Plan of changes to the Catechism of Christian Doctrine by St. Pius X]. This draft was followed immediately by another, bearing the title *Catechismo della Dottrina Cristiana. II Progetto* [Catechism of Christian Doctrine. Second Plan]. This text, however, was no longer the formulary of Pope Sarto [Pius X], or even a revision, but a real and totally new universal catechism, composed of 1060 questions and answers collected in 240 pages.

IV. The Problem of the Catechism Text in Vatican II

The *Second Plan* cited above also had no successor because in the meantime the announcement of the Council had come.

The consultation carried out in the preparatory phase before the session led to the filing of 160 propositions pertaining to catechetical ministry; these were combined, along with "votes" on other material, in a voluminous *Analyticus conspectus*.

These propositions pertaining to catechesis ranged broadly from binding references to the norms in force on religious instruction to rather timid and generic openness to suggestions introduced to local Churches by the catechetical movement active then, as the request for a *kerygmaticus* catechism shows.

Of the 160 propositions, at least 41 took the catechism understood as text as their topic, suggesting various possible typologies of universal catechism.

Only three requests showed a decisively different orientation, inasmuch as one asked that no universal catechism be produced for the faithful; another looked for the statement of directives at the level of principles, typical of a directory; a third proposition, formulated by the bishop of Beauvais (France), Mons. Pierre-Marie Lacointe, is the only one that explicitly suggested the publication of a "directory."

And it was just this instruction that won the approval of the Council Fathers. They were seen to advance three hypotheses in the course of their work on a possible catechetical text, at the level of assemblies or commissions. Some wanted a real catechism drafted; those opposed wanted a directory. Between the two extremes the idea of a *catechismus fons* made its way, that is, a compromise text between the two other hypotheses: hence a document intended to outline at least the fundamental content of all catechisms, together with principles that should guide it. As is well known, in *Christus Dominus* the Council made the clear choice of a directory, which would come to light as the *General Catechetical Directory* in 1971; it would be the work of the Congregation for the Council, which in the meantime (1967) had become the Congregation for the Clergy.

V. The Catechism in the Post-Conciliar Period: Between "Text" and "Commentary"

The fortunes of catechesis since the Council are too well known to need to dwell on them for long; moreover, the following pages will take them up with greater attention, as providing the immediate and specific context in which the *CCC* was born.

Here it will suffice to state briefly that the Council, which did not deal with catechesis at all in specific terms and left no *ad hoc* document about it, also led all of catechetical practice to a profound renewal.

On the wave of the spirit of the Council, the local Churches in various countries elaborated their own directories that gave orientation to the writing of national catechisms for various ages. In other situations such as in the Church in France, through what we call catechisms of "initiation" today, preparations for a national catechism were abandoned; instead a sort of *catechismus fons* was written for every age-level, leaving to various local teams the elaboration of catechetical aids more "incarnated" in the diverse existential situations of those being catechized. Nor should we forget that in yet other nations, where church forces are weaker, they have been limited to finally opening up to the ideas of the pre-conciliar catechetical movement, while they also continue catechesis with the classic question and answer book.

"Experiential" Catechesis for a Catechism More and More "Commentary"

Staying at the level of a general overview of the post-conciliar evolution of catechesis, it is important to observe that a choice was made, everywhere to some extent but especially in the West and in Latin America, to emphasize the properly "anthropological," or rather "experiential" dimension.

The choice was motivated substantially by the fact that the Church became acutely aware that modern man, radically marked by individualism, subjectivism, and relativism (or—to use a summary term that was especially at its peak in the immediate post-conciliar era—marked by a radical "anthropological turn" of a cultural type), has been adopting more and more negative attitudes about any religious discourse and about specific proposals of faith, even in so-called Christian societies. Such stances can manifest themselves as opposition, active or peaceful, asserting that religious pronouncements are "not credible" or as "indifference" toward them, based on their "meaninglessness" for modern man.

In such a context, the traditional pastoral practice of many centuries, including catechetical practice, shows very obvious signs of crisis. In the search for a solution to the macroscopic problem, the Church places herself in a positive attitude toward man, who is contemporaneous with her, who is a child of modernity, and the Church devotes herself to show him the "meaning" that the Christian message has "for his existence".

In our perspective, this complex intention leads to the conviction that catechesis—in the evocative image of J. Goldbrunner—having been concerned about the "seed," the Christian message, for a long time, had to take interest during the years that followed the Council in the "land" on which the seed itself had to fall, the human being.

From this a type of catechetical activity was derived which developed some choices already present in pre-conciliar French catechesis and began to subject the anthropological data to innovative treatment: man, with his concrete existential, personal, and social experience, changes from being the simple recipient into being the source and context of the catechetical journey. In an obvious analogy with the anthropological turn in theology favored in the 1930s by Karl Rahner, all the classic arguments of the catechism are dealt with, worked out again, and proposed with the person as starting point, that is, in continual dialogue with the human experience and in service of the meaning they can assume for the person himself.

Catechetical reflection, united with more general theological-pastoral reflection, is naturally involved in the theoretical foundation of this radical choice. So while it confronts the difficult concept of "experience" in a philosophical way, the various reasons that can justify a pastoral approach and catechesis of existential or "experiential" type are explained from a theological viewpoint. For example, these reasons are identified in the objective relations that connect revelation and human experience, or experience and salvation; relations that show an obvious convergence and correlation between the theological pole and the anthropological. The point of synthesis of the argument is found in the event of the Incarnation which becomes the principle of pastoral and catechetical action, as the *DB* for the post-conciliar renewal of Italian catechesis (1970) amply documents.

Supported by well-founded reasons of the theological order, the orientation to an experiential catechesis spread rapidly in vast areas of the Church. In this sense, The International Catechetical Weeks, which took place successively in the 1960s at Eichstätt (Germany, 1960), Bangkok (1962), Katigondo (Uganda, 1964), Manila (1967), Medellín (Colombia, 1968); the last being a week in which the anthropological orientation in the field of catechesis certainly marked its high point.

The Magisterium itself, although it obviously did not absolutize a particular pastoral option like the experiential model, still recognized its validity and importance. It is a fact that can be grasped easily with an analysis of the catechetical documents worked out at the episcopal level, such as the *DB* cited above, which was adopted by, among others, the Church in Australia. And analogously one can cite pontifical and curial pronouncements such as the *DCG* (April 4, 1971) and *EN* (December 8, 1975). The same *CT* (October 16, 1979) which also suggested some caution in its regard, approved the perspective of an experiential-type catechesis.

On the basis of all these theological and magisterial indications, a luxuriant flowering of catechetical projects, catechisms, and aids was born, in which the person and his daily experience came into their own. Catechisms as "texts," Cardinal Ratzinger would say in France in 1983, that is, precise and complete collections of the truths of the faith, changed more and more into "commentaries," that is, instruments involved in translating *hic et nunc* the content of the Christian message, at times to the detriment of accurate communication of the data of the faith.

The Recovery of the "Text" Catechism

The experiential-anthropological orientation therefore became emblematic of post-conciliar catechesis, so much that it appeared to indicate a third great step carried out in its journey of renewal; after having been renewed on the methodological plane at the beginning of the catechetical movement and then in its contents in the wake of kerygmatic theology, it continued its progress by giving due attention to its proper reference, the person being catechized.

Yet the choice, although widespread, was not shared universally or placidly. Many in the Church were concerned that catechesis should continue to insure an integral and orthodox communication of Christian truths. Justified by the weak effectiveness and insufficiency that followed the concrete practice of experiential catechesis, they made it the target of various accusations: there was excessive concern about the *fides qua* to the detriment of the *fides quae*, some truths were only partially communicated, memorization was abandoned, it was responsible for religious ignorance, and similar complaints.

The criticism of these deficiencies and the reaction against them was manifested at all levels of the ecclesial community.

At the "base" level, for example, in opposition to catechisms accused of "ignoring the Creed" or the "Our Father," the *Catechismus ad parochos* or the formulary of Pius X were reprinted and promoted; choices that go hand in hand with the rejection of catechisms promulgated by the episcopal conferences, or the adaptation of their contents suitably integrated into the traditional question-answer schema.

Various signs of critical attention to post-conciliar catechesis also emerged at the level of the Magisterium. We can take them starting with the case of the *Dutch Catechism* (1966) and the first *Synod of Bishops* (1967), when authoritative exponents of the Church hierarchy suggested the writing of a "universal" catechism, naturally understood as a "text," not a "commentary," with the aim of a more exact catechesis and as a remedy to the errors snaking through the Church of that era. We also find an analogous indicator in the 1971 *DCG*, which, while remaining a Directory, a document that only enunciates principles in the realm of method and content, takes the trouble to propose a list of specific content, at paragraphs nn. 47–69, that every catechism should convey. Equally indicative was the debate that developed between the Synod of 1971 and that of 1974 on the relation between evangelization and human promotion; a debate that ranged between the extremes of considering human promotion "constitutive" of the process of evangelization, and at the opposite, as "secondary" and therefore not essential. Important and decisive calls to return to a catechesis that, while faithful to man, should not forget fidelity to God were expressed later in *CT* and in the famous conference of Cardinal Ratzinger, to which we have referred above. Last of all, we should add the recurring call which emerged, in fact, from all the Synods up to 1985, to write a "text" catechism of universal value, and one will have a clear enough vision of the playing field in which the fortunes of the *CCC* developed; a history, however, that calls for its own treatise.

HISTORY AND STRUCTURE OF THE CATECHISM

Raffaello Martinelli

I. The Elaboration of the Text

The journey of developing the *CCC* passed through various salient stages. We can describe the path in summary form through the following schema.

From the Extraordinary Synod of 1985 to November 1986

Accepting the proposal made by the Extraordinary Synod of 1985, the Holy Father Pope St. John Paul II established a limited Commission, representing pastors from various continents and officials from the competent dicasteries of the Roman Curia. The aim of the Commission, specified by the Holy Father, was to work out a plan for a *Catechism for the universal Church* or *Compendium of Catholic doctrine* (on faith and morals) that "can be a point of reference for catechisms prepared, or to be prepared, in the various regions." It was also desired by the Pope that "the preparation of the catechism be made in the style and the manner hoped for by the Synod Fathers and required by the pedagogical, psychological and technical needs of society and modern culture" (*Address to the Roman Curia*, June 28, 1986).

The Synod Fathers had expressed themselves on the subject in their 1985 Final Report in the following terms: "Very many have expressed the desire that a catechism or compendium of all Catholic doctrine regarding both faith and morals be composed, that it might be, as it were, a point of reference for the catechisms or compendiums that are prepared in the various regions. The presentation of doctrine must be biblical and liturgical. It must be sound doctrine suited to the present life of Christians" (*Final Report*, II, B. 4). The Commission of cardinals and bishops named by the Pope decided in the first session of November 1986 to avail itself of the help of an Operations Secretariat (composed of personnel from the Congregation for the Doctrine of the Faith), an Editorial Committee (seven diocesan bishops belonging to various linguistic areas), a Secretary Editor, and a College of Consultors (forty experts, chosen according to either their specific competence in various theological disciplines or their belonging to various cultures and languages).

From December 1986 to October 1989

First the Commission proceeded to the preparation of a general schema of the *CCC* and, following that, to various plans for the catechetical text, seeking to implement some basic editorial principles such as, for example: brevity and concision; attention to cultural context and to the tradition of the Eastern Churches; frequent use of the traditional terminology of the Church; a "no" to theological options and to methodological-didactic applications.

In July 1989, they reached the preparation of the *projet-révisé* as planned, which was considered mature enough to be submitted for the consultation of all the bishops. After translations into the four main vernacular languages (English, French, Spanish, German) had been made, consultation took place from November 1989 to November 1990 with all the bishops of the world as well as the episcopal conferences and, through them, the principal university-level Catholic institutes. The text, which was sent out in about 5,000 copies, stands fourth in the series of nine versions.

Examination of the Responses of the Episcopate

The work of examining the responses of the bishops proved not to be easy and was even a little laborious. The incoming material was indeed most abundant: 938 responses with over 24,000 comments, all to be examined and catalogued, with the aim of preparing the most complete and objective "X-ray" possible and a summary about the general questions, the individual parts, and a few particular topics, with possible proposed solutions.

Almost unanimously, those who had sent their judgment had been in agreement, thinking it necessary and relevant, indeed urgent, to have a single catechetical text for the whole Catholic Church which would serve as a "point of reference" for the writing of national and diocesan catechisms. In general, the number and the tenor of the responses showed that the *projet-révisé* had been well received by the bishops, who considered it a "valid base," able to receive the great number of improvements suggested in view of the definitive writing of the text. In various meetings the Commission, assisted by the Editorial Committee, proceeded to the drafting of the definitive text. For this the text was reviewed by a mixed group of experts, theologians and exegetes in regard to its use of sacred Scripture, taking into account both the specific purpose of the *CCC* (which is not a study of scholarly exegesis), and the methodology indicated in *DV*. On February 14, 1992—the feast of the co-patrons of Europe Cyril and Methodius, named by the Holy Father in the Encyclical *SA* as "true models for all missionaries" (n. 11)—the members of the Commission expressed their comprehensive evaluation of the entire text in a secret vote: the favorable result was unanimous. Applause from all present marked the happy completion of the effort undertaken in 1986.

St. John Paul II, who had accompanied the preparation of the text regularly in its various phases, attentively examined the final plans for the text, and had presented his own improvements, approved the text, naming it the *CCC* on June 25, 1992, close to the solemnity of SS. Peter and Paul, with a ceremony that was simple but of notable importance. An Apostolic Constitution titled *FD* was placed at the beginning of the text with the date October 11, 1992, the thirtieth anniversary of the opening of the Second Vatican Ecumenical Council, which had been the constant guide during the construction of the *CCC*. Thus the solemn ceremony of the promulgation of the *CCC* followed on December 8, 1992, the solemnity of the Immaculate Conception.

In summary, therefore, we can identify the following phases in the preparation and writing of the Catechism: *Adumbratio schematis* (February 1987); *Avant-projet* (December 1987); *Plan* (February 1989); *Revised plan* (November 1989); *Textus emendatus* (March 1991); *Pre-definitive text* (May 1991); *Corrected pre-definitive text* (August 28, 1991); *Definitive plan* (December 8, 1991); *Definitive text* (February 14, 1992).

II. The Structure of the *CCC*

The structure of the *CCC* appears with a few characteristics that deserve to be analyzed briefly now. The configuration can be subdivided by a "quadripartite," "symphonic," "veritative" structure.

Quadripartiite

A particularly important hermeneutical criterion for an adequate approach to the Catechism and for a correct understanding of its content is its structure, characterized by the "inseparable unity of the four parts." Those parts prove to be interwoven like a fabric, harmonized like a symphony, set in place like the tiles of a mosaic. The numerous cross-references noted in the margins are only one demonstration of this. As *FD* shows: "The four parts are related one to the other: the Christian mystery is the object of faith (first part); it is celebrated and communicated in liturgical actions (second part); it is present to enlighten and sustain the children of God in their actions (third part); it is the basis for our prayer, whose privileged expression is the Our Father, and it represents the object of our supplication, our praise and our intercession (fourth part). The Liturgy itself is prayer; the confession of faith finds its proper place in the celebration of worship. Grace, the fruit of the sacraments, is the irreplaceable condition for Christian living, just as participation in the Church's liturgy requires faith. If faith is not expressed in works, it is dead (cf. Jas 2:14–16) and cannot bear fruit unto eternal life."

This unity among the parts implies and justifies the following statement: the treatment of a single basic theme within the *CCC* in a single part, and in some cases in all four parts, is closely connected to and complementary with the treatment of other basic themes: they explain and illuminate one another. Because of this there is also a close connection in the *CCC* among the *lex credendi, lex orandi, lex agendi*; among *quid credas, quo tendas, quid agas*.

Moreover, this interconnection of the parts of the *CCC* is also given by the editorial commission's choice of a well determined proportion among the parts: 39% for the "Credo," 22% for the second part (whose second section, the sacraments, constitutes 16% of the whole *CCC*), 27% for the commandments, and 12% for the "Our Father."

The harmonious complementary of the various subjects is also an expression, a concretization of the profound unity of the Christian mystery itself. Again it is this unity that characterizes the *CCC* as a whole: "In reading the *CCC* we can perceive the wondrous unity of the mystery of God, his saving will, as well as the central place of Jesus Christ, the only-begotten Son of God, sent by the Father, made man in the womb of the Blessed Virgin Mary by the power of the Holy Spirit, to be our Savior. Having died and risen, Christ is always present in his Church, especially in the sacraments; he is the source of our faith, the model of Christian conduct and the Teacher of our prayer" (*FD*).

Symphonic

This quadripartite structure, with its interconnection of parts, makes it possible to describe the *CCC* as a "symphony," as St. John Paul II does in various discourses and especially in *FD*. There are numerous and complementary aspects and meanings of the *CCC* that characterize it as a symphony. The catechism as a complete exposition of the essential and basic content of the *depositum fidei*: this itself is a symphony, inasmuch as it constitutes a choral and organic presentation of the principal truths of Catholic faith and morals. The catechism is symphonic in the sense that it is a collegial work (willed by a Synod of bishops, drafted by bishops, the fruit of consultation with the whole Catholic episcopate and of collaboration with vast numbers of experts and specialists in the various theological, pastoral, pedagogical, and other disciplines). It is symphonic in the interconnection of the four parts (it suffices to check the quantitative proportional relationship of the various parts; the theological-doctrinal link among them, shown also by the cross-references). The symphony of the Catechism reflects the unity of the Christian mystery (cf. *FD*), and also the circularity of the theological virtues: faith, hope, charity. It is a symphony that is also manifested and realized in the interconnection of the sources of the *CCC*: biblical, patristic, liturgical, magisterial, testimonial. Also prominent is the symphony of the two "lungs" of the Church which interact in the *CCC*: western and eastern Tradition. Nor can we forget that there is a profound and mysterious correspondence between the symphony of truths of the faith and the symphony of the unity of the faith. The symphony is also performed by presenting the harmonious beauty that characterizes Catholic truth (as results from the style and language of the Catechism, which pursues these characteristics). The symphony of these truths, which derives from their hierarchy and is realized in respect for it, is also relevant. The *CCC* is symphonic in the sense that it seeks to combine enduring truth with the ecclesial and social reality of today. The *CCC*, as a point of reference for the elaboration of local catechisms, promotes the symphonic unity of catechesis, or rather of catechesis that seeks balance and integration between the universal dimension (catholic) and particular characterization, between the diverse dimensions that compose the catechetical act. The need for a dimension that expresses a symphonic mentality not just for the individual Christian, but also for the ecclesial community at various levels, is derived from this symphonic concept of the truth and of the Church, presented by the *CCC*.

Veritative

This quadripartite and symphonic structure is also characterized by a special attention to the content of the Christian faith that makes the *CCC* a compendium of the essential and basic content of the Catholic faith. The *CCC*, putting the exposition of content (*depositum fidei*) foremost, belongs more to the genus of veritative catechesis (*fides quae*, the truth of catechesis), rather than to the genus of communicative catechesis (*fides qua*, more attentive to the recipients and to pedagogical and didactic methods). It sets out to state what is essential and basic to guarantee the unity of the faith: certain, secure, believed, celebrated, lived, prayed by the Catholic Church; carrying out a number of principles, such as: completeness, integrity, orthodoxy, certainty of faith, systematicity, essentialness, clarity, simplicity, concision. The *CCC*, therefore, proclaims the truth of the Church: what the Church believes, celebrates, lives and prays; it is the memory of the faith of the Church in all its rigor, its vigor, and its beauty. The *CCC* expresses a special attention to the truth. It is fidelity to Christ and the mandate-mission entrusted to the Church: in fact the Church is the treasury, custodian, interpreter, witness of the truth of Christ. It is service to the person, who himself is fulfilled in the truth, is called to the truth that "makes you free," and therefore it is service to the building of a new person and a new humanity. In short, it is the carrying out of the mission received, by proclaiming the truth of Christ, as it is believed, proclaimed, celebrated, lived, prayed by and in the Church.

THE CATECHISM OF THE CATHOLIC CHURCH IN THE DYNAMIC OF THE RENEWAL OF CATECHESIS

Joël Molinario

The *CCC* and the Renewal of Catechesis

Pope Benedict XVI, in the 2012 *Motu proprio PF*, wanted to create a connection among the Second Vatican Council, the Year of Faith, the Synod for the New Evangelization, and the *CCC*, to create a better understanding of the *CCC* and bring it into the catechetical activity of the Church. The *CCC*, therefore, is not a document that can be isolated from the life of the Church, nor is it a static expression of her doctrine. It came in order to reaffirm that Vatican II, in the name of Tradition, is the true theological expression of today, as Pope Paul VI already said.

So it isn't possible to understand and accept the *CCC* for catechetical activity without caring for the organic link that joins it to the Second Vatican Council, integrating the principles of the *CCC* with the faith which the Church lives and teaches; and finally interpreting it as an instrument of service to the new evangelization.

The *CCC* and the Second Vatican Council

From the announcement of the writing of a universal catechism, which happened during the Synod of 1985, two attitudes took shape, both of them excessive: on one hand, among many people responsible for catechesis, especially in the West, an indifference to the *CCC* arose, if not an outright rejection. This indifference can be traced back as far as the beginning of the 20th century. On the other hand, there was an enthusiasm that saw in the *CCC* a solution for every problem. These two attitudes did not allow for a right and serene reception of the *CCC* and created an ambiguity about the role it should carry out in the life of the Church and particularly in catechesis.

The *CCC's* enthusiastic reception into catechesis, particularly in Europe and in America, and the diffidence in other countries, came to exist because of a distorted image of the catechism which was propagated in Europe in the course of the 19th and early 20th centuries. We cannot develop the historical argumentation here (cf. the works of the great historian Sr. Elisabeth Germain), but we hold that the notion of catechism had changed its meaning in the Church between the Council of Trent (1545–1563) and Vatican I (1870). The *Roman Catechism*, called the "Catechism of Trent," intended to be an instrument to foster the desire to know Jesus Christ, assigning to pastors the task of adapting the pedagogy to various types of believers, in the spirit of the Renaissance humanists, and in view of building up individual believers. That is what St. Charles Borromeo expressed in the oft-cited introduction to the *Catechism of the Council of Trent*. The catechisms of the 19th century, for their part, insisted on a text to be learned out of obedience, thought of as a guarantee for salvation and eternal life. In effect, the catechisms of that era were on the defensive and had become rigid about three areas of controversy: against Protestants above all, which caused a considerable retreat in the role of sacred Scripture and a conception of faith as a collection of truths to believe; then against the Jansenists, which led to a strong tendency toward moralism, with the development of catechisms around three "musts": one"must believe," one "must observe the commandments," one "must receive the sacraments"; and finally argument against ideas of the Enlightenment, which led to a spiritual impoverishment and an intellectualism constrained by responding to the 18th-century philosophers who asserted that faith is irrational (cf. J. Molinario, *Le catéchisme, une invention moderne. De Luther à Benoît XVI*, Bayard, Paris 2013).

It was during the 1985 Synod that Pope John Paul II and Cardinal Ratzinger relaunched the idea of writing a Catechism for the Catholic Church. At the time, two constant references appeared: the *Catechism of the Council of Trent*, with the preface by St. Charles Borromeo, and the Second Vatican Council, which Paul VI called the "Catechism of the 20th century." The magisterium rightly avoided reference to catechisms of the 19th and early 20th centuries, to write a catechism that would be the fruit of Vatican II.

This wish to write the *CCC* as a fruit of Vatican II was not something obvious to carry out, since the Council Fathers had not desired to promulgate a universal catechism, out of fear of "freezing doctrine," according to Cardinal Ciriaci. In effect the Council Fathers had in mind the majority conception of catechisms whose reference model came from the 19th century. Because of that, they hesitated about rewriting a catechism at a time when a new concept of the relation of the Church with the world was taking shape, and especially when new and great figures of theology (we can think of de Lubac, Congar, Geseilmann, Balthasar, Rahner…) and of the catechetical renewal (J.-A.

Jungmann, J. Colomb) were taking up the question of the supernatural and revelation in a new way. While the question of a catechism had been posed at the beginning of the Council, that interest was transformed bit by bit in the course of four sessions, in the direction of catechesis and the catechumenate (*SC* 64; *AG* 14; *CD* 14; *LG* 19).

The *CCC*'s organic link with Vatican II was underscored pastorally by Pope John Paul II. In *FD*, the Apostolic Constitution for the publication of the *CCC* which serves as an introduction to it, John Paul II returns insistently to Vatican II and the anniversary of its opening, to the happy memory of John XXIII and to the joy he had in participating "in that session of the Church" that nourished the present *CCC*.

The organic link to Vatican II is emphasized in a more theological way in the two introductory chapters of the *CCC*, which had the aim of clearing away any theological misunderstanding about the principles and doctrine espoused in it. "Faith," says the *CCC*, "is a personal adherence of the whole man to God who reveals himself" (n. 176).

The text deals with the theology of Vatican II, following the long Tradition of the Church. After affirming just that, the first chapter takes up *GS* again to underscore that man is capable of God (nn. 27–30) and is restless until he rests in him. The second chapter then takes up the doctrine of revelation from *DV* to express how the revelation of God in Jesus Christ is met as human desire; and that the fullness of this revelation makes human beings partakers of the divine nature, thanks especially to the mediation of the holy Scriptures (nn. 51–53). In this beginning of the *CCC* we find confirmed the great theological advances that Vatican II realized. *GS* and *DV* renewed the very nature of our understanding of a catechism: this is what the first two chapters of the *CCC* convey.

The *CCC* and Faith

Benedict XVI wrote in *PF* that "there exists a profound unity between the act by which we believe and the content to which we give our assent" (*PF* 10). Faith is an opening of the heart to the gift of God and an attachment to the word of God with the confession of our lips. Knowledge of the teachings is therefore insufficient, Benedict XVI points out, without the opening of the heart which converts the person (*PF* 10).

This interpretive key for the Year of Faith turns up a few lines later when the *CCC* is the topic: "In order to arrive at a systematic knowledge of the content of the faith, all can find in the *Catechism of the Catholic Church* a precious and indispensable tool" (*PF* 11). Benedict XVI continues: "In its very structure, the *Catechism of the Catholic Church* follows the development of the faith right up to the great themes of daily life. On page after page, we find that what is presented here is no theory, but an encounter with a Person" (*PF* 11). So this interpretive key opens the way to a good use of the *CCC* in catechesis. The *CCC* fulfills its task as an "instrument to support faith" when the understanding of the words leads to the opening of the heart; and also conversely, when the grace of opening the heart leads to the desire to know him in whom the believer has placed his trust. The knowledge dealt with in the *CCC* is therefore not abstract; there is a structure that harmonizes the faith professed, celebrated, lived, and prayed: the four parts of the *CCC* that enable us to meet Christ. So the faith contents in the *CCC* are at the same time words of understanding the faith and human experiences of faith. Catechesis, then, consists of uniting understanding and experience of the mystery of God, although no one can grasp him totally.

Saint Augustine left us a formula with a surprising clarity to understand this. Commenting on the Apostles' Creed (the first part of the *CCC*), he writes: "If you believe 'in' him, also believe him; yet he who believes God (*credere Deo*) does not necessarily believe in him. The demons believe him, but they don't believe in him." (*In Evangelium Ioannis Tractatus*, 29, 6). And the bishop of Hippo explains that we become Christians from the moment in which we believe in God (*credere in Deum; "Hoc est etiam credere in Deum quod utique est quam credere Deo": Enarrationes in Psalmos, 77, 8*). Without the grace of a relation with Christ, proclamation remains arid and dogma does not achieve its purpose of designating the mystery of the living God for every man. According to the beautiful expression of Fr. de Lubac, it is a doctrine of life that catechesis must promote, with the help of the *CCC*. In this regard, the great innovators of catechesis of the mid-20th century and the great theologians who inspired Vatican II agree perfectly.

Pope Francis—with Benedict XVI—takes up this fundamental key in *LF* and adds this further explanation: "Faith, in fact, needs a setting in which it can be witnessed to and communicated, a means which is suitable and proportionate to what is communicated. For transmitting a purely doctrinal content, an idea might suffice, or perhaps a book, or the repetition of a spoken message. But what is communicated in the Church, what is handed down in her living Tradition, is the new light born of an encounter with the true God, a light which touches us at the core of our being and engages our minds, wills and emotions, opening us to relationships lived in communion" (*LF* 40).

The *CCC*, the New Evangelization, and Christian Initiation

Once any misunderstanding about the foundations of the *CCC* is clarified, thanks to Vatican II and the Year of Faith, we can better understand its place in the new evangelization. Let us take up an element cited as evidence at the time, the catechumenate, mentioned in Proposition 38 of the Synod on the New Evangelization and in *LF*, texts that help us catch sight of the link among the three elements of the catechism text. On one hand, the faith is transmitted first of all with baptism, which is not an isolated past event, because it involves the whole life of the Christian. Pope Francis writes: This dynamic of transformation "which takes place in baptism helps us to appreciate the singular importance of the catechumenate […] for the new evangelization" (*LF* 42). On the other hand, the search for God is presented in the encyclical as the road which the Magi followed: "For them God's light appeared as a journey to be undertaken, a star which led them on a path of discovery" (*LF* 35). This image relates naturally to the experience of the catechumen.

How does this matter for the *CCC?* We need to return to the theological structure of the catechism in four parts organically connected among themselves (cf. the conferences of Cdl. Ratzinger at Lyon and Paris on *"Transmission of faith and wellsprings of faith"*): the faith proclaimed ("The profession of faith", nn. 144–1065), the faith celebrated ("The celebration of the Christian mystery," nn. 1066–1690), the faith lived ("Life in Christ," nn. 1691–2557) and the faith prayed ("Christian prayer," nn. 2558–2865); this is the theological structure used by the Council of Trent, common to Luther's catechisms (Little and Great Catechism, 1529) and whose origin traces back explicitly to the catechumenate which the Church developed between the third and fifth centuries and to the apostolic life as it is presented to us in the Acts of the Apostles: "They devoted themselves to the teaching of the apostles and to the communal life, to the breaking of the bread and to the prayers" (Acts 2:42). In effect, for the Christian initiation of adults, a participation in the liturgical life of the Christian community is necessary, the call to conversion and to live a Christian life with reference to the biblical commandments is permanent; finally, when the *traditio-redditio* of the Apostles' Creed and of the Our Father is accompanied by appropriate catechesis, they articulate the final preparation for the sacraments that will be received at the Paschal vigil (*RICA* 175–178). And the Second Vatican Council wanted the restoration of the catechumenate for the current era and invited the bishops to organize a baptismal itinerary for adults articulated in various stages (*SC* 64, cf. *CCC* 1232). The *DGC* sees them as the reference point and inspiration for all catechesis (nn. 59 and 88–90). This means that there is a theological structure common to the Christian initiation of adults (*OICA* 53 and 55), the catechetical practice of every era, the *CCC*, and the apostolic life.

The four parts of the *CCC* do not thereby correspond to a program to be followed word for word like a manual. They are, rather, comparable to lighthouses and signal buoys that guide sailors in the essential passages of their crossing. Hence the varied usage of this theological structure in catechesis: if in the baptismal catechumenate there is the ritual character that guides the order and articulation of the four elements, then in the *CCC* the catechesis of children needs to be considered as a post-baptismal catechumenate (n. 1231). This means that children or adolescents already baptized also need to live the essence of the journey of Christian initiation. This is based on a theological understanding of baptism that does not limit it to its isolated liturgical celebration, because the sacramental grace extends for the whole length of the itinerary of becoming a Christian, before and after the sacrament. In this, the catechumenate's "dynamic of transformation" can be considered a reference for the new evangelization. Here too the *CCC* furnishes the needed guidance. Even if, unlike what happens with adults, where the *traditio* of the Our Father is only foreseen at the end of the catechumenal process (*OICA* 188–192), the Christian initiation of baptized children often begins with the Our Father. Is it not normal to introduce children immediately to a filial relation with God? (*CCC* 2765–2766). Equally, conversion of the heart and change of life in the name of the Gospel are at the center of becoming mature in faith. Now, one cannot ask children to change their life when they are in a time of building their personality; therefore the lighthouses and signal buoys proposed by the *CCC* remain the same, but the encounter with the four parts of the *CCC* and their articulation are made in differing order and manner, according to common sense and the age of those being catechized. The essential and combined contribution of the catechumenate and the *CCC* to catechesis and the new evangelization is in understanding that every catechetical itinerary is sacramentally structured, and that baptismal grace is not isolated, but extends before and after having received the sacrament. So the *CCC* plays the role of a concrete means in the form of a theological structure of the Church's faith, and, as such, is suited to inspire and nourish every itinerary of faith for the life of every person. In this way, the exposition of the faith contained in the *CCC* refers to the lived experience of faith and points forward to its continuation. (Fr. Moog and J. Molinario, eds., *La cathéchès et le contenu de la foi*, Paris: DDB, 2011).

The *CCC* and the Living Faith of Believers

The *CCC* fulfills its role completely when its theological expression succeeds in describing the human experience of believing in God, when its language is able to let us sense the Gospel that shapes a life, when its dogmatic expression defines the believing experience. In short, therefore, the often-asserted opposition between dogmatic language and the language of experience is empty, while their mutual articulation proves vital. Our modern era has separated what was originally united in apostolic life. The four parts of the *CCC* are only the re-appropriation of the life of the Church, which comes first of all. It is the life of faith of the apostles that raises this theological structure of the *CCC*. So in the *CCC* the life of the Church and the catechists are not applying an abstract dogma given by the Magisterium of the Church, but rather the Magisterium sets itself to listen to the apostolic life, to discern elements that structure every Christian life. In this way we can better understand the idea that the contents of faith expounded in the *CCC* refer to how the Church lives her faith, to such an extent that the two are not separable. This is why, in reading every chapter of the *CCC*, it is right to ask oneself about the experience of faith that it describes (M.-L. Rochette and J.-L. Souletie, *La resurrection de la chair*, Paris: Le Sénevé-ISPC, 2011, 7–15). Without this work, we risk confusing the *CCC* with an abstract theory that would not take account of the experience of the believer's encounter with Jesus Christ (*EG* 7–8).

Another aspect of the *CCC* is suggested by Charles Borromeo, who explained that the catechism is an instrument at the service of catechists ("Doctors of the Church") because it "is applied [will be applied] first of all to make the sincere desire to know Jesus Christ be born in the soul of the believer," Thus the purpose of the *CCC* is not only to nourish and clarify the believing experience, but also to arouse a desire (nn. 2541, 2589). This desire has two dimensions: a theological one, the desire to see God, of which St. Thomas Aquinas spoke so well, the other pastoral and pedagogical. There is indeed a catechetical pedagogy of desire in absolute consonance with what a French writer said about great works: "One of the great and marvelous characteristics of beautiful books [...] is that what the author could call "conclusions" can be called "the outset" by the reader" (Marcel Proust, *Days of Reading*). He went on to explain that great works are great, above all, by giving desire. Setting the desire for Jesus as the purpose of the Catechism, Charles Borromeo has anticipated our initiative for a new evangelization. In effect, without the desire for God, the Gospel will always appear old, because it is desire that opens us to a renewal of faith and of our relationship with Christ. Hence the *CCC* will evangelize all the better, the more it will make the believer become aware that God also desires the salvation of man.

THE CATECHISM OF THE CATHOLIC CHURCH IN THE PARTICULAR CHURCHES

Christoph Schönborn

Introduction

The *CCC* was promulgated twenty-five years ago. The catechism preceding it, the *Roman Catechism* (1556) which fulfilled the directives of the Council of Trent, remained for four hundred years the principal reference work for the transmission of the faith in the Catholic Church. After twenty-five years, it is not yet possible to evaluate precisely whether the *CCC* will be able to play a similar role. Yet one particular thing can be taken as established. The *CCC* has become "the" principal reference text when questions arise regarding Church teaching. John Paul II, in his Apostolic Constitution *FD* (October 11, 1992), made clear: "I declare it [the *CCC*] to be a valid and legitimate instrument for ecclesial communion and a sure norm for teaching the faith."

In the reflections that follow I will try to trace the major principles on the basis of which the *CCC* was conceived and written. To this end I have set seven criteria, which were also guiding criteria for the whole of the catechism, as well as the individual sections.

The first criterion (1) necessary for the drafting of a catechism is the acknowledgement that the faith presents itself as a unity, and as such can be used to profess itself; in second place, (2) the distinction between the doctrine of faith and theology must be clear, as appears from the *Prologue* of the *CCC*; then it is a matter (3) of taking the hierarchy of truths of the faith into consideration, for the sake of presenting the unity of the doctrine of the faith as an organic whole; (4) beyond any other aspect, the primacy of grace must be shown; (5) doctrine is to be presented clearly in its trinitarian structure; (6) everything must be oriented to Christ; (7) in every topic, it is also important to make clear the intimate union existing between Scripture and Tradition. Having listed these guiding principles of the *CCC*, I will expound them briefly.

I. The Faith: An Organic Whole

The very concept of Catechism implies that the faith can be received and accepted as a whole, and likewise, that the faith is presented and understood as an organic whole. From this perspective, the key points are the quotations from St. Irenaeus at nn. 172–175. It is indeed a matter of the question of unity: "Through the centuries, in so many languages, cultures, peoples, and nations, the Church has constantly confessed this one faith, received from the one Lord, transmitted by one Baptism, and grounded in the conviction that all people have only one God and Father" (n. 172). A fundamental principle of the *CCC* is the unity and the trinity of God and, from this, the unity of the human race, by which all men are recipients of a supernatural call to communion with God. St. Irenaeus of Lyons adds: "Indeed, the Church, though scattered throughout the whole world, even to the ends of the earth, having received the faith from the apostles and their disciples…guards [this preaching and faith] with care, as dwelling in but a single house, and similarly believes as if having but one soul and a single heart, and preaches, teaches, and hands on this faith with a unanimous voice, as if possessing only one mouth" (n. 173).

The conviction that the faith is one, even in the passing of centuries, is the essential by which we today can also proclaim the same faith that the apostles in turn transmitted to us. Irenaeus continues: "For though languages differ throughout the world, the content of the Tradition is one and the same. The Churches established in Germany have no other faith or Tradition, nor do those of the Iberians, nor those of the Celts, nor those of the East, of Egypt, of Libya, nor those established at the center of the world." We do not have the benefit of knowing what Irenaeus intended by 'center of the world,' whether Antioch or his own Lyons, but in any case he reveals to us that the good News was also taught there. The Church's message, then, "is true and solid, in which one and the same way of salvation appears throughout the whole world" (n. 174). And finally: "We guard with care the faith that we have received from the Church, for without ceasing, under the action of God's Spirit, this deposit of great price, as if in an excellent vessel, is constantly being renewed and causes the very vessel that contains it to be renewed" (n. 175). The faith itself remains young and keeps the Church young.

The faith is one. Not only at the time of Irenaeus, but also twenty centuries later. And the whole history of the *CCC* got underway precisely with this argument. On the first day of the Synod of 1985, Cardinal Bernard Law, then the archbishop of Boston, expressed himself with these words in Latin: *"Juvenes Bostoniensis, Leningradendis, et Santiago de Chile easdem blue jeans induti sunt et eandem musicam audiunt et saltant."* The argument was probably not of the theological height of Irenaeus, and the Latin certainly did not have the polish of Cicero's; but it dealt with a particularly illuminating intervention anyway. The question runs as follows: why, in a world where all the youth wear the same blue jeans, do they not profess the same faith in a single language, given that this faith remains the same in all the languages and nations? Today, in short, it is a matter of confessing the faith together. This is certainly the main theme that forms the background of the *CCC*. Where pluralism is taken into consideration as a last resort for the faith, then it happens that the *CCC* appears true.

II. Theology and Doctrine of the Faith

First of all and naturally, it is necessary to create a distinction here between theology and the doctrine of the faith. By my way of seeing, it is a fundamental problem of contemporary debate, given that the differentiation between theology and doctrine of the faith is not sufficiently clear. Here and there the suspicion emerges that this *CCC* would represent only one theology among others. It would supposedly be "Ratzingerian," or as Hans Küng has said, "Roman theology." Naturally the bishops do have their own personality which is also present in their contributions—of which there were many—a theology of their own, their own culture, their language, their own character. In the Church there is a legitimate plurality, which will always exist. Bonaventure and Thomas differed from one another, as did John and Matthew. And certainly this diversity for forms is made possible when it does not become opposition or contradiction, precisely on the basis of the unity of the faith. These theologies need to presuppose that unity of faith precedes the plurality of theologies. Whenever it should no longer be possible to speak of the same faith among diverse theologies, then these diverse theologies are no longer at home in the Catholic Church. The *CCC*, considering this is one of the most important criteria for its writing, has always tried to formulate its understanding through the sharing of the one faith, obviously not by a mere definition, but also taking account of what the Magisterium of the Church says, and how much it expresses the mind of the faith of the Church.

In the various phases of writing, there was always attentive consideration to various theological theses, including controversial ones, though these were always kept apart from the *CCC*. An example: in a preliminary phase of writing, the chapter on the *descensus ad inferos* was labeled as "Balthasarian." In reality, an attempt was made to include the insights of Hans Urs von Balthasar and other theologians about this mystery of the faith and incorporate them into the *CCC*. During the editing process, these expressions were removed, because—it was said—they dealt with a theological thesis still under debate, as much as it was also analyzed in a rather spiritual way and therefore worthy of attention, it did not, however, form part of the Church's teaching of the faith. Just to show another example, no one will find St. Augustine's psychological analogy of the Trinity in the *CCC*, as much as several bishops and experts considered it important, at least because it was a distinctive mark of Western theology for centuries. This theory is not part of the doctrine of the faith, and remains a theological hypothesis to this day, certainly worthy of attention, but always a theological hypothesis not bound to the doctrine of the faith. So the distinction between doctrine of the faith and theology is a useful requirement, whenever one wants to compose or present a book on the faith without thereby depriving theologies of their prior right to diversity, and with the affirmation, despite this, that there is something here to do with a fundamental level, the level of doctrine of the faith.

III. Hierarchy of Truths

The plan that was submitted to the attention of all the bishops in 1989 became the object of many complaints, for various reasons, particularly from the English-speaking world, because they noticed an obscuring of the principle of the hierarchy of truths. Some said that the truths of the faith suffice well enough on their own, without needing to order them according to a more or less clear enough central truth.

How does today's *CCC*, in its *conclusions*, treat this principle of the hierarchy of truths from Vatican II? Cardinal Ratzinger has always pointed out that "hierarchy of truths"—certainly a controversial term also used in the Decree on Ecumenism—cannot be considered a principle of subtraction, as though one could say, "this is essential; the rest, so to speak, is presented as a positioning and thus can be omitted." The hierarchy of truths cannot be mistaken for degrees of certainty understood in some way, since under that condition the doctrine of the faith appears to be a precise teaching for which some certainties are less certain than others.

The hierarchy of truths enters into the *CCC* through the Catechism's own expression and structure. In the debates on the *CCC*, Cdl. Ratzinger always pointed out that it was present from the beginning of the Catechism's birth, since it begins with the Credo, and then the sacraments are dealt with, and thus Christian morals, and finally prayer; these four sections coming from the primitive Church themselves constitute an expression of the hierarchy of truths.

It is fitting here to make note of the critical edition of the *Roman Catechism*, a valuable and enriching scholarly work, prepared by two scholars, members of Opus Dei. In the Vatican Library, Pedro Rodríguez and Raúl Lanzetti found the original manuscript of the *Roman Catechism*, which was thought to have disappeared, and starting from this basis they prepared the first critical edition of this catechism. In the research prior to this edition, they made clear some rather important elements which are also valid for the new

CCC. It is well known that the *Roman Catechism* has been the model for the structure of the *CCC.* Pedro Rodríguez and Raúl Lanzetti have shown that this structure is more than justified. For example, it is not justifiable that the ten commandments would appear first within the third section. In the Latin American catechetical tradition and also the French, there is a clear tendency to deal with the commandments before the sacraments, precisely as Luther did in his *Catechism.* The *Roman Catechism* follows another model here, a direct application of the hierarchy of truths: faith and sacraments, the *fides* and the *fidei sacramenta* come first of all, then, following, the commandments and prayer. Raúl Lanzetti and Pedro Rodríguez have shown that the *Roman Catechism,* in reality, is not subdivided in four but rather in two sections, two equal wings of a diptych: one wing of which opens to expose the action of God, as it is presented in the Credo, and the great works of the triune God, communicated to us in the sacraments. The second wing of the diptych represents the response of man. It is a particularly meaningful fact, as the two researchers have shown, that in this case the Council of Trent, or rather the Commission assigned to write the Catechism, chose to respond to the provocations of the Reformation.

IV. Primacy of Grace

The primacy of grace is also addressed. Again, before speaking about man's actions and obligations, first the story is told of what God has done for men, and that what God has made possible has been realized through human action and his grace. So the primacy of grace is expressed again in a second step: the proportion of the first two parts is measured in relation to the third and fourth part. These proportions correspond with a certain precision to those of the Catechism of Trent, except for one variation: in the new *CCC* the Credo occupies about 39% of the whole text, while in the Catechism of Trent 37% of the whole text is dedicated to the treatment of the sacraments. In any case, the whole of the two sections, the first and second, about the action of God with men, constitute two-thirds of the whole *CCC.* Comparing these proportions should not be interpreted as a game or a gimmick. Rather, it is a catechetical proclamation. Or rather, this way, the catechism specifies that the working of God with men, and therefore God himself, must take the first place, and that human action always takes shape in the nature of a response made possible by the impulse of grace. When we read the first statement of the third part, it is easy to see a precise parallelism with the *Roman Catechism,* precisely in the view of man's response to God: "Christian, recognize your dignity and, now that you share in God's own nature, do not return to your former base condition by sinning" (n. 1691). The imperative follows the indicative.

It concerns me that theologians do not notice clearly, or only rarely, that this important catechetical proclamation only has its effect if we look at the structure of the *CCC*. The *CCC* does not prescribe any catechetical method, as is clearly stated in the *Prologue*. Notwithstanding that, this proclamation certainly holds a central position in the whole *CCC*, thanks to the fundamental intuition that grace holds absolute primacy in the proclamation of the faith. In this way the affirmative style of the *CCC* is made clear also. The basic model runs diagonally through all the texts, especially as an affirmation of the faith on which they are based, so that from the indicative of the faith an imperative for the Christian life emerges. John Paul II intervened directly in the pages of the *CCC* rather rarely, given that he always showed a great personal interest in it. Except for one single time when he directly intervened with a significant suggestion: use affirmative language! This does not mean: "The Church affirms that Christ is risen," but much more directly, "Christ 'is' risen." Proclaiming the faith does not fit with hiding behind another authority, even that of the Church, but rather more with affirming and recognizing the proclamation itself. And not out of pride but with that humble awareness of having received in faith what was handed on to us. Yes, Christ is truly risen! From this indicative follows the imperative for the Christian life.

V. Trinitarian Structure

The topic of the hierarchy of truths appears clearly, as seldom before, in the language of the Catechism's internal structure. Already in a first glance at the table of contents, one can see that in the hierarchy of truths two fundamental points appear, as though they were the two foci of an ellipse: they are the two principal mysteries of the faith: the unity and trinity of God and the human-divinity of Jesus Christ, as they should also be for the proclamation of the faith.

The Trinity, mystery of God one and three, is presented as the central point in the hierarchy of truths: "The mystery of the Most Holy Trinity is the central mystery of Christian faith and life. It is the mystery of God in himself. It is therefore the source of all the other mysteries of faith, the light that enlightens them. It is the most fundamental and essential teaching in the 'hierarchy of the truths of faith'" (n. 234). A quotation follows from the General Catechetical Directory (47): "The whole history of salvation is identical with the history of the way and the means by which the one true God, Father, Son and Holy Spirit, reveals himself to men 'and reconciles and unites with himself those who turn away from sin.'" If anyone should wish a good summary of the whole *CCC*, composed of over 800 pages, they would find it in this affirmation. It is really the synthesis of the entire *CCC*.

A similar summary can be traced down to the first article of the CCC, which offers, so to speak, a preliminary vision of the whole: "God [is] infinitely perfect and blessed in himself." Once I happened to hold a conference for a group of young people, composed mostly of children, about the *CCC*. Obviously is not easy to talk about the *CCC* to little children. One among them was drawing while I was speaking. At the end she gave me what she had drawn as a present. It struck me greatly that this nine-year-old girl had summarized my conference with a balloon at my mouth: "God is infinitely blessed." It seemed a marvelous and theological impossibility: the response of faith of a nine-year-old girl.

This first affirmation of the *CCC*: "God is infinitely perfect and blessed in himself" leads to the second: "In a plan of sheer goodness [he] freely created man to make him share in his own blessed life." Once again I think the hierarchy of truths is here, expressed in a summary form. It speaks of sharing in the divine nature, as the Second Letter of Peter affirms about *théosis*, as they say in the Eastern Church. In fact the mystery of God one and three is the fundamental melody that runs through all the book. Only with this theme we can show how it passes through everywhere, like a *fil rouge*, to reach the light of day where the weaving of the text becomes clear, like hidden stitches in a fabric.

If we take the Creed, we notice that it has a clear trinitarian accent. But also in the various chapters it is continuously underscored that the works of God are works of the triune God. I would only like to point out that in the chapter on the Trinity the topic of the trinitarian economy is presented as an opening perspective for the remainder and for the whole text of the *CCC*: "*O lux beata Trinitas et principalis Unitas*: 'O blessed light, O Trinity and first Unity!' God is eternal blessedness, undying life, unfading light. God is love: Father, Son and Holy Spirit" (n. 257) Hence this shows how the whole divine economy, the whole divinity, and also salvation and all of created reality is a work of the three divine persons and how this work ultimately seeks to incorporate the human being into the intimacy of the communion of trinitarian life. This is well demonstrated by n. 260, which ends with the prayer of St. Elizabeth of the Trinity: "O my God, Trinity whom I adore…" This is a first focus of the ellipse.

VI. The Mystery of Christ

The second focal point of the ellipse regards the mystery of Christ. I take the liberty of pointing back, again in this case, to the *Prologue* that recalls the Christological articles of faith in the Credo. It is important here to take into consideration nn. 426 and those following, where, in harmony with *CT* the central place of Christ in catechesis is emphasized: "'At the heart of catechesis we find, in essence, a Person, the Person of Jesus of Nazareth, the only Son from the Father…who suffered and died for us and who now, after rising, is living with us forever.' To catechize is 'to reveal in the Person of Christ the whole of God's eternal design […] It is to seek to understand the meaning of Christ's actions and words and of the signs worked by him.' Catechesis aims at putting "people…in communion…with Jesus Christ: only he can lead us to the love of the Father in the Spirit and make us share in the life of the Holy Trinity'" (n. 426). There is much to say about this Christocentric perspective; I would just like to demonstrate two points. The first relates to the "mysteries of the life of Jesus," which often seems neglected among the fundamental sources of Christology. I am convinced that a rich perspective of 20th-century Christology is hiding here, and we can make new use of it. I am thinking of Hugo Rahner's words in the 1930s and of the proposal by Karl Rahner and Hans Urs von Balthasar to conceive a dogmatic theology from the viewpoint of salvation history. It has become rather clear that there has been a considerable accent on exegesis basing itself on the historical-critical method; related to that, the connection between the life of Jesus and his realization in our existence has been somewhat lost in part along the way. Naturally the question of the historical Jesus has remained, at least for the adepts of exegetical work, as has the connection to liturgical-sacramental life, to the point that we celebrate the entire life of the Lord annually within the cycle of the liturgical year, to make it present and to bring ourselves into it. Now, following a choice by the Commission for the *CCC* which emerged already in the first meeting, it was fairly clear for the *CCC* to set out to present the life of Jesus from the perspective of the theology of the mysteries (broadly speaking). When we read the paragraph titled "Mysteries of the life of Jesus" seen from a Christological viewpoint, we have to perceive the corresponding attempt to create bridges to the liturgy, and to the sacramentary and morals, because in fact Christian life is the life of Christ in us. Christ wants to live his own life in our life (cf. n. 521).

These are two focal points that clearly show the sacramental framework in which they are placed. The first four sections are presented like a picture, and the first three of them can be found in proto-Christian art. At the front of the second section stands a fresco image from the catacombs of Saints Peter and Marcellinus. It depicts the woman suffering from a hemorrhage who touched the hem of Jesus' garment. When we read the story of this image, we also understand the perspective from which the whole sacramental section was conceived. "The sacraments of the Church now continue the works which Christ had performed during his earthly life." In the same text there is a reference to St. Leo the Great: "What was visible in our Savior has passed over into his mysteries" (n. 1115). The mysteries of the life of Jesus are made present to us in the sacraments. Continuing the narration of the fresco image:

"The sacraments are as it were 'powers that go forth' from the Body of Christ" (as was said in the Gospel of Luke: "power came forth from him," and in the Gospel of Mark: "power had gone out from him") "to heal the wounds of sin and to give us the new life of Christ." "This image thus symbolizes the divine and saving power of the Son of God who heals the whole man, soul and body, through the sacramental life."

When the *Prologue* opens in the third section, here too we notice the perspective of the mysteries of the life of Jesus. Here we read at the end of the *Prologue*: "The first and last point of reference of this catechesis will always be Jesus Christ himself, who is 'the way, and the truth, and the life' (Jn 14:6). It is by looking to him in faith that Christ's faithful can hope that he himself fulfills his promises in them, and that, by loving him with the same love with which he has loved them, they may perform works in keeping with their dignity" (n. 1698). The whole is clarified further with a quotation from St. John Eudes: "I ask you to consider that our Lord Jesus Christ is your true head, and that you are one of his members. He belongs to you as the head belongs to its members; all that is his is yours: his spirit, his heart, his body and soul, and all his faculties. You must make use of all these as of your own, to serve, praise, love, and glorify God. You belong to him, as members belong to their head, and so he longs for you to use all that is in you, as if it were his own, for the service and glory of the Father" (ibid.). Here we can see the kind of perspective in which the hierarchy of truths is being considered, always remaining fixed on the Christological pole as a focal point of the ellipse, to reach the concrete questions about morality.

VII. Unity of Scripture and Tradition

Let us devote another word to the use of Scripture by the *CCC*. The exegetical work imprinted on the *CCC* was overseen by excellent experts and exegetes. It is not at all the case that if you look at the text of the *CCC*, the exegesis of the past thirty or fifty years has been bypassed. The text about the relation of Jesus and the Jewish people, for example, between Jesus and those favored by the crowds (nn. 574–591) presupposes different and rather nuanced exegetical studies. Anyone who has had to devote himself to exegesis, even only a little, will notice that the exegetical work is ample and of the highest quality. So when the exegetical work is criticized as "carried out unscientifically" because the *CCC* affirms "Jesus said"—followed by a quote from the Gospel of John—it seems to me, then, that the objection rebounds on itself. We are dealing here with a Catechism, not an exegetical monograph, but rather a book of the faith. So it is legitimate when we say in the liturgy: "Word of our Lord Jesus Christ," when we read the Gospel of John. On this point, almost no one says that the Gospel of John is an *ipsissima vox*. In a similar way, the criticism aimed at the Pastoral Letters, when they are cited with the *incipit* "Paul says," before a quotation from the First Letter to Timothy, is equally unserious. In reality one makes a distinction between a monograph of scholarly exegesis and the catechetical use of Scripture. Rather, we must say, and based on the Church's exegetical criteria, we have the right to say, "Paul writes in the First Letter to Timothy. ..." This does not mean that he delivered the Letter, let alone that the First Letter to Timothy is the *ipsissima vox* of the apostle Paul. However, when the Church, in her own liturgy, declares this Letter to be from Paul, this is not done without an authentic justification. The criteria with which Scripture is used in the *CCC* are those indicated in *DV* 12. Whenever we study the Sacred Scriptures by exploring the intention declared by the sacred authors, it is legitimate and necessary that attention be given to the culture, the idioms, the thought, and the literary genre of that time. Moreover, there is an important principle for correct interpretation, without which the Scripture remains a dead letter, and it is this: Scripture is read and interpreted with the same Spirit by whom it was inspired (cf. *CCC* 111). This is about the intimate relation between scholarly and spiritual interpretation. It is about accurately paying attention to the content and to the unity of the whole Scripture. Scripture is interpreted within the common tradition of the Church and cannot be read in a way detached from the interpretive history which precedes it. This is done precisely out of consideration for the analogy of faith, which is also based upon the experience of faith through the centuries that have preceded us. Thanks to this, Francis of Assisi is a living commentary on the Gospel. And it is just this that the *CCC* seeks to expound: Scripture and Tradition mutually interwoven in unity.

A complaint has also been raised that various citations in the *CCC* follow one after another: Augustine, then Thomas, then the Councils, then citations from the liturgy. About this criticism, some considerations can be offered. The basic idea being consciously carried out is to perceive the Tradition of the Church which presents itself as a living unity. Because of this, I have the right and the possibility of reading Augustine today without being an anti-Pelagian specialist, and to read Thomas without being a profound connoisseur of Aristotle. This means that alongside the scholarly interpretation of Church teaching there must also appear a reading performed within the unity of the Tradition of the faith, in which I, for example, can read Augustine as among the first witnesses of the faith. Because of this, Thomas, Augustine, Irenaeus, and little Thérèse of Lisieux can be considered companions close to one another. Indeed, this is about the contemporaneousness of the faith.

Finally, the decisive experience of the saints also pertains to this proposition. In all the important passages of the *CCC* there has been a conscious attempt to leave the last word to the saints, to make it clear that this is not merely a dry teaching, but a living experience of faith. It would have been impossible for this Catechism to represent the diverse faith experiences of the present day in an articulated manner, given that they are rather varied from a cultural point of view. However, one experience can be universalized like no other: the experience of the saints. It is no accident that no saint is as popular today, even outside the confines of the Church, as St. Francis of Assisi. Similarly, it is no accident that little Thérèse is the most popular saint at a worldwide level. The fact that little Thérèse, Teresa of Avila, Catherine of Siena, and other saintly women have the last word in the *CCC*, does not meant that women in the Church have to have the last word, but that the saints have a last word to say. It is the more important word, exactly the Word in which it becomes clear that the doctrine of the faith ultimately possesses something that has to do with life. And this needs to become evident with the testimony of the saints.

RECEPTION OF THE CATECHISM OF THE CATHOLIC CHURCH

Caroline Farey

Introduction

The concept of "reception" and the proof of its importance can be found already in the New Testament (cf. 1 Cor 12; 1 Cor 15). The baptized Christian is sanctified by the Holy Spirit, by means of whom each one will be able to receive and adhere to the truths of the faith for "the renewal and building up of the Church" (*LG* 12). The reception by the people of God of "what is proposed as belonging to the faith of the Apostles" (*SF* 74) is taken seriously: "because it is by the Church as a whole that the apostolic faith is borne in the power of the Spirit" (*SF* 74).

A working definition of the Church's concept of reception is contained in the recent document on the *sensus fidei* developed by the International Theological Commission (2014). It is described as "a process by which, guided by the Spirit, the people of God recognizes intuitions or insights and integrates them into the patterns and structures of its life and worship, accepting a new witness to the truth and corresponding forms of its expression, because it perceives them to be in accord with the apostolic Tradition" (*SF* 78). An important concept stands out here: that the believer is already in accord with apostolic Tradition in order to be a legitimate part of the ecclesial "process" of reception.

A lack of reception of magisterial teaching, then, "may indicate a weakness or a lack of faith on the part of the people of God, [...]. But in some cases it may indicate that certain decisions have been taken by those in authority without due consideration of the experience and the *sensus fidei* of the faithful" (*SF* 123). In the case of the Catechism, some have raised the suggestion that the apparent non-reception of some elements of its content is a clear sign of these last two possibilities.

Another element related to reception and relevant for our purposes is found in the same document: "The Eucharist shapes and forms" the people of God, since it is here that the mystery of the faith is received most fully, is "encountered and celebrated" (SF 75). This is clearly a significant condition that implies, along with the need to be in accord with the apostolic Tradition which reaches us through the Magisterium, that the attitudes and theological positions of those who have not fully received the *CCC* (or those who maintain their non-reception) must be taken into consideration.

This analysis of how reception is connected to the *CCC* is presented here in three parts: first of all, questions related to reception of the *content* of the document are considered; second, the reception of the *nature* of the *Catechism* is examined; and third, evidence of reception is described in terms of the catechetical usefulness of the *CCC*; for example, the number of translations, the spread of local catechisms and all the other types of publications, including those related to electronic media.

I. Reception of the Content of the CCC

The most significant element to note, when we face the whole question of reception of the doctrinal content of the *CCC* is that the content consists expressly of an "already" "received doctrine." Therefore, the content is presented as "an organic synthesis of the essential and fundamental contents of Catholic doctrine, as regards both faith and morals" (*CCC* 11), drawing from "the Sacred Scriptures, the Fathers of the Church, the liturgy, and the Church's Magisterium" (ibid.).

The authors of the various parts and the Commission that supervised the project followed several editorial criteria, among which was one that "claims the first rank: everything that can be considered as pertaining to a school of theology should be set apart from the *CCC*." This, explained Cardinal Schönborn, was due to the fact that "the *CCC* is not situated at the level of the theologies, which are necessarily plural, but at the level of the *regula fidei* which is necessarily one." Its content "is at a level that precedes theological concepts and provides for their foundation" (Cardinal Christoph Schönborn, *"Il concetto teologico del Catechismo della Chiesa Cattolica"* [conference address], October 9, 2002). In this essay, presented on the occasion of the tenth anniversary of the *CCC*, Schönborn provides the example of St. Augustine's explanation of the most holy Trinity. While Augustine is the most cited ecclesiastical writer mentioned in the *CCC*, his explanation of the most holy Trinity was deliberately not included, because it was judged as a "particular" theological explanation rather than something that can be considered normative in "apostolic Tradition."

In the same tenth-anniversary conference, Cardinal Ratzinger emphasized that "the goal of the *CCC* is precisely that of presenting this 'given' that precedes us, whose developing doctrinal formulation of the faith is offered in the Church; it is a proclamation of faith, not a theology." He continued: "the faith is not primarily the matter for intellectual experimentation, it is rather the solid foundation—the hypostasis, as the Letter to the Hebrews (11:1) tells us—on which we can live and die" (Congregation for the Doctrine of the Faith, Address of Cardinal Joseph Ratzinger: "Current Doctrinal Relevance of the Catechism of the Catholic Church," October 9, 2002).

The changes introduced by the definitive edition of 1997, therefore, were intended to guarantee that the content present in the *CCC* truly *be* and *only* be the "doctrine already received," which flows from Scripture and Tradition and which has been confirmed by the Magisterium. Hence we see an emendation made in the 1997 definitive edition of the *CCC*, for example, by removing a phrase that had been included in the 1992 edition about nations "entrusted by divine providence to the guardianship of angels" (*CCC* 57, 1992 edition).

It is useful to think in terms of authentic Christian culture being an "expression of received doctrine," showing this reception in the four dimensions of Church life, "profession of faith," the "sacraments of the faith" celebrated in the liturgy of the Church, the "life of faith" in its moral positions and commitments, and the "prayer of the faithful" (cf. *CCC* 13–17). These appear in the Catholic cultural heritage of writings, the arts, architecture, liturgical practices, mores and social laws, and in the Church's prayers, hymns, and devotions. These expressions of reception through the centuries—from various nations, by women and men saints and writers, and from diverse historical periods—notably enrich the *CCC*. The four works of art included in the *CCC*, for example, together with the full range of sources attested in the index of citations, reveal something of the contribution of these expressions of received doctrine.

Social doctrine was the section most difficult to structure in regard to "received doctrine," as Cardinal Ratzinger explained, "on the one hand, on account of the differences that are debated about the structural principles of Christian morality, and on the other by reason of the difficult problems in the realm of political, social ethics, and bioethics" (Ratzinger, 2002). The Church has a prophetic voice about the current state of events connected to the present time, and only with a sense of the time it is possible to distinguish more easily what is truly perennial.

Differing visions about the relation of doctrine and theology have also influenced the reception of the content of the *CCC* in a variety of ways. For example, it is clear that some problems are rooted either in the failure to recognize some significant difference between doctrine and theology or in not accepting the Church's basic understanding of theology. Those who do not acknowledge any distinction between doctrine and theology, who hold that so-called "doctrine" is in reality "another theology," one among many, do not see any reasons to offer a preferential treatment to one rather than another theology and would prefer to observe a variety or a balance among the theological viewpoints presented. On the other hand, those who embrace a patristic and ecclesial vision of theology (cf. *CCC* 236), according to which the self-revelation of God constitutes a mystery into which we are called to enter, understand that "theology [is…] the effort to recognize the gift of knowledge that precedes […] reflection" (cf. Ratzinger, 2002), and so they can build their theological reflection on the solid base of transmitted doctrine present in the *CCC*.

Another reason in support of non-reception of the content of the *CCC*, on the ground of its apparent irrelevance, is advanced by theologians involved in the fragmentation of the traditional discipline, in theologies based on hermeneutical keys. Scripture and Tradition are thus read from a specific perspective—feminist, Black, liberation, and so on. In general, doctrine is considered fixed, static, and ahistorical, and necessarily limiting the freedom of expression required for creative theological exploration. Cardinal Piacenza, clearly considering the way in which such theologies have distanced themselves from the deposit of faith, speaks of a theological understanding that needs to invest "its own energies in a less centrifugal and somewhat sadly marginal way, with respect to the essential truths of our faith" (Piacenza, 2012).

For Cardinal Avery Dulles, the *CCC* is "the boldest challenge yet offered to the cultural relativism that currently threatens to erode the contents of Catholic faith" (A. Dulles, "The Challenge of the Catechism," in First Things 1/1995). He maintains that among theologians there are some who consider doctrinal affirmations "so culturally conditioned that they cannot be transferred from one age or one cultural region to another. Every theological affirmation that comes to us from the past must be examined with suspicion because it was formulated in a situation differing markedly from our own." For these thinkers there is only the forward-looking dimension, with the *CCC* considered as only one perspective, under the best of hypotheses a model, but without occupying a privileged position.

Once again, some have maintained that some doctrines contained in the *CCC* are simply outmoded and obsolete (for example, certain eschatological teachings or those on original sin.) They maintain that the weak reception of the *CCC* was caused by contemporary theological re-examination of those concepts in some environments. Here the doctrinal consensus is considered as "a threat to the creativity of local churches" (Dulles, cit.) Here too the *CCC* is not received due to a misunderstanding about the nature of what is contained in the *CCC*.

The acceptance of the Second Vatican Council also influences the reception of the content of the *CCC*, which depends strongly on it (cf. the index of citations). Those who read the Second Vatican Council with a hermeneutic of continuity and reform receive the *CCC* as the combination of the Council's work with the continuity of Tradition. Those who consider the Council under a hermeneutic of discontinuity and rupture from a past which is unfortunately lost now, as well as those who see in the Council a necessary and valuable break from the preconciliar Church, both find it difficult to see the texts of the Council used with a hermeneutic of continuity with apostolic Tradition.

Some Scripture scholars, moreover, have rejected the content of the *CCC* for its failure to incorporate some conclusions typical of contemporary exegesis. However, this rejection is caused in large part by a misunderstanding about the specific nature of a catechism and on the role of Scripture in teaching the faith that comes from the Apostles and which "is the foundation of Christian life." Ratzinger responded to this type of criticism of the *CCC*, recalling that "relative to a work which must present the faith—not hypotheses [...] we must keep in mind how rapidly exegetical hypotheses change and, to be honest, how great is the dissent, even among scholars, regarding many theses." He continues with a threefold defense of the use of Scripture in the *CCC*, which is worth quoting in its entirety: "The canonical method of exegesis emphasizes the unity of the Bible as the principle of interpretation; synchronic and diachronic interpretation are being increasingly recognized in their equal dignity. The essential connection of Scripture and Tradition is emphasized by the famous exegetes of all confessions; it seems clear that an exegesis separated from the life of the Church and from her historical experience is not binding and cannot go beyond the category of hypothesis" (Ratzinger, 2002).

Probably the most deeply rooted source of non-reception of the *CCC* is the rejection of the premise of a unique deposit of faith and of the "interior certainty" of only one faith. To receive the *CCC* in accord with apostolic Tradition means accepting revelation as a "divine deposit committed to the spouse of Christ to be faithfully protected and infallibly promulgated" (*DF* IV; cf. *DS* 3020).

Cardinal Müller speaks of the unity of the faith in his exposition on the "*Ecclesiality of the Catechism*" (Cdl. Müller, Ecclesiality of the Catechism, Ireland, 2014) in which he speaks of the "ecclesial character of the *Catechism of the Catholic Church*, [...] that in its origin, content and structure it reveals itself to be intrinsically *of the Catholic Church*." It is the Church's instrument at the service of her fundamental evangelistic mission. The very first words of the *CCC* express this: "Father, [...] this is eternal life, that they may know you, the only true God, and Jesus Christ whom you have sent" (Jn 17:3).

To respond to the relativism and perspectivism of certain theologies, Pope John Paul II, in his encyclical *FR*, speaks of the indispensable requirements of the Word of God. He affirms these requirements in a precise way because they are frequently denied. Without these three requirements, the Word of God cannot be fully grasped or understood and the *CCC* often is not received when these elements are missing. The requirements are philosophical, in the sense that certain fundamental positions need to be maintained to be able to fully attest the truth of the Word of God. The first requirement is an all-encompassing meaning of life. It is not possible to teach the Catholic faith as one equally valid system of beliefs among others, if Jesus is the only-begotten Son of God. The second requirement is that of trusting in the human capacity to know objective truth. In the transmission of the Word, our trust can be placed legitimately in Scripture and apostolic Tradition as objectively true for all of humanity. The third requirement is the maintenance of a genuine "metaphysical range" that allows man "to move from phenomenon to foundation," transcending empirical data to attain to something absolute, ultimate and fundamental in the search for truth. This passage from phenomenon to foundation is described as "a step as necessary as it is urgent" (*FR* 81–83) and its absence has also influenced the reception of the *CCC*.

II. Reception of the Nature of a Catechism

"The Catechism is not a theology book, but a book of the faith, for the teaching of the faith. In present day theological consciousness this fundamental difference is often not sufficiently present" (Ratzinger, 2002). The *CCC* is at the service of catechesis, which is not "less than" theology or an "impoverished level" of theology; rather it is theology which is to be of service to catechesis. Given that the Church exists to evangelize (*EN* 14), it is well to recall that "theological work in the Church is first of all at the service of the proclamation of the faith and of catechesis" (*FR* 99). A catechism is intended by its nature, structure, and purpose to be an instrument of transmission; it is, so to speak, explicitly intended to "promote the reception of the faith."

Transmission and reception are like two faces of the same coin; only what is received can be transmitted, and only what is transmitted can be received. As St. Paul says, "faith comes from what is heard" (Rom 10:17). The transmission is not complete until there is a corresponding reception. Both of these take time and human attention; both are living processes in the life and growth of the Church. Therefore to pose the question of the reception of the *CCC*, we have to ask if it is fulfilling its nature and its own aim, because it is a document intended for the constant mission of the Church to "hand on" (*traditio*) the fullness of faith in Jesus Christ which leads every person to the home of the Father.

The lack of reception of the *CCC* can derive simply from the lack of understanding of the nature of catechesis. Those who think that catechesis is "merely [a question] of eliminating ignorance" (*DCG* 9) and who correspondingly expect the Catechism to be a compendium of information as one finds in the work of Ludwig Ott or in Denzinger remain disappointed at bumping into a pedagogical instrument.

There are also those who understand that catechesis relates to something more than the simple imparting of knowledge, but also nonetheless think that the *CCC* has only that aim. Publishers who remove the works of art and the index of citations from the *CCC*, in effect, are removing two key instruments of teaching with regard to the transmission of the Tradition and the patrimony of the family of God. Such publishers, deciding to remove the indexes of citations of works from the cultural, historical, and pastoral areas, have treated the *CCC* as if it were simply a reference text for the knowledge of the material.

Thus the *CCC* is intended to help in the recovery of the *traditio Evangelii* (cf. *Instrumentum Laboris* for the 13th Ordinary General Assembly of the Synod of Bishops, dedicated to "The new evangelization for the transmission of the Christian faith," Vatican City: Libreria Editrice Vaticana, 2012, n. 26), in order to be a faithful transmission of the good News and the four dimensions of the Christian life, and a complete formation in the faith. Those who seek a catechetical instrument to support a more "experiential" catechesis are disappointed to find the *CCC* so exhaustive from a doctrinal point of view. In presenting this "dogmatic spirituality," the *CCC* also incarnates the healthy tendencies of the catechetical renewal of the 20th century—including the liturgical and scriptural elements from the renewal of Jungmann and the kerygmatic structure developed by Hofinger. Whoever is unaware that the intuitions of these important figures of the catechetical renewal are found in the *CCC* cannot take account of the importance of the role the *CCC* can play, and is playing, in the renewal of catechesis (cf. the analysis in P. de Cointet, B. Morgan, P. Willey, *The Catechism of the Catholic Church and the Craft of Catechesis*, San Francisco: Ignatius, 2007). In the *CCC* content is presented in a way that manifests and demonstrates the pedagogy of God. It is the presentation of a doctrine that honors the pathways of God and man (cf. C. Farey, W. Linnig, M.J. Paruch, *The Pedagogy of God. Its Centrality in Catechesis and Catechetical Formation*, Steubenville: Emmaus Road, 2011).

III. Translations, Local Catechisms, and Other Publications

We notice that where the *CCC* has been presented well, its reception has been extremely widespread and widely felt. For example, the largest religious network in the world, EWTN (Eternal Word Television Network), which broadcasts in 145 countries today, promotes the *CCC* to its television viewers in all areas of life and in different languages. It also promotes the entire *CCC*, all four parts, as an organic and integrated whole, and has done so continually and as a policy over the last twenty-five years in many of its programs specifically dedicated to the *CCC* itself. In a similar way, Shalom TV of India has a constant promotion of the *CCC* in its schedule. These examples remind us that "reception" in the 21st century has to include not only the printed page but also Catholic radio, various electronic programs and markets of the digital world.

Considering reception, one has to recall the great number of translations into various languages that have taken place since the first publication in 1992 in French, the language of the editorial committee, and the two million copies sold. The first fruits of reception were evidenced by the rapid translations into other European languages, two years later into English, and gradually into another 35 languages such as Arabic, Chinese, Persian, Malay, Vietnamese, Swahili, and Ethiopian, just to name a few. Publication has continued in all the European languages except German.

As recommended by the *CCC* itself (n. 24) for the purpose of understanding, local catechisms, resources for the formation of catechists and for the spread of catechesis, have begun to be produced in various parts of the world, as was requested of the Episcopal Conferences. However, the process is not simple. The Congregation for the Doctrine of the Faith and the Congregation for the Clergy compiled the text *"Orientamenti circa le 'opere sintesi' del CCC"* [Instructions regarding works derived from the *CCC*] (December 20, 1994), on local catechisms whose authoritative reference text is the *CCC*. The document speaks of the need for an adequate assimilation of the *CCC*. Even in the case of a "prolonged time for assimilation of the *CCC*, there will be preparation of the theological, catechetical, and linguistic terrain for a real work of inculturation of the content of the *Catechism*" (*Orientamenti* 3).

In other words, a period of reception is needed, above all, so that the local catechisms can be prepared truly. Others have been published, but it would be interesting to note: how many have included, for example, the way of beauty? How many have included or excluded the index of citations from Scripture and from Tradition, or have they presented only an index of citations from Scripture? How many are kerygmatic, with a presentation always linked to the fundamental truths? How many are attempting an organic presentation and how do they explain it? How the *CCC* does this is explained in nn. 18–22. How well is doctrine expressed in life, as is done in the *CCC* through the words of saints? Are events such as the Year of Faith and other occasions and conferences on the anniversary of the date of publication efforts intended to promote "a little more detailed reception of the Catechism, as an instrument of sure doctrine and, at the same time, of a correct hermeneutic of the Second Vatican Council"? (Piacenza, *Lectio magistralis su Catechismo e nuova evangelizzazione*, May 19, 2012).

Pedagogical texts: Cardinals Ratzinger and Schönborn have written various explanatory works that introduce the text and its pedagogical characteristics. This topic has only been taken up in the works of Petroc Willey at Franciscan University of Steubenville and at the Institute of Notre Dame de Vie in France.

Homiletic texts: The index of scriptural citations in the *CCC* has been used to compile model texts for catechetical homilies that connect passages of Scripture from the Liturgy of the Word to the doctrine of the Church supported by the same passages of Scripture.

Catechetical texts: The Committee for Catechesis of the United States Conference of Catholic Bishops has been able to influence the publishers of catechetical works who have brought many publications to press in English, Spanish, Portuguese, and French with a major and direct reference to the content of the *CCC*, and to its structure in four parts. Bibles, both for adults and for adolescents, have been published making reference to the *CCC* to help catechists keep Scripture, Tradition, and Magisterium united.

Texts for youth: The YouCat series, produced in many languages, brings the *CCC* closer to the young through digital tools and traditional printed books.

Doctrinal texts: In various languages, especially Portuguese, Spanish, and English, internet searches show works based broadly on the *CCC* in support of the *traditio Evangelii*.

As Cardinal Piacenza has said, "much has been done, but certainly much still remains to be done for the correct reception of the *CCC*": to obtain this, we will do well to turn to the perfect model of receptivity of the Word made flesh, the blessed Virgin Mary, Mother of the Incarnate Word. Posing the question of the reception of the *CCC* means asking if it has been received analogously to Mary's reception of the message of the archangel Gabriel. By reason of her perfect reception of the Word of God, Pope St. John Paul II defined her as "a living catechism" (*CT* 73). Receiving the Blessed Mother into our own lives enables the faithful to also receive the *CCC*.

PART ONE

THE PROFESSION OF FAITH

Section One

"I BELIEVE"—"WE BELIEVE"

Chapter One:
MAN'S CAPACITY FOR GOD

Ramón Lucas Lucas

The *imago Dei* is a core expression of sacred Scripture to define the human being, and it is affirmed in the *CCC* from the beginning (nn. 31, 36). Starting from the book of Genesis, man is described as one who can enter into communion with God and listen to his voice. According to Rousseau, man is distinguished from other animals not by perfection but by perfectibility; that is, perfection in man is not having reached the highest level of development among the primates, but being conscious that his life is a task and a responsibility, because he perceives an absolute perfection and aims to reach it. The intention at the basis of the first chapters of Genesis, from which the *CCC* takes the expression *imago Dei*, is nothing to do with making a cosmological description, but rather to clarify the meaning and significance of human existence and to place "man [...] before God [...] in search of his own identity; it could be said he is in search of the definition of himself" (John Paul II, Wednesday catechesis, October 10, 1979). His is not a static perfection, but dynamic: he is *capax Dei*, or as the philosophers say, *quodammodo omnia*. In fact, by his nature, inasmuch as he is *imago Dei* and *capax infiniti*, he tends to desire God, to search for truth and to aspire for the infinite (n. 27). "Man infinitely transcends man" (Pascal, *Pensées*), feeling he is truly himself when he is surpassing the limits of finitude, *trasumana* (Dante, *Paradiso*, I, 70), beyond human. His finite being transcends itself while remaining itself because "in fact, what is man in nature? A nothing in comparison with the infinite, an all in comparison with the nothing, a mean between nothing and everything" (Pascal, *Pensées*, 72). Benedict XVI expressed it well: "The person who turns to God does not become smaller but greater, for through God and with God he becomes great, he becomes divine, he becomes truly himself" (Cappella Papale on the 40th anniversary of the closure of the Second Vatican Council, Homily, December 8, 2005) inasmuch as he is *imago Dei*. To be a man is not to exist, but to ask oneself about existence. Since the time of Socrates we have testimonies that the human being is the only being that wonders about the why of things.

From these first reflections, it is already evident that the *CCC* seeks to bring together the doctrinal dimension and the moral and pastoral dimension. To be *capax Dei* is not only an ontological constitution, but also a calling to the coherence of freedom and a demand of moral life. For the Christian, the connection between ethical life and Christian faith is not necessary from the point of view of ethics, but from that of faith. It is that faith that needs morality to verify its authenticity. Only when a person has Catholic faith, an ethic arises in him that necessarily takes shape in reference to the faith he professes. So this ethic is "religious" not for the sake of an intrinsic requirement, but due to the necessary interaction of faith with the moral life. "If you love me, you will keep my commandments" (Jn 14:15), Jesus says. Openness to faith does not deprive man of his absolute value; rather, it leads him to discover fully why "only in the mystery of the incarnate Word does the mystery of man take on light" (*GS* 22). It is precisely God who makes a human being be the one he is. In this way, the fulfillment of man is always inclination to God and participation in his perfection. Because of this *VS* speaks of "participated theonomy" (n. 41).

I. The Desire for God

The "desire for God" of which the *CCC* speaks is not a feeling, nor an act of will; rather it is a basic structure of the person. One of the essential characteristics of the revealed Christian message is its universality. If it is directed to all men (n. 51), that means that in everyone there is the capacity to receive it as the foundation of universality. Such a message calls for the anthropology or vision of man that has become traditional in the Catholic Church and has imprinted itself on the expression "human nature," There is a human nature, shared by all men, in which we recognize the prerequisites for the universal call to salvation and the point of contact with the Absolute. If all men had not been equal, if they had not possessed a nature or essence, that is, a common ontological structure that is realized in the uniqueness or particularity of each of them, they would not be called to salvation nor could they receive revelation (n. 36). The vocation of all to supernatural life requires that in every man there be a common basis that stands to mean what man is, what is essential to him. This common basis is precisely the ontological constitution traditionally called "human nature." Only one particular ontological constitution, a "natural desire for God," is a condition for the possibility of being "beyond human" and being the recipient of revelation, enabling him to respond to it in a personal way.

The Christian revelation is the call to a dialogue of love between God and the human being. This is possible only if man is structurally capable of hearing the said call and establishing the relationship of a dialogue of love. There must be within man, not only in his conscious and free acts, but also in his very ontological structure, an anchoring point with God. As Emil Brunner says, "no one who agrees that only human subjects but not sticks and stones can receive the Word of God and the Holy Spirit can deny" this. "The Word of God does not have to create man's capacity for words. He has never lost it: it is the presupposition of his ability to hear the Word of God. But the Word of God itself creates man's ability to believe the Word of God, i.e., the ability to hear it in such a way as is only possible in faith" (Brunner, *Natural Theology*, 1946, translation of *Natur und Gnade*, 1934).

Brunner sees this point of contact in the biblical concept of the *imago Dei*, thereby following a consolidated theological tradition, as can be derived from the writings of St. Irenaeus and St. Thomas Aquinas, who take up the thought of St. Augustine and bases this capacity on the fact that man is created in the image of God: "the soul is naturally capable of grace; since, from its having been made in the likeness of God, it is fit to receive God by grace, as Augustine says [*De Trinitate*, 14, 8]" (*Summa Theologica*, I–II, 113, 10). This is also confirmed by the *CCC*, which, recalling *GS*, places it as the foundation of human dignity: "The desire for God is written in the human heart, because man is created by God and for God; [...] 'The dignity of man rests above all on the fact that he is called to communion with God'" (n. 27); "Created in God's image and called to know and love him" (n. 31). In any case, it seems fitting to underscore that the essence of the *imago Dei*, and therefore of the "desire for God," is found in the open and spiritual nature of man who, precisely because of this, is capable of hearing the Word. This human spiritual nature is the foundation of man's possibility of establishing a dialogue with God, the reason by which we can affirm that the human being is by his nature "religious." This is the anthropological basis of the vocation of all men to salvation. Only an anthropology in which man is a spiritual being, structurally open to the Absolute, can be compatible with revelation (n. 36). We can do well to recall Nietzsche's expression, "the greatness of man is in being a bridge, not an end"; in his very structure man has a contact/anchorage with God.

The academic vicissitudes that brought the young Karl Rahner to study theology did not stop him from researching the anthropological roots of the possibility man has to be a "hearer of the Word". To hear the revealing word implies and attests to a fundamental constitution of the hearer. "This fundamental constitution of man, which he implicitly affirms in all of his knowledge and actions, we call, in a word, his spirituality. Man is spiritual, that is, he lives his life in a continual striving toward the Absolute, in an openness to God. And this openness to God is not a happenstance that, so to speak, can appear or not appear in man here and there at his pleasure. It is the condition that enables man to be what he is and must be and it is always present, even in the least actions of everyday life. He is man only because he is already on a journey toward God, whether he knows it expressly or not, whether he wants it or not, because he is always finite being's endless openness to God" (*Hörer des Wortes* [Hearers of the Word], in *Sämtliche Werke* [Collected Works], vol. 4, Benziger, 1997, 103). Rahner's text is significant: man can hear and adhere to the call of God, because he is structurally open to him. His spiritual nature is precisely this openness to the Transcendent.

II. Ways of Coming to Know God

Man, *capax Dei*, feels the need to know the one of whom he is the image (*CCC* 31). *Fides quaerens intellectum* is the famous title Anselm gave to the *Proslogion*, written for "one who is trying to raise his spirit to contemplate God and seeking to understand what he believes" (*Preface*). The expression has become classic to indicate, on one hand, the possibility for human reason to know God; on the other, the need for reason to be involved with faith, which thus becomes theo-logy; *"Oportet philosophari in theologia,"* says Fisichella (cf. Gregorianum 76 [2/1995] 221–262 and 76 [3/1995] 503–534). A *fides quaerens intellectum* flees from superstition, seeks understanding, and cannot neglect to give a reason for what it believes. A believer does not nullify reason, but rather exalts it, seeking as much as possible to give "a reason for one's faith," yet without being able to prove it. What Camus said is not true: that a believer only has dogmas. Faith seeks intelligibility: *credo ut intelligam.* I believe in order to understand, to deepen the reasons that are present in the contents of the faith. But "the motivations for faith are sufficient, because the understanding adheres to them without this appearing absurd; but they are not sufficient to produce a forced adherence, as, for example, the proof of the Pythagorean theorem does. For this adherence to take place requires, under the influence of grace, a free and personal act of the will" (F. Hadjadj, *La fede dei demoni ovvero Il superamento dell'ateismo* [The faith of the demons, or Overcoming atheism], Genoa and Milan: Marietti, 2010, 82).

FR highlights the metaphysical openness that allows man to pass from phenomenon to foundation: "Wherever men and women discover a call to the absolute and transcendent, the metaphysical dimension of reality opens up before them: in truth, in beauty, in moral values, in other persons, in being itself, in God. We face a great challenge at the end of this millennium to move from *phenomenon* to *foundation*, a step as necessary as it is urgent. We cannot stop short at experience alone; even if experience does reveal the human being's interiority and spirituality, speculative thinking must penetrate to the spiritual core and the ground from which it rises. Therefore, a philosophy which shuns metaphysics would be radically unsuited to the task of mediation in the understanding of Revelation" (*FR* 83).

Equilibrium between faith and reason is always necessary. As Thomas Aquinas says, "when a man's will is ready to believe, he loves the truth he believes, he thinks out and takes to heart whatever reasons he can find in support thereof" (*Summa Theologica*, II–II, 2, 10). Understanding, however, is not really possible without faith; therefore *intellectus quaerens fidem* is also necessary: "I [...] desire to understand your truth a little, that truth that my heart believes and loves. For I do not seek to understand so that I may believe; but I believe so that I may understand. For I believe this also, that 'unless I believe, I shall not understand' (Is 7:9)" (*Proslogion*, 1). These expressions are already present in St. Augustine who had the experience before Anselm: "Unless you believe, you will not understand" (*Sermons*, 41, 9). "Do not forsake me when I call on you, who, before I called on you, anticipated me" (*Confessiones*, XIII, 1, 1). Augustine is very astute. He had sought the truth everywhere, and once he had found it in the faith, he does not give up understanding what reason is able to reach (n. 35). It is enough to cite two very incisive texts: "But we desire to have knowledge and learning of what we accept by faith" (*De libero arbitrio*, II, 2, 5). "We seek him in order to find him, and we seek him again after having found him. For finding him requires seeking him, because he is hidden; and after having found him, we must seek him again, for he is immense" (In *Evangelium Ioannis Tractatus*, 63, 1).

In this context the acceptance of faith is not a humiliation for reason, but the light that guides it to recognize its own limits and the many difficulties it finds (n. 37), in accord with Pascal's statement that reason reaches its summit by admitting that infinitely many things surpass it and that it cannot set itself up as the one sole measure of truth: "The last proceeding of reason is to recognize that there is an infinity of things which are beyond it. It is but feeble if it does not see so far as to know this. But if natural things are beyond it, what will be said of supernatural?" (Pascal, *Pensées*, 267). *Credo ut intelligam*, reason is not sufficient by itself: it has to make recourse to faith to have the final explanation of reality. Thus the *fides quaerens intellectum* becomes an *intellectus quaerens fidem* (n. 35).

Man has the *possibility* of establishing a dialogue with God through the sole fact of being man. It is true that to love God "with all your mind and all your strength" (Mk 12:30), *is realized* only through divine grace. But it is nonetheless true that man is [has the] *possibility, capacity* for this love as a structural given of his nature (n. 35). With his usual precision, St. Augustine rightly distinguishes *capacity* from *realization: "Posse habere fidem, sicut posse habere caritatem, naturae est hominum; habere autem fidem, quemadmodum habere caritatem gratiae est fidelium" (De praedestinatione*, V, 10). Lonergan comments that this capacity is only *quaestio iuris* and not *quaestio facti*, that is, it "is not fact but possibility, not act but potency" ("Natural Knowledge of God." In *A Second Collection,* by Lonergan Bernard J. F., 118. University of Toronto Press, 1974). Man finds himself in regard to the message of salvation, as potency in regard to act. As potency he is capable of receiving the revealed message, but with only his natural capacity he cannot receive it effectively and possess it in act; to realize it, supernatural grace must intervene. In a sound interpretation, one could say that it is a passive potency, not an active one. Hence the supernatural yes presupposes the spiritual dimension of human nature, in which it can exist and act. That spiritual dimension is none other than the structural openness of human nature to the totality of being, and thereby, to Absolute Being and supernatural mystery (n. 33). The famous *potentia oboedientialis,* as a capacity to receive supernatural grace from God, refers precisely to this. Therefore the revealed message presupposes human nature. It is not something added externally to it but forms a unitary whole with it.

III. The Knowledge of God According to the Church

This capacity of man to place himself in relationship with God, based on his own essence, constitutes the foundation of the religious dimension of the person. Man's relation with God and its diverse expressions (n. 28) occupy a prominent place in the history of humanity. Goethe used to say that the mother tongue of Europe is Christianity. The culture, the art, the wars, the historical events of all the peoples were marked by this relationship. Inspired by religion, splendid cathedrals, mosques and pagodas were built; literary masterworks were written, symphonies and musical works of the highest merit were composed, high acts of generosity were completed, even to the point of martyrdom, wars were fought, and the worst injustices were committed. This massive presence leads us to believe we stand before a fundamental dimension of man, present always and everywhere, connected with his ontological structure and not a mere result of contingent situations. This makes possible a dialogue with all human beings, including non-believers (n. 39).

Despite the opposition of contemporary thought, technological development and certain forms of militant atheism that developed energetically in the last centuries (n. 29), the religious dimension is not burning out; rather, the signs of religiosity are awakening, and the teeming of sects and religious movements is obvious. How to explain this fact? Why is there, notwithstanding the variety of interpretations, a common accord in recognizing that man presents himself everywhere as *homo religiosus;* or rather, that in all men there is a point of contact that makes this relationship possible? This anchorage is what we call human nature. Man is by nature "a religious being" (n. 28) who speaks of God and with God. This means that in his constitutive essence this dimension belongs to him unalienably. As Viktor Frankl says, "Within the specifically human dimension, we need to localize, among other phenomena, that of the self-transcendence of existence toward the Logos. In fact, human existence always tends to go beyond itself, always tends toward a dimension of meaning" (*Das Leiden am sinnlosen Leben* [1977]).

The problem of God is not the problem of a Beyond. The religious dimension is a "human dimension," inasmuch as it constitutes the very possibility of man's existence. The solution of the problem of God, moreover, is not primarily a preparation for another world, but for this world itself, to be able to "be in reality." The religious dimension is primarily a problem of this side, because it is the explanation of human reality. It is enlightening that Xavier Zubiri had not wanted to pose the problem of God as a question that fell from above, but as a question emerging from the heart of our human reality itself. "Man does not 'have' experience of God, rather man is experience of God" (*El hombre y Dios* [1984]).

Man is religious in his very structure or nature because it is a spiritual nature, open to the infinite, that has the infinite as its origin and foundation. The religious dimension is a "movement toward," an "adherence to" a being that calls, "rooted" in a foundational being; an "invocation" of an infinity that is a personal You, endowed with intelligence and will, a "tendency toward" grasping God and entering into relation with him, because every capacity creates a tendency; a cognitive, affective, psychological and spiritual "need" for a transcendent you, rooted in the most intimate part of man (n. 33). This transcendent you stands within man as the foundation of that essential openness toward the Other, that tends toward communion.

IV. How Can We Speak about God?

"The desire for God is written in the human heart, because man is created by God and for God; and God never ceases to draw man to himself. Only in God will he find the truth and happiness he never stops searching for" (n. 27). Benedict XVI, the mind behind the *CCC,* commenting on this passage, highlights the existential paradox. "A statement like this that even today in many cultural contexts seems quite acceptable, even obvious, might however be taken as a provocation in the West's secularized culture. Many of our contemporaries might actually object that they have no such desire for God. For large sectors of society he is no longer the one longed for or desired but rather a reality that leaves them indifferent, one on which there is no need even to comment" (General Audience, November 7, 2012).

In other cases the "desire for God" is interpreted as a psychological and social projection of unconscious tendencies, hidden aspirations, frustrated hopes, profound complexes. Religiosity becomes a psychological, sentimental, irrational fact, a real flight from reality. Not to mention the "fathers" of this position (Feuerbach, Marx, Freud; also Schleiermacher and R. Otto), you can recognize quite a few of our contemporaries in it. A position of this kind presents itself as the antithesis of a real desire for God; indeed, nothing is farther from the experience of the sacred than such this-worldly opinions. A believer relates to realities that totally transcend him and which he loves, reveres, fears, beseeches, and so on, in a very personal experience. Religion is, by definition, is a relationship with a you; the other you, however, is not a human person, but Absolute. Reductive interpretations have their weakest point here. "As soon as religion is conceived as a relationship only within the human sphere, its specificity is eliminated, its problems are falsified, its whole reason for being is taken away. For the phenomenon of religion to operate, one has to accept that one of the sides in the relation is by nature not human" (Y. Ledure, *Transcendances: essai sur Dieu et le corps,* Desclée de Brouwer, 1989).

Often the desire for God and religiosity are understood as the sum of external forms: religious language, forms of prayer, religious institutions and associations. This is the meaning Bonhoeffer presents when he calls for a "Christianity without religion." Authentic religion is neither formalism nor irrationality. If religion is "humanity's illusion," created to find a consolation in the miseries of life, why do people hold to it even when it is unable to console or when it cannot save man from suffering and death? If religion is a sign of "mental weakness," why do believers show greater strength of spirit in the difficulties of life, and even some who have the courage to face martyrdom? If religion is a "sickness of the spirit," an "obsessive neurosis," why is it the most deeply religious people that show spiritual sanity, balance, honesty, goodness, ability to understand and give to others, solidarity?

The desire for God, then, does not depend on states of mind or subjective attitudes, but is a need that presupposes an ontological foundation, whose value the philosopher has the duty to examine. Subjective factors of a psychological nature can be involved in the way the phenomenon of religion is manifested, even expressed as denial, but it goes beyond them and is fundamentally rooted in the ontological nature of the person (n. 36). There is no doubt that the sense of crisis and disorientation, danger and anguish, frustration and emptiness can press people toward inauthentic forms of relationship with God. Yet we do not need to confuse the need for peace, much less psychic equilibrium, with the authentic religious dimension of the person. The frustration that manages to become mental illness and dresses itself in religiosity, is not authentic religiosity, but as Viktor Frankl says, commenting on Freud, "obsessive neurosis is mentally ill religiosity" (*Dio nell'inconscio. Psicoterapia e religione,* 5th ed., Brescia: Morcelliana, 2014, 82). At the same time we should not lose sight of what is positive in these attitudes. Because of this, as F. M. Schiacca says: "When the sense of crisis and disorientation is felt as an interior crisis of conscience, as an awareness that earthly life as an end in itself and considered only in the natural order is incomprehensible, that this order is contingent, then demands, anxiety, labor become filled with a spiritual content and are truly sincere, religious, need for faith" (*Il problema di Dio e della religione nella filosofia attuale,* 2nd ed., Brescia: Morcelliana, 1946, 15). This was the experience Augustine lived. Since nothing finite could fill his heart, it was restless until it could rest in God.

Today too, secularized man experiences the "desire for God" in many ways that apparently seem to be a rejection (n. 29). Starting with the Renaissance, and particularly with the Enlightenment, there was an opening to the human sciences and unexpected natural horizons, which regained their own autonomy. Natural science, technological development, and immanentist philosophical thought acquired an extraordinarily seductive prestige that provoked a break with the preceding theistic thought before long. At first, this separation only meant a divergence in intellectual orientation within a common religious faith; but before long it acquired a hostile orientation that led to well-known conflicts—such as the Galileo case and the anti-evolutionist campaign—thanks to which it seemed that religion was slowing or even blocking science, thereby creating a new gap between scientific/rational truth and the truth of the faith.

The splitting of rationality from faith is more meaningful when the faith is the Christian faith. J. Ratzinger, who has studied this topic in depth, poses the problem pointedly in *Truth and Tolerance:* "The power of Christianity, which made it into a world religion, consisted in this synthesis of reason, faith, and life; [...] Why is this synthesis no longer convincing today? Why, on the contrary, are enlightenment and Christianity regarded today as contradicting each other or even as mutually exclusive? What has changed in enlightenment, or in Christianity, that it should be so?" (San Francisco: Ignatius, 2004, 175). Today we are living this apparent division between science and faith again. The desire for God seems to be cancelled by scientific consciousness and finds"many difficulties" (*CCC* 37). But again Pascal, in his *Pensées*, speaking of the design and order of apologetics, seeks to show how this is not true: "Men despise religion; they hate it, and fear it is true. To remedy this, we must begin by showing that religion is not contrary to reason." It is eloquent to reread the letter of Galileo to the priest Benedetto Castelli in its entirety. Written on December 21, 1613, it constitutes the programmatic text of autonomous scientific research postulated by the modern era, and it faces and resolves the difficult problem of the relations between science and faith in an unprejudiced, advanced way, maintaining that natural science and sacred Scripture express the same truth with two different languages. In any case, each has its own autonomous method that calls for rigor. And "although Scripture cannot err, some of its interpreters may err sometimes nonetheless." Because of this, there is no danger that valid, effective scientific doctrine could ever conflict with the firmness of truths concerning the faith and sacred Scripture: "Since sacred Scripture and nature both proceed from the divine Word, [...] and it is obvious that two truths cannot contradict one another, wise expositors have the duty to make efforts to find the true meaning of the passages."

Faith is not opposed to reason, and "there is thus no reason for competition of any kind between reason and faith: each contains the other, and each has its own scope for action." (*FR* 17). Moreover, the Christian knows that faith does not mortify reason; rather it perfects and uplifts it. So he also knows that the rejection of the "desire for God" can be only apparent, and in a paradoxical way, reaffirm it. It seems that men no longer believe in God (*CCC* 29); they have become adults; scientific-philosophical knowledge has replaced the voice of God, who is no longer heard because he is dead. But God has not disappeared definitively and "does not tire of calling every man'" (n. 30) from the depths of the heart. He is still present as hidden desire and is perceptible and tangible, even as a corpse. That is the drama. "This silence of the transcendent, in the face of the patent religious need and demand of modern man, is the problem that torments Nietzsche, Heidegger, Jaspers" (M. Buber, *Religion und modernes Denken,* in Merkur 48 [1952], 101–120). It is the anguish that tormented Camus, Sartre, and Freud. It is the anguish that does not leave those who deny it indifferent. Atheists build up a high idea of religion; they could not understand it any other way, because they fight it with such determination. The more one devotes himself to denying God and criticizing religion, the less plausible it is that this denial and criticism is a sign of the absence of the desire for God. "You have made us for yourself, and our hearts are restless until they rest in you" (*Confessions,* I, 1, 1).

Chapter Two, Article 1:

THE REVELATION OF GOD

Rino Fisichella

I. God Reveals His "Plan of Loving Goodness"

One can make a fair argument that the true beginning of the *CCC* is in these lines (51–73). Indeed, only by starting from the revelation of God can one understand the content of the Christian faith. The *CCC* presents the fundamental traits of revelation in just three paragraphs, following a classic formulation: what constitutes it, the contents that shape it, and the end to which it is directed.

The citation from *DV* which opens the chapter sets the stage on which the concept of revelation is placed: "It pleased God, in his goodness and wisdom, to reveal himself and to make known the mystery of his will" (*DV* 2). It follows from this expression that the act of revelation is conceived as the self-communication of God. From the silence of his mystery he goes forth to make himself known and to communicate his very self, for the sake of a communion of life with humanity. These lines are set in the context of the *Preface* of the Dogmatic Constitution *Dei Verbum*. The Council, quoting 1 Jn 1:2–3, shows its intention to lead into the mystery that made salvation possible for mankind. In this context, it is easy to understand that the best expression for what the Council means by revelation is love.

The revelation of God is indeed a free, gratuitous act of love that desires nothing but the good of the beloved person. It is the kind of love that loves without any possibility of repayment. To understand the effect of this statement fully, one need only look up the references the *CCC* places in the margin of the text. On one hand, there is a reference to the prayer of the Our Father, in which the faithful ask that the will of God be done (*CCC* 2823); on the other, a reference to grace and to the moral law (nn. 1996; 1950). Conceiving revelation in the light of love as the principle that informs it lets the believer set out to follow Christ, to become his disciple, taking on his law which is none other than love. This choice does not abase him in any way, but realizes him because the human vocation is love. At the same time, the believer can turn to the Father with full trust and abandonment, asking that his will be done always. Indeed, he is aware and sure that the will of God can express itself always and only in the light of love.

The content of revelation is God in his trinitarian mystery. The "inaccessible light" in which he dwells is clarified by the event of the Incarnation in which one of the Trinity becomes man. In this unique and unrepeatable event, the act with which God reveals himself is no longer separable from the very content that is revealed. Revealer and revelation become identical in the person of the Son made flesh, who becomes the true "interpreter" of the divine life (Jn 1:18). This dimension will be clarified in the succeeding items, where the *CCC*, on the same wavelength as *DV*, reviews the various stages of the economy of revelation, to reach its peak: Christ Jesus, "the mediator and the fullness of all revelation" (*DV* 2).

The end of revelation is the salvation of man or, rather, his participation in divine life. The act with which God reveals himself is an act of love, extended to all humanity and to every person as a call of grace, a call to sharing. Salvation is explained in the light of the words of John: "This is eternal life: that they may know you the only true God, and Jesus Christ whom you have sent" (Jn 17:3). Revelation in Jesus Christ, therefore, surpasses the revelation made visible in creation. In the creation everyone is called to recognize and praise God as creator; in Jesus Christ, in turn, the human being is invited to a participation in divine life as a son. In short, what is being revealed is a total participation, made possible by the fact that God has given himself first.

N. 52 of the *CCC* lets us understand the different order on which this revelation is based: "By revealing himself God wishes to make them capable of responding to him, and of knowing him and of loving him far beyond their own natural capacity." An expression like this brings to mind the great questions that revolve around the theological topic of the *potentia oboedientialis* which is good to bear in mind in catechesis, for the great perspectives into which it leads. In the preceding chapter, the *CCC* presented the theme of man who is "open" to the knowledge of God. It is revealing that the introductory passage for this second chapter should be a quotation from the constitution *DF* from the First Vatican Council, where it is affirmed that "God [...] can be known with certainty from the things that were created, through the natural light of human reason" (*DS* 3004). However, the *CCC* is obliged not to stop with this point, but to go further. Indeed it states that with creation God has placed in every person the "capacity" and the "possibility" to know him, even if only at a level of potentiality *(potentia)*. Indeed it is necessary to follow the call, which is grace, with which man abandons himself to him in the obedience of faith *(oboedientialis)*. A full knowledge of God, therefore, is not to be had on the basis of creation; one needs to reach the event of the incarnation, with which God makes his very self known as a person who comes to encounter man, asking for the response of faith in him. The reference to St. Paul's Letter to the Romans lets us understand this perspective better. The Apostle, explaining why the pagans are without excuse in failing to recognize and honor the Creator, clarifies how one can know God. He maintains that every creature has a concrete possibility to know God through the creation. For this reason the pagans are without excuse, because while they were able to know God in the works of creation, nonetheless they did not want to accept him or praise him. Therefore creation is a true revelation by God to make himself known, but it is still a first stage that requires us to go further, dynamically, to reach its fullness.

N. 50 is a quotation from *DF* that lets us complete a twofold transition. On one hand, it connects the topic of revelation with the preceding chapter, which presents the natural knowledge of God, starting from the text of Rom 1:18–24, and the possibility for every creature to reach an understanding of God the creator through reason. On the other, it shows that revelation cannot be reduced to the simple rational order; it first requires the free and transcendent act with which God decides to reveal himself. From this perspective one can better understand the transition that was carried out between the two Vatican Councils, around the idea of revelation. Under the influence of two extreme tendencies, rationalism and traditionalism, the conciliar Fathers presented the idea of revelation at Vatican I in the light of a twofold principle: "truth" and "authority." With the first, it was shown that revelation was a complex of truths that are knowable only in the light of a supernatural knowledge; from this the second principle was derived: the truths of revelation are such because their guarantor is God in the very act of communicating them. In other words, revelation was presented as a complex of truths that form a doctrine, whose truth nonetheless cannot be subjected to the rigid inspection of reason alone. In effect, reason is able to accept revelation by analyzing the "signs" that it expresses. In fact the signs guarantee reason the freedom of understanding the truth of revelation, notwithstanding its evidence. In short, the perspective into which Vatican I was placed turned principally on emphasizing the supernatural character of revelation; the Fathers in that Council, however, did not address, nor did they want to deal with the topic of the nature of revelation. It fell to Vatican II to fill this void, looking to a truly innovative concept of revelation.

With *DV* the Council addressed the topic of revelation in the framework of a strongly biblical-patristic understanding, causing the element of salvation history to emerge to the foreground. Rereading revelation in light of the history of salvation rather amounts to completing a twofold movement: on one hand there is a return to the original source of revelation, the Word of God; on the other, the originality of the Christian revelation appears in comparison to every other possible revelation. Returning to the biblical perspective goes hand in hand with recovering the salvific horizon of revelation. The God who reveals himself is the Father who enters human history to communicate his love and to enter into a relationship of friendship and communion. This expression confirms it forcefully: "God, out of the abundance of His love speaks to men as friends and lives among them, so that He may invite and take them into fellowship with Himself" (*DV* 2, with references to Ex 33:11, Bar 3:38, Jn 15:14–15). In few words the conciliar Fathers affirm the primacy of God in revealing himself; at the same time, they express the method of revelation. It is the fruit of love and enables God to have a constant, permanent, and continuous presence for the sake of participation in his life of love. God, therefore, not only reveals himself, but "dwells among" mankind: that is, he remains for the duration, because the invitation to participate in divine life is a true act of personal freedom with which every person realizes himself in communion of life with God.

As for what concerns the event of revelation more directly, we must note an extremely important passage completed by *DV* in regard to *DF*: revelation changes from a presentation of the "gnoseological" order to one of the "salvific" order. While in *DF* revelation was interpreted in the light of a teaching given by supernatural means, *DV* recovers the truth-affirming dimension in the perspective of salvation history: God communicates himself, but does so by entering into history and subjecting himself to it within its limits. The *kénosis* of God is the metric with which revelation can and must be read in the process of the economy of salvation. We should remember in this regard that at the level of terminology Vatican II is working to let us grasp the most original meaning of the expressions. For example, we can think of the use of "economy" which, in the Fathers of the Church, was used to explain the mystery of the Incarnation, distinguishing it from "theology," which at the time was meant to identify the trinitarian mystery of God. The truth of revelation, as we know, is offered in the historicity of the event of the incarnation; this involves a permanent dynamic that lets us enter progressively into the mystery of the revelation of God. What was revealed in Jesus Christ is the whole truth that God wanted to make known to humanity for its salvation; or rather, this truth of love is expressed in a "dialectical" form proper to revelation: while it manifests something in a clear way, at the same time it hides ("re-veils") it for a higher stage of progress in deeper understanding.

II. The Stages of Revelation

Following this path, the *CCC* progressively enters the various phases that mark the economy of revelation: from the revelation in creation, to the historical revelation among the people of Israel, and then to the definitive one in Jesus of Nazareth. There have been various ways in which the stages of the economy of revelation have been described. Following in the footsteps of Paul, some of the Fathers and especially St. Augustine proposed landmarks with reference to the law; thus one speaks of revelation *ante legem, sub lege, sub gratia.* Other authors distinguished rather a trinitarian tripartite division, for which the "creation" would correspond to the action of the Father; "redemption" to that of the Son; eschatological "waiting" to that of the Holy Spirit. The subsequent theology at Vatican II preferred a division that seeks more to recover the Old Testament data and is the one taken up by the *CCC.* Now it is customary to establish three major phases: 1) revelation through nature; 2) through the history of Israel; 3) through the prophets. Any kind of subdivision clearly involves limitations and merits; but beyond this, it is easy to glimpse the underlying idea: a continual and enduring progress by God, as it were a pedagogy of his own, leading to the final event: Jesus Christ.

So that these texts not be read in a reductionist manner, it is good to emphasize that the *CCC,* following the trail traced by *DV,* cannot prescind from placing these various stages in light of the incarnation. *DV* 2, repeatedly cited in the three paragraphs in question, and para. 53, which concludes with the prospect of revelation that "shines out" in its fullness in Christ, serve only to express this centrality. The same can be observed for the quotation from *DV* 3, which leads into the paragraph on revelation through the creation, which finds its full light in the mystery of the incarnation: "God, who through the Word creates all things." These references show that the foundation of this teaching traces back to Christological principle. Hence the Christian understanding of revelation, in its diverse manifestations, can effectively be recognized as history of the salvation wrought by God, based on its end, where the fulfillment of revelation itself is realized: Jesus of Nazareth in his paschal mystery.

The Creation

The "creation," once again, is positioned as the necessary stage on which to place the first revelation of God. It remains in history above all as the initial act with which the Triune God begins the revelation of his saving plan, which neither sin nor betrayal can ever destroy (n. 55). At the same time, creation remains a dynamic and living act within history, and will continue until the end of time, when all will be recapitulated in Christ (Eph 1:10; Col 1:16,20). This perspective can be better understood if one returns to a more precise reading of the conciliar quotation that is placed in the text of the *CCC.* Correcting a first redaction, *DV* speaks of the creation as a continuous act; the use of "creates…and keeps in existence" gives evidence that the creation is an act in continual *fieri*; that the universe is open to a fulfillment and an evolution that is always progressing, until the end. Whoever wants to meet God in creation will see him always and constantly at work, endlessly expressing the infinite openness of his love. For the *CCC* also in this case the Christological intent remains unchanged. The mention of the fact that the Father creates all things through the "Word" emphasizes that the created world is under the Word of God and lives in its shadow; the Word is creative word: he speaks, and all is created.

The insistence on the natural and cosmic dimension of revelation is not without significance for contemporary sensibilities, which seem to return to seeing the relationship with nature at a level that is more direct and immediate and no longer metaphysical as in preceding centuries. It can become a valid instrument for a more universal understanding of the fact of revelation, without thereby falling into strained forms of immanentism. Through the creation, man can verify, if he wishes, at every stage of his history and in every moment of his existence, the constant presence of God. The *Roman Canon* makes note of this with a revealing expression: "you continue to make all these good things, O Lord; you sanctify them, fill them with life, bless them and bestow them upon us." In creation the mystery seems to come to each of us with a fascination all its own; on one hand, although the human being is placed at the head of all creation (Gn 1:26; Ps 8:4–5), he sees the greatness of the cosmos and its infinity, even if he experiences its limits. On the other, however, he sees that in the cosmos his intelligence has room to transcend, and seek to discover the mysteries it contains, through a continuing dynamic, even if they are hidden.

The revelation that comes through the cosmos lets us recognize, above all, that the creation is a free gift of God, and he is at the origin of everything. The prophet expresses this clearly when he says, "I, the Lord, am first" (Is 41:4); or again: "I made the earth, and created man upon it; it was my hands that stretched out the heavens, and I commanded all their host" (Is 45:12). Moreover, at the same time, it becomes apparent that man is created in the image of the Creator and carries the reflection of divinity within himself. In short, through the creation, the human being gives glory uninterruptedly to God, taking the very works God has created as an instrument to express gratitude: "The heavens are telling the glory of God; and the firmament proclaims his handiwork. Day to day pours forth speech, and night to night imparts knowledge" (Ps 19:1–2; 104; 136).

As a gift and fruit of love, the revelation of God cannot be defeated by the presence of evil and sin; to the contrary, it conquers that. The revelation of God who creates is at the same time a manifestation of God who goes beyond the limit of evil and human disobedience, to place within history the principle of a promise of salvation that will never fail. Sin does not take away the aspect of grace from revelation; rather, to use the words of the Apostle, "where sin increased, grace abounded all the more" (Rom 5:20).

This part of the *CCC* finds a meaningful explanation in the Encyclical Letter LS by Pope Francis. While the Pope analyzes the "mystery of the universe," he reads and interprets it in the light of love (cf. n. 76). The creation is a "caress of God" (n. 84) and in its contemplation it is possible to grasp the newness of divine revelation: "This contemplation of creation allows us to discover in each thing a teaching which God wishes to hand on to us, since 'for the believer, to contemplate creation is to hear a message, to listen to a paradoxical and silent voice.' We can say that 'alongside revelation properly so-called, contained in sacred Scripture, there is a divine manifestation in the blaze of the sun and the fall of night.' Paying attention to this manifestation, we learn to see ourselves in relation to all other creatures" (n. 85).

Covenant

Now the *CCC* carries out another phase, presenting the second stage in the history of revelation: the "covenant". Its strong emphasis on the covenant with Noah and the space devoted to it will be no surprise. The figure of Noah is charged with characteristics offered by the Old and the New Testament. In the person of Noah in particular appears the universal character of God's covenant with humanity and the social character of that covenant. The covenant with Noah, in fact, is the prefiguration of a covenant that will reach the "nations," that is, the peoples, for ever (cf. n. 58). The revelation of God offered with the covenant to Noah will no longer be limited to a single person or a single nation but will be open to entire peoples and nations. This lets us see an underlying idea which is explained in n. 57: the division among the peoples is an objective evil; it is always on the lookout whenever man's face is turned away from God, the source of unity and peace. Forms of idolatry or polytheism that assume new names and new faces in various societies today point to a merely provisional path and they do not let us complete either a personal or a universal history.

The figure of Noah is particularly meaningful in this regard. He is taken up as the prototype of the just person who bears fruit of salvation despite the sin and evil of humanity (Sir 44:17–18). Noah, as his very name attests, is a sign of consolation for having listened to the word of YHWH. In a sense, he becomes foremost an image of all humanity, with whom God reconciles himself for ever: "I will never again curse the ground because of man…neither will I ever again destroy every living creature as I have done" (Gn 8:21). The universality of this covenant made with Noah will remain in the history of the people as the sign of a patient mercy which God feels toward it: "This is like the days of Noah to me: as I swore that the waters of Noah should no more go over the earth, I have sworn that I will not be angry with you and will not rebuke you" (Is 54:9). This covenant will remain as a constant memory that a "remnant" of Israel will at all times be ready to assume the responsibility to be a partner of a new covenant with YHWH, until his promise will be fulfilled.

In light of a New Testament reading, the figure of Noah, placed at this point in the *CCC*, must also remind us of the permanent vigilance which the believer must have in view of the expectation of the return of the Lord (Mt 24:37). In a world in which the Christian often becomes an isolated but nonetheless prophetic voice, the figure of Noah records the courage of testimony (2 Pt 2:5) and integrity in faith (Heb 11:7). The universal and eternal alliance that is set forth here lets us see a further salient trait of revelation: sin will never again have the upper hand over the love of God, because in the death of the Crucified every man is saved from the flood of death and self-destruction. Passing through the waters of Baptism, indeed, everyone can be reborn to a new life.

The aim of revelation, as was indicated above, is to lead all humanity into the hands of Christ, who will offer it to the Father. This movement of synthesis, in which all creation, the cosmos, and man within it will be reconciled definitively with God, already finds concrete realizations within history that prefigure the future reality. In this horizon we can read a further stage of revelation which the *CCC* presents in nn. 59–61: the covenant that God completes with Abraham, "father of all who believe" (Rom 4:11,18).

The figure of Abraham, as it emerges from the three biblical traditions—Elohist, Yahwist, and Priestly—that converge in Gn 12–25, is the image of the man called by God to enact the covenant that would be handed on for entire generations. Put to the test, but filled with blessings, Abraham responds with trusting and total abandonment to this call, trusting only in the promise made to him. The character of freedom present in God's calling emerges immediately and effectively from the text: "In order to gather together scattered humanity God chose Abraham" (*CCC* 59). God is always the first to intervene. This primacy is recognized in the call to follow his will, as well as in setting forth the covenant. There is no alternative; it is God who chooses Abraham; his is the proposal of the covenant; his the promise. The expression "I will give you" resounds like a refrain in all the texts about Abraham: the "land", the "fruitfulness of Sarah", the "son Isaac", "descendants as numerous as the stars of heaven" …all is gift and grace placed before Abraham because "the Lord had blessed Abraham in all things" (Gn 24:1).

What derives from this, as a determining factor, is that the vocation of Abraham is directed toward his "fatherhood". The call is not individual, but universal: "By your offspring shall all the nations of the earth gain blessing for themselves" (Gn 22:18). What makes Abraham significant for the history of revelation is being "father of a multitude of nations" (Gn 17:5). On the strength of this, the priestly tradition changes his name: "No longer shall your name be Abram, but your name shall be Abraham" (Gn 17:5), which in fact means "father of a multitude."

As with Noah, God had promised a universal and eternal covenant, according to which he would never again destroy the fruit of his creation, so with Abraham, God makes visible the first sketch of this blessing and promise. While in Noah the blessing of God bore generic traits, because it was extended to all, in Abraham on the other hand, it becomes concrete, because it is focused on the man who has faith in him. The marginal note referring to n. 145 lets us see that the relationship "Abraham—faith" will require a more exact discussion in another context; here, in a sense, we are anticipating its prefiguration of the true faith that man must place in God. Put to the test at the crucial moments of his existence, he proves to be the one who "believed the Lord, and he reckoned it to him as righteousness" (Gn 15:6).

What the *CCC* seems to emphasize strongly in this passage at n. 60 is that Abraham anticipates the recapitulation that "one day, in the Church" will be carried out among all the children of God. There is a recurring idea in these paragraphs, starting with the presentation of the covenant made with Noah, that finds a further explanation here. The universal dimension of revelation, the text seems to suggest, is not negated by the fact that it enters into a particular history, that of the people of Israel, but to the contrary. The promise made to Abraham to bring together all the nations prefigures the universal call that was realized by the death and resurrection of Christ. The text of John 11:52, cited here as a reference, leaves no doubt about the matter.

According to John, the high priest, without intending it, spoke a prophecy: "He did not say this of his own accord, but being high priest that year he prophesied that Jesus should die for the nation, and not for the nation only, but to gather into one the children of God who are scattered abroad" (Jn 11:51–52). Johannine theology, through the mouth of the high priest, records in this step the salvific value of the death of Jesus: no longer the one people limited within the confines of Israel, but the future eschatological Israel in which, as a new people, Jews and pagans will be joined together.

This Old Testament prophecy recurs in various sacred books (Is 11:12, Mi 2:12; 4;6; 7:11; Jer 23:3; Ez 11:17; 20:34; 28:25; 34:16); but here John brings in an ecclesiological understanding of fundamental importance: no longer are the tribes of Israel to be gathered, but the "children of God." In the death of Jesus, therefore, believers have become truly children of God; their condition is real, even if what it shall be in the future is not yet clear (1 Jn 3:1–2). They shall be scattered in the world, and yet the glory that flows from the Cross shows the point of unbreakable unity. The one flock of Christ is gathered and united, even if it is composed of "Jews and pagans": what becomes decisive now is being "children of God." Therefore, starting from Abraham, again opens the universal perspective of God's revelation that has called and chosen all men, especially those who are far away, to share at his table. No one shall be excluded (cf. Jn 12:20), for the death of the Son bears a universal value: "I, when I am lifted up from the earth, will draw all men to myself" (Jn 12:32). Engrafted upon the "cultivated olive tree," the Church cannot renounce the history of the people to which she is joined. Thereby she shares with the ancient people the patriarchs and the prophets, venerates them and considers them saints, that is, partakers in the promise and in the sharing of the kingdom of God.

From a more theological perspective, nn. 62–64 form the foundation of what has been expressed heretofore about the cosmic revelation of God. Biblical reflection indeed began to think of God as creator only after it had known him as the God of Abraham, Isaac, and Jacob. The God who had made a covenant with Israel, from whom it had received the "ten commandments" (Ex 34:28) to observe for ever, was the same God experienced as he who "with strong hand and mighty arm" had freed the people from slavery in Egypt. A God so great and powerful, therefore, must have created the heavens, the earth, and everything that dwells in them.

In history, and in the various circumstances that compose it, Israel has known the revealing and saving action of YHWH. Based on that, the history of revelation as we know it today got underway, even if revelation has known differing phases, chronologically. In this sense revelation is described as "historical," to indicate God's entrance into the circumstances of the chosen people and moreover to specify the means of revelation. The word with which God had created the heaven and the earth now becomes a word that asks man and the chosen people to assume their proper responsibilities. God intervenes, causing them to recognize the signs of his presence, and based on them, he asks each one to live according to the canons of the covenant.

In the history of Israel, the covenant will remain as the vital point in which God's plan for salvation is expressed. The covenant *(berît)* at Sinai will condition the entire life of the people: all the political, family, social, military and above all religious institutions will be developed and seen in the light of this covenant. Revealing his name to Moses (Ex 3:7, 14), God indicates also the plan of his revelation: to free Israel, to lead it into the land where "milk and honey" flow (Ex 3:16–17). The exodus from Egypt comes to confirm God's choice of Israel and marks the first confirmation of his fidelity to his word. The people respond to YHWH with faith, accepting his words and putting them into practice. The text of Exodus expresses, in a single act, the essence of the covenant: "If you will obey my voice and keep my covenant, you shall be my own possession among all peoples; for all the earth is mine, and you shall be to me a kingdom of priests and a holy nation" (Ex 19:5–6).

Starting from here, Israel will be established as a holy people that renders worship only to YHWH its God (Ex 20:3). To make its consecration evident, it will be separated from the pagan peoples and from every form of idolatry (Ex 23:24; 34:12–16)—which will always be considered the gravest sin, as a form of betrayal–and it will be established as the kingdom of the Lord. The commitment of Israel corresponds to the choice on God's part: "All that the Lord has spoken we will do" (Ex 19:8). Whether faithful or not to this commitment, the people will decide its own destiny, whether life or death; whether to remain free or fall into slavery again.

At the covenant with Moses, revelation expresses one of the essential traits of its purpose: God's plan to unite all human beings to himself, realizing a community fit to offer worship, the recipient of his promise, and able to put into practice his commandment of justice and love. Yet the covenant at Sinai does not bear traits of definitiveness; the partners are placed on a different level: God and the people cannot be placed on the same level. The face of being "elected," "called," "chosen" always places Israel before a pre-eminent freedom of God which reflects his absolute transcendence. Only in light of the New Testament is the value of the Sinaitic covenant fully understood. Jesus who celebrates the Passover with his disciples expresses the same authority of God; he alone, therefore, is able to realize the covenant in his "blood" (Mk 14:24; Mt 26:28; Lk 22:20; 1 Cor 11:25) that thereafter will have universal salvific value. In place of the sacrifice made at Sinai, in which animals were immolated, with whose blood Moses had sprinkled the people (Ex 24:8), now the blood of the innocent lamb is substituted, which makes the sacrifice completely and radically new. Only then does the new covenant assume the traits of definitiveness, because it conjoins and summarizes in a single act the sacrifice of the covenant, expiatory sacrifice, and new Passover of God in the midst of his people.

Prophetic Revelation

N. 64 is always to be understood in the context of the covenant, which marks the phase of "prophetic" revelation. Prophecy accompanies the entire history of the people. In moments of betrayal the prophet remains as a vigilant "sentinel" to recall them to fidelity to the pact; in the exile, he makes his voice heard as consolation and hope; on the return to the land, he becomes an instrument of renewal and mercy that touches man in the deepest roots of the heart and does not let him be satisfied with only formal observance of the law. The role of the prophets in the history of revelation is essential, because it shows the privileged means that God assumes to communicate with his people. He speaks through the prophets (Jer 1:9; Ez 3:1–3); his very voice resounds in the signs the prophet enacts; the obedience asked of the prophet is total and his death shows extreme and unconditional devotion to the word that has been addressed to him. In short, the prophets form a synthesis of all the constitutive elements of the Old Testament people and renew them in light of a new experience of revelation.

The covenant at Sinai is the stage on which to place the stance of the prophets; whether they denounce infidelity, whether they proclaim curses or words of mercy, Sinai will remain as the permanent and indelible memory. Against an overly juridical interpretation of the covenant, the prophets add notes that encourage its interiorization. The relationship between God and his people will be read symbolically with images of pastor and flock, of vineyard and vine-dresser, of husband and wife, of father and son. In a word, the covenant acquires the progressive traits of a personal relationship, where love emerges as a basic dimension, that goes beyond the sphere of juridical observance of the Law (Ez 16:6–14). But Israel "trusted in her beauty" (cf. Ez 16:15) and on the strength of that, betrayed the pact. The infidelity of the people to the covenant is the sin shouted by the prophets; it displays the drama of a people that wants to live without God and his law (Jer 22:9). As a husband is betrayed by his wife, so YHWH is betrayed by Israel and the pact is broken (Hos 2:4; Ez 16:15–43; Jer 31:32). God is not at the origin of this breach; rather, he is obliged to make the people aware of the consequences of betrayal: exile, the destruction of Jerusalem, and the dispersal of the chosen people.

Despite sin and betrayal, the love of God and his faithfulness to his Word maintain their primacy. Prophetic revelation rereads the themes of the Exodus, seeing in the future of the people a new exodus and a new covenant. The time of betrothal stands for return (Hos 2:21–22) and Israel will be the spouse of her Lord for ever; justice, peace, faithfulness, joy and deep knowledge of YHWH will be the characteristics of these new times. The greatest transformation, in a way, will be the one God himself will work in the deepest part of the person: he will write his law on their hearts (Jer 31:33), will unite them from every country where they had been dispersed and will establish them again as a new and unique people (Jer 32:37–41; Ez 36:24). The covenant of Sinai will be renewed definitively, as it will be purified and made actual by the mediation of the Spirit (Ez 36:27). The seal that will conclude the old covenant will be the same that concludes the new one: "You will be my people and I will be your God" (Ex 36:28; 37:27; Jer 31:33; 32:38). In the proclamation of the last Isaiah, even the renewal of the covenant of Noah will appear (Is 54:9). The circle, therefore, will be completed, returning to the initial plan of an eternal covenant made with all of humanity, one of universal value, because the love with which God reveals himself cannot be enclosed in the strict confines of one single nation; it extends itself seeking to embrace every man in every land and in every place.

The Great Women of Revelation

It is meaningful that at this point the *CCC* points to the images of great women who have shared in revelation and constitute a mediation of revelation which cannot be considered as only symbolic. The names of these women recall examples which express the fact that the distinction of sex does not constitute an obstacle to the action of the Spirit; to the contrary, Scripture freely takes up the figure of woman often to express divine wisdom. "Sarah" is a sign of faith who knows how to make life fruitful despite advancing age (Gn 18:9, 15). "Rebecca" is an instrument of God who freely, even if mysteriously, chooses Jacob, preferring him over Esau (Gn 27:7–17). "Rachel", the one who in anguish does not despair of the Lord, but, tenacious and constant in her request for a son, will be at the founding of the house of Israel (Gn 30:22–24; Ru 4:11). "Miriam" the prophetess sister of Aaron who invites the people to prayer and praise with every instrument (Ex 15:20–21). "Deborah," judge and prophetess in Israel who calls for war and sings the victory of YHWH over the enemy (Jdt 4–13). "Esther" who remains faithful to the law of the Lord even in a foreign land and saves her people from destruction (Est 2–8).

All the women form a choir around Mary and, in a sense, anticipate her fundamental traits of obedience and fidelity that make her mother of the Lord. The *CCC* will take up this theme again with a particular section at nn. 963–972.

III. Christ Jesus—"Mediator and Fullness of All Revelation"

The presentation of revelation in Jesus Christ allows the *CCC* to reach the high point of its teaching on revelation. With the presence of Jesus in history, God has visited his people without any other mediation and has carried out the promise he repeatedly made (cf. n. 422). Opening the paragraph with the initial quotation from the Letter to the Hebrews, attention inevitably falls upon the dialectic which the sacred author desired to place among the elements expressed in the various stages of revelation in the Old Testament and the newness expressed by that of Jesus: "In many and various ways God spoke of old to our fathers by the prophets; but in these last days he has spoken to us by a Son, whom he appointed the heir of all things, through whom he also created the ages" (Heb 1:1–2). In these few verses we are swiftly introduced into the heart of the discourse, and the essence of the content of the Bible has been displayed: now everyone is in a relationship with God and can finally enter into dialogue with him (cf. Heb 7:19; 10:19). The astounding fact of the whole story is marked by these words: "God spoke." He has entered into a peculiar dialogue with man, made of communication and interpersonal relationship. What the author of the Letter to the Hebrews wants to teach, in fact, is that God has tirelessly sought a dialogue of true love with man, as between two persons; a detail of the language expresses this directly. The content of the divine communication is not specified, while on the other hand the subjects of the communication are presented: God, the fathers, the prophets, us, the Son. Revelation is not primarily a collection of doctrines or facts, but an encounter with a person. The various and differing ways in which God had revealed his will to the fathers and the prophets then find their peak in the very person of the Son. In the previous stages, the word was fragmentary and multifarious, marked by differing mediations that ultimately led to a partial vision of revelation. Now, since it is the Son who reveals, the original plan of the Father is expressed in unity and fullness. Even stylistically, the author of the letter makes this peculiarity and uniqueness of the revelation of Jesus stand out; he places the Son at the ending of the verse. The whole thing has been said before, to be brief: it has been extended to him because he himself is the peak of revelation. The Son is the "heir," by means of him everything was made; he participates in the same divine nature and hence is qualitatively distinct from every preceding mediation. His relationship with the Father is unique, typical of him who was begotten as Son and "brightness of his glory": fullness and definitiveness rest in him.

The revelation of Jesus Christ is the complete and definitive synthesis of all the actions of God in history because it is realized in God's own sharing of human nature.

The brevity with which the *CCC* treats this section is somewhat surprising. It is true that the Christological part will be explained in the section comprising nn. 422–679; the topic, however, is so highly vital that it would have deserved a more ample treatment.

The same quotation from Heb 1:1–2 is also found in *DV* 4, and at this point, we need to turn to it if we wish to reach a global comprehension of the theme. In *DV*, in fact, we can see a step-by-step presentation of revelation in Christ which, starting from the *Preface,* reaches to n. 4 where the council fathers made a complete identification of the content of revelation and the one who reveals. Since Jesus is the "Word made flesh" and "speaks the words of God," there is no longer any difference to be found between what he is as revealer and as the content of revelation itself. His word differs in nothing from that of the Father, because he has heard it pronounced from within the Father himself (cf. Jn 5:38); the works he carries out are the same that he has seen the Father perform (cf. Jn 5:36); the witness that he offers is confirmed by the Father himself of whom he bears witness, because to him and him only does Jesus refer constantly to make his life understood as a mission of obedience which he received from God (cf. Jn 5:31–34).

This revelation has its fullness and definitive character because Jesus is the second person of the Trinity, the Word that became man; he is God, as is the Father, who speaks in human language through the incarnation. No one could express the mystery of God better than he, since only he knows it perfectly inasmuch as he is God. This quotation from the words of John let us reach his identity: "He who has seen me has seen the Father" (Jn 14:9). With this consciousness he outlines the definitive character of revelation; earlier mediators and various historical forms of mediation have finished their role by now. Everything that preceded the Son who speaks communicating the mystery of God is referred to him and in him finds its full meaning. Before him even the Sacred Scriptures that had guided the life of the people become "old," because the "new" pact is being made. "Through his whole work of making Himself present and manifesting Himself" (*DV* 4) expresses the council's teaching clearly: in Jesus, God is present in fullness; thereby the manifestation of his revelation is itself definitive, because in the Word the trinitarian mystery of God, Father, Son, and Holy Spirit becomes visible.

The gradual approach that *DV* creates in showing the revelatory work of the Son deserves particular attention, because it lets us see a "hierarchy" of revelatory significance that determines the assent of faith. What is presented as the object of revelation is, in the first place, the person of Jesus Christ, the Word among men. Meeting him, hearing his word, and accepting his testimony generate faith. He is credible in himself, because his life is totally coherent with the mission he received from the Father.

The fact that he "points" only to the Father places him in a situation of self-attestation which needs no justification. His Word and his actions are true because the power *(dýnamis)* of the Father rests in him, and the Father's glory *(dóxa)* shines within him. The fullness of the Spirit which clothes him is the guarantee that every man can entrust himself to him totally as to God himself. The signs that flow from his person let us verify his action as the act of God himself. His words and his deeds "intimately linked" shape the originality of the person; the signs and miracles he performs express the love of the Father and his power that conquers evil. His paschal mystery, in a particular way, renders full evidence of how he loves God. Death and resurrection mark the crowning expression of revelation, as they constitute the definitive event of salvation. Once again it becomes evident that it is not possible to separate the content of revelation from the achievement of its aim: salvation as communion of life with God.

What has been said up to now about the new and definitive covenant finds confirmation in n. 66 which, quoting *DV* 4, lets us grasp why this revelation is now definitive. Yet fullness and definitiveness are not equivalent to "completeness" of revelation. The historical dimension in which the revelation of Jesus is placed lets us verify a twofold dimension. On one hand, revelation is definitive because it was carried out by God himself, and no other manifestation will be able to change its truth. On the other, it is obliged to go through a continual and dynamic progression of its truth which will find fullness only under the action of the Spirit who leads the Church within time to the entire truth (cf. Jn 16:13). In this space of history that constitutes the history of the Church, revelation is understood more and more, is related to the various situations in which the community finds itself, and grows in the dynamic of the truth which is proper to it.

Revelation in Jesus, in fact, is offered in its natural dialectic: it unveils mystery but at the same time hides it again, to prod faith into being more and more itself; that is, to go beyond what it has understood, to seek the truth in which it believes, ever more in depth. The axiom of St. Anselm, at this point, is the key to understand the revelatory dynamic: God is always greater than what we can think of him, and with reason we understand that he is incomprehensible. Our gaze, therefore, is pointed to the eschatological view and to the parousia which will reveal fully the true face of God, inasmuch as we shall contemplate him as he is (cf. 1 Jn 3:2).

N. 67 concludes this chapter, suggesting two problems of vast contribution and contemporary relevance: the problem of revelations after Christ and the specificity of Christian revelation in view of other religions that advance their own revelatory claims.

It would probably be fitting to abandon the terminology of "private" revelations, which seems unsuitable. It was probably necessary when messages, whether they be true or alleged, were presented with apocalyptic language which often led the faithful into great errors, misunderstanding the true and real meaning of the manifestation. However, once there is a real and confirmed revelation, it should have a significance for the entire Church; so to say that it is "private" becomes improper. Various theological problems tend to arise in view of revelations after the revelation of Christ. Logically, one can say that such revelations require a serious and dispassionate analysis to verify their supernatural character. Moreover, it is necessary to evaluate the "message" which is often presented together with the vision and which often enough needs to be interpreted in light of the category of "prophecy." In short, such a manifestation needs to be submitted to a set of criteria able to ascertain the truthfulness as well as the credibility of the seer. In any case, such a manifestation will never be able to add anything to the revelation made by Jesus Christ; it can only be a faithful and coherent echo of his Word. Apart from these elements, any other manifestation excludes itself from having a revelatory character.

As regards the specificity of the Christian revelation in view of other religions, it is opportune to recall what Vatican II taught in *NA:* "The Catholic Church rejects nothing that is true and holy in these religions. She regards with sincere reverence those ways of conduct and of life, those precepts and teachings which, though differing in many aspects from the ones she holds and sets forth, nonetheless often reflect a ray of that Truth which enlightens all men" (n. 2). Because of revelation, in any case, the Church cannot neglect her mission to announce that Christ is "the way, the truth, and the life" (Jn 14:6).

Yet it is necessary to distinguish among religion and sects. While the former make an effort to respond to the great questions about man and the mystery of God, the sects tend to absolutize a few aspects, radicalizing their eschatological component and falling easily into forms of fanaticism or fundamentalism. Interreligious dialogue is open to the acceptance of positive and true elements present in diverse religious experiences, though not renouncing the normative and salvific value which the revelation of Jesus Christ possesses for the Christian faith.

Chapter Two, Article 2:

THE TRANSMISSION OF DIVINE REVELATION

Jared Wicks

The article on the transmission of revelation begins with a classic text, 1 Tm 2:4, which ties the Church's communication of revelation to God's universal salvific will. This transmission is intended to realize the divine intention to lead every human being, without exception, into the community of adoptive sons who, through the mediation of Christ and in the Spirit, gain access to the Father (nn. 51–52). Our entire humanity is thus the intended recipient of the divine plan of salvific revelation.

The teachings offered on transmission can be grouped around three principal themes: the apostolic Gospel, Tradition, and the Magisterium that interprets the original apostolic gift.

I. The Apostolic Tradition

In the center of the economy of revelation stands the person of Christ, in whom God the Father has shown us his whole loving will to save man (n. 65). But so that the plan of God would realize its universal aim, Christ himself began a further phase of communicating what he had revealed. The primordial means of this transmission, according to n. 75, is the Gospel of salvation that Christ entrusted to his apostles with the solemn mandate to proclaim it universally (Mk 16:15; Mt 28:18–20; Lk 24:46–48; Acts 1:8).

The apostolic Gospel was and is the essential mediation between Christ and every person who receives salvation from him who "died for our sins… [and] was raised on the third day" (1 Cor 15:3–4). Already before Christ, in Israel a word of the Gospel resounded, in which the apostolic message has its own prior history, especially in the prophetic announcement of the end of the exile and the return of the chosen people to the Land of the promise (Is 52:7–12). Jesus himself, in his public ministry, was the itinerant herald of the

Gospel of the Kingdom of his Father, with a call to conversion and faith (Mk 1:15; Mt 4:17, 23; Lk 4:16–21; Acts 10:35–38; cf. nn. 541–550).

We find formulations of the apostolic Gospel in the Letters of St. Paul, especially in the passages on Christ dead and arisen, which stem from the work of those who were apostles before Paul (Rom 1:2–4; 4:24–25); 1 Cor 15:3–5; Gal 1:3–4; 1 Th 1:9–10). Other expressions of the evangelical message resound in the apostolic discourses of Peter in the book of Acts (2:14–36; 3:12–26; 4:8–12; 5:29–32; 10:34–43). This proclamation is "the power of God for salvation to every one who has faith" (Rom 1:16), which reaches to us "not only in word, but also in power and in the Holy Spirit and with full conviction" (1 Thess 1:5). The Gospel is "the word of faith which we preach. Because if you confess with your lips that Jesus is Lord and believe in your heart that God raised him from the dead, you will be saved" (Rom 10:8–9).

The Gospel entrusted to the apostles and then proclaimed until their witness of martyrdom is in substance an account of Jesus Christ that highlights the meaning of his death and resurrection for the good of all humanity. The apostolic Gospel is "according to the Scriptures," as the luminous fulfillment of everything that was written in the holy books of Israel (Lk 24:44). In the Church the Gospel received with faith is the fundamental content of what unites Christians in their profession of faith.

The preached Gospel was a fruitful message open to expansions, which were brought about with accounts about Jesus that were eventually put into writing in the four Gospels, the "memories of the Apostles" (St. Justin) that are really "the heart of all the Scriptures" (n. 125). But faithful reading of the Gospels looks in every passage for the resonance of the Gospel, which announces that Christ died for our salvation but now lives "designated Son of God in power according to the Spirit of holiness by his resurrection from the dead" (Rom 1:4).

The Gospel, being the announcement of salvation, is the "source of all saving truth and moral teaching" (*DV* 7, drawing from the Council of Trent, *DS* 1501) and the vital nucleus of Tradition, that is of "everything which contributes toward the holiness of life and increase in faith of the people of God" (*DV* 8).

Catholic doctrine on the transmission of the Gospel, formulated densely by the Council of Trent, is not principally articulated in terms of the often-heard duality between written and oral modes of communication, but of a deeper duality, formulated at Trent by the cardinal legate Marcello Cervini (February 18, 1546). It deals with the distinction between the oral Gospel of public preaching by Jesus and the apostles and the Gospel that was sown in hearts through the interior work of the Holy Spirit. The interior dimension of transmission is often forgotten but remains the true foundation of all discussion about the transmission of the Word of God and faith (cf. nn.

91–93, on the "sense of faith"). Also at work today, perhaps in readers of the *CCC*, is the Spirit who writes in hearts to support the hearing of the Gospel with joy amid tribulations and faith in the Word of God transmitted with human words (1 Thess 1:4–6; 2:13).

II. The Relationship between Tradition and Sacred Scripture

The second key topic of this article is Tradition, the subject of a profound teaching given by the Second Vatican Council in *DV* 8. Based on that text, Tradition is defined in n. 78 as the living extension, through the Church's doctrine, life, and worship, that prolongs to all generations what the Apostles created under the guidance of the Holy Spirit: a coherent form of existence and faith, in the churches of apostolic foundation. "Tradition" is a global notion connected to the Church, with reference to the way this community, as a corporate subject, perpetuates what she is and what she believes, continuing ceaselessly to accept and communicate further the original apostolic gift.

In the New Testament, "tradition" is first of all the apostolic modality of oral transmission, but more precisely, the rite of the Lord's supper (1 Cor 11:23) and the Gospel itself (1 Cor 15:3). The "traditions" that guide the life of the faithful can be oral or written (2 Thess 2:15), but are to be observed accurately. In the later Letters of the New Testament, "tradition" has the more global and objective meaning of the apostolic "deposit" that must be preserved intact by virtue of the Spirit who dwells in the faithful and in her pastors (1 Tm 6:20; 2 Tm 1:14). This "deposit" is the complete cell of the Church's life, whose nucleus is the Gospel, and which is to be received, protected, and faithfully communicated to integrally perpetuate what the apostles shaped in the churches ever since their foundation.

While the biblical understanding of Tradition joins together elements of living transmission and of a coherent complex of community life, the first Fathers identify Tradition with the fundamental doctrine that unites the catechesis and the profession of faith of the various Churches (cf. nn. 173–175). The Tradition of truth left by the apostles expresses the true meaning of the Scriptures and serves as a "rule" of faithful and fruitful reading of the sacred books (cf. n. 113). The symbol of faith, the creed, summarizes this doctrinal tradition in its principal and constitutive elements or "articles."

However, Tradition is not a complex of doctrines that the apostles communicated at first secretly and unwritten. Such a notion of unwritten tradition was the basis of the "gnostic" doctrine advanced during the second century with the claim of being a secret teaching of the risen Jesus. Against the gnostic heresy, Fathers such as St. Irenaeus had insisted on Tradition as the "rule of faith" transmitted and taught publicly in the churches of apostolic foundation. At the threshold of the modern era, however, the Council of

Trent insisted on a number of "unwritten traditions" that transmitted certain values of the Gospel. These are ecclesial practices of great antiquity, such as the observance of Sunday and the baptism of infants, while Tradition as the comprehensive rule of faith was asserted by the Council of Trent, in its declaration on the normative manner of interpreting "the meaning [of Scripture] that Holy Mother the Church has held and holds" (*DS* 1507).

In the Church, Tradition is creative in the community environment of liturgy, spirituality, and lived testimony. This environment, according to Catholic conviction, has a natural affinity with sacred Scripture, through a relation of mutual coinherence, due to the common elements listed in nn. 80–81 of the *CCC*. Tradition, therefore, creates the context where the sacred text is read, understood, and lived as a prophetic and apostolic witness that supports faith. At a deeper level, this dialogue of the Word of God and faith is the way in which revelation, in the Church's time, becomes a present-day communication of the *viva vox evangelii* for the salvation of the world (cf. n. 79).

III. The Interpretation of the Heritage of Faith

The transmission of revelation is effectuated with the triangular and mutual interaction among Scripture, Tradition, and the Church's Magisterium (n. 95). Each member of this "triad of transmission" contributes to the understanding of the other two members, with the Magisterium in the role of the living and authoritative exponent of the content and meaning of revelation for the present moment of ecclesial life and testimony (nn. 85–87).

The basis, the role, the aim, and the authority of the Magisterium are expounded in a more articulated manner elsewhere In the *CCC* (cf. nn. 67, 688, 861–862, 888–892, 1558, 2032–2040, 2663). The present article deals with the relation of "teachers of the faith" (n. 1558) to Scripture and their service of the living Tradition. It highlights the hermeneutical office of the Magisterium that interprets the written Word and promotes the Tradition by deploying the riches of truths and norms of life contained in the original apostolic heritage.

Certain books of the New Testament show the concern, strongly felt toward the end of the apostolic era, to faithfully preserve what the apostles taught and instituted and to communicate it in its integrity. The last discourse of St. Paul's apostolate gives the elders and "bishops" of Ephesus the task of watching over the flock of Christ in which the Apostle had preached and taught the Gospel of God's grace in its entirety (Acts 20:18–35). The pastors are to teach the content of the apostolic heritage consistently and accurately maintain the structures and worship of their communities (1 Tm, 2 Tm, Ti), which form a precious "deposit" (cf. 1 Tm 6:20; 2 Tm 1:14). A rudimentary indication of a post-apostolic Magisterium is found in the admonition given to Timothy: "what you have heard from me before many witnesses entrust to faithful men who will be able to teach others" (2 Tm 2:2).

In the early Church, bishops carried out their magisterial service by transmitting the "rule of faith," especially with relevant explanations to catechumens. Bishops like St. Athanasius of Alexandria and St. Augustine were among those who spread and defended the specifications of the official canon of Scripture. The bishops, meeting in synods, resolved various doctrinal controversies with the first declarations of dogmatic force, as at the Council of Nicea in the year 325 (n. 465). Such magisterial acts specified the contours and detailed some contents of the apostolic heritage that have marked the life of the Church through its entire history.

Twice the *CCC* connects the action of the Magisterium with discernment of what conforms to the word of Christ and is faithful to his teaching, for the good of the Church (nn. 67, 2663). In a similar way, Paul VI explained to Mons. Lefebvre that the Pope and Council must discern between the authentic heritage of the apostles and reformable traditions that sometimes can be updated to serve the mission of the Church better (letter of October 11, 1976; cf. n. 83). With his customary perception, St. Thomas specified the magisterial role of the Pope as that of *"determinare ea quae sunt fidei,"* that is, confirming the "articles" that express saving revelation authentically and therefore require the adherence of faith (n. 88; but cf. n. 170).

The Magisterium, however, has a larger field of action than the definition of dogmas of divine and catholic faith, as the *CCC* explains, for example, in n. 67 (judgment of private revelations), 2032–2040 (moral teaching) and 2663 (evaluation of forms of prayer). The fundamental service of the Magisterium, in any case, remains the promotion of the integral and living preaching of the Gospel in every era. Precisely for this reason, "the apostles left bishops as their successors. They gave them their own position of teaching authority" (n. 77, quoting *DV* 1 and St. Irenaeus).

A fundamental reason for the existence and working of the Magisterium is the very fruitfulness of the Gospel and the immanent dynamism toward progress found within the apostolic heritage (cf. n. 175). Cardinal Newman wrote that what the apostles left cannot be contained in a number of documents, being "too vast, too minute, too complicated, too implicit, too fertile, to be put into writing." In the Church, Tradition "was manifold, various and independent in its local manifestation" (*Essays Critical and Historical,* London, 1871, 1, 126f.) Moreover, the interior dimension of transmission adds to the potential for further development of doctrine, liturgy and other forms of witness (nn. 91, 94). Yet who is to judge, to confirm the origin of new forms of understanding and expression of the faith and life coming from the original deposit? This service of discernment of authentic progress is the proper contribution of the Magisterium.

The Church has also received various charisms of witness and teaching that are documented in Pauline references to the "word of knowledge" and to "teachers" *(didáskaloi)* in 1 Cor 12:8,28; Rom 12:7; Eph 4:11. In addition, the importance of scientific exegesis is recognized in nn. 101–110 and 111 of the *CCC*, as is theological research in n. 94. Considered among the most important tasks of theologians are explaining the origin of doctrines of the faith and making plain the "hierarchy of truths" (n. 90), that is, the order and configuration of particular articles around the great truths of the baptismal creed, which confesses faith in the creating Father, the redeeming Son, and the sanctifying Holy Spirit and thus brings to fulfillment the Father's plan and the work of the Son (cf. nn. 189–191).

Because of this abundance of ministries of the word in the Church, the magisterium of bishops does not exhaust the entire function of teaching. It cannot operate alone, in the final analysis, as it is part of the community in which all have received the interior anointing of the Spirit of truth (n. 91). However, the Magisterium possesses the key role of "direction", through acts of discernment, evaluating what emerges from the various activities in the Church aimed at promoting the understanding and present-day relevance of divine revelation.

Chapter Two, Article 3:
SACRED SCRIPTURE

Ignace de la Potterie

To understand the importance and the relative newness of this section of the *CCC* well, it is very useful to make a brief comparison with previous documents of the Magisterium.

In the three biblical encyclicals of the past century—by Leo XIII (1893), Benedict XV (1920) and Pius XII (1943)—almost nothing was said about revelation. The perspective these encyclicals took was completely overturned at Vatican II in the Dogmatic Constitution on Divine Revelation: its title *DV* does not indicate the written "word of God," that is, Scripture, but the event of divine revelation itself: now this revelation "shines out for our sake in Christ, who is both the mediator and the fullness of all revelation" (*DV* 2). By this the Council was propounding a strong "Christological concentration" of revelation (cf. the text of St. John of the Cross, at *CCC* 65). Something analogous can be said for the Holy Spirit: the biblical encyclical of 1943, which intended above all to promote philological and historical study of the Bible, still did not explain the theological importance of inspiration, despite its title *DaS*. This changed anew in *DV*, which introduces a formal connection between the dogmatic fact of inspiration (which consists in the action of the Holy Spirit in the development of Sacred Scripture) and our interpretation of it: sacred Scripture "must be read and interpreted in the sacred spirit in which it was written" (*DV* 12:3). Hence it is rightly said that the heart of the Council is truly located in this: it reopened the problem of "interpretation" of the "faith." Now this double perspective opened by *DV*, both the Christological, and more so, pneumatological, is not only reused, but also reinforced in the *CCC*. In our analysis of the article on sacred Scripture, we shall distinguish three aspects, following the divisions indicated in the text: (a) Christ and sacred Scripture; (b) the Holy Spirit and sacred Scripture; (c) sacred Scripture in the Church (an extension of the preceding section).

I. Christ—The Unique Word of Sacred Scripture

This meaningful title expresses a teaching common to all of Tradition (cf. nn. 65; 134). St. Augustine comments on it profoundly (n. 102), with a reference to the Prologue of the Gospel of John; we cite it here in a new version, adhering more to the Latin original: "Remember that one single Word of God extends through all the Scriptures and that from the many mouths of the holy [writers] a single Word resounds, he who 'in the beginning was God with God' (Jn 1:1): in him there are not multiple syllables because there are not multiple times" (*Enarratio in Psalmum,* 103, 4, 1: *PL* 37, 1378).

Therefore, this unique Word of God was called the *Verbum abbreviatum: "Eloquium Dei, Verbum Dei; Verbum Dei, Filius Dei"* (cit. from de Lubac, *Esegesi medievale,* I, Rome, 1972, 340). Jesus himself had already said that the Scriptures bear witness to him (Jn 5:39); after the resurrection, in the encounter with the disciples at Emmaus, "beginning with Moses and all the prophets, he interpreted to them in all the Scriptures the things concerning himself" (Lk 24:27).

Paul taught the Corinthians that the rock from which Israel drank in the desert was in reality a spiritual rock: "the rock was Christ" (1 Cor 10:4); and with the death of Jesus on the Cross, the Scripture was fulfilled perfectly (cf Jn 19:28). But if Christ is at the center of the Scriptures, if he is the principle of their unity, the reason is really that he is "the fullness of the whole of revelation," that the revelation of God is made in the man Jesus; in the heart of Christ, the heart of God is revealed.

A medieval author, Gottfried of Admont (1165), explained this: "The breast of Jesus is sacred Scripture.... Those who love God and want to imitate John must work to know sacred Scripture with the sole aim of...finding in it the heart of God, a sense for God" (*Homilia LI in Dominicam IV post Pascha prima: PL* 174, 339; cf. also St. Thomas, n. 112).

During the Second Vatican Council an African bishop, the cardinal P. Zoungrana, took up this teaching, which is more relevant than ever: "Fundamentally, Christ himself is the revelation that he brings. The truths to believe and the duties to carry out must be considered mainly in their relation to a living person. Tell the world that the divine revelation is Christ" (cit. from de Lubac, *Entretiens autour de Vatican II,* Paris: Cerf, 1985, 51).

Keeping in mind, then, that "all truth is contained in the mystery of Christ" (*DV* 24), one can deduce that this doctrine from the great Tradition of the Church was already summarized in the Johannine Prologue: "grace and truth came through Jesus Christ" (Jn 1:17), because he, the man Jesus, revealed the incarnate Word in himself, "the only-begotten Son, who is in the bosom of the Father," who has thus opened for us the way to the Father (Jn 1:14–18).

We can only discover this fullness of revelation present in Jesus Christ, however, through the mediation of Scripture, the Word of God. And here the relation of Scripture with the Holy Spirit is essential.

II. Inspiration and Truth of Sacred Scripture

John had quoted the decisive word of Jesus: "I am…the truth" (Jn 14:6), but he says also that "the Spirit is the truth" (1 Jn 5:6), and he alone in the New Testament uses the formula "the Spirit of truth" several times (for example, Jn 14:17; 1 Jn 4:6). Only the Spirit, Jesus had said, would be able to guide us "into all the truth" (Jn 16:13). What is then the function of the Holy Spirit, first in the elaboration of sacred Scripture, and then in how we can understand it and are to interpret it? We shall see through the following observations.

The Dogma of Inspiration

The dogma of the inspiration of the sacred books is almost forgotten in contemporary theology. Rather, a sort of challenge has been launched: "The end of the theology of inspiration" (O. Loretz). Such a claim, however, would have grave consequences for biblical exegesis, which would risk being reduced to a simply philological and historical science.

The *CCC*, following *DV* attentively, presents the essential facts of the traditional doctrine again in nn. 105–198, but with a greater insistence on its implications for the Christian interpretation of sacred Scripture. Above all the fundamental dogmatic fact is reaffirmed: "the books of the Old and the New Testaments, whole and entire, with all their parts, [were] written under the inspiration of the Holy Spirit," and because of that, "they have God as their author, and have been handed on as such to the Church herself" (n. 105).

Yet in the following paragraph (n. 106) it is stated that the human authors of the sacred books wrote "as true authors": it is the first time in a magisterial document that the word "author" is applied to the sacred writers. Here the doctrine of *DaS* (*EB* 556–557) is implicitly taken up (though it is not cited): that the human author, as an instrument of the Holy Spirit, maintains his own nature and the use of his faculties intact. But it would be mistaken to conclude from this—as is sometimes advanced—that the conciliar text is thus focused on the linguistic sciences: these linguistic sciences are human sciences; they cannot be the theological explanation of the doctrine of inspiration, since inspiration is a divine action on human authors. So it remains essential that the sacred books "have God as their author." The *Deus auctor* cannot be traced back to the *hagiographus auctor* (cf. our article "L'esegesi biblica scienza della fede," in *L'esegesi Cristiana oggi,* Casale M.: Piemme, 1991, 141–144). In the *CCC*, the true sense of *Deus auctor* is indicated three times: it means that, by reason of inspiration, the sacred books contain "the divinely revealed realities" (n. 105), "whatever he [God] wanted written" (n. 106), which is to say, "that truth which God, for the sake of our salvation, wished to see confided to the Sacred Scriptures" (n. 107). Each time the idea of revelation in the sacred books is emphasized.

The "Truth" of Scripture

This is how we understand wherein the "truth" of the Scripture consists. There were bitter debates about this during the Council. The problem of biblical inerrancy was involved, which in the time of modernism in France, stood at the center of the *"question biblique."* The so-called "obsession with inerrancy" was alive again at the beginning of Vatican II. The text presented to the Fathers at first re-proposed the old issue of "absolute immunity from error in all of sacred Scripture…in any matter, religious or secular." But that first draft, really unfeasible, was immediately rejected by the Council. Five schemas were worked out in succession. The next to last one said, on our topic: "The entire books of Scripture…teach firmly and faithfully, integrally and without error 'the saving truth' *(veritatem salutarem).*" This formula also brought forth strong reactions: it was feared that inerrancy would thereby be limited to the *"res fidei et morum"* (a condemned doctrine). The doctrinal commission explained, however, that *"veritas salutaris"* was not introducing any material limitation on the truth of Scripture, but indicated its formal specification. In any case, to take away any ambiguity, a final change was made, and so they came to the definitive formula which says the same thing more clearly. The "without error" therefore remained, but is to be put in correlation with "truth," which already excludes the contrary. And the term "truth" itself is to be understood in its biblical meaning, used elsewhere in various texts of the Council (cf. *DV* 2, 8, 24; *LG* 17; *DH* 11), or rather it designates divine revelation itself, salvific revelation.

In short, how is it to be understood that Scripture teaches the truth? It means that everything in Scripture is connected with revelation, which is oriented toward our salvation; this does not rule out that there can be "errors" in the Bible, from the specific point of view of historiography or of modern science. But communicating precise data of "this" type was not and is not the aim of sacred Scripture.

III. The Holy Spirit, Interpreter of Scripture

This section takes up and develops n. 12 of *DV*. Right away, however, we notice a strong disproportion between the two parts: only in nn. 109–110 is there a recommendation to highlight the literal sense of Scripture, that is, to grasp the human intention of the sacred authors exactly; for this purpose, the text explains, one needs to take account of the "literary genres" they used and the historical context in which they lived and spoke (here, the teaching from the encyclical of Pius XII is summarized without being cited). Without a doubt, the search for the literal sense will always be the basis of all exegesis. Yet it remains that in all the rest of the section (nn. 111–119) there is more insistence on the fact that sacred Scripture "must be read and interpreted in the light of the same Spirit by whom it was written" to be rightly understood. Perhaps this is meant to explain the paradox that this whole section is given the less-than-ideal title "The Holy Spirit, Interpreter of Scripture," whereas in the conciliar formula on which the title depends, these three verbs were used more rightly in the passive form *(legenda est, interpretanda est, scripta est),* because to "write" the biblical texts, to "read" them and "interpret" them are human activities, not those of the Holy Spirit; yet it remains true that they must be practiced *eodem Spiritu quo…* In other words, the Spirit in which the sacred books were once "written" and in which they are today "read" and "interpreted" must be the same Spirit. So it is clear that the dogmatic fact of biblical "inspiration" is presented as the true hermeneutical norm of the "interpretation" of Scripture. Here we have the basic principle of the search for the spiritual sense of the biblical text (on all of this, cf. our article "L'interpretazione della Sacra Scrittura nello Spirito in cui è stata scritta [*DV* 12, 3]" in *Vaticano II. Bilancio e prospettiva venticinque anni dopo, 1962–1986,* Assisi: Cittadella, 1987, 1, 204–242).

What, in specific, does such an interpretation "in the same Spirit" mean? It means: to interpret in the light of the faith; that is, to seek the deep meaning in Scripture, its spiritual meaning, because, as St. Jerome said, only the spiritual man "discovers Christ in the divine books" *(Commentaria in Epistolam ad Galatas,* 4. 24: *PL* 26, 417A). *DV* (12, 3) used here in the *CCC* and at nn. 112–114, indicates three concrete means to make such an interpretation: "No less serious attention must be given to the content and unity of the whole of Scripture [….] The living tradition of the whole Church must be taken into account along with the harmony which exists between elements of the faith." The first means, already explained in the *CCC* (cf. nn. 101–104), was illustrated in the well-known words of Hugo of Saint-Victor: "All Sacred Scripture is but one book, and that one book is Christ" (n. 134). It is the Christological principle that creates the unity of all sacred Scripture. The second means is the living Tradition of the whole Church. There is a short compendium on the classic principle of Catholic exegesis, almost ignored today, on the mutual relation between Scripture and Tradition (cf. nn. 9–10). The text from Origen quoted in the note (n. 113) explains the meaning of this principle well: "according to the spiritual meaning which the Spirit grants to the Church" (*Homiliae in Leviticum,* 5,5: *PL* 12, 454). The third means is the analogy of faith: the interpretation must be such that it fits well in the overall movement of all revelation; it requires that the interpreter be sensitive to this full development of the history of salvation and of the faith.

Up to this point the *CCC* has followed *DV* closely. But we notice with some surprise that a little section is inserted here (nn. 115–118) under the subtitle "The senses of Scripture," inasmuch as this was not in the conciliar Constitution, but develops the interpretive principle just explained, that of interpretation "in the Spirit," from *DV.* Therefore, it seemed to the writers of the *CCC* that the fundamental principles of scholarly exegesis in the 1943 encyclical could be considered today as accepted, but now it was worthwhile to go further, even beyond *DV,* with the invitation to deepen the search for the "senses of Scripture." In a thought-provoking article recently published ("Il senso spirituale della Scrittura," in Communio (Italian edition) 126 [1992] 82–87), Hans Urs von Balthasar noted just the same that in contemporary theology there is almost nothing more needed than "a radical reflection on the meaning of Scripture."

To illustrate this doctrine on the "senses" of Scripture, the famous medieval couplet is then quoted (cf. n. 118), which was amply studied by Henri de Lubac in his time (*Esegesi medievale. I quattro sensi della Scrittura,* 3 vols., Rome: Paoline, 1962–1972). He particularly insisted on the importance of the order of the first two spiritual "senses" (that is, whether the "moral sense" comes before or after the "allegorical"): according to the great Tradition, the "allegorical" sense must precede the "tropological" (i.e., the moral); that is, what we must "believe" on the basis of the biblical accounts *(quid credas)* must always precede what we must "do" *(quid agas),* to avoid the danger of wanting to draw moralizations immediately from Scripture: Christian morality must always be a morality of the faith; otherwise Christianity risks being reduced to an ethic. It is also useful to recall that in the Middle Ages the three spiritual senses were connected with the three theological virtues: allegory, with faith (*quid credas*), which discovers the depth of mystery in historical events; the moral sense (*quid agas*) was centered on charity; but it was considered as a fruit of the hope of finding the eschatological fulfillment of biblical revelation (*quo tendas*).

IV. The Canon of Scripture

This relatively long section (nn. 120–133) does not require as much explanation. It will suffice if we point to its meaning accurately. The biblical canon is the collection of books recognized as inspired, and thereby considered as a "rule" for the faith (the term "canon" means "rule"). On this point there have been various opinions in the course of the centuries. In Catholic terminology it is customary to distinguish between the "protocanonical" and "deuterocanonical" books; these last are the books whose inspired character is not always accepted by all; among the Jews (for the Old Testament) and among the Protestants (for both Testaments) these books are called "apocrypha." In the Church, the definitive demarcation of the biblical canon was fixed only at the Council of Trent, at the time of the Reformation (cf. *DS* 1502–1503).

In this section of the *CCC*, all the doctrine is taken up again, point by point, from *DV*, in chapter IV (Old Testament) and chapter V (New Testament). Two points deserve emphasis here. The first is that in the history of the Church, the temptation to exclude certain parts of Scripture recurs regularly: the gnostics rejected the texts that spoke of the *"Verbum caro factum"* (Jn 1:14), as had the "antichrists" of the Johannine church; Marcion rejected the Old Testament; from the time of the Reformation to our day an analogous tendency has been present, to distinguish "a canon within the canon," that is, to neglect various parts of the New Testament (for example, the pastoral letters), in which traces of "proto-catholicism" are thought to be found, which are thus considered deviations from the *"puritas evangelii."* The other point that is strongly reemphasized in the *CCC* (nn. 128–130) is the unity of the Old and the New Testament (which was already discussed in *DV* 12, 3). This doctrine is common to the whole Tradition, the patristic as well as the medieval (cf. "I due Testamenti" in H. de Lubac, *Storia e Spirito,* Milan: Jaca Book, 1985, 185–198; *Exégèse médiévale,* I/1, 305–365; "L'unità di tutta la Bibbia," in D. Barsotti, *La parola e lo Spirito,* Milan: OR, 1971, 38–42). And this unity finds its center in the person of the incarnate Son of God. Here one can apply the famous word of St. Irenaeus, who responded to Marcion and the Valentinians, according to whom Christ had brought nothing new: *"Cognoscite quod omnem novitatem attulit semetipsum afferens"* (*Adversus Haereses,* IV, 34, 1).

V. Sacred Scripture in the Life of the Church

In the concluding items, nn. 131–133, there is a brief summary of chapter VI of *DV*. With this new orientation due to the Council, it is said that "the centrality of the Word of God" has been realized today in the Church (E. Bianchi). Rather, there is talk about the primacy of the Bible. But if this were true, it could expose the Church to the danger of a certain biblicism. Hence one must always remember the insistence of Vatican II on the unity between Scripture and Tradition.

But what it affirms on the relation between Scripture and theology is especially important: "The study of the sacred page should be the very soul of sacred theology" (n. 132). This principle, at the time of the Council, had an almost revolutionary character. But today one must ask: what hermeneutic does this suppose? One can only answer that it is necessary to respect everything that has been said previously on the interpretation of sacred Scripture, and that it is also stated here (*DV* 24): whether in biblical or theological exegesis, we must be "scrutinizing in the light of faith all truth stored up in the mystery of Christ." Each of these words must be pondered at length.

Along with the various texts listed here, it is fitting to add a prophetic passage from the Council (*DV* 8), which has not been quoted yet; it seems to be directly inspired by Jn 16:13, where Jesus says that the Spirit of truth will lead the disciples into all the truth; on the subject of Tradition, the Council says: "For as the centuries succeed one another, the Church constantly moves forward toward the fullness of divine truth until the words of God reach their complete fulfillment in her." The same Johannine text had struck Tertullian greatly and had inspired him to give the Holy Spirit various titles *"doctor veritatis"* (*De Praescriptionibus Adversus Haereticos,* 28, 1); *"deductor omnis veritatis"* (*Adversus Praxean,* 2, 1; 30, 5); *"dux universae veritatis"* (*De Ieiunio Adversus Psychicos,* 10, 6).

Chapter Three:
MAN'S RESPONSE TO GOD

Rino Fisichella

The topic of faith in the *CCC* lets us go deeply and with confidence into an issue that touches every believer firsthand. Indeed, with faith, each one makes the choice to trust in God, putting everything on the line, one's whole self, in the name of love. Pascal mentioned this also, with the force of his argument: "Yes, you must wager; it is not optional.... what harm will befall you in taking this side? You will be faithful, honest, humble, grateful, generous, a sincere friend, truthful.... I will tell you that you will thereby gain in this life, and that, at each step you take on this road, you will see so great certainty of gain, so much nothingness in what you risk, that you will at last recognize that you have wagered for something certain and infinite, for which you have given nothing" (Pensées, 233).

The quotation from *DV* 2 with which the third chapter of the *CCC* opens supports an understanding of faith as a true interpersonal "encounter" with God who reveals himself. In answer to the revelation of God, with which he chooses to dwell with and "move among" humanity in "the fullness of his love" and to invite them to communion, human faith corresponds, abandoning itself to him. So to understand revelation in a coherent way, faith is necessary.

Article 1:
I BELIEVE

I. The Obedience of Faith

The favored expression with which the *CCC* defines faith is that of "obedience." The mind turns instantly to the classic text of Paul: "How are men to call upon him in whom they have not believed? And how are they to believe in him of whom they have never heard? And how are they to hear without a preacher? And how can men preach unless they are sent? As it is written, 'How beautiful are the feet of those who preach good news!' But they have not all heeded the gospel; for Isaiah says, 'Lord, who has believed what he has heard from us?' So faith comes from what is heard, and what is heard comes by the preaching of Christ" (Rom 10:14–17). The apostle plays on the double meaning of the Hebrew word *shemâ* which is translated in Greek as "to listen" and "to obey"; the meaning of his thought, however, is fully expressed precisely by the relation of the two verbs: faith consists in listening to the word of preaching which leads to obedience, and conversely, obedience leads to listening to the word proclaimed.

It will be worthwhile, before entering into the specific analysis of the act of faith, to recall the semantic value the term possesses in sacred Scripture, knowing that underlying the term is a vast range of meanings that can encompass the global meaning of faith only in their complementarity.

The Hebrew language possesses a range of terms to describe "faith." The nearest basic expression refers to the root *'aman* which has the meaning "to be steady", "stable", "secure"; starting from this center, other words can be found that add to it or make it more specific: to "take refuge," "entrust," "find shelter", that express the attitude of the reverent and religious man. One must also add the meanings of to "hope" and "wait," no less important. The shadings that these terms express find confirmation in the concrete attitude of biblical man which, from time to time, becomes one of "fear" or "wonderment," of "trusting abandon" and "veneration."

If in common use "to believe" amounts to relying on someone who offers guarantees (cf. Gn 45:26), when it is applied to YHWH, instead it expresses the act of total and trusting abandon, knowing that God is jealous and faithful. For the whole biblical tradition, the classic example of faith will be the attitude of Abraham, in which the peculiar characteristics of faith come together, as they are expressed in the *CCC* in nn. 145–147. In Gn 15:1–21—especially in the interpretation Paul will provide in Rom 4:18–25—three attitudes are found, condensed, that determine the understanding of biblical faith: full "trust" in the promises that YHWH makes, the "obedience" of Abraham to the word and the command addressed to him, and finally, the "knowledge" of God in the events of his life. Abraham believes in God who promises him descendants despite the advanced age of Sarah. Believing, he trusts in him and abandons himself to his promise; but, at the same time, he has full conviction, that is, the certainty that the promise made would be realized. The same characteristics can be found also in Ex 4:31 where it is told that the people believed in the words YHWH had addressed to Moses, accepting his mission and living in the certainty of liberation.

For the Old Testament, believing appears as an act with which one "knows" God in his concrete historical action; one "acknowledges" the truth of his promise, and "abandons" oneself to him with an unshakable obedience, knowing that he is a faithful God. Therefore believing is not an isolated, let alone a merely theoretical, act. It is expressed in a basic attitude of trust and certainty that involves the believer in his whole existence. The culminating expression of this attitude is found in a strongly controversial text from an exegetical point of view, one which constitutes a classic reference point: "If you do not stand firm in faith, you will not stand at all" (Is 7:9). The prophet indicates, at a stroke, the essence of faith: faith is being "rooted" in the Lord and all existence is only realized in this awareness of being "rooted" in him. It is no accident that the Greek version, the Septuagint, translates this passage: "If you do not believe, you will not understand": that is, life will not be comprehensible without faith. The same prophet Isaiah again presents a revealing text that leads to a valuable synthesis on the topic of faith: "'You are my witnesses,' says the Lord, 'and my servant whom I have chosen, that you may know and believe me, and understand that I am He" (Is 43:10). Of course, for biblical man, knowing is not the same as a form of theoretical thinking, as it is for our contemporary man. Rather, to know is to verify the fulfillment of promises, in the concreteness of one's own life and in the history of the people. However, this text by itself helps us understand the cognitive value faith possesses. It is not a sacrifice for the mind; to the contrary it is so involved with knowledge as to reach certainty.

The Psalms give further proof of this dimension in several places: "I know that the Lord maintains the cause of the afflicted, and executes justice for the needy" (Ps 140:13); "This I know, that God is for me" (Ps 56:9); "I know that the Lord is great, and that our Lord is above all gods" (Ps 135:5); "I know, O Lord, that your judgments are right and in faithfulness you have afflicted me" (Ps 119:75)… this *knowing* on the Psalmist's part expresses the certainty of a knowledge of the presence of God that brings strength to his faith.

The New Testament further deepens the data expressed so far and confers greater concreteness on them, directing the gaze to the event of the incarnation. The mere count of the uses of *"pístis"* and *"pistéuein"* (about 240 times) indicates the value it possesses for the theology of the New Testament. The appeal to be "ready," "patient," "vigilant" in faith and to have hope, indicates the consistent religious attitude that imprints its decisive orientation on life. In the many expressions found in the various sacred writers, the act of believing maintains a privileged form that amounts to "accepting the preaching of Jesus of Nazareth." Various notable texts in Acts (2:14–36; 3:12–26; 4:8–12; 5:29–32; 8:5–35; 9:20–22; 10:34–43; 13:16–41; 17:1–3; 18:5…) that report the preaching of Peter, Philip, and Paul show with obvious clarity that believing involves an act by which one agrees, after hearing the preaching of the apostle, to live in conformity with that message.

The Synoptic Gospels express the theology of faith as "trust" that the disciple has toward the Master. Faith is the act by means of which a person entrusts himself fully to God and to his Word, radically changing his way of life. The proclamation of the Kingdom being fulfilled, in the very person of Jesus (cf.

Lk 11:20) is directed toward the acceptance of his person in the concreteness of life. Whoever accepts the Lord is simply called a "believer." The preaching of Jesus gives clear encouragement to take on the risk of faith as giving oneself up to the word that the Father makes heard (cf. Mt 6:25–34). In short, for the Synoptics the darkness of waiting has ended, and the signs that Jesus works are demonstrations that the Kingdom is finally come in our midst. The time of fulfillment calls for definitive choice, whatever fate it may bring (cf. Mk 10:38–40; Lk 9:23–24).

The evangelist John provides a more elaborated reflection on the topic of faith, as it represents an all-encompassing theme in his Gospel. Through John a reflection of deep theological value develops, especially with the twinned concepts "to believe"/"to know." It is easy to show how all of his Gospel finds its synthesis in the verse that concludes his writing: "that you may believe that Jesus is the Christ" (Jn 20:31). This conclusion is so decisive that chapter 21, written afterward, does not dare to suppress or modify it. Starting from this text, one retrospectively can read the whole Gospel, where the drama between "believing" and "not believing" (3:36) emerges in a clear way.

Faith, for John, is the principle of Christian life and the synthesis of man's participation in the life of communion with God. The trinitarian life of God is the content of faith, and faith only reaches it if the Father calls and offers the means to reach it (cf. 6:29, 40). Jesus teaches the "skeptical" Nicodemus that one needs to be "born from above" (Jn 3:7); hence the way to come before him must be different, because only "he who comes from above is above all"; he who comes from the earth "belongs to the earth, and of the earth he speaks" (3:31). Moreover, the evangelist emphasizes that faith is already part of the earthly work of Jesus and it becomes explicit in an encounter with him. A look at the construction of the verb indicates the meaning toward which it tends: "believing about," "believing in," "believing that," "believing in the name of Jesus," express the various functions faith addresses.

Believing and knowing, in his Gospel, are similar and at times even interchangeable; the underlying meaning, however, is different and discouraging for anyone who may want to pursue modern gnoseological theories. To "know" indicates a more conscious faith (cf. 6:69; 10:38; 14:20), not in the sense of a greater intellectual clarity; rather, more of an understanding of one's own life, opening itself more and more toward the new. It is this form of knowledge that creates communion with the Father; because of this, we can understand the greater use of the verb "to know" in the farewell discourse (cf. chap. 14, 17). In other words, for John, believing is a concrete attitude in which "knowing," "recognizing," "seeing," "accepting," "listening," "touching" come together…in all its dimensions the believer opens himself to the Spirit to accept the Spirit's life of grace and his truth. Therefore, to believe is to see the Son and the works he performs that reflect the glory *(dóxa)* of the Father. Indeed, listening to his Word and seeing his works have led us to know him and recognize him as the revealer of the Father, and therefore to enter into a relationship of love with him.

Faith, in other words, is open to an ever greater knowledge and understanding and an ever closer communion, so as to lead us to love. At the same time, this knowledge, because it is realized in the light of faith, is protected from any possible mythic or gnostic misunderstanding. It remains tied to historical fact and to the historicity of a person with whom one has such a relationship of life, that one leaves everything for him and follows him (cf. Jn 1:35–51) always, even though one can no longer "see" him directly (cf. Jn 20:24–29). So to believe, for John, indicates a concrete commitment of life which implies a decision that embraces all of existence. Because this is "light" coming into life, it implies a break with the world of "darkness," with "lies" and "sin"; this explains why John never uses the verb "convert" or the noun "conversion," because believing *per se* amounts to being a new creature that enters into the very life of God, who is addressed as Father.

In the theology of Paul, then, the topic of believing takes up a significance with further originality. Here is expressed the soteriological dimension, which sees the high point of salvation in the mystery of the Lord's passion, death, and resurrection. Certainly one can say that for Paul the theme of faith plays an essential and decisive role in his Christian vision. Faith, for the Apostle, defines a Christian's being and his personal identity. It is a dynamic reality; it begins with baptism but lasts all of life without knowing any interruption or alteration of its involvement. Moreover, faith has a universal dimension; everyone has access to it and no one is excluded from it: barbarians, Greeks and Jews; free men or slaves; men or women; all are called to salvation by means of the act of faith (cf. Gal 3:26; Rom 10:12). Through the proclamation of the Gospel, all are invited to accept Christ to obtain salvation. The proclamation of the Gospel, however, opens to a missionary dimension; whoever becomes a believer is called in turn to share the joy of meeting Jesus with others (cf. Col 1:4–6). Faith, in short, has the whole believing community as its subject. It is the Church that believes, in her various actions: the testimony of liturgical prayer only bears witness to the communitarian dimension of faith.

All of this depends on the fact that Paul thinks of faith as *fides ex auditu* (Rom 10:17). It depends on the preaching of the Apostle, but in turn, it becomes actual and is based in the word of the Lord Jesus. For Paul, then, faith is centered on the Christological formulation that synthesizes the paschal mystery: the passion, death, and resurrection of the Lord. In that sense, a text from 1 Cor takes on a programmatic value: "so we preach and so you believed" (1 Cor 15:1–19). In a few strokes Paul provides the originality of the Christian faith: the paschal event has direct witnesses. Faith is transmitted by means of the proclamation of the Church, it is real and true; otherwise missionary work would end up destroying itself.

So in Pauline theology, "believing-knowing" and "believing-entrusting" become a duality set in ongoing parallelism because only in their mutual interrelation do they point out the global sense of the one act and make it explicit. Indeed, man can understand himself only if he believes. His life becomes meaningful only if it is placed on a road marked with a starting point—the justification received from the paschal event of the Lord—and a point of arrival—the glorious return of the Lord. All the believer's existence is placed between these two pillars; it seems to "fluctuate" between these two moments; without creating any anguish or anxiety; to the contrary, it is precisely waiting for the Lord that adds trust in him because the knowledge of his mystery grows.

It will seem paradoxical, and yet Paul is never afraid to use the verb "know" with complete ease, just when he is speaking about the greatest and most unreachable mysteries of the faith and of human life. Some quick examples make this plain: "If we have died with Christ, we believe that we shall also live with him. For we know that Christ being raised from the dead will never die again" (Rom 6:8–9); "We know that if the earthly tent we live in is destroyed, we have a building from God" (2 Cor 5:1); "Knowing that he who raised the Lord Jesus will raise us also" (2 Cor 4:14). The Apostle's sure knowledge is an expression of faith that has no fear of entering into the mystery with the strength of reason illuminated by grace.

As we can confirm from this quick glance, "believing," for Scripture, is a peculiar form of knowledge. Faith is a concrete attitude and implies "recognizing," "accepting," "seeing," "hearing," and "listening," in a word, a personal contact. These are all verbs that anticipate, accompany, or lead to the act of "believing" as a form, by means of which each one expresses itself fully, even through the senses. In a word, we are faced with understanding a fully personal act in which the whole person is entirely taken up: the intellect, will, understanding of self, and decision.

In nn. 148–149 the *CCC* fittingly identifies the most coherent expression of New Testament faith in Mary. The "marian principle" becomes the form through which the Church can see the act of believing in the person of Jesus realized and directed to its purpose. "The Church finds her personal center in Mary as well as the full realization of her idea as Church" (H.U. von Balthasar, *Explorations in Theology II: Spouse of the Word,* San Francisco: Ignatius, 1991, 161), because in the Mother of the Lord the Church sees enacted the most coherent response that humanity has given to Christ. Mary marks the highest point of the action of grace when a believer lets herself be shaped and defined. So Mary's act of believing makes clear, in the best way possible, the Christian conception of faith; it stands under two aspects: virginity and fecundity. In its origin, faith is always a grace and gift of God; the immaculate being of Mary points this out. In its purpose, it aims toward fruitfulness because it gives birth, like the Church that gives birth in the faith to new believers.

Beside Mary's exemplary role for the faith, it is also fitting to place that of Peter, since he too becomes a sign of how a sinner believes; or that of John, the disciple who in loving believes and in believing loves. These are different perspectives of how a person who accepts faith meets its gratuitous nature and knows how to respond. Peter, who in the name of the Twelve professes the Lord's messianic identity first (cf. Mk 8:25–30) and who is capable of great promises (cf. Mk 14:30), falls, however, into betrayal (cf. Mt 20:30–35). John manages to believe, even in the sorrow of his trial at the foot of the cross and still will be first to recognize the resurrection (cf. Jn 21:7). Faith touches all in the weakness of their own lives, but also is able to bring trust and strength, as the fruit of grace, which makes what is weak strong (cf. 1 Cor 1:28).

II. "I Know Whom I Have Believed"

According to a classic expression, the act of faith is specified by its object *(actus fidei specificatur ab obiecto).* Behind this formulation an incalculable richness is hidden that lets us see in detail the specificity of faith in God. In common language, the word "believe" is used in disparate contexts: "I believe the weather will be good tomorrow," "I believe that a market economy allows for a diversified use of riches," "I believe that my friend is telling the truth".... Each time it is used, the person is involved in a different way, according to the content that completes it. To say that one "believes in God" implies the assumption of an attitude that touches the person in his depths and determines his whole existence inasmuch as it refers to the transcendent.

In theology two expressions are used that support the understanding of the unity between the act of faith and the content which is believed: *fides qua* and *fides quae.* The first describes the act with which one believes; the second, the content that is believed. Faith consists inseparably of these two moments that form a substantial unity, but are theologically distinguished for analysis. In nn. 150–152, the *CCC* turns first to the topic of *fides quae*, showing its trinitarian content. Christian faith is in fact defined as faith in the Trinity. Nothing has so transformed human intelligence as the mystery of the Trinity, and at the same time nothing of the Christian faith in that mystery can be replaced. It constitutes the foundation of our believing and the ultimate end the believer desires to reach. Only in this perspective does Christology assume its full value and revelation its final meaning. What Jesus of Nazareth reveals of himself as the ultimate and definitive expression of the Word of God (cf. *DV* 4) is still always the consciousness of a "pointing" to the Father and his mystery of love. Faith becomes clear in this profession of the Trinity and becomes fruitful only in it. It is impossible to separate Jesus Christ from the Trinity; it is harmful to think of God while leaving aside Jesus Christ. The mystery of Christian faith gains all its originality and uniqueness only to the extent that the mystery of the Triune God is explained and revealed in the incarnation of the Son, in its "deeds and words having an inner unity" (*DV* 2) (historical dimension); and from this each one's personal existence regains its ultimate meaning for a full significance (soteriological dimension).

God, revealed by Jesus as Father, Son, and Spirit, is therefore the center of the faith and its specific mystery. Around this the other mysteries of Christianity are articulated and explained: the incarnation of the Son and his obedience to the Father even to death on a cross, to be raised by him; the origin of the Church in the dynamic power of the Spirit of the Risen One, who leads the faithful to the definitive encounter with the glorified Christ; the Church as institution marked by the "kenosis of the Spirit" (von Balthasar), and the ministers in her provided as gifts of the same Spirit for the upbuilding of the community (cf. nn. 748–750); dogma as ever greater understanding of the mystery of faith in openness to all the truth (cf. Jn 16:13). So around the one mystery of the Triune God a hierarchical articulation is created that lets us see the one truth as a symphony, harmonized and played with the intention that everything be *ad maiorem Dei gloriam.*

While explaining the articles of the Creed, which like all the creeds of the faith possesses a "trinitarian structure," the *CCC* will make explicit the main contents that are only hinted at in these three paragraphs of the *CCC*. So one can refer to the marginal numbers that appear throughout the first part of the *CCC* to have a more complete and coherent vision.

We will do well to emphasize the use which the *CCC* often makes, of faith as "assent." Assent indicates a particular attitude of the subject that implies an absolute commitment in the acceptance of some point of content. It was particularly the great nineteenth-century convert, Blessed John Henry Newman, who explained theologically the intuitions of St. Augustine on this subject. In his *A Grammar of Assent,* he distinguishes between "real" and "notional" assent and defines it as "the absolute acceptance of a proposition without any condition" (New York: Longmans, 1947; 11). Particular attention is given to St. Augustine who affirms, in a famous passage: "Belief itself is nothing else than to think with assent. For it is not every one who thinks that believes, since many think in order that they may not believe; but everybody who believes, thinks—both thinks in believing and believes in thinking.... Because if faith is not a matter of thought, it is of no account; and we are not sufficient to think anything as of ourselves, but our sufficiency is of God" (*De predestinatione sanctorum,* 2, 5; *PL* 44, 962–963).

Starting from the Augustinian tradition, in a passage of the *Sermon on the Creed,* we read: "It is one thing to believe about him, another to believe him, another to believe in him. To believe about him amounts to believing that everything he has said is true; to believe him amounts to believing that he himself is God; to believe in him means to love him" (*PL* 40, 1190–1191).

As we can see, all believing is gathered around a threefold expression that sums up the entirety of the biblical richness about the subject: *credere Deo, credere Deum, credere in Deum.* With *credere Deo* (believing "about" God), the aim is to underscore the formal dimension of the faith; what constitutes its foundation, which is to say, the authority of God in revealing himself. By believing one accepts the very testimony which God gives about himself and which is based on the same authority; thus the believer accepts the truth of revelation because God himself is its guarantor. With *credere Deum* (thus believing God as the object of faith), there is emphasis on the mystery believed and what the whole divine life revealed in Christ is. This expression aims to emphasize that the center of faith is God himself and his mystery which cannot be fully grasped by the mind, but which indeed call for assent. With *credere in Deum*, lastly, the dynamic dimension of faith and the interpersonal element are emphasized. To believe in God amounts to accepting a person; in the horizon of faith this implies deciding to do so and entering into a permanent relationship of communion which is love. So faith is seen here in light of the relation of love which commits the believer to give himself fully to God, knowing that he is totally committed in making himself man.

III. The Characteristics of Faith

An interesting paragraph opens in the *CCC* now at nn. 153–160. It attempts to describe the structure of the act of faith and the various elements that come into play. It is known that for many verses this topic constitutes the *crux theologorum;* objectively it is difficult, and the topic calls for knowing how to grasp the various aspects present in a single act. In any case, we will need to emphasize the extreme importance of the content of these paragraphs for Christians of today and its urgency in pastoral practice. It is above all in this section that the question must be posed: "Why do I believe?" The question can no longer be treated as obvious; that suffers from weakness of faith itself. The question "why do I believe?" is a qualifying stage on the road of faith, and on it faith works out as a "personal" and "free" choice in view of the truth accepted into the self as a condition of life. Without the answer to this question, given at various levels but corresponding to the person's age and formation (cf. nn. 23–24), it will be difficult for the Christian to think he has made a full act of faith.

We live in a cultural context, above all with regard to the West, in which great difficulties seem to emerge in explaining the act of faith. These can be described under two aspects: ideological and ecclesial. In the first aspect, it is easy to identify the presence of certain behaviors that, as such, threaten the understanding of the faith. The conviction seems to grow more and more that it is impossible to carry out choices that are definitive. The overly fragmented nature of everything, and behavior that is often only functionalistic—even in what characterizes the person's ultimate identity, such as love—these set up a preconception in which everything seems limited to the commitment of a moment, but not a whole life. Besides this, the supremacy of subjectivity over every form of objectivity, especially in regard to the dimension of truth, drives the person to the point where he calls himself back to his own convictions and certainties as the only criterion of truth, losing sight of the very horizon on which to place the question about truth and meaning. At the level of the Church, it is easy to verify how often pastoral practice is not up to adequately meeting the question of "why do I believe?" Avoiding this question risks that faith may be understood only as a series of propositional contents that have no bearing on one's personal life. Thus it is fundamental that catechesis spend a lot of energy to recover the presentation of the act of faith, by analyzing various proposals able to give flesh to an answer to this deep question.

In this horizon it is opportune to recall, first of all, the specific topic that is known under the name of *motivum fidei,* that is to say, the "motivations" that lead one to believe. On this aspect the *CCC* makes reference only to *DF* from Vatican I and directly to the classic signs of credibility such as: miracles, prophecies, holiness, and the spread of the Church (n. 156). To understand the text from Vatican I in the right framework. we need to think back to the context in which those affirmations were placed. The Council had before it two extreme positions to which to respond: rationalism and traditionalism. It argued against the first that, although it was possible to arrive at the knowledge of God through natural means, he had nonetheless revealed himself in another, supernatural way, that constituted the coherent and correct expression for true knowledge of himself (*DS* 3004). It responded to the second that faith could not be a "blind movement of the spirit" (*DS* 3010), but required intelligence as the capacity able to verify the coherence between the content of the faith and reason itself. In this sense, the signs of revelation, as historical events, are entrusted to reason that it may evaluate them and verify in them not only that they do not contradict reason, but especially verify the possibility of grasping in them the very action of God in history. Miracles, prophecies, and the soundness of the Church, at each level, showed the divine origin of Christianity and allowed reason to choose in a free way, because it was reaching the certainty of truth through the analysis of these signs.

In the current cultural horizon it is necessary to broaden the teaching proposed by the *CCC* to place the motive for faith more in light of the "search for meaning," which is much more significant to our contemporaries. The search for an ideal of life is particular to the person, and to see the self directed toward this ideal is a form of actualization of the personality; it allows the person to give meaning to existence. This means that all of life is seen primarily in its totality and not in the fragmentary nature of individual gestures or moments. Faced with the meaning of existence, each one reflects on himself, searches and chooses, because he needs to give some certainty to his own life. No one indeed could live a personal existence if he did not have certainties; at least the certainty of his own existence is required. By this requirement, everyone is placed in the condition of having to choose in a definitive way at least regarding his own life. This is not left to arbitrariness and no one can remain neutral. In the choice of directing one's own existence toward an aim so that it could have a meaning, no one can have absolute certainty that all of life will gain meaning in that ideal; nevertheless, one "believes" that what one has placed as an ideal can satisfy it. In this framework, faith shows itself as a form of knowledge that goes beyond the factual, but also as an authentic capacity of the person to entrust himself to another to obtain a complete meaning.

The motive for believing, therefore, is joined not with an external dimension of the person, but is profoundly tied to his life and above all with the true motive which existence poses: the meaning for which one lives. Not only that: in the moment when the encounter with the whole person of Jesus Christ presents itself as what "fully reveals man to man himself and makes his supreme calling clear" (*GS* 22), then it becomes evident that the motive for faith is above all the encounter with a person and not just with a manifestation of him, as happened in the past with the reference to miracles.

Having presented the motive for believing, it is necessary to proceed to the analysis of the act of faith, which involves the treatment of at least three topics: the action of grace, the certainty of the truth, and the condition of personal freedom.

The Action of Grace

"Believing is possible only by grace and the interior helps of the Holy Spirit" (n. 154). God is always at the origin of every action; so in our faith also, he is the author of our believing through the gift of grace. In the creation, God has made every person in his "image and likeness" (Gn 1:27). He has placed in each one a *"potentia oboedientialis"* as the capacity *(potentia)* that allows us to receive determinations that one does not possess per se but can only accept as a gift, obedientially *(oboedientialis)*. So in every person there is the possibility of being able to accept the grace that propels one to acts which one could not expect to carry out at only the human level. The action of grace does not contradict man's freedom; in fact, one is free only to the extent to which one is open to a horizon of meaning that personalizes this freedom, bringing it to carry out acts of authentic self-transcendence.

A text from the First Letter of John can make it easier to understand this relation: "If we receive the testimony of men, the testimony of God is greater: for this is the testimony of God that he has borne witness to his Son. He who believes in the Son of God has the testimony in himself. He who does not believe God has made him a liar, because he has not believed in the testimony that God has borne in his Son" (1 Jn 5:9–10). In this text, it seems that the sacred author wants to express the idea that the testimony of God is at the same time internal and external. It is a testimony for Jesus Christ who is accredited as Son (cf. Jn 5:32,37); therefore it is a testimony that places itself in history, and makes itself visible through the whole life of Jesus, and enables us to accept all of this as his very revelation. Yet here the author adds another particular: the testimony of God is greater than that of men and cannot be placed on the same level. Indeed it is given within man himself, in his depths, where he receives and perceives the very presence of truth. Paul expresses the same concept in clear words when he declares: "For what person knows a man's thoughts except the spirit of the man which is in him? So also no one comprehends the thoughts of God except the Spirit of God. Now we have received not the spirit of the world, but the Spirit which is from God, that we might understand the gifts bestowed on us by God" (1 Cor 2:11–12). Therefore to the extent man believes, the testimony of God in him becomes "faith"; this, to again use an expression of the Apostle, is nothing other than the light of God "who has shone in our hearts" (2 Cor 4:6). Therefore God, in his intra-trinitarian nature can be known and accepted by man only if he lets himself be moved by the Spirit of God, the only one who can know him. The patristic and scholastic tradition have called this interior testimony from God and the grace that acts in us *lumen fidei,* the light of faith. God, therefore, is at the origin of every act of faith in him and constitutes the most intimate point of the very foundation of faith. As the text of Acts bears witness in summary form: "by the work of grace many became believers" (cf. Acts 18:27).

The dimension of grace present in us that spurs us to faith is directed toward the horizon of the Son, the revealer of the Father. He not only makes possible the light of grace in us, but at the same time stands as the true light for all who want to reach the Father (cf. Mt 11:27; Jn 1:4–9; 9:5; 12:36). Here the Christological dimension of faith is expressed again, faith which is the indispensable way of access to the God of Jesus Christ. To accept and believe in Jesus Christ, visible presence and "image-icon" (Col 1:15) of the Father, amounts to accepting and seeing God himself (cf. Jn 14:9). This inseparably involves believing in the Word and becoming sons, and therefore sharers of divine life. To use a beautiful image from Pope Francis, "Faith does not merely gaze at Jesus, but sees things as Jesus himself sees them, with his own eyes: it is a participation in his way of seeing" (*LF* 18).

The Certainty of Faith

A second element to evaluate is the dimension of the certainty of faith (n. 157). Without this certainty one cannot conceive the act of believing, because it could not correspond to human nature itself. Really, no one could carry out a definitive act based on a premise that, as such, appears provisional and uncertain. Life would be marked with its negative traits and would develop in the shadow of instability and hence constant doubt and anguish. The certainty of faith is based on knowledge of the truth acquired in the very act with which one believes. So it is fitting for catechesis to value some elements that are the particular possession of the Christian tradition under this aspect. First among them is the theme of truth.

One should not forget that influential misunderstandings caused by philosophical and cultural preconceptions play a role with this topic. Two worlds meet and, as it were, collide in the understanding and explanation of the truth: the Greek world and the Christian. To be sure, for both of them truth is in being itself and therefore in the manifestation of being; but the revelation of being for the Greeks (and those who follow them; that is, essentially all of Western philosophical thought) is not the same as among Christians. Here the first great problem arises, and it is about this that the great difference begins to play out: the meaning of truth will be different because the way being is manifested is different. In the Greek world, what prevails is experience of the direct rootedness of truth in being, which leads to the very necessity of being; so the Greek meaning of truth is considered a perfection of the world. In the face of this concept, the philosopher is forced to confront truth alone in intellectual contemplation.

In contrast, the Christian world conceives truth as the manifestation and revelation of God in a "historical event" that brings with it the characteristic of final fulfilment. The biblical preconception of "*alethéia*-truth" not only means "manifestation" but much more; it expresses first of all the fidelity of YHWH to the promises he has made. Truth for biblical man essentially equates to confirming that YHWH is a God who keeps the promises he has made, because man experiences it directly in his personal history. In a word, he understands the truth in light of the revelation God makes in history, giving it an eschatological direction that aims toward a definitive encounter with him. In the Christian perspective, therefore, truth cannot prescind from this supporting idea; it is conceived as an event of revelation that will be ever fuller and more total but which for the moment has traits of hiddenness because "no one can see God and remain alive" (cf. Ex 33:20). So in Christian thought the truth is united, for the first time, with temporal and historical categories.

On the other hand, placing truth within time and history implies seeing it related with the typical temporal movement which is structured of past-present-future. In this historical-temporal perspective, the revelation of God also brings into effect a dialectic between "disclosing and concealing." So there will be a truth in the past, established by the event of creation, that bears witness to the goodness of God and confirms the possibility of knowing him (cf. Rom 1:20). However, there is the truth of the present which, for the believer, is expressed in the entire event of the Incarnation which imprints upon all of history the ultimate and definitive synthesis of every possible revelation of God (*DV* 2:4). This truth is also tied to the future, inasmuch as it implies the total realization of the Kingdom proclaimed by Christ and, with that, full knowledge of God (Jn 16:13).

These premises lead directly to confirming the dimension of faith as a form of knowledge that possesses the certainty of truth. Access to God and to his truth is given through the historicity of the Christ event, which finds its own objectivity in itself and not in decisions which the believer might give based on his "believing" in him. Faith and revelation indeed are none other than two poles of the one revelatory structure that refers to his historical manifestation, which makes real the truth about himself and therefore about the world and makes it visible. In this framework, it is understood how certainty does not come to man from himself, as much as it points back to the evidence of the revelation he encounters historically in the person of Jesus of Nazareth. In him, truth is offered in the present of every day, because it possesses—once for all in the history of mankind—the traits of universality but in the concreteness of his historical person *(universale concretum)*. The truth that emerges from the person of Jesus Christ necessarily requires that we read and interpret it in the light of love that remains as the intimate nature of the divine mystery. Love, therefore, is the coherent criterion of truth to enter into revelation and is the fundamental content that gives impetus and strength to faith.

The evidence of revelation is the evidence of love that asserts itself on its own, without any other motive but love itself. A beautiful explanation along this line is found in *LF*, where Pope Francis writes: "Love and truth are inseparable. Without love, truth becomes cold, impersonal and oppressive for people's day-to-day lives. The truth we seek, the truth that gives meaning to our journey through life, enlightens us whenever we are touched by love. One who loves realizes that love is an experience of truth, that it opens our eyes to see reality in a new way, in union with the beloved. In this sense, Saint Gregory the Great could write that '*amor ipse notitia est,*' love is itself a kind of knowledge possessed of its own logic. It is a relational way of viewing the world, which then becomes a form of shared knowledge, vision through the eyes of another and a shared vision of all that exists. William of Saint-

Thierry, in the Middle Ages, follows this tradition when he comments on the verse of the Song of Songs where the lover says to the beloved, 'Your eyes are doves' (Song 1:15). The two eyes, says William, are faith-filled reason and love, which then become one in rising to the contemplation of God, when our understanding becomes 'an understanding of enlightened love'" (*LF* 27).

What faith confirms, in this perspective, is the possibility of offering further motives to the understanding which questions the mystery to be certain of its truth. The instruments that exegesis and hermeneutics offer today, with the assistance of historical and archaeological sciences, let us reach secure facts about the person and personality of Jesus of Nazareth. Obviously these facts do not offer faith; it is always the fruit of grace which converts the heart, but they guarantee the believer that what he believes can also be reached and analyzed by reason and is not therefore a simple product of the faith of a few men and women in the past; let alone the fruit of their imagination. Their testimony, in sum, is based on verifiable historical facts and subject to critique.

Personal Freedom

At the conclusion of the topic of grace and of the certainty of truth comes the inevitable question of how the act of faith can be considered a free and personal act. If we come face-to-face with the certainty and evidence of the truth, how can one still be free to choose? Is one not likely obliged by the evidence? Paragraph n. 160 of the *CCC* only outlines a response to this, and the quotations from *DH* (cf. nn. 10–11), by themselves, do not deal with the topic being raised. Those passages speak of the nature of the act of faith in a context focused on explaining religious liberty, and hence focused on the freedom to adhere to religion; however, its aim is not to establish a relation with the truth of the faith as, in contrast, our case seeks. Certainly it would have been better to make use of n. 2 of the same document where it is written that all men are "bound to adhere to the truth, once it is known, and to order their whole lives in accord with the demands of truth" (*DH* 2). In this way, the issue would have been more coherent and the reference and connection to nn. 1730–1742, in which the *CCC* outlines the theme of freedom in the sphere of the moral life, would have become more logical and consequential.

No one can think that the topic of freedom in faith could be presented only with the example that no one obliges anyone to believe in God and therefore one is free. Such a stroke only reflects a part of the truth and could easily be shown false with a deeper analysis. *True* freedom is not revealed in the confrontation between two created beings, but in relation to a freedom that goes beyond one's own inconsistency. Freedom is always a space of choice that includes overcoming one's own limitations, one that realizes the person, allowing him to carry out gestures that transcend the finite. Now, an authentic freedom is realized in the moment when one discovers the presence of the infinite and abandons oneself to it. Christian faith lives on the supreme paradox that God the creator respects the creature, to the point of leaving him free to choose against him. Yet a choice like that would not correspond to personal freedom, since it would impede man from reaching a space that goes beyond his own limits. In a word he would remain enclosed within his own inconsistency, without any possibility to really overcome himself and therefore reach an absolute space of freedom.

In the act of faith no one is obliged to believe by the evidence of the truths of revelation, because, as has been indicated, Christian revelation identifies truth in the person of Jesus Christ. Yet this truth is given in the dialectic of revelation itself that develops between knowledge and hiddenness. This means that we, always and everywhere, come face-to-face with the mystery of faith that spurs the mind and the intelligence to constantly discover the truth of God, and in it the truth about ourselves. The truth discovered is always a truth that sends us to a further truth, because this is what the revelation of God consists of: once "revealed", it remains "hidden" and in "hiddenness reveals" itself further. So the believer reaches his own sphere of personal freedom, because he places himself before the truth of the faith, in the act of a continual discovery that commits him to seeing God always present in his life and for all his existence. His freedom will be what will permit him, in the light of grace, to perceive the plan of salvation and to choose it.

The fact that revelation enters into personal life with the dialectic of hiddenness and disclosure demands that the choice to accept it and entrust oneself to it be the fruit of *faith*. This means a knowledge able to risk and wager, not so much on a concept of truth in itself as pure theory as on the choice, rather, of a personal obedience that entrusts one's own existence and its ultimate meaning to this revelation, even though one may perceive and know it always in a movement which is that of mystery. So freedom consists in agreeing to recognize one's own dependence on the revealed truth and on the form that is able to make it known: faith. Without faith, therefore, no one could know the truth of God and so no one could be authentically free (cf. Jn 8:32).

We will not have completed our overview on the act of faith, if the inexplicable void left by the *CCC* on the point is not filled, about the relationship of faith and love and the circularity between the two. The primacy belongs to St. Thomas for having organized the unity between them in a systematic way. On several occasions he proposes *caritas* as the form of faith: "Charity is called the form of faith in so far as the act of faith is perfected and formed by charity" (*Summa Theologiae*, II–II, 4,4). Yet this circularity is carried out in a relation that puts faith in the first place in the *ordo generationis,* but can grant the primacy to love in the *ordo perfectionis.* Theological reflection on this topic needs further development. Based on the words of the First Letter of Peter: "You love him; though you do not now see him you believe in him" (1 Pt 1:8), the primacy of love in generating faith, too, could easily be accepted. The perspective which von Balthasar opened with the *pulchrum* would fit coherently in this environment, where love would find its constitutive value restored as the very form of revelation.

Faith, particularly in Johannine and Pauline theology, is seen as a road that leads to love; under this aspect, both John and Paul derive from only faith a second fundamental requirement, that of love. Indeed for Paul faith becomes active in love (cf. Gal 5:6); for John, love of neighbor becomes a new commandment that will make it possible in the future to recognize the true disciples of Christ. For both, believing and loving are two demands that summarize all the others and assert themselves for anyone who wants to be a disciple of Christ. No one could have faith if that faith did not advance and evolve into love; but no one could have love either if it did not have its start from a faith that knows how to recognize the never seen face of the Master who has been proclaimed.

Love and faith, therefore get their life from a cyclical relationship that lets us explain how each one proceeds from the other, but both together fundamentally constitute Christian life. The saving event that Jesus of Nazareth represents can only be recognized on the basis of the two, because together they form the authentic and coherent response that can be rendered to revelation. Certainly in the distinctiveness of New Testament usage, faith and love lead to identifying their complementary aspects by which, especially in Paul, faith will point to a new relationship that comes to be established with God through Christ; while love, rather, will evoke the intensity, the openness, the totality, and the full abandon that are due in this relationship, but both describe and determine the act of faith in its entirety. Faith cannot be limited to the moment of conversion: it opens into love; it seeks it because, in the end faith finds love to be its origin, to which it owes everything, its *raison d'être.* (For a more systematic vision, cf. R. Fisichella, *"Fides quaerens caritatem,"* in M. Kessler, W. Pannenberg, and H.J. Pottmeyer, *Fides quaerens intellectum. Beiträge zur Fundamentaltheologie,* Tübingen, 1992, 414–426).

In this cyclical framework between faith and love, we will need to do everything, in catechesis, to recover the unitary character of the act of faith that cannot be divided into a "before" and "after." It would not be right to think that "'first' one believes" and "'then' one lives as a Christian." To believe is already, in itself, to live according to the distinctive modality of love. It becomes still clearer, in this sense, that the act of believing is fundamentally a decision that encompasses all of life, and nothing of life is excluded. So to believe implies the concreteness of a praxis that becomes a testimony of faith as James explicitly affirms: " 'You have faith and I have works.' Show me your faith apart from your works, and I by my works will show you my faith" (Jas 2:18). This same teaching finds confirmation in Paul when he speaks of "commitment of faith" (cf. 1 Thess 1:3; Eph 4:15). According to all of biblical thought, knowing God amounts to "carrying out his righteousness" and "his will"; because "Not every one who says to me, 'Lord, Lord,' shall enter the kingdom of heaven, but he who does the will of my Father" (Mt 7:21).

CCC n. 158, which bears two classic quotations as opening and conclusion, the first from Anselm *("Fides quaerens intellectum")* and the second from Augustine *("Credo ut intelligam et intelligo ut credam"),* gives us the opportunity to devote two further words to the value of knowledge and of seeking in faith. Faith by its nature seeks understanding of its own content and wants to convey it. All of Christian tradition, in various ways, has done nothing but seek understanding of what it believes. The Eastern Fathers first and then the West made a toolkit of concepts and language out of their traditions and from forms of philosophical thought, to seek to understand, explore, and convey the content of the faith. What remains as common patrimony of all this uninterrupted tradition is the constancy of *"quaerere"* of the faith. If faith were not seeking, it would not be Christian faith, but only a gnosis.

Seeking understanding of what one believes is not motivated by causes external to faith, but by internal factors. At least three can be recognized: the first is in the realm of the certainty of truth, as was previously said. The second is in the realm of apologetics, because the content of faith must be transmitted and thus one has to find the proper means to communicate, that they may be as universal as possible; in this sense, arguments capable of defending the faith must also be presented when there are erroneous interpretations. The third is what St. Bonaventure expressed in summary form: "When faith does not give assent due to reason, but due to love, it still desires to have reasons; this does not take away the merit of human reason, but it adds consolation" (*Proemium I Sent.* 2 ad 6).

So faith is not afraid to face the results of the sciences (cf. n. 159); to be sure, their areas of competence are different, yet the Church "affirms the legitimate autonomy of human culture and especially of the sciences" (*GS* 59). It will be useful to integrate the quotation from GS 36, which concludes n. 159, with another extremely significant statement of the Council. In the context of difficulties about harmonizing the results of the sciences with Christian teaching, the Council writes: "These difficulties do not necessarily harm the life of faith, rather they can stimulate the mind to a deeper and more accurate understanding of the faith. The recent studies and findings of science, history and philosophy raise new questions which effect life and which demand new theological investigations. Furthermore, theologians, within the requirements and methods proper to theology, are invited to seek continually for more suitable ways of communicating doctrine to the men of their times; for the deposit of Faith or the truths are one thing and the manner in which they are enunciated, in the same meaning and understanding, is another. In pastoral care, sufficient use must be made not only of theological principles, but also of the findings of the secular sciences, especially of psychology and sociology, so that the faithful may be brought to a more adequate and mature life of faith. Literature and the arts are also, in their own way, of great importance to the life of the Church. They strive to make known the proper nature of man, his problems and his experiences in trying to know and perfect both himself and the world. They have much to do with revealing man's place in history and in the world; with illustrating the miseries and joys, the needs and strengths of man and with foreshadowing a better life for him. Thus they are able to elevate human life, expressed in multifold forms according to various times and regions" (*GS* 62).

So the call for permanent education in the faith, which is performed by catechesis, will never be sufficient. Faith requires the effort of constant and systematic study because the mystery before us perennially sets personal existence in play. Theology, in this perspective, is not an optional item for the faith, but is its proper form through which the Church herself studies, searches, and teaches in suitable ways the revelation in which she believes (cf. *CT* 20–21:61). So a road opens for the faith; it lasts all of life, but is lived with courage and passion by the one who knows he is having a foretaste of what will constitute eternal happiness: the contemplation of the love of the Triune God.

Article 2: WE BELIEVE

The second article of this third chapter deserves great attention, because if its meaning were taken into serious consideration, it could be capable of making an important impression on the formation of believers. Above, there was emphasis on the difficulty that explaining and understanding the act of faith involves in contemporary culture. A strong subjectivism has entered not only into behavior, but into the very mindset of individuals who no longer seem to notice the drama of such behavior. When contact with the truth is lost, personal conscience is weaker and is tempted to become autonomous, with the risk of closing the self into one's own little world.

The recovery of an "ecclesial conscience" is one of the commitments that should be proposed as an objective, to break the circle of subjectivism and fully recover the genuine meaning of the faith and the commitment to solidarity for all. Christian faith is an ecclesial faith not only because its subject is above all and primarily the Church, but also because this itself is a part of the content of the faith. It is amazing that the Italian edition of the *CCC*, transcribing the two texts of the Creed, insists on presenting an erroneous translation of the Nicene-Constantinopolitan Creed, especially after the *CCC* emphasized the importance of "we believe" with a whole article (cf. nn. 166–175). Even in the Sunday liturgy, the Italian Church has remained nearly alone in maintaining the wording "I believe," while in the other Churches the faith is rightly proclaimed with "'we' believe." The original of this profession of faith, in fact, is "we believe" (*DS* 125,150) and with good reason. That is what we propose to expound briefly in the following considerations.

The rise of the professions of faith (the Creed, cf. nn. 185–197) took place in a context that was not unitary; at least two contexts can be recognized: "liturgical" and "theological." The first has its reference point in the baptismal liturgy and is always expressed in the first person singular, because it aims to show direct knowledge of the content of the faith and the decision to live in it. The second, which arises probably to resist early errors and heresies, has its specific environment in the Councils, and wants to emphasize the faith professed by the whole Church. Certainly there is not necessarily any opposition between the two; rather, they confirm a characteristic of the act of Christian faith, which is at once a personal and ecclesial act. In this process, the "I" of the individual believer is not dissolved by the ecclesial "we" but finds its full sense and possibility of meaning in it. We shall propose a few theological lines that can, suitably developed, support the understanding of the basis of "we believe." We have already insisted on the fact that the act of faith is determined by its content *(actus fidei specificatur ab obiecto)* and we have seen how the content of the faith is the mystery of the Trinity (cf. nn. 150–152). Starting from this datum it is possible to think of the act of faith in its ecclesial dimension.

To affirm that the Church professes all her faith in the Trinity cannot but have consequences from the theological point of view. Trinitarian faith, in fact, implies an affirmation about the very essence of the Christian God, which is precisely unity of nature and trinity of persons. A first consequence is one that leads into an understanding of God as a tripersonal God. This affirms, in a word, that in the image of the Christian God, the communitarian dimension is constitutive. The knowledge that faith receives is not of an isolated God, closed in his Olympus, but of a God who is "relation" and who therefore enters into relation and is interested in the other. In our opinion, this is the fundamental theological element, because it creates a first basis for the ecclesial dimension of believing. The God of faith, as he is professed in the faith of the Church, is imprinted on the image of God who is community and who lives communion. In the economy of revelation, the conduct of Jesus of Nazareth, who interests himself in the other and gives himself to the other—especially when the latter is weak and defenseless, or more so when he is under the indifferent gaze of everyone (cf. Lk 10:29–37)—is among the most expressive and coherent, to reveal the nature of God. Consequently, we must say, then, that the content of trinitarian faith determines the very structure of the act of faith, and makes it an act that needs to be "trinitarian" by its own nature. Above all, that means a communitarian act and hence an act of communion. The centrality of the Trinity for the act of faith equates to admitting the principle of community-communion as the basis of the act of faith itself.

In a perspective of Christian anthropology, the Trinity determines the understanding of being a "person," because this gains its ultimate value, capable of discovering personal being as a communional being, on the basis of relationality. Now, being a "person" in Christian anthropology becomes evident, with the revelation that Jesus historically carries out. The text of Philippians clarifies this dimension significantly: Christ Jesus "though he was in the form of God, did not count equality with God a thing to be grasped, but emptied himself, taking the form of a servant…and became obedient unto death, even death on a cross" (Phil 2:6–8).

As can be seen, in this text the Apostle speaks of the second person of the Trinity; he who became incarnate is the Son; he is qualified to express the "nature" of God, because he is God like the Father. He constitutes the first communication by means of which the love of God becomes evident. It is revealed that the divine nature consists in the Father's "giving all"—thereby the Father is "father" in the intra-trinitarian relationality—and in the Son's "receiving all"—and thereby he is "son" within the same dynamic. The "giving all" is what constitutes the divine nature. The "keeping 'nothing' for oneself" but giving all to the "other" is what makes possible the differentiation of the three persons. They are "person" because of this, that they are characterized by "giving all" until the end and "receiving all." In human language, this "giving all" by God becomes visible in the assumption of a reality that cannot pertain to him properly because he is God. The Apostle, therefore, sees the incarnation—and its culminating expression, revealed in the death of the innocent man nailed upon the cross—as the ultimate and definitive sign given to man so he may understand that here God gives his whole self. For us, impenitent Cartesians, used to seeing the "end" as the process that goes as far as possible from the "beginning" (Plotinus), it becomes difficult to understand the logic of revelation in which the end is not the end, but remains beginning, source, and very spring of the being of God, therefore love that gives its whole self.

When God loves, he loves according to his nature: giving "all"; without letting himself be conditioned in this by the creature that would want to hold back in the face of death. The message revealed in this event is, however, the ultimate possibility for the understanding of our being "person." Only in carrying out this "giving all" can we also discover the true face of being man and woman in the "image of God."

It is in this context that a point made above, on the topic of personal freedom, becomes clearer. Johannine theology provides a help where the intention of Jesus is shown before his death: "I lay down my life, that I may take it again. No one takes it from me, but I lay it down of my own accord. I have power to lay it down, and I have power to take it again" (Jn 10:17–18). Only to the extent one is capable of realizing this act of freedom, anthropologically the most meaningful, that is, "giving one's own life", will one be able to "take life up again". Self-abandonment is therefore undertaken in view of gaining a personal identity that involves going out of the self to enter into a broader process, the one that leads into relationality of persons and communion.

From all this, we can conclude that being "person" amounts to assuming the same trinitarian structure that allows for the ultimate dimension of the expressivity and identity of the "person." In the perspective of the act of faith, it follows that to assume the object professed as normative implies substantial unity with the subject who professes it. The "I" who professes the faith, therefore, needs to inscribe himself in that Christological optic that makes him a communional "I," an "I" in whom all the Church meets herself and finds herself.

At this point, the understanding of the mystery of Christ becomes evident in light of his "self-expropriation" to receive the other. This ontological dimension, even prior to the psychological, has to become the "being" of the believer, who becomes a "believer" only by its strength. He is a believer only to the extent he expropriates himself to receive the other. As in Christ there is nothing of the "individual," therefore likewise for the believer everything becomes "ecclesial."

Yet to become believers, understood as a reality by which one abandons oneself to God and lives for him, can only happen by means of "being-for-Christ"; this implies the presence of the Church which transforms the single subject into an "ecclesiastical soul." So the possibility that the single believer can be understood as such becomes real, because believing has an ecclesial nature that expresses communion, the form by which the Spirit constructs the Church.

Being a believer, in other words, amounts to the ability to expropriate oneself of what is most personal; to the point of allowing that the "other"—including the Church as institution—becomes able to judge even my charism, the personal gift that God makes to me, so that the act of believing becomes obvious to the extreme as "abandoning oneself" in obedience. Since the act of faith is also always an act of love, and this must always be measured by the love of Jesus Christ, it amounts to a full and total act of self-expropriation. By means of this the believer, depriving himself, makes room for the other whom he loves, so that he may take possession of him and enable him to find a completely new identity, at first unhoped-for, but now achieved: personal identity so new and real that he will no longer be able to understand himself but in relation to the beloved person. Since the revelation of God is given in the incarnation of the Son, and this continues with his saving presence of grace in the life of the Church, now the believer can, through the power of this act which is no longer his alone but communitarian, "live, feel, experience the subjectivity of the Church and that of the Son, as if it were one's own" (Hans Urs von Balthasar, *Gloria. Un'estetica teologica* I. Milan: Jaca, 1970, 237). In a word, the act of faith personalizes while ecclesializing.

The Apostle clearly shows how this passage becomes concrete when he writes: "I have been crucified with Christ; it is no longer I who live, but Christ who lives in me, and the life I now live in the flesh I live by faith in the Son of God, who loved me and gave himself for me" (Gal 2:20). Unlike many texts in which Paul interchangeably uses "I" and "we," in this case the usage is specific to express the personal condition of the Apostle; the "I" of which Paul speaks is he himself; it indicates the concreteness of his personal existence.

If we wanted to, with this text we could find all the necessary elements that underlie the considerations made so far. The believer, in his personal identity, lives a historical existence that is already marked, per se, by an ontological union with Christ, through the power of faith. This union which takes place through grace, inasmuch as one is incorporated into Christ through conversion and baptism, is necessarily mediated by the Church, because the proclamation of Christ and baptism come through her. So the believer always lives his personal existence "in the flesh", but it is a life now marked by being "in faith in the Son of God"; that is, in a condition where something of oneself has been surrendered, and one has been placed in a new existence that realizes a new creature. So the act by which the subject believes implies therefore that the "I" is an "ecclesial I" outside of which faith could not be fruitful.

This characterization of the act of faith, in other words, places the believer into that "we" which is a condition for future faith. The act of personal faith is an act that creates a twofold relation with the Church. First, because it proclaims and transmits the content of the faith to everyone. So the personal act is an act "participating" in the Church's more global and total act, which continues forever. The faith professed is not only what the Church believes as its content, but even before that, "faith of the Church" It is the Church that communicates baptism (cf. n. 168); this new creation that makes the personal choice of believing evident and effective; it constitutes entry into the Kingdom. By baptism, indeed, each one is added "into Christ" (1 Cor 12:13); and as is usual for Pauline theology, being "in Christ" is interchangeable with being "in the Church" (Rom 16:7, 11; 1 Cor 1:30; Gal 1.22; 1 Thess 2:14). Being "in Christ," far from being a formula of mystical union, is first of all an "ecclesiological formula" and designates being added to the body of Christ through baptism (cf. Rom 8:1; 2 Cor 5:17, Gal 2:17).

A faith conceived in this way does not aim to depersonalize the individual but rather to make him conscious of a dimension that goes beyond the individualistic sphere and makes possible the reception of an ecclesiality as an essential element for faith itself. In this way, the life of the believer becomes a continual dynamic, in which the movement between "already" and "not yet" (cf. nn. 163–165) is concretely realized. This means that the act of faith with which the believer is incorporated into the Church is not a static process. It constitutes, rather, the decisive act, by which he abandons himself and is added to Christ and his body, and at the same time an act open to the future: an act in which becoming Church involves a constant dynamic of his personal life, through which he identifies in his whole self ever more with the Church of which he is a part, and at the same time makes the Church ever more evident before the world as a reality that is constitutive and meaningful for his life.

A concluding note to this long discourse on the act of faith could be summarized through a few expressions of synthesis that can be condensed in this way:

1. As the *CCC* rightly points out, bringing in a clear formula by St. Thomas Aquinas: "The act of faith does not end at the formula, but reaches the essence that is professed" (*Summa Theologiae,* II, 1, 2 ad 2: *"Actus autem credendi non terminatur ad enuntiabile sed ad rem"*). The essence is the mystery of God who has revealed himself as Father, Son, and Spirit in Jesus Christ. The Trinity is the center of the faith and trinitarian love is the norm of Christian existence.

2. A second expression of St. Thomas, in his treatise on faith, says that "the article of faith is perception of divine truth, that tends to grow in it" (*Summa Theologiae,* II–II, 1, 6: *"Articulus fidei est perceptio divinae veritatis tendens in ipsam"*). There is a continual progress in faith and it is in a single act: in the knowledge of the revealed truth that the Church will receive until the end as a gift of the Spirit (Jn 16:13); progress in the life of faith that will have to be borne out in coherent witness.

3. The content of the faith is "catholic": that is, universal. Languages may diverge but the "language" of the faith will remain one as a sign of communion and of a single community, believing, praying, and loving, that testifies to the unity of what it professes (nn. 170–171).

4. The act of faith is not an end in itself; it is completed in the vision of salvation. The evangelist John teaches this clearly: "these are written that you may believe that Jesus is the Christ, the Son of God, and that believing you may have life in his name" (Jn 20:31; cf. nn. 163–164). Eternal life, and thus salvation, is the ultimate end toward which it aims, because it is the life of communion with God.

5. Faith is the serious matter of life. It is sad not to see in this section the word that would have given an overall meaning to the whole of faith: martyr. Martyrdom is the sign of the greatest love because, for faith, it gives supreme testimony which freely chooses the death inflicted, for the certainty of being in the truth and having life.

"'I believed, and so I spoke'; we too believe and so we speak" (2 Cor 4:13); with these words the Apostle expresses his conviction that once we have become believers it is no longer possible to conceive of existence closed in oneself; to the contrary, one opens to communion and participation. So from faith derive the various forms of involvement in the world, in society, in culture, in the workplace, where man lives and needs a word that gives a reason for hope without taking away his responsibility.

Faith, the Apostle always teaches, can be measured only with the "measure of faith" that God has assigned to each one (Rom 12:3). This "measure" is built on the form of *agápe*, which, by definition, can never be possessed by an individual (cf. Gal 5:6). It is love, in the end, that makes us understand how the act of faith cannot be limited to a single individual and why it will never be able to be classified alongside the multitude of all other acts. As a fruit of love, and corresponding to love, faith remains as the constitutive act of one's own being, and as such is considered unique. So one can understand why ancient tradition wanted the profession of faith not to be written but maintained alive, learned by memory, by an understanding to make it always present in the various situations of life. The act of faith in effect, marks the whole life of the believer, placing itself in that moment of time in which he begins to participate in the eternity of the love of the Triune God.

Section Two

THE PROFESSION OF THE CHRISTIAN FAITH

THE CREEDS

Jared Wicks

Before the detailed exposition of the content of the faith, the *CCC* discusses the formulas with which the believer confesses the faith of the Church. This section explains the terms that refer to these formulas (nn. 187–188), their connection with baptism and their trinitarian structure (nn. 189–191), and the principal professions of faith particular to the Catholic tradition (nn. 192–196).

A particular accent of the *CCC* is the connection between the profession of the Creed and baptism, especially in nn. 189 and 197. Indeed a close relationship links the declaration of adherence to God and to his revealed truth (n. 150) and the sacramental consecration of the person "in the name of the Father and the Son and the Holy Spirit".

The New Testament indicates various formulations of the confession of faith, from the simple proclamations, "Jesus is Lord" (1 Cor 12:3) and "Jesus is the Son of God" (1 Jn 4:15), to the statement of the essential content of the preached gospel, "if you confess with your lips that Jesus is Lord and believe in your heart that God raised him from the dead, you will be saved" (Rom 10:9). Elements of an archaic creed resound also in St. Paul's reference to the beginnings of the church of the Thessalonians, "you turned to God from idols, to serve a living and true God, and to wait for his Son from heaven, whom he raised from the dead, Jesus who delivers us from the wrath to come" (1 Th 1:9–10).

Around the year 200 A.D. in North Africa, according to what the writer Tertullian relates, whoever was baptized first renounced Satan and then professed the faith in response to three questions about God as Father, Son, and Holy Spirit. Around the year 215, Hippolytus describes the baptismal rite of the church of Rome, reporting a text that should be considered a fixed formula. In the water, before each immersion, the minister addresses these questions: "Do you believe in God the Father almighty? Do you believe in Jesus Christ, the Son of God, who was born of the Holy Spirit from the Virgin Mary, was crucified under Pontius Pilate, died and was buried and rose alive from the dead on the third day and ascended into heaven and is seated at the right of the Father and will come to judge the living and the dead? Do you believe in the Holy Spirit, in the holy Church, and the resurrection of the body?" (*Traditio apostolica,* 21).

Let us note the dialogical structure in this formula of faith. So the faith takes form in the "I believe" responses to the questions that present the convictions of the Church. The trinitarian structure demonstrates how the individual, with his profession, entrusts his own life to the Father's saving plan realized in Christ and in the Holy Spirit. In this way the Creed becomes part of the liturgical expression of conversion to the Triune God. The further development of the early Church produced a number of declarative creeds in the various local churches. While the question-and-answer formula remained central in baptism itself, the handing-on or *traditio* of the Creed to catechumens marked their passage to an advanced stage of preparation for baptism. They were asked to learn it by memory, while the bishop imparted instructions on the meaning of each article, as in the discourses of St. Cyril of Jerusalem and of St. Ambrose, cited in the text of the *CCC* (nn. 186, 191 note 6, 194 note 11, 197). Shortly before being baptized the candidates reached the end of pre-baptismal instructions with the rite of the *redditio* or open profession of the Creed. St. Augustine recounts in his *Confessions* (Book VIII) how this took place at Rome around the year 350, when the famous rhetorician Marius Victorinus became a member of the Church; "At Rome those who are about to approach to your grace normally make the profession of faith in a set form of words committed to memory, which they then recite on a podium before the faithful." Marius refused the possibility of a private profession. "He made his profession of the true faith with immense confidence and everyone wished they could have embraced him and drawn him to their heart." After the Council of Nicea (cf. n. 465), the Creed assumed a new function, becoming the expression of orthodox faith with the exclusion of erroneous positions. In this way it begins to serve as the criterion of belonging to the college of bishops and thus to the communion of their Churches. These elementary points of the history of the Creed demonstrate how the Church possessed and transmitted her faith to her members. This faith is anything but a vague sentiment of sincerity, because it comes from the preaching and teaching of the apostles of Christ in the churches, ever since their foundation. Hence the primary subject of the profession of faith is the "we" of the community formed in response to what the apostles saw and testified (cf. 1 Jn 1:1–3). The dialogue of the baptismal Creed is, above all, the offer of the Church's faith to a new member and then the voluntary appropriation of this faith on the part of one who is entering into the community and beginning to share its faith. In this act the revelation of God reaches its end, when by baptism the believer receives new life through Christ and can approach the Father in the Holy Spirit. The daily mediation of the Creed, moreover, supports and deepens this personal communion with the Triune God and with the Church that perpetuates and transmits everything she believes to all the generations (*DV* 8:1).

Chapter One: I BELIEVE IN GOD THE FATHER

Thomas Joseph White

The *CCC* begins its teaching on the mystery of God by emphasizing the centrality of faith in God for the Christian life. "I believe in God" is the most fundamental statement of the Apostles' Creed and all the other statements must be interpreted on the basis of it. The human being and all of creation, ultimately, is understood best in relation to God, the transcendent source of all that exists. All the articles of faith are intelligible in the light of the first one: the confession of faith in God the Trinity. The perspective of the *CCC* on this point greatly resembles the teaching of Thomas Aquinas (cf. *Summa Theologiae*, I, 1, 7), which notes that God, who reveals himself to humanity, is himself the principal subject of the science of theology. In other words, Catholic doctrine teaches human beings to interpret all things (the creation, the explanation of the divine economy, the mystery of life in Christ) in relation to God the Trinity. In the same way, the Catholic faith allows the human person to scrutinize the mystery of God himself, albeit in the obscurity of this life (cf. *Summa Theologiae*, II–II, 1,1). In her confession of faith, the Church teaches humanity who God really is.

The theological perspective of the *CCC* is decisively theocentric, but not so as to cast doubt on the intrinsic dignity of the created world. On the contrary, the confession of the mystery of God provides an ultimate foundation for affirming the dignity of creation and in particular of the human person, whom God created in his image and redeemed in Jesus Christ.

Chapter One, Article 1, Paragraph 1:
I BELIEVE IN GOD

Thomas Joseph White

I. "I Believe in One God"

The first utterance of the Nicene-Constantinopolitan Creed is the statement of the unicity of God. Here the *CCC* emphasizes the normative character of monotheism for the Christian life, and notes that the unicity of God has its origin in the revelation of the Old Testament. At the same time, biblical teaching does not exclude the contribution of philosophical reasoning about God, but on the contrary invites such reasoning to the service of divine revelation. Items nn. 2 and 3 of the *Roman Catechism* commissioned by the Council of Trent are quoted precisely to demonstrate this point. In the sections quoted, the *Roman Catechism* observes that unaided human reason often finds great difficulty in reaching a right knowledge of God; it needs time, is mixed with error, and is, in a way, very limited. Natural reason fortified by supernatural grace, in contrast, can lead to understanding God in a true and realistic way, most of all by the grace of divine revelation, but also by the salutary contribution of sound philosophical reasoning. N. 200 cites the statement of the *Roman Catechism* that God is "one by nature, by substance, and by essence." This teaching is significant because it shows that the biblical revelation of the unicity of God is rightly interpreted in the classic teaching of the great patristic figures who made a moderate use of classic terms derived from Hellenistic philosophical traditions. These terms were used in meaningful ways in the Church's definitions from the first Councils and to this day remain a normative part of the Creed's confession of faith, as when we say that the Father and the Son are "consubstantial" (as at the Council of Nicea) or that God the Son subsists personally in his incarnation in two "natures," both divinely and humanly. In an inadequate but direct way, the Catechism here indicates the normative place of traditional practices in Catholic theology, inasmuch as it seeks to interpret the revelation of the Old and New Testaments in profound agreement with perennial philosophy and to understand the development of Christian doctrine historically, according to a hermeneutic of continuity, from the Patristic and Scholastic periods to the modern era.

With that structure in place, the *CCC* proceeds to anchor the affirmation of the unicity of God in the teaching of Sacred Scripture. The scriptural formulation of Dt 6:4–5 is quoted because it represents the central affirmation of the Creed in the Pentateuch. In these words, the sacred author wishes to incarnate the heart of the Mosaic revelation. "Hear, O Israel: the Lord your God is one Lord, and you shall love the Lord your God with all your heart, and with all your soul, and with all your might." The content of this "*Shema* prayer" is all at once theoretical, historical and ethically imperative. Theoretically, the prayer refers to the fundamental faith of Israel in one God, whom both the Pentateuch and the prophets depict as the one Creator of heaven and earth. Historically, the prayer cites the divine fact that God has willed to reveal himself as "the Lord" (YHWH), to bring the people of God into a covenant of fidelity, characterized by the distinctive witness of monotheism and the rejection of false gods. Ethically, this teaching is seen as binding in the hearts of all who profess faith in the one God of the Bible. Only God is adored, he who is to be loved above all things, and moreover to be confessed before the rest of humanity, as testimony of the truth about God.

This same vision of biblical monotheism is deepened by the reference to Is 45:22–24 and likewise to Phil 2:10–11 (n. 201 and note 2). Isaiah's prophecy in the passage was given in its original context to the people of Israel, who were suffering through the crisis of the Babylonian exile and cultural subjugation by political and religious forces against the truth of biblical teaching. The revelation of God given by the prophet states in very explicit terms that the God of Israel is the sole Creator of the world, who alone can save the pagan nations and that he will reveal himself (his holy name "the Lord") to all the nations through Israel his chosen people, despite their apparent insignificance. In Phil 2:10–11, St. Paul recalls this same passage of Isaiah, interpreting the monotheism of the Old Testament in a characteristically Christological way. He reveals that the promise of God made by Isaiah is proven in the incarnation, death and resurrection of Jesus Christ. It is Christ the Lord, physically raised from the dead, who has revealed the identity of the God of Israel to all the nations. In the death and resurrection of Jesus, the salvific power of the Creator is shown to all.

The doctrinal teaching of the Catholic Church clearly maintains, therefore, not only the potential harmony of biblical revelation and human philosophical reason, but also profound consistency within the very revelation of God's intention in the Old as in the New Testament. A serious theological error arose in the second century A.D. with the teaching of Marcion. He took the position that the God of the New Testament was in some way fundamentally different from the God of the Old Testament. Fathers of the Church such as Irenaeus (*Against the Heresies,* Book IV) demonstrated convincingly that the New Testament revelation of God presumes and completes the teaching about God given to Israel in the Old Testament Scriptures. In this way, neither of the two Testaments can be grasped adequately without referring one to the other.

Hence the *CCC* proceeds to examine (n. 202) the way Jesus Christ appeals to the revelation of the Old Testament, as something central in his own teaching and ministry, and to the revelation of his identity as Son of God. In Mk 12:29–30, Jesus invokes the *Shemâ* of Dt 6:4–5 as a normative understanding of God for every human being. At the same time, only a few verses later in Mk 12:35–37 Jesus helps us to grasp that he himself is "the Lord" to whom the Old Testament prophecy of Ps 110:1 refers. It is essential to the Christian faith that we confess that Jesus Christ is Lord, that is, that Christ is one with God the Father, and he himself is the God of Israel who became man. And in the same way the Church confesses that the Holy Spirit is "the Lord and giver of life": the Holy Spirit also is the one God of Israel together with the Father and the Son. The Church's confession of faith in the divinity of Christ and in the divinity of the Holy Spirit is not contrary to faith in the one God, nor does it introduce any division in God. To the contrary, the confession of a rigorous and unequivocal monotheism is central in the Church's understanding of the mystery of the Trinity. The New Testament is a totally trinitarian and totally monotheistic document.

To emphasize the monotheistic character of New Testament teaching, the *CCC* completes this first section on the unicity of God, making appeal to the Fourth Lateran Council (1215). That Council solemnly affirmed that the one God is "eternal, infinite, and unchangeable, incomprehensible, almighty, and ineffable, the Father, the Son, and the Holy Spirit, three Persons, indeed, but one essence, substance or nature entirely simple" (*DS* 800). The teaching on the unity of the two Testaments, Old and New, is presented here in dogmatic terms: the Trinity is the one God of Israel. And what was noted above, methodologically, is highlighted here: the philosophical heritage of scholastic thought is essential for a right understanding of the mystery of God. This is why the Church speaks dogmatically about the divine attributes of God that denote the divine essence: simplicity, eternity, infinity, immensity, immutability. A profound theological reflection on the divine attributes is important for at least three reasons. In the first place, it helps Catholic theology to emphasize correctly that the God of the Bible must not be confused with the finite and temporal world that he created. Every form of pantheism is excluded, since God totally transcends the order of the creation, he is the cause of everything there is, and he is intimately present in everything that he sustains in being. Second, an extended reflection on the divine attributes is a requirement for trinitarian theology, so that one can really grasp what it means to affirm that the three persons are one in essence. Trinitarian monotheism depends on a theology of divine attributes so that we can speak coherently of the divine nature possessed completely by each of the divine persons. Yet, finally, such a reflection makes plain that the God of the Bible is also the God of the philosophers. The revelation of God respects the natural aspirations of human reason and invites us to cooperate actively with grace in the making of theology. Reflection on the divine attributes arises from this form of Christian collaboration between revelation and human philosophical reason. This lets us speak properly of what God is and is not, but also lets us recognize the transcendence and the hiddenness of God. God is also known by us imperfectly, through the veil of his creation and by faith in the mystery of his self-revelation. His greatness can never be totally comprehended by our finite understanding.

II. God Reveals His Name

The biblical revelation of God is profoundly rooted in the revelation of the divine name, given to Israel through Moses in Ex 3:13–15. The *CCC* observes how there is an analogy between the natural role that interpersonal names play among human persons and the supernatural role that the divine name plays in establishing a relationship between God and humanity. Names can reveal the nature of something or the individual identity of a person. They also establish a basis for interpersonal communication and can indicate the intimacy of friendship and personal love. All this takes place at the divine level in a distinctive manner through the revelation of the name of God to humanity in the biblical revelation. The name of God reveals the essence of God and his individual identity as well. This name gives access to God in interpersonal terms, within the covenant of supernatural faith and makes it possible for human beings who invoke God to trust in his intimate presence as Father and Savior.

The self-revelation of God in all of biblical history is progressive. It develops through the teachings of the prophets of the Old Testament and then in the revelation of Christ and the teaching of the apostles. Despite this, the foundation of the whole inheritance of divine revelation is found at the beginning, in the giving of the name of God in Exodus. In emphasizing the centrality of the Mosaic revelation, the *CCC* affirms the implicit historicity of the Exodus event and the reality of inspired prophecy as a gift to the people of ancient Israel. The divine name of God is seen as central in the historical covenant formed by God with Israel at Sinai (n. 204). At the same time, the *CCC* recognizes that the revelation of God given in Exodus is expressed in strongly soteriological terms. God is the living God of the patriarchs Abraham, Isaac, and Jacob, who comes to his people in Egypt to free them from slavery and the threat of extinction. The compassionate action of God in history reflects who God really is, in his eternal nature. His fidelity to the covenant has its transcendent foundation in the eternal identity of God and in his unchangeable goodness. Interpreting Exodus in this way, the *CCC* offers a solution to contrasting problems that are found at times between a theology of the ontological attributes of God and a theology of God's action and saving work in history. The whole development of the cosmos and of human history needs to be interpreted in light of the eternity of God who has revealed himself in Scripture and whose self-revelation culminates in Christ.

Nn. 206–209 offer an extended commentary on the meaning of the divine name revealed in Ex 3:13–15. N. 206 presents three differing interpretations of the divine name. "I am he who is" denotes the divine essence: God is he who exists in virtue of his own nature. He cannot not exist and it is he who gives being to everything else that is. "I am who I am" suggests the mystery of the present eternity of God. God is an eternal act of perfection, and hence there is no time of evolution in God. His eternity consists in a perfect and infinite possession of divine life. "I am who I am" denotes the apophatic content of revelation. God remains hidden even while he reveals himself. His essence exceeds the measure of human understanding. Whoever draws near to God must prepare himself to enter a cloud of unknowing. It is significant that the *CCC* assumes the fundamental compatibility of all three interpretations. All are very common in the Christian tradition and can be seen as mutually complementary and defining.

N. 207 marks the soteriological importance of the divine name. As God is "he who is" eternally, God can be present to Israel for all her history as the God of the patriarchs as well as the God of the covenant. He remains faithful to his people for ever, both in the past and the future. Once again here we see the rejection of a false opposition between the ontological and soteriological dimensions of the Bible; the idea of God as eternal and the idea of God as one who is present in history. God can govern history effectively with his providence to save us precisely due to the fact that he is God in his eternal and immutable identity. The eternal identity of God manifests itself precisely in and through his activity and his presence among us in sacred history. At the same time, God is a hidden God (Is 45:15). The presence of God among us does not render God automatically accessible or controllable. Still less does it abolish the irreplaceable role of free human will, because God rarely imposes a sensation of his presence on his rational creatures. He must be sought freely, and indeed God is never far from those who seek him.

The revelation of the divine name is also accompanied by a revelation of the holiness of God. This is symbolized by Moses who removes his sandals in the presence of the Lord in Ex 3:5–6. Before God the human person more and more recognizes his relative littleness and moral unworthiness (Is 6:5;

Lk 5:8; Hos 11:9). The holiness of God suggests the transcendence, moral purity, splendor or radiance, and infinite power of God. The name of God [YHWH] is not pronounced by the people of Israel out of respect for the holiness of God and is frequently replaced in Scripture itself by euphemistic titles such as *Adonai* in ancient Hebrew or *Kýrios* in the LXX. When Jesus is called "Lord" *(Kýrios)* in the New Testament, it also denotes the holiness of Christ. He is the Lord of glory who was crucified (1 Co 2:8), he who is most holy. Contemplating the mystery of the crucifixion, the Church is called to recognize the transcendence, the beauty, and the power of God, who has revealed himself personally present even in the suffering and the human death of Christ.

Our understanding of the name of God revealed in Ex 3:13–15 must be described in reference to a later revelation, given in Ex 34:5–7 (cf. notes 10–11), where the name originally given is restated. God speaks to Moses a second time. This final revelation happens after Israel's fall into the sin of adultery (Ex 32), immediately after the declaration of the covenant. The people violates the first commandment (Ex 20:4) and makes a god for itself with a representation, worshipping the golden calf (Ex 32:4). This act of betrayal certainly is meant to symbolize Israel and humanity both in their systemic weakness and in their lack of fidelity to God; in any case, the response of God is also represented in symbolic and universal terms. God reveals his name to Moses again as "YHWH," but now qualifies the name with the addition "a God merciful and gracious, slow to anger and abounding in mercy and faithfulness" (Ex 34:5–6). Here the revelation of God, as he who is, is completed by the revelation of divine mercy. God is he who is free to be eternally faithful and kindly, due precisely to the fact of being God in his being, in his goodness, and his eternal power. The *CCC* underscores the fact that this profound connection between being and the merciful compassion of God is brought back in the New Testament and recapitulated there in Christological terms. Jesus Christ says in Jn 8:28: "When you have lifted up the Son of man, then you will know that I am he," Here the Lord applies the divine name "I am" to himself, denoting his identity with the God of Israel and the fact that he possesses the name reserved only to God. Yet he indicates that the mercy of God will be revealed particularly in the crucifixion, as a direct response to human sinfulness, which has crucified God made man. God has the power to pardon sins and redeem his creation, even when he himself suffers in his human nature at the hands of men. The divine name has the power to reveal this mystery of God crucified, especially when it is pronounced by Jesus Christ himself.

Obviously the statements made to this point presuppose that the biblical revelation of God has metaphysical or ontological dimensions, while being profoundly personal and theologically numinous. But here one can pose a question or place an objection. Is it not possible that the tradition of the Church may have later imposed a philosophical and Hellenistic concept of God on a prior Hebrew tradition that was originally more symbolic and affective? The *CCC* responds to this concern, observing that there is a historical development of the concept within the Scriptures themselves. The formulation is nuanced enough: "Over the centuries, Israel's faith was able to manifest and deepen realization of the riches contained in the revelation of the divine name" (n. 212). In a certain sense, it is clear that the revelation of God proceeds from a less perfect state to a more perfect state as one moves from the Old Testament to the New. However, it is also possible to observe a contrary movement: what was given originally in fullness in a higher and more implicit way can be manifested or rendered more explicit conceptually in time (on this point, see Thomas Aquinas, *Summa Theologiae*, II–II 1,7). The Catholic Church in the post-apostolic age adds nothing to the intrinsic content of divine revelation, but articulates her understanding of this revelation in a manner that is conceptually more explicit with time, and doing that deepens her theological understanding of the mystery originally revealed in the apostolic age (cf *DV* 23). Thus "analogically," after the era of divine revelation itself, Israel succeeds in understanding more perfectly in time what was initially revealed to the greatest prophets in a higher but also more hidden sense (cf *DV* 14).

The *CCC* suggests that this evolutionary form of biblical thought is what is present in Exodus with the divine name. What was present in a less manifest and implicit way is made clear and rendered conceptually more explicit in time, because the prophets and later inspired authors represent the original revelation within successive epochs. The text appeals particularly to Isaiah 44, where the name of God revealed to Moses clearly has a universal ontological significance. The "Lord" is the one and eternal God, the source of all things and the sovereign of all the nations. This universalistic understanding of the divine name is presupposed in the Greek wisdom literature both of the Old and the New Testament. In these texts, the God of Israel is described by the sacred authors who make inspired use of Hellenistic concepts to illustrate the perennial truths of revelation. Jas 1:17 notes therefore that in God "there is no variation or shadow due to change," from which one can correctly infer the numinous mystery of God's divine immutability. The God of the Bible is forever the same in his identity, fidelity, and goodness.

At the same time, the translation by the LXX of the divine name in Exodus is reaffirmed by the *CCC* with a legitimate development of the ancient tradition of Israel, which had great influence in the early Church and in later Catholic theology. The translation of Ex 3:14 from the LXX as *"ego eimi ho on"* has distinctive ontological implications: "I am he who is" or "I am he who is Being." Patristic thinkers such as Augustine (*De Trinitate,* V, 3) and Gregory of Nyssa (*De Vita Moysis,* II 22–26) saw in this text a sign of divine perfection: God is incomprehensible to us because he possesses changeless and perfect fullness of being in himself. Similarly, Thomas saw in the divine name the foundation for a Catholic theology of creation. Only God possesses being by himself. Everything else receives its being from God as a gratuitous gift and therefore participates in his being (cf. Thomas Aquinas, *Summa contra Gentiles,* I, chap. 22). The *CCC* affirms this tradition, saying that "God is the fullness of Being and of every perfection, without origin or end" (n. 213). What follows from that is a irenic affirmation of the simplicity of the divine essence. "All creatures receive all that they are and have from him; but he alone is his very being, and he is all that he is from himself." In every creature, existence is a gratuitous gift of the Creator. Being does not belong necessarily to the essence of a certain creature; the creature can exist or not exist. To the contrary, it is of the essence of God that he necessarily subsists, but in God "properties" such as wisdom or goodness are identical with the divine essence. God is his goodness and his wisdom, and his wisdom and his goodness are in some way identical, one with the other. God is a good eternal wisdom or a wise eternal goodness. To say all this is not an attempt to reduce what God is to the measure of our human understanding or to capture God in an abstract human structure. To the contrary, the affirmation of the perfection and the simplicity of God help to safeguard a right sense of the divine ineffability and transcendence.

III. God, "He Who *Is,*" Is Truth and Love

In the modern era, Christian theologians have debated about the order in which trinitarian theology should be approached. Should Christian reflection begin from the unity of God and then consider the distinction of the persons; or rather should it begin with a consideration of the three persons in communion and then reflect on their unity of essence? There are various biblical and theoretical approaches presented among the doctors of the Church, with figures such as Augustine (*De Trinitate,* I, 2) and Bonaventure (*De mysterio Trinitatis,* I–II) who start from a consideration of the distinction of the three persons, while thinkers such as Gregory of Nazianzen (*Oratio,* 27–31) and Thomas Aquinas (*Summa Theologiae,* I, qq. 3–43) start from a consideration of the divine essence as a prelude to reflection on the unity and the distinction of the persons. Evidently, approaches so distinct can be profoundly convergent. The Father, the Son, and the Holy Spirit must be one in being and in essence, and therefore a sustained reflection on the communion of the persons requires a consideration of the unity of the essence of God as a necessary condition for trinitarian theology. Analogously, a consideration of monotheism in Christian theology aims to serve as a prelude to sustained reflection on the persons of the Trinity, precisely because the three persons are one in being and in essence. This final approach also reflects the history of revelation in a basic sense, inasmuch as the Old Testament revelation of the one God of Israel is a prelude to the New Testament revelation of the Trinity.

Without seeking to propose any definitive solution to the aforementioned theological debates, the *CCC* will adopt in practice a Thomist order of reflection on such questions. After the treatment of the one God in his transcendent being there is a consideration of the life of God as knowing and loving. This presentation is, as we shall see, a thematic prelude to the consideration of the Trinity in the following section of the *CCC*.

Affirming that God, who is "He who is," is also truth and love, the *CCC* denotes the personal characteristics of God. A theology of the divine aseity that emphasizes the perfection of the divine being is not opposed to a personalistic concept of God. Indeed, the former is the foundation for a correct understanding of the latter. God is personal in a way that transcends our normal comprehension of human personal being and is not subject to our all too human anthropomorphic conceptions or sense representations. God is truly personal and the Scriptures reveal it, speaking of the moral qualities of God: his goodness, his steadfast love, his fidelity, and his truth. While the Old Testament certainly attributes such qualities to God, they are confirmed in New Testament revelation, which teaches that "God is light and him there is no darkness at all" (1 Jn 1:5) and that "God is love" (1 Jn 4:8). The two Testaments together give witness of the personal character of God as truth and love. At the same time, this affirmation is also open to our natural understanding. According to the Scriptures, being a person is at the heart of all ontology. The physical universe is not simply a product of chance or a lucky but meaningless break. It was created fundamentally for the incarnate person: human persons are spiritual animals of truth and love, made in the image and likeness of God. The ultimate principle of our existence is a hidden and mysterious personal God who created all things and revealed himself to Israel. God reveals his personal identity as the Trinity to each of us, in the mystery of Jesus Christ, so that we can live in personal intimacy with God.

When all is said and done, Christianity is irreducibly in contrast with all religious or metaphysical assertions that imagine the ultimate principle of reality as something impersonal or with the statement that the personhood of human beings is ephemeral or not real. Also it is in contrast with all the philosophical forms of materialism, atheism, or agnosticism, especially with the latter when it states that we cannot truly know who God is or encounter God definitively in his own personal mystery. Divine revelation serves as a supernatural correction to various mistaken conceptions of reality that lead people to grave errors or to philosophical despair. The *CCC*'s consideration of the personal and spiritual attributes of God follows the consideration of the being and essence of God. Personal being belongs to the essence of the eternal God in a transcendent and mysterious divine life of truth and love.

The teaching on divine truth *per se* starts from soteriological principles. The commandments and the instruction of God are truthful and worthy of trust. If we follow the road traced by God for us we cannot be led astray because God is truth itself. His word cannot deceive. These teachings are immersed in Scripture (2 Sm 7:28; Dt 7:9). At the same time, the original temptation of the devil portrayed in Gn 3:1–5 consists in the use of deception. Human doubt regarding the truth of the teaching of God stands at the origin of the original sin of humanity and, more generally, of human sin.

The foundation for this soteriological truth is of an ontological type: God acts on the basis on what he is in himself and according to his divine identity. We noted above, regarding the doctrine of the divine simplicity (stated by the Catechism and *DF* from Vatican I as precedent), that it is true to say that God is in some way identical to his attributes. God simply is his goodness, for example, or is subsistent goodness. So the Church also teaches that "God's truth is his wisdom, which commands the whole created order and governs the world" (n. 216). The wisdom literature of the Bible says just that, in various ways. God is wise in himself, "before" the creation, and it is from this wisdom that the created world derives its existence, its order, and its ultimate end (see, for example, Wis 7:24–29). This teaching implies that he possesses self-awareness from all eternity and that this self-awareness is the source of everything else, which is everything that God carries out "outside" himself. At the most fundamental level, this includes giving existence to finite creatures: everything that God creates is a product of his wisdom and his self-understanding. It is important to underscore that the wisdom of God is at the origin of everything that exists, and not the contrary. Creatures that depend on God for their own being do not add to the actuality and the perfection of God's eternal self-awareness. Instead, as St. Thomas affirms, it is in the light of God's perfect awareness of himself that he freely creates, and in understanding himself God also understands the reality of all creatures (cf. *Summa Theologiae,* I, 14, 5). Analogously, the divine economy is visible in God, who is all-knowing and "can alone impart true knowledge of every created thing in relation to himself" (n. 216).

It follows from this that God is totally worthy of trust in his self-revelation, particularly in sending into the world his Son, who renders testimony to the truth (cf. Jn 18:37) and who is himself true. "I am the way, the truth, and the life" (Jn 14:6). In Christ, the internal truth of who God is has been manifested to creatures in an absolute sense, in human history. Consequently we must not wait for a further revelation of God regarding his mystery and his identity. Who God eternally is has truly been given to us to know in the divine economy. Accepting the grace of faith, Christians progressively learn to live with the revelation of the fullness of truth about God and about themselves. By means of grace they can participate in the very life of God, a life of truth that is intimate with the Trinity (cf 1 Jn 5:20).

The *CCC*'s discussion of divine life is presented above all in biblical terms, recalling the gratuitous choice of Israel by God. God freely chooses Israel, based on the love he has for human beings, and continues to maintain the covenant with Israel, despite religious infidelity, precisely by his enduring love (cf. notes 18–19). The soteriological dimension of divine love is seen here as the entrance that invites us to think more profoundly about the identity and the essence of God as love. It is the eternal love of God in himself that is revealed in the gratuitous election of the human being. This anti-pelagian point can be expressed both positively and negatively. We are saved by the free initiative of the grace of God and not by our own natural efforts or by human initiatives without being helped by grace. Israel did not deserve the gift of divine election but was shaped as a chosen people by God's initiative, a dynamic that continues to be confirmed in the Catholic Church and in the gift of election to life in Christ. This gratuitous gift of love is seen here as revelatory of who God eternally is, in his transcendence and his freedom.

The Old Testament uses various metaphorical images to represent this divine transcendent love: fatherly love, motherly love, husband and wife, a love that is victorious over every evil and human infidelity and is eternal. The soteriological hope of Israel will become that of the Catholic Church through the manifestation of Christ. The New Testament promise of the eternal victory of God's love has its foundations in the Old Testament promises that are confirmed and brought to fulfillment in the incarnation, death, and resurrection of the Son of God.

Finally, the *CCC* turns to the topic of the one God, speaking of the nature of the eternal, immanent and uncreated love of God (n. 221). New Testament revelation teaches that "God is love" (1 Jn 4:8). In a certain sense, this teaching incarnates Christianity and distinguishes it historically as a religion and "philosophy" or way of life. There is an immanent life of love in God. Believing in this love is not something irrational or existentially inaccessible to men. To the contrary, divine love is the foundation of the created order and is the highest reality that the person can aspire to know and encounter. *In principio* there was the mystery of divine love. Hence believing in an ontology of love is eminently rational and in a certain sense even the proper characteristic of any true philosophy.

The *CCC* uses this language of divine love in various senses. The word can serve not only as what Thomas Aquinas calls an "essential term" regarding God (pertaining to the divine nature common to the three persons of the Trinity), but also as a "notional term" that can indicate one of the three persons in his eternal activity and in his distinct personal being (cf. *Summa Theologiae,* I,

37, 1). In sending the Son and the Spirit into the world, "God has revealed his innermost secret: God himself is an eternal exchange of love..." (n. 221). The Father eternally generates the Son with the power of generation that he possesses as God, which is also a power of eternal love. He communicates to the Son in love all that he has in himself, including the power of divine love, by means of which the Trinity creates the world. The Son in turn loves the Father, and with the Father (in their mutual love) is at the origin of the eternal spiration of the Holy Spirit, a divine person who is love, proceeding from the Father and his Word.

God has shown this truth in the New Testament not only so that we can truly know who God is, but also so that we can participate in the divine life of God by means of grace. Our participation in the charity of Christ is a participation in the very life of God. The revelation of the Trinity means that the one God desires to make us participants in what is primary in the order of reality: a communion with the intimate life and mystery of God as he is in himself.

It should be clear from the discussion of monotheism offered above that the *CCC* is already seeking to anticipate a theology of the Trinity, in the way it presents the attributes of the one God in its discussion of the revelation of the Old and the New Testament. This is particularly significant in the discussion of the section we are considering, about the truth and the love of God. These certainly are essential terms that pertain to God in his eternal essence and his divine unity. Yet they are also terms that can be used in analogous senses to express the distinction of the persons of the Trinity in God. The Son is the Word of God eternally generated, and Jesus Christ himself speaks of himself as the truth of the Father, as we have noted. The Spirit is traditionally understood as the eternal love of the Father and the Son. This means that the discussion of the truth and love of God in his unity here anticipates the mystery of the Trinity. What the Old Testament reveals as pertaining to the essence of God, the New Testament reveals as pertaining to the mystery of the Trinity and the life of God previously hidden. The "psychological analogy" of truth and love (drawn from the human spiritual acts of knowledge and of love) can be used, by way of similarity, to speak of the life of God, totally other in his essence. But this analogy itself can be used, by way of similarity, to speak of God in his trinitarian identity as Father and Son and Holy Spirit. The point of this last section on the consideration of the divine life is that of anticipating the treatment of the Trinity in the following section. What we know of the intimate life of God "essentially" as the mystery of eternal knowledge and love comes to perfection in what we know of the life of God interiorly-personally, as the mystery of the eternal generation of the Word by God the Father and his eternal spiration of the Holy Spirit, which is a spiration of love, with and by means of his Word.

IV. The Implications of Faith in One God

The final section of the teaching of the *CCC* about belief in God pertains to the practical implications of the Church's confession of faith. As God is the principal origin and the end of all created reality, any realistic recognition of God on our part should progressively define our entire life and the integral exercise of our reason in practical concrete actions. Such a teaching is certainly a challenge. But the grace of Christ raises our inclinations and our spiritual instincts to enable them to recognize the truth about God and integrate our whole life in the service of God, animated by charity. This instinct of Christian life to serve God faithfully can give human existence its true nobility and inspire everything we do with a salutary religious stability. The *CCC* quotes the great words of Joan of Arc on this subject: we must "serve God first" (n. 223).

The religious imperative to love and serve God is given here in hierarchical and organically united terms. We should seek above all to recognize the greatness and the majesty of God and live in thanksgiving to him, in gratitude for our existence, for his divine providence and for the many various gifts that are in the order of grace and nature. Then, in the light of God, we should recognize the unity and true dignity of all human beings, who are made in the image and likeness of God and are called to unity in communion and in the life of the Catholic Church. Finally we should recognize the goodness of all created things, which always reflect something of the divine goodness and the wisdom of God that gives order. Created realities can be used in the service of God and of one's neighbor and should be kept with respect, appropriate love, necessary detachment, and in thanksgiving to God. Lastly, a recognition of the truth of God should motivate us to trust in God in every circumstance. The *CCC* quotes St. Teresa of Avila: "Let nothing trouble you; let nothing frighten you. Everything passes; God never changes. Patience obtains all; whoever has God wants for nothing. God alone is enough" (n. 227 and note 29). Our deepest peace and our stability are derived from unconditional trust in God, because only he has the power to save us in all circumstances and only he is eternal in his wisdom, in his goodness, and in his love.

Chapter One, Article 1, Paragraph 2: THE FATHER

Thomas Joseph White

In this section of the *CCC*, the dogmatic teaching of the Church regarding the Trinity is presented in a more detailed way. The first part considers (I) the trinitarian name of God and the centrality of the mystery of the Trinity for all of Christian life and for doctrine. The second through fourth parts offer a succinct presentation of the Church's doctrine of the Trinity. Respectively they consider (II) how the mystery of the Trinity has been revealed, (III) how the Church has articulated the doctrine of faith regarding this mystery, and (IV) how God the Father carries out the plan of creation, redemption, and sanctification by means of the divine missions of the Son and the Spirit who are sent into the world.

I. "In the Name of the Father and of the Son and of the Holy Spirit"

The doctrinal presentation begins with a consideration of the name of God as "Father and Son and Holy Spirit." This title for God is revealed at the culmination of the Gospel of Matthew during the final appearance of the risen Lord, in Mt 28:19. Jesus Christ gives the command to go to all nations, baptizing them in the name of the Father and of the Son and of the Holy Spirit. Why is it so important? Christian worship has its foundation in baptism, the primary sacrament of initiation, and it is administered in the name of the Trinity on the basis of the teaching of Mt 28:19: "I baptize you in the name of the Father and of the Son and of the Holy Spirit." From this it follows that Christian identity is radically trinitarian. Believing in this mystery is proper to all of Christian life, because one must be baptized in the name of the Trinity to be able to receive all the other sacraments. Baptism is also essential for the unity of the Church. Since Catholics are baptized, they can take part in the Holy Eucharist and share in the sanctifying communion of the faithful.

The name of God is in the singular and not in the plural (n. 233). There are not three gods but one God who is Father and Son and Holy Spirit. When the Lord Jesus reveals this name for God in Mt 28:19, he is recapitulating and redefining the use of the divine name in Ex 3:13–15. Just as the resurrection reveals that he is one with the Father and the Holy Spirit, the "I am" of God is revealed as having a trinitarian content that was previously hidden. The Trinity is the final revelation of the name of the one God of Israel. As the *CCC* notes, Pope Vigilius I solemnly recognized this biblical truth in the sixth century, formulating the teaching as a doctrine of the Church (note 33).

The mystery of the Trinity is the central mystery of all Christianity. All the other mysteries, such as the incarnation, the life of the Church or the Eucharist draw their intelligibility in relation to this principal mystery. Here the *CCC* speaks of the doctrine of the Trinity as the highest in the hierarchy of truths. In other words, this teaching casts light on everything else, as the ultimate foundation, from the highest perspective. The notion of the hierarchy of truths is meant, in Catholic theology, to illustrate the way in which the various teachings of supernatural life depend on one another and how they are related to one another in an intelligibly ordered way. This does not mean that some mysteries are essential for the faith while others can be dispensed with, because all the supernatural mysteries are revealed by God and to reject any aspect of the revelation of God implicitly leads to a rejection of the whole (see the analysis by Thomas Aquinas, *Summa Theologiae,* II–II, q. 1). Yet it is extremely important to communicate the truths of Christian doctrine in an order of objective priority, keeping to the teaching of Christ himself, making visible how the most central mystery of all is about the identity of God. Trinitarian doctrine does not relativize or obscure the other teachings of the faith. To the contrary, it allows us to grasp them more profoundly. Mysteries such as the Incarnation, the Church or the Eucharist aim to reveal to us more profoundly who God is; so faith in the trinitarian God organically leads to a deeper understanding of these other sacred truths, as they themselves reveal truth about God. The entire history of salvation has its basis in the revelation of the mystery of the Trinity.

To illustrate this point, n. 236 introduces the traditional distinction between *theologhía* and *oikonomía,* which was articulated for the first time by Origen in the third century (*Homilies on Jeremiah,* n. 18) and subsequently was used by Fathers of the Church such as Basil, Gregory Nazianzen, Maximus the Confessor and John Damascene. The distinction aims to denote what is proper to God in himself (*theologhía*: the intimate life of the Trinity) as distinct from *oikonomía,* the divine economy in which God reveals himself and communicates his life. The two are related but also distinct: "Through the *oikonomia* the *theologia* is revealed to us; but conversely, the *theologia* illuminates the whole *oikonomia*." An analogy is taken from the human person. On one hand, the exterior acts of a person reveal his interior identity; on the other, the more we know who a person is interiorly, the more we understand his decisions and exterior acts. In a similar way, we can say that God the Trinity truly reveals himself to us in the divine economy of creation, redemption, and sanctification. The revelation that is opened to us in history teaches us who God is in his eternal immanent life as Father, Son, and Holy Spirit. At the same time, God is immutably triune in his perfect and eternal being, distinct from and without any ontological dependence whatsoever on the created world. So God is in no way built up in his trinitarian identity by his historical revelation and by his self-communication to human beings. God is God independently of the gratuitous gift of creation, which he made and independently of his redeeming grace given to us in human history.

If we understand this distinction correctly, it lets us avoid two opposing but related errors that arose in the early times of the Church. One is the error of "Arianism" which states that the person of the Father is truly God, but that the Son and the Holy Spirit are mere creatures. This erroneous statement sees the Son and the Spirit as produced by God in the divine economy and not prior to it. The contrary error of "Sabellianism" (or "modalism") states that the Father, the Son, and the Holy Spirit are mere imperfect significations of the one God, given to us in the divine economy, but that there is no real eternal distinction of persons in God. God appears under these three aspects or modes within the economy, but they do not characterize who God truly is in himself. Arianism affirms a distinction of persons, but not a unity of essence common to the three persons. Modalism affirms a unity of essence of the three persons but denies that there is a real distinction of persons. These errors have two presuppositions in common: (1) a distinction of persons does not exist eternally in God, in which each person fully possesses the one divine being and essence; (2) hence, the distinction of persons arises solely in the economy, but is not proper to the eternal identity of God. The *CCC* uses the patristic distinction between *theología* and *oikonomía* precisely to avoid these twin errors. God is truly triune from all eternity: three persons truly distinct who are one in being and essence. God truly reveals to us who he is, in and through the economy of salvation.

This first section ends by noting that the mystery of the Trinity is a mystery of the faith in the strict sense and therefore it is inaccessible to natural reason. Thomas gives a clear articulation of this idea (cf. *Summa Theologiae,* I. 32, 1). The identity of God as Trinity can neither be proved or disproved by natural philosophical reason. The reason for this is that our natural knowledge of God is indirect and derived from the natural created effects of God. But all these effects have their origin in God in his unity. We could say that they are all effects of the three trinitarian persons acting in unity and that, due to the type of effects that they are, they do not manifest the real distinction of the persons in God. By means of natural reason we can come to the knowledge that a transcendent creator exists, who is the primary origin and ultimate end of all things (cf. *DF*). This knowledge, however, does not gain anyone direct perception of the essence of the hidden identity of God. To know God personally as Trinity, God must reveal himself to us by means of a new initiative of grace. There are traces of the trinitarian mystery imprinted in creatures. The *imago Dei* in human beings, for example, in which we perceive knowledge and love "proceeding" from a personal subject, furnishes a certain imperfect analogy to the Trinity. Such analogies are fully perceptible by human reason only after the fact of the trinitarian revelation in Christ. So the Church is opposed to all forms of rationalism that seek to demonstrate or refute the reality of the Trinity philosophically. We are illuminated by grace alone to discover this mystery. But the supernatural character of knowledge of the most holy Trinity is not a source of alienation for human reason. It is part of the Good News. In revealing himself freely to us, God addresses (and perhaps awakens in us) our interior desire for direct and personal knowledge of God. What natural reason can desire but not obtain by itself, divine revelation provides. In this way, revelation invites human reason to find its own interior completeness, starting from faith, by receiving the gift of truth about the Trinity, in personal friendship with God.

II. The Revelation of God as Trinity

The Father Revealed by the Son

Then the *CCC* considers how the mystery of the Trinity was revealed. The presentation begins with a consideration of what it means to speak of the fatherhood of God. It observes that the notion of God as a Father arose in various non-Christian religious traditions and is, from certain points of view, a natural characteristic of human religiosity. Yet the notion takes on special meanings in Old Testament revelation, where the fatherhood of God is discussed in a variety of ways. They can denote God as Creator of the world and as the source of the election of Israel, because God begets it as his "first-born son" through the gift of the law (Ex 4:22). God is the Father of the king of Israel (his son) and is also the Father of the poor, governing the world providentially in view of the good of his people (cf. Is 66:13; Ps 131:2). These various Old Testament images of fatherhood prefigure the revelation of the eternal fatherhood of God in the most holy Trinity, made manifest in Christ.

It is important to take into account that nn. 239 and 240 follow one another in the *CCC* to suggest a comparison and a contrast. N. 239 explores the general meaning of the divine fatherhood in the broad sense of the term, as enunciated in the Old Testament. Here we are speaking of the fatherhood of God according to a certain metaphorical similarity. God is like a human Father inasmuch as he produces effects that resemble human fatherhood: God is the origin of everything that exists and is a transcendent authority. He governs creation in a personal manner, to direct human beings to their well-being and their fulfillment. In the same way, the Old Testament speaks of God metaphorically as a mother who takes care of her children (cf. Is 66:13; Ps 131:2). Where the metaphor of fatherhood means the transcendence and authority of God, the metaphor of motherhood suggests the divine immanence of God to his creation and his compassionate governance of the world. These comparisons, like the human parents who are present in divine revelation, presuppose our common experience of fatherhood and motherhood in society. Yet for the same reason, such metaphors are profoundly imperfect and wanting. They have to be qualified conceptually by metaphysical and moral realism. God is neither masculine nor feminine. He is God who gives being to all things and who transcends all human images. Human beings can fall short as parents and distort in us a deeper meaning of a true fatherhood and a true motherhood, but God can never fall short in his eternal goodness. Thus his fatherhood is the origin and the standard that transcend all created fatherhood.

N. 240 traces a deeper and more proper meaning of divine fatherhood which is revealed explicitly and perfectly only in the New Testament, against the background of both human religious traditions and Old Testament revelation. There we find the newness of the revelation of the fatherhood of God, starting from Jesus. God is eternally Father in virtue of his relation with his only Son, who is Son only in relation to the Father. No longer are we speaking of metaphorical similarities with the divine fatherhood, like those we find in the inspired authors of the Old Testament. The revelation of God the Father that is given to us uses its own analogous terms that mean truly, although imperfectly, what God is in his immanent life. God the Father eternally generates his Son, the eternal Word of God, and is eternally constituted by his relation to the Son. This distinction of divine fatherhood and filiation is proper to God who immanently is for all eternity. Certainly God does not generate in the way of human fathers and therefore the comparison is merely analogous, but there truly is fatherhood, generation, and filiation, and so the meanings conveyed in the New Testament indicate something more than the metaphorical images of the Old Testament. They reveal in a deeper way what God is in himself.

Biblical revelation provides the foundations for the later trinitarian theology of the Church. God the Father and God the Son can be understood only in the relation between them. "No one knows the Son except the Father, and no one knows the Father except the Son" (Mt 11: 27). We hear in the Prologue of the Gospel of John that the Son is the eternal *Lógos* or the "Word" of God. The Son is the eternal Wisdom of God that comes from the Father as the image of the invisible God (Col 1:15; Heb 1:3).

Let us observe what these terms suggest. 1) The Son has an eternal pre-existence that precedes the creation. All things were made by means of him. 2) He is generated eternally by the Father and is characterized by this relationship of origin from the Father. The generation of the Son is of a spiritual type, not physical or temporal. There is an analogy with human spiritual activity. As thought proceeds from the thinker, so the Son proceeds from the Father as his only-begotten Word. 3) The Son is a totally adequate reflection of the Father, which means that everything that is in the Father is communicated to the Son. Hence they are one in essence, in attributes, and in power.

In the early Church, the Councils of Nicea (325) and Constantinople (381) formulated this biblical teaching in dogmatic terms using the Greek term *homoúsios* (Latin: *consubstantialis*). Against the ancient heresy of Arianism, the Church proclaimed that the Son is not a creature but is the uncreated Word of the Father and is "one sole God with him" from all eternity. All things were made by means of him. Hence we speak of the Son as "consubstantial with the Father" and as "God of God, Light of Light, true God of true God." The Son is one sole God with the Father, and the Son has his origin eternally from the Father. The notion of consubstantiality denotes identity of essence. There is one sole God. The concept of "to generate" denotes the equality of the Son derived from the Father. In the generation of the Son, the Father communicates to the Son everything that he has and is as God, so that all that pertains to the divine essence (divine wisdom, goodness, power, etc.) is communicated to the Son. He possesses it in unity of being with the Father, as the one true God.

The Father and the Son Revealed by the Spirit

The Church also affirms, based on biblical revelation, that the Holy Spirit is a divine person distinct from the Father and the Son. The revelation of the Spirit as a divine person is present in many texts of the New Testament, but especially in the Gospel of John, where Christ promises to send "another Paraclete" (Consoler) who will remain with the apostles to guide them "into all the truth." It is the Spirit who will guide and instruct the Church (cf. Jn 14:26; 15:26; 16:14).

N. 244 makes a profound observation on the nature of trinitarian theology based on the temporal mission of the Holy Spirit (his being sent by the Father and the Son upon the Church). It is said that this temporal mission reveals to us who the Spirit truly is, as one who originates eternally from the Father and the Son. What is affirmed implicitly in this item of the *CCC* is that the relations of the persons, revealed to us in the divine economy, reflect the true identity of who God is eternally. The trinitarian relations within the life of God cannot undergo any development or chronological alteration as a result of the economy. If this were the case, the Trinity would be born historically, or would be constituted in some way internal to the act of God's self-revelation in history. Such notions are absurd. In contrast, we must say that the economic revelation of the relations of the Persons, which happens in time, reflects who God truly is in his intimate life from all eternity. The Spirit is sent into the world both by the Father and by the Son, and so we must also say that he proceeds eternally both from the Father and the Son, through a common spiration.

The divinity of the Spirit was defined dogmatically at the Council of Constantinople (381), following the theological arguments of Basil the Great (*De Spiritu Sancto*) and Gregory of Nazianzen (*Oratio* 31). They said that according to the New Testament, the Holy Spirit saves and divinizes, but only God can do these things, and hence the Spirit is truly God. The Council stated that he is consubstantial (*homoúsios*) with the Father and the Son. "We believe in the Holy Spirit, the Lord and giver of life. With the Father and Son he is adored and glorified." The *CCC* observes that this reflection was further developed in a logically organic way at the sixth Council of Toledo (638) and at the eleventh Council of Toledo (675). The first of these Latin councils affirmed that the Father is the primary source and origin of the whole Godhead, because the Son and the Spirit proceed from him. The second stated that the Spirit proceeds from the father as Spirit of the Father, but to the same degree as the Son who is one with the Father. This is the traditional Latin doctrine of the faith known as the *Filioque:* the Holy Spirit proceeds eternally from the Father and the Son. He does so from the beginning and through a spiration.

The Church's doctrinal formation of the *Filioque* is theologically important for at least three reasons. First, it helps to understand the real distinction of the persons in God. The divine persons are identical in being and participate equally in the divine essence. Hence the distinction between them becomes intelligible only in light of their relations of origin. If the Son and the Spirit proceed only from the Father, it is not clear how we can truly distinguish them theologically. The teaching that the Spirit proceeds from the Father and the Son as from a single principle helps us to understand the distinction between the Spirit and the Son. The Spirit is the Spirit of the Father and the Son.

Second, this teaching is important for maintaining an authentic biblical monotheism. Only if there is a real distinction of persons, from their origin, can we affirm how each of the three persons possesses in himself the fullness of deity while remaining distinct from the others. The Son is eternally God, the Word generated by the eternal wisdom of the Father. The Spirit is eternally God, the spiration of love, originating from the mutual love of the Father and the Son.

Third, this doctrine provides a much deeper understanding of the psychological analogy revealed in the Prologue of the Gospel of John, which was discussed in the previous section of the *CCC*, speaking of the one God. The Son is the Word of God eternally generated, who proceeds from the Father as an emanation of the eternal wisdom of the Father. The Spirit is the eternal spiration of love who proceeds from the Father as the emanation of his eternal goodness. But, as love between human persons presupposes knowledge and proceeds from knowledge (since we cannot love what we do not first know), so in God, by analogy, the Spirit who is love proceeds from the Father "by means of" the Son, who is the eternal Word of the Father. The dogma of the Church about the procession of the Holy Spirit emphasizes the fact that the human soul is a created image of the Trinity.

Numbers 247 and 248 formulate an important ecumenical consideration on the doctrine of the *Filioque* in view of the relationship between the Catholic Church and the Orthodox Churches which do not accept this doctrine. The Orthodox view commonly expresses the concern that the *Filioque* represents a particular doctrinal innovation of the medieval Latin Church. It also states that the teaching compromises the primacy of the Father in the trinitarian relations. N. 247 is historical in nature and seeks to relate to the first concern sensitively. It notes the antiquity of the statement of the Filioque in the Latin and Alexandrine traditions, originating from a time even earlier than the undisputed ecumenical council of Chalcedon, and also clearly recognizes that in time the idea was introduced into the Latin liturgy and into the Latin formulation of the Nicene Creed. This happened especially from the eighth to the eleventh centuries and remains a point of dispute with the Orthodox Churches, because the Catholic Church upholds the conviction that it is a case of legitimate doctrinal development.

N. 248 then offers a profound and irenic analysis of the convergence of the Eastern and Western concepts of the spiration of the Holy Spirit. Theologians of the Orthodox tradition often affirm that the Spirit proceeds from the Father through the Son. This is entirely compatible with the Catholic teaching, because the affirmation that the Spirit proceeds from the Father and the Son as one principle does not deny the affirmation that the Spirit proceeds principally from the Father by means of the Son. The Father maintains his primacy in relation to the Son because the Father is the eternal origin of the generated Son, the principle without principle. Similarly, Catholic theologians are in agreement with the Orthodox that the Father is the principal source of the Spirit but they note that the Father is Father himself because he is always and already the eternal principle of the Son who dwells in him, in virtue of his eternal generation as the Word. By the mutual interpenetration (*perichorésis*) of the Father and the Word, the Father is only the eternal origin of the Spirit as he who is one with the Son. As Maximus the Confessor noted already in the seventh century, the teachings of the Western and Eastern traditions on the Holy Spirit are profoundly convergent and theologically compatible if each is treated with understanding and mutual charity.

III. The Holy Trinity in the Teaching of the Faith

The Formulation of Trinitarian Dogma

Having dealt with the revelation of the Trinity in Scripture, the *CCC* seeks to delineate the essential elements of trinitarian dogma. What follows in this section therefore is a clear, succinct, and beautiful exposition of trinitarian doctrine. The first part of the section is dedicated to considering the historical development of the trinitarian dogmas. How did they arise? The *CCC* notes that there are trinitarian formulas present in Scripture itself that are implicitly doctrinal in structure. "The grace of the Lord Jesus Christ and the love of God and the fellowship of the Holy Spirit be with you all" (2 Cor 13:14). Such confessional phrases are often incorporated into the eucharistic liturgy and correspond to the baptismal formula that uses the name of the Father and of the Son and of the Holy Spirit. In other words, the explicit confession of the three Persons of the Trinity is present in the New Testament and is inscribed in the sacramental life of the Church. This is the historical case that precedes all the subsequent doctrinal explanations. The apostolic deposit of the faith and the original sacramental life of the Church remain the foundation for the later proclamation of dogmatic affirmations regarding the Trinity.

In the first four centuries of the Church, she faced a great number of relevant controversies regarding the identity of Christ and the mystery of God. In this process she faced a series of erroneous teachings or heresies such as the Arianism and Sabellianism already mentioned. The dogmatic teaching of the Church developed to advance a true understanding of the New Testament regarding the mystery of the Trinity. To do this, the Church made use of a great number of explanatory terms or expressions such as "substance," "person," and "relation." These notions were used to safeguard a correct interpretation of Scripture and the Apostolic Tradition under the vigilant care of the living Magisterium of the Church (cf. *DV* 23). Such explanatory terms are not meant to be unfaithful to the luminous character of the revelation of God. To the contrary, they help to safeguard the meaning of the mystery of the Trinity, which remains "infinitely beyond all that we can humanly understand" (n. 251).

The terms "substance," "essence" and "nature" are all used in trinitarian dogma to speak of divine being in its unity. God is one and so we rightly say that the Trinity is one in substance, essence, and nature. The terms "person" and *hypóstasis* refer to the Father, to the Son, and to the Holy Spirit in distinguishing among them. *Hypóstasis* is an ancient Greek term that designates a person as a concrete subject distinct from others. It is used to denote the distinction between persons. The notion of relation is used in trinitarian dogma to denote the fact that the distinctions among the persons arise from the relations that exist among the persons. As we have already observed, the relations in the Trinity are principally relations of origin, a point to which we shall return.

The Dogma of the Trinity

The fundamental principles of trinitarian dogma are articulated by the *CCC* in a clear and direct manner from nn. 253 to 256. Here we find basic principles that add clarity to the perennial teaching of the Church.

The Trinity is One

"We do not confess three Gods, but one God in three persons, the 'consubstantial Trinity'" (n. 253). Obviously, by this statement monotheism is affirmed and any idea of tritheism is excluded; however, the affirmation of the unity of the Trinity also excludes Arianism (which asserts that the Son and the Holy Spirit are merely created and not divine). The three Persons of the Trinity are said to be "consubstantial" precisely because they are one in essence and in being. Does it mean that the three persons "have a share" in divinity, each one taking different parts of divinity in separate ways? Clearly not. Instead, each of the persons participates fully in the one divine essence and is entirely God. The Father is the one God, the Son is the one God, the Holy Spirit is the one God. The deity of the Father (the divine essence) is communicated to the Son by means of generation in such a way that the Son possesses in himself everything that is in the Father. The truth of the Father and the Son is communicated to the Holy Spirit by means of spiration in such a way that the Holy Spirit possesses in himself everything that is in the Father and in the Son.

To underscore the unity of the Trinity, the *CCC* quotes the Second Council of Constantinople, the Eleventh Council of Toledo, and the Fourth Lateran Council in n. 253. An important hermeneutical point is being indicated here. The Councils of the Catholic Church must be read in harmony among each other according to the logic of historical development, so that it is understood that the successive teachings are in theological continuity with prior teachings. Later teachings make more explicit what is contained potentially and implicitly in earlier doctrines. Moreover, the Church's intentional use of terms that come from ancient philosophy (such as "substance," "essence," "nature") is never something that tradition abandons or discards. To the contrary, these terms are part of the doctrinal patrimony of the Church because they give us a way to clearly designate the biblical mystery of the unity of God and the fact that our trinitarian faith is decisively monotheistic. Also they have a devotional element: we must serve only the one God, who we know is one in essence and substance. The undivided Trinity is the source of our heart's undivided devotion.

The Divine Persons are Really Distinct Among Themselves

While the dogmatic affirmation of the divine unity is meant to exclude tritheism and Arianism, this affirmation means to exclude modalism. "Father," "Son," and "Holy Spirit" are not merely names that designate modalities of the divine being or the way in which God appears to us in the economy. They designate who God truly is in his eternal identity. Hence, the Eleventh Council of Toledo can affirm simultaneously that "The Father is that which the Son is,...the Father and the Son that which the Holy Spirit is," thanks to the unity of the divine nature, and also that "He is not the Father who is the Son, nor is the Son he who is the Father, nor is the Holy Spirit he who is the Father or the Son." These two affirmations are not contradictory and are indeed profoundly consistent. The Father, the Son, and the Holy Spirit are truly distinct as persons and truly identical in nature. This truth is deeply mysterious, but in fact not intellectually incoherent. Indeed, it represents the deepest ontological mystery of all reality. In God, there is a communion among persons that involves an essential unity of being. The three persons are really distinct, but also absolutely immanent one to another because each possesses the unique essence and fullness of the divine being.

The trinitarian persons are distinct by their relations of origin. The Father generates the Son and communicates to him the fullness of divine being. The Father and the Son spirate the Holy Spirit and communicate to him the fullness of divine being. "The divine Unity is Triune" (n. 254). This means that there are modal realizations of the divine essence. For example, one can say that the one God is all-powerful, but the omnipotence is fatherly in the Father, filial in the Son, and spirated in the Spirit. The one omnipotence of God subsists in three distinct modes of being, in the three really distinct persons of the Trinity. If the Father acts in his divine omnipotence, he does so as the Father who is the eternal origin of the Son and the Spirit. If the Son acts in his divine omnipotence, he does so as one who has received everything he has in his divine power from the Father, as the Word generated by the Father. If the Spirit acts in his omnipotence, he does so as one who receives everything he has from the Father and from the Son as their Holy Spirit of love.

The Divine Persons are Relative One to Another

It follows from the first two dogmatic principles noted above that the persons of the Trinity are solely persons in relation among one another. "The real distinction of the persons from one another resides solely in the relationships which relate them to one another" (n. 255). Therefore one can only think of each of the divine persons in a twofold manner: as from the others or for the others, and as totally God. The Father is only Father as the eternal origin of the Son and the Spirit, and is only Father as he who possesses the fullness of truth in himself, communicating it to the Son and to the Spirit by generation and spiration. The Son is only Son as one eternally generated by the Father, and is only Son as one who possesses the fullness of deity in himself having received it from the Father. The Spirit is only Spirit as one spirated by the Father and by the Son, and as he who possesses the fullness of deity in himself as communicated to him by the Father and by the Son.

The *CCC* proceeds to quote the Council of Florence to emphasize that the three persons dwell each within the others by interpenetration, or *perichorésis* in Greek (n. 255, note 69). The teaching expressed here is very close to the understanding of St. Thomas (cf. *Summa Theologiae,* I, 42, 5). The mutual interpenetration of the persons follows from their common possession of the divine nature. Everything that the Father has within himself as God he communicates to the Son by generation, and they in turn to the Spirit by spiration. Consequently, everything that is in the Father is in the Son and in the Spirit, in the same way. Nothing is to be found in one of the persons ontologically alien in any way to the others, even if the three persons remain eternally distinct one from another. "I am in the Father and the Father is in me" (Jn 14:11).

This section of the *CCC* ends with a long quotation from Gregory of Nazianzen from the *Theological orations* (*Orationes,* 40) articulating the theology of what could be called "derived equality." The Son and the Spirit come from the Father, but are not less than the Father. They are eternally identical and equal to the Father, possessing the fullness of the divine essence from the Father. "I give you but one divinity and power, existing one in three, and containing the three in a distinct way. Divinity without disparity of substance or nature, without superior degree that raises up or inferior degree that casts down…the infinite co-naturality of three infinites. Each person considered in himself is entirely God…the three considered together…I have not even begun to think of unity when the Trinity bathes me in its splendor. I have not even begun to think of the Trinity when unity grasps me."

This presentation of the trinitarian persons brings to light the notion that the principal truth of all reality is an eternal communion of divine Persons that is ineffably perfect. There are implications here for all human beings, who are created in the image of God and are called to communion with God the Trinity. Each of us is invited to participate by grace in the eternal communion of the three Persons. By this same grace we are also united to one another in the visible life of the Catholic Church, which is a communion of human persons in charity. This communion of persons in the Catholic Church reflects the eternal life of the Trinity by means of a created similarity.

IV. The Divine Works and the Trinitarian Missions

The final part of the teaching of the *CCC* on the Trinity deals with the missions of the divine persons. Thomas Aquinas defines a divine mission of a trinitarian person with a twofold meaning: procession of origin from the person sending, and a new way of existing in another (cf. *Summa Theologiae*, I, 43, 1). What this means to say is that when the Son is sent by the Father into the world, this presupposes ontologically that the Son proceeds eternally from the Father but implies a new way of existence for the Son among us (in virtue of the incarnation of the Son in a human nature). When the Spirit is sent by the Father and by the Son on the apostles and on the Church, he comes as one who proceeds eternally from the Father and from the Son. But now he is present in a new way among us as the author of grace. We speak of the missions, therefore, because we have to clearly say that the temporal effects of the Son and of the Spirit among us are fundamentally rooted in the life of God himself. The missions reveal to us who God really is, and they serve to communicate the eternal life of God to us by means of grace. Hence there is a deep significance in the trinitarian missions. The Father sends the Son and the Spirit into the world to redeem and sanctify man. This sanctification, when all is said and done, consists in our assimilation of the very life of God, a life of divine truth and love. God seeks to communicate the glory of his blessed life to man by means of the visible missions of the incarnate Word and by means of the sending of the Holy Spirit on the apostles and on the Church.

As n. 258 clearly says, the whole divine economy is the common work of the three Persons. The Persons are of one and the same essence and of one and the same operation. So Catholic theology traditionally affirms that all the works *"ad extra"* of the Trinity (all the effects of God outside of himself) are always and only acts of all three persons. It is the Father, the Son, and the Holy Spirit who act together as a unity, who create and redeem the world. Each of the Persons truly acts according to his personal way of being. The Father creates the world by means of the Word and in the Spirit. The Word creates the world as the wisdom generated by the Father. The Spirit creates the world as the love spirated by the Father and the Son. However, there are *no* actions of the Father that do *not* involve the Word and the Spirit, or of the Word that do not involve the Father and the Spirit, and so on. Trinitarian actions are all interpersonal and in each of them the Persons act as one.

The apex of the divine economy is the incarnation of the Son and the sending of the Holy Spirit. The sending of the Son and the Spirit into the world are also works of all the three Persons, actively willed by all three Persons. The Father, the Son, and the Holy Spirit all will that the Son be made man for our salvation. Only the Word is incarnated and becomes man. Only the person of the Word suffers a human death and is risen and glorified in his human nature. But when Jesus Christ acts in virtue of his divine nature, he acts in unity with the Father and the Spirit. When Jesus extends his hand to heal someone it is solely the Son who acts in a human nature, with human gestures. But when he miraculously heals the person whom he touches in virtue of his divine power, he acts in unity with the Father and the Spirit, who also effect this healing. It is only the Spirit who is sent by the Father and the Son on the apostolic Church. Yet when the Spirit acts divinely to sanctify the members of the mystical body of Christ, he does so only acting with the Father and the Son, with whom he is one in being and in nature, as God. Hence the actions of any of the Person in the divine economy necessarily reveal to us the other two persons. The Holy Spirit illuminates us and brings us into knowledge of the incarnate Word. And the incarnate Word leads us to the Father. When the persons act in the divine economy, they act in unity as Trinity by revealing themselves to us in their unity as well as in their personal identities. There is a deeply spiritual character of this teaching that touches our Christian lives in a very concrete way. The more we learn to recognize Jesus Christ, the Son of God, personally, the more we also meet the Father and the Holy Spirit as acting personally in our lives. A profound personal trust in God the Trinity stands at the heart of the spiritual and mystical life of the Christian.

The teaching of the *CCC* about the doctrine of the Trinity ends with two meaningful affirmations in n. 260. First, based on Jn 17:21–23, the text states that "The ultimate end of the whole divine economy is the entry of God's creatures into the perfect unity of the Blessed Trinity." The beatification of spiritual creatures, of men and angels, is the primary aim of all God's work of creation and sanctification. As this beatification has a communitarian nature, we can say in truth that the principal reason for which God created all things is the communitarian life of the celestial Church. The Trinity wishes to dwell in his spiritual creatures by means of grace and communicate his divine life to them, to shape in us an eschatological communion of human persons.

Second, the *CCC* notes that this life of communion with the Trinity can begin already in this life by means of the spiritual indwelling of the Trinity in the souls of the Christian faithful. This teaching has a scriptural basis in Jn 14:23 (n. 260) and was emphasized by Pope Leo XIII in his encyclical *Divinum illud munus* (May 9, 1897). God desires to offer to each man who lives in the heart of the Church a real participation in the life of God and an intimate knowledge of the Persons of the Trinity. The *CCC* appropriately concludes with a quotation from a prayer of Elizabeth of the Trinity, a modern Carmelite saint for whom reflection on this mystery of the divine indwelling was a theme. "O my God, Trinity whom I adore, help me forget myself entirely so to establish myself in you, unmovable and peaceful as if my soul were already in eternity. May nothing be able to trouble my peace or make me leave you, O my unchanging God, but may each minute bring me more deeply into your mystery! Grant my soul peace. Make it your heaven, your beloved dwelling and the place of your rest. May I never abandon you there, but may I be there, whole and entire, completely vigilant in my faith, entirely adoring, and wholly given over to your creative action." Fundamentally, we are studying the mystery of the Trinity to live in a contemplative friendship with the Trinity, in this life and in that to come.

Chapter One, Article 1, Paragraph 3:
THE ALMIGHTY

Thomas Joseph White

The Catholic Church confesses in the Nicene Creed that God is almighty: he has infinite power and can do anything. Of all the divine attributes, only omnipotence is mentioned in the Creed. This confession of the omnipotence of God has an important practical value in our life. At the heart of our expectations and of our hope in God as our savior is the conviction that God can save us and has the power to do so. How, then, are we to understand the nature of God's omnipotence? First of all, the power of God has a universal range. Second, it is *fatherly* and thus *loving*. Third, it is mysterious, and acts in accord with the providential designs of God in the midst of our weakness and our human limitations. This section of the *CCC* dedicates a paragraph to considering each of these three aspects of divine omnipotence.

I. "He Does Whatever he Pleases"

Biblical revelation emphasizes the *universal range* of the divine power (Gn 49:24; Is 1:24). The fact that God is omnipotent is manifested in the most fundamental way by the very existence of the created world. That is to say, God creates all things out of nothing without any pre-existing material and without the use of any instrumental agent. He simply gives being to all things directly. Only one who has infinite power can act in this way (cf. Thomas, *Compendium Theologiae,* I, cc. 69–70). Hence God can not only create out of nothing, but also can do miracles, as he can also govern the universe by means of his wisdom. Nothing is impossible to God, who disposes of his work as he pleases (cf. Lk 1:37). He is the Lord of all the universe and his providence is detailed and specific, reaching all things. In the same way, the Church affirms that God is the lord of history and the governor of the human heart. This means not only that God knows what happens in the heart of every person, but also that he is the transcendent cause of our human freedom itself, the one who gives existence to us as creatures endowed with free will.

If understood rightly, there is no possible rivalry between the omnipotence of God and human free will. To the contrary, the omnipotent action of God is the transcendent source of our freedom, because he gives being to truly free human creatures (see, for example, *Summa Theologiae,* I, 19, 8).

II. "You Are Merciful to All, for You Can Do All Things"

The power of God is characterized by *fatherly love.* The fatherhood of God is manifested in his all-powerful action: he gives being to all creatures and provides for their needs. It is also reflected in his election of human beings as sons of God in Christ. Perhaps the all-powerful love of God is manifested above all in the activity of the infinite mercy of God. God uses his omnipotence in the service of his mercy. Why is the mercy of God particularly expressive of his omnipotence? Because it reveals the redemptive power of God, which is never defeated by evil or sin. God does not want moral evil in creatures, but mysteriously permits it and tolerates it, in view of a greater good he intends to draw. St. Augustine says that in a certain sense, God does a greater work in making a sinner just by means of the merciful gift of a relationship with him than in creating the heavens and the earth (*In Evangelium Ioannis,* tractatus 72). This is due to the fact that God, who is merciful, uses even the weakness of morally erring human beings as an occasion to offer them the greatest of all possible goods: participation in the life of God.

The use that God makes of his omnipotence is in fact not arbitrary. In n. 271, the *CCC* cites Aquinas: "In God, power, essence, will, intellect, wisdom, and justice are all identical. Nothing therefore can be in God's power which could not be in his just will or his wise intellect" (*Summa Theologiae,* I, 25, 5, ad 1). The idea expressed here is significant and refers implicitly to the doctrine of the divine simplicity. In God, the attributes that we denote with distinct names are in reality ontologically one. Human beings can possess knowledge, justice, and power as properties or attributes. But in his eternity and his divine perfection, God is his wisdom, his justice, and his power, which are mysteriously infinite. Moreover, his wisdom, his justice, and his power are identical. The attributes of divine nature of which we speak in distinct ways are in reality one in God. From this it follows that there are two extremes we must avoid when we think of the fatherly omnipotence of God. One of the extremes would emphasize the objectivity of divine wisdom and justice, to the detriment of the free omnipotence of God, as though God were always constrained to act according to a pre-existing ideal of justice that would transcend God, to which he would be subject. Such a way of thinking is obviously absurd. The other extreme is to think that the free omnipotence of God were potentially empty of wisdom and justice, as if something could be good simply because God willed it so, without reference to any criterion of wisdom or goodness. If we think of the power of God in this way, his action could appear morally arbitrary and ultimately free from any reference to his wisdom and justice itself, which is equally absurd. The true *via media* is based on the affirmation of the divine simplicity. God is eternally wise and just, just as God is all-powerful in his divine acts. Therefore, when God is acting, he does so according to his eternal wisdom and justice. The use of his almighty power, always good and wise, is never arbitrary or unjust. This activity is the expression of the eternal identity of God, because God is sovereignly good and perfectly wise and in him there is no variation or shadow of change (cf. Jas 1:17).

III. The Mystery of the Apparent Impotence of God

The exercise of God's power is *mysterious*. "Faith in God the Father Almighty can be put to the test by the experience of evil and suffering. God can sometimes seem to be absent and incapable of stopping evil" (n. 272). Human beings naturally seek to understand why God permits evil and suffering and how he could in some way draw good from them. Only in light of divine revelation can we gain a reliable perspective in regard to these questions. The key to understanding the apparent impotence of God in the face of evil is found in the voluntary humiliation and the resurrection of the Son of God. God has defeated evil in a mysterious way, particularly by making himself subject to evil and suffering in solidarity with human beings, as one who is fully human himself. He conquered evil in a definitive way by means of the victory of the resurrection of Christ, in the glorification of his body and his soul. St. Paul makes reference to the seeming impotence and folly of the cross that in truth reveal the immeasurable power and wisdom of God the Father (cf. 1 Cor 1:24–25; Eph 1:19–22). Christian life is animated by the hope we have in Christ crucified and risen. In virtue of our union with Christ in love, even our sufferings now can be a source of spiritual life in the greater body of the Church (cf. Col 1:24). St. Paul assures us that no matter what evils we may encounter in this life, "neither death, nor life…nor anything else in all creation will be able to separate us from the love of God in Christ Jesus our Lord" (Rom 8:38–39).

It is the knowledge that comes by means of the one supernatural faith that gives final access to the mystery of God's almighty governance of the world. "Only faith can embrace the mysterious ways of God's almighty power. This faith glories in its weaknesses in order to draw to itself Christ's power" (n. 273). Here it can seem that the *CCC* is engaged in special pleading, as though it were saying that we must simply accept our impotence by entrusting ourselves to the power of God by a voluntaristic act of will. But the idea expressed is much deeper and has a great spiritual and logical depth. For this faith glories in human weaknesses as a means of emphasizing its real collaboration with the divine power. St. Paul teaches this, quoting the words Christ spoke to him: "My power is made perfect in weakness" (2 Cor 12:9). The idea is not that Jesus Christ wants to diminish man. Rather, Christ offers men who are truly limited, sinful, and weak the possibility of a genuine spiritual friendship with one who is almighty and can give him the strength to do anything (cf. Phil 4:13). God uses his omnipotence in the service of his love, to unite us even in the midst of our weaknesses with the redeeming power of Christ crucified. The Virgin Mary is represented here as the model of Christian trust in the goodness and omnipotence of God. She believed in the word of the Archangel that nothing is impossible to God and lived with this conviction not only for the time of the infancy and the hidden life of Christ, but also in the course of his public ministry and in the hour of his crucifixion and death. She was also assimilated by Christ to the power of his resurrection in the mystery of her Assumption into glory. The Virgin Mary demonstrates the virtue of absolute trust in the power of God by her humility, her hope to magnify God and her grateful reception of God's initiatives.

The treatment of omnipotence by the *CCC* ends with a quotation from the *Roman Catechism* (I, 2, 13): "Nothing is more apt to confirm our faith and hope than holding it fixed in our minds that nothing is impossible with God. Once our reason has grasped the idea of God's almighty power, it will easily and without any hesitation admit everything that [the Creed] will afterwards propose for us to believe—even if they be great and marvelous things, far above the ordinary laws of nature."

This passage implicitly touches upon the relation of faith and reason with respect to the mystery of divine omnipotence. On one hand, belief in the omnipotence of God is reasonable. God has given being to all things and is therefore infinitely powerful. We could say, following the First Vatican Council (*DF*), that the Church's confession of the omnipotence of God forms part of what we traditionally call the *praeambula fidei*. The "preambles of the faith" are teachings contained in divine revelation to which one can accede by natural human reason, in the state of fallen nature. To be precise, it is possible for natural human reason to arrive at the knowledge that God exists and that God is omnipotent.

On the other hand, no one can demonstrate by means of natural reason alone that God, who is omnipotent, initiated the mysterious, supernatural, or miraculous things that are attributed to him in Scripture, such as the Incarnation, the founding of the Catholic Church, or the institution of the Eucharist. They are mysteries of the faith that are revealed, not conclusions of natural reason that human beings could discover on their own. Having said this, divine revelation and natural reason can cooperate harmoniously. If we consider the mysteries revealed in light of the rational acceptance of

God's omnipotence, we can see that God "can in principle" do the things attributed to him in sacred Scripture. The affirmations of the Catholic faith in the Creed, therefore, are in no way contrary to natural reason. God can become incarnate as a person, rise from the dead, found the Church, preserve her from error, and change bread and wine into the body and blood of Christ. If we believe in God, we can see that everything the Catholic faith affirms is rationally feasible in principle, because God truly exists and because truly "all things are possible to God."

If we consider the omnipotence of God in light of divine revelation itself, however, we can say much more. The omnipotent actions of God in the divine economy are manifestations of the mystery of the identity of God. His power expresses his goodness, love, and mercy. Through the initiatives that God freely undertakes for our salvation we can intimately know who the Trinity is. As we confess in the Creed: "For us men and for our salvation he came down from Heaven." The incarnation, life, and resurrection of Christ reveal most profoundly the mystery of the omnipotent wisdom and love of God. Trust in the power of God given to us by supernatural faith, hope, and charity are of a higher and more perfect order than any kind of conviction derived simply from human reason. The revealed truth of the omnipotent love of God should be a fundamental reference point for us in all the moments of our Christian life. God who is almighty has done great things for us and holy is his name (cf. Lk 1:49). We can confide ourselves to him with absolute trust, therefore, as our perpetual help and as the author of our salvation.

Chapter One, Article 1, Paragraph 4:
THE CREATOR

Luis F. Ladaria

The Catechism's text about God the creator begins by quoting Gn 1:1, the first phrase of sacred Scripture. Faith in the creation deserves a place of honor by that very fact. Everything that exists, heaven and earth, are works of God the creator. All the divine action in the world and the economy of salvation which will have its final fulfillment in Jesus begins from this assumption. The Creed takes up the same idea from Genesis. But a simple comparison between these two texts will suffice to discover a fundamental difference. According to the confession of Christian faith, God the creator of all is the Father. Below, in part II of this paragraph 4, there will be reference to the Trinity as such acting in the work of creation. It is also useful to note that this perspective is already present in these introductory indications.

In n. 280, the relationship of the creation with Christ is presented in summary.

In fact, in two directions: on one hand, the creation is the beginning of the history of salvation that will reach its peak in Christ. We must not think that the creation is a simple neutral background that God puts in place, on which to then bring about the salvation of men. According to Gn 2:7, God creates man with his own hands: according to Gn 1:26f, he creates man in his own image and likeness. Other things have meaning in relation to the human being, with whom the work of creation culminates. From the first moment God is already close to men.

This is why the creation culminates in Christ; in creation begins the dialogue between God and man which is to reach its summit in Jesus. Yet at the same time we are told that the mystery of Christ is the definitive light for understanding the mystery of creation. Indeed according to the New Testament, Christ is the mediator in the work of creation, as he was in the work of salvation (cf. 1 Cor 8:6; Col 1:15; Jn 1:3,19; Heb 1:2).

N. 281 makes evident how the liturgy, and in particular the celebration of the paschal vigil, sets the creation as the first moment of the history that will culminate in the resurrection of Jesus.

I. Catechesis on Creation

The importance of this topic will escape no one, though sadly it has been somewhat forgotten in the theology of recent times. Currently, a growing interest has returned for the theology of the creation. Many important questions on the meaning of our life and of the world are intimately related with the truth of creation. Is our being the fruit of the free and loving will of a good God? Or is it the result of a blind fate? Naturally many consequences in human life, including concrete ones, depend on the answer we give to these questions. The theological question, as nn. 283–284 indicate, is not placed on the same level as questions of the sciences, even if there may be a certain relation with them. Rather, it is the question of the meaning of the universe, of God its permanent foundation, which interests us.

N. 285 reviews a series of answers to the question of origins, understood in a sense that is not only chronological. We cannot comment here on these solutions one by one. But we can state positively: the Christian faith says that the world depends totally on God but also has a consistency of its own and its own creaturely good (it is not God), which is not the fruit of a fall; that there is not a good higher world and a bad lower world; that it is not a reality from which we need to liberate ourselves, but it is radically good inasmuch as it reflects the goodness of the Creator: and that it is not a work about which God is disinterested once he has set it in motion, but that it continues to be the constant object of his loving care. Some of these questions will become clearer in the development of the points to follow.

According to the First Vatican Council, man can attain to certain knowledge about God the creator through created things (cf. *DS* 3004; 3026). This teaching has its foundation in Wis 13:1–9. In the New Testament, the idea is repeated in Rom 1:19–20 and Acts 17:24–29. The text of the *CCC* follows the line of Vatican I, which affirms that divine revelation comes to confirm and clarify truths that, even if in themselves they can be reached by human reason, nonetheless in the current human condition they cannot in fact be known easily with total certainty and without an admixture of error (cf. *DS* 3005). This is applied concretely to the creation.

In effect, many centuries of Judeo-Christian tradition can make us think that the creation is an evident truth, at least for those who believe in God. In reality, the experience which the people of Israel had, of closeness to God manifested in the covenant, was fundamental for the development of faith in the creation. Even if to this day not all accept that the idea of creation attained a theological meaning only as a development from the idea of the covenant (this was the thesis of Karl Barth, as is known), there is no doubt that the idea of the covenant of God with his people played a determining role in deepening the idea of creation. Echoes of the covenant can be discovered in the Yahwist story of creation and sin itself: God manifests his power in the benefits he grants to man: the creation and placement of man in the paradise prepared for him, an event similar to when God has his people leave Egypt and gives them the promised land. The duty of Adam and Eve to observe God's command not to eat from the tree of knowledge of good and evil; the duty to observe the precepts of the covenant. Divine reward or chastisement according to human behavior; yet chastisement is not the last word. In the prophets, particularly in Deutero-Isaiah (cf. Is 41:20; 43:1,7,15; 44:1–2; 45:8, etc.), the works that God performs to aid his people are explained in terms of creation. This explains, as the text indicates, that the idea of love for the people is deepened in the idea of creation (Is 44:24). The God of Israel manifests himself in this way as the one God of all men, he who created heaven and earth. On the other hand, the power to create is the guarantee of God's ability to save his people, to return the people from exile (Jer 31:35f; 32:17f; 33:2, 23–26). The two accounts of the creation, the first three chapters of Genesis, have a central role in the Old Testament. They present fundamental ideas about man and the world, creatures of God, the original fall and divine pardon. The fundamental coordinates of man's relationship with God are found already established there, but, the text rightly indicates, "read in the light of Christ" (n. 289). The creation is a Christian truth, not only one of the Old Testament. The continuation of the text will give us occasion to return to this question below.

II. Creation—Work of the Holy Trinity

We can only praise the fact that the text of the *CCC* gives special attention to this point. At times it is said, somewhat one-sidedly, that the creation is the work of the one God. Certainly this is so. But perhaps the whole truth is not said in that. The biblical, liturgical and patristic texts that the catechism text presents are eloquent in this regard. Here are only a few examples among the many that could be cited.

The first statement of n. 290 makes mention of the specificity of the creative act. Everything that exists outside of God depends totally on him. "To create" is something that only God can do. The Old Testament itself, in Hebrew, has a word that shows this particularity (it is used especially in the priestly document, and concretely in the account of creation in Gn 1:1–2:4a) and can only have God as its subject. Continuing, the involvement of various persons in the creation will be specified further.

We have already made reference above to the mediation of Jesus in the creation, dealing with the new vision that we have of it in the light of Christ. Jn 1:3 and Col 1:16–17 are quoted (n. 291). The intervention of the Holy Spirit in creation is not directly indicated in the New Testament, but it is well attested in the tradition of the Church. The Council of Constantinople speaks in generic terms of the "vivifying" function of the Spirit. The liturgical hymns that speak of the Spirit as "creator" are famous. The patristic apologists had seen the intervention of the Holy Spirit in the creation (cf. Athenagoras, *Legatio pro Christianis,* 6; Theophilus of Antioch, *Ad Autolycum,* 7). Worthy of special mention is the doctrine of St. Irenaeus, reported in n. 292, which describes the Son and the Holy Spirit as the hands of God. The idea became so common that it was crystallized in the canons of the Second Council of Constantinople, in the year 553: "one God and Father from whom all things are, and one Lord Jesus Christ, through whom all things are, and one Holy Spirit in whom all things are" (*DS* 421; cf. *CCC,* n. 258). N. 292 aptly indicates that the action of the three persons is a single action. Father, Son, and Holy Spirit are not three principles of the creation but one single principle. For this reason, the creation is a "common" work of the Trinity. The biblical texts and texts of Tradition which are presented themselves make it possible to go a step further, which the *CCC* prudently seems to leave open: the action of the three persons, being common, is at the same time "differentiated": the ultimate initiative is attributed to the Father, mediation to the Son, etc. We can observe a certain parallelism between the action of the Trinity in creation and the action that will be accomplished in the salvation of man: the Father realizes the salvific work with the unique mediation of the Son and in the Holy Spirit. In this way, the relation between the act of creation and that of salvation is made evident. Both respond to a single plan of the only God, one and three. God, one and three, who has the fullness of life in himself and therefore has absolutely no need of any creature for his perfection, creates so that he can communicate his goods to creatures.

III. "The World Was Created for the Glory of God"

The communication of the divine glory is what moved God, one and three, to create. The formulation from Vatican I, a bare skeleton, is filled with content through the quotations from St. Bonaventure and St. Thomas. For Vatican I creation for the glory of God (*DS* 3025) and creation to "manifest … [his] perfection through the benefits which he bestows on creatures" (*DS* 3002) seem to coincide. In both cases, the idea that the creation serves to perfect God is excluded.

The glory of God is a notion with strong biblical roots. Already in the Old Testament it is used to indicate the manifestation of God through the creation (Ps 19:2 "the heavens are telling the glory of God"), and in the prodigy of the Exodus (cf. Ex 16:7, 10; 40:34). In the New Testament the idea of glory is joined to the revelation of the Father that takes place in Jesus (cf. among other texts, Jn 1:14; 2:11; 17:1f; 2 Cor 4:4). The glory that the Father has given to Jesus is a good communicable to man (cf. Jn 17:22). The salvation of man, the attainment of divine filiation, is what glorifies God. Both the text from Ephesians and the well-known words of Irenaeus of Lyons are presented fittingly in n. 294. The glory of God is the manifestation of his love in the salvation of man. And at the same time it consists purely of participation in the divine life that is given to us in Jesus. The end of the creature, of man in particular, is only God himself (cf. 1 Cor 15:28, "that God may be all in all"). For this reason, St. Thomas was able to write that God does not seek his glory for his own sake, but for us (*Summa Theologiae*, II–II, 132,1).

IV. The Mystery of Creation

The creation flows from the free will of God, from his wisdom and from his love. The biblical texts that are quoted are clear enough. The fact that the world is sustained by the free will of God gives meaning to human freedom. It would make no sense to speak of it in the context of a world governed by blind necessity. The First Vatican Council emphasizes in *DF* that God created the world by his goodness and his almighty power (*DS* 3002). The prominence given to love is very significant. This is why God can pour out his love on all his creatures. It is love that moves the world, "the sun and the other stars," as the unsurpassable verse of Dante says.

God has no intrinsic prerequisite for creation other than his own love, which is free. Nor is there any extrinsic prerequisite that would limit his freedom. He creates "out of nothing": that is, the world is not an emanation from him, and on the other hand, there is nothing extraneous to him that places conditions on him. Everything that exists depends radically on him, according to all that it is (cf. Vatican I, *DS* 3025). In Scripture the positive formulations predominate: God has created everything that exists. Yet in two texts quoted by the Catechism, 2 Mac 7:28 and Rom 4:17, creation out of nothing appears. The Catechism indicates rightly that this is a truth of hope. In effect, these two texts unite creation out of nothing and faith in the resurrection.

In n. 298 an allusion is made to creation "by means of the word." The idea is frequently repeated in the Bible, starting from Gn 1:1f. God who creates out of nothing can, entirely freely, "speak," "express himself," or as Vatican II says (*DV* 3), give "an enduring witness to himself." This divine power can also give light to faith in the hearts of men.

The world is not a chaos, but a cosmos, an ordered and coherent whole. From this comes the Creator's affirmation at the end of each day: "And God saw that it was good." With the appearance of man the good world becomes "very good" (Gn 1:31). The creation is consigned to man so that by means of it he may know and honor his Creator. Given that everything has flowed from the free will of God and from his hands, the created world is radically good. The Church has always rejected every pessimistic idea about the created world (cf. the references at the end of n. 299). The goodness of created being proclaims that of the Creator. We do not recognize the greatness of God when we diminish the value of his creation. The latter certainly depends on God, but in its dependence it has a goodness and consistency of its own (GS 36). These two truths, opposed at first glance, must always be held together: God is transcendent to the world and at the same time immanent to it. He is not confused with the world, he surpasses it, because he created it freely. But as created things have no consistency if not in him, he is the most intimate thing about the things themselves. St. Augustine expressed this paradox in the famous sentence which is quoted, saying that God is more intimate to us than we ourselves are (*Confessions,* III, 6, 11). St. Bonaventure underscored that God is more intimate to any thing than it is to itself (*In Sententiarum,* III, d. 29, q.2). And St. Thomas says that things are more in God than God is in them (*Summa Theologiae,* I, 8, 3). The creature can never attain a self-sufficiency before the Creator, unlike human works, which, once they are completed, subsist independent of their author. God is faithful to himself and to his works. Therefore he keeps in being what he has freely created. He loves everything he has made, because otherwise he would not have made it. The "conservation" in being of what God has made is the continuation of the creative act (*Summa Theologiae,* I, 104, 1). To recognize this dependence amounts to seeing God who acts in creatures, so as to discover his active presence in the world. The text indicates that this is the source of wisdom and freedom, of joy and trust. The reason for everything can be in the nearness with which God is experienced: God who is the source of every good.

V. God Carries Out His Plan: Divine Providence

The topic which the Catechism addresses now is immediately related to the one it just finished explaining. In both cases it aims to underscore the constant action of God in the world he created. The fact that God holds the world in being does not mean that his presence is merely static. This maintaining is at the same time guiding creation toward its destiny. This more dynamic dimension of God's constant action is what is highlighted when we speak of *providence*. The creation will reach its end only when God will be all in all (1 Cor 15:28). In the meantime, God leads it to perfection with his providence. Vatican I, in *DF,* presents these ideas, even if it does not specify the concrete end toward which God wants to lead creation in the paragraph dedicated to providence.

God's solicitude for the good of creatures in his "providence" is not limited to direction and guidance of the world in its totality. Scripture makes plain the immediacy and concreteness of this divine care (n. 303). Nothing escapes the eye of God. Every man, every concrete event, has a relevance for God, no doubt very different from what we give it in our valuation. The primacy of God's action in guiding history and the world is manifested in sacred Scripture in attributing specific actions *to* God without mention of secondary causes (n. 304). It is the result of the vision of faith with which the world is contemplated in the Bible. Actually, God the Lord of all is also working in the actions of "secondary causes," even in those of free beings. We shall return to this particular point below. But first the call of Jesus to filial trust in divine providence is highlighted (n. 305). God who provides, in the care he has for creatures, manifests his fatherhood. The words of the Sermon on the Mount are eloquent in this regard. In this context Jesus frequently refers to God his Father as the Father of the disciples: "*Your father* knows what things you need...." The greatness of the Creator is manifested in the capability he gives to his creatures. This is why the "competition" of God and his creatures in fulfilling the divine plan is not a sign of weakness, but the utmost expression of the Creator's greatness. In their condition as "secondary causes" creatures participate in the fontal causality of God. It is a perfection especially marked by the fact that God is able to make his creatures participate in it. If this is already true for blind, natural secondary causes, it must apply even more so for the human being. From his first instant he is called to dominate the earth. Man, with his intellect and freedom, is able to be an authentic cooperator with the work of God. Man was created, and at the same time God made him a "creator." With his free action man makes the potentialities of nature develop in a way it could never reach, left to its own. If God always has the primacy in the works of secondary causes, he has it supremely in human action. God is also the sustainer of freedom, not a brake or limitation upon it. Conversely, in man's free response to the divine invitation, the greatest power of the Creator appears. If there is no opposition between Creator and creature, given that the latter receives everything from God, there can also be none between man and God. God the giver of life can never be presented as the one who limits my freedom. Human greatness is manifested in its capacity to cooperate not only with the creation, but also in the Kingdom, in the salvation of man (n. 307, at the end). Once again in the text of the *CCC* we observe the unity of the divine design that inseparably embraces creation and salvation. Both can and must be distinct, but not separate. Creation, as was indicated above, is the beginning of the work of salvation.

The same ideas recur in n. 308. God is the beginning of every action, including and principally that of man. God rouses us to will and to work for the realization of his designs (cf. Phil 2:13). In his ability to rouse the free cooperation of his creature, the Creator shows his utmost greatness; at the same time, the dignity of man is highlighted. Here too, the explicit consideration of salvation is present. The creature does not disappear with the

Creator, because he alone is the one who sustains it in being; and moreover, the creature cannot reach its end without the help of grace. This must also be applied specifically to the human being. The question of evil is an ancient one. It is the objection which is always repeated in the face of the message Christianity proclaims, of the good God who provides. The existence of evil, the suffering of the innocent…, does it not refute what has been said up to this point? We must acknowledge that a rational explanation of evil that proves fully satisfactory will probably never be found. The *CCC* wisely indicates that, in some sense, the whole Christian faith is a response to the question of evil. It is, especially if we keep in mind that by his incarnation the Son of God has suffered evil, including the consequences of human sin, and with that he opened to us the hope of the joyous resurrection. Truly, the Christian faith is a response to the question of evil: it has been taken on by God himself. Jesus became like us in all things but sin (cf. Heb 4:15). Naturally, God could have created a better world than ours. He could have created "everything at once," without the process of improvement and change to which we are subject. He did not do it that way. We cannot enter into God's intentions. But it is licit for us to think that with this "perfectibility" which God wanted to leave open to his work, he wanted to give man the possibility of cooperating in the work of creation. Man in his freedom, improves himself and, at the same time, the world surrounding him also. The world is a challenge for man and his creativity. This is because he is limited, capable of improvement. It is also why what is called "physical" evil exists, the type that derives from natural causes and from creaturely limits. Living beings are born and die, they are built and they are destroyed. This evil can be a motive for greater goods, though it should not be trivialized and it will always be a question for man, who will only find a light for this mystery in the cross of Christ.

Yet intelligent and free creatures must reach their purpose by the choice of their loves. This is the greatest improvement: to be able to reach their purpose freely, with their will, unconstrained. But angels and men have sinned. Moral evil, the free rejection of God, sin, is an infinitely greater evil than physical evil. The very eternal destiny of the creature is at play. Because of this, one must say that God does not will this evil and cannot be considered its cause. St. Augustine said that everything we are and have comes from God, excepting sin; this comes only from us. The Church has always rejected predestination to evil, because God wants that all men be saved. Given that we cannot imagine a "space" in the world in which God does not intervene in some way, nor that things could happen absolutely against his will, we traditionally turn to the solution that evil is "permitted" by God who respects the liberty of the creatures he himself has made. If God has created us free, he cannot prevent that freedom from being exercised. From this comes the risk of evil and of sin, the risk that God runs, so to speak, by creating us free.

Naturally God, always omnipotent in his love, is able to draw good from evil. The sin of men made room for the Son of God to be delivered even to death. So God has manifested his love in a way that we could not have suspected, if human sin had not been: the proof that God loves us is that, while we were yet sinners, Christ died for us (cf. Rom 5:8). From the very death of Jesus, the most horrible crime that humanity could have committed, as the text relates, has come the greatest good possible, the glorification of Jesus, the redemption of man. The fact that the all-powerful love of God can draw good even from the worst evils does not mean that moral evil is no longer evil and that therefore it is willed by God. This principle must remain clear.

All things work together for the good of those who love God, says Paul. This (n. 313) seems to refer to the physical evil that can happen to us. Sin does not work to the good of anyone, and besides, because of sin, we refuse the love that God always has for us. Hope is a theological virtue, one of the fundamental attitudes of Christian life. Anyone who believes in God the provident Father has to think that everything God sends is for our good. The ways of God are mysterious for us now. They are the same ways by which he guides us in each of our days. But God is the Lord of history. Neither evil nor sin have rent this lordship. By this we know that he will lead his creation to its end. It is called to the final consummation in definitive rest, of which the sabbath rest of Gn 2:2 is only a prefiguration: the fullness of all men and also of the creation itself, sharing the glory of the risen Lord. The eighth day, the day of the resurrection, is the beginning of a new world (cf. *Letter of Barnabas,* XV, 8). The creation opens to us an eschatological perspective to which the final part of our confession of faith is dedicated.

Chapter One, Article 1, Paragraph 5: HEAVEN AND EARTH

Paul O'Callaghan

I. The Angels

The *CCC* teaches that all things were created by God, both spiritual and material things, including man "who, as it were, shares in both orders." In this teaching, it follows the Fourth Lateran Council (*DS* 800, *CCC* 326). This doctrine is mentioned in the Apostles' Creed, which professes that God is the "creator of heaven and earth" and in the Nicene-Constantinopolitan Creed, which adds: "of all things visible and invisible." The first designates the material world inhabited by men; the second can refer to "the firmament and God's own 'place'...and the 'place' of the spiritual creatures, the angels, who surround God" (n. 326).

The term "angel" derives from the Greek *ánghelos* (from which comes *angelus* in Latin) which means "messenger." Scripture, both the Old and the New Testament, speaks of the angels frequently. "Nearly every page of the sacred Scriptures gives witness of the existence of the angels and archangels," observes Gregory the Great (*Homiliae 34 in Evangelia,* 7).

The expression "angel of the Lord" *(malak YHWH)* is often found in the Old Testament. The close relation between the angels and God is much emphasized in the Old Testament, to the point that the precise identity of the "angel of the Lord" is not always clear; at times, the expression seems to refer to the actions of God himself and not to a separate subject.

The closeness of their relationship with God is expressed mainly in two ways in Scripture. The first, in praise to God: "Praise the Lord! Praise the Lord from the heavens, praise him in the heights! Praise him, all his angels, praise him, all his host" (Ps 148:1–2). "Bless the Lord, O you his angels, you mighty ones who do his word, hearkening to the voice of his word!" (Ps 103:20). And the second, in their care for the rest of creation and especially for man. The angels, "since creation and throughout the history of salvation," have been "announcing this salvation from afar or near and serving the accomplishment of the divine plan: they closed the earthly paradise; protected Lot; saved

Hagar and her child; stayed Abraham's hand; communicated the law by their ministry; led the People of God; announced births and callings; and assisted the prophets, just to cite a few examples" (*CCC* 332).

Clearly the two expressions go together and explain one another: the angels assist men, with the aim of directing their lives toward God, joyfully fulfilling his will, in praise and thanksgiving.

At the time of the New Testament there were some doubts about the existence of angels, both among the Jews and among the Greeks. They were abandoning the spirits, gods, and deities. On the other hand, Jesus, in the Scriptures, besides affirming the existence of angels, contrary to the Sadducees (Mt 20:30; Acts 23:8), clarifies two things. First, that the angels and spirits of any kind are strictly subordinate to him. In fact, the *CCC* says that "Christ is the center of the angelic world" (n. 331). They are, after all, "his angels" (Mt 25:31). This teaching can be found particularly in the Pauline writings. Like all other things, the angels were created "through and for him": "He is the image of the invisible God, the first-born of all creation; for in him all things were created, in heaven and on earth, visible and invisible, whether thrones or dominions or principalities or authorities—all things were created through him and for him" (Col 1:15–16; cf. Heb 1:14). With all likelihood Paul was alluding to gnostic teachings common at the time, which considered Jesus more as one angel—or deity or spirit—among others. Second, the whole life and ministry of Jesus are surrounded and inspired by angels. "From the Incarnation to the Ascension, the life of the Word incarnate is surrounded by the adoration and service of angels. When God brings the Firstborn into the world, he says: 'Let all God's angels worship him.' Their song of praise at the birth of Christ has not ceased resounding in the Church's praise: 'Glory to God in the highest!' They protect Jesus in his infancy, serve him in the desert, strengthen him in his agony in the garden, when he could have been saved by them from the hands of his enemies as Israel had been. Again, it is the angels who 'evangelize' by proclaiming the Good News of Christ's Incarnation and Resurrection. They will be present at Christ's return, which they will announce, to serve at his judgment" (*CCC* 333). The appearance of angels at the moment of the Ascension is particularly significant: when Jesus leaves the sight of the apostles, the angels explain to them what the disappearance of the Master means (Acts 1:10).

Given that the Christological teaching of the Church has developed and become consolidated through all the centuries, likewise devotion for the angels and the resulting theology have progressed and matured solidly, becoming an essential element in ecclesiology and Christian spirituality. Since the very first days of the Church the angels have taken care of believers, and the latter have expressed their devotion toward them. "The whole life of the Church benefits from the mysterious and powerful help of angels" (*CCC* 334). When the apostles were put in prison, "at night an angel of the Lord opened the prison doors and brought them out and said, 'Go and stand in the temple and speak to the people all the words of the Life'" (Acts 5:19–20). Precisely because the angels have taken part in the mission of Christ, so they also participate in that of the Church, his Body. And the faithful have recognized their power and action. When Peter is released from prison by the power of an angel and presents himself at the house where the Christians were living, they exclaim: "It is his angel" (Acts 12:15). Paul, too, is saved by the angels when he was drowning (Acts 27:23–24). Peter becomes involved in the conversion of Cornelius because of the invitation of an angel (Acts 10:3–12). The same thing happens to Philip on the road from Jerusalem to Gaza (Acts 8:26–29).

Because of this, it is no surprise that Origen can state that there are two churches: one of men and one of angels, visible and spiritual, each united closely to the other, each governed by a bishop of its own, one angelic and the other human (*Homiliae in Lucam,* 13). Their presence is particularly intense and powerful during the celebration of the Eucharist. "In her liturgy, the Church joins with the angels to adore the thrice-holy God. She invokes their assistance (in the Roman Canon's *Supplices te rogamus*...['Almighty God, we pray that your angel...']; in the funeral liturgy's *In Paradisum deducant te angeli*...['May the angels lead you into Paradise...']). Moreover, in the 'Cherubic Hymn' of the Byzantine Liturgy, she celebrates the memory of certain angels more particularly (St. Michael, St. Gabriel, St. Raphael, and the guardian angels)" (*CCC* 335).

Many Fathers of the Church and renowned theologians have taught that God provides every man an angel as protector (or "guardian"). In addition, it is commonly held that houses, institutions, and entire countries are under the protection of angels. Origen says this rather clearly: "Each member of the faithful, even the least of the Church, is guarded by an angel who, according to the words of Christ, beholds the face of God" (*De principiis II,* 10, 7). Thomas Aquinas also teaches that men are guarded by angels during their earthly sojourn, and that after they arrive in heaven they no longer have an angel guardian but rather an angel "to reign with him" or (in the case of damnation) a demon to punish him (*Summa Theologiae,* I, 113, 4).

The Fathers also were conscious of the Christological point of view on the life and activity of the angels. Gregory the Great says that we lost the friendship of the angels by the guilt of sin: "we were distanced from their luminous purity". However, "starting from the moment we begin to recognize our King, the angels recognize us as their compatriots. From the moment when the King of heaven assumed our earthly flesh, they no longer distance themselves from our misery. Still less do they dare to consider him whom they adore inferior to their nature, seeing it exalted above them in the Person of the King of heaven" (*Homiliae in Evangelia,* 8, 2). And the *CCC,* obviously, accepts this tradition: "From infancy to death human life is surrounded by their watchful care and intercession. 'Beside each believer stands an angel as protector and shepherd leading him to life' (St. Basil the Great, *Adversus Eunomium,* 3, 1). Already here on earth the Christian life shares by faith in the blessed company of angels and men united in God" (n. 336).

But the question we raise is this: are the two statements from the New Testament consistent with one another, that is, that on one hand the angels are subordinate to Christ, and, on the other, Jesus and the Church, his Body, need them in the exercise of their ministry and the work of salvation? This brings us to the question of the "mediation" exercised by angels. After all, Jesus Christ is "the one mediator" (1 Tm 2:4). On the basis of this affirmation, therefore, where are the angels to be placed? If Christ, the only-begotten Son of God, the Word in whom all things came to be, is the one mediator of God's word and his power, why should we attribute a relevant role to the angels in this process as mediators of the divine? We can make five observations.

1. To begin with, the mediation of the angels is not in competition with that of Christ. They share his one mediation. St. John Paul II, in his catechesis on the angels, observes that "the existence and activity of the angels (good and bad) is not the central content of the word of God [....] The truth about the angels is in a certain sense 'collateral,' though inseparable from the central revelation, which is the existence, the majesty and the glory of the Creator which shine forth in all creation ('seen' and 'unseen') and in God's salvific action in the history of mankind" (Audience, July 9, 1986, n. 3).

2. The nature and role of the angels have been put in doubt often in recent centuries. This is due in part to the program of demythologization from Bultmann and others, who contended that the angels do not belong by right to sacred Scripture, but are, rather, simple figments of our imagination, as Hobbes and Voltaire had said. Science has banished them from the Christian religion, Bultmann would say, along with miracles and other mythological figures. Doubts about the existence and the activity of angels arise also from the fact that Protestant theology is moving away completely from the Christian view of mediations of any kind, fearing that believers' attention to them—and to the other mediations such as the Church, the sacraments, the word, ministers—can promote idolatry and limit the mediation of Christ. It proves interesting to note that Calvin considered belief in the angels to be of great importance (*Inst. Christ.* I, 14,3), and Luther called them "the sentinels of God" (*Weimarer Ausgabe* 30/2 597). In the same way Karl Barth insisted on the importance of the angels as mediators in the history of salvation, even if he considered them inferior to man (*Church Dogmatics* III/3, §51). In any case, the bottom line is that Protestantism typically sets the mediation of Christ in opposition to that of creatures, and this has left its mark. With Scripture in hand, their existence cannot be denied, but in modern theology

both Protestant and Catholic, they are commonly considered irrelevant at both the pastoral and spiritual level.

3. Angels are purely spiritual beings. Origen, Augustine, and others thought that they were at least in part material beings. In this way it would be possible to explain how they were created and finite before God who is the only pure Spirit. Thomas Aquinas, however, insisted on the fully spiritual nature of angels, in which they reflect the infinite perfection of God who is Spirit, within the created order (*Summa Theologiae*, I, 50, 2). He states that their way of being created and finite is guaranteed by the composition in them of act and potency (*Summa Contra Gentiles,* III, 53). Unlike God, they are unable to express their own entire nature in a single act, because only God is "pure act." Indeed the *CCC* teaches that angels are "purely spiritual creatures" (n. 330). Hence we men are not able to interact with them at the empirical level. We believe in them, but we cannot be sure of seeing them, touching them, or hearing them. Although there is a crisis today in devotion to the angels, this is not due to an excess of science or a defect of idolatry, but rather a lack of faith. Historically, it is interesting to note that when faith in the angels has decreased, faith in God is also diminished. When we try to eliminate the angels, Scripture has to be completely reinterpreted, and with that the very history of salvation becomes empty (J. Auer, A. Winklhöfer).

4. If the mediation of angels is not necessary, as that of Christ is, in contrast, what role do they play in the lives of believers and in the world in general? Their mediation will not be necessary "for God," but is still very appropriate "for us." God makes use of mediations of various kinds to communicate his grace and strength, which are (or ought to be) a reflection of his trinitarian communion itself, to rouse a free, conscious and generous response to his gifts. The angels who praise God incessantly communicate their own spirit of service and praise to the rest of creation. In doing this they teach believers the true essence of charity, humility, and praise. Paradoxically the perfection of their mediation can be seen in the fact that they disappear when they carry it out, whatever it is, and do not require any repayment but that God's glory be proclaimed and his majesty praised forever. In them the words of Jesus to the disciples are fulfilled to the letter: "Let your light so shine before men, that they may see your good works and give glory to your Father who is in heaven" (Mt 5:16).

5. Because of their discreet mediation, we know little of the nature of angels, even if we are aware of the fullness of their mission through the testimony of Scripture. "The word 'angel' designates office, not nature. If the question is about the name of this nature, the answer is that it is spirit; if the question is about the office, the answer is that it is angel" (Augustine, *Enarratio in Psalmum* 103, 1, 15).

But we must say something further about their nature. The *CCC* says: "As purely spiritual creatures angels have intelligence and will: they are personal and immortal creatures, surpassing in perfection all visible creatures, as the splendor of their glory bears witness" (n. 330). Regarding their pure spirituality, Thomas Aquinas (*Summa Theologiae,* I, aa. 50–61) teaches that (1) given that the angels do not occupy any space, there is no reason why a vast number of them could not exist, as Scripture seems to indicate (Dn 7:10; Rv 5:11); (2) their identification is not derived from matter as is the case for other creatures; so it can only be derived from their species: for this reason, each angel has its "own" species, unlike men who have a common nature and thereby all belong to the same species; (3) angels are immortal given that they are not composed of matter and spirit: Jesus in fact says that the resurrected "cannot die any more, because they are equal to angels" (Lk 20:36); (4) although spiritual and immortal, angels are creatures and live within a certain temporal structure, called *aevum,* in which their actions occur one after another in succession; (5) angels are not localized within a material and spatial circumscription, as is the case with men: they are not omnipresent like God, but their presence in the created universe is "operative" more than circumscribed; (6) the angelic intellect is different from human intellect, which is discursive and dependent on matter: they know things through divine illumination, in a way that is intuitive, direct, and clear; and (7) the will of angels follows their intellect, without the dark and cloudy imperfections that weigh on the human being: they act in a way that is completely clear, lucid, instantaneous and definitive, so much that they are incapable of repenting of their actions, as limited human beings, in contrast, can do.

Paul Claudel expresses this teaching very powerfully: "The angel…has nothing to learn: he knows and exists in guarding…There is no veil. Nothing in the angel is opposed to the realization of the person, of the things for which he was created, neither ignorance, nor weakness, nor any obstacle. His knowledge reaches everything and is immediately transformed into will, as a circle is transformed into a circuit. The role he carries out is, for him, existence itself. He breathes his inspirer inexhaustibly. In him, vision causes such a pull on the will, the Spirit pulls the Spirit with such a strictness that in the coherence of all his infinitely complex rhythmic elements, out of nothing bursts the utterance of this marvelous name, this inextinguishable being" (*Presenza e profezia,* Milan: Edizioni di Comunità, 1947, 147f).

II. The Visible World

In the Christian economy there are not only spiritual mediations, like the angels, but also material ones. Since the most ancient times, Christians have resisted gnostic teachings that considered matter as disordered or outright opposed to God, a category of evil and perversion. Repeatedly the Church has insisted on the goodness not only of the soul but also of the body, of matter, the world, of marriage, of procreation, of the stars and the whole universe. This was done on the basis of many fundamental doctrines. In the first place was that of the *creation*: God brought all things into being, without exception, even the most humble. "Nothing exists that does not owe its existence to God the Creator. The world began when God's word drew it out of nothingness; all existent beings, all of nature, and all human history are rooted in this primordial event, the very genesis by which the world was constituted and time begun" (*CCC* 338). Second, the value of matter is confirmed in the incarnation of the Word (God became man, and moreover, became flesh: Jn 1:14). Similarly the material world is valued positively on the basis of the sacramental economy (the grace of God reaches man infallibly through material elements such as water, oil, bread, and wine). Finally the future vocation and endurance of matter in the plan of God can be found in the doctrine of the final resurrection, when men will rise in the flesh at the end of time. To sum it all up, one can say that God loves matter and takes it into consideration. Actually, as Tertullian says: *caro cardo salutis,* "the flesh is the hinge of salvation" (*De carnis resurrectione,* 8).

So we can make six affirmations about the material world from a theological point of view.

1. The goodness of material creatures derives from God, in the sense that hypothetically, if God had not created them, they would not be "goods." "Each of the various creatures, willed in its own being, reflects in its own way a ray of God's infinite wisdom and goodness. Man must therefore respect the particular goodness of every creature, to avoid any disordered use of things which would be in contempt of the Creator and would bring disastrous consequences for human beings and their environment" (*CCC* 339). Consequently, all creatures are willed to glorify their Creator. This is the true meaning of the *shabbath* day that concludes the work of God's creation: "God 'rested' on this day and sanctified and blessed it" (n. 345). "Creation was fashioned with a view to the sabbath and therefore for the worship and adoration of God. Worship is inscribed in the order of creation" (n. 347).

2. Material beings belong together in harmony, in unity, in symphony. They are found in mutual relations, interacting, interdependent, enriching each other. "The sun and the moon, the cedar and the little flower, the eagle and the sparrow: the spectacle of their countless diversities and inequalities tells us that no creature is self-sufficient. Creatures exist only in dependence on each other, to complete each other, in the service of each other" (n. 344).

3. All creatures, by the fact of having their own origin in God, can be considered beautiful, attractive, fascinating, with a beauty that is not cold, solitary, or competitive, but shared and mutually increasing. "The order and

harmony of the created world results from the diversity of beings and from the relationships which exist among them. Man discovers them progressively as the laws of nature. They call forth the admiration of scholars. The beauty of creation reflects the infinite beauty of the Creator and ought to inspire the respect and submission of man's intellect and will" (n. 341).

4. God has established material beings in a hierarchy whose summit is occupied by man. "The hierarchy of creatures is expressed by the order of the 'six days,' from the less perfect to the more perfect. God loves all his creatures and takes care of each one, even the sparrow. Nevertheless, Jesus said: 'You are of more value than many sparrows' (Lk 12:7), or again: 'of how much more value is a man than a sheep!' (Mt 12:12)" (n. 342). The *CCC* insists on the fact that while all the creatures are made by God, man occupies a superior position, having been formed in his image and likeness. "Man is the summit of the Creator's work, as the inspired account expresses by clearly distinguishing the creation of man from that of the other creatures" (n. 343).

5. The fact that God created the world, down to the last detail, means that he "laid a foundation and established laws that remain firm, on which the believer can rely with confidence, for they are the sign and pledge of the unshakeable faithfulness of God's covenant" (n. 346). Our grateful acceptance of God's work of creation consists in that we "remain faithful to this foundation, and respect the laws which the Creator has written into it" (ibid.) The joyful Christian appreciation of the material world brings us to investigate and accept the natural law.

6. The material world is not closed and infinitely repetitive, as the Greek doctrine of eternal return suggests. Rather it is open to the newness of the creation in Christ. This is often indicated in Scripture as the "eighth day." "But for us a new day has dawned: the day of Christ's Resurrection. The seventh day completes the first creation. The eighth day begins the new creation. Thus, the work of creation culminates in the greater work of redemption. The first creation finds its meaning and its summit in the new creation in Christ, the splendor of which surpasses that of the first creation" (n. 349).

Chapter One, Article 1, Paragraph 6:
MAN

Luis F. Ladaria

Having spoken of the mystery of creation, the invisible world (including the angels) and of the visible world in general, the *CCC* turns its attention now to man. It is easy to recognize the importance of this paragraph. Who are we according to the Christian faith? We can know many things about ourselves that do not come from divine revelation. But Jesus, the perfect man, revealing the love of the Father to us, has told us who we are (*GS* 22). Faith gives us the vision of man according to the thing that characterizes us most radically, in the final analysis: our relationship with God. Gn 1:26f points to the special dignity of man in the creation thanks to his status as the image of God. Therefore this will be the first point to develop. A further three sections follow, dedicated to man inasmuch as he unites the material and spiritual worlds; as man exists as male and female; and as God has established man in his friendship.

I. "In the Image of God"

A great many interpretations have been given in the course of history about the statement in Genesis: man was created in the image of God. The Second Vatican Council, in *GS* 12, points to man's condition as the image of God as the thing most proper to the Christian vision of the human being, above all, that sets it apart from the numerous visions of man that are offered. And it particularly defines this image as the capacity to know and love his Creator. The idea is found already in St. Thomas (*Summa Theologiae,* I, 93, 3; even if only the soul were properly the image of God for Thomas, following St. Augustine, and the body would not share that dignity, neither Vatican II nor the Catechism text on which we are commenting apply that restriction: they speak, and rightly so, of the whole man.) Also, there is mention of the task God has given human beings, to rule over the creation. The text of *GS* 12 ends with an allusion to the social condition of man. The *CCC* favors the first point from the Council, I think rightly; it obviously does not exclude the other dimensions. Yet they acquire a new force if they are considered as consequences of this fundamental condition: the human being is a privileged creature of God inasmuch as he is created in God's image and likeness, called to communion with him and to participation in his life, in knowledge and especially in love. The Christological considerations that follow will help us to explore this question.

The *personal* condition of man is placed in relation with his condition as image (n. 357). There are good reasons for this once the question of the image is centered on man's relationship with God. Two characteristics of personal being are highlighted: on one hand, the capacity to know and possess oneself; second, the possibility to give oneself freely and enter into communion with others. The two aspects are equally important. The latter gives us the ultimate reason for this peculiar dignity of the human being: the call to a covenant with the Creator, to a response of faith and love. Man's personal condition as "subject" cannot be disconnected from this call to divine life. Man is "someone" and not just "something," above all because God has willed to create man as his interlocutor. If God has created us with this capacity of self-possession and self-donation, it is because we can give ourselves freely to him and to our brothers. Our personal being reaches its fullness in gift and in love, in the following of Jesus. Man was created by God for this. He is the only creature in this world that can know him and love him, praise him, and give him thanks. This is why man, in praising, as the liturgy says, becomes the voice of all the creatures. Other things are for man's sake (n. 358). Man is not a means, he is an end in himself. For his sake, God delivered up his Son.

N. 359 uses a felicitous phrase from the Second Vatican Council, *GS* 22, although it does not develop it: "In reality it is only in the mystery of the Word made flesh that the mystery of man truly becomes clear." The beautiful words of Peter Chrysologus use the Pauline parallelism between Adam and Christ. With great fidelity to the Pauline spirit, though not a directly literal fidelity, the holy doctor tells us that the second Adam, Jesus, is really the first. He is the first and the last. That is how the words of the book of Revelation present it (1:17; 21:6; 22:13; cf. 1:8). I would like to call attention to a phrase in the quote: "The second Adam stamped his image on the first Adam when he created him." This takes up an ancient tradition that traces back to St. Irenaeus and Tertullian, which St. Hilary of Poitiers also transmits, according to which God's model in creating man had been his Son who was to become incarnate. Or rather the Son of God himself, being the mediator of creation (we have spoken of St. Irenaeus' doctrine, about the hands of the Father), molding man, impressed upon him then the traits he, the Son, had to assume in his incarnation. According to this line of thought, man was created in the image of God because he was created according to the model of Jesus (the only one who properly is the image of God: 2 Cor 4:4; Col 1:15) who was due to become incarnate. This is not the only interpretation given in history to this biblical truth; but it is particularly suggestive and deep, with a strong New Testament inspiration (cf. 1 Cor 15:45–49). We should be happy for the fact that the *CCC* has taken it up and made use of this text of St. Peter Chrysologus to comment on the statement from GS 22. According to this conciliar text, all the affirmations which the Council itself made about man in chapter 1 of the Constitution find their source and reach their summit in Jesus, including the truths about man created in the image of God.

The final numbers of this section (360–361) relate to us the unity of the human race. And this is a theological truth of great importance. It is certainly based on our common origin, as was indicated, but also on our common vocation in Christ. Or rather, if the first Adam is already the image of the second, we should think that this Christological foundation of the unity among us cannot be secondary in any way. Only in the revelation of the "fatherhood" of God, which is manifested in Jesus, can we understand the full meaning of the "brotherhood" of all men, in respect and in the acknowledgement of variety.

II. "Body and Soul But Truly One"

Man is one in body and soul. All of him was willed by God, all was created in the image of God. In his unity, there is a need to recognize a diversity of aspects and dimensions. With a language different from ours, Genesis itself shows the bodily condition of man, and at the same time, his participation in the life of God.

The term "soul" has multiple meanings (n. 363). In Scripture particularly, it means life, and also the whole human person. But it can also mean what is most intimate in man, the principle in him transcending this world, his "spiritual" principle, and this has been the meaning which has had the most development in the succeeding tradition. It is said that by his soul man is "more particularly" the image of God. After what has been said so far, and what will be said to follow, this cannot mean the exclusion of the body from that status. Naturally it is by means of his spiritual principle that man can know God and enter into a communion of love with him.

Given that the being created in the image of God is "man," as was stated previously, his body cannot fail to participate in the dignity of that image. Since the soul is the form of the body (cf. n. 365), the body is human only because it is animated by the soul. In turn, for the soul, being the form of the body is a dimension of its very nature. In this way the distinction between body and soul does not corrode the deep substantial unity of the human being. He is one precisely inasmuch as he is soul and body. The distinction between the soul and the body is shown in the final destiny that awaits us: according to Christian faith, this destiny is the resurrection, which involves the whole man. Any scorn for the body is therefore contrary to our faith. Faith in God the Creator means the affirmation of the goodness of all the creation, including the material world, and consequently the human body. So we do not have first a soul and then a body, which unite and constitute man. It is not a case of two united natures, but of one single corporeal-spiritual nature. The Council of Vienne insisted on this unity, affirming that the rational soul is the one form of the body. The Council made use of a formula that St. Thomas had already coined. Naturally no one formula will be able to totally embrace the human mystery, a reflection of the mystery of God, inasmuch as it was created in his image. But we need to remain clear that for the faith of the Church, man is substantially one, in the necessary distinction of the spiritual and bodily dimensions. Both the soul and the body are soul and body "of man."

In n. 366 some important affirmations are stated on the creation of the human soul and its immortality. First, the immediate creation of the soul by God. Pius XII, in the encyclical *HG*, reaffirmed this traditional teaching of the Church. The unrepeatability of the human person in his relation with God, in effect, requires this direct intervention. Inasmuch as man transcends this world, or rather is called to communion with God, the origin of man cannot be only in this-worldly causes. The teaching of the direct creation of the soul by God cannot make room for contempt toward the body: the soul created by God directly is at the same time the "form of the body." The immortality of the soul was affirmed multiple times, especially at the Fifth Lateran Council in 1513. This immortality that belongs to one of the two co-principles of the human being, is the guarantee of the continuity and identity of the human subject between the present life and the life of the resurrection, the ultimate end of man.

N. 367 alludes to an important distinction, the one it establishes between "soul" and "spirit." Certainly the two notions are not identified in the New Testament (there is a reference to 1 Thess 5:23), nor in the first Fathers of the Church (for example, Irenaeus of Lyons). It is not a matter of a duality in the soul. The distinction emphasizes something much deeper. Man is a being that does not have its finality in itself; he is called, since his creation, to a unique divine vocation, as the Second Vatican Council states (*GS* 22). Thus he lives in the "supernatural" order. Without the gift of the divine Spirit who transforms him interiorly, he cannot reach his ultimate end. The salvation of man does not come from his own anthropological components (though it is not realized altogether apart from them), but from God himself. The notion of "spirit" shows us this essential relation of man to God; inasmuch as he is united to Jesus and guided by the Spirit, man becomes "spirit" (cf. Rom 1:10;

1 Cor 6:17). The heart (n. 368) is the expression of man in the depth of his being, in which he decides in his liberty for or against God. According to biblical language, God also has a heart in which he decides in favor of man (cf. Ps 33:11).

III. Male and Female He Created Them

Genesis emphasizes that, as much for woman as for man, they are created in the image of God. With this fundamental affirmation it is made clear that the two are equally willed by God and that their dignity as images and as human persons, in the individuals and in both sexes, is the same. Given that God willed this distinction, the text emphasizes, it is good. Man exists, necessarily being male or being female. The difference is not an obstacle to their common dignity.

God is obviously neither male nor female. But they come from him and are participations in his most perfect being: however great the qualities or "perfections" are that characterize man, those that characterize woman are likewise. So there is nothing strange in the fact that in the Bible God appears with masculine and feminine traits, those of a mother on one hand, of a husband and father on the other. In the Virgin Mary we have an icon of this "motherhood" and therefore of these feminine traits of God.

Man and woman were not created alone together, but each for the other. Already Genesis shows us this truth. The text (n. 371) evokes the high point of the Genesis account of the creation of woman. Man, discovering woman as flesh of his flesh, following the meaning of the biblical expression, discovers her as a being with whom he is united by a bond that does not depend on his will, but on the divine design itself.

This is why man and woman are made for each other. The text puts us on guard against a false interpretation of this truth. It is not the case that man and woman, considered in themselves are incomplete. No: in their being as intelligent and free persons, created in the image of God, each of them has an unrepeatable vocation, and is for God a "you," responsible for the self. Only if we consider them as persons in the full sense of the word, in their self-possession and capacity for gift, then does the gift of themselves, made to one another mutually in marriage, have meaning. With this union they form "one flesh," not in the sense that their personal being disappears or remains absorbed in a higher unity, but in the sense that the personality of each receives a new connotation from this union with the other. In virtue of this union they can transmit human life and they cooperate in a unique way with the work of the Creator. Actually, there is no greater cooperation in the work of creation than what is realized in procreation: the human being is the apex of the creation, the only being in this world that God willed for its own sake.

In the creation of man as male and female we find the essential nucleus and a highly defined expression of human sociability: but certainly this quality of man is not reduced to this aspect. In Genesis man, male and female, has been given the assignment to dominate the earth, as well as to grow and multiply. Naturally, this dominion cannot be made without reference to the Creator. This dominion must take account of the other creatures, which certainly serve man according to the design of God; but man is not their master. Not only is there concern for other beings, man must also have care for future generations. This problem today is of great contemporary relevance, with the ecological crisis set before humanity. In his enormous anxiety to dominate the world without reference to the Creator, man can destroy himself. Pope Francis, in his encyclical *LS,* has addressed this problem.

IV. Man in Paradise

As we have indicated previously, man, ever since his creation, has a unique divine vocation. From the first moment, he was established in friendship with the Creator, in "grace." From this harmony in his relationship with God was meant to come harmony with himself, harmony with others, and with all creation. This situation of peace in which God created man is destined to be surpassed only in the glory of the new creation in Christ. The relationship between the beginning and the end is an ancient one. In ordinary theological language there follows mention of heaven, of eternal life, as of "paradise": as does the New Testament already. Images from the beginning are used to illustrate the fullness of the end.

Without a doubt, the fundamental point of the teaching of the Church about man in paradise is about the "holiness and justice" (the expression is from the Council of Trent) granted to our progenitors. This gratuitous gift signifies participation in divine life. Man, creature of God, has been placed in a superior state to what would be due him on the basis of this creaturely situation.

All the other goods man enjoyed in paradise are the radiance of this grace. They must never be seen without an intimate relation to it. "Original justice" especially is founded on it, embracing all the other gifts of which the Bible and the Tradition of the Church speak: immortality, the lack of suffering, interior harmony of man in himself ("integrity" or the absence of concupiscence), harmony in relations between man and woman, and harmony of man with the world. The relationship with God necessarily articulates itself in all these this-worldly spheres.

N. 377 emphasizes well how dominion over nature cannot be separated from man's dominion over himself. On the contrary, perhaps one could say that only if man is really master of himself can he exercise dominion over other creatures in an orderly way. Otherwise this lack of interior harmony will reflect upon creation. It is what happens after sin. Concupiscence has obscured man's ability to grasp the truth and follow reason and the good in our actions. The Councils of the early Church spoke of the "freedom" of man before sin. If we understand freedom as the capacity to carry out the good, we understand how sin reduced the human will to slavery. In the state of friendship and familiarity with God, man was to cultivate and have care of the paradise in which he had been placed. It is an erroneous interpretation to think that work is a punishment, a consequence of sin. Genesis clearly affirms the contrary. By means of his work, man cooperates with God in the work of creation; or rather, he humanizes the creation itself (cf. John Paul II, *Laborem exercens*). The last paragraph (n. 379) opens the passage to the next chapter: the sin of man which causes the loss of these goods. Altogether we ought to appreciate the sobriety with which the text of the *CCC* speaks of paradise. The theological elements are emphasized particularly: grace, participation in the life of God, man's internal and external harmony, contemplated in their intrinsic intimate relation. Without a doubt, Genesis means to refer to these profound truths with its very rich symbolic language.

Chapter One, Article 1, Paragraph 7:
THE FALL

Luis F. Ladaria

N. 385, which introduces the topic of original sin, shows the way to approach this mystery. The experience of evil is general: we all do it. But if we remain in this experience, that is not a solution to the problem. Only the revelation of the mystery of divine mercy, making known the superabundance of pardon and grace, tells us what the extent of evil is. It is the revelation of Jesus that makes known to us in depth what human sin means. Only when we know the immense love of God for men, do we know what sin, which is opposed to this love, means. This does not mean that we cannot have a certain idea of this sin already. We find that in the Old Testament. However, with the definitive revelation of grace, sin gains all its gravity. The title of the first section of this paragraph is already eloquent by itself (cf. Rom 5:20).

I. Where Sin Abounded, Grace Abounded All the More

Sin is present in human history, and it is useless to try to mask it. It can happen because man is essentially directed to God, who has called him to friendship with him, as we have seen in the last section of the preceding paragraph. Only if we start from this relationship with God can we understand sin as the refusal and rupture of that friendship.

Sin implies human freedom, or personal freedom (in the case of personal sin which we all commit), or the freedom of those who went before us (this is the case of original sin). The text, in n. 387, makes reference to some attempts to explain sin as a defect of growth (primitive states of evolution, as an explanation of original sin), or errors, or unfavorable social conditions. It is better to call sin by its right name. It is the abuse of the freedom that God has given us, for us to love him and our neighbor. Paradoxically, sin shows us negatively the greatness of human freedom: while it was made for receiving God, it also can turn against him. We have already given some attention to the question of evil previously; here it is possible to address the topic more directly.

At the beginning of the Old Testament we find the account of the first sin. A certain awareness of the "original sin" existed prior to Jesus. Some other books of the Old Testament, but relatively few and late, make reference to the sin of Adam and Eve and the consequences they had for humanity (cd. Wis 2:23f; Sir 2:24). But the importance of what Genesis tells us cannot be known until the full revelation of the redemption and the pardon which Christ brings us. The most important text of the New Testament for understanding the mystery of original sin is Rom 5:12–21. Paul uses the parallelism between Adam and Christ, which he used before in 1 Cor 15:20–28, 44–49, to make visible how, in Christ, there begins a new life of grace and pardon that abounds all the more in the face of the situation of sin, in which all humanity finds itself as a consequence of Adam's sin; hence "sin came into the world through one man, and death through sin, and so death spread to all men because all men sinned" (Rom 5:12). Consequently, one cannot understand the doctrine of original sin except as the reverse side of the Gospel. It shows us from what thing Christ has freed us, and how great is the reach of his salvation and the superabundant grace he gives us. In this sense the doctrine of sin, and specifically the doctrine of original sin, is of fundamental importance for the faith. An inadequate understanding of it leads to an inadequate understanding of the mystery of Christ and the salvation he offers us. The Church is not interested in the doctrine of original sin in isolation, "by itself," but in its inseparable relation with Jesus who redeems us and frees us from this sin. It is clear that the account of Gn 3 is symbolic, but that does not mean that it is not presenting a real event that took place at the beginning of history. Therefore, even if the details of this sin from our first parents remain unknown, we do know that it took place and that, with its negative influence, it has marked and continues to mark all of human history. Only by placing this sin at the beginning of history can one understand the universality of sin which embraces everyone and, consequently, the universality of Jesus' redemption in which the Father has reconciled the world with himself.

II. The Fall of the Angels

Behind this event, which took place at the beginning of history, another one is placed, whose contours are more mysterious yet. At the origin of temptation and sin there is a being who opposes God. The serpent of Genesis is identified, on the basis of Wis 2:24, with Satan. The New Testament and Tradition present him as a fallen angel. Actually, the angels, as spiritual beings, have freedom in common with man, and since it is also a finite freedom in their case, it can be badly used. The New Testament speaks of this sin of the angels, at 2 Pt 2:4: "God did not spare the angels when they sinned, but cast them into hell and committed them to pits of deepest darkness." In this case also, sin is a rejection of God. They did not want to submit themselves to him; they wanted to "be like God." Because those words were said in the tempting voice of the serpent, we can recognize what had been, in its kernel, the sin of the angels. Naturally, if we do not know the specific details of the first sin of man, still less can we venture to imagine those of the sin of the angels. But I think it is interesting, by way of curiosity, to mention that one tradition of early Christian times, which finds an echo, for example, in the writing of St. Irenaeus, sees the manifestation of this sin (the "apostasy") in envy (cf. Wis 2:24) for the goods that God wanted to grant to man and which were to have their greatest expression in the glorious humanity of Jesus. Bearing a grudge against God for these goods, Satan wanted to prevent human beings from enjoying them, by means of temptation.

The sin of the angels, their free decision against God, is, by its very nature, irrevocable. The explanation traditionally given for this fact is that, since an angel has a purely spiritual nature, he disposes entirely of himself in his free choice; so he determines himself in an irrevocable manner. Man, too, in his free choice, disposes of himself. But given his conditioning, this disposition is not total; so he can repent and change his conduct, while he is in this world. Thus the gravest result of the influence of Satan, a murderer since the beginning and father of lies (cf. Jn 8:44), has been inducing man to commit the original sin. He continues to be a negative influence upon us. As he tempted our forebears and triumphed in his mission, so he also tempted Jesus. But whereas Adam and Eve yielded to the temptation of wanting to be like God, Jesus, who was in the form of God, did not count equality with God a thing to be grasped, but emptied himself of his rank (Phil 2:6f). With his coming into the world, with his obedience to the Father, he destroyed the works of the devil. The final number of this section puts us on guard against false interpretations that tend to exaggerate the power of the devil. He is a creature of God. His action and the harm it causes are always permitted by God. So there is no evil principle opposed to the principle of good and at the same level. There is only one Creator of everything, the good God, who can draw good even out of evil.

III. Original Sin

Having dealt with the sin of the angels, the *CCC* returns to the story of man's origins. What was said earlier in n. IV of paragraph 6 on man in paradise (nn. 374–379) is taken up again. God established man in his friendship. This friendship cannot be imposed; man must accept it freely. Given that man has received everything from God, this friendship has the meaning of grateful submission. The divine prohibition against eating from the tree of knowledge of good and evil has a profound significance: man will die if he wants to rebel against God, if he wants to become, as it were, the one who knows what only God is supposed to know (cf. Gn 3:5,22). The divine command is thus not arbitrary. It shows that man can only live in dependence on the Creator.

Man disobeyed God, because he failed to have trust in him. After the instigation of the serpent, he wanted to live while being like God, that is, without reference to the God who made him. The first sin, beyond being the source of such great evils, is at the same time the example, the paradigm of every sin: man wants to assert himself against God; by doing so, he disobeys, forgetting the fact that he can only live if he abandons himself trustfully to God who loves him. This self-assertion leads to disobedience because the human being is not convinced that his happiness lies only in God.

Trying to be like God, eating from the forbidden tree, man is not claiming a greatness that was not offered to him: he was created in the image and likeness of God, in the grace of God, being a "god" was and is his destiny. But, as Maximus the Confessor says expressively, he wanted to be God without God and not according to God. He wanted to be that by his own conquest and not by the acceptance of a gift. The source of such great evils for man derives from this.

Genesis shows the consequences of man's sin. N. 399 concentrates on the essentials: the loss of friendship with God and his "grace," which constituted the essential nucleus of the condition of man in paradise. We note that the remaining observations in this number refer to the deterioration of man's relationship with God: man and woman fear him; they have made a false image of their Creator. Holiness and justice consist in friendship with God, and the loss of this condition constitutes the destruction of this harmonious relationship.

If the holiness and grace of paradise were the source of all the other gifts man enjoyed, as we have observed in speaking of the original state of man and of paradise, we cannot be surprised by the fact that, with the loss of this harmony in man's relationship with God, all the other goods were lost (n. 400). In first place, man's harmony with himself, his self-mastery, the control of his passions, etc., were lost. Harmony with the neighbor is broken, already in conjugal life itself (cf. Gn 3:11–13,16), and from here in all the other manifestations of social life. Lastly, harmony with creation and nature. Although God did not punish sinful man and woman immediately with death, according to the account of Gensis, despite this one of the most terrible consequences of sin is that man must return to the dust from which he was made. The chastisement announced by the Lord is realized, although its execution is postponed. "Sin came into the world because of one man and death through sin," says Paul in Rom 5:12. We must keep in mind that in the biblical mentality death means not only the biological fact, but also the separation from God that is expressed in physical death. If we take account of this fact, it appears more clearly how, for the sacred authors, death is intrinsically united with the loss of holiness and original justice and of friendship with God.

Sin begets sin. This appears already at the beginning of history. The consequences of the sin of Adam and Eve, beyond their expulsion from paradise and the new life situation in which they then found themselves, are also manifested in new sins that are committed, doubtlessly a consequence of the new state of isolation from God in which the human being finds himself outside of paradise: most of all, Cain's fratricide, in which he kills his brother Abel and which, after the growth of the mass of sin, goes so far as to provoke God to say he "repents" of having created man on the earth; then comes the flood, from which only a few are saved, but the history of sin in the world does not stop with that. The sin of Adam and Eve is the beginning of a history and a chain of sin that will sweep away all of humanity. We said a little while ago that the sin of Adam is the paradigm and model of every sin. Now we see that it is more than that: it is at the same time what unleashed a force of sin that sweeps away and envelops all men. It seems very significant to me that the *CCC* makes reference to this problem. At times, in the context of the doctrine of original sin, the only problem dealt with is how it is possible that a child who comes into the world has contracted sin, etc. These questions are not being forgotten, as we shall see later. Moreover, we see that even this concatenation of sins, this universality of sin, must be seen in relation with the original breach of friendship with God because of the sin from the origins of humanity. We recall that the Magisterium of the Church has spoken of "structures of sin" (cf. John Paul II, *SRS*). Even if it is not exactly about the same thing, there is, no doubt, a relationship between the universality of sin in human history and the fact that "sin" introduces itself into the structures of society and human habitation. The quote from *GS* that closes the section is eloquent. Divine revelation explains the deep meaning of the experience man has in himself and in the world around him: division, the inclination to evil, which good sense refuses to attribute to the good Creator who gave everything its origin.

In reality, the text already began to speak of these consequences in the last number. It indicated that after the sin of Adam, an invasion of sin into the world was produced. Now it deals with making a step forward, that is, to see the close link that exists between Adam's sin and sinful men. As was said at the beginning of this paragraph, the doctrine of original sin becomes part of the doctrine of the redemption and stands in relation to it. Hence the Pauline quotations of n. 402: the universality of sin as a consequence of the sin of Adam, and at the same time, the universality of salvation in Christ. So the Catechism is moving in Pauline coordinates. These need to be kept in mind, for the sake of interpreting all the concrete affirmations rightly.

N. 403 repeats some statements that we already know. The evils that afflict man, particularly his inclination to evil, are not understood without the link with Adam's sin, or prescinding from the fact that he "transmitted a sin to us" that relates to us all from our birth and is the "death of the soul". In the commentary, we must dwell on this affirmation of undoubted theological interest. Following the teachings of the Church, in particular of the Council of Trent, the text says that, as a consequence of the sin of Adam, man is a "sinner" even before a free choice on his part. Later the meaning of being a sinner in this way will be defined further. For now, we hold this: because of the sin of Adam, and by the fact of birth itself, a sin is transmitted to man. Because of this, a child, who cannot yet have sinned personally, is really baptized "for the remission of sins." The Council of Trent affirms that this formula is true and not false, including the case of a child (cf. *DS* 1514).

N. 404 addresses the more difficult point of the doctrine of original sin, how the sin of Adam can be the sin of all. The answer is naturally very nuanced and is given at various times. First, the Catechism speaks of the unity of human nature, to which the *CCC* has referred previously (we recall n. 360–361); unity in Adam and also unity in Christ. So the unity of all men is what makes it possible for us all to be implicated in the guilt of Adam as in the justice of Christ. This first observation, a necessary one, opens the passage to the second: we cannot find a totally rational, comprehensible explanation of the way original sin is transmitted to us. In the third passage, presupposing the other two, the fact of revelation is taken up: Adam and Eve received original justice not only for themselves, but also for their descendants. That is, in their obedience to God's plan, and by personally possessing grace; they had to be, somehow, "transmitters" of this state of justice and holiness. With the sin that was "personal" in them, they caused others to be deprived of grace, as the human nature they transmitted was lacking it. Here we have a very special case of something that also happens at more normal and unimportant levels. Since the unity of the whole human race is presupposed in God's plan, the good and the evil each of us carries out is not only important for us. It also relates to others, in one way or another. So original sin was able to provoke this privation of grace in all, because our progenitors had been called to transmit grace and divine friendship, in obedience to God, to everyone, by transmitting human life and human "nature." Given that this "mediation" failed, we say that man comes into the world deprived of holiness and justice. The sin from our origins interrupted this communication of his love, which God wanted to make to us, with the mediation of Adam and Eve. The explanation of the last lines is most important: original sin is real in us, but is sin in an "analogous" way, in comparison to personal sin: that is, it is not a sin that we "committed"; we "contracted" it in the way we have just finished seeing. It is not an act, but a "state" in which we find ourselves, regardless of our will. But we can add, if the grace of God does not help us, we, in our personal sins, ratify, we make our own in some way, the sinful decision of our forebears: we too rebel toward God.

Original sin relates to us not just "externally," as we sometimes have the temptation to think. And there is no lack of theological interpretations that only go in that direction. They do not seem to be sufficient. The Council of Trent, as the text fittingly mentions (n. 405), states that this sin is in everyone as his own. The Council wanted to oppose precisely the attempts to explain original sin as merely extrinsic. But at the same time, the text insists on what has been stated already at the end of the preceding number: original sin does not have the character of personal guilt in us. This too is a statement to which the *CCC* wants to give weight, doubtless to avoid misunderstandings that can lead to the rejection of the whole doctrine of original sin. In effect, it is possible to argue in the following way: "Given that it is not possible for another's sin to be mine, what is taught about original sin makes no sense." After what we have said it is clear that the assumption from which this reasoning begins is not correct: the Church does not teach that the sin of Adam is ours in the same sense in which it is his. The privation of holiness and original justice is related, without a doubt, to nature, it has wounded it: but it has not corrupted it totally. The *CCC* alludes briefly to the Catholic doctrine of concupiscence, which comes from sin and inclines toward it, according to what the Council of Trent states (cf. *DS* 1515), but is not sin in the strict sense (at least in the baptized person). Baptism, giving us grace, cancels original sin, and makes us turn to God anew. The baptized person remains interiorly transformed, sanctified. There is nothing in him that God hates. But this does not mean that all the effects and consequences of sin have disappeared. Christian life has been compared many times to a combat. The text mentions it, but with trust placed in God and in his grace the Christian can come forth victorious from this struggle.

N. 406 gives some interesting historical information. There are two key moments for understanding the development of the doctrine of original sin: St. Augustine's struggle against the Pelagians, and the Catholic reaction at the Council of Trent to Protestant doctrines. The former reduced Adam's influence over us to a bad example. And they tended also to consider Christ as also only a good example, and that therefore we have no need of his grace to be good. The first Protestant reformers, in contrast, were inclined to the extreme opposite, that is, to consider human nature totally corrupt and incapable of any good. Faced with these extremes, the doctrine of original sin which the Church propounds to us (Council of Orange in 529, and earlier in the council of Carthage in 419, and, above all, the Council of Trent in its fifth Session in 1546), follows a moderate, balanced line. It insists on the reality of original sin and the impossibility of escaping it with our own strength:

only by the merits of Christ, which are applied to us in baptism, can we see ourselves freed from it. On the other hand, it does not consider man totally corrupt. Sinful man continues to be a creature of God, continues to be loved by God even if the creature refuses him. Its creaturely goodness, certainly wounded, remains. This is why it is able, always moved by God and his grace, to receive the gift of pardon which God offers him and to cooperate in his own justification.

The idea of combat, which we have already seen introduced, reappears. This n. 407, rather than moving on to new doctrinal material, is a call to realism. The doctrine of original sin helps us to understand man and the world. Pascal said that original sin is certainly difficult to understand. But without it, numerous things become even more incomprehensible. Many of us subscribe readily to this acute observation. Forgetting the situation in which sin has placed man, and a certain dominion that its power exercises over us, our inclination to evil, etc., does not lead to any good result. The call to sane realism is not pessimistic. As we have noted many times, the *CCC* does not separate sin from redemption. Here, their profound union is reported once again.

In n. 408, after this reminder of the real condition of man, the text returns to make some notable theological observations. Adam's sin has had consequences for humanity. As previously noted, other sins are consequences of the power of sin, unleashed by the first sin; these also have consequences. The privation of holiness and original justice has made easier the fact that all men have fallen into personal sin, and this, in turn, cannot fail to have negative consequences for other human beings. Starting from the first sin, the "sin of the world" increases like a ball of snow rolling down a slope. So the sinful state of the world and humanity encompasses all these sins. Personal sins create situations and structures that are sources of new sins. I think it is very perceptive that the Catechism mentioned these theological and magisterial intuitions in the context of the doctrine of original sin. In this way it gains a great existential strength: it is not only about the fact that we suffer the consequences of the sin from our first parents: our neighbor also suffers the consequences of our sin and our infidelity to God. We all contribute to increase the power of sin in the world. The "sin of the world" helps us understand the doctrine of original sin and at the same time is a chapter in it. The *CCC* has already referred to the power of the devil and his limitations in this same paragraph. We cannot interpret the statement of n. 409 in an absolute sense, without taking account of what has been said before. But this real power is the cause of the combat against the power of evil, a combat that Christ began and that will last until the end. Every man is involved in this struggle.

IV. "You Did Not Abandon Him to the Power of Death"

With this phrase, the liturgy (cf. the fourth Eucharistic Prayer) summarizes the teaching from Scripture and Tradition: God did not abandon man after sin. N. 410 mentions the fundamental points from Gn 3 in regard to this: God goes in search of the man who has hidden himself, and calls him: he does not curse the man or the woman, as he does the serpent. And above all he announces salvation in a mysterious way. Christian tradition calls Gn 3:15 the "Protoevangelium." Only in the light of Jesus is the ultimate meaning of this initial promise of salvation understood.

Jesus, with his obedience, inaugurated a new way of being man, set against the way of disobedience that marked the life of Adam and the men who came after him. In his obedience to the Father, giving himself over to death on the cross, he is the redeemer of men, he who is free of sin. Intimately united with Jesus, who does not know sin and who has freed us from it, the tradition of the Church contemplates Mary. She is the "new Eve" who, with her obedience to the plan of God, has made possible the incarnation of the Word, the new Adam (in contrast to Eve who, with her disobedience, induced Adam to disobey). In this way Mary appears intimately associated to the work of Jesus. As regards her being exempt from original sin, the dogmatic definition of the Immaculate Conception was promulgated in 1854 (cf. *DS* 2803). Other magisterial declarations prepared the way for it. The decree of the Council of Trent on original sin is important: in canon 6, it says that what is stated in this canon about all human beings does not apply to Mary (cf. *DS* 1516). As the text mentions, the same council indicates that Mary, by a divine privilege, did not commit any sin in her life (*DS* 1573).

Why did God permit sin? We return to face the problem of evil, which the Catechism has already addressed. God created man free and respects his freedom. Moreover, nothing prevents God from drawing good from the worst sins. The revelation of his immense love, giving the Son over for us while we were yet sinners (cf. Rom 5:6f), could not have been produced without sin. Now we can know the infinite greatness of his mercy. The grace of Christ is stronger than sin: where sin abounded, grace abounded all the more (Rom 5:20). Additionally, the *CCC* mentions the teaching of St. Thomas, that nothing prevents God from having decided to give man greater goods even after sin, as in the beautiful exclamation of the paschal praeconium, the Exsultet: *"O felix culpa…!"*

Chapter Two:

I BELIEVE IN JESUS CHRIST, THE ONLY SON OF GOD

Vincenzo Battaglia

I. Didactic and Pedagogical Criteria

1. The Christological content of the Christian faith is confessed in the second part of the Apostles' Creed, in six articles, from the second to the seventh, whose formulation gathers the normative transmitted essentials pertaining to the mystery of Christ, from the deposit of faith "contained in Sacred Scripture and Tradition" which "the apostles entrusted [...] to the whole of the Church" (n. 84).

After the second article, centered on three major titles with which the Church confesses faith in Jesus of Nazareth and expresses his identity and his work of salvation: Christ, Only/Only-begotten Son of God, Lord; the four articles that follow, from the third to the sixth, set forth the absolutely decisive reference, in terms of revelation and salvation, to those "mysteries" of the life of Christ which are the historical foundation of the Christological titles treated in the second article. Those mysteries are: the incarnation—Christmas—bringing us to the divine and virginal maternity of Mary, which took place by the Holy Spirit (third article); the paschal mystery, which goes from the passion Jesus suffered in the time of the Roman procurator Pontius Pilate, to the resurrection, culminating in the ascension/exaltation to the right hand of the Father (fourth, fifth, and sixth articles). Finally, the seventh article looks to the event of the Parousia—the second coming of the Lord Jesus, his coming in glory—of which Easter is the anticipation, guarantee, and promise. The Parousia will seal the exercise of the universal and eschatological judgment; judgment that belongs by right to the Lordship of Christ, as Redeemer/Savior of all, and will involve the definitive fulfillment of salvation with the resurrection of the dead, an affirmation which is implicit in the fact that he "will come [...] to judge the living and the dead."

In this way the mystery of Jesus Christ, the Only-Begotten of the Father, Lord of the Church and Savior of the world, stands "at the center of catechesis" and evangelization (nn. 426–429). This statement is derived from certainty about the unicity and universality of Christ's revelatory and salvific mediation, exercised in the power of the Holy Spirit, according to God's plan. The necessity of Jesus Christ, imposed by God, now implies that the only valid and effective condition for obtaining salvation, equally imposed by God, is faith in Jesus of Nazareth, "the eternal Son of God made man" (n. 423).

2. Having taken note of this fundamental doctrinal principle, it is opportune to set forth a preliminary explanation about the inseparable unity between faith in God and faith in Jesus, to guide the faithful to an ever more exact comprehension of the fact that Christian doctrine about God is determined by Jesus Christ as its founder: we believe in God because of him, according to the revelation he carried out, and thanks to him. "The deepest truth about God and the salvation of man shines out for our sake in Christ, who is both the mediator and the fullness of all revelation" (*DV* 2). At the same time, we believe in Jesus Christ, convinced that faith in him is not different from faith in God in any way, as to its necessary and binding character, and the total involvement of the person.

The Apostle Paul testified "both to Jews and to Greeks of repentance to God and of faith in our Lord Jesus Christ" (Acts 20:21). We Christians indissolubly unite God and Jesus Christ, theo-logy and Christo-logy, in the certainty that, in Jesus Christ, God has revealed himself, and therefore, has made himself known to us, and has communicated himself to us in a definitive way in history, for the salvation of humanity. He revealed himself for who he really is, in his identity as God who is both one in substance and three in persons. In principle, Christian language about God is regulated and mediated by the event of Jesus Christ, made accessible in fullness by the Holy Spirit; it is a Christocentric and trinitarian language. Trinitarian monotheism is the essential and normative content of Christian faith about God: "The mystery of the Most Holy Trinity is the central mystery of Christian faith and life. [...] It is therefore the source of all the other mysteries of faith, the light that enlightens them" (n. 234): this also applies to the mystery of Jesus Christ, in the harmonious and inexhaustible reciprocity between the one and the other. Therefore, if contemplating the mystery of Christ immerses the believer seamlessly into the mystery of the Trinity, it is just as true that contemplating the latter leads the believer more and more to immerse himself in the mysterious depth of the Word incarnate, crucified, and risen.

3. A commitment and desire to advance in "the loving knowledge of Christ" (n. 429), therefore, cannot fail to accompany and corroborate catechetical and evangelizing activity, as we read in nn. 428 and 429. Taking up a word

of Pope Francis, it is helpful to emphasize that "The primary reason for evangelizing is the love of Jesus which we have received, the experience of salvation which urges us to ever greater love of him" (*EG* 264).

Progress in the loving knowledge of Christ is inscribed in the dynamic rapport between intellectual life and spiritual life, between study and contemplation, between knowledge and holiness, a rapport that leads to growth in real Christian wisdom, based on the harmonious and progressive interaction, which can never be exhausted, between intellectual activity and affective sensitivity. This approach thoroughly pervades the Christological part of the Apostles' Creed.

It is useful to specify here that the experience that one has of Jesus Christ is a type of global and complete knowledge, which implies that awareness/consciousness of faith in him involves both reason and will, knowledge and love: indeed faith involves full submission of the intellect and the will to God who reveals himself (cf. *DV* 5). It is with the entirety of his acts that the Christian lives communion with Christ under the guidance of the Holy Spirit and, thanks to this communion, lives the condition of being an adoptive son of God, belonging to the Church, and neighborly love. Into the foreground emerges the absolutely gratuitous initiative of the Lord Jesus, an initiative extended by virtue of his presence, offered in gift and intrinsically open to relationship. "From his fulness have we all received, grace upon grace" (Jn 1:16). Moreover, Christian experience cannot go without a permanent process of conversion, a growth toward holiness, whose fullness and fulfillment must be considered in an eschatological perspective. Now we can understand clearly in what sense the Holy Spirit acts to transform and shape Christians into the image of Christ Jesus crucified and risen; toward what aim he creates a new heart and a new spirit in them, and pours his gifts into them, making them partakers of holiness—and therefore of the "sentiments" and "way of life"—of their Lord. That Spirit of truth (Jn 16:13) is the authoritative interpreter, the trustworthy exegete of the mystery of Jesus Christ, who is the one trustworthy interpreter of the mystery of God the Father (cf. Jn 1:18). All of this happens through the joint mission of the Son and the Spirit, a mission that, once the glorification of the Son has come, "will be manifested in the children adopted by the Father in the Body of his Son: the mission of the Spirit of adoption is to unite them to Christ and make them live in him" (n. 690).

4. Finally, the thematic argument in this second part of the Apostles' Creed teaches us to give the right place and the right prominence to the story of Jesus of Nazareth in the construction of Christological language. It is treated according to a narrative method, following the progressive course proper to the gospel accounts, one which is characterized and pervaded by a balanced interaction between history and interpretation, between the historical hermeneutic and the hermeneutic of faith. This hermeneutic, typical of a

methodologically integrated and complete approach, guarantees theological reflection a rigorous, systematic knowledge of the saving truth, oriented toward education in the faith, according to the demands and the duties of permanent formation.

In this sense, the text of the *CCC* teaches us to attentively appreciate and, with a spirit of wisdom, learn to integrate all the gospel material related to what Jesus said and did during the days of his earthly life, culminating in his Pasch, and also to the events that compose his singular and unique history. In light of these considerations, we can better appreciate the fruitfulness of contemplative, prayerful reading of the Word of God, especially of the Gospels. Now the prayer of the Collect of the feast of the Apostle John proves very instructive: "O God, who through the blessed Apostle John have unlocked for us the secrets of your Word, grant, we pray, that we may grasp with proper understanding what he has so marvelously brought to our ears." The gift of a proper understanding of the Word of life is the result of a continual acceptance, born by "remaining" in the love that the Lord Jesus fosters for the Church, for each of his disciples, as we learn from the wonderful passage of the vine and the branches (cf. Jn 15:1–11). The invitation, the call addressed to disciples of all times, becomes concrete in the gift given to the Church, his Body and his Bride, of a real communion with him, fed day by day with his Word and the sacraments, with the Eucharist at its center, in which the sanctifying action of the Holy Spirit is at work, with the aim of rendering glory to the Father.

Chapter Two, Article 2:

AND IN JESUS CHRIST, HIS ONLY SON, OUR LORD

Vincenzo Battaglia

The second article of faith begins from the name and with the name Jesus, to whom are attributed the titles Christ, his (God's) only Son, our Lord. This means, above all: Jesus of Nazareth is at the origin and the foundation of the confession of faith, of the Christology of the New Testament, of every Christology of the New Testament. In this respect, the memory and narration of his history are present in the other Christological articles of the Apostles' Creed, flowing into the Passover and into Pentecost, and reaching out to the Parousia. A singular, unique, and unrepeatable history. Moreover, the expression "and in Jesus Christ" is already, in itself, a complete and authoritative confession of faith according to the New Testament tradition. That is inasmuch as the title Christ contains and comprehends both the identity of Jesus in relation to God (the Messiah of God, sent, attested, and confirmed by God "according to the Scriptures"), and his redemptive and salvific mission for the good of humanity and the whole creation (Messiah according to the plan of God, which is narrated by and in the history of salvation, "according to the Scriptures").

The aforementioned expression is the basis, the justification, of the two successive Christological titles of divine character, which make it specific—though always with a style that is both profession and narration at once—particularly stating his identity in relation to God: his only Son, the Only-begotten; and his saving function in relation to humanity and to the Church in particular: our Lord. Here the possessive adjective "our" states clearly that the subject confessing the faith is the Church; but it says with equal clarity that every single subject who confesses the faith carries out this act as a member of that Body in which only Jesus Christ, the only Son of God, is the Lord. Moreover, from the exposition constructed with a wise and continual reference to numerous biblical passages, gathered above all from the Gospels and other writings of the New Testament, it follows that the pedagogical purpose is that of teaching believers to confess the faith, making their own the formulas and the words handed on from the apostolic Tradition, based on the authority of Jesus and the Fathers.

The second Christological title is presented with a unique linguistic and doctrinal characteristic. It refers back to the first article of the Creed, by confessing the eternal intratrinitarian relations of the fatherhood of God in respect to Jesus Christ, and the sonship of Jesus Christ in regard to God the Father. This title contains a further specification of the fatherhood of God, because this fatherhood is expressed, is revealed in all of its truth in the relation with Jesus, who is the only Son of the only God. As such, as the Only-begotten of the Father, he is the Firstborn of a multitude of brethren. If it is justified to interpret the title in connection with the first article of the Creed, it is equally justified—and necessary—to interpret it in connection with the third article of the Creed: "He was conceived by the Holy Spirit and born of the Virgin Mary," which contains the confession of the event of the incarnation. Finally, the central position of this title—standing between the titles Christ and Lord—stands to bear witness also that the confession of the divine sonship of Jesus "will be the center of the apostolic faith, first professed by Peter as the Church's foundation" (n. 442).

The third Christological title teaches us to join the lordship of Jesus with the lordship and kingship of God: "the power, honor and glory due to God the Father are due also to Jesus" (n. 449), and the saving power that Jesus exercises as Lord is a power of the divine order, it comes to him from God, being his Only-begotten Son, he exercises it in communion with him and by his command, and therefore it has the very effectiveness of the power of God. Besides, the wording "our Lord" implies, first, the truth that only Jesus of Nazareth is the Lord recognized, confessed, adored and proclaimed by the Church. This is significant, as an example of the critical-prophetic witness that Christians must give in the face of the absolutist pretensions of every form of human and earthly power; it underscores that confessing the lordship of Jesus "has implicitly recognized that man should not submit his personal freedom in an absolute manner to any earthly power, but only to God the Father and the Lord Jesus Christ: Caesar is not 'the Lord'" (n. 450). Second, the fact that the kingdom of God has come, is coming, and will come definitively in and through Jesus Christ, by the power of the Holy Spirit, can be justified only on the basis of what is stated by the titles of Christ and only Son of God. The Father has entrusted, consigned all power in heaven and on earth to him (cf. Mt 28:18). What is confessed about the universal salvific lordship exercised by Jesus is further augmented and justified by the confession of his divine/filial identity, precisely by the fact that "After his Resurrection, Jesus' divine sonship becomes manifest in the power of his glorified humanity. He was 'designated Son of God in power according to the Spirit of holiness by his Resurrection from the dead' (Rom 1:4)" (n. 445).

Given this thematic direction, once again the unifying, anticipatory, and programmatic character of the second article of faith is firmly established with regard to the Christological articles that follow. The universal lordship of Jesus Christ as absolute mediator of the coming of the kingdom of God is founded, ultimately, on the incarnation and on the Pasch, on his exaltation to the right hand of God the Father almighty, on his second coming in glory, and on the certainty that "he will come to judge the living and the dead."

Finally, we note that the title "our Lord," read in the same hermeneutical direction, demands that we return to the statement of the omnipotence of God the Father, the object of the third paragraph of the first article of the Apostles' Creed (nn. 268–278). Jesus Christ, Only Son/Only-Begotten of God, and Lord "seated at the right hand of God the Father almighty." In the exercise of his lordship, he participates in the universal, loving, and mysterious omnipotence of God, (cf. n. 268). At the same time, because "faith in God the Father Almighty can be put to the test by the experience of evil and suffering" (n. 272), the Christocentric principle proves decisive again, as I explained earlier while illustrating the didactic and pedagogical principles. The fatherhood and the omnipotence of God—"his fatherly omnipotence" (n. 270)—do indeed bear a precise and definitive Christological imprint, inasmuch as "in the most mysterious way God the Father has revealed his almighty power in the voluntary humiliation and Resurrection of his Son, by which he conquered evil. Christ crucified is thus 'the power of God and the wisdom of God'" (n. 272).

With the reflection on the second article concluded, the doctrinal and spiritual significance of the name "Jesus," which in Hebrew means "God saves" (n. 430), and which is "at the heart of Christian prayer" (n. 435), stands out in its fullness. Indeed, attentively appreciating the doctrinal content of the three Christological titles in question and recognizing their interaction, we learn and contemplate with ever greater conviction that in Jesus and only in him, "God recapitulates all of his history of salvation on behalf of men" (n. 430). Christ Jesus is the cornerstone on which the Church is built, on which every Christian community stands firm: "built upon the foundation of the apostles and prophets, Christ Jesus himself being the cornerstone" (Eph 2:20).

Chapter Two, Article 3: "HE WAS CONCEIVED BY THE POWER OF THE HOLY SPIRIT AND BORN OF THE VIRGIN MARY"

Vincenzo Battaglia

The treatment of the third article of faith is very dense and it begins to take up the topic of the historical event of Jesus of Nazareth. The items of the *CCC* that relate to it have a notable pedagogical impact in this sense, inasmuch as they present a reading of the Gospels understood as theological biography of Jesus, and also due to their meaningful reference to the "mysteries" that characterize that event. The gospel accounts teach that the identity of Jesus is inseparable from the itinerary that reveals it in all its truth and fullness of grace.

The three paragraphs that compose the exposition provided for the third article contain, in a progressive form, teaching about the reason for the Incarnation and about the person, about the ontological constitution, of the Incarnate Word, true God and true man (par. 1); about the intervention of the Holy Spirit in the event of the Incarnation, considered from the perspective of the divine and virginal motherhood of Mary (par. 2); about the mysteries of the life of Christ from his infancy to his public life (par. 3).

I. The Son of God Became Man

The object of the first paragraph is notably important for formation: the treatment of the multiple salvific aspects of the mystery of the Incarnation. The response to the question of why God became man, a question that is always relevant and more so today than in the past, is summarized in four essential statements that make it possible to gather the multiple aspects of the soteriological narrative into a single square, as it were. First is reconciliation with God, which involves the redemptive purpose of the event of the Incarnation (n. 457). Then the revelation and gift of God's love, in its definitive form and unsurpassable measure (n. 458). Third there is the foundational reference to Jesus Christ as the model of holiness, inasmuch as the life of disciples requires commitment to following and imitating him, which leads to being conformed to him (n. 459). Finally, participation in the divine life, by grace, by virtue of the *admirabile commercium* (the marvelous exchange), a participation that is configured as participation in the divine sonship of the Only-Begotten Son of God, following his assumption of our human condition (n. 460).

So we are given an introduction that leads us to read, understand, and confess the mystery of Jesus Christ, giving due prominence to its importance and its soteriological effect, as follows initially from the phrase placed at its beginning: "for us men and for our salvation" (n. 456), taken from the Nicene-Constantinopolitan Creed, a phrase connected first of all with the mystery of the Incarnation.

In the formula "for us men and for our salvation" the preposition "for" (expressed in the original Greek text with *dià,* and in the Latin translation with *propter*) is found many times in the New Testament, and here in the conciliar text it basically means "for our benefit, for our sake, to realize our salvation." Less obvious and somewhat in a subordinate position, there is also a third meaning: "in our place." In reflecting on the reason for the Incarnation, the road to follow is to consider in a precise way the initiative which the Only-Begotten Son of God assumed, in communion with the Father, by the power of the Holy Spirit. But to be able to understand the motivation for it, to know its meaning and its purpose "for us men," we have no other criterion to adopt but that of the history of salvation, culminating in the event of Jesus Christ, whose saving mediation is universal and embraces all time: past, present, and future, reaching out to an eschatological perspective and a protological perspective. The book of Revelation pronounces this essential truth in lapidary form: "I am the Alpha and the Omega, the first and the last, the beginning and the end" (Rev 22:13; cf. 1:8; 21:6). The *CCC* teaches, in a pellucid expression, that "The Church calls 'Incarnation' the fact that the Son of God assumed a human nature in order to accomplish our salvation in it" (n. 461).

But, in order to avoid the risk of thinking about the mystery of Jesus Christ in only a functional manner—this happens when we do not take account fittingly of his divine/filial identity, or fail to join it with the fact of his eternal pre-existence in God as Word and Only-Begotten Son of the Father—in the continuation of the paragraph, the doctrinal exposition on faith "in the true Incarnation of the Son of God" is given the right prominence: it is "the distinctive sign of Christian faith" (n. 463). The exposition makes use of the authoritative and decisive contribution from the history of Christological dogma in the patristic era, especially from the dogmatic formulas of the first seven ecumenical Councils, which are mentioned with clear and summary explanations in the items that form part of paragraph 1 (cf. nn. 456–483).

In this first paragraph the *CCC* focuses attention above all on the heresies such as Apolliarianism, Nestorianism, and Monophysitism, which theorized an erroneous explanation of the event of the Incarnation in regard both to the ontological constitution of the Incarnate Word, in his condition as true God and true man, and also to the integrity and concreteness of the human nature (rational soul and body), the human condition assumed by the Son of God. As regards the definition of the divinity of Jesus made by the Council of Nicea, in contrast, it is given only a single numbered item (cf. n. 465). Given the numerous difficulties which many find in understanding and then accepting this truth, which is the central datum of the faith handed on by the Apostles, I think it is useful to propose a little more detailed explanation of the Nicene Creed, which was then the indispensable point of reference of the other Councils of the patristic age. In this way we will be able to appreciate further how much the *CCC* says in the preceding items on the title of Only Son/Only-Begotten of God.

The question confronted and resolved at Nicea, in response to the erroneous theses of the Arians, touched on two sides of doctrine: Christological and trinitarian. The Arians had an interpretation of the divinity of Jesus Christ and his relation with God that confused generation and creation; Nicea defined the difference between the two concepts. The concept of "created" is applied to the relation between the world (men) and God; "generated" is applied to the relation between Jesus Christ and God. The world comes from God by way of creation; Jesus Christ comes from God by way of generation: he is generated by the substance of the Father, the Fathers of Nicea say, teaching that the existence of the Son is necessary, unlike the creation of the world, as it exists by the will of God. From the combination of the two phrases "generated…from the substance of the Father" and "consubstantial with the Father" one reaches the understanding that coming from the Father by way of generation implies, for Jesus Christ, a perfect equality with him as being God, and therefore coeternal. The Son exists from eternity and necessarily exists, together with the Father and on par with him. In the last analysis, Nicea definitively clarifies that to express the personal identity of Jesus of Nazareth, one must confess that he is a divine person and, because of his eternal and unchangeable relation with God, he is the divine person whose name is Son and Word of God. Second, the creed attributes to the very same subject, the Only-Begotten Son of God, both his eternal procession from the Father and the Incarnation and the events that follow from it, until the Pasch and the Parousia.

The declaration of faith that the Son is truly God, that is, God as is the Father who generated him, imposes a radical turn in theological language: "true God" is now a common name for more than one person: the Father and the Son. While Arius had considered it unacceptable to think that God, the one eternal God, had communicated the divine substance, his being God, to another, to the Son, the Council of Nicea affirms the exact opposite, teaching that the Father and the Son have the same substance by the term *homoúsios* (of the same substance as the Father), without thereby eroding the monotheistic creed.

Then for clarifying the ontological constitution of the Incarnate Word, true God and true man, the story of the contribution of the Council of Chalcedon proves indispensable. One must consider the unity of Christ's person, in whom coexist two natures distinct but not separate. This is the "hypostatic union" as the Council of Ephesus declared. The union is an act carried out by the Word: it relates to and involves his person.

The Word is not transformed into flesh losing his own divine identity, nor is the flesh absorbed and thus altered or compromised by the Word. The Incarnation is not explained as though it were a fusion or mixing between the two natures. The distinction remains unchanged by which we can confess that Jesus Christ is true God and true man, and confess it because he is known to be so, by reason of the testimony offered in the gospel accounts and in the revelation made by Jesus Christ himself with his words and actions. Moreover, to speak of duality in Christ does not mean accepting the idea of two individuals, two subjects placed beside one another or joined to each other. With the Incarnation a real communication takes place between the Word and the human nature which he assumed: the Word transmits his own personal specificity to that human nature and takes on its identifying properties. It remains certain that "Christ's humanity has no other subject than the divine person of the Son of God, who assumed it and made it his own, from his conception" (n. 466). If, to the contrary, one were to insist on the error of maintaining an imperfect communion and communication between the Word and human nature, it would be inevitable to think of two subsistent subjects, with the result that there could be a separation, that is, a distance, so that union between the Word and the flesh animated by the rational soul could no longer be contained within the unity of the person. One single person, and precisely the Incarnate Word, is the subject of the words, the acts, and the event of Jesus of Nazareth.

In this sense, catechesis must favor an exact understanding of the human experience made by the Word of God, in whom all the characteristic elements are present: soul, knowledge, activity, will, corporeality. For the purposes of this commentary, it seems useful to place the emphasis especially on the human will of Christ, according to the doctrinal decree of the Third Council of Constantinople (681).

The statement that the human will of the Incarnate Word is perfectly submitted to his divine will belongs to the ontological side of the mystery of the hypostatic union, and thus amounts to saying that all the obediential acts placed by Jesus of Nazareth, who always made reference to the will and the love of the Father, are the salvation-historical translation, the concrete and visible revelation of his divine-filial identity and of his eternal communion of love and intention with the Father in the unity of the Holy Spirit.

Second, in specifying that his human will, although divinized, preserves its full autonomy and its specific way of being and acting, the Third Council of Constantinople invites us to reason about the harmonious correspondence between the salvific efficacy of the obedience of Jesus of Nazareth and the real participation, the necessary cooperation, required and due from the human nature assumed by the Word. In this context, it is good to recall that the divine will and the human will, as well as the two types of acts, do not stand on the same plane. In respect to the difference between the two properties and therefore with respect to the twofold principle "without confusion or mixing" (against Monophysitism) and "without division or separation" (against Nestorianism), we can understand that the salvific potential of the human nature is different from that of the divine nature, and the first would be nothing without the second.

Third, we are able to understand the truth of the incarnation and the full humanization of the Son of God better still, thanks to the continual recourse to the evangelical story of Jesus of Nazareth, especially to his passion and death on the Cross, the specific object of the fourth article of the Apostles' Creed, treated in suitable and deeper measure in the text of the *CCC*. In other words, only by fully respecting the authenticity of the human experience chosen and made by the incarnate Word of God is it possible to adequately take in the soteriological meaning of the divinization of the human creature as the aim and fulfillment of his humanization. Indeed, the human person is promoted in his dignity as a creature of God precisely because he is placed in the condition of cooperating, with full consent of the intellect and will, in his own salvation, receiving it freely as a gift that only God can realize and place at his disposition, through the Savior Jesus Christ and by the sanctifying grace of the Holy Spirit.

II. "Conceived by the Power of the Holy Spirit and Born of the Virgin Mary"

The language of faith about blessed Mary, Virgin and Mother of God, is a full-fledged part of the intellectual, spiritual and pastoral formation of the faithful.

The doctrinal content of this second paragraph is connected and completed with the doctrinal content of paragraph 6: "Mary, Mother, of Christ, Mother of the Church", which forms part of the ninth article of the Apostles' Creed: "I believe in one holy, catholic, and apostolic Church". The teaching on the person and the role of the blessed Virgin Mary in the history of salvation thus becomes organized in two sections, according to the structure presented in the title of Chapter Eight of *LG*: here the *CCC* speaks of the blessed Virgin Mary, Mother of God, in the mystery of Christ; in the other paragraph it speaks of her in the mystery of the Church. The doctrinal principle that guides the present paragraph is expressed well as follows: "What the Catholic faith believes about Mary is based on what it believes about Christ, and what it teaches about Mary illumines in turn its faith in Christ" (n. 487). Connected to this is another principle, deriving from the dogma of the divine and virginal maternity of Mary, which took place by the work of the Holy Spirit: "The mission of the Holy Spirit is always conjoined and ordered to that of the Son" (n. 485). This assertion constitutes an interpretive key of prime importance for everything concerning the fulfillment of the mystery of Jesus Christ, and at the same time, it offers the impulse and motive for deepening our reflection on the relation between Christology and pneumatology.

The language of faith about the blessed Virgin Mary has to be elaborated and set forth in a way that avoids all false exaggerations as well as undue reductionisms. It touches upon a rich heritage: the common sources of every essential truth of the Christian credo and every theological discipline. The Dogmatic Constitution on the Church *LG* expresses it with precision when it states, addressing theologians and preachers: "Following the study of Sacred Scripture, the Holy Fathers, the doctors and liturgy of the Church, and under the guidance of the Church's magisterium, let them rightly illustrate the duties and privileges of the Blessed Virgin which always look to Christ, the source of all truth, sanctity and piety" (*LG* 67).

Theological reflection and interventions of the Magisterium interact to an effective degree, as we can deduce, especially from the history of magisterial definitions about the four Marian dogmas, whose authoritative character calls for the adherence of faith. Three of them are mentioned with commentary in this second paragraph: the Immaculate Conception, the divine Maternity, and the Virginity. The fourth, the Assumption body and soul into heaven is the subject of commentary in the context of the ninth article (cf. n. 966). The first and fundamental dogma, to which the others are correlated, and on which they depend, is that of the divine and virginal maternity of Mary, based on the gospel texts of Mt 1:16,18–25 and Lk 1:26–38: she conceived the only-begotten Son of the Father as man, he who was filled with the Holy Spirit of God from his mother's womb. From this starting point, the text emphasizes the fact that the Incarnation is an event in which we contemplate, in a sublime relationship, the action of the Word of God who unites to himself the human nature received from his mother Mary, and the anointing of the Word performed by the Holy Spirit, according to the initiative of the Father who sends the Son and the Holy Spirit. As I indicated above, the act of becoming flesh by the Word, the Only-Begotten Son of God, is carried out by the Holy Spirit, through the work of the Holy Spirit along the whole arc of the Son's historical-earthly life that flows into the paschal event.

Continuing the treatment of this subject, the *CCC* teaches that the faith of the Church recognizes an intrinsic connection between the divine maternity of Mary and her virginity. Her virginity—before, during, and after the birth—has a primarily Christological meaning, related to the identity of Jesus as the only-begotten Son of God, but also Mariological meaning. The Mariological meaning makes plain the total self-giving and consecration of the handmaid of the Lord to the saving plan of the Trinity, as the favored daughter of the Father, the mother of the Son of God, the dwelling-place of the Holy Spirit (*LG* 53) and, consequently, to the person and work of the Son: that is, her self-giving and consecration that highlight her status as the woman "full of grace" and "all holy," her perfect obedience in faith to the will of God, her capacity for a radical oblative love, which she was able to put into action thanks to the Holy Spirit working in her; being the first person redeemed, and redeemed in a most sublime way, relative to other human beings, because she was preserved immune from original sin; the humble Handmaid of the Lord shows in herself all the effectiveness of the saving work realized by Christ Jesus, the most perfect Mediator and Redeemer/Savior. Moreover, by reason of the obedience evidenced in the story of the Annunciation, she is "the supreme model" of faith, for "only faith can embrace the mysterious ways of God's almighty power" (n. 273).

The *CCC*, incorporating the guidance of contemporary Mariology, which is also the fruit of a prolific harvest of scriptural truths about the role of the blessed Virgin Mary in salvation history, as the Second Vatican Council taught authoritatively, offers many suggestions for looking to the Virgin Mary as a model of Christian life. It does this by outlining the salient characteristics of the "pilgrimage of faith" (*LG* 58) she led as mother, faithful disciple, and generous cooperator of her Son: a pilgrimage that reached its decisive turning-point in the tragic and glorious hour of the Passion, when, suffering together with her Son, "in this singular way she cooperated by her obedience, faith, hope and burning charity in the work of the Savior in giving back supernatural life to souls. Wherefore she is our mother in the order of grace" (*LG* 61). That is how we interpret the observation found later in the context of the fourth article, when the Catechism, emphasizing that Christ wanted to associate his own sacrifice with the people who were its prime beneficiaries, that is, all the members of the Church, says that "this is achieved supremely in the case of his mother, who was associated more intimately than any other person in the mystery of his redemptive suffering" (n. 618).

The Virgin Mary's dependence on Christ Jesus is of such an order that it was set in place before time began. The Trinity decided from eternity to create and save the world by means of the Son/Word of God and in the Holy Spirit, and because of this, his predestination to the incarnation also involved the predestination of the woman who was to be "the virgin Mother of the Redeemer, and above all others and in a singular way the generous associate and humble handmaid of the Lord" (*LG* 61). This truth is fittingly placed in the commentary on the phrase "born of the Virgin Mary" (nn. 488–489). Mary of Nazareth was foreordained from eternity to be the first human person filled with grace: this grace coinciding with her vocation and mission as Mother of the Son of God, by the work of the Holy Spirit. "Hail, full of grace, the Lord is with you" (Lk 1:28). The theological meaning of the angel's greeting can be explored more deeply by recourse to what the prologue of John states about the Incarnate Word, full of grace and truth: "from his fulness we have all received, grace upon grace" (Jn 1:16). This affirmation applies in a unique way to her who gave birth to the author of life, the one perennial source of grace for all humanity, as a man (cf. LG 61). So the sending and the gift of the Son that took place in the fullness of time (cf. Gal 4:4), reveal the immeasurable love of God for humanity, while they also reveal the immeasurable love of God for Mary of Nazareth. The gift, the grace extended by God to Mary are the measure of his love for her who declared herself the lowly handmaid of the Most High (cf. Lk 1:38).

III. The Mysteries of the Life of Christ's Life

Setting aside a place for the mysteries of the life of Christ corresponds to a truly valid principle from the doctrinal point of view: although the Apostles' Creed only mentions two mysteries, the Incarnation and the Pasch, and it "says nothing explicitly about the mysteries of Jesus' hidden or public life," the articles about those two mysteries do "shed light on the whole of his earthly life" (n. 512). The qualifying word "whole" suggests that the Incarnation and the Pasch encompass the entire earthly course of Jesus' life with their revelatory and salvific effect; at the same time, they constitute the most coherent historical and theological inclusion from it. Therefore, if the light of the Pasch reverberates on the whole history of Jesus to make us contemplate what took place for God in the hiddenness and the silence of the virginal conception and birth of Jesus, at the same time, the light of the Incarnation reaches all the way to the fulfillment of Jesus' earthly history, making us understand that the Pasch contains the definitive answer about the reason for the Incarnation. Again, by virtue of the harmonious and progressive relationship between the Incarnation and the Pasch, we can understand that the humanity of Jesus "appeared as 'sacrament,' that is, the sign and instrument, of his divinity and of the salvation he brings: what was visible in his earthly life leads to the invisible mystery of his divine sonship and redemptive mission" (n. 515).

The formative program about the development of "all the richness of the mysteries of Jesus" (n. 513) must stress the traits they share, above all. The *CCC* names three of them, but reaffirming a concept I emphasized above, i.e., that these traits emerge from "Christ's whole earthly life". They are "revelation of the Father," "a mystery of redemption," "a mystery of recapitulation" (nn. 516–518). This insistence on the entirety of the life of Christ functions to make us recognize the revelatory/salvific character of every narrative fact contained in the gospels, which are also the result of a quite accurate selection from the tradition of and about Jesus, aimed at transmitting in narrative form everything that has authoritative power to lead us to faith in Jesus as Christ, Only/Only-Begotten Son of God and Lord. This criterion was enunciated by the author of the fourth Gospel: "Now Jesus did many other signs in the presence of the disciples, which are not written in this book; but these are written that you may believe that Jesus is the Christ, the Son of God, and that believing you may have life in his name" (Jn 20:30–31). Because of this, one really must not let any narrative detail of the Gospels fall to the side or be omitted through neglect or ignorance; in them everything is concentrated that one needs to know about Jesus, to believe in him. Truly, as the Catechism puts it incisively: "All Christ's riches 'are for every individual and are everybody's property'" (n. 519). So "Christ enables us *to live in him* all that he himself lived, and *he lives it in us*" (n. 521). The experiential perspective and basis regarding the life of Christ are outlined absolutely clearly.

Here, rather than to go into commentary on the various mysteries of the infancy, the hidden life, and the public life of Jesus, I think it suitable to outline some considerations of a general order.

The event of the Incarnation, culminating in the Pasch, guarantees the absolute, normative and eternal value of the life in the flesh assumed, once and for all, by the Only-Begotten of the Father. The Lord Jesus, wherever he found himself, before God, before the world, and before the Church, was there with his whole "mystery" which the Church commemorates, waiting for his coming in glory, celebrating and contemplating the "mysteries" of his life, of which she has been made a sharer by the Holy Spirit. I would like to observe that contact with the mysteries of the life of Christ—and with the grace proper to them—takes place in the time of the Church, especially through the liturgy and the cycle of the liturgical year. In particular, the Church "within the cycle of a year, [...] unfolds the whole mystery of Christ, from the Incarnation and birth until the Ascension, the day of Pentecost, and the expectation of blessed hope and of the coming of the Lord. Recalling thus the mysteries of redemption, the Church opens to the faithful the riches of her Lord's powers and merits, so that these are in some way made present for all time, and the faithful are enabled to lay hold upon them and become filled with saving grace" (*SC* 102).

With the cooperation of the Holy Spirit—who acts in the Church and in the world on behalf of Christ and on the basis of Christ—the Lord Jesus continually makes present and effective everything he said and did during the days of his earthly life, to lead humanity and the world toward the eschatological fullness of salvation already achieved once and for all, toward that final destination, that eschaton of history that coincides with his Parousia. He is "the First and the Last, and the Living One" (Rev 1:17; 1:8; 21:6) who gave the whole history of man its beginning, and will give its fulfillment, as the one perfect Mediator between God and men. History receives its definitive meaning from him: he alone is the Way, the Truth, and the Life (Jn 14:6). If he already realized the definitive beginning of the kingdom of God in history with his earthly mission leading into the Pasch, if he has acted to reveal the sovereignty and fatherhood of God, whose omnipotence is manifested above all in mercy and pardon, if he has wrought salvation by means of his *agápe* exercised in the Holy Spirit, this way of his, in relating to the world and humanity, is universally valid, and is valid unto eternity.

It is in this full theological context that both the normativity of discipleship and imitation to which Christians are called and also the grace of being conformed to the Lord Jesus, the high point of spiritual experience, enter and are understood: "In all of his life Jesus presents himself as our model" (n. 520). A conformity that is participation, in the Spirit, in the Jesus event, in his sentiments and his way of life, especially in his affectivity. The last is a sign and a concrete realization of how the Son of God entered into the human condition, and into such a close and definitive contact with the world, in order to take on the expressive gamut of human sensibilities borne from the body and in it. In that regard, we must give due prominence to the biopsychological, historical, and theological fact of the maternity of the Virgin Mary, and consequently to the thesis that the human sensibility of the Son of God also bears the imprint of the "flesh" of Mary, in the context of the affective relationship he lived at Nazareth with his mother and Joseph.

The affectivity, sensibility, prayer, sentiments, and way of life of the Lord Jesus are now definitively transfigured by the glory and the power of the Holy Spirit, which characterized the event of the resurrection and the exaltation to the Father's right hand. For this reason, Christians can experience them to the extent in which they become ever more the Body of the Lord Jesus—the Body which is the Church, filled with his Spirit—gradually being immersed into the totality of his "mystery," above all and first of all through the prayerful reading of the Word, the liturgy and the sacraments, with the Eucharist, the personal and communitarian prayer, at the center.

Chapter Two, Article 4:

"JESUS CHRIST SUFFERED UNDER PONTIUS PILATE, WAS CRUCIFIED, DIED, AND WAS BURIED"

Vincenzo Battaglia

The narrative of the mysteries of the life of Jesus, the object of the third paragraph of the third article, concludes with the messianic entrance into Jerusalem. Now in the fourth article of the Apostles' Creed, the narration continues with the account of the passion, following a subdivision in three phases: the relation of Jesus and Israel (par. 1); the death upon the cross (par. 2); the burial of Jesus (par. 3).

Taking into account that "God's saving plan was accomplished 'once for all' [Heb 9:26] by the redemptive death of his Son Jesus Christ" (n. 571), it is necessary to recognize that only an accurate and well documented historical study on the circumstances and therefore the causes of the death of Jesus, according to the gospel narratives and the contribution of other historical sources, supports and ensures a better understanding of the meaning of the Redemption (cf. n. 573). Because the relevance of such a detailed methodological approach is established, one will keep in mind that the *CCC* proceeds to elaborate the historical-theological narrative of the course Jesus travelled in the unfolding of his earthly mission, and does so on the basis of an integral hermeneutic that joins together history and faith, moving from the first opposition of his adversaries to his death on the cross and his burial. Appreciating as well as is possible the didactic and pedagogical resources found both here and in the part dedicated to the mysteries of the life of Christ, it is useful to sketch out a connection between the two parts, to grasp the continuity and progressive relation of the doctrinal teaching, especially in reference to the interior attitudes that characterize the way in which Jesus completed his messianic and salvific mission. Above all, I am referring to his obedience and his sacrificial-oblative love which led him to give everything he had and his whole self for the salvation of the world.

For example, recalling the temptations he faced and overcame in the desert, out of his obedience, with which he made reparation for our disobedience, the text says quite clearly that "Jesus is the new Adam who remained faithful just where the first Adam had given in to temptation. [...] Christ reveals himself as God's Servant, totally obedient to the divine will" (n. 539). Equally, considering the self-offering he made to the Father for our sins, it states that "By his obedience unto death, Jesus accomplished the substitution of the suffering Servant, who 'makes himself an offering for sin,' when 'he bore the sin of many', and who 'shall make many to be accounted righteous,' for 'he shall bear their iniquities'" (n. 615). Also, by virtue of his sacrificial-oblative love, the most concrete sign of Jesus' love for the Father, and the Father's love for humanity in need of redemption and salvation, it is fitting to draw attention to the proclamation of the kingdom of God as the center and aim of the mission Jesus carried out, a topic dealt with extensively in the context of the mysteries of his public life. In this way it is possible to emphasize both the fact that Jesus reveals the lordship/kingship of God in the form of divine fatherhood, full of mercy, compassion, and pardon for all, especially for the poor, the little, sinners, the marginalized, and persons stricken with various illnesses and sufferings, and the fact that "The kingdom of God will be definitively established through Christ's cross: 'God reigned from the wood'" *["Regnavit a ligno Deus"]* (n. 550). Truly "the mystery of the cross" is not only part of the saving plan of God and his universal salvific will, as the writings of the New Testament witness unanimously—in them, everything that happened to Jesus was "according to the Scriptures," especially his passion, death for our sins, and resurrection (e.g., cf. Lk 24:26–27,44–48; Acts 2:22–24; 1 Cor 15:3–5)—but, as a consequence, it is fully part of the construction of Christian language about the mystery of God.

Therefore having recourse to the many points of reflection that a continual and ever deeper reading of the *CCC* can suggest, we make room, foremost, for the theology of the consignment, of sacrificial-oblative love, giving due emphasis also to the presence and the intervention of the Holy Spirit. Given that the Father sent, consigned, and gave the only-begotten Son with an extreme act of love which makes known the cooperation enacted by the Holy Spirit, it follows that the gift of self, made by Jesus on the cross, not only happened in the Holy Spirit (cf. Heb 9:14), but constitutes the beginning of the consignment, the gift and the sending, of the Holy Spirit upon the newborn Church, to as many as believed in Christ Jesus (cf. Jn 19:28–37).

Second, the mystery of the cross, by force of its redeeming effect, leads us to believe firmly that God is and will remain faithful for ever to his saving plan centered on his loving and spousal covenant with humanity, in the Church and by means of the Church. God, who is absolutely free and gratuitous Love, is so faithful to himself and to humanity, created because it was loved from eternity, as to eliminate any obstacle that human beings have placed and still do place in the way of loving communion with him, first and foremost sin. Making use of the systematic contribution offered by the trinitarian theology of the Cross, which invites a reading of the story of the Crucified in a kenotic-agapic perspective—a perspective that can be easily found in the numbers of the *CCC* under discussion—there is well-founded and valid reason to attribute to the preexisting Son of God a disposition to become man not in an abstract way, removed from the real human condition, but in the only way able to put humanity and every human person in the position of knowing and receiving the Love that God Three-in-One cherishes for ever for his creatures. The way perfectly consonant with the wisdom, omnipotence, and goodness of God, and therefore, truly effective for human salvation, is the one revealed and transmitted in and by the story of the passion, in light of what is proclaimed in the first part of the hymn in the Letter to the Philippians (Phil 2:6–8). In the last analysis, we cannot fail to admit also that "from the first moment of his Incarnation the Son embraces the Father's plan of divine salvation" (n. 606), on the basis of what, e.g., the Letter to the Hebrews attests (Heb 10:5–10).

With regard to that last thesis, the following affirmation deserves attention, as it justifies the destination and thus the universal effectiveness of the redemptive sacrifice: "It is love 'to the end' that confers on Christ's sacrifice its value as redemption and reparation, as atonement and satisfaction. He knew and loved us all when he offered his life. [...] The existence in Christ of the divine person of the Son, who at once surpasses and embraces all human persons, and constitutes himself as the Head of all mankind, makes possible his redemptive sacrifice for all'" (n. 616). Based on this objective and fundamental truth, the observation about the relation between God and Israel, which was treated in par. 1, assumes a particular importance: "If the Law and the Jerusalem Temple could be occasions of opposition to Jesus by Israel's religious authorities, his role in the redemption of sins, the divine work par excellence, was the true stumbling-block for them" (n. 587). In the perspective of the interpretative synthesis outlined above, it becomes necessary to answer a crucial question: to speak completely, rigorously, of the event of the Incarnation, one cannot fail to appreciate as much as possible the inseparable relation between the fact that the Word, the Only-Begotten Son of God, became man, and his entering into a particular history that becomes part of universal history, and the history of first-century Palestine, with all the thickness of the multiple relationships he lived, starting with the affective-filial bond with his mother Mary and with Joseph.

Moreover, recognizing and appreciating the dramatic implication of his earthly life, marked by his condemnation to death and the torment he suffered on the scaffold of the cross, one cannot fail to acknowledge once again that a non-abstract theological discourse on the incarnation of the Son of God must incorporate the fact that for the only-begotten Son of God to become "flesh/man/body" meant also to enter into the most dramatic, the most distant from God, the darkest turns of human history and human freedom: to take account of man's sin, rejection, hostility, his death-wish; of those who condemned him as a "blasphemer" and "false messiah," as one who would be considered a dangerous, subversive person, guilty of *lese-majesté* toward Roman rule.

Here emerges the connection with several centuries of theology and spirituality of the kenosis of God in the person of Christ Jesus, come in the Holy Spirit. Christ Jesus "though he was in the form of God, did not count equality with God a thing to be grasped, but emptied himself, taking the form of a servant, being born in the likeness of men" (Phil 2:6–7). The Church will never cease to reason, in faith and according to the faith, on these few lines of a liturgical hymn that announce, in sober but most incisive form, an event that, by its paradoxical nature, will never cease to amaze and scandalize. Paraphrasing it, one can say that only Christ Jesus, being God himself, was in a position, was capable, to enter into the likeness of men. "Being found in human form he humbled himself and became obedient unto death, even death on a cross" (Phil 2:7–8). Entering into the likeness of men was not an end in itself: it was the way, the "place," the act of a saving solidarity that he willed, even to its extreme consequences, absolutely inclusive. He is the One who has wanted, and known how, to stand on behalf of each and all, excluding no one; to stand with the least of the least (cf. Mt 25:31–46). He wanted and knew how to immerse himself in the most dehumanized of human beings: dehumanized by suffering and sin; and wanted to take them upon himself, to heal and save. Bringing to fulfillment what was said by the prophet Isaiah in the fourth song of the servant of YHWH: "He took our infirmities and bore our diseases" (Mt 8:17; cf. Is 53:4). "He himself bore our sin in the body on the tree" (1 Pt 2:24; cf. Jn 1:29). Christ Jesus, the Lamb without spot or blemish who redeemed us at the price of his blood "was destined before the foundation of the world, but was made manifest at the end of the times for your sake" (1 Pt 1:19–20).

Chapter Two, Article 5: "HE DESCENDED INTO HELL; ON THE THIRD DAY HE ROSE AGAIN"

Vincenzo Battaglia

Descent and ascent, abasement and exaltation: in the fifth article the Apostles' Creed takes up and reflects a Christological model in two stages, in which the universal extension of Christ's victory over sin and death, in time and in space, is highlighted. If Jesus "like all men, experienced death and in his soul joined the others in the realm of the dead" (n. 632)—the *CCC* proposes the traditional definition of death as the separation of soul from body—it is equally true that by his experiencing it, his sojourn in the world of the dead, he was able "to free the just who had gone before him" (n. 633). This affirmation is based on the truth that "the divine person of the Son of God necessarily continued to possess his human soul and body, separated from each other by death" (this is stated in regard to the burial of Jesus in the mystery of Holy Saturday: n. 626). It belongs to God to give life and to defeat death, freeing man from death: thus the wise connection made by the fifth article of the Apostles' Creed highlights the whole function of Christ as author of life, who exercises his own power over death and over the underworld. And not only that:"By his Resurrection, he opens for us the way to a new life" (n. 654), open to that definitiveness which coincides with our future resurrection, of which he is the "principle and source" (n. 655), precisely because in his risen body, by the power of his new state of being glorified/exalted by God, he passed to another life, the life filled with glory, proper to God, "beyond time and space" (n. 646). Lord and Ruler of time and space, he exercises his own power as God, the power to give life, in the first creation as in the new creation.

In light of these preliminary details, the explanation enters into the merits of numerous aspects of a systematic discourse on the resurrection of Christ, received as the culminating and central truth of faith in him (cf. n. 638).

The event of the resurrection of Jesus from the dead and his exaltation to the right hand of the Father by the power of the Holy Spirit uncovers and definitively confirms the truth inherent in his mission, in his words and works, and in all his conduct. There is a long-running continuity between the pre-paschal phase and the post-paschal phase of the events surrounding Jesus; at the same time, there is also a discontinuity, a difference, inasmuch as the first phase is perfected and brought to fulfillment, to the eschatological fullness of the event of the resurrection, which confers on Jesus crucified a new condition in contrast to his earthly condition. The language of the New Testament authors is as essential as it is precise in this regard, through its use of concepts set in relation to one another: humiliation, abasement, weakness, and exaltation, glorification, power.

The faith of the Church confesses that, with the power of the Holy Spirit, God has definitively confirmed and convalidated the person and the mission of Jesus of Nazareth "crucified under Pontius Pilate." His resurrection, hence, has a unique and eschatological character. It is the event in which God has wrought what Israel awaited and hoped for the end of time: the resurrection of the dead. God has realized it in this world and in this history for Jesus of Nazareth, and through him and in him, for humanity and the world, in the way described by the New Testament authors and attested by the faith and the experience of the Church. Testimony that is condensed into the confession of faith regarding the unicity and salvific universality of Jesus, established by God as Lord and Christ (cf. Acts 2:36). Consequently, the resurrection-exaltation of Jesus Crucified is and involves the definitive turning point of time and of history. The risen Lord constitutes and is the beginning of humanity renewed and of the new creation, freed from the corruptions of sin and death and set out toward final perfection: he, "the Lord of glory" (1 Cor 2:8), is the first-fruits, the first-born of those who rise from the dead (cf 1 Cor 15:20–23); Col 1:18; Rev 1:5). Therefore, the Church, trusting and vigilant, awaits the Parousia, the coming in glory, when he will bring the kingdom of God to fulfillment (1 Cor 15:24–28).

Within this broad horizon of meaning, is it very necessary to propose a rigorous evaluation of the relationship between the "signs" that led the New Testament authors to bear witness to the truth of the apostolic faith they confessed about the resurrection of Jesus: the discovery of the tomb found open and empty; the appearances of Jesus; the vitality and the evangelizing work of the Christian community. Logically, the turning-point is established by the appearances of Jesus. The authors of the New Testament are in agreement in affirming that it was the same Jesus of Nazareth who had appeared, who was seen "living" by the disciples after his death (cf. Acts 1:3; Jn 20:19–20; 1 Cor 15:5–8). Therefore, in the words pronounced by the Eleven and by the others who were with them: "The Lord has risen indeed, and has appeared to Simon" (Lk 24:34), we have the transcription of a traditional formula of faith which can also be found in the Pauline epistles. Constructed by the linking of two verbs in the past tense ("he has risen"—"he has appeared"), to which the adverb "indeed" is affixed, it explicitly affirms that the encounter with the risen Jesus was real. Moreover, the accounts of the appearances are constructed according to a structure that foresees three converging facts: the free and gratuitous initiative taken by Jesus that, in this way, reunites the disciples around him and leads them to full and definitive faith in him; the recognition of Jesus on the part of the disciples, which is brought forth and enabled by the Lord through gestures familiar to them and by his Word; the conferral of the mission to announce the Gospel to all peoples.

The experience of the appearances of Jesus leads to giving the right explanation for the fact that the tomb was found open and empty, and thanks to this experience the disciples are now in a position to grasp, to accept, to believe that Jesus, already during his earthly life, was, albeit in concealed and hidden form, the Christ, the Son of God, the Lord. Thus they are now ready to carry out the universal mission entrusted to them by Jesus. This mission constitutes the outflowing and the purpose of the call to discipleship they had received in the days of his earthly life.

For all these reasons, as follow from nn. 639–647 of the *CCC*, the Resurrection is classified as an objective fact that really took place within the history of the world and that maintains a permanent connection with this history and, at the same time, as a transcendent event that surpasses history, inasmuch as it is only made accessible in faith and thanks to the initiative of the Lord who shows himself only to the disciples and to those who are called by him to be his witnesses in the world, unto the ends of the earth.

Chapter Two, Article 6: "HE ASCENDED INTO HEAVEN AND IS SEATED AT THE RIGHT HAND OF THE FATHER"

Vincenzo Battaglia

The sixth article of the Apostles' Creed, in a lapidary phrase, states what happened to Jesus crucified following his resurrection from the dead: the intervention of God in his favor has included his elevation/exaltation to the right hand of God. This is the fact that, more than any other, lends itself to understanding and confessing the divinity and lordship of Jesus, in all their integrity as true doctrine. Given that the risen Jesus occupies that position at the right hand of God (among the many related passages in which it appears: Ps 110:1, cf. Mk 16:19; Acts 2:33–34; 5:31; 7:55–56; Rom 8:34; 1 Cor 15:25; Col 3:1; Eph 1:20; Heb 1:3–4, 13), it all amounts to saying, interpreting the symbolic/local language in an ontological and functional sense, that he has been confirmed by God in his identity as only-begotten Son and fully shares his glory. In regard to this, the *CCC* makes note that there is "a difference in manifestation between the glory of the risen Christ and that of Christ exalted to the Father's right hand" (n. 660). Being equal to God, he can stand beside him, that is, can live perfect and eternal communion with him in the unity of the Holy Spirit; moreover, he receives from the Father the task and the power to share his salvific lordship and to exercise it for the good of humanity and the world, forever. Indeed God has exalted him in an eminent and unique way (highly exalted him: Phil 2:9). Consequently, he conferred on him "the name which is above every name," that is, his own divine name of Lord, by which all creatures are subject to him and all peoples, "every language," must give him honor, proclaiming him Lord "to the glory of God the Father" (Phil 2:9–11; cf. Eph 1:20,21).

In this regard, the language of ascension, which is undoubtedly more recent than that of exaltation, affirms the idea that the Risen One was assumed, raised (by God) into heaven (cf., for example, Acts 1:2,11, 22) and sits forever at his right hand (cf., for example, Mk 16:19), but also adds information on a very important fact: at a certain point no more appearances are confirmed. The Lord Jesus, however, is not absent! He has not distanced or separated himself from the world. From now on his presence will be experienced only through the signs he produced with the power of the Holy Spirit, signs that stand to attest that he is working effectively for the salvation of the world; the fact that he, in heaven, "permanently exercises his priesthood" for our benefit (n. 662). The sign *par excellence* is the Church: the Church is his Body (cf. Rm 12:5; 1 Cor 6:15; 12:27; Col 1:24; Eph 1:23; 4:12; 5:30), of which he is the Head (cf. Eph 1:22; 4:15–16; Col 1:18; 2:19); the Church is his Bride (cf. 2 Cor 11:2; Eph 5:21–33; Rev 19:7–9; 21: 2,9; 22:17). Indeed with the Ascension begins the time of the Church, "the Messiah's kingdom" (n. 664), of which the Church is truly the beginning, seed, and instrument (cf. n. 669). In the sphere of the Church, the other signs take shape: the Word, the sacraments, above all the eucharist, which feed evangelization, testimony, contemplation, and action. As "high priest of the good things that have come" (Heb 9:11), the Lord Jesus "is the center and the principal actor of the liturgy that honors the Father in heaven" (n. 662).

Exalted and glorified by God, ascended to his right hand, the Lord Jesus is also in the position of living a new relationship with humanity and the whole creation. Indeed, by virtue of his risen corporeality, spirit-filled and glorious, he is absolutely free not only to communicate with humanity and with the cosmos, but also to share his Spirit with humanity and the cosmos and, through the Spirit, to communicate his new and glorious life. He, no longer subject to space and time as in the days of his earthly life, is now the Lord of space and time who wills to give himself and give his saving love to all, to lead all creation, whose Mediator he is, to the fullness and perfection inscribed in it by God from the beginning. This kind of conclusion allows us to better appreciate the central truth of communitarian and final eschatology: the resurrection of the dead is understood as the extension of the resurrection of the Lord to those who belong to him. "And so we shall always be with the Lord" (1 Thess 4:17).

Chapter Two, Article 7: "FROM THENCE HE WILL COME AGAIN TO JUDGE THE LIVING AND THE DEAD"

Vincenzo Battaglia

The closing part of the commentary on the sixth article of the Apostles' Creed preceded and prepared the way for the commentary on the seventh article. The *CCC*'s exposition begins in this case with, among other things, a well-timed connection to the mystery of the Ascension; and it closes this introduction by opening its gaze on the role of Lord Jesus as the future of history and its recapitulator: "In him human history and indeed all creation are 'set forth' [Latin: '*inveniunt recapitulationem*', find recapitulation] and transcendently fulfilled" (n. 668). Because of this, the truth that the Lord Jesus "will come again in glory," our faith in his Parousia with its salvific consequences which will involve the resurrection of the dead, the final/universal judgment, the definitive establishment of the new creation; these contain the ultimate answer about the reason for the Incarnation. But, at the same time, only the realism of the Incarnation guarantees the realism of the Parousia: the one event and the other are tied together by the paschal mystery, which is the center of salvation history.

The features of eschatological discourse taken up in this last article of the Christological section of the Apostles' Creed serve principally to give a foundation and support to Christian hope, which is marked by vigilance and waiting: the vigilance and waiting that run through the life of the historical Church, committed to face the struggle against the unleashing of evil and against any falsification of the future Kingdom, "especially the 'intrinsically perverse' political form of a secular messianism" (n. 676). Fittingly, it continues: "The Church will enter the glory of the kingdom only through this final Passover, when she will follow her Lord in his death and Resurrection." Hence there are no triumphalisms on which to build illusions. The Kingdom will be fulfilled "by God's victory over the final unleashing of evil, which will cause his Bride to come down from heaven" (n. 677).

"His Bride." Sacred Scripture has the book of Revelation as its seal and stamp: its last prophetic pages proclaim the eschatological wedding of the sacrificed and glorified Lamb with the Church and the humanity of whom he is the Lord and Savior, but also the Judge. "Christ is Lord of eternal life. Full right to pass definitive judgment on the works and hearts of men belongs to him as redeemer of the world" (n. 679). "The Spirit and the Bible say, 'Come.' And let him who hears say, 'Come.' [...] He who testifies to these things says, 'Surely I am coming soon.' Amen. Come, Lord Jesus" (Rev 22: 17, 20). "Our Lord, come!" (Greek: *Maranatha*) (1 Cor 16:22). "The voice of my beloved! Behold, he comes..." (Song 2:8). Brought near by love infused and fed by the Holy Spirit, by the love that makes room for his welcome and enflames desire, the Church is committed to remain ever watchful and faithful, so as to find herself ready when the Lord Jesus will come to bring her "into his chambers" (cf. Sg 1:4), to celebrate with her the feast of the eschatological wedding (cf. Mt 25:10), that she may enjoy in eternity the joy and delights of his love that will never pale. One can say that the last prophetic word—the word that will be fulfilled in the fullness of an eternal life and a beatitude without end—will be the word the Bridegroom of the Church will say to his bride, and to every person that belongs to him as a member of his Body: "Arise, my love, [...] my fair one, and come away; [...] I will espouse you for ever [...] and you shall know the Lord" (Song 2:10; Hos 2:21–22). Then, it will be given to the beloved bride to experience perfectly the truth inherent in the words which the beloved addresses to her lover at the beginning of the Song of Songs: "Rightly do they love you" (Song 1:4).

A love that is educated by spousal sensibility disposes one to accept the risks, the fatigue, the martyrdom coming from the choice to share the Church's mission, placed at the service of the saving mission carried out by the Lord Jesus. In the life of the Church who is Bride, one learns to share everything of the Lord. Love, therefore, gradually produces the courageous acceptance to live in history, to be in solidarity with brothers and sisters who suffer and hope, to confront the great, at times unequal, challenges posed both by the rapid and profound transformations under which contemporary society labors, and also by the worrisome spread of violence and the decline of values. For any Christian who wants to live the vocation of a member of the Church, the Bride of the sacrificed and victorious Lamb, he must be convinced that the key to completely interpret Christ's life according to the criterion of sacrificial/oblative love always corresponds to two radical demands contained in the Gospel. The first is this: "If any man would come after me, let him deny himself and take up his cross and follow me. For whoever would save his life will lose it, and whoever loses his life for my sake will find it" (Mt 16:24). The other points to the rule contained in the parable of the universal judgment: "Truly I say to you, as you did it to one of the least of my brethren, you did it to me" (Mt 25:40).

Chapter Three, Article 8:

"I BELIEVE IN THE HOLY SPIRIT"

Giulio Maspero

Introduction (nn. 687–688)

The first point of the eighth article, in this third part, presents the Holy Spirit right away in relation to the Father and the Son: one might say "between" the Father and the Son. Two images that Tradition has identified for approaching this mystery are air and love. The Spirit is like the air in which the Father pronounces his word, or like the love in which he generates his own Son and in which he is loved by him in return. We do not see air, but without it there is no life, and good air is good for our health. Likewise, love is not seen or touched, but its existence is very real and essential.

This seeks to explain first of all that the mystery of God is not simply gnoseological, not just a matter of information, as in a crossword puzzle, where the solution exists and only the limits of the knower impede access to it. In contrast, precisely through the Holy Spirit one discovers that the mystery of God is ontological, in the sense that it cannot be comprehended, due to the infinite nature of the known object itself, as is the case analogously for us with the immensity and depth of the sea.

This is also the doctrine of the saints, who defined the third Person as "the Great Unknown" (J. Escrivá de Balaguer, *Christ is passing by*, New York: Scepter, 1974, nn. 127–138) or who highlighted the difficulty in speaking of him because when speaking of love we experience a true poverty of words (Thomas Aquinas, *Summa Theologiae,* I, q. 37). Thus to express human love we make use of art, for example, poetry and song. Love indeed is always a mystery, so much so that the love of God, that is, the love of the Father and the Son, must be mystery *par excellence* (J. Ratzinger, *Introduzione al cristianesimo,* Queriniana, Brescia 2005, 121). The question of why two persons love one another is indeed mysterious: to answer "because this person is rich" or "is beautiful" does not hold up. The only reason is that one loves the other because the person is who she is; because she is herself.

Now we can understand the decision to begin by quoting 1 Cor 2:11, which states that only the Spirit of God knows the secrets of God (n. 687). There is an analogy here to the human being, whose intimate depth and whose heart cannot be grasped "from the outside," but only "from within." So the Spirit never speaks of himself, but is like the light passing through stained glass to reveal the face of Christ; or like the gold of icons. The third Person, as Person-Communion and Person-Relation who unites the first two, as Person-Love and Person-Gift (John Paul II, *DeV* 10), does not draw attention to himself, because his personal characteristic itself is to be Love which unites the other two Persons. This hiding, which in n. 687 is called "properly divine self-effacement," reveals his distinctive characteristic as a divine Person.

This also helps us understand why the Spirit cannot be known through unaided reason or a philosophical process carried out alone. In contrast, it is in the communion of the Church and in history that one can recognize his presence and enter into relation with him. So the list in n. 688 presents "places" where we meet the third Person: Scripture, the living Tradition of the Church, in particular the Fathers, the Magisterium, and the sacramental liturgy, prayer and charisms, apostolic and missionary life, the testimony of the Saints. Indeed the Spirit who is communion between the Father and the Son is known in communion; the Spirit who is the life of the Father and the Son is known in life. Thus communion and life are two privileged keys for reading the *CCC* in its presentation on the pneumatological article of the Creed.

I. The Joint Mission of the Son and the Spirit

This reference to the identity of the third Person as communion of the Father and the Son seems to acquire a structural role in the organization of this article of the *CCC*. In fact, communion and relation bespeak union and distinction at the same time. Now, tracing back from the history of salvation, which n. 688 indicates as the one way of access to knowledge of the Spirit, to the intimate depth of the triune God; that is, in tracing back from his action to his immanence, the dimension that pertains to his eternal being, one confirms that the third Person is one single thing with the first two, the one substance or nature that simply and absolutely is, as the fontal fullness of Being itself. Yet at the same time, the distinction of persons is also recognized in this passage. So in the New Testament there are many expressions in which the Spirit is the subject of personal verbs, until he is mentioned by Jesus himself as "another Paraclete," another Consoler whom the Father sends to the world in the name of the Son to recall and make present in history the Word who became flesh once and for all (cf. Jn 16:12–14).

So the line of thought that developed especially in 20th-century theology, thanks to the rediscovery of Scripture, of the liturgy and the Fathers, and taken up in the general approach of Vatican II—that the life of the Church is founded on the trinitarian missions, which are in turn rooted in the eternal processions—flows together in n. 689. The unity of the people of God gushes from the Trinity, because its life is that of the Trinity (*LG* 4). From the divine action, which technically is defined as "economia," we can trace back to "immanence," that is, to that eternal dimension of God consisting of personal distinction in perfect unity of the one nature (cf. *CCC* 236).

God, obviously, continues to be a mystery, but the action of God truly reveals his Being, because in the divine missions the very Trinity shares itself with man in its personal depth, establishing real relations, between its own immanence and that of the human person. With the trinitarian revelation, through Scripture, the liturgy, the charisms, etc., that is, through the "places" seen in n. 688, we can truly speak the word "you" to each of the divine Persons.

This approach leads, then, to a unitary and relational reading of the two missions of the Son and the Spirit, which points to a corresponding conception of the relation of the two eternal processions in the divine immanence. Based on Jn 16, in fact, the missions of the second and the third Person can be considered as a single "joint mission." In the Incarnation the Spirit covers Mary with his shadow (Lk 1:35) and Jesus pours out his Spirit upon the disciples. To distinguish a priority in time or degree between the one mission and the other would be mistaken. Hence the two missions are distinct but inseparable, as in communion and relation themselves. And this can be traced back to the relation of the two processions in God: of distinction without separation and union without confusion.

In the history of theology this has been a critical point, because existentially and historically it is easier for man to perceive and thus to speak of the mission of the Word, inasmuch as He became flesh. Because of this at times the tendency has been felt to conceive of the second procession as separate from and secondary to the first. It can seem an abstract question, but the consequences of this different approach are extremely relevant at the anthropological and ecclesiological level. If the two processions are conceived as independent and relationally unconnected with one another, then the missions of the Son and the Spirit can be considered as unconnected. The action of the second Person in history would be translated into a visible and institutional dimension, while the presence of the third Person would indicate the primacy of what is invisible, spiritual, and charismatic. This way would create room for a dialectical interpretation of the two missions, which contradicts the scriptural data.

Analogously, at the level of anthropology, the separation of the procession of the divine Word, which in the created human image corresponds to thought, from the procession of the Holy Spirit, could lead to the terrible misunderstanding of opposing intellect and love. Rather, for St. Thomas, the second Person of the Trinity is not just any utterance of the Father, but is the Word who breathes Love (*Summa Theologiae,* I, 43, 5, ad 2). And also at the human level, one cannot really know without loving; that is, one cannot enter into a real relation with the other, nor can one will good for someone, without seeking to know what the good is.

The intimate bond between the two missions was already highlighted at the magisterial level by St. John Paul II, in *DeV* n. 7, but at n. 690 of the *CCC* it reaches a particularly effective formulation and synthesis, introducing the definition of "joint mission of the Son and the Spirit."

This expression is a particularly felicitous one and, it seems, can be considered a genuine key for reading the pneumatological doctrine offered in this article of the *CCC.* In fact the formula of joint mission and references to the reality it indicates return several times in the items we are commenting upon (e.g., nn. 702, 721, 727, and 737) until the final summary, where it is explicitly used again at n. 743.

The patristic inspiration for this interpretive dynamic is uncovered in n. 690, which presents a particularly effective quotation from Gregory of Nyssa. In the last quarter of the fourth century an intense confrontation arose with the Pneumatomachians or Macedonians, who recognized the divinity of the Son but denied that of the third Person, based on the principle, derived from a literalist concept of exegesis, that in sacred Scripture it is not stated that the Spirit took part in creating anything. Hence they, being opposed to the Arians, who also denied the divinity of the Son based on Jn 1:3, which states that everything was created by means of him, stated that the third Person, if he was not Creator, must be a creature. In this context the formulation of orthodox trinitarian doctrine necessarily had to tend to present the processions of the Son and the Spirit as distinct, but at the same time inseparable.

It is this which leads Gregory of Nyssa to take for his starting point the meaning of the term "Christ," which refers to being anointed. This name would therefore point immediately to the Holy Spirit who is unction, so as to exclude any possibility of drawing near to the second Person without entering into relation with the third also, just as one cannot touch an anointed body without coming into contact with the oil, and thus becoming anointed oneself (Gregory of Nyssa, *Adversus Macedonianos,* 16). The style is typical of the Cappadocian Fathers, who love to illustrate Johannine theology through physical metaphors. Thus the interplay of the Son and the Spirit is reread in a relational key, in such a way that everything in the Incarnation is presented on the basis of the fullness of the Holy Spirit, and in turn the Spirit is fruit of the fulfillment of the paschal mystery, when the Son shares his glory, i.e., his Spirit, to those who believe in him.

In this way, the action of the third Person in salvation history is presented precisely as coming from his personal identity in relation to the Son. In fact he makes the baptized sons in the Son, imparting to them salvation, that is, participation in the eternal life that gushes from the bosom of the Father.

II. The Name, Titles, and Symbols of the Holy Spirit

From what has been said, the very possibility of referring to the Holy Spirit with a name or with images depends precisely on the joint mission. For this reason, the name, the titles, and the symbols that are related to the third Person recall communion, relation with the Son and the diverse manifestations of the Spirit in the history of salvation.

So the name proper to the third Person, which Christ indicated in the great commission presented at the end of the Gospel of Matthew (Mt 28:19), is "Holy Spirit," that is the combination of two names that can be attributed to God *per se* and thus to each of the divine Persons. Augustine notes that, precisely because the third Person is communion or the *caritas* of the Father and the Son, it is logical that his name should be a form of union of terms that also correspond to the other two divine Persons (Augustine, *De Trinitate*, VI, 5, 7).

To grasp the full significance of this name, it is essential to consider the Hebrew meaning of the term to which it points: *Ruah* not only refers to the intelligible or intellectual dimension, which was typical of Greek metaphysics, but first of all refers to the force of the wind, the power of life (n. 691). The Christian pneumatological reflection must therefore purify this name and invest it with new meaning, at the same time recognizing the Spirit's immateriality and power of giving, preserving, and transforming material life. This means that real force or power is not a question of solitude, that is, a dialectical possibility of surpassing others, but communion, the capacity to unite others and bring them into relationship.

Therefore one can understand why the titles of the Holy Spirit make reference to the Son, starting with "Paraclete," a term explicitly attributed both to the second and to the third Person. He is the Consoler who consoles by uniting to Christ, who in turn is the Consoler because he leads to the Father, the source of life, of every life (n. 692). In the same way the Spirit promised is the Spirit of glory, that is, the Spirit of Christ and the Spirit of the Lord (n. 693).

The way all the symbolism of the Spirit refers to salvation history also corresponds to this dimension of communion, which recalls the joint mission. "Water" is listed as the first symbol of the third person by direct reference to baptism: as in nature human birth takes place in water, so the water of baptism communicates supernatural life. This line of interpretation unites the rock from which water gushes in the desert to the water and blood that flow from the ribs of Christ, and, in passing, the water that springs up for eternal life in the encounter with the Samaritan woman.

If the first symbol points to baptism, the second alludes to the sacrament of confirmation. The Spirit, as we have already seen, is tied to "unction" and thus to the very name of Christ. Here too the line of interpretation connects back with the Old Testament, with the anointing of David. The full and definitive communication of the anointing of the Spirit takes place, however, only with the Incarnation, when Mary conceives Christ, that is, the Anointed One, by the work of the Holy Spirit. From this moment the presence of the third Person, as it were, exploded into history through the humanity of Jesus. Wherever he passes or is brought, as in the Visitation and the Presentation in the Temple, the Spirit is poured out on those who enter into relation with Mary and the Infant, as happens with Elizabeth and Simeon. In this way holiness passes through the flesh and the physical presence of Christ, until the extreme of the resurrection, where the Spirit acts even in the sepulcher and on the dead body of our Lord, raising him. From here, it is as though the third Person overflowed from the crucified-and-risen Christ upon all, to sanctify men, rendering them one single body with their Redeemer, so as to form the *Christus totus* (Augustine, *In Epistolam Ioannis,* I, 2).

Beyond the water and the unction, a third element that indicates the Spirit in biblical symbolism is "fire." Here the meaning connected with power, including the Hebrew *Ruah*, is in the foreground. Indeed the Spirit transforms what he touches into himself, because uniting man to the Son brings him into the bosom of the Father; that is, divinizes the created person. He is transforming energy that reveals himself in the Old Testament through the fire that ascends to heaven or the fiery words of the prophets, such as Elijah. In the New Testament he begins to be presented in his personal individuality through the figure of the Baptist who announces the baptism in the Holy Spirit and fire (Lk 1:17). Jesus himself defines his own mission as having come to bring fire upon the earth (Lk 12:49). One sees how, in the interweaving of the various symbols, the missions of the Son and the Spirit cannot be separated, but continually invoke one another.

This is also evident for the further symbol of the "shining cloud." It is present from the Exodus through the desert, in the form of the presence of the Most High, to his people in flight from Egypt to the promised land and in the encounter of Moses with God on Mount Sinai. Therefore one can say that it is the symbol *par excellence* of the presence of God in the Old Testament, presented again in the New Testament at the moment of the greatest trinitarian theophanies, in the baptism of Jesus at the Jordan and in the Transfiguration. Here the unity of its meaning with the Law and the Prophets is explicitly shown in Christ's dialogue with Moses and Elijah.

Then, in the New Testament, from the Annunciation until the Ascension of Jesus into Heaven, the cloud accompanies the humanity of Christ in the most significant moments, as if to indicate the dimension of that ontological mystery of which we spoke above. The knowledge of God in his trinitarian depth, indeed, cannot be obtained only through the light of the intellect, but always requires the veil of the flesh assumed by the Son with the power of the Spirit in the Incarnation. The Greek Fathers such as Gregory of Nyssa, cited above, affirm that God in his transcendence and infinity is like the sun that cannot be viewed directly by the creature; this means that man could not have known him if not through the missions of the second and the third Person, that is, in the flesh and the life of Jesus. This statement of the impossibility of knowing God, one and three, except through his body and his history is so radical that the Cappadocian Father reaches the point of saying that even the angels can know the Trinity only through the humanity of Christ and hence through the Church (Gregory of Nyssa, *In Canticum Canticorum,* 8).

Because of this, there is no need to be surprised at the materiality of the last four symbols listed in these items of the *CCC.* The "seal," in John and in the Pauline writings, is a figure semantically close to anointing, and expresses the definitive state of anointing more explicitly, in such a way as to offer itself as the principal point of symbolic reference for affirming the indelible character of baptism, of confirmation, and orders (n. 698). The "hand" is thus also a symbol of the third Person, as follows from the gestures of Jesus who cures the sick and blesses. The same communication of the Holy Spirit will take place through the imposition of hands, as is found today also in the liturgy. In the celebration of the sacraments the epiclesis appears, that is, the invocation of the Spirit so that he may descend on the person or the offerings. This takes place at times through the simple gesture unaccompanied by an explicit formula. An example of this is the Roman Canon, when the priest covers the offerings with his hands at the time of the consecration, creating a shadow over them. This has a function of beseeching the presence of the Spirit, connecting with the symbol of the cloud. Connected to the hand is the figure of the "finger," which expresses divine force and power better, as Jesus shows, casting out demons with the finger of God (Lk 11:20). This expression is at the basis of the image that appears in the hymn to the Holy Spirit, *Veni Creator Spiritus.* Finally, the "dove" is a further symbol that, ever since the flood and the covenant with Noah, runs through the history of salvation. According to some patristic exegeses, this symbol could be made to trace back even to the moment of the creation, when Scripture speaks of the Spirit who hovered over the waters (Gn 1:2). Such prefigurations find their complete fulfillment in the descent of the Spirit under the form of a dove during the baptism of Jesus. The *CCC* shows its attention to the liturgical element and to iconography by recalling the vessel for the Most Holy Sacrament in the form of a dove, called a *columbarium,* placed above the altar.

III. God's Spirit and Word in the Time of the Promises

The same list of symbols tied to the Holy Spirit can be considered a sketch for reconstructing the history of salvation in a pneumatological key. This history is illustrated in an articulated way in the last three sections, where the joint mission of the Son and the Spirit is presented first in the time of the promises (III), then in the fullness of time (IV), to conclude with eschatology (V).

Significantly, n. 702 opens this reconstruction by once again recalling the joint mission, which is hidden in the Old Testament but already at work. From the theological point of view the question of the relation between the God of the Old Testament and the triune God, revealed fully only in the New, is crucial. Since the first era of the Church, one of the most difficult challenges which Christian thought had to face was the opposition, proposed by gnostic milieus, between the bad god who supposedly had created and had given the Law, and the good god of Jesus. Such a position would have radically deprived the material world of value, as opposed to the vision of the Flesh of Jesus as the one possibility of access to God in his personal depth. So creation and salvation would be in dialectical relationship. Because of this the *CCC*, with great precision and clarity, shows the Spirit who prepares from the beginning for the coming of the Messiah, in such a way that both he and the Son are not yet fully revealed, but already promised. This is the foundation for the possibility of reading the Old Testament in light of the New, as the Fathers taught.

This passage, so effectively presented in the *CCC*, is the fruit of great theological work of the 20th century, whose fruitfulness also flowed together in the Second Vatican Council. In the Middle Ages, there was particular accent on the distinction between the substantial dimension of God, that is, of his unity, omnipotence, eternity, etc., which can be known with reason, and the properly personal and trinitarian dimension, to which one only has access by revelation. This approach was dictated by the desire to safeguard the transcendence of God and underscore the role of grace. At the same time this method needed to be completed, in a way, by the observation that God is always and only Trinity. Likewise Karl Rahner specifically highlighted that the God of the Old Testament is always the Father. This is in harmony with the exegesis of the Church Fathers, who identified the one who appeared to the Patriarchs in theophanies with the Word. The insertion of "who has spoken through the prophets" into the pneumatological article of the Nicene-Constantinopolitan Creed, referring to the Spirit, goes in the same direction. N. 702 specifies significantly that "prophet" therefore should also be understood to include those who composed the sacred books, both of the Old and of the New Testament.

The reconstruction proposed by the *CCC* aims to powerfully bring forth a principle of unity in the history of salvation. For this reason it places its beginning in the very act of creation. It is explained by citing, in the first place, a text from the Byzantine liturgy, which states with clarity and beauty that the Spirit is Creator together with the Father and the Son. This was a truth denied by the Pneumatomachians or Macedonians, as seen above.

Hence, in the text the joint mission of the Son and the Spirit is already connected at the creation of man, recalling the beautiful metaphor of Irenaeus, who defines the second and the third Person of the Trinity as the two hands of the Father, that impressed the invisible divine image into visible human material. This perspective is particularly effective because it presents all of history as a great embrace in which God the Father draws the world to himself through the missions of the Son and the Spirit, distinct but inseparable.

The distinction between image and likeness has always come from the Fathers: typically, for example, from Origen. Man had lost the likeness by original sin, but had retained the image, inasmuch as the Son remained the model and the meaning of man, even when man had injured his relationship with him. The content of God's promise to Abram is the restoration of likeness, through the Incarnation and the gift of glory which is the Spirit himself. Hence the descendant of the Patriarch is Christ with his Spirit, from whom a limitless fruitfulness takes origin, a fecundity stronger than death.

So the relation between the Word and the Spirit is already at the heart of the Old Testament theophanies, inasmuch as they are attributed to the second Person while the third is symbolically foreshadowed in them. The Law itself is presented in this light, as a gift of divine pedagogy, to dispose man to the encounter with Christ: its purpose would be to bring awareness of human powerlessness and therefore the need to be redeemed. The end of the Law, therefore, would be to awaken the desire for the Spirit.

The relation between the Law, man's perception of his own limits, and openness to the spiritual dimension is also found in the journey of the people of Israel, in particular in its wavering in regard to institutional structure. The Kingdom promised by God is not a solely human reality in which to shelter, transforming it into an idol. This is a temptation that recurs continually in the history of the Church. The presence of God produces fruits and works, but they are not the end itself to which the human heart must turn. When the people of Israel chooses, for example, the political kingdom instead of the apparent uncertainty of their relationship with God, it is necessarily exposed to a purification. This will happen in the exile.

The cross of Christ is revealed in this way as the meaning of the Old Testament also, as the way of access to man's true identity in the gift of divine filiation, the fruit of the joint mission. N. 711, then, presents the convergence of a prophetic line whose center is in the Messiah, and another prophetic line that speaks of a new Spirit able to render all things new, to recreate them. But this happens through the remnant of Israel, through the poor, the few who remain faithful. These point toward the Messiah, who does not come to establish a political kingdom but to generate a spiritual Kingdom.

So the disposition to accept the promised Messiah is based precisely on the recognition of his unbreakable connection with the Spirit. The prophecy of Emmanuel, in Is 11:1–2, is brought as an example of this central nucleus of Old Testament preparation: the spirit of the Lord will be placed upon the shoot that will sprout from the trunk of Jesse, filling him with the Spirit's gifts. Analogously, the Savior who must come is described in the Songs of the Servant as suffering man, pointing to the cross from which the Holy Spirit will be poured forth. The connection with this teaching in Isaiah is indicated by Christ himself when, in the synagogue at Nazareth, he applies Is 61:1–2 to himself, stating that he has been consecrated with anointing, inasmuch as the Spirit of the Lord was upon him (cf. Lk 4:18–19).

Pentecost will be the definitive fulfillment of these promises, since, thanks to the fullness of the outpouring of the Spirit, made possible by the paschal mystery, a new Law is sent into the human heart, capable of bringing him to life. The external Law, impossible to fulfill, is replaced with an immanent Law, which is the very Life of the Trinity in man. In this fulfillment mercy is revealed as the heart of the Good News, because the gift can be accepted only by those who recognize themselves as poor, sinners, unable to save themselves alone. The Spirit disposes man, therefore, to recognize the need to be redeemed, which dwells in the heart of every man.

IV. The Spirit of Christ in the Fullness of Time

The Baptist, Mary, and Christ represent, as it were, a triptych that offers the fulfillment of the promise to the wonder of the faithful. The third Person is characterized here as the Spirit of Christ.

John the Baptist is presented precisely as the remnant of Israel, leading his hearers by his own testimony and his own preaching to recognize the need of salvation in their own sins and their own miseries. The temptation to self-sufficiency, which at times can strike specifically those who are more attentive to the Law, is radically dismantled here. And this happens in the very person of the Forerunner more than in his teaching.

We note how this section begins with a quotation from the Prologue to the fourth Gospel, where it is stated that there was a man "sent" from God. The connection with the joint mission is again in action. Indeed the Baptist, sent to point out to Israel the Word who became flesh, is filled with the Spirit from the womb of his mother, before he ever did anything. It is particularly interesting to notice how, in the Visitation, the continual intersection of the personal histories emerges with clarity as the universal history of Israel and of humanity. N. 717, in fact, makes clear that the encounter of Mary and her cousin is at the same time the encounter of God with his people.

The journey of this people's preparation to meet the coming Lord thus is fulfilled in the life of John the Baptist. That fire which burned in Elijah breaks out in the life of the Forerunner, purifying the remnant of Israel and disposing him to receive the Christ. So in him the cycle of the prophets closes, since he can point out directly for his disciples the Messiah present in their midst, in such a way that those very disciples will also be the first disciples of Jesus.

In this sense, the example of John shows powerfully the perfection of being pure relation: he is the voice of him who comes, he is witness of the Light. Everything in him is reference to Christ and to the Kingdom that Christ has come to institute, giving back the divine likeness that man had lost with sin. N. 720 is particularly important for this reason: the Baptist is not simply an envoy whose task is exhausted with the beginning of Jesus' preaching. Such a point of view would be merely functionalistic and dialectical, projecting human logic into the action of God. Instead, the action of the Trinity conforms to its being, where relationship is eternal and absolute. Thus in what is called the "poverty" of the Baptist, whose life is totally defined by Jesus and at the service of Jesus, the very core of his identification with Jesus is revealed, as his own death indicates.

This is made evident by the other two elements of the "triptych," inasmuch as the life of Mary also is pure relation to God. And her unsurpassable perfection consists in that very thing, inasmuch as the Son of the Father, who became flesh in her womb by the work of the Holy Spirit, is also pure "being from" the Father and "being for" the Father, according to a beautiful expression of Ratzinger's (*Introduzione al cristianesimo,* cit., 180). The Baptist, thanks to the gift of the Spirit received in his mother's womb, then, acquires the characteristics of the Son who became flesh in the womb of Mary. Therefore he is divinized, that is, becomes totally relation and totally communion.

What is proclamation in John is fulfillment in Mary. N. 721, turning to the essential theological key of this eighth article, defines her "the masterwork of the mission of the Son and the Spirit". This is explained in the following sense: given that the joint mission has the Father as its origin and the created person as its end, in Mary that end point takes the form of being the dwelling place of the Trinity. Indeed, "the Father found the dwelling place where his Son and his Spirit could dwell among men." Because of this, Tradition has attributed to her the most beautiful titles related to Wisdom and, in particular, the title "Seat of Wisdom."

She is, therefore, completely "trinitarianized," inasmuch as she is totally relationship with each divine Person. The saints have perceived this reality powerfully. For example, Francis of Assisi called our Lady "Daughter of God the Father, Mother of God the Son, and Spouse of God the Holy Spirit"

(*Scritti,* 163) and Louis Marie de Montfort wrote: "Mary is entirely relative to God. Indeed I would say that she was relative only to God" (*True Devotion to the Blessed Virgin,* 225). This doctrine is also taken up in the Second Vatican Council: "The Virgin Mary, who at the message of the angel received the Word of God in her heart and in her body and gave Life to the world, is acknowledged and honored as being truly the Mother of God and Mother of the Redeemer. Redeemed by reason of the merits of her Son and united to Him by a close and indissoluble tie, she is endowed with the high office and dignity of being the Mother of the Son of God, by which account she is also the beloved daughter of the Father and the temple of the Holy Spirit. Because of this gift of sublime grace she far surpasses all creatures, both in heaven and on earth" (*LG* 53).

This last text is particularly important, because it clearly expresses how the profound relationship with each divine Person that characterizes Mary does not imply a separation from men. Precisely to the contrary, this relationship with God places her in a relationship with every man, unique in intensity. Indeed the Virgin has received a gift far superior to any other creature, but this gift is the fruit of redemption. She is not unreachable, but was the object of divine mercy more than anyone else, having been redeemed at the moment of her very conception in the most radical way. In this way what God is accomplishing in history is revealed to men in her. In her the omnipotence of divine mercy is shown in its fullness.

The *CCC* expresses all this through four verbs that dynamically show the relation of Mary with the Holy Spirit. He "prepared" her, filling her with grace, so that the divinity could dwell bodily in her (Col 2:9), to bring all things to the Trinity (n. 722) The movement of salvation history, then, has its origin in the bosom of the Father, and has as its immediate end the womb of Mary, from which it returns to the bosom of the Father, bringing all the world to him. Hence in our Lady the Spirit "fulfills" the merciful plan of the Father, who pours out his own infinite fruitfulness in the virginity of the mother of his Son (n. 723). For this reason, the Spirit himself "manifests" the Son of the Father as Son of the Virgin, in her, the true and definitive burning bush (n. 724). So the whole being of our Lady, her whole life and existence are at the service of this communion which is truly the code of the Spirit, who begins to "bring men…into communion with Christ" through her, starting with the last and the least (n. 725). So in her the nearness of God to those who suffer becomes evident. The Trinity does not await man on high, standing to see whether he overcomes difficulties and raises himself above the darkness of the world. Rather, the Father sends the Son and the Spirit into the darkness, to transform it with his light. There the sun shines; indeed, the darkness is dispelled, even in tight places. What is revealed to every man, in Mary, is that

God makes himself present in the clefts, in the limits, the sorrows, to the end, at the hour of our death.

The mission of Mary, whose existence is totally directed toward and permeated by the joint mission of the Son and the Holy Spirit, is universal. This is why n. 726 takes up the patristic image of the new Eve: Mary is the "Woman," as Christ calls her in the Johannine narration, the Mother of the living, the dawn of the new creation that reflects back the light of day she announces (H. de Lubac, *Cattolicesimo,* Milan: Jaca Book, 1992, 123).

In this way we reach the central element of this triptych, which presents the Christ as the fullness of time in the light of the Holy Spirit. Once again the joint mission emerges, shown to be the authentic key for reading both the second and the third article of the Creed. Jesus, as Christ, in his own deepest identity, points to the Spirit. Throughout his life he lets the Spirit be glimpsed more and more, as follows from the encounters with Nicodemus and with the Samaritan woman. But it is in his hour that Jesus promises the coming of the third Person through his death and resurrection. The Spirit is the other Paraclete, whom Jesus has besought from the Father, and whom the Father sends in the name of Jesus himself. Thus, his being always with us, which etymologically defines Emmanuel also, speaks a reference to the third Person, as the very name of Christ already does. It is the Spirit indeed who teaches and recalls everything that Jesus has said and done, leading us into all the truth.

So in the hour of Jesus, that is, on the Cross, he renders his Spirit to the Father, giving back in his humanity that very Spirit which eternally belongs to him in his divinity. The third Person, in fact, as we have seen, is the Life or the Love with which the Father generates the Son and which the Son gives back to the Father. The first Person does not give just "something" of himself, in giving origin to the second, but gives himself, that is the Life and Love that are God himself. And the second Person, in turn, is the perfect image of the Father precisely because he does not "keep for himself" this Life and this Love, but gives them back to the first Person, giving himself back to him. The Holy Spirit, therefore, is that Life and that Love originating from the Father which he exchanges with the Son. This act of self-giving and regiving is so perfect and absolute that the three are one single thing, that is, infinite unity and eternal divine substance.

When Jesus is on the Cross and he is told to show his power by descending from it, that is, to demonstrate that he is truly the Son of God through an act of power, freeing himself from the nails and the talons of death that bit by bit were gaining possession of him, the incarnate Word remains faithful to the Love of the Father unto the very end, *usque ad summum,* that is, until the completion of the gift of his humanity. The offering of his finite human life takes form thus as the translation into time of his being Son in eternity.

Perfectly uniting his own human will to the divine will, Jesus makes it possible for his humanity to be filled with the Spirit of God, overflowing upon the world and upon history. The Holy Spirit, therefore, is the fruit of the cross, because the offering of his finite life makes possible the eruption of infinite life into humanity. From this gift, from this effusion, the mission of the Church is born, as from the blood and water that gushed from the pierced heart of Christ. There is, therefore, a single line that connects the joint mission of the Son and the Spirit to the mission of the disciples and of the Church, not just ideally but before that, ontologically.

V. The Spirit and the Church in the Last Days

The Pasch of Jesus is really completed, then, at Pentecost, when the Spirit is poured out fully as a divine Person upon the disciples. On this very day the most holy Trinity is revealed fully; that is: the kingdom of God, which is the very life of the triune God, is disclosed to men (n. 732). The joint mission, more than God's going out from himself, is the attraction of men into the Trinity. With a further reference to the Byzantine liturgy, the *CCC* presents this dynamic as an introduction of the world in the last days to the work of the Spirit.

Now, in the eschatological anticipation realized by the third divine Person, it becomes possible for man to live from the life of God and love with the love of God (n. 735). The Spirit, then, is like the sap that joins branches to the life which is Christ, communicating divine fruitfulness itself to the sons of God. So eternal glory and the fullness of sonship to the Father in the Son by the Holy Spirit are one and the same thing, according to the doctrine of Basil, elder brother of Gregory of Nyssa, cited above. Once again the Eastern attention which inspires the pneumatological perspective of the *CCC* is evident.

The end of the joint mission of the second and the third Person is, then, the Church, presented as the body of Christ and temple of the Holy Spirit. Men thus are led into divine communion through the action of the Paraclete, who directs to them the actions described by the four verbs applied to Mary: he "prepares," he "manifests" the Risen One to them, "makes present" the mystery of Christ to them, especially in the Eucharist, and "brings [them] into communion" with God (n. 737).

The journey is completed, then, in presenting the mission of the Church in intimate union with the joint mission of the Son and the Spirit. With the help of a quotation from another Greek Father, Cyril of Alexandria, it is shown how the mission of the Church is not an addition to the divine missions, but rather is their prolongation (n. 738).

In this way the last four points of the article refer organically to what follows in the *CCC*, first to the eschatological section (article nine), which immediately follows the pneumatological. The relation between the third Person and the sacraments, presented as anointing which spreads into the various members of the body of Christ, points back, on the other hand, to the second part of the *CCC* (n. 739). Hence the new life that has his origin from that relation is indicated as the object of the third part of the *CCC* (n. 740), just as the prayer which animates this life is the theme of the last part of the *CCC* (n. 741).

As the summary points also reveal, everything is organized according to the joint mission of the Son and of the Spirit (n. 743), whose purpose is to attract human beings to that communion "with" God which in the Holy Spirit is communion "in" God. The quotation of Gal 4:6, placed as the *incipit* of the summary section, can well serve as a compendium of the whole journey, inasmuch as it makes explicit the connection between the joint mission and divine filiation: man, who *per se* is a creature and cannot call God Father in the proper sense, that is, *Abbà*, as Jesus in contrast does, can pray, live and love in the very Trinity itself, like Mary, thanks to the presence of the Spirit of the Father and of the Son in his own heart.

Chapter Three, Article 9: "I BELIEVE IN THE HOLY CATHOLIC CHURCH"

Manuel José Jiménez R.

Since the time of the Council, people have spoken of the "Church of the Trinity." Sustained by sacred Scripture and patristic writings, the trinitarian ecclesiology of Vatican II, which is that expressed in the *CCC*, underscores a relationship of the Church with the Trinity on three principal fronts: (a) the trinitarian origin of the Church; (b) the trinitarian form of the Church; (c) the trinitarian objective or destiny of the Church. Countersigned with the seal of the Trinity, the Church has her origin, her model, and her end in God One and Three.

When Cardinal Schönborn, at the time Secretary of the Commission for the preparation of the Catechism, presented the *CCC*, he said that "the trinitarian mystery is its common thread." To explain this, he referred to n. 234 of the *CCC*: "The mystery of the Most Holy Trinity is the central mystery of Christian faith and life. It is the mystery of God in himself. It is therefore the source of all the other mysteries of faith, the light that enlightens them. It is the most fundamental and essential teaching in the 'hierarchy of the truths of faith.'"

The *CCC*, in the article on God, makes clear from the start the imprint of the Trinity upon the Church also: "The whole divine economy is the common work of the three divine persons. For as the Trinity has only one and the same nature, so too does it have only one and the same operation" (n. 258). "Being a work at once common and personal, the whole divine economy makes known both what is proper to the divine persons, and their one divine nature" (n. 259).

This trinitarian orientation inspires the structure of the commentary that we present. Use will be made of expressions taken from the *CCC*, from article 9 of chapter 3: "The Church is one, holy, catholic, and apostolic" (nn. 811–870). Presented in this way, the commentary takes on the formula of the Nicene-Constantinopolitan Creed as the articulating principle of the whole reflection. Also present in this reflection is a principle of trinitarian ecclesiology drawn from the same *CCC*: "We begin our investigation of the Church's mystery by meditating on her origin in the Holy Trinity's plan and her progressive realization in history" (n. 758).

Similarly another trinitarian theological principle of the *CCC* is related: "To believe that the Church is 'holy' and 'catholic,' and that she is 'one' and 'apostolic': (as the Nicene Creed adds)" (n. 750).

For reasons of space and due to the limitations proper to this type of commentary, it is not possible to explore each of these attributes of the Church in depth. We shall put them together under the attribute: the Church is one. And from this premise, the other contents in reference to the Church will be highlighted and set in relation.

I Believe the Holy Catholic Church

The first part of the *CCC* is a clear reference to the trinitarian dimension of the Church. In n. 74–79 the action of the three divine persons is put on display: "The Father's self-communication made through his Word in the Holy Spirit, remains present and active in the Church" (n. 79). This argument returns in article 8. "The article of faith about the Church depends entirely on the articles concerning Christ Jesus" (n. 748), and "depends entirely on the article about the Holy Spirit, which immediately precedes it" (n. 749). In this way the *CCC* takes what the creeds of the first centuries of the Church share: the Church becomes part of the Creed, in the articles on the profession of faith in the Holy Spirit, much as believing in the forgiveness of sins, the resurrection of the body, and life everlasting become part of the Creed.

In the Creed, the early Church discovered the mystery of the Trinity in the light of Christian life, and in particular the Holy Spirit as the giver of all life. Therefore, the Creed proclaims the Church's faith in the Father who creates, the Son who saves, and in the Holy Spirit who gives life and works principally in the Church and through her. When the Creed has us say: "I believe the Church" it is not introducing a fourth proposition complementary to the three trinitarian propositions. The Church is, in this case, the first work of the Holy Spirit, whose active presence in the heart of persons has just been professed.

The *CCC* assumes all this, and leads into the articles on "I believe the Holy Catholic Church" (nn. 748–975), "I believe the forgiveness of sins" (nn. 988–1019) and "I believe in life everlasting" (1020–1065), within the article on "I believe in the Holy Spirit" (nn. 633–1065). These articles are article 8 (I believe in the Holy Spirit); article 9 (I believe the Holy Catholic Church); article 10 (I believe the forgiveness of sins); article 11 (I believe the resurrection of the body), and article 12 (I believe life everlasting).

This makes it necessary for us to understand adequately the meaning of "believing the Church." To do this, we point out two ways present in the *CCC*. First of all, we do not speak of believing "in" the Church, while we do speak of believing "in" God; because we only believe in God, but we believe that the Church exists by the will or plan of God. She has her origin in the mystery of God one and three, in his plan of salvation for humanity, calling it to communion of life with him, by the mediation of his Son and in the Holy Spirit. The object of faith is God: the revelation of God that we find in the Church through the Church's faith. Consequently the Church, in the first place, is not the object, end, or content of the faith, but an intrinsic dimension of the faith. The Church does not form part of the faith as just any object, but rather as the principle and organ of discernment of what we must believe. The importance of the Church resides in her participation in Christ as a mediatrix and therefore becomes the road for reaching God. The role of the Church is to be the mediatrix and communitarian context of the faith. The *CCC* refers to this first meaning of "I believe the Church" when it states: "To believe that the Church is 'holy' and 'catholic,' and that she is 'one' and 'apostolic' (as the Nicene Creed adds), is inseparable from belief in God, the Father, the Son, and the Holy Spirit. In the Apostles' Creed we profess 'one Holy Church' *(Credo…Ecclesiam),* and not to believe "in" the Church, so as not to confuse God with his works, and to attribute clearly to God's goodness all the gifts he has bestowed on his Church" (n. 750).

In a second sense, "I believe the Church" means that the Church is not part of the center of the faith nor is its end, but is the place and the right context of faith, being a sacramental community. So it shows the way of being community proper to the profession of the Christian faith, as the ecclesiastical expression of faith in God. It also expresses being community convoked or called, and community that itself convokes and calls; or community that listens and proclaims as established in the Constitution *DV*. To receive the Christian revelation it is necessary to have faith in the Church, and this in two aspects: as the space or place of revelation, and inasmuch as the Church is part of the object of faith. It is the Church that gives the faith we profess. God gives faith to the Christian through the Church. Faith is not a personal invention, because it is received and lived in the community of the Church. The ecclesial aspect of faith does not depend on the subject called to believe in the Church, but on divine revelation. With regard to revelation, the mission of the Church is that of preserving and transmitting it. From this point of view, the Church understands herself in God's will to communicate himself. The existence of the Church depends entirely on the revealing action of God. According to César Izquierdo, to believe the Church means to find Jesus Christ in her. It is recognizing that the Church is the place of faith, because she also is a believer. And therefore believers are believers to the degree as they share the faith of the Church. But, as we have already said before, to have faith in the Church is not on the same level as having faith in God, but a faith in relation with God, dependent on him. Faith in the Church is faith in the action of God in the Church. To believe the Church therefore means to recognize her essential relationship with revelation and God's will to communicate himself.

In a certain sense the Church can be called "the great believer," the place where individual believers unite in a single faith, which is the faith of the Church. From the Church every believer receives the contents of the faith and how to believe. In appropriating the faith of the Church, every believer becomes Church, builds her, and contributes to the birth of new believers. In transmitting revelation the Church invites Christians to make her faith their own "by her mediation", but also to become one entity "together with the Church and in the Church". The creed of the faith of the individual is the creed of the faith of the Church. The faith of the Church is expressed and exists in the act of faith of those who live the faith in communion with her. The believer is an object of faith, to the extent that he forms part of the communion of the faithful, and not separately or autonomously from that. What has been said is not in contradiction with the necessary personalization of the faith, because only in communion with the Church is the personalization of the faith authentic and mature. Otherwise it would be subjectivization rather than personalization of the faith. To believe the Church is, in the last analysis, to believe in an ecclesial manner. The Church is the communitarian and sacramental environment where the Christian faith is professed, celebrated and witnessed.

This second meaning of "believing the Church" also appears in the *CCC* when, in the first part, it explains the meaning of faith: "Faith is a personal act—the free response of the human person to the initiative of God who reveals himself. But faith is not an isolated act. […] You have not given yourself faith […]. The believer has received faith from others and should hand it on to others. […] Each believer is thus a link in the great chain of believers. I cannot believe without being carried by the faith of others, and by my faith I help support others in the faith. […] 'I believe' is also the Church, our mother, responding to God by faith as she teaches us to say both 'I believe' and 'We believe.' It is the Church that believes first, and so bears, nourishes and sustains my faith. Everywhere, it is the Church that first confesses the Lord: […] Salvation comes from God alone; but because we receive the life of faith through the Church, she is our mother: […] Because she is our mother, she is also our teacher in the faith" (nn. 166–168).

The Church is One, Holy, Catholic, and Apostolic

Regarding the Church, the Apostles' Creed speaks only of the "holy catholic Church," and the Nicene Creed states: "We believe in one holy catholic and apostolic Church." For the Council of Constantinople, these four dimensions or four attributes of the Church are the sign of authenticity of the Church. The Second Vatican Council spoke along the same lines: "Christ, the one Mediator, established and continually sustains here on earth His holy Church, the community of faith, hope and charity, as an entity with visible delineation through which He communicated truth and grace to all. [...] This is the one Church of Christ which in the Creed is professed as one, holy, catholic and apostolic, which our Savior, after His Resurrection, commissioned Peter to shepherd, [cf. Jn 21:17] and him and the other apostles to extend and direct with authority, [cf. Mt 28:18f.] which He erected for all ages as 'the pillar and mainstay of the truth' [1 Tm 3:15]. This Church constituted and organized in the world as a society, subsists in the Catholic Church, which is governed by the successor of Peter and by the bishops in communion with him, although many elements of sanctification and of truth are found outside of its visible structure. These elements, as gifts belonging to the Church of Christ, are forces impelling toward catholic unity" (*LG* 8).

Along the same line, the *CCC* has it: "These four attributes, inseparably linked with each other, [cf. *DS* 2888] indicate essential features of the Church and her mission. The Church does not possess them of herself; it is Christ who, through the Holy Spirit, makes his Church one, holy, catholic, and apostolic, and it is he who calls her to realize each of these qualities. Only faith can recognize that the Church possesses these properties from her divine source. But their historical manifestations are signs that also speak clearly to human reason" (nn. 811–812).

Avery Dulles, in relation to these four attributes, focuses on differences in the way of interpreting them in light of diverse ecclesiological models. For the purposes of the present text, we highlight the meaning that they take in the institutional model, before Vatican II, and in the communitarian and sacramental models proper to Vatican II. In the "institutional" model of the Church, it is seen in a static way, as a society that has had some specific attributes which were given to her in a definitive way by Christ. The institution was necessarily considered in the sense that man was constrained to belong to it to have any hope of saving his soul. Consequently, it was a question of life or death for the people to be able to recognize the true Church. The four attributes were understood as distinctive notes of a visible society. Hence unity, for example, was conceived as "the subordination of all believers to one single spiritual jurisdiction and to one single Magisterium." The connotation of catholicity is secondary, because it is strongly linked to unity. In the institutional theory it was understood as highly visible and measurable in geographical and statistical terms. In relation with unity, catholicity stands to mean that one Church, germinating in all the world, must have the same creed, the same cult, and the same juridical system. The immense development of the Church and the multitude of her followers were considered as a particular reason for her splendor, her cohesion and her discipline. The third note, holiness, was interpreted as a characteristic of the Church as a visible society. Hence it was not principally connected with the interior union of believers with God, but rather with its visible holiness. Many apologists of this period drew attention *in primis* to the sacrality of the Church's means, in particular of those lacking among her adversaries. The last note, apostolicity, was interpreted as belonging to the institution as a means of salvation. Great importance was given to the maintenance of the apostolic deposit of doctrine, the sacraments, and the ministry. For practical purposes, priority was given to governance or to office. By office was meant the capacity and the power to declare what was true doctrine and what were true sacraments. For these apologists, apostolicity therefore had the meaning of legitimate succession of pastors, and the approval of pastors was seen as coming from Rome.

In the "communitarian" model of the Church, the attributes are no longer interpreted as visible signs of a specific society, but rather as the qualities of a living community. Consequently, the Church is described in dynamic categories, vitalistic and with a perspective of continual growth toward the reaching of perfection. In this way her participation in the attributes that define her will only be partial and orientating, until the end of time. The attributes are seen as an assignment to be carried out on the part of each of the Christian communities rather than as the exclusive property of one society. The aspiration of the Church is to become in fullness one, holy, catholic and apostolic. The unity to which reference is made is not the external unity of an organized society; rather the interior unity of reciprocal charity which builds a community of friends. Holiness is not so much the holiness of the means of sanctification, or an external holiness able to be measured statistically, but refers in first place to a holy life, an interior communication with God that raises communion with one's neighbor. Fundamental catholicity, for this ecclesiology, is not so much the fact of having many members scattered in various latitudes, but rather the catholic dynamism of a love that seeks everything and excludes no one. This "catholic" charity makes the Church become, in the terminology of Bergson, an "open society." The apostolicity that counts in this theology is not so much legal succession of the prelates duly ordained; rather it is the enduring magnanimity of the Holy Spirit that has soaked in since the origin of the apostolic Church at Pentecost.

In the third model, the Church as "sacrament," the four attributes are traditionally used sometimes as foundational criteria of the true Church, but the perspective is very different from that of the two preceding models. The operative category will be the sacramental sign. Christ is the sign *par excellence* of the redemptive purpose of God. The Church exists to make Christ really present as the sign of the redemptive love of God which extends to all humanity, which implies the existence of a community that has certain definite attributes. In the first place, the sign of Christ should be extended in time in such a way that it becomes definitive and involves everything or, with a more technical term, must be eschatological. For the sake of perpetuating the sign of Christ until the end of time, the Church of every historical moment must remain in evident continuity with Christ and with the apostolic Church, or, in other words, must have apostolicity. Second, the sign of Christ should expand in space to manifest and make actual the salvific will of God toward all regions and toward all cultural and ethnic diversities. To put it another way, it should express the response of all these peoples to divine grace; which means that the Church must be catholic; or expand into all the world, and not only according to the culture of western Europe. As the Second Vatican Council says in reference to catholicity: "This characteristic of universality which adorns the people of God is a gift from the Lord Himself. By reason of it, the Catholic Church strives constantly and with due effect to bring all humanity and all its possessions back to its source in Christ, with Him as its head and united in His Spirit. In virtue of this catholicity each individual part contributes through its special gifts to the good of the other parts and of the whole Church" (*LG* 13). Finally, the Church must be characterized by holiness; otherwise it could not be a sign of Christ. The Church, inasmuch as it is earthly, will never be able to be completely holy. However, in virtue of her formal principles and under the guidance of the Holy Spirit, the Church works constantly to purify man from his sins and lead him to conversion and penance. The awareness that her members have of not being worthy of their high vocation and of committing sins every day is a testimony of holiness coherent with the nature of the Church. In the sacramental model, therefore, the four notes or attributes assume greater importance than in the communitarian model. They must be the visible qualities of the Church in her actual form, or in a contrary way, the Church will not be a sacrament of Christ, a visible expression of his invisible grace that triumphs over human sin and alienation. Her visibility is necessary as in the institutional model, but it is necessary to emphasize a significant difference. The first model proposes a visibility manifest to the eyes of all, measurable and accessible to statistics, and able to be used in a rational way in an apologetical argument. The third model, however, proposes a special model of visibility adequate for a sacrament, which is to say, the physical expression of a divine mystery.

When the *CCC* speaks of the attributes, it highlights in them both the dimensions of gift and reality toward which the Church tends, and her dimension as concrete historical reality in the models of communion and sacrament, according to Dulles' way of understanding them. A clear example is the way in which the *CCC* refers to the holiness of the Church: "The Church on earth is endowed already with a sanctity that is real though imperfect. In her members perfect holiness is something yet to be acquired" (n. 825). Thus the *CCC* shows that the Church is at the same time a spiritual and visible reality: "The Church is in history, but at the same time she transcends it" (n. 770).

The Church is One

Vatican II speaks not only of unity. In the decree on ecumenism it uses the terms "unity and unicity of the Church" (*UR* 2). In this way it states that Christ founded one single Church and that he wanted her perfectly united. The divine plan of unity was shown in the actions of Christ during his earthly life and reached its high point after the glorification of Jesus, with the coming of the Holy Spirit, divine principle of unity of those who believe in Christ. Unity is a specific connotation of the Church of Christ: "Unity is of the essence of the Church" (n. 813). As Pope St. John Paul II said: "In effect, this unity bestowed by the Holy Spirit does not merely consist in the gathering of people as a collection of individuals. It is a unity constituted by the bonds of the profession of faith, the sacraments and hierarchical communion. The faithful are one because, in the Spirit, they are in communion with the Son and, in him, share in his communion with the Father: 'Our fellowship is with the Father and with his Son Jesus Christ' (1 Jn 1:3). For the Catholic Church, then, the communion of Christians is none other than the manifestation in them of the grace by which God makes them sharers in his own communion, which is his eternal life. Christ's words 'that they may be one' are thus his prayer to the Father that the Father's plan may be fully accomplished, in such a way that everyone may clearly see 'what is the plan of the mystery hidden for ages in God who created all things' (Eph 3:9). To believe in Christ means to desire unity; to desire unity means to desire the Church; to desire the Church means to desire the communion of grace which corresponds to the Father's plan from all eternity. Such is the meaning of Christ's prayer: *'Ut unum sint*" (*UUS* 9).

The trinitarian structure of the Church's unity stands out from the quotation. The *CCC* explores "the sacred mystery of the Church's unity" from this clearly trinitarian perspective: "The Church is one because of her source: 'the highest exemplar and source of this mystery is the unity, in the Trinity of Persons, of one God, the Father and the Son in the Holy Spirit' (*UR* 2). The Church is one because of her founder: for 'the Word made flesh, the prince of peace, reconciled all men to God by the cross,...restoring the unity of all in one people and one body' (*GS* 78:3). The Church is one because of her 'soul': 'It is the Holy Spirit, dwelling in those who believe and pervading and ruling over the entire Church, who brings about that wonderful communion of the faithful and joins them together so intimately in Christ that he is the principle of the Church's unity' (*UR* 2)" (*CCC* 813).

The Church is "One" Because of Her Source

The trinitarian ecclesiology of the *CCC* takes the category of "mystery," from Vatican II, as a reference point that guides its reflection: "We begin our investigation of the Church's mystery by meditating on her origin in the Holy Trinity's plan and her progressive realization in history" (n. 758). And therefore it states that the Church is "a plan born in the Father's heart." Starting with the prologue, the *CCC* assumes this structure of the trinitarian mystery of the Church. The text begins by contemplating God in eternity, enjoying perfection and infinite happiness. All his actions for the good of human beings are attributed to the Father. The Father performs them "through the Son" "in the Holy Spirit." This is why it proclaims from the beginning: "The profession of faith summarizes the gifts that God gives man: as the Author of all that is good; as Redeemer; and as Sanctifier. It develops these in the three chapters on our baptismal faith in the one God: the almighty Father, the Creator; his Son Jesus Christ, our Lord and Savior; and the Holy Spirit, the Sanctifier, in the Holy Church" (n. 14).

In the section dedicated to God the Father, the *CCC* confirms that God is the source and origin of all, including the Church, since the articles about the Church depend on the articles about God the Father. God is the beginning and the end of all. "'I believe in God': this first affirmation of the Apostles' Creed is also the most fundamental. [...] The other articles of the Creed all depend on the first, just as the remaining Commandments make the first explicit. The other articles help us to know God better as he revealed himself progressively to men" (n. 199).

Regarding the Church, in dealing with her origin, foundation, and mission, the *CCC* affirms that she is a plan present in the heart of God from the beginning of time, present in his heart before the creation of the world. As Bruno Forte says, "the origins of the Church are hidden in the depth of the mystery of God. The Church is from the Father, beloved since the beginning of time. She has always existed in the heart of God. If the Church is the bride of Christ Jesus, she has been ready for him since before the creation of the world (Eph 1:3–6). The Church is from the Father, beloved by him from all eternity by virtue of his love, and exists in his heart as the community of salvation. The Church willed by the Father is, then, the work of the Son (the work of the Word of God), animated by the Holy Spirit: truly the work of the Trinity." The Church is not a human initiative, but the initiative of God: an initiative that maintains profound relationship with the creation of all things and the creation of human beings (*CCC* 759). Since the beginning of time, the will of God is to raise human beings to participation in the divine life: "The glory of God consists in the realization of this manifestation and communication of his goodness, for which the world was created. God made us 'to be his sons through Jesus Christ, according to the purpose of his will'" (n. 294).

It is the will of God to save human beings, calling together a people. He has willed to call together believers in Christ into the holy Church (n. 759). The Church exists by the divine plan and will as an instrument of salvation for all of humanity, to save them in Christ and with Christ. The Church must be grasped in her interior nature, as an expression and manifestation of the universal saving will of God. The Church is a plan from the heart of the Father. It is an intention that is realized and made present in the history of humanity. "'The Father...determined to call together in a holy Church those who should believe in Christ.' This 'family of God' is gradually formed and takes shape during the stages of human history, in keeping with the Father's plan. In fact, 'already present in figure at the beginning of the world, this Church was prepared in marvelous fashion in the history of the people of Israel and the Old Covenant. Established in this last age of the world and made manifest in the outpouring of the Spirit, it will be brought to glorious completion at the end of time' (*LG* 2)" (n. 759).

The *CCC*, in the subtitles, leads us to understand what is called "the gradual realization" of the Church through the centuries: "A plan born in the Father's heart"; "The Church, foreshadowed from the world's beginning"; "The Church, prepared for in the Old Covenant"; "The Church, instituted by Christ Jesus"; "The Church, revealed by the Holy Spirit"; "The Church, perfected in glory" (nn. 751–769).

It takes up the gradual realization of the Church through the centuries, in the part dedicated to "believing in the Holy Spirit". It does so by highlighting the divine person of the Holy Spirit who acts and is manifested in the whole history of salvation, in three great moments: "God's Spirit and Word in the time of the promises" (nn. 702–716); "The Spirit of Christ in the fullness of time" (nn. 717–730); "The Spirit and the Church in the last days" (nn. 731–741).

The *CCC* speaks of a remote preparation for the gathering together of the People of God, which begins with the call of Abram, and the immediate preparation with the election of Israel as the people of God and with the proclamation of a new and eternal covenant (n. 762). In this way it is affirmed that the Church can be understood only in close relation with Israel and with the First or Old Covenant. To express this relationship, theological reflection makes use of three categories: continuity, complementarity, and newness, between the Church and Israel. In regard to continuity, it highlights the condition of being the "people of God" (n. 781). In current-day theological reflection thinking of the Church as people of God is a prominent characteristic, complementary to others such as "body of Christ" and "sacrament of salvation." According to Antonio María Calero, the category "people of God" is central and foundational for the ecclesiology of Vatican II because it sheds light on the following dimensions of the life of the Church: the historical dimension of the Church, the biblical category of covenant, continuity and discontinuity of the Church vis-à-vis Israel, the relationship of the baptized within the ecclesial community, the fundamental equality and dignity of all as baptized persons, the distinction between the Church and kingdom of God, the eschatological nature of the Church and a new way of understanding the relation between the Church and the world.

The *CCC* is not extraneous to this subject. As mentioned above, the category of people of God is fundamental for how the *CCC* presents the Church. It quotes the Council, in particular *LG* 9: "At all times and in every race God has given welcome to whosoever fears Him and does what is right. [cf. Acts 10:35] God, however, does not make men holy and save them merely as individuals, without bond or link between one another. Rather has it pleased Him to bring men together as one people, a people which acknowledges Him in truth and serves Him in holiness. He therefore chose the race of Israel as a people unto Himself. With it He set up a covenant. Step by step He taught and prepared this people, making known in its history both Himself and the decree of His will and making it holy unto Himself. All these things, however, were done by way of preparation and as a figure of that new and perfect covenant, which was to be ratified in Christ, and of that fuller revelation which was to be given through the Word of God Himself made flesh."

An expression of this continuity is the common use of images for speaking of Israel as the people of God in the Old Covenant and of the Church as people of God in the New Covenant. Among these, the *CCC* uses the following images: the sheepfold, the flock, the farm or field of God, the building of God, house of God, family of God, holy temple (nn. 753–757). But the continuity shown and supported by these images draws attention to a newness besides: "In Scripture, we find a host of interrelated images and figures through which Revelation speaks of the inexhaustible mystery of the Church. The images taken from the Old Testament are variations on a profound theme: the People of God. In the New Testament (cf. Eph 1:22; Col 1:18), all these images find a new center because Christ has become the head of this people (cf. LG 9), which henceforth is his Body. Around this center are grouped images taken 'from the life of the shepherd or from cultivation of the land, from the art of building or from family life and marriage' (LG 6)" (n. 753).

The *CCC* also shows the newness in continuity of the Church as people of God, when it makes note of some characteristics proper to the Church as people of God, highlighting them with the use of italics: "One becomes a *member* of this people not by a physical birth, but by being 'born anew,' a birth 'of water and the Spirit' (Jn 3:3–5), that is, by faith in Christ, and Baptism. This People has for its Head Jesus the Christ (the anointed, the Messiah). Because the same anointing, the Holy Spirit, flows from the head into the body, this is 'the messianic people.' 'The *status* of this people is that of the dignity and freedom of the sons of God, in whose hearts the Holy Spirit dwells as in a temple' (*LG* 9). 'Its *law* is the new commandment to love as Christ loved us' (cf. Jn 13:34). This is the 'new' law of the Holy Spirit (Rom 8:2; Gal 5:25). Its *mission* is to be salt of the earth and light of the world (cf. Mt 5:13–16). This people is 'a most sure seed of unity, hope, and salvation for the whole human race' (*LG* 9). Its *destiny,* finally, 'is the Kingdom of God which has been begun by God himself on earth and which must be further extended until it has been brought to perfection by him at the end of time' (*LG* 9)" (n. 782). The fundamental newness is given by the event of Christ and by the Church's faith in him as Messiah, Savior, and Son of God (nn. 422–682). The complementarity is explained through the close linkage between the two covenants and the religious significance of Israel (nn. 839–840).

The Church is "One" Because of Her Founder

In addressing the question the *CCC* uses various expressions: "Christ founded the Church," "The Church instituted by Jesus Christ," "The Lord Jesus gave his Church its beginning," and "The Church was born principally from the total gift of Christ". In this way it is affirmed that the Church is the work of Jesus Christ, the Word made flesh, which means, as we said previously, that she is also the work of the Father and the Holy Spirit. Her trinitarian origin presents itself in describing the economy of salvation. To summarize, the *CCC* shows, in various forms and in a diversity of words that the Church is the work of the Trinity: she is the will of the Father, fulfilled by Christ Jesus, with the power of the Holy Spirit. She is the result of a plan and initiative of the Father and of the missions of the Son and the Holy Spirit. This is the approach of Vatican II, following in the footsteps of Cyprian's *Ecclesia de Trinitate* (cf. *LG* 2–4).

How, then, should one understand that the Church was instituted or founded by Jesus Christ? Antonio María Calero speaks on this question: "One can say, therefore, that Jesus founded the Church, but explaining this expression rightly and specifically, in the sense that what was done by

Jesus was done, on one hand, a result of the eternal plan of the Father to save all of humanity through an instrument that existed prior to Christ, thanks to the reality and the institution of the Old Covenant; it took place, moreover, during the earthly life of Christ, thanks to his unique and unrepeatable mediation; and, after Christ, it is directed to the people of the new and definitive covenant. In another sense, Jesus instituted the Church by building its foundations: the establishment of a group to which he entrusted the mission that he himself had received from the Father, and on which he conferred the elements necessary so that salvation by means of him would not slip away [...]. Hence the answer to the question posed earlier not only goes beyond a completely isolationist vision of the Church, as something connected exclusively to the historical Jesus, but consequently implies the presence and action of the three divine persons. The relation of the Church with the person of Christ is much more detailed today, and is found in a theologically much richer perspective (the Trinity), and historically much more dynamic as a reality that is constructed gradually until reaching its historical completion starting at Pentecost."

The International Theological Commission (1984), along the same lines as the Second Vatican Council, lists the process of the founding of the Church in this way: (a) the Old Testament promises in regard to the people of God; (b) Jesus' broad invitation to all men to repent and believe in him; (c) the call and the institution of the Twelve; (d) the renaming of Simon Peter; (e) the rejection of Jesus by Israel and the split between the Jewish people and the disciples of Jesus; (f) the institution of the supper and the passion and death; (g) the resurrection; (h) the sending of the Holy Spirit at Pentecost; (i) the mission of the disciples to the pagans; (j) the definitive break between the "true Israel" and Judaism. In conclusion, it states, "No single step, taken in and by itself, could constitute the total reality, but the entire series, taken as a unity, shows clearly that the Church's foundation must be understood as a historical process, that is, as the becoming of the Church within the history of revelation.[...] As this process unfolds, the permanent and definitive fundamental structure of the Church comes into being."

Salvador Pié-Ninot draws this conclusion on the subject: "Founding, origin, and foundation are three specific and complementary terms for the understanding of the Church rooted sacramentally in Jesus: (a) the founding of the Church by Jesus is manifested in the implicit and procedural ecclesiology that bears witness that, even before the Pasch, Jesus began a movement of restoration of the whole people of God; (b) the origin of the Church is in Jesus, because after the Pasch the movement begun during his ministry was rebuilt and broadened powerfully; (c) the foundations of the Church are located in Jesus Christ, because he is acting and is still present in the Word of God, in the sacraments, in the ecclesial community, and in the life of believers."

The foregoing is important in the structure of the *CCC*. Even if it is true that it dedicates only one numbered item to the Church as instituted by Jesus Christ (n. 763), this should be read and interpreted in light of the second point of article 9 ("The Church's origin, foundation, and mission," nn. 758–769). And better yet, in light of the whole second section of the *CCC*. In both cases, the *CCC* speaks of the origin of the Church and of its foundation in the context of the history of salvation and its various phases. For that purpose, it is sufficient to recall a declaration—a theological and structural principle of the *CCC*—"the article of faith about the Church depends entirely on the articles concerning Christ Jesus" (n. 748).

The Church is One Because of Her Spirit: the Holy Spirit

"The Church is the temple of the Holy Spirit" is one of the titles which the *CCC* gives to the Church. "The Spirit is the soul, as it were, of the Mystical Body, the source of its life, of its unity in diversity, and of the riches of its gifts and charisms" (n. 809). It is clear in the *CCC*, in its trinitarian concept of the Church, that "The article concerning the Church also depends entirely on the article about the Holy Spirit, which immediately precedes it. 'Indeed, having shown that the Spirit is the source and giver of all holiness, we now confess that it is he who has endowed the Church with holiness.' The Church is, in a phrase used by the Fathers, the place 'where the Spirit flourishes'" (n. 749).

This dependency is so obvious that the end of the third chapter of the *CCC* ("I believe in the Holy Spirit") speaks of the Church of the Holy Spirit, emphasizing the promise of Jesus to his disciples to send the Holy Spirit on the day of Pentecost: "From this hour onward, the mission of Christ and the Spirit becomes the mission of the Church" (n. 730). "By his coming, which never ceases, the Holy Spirit causes the world to enter into the 'last days,' the time of the Church, the Kingdom already inherited though not yet consummated" (n. 732): in such a way that if "the mission of Christ and the Holy Spirit is brought to completion in the Church" (n. 737), "the Church's mission is not an addition to that of Christ and the Holy Spirit, but is its sacrament: in her whole being and in all her members, the Church is sent to announce, bear witness, make present, and spread the mystery of the communion of the Holy Trinity" (n. 738). This, according to the *CCC*, is the subject of the entire ninth article.

Cardinal Walter Kasper, in one of his latest writings, explores the fundamental characteristics of an ecclesiology of communion or the characteristics of a catholic ecclesiology. One of these writings is dedicated to the Church as temple of the Holy Spirit and another to the Church as sacrament of the Holy Spirit. Consequently, as the Creed indicates, ecclesiology is framed within the context of pneumatology, the doctrine of the Holy Spirit. According to the testimony of the Acts of the Apostles, at Pentecost the Church appears in public for the first time as the work of the Holy Spirit. The rest of the Church's journey has been made in the light of, and under the guidance of, the Holy Spirit. To explain the relationship of Spirit and Church, the *CCC* draws attention to a phrase of Irenaeus of Lyons: "For where the Church is, there also is God's Spirit; where God's Spirit is, there is the Church and every grace" (n. 797).

We have said that it proves difficult to show the explicit foundation of the Church on the part of Jesus, but it is possible to give a special prominence, as the *CCC* does, to the event of Pentecost in the first public manifestation of the Church: "'When the work which the Father gave the Son to do on earth was accomplished, the Holy Spirit was sent on the day of Pentecost in order that he might continually sanctify the Church' (*LG* 4). Then 'the Church was openly displayed to the crowds and the spread of the Gospel among the nations, through preaching, was begun' (*AG* 4)" (n. 767). "From this hour onward, the mission of Christ and the Spirit becomes the mission of the Church" (n. 730). On this topic, Cdl. Kasper says that "the Church is, by her origin, the work of Jesus and its fulfillment in the Holy Spirit. She is born in the moment when the disciples of Jesus decided, in the Holy Spirit, to begin the eschatological gathering of all the nations, proclaiming the death and resurrection of Jesus and the sending of the Holy Spirit, evoking this unique event of the Spirit by preaching and the celebration of the sacraments." This justifies, again in the words of Cdl. Kasper, understanding the Church as sacrament of the Spirit. Confirming that it is by the action and mediation of the Holy Spirit that we can succeed in updating and understanding our Church today as the Church of Jesus present in a real and existential way in the community of believers. The Church must be understood in her mission: "The Church on earth is by her nature missionary" (cf. nn. 849–856).

The *CCC* brings all the riches of Scripture, the Church Fathers, the Magisterium, and the theology of the Holy Spirit to memory. It is common to all these sources to refer to the Holy Spirit as the soul of the Church. To be "soul" means that he is the one who builds, preserves, animates, grows, and guides the Church. This explains why the *CCC* maintains a trinitarian perspective of the mission and the missionary nature of the Church. In the first place, by her origin: "The Lord's missionary mandate is ultimately grounded in the eternal love of the Most Holy Trinity: 'The Church on earth is by her nature missionary since, according to the plan of the Father, she has as her origin the mission of the Son and the Holy Spirit' (*AG* 2). The ultimate purpose of mission is none other than to make men share in the communion between the Father and the Son in their Spirit of love" (n. 850). Third, by reason of her mission: "It is from God's love for all men [...] Indeed, God 'desires all men to be saved and to come to the knowledge of the truth' (1 Tm 2:4)" (n. 851). Fourth, for the life of mission: "The Holy Spirit is the protagonist, 'the principal agent of the whole of the Church's mission' (*Redemptoris missio* 21). It is he who leads the Church on her missionary paths. 'This mission continues and, in the course of history, unfolds the mission of Christ, who was sent to evangelize the poor; so the Church, urged on by the Spirit of Christ, must walk the road Christ himself walked, a way of poverty and obedience, of service and self-sacrifice even to death, a death from which he emerged victorious by his resurrection' (AG 5)" (n. 852).

At this point it is clear that for the *CCC* the trinitarian life of God is the wellspring and origin of the Church's mission. This is a matter of fact in the Scriptures, in particular in the Gospel of John. For the evangelist John, mission is the result of the Father's initiative by means of Christ, through the action of the Holy Spirit (Jn 16:7; 16:13–15; 14:25–26). To the questions: whence did the mission of the Church begin? What is its one true source? Antonio María Calero responds: "Keeping in mind that the mission of the Church is the continuation in history of the mission of Christ, and that the mission of Christ was received from the Father and is carried forward through the centuries with the power of the Holy Spirit (Lk 4:14), we must respond to those questions that the Trinity is completely at the root and the origin of the mission of the Church." Hence the mission of the Church is not to be understood as an addition to that of Christ and of the Holy Spirit, but is its sacrament. "In her whole being and in all her members, the Church is sent to announce, bear witness, make present, and spread the mystery of the communion of the Holy Trinity" (n. 738).

The Church is "One" in Her Diversity

"From the beginning, this one Church has been marked by a great diversity which comes from both the variety of God's gifts and the diversity of those who receive them. Within the unity of the People of God, a multiplicity of peoples and cultures is gathered together. Among the Church's members, there are different gifts, offices, conditions, and ways of life. 'Holding a rightful place in the communion of the Church there are also particular Churches that retain their own traditions' (*LG* 13). The great richness of such diversity is not opposed to the Church's unity. Yet sin and the burden of its consequences constantly threaten the gift of unity" (n. 814). This item of the *CCC* can be defined as an ideal synthesis, as it gathers and presents various elements of the Church's essence present in other sections of the same article 9. In the background of this vision of the being and the mission of the Church, there is a concept from Vatican II that understands the Church as mystery, reaffirmed by the Extraordinary Synod of Bishops of 1985. The *CCC* utilizes the expression "the mystery of the Church" (n. 770) in this case. According to this understanding of the Church as mystery, we can affirm that the Church is the revelation of the mystery of God and his plan to save all men in the course of history until the end of time, in Christ and through Christ. The Church is also the place in which this plan of salvation is carried out, by being a historical realization of salvation by God in Christ.

The trinitarian nature of the mystery of the Church must be understood in two ways: (a) the Church is the work of the three divine persons; (b) the Church is a manifestation, an epiphany, the presence in history of the mystery of God One and Three. On the first aspect, this commentary on the *CCC* has referred to it at length. On the second, there is emphasis on how the Church is called to be a visible manifestation of the trinitarian mystery within history. Above all, there is a need to say that as the Trinity is a communion of life and love, the Church must also be likewise. Therefore, everything within the Church: the people, the ministers, the charisms, the structures at all levels (universal and local Church), in her relationship with the world, and in her relation with non-believers and with other believers; everything should be recognized in its character of communion, dialogue, and service, in resemblance to the Trinity. On this point Bruno Forte affirms: "The Church remains understood as *communio,* as an icon of the Trinity, structured in the image and likeness of the trinitarian communion: one in diversity of persons, in a relationship of fruitful exchange. The Church structured as icon of the Trinity will be obliged to stay far from a uniformity that crushes and mortifies the richness and originality of the gifts of the Spirit, and equally far from an extreme opposition of elements. The Church is articulated communion of charisms and ministers in local unity and catholic communion of the particular Churches in the unity of the universal Church, which is present in them and lives in them, joined around the bishop of Rome, who presides in love."

Various items of the *CCC* contained in article 9 must be read in this perspective of being an icon of the Trinity, unity in diversity, communion and participation: the Church is "a priestly, prophetic, and royal people" (nn. 783–786), "each particular Church is catholic" (nn. 832–835), "the Church, body of Christ" with diversity of members (nn. 787–795) and "the Church is apostolic" (nn. 857–865). The first items recall the common dignity of all the baptized in Christ, the common priesthood of the faithful. For Bruno Forte and others, this is how Vatican II overcomes the clericalist (or hierarchological) conception of the Church that sees ecclesial reality articulated in the separation of two types of Christians (clergy and laity), one active, the other passive. With this way of speaking, Vatican II describes the unity of baptism of the people of God, rich in charisms and various ministers, as the pre-existing basis of any individual articulation.

In regard to the second we can cite what the *CCC* presents on the topic: "The body's unity does not do away with the diversity of its members: 'In the building up of Christ's Body there is engaged a diversity of members and functions. There is only one Spirit who, according to his own richness and the needs of the ministries, gives his different gifts for the welfare of the Church'" (n. 791).

Article 9, which follows the Apostles' Creed, and in which the apostolicity of the Church is professed, highlights the apostolic ministry of the Church, and within it the Pope and the bishops as successors of the apostles. The *CCC* places particular attention on unity in diversity and on understanding the particular Churches: "'Let us be very careful not to conceive of the universal Church as the simple sum, or…the more or less anomalous federation of essentially different particular churches. In the mind of the Lord the Church is universal by vocation and mission, but when she puts down her roots in a variety of cultural, social, and human terrains, she takes on different external expressions and appearances in each part of the world' (n. 835).

Salvador Pié-Ninot emphasizes how the Second Vatican Council treated the reality of the particular Churches in a special way and provides an adequate understanding of them: "According to Vatican II, the catholic Church is born out of a double movement, concomitant and reciprocal: on one hand, she exists concretely to the extent she exists in the local churches; and on the other, she becomes a concrete and historical reality in the local churches. And so, the catholic Church that is realized in the local churches is the same one that is made up of the local churches; hence the formula "in them" and "of them" *(in quibus et ex quibus)* renders the mystery of the Church in her institutional essence according to the logic of the mutual immanence between the local-particular dimension and catholic universality and vice versa."

Toward Unity

In regard to the adjective "catholic" within *LG* 8, Salvador Pié-Ninot writes: "It should be noted that the adjective 'catholic' takes on two different connotations: a qualitative one, and the other, confessional. Initially it is useful to qualitatively specify the one Church of Christ as catholic, as the Creed professes […]. On the other hand, this expression is used in a confessional sense to indicate the concrete Roman Catholic Church, governed by the successor of Peter and the bishops in communion with him. It is obvious that the connection between the two connotations is found in the meaningful formula "subsists in" *(subsistit in)*, which highlights how the one catholic Church is present in the Roman Catholic Church, even if there are elements of catholicity outside her visible structure which, as gifts proper to the Church of Christ, give impetus toward catholic unity. So the Council also expresses the wound within the fullness of catholicity which the Church of Rome has, since the lack of unity among Christians is a wound; not in the sense that she is deprived of unity, but as an obstacle to the full realization of her universality [...]. In this way there is an allusion to the deficit present in the Roman Catholic Church and that therefore there is a duty on the Roman Catholic part, as one who is not doing her part toward the attainment of unity."

The expression "subsists in" replaces the word "is," the use of which would have denied the existence of elements of the Church outside the Catholic Church. For Pié-Ninot "subsists in" must be understood as "being present" or "continuing to be present" in the Catholic Church: the fullness of the means of salvation (*UR* 3), the fullness of revealed truth (*UR* 4) and the essential elements of the Church of Christ (*LG* 8). In this way it is said that the Catholic Church is not one among many Churches. It states that the Church of Christ has her concrete place in the Roman Catholic Church and therefore she exists in history and becomes visible in it.

Although the *CCC* may explain clearly that "the Church is ultimately one, holy, catholic, and apostolic in her deepest and ultimate identity" (n. 865), it recognizes also that within the Church in her historical form there exist "wounds to unity": "ruptures that wound the unity of Christ's Body," which do not happen without the sins of men (cf. n. 817). From this follows the importance and the prominent place which the expression "subsists in" occupies in the presentation of the *CCC* (n. 816) and in other correlated topics, as for example: "who belongs to the Catholic Church," the phrase "outside the Church there is no salvation" and the ecumenical dialogue (nn. 811–822; 836–848).

Regarding the first, the *CCC* refers to various forms of belonging, just as Vatican II emphasizes. The Council, in the words of Pié-Ninot, maintains a circular and concentric position in ecclesial communion. The modalities in which the Council refers to this material speak also of gradualness: full, integral, not full, imperfect, gradual, in various ways. All this supports a communional and processual vision, as follows from the fact that the Council does not use the term "member." This expression is replaced in the Council with adjectives such as: full communion, integral, not full, not perfect (*LG* 15; *UR* 2,3,4,14,17; *Orientalium ecclesiarum* 4,30); such as the expressions: ordination, orientation, incorporation, belonging (*LG* 13,14,16; *UR* 3,22). The *CCC* takes up this processual and gradual approach in the two items dedicated to this subject. Not only does it not use the expression "member," but in each of them it expresses gradualness. In n. 836, in line with *LG*, it says:

"All men are called to this catholic unity of the People of God....and to it, in different ways, belong or are ordered: the Catholic faithful, others who believe in Christ, and finally all mankind, called by God's grace to salvation." And in the succeeding item (837), again in line with the teachings of the Council the *CCC* refers to those "fully incorporated into the society of the Church," emphasizing the three visible bonds that conform to it: the profession of faith, the sacraments, and the ecclesiastical governance of the communion (n. 837). According to Pié-Ninot, it is necessary to make a discernment about these three bonds, inasmuch as they have a diverse role in the constitution of the Church. The first two (profession of faith and sacraments) constitute, found, and cause the Church. The third, on the basis of the hierarchical and ordained ministry, is to be understood as a service to what God has given and disposed. The ministry is not the cause or foundation, but the witness, condition, service of the profession of faith and the sacraments. This is why the theological tradition points to the Church at the service of "the object of faith," and therefore as a condition and not a cause of assent. On the other topics, the *CCC* highlights the call to unity: "The desire to recover the unity of all Christians is a gift of Christ and a call of the Holy Spirit" (n. 820). This requires, on the part of everyone, a continual renewal, conversion of heart, common prayer, mutual brotherly recognition, dialogue among theologians and collaboration among Christians in various fields of service to humanity (cf. n. 821).

The Church Perfected in Glory

In this commentary it has been set forth that according to the *CCC*, "We begin our investigation of the Church's mystery by meditating on her origin in the Holy Trinity's plan and her progressive realization in history" (n. 758). The *CCC* structures this approach in this way: "a plan born in the Father's heart" (n. 759); "the Church, foreshadowed from the world's beginning" (n. 760); "the Church, prepared for in the Old Covenant" (nn. 761–762); "the Church, instituted by Christ Jesus" (nn. 763–766); "the Church, revealed by the Holy Spirit" (nn. 767–768); and "The Church, perfected in glory" (n. 769).

With this structure the *CCC* displays what was said at the beginning of this commentary with the words of Bruno Forte: (a) the trinitarian origin of the Church; (b) the trinitarian form of the Church; (c) the trinitarian objective or destiny of the Church. On the trinitarian destiny of the Church the words of Bruno Forte are meaningful: "The Church, which comes from the Trinity and is made in the image of the trinitarian community, does not have its completion in this world, but moves toward the Trinity in the journey of time. The Church aims upward to reach the eschatological day in which God will be all in all. The time of the Church is the "in-between," between the gift received and the promise yet to be reached. This is why everything in the being and working of the people of God is marked by the "already" and the "not yet." So the whole eschatological dimension permeates the entire life of the Church; an eschatological character that lets the pilgrim Church recognize her status as an instrument, of being service, of not identifying with the kingdom of God."

This eschatological nature allows us to conclude this commentary on article 9 of the *CCC* with a sort of Creed in reverse, in the sense that it starts from the mystery of Christ and from the action of the Holy Spirit in the Church, to turn back to the Father, the ultimate end of every thing. Once again with the words of Bruno Forte: "The Church generated by Christ in the Holy Spirit journeys toward the Father through the Son in the one Spirit of life.

Chapter Three, Article 9, Paragraph 4/I–II:
CHRIST'S FAITHFUL—HIERARCHY, LAITY, CONSECRATED LIFE

Salvador Pié-Ninot

The nature of the Church, in its visibility, makes manifest the deeper reality to which it leads: the life of the Trinity itself. From here flows the twofold dynamic of communion and mission proper to the Christian faithful, based on baptism, the sacramental foundation of incorporation into Christ. N. 871 describes this sacramental foundation powerfully when it recalls the four patristic and scholastic descriptions of the sacramental character conferred by baptism, which integrates the Christian believer into the people of God (*signum distinctivum*), conformed to the image of Christ (*signum configurativum*), called to exercise the mission that God has entrusted to his Church (*signum dispositivum*), so that he realize it in the world (*signum obligativum*) (cf. John Damascene, De fide orthodoxa, IV c. 1).

The conformation of the Christian believer to Christ is articulated with his threefold mission or ministry (*triplex munus*) as Prophet, Priest, and Lord/King, which constitutes the vertical axis of the whole paragraph dedicated to the hierarchy and to the laity. In this sense, the text is placed in the perspective of Vatican II, which describes the mission of the Church precisely based on the threefold saving mission of Christ, "priestly, prophetical, and kingly," in such a way that the threefold mission of Christ shapes the threefold mission of the Church—the *munera Ecclesiae*—a theological formulation that, by its significance, attains the category of common doctrine in the Council (cf. *AS* III/1, 285). In fact, the pastoral ministry of bishops is structured around it (cf. *LG* 25–27); *CD* 12–16), as well as that of their collaborators, the presbyters (*PO* 4–6) and the mission of lay people (cf. LG 34–36; *AA* 2), and it is also treated this way in our text: hierarchy (nn. 888–896) and lay faithful (nn. 901–913). First, this category is used to describe the characteristics of the people of God as "a priestly, prophetic, and royal people" (nn. 783–786), and then, expanding on the grace of baptism, it is mentioned once again (nn. 1268f.). This theological formula is used consistently for the first time in

Catholic teaching in the *Roman Catechism* which not only states and justifies it, as ancient tradition had already done, including the scholastic era, but also seeks to imbue it with content, for "when Jesus Christ our savior came into the world, he assumed these three characters of prophet, priest, and king, and therefore was called Christ" (art. 2). In addition, it confirms these three titles and explains how this threefold function takes in the whole redemptive work of Christ, as he was anointed to fulfill these ministries which in turn are "three eminent offices and functions" for the good of his Church (art. 7).

Because of its considerable similarity, this exposition seems to stem from the *Catechismo Cristiano* by Cardinal Bartolomeo de Carranza, archbishop of Toledo, who was one of the bishops to whom the preparation of the first part of the Creed in the *Roman Catechism* was entrusted. On the other hand, it seems clear that Carranza was inspired in turn by the *Institutes of the Christian Religion* by the reformer Calvin, who articulates the redemptive work of Christ around the threefold mission entrusted to him by the Father, contrary to the Roman theologians who accused him of having obscured the mission of Jesus, citing it only "with empty words and cold language" (cf. *Roman Catechism,* ch. 3, n. 26). Carranza, therefore, takes advantage of these doctrinal points which the Reformation authors had highlighted—they had fought against Roman-Catholic theology for having abandoned them—and, given that the doctrine of the "threefold mission" had crept into tradition, he developed it accurately.

The *Roman Catechism* makes the concept its own, for the same reasons, so that for the first time this theory was structured consistently as a part of Catholic teaching (cf. R. Donghi, *Credo la Santa Chiesa Cattolica. Dibattiti pretridentini e tridentini sulla Chiesa e formulazione dell' articolo nel Catechismo Romano,* Rome: PUL, 1980). In the Second Vatican Council, the "threefold mission of Christ" will be extended more clearly to the mission of the Church, doubtlessly because of the important analogy between the incarnate Word and the Church (cf. *LG* 8; *DV* 13), and for the decisive theology of the Church as the sacrament of salvation in Christ (cf. *LG* 1,9,48,59; *SC* 5,26; *GS* 42,45; *AG* 1,5).

The two following numbers—872 and 873—emphasize, on one hand, the radical equality of all the Christian faithful in virtue of their baptism, by means of which the gift of faith is received, the one thing necessary for salvation. And, on the other hand, there is the difference among the Christian faithful that is established thanks to the various functions and ministries which each is called to realize within the Church. These differences in the Church depend fundamentally on the will of God for each one, and, expressing themselves visibly in life, reveal the condition proper to each one in the Church (baptism, matrimony, orders, consecrated life….)

In this way, therefore, our texts bring together our understanding of the Church as communion and mission. Communion truly accents the radical equality of all by virtue of baptism, and mission highlights the various functions and ministries which the Christian faithful are called to exercise in the Church, something that implies a functional difference, ontologically rooted when it is the fruit of a sacrament, and all of this oriented to unity in mission.

I. The Hierarchical Constitution of the Church

The general theological justification of ecclesial ministry arises from Christ himself as the source who is expressed here (cf. nn. 874–875) with five key words: he is the one who has "instituted" the Church, given her "authority" and "mission", "orientation" and "goal" (cf. the recent edition of the classic K. Rahner, *La gerarchia nella Chiesa. Commento al capitol III di Lumen gentium* [= original in *LThKVat.II* 1, 514–528], ed. and with introduction by G. Canobbio, Brescia: Morcelliana, 2008). This theological justification is expressed after developing two technical expressions used by Vatican II to describe the actualization of sacramentally ordained ministry: it receives "mission and faculty" ("sacred power") to act "in the person of Christ the Head" *(in persona Christi Capitis).*

Sacred power is the specific expression of the mission and the faculty of Christ entrusted to the ordained ministers just as our text affirms, citing *LG* 18. This expression is used initially in *LG* 10, to signify the essential difference (*essentia non gradu tantum*) between the common priesthood of the faithful and the ministerial or hierarchical priesthood, in accord with the presentation in the encyclical *MD* by Pius XII (*DS* 3850–3852) and made explicit in his allocution *Magnificate Dominum* of November 2, 1954. This means that the ministerial priesthood does not stand on the level of the essential ontology of the common priesthood of Christians, but on the level of "ministerial service." Therefore it is a functional participation, but one that includes an ontological basis on the level of function, by being a tangible manifestation of the personal and priestly "mediation" of Christ.

This "sacred power" gives mission and faculty, right and capacity to act in the person of Christ the head (*in persona Christi Capitis*), as Vatican II says (*LG* 10, 28; *PO* 12; only *"in persona Christi"* in *SC* 33; *LG* 21; *PO* 2, 13), following a broad theological tradition. For this reason, this ministry can only be exercised in virtue of the gift of God conferred by a specific sacrament: the sacrament of order.

It will be useful to recall the recent considerations by Pope Francis on this topic, emphasizing that "it must be remembered that when we speak of sacramental power 'we are in the realm of function, not that of dignity or holiness'.... Even when the function of ministerial priesthood is considered 'hierarchical,' it must be remembered that 'it is totally ordered to the holiness of Christ's members'" (*EG* 104).

We note, as well, that on the question of "sacred power" in the Church there exist two great interpretations based on the origin of the power of bishops. On one hand, the concept of sacred power as having originated from the sacrament of order (cf. authors such as W. Bertrams, G. Philips, K. Mörsdorf, W. Aymans, K. Rahner, Y. Congar, E. Corecco, J. Manzanares...); and, on the other, as being shared through the sacrament and the Church's mission (cf. authors such as D. Staffa, A. Gutiérrez, U. Lattanzi, A.M. Stickler, J. Beyer, G. Ghirlanda...). But, based on an ecclesiology of communion and on a better understanding of the *Decretals* (1120–1140) of Gratian, the father of canon law, one could overcome the dualism of *"ordo/jurisdictio"* with the distinction *"potestas/executio,"* in which the *potestas* is transmitted entirely by the sacrament of order, but its *executio* depends on whether the minister remains in the communion of the Church (this is why the orthodox Churches, although separated from the Catholic Church, have an episcopate recognized as valid; cf. the *Nota explicativa praevia* to *LG*).

The text of n. 876 forcefully emphasizes the character of service proper to the sacramental nature of ecclesial ministry, with a threefold mention of the New Testament term "slave": "slaves of Christ" (Rom 1:1), "the form of a slave" (Phil 2:7) and "slaves of all" (1 Cor 9:19). The vocabulary of service/slavery is typically Pauline, to express the apostolate as disinterested mission of the Gospel (*2 Cor* 4:5; 11:8), with which his co-workers are associated (*Phil* 2:22; *Col* 1:7; 4:7; cf. *Rev* 6:11). In the liturgical tradition the expression "service" is used both to describe the priestly ministry of the "servants" of God and to denominate the ministers themselves (cf. *Verona Sacramentary,* 767.1114, and the *Gelasian,* I: 25, 71, 181).

Furthermore, on the basis of the identification made by Heb 8:6 between priesthood and ministry, this further term, used frequently in the *Vulgata* and in the Latin tradition, will assume a preeminent place to describe presbyters as "priests." The Second Vatican Council, in contrast, prefers to speak in key moments, rather, of "service of the community" (*LG* 20) and of "true service, which in sacred literature is significantly called 'diakonia' or ministry" (*LG* 24), as is seen in the title itself of the Decree on the "ministry and life of priests" (*PO*).

Moreover, the sacramental nature of ecclesial ministry shows itself to have a collegial character. The ecclesiology of communion emerges here again as the strong backbone of ministry, in line with what was stated by the extraordinary Synod of 1985 (II. C. 1, in *EV* 9, 1800) and by Pope John Paul II (cf. *ChL* 19).

The text, quoting from Vatican II, recalls the institution of the Twelve, who "were the first budding-forth of the New Israel, and at the same time the beginning of the sacred hierarchy" (*AG* 5). It is, in effect, a fact recognized as pre-paschal by current research, and one that the International Theological Commission has mentioned as fundamental in discussing the process of the Church's founding (cf. *Select Themes of Ecclesiology,* 1985, n. 1,4, in *EV* 9, 1677–1679). And in this institution of the Twelve a correlation is shown between the reign of God and the people of God, one without which Jesus cannot be understood. The reign of God requires a people in whose midst it can impose itself, and from whom it can radiate outward, given that otherwise it would be neither historical nor localizable. In this sense, the institution of the Twelve, beyond being a symbolic gesture that announces the definitive reuniting of Israel, points to a foundational and juridical dimension, since by including that nation it also embraces the Church as the eschatological Israel.

The collegial character of the Twelve flows from their fraternal unity, on the basis of the fraternal communion of all the faithful, as a reflection of the most definitive communion, that of the divine persons, as it is expressed in the text quoted from Jn 17:21–23. So it is not strange that these Johannine verses are used as support for an organization of the Catholic Church that takes account of episcopal collegiality, where the situation they presuppose is close to that reflected in the Letter to the Ephesians, in the Pastoral Letters, and in *1* Jn, for which the ideal of unity becomes an ideal of community. From this the concrete collegiality of the ministry of the bishop and the ministry of the presbyter also follows, as an expression of the hierarchical communion to which they are due, as is mentioned in *LG* 22, 23 and *PO* 2,7,8, and which is more extensively developed in our text below (nn. 880–887).

Finally, the *CCC* (n. 878) also underscores the personal character of ecclesial ministry with a reference to the New Testament expression: "Follow me". It is a unique and exclusive formula to express the personal following of Jesus, which appears only in the mouth of Jesus and in the four Gospels (it also is used in Rev 14:4, as an application of Mt 10:38, speaking of the *"imitatio Agni"*), and includes two aspects: closeness with him—vital communion—and the spreading of the Gospel—mission. Indeed, the fourth Gospel points to the equation between following him and serving him (12:26), which is the fruit of a gift of God (21:20–22) and not of one's own self-determination ("Peter said to him, 'Lord, why can I not follow you now?'" 13:36–38), and because of this the culmination of Peter's discipleship consists in "following" the Lord, even materially (21:19,22).

The institution of the *Apostolic college* "by the disposition of the Lord" *(statuente Domino)*, which n. 880 affirms by citing *LG* 19,22, was confirmed by an explicit judgment of the Pontifical Biblical Commission which attested to its biblical foundation during the conciliar sessions, at the request of the Pope himself. On the succession of the apostolic college with the episcopal college, that judgment declared that Scripture alone did not suffice for its concrete realization (cf. *AS* III/1, 13f.). The expression "by the disposition of the Lord" must therefore be seen in light of the famous statement in *DV* 9 on the Catholic principle of tradition: "So it happens that the Church does not attain her certainty about all things that have been revealed from sacred Scripture alone" (cf. "La chiesa radicata in Gesù" in our *Ecclesiologia,* Brescia: Queriniana, 2008, 103–139).

To explain the primatial ministry of Peter, n. 881 cites two classic gospel texts, Mt 16:18f and Jn 21:15–17, as in Vatican I, which, relating them to the institution of St. Peter's apostolic primacy, observes that this is a "very clear teaching of the Holy Scriptures, as it has always been understood by the Catholic Church" (*DH* 3054). These texts, therefore, even if they do not themselves fall under the dogmatic definition, obviously stand at the origin of this authoritative ecclesial interpretation.

Mt 16:16–19 deserves particular attention, given its decisive importance in the history of the theology of the primacy. It is, in fact, an original, not an interpolated, pericope, clearly of Aramaic origin, according to the studies of specialists from every school of thought. The opinion has also been advanced, including among Catholics, that it is a text likely to be of post-paschal origin, probably connected to the protophany of 1 Cor 15:5 and Lk 24:34 (thus exegetes such as R. Schnackenburg, A. Vögtle, R. Pesch, X. Léon-Dufour, R.E. Brown, P. Grelot, R. Fabris, R. Aguirre…, and theologians such as H. Fries, F.S. Fiorenza, J.P. Tillard, M.M. Garijo-Guembe, W. Kasper, M. Kehl, S. Pié-Ninot…): a hypothesis that cannot be excluded, provided there be a guarantee of the historical validity of this promise, based on an authentically Christian faith in the event of the resurrection of Jesus Christ.

Our text also, citing *LG* 22, makes reference to the power of the keys, with the mission of loosing and binding entrusted to Peter and the apostles and continued by the bishops under the primacy of the Pope. For Judaism the power of the keys of the kingdom evokes a consolidated authority over an objective reality, and the power of binding and loosing makes it possible to exclude from, or in turn admit into, the community, and also implies a power to declare what it is necessary to believe and do to enter into the Church of God and remain in her.

All of n. 882 is dedicated to the ministry of the bishop of Rome and successor of St. Peter, the Pope, based on *LG* 23, which draws on the dogmatic constitution *Pastor Aeternus* of Vatican I, as "a perpetual principle and visible foundation of […] unity" (*DH* 3051), for the sake of which he "has full, supreme, and universal power over the whole Church, a power which he can always exercise unhindered," as is quoted from *LG* 22, cf. *CD* 2,9 (cf. *UUS* 95, and the extensive commentary on "Ministerio petrino" in our *Ecclesiologia,* 454–584).

The last text quoted from *LG* also serves as a starting point to deal with the power of the college of bishops with its head (cf. nn. 883–885), which notably shares in the same adjectives attributed to the Pope alone, even if the order is different, a point that is undoubtedly not accidental. It has a "supreme and full power over the universal Church" (*LG* 22; cf. *CIC* can. 336). Furthermore, in the succeeding items, two important aspects of the college of bishops are emphasized: first (n. 884) the exercise of its power in solemn form in an ecumenical Council, confirmed or at least accepted by the Pope (cf. *LG* 22; *CIC* can. 337); and second (n. 885), the expression of universality and unity shown by the varied composition of the college of bishops itself (cf. *LG* 22 and the document of the Pontifical Biblical Commission, *Unity and diversity in the Church* [April 11, 1988], found in EV 11, 554–643).

All of n. 886 is dedicated to the bishops, based on *LG* 23; they are "the visible source and foundation of unity in their own particular Churches," which are described as a "portion of the People of God" and not as a "part," because they could be interpreted then as partial Churches. Perhaps for this reason the adjective "particular," which the new *CIC* has consecrated as the prevailing term for the definition of dioceses (can. 368f.), marginalizing the term "local Church" which Vatican II used in a similar manner, raises certain ambiguities, since it runs the risk that the dualism "particular/universal" may generate a bipolarity that makes it difficult to articulate their essence and their "mutual inclusion" by nature. In this sense, it would surely be better to retain the expression "local Church," for its multiplicity of meaning and for its easier articulation along with the adjective "universal."

On the relation of the universal Church and local Churches, theological reflection continues to explore the meaning of the conciliar affirmation that the particular Churches "are constituted after the model of the universal Church; it is in these and formed out of them *(in quibus et ex quibus)* that the one and unique Catholic Church exists" (*LG* 23, quoted in n. 833 of the *CCC*).

On the topic of the priority between local Church and universal Church various authors have mentioned that it is a debate "leading to a blind alley," and therefore it is preferable to speak along the lines of "mutual presence and reciprocal inclusion" (W. Aymanns, Y.M. Congar, H. Légrand, A. Anton, D. Valentini, S. Pié-Ninot…). The Congregation for the Doctrine of the Faith, in the document *Communionis notio, "On some aspects of the Church understood as communion"* (May 28, 1992), affirms that the particular Churches have a particular relation of "mutual interiority" with the universal Church (cf. International Theological Commission, *Select Themes of Ecclesiology,* 1985, n. 5.2, found in *EV* 9, 1714). Because of this, the universal Church is "a reality ontologically and temporally prior to every individual particular Church." This is why the formula of the Second Vatican Council, "the Church, in and from the Churches" (*"Ecclesia in et ex Ecclesiis,"* from *LG* 23, which develops what is stated by *MC: "Ex quibus una constat Ecclesia Catholica"*), is inseparable from this other expression: "the Churches, in and from the

Church" *("Ecclesiae in et ex Ecclesia").* It is important to note, in this sense, that the conciliar text places the formula *"in quibus et ex quibus"* after the statement that the particular churches are "fashioned after the model of the universal Church" (*LG* 23). Perhaps the analogy with the relation between head and body could give a useful orientation for understanding this inclusive articulation and this mutual interiority of the local Churches and the universal Church for the sake of an ecclesiology of *"communio Ecclesiarum"* (*AG* 38, and *"corpus Ecclesiarum": LG* 23; cf. the remainder of our *Ecclesiologia,* cit., 375–383). It also indicates that the bishops, as members of the college, must have a solicitude for all the Churches. It recalls an expression proposed in the encyclical *Fidei Donum* by Pius XII in 1957, through which he invited the bishops to support missionary activity with prayer, charity, and the development of missionary vocations. The newness of this perspective was based on defining the solicitude of bishops not only as a "participation" in the Pope's solicitude, but more prominently, as proper to the apostolic succession based on its institution by Christ. The expression *"sollicitudo pro universa Ecclesia"* was expanded in *LG* 23 and *CD* 6 to show in turn the function of unity, proper to the promotion and care for the *"communio"* of the *"corpus Ecclesiarum"* which the bishops are to realize. This "sollicitudo," which must be translated into reality in their behavior and pastoral practice, is made significantly visible by the presence of various bishops at their episcopal ordination, as the *Apostolic Tradition* of Hippolytus (ch. 3) testifies, along with the Council of Nicea (can. 4). Canonical legislation makes concrete the aspects of this solicitude of every bishop for the universal Church, both in the exercise of his ordinary power, especially evident in the canons that would call for "vigilance" in the bishop's own diocese (c. 305, 392, 804, 823f), and in the specific institutions created for this purpose, such as the episcopal synod, particular councils, episcopal conferences (c. 342; 439–459). Our text specifies particularly the intended beneficiaries of this solicitude for the universal Church: the poor, those persecuted for the faith, and missionaries.

The last point (n. 887) specifies the synodal structures of communion among the particular/local Churches. In the first place the ecclesiastical provinces, patriarchates, and regions are cited. Already from the third century the Church was organizing herself in this way under the presidency of the Metropolitan or Patriarch, as was attested in the fourth century by the *Canons of the Apostles*, n. 34 (*PG* 137, 103–106), cited in our text, who had certain prerogatives recognized by the Councils of Nicea in 325 and Chalcedon in 451, later circumscribed by the Council of Trent. In *LG* 23, Vatican II clearly distinguishes between the ordinary power of every bishop, who cannot "exercise their pastoral government [...] over other churches" and, on the other hand, the obligation "to be solicitous for the whole Church," as a fruit of the "unity and collegial affection" of all the bishops, given that "in these days especially bishops frequently are unable to fulfill their office effectively and fruitfully unless they develop a common effort involving constant growth in harmony and closeness of ties with other bishops" (*CD* 37).

Second, the forms of synodal cooperation are mentioned: particularly the provincial synods or councils, frequently celebrated in the early Church and in the Middle Ages, that became rarer after the Council of Trent. The *CIC* of 1917 stabilized their celebration every twenty years, and the new *CIC* leaves them to the pastoral prudence of the Metropolitan. Finally, there is mention of the episcopal conferences as indicated in *LG* 23. The 1973 *Directory for the Pastoral Ministry of Bishops* (*EV* 4, 1945–2328) presented a first set of norms on their theological and juridical status. But later in the 1983 *CIC* their "pastoral office" (*CD* 38) anticipated by Vatican II, was restricted to only "certain pastoral functions" (c. 447), a specification confirmed in *Apostolos suos* (May 21, 1998), n. 15 (*EV* 17, 834), in *Pastores gregis* (October 16, 2003), n. 63 (*EV* 22, 910f) and in the 2004 *Directory for the Pastoral Ministry of Bishops* (October 22, 2004), nn. 28–32 (*EV* 22, 1636–1649). The recent and new reflections of Pope Francis appear against this background, when he states that "a juridical status of episcopal conferences which would see them as subjects of specific attributions, including genuine doctrinal authority, has not yet been sufficiently elaborated. Excessive centralization, rather than proving helpful, complicates the Church's life and her missionary outreach" (*EG* 32).

The development of the *"triplex munus"* of the Church begins with the teaching office, which is given more space, as corresponds to what is proper to a Catechism principally set in the sphere of doctrine, as was indicated in *FD* from John Paul II, who promulgated it. It is emphasized that the first duty of bishops, with their co-workers the presbyters, is to proclaim the Gospel according to the missionary text with which the Gospel of Mark ends (16:15). The bishops are described, significantly, as "authentic teachers"; the Latin is translated more precisely as "authoritative," according to the editors of the conciliar text, who wanted to emphasize that the magisterium of bishops is carried out "with authority/authoritatively," as the explanation in the quoted text indicates: they are "authentic teachers [...] endowed with the authority of Christ" (*auctoritate Christi praediti*: *LG* 25) (cf. F. A. Sullivan, *Il Magistero nella Chiesa Cattolica,* Assisi: Cittadella, 1986; "Magistero," in *Dizionario di Teologia Fondamentale,* edited by R. Latourelle and R. Fisichella, Assisi: Cittadella, 1998, 653–661). The purity of the faith in which the Church is to maintain herself arises from Christ the Truth himself, who makes her a sharer in his own infallibility. Hence this infallibility appears as proper to the whole Church because of her rootedness in Christ; because of this, thanks to the "supernatural sense of the faith," the people of God "adheres unwaveringly to the faith" under the guidance of the living magisterium of the Church. This *"sensus fidei,"* which *LG* 12 locates in the "entire body of the faithful, [...which] cannot err in belief," is an echo of the famous "infallibility in believing" used in the conciliar debate (cf. *AS* III/1, 198). Our text—n. 889—refers to two moments in which Vatican II cites this *"sensus fidei"* (*LG* 12; *DV* 10), although *LG* broadens the range of its meaning, referring not only to its function of adherence, but also to the deepening of knowledge *(recto iuditio in eam profundius penetrat)* and application to life *(in vita plenius applicat),* as an expression of the way "this tradition which comes from the Apostles develops in the Church," as it is neatly described in *DV* 8 (cf. our "Sensus fidei," in *Dizionario di Teologia Fondamentale,* cit., 1131–1134, and the recent document of the International Theological Commission, *The sense of faith in the life of the Church* [June 10, 2014]).

In an innovation for an ecclesial text, n. 890 analyzes the mission of the Magisterium as a sign of the "definitive nature of the covenant established by God with his people in Christ." One of the great contributions by the theologian K. Rahner mentions such an analysis when he states: "The Church would not be the eschatological community of salvation if she did not possess the truth of Christ infallibly" (cf. *Sacramentum mundi,* 8 vols., Brescia: Morcelliana, 1974–1977; *Corso fundamentale sulla fede,* Alba: Paoline, 1977). At the same time, n. 890 emphasizes precisely that the pastoral mission of the Magisterium is in the service of "the truth that liberates," an echo of the Johannine expression "the truth will make you free" (Jn 8:32). Let us recall that *DV* 8 shows that this kind of teaching is based on the "sure gift of truth" communicated with apostolic succession. This charism of infallibility is exercised in "matters of faith and morals" *(fides et mores),* as an expression of the content of the "deposit of revelation," which embraces not only "the faith" but also "every rule, norm, and command of morality," according to the nuanced expression of the Council of Trent used by Vatican II: *"morum disciplina"* (*DH* 3006; *DV* 7: "all [...] moral teaching"). The theological commission of Vatican II explained that the object of infallibility "extends as far as the deposit of divine Revelation itself"—as our text concludes by citing—and therefore extends directly to that deposit, or to whatever is required to protect it and expound it faithfully (cf. *AS* III/1, 251).

The declaration *ME* from the Congregation for the Doctrine of the Faith, directly addressing the topic of the secondary object of the Magisterium, speaks of "those matters without which that deposit [of faith] cannot be rightly preserved and expounded, and which must be expounded—not as revealed truths proper to the primary object, but—as in accord with Catholic doctrine" (n. 3, in *EV* 4, 2572; cited later in our text at n. 2035). The exercise of infallibility on the part of the Roman Pontiff and the body of bishops in union with him, is described (n. 891) as the "supreme magisterium"—beyond "extraordinary"—and is expressed with the formula "definitive act," avoiding the more famous but surely less immediately comprehensible term, to speak *"ex cathedra"* (cf. Vatican I; *DH* 3074; in Vatican II: *LG* 25, both are used). The adherence required by such definitions is the "obedience of faith" (*"obsequium fidei"*: *LG* 25; *AG* 15; *DH* 15; cf. *CIC* 750), which, according to the conciliar explanation, is more than a sincere adherence of the mind, because, in regard to definitions, it reaches the level of acceptance by faith (cf. *AS* III/I, 251).

The following text (n. 892) concentrates on the ordinary Magisterium, which is described as "a teaching that leads to better understanding of Revelation in matters of faith and morals." To distinguish this type of Magisterium, *LG* 25 itself offers three criteria that must be presupposed: "the character of the documents, [...] frequent repetition of the same doctrine, or [... the] manner of speaking." The adherence required by the Magisterium is "religious assent" (the *"obsequium religiosum"* of *LG* 25). Our text, placing it in relation to the "assent of faith", indicates a fine hermeneutical criterion based on both the distinction and the coherence between these two formulations: "religious assent, [...] though distinct from the assent of faith, is nonetheless an extension of it" (cf. the important document *De interpretatione dogmatum* [1989] from the International Theological Commission, in *EV* 11, 2717–2811). It should be noted that subsequently John Paul II promulgated the *motu proprio Ad tuendam fidem* (May 18, 1998, in *EV* 17, 801–897), specifying a new distinction in the ordinary Magisterium between the definitive and the non-definitive (cf. this topic in our *Ecclesiologia,* cit., 532–538).

Briefly—perhaps too briefly, even if the second part of the *CCC* dedicated to the sacraments justifies it—there is mention of the sanctifying office of the Church, by reason of the fact that the bishop is "the steward of the grace of the supreme priesthood": the *oeconomus,* says the Latin text of *LG* 26. This expression is characteristic of the *Apostolic Tradition* of Hippolytus and the Veronese *Sacramentary* to describe the bishop, and is taken up by Vatican II to explain the teaching that "by episcopal consecration the fullness of the sacrament of orders is conferred" (*LG* 21). Because of this the new *Prex ordinationis* of the bishop incorporated it into the 1968 postconciliar *editio tipica,* and it remains in the 1989 second *editio tipica.* The text concentrates on the exercise of this priesthood in the "Eucharist which is the center of life of the particular Church." Vatican II stands in this same perspective, tracing the theological notion of the diocesan Church (*CD* 11, which the new *CIC* substantially takes up in c. 369). In effect, the Eucharist is "the fount and apex of the whole Christian life" (*LG* 11) and "of all evangelization" (*PO* 5) and therefore, of the Church's mission, as well as the "source of the Church's life" (*UR* 15). The same Council affirms that the eucharist is the "center and summit" of the sacraments (*AG* 9) and, in turn, "the center and culmination of the whole life of the Christian community" (*CD* 30). Because of this,

LG 26 describes the diocesan Church as the community united around the bishop "in the Eucharist, which he offers or causes to be offered, and by which the Church continually lives and grows," and in turn concludes: "in any community of the altar, under the sacred ministry of the bishop, there is exhibited a symbol of that charity and 'unity of the mystical Body, without which there can be no salvation.' In these communities, though frequently small and poor, or living in the Diaspora, Christ is present, and in virtue of His presence there is brought together one, holy, catholic and apostolic Church" (cf. Augustine, *in loco*).

With this formulation and following Vatican II, our text takes up a principle present in the ecclesiological-theological tradition that sees how the Church makes the Eucharist and the Eucharist makes the Church, found in the "eucharistic ecclesiology" that is especially developed in Orthodox theology (cf. the reference to N. Affanassief in the same conciliar *relatio* on *LG* 26; cf. *AS* III/1, 254); in addition, J. Meyendorff, A. Schmemann, J.D. Zizioulas…). Significant echoes of this ecclesiology are also found in the Catholic sphere (cf. J. Hamer, and after Vatican II, J. Ratzinger, B. Forte, G.J. Békés, J.M. Tillard, M.M. Garijo-Guembe…). So it is not strange that the connection between eucharist and Church is fundamental in the official commissions between Orthodox and Catholics (cf. "Il mistero della Chiesa e dell'eucharistia alla luce della santa Trinità," in *EO* 1, 2183–2197), as also between Orthodox and Anglicans (*Moscow Declaration* [1976]; *Dublin Report* [1984], in *EO* 1, 409–415; 552–558). This Catholic recovery of ecclesiology needs to include "the existence of the Petrine ministry, which is a foundation of the unity of the episcopate and of the universal Church, [and] bears a profound correspondence to the eucharistic character of the Church" (Congregation for the Doctrine of the Faith, *On some aspects of the Church understood as communion,* May 28, 1992, n. 11).

Finally, the pastoral or governing office (*munus regendi*) is described more generically with prayer and work, and around the ministry of the Word and the sacraments, being "examples to the flock," as 1 Pt 5:3 expresses the relation of pastors and faithful, which is a clear classic witness of ministry and the ecclesial order in the primitive Church (cf. our *Ecclesiologia,* cit., 117–139). The designation given to bishops as "vicars of Christ" was found already in the third century in the Latin Fathers (Cyprian, Hormisdas, Braulius, Catulfus, Amalarius…). Following St. Ambrose and the Roman synod of 495, the term is applied to the Roman Pontiff, although he is preferentially called *"Vicarius Petri"* until the 11th century. The title of *"Vicarius Christi"* applied to the bishop of Rome became widespread due to St. Bernard and is used officially at the Council of Florence (*DH* 1307) and at Vatican I (*DH* 3059): *"Verus Christi Vicarius."* Nonetheless, it continues to be applied to the bishops, as indicates St. Thomas, who describes the apostles and their successors as *"vicarios Dei quantum ad regimen Ecclesiae constitutae per fidem et fidei sacramenta"* (*Summa Theologiae,* III, 64, 2 ad 3).

Our text, citing *LG* 27, strongly emphasizes the "proper, ordinary, and immediate" power of bishops in their particular Churches, and afterward notes that "the bishops should not be thought of as vicars of the Pope. His ordinary and immediate authority over the whole Church does not annul, but on the contrary confirms and defends that of the bishops." This last part is a summary of the second paragraph of *LG* 27, whose three observations complete its meaning: first it recalls the response of Pius IX to the German bishops in which he emphasized this point in response to Bismarck (cf. *DH* 3112–3117), and on the other hand, it cites Vatican I with its explanatory *relatio* on this point (cf. *DH* 3061; the conciliar *relatio* published in *Mansi* 52, 1114D) and finally *LG* 27 adds that the "proper, ordinary, and immediate" power of bishops "is ultimately controlled [*ultimatum regatur*] by the supreme authority of the Church," emphasizing with this formulation the proper role of the ministry of the Pope, and not describing the power of the Pope again with the same adjectives "ordinary and immediate" as Vatican I did (*DH* 3064), creating certain hermeneutical difficulties. This is why these adjectives are not used in the Dogmatic Constitution of the Church *LG*, even if they are cited secondarily in a conciliar disciplinary decree such as *CD* 2.

In addition, it is undeniable that here we find one of the points, perhaps not easily seen, but whose repetition—both the affirmative in n. 894: "The bishops are vicars of Christ," and the negative in n. 895: "The bishops are not vicars of the Pope"—represents an important statement of the theology of Vatican II on the episcopate and the local Church, in the name of an unmistakable ecclesiology of communion *"cum et sub Petro"* (cf. *LG* 22 and the *Preliminary Note of Explanation* for *LG*). Finally, with the image of the Good Shepherd, presented as "the model and 'form' of the bishop's pastoral office," our text concludes its part on the hierarchy at n. 896. It is known that the symbolism of the shepherd who guides and protects his flock became traditional in the primitive Church, and so we find it described in the message of Paul to the "presbyters" from Ephesus at Miletus (Acts 20:7–38), which seems to be the background for our text. In Luke's intention this message contains a decisive teaching for those who have a ministry in the post-apostolic era; indeed, thanks to the parallelism between Paul and Jesus, it is made plain to what extent ministry for the community can constitute a *"diakonía"* (v. 24) and a "happy giving" (v. 35), and therefore, as with Paul himself, the "guardian" (v. 28) has a duty of vigilance (v. 31f.) in the community. This last point presents a strong parallelism with the discourse on the Good Shepherd in Jn 10:11–18, in which the importance of "personal knowledge" of the sheep is emphasized, after the image of the "knowledge" that exists between the Father and the Son. This parallelism would prove more obvious yet if these two New Testament texts were both to have arisen from Ephesus, a hypothesis not to be dismissed (cf. also 1 Pt 2:2,25; 5:1f).

In addition to the image of the Good Shepherd, the text closes its description of the figure of the bishop and his "threefold mission" with the well-known and incisive statement of St. Ignatius of Antioch: "Let no one do anything connected with the Church without the bishop" (Epistle to the Smyrnaeans, 8, 1). With this as background, the recent reflection of Pope Francis is worthy of attention, when he writes: "The bishop must always foster this missionary communion in his diocesan Church, following the ideal of the first Christian communities, in which the believers were of one heart and one soul (cf. Acts 4:32)" (*EG* 31).

II. The Lay Faithful

N. 897 takes up the first part of the famous definition of the lay faithful from *LG* 31, which starts from the negative dimension: the laity are all the faithful who are not members in either sacred orders or in the religious state; and turns toward the positive dimension: lay people are all those who are incorporated into the Church with baptism, who form the people of God, and share "in their own way" in the priestly, prophetic, and kingly functions of Christ, and who "carry out for their own part the mission of the whole Christian people in the Church and in the world."

This definition, taken literally from *ChL* 9, and also from the *CIC* itself in c. 224f., prescinds from the second part of the text of *LG* 31, in which the specific "way" and "part" pertaining to their identity are specified more positively: the famous "secular nature," seen as "proper and particular" to the laity. One cannot deny that although this is not a formal definition by Vatican II, this secularity opens new ecclesiological perspectives and makes it possible to get beyond the problem of attributing competences to the laity ever closer to those of the ministerial priesthood, with the subtle risk of clericalization which changes the character of secularity. Specialists in the theology of the laity propose three interpretations of this "secular nature."

1. The sociological interpretation by canon lawyers of the German school (K. Mörsdorf; W. Aymans), and by important Italian theologians (S. Dianich, B. Forte), who hold that the category of laity has been surpassed in ecclesiology. This interpretation supports a twofold partition of the Christian faithful: clergy and laity, according to c. 207.1.

2. The theological interpretation of the secular nature, particularly prominent in E. Correcco, as it appears in his intervention at the Synod on the laity, in which he defined the constitutive elements of secularity as property, marriage, and liberty. From elsewhere it was also supported by the greater part of the participating authors at the International Symposium on

the laity at the University of Navarre (1987). This interpretation takes up the threefold partition of the faithful: clergy, laity, and religious, as canons 225.2, 1427.3, and 711 suggest.

3. Finally, there is an intermediate position that assumes elements of the preceding two and could be characterized as ministerial-missionary: the later writings of Y.M. Congar on the ministerial dimension of the layman are situated along this line, as are W. Kasper, who emphasizes service to the world (*Weltdienst*), and the canonists J. Beyer and G. Ghirlanda who speak of the "charism of secularity" and that it would certainly be desirable (thus also our *Ecclesiologia,* cit., 308–325).

The three following numbers, 898–900, make explicit the vocation of the laity precisely in its "secular nature," again prescinding from this expression with the phrase that is the most important of everything in chapter IV, and which constitutes, as it were, the keystone: "By reason of their special vocation it belongs to the laity to seek the kingdom of God by engaging in temporal affairs and directing them according to God's will" (G. Philips, *La Chiesa e il suo mistero nel Concilio Vaticano II. Storia, testo e comment della Costituzione Lumen Gentium,* Milan: Jaca Book, 1969, citing *LG* 31). The ultimate end sought is "to illuminate and order all temporal things." The term "illuminate" shows that if temporal values are not respected or if they are despised, they do not become illuminated. It is not enough to accompany work with a good intention: it must be "illuminated" from within, to be ordered according to the will of Christ, to "be to the glory of the Creator and Redeemer." This involves a synthesis between creation and salvation with a Christological focus that recalls the great lines of *GS*. With great courage, the text accents the necessary "initiative" of the laity, described as "a normal element of the life of the Church," "discovering or inventing the means for permeating social, political, and economic realities." This rests upon the expressive statement that "lay believers are in the front line of Church life," drawn from Pius XII and cited by John Paul II in *ChL* 9, which has a clear resonance in his concluding homily at the Synod on the laity, exclaiming: "So here is the lay believer, facing the frontiers of history: the family, work, culture, the world of work, economic goods, politics, science, technology, social communication; the great problems of life, solidarity, peace; of professional ethics, of human rights, education, religious liberty" (October 30, 1987; cf. our commentary in Pontifical Council for the Laity, "Presenza e missione dei laici nel mondo: Christifideles Laici: spunti per uno studio," in *I Laici oggi,* 32/33 [1989/1990] 95–101).

The call to apostolate concludes the topic of the vocation of the lay person. it is emphasized that this basic obligation and this right, both individual and in association, have their sacramental foundation in baptism and confirmation, and that this obligation becomes ever "more pressing" when lay people are the only way in which men can hear and know the Gospel and Jesus Christ (cf. *LG* 33). It is not unusual that quite recently Pope Francis emphasized the great challenge which consists in the Church "going out", where "the formation of the laity and the evangelization of professional and intellectual life represent a significant pastoral challenge" (*EG* 102).

Following the three-part schema used above in speaking of the hierarchy, and in accord with Vatican II, the mission of the laity is studied in depth in three blocks. In the first, on the priestly mission, the sharing of lay people in the priestly office of Christ is spelled out. It begins by citing *LG* 34, in which the two fundamental elements of the priestly function are summarized: worship "in spirit and truth," and witness, the two axes of the theology of the priesthood in the New Testament (cf. Heb 1; 1 Pt 2:4–10). Under the rubric of witness, the formula coined by Pius XII in 1957 at the second world Congress for the lay apostolate is mentioned: "consecration of the world to God," which characterizes the illuminating and permeating mission of the Gospel in the world, in the sense of "a Christian service in the temporal sphere" (Y.M. Congar). The next point touches upon this direction, referring to conjugal life and the Christian education of children, with a citation of the *CIC*, c. 835.4. This block ends with a reference to the ministry of lay people according to the *CIC*, c. 230. It deals both with stable ministries and the extraordinary ministries of lector and acolyte. According to the *motu proprio* of its institution by Paul VI, the ministry of lector is not limited to the liturgical realm, since it includes the proclaiming the Word of God, leading the liturgy, and preparing the faithful for the sacraments, and therefore catechesis (*MQ* V, found in *EV* 4, 1761). This *motu proprio* also allowed episcopal conferences to institute other ministries, as for example, that of charity, something that will later makes its way into *ChL* 41. Despite this, the Synod of the Laity expressed the desire that this *motu proprio* be revised (*Propositio* 18) and that a specific commission be created to this end (cf. *ChL* 23). On this point it is appropriate to take account of the post-conciliar fluctuation of the term "ministry," which can be an occasion of confusion, given that in Vatican II and various subsequent documents (*MQ* V; *EN* 73 and *FC* 28,32,38f.) this term also expresses the ecclesiological concept of lay "ministry" in the world: of the 16 times when the term appears in Vatican II, 7 are applied to the laity. On the other hand, in the *CIC* (c. 230, 759, 910, 943, 1481, 1502, 1634), "ministry" is applied only to the Church. For the sake of the development of lay ministries, one might hope, therefore, to get a clarification of the doctrine about their nature as well as a canonical clarification, to situate them and protect them with socio-pastoral clarity, in order not to proceed on the basis of improvisation and impulse.

In the second mission the sharing of the laity in Christ's prophetic office is assessed. The prophetic function of the laity is described in nn. 904f, on the basis of *LG* 35, as the exercise of the prophetic office of Christ at two levels: the first is to be "witnesses," a constant point of reference from Vatican II in its concrete search for the concrete credibility of the faith. The text takes an interest in emphasizing the complementarity between witness of life and proclamation of the Word, also citing *AA* 6 and *AG* 15, and articulated well in the famous text of *EN* 20f.

Second, the "prophetic" office is expressed in "the sense of the faith and the grace of the word," a formula developed in *LG* 12, and used again in *ChL* 14, and also cited previously in n. 92 of our text. This *"sensus fidei"* must be placed in the context of ecclesial communion, which makes possible the vast articulation between the "exterior" Magisterium, proper to the apostolic college with its head and its successors, which has "the task of authentically interpreting the word of God, whether written or handed on" (*DV* 10; cf. *LG* 25) and the "interior" Magisterium of the Spirit, present in all the baptized, which is manifested in their sharing in the prophetic role of Christ and the Church (cf. *LG* 12, 35, 37; *DV* 8), as an empirical means of the Church's living tradition (cf. our *Sensus fidei,* in *Dizionario di Teologia Fondamentale,* ed. by R. Latourelle and R. Fisichella, cit., 1133f). The last two points on the prophetic function, nn. 906–907, describe the pertinent canonical norms that embrace this prophetic function: catechesis, the teaching of sacred sciences and the means of social communication, as well as the importance of manifesting to the sacred pastors "their opinion on matters which pertain to the good of the Church" (*CIC,* c. 212.3). It deals with what was suggested by *LG* 37, which cites two memorable texts from Pius XII, that mention on one hand that "in the decisive battles the initiatives of greatest value arise from the front-line," and on the other, there is emphasis on the importance of a healthy public opinion in the life of the Church (*LG* 37, note 7).

Finally, as the third aspect, the sharing of the laity in the "kingly" office of Christ is explained, following *LG* 36. In n. 908, our text introduces this kingly office in an innovative way, as based on Christ's obedience even unto death, which thus communicates "the gift of royal freedom," described finely with a literal quotation from St. Ambrose. Based on this, two central expressions appear for the presence of the Christian in the world, that is, for his "kingly office": to "heal" everything that is sin, and in turn to "permeate" reality with moral values; two expressions that recall the theology of grace as purifying and liberating (the *"gratia sanans"* of Augustine), and as elevating and divinizing (the *"gratia elevans"* of the 13th century), and which unite the mission of the Church according to *LG* 13, 17 (*"sanans-purificans/ elevans-roborans/consumans"*). The next two items, nn. 910–911, address the participation of the laity in the exercise of the governance of the Church. The possibility of exercising "ministries" in the Church is noted with the quotation from *EN* 73, which we have already commented upon. Then the canonical norm makes clear that they can "cooperate in the exercise of this power" of governance in particular councils, synods, pastoral councils, and councils for economic affairs, pastoral care of a parish, and participation in ecclesiastical tribunals. Let us note that, by citing c. 129.2, which uses the term "can cooperate" as its basis, and not *LG* 33, which speaks of a further "capacity to assume from the hierarchy certain ecclesiastical functions," it appears clearly that the passage is about an extrinsic cooperation in the power possessed by others, i.e., the hierarchy, and not about a native and proper capacity for the exercise of governance in the Church.

To conclude, our text on the laity mentions *LG* 36, emphasizing the "indispensable distinction" (G. Philips) between members of the Church and members of human society. Far from falling into a split personality, it notes that the "harmonious" unity between these two spheres is based on the guidance "of a Christian conscience," which brings unity to the person and always has a word to speak to human reality. So this unity is established thanks to the ethical-moral dimension and this is what exercises its dominion—which is the dominion of God written in the heart of the believer—on temporal activity. The reference to "Christian conscience," cited only once in *LG* 36, is multiplied in *GS*, on the subject of the presence of the Church and Christians in the world (21 times).

The concluding item on the laity cites *LG* 33, which affirms the lay vocation and mission, which must be described clearly as being of the Church, since it "is at the same time a witness and a living instrument of the mission of the Church itself," thanks to the radical equality that exists from having received the sacraments of initiation "according to the measure of Christ's bestowal" (Eph 4:7; cf. the commentary and bibliography by D. Vitali, "*LG. Capitolo IV. I laici,*" in *Commentario ai Documenti del Vaticano II: 2, Lumen Gentium,* Bologna: EDB, 2015, 315–321, and *Lumen gentium. Storia—Commento—Recezione,* Rome: Studium, 2012).

Chapter Three, Article 9, Paragraph 4/III: "THE CONSECRATED LIFE"

Pier Giordano Cabra

Foreword

After the publication of the *CCC* (1992), the Synod of Bishops on consecrated life was held (1994), which concluded in 1996 with the publication of the Apostolic Exhortation *VC,* which can be considered the most authoritative commentary on our topic.

The Origins of Consecrated Life

In the history of the Church, the forms of consecrated life are numberless and most varied, but they all can be traced back to the Lord Jesus who, while preaching the kingdom of God to everyone, only asked some to leave everything to stay with him, to live as he lived. Although he asked everyone to follow him in living the demands of the Kingdom in the normal conditions of life, he did not ask all to follow him in his "abnormality" of celibacy, without material resources, without the prestige of power, dedicated fully to the Father's business and the proclamation of the Kingdom. "In every age there have been men and women who, obedient to the Father's call and to the prompting of the Spirit, have chosen this special way of following Christ.... Like the Apostles, they too have left everything behind" (*VC* 1). One can understand how this "special way of following" would also continue after the resurrection, which had manifested the glory of divinity present in the man Jesus. Everything in Jesus was a manifestation of God: not only his deeds and words but also his way of life, which placed itself at the summit of the Christian ideal, being understood as the divine form of living human life or the human form of living divine life. Consequently we can understand the importance given to virginity "in honor of the flesh of the Lord." From St. Paul to St. Ignatius of Antioch, virginity (or celibacy) was esteemed as an expression of a special love for the Lord, virgin and bridegroom, with a passion for every person who does not refuse his love. The "special way of following Christ" was soon practiced and made visible in monasticism of the most varied forms and with various rules, but all characterized by the consistent common denominator of virginity or celibacy, from its origins to our day.

In the second millennium the theology of the three "evangelical counsels" was affirmed, as an interpretive summary of the "special way of following Christ." In practice it is the thematic presentation of the ideal of total dedication to God, around the three evangelical counsels of poverty, chastity, and obedience, present in all the preceding *Rules.* A decisive contribution to the affirmation of this triad is the unique personality of St. Francis who synthesized his ideal in this way: "The rule of the brothers is this, that is, to live in obedience, without any property and in chastity" (*Regola non bollata* I, 1). For the love of Christ one wants to live like him. A few decades later, St. Thomas will defend the profession of the evangelical counsels before the theologians of the University of Paris, illustrating their anthropological dimension, in which the three counsels remove the principal obstacles to the attainment of perfect charity, posed by threefold concupiscence. From then on the "special way of following Christ" will be called religious life or regular life or consecrated life, assumed through the profession of the evangelical counsels.

Consecrated Life

This article can be understood better if we keep in mind two dimensions of the Church, the Petrine and the Marian. *VC* 34, presenting the group of disciples gathered in the Cenacle to await the Holy Spirit, states: "In Peter and the other Apostles there emerges above all the aspect of fruitfulness, as it is expressed in ecclesial ministry, which becomes an instrument of the Spirit for bringing new sons and daughters to birth through the preaching of the word, the celebration of the Sacraments and the giving of pastoral care. In Mary the aspect of spousal receptivity is particularly clear; it is under this aspect that the Church, through her perfect virginal life, brings divine life to fruition within herself. The consecrated life has always been seen primarily in terms of Mary—Virgin and Bride. This virginal love is the source of a particular fruitfulness which fosters the birth and growth of divine life in people's hearts." Peter and Mary, institution and life, gift and response, two "coessential" dimensions, indisputably and indissolubly united, at the service of the people of God.

Evangelical Counsels and Consecrated Life

The New Testament presents numerous counsels that aid in leading a life inspired by the Gospel, such as continual prayer, generosity in giving, the sharing of goods, the acceptance of injustice to oneself, offering one's life for one's enemies. We can also think of the evangelical counsels contained in the Beatitudes. The expression "evangelical counsels" evokes the triad of chastity, poverty and obedience, a triad considered as summarizing gospel behavior with regard to the body, to goods, and to self-affirmation. Aiming ourselves toward God, following the example of Christ, in the power of the Holy Spirit, these three fundamental forces mean to start the re-orientation of the whole human person toward perfect communion with God.

VC presents some explanations on the subject of our two articles:

1. *Evangelical counsels and Christian perfection.* "In fact, all those reborn in Christ are called to live out, with the strength which is the Spirit's gift, the chastity appropriate to their state of life, obedience to God and to the Church, and a reasonable detachment from material possessions: for all are called to holiness, which consists in the perfection of love. But Baptism in itself does not include the call to celibacy or virginity, the renunciation of possessions or obedience to a superior, in the form proper to the evangelical counsels. The profession of the evangelical counsels thus presupposes a particular gift of God not given to everyone, as Jesus himself emphasizes with respect to voluntary celibacy (cf. Mt 19:10–12)" (*VC* 30).

2. *Christian life and consecrated life.* Whereas every Christian worthy of the name is called to be conformed to Christ, based on his attitudes in regard to things and extending to his way of feeling and thinking: "Have this mind among yourselves which was in Christ Jesus" (Phil 2:5), the vocation of conforming to his way of life has been given to some also. "The profession of the evangelical counsels is intimately connected with the mystery of Christ, and has the duty of making somehow present the way of life which Jesus himself chose and indicated as an absolute eschatological value" (*VC* 29). The values of Christ's "way of life" are an unrenounceable part of the revelation and the spiritual inheritance that the Church is obliged to hand on to all generations (cf. *DV* 7). The transmission of this spiritual treasure cannot be carried out by words alone. It is necessary that certain people, consecrated to the Father, continually represent the "way of life" Jesus embraced, within the Church. It is necessary that some people, enabled by the Spirit, offer the world a typical and permanent visibility of the characteristic traits of Jesus, with their Christ-shaped presence (cf. *VC* 1).

From this comes the illuminating and exacting statement: "The consecrated life truly constitutes *a living memorial of Jesus' way of living and acting* as the Incarnate Word in relation to the Father and in relation to the brethren" (*VC* 22). This is a great gift and a great duty, which is made possible by loving, prayerful attention to the person of the Lord Jesus, by contemplating him as a concrete person, that is, the "sacred humanity" of the Lord Jesus, and a commitment of "striving to conform," given the very high goal presented to fragile human nature. But this is very important, to keep alive in the Church and before the world the true memory of the Lord Jesus, a memory that can be easily deformed by aspirations that are all too human, which are present today as yesterday. It is too easy to project our expectations on the figure of Jesus, instead of letting him shape us through his words. Consecrated life, with its own presence, affirms that he came without power, in the form of an obedient servant. He came without riches, with only the disarmed power of the Word. He came celibate, with only the gratifying power of the love of God, to tell us that God is his and our realization; to remind us that God is his and our timeless riches, to convince us that God is his and our love, the only one that can fill the heart definitively.

One Great Tree with Many Branches

Consecrated life does not exist in the abstract, but many concrete forms do exist: Orders, Congregations, Institutes of various denominations: Jesuits, Franciscans, Salesian Sisters.... The multiplicity of Institutes depends on the needs of the Church, to which the Spirit has listened and intends to respond through a new form of consecrated life. When we needed to have the seriousness of following Christ reaffirmed, the desert became populated with ascetics who reminded the Church that we need to know how to renounce ourselves for the sake of Christ. When the so-called barbarians sowed material and spiritual destruction in the West, St. Benedict created the foundations for spiritual and civil reconstruction in the society of his time. Francis and Dominic remind us that the Gospel is preached with humility and not imposed with force or other forms of pressure; and so on, up to the male and female Congregations of *diakonia* that have served the poor, exercising the various works of mercy, so much that it is impossible to write the history of many countries if we forget the history of consecrated life, so much has it contributed to the humanization of life, as well as to personal sanctity and the life of the Church.

But who is to say if a new proposal for consecrated life comes from the Spirit? N. 919 has a clear indication: the first discernment belongs to the local bishops and definitive approval belongs to the Holy See. While the Church does not create consecrated life, the authentication of charisms that define consecrated life belongs to her.

The Eremitic Life

Describing the various branches of the plant "which sinks its roots into the Gospel and brings forth abundant fruit in every season of the Church's life" (*VC* 5), begins with eremitical life, celebrated in the *Life of Anthony* (251–356), written by St. Athanasius, who had known Anthony personally. Reading this spiritual biography, which was decisive for St. Augustine and many others in their choice of life, bespeaks the fascination of a life totally dedicated to God alone (*solus cum Solo*). Indeed it appears true that "God is all" for him who has left everything, thereby reminding people like himself and the ecclesial community "'never to lose sight of the supreme vocation,' which is to be always with the Lord" (*VC* 7). But this biography itself, far from presenting a romantic vision of eremitical life, shows the need and the difficulty of spiritual combat, to create order within oneself. The desert and solitude unmask our illusions about our so-called "innocence," sharpening the need to undertake the difficult road of purification to return to the Father.

Consecrated Virgins and Widows

For the Christian, Christ is everything: Lord, Friend, Bridegroom. He has loved the individual human person and the Church "to the end": he is the eschatological and definitive Bridegroom who desires to be loved "with the whole heart." Virginity for "the kingdom of heaven" recalls this spousal reality of Christian life. It is understandable how since apostolic times there have been Christian virgins who, called by the Lord to dedicate themselves exclusively to him in a greater freedom of body and spirit, have made the decision to live in the state of virginity for the "Kingdom of heaven" (Mt 19:12). "It is a source of joy and hope to witness in our time a new flowering of the 'ancient Order of Virgins'[…]. Consecrated by the diocesan bishop, these women acquire a particular link with the Church, which they are committed to serve while remaining in the world" (*VC* 7). The same apostolic exhortation also notes the order of *widows:* "Again being practiced today is the consecration of widows, known since apostolic times (cf. 1 Tim 5:5, 9–10; 1 Cor 7:8), as well as the consecration of widowers" (*VC* 7). These consecrate their condition through the vow of perpetual chastity to dedicate themselves to prayer and to the service of the Church. The renewal of this most ancient, even apostolic, form of consecration had its beginning in the Second World War, when a number of women who had lost their husbands joined together both to support one another in their widowhood and to consecrate themselves to God in supporting their children.

Secular Institutes

In the past century the Holy Spirit has continually raised up new expressions of consecrated life. "One thinks in the first place of members of Secular Institutes seeking to live out their consecration to God in the world through the profession of the evangelical counsels in the midst of temporal realities; they wish in this way to be a leaven of wisdom and a witness of grace within cultural, economic and political life. Through their own specific blending of presence in the world and consecration, they seek to make present in society the newness and power of Christ's Kingdom, striving to transfigure the world from within by the power of the Beatitudes" (*VC* 10). Though being in the state of consecrated life, the members of these institutes nonetheless do not change their canonical condition, lay or clerical, precisely to make possible their full apostolic insertion in the structures of secular and ecclesial life, without being distinguished in any way from other lay or clerical faithful. In fact they lead their lives in the ordinary situations of the world, without any external sign, alone or each in his or her own family. Yet they can also live in groups of fraternal life, without taking up the forms of religious common life, in order to be a discreet leaven in the world.

Societies of Apostolic Life

Societies of apostolic life, or societies of common life, "pursue, each in its own particular way, a specific apostolic or missionary end" (*VC* 11). These trace their origin to St. Philip Neri who gathered priests around himself, with only the bond of obedience, without vows. Widespread, especially in France (Lazarists, Eudists), at times they also take up the evangelical counsels. Still, the particularity of their consecration distinguishes them both from religious institutes and secular institutes. "In recent centuries it has produced many fruits of holiness and of the apostolate, especially in the field of charity and in the spread of the Gospel in the Missions" (*VC* 11).

Religious Life

While the Christian East concentrated on monastic life, the West saw rather diversified forms of religious consecration arise, most of them born to respond to the needs of the Church and also of society. This diversity could be interpreted with a special reference to two distinct Beatitudes. The East is organized around the Beatitude of "the pure of heart, for they shall see God." From this comes the importance of ascetical commitment, the purification of the heart, the contemplation of divine realities, of keeping the theandric or divine/human dimension of the Christian vocation alive and active. The West seems to have as its pole star the Beatitude of "the merciful, for they shall find mercy." From this comes a more accentuated attention on the neighbor, on God who comes through the poor, the suffering, the marginalized. In this context, religious life is fundamentally present under two forms: *contemplative religious life,* which reveals and imitates Christ praying on the mountain, becomes a sign of the presence of the kingdom of God, of its having already been inaugurated by Christ, as being also a sign of the pilgrim Church in a passing world. It dedicates itself to the glorification of God through *lectio,* continual prayer, and the cultivation of the liturgy. It declares the absolute primacy of God in everything, starting with the organization of time. It groups together many various forms: from cloistered monasteries to contemplative monks and other forms, sign of an indisputable vitality. The *active apostolic life* imitates Christ who teaches, heals, evangelizes. In history it has created schools, hospitals, and works of assistance for every type of need. It is a sign of a Church sent to serve and save.

Vocation and Profession

The vocation of a person to consecrated life is a gift which the Trinity makes not only to the person, but also, and especially, to his Church. The Father draws a person to himself so that the person may be dedicated exclusively to his Kingdom. He introduces him to following the Son, to learn from Him to dedicate himself to the matters of the Kingdom. The Father sends the Spirit to make these things attractive and comprehensible, as they are unaccustomed, and to give the courage and strength to carry out the renunciation of goods so rooted in nature. In the light and strength of the Spirit, the person called discovers what it means to dedicate himself to the Kingdom as did the Lord, who though rich made himself poor, though powerful made himself defenseless, though glorious he became humble; and wanting to place himself at the Lord's disposition, he agrees to share the chaste, poor, and humble life of his Lord, deciding to profess the evangelical counsels in a charismatic project, that is, in an institute approved by the Church.

The evangelical counsels are professed as vows and received in the Church and by the Church, which sees its reality as Bride, totally dedicated to her Lord, realized here in a higher form. The term "profession" of the evangelical counsels is understood both as the liturgical act with which the obligation of practicing the evangelical counsels is assumed, during the celebration of the Eucharist, and also as the practical enactment of the evangelical counsels so as to be perceived publicly, that is, it must take place openly before the Church and society, with a certain separation from the world. Those who profess the evangelical counsels "receive a new and special consecration" to be able to make "the way of life practiced personally by Jesus and proposed by him to his disciples" their own (*VC* 31). Let us note that this is not a distinction of degree, as though the consecrated person were more consecrated than the layman is by baptism, but a consecration of a different nature, as the special way of following Jesus, requested of some by the Lord, is different. In the profession of the evangelical counsels a threefold consecration takes place: *God,* who consecrates, setting apart a person for himself; *the person* who is consecrated; *the Church* who, accepting this consecration, consecrates herself to God in certain of her children.

Canonical Regulation

Religious life is regulated accurately by the *CIC,* which makes it recognizable by three elements: religious profession, fraternal life in community, specific mission.

a) Men and women religious make temporary "public vows," to be renewed periodically, or perpetual vows, and according to the proper law of the Institute.

b) "Fraternal life in community," in a house legitimately established, under the authority of a superior designated by the norm of law, in which there is to be at least an oratory where the Eucharist is celebrated or reserved.

c) "A specific mission" that involves a "public witness" to Christ and the Church, represented also by enclosure and the habit, according to the nature and purposes proper to each institute (dedicated entirely to contemplation, monastic, canonical, conventual, apostolic).

Moreover, religious institutes, in various degrees according to their type (of diocesan right, of pontifical right), enjoy an autonomy, especially of governance, which the bishops and their collaborators must preserve and foster. Relations between bishops and religious are regulated by particular documents and local agreements, based on the principle of mutual respect. While the local Church must respect the charisms of institutes, these must respect the pastoral plans of the local Church. The essential elements of religious life's mission also come from these essential facts that fix its canonical identity.

Consecration and Mission: Proclaiming the King who is Coming

Consecrated life participates in the mission of the Church with all its being: with its special consecration, with its fraternal life, with its specific mission.

Consecration

The special consecration means that the mission, above all, is to make the Lord Jesus, the true way that leads to the Father, present through the particular person, in various contexts, thanks to the working of the Holy Spirit.

a) "Consecrated persons make visible, in their consecration and total dedication, the loving and saving presence of Christ, the One consecrated by the Father, sent in mission. Allowing themselves to be won over by him (cf. Phil 3:12), they prepare to become, in a certain way, a prolongation of his humanity. The consecrated life eloquently shows that the more one lives in Christ, the better one can serve him in others" (*VC* 76). Christ's way of life implies an emptying of self to let oneself be taken over by "the Father's business," by his desires, by his will that all human beings know him, feel themselves loved by him, and love him in return. The extraordinary display of the fruits borne of consecrated life in history, in the most diverse fields (from the spread of the faith to the works of charity), stands to demonstrate the fruitfulness of being in mission, without ties or interests or worries or personal programs, full-time and unconditionally. Truly whoever is taken over by the love of God has no other desire than that he be loved: "To love thee and make thee loved!"

b) The evangelical counsels make man not only a disciple who follows Christ more closely, but rebuild in him the image of God as it was formed in creation. The three vows only function to dominate the three instincts that characterize the profound being of man: the desire to possess, to procreate, and to govern oneself. These three values form part of creation and are therefore fundamentally good. Sin, however, which hides in the human heart tends to absolutize these vital instincts, making them works of death. People who profess and practice the three vows, through their voluntary and joyful renunciation, are not only imitators of Jesus, but are also therapists for humanity wounded by the intoxication of self-determination.

c) Consecrated life is realistic. While on one hand it knows that "men are brought to their destiny of beatitude through the humanity of Christ" (*Summa Theologiae,* III, 9), on the other hand it knows that, in order to rebuild man in the image of Christ, it is necessary to accept the uncomfortable pages of the Gospel, where it speaks of denying oneself and bearing one's cross daily. The evangelical counsels involve renunciations, neither little nor brief, that however, if practiced with good will, can sustain parting from brothers and sisters. It is by looking to the heights that one is lifted up, or least, that one desires to be lifted up. It is by looking to him who renounces much that one can renounce anything, to be "brought to the destiny of beatitude."

Fraternal Life in Community

Religious life has always cultivated fraternal life in community, with greater or lesser intensity, with various results and in various ways. The ideal of living the *apostolica vivendi forma* (i.e., the way of life of the apostles who, leaving everything, lived with Jesus, forming a new family with him) has been cultivated continually and taken up anew in moments of reform, giving impulse to new, original forms of fraternal life. Other points of reference have been "the first Christian communities," described by the Acts of the Apostles, more recently the Holy Family of Nazareth; and also reflection on the Trinitarian communion and on the corresponding spirituality of communion has been and is ever more relevant.

a) Fraternal life is one of the fundamental teachings of the Lord Jesus, and has been one of the most effective causes for the spread of Christianity. Even today, in the climate of widespread individualism, it becomes one of the most sought-after and needed forms of witness for Christians. Religious, who have been called "experts in communion," have a relevant function in the Christian community and in the Church where the awareness and need grow every day for a theology, a praxis, and a spirituality of communion. Christian fraternity is a gift that begins with the coming of the Holy Spirit who has made it possible to build fraternal communities. The gift of fraternity is particularly felt in the religious community, which not only gathers people around apostolic purposes or projects, but unites and grounds their existence in the name and for the love of Christ. Without the Holy Spirit the dissipating forces of self-referentiality are not defeated, and a fraternal community is not built. But the Spirit is a gift that is sought "with one accord and in perseverance" (cf. Acts 2:46).

Religious community is the place where "initiation into the hardships and joys of community life takes place" (*VC* 67), to show that where the Gospel arrives fraternity grows. This contributes to keeping alive the fraternal dimension in the Church, the "sign and instrument both of a very closely knit union with God and of the unity of the whole human race" (*LG* 1). The art of making fraternity is part of mission, especially today, when it seems that egoisms are globalized more than solidarity.

b) Consecrated life, including eremitical life, has always had a strong sensitivity to the "communion of the saints." The early Fathers of the desert faced solitude, sure of participating in the mission of the Church in that way, given that every victory of theirs over evil in themselves weakened the forces of evil in the world, by the close connections among all the members of the body of Christ. Austerity and the penitential life were considered a reservoir of spiritual energies for all the Church and not only a means of personal purification. Whoever prays, whoever suffers for love, is found in the heart of the Church, as saints of every age have testified, especially in cloistered life. And not alone, for whoever draws near to God is not distanced from men, but becomes truly close to them with a merciful and constructive love.

c) Today communities of consecrated life experience the challenge of living together for people who come from different cultures, a challenge that touches all of society. The commitment to build "multi-colored" fraternal communities is not only an internal duty, but a true missionary act that shows that the new commandment of the Lord is the secret for building a new world, a new society, where potentially explosive situations can be factors of mutual enrichment and human growth.

Specific Mission

a) Many charisms, many institutes, many specific missions. "The same Spirit, far from removing from the life of humanity those whom the Father has called, puts them at the service of their brothers and sisters in accordance with their particular state of life, and inspires them to undertake special tasks in response to the needs of the Church and the world, by means of the charisms proper to the various institutes. Hence many different forms of the consecrated life have arisen" (*VC* 19). Through the various specific missions (foreign missions, education, the sick, hospitality, etc.), consecrated life has made the Church present in the various areas of the world and in various vital spheres, not only with works of assistance and promotion, but also offering forms of spirituality linked to the charism. A glorious, at times heroic, history of lives spent to announce the coming Kingdom: it will suffice to think of the recent impact of the evangelization of Africa, primarily by the work of missionary institutes.

b) Elijah and prophecy. Elijah is constantly present in consecrated life as a model of an ever needed prophecy. "Courageous prophet and friend of God, he lived in God's presence and contemplated his passing by in silence; he interceded for the people and boldly announced God's will; he defended God's sovereignty and came to the defense of the poor against the powerful of the world (cf. 1 Kg 18–19)" (*VC* 84). Consecrated life, moreover, has been seen as prophetic when it knew how to anticipate innovative solutions for the life of the Church, both in the field of spiritual realities (calling people strongly to God) and in social realities (particularly forms of assistance or promotion, or defense of the poor and the marginalized). It should be noted that "prophetic witness requires the constant and passionate search for God's will, [...] to apply the Gospel in history, in expectation of the coming of God's Kingdom" (*VC* 84).

c) Peter and John running to the tomb. The morning of Easter, Peter and John run toward the tomb. In their running, the Church has seen her own eschatological tension, her own desire to see the face of God, to enjoy the promises of Christ to enter "into the joy of her Lord." The consecrated life is seen in John, who runs faster, who desires to see the heart's beloved, by whom he feels himself particularly loved, and for whom he has given up so many other things. And thus his running supports that of Peter, of the whole Church. In a moment when heaven seems closed or irrelevant, consecrated life has the task of recalling the decisive importance of the resurrection to the world, keeping alive the desire for God and bringing a little bit of heaven into the hells of the world. "The people of God have no lasting city here below [...]. The religious state [...] more fully manifests to all believers the presence of heavenly goods already possessed here below. Furthermore, it not only witnesses to the fact of a new and eternal life acquired by the redemption of Christ, but it foretells the future resurrection and the glory of the heavenly kingdom" (*LG* 44). Never give up running, so that others do not tire of walking! Never give up calling out: "Christ, king of glory, come and bring us peace!"

Chapter Three, Article 9, Paragraph 5:
THE COMMUNION OF SAINTS

Salvador Pié-Ninot

The formula *"communio sanctorum"*—the last of the articles incorporated in the Apostles' Creed (*DH* 30)—is mentioned for the first time in the context of the Creed by the Commentary of Nicetas of Remesiana (†c. 420; cf. *Explanatio Symboli,* 10: *DH* 19; cf. his history in D. Sorrentino, "Comunione dei santi," in G. Calabrese *et al.*, *Dizionario di Ecclesiologia,* Roma: Citta Nuova, 2010, 292–307). This formula possesses a double meaning: on one hand, it expresses the Church as the "community of holy things," especially the Eucharist (*"sanctorum,"* from *"sancta/sanctorum,"* neuter plural); on the other hand, it also points to the Church that is made visible as the "communion of the saints," the "sanctified people" (*"sanctorum"* from *"sancti/sanctorum,"* masculine plural): in regard to those already glorified, and equally to those still on their pilgrimage.

The formula *"communio sanctorum"* became widespread by Luther to define the Church as the "invisible" communion of saints, separate from the visible and empirical Church equipped with ministers. It is necessary now to point out that early Christianity did not separate these two aspects, since the *"communio"* was based on the sacrament of the Eucharist and equally on the bond of unity with the bishop—the *"ius communionis"* (cf. Cyprian, *Epistula,* 16,2)—, understood as "Communion as the bond of unity between bishops and faithful, bishops among each other, faithful among each other, that is effectuated and at the same time made manifest by eucharistic communion" (cf. L. Hertling, *Communio. Chiesa e papato nell'antichità cristiana* [1943], Rome: PUG, 1961).

For good reason the *Roman Catechism*, implicitly responding to Luther, reaffirmed its sacramental-ecclesiological character, given that "the communion of the saints is a new explanation of the very concept of Church, one, holy, and catholic. The unity of the Spirit, who animates and governs her, causes that everything the Church possesses be communally possessed by those who form her. And thus the fruit of all the sacraments belongs to all the faithful, who are united by means of them and incorporated into Christ. This applies especially for the sacrament of baptism, the gate through which Christians enter into the Church. Baptism is followed by the Eucharist, which produces this communion in a most special manner" (I, 9, V).

Already at the start of the 20th century, the Lutheran D. Bonhoeffer brought the topic of the Church to the attention of contemporary theology powerfully in his work *Sanctorum Communio* (1930; in the *Opere di Dietrich Bonhoeffer,* Brescia: Queriniana, 1994). More recently, in the wake of the Second Vatican Council, and in the ecumenical sphere the expression "communion of saints" has been promoted particularly as a description of the Church by the "Bilateral Working Group of the German Bishops Conference and the Leadership of the United Evangelical Lutheran Church in Germany" in the Document *Communio Sanctorum* (2000). In this document the same concept is proposed as a point of encounter toward which the conceptions of Church developed in Catholic and Evangelical tradition can converge (cf. *Communio Sanctorum: The Church as the Communion of Saints.* Collegeville: Liturgical Press, 2004).

I. Communion in Spiritual Goods

As an introductory scriptural reference point, at n. 949 the text presents the famous summary from Acts 2:42 on the *koinonía* of the primitive Christian community, described with four concepts: the dynamic "teaching of the apostles," the fundamental "communion," the innovative "breaking of the bread," and the traditional "prayer."

It deals with four concepts that describe the particular constitution of the life of the new messianic group of converts to the Christian faith, presented as a binding model for the community of its time. This description of fraternal communion, surely augmented with a certain idealization, is shown in an ascending manner: based on the seed of local unity, it moves up to social unity based on the faith, also becomes spiritual and eucharistic unity, and is implemented as communion of goods. This text structures *koinonía* in five aspects.

The first (n. 949) is *communion in the faith* of the Church, received from the apostles, seen as a treasure of life that is enriched while it is shared, and in this way emphasizes the needed apostolic-hierarchical communion.

The second (n. 950) is *communion in the sacraments,* the axis of which is centered on the Eucharist, which "brings this communion to its apex" and has the episcopate as its "principal minister." Indeed, these two first aspects are united in the document "On some aspects of the Church understood as communion" (May 28, 1992) from the Congregation for the Doctrine of the Faith, with this assertion: "The unity of the Eucharist and the unity of the Episcopate with Peter and under Peter are not independent roots of the unity of the Church, since Christ instituted the Eucharist and the Episcopate as essentially interlinked realities" (n. 14).

The three remaining aspects follow, under the axis of communion-participation: *communion of charisms* (n. 951), seen as gifts of the Spirit to promote the edification and well-being of the Church; *participation in common* (n. 952), with the accent on the more material aspect; and *communion of charity* (n. 953), a synthesis of profound solidarity with all men, living and dead, as members of the Body of Christ, and the greatest expression of the communion of saints.

II. Communion of the Church of Heaven and Earth

While using the expression "Church of Heaven" and "Church of Earth," the text does not intend to promote any sort of dualism, as through two Churches existed, and for this reason it speaks in a nuanced way of "three states of the Church." These recall the categories which the *Roman Catechism* used in speaking of the Church militant, suffering, and triumphant, terms which are forgotten here, following *LG* 49–51. In this way, the axis which unites them appears so that they form "one and the same Church," in that they "are in communion in the same charity of God and neighbor."

This communion is manifested, in the first place, by "the intercession of the saints" (n. 956). Following *LG* 49 in summary form, it emphasizes that the intercession of the saints is due to graces received from Christ, the one mediator (cf. 1 Tm 2:5; also strongly present in Vatican II: *LG* 8, 28, 41, 49, 60, 62; *UR* 20; *PO* 2; *AG* 7). The conciliar text mentions in turn that the saints fulfill in their flesh what was lacking in the sufferings of Christ, on behalf of his Body which is the Church, citing Col 1:24 and *MC* from Pius XII, which develops this point with obvious compassion.

Second, at n. 957, our text concentrates on the "invocation of saints," following *LG* 50, seen not in the manner of a mere recollection of them as models, but as an expression of the "community of love" among the members of the Body of Christ, in whatever state they may find themselves. Now, not only is the imitation of saints to be given a Christological orientation, so is the invocation addressed to them, assuming that it "tends toward and terminates in Christ." Here again *MC* is recalled, which gives special attention to "Christ the fount and author of all sanctity," which our text reaffirms with a quotation from St. Polycarp. It is obvious that various judgments may be given in regard to popular customs in the cult of saints, but the core of the matter is doubtlessly in accord with the biblical and Christian tradition, when it concentrates on venerating the mystery of God in human holiness.

Third, in n. 958, our text develops "communion with the dead," following *LG* 50. Truly the concept of "communion" has a relevant place here, since it applies to union with those brethren who have preceded us. Their memory will progressively become a cult and an invocation. The text refers to the story of 2 Mac 12:45—a classic quotation and basis for the Christian teaching on purgatory (cf. n. 1032)—in which we read that to pray for the dead, so that they be freed from their sins, is a sound and salutary thought. The biblical text also establishes an explicit relationship between this gesture of piety and the hope of future resurrection. Our text adds the reciprocity of such prayer, affirming that "Our prayer for them is capable [...] of making their intercession for us effective," just as the same cited biblical text confirms about the intercessory power of the righteous dead for the living (cf. 2 Mac 15:11–16).

The conclusion takes up the final words of the chapter on the eschatological nature of the Church from *LG* 51, in which it is stated that the "sons of God [...] constitute one family in Christ." In the conciliar text cited it is easy to recognize the radiance of the heavenly liturgy of the Book of Revelation, described so beautifully in *SC* 8: "In the earthly liturgy we take part in a foretaste of that heavenly liturgy which is celebrated in the holy city of Jerusalem toward which we journey as pilgrims, where Christ is sitting at the right hand of God, a minister of the holies and of the true tabernacle (cf. Rev 21:2; Col 3:1; Heb 8:2); we sing a hymn to the Lord's glory [...]; venerating the memory of the saints." This is why the invocation of saints is a singular expression of the "communion of the saints," particularly "supplications to the Mother of God and Mother of men that she [...] may now, exalted as she is above all the angels and saints, intercede before her Son in the fellowship *[communio]* of all the saints" (*LG* 69).

Chapter Three, Article 9, Paragraph 6:
MARY—MOTHER OF CHRIST, MOTHER OF THE CHURCH

Regina Willi

The topic of "Mary, Mother of God, Mother of the Church" is found in the third chapter of the profession of Christian faith: "I believe in the Holy Spirit". There subsists an intrinsic and special relation between the Holy Spirit and the subsequent articles of faith: "It actually is a matter of the works proper to the Spirit, or better (given that they constitute an entirety, regardless of their number) the Spirit's own works" (H. de Lubac, *Credo,* Einsiedeln, 1975, 86–87). Yet at the same time the one God reveals himself in the history of salvation. This is why St. Ambrose writes: "Every creature exists both of the will, and through the operation and in the power of the Trinity" *De Spiritu Sancto,* book 2, ch. IX [*CSEL* 79, 125; *PL* 16, 764]). Everything comes "from" the Father, "through" the Son, "in" the Holy Spirit. The third chapter of the Creed is subdivided into five articles. The paragraph on "Mary, Mother of God, Mother of the Church" belongs to the article titled: "I believe in the holy Catholic Church."

Indeed, all four parts of the *CCC* speak of Mary. This fact lets the Marian dimension of the entire Christian mystery be heard. On the other hand, this Marian dimension is not the only one that characterizes the *CCC,* even if it spans a fundamental meaning. Here is how Pope Paul VI expressed it: "Understanding the true Catholic doctrine about the Blessed Virgin Mary will always be an effective help in rightly grasping the mystery of Christ and the Church" (*Allocution* [November 21, 1964], in *AAS* 56 [1964] 1015). Pope Benedict XVI took up this thought and illustrated it: "Indeed, with this title the Pope summed up the Marian teaching of the Council and provided the key to understanding it. Not only does Mary have a unique relationship with Christ, the Son of God who, as man, chose to become her Son. Since she was totally united to Christ, she also totally belongs to us. Yes, we can say that

Mary is close to us as no other human being is, because Christ becomes man for all men and women and his entire being is 'being here for us.' Christ, the Fathers said, as the Head, is inseparable from his Body which is the Church, forming with her, so to speak, a single living subject. The Mother of the Head is also the Mother of all the Church; she is, so to speak, totally emptied of herself; she has given herself entirely to Christ and with him is given as a gift to us all" (Benedict XVI, *Homily* [December 8, 2005], in AAS 98 [2006] 15).

Items 963–975 of the *CCC,* which we are to explore here, complete the discourse on the Church, on her origin, her mission and purpose, by directing our attention to Mary. As model of the Church as *Ecclesiae typus,* we can see in her what the Church is in mystery, in the "pilgrimage of faith," and what she will be at the end of her journey to her homeland (n. 972). These twelve items primarily include the text of the conciliar constitution *LG* chapter VIII, "The Blessed Virgin Mary in the mystery of Christ and of the Church" (nn. 52–69). In addition, the title of "Mother of the Church" is explicitly accepted.

In n. 963, attention is brought first to "her place in the mystery of the Church," after nn. 484–507 and nn. 721–726, which spoke of "the Virgin Mary's role in the mystery of Christ and the Spirit." As suggested by n. 963, which introduces them and looks ahead to them, nn. 964–972 can in turn be subdivided into three parts:

I. Mary's motherhood with regard to the Church (nn. 964–970)
II. Devotion to the Blessed Virgin (n. 971)
III. Mary, eschatological icon of the Church (n. 972)

Nn. 973–975 repeat the presentation in summary form.

While the "role and function of Mary in relation to the Church" is principally the topic in the first part, the Church's devotion to the Virgin Mary in addressed, symmetrically, in the second part.

In the texts of Vatican II Mary is only indirectly noted as Mother of the Church. However, Pope Paul VI, in the closing address on November 21, 1964, after the promulgation of the *textus approbatus* of the conciliar constitution *LG,* reserved for himself the act of declaring Mary as "Mother of the Church" and therefore, realizing a desire expressed many times. Against the criticism that this title was rarely used, Paul VI emphasized that it was "by no means unfamiliar to Christian piety" and that it "belongs to the very seed of Marian piety." Paul VI explained: *"Mater Ecclesiae, hoc est totius populi christiani, tam fidelium quam Pastorum"* "Mother of the Church, which is of the whole Christian people, both the faithful and the pastors."

The Maternal Duty of Mary with Regard to the Church (n. 963)

LG speaks of the maternal duty of Mary toward members of the Church, even if the title "Mother of Church" is not mentioned explicitly: indeed she "cooperated by charity that faithful might be born in the Church" (*LG* 53). This declaration—basically a quotation from Augustine in *De Virginitate,* ch. 6 (*PL* 40, 399)—was added to the *CCC* at n. 963. But what does this statement mean? In what way did the Virgin Mother of God cooperate that the faithful might be born in the Church? The motherhood of Mary toward the Church is rooted in her divine motherhood.

In Lk 1:26–27 we read: "In the sixth month the angel Gabriel was sent from God to a city of Galilee named Nazareth, to a virgin." The title "Virgin" is the first title of Mary. Later, at the Council of Ephesus (431), Mary was solemnly honored with the title of *"Theotokos"* (Gk. *Theotókos,* Lat. *Dei Genitrix*) or "Mother of God." The most ancient Marian prayer known, *Sub tuum praesidium,* which goes back to the third century, uses the phrase *Dei Genitrix* "Mother of God," to say that the Virgin Mary really conceived and brought to light the Son of God through the creating work of the Spirit of God. This is the starting point for all Mariological discourse and all Marian spirituality. "Given that the incarnation itself belongs to the work of salvation that God carries out in His Son for the good of mankind, Mary also took part in this event of salvation, not only passively, but also actively as mother. Therefore [...], especially since the second century, she is praised as the new Eve, who brought life to light. The salvation-historical meaning of the motherhood of Mary has grown through the parallelism Eve/Mary" (A. Ziegenaus, *Maria in der Heilsgeschichte* in *Katholische Dogmatik* V, Aachen, 1998, 205–206.

In the course of her life, the physical motherhood of Mary to the Son of God became extended to spiritual motherhood toward the disciples of Jesus Christ. At the wedding of Cana, she presented the "need" of the spouses to her Son Jesus Christ (Jn 2:3) and addressed the servants: "Do whatever he [Jesus] tells you" (Jn 2:5). "In the evangelist's representation of Mary in the pericope of Cana, her participation in Christ's earthly suffering and in the revelation of 'his glory' is described" (A. Ziegenaus, *Maria in der Heilsgeschichte,* cit., 218). And so on Golgotha, under the cross, where Jesus entrusts his mother to the apostle John and vice versa, the spiritual motherhood of Mary becomes particularly evident.

The text of St. Augustine quoted at n. 963 speaks of how Mary "joined in bringing about the birth of believers in the Church." So we read in the Letter to the Ephesians: "the God and Father of our Lord Jesus Christ [...] destined us in love to be his sons through Jesus Christ, according to the purpose of his will, to the praise of his glorious grace which he freely bestowed on us in the Beloved. In him we have redemption through his blood, the forgiveness of our trespasses, according to the riches of his grace" (Eph 1:3, 5–7). The "birth of believers in the Church" is based on the death and resurrection of Jesus Christ and is brought to fulfillment in the sacrament of baptism of individual persons. Mary stood by the cross of Jesus Christ and suffered the darkness and cruelty of those events with him, in her heart, and thus showed herself to be truly the mother of Jesus Christ, the Savior of the world, mother not only according to the flesh (cf. Mt 12:50; Mk 3:35). With Jesus she accepted the will of the heavenly Father and gave herself over entirely to his work of salvation: "Yet it was the will of the Lord to bruise him; he has put him to grief; when he makes himself an offering for sin, he shall see his offspring, he shall prolong his days; the will of the Lord shall prosper in his hand, he shall see the fruit of the travail of his soul and be satisfied; by his knowledge shall the righteous one, my servant, make many to be accounted righteous, and he shall bear their iniquities. Therefore I will divide him a portion with the great, and he shall divide the spoil with the strong, because he poured out his soul to death, and was numbered with the transgressors; yet he bore the sin of many, and made intercession for the transgressors" (Is 53:10–12).

With her profound union with her Son upon the Cross, she truly became the new Eve, the help of the new Adam, Jesus Christ. So we read in *LG:* "Rightly therefore the holy Fathers see her as used by God not merely in a passive way, but as freely cooperating in the work of human salvation through faith and obedience. For, as St. Irenaeus says, she 'being obedient, became the cause of salvation for herself and for the whole human race' (*Adversus Haereses,* III, 22, 4; *PG* 7, 959). Hence not a few of the early Fathers gladly assert in their preaching, 'The knot of Eve's disobedience was untied by Mary's obedience; (*Adversus Haereses,* III, 22, 4; *PG* 7, 959) what the virgin Eve bound through her unbelief, the Virgin Mary loosened by her faith.' Comparing Mary with Eve, they call her 'the Mother of the living,' and still more often they say: 'death through Eve, life through Mary' (Jerome, *Epistula,* 22, 21: *PL* 22, 408. Cf. Augustine, *Sermones,* 51, 2, 3: *PL* 38,335; *Sermones,* 232, 2: *PL* 38, 1108; Cyril of Jerusalem, *Catech.* 12, 15: *PG* 33, 741AB; John Chrysostom, *Hom. 2 in dorm. B.M.V.,* 3: *PG* 96, 728)" (*LG* 56).

Mary is Mother of the Church because she is Mother of Christ (n. 964)

The Marian title *Mater Ecclesiae* makes its appearance relatively late, specifically only in the ninth century, thanks to Berengar of Tours. In the Woman of the Apocalypse (Rev 12), he sees Mary, along with the Church: *"Possumus per mulierem in hoc loco et beatam Mariam intelligere, eo quod ipsa mater est Ecclesiae; quia eum peperit, qui caput est Ecclesiae"* ("… for she gave birth to him who is head of the Church") *"et filia sit Ecclesiae, quia maximum membrum est Ecclesiae"* (*Expositio Berengaudi, PL* 17, 876 [2nd ed. 1879]). As Mother of Christ, Mary is also Mother of the Church, and because of this nearness to her Son, she is predestined for the Church, while nonetheless she is seen to be a redeemed woman (as the "first of the redeemed") and a "daughter," even within the Church. The head and his body are in close connection, and from this the title of Mary, Mother of the Church, gains its legitimacy. Pope Leo XIII used the title in an official text for the first time in the "Rosary encyclical" *Adiutricem populi* (September 5, 1895), in which the Pope characterized Mary as the spiritual mother of the faithful, and concludes that she is truly "Mother of the Church," as well as "Teacher and Queen of the Apostles" (*Mater Ecclesiae atque magistra et Regina Apostolorum,* in *AAS* 28 [1895/1896] 130).

The spiritual motherhood of Mary in relation to the Church and her position as an (eminent) member of the Church should not be seen as in opposition, as though her freedom from original sin and her classification among the redeemed were opposed to one another. "As a believer and the first-fruits of the Redemption, Mary is classified in the community of the redeemed; as servant and spouse of Christ she is classified, with respect to Christ, at the summit of the Church. She was chosen in her spiritual motherhood, which continues the Son's work of redemption from Heaven, in a maternal way and is involved in the birth of the members of Christ to divine life" (L. Scheffczyk, *Maria, Mutter und Gefährtin Christi,* Augsburg, 2003, 175).

While the title of *Theotókos* indicates the unity of the two natures in Jesus Christ, the title *Mater Ecclesiae* shows the intimate interweaving between the mystery of Christ and the mystery of the Church. At the same time, the title *Mater Ecclesiae* suggests the most profound connection and unity of the faithful among each other through their common mother. Benedict XVI explained it this way: "Looking down from the Cross at his Mother and the beloved disciple by her side, the dying Christ recognized the first-fruits of the family which he had come to form in the world, the beginning of the Church and the new humanity. For this reason, he addressed Mary as 'Woman,' not as 'Mother,' the term which he was to use in entrusting her to his disciple: 'Behold your Mother!' (Jn 19:27). The Son of God thus fulfilled his mission: born of the Virgin in order to share our human condition in everything but sin, at his return to the Father he left behind in the world the sacrament of the unity of the human race (cf. *Lumen Gentium,* 1): the family "brought into unity from the unity of the Father and the Son and the Holy Spirit" (Saint Cyprian, *De Orat. Dom.*, 23: PL 4, 536), at whose heart is this new bond between the Mother and the disciple. Mary's divine motherhood and her ecclesial motherhood are thus inseparably united" (Homily before the Marian shrine of Meryem Ana Evì in Ephesus [November 29, 2006], in *AAS* 98 [2006] 910–911).

Mary as a Member of the Church (n. 965)

After the Ascension of Jesus Christ, Mary remained united with the apostles in prayer at the Cenacle (cf. Acts 1:14). Together with the apostles and several women, "we see […] Mary by her prayers imploring the gift of the Spirit, who had already overshadowed her in the Annunciation" (*LG* 59).

Mary Participates in the Resurrection of the Son in a Unique Way (n. 966)

Here two dogmas come into our topic, that of the Immaculate Conception of Mary and that of her bodily Assumption, with the citation of an excerpt from the Apostolic Constitution *Munificentissimus Deus* by Pius XII (*AAS* 42 [1950] 753–773). The Pope takes into consideration the preservation of Mary from original sin and recalls the faith and the long liturgical tradition of the Church of the East and the West from time immemorial.

So St. John Damascene, distinguished among all as an eminent witness of this tradition, considering the bodily assumption of the dear Mother of God in light of her other privileges, exclaims with vigorous eloquence: "It was fitting that she, who had kept her virginity intact in childbirth, should keep her own body free from all corruption even after death. It was fitting that she, who had carried the Creator as a child at her breast, should dwell in the divine tabernacles. It was fitting that the spouse, whom the Father had taken to himself, should live in the divine mansions. It was fitting that she, who had seen her Son upon the cross and who had thereby received into her heart the sword of sorrow which she had escaped in the act of giving birth to him, should look upon him as he sits with the Father. It was fitting that God's Mother should possess what belongs to her Son, and that she should be honored by every creature as the Mother and as the handmaid of God (*Hom. II in dorm. B. Virginis Mariae,* 14: *PG* 96, 742)" (Pius XII, *Munificentissimus Deus,* in *AAS* 42 [1950] 761).

The Assumption or Dormition of the Blessed Virgin Mary is not only a unique sharing in the resurrection of the Son, but also an anticipation of the bodily glorification of the just. The truth of the bodily Assumption of Mary into Heaven must imply a consolidation of mankind into her existential journey, making the value of human life and the noble end to which each man is destined shine forth. The Blessed Virgin Mary has not left the world with her Dormition. She is and remains truly mother in the order of grace.

Mary as Archetype and Model of the Church, as *Ecclesiae Typus* (n. 967)

"By her complete adherence to the Father's will, to his Son's redemptive work, and to every prompting of the Holy Spirit," or rather, thanks to her complete devotion to the Trinity, the Virgin Mary is an archetype for the Church (cfr. n. 967). St. Ambrose expressed it in this way: "The Mother of God is the type of the Church, in the order of faith, of love, and of perfect union with Christ" (*Expositio Evangelii secundum Lucam* II, 7: *PL* 15, 1555). Therefore, she is "hailed as a pre-eminent and singular member of the Church" (*LG* 53). She is "archetype of the Church," *Ecclesiae typus.* While patristic theology points out Mary as týpos of the Church, this means that it recognizes in the Virgin Mary the personification and, as it were, the anticipation, of everything that was to develop in the Church, in her essence and ability (cf. H. Rahner, *Maria und die Kirche,* Innsbruck, 1951, 15).

John Paul II writes in his encyclical *RM,* at n. 44: "Given Mary's relationship to the Church as an exemplar, the Church is close to her and seeks to become like her: 'Imitating the Mother of her Lord, and by the power of the Holy Spirit, she preserves with virginal purity an integral faith, a firm hope, and a sincere charity' (*LG* 64). Mary is thus present in the mystery of the Church as a model. But the Church's mystery also consists in generating people to a new and immortal life: this is her motherhood in the Holy Spirit. And here Mary is not only the model and figure of the Church; she is much more. For, 'with maternal love she cooperates in the birth and development' of the sons and daughters of Mother Church. The Church's motherhood is accomplished not only according to the model and figure of the Mother of God but also with her 'cooperation.' The Church draws abundantly from this cooperation, that is to say from the maternal mediation which is characteristic of Mary, insofar as already on earth she cooperated in the rebirth and development of the Church's sons and daughters, as the Mother of that Son whom the Father 'placed as the first-born among many brethren' (*LG* 63)."

For us Mary is Mother in the Order of Grace (n. 968)

The Blessed Virgin Mary is therefore not only a model for us thanks to her personal journey of faith, but she also "cooperated" in a completely unique way and with ardent love in the work of the Redeemer: that is, in recreating the supernatural life of souls, as was already discussed above (n. 963).

"'Woman, behold your son' and to the disciple: 'Behold your mother' (Jn 19:26–27). They are words which determine Mary's place in the life of Christ's disciples and they express [...] the new motherhood of the Mother of the Redeemer: a spiritual motherhood, born from the heart of the Paschal Mystery of the Redeemer of the world. It is a motherhood in the order of grace, for it implores the gift of the Spirit, who raises up the new children of God, redeems through the sacrifice of Christ that Spirit whom Mary too, together with the Church, received on the day of Pentecost" (*RM* 44).

Moreover, Mary is the type of the Church not only from the perspective of faith and love, but as Ambrose said, also of perfect union with Christ. Pope Francis explained this fact in these words: "The life of the Holy Virgin was the life of a woman of her people: Mary prayed, she worked, she went to the synagogue [...]. But every action was carried out in perfect union with Jesus. This union finds its culmination on Calvary: here Mary is united to the Son in the martyrdom of her heart and in the offering of his life to the Father for the salvation of humanity. Our Lady shared in the pain of the Son and accepted with him the will of the Father, in that obedience that bears fruit, that grants the true victory over evil and death" (*General Audience,* October 23, 2013).

The Motherhood of Mary in the Economy of Salvation Continues Still (n. 969)

Mary's cooperation in the work of salvation does not belong only to the past: it is and remains prominent by reason of Mary's participation in the power of the risen Christ through her Assumption into Heaven. In this way, after her Assumption into Heaven, she continues to impart the gifts of eternal salvation, through her manifold intercession, mediating divine grace for us (cf. nn. 968–969). In her motherly solicitude, she trains the faithful in true divine sonship with her example of faith and love and "cares for the brethren of her Son, who still journey on earth surrounded by dangers and worries, until they are led into the happiness of their true home. Therefore the Blessed Virgin is invoked by the Church under the titles of Advocate, Auxiliatrix, Adjutrix, and Mediatrix" (*LG* 62).

Mary's *Fiat* at the moment of the Annunciation by the angel (Lk 1:38), joined to her dedication and cooperation at the Cross of Jesus Christ, has an impact on all humanity. Mary accepts the message that the angel announced to her, and her agreement has a universal salvific effect. Based on this, St. John Damascene was able to write: "So it is just and true that we call the Virgin Mary *Theotókos* (Mother of God). Indeed this name summarizes the whole economy of salvation" (*De fide orthodoxa,* III, 12: *PG* 94, 1029). It is her motherly consent for the good of all mankind that has been redeemed by Christ. Mary is defined as mother, as helper and permanent collaborator of Christ for the good of all the Church. Her motherly charity intercedes before

God for the Church, protects her and is present in her pilgrimage. Mary is an eminent sign of the nearness of God.

Through her unconditional fidelity to her son Jesus Christ, Mary contributed to the birth of the faithful in the Church (cf. Augustine, *De Virginitate,* ch. 6: *PL* 40, 399). "From this community of will and suffering between Christ and Mary she merited to become most worthily the Reparatrix of the lost world (Eadmer, monk, *De Excellentia Virg. Mariae,* ch. 9) and Dispensatrix of all the gifts that Our Savior purchased for us by His Death and by His Blood" (Pius X, *Ad diem illum laetissimum* [February 2, 1904]). St. Louis Marie de Montfort explained: "God the Son imparted to his mother all that he gained by his life and death, namely, his infinite merits and his eminent virtues. He made her the treasurer of all his Father had given him as heritage. Through her he applies his merits to his members and through her he transmits his virtues and distributes his graces. [...] God the Holy Spirit entrusted his wondrous gifts to Mary, his faithful spouse, and chose her as the dispenser of all he possesses, so that she distributes all his gifts and graces to whom she wills, as much as she wills, how she wills and when she wills. No heavenly gift is given to men which does not pass through her virginal hands. Such indeed is the will of God, who has decreed that we should have all things through Mary" (*True Devotion to the Blessed Virgin,* Bay Shore, NY: Montfort Publications, 1980, nn. 24–25).

Mary Guides the Eyes and Hearts of the Faithful to Christ (n. 970)

Mary's maternal role for men does not obscure or diminish the unique mediation of Christ in any way, but shows us its efficacy. Each salutary influence of the Blessed Virgin toward men is not born from objective necessity, but from a purely gratuitous disposition by God, and pours out from the overflowing abundance of the merits of Christ; hence it is based on his mediation, absolutely depends on it, and draws all its efficacy from it, and does not in the least impede direct union of the faithful with Christ, but rather facilitates it (*LG* 60).

In the first letter to Timothy, St. Paul writes: "There is one God and there is one mediator between God and man, the man Christ Jesus, who gave himself as a ransom for all, the testimony to which was given at the proper time" (1 Tm 2:5–6). And in the Letter to the Galatians we read: "But when the time had fully come, God sent forth his Son, born of woman, born under the law, to redeem those who were under the law, so that we might receive adoption as sons" (Gal 4:4–5). The Church considers Mary to be at the center of the revelation of the divine plan for the world. The revelation of salvation in Jesus Christ is inseparable from the fact that the Son of God came through Mary in history, by the work of the Holy Spirit. Only the Holy Spirit, the power of the Most High, will allow her to receive the Son of God, Jesus Christ (cf. Lk. 1:35). Both the evangelist Matthew and the evangelist Luke explain the motherhood of Mary as the work of the Holy Spirit. The creator Spirit, the spirit of Genesis, worked in her and through her, overshadowed her with the power of God. Hence, he whom she conceived in her womb was called holy and the Son of God (cf. Lk 1:35).

It was all accomplished in Christ and for Christ, but to really understand the mystery of Christ one cannot leave aside the mystery of Mary, who is totally at the disposal of God and Christ, our one Mediator and Savior (cf. Paul VI, *Allocution* [November 21, 1964], in *AAS* 56 [1964] 1017: *"Praesertim exoptamus ut id praeclara in luce collocetur: scilicet Mariam, humilem Domini ancillam, ad Deum et ad Christum Iesum, unicum Mediatorem Redemptoremque nostrum, totam spectare"*). By the very nature of things, the mystery of Mary, Mother of God, imposed itself on the great Christological debates of the fourth and fifth centuries. This is obvious, if it is true that without Mary Jesus Christ would not have existed in his concrete and living reality, and that without her the fullness of the mystery of Christ could not have been.

"He is the image of the invisible God, the first-born of all creation; for in him all things were created, in heaven and on earth [...]. All things were created through him and for him. He is before all things and in him all things hold together. He is the head of the body, the Church" (Col 1:15–18). In this body the baptized are the members (cf. 2 Tm 2:10–11; Eph 2:4f; Col 2:12–13 and *LG* 7). Christ is the head of the body. "As the assumed nature inseparably united to Him serves the divine Word as a living organ of salvation, so, in a similar way, does the visible social structure of the Church serve the Spirit of Christ, who vivifies it, in the building up of the body (cf. Eph 4:16)" (*LG* 8).

Through this nexus between Christ and the Church, the title of "Mary, Mother of the Church" is explained finally, even more clearly: if Mary is the mother of Jesus Christ, the incarnate Word of God, then she is also mother of the "whole Christ," or as Augustine said, the mother of Christ will also be mother of the members, mother of the Church. Pope Paul VI explained it thus: "It is precisely by this title, in preference to all others, that the faithful and the Church address Mary. It truly is part of the genuine substance of devotion to Mary, finding its justification in the very dignity of the Mother of the word Incarnate. [...] Since she is the mother of Him who, right from the time of His Incarnation in her virginal bosom, joined to Himself as head His Mystical Body which is the Church. Mary, then as mother of Christ, is mother also of all the faithful and of all the pastors" (*Allocution* [November 21, 1964], in *AAS* 56 [1964] 1015).

And like Mary, every member of the Body of Christ, every member of the Church, has a further task and a further vocation. "As the one goodness of

God is really communicated in different ways to His creatures, so also the unique mediation of the Redeemer does not exclude but rather gives rise to a manifold cooperation which is but a sharing in this one source" (*LG* 62).

Devotion to the Blessed Virgin (n. 971)

"The Church's devotion to the Blessed Virgin is an intrinsic element of Christian worship" (*Marialis cultus* [February 2, 1974] 56). She has been venerated as well since ancient times with the title of Mother of God, under whose protection the faithful implore shelter in every danger and necessity: "Under your protection we find refuge, holy Mother of God." For lovely moments of Marian devotion, it refers to the liturgical feasts dedicated especially to the Mother of God (cf. *SC* 103), and also to the Marian prayer of the Rosary, the "compendium of the entire Gospel" (*Marialis cultus* 42). In the Rosary we contemplate the face of Christ with Mary. Pope John Paul II wrote in his Apostolic Letter *Rosarium Virginis Mariae* [October 16, 2002] (n. 11): "Mary lived with her eyes fixed on Christ, treasuring his every word: 'She kept all these things, pondering them in her heart' (Lk 2:19; cf. 2:51). The memories of Jesus, impressed upon her heart, were always with her, leading her to reflect on the various moments of her life at her Son's side. In a way those memories were to be the 'rosary' which she recited uninterruptedly throughout her earthly life. Even now, amid the joyful songs of the heavenly Jerusalem, the reasons for her thanksgiving and praise remain unchanged. They inspire her maternal concern for the pilgrim Church, in which she continues to relate her personal account of the Gospel. Mary constantly sets before the faithful the 'mysteries' of her Son, with the desire that the contemplation of those mysteries will release all their saving power. In the recitation of the Rosary, the Christian community enters into contact with the memories and the contemplative gaze of Mary."

For the practice of devotion to the Blessed Virgin, Paul VI especially recommended the *Angelus Domini* in the Apostolic Exhortation *Marialis cultus,* alongside the Rosary (cf. nn. 40–41). It goes without saying that childlike attachment to the Virgin Mother of God cannot suffice by itself. Rather, that kind of attachment should be considered as a help which by its nature leads people to Christ and connects them with the eternal Father in Heaven, through the bond of love of the Holy Spirit. The Church, considering the fact of Mary "in light of the Word made flesh" (*LG* 65), becomes sensitive to the working of God, which chose Mary to realize our salvation in her beloved Son. Mary followed the call of God: she believed in the word which the Lord addressed to her by means of the angel and she placed herself totally at the disposition of God's will. So Paul VI writes in *Marialis cultus:* "Finally,

[…] we would like to repeat that the ultimate purpose of devotion to the Blessed Virgin is to glorify God and to lead Christians to commit themselves to a life which is in absolute conformity with His will. When the children of the Church unite their voices with the voice of the unknown woman in the Gospel and glorify the Mother of Jesus by saying to Him: 'Blessed is the womb that bore you and the breasts that you sucked' (Lk 11:27), they will be led to ponder the Divine Master's serious reply: 'Blessed rather are those who hear the word of God and keep it!' (Lk 11:28) […] This reply is […] an admonition to us to live our lives in accordance with God's commandments. It is also an echo of other words of the Savior: 'Not every one who says to me, Lord, Lord, will enter the kingdom of heaven, but he who does the will of my Father who is in heaven' (Mt 7:21); and again: 'You are my friends if you do what I command you' (Jn 15:14)."

True devotion to Blessed Mary, Virgin and Mother of God, impels us to start listening to the Word of God and to observe it, just as she did. At the same time, she also teaches the Church how to become a praying community: "To venerate the Mother of Jesus in the Church means, then, to learn from her to be a community that prays: this is one of the essential notes of the first description of the Christian community delineated in the Acts of the Apostles (cf. 2:42). Often prayer is dictated by situations of difficulty, by personal problems that lead us to turn to the Lord to gain light, comfort, and aid. Mary invites us to open the dimensions of prayer, to turn to God not only in need and not only for oneself, but in a way that is united, persevering, faithful, with "one heart and mind" (cf. Acts 4:32)" (Benedict XVI, *General audience* [March 14, 2012]).

One could cite countless more devotions that are practiced by the faithful, in the veneration of Mary the Mother of God; if nothing else, the rich treasury of hymns and chants, of Marian icons and representations, sermons and litanies. In recent decades, in particular, the practice of pilgrimages has returned to a high level.

Mary as Eschatological Icon (n. 972)

The dogma of the Assumption of Mary into Heaven explains and defines, "to the glory of the holy Trinity" that "the Immaculate Mother of God, the ever virgin Mary, the course of her earthly life having ended, was assumed into heavenly glory, soul and body" (Pius XII, *Munificentissimus Deus* [November 1, 1950], in *AAS* 42 [1950] 770). In her we are able to look at what the Church is in her mystery, in her "pilgrimage of faith," and at what she will be in her fatherland, at the end of her journey (n. 972). "Redeemed first of all by her Son, she participates fully in his holiness. She is already that which the whole Church desires and hopes to be. She is the eschatological icon of the Church" (John Paul II, *Homily* [December 8, 2004]). Mary is the eschatological "icon of the pilgrim Church in the wilderness of history but on her way to the glorious destination of the heavenly Jerusalem, where she will shine as the Bride of the Lamb, Christ the Lord. The Mother of God, as the Church of the East celebrates her, is the *Hodegetria,* she who 'shows the way,' that is, Christ, the only mediator for fully encountering the Father. [...] In her glorious Assumption into heaven Mary is the icon of the creature who is called by the risen Christ to attain, at the end of history, the fullness of communion with God in the resurrection for an eternity of bliss. For the Church, which often feels the weight of history and the assault of evil, the Mother of Christ is the shining emblem of humanity redeemed and enveloped by the grace that saves" (John Paul II, *General audience* [March 14, 2001]). In this way, she enlightens us, the pilgrim people of God on this earth, until the coming of the day of the Lord (cf. 2 Pt 3:10) as a sign of sure hope and consolation (*LG* 68).

In Summary (nn. 973–975)

In the three items what has been set forth in the preceding paragraphs is summarized in brief texts. In n. 975 the solemn profession of faith of Pope Paul VI is cited, the *Credo of the People of God* of June 30, 1968 (*AAS* 60 [1968] 436–446). This confession of faith, articulated in 30 points, speaks of the Blessed Virgin Mary principally in sections 14–15: "We believe that Mary is the Mother, who remained ever a Virgin, of the Incarnate Word, our God and Savior Jesus Christ, and that by reason of this singular election, she was, in consideration of the merits of her Son, redeemed in a more eminent manner, preserved from all stain of original sin and filled with the gift of grace more than all other creatures. Joined by a close and indissoluble bond to the Mysteries of the Incarnation and Redemption, the Blessed Virgin, the Immaculate, was at the end of her earthly life raised body and soul to heavenly glory and likened to her risen Son in anticipation of the future lot of all the just; and we believe that the Blessed Mother of God, the New Eve, Mother of the Church, continues in heaven her maternal role with regard to Christ's members, cooperating with the birth and growth of divine life in the souls of the redeemed."

Chapter Three, Article 10:
"I BELIEVE IN THE FORGIVENESS OF SINS"

Antonio Miralles

To confess faith in the forgiveness of sins, which is closely tied to faith in the preceding articles of the Apostles' Creed, means to believe in the efficacy of the work of redemption—the victory of Christ over sin—which reaches, in the Church and through the Church, to men of all times and all places; to believe, then, in the presence of Christ and the sanctifying action of the Holy Spirit in the Church. Jesus Christ arisen shows how he has associated the Church with his victory over sin, conferring on the apostles the power to pardon sins, together with the mandate to continue his mission; and with the gift of the Holy Spirit: "As the Father has sent me, I also send you." Having said this, he breathed on them and said: "Receive the Holy Spirit. If you forgive the sins of any, they are forgiven, if you retain the sins of any, they are retained" (Jn 20:21–23). The gift of the Spirit constitutes the power that enables the apostles to continue the mission of Christ and to destroy sin. Their intervention which destroys sin is revealed as an action filled with the power of the Holy Spirit.

The Church on earth is not a community of the sinless and perfect, but the forgiveness of sins is found in her, precisely because the apostles and their successors received from Christ the power to judge sins and pardon them. The Church can never give up her activity of frontal opposition to sin, because doing so would betray her nature as the universal sacrament of salvation.

I. One Baptism for the Forgiveness of Sins

In the Church the remission of sins is obtained first of all by means of baptism (nn. 977–978), which makes us sharers in the death and resurrection of Jesus Christ, to the extent that "the Passion of Christ is communicated to every baptized person, so that he is healed just as if he himself had suffered and died" (*Summa Theologiae,* III, 69, 2). As St. Cyril of Jerusalem explained to the newly baptized: "Christ received nails in His undefiled hands and feet, and suffered anguish; while on me, without pain or toil, by the fellowship of His suffering He freely bestows salvation" (*Catechetical Lectures* 20, 5, found in *Nicene and Post-Nicene Fathers, Second Series,* vol. 7). So there remains no guilt to pardon, no penalty to be paid in purgatory, we are made partakers in the resurrection of Christ, which starts a new life, like a new birth; baptism indeed is a "washing of regeneration and renewal in the Holy Spirit" (Ti 3:5). But the consequences of sin remain, which do not constitute a guilt, but rather a penalty to overcome: the inclination to sin, which demands effort and struggle in order to maintain oneself in the good; suffering, fatigue, sickness, and death. The newly baptized are not transported to a state of paradise: our participation in the resurrection of Christ, here on earth, is only inchoate in relation to the spiritual life, and it will become complete in the final resurrection of the body. The sufferings of the present life allow the baptized to be conformed to Christ, following the way that he opened, the way that passes through the Cross before reaching the glory of the resurrection, that is, being "fellow heirs with Christ, provided we suffer with him in order that we may also be glorified with him" (Rom 8:17).

Through baptism sin is defeated, but not completely overcome, since in this life the will is always changeable, even in respect to its most radical determinations, and can resist the divine action that leads us to eternal life. Furthermore, the inclination to sin continues to be present in the baptized. Still, they can emerge victorious from the battle against sin, because in baptism they have been endowed with all the arms to conquer, according to the image of St. Paul, who sees the Christian as a soldier, well-armed to bring him to victory over evil (cf. 1 Thess 5:8; Eph 6:14–17).

Even if the Christian, is wounded in the struggle against sin, and gravely so, he can always rise up again penitent and obtain the pardon of sin by means of the Church, specifically through the sacrament of penance (nn. 979–980). As baptism is necessary for the remission of sins prior to the regeneration of baptism, so penance is necessary for the remission of grave sins by the baptized. The grace of baptism is restored, but this time it is a case of a "laborious baptism." Whoever has attained the use of reason and seeks to be baptized, must have interior penitence for sins—repentance and the intention to change one's life and follow a Christian way of acting—, but there is no obligation to carry out particular works of penance.

In contrast, "the repentance of a Christian after his fall into sin differs vastly from repentance in the time of baptism. It includes not only giving up sins and detesting them, or 'a broken and contrite heart,' but also their sacramental confession or at least the desire to confess them when a suitable occasion will be found and the absolution of a priest; it also includes satisfaction by fasts, almsgiving, prayer, and other pious exercises of the spiritual life" (*DS* 1543).

II. The Power of the Keys

The power of the keys, which the apostles and their successors have—the bishops assisted by presbyters—and by whose strength the sins of the faithful are remitted, is named in reference to the promise of Christ made to St. Peter (n. 981): "I will give you the keys of the kingdom of heaven, and whatever you bind on earth shall be bound in heaven, and whatever you loose on earth shall be loosed in heaven" (Mt 16:19). It is a power conferred not only to Peter, but to all the apostles (cf. Mt 18:18), which encompasses the authority to govern, to pronounce judgments on matters of doctrine, and above all, the characteristic of greatest value, the authority to judge sins and pardon them (cf. Jn 20,23).

The power of the keys extends to all sins committed after baptism, excluding none (n. 982). Not even the severe admonition of the Lord: "Whoever blasphemes against the Holy Spirit never has forgiveness" (Mk 3:29) constitutes a limit on the power of the keys. The sin against the Holy Spirit shows itself to be unforgivable inasmuch as it itself constitutes impenitence, that is, the refusal of the offer of salvation and pardon that come from the Spirit (cf. n. 1864). Pope Gelasius I interprets the words of the Lord this way and concludes: "There is no sin for whose remission the Church does not pray, or which she cannot forgive those who desist from that same sin, or from which she cannot loose for those who repent" (*DS* 349). The conversion of the impenitent sinner requires a special gift from God to make opposition to the grace of repentance bend.

Chapter Three, Article 11:
"I BELIEVE IN THE RESURRECTION OF THE BODY"

Luis F. Ladaria

Creation, salvation, and the sanctification of man, works of the Trinity, culminate in the resurrection from the dead and to eternal life. The action of God for our good has no temporal limits as our life in this world has. Creation is called to be consummated in the second creation; the salvation of man is for ever; his sanctification means participation in the life of God himself. Faith in the resurrection of the dead proclaims that what God has done for our good is for ever and moreover embraces our entire being. Not with the limits proper to this life and our earthly condition, but in a transfigured and heavenly state, whose first-fruits we already have in Christ arisen who has made us sharers, already in this life, in the gift of his Spirit.

Faith in the resurrection of Christ is central for every Christian. This truth, which is the foundation of the final articles on which we are commenting now, is proclaimed elsewhere in the Creed. In the New Testament the resurrection from the dead at the end of time is seen in relation with the resurrection of Jesus (at the text cited in n. 989, to which others could be added: 1 Cor 6:14,15,20–23,45–49; 2 Cor 4:14; Phil 3:20). The basis of our future resurrection is therefore Jesus, who conquered sin and death. He is the resurrection and the life, according to Jn 11:25. As the Father raised Jesus from the dead, the initiative of our resurrection lies with the Father, after the image of his Son's. And as Rom 8:11, cited very fittingly in this context, indicates, the Holy Spirit is also at work in our resurrection: his present dwelling in us, as the gift of the risen Lord, is like a guarantee of the future resurrection of our mortal bodies; they will receive life by virtue of the Spirit.

The resurrection means new and definitive life for the whole man, including the "carnal" dimension of weakness. Christian hope is not reduced to the life of the immortal soul. The words of Tertullian which we find in n. 991 (*De Resurrectione,* 1), "The faith of Christians is resurrection from the dead; we are what we are, by believing in that," show us the importance that this article of faith had in the early Church. Christians are who they are, to the extent that they believe in the resurrection of the dead. The idea of the immortal soul, shared by many in those times, is not sufficient for Christians, who have the risen Lord before their eyes. The same Tertullian will say that those who only believe in the immortality of the soul believe in "half a resurrection" (*De Resurrectione*, 2): it is the only kind that the gnostics know. Christian hope therefore refers to the definitive life of the whole human being. Christ is contemplated as the fruit-fruits of this resurrection. The following section goes more directly into this point.

I. Christ's Resurrection and Ours

We know that it was not easy for the Old Testament to reach the idea of the resurrection. As in other points, the revelation of God to his people about this was "progressive." And as the text shows, faith in the resurrection reached the consciousness of the chosen people in their reflection on God the creator and savior. God who created all things, who established his covenant with Abraham and his descendants, is the God who can do anything and who therefore will save man and not let him perish. Faith in the resurrection of the dead, at least for the just, is formulated already in some late texts of the Old Testament, 2 Mac 7 and Dn 12:1, as full salvation of the faithful Israelite.

At the time of Jesus, the Pharisees hoped in the resurrection, while the Sadducees denied it. The New Testament shows us this diversity of opinions. Jesus, in the time of his public life, taught the resurrection. The fact is well known and the *CCC* offers classic texts about this.

But what is decisive is that in the New Testament the Resurrection appears joined to the very person of Jesus. In the proclamation Jesus himself makes about his Passion, the proclamation of his resurrection on the third day is already there (cf. Mk 8:31; 9:31; 10:34, and parallels).

In the Synoptics there are other allusions to the resurrection which the text indicates. But especially according to the fourth Gospel, Jesus proclaims the resurrection of those who believe in him. The miracle of the raising of Lazarus is interpreted explicitly in this sense. So it is no longer a matter of a generic faith in the resurrection of the dead, as with the Pharisees. In the New Testament the resurrection of Jesus becomes the center of the proclamation. Though on one hand the general outlook of hope in resurrection was able to help in understanding the resurrection of Jesus, on the other hand it is the fact itself of this resurrection that has already taken place that orients our definitive grounding toward hope. The hoped-for resurrection is consequently participation in the resurrection of Jesus: we shall rise like him, with him, by means of him (n. 995).

The proclamation of Jesus risen is the hinge of Christian witness. Testimony about Jesus and about the resurrection necessarily go together. The apostles ate and drank with him after his resurrection, according to the Acts of the Apostles. The insistence on eating and drinking with the Risen One shows the realism with which the New Testament saw the resurrection of Jesus. N. 996 alludes to the difficulties and the opposition which the very proclamation of the resurrection encountered from the first instant. We have indicated above that, in the time of Jesus and the early Church, the immortality of the soul was commonly accepted, but the idea of resurrection provoked scandal. Only faith in the infinite power of God, manifested in the resurrection of Jesus, can open us to this hope. N. 997 begins with a "definition" of resurrection. The traditional categories are used, of death as separation of body and soul, and of the further reunion of these two principles of man. It is interesting to note that even without it being said explicitly, it seems that resurrection is being spoken of here in the fuller and more positive sense of the term. In effect, it is saying that the soul remains awaiting the reunion with "its glorified body." It might be useful here to note here that the New Testament and tradition use the term resurrection in two senses, intimately related but not identical: the first is what is suggested here, the human being's full participation in the life of the glorified Jesus. In most cases in which the New Testament speaks of resurrection the term is used in this full and positive sense. The second sense is what we find in n. 998: the resurrection as the reuniting of the body and soul is for everyone, for those who have done good and those who have done evil. The New Testament also knows this more neutral concept of resurrection, and the text cited demonstrates this itself (cf. also Ac 24:15). It is important to take account of this distinction to understand the biblical texts well and even those of the Catechism itself. Naturally, given the way in which we speak of the resurrection in the context of Christian hope in salvation, it is the first sense that predominates. Even when one tries to speak in "neutral" terms, it is not rare that the expressions used lead imperceptibly toward the first of these meanings.

Already in the New Testament the question is posed: how will we rise? We have already referred to the realism with which the New Testament speaks of the resurrection of Jesus. At the same time we know that immediate recognition of the risen Jesus was not always easy for the disciples. This explains why, on one hand, magisterial texts have insisted on the identity of the present body and the resurrected body. On the other hand, however, we find ourselves with the impossibility of describing the phenomenon. There is a transfiguration into a glorified body (and we note how imperceptibly the text of the *CCC* passes from the second meaning of resurrection to the first). The text cited from 1 Cor, one of the most important texts of the New Testament for relating the resurrection of Jesus with ours, is significant. Paul does not answer the question of how. He points to various analogies, and lastly (and it is unfortunate that these verses are omitted in the citation) refers to the comparisons between the two Adams: if now we bear the image of the earthly body of the first Adam, later we will bear the image of the spiritual body of the second, the risen Christ: filled with the Holy Spirit, not an "immaterial" body, which would clearly be a contradiction (cf. 1 Cor 15:44–49). As n. 1000 indicates, the how of the resurrection surpasses our understanding and our imagination. Rather, if we were to believe we understood it or imagined it, we would continue to follow the categories of our world; and the resurrection, by definition, surpasses them. We have to recognize that for many questions we do not have a rational answer; for example, how to explain the physical identity between the mortal body and the resurrected body, taking account of the changes that arise in the material world. Yet the fact that the reality of our future being goes beyond our categories does not mean that we cannot already have a foretaste of heavenly goods. In faith we have a sure access to them. This happens above all in the celebration of the Eucharist. Already in the New Testament Eucharist and resurrection are related (cf. Jn 6:52f). Participation in the Eucharist makes us incorruptible, according to St. Irenaeus.

The resurrection of the dead in the New Testament is intimately united to the Parousia of the Lord; cf., besides the texts cited by the Catechism, 1 Cor 15:22f. The Resurrection is the effect in us of the full manifestation of the lordship of Jesus over everything, the destruction of all foes, and in a special way sin and death. It is the final consummation of the salvific work of Christ, the moment in which, victorious over all, he will render the kingdom to the Father, so that God will be all in all things (cf. 1 Cor 15:24–28). Even if we await the resurrection on the last day, the New Testament teaches that the baptized person has already shared in the death and the resurrection of Jesus. With baptism we cease to be slaves of sin and begin to live the new life. The resurrection of Jesus, which will show the fullness of its effects at the end, is already effective in us, because Jesus, exalted at the right hand of the Father, has given us his Holy Spirit. But this resurrection is still "hidden," as that of Jesus still is, in a way, as he has not revealed its power nor manifested his glory to all men. Hence the full manifestation of Jesus will also be ours. Our life as resurrected persons is now hidden with Christ in God. Christian hope, which relates to the whole man, since he is one in soul and body, determines the respect which every man deserves already now, in all the dimensions of his being, including the corporeal and material. His conformation to Christ which will be full in the resurrection means that already now we must see ourselves and others as "members of Christ." Jesus himself is identified especially with those who suffer (cf. Mt 25:31f).

II. Dying in Christ Jesus

Christian death means going and living in the presence of the Lord, as Paul says in 2 Cor 5:8. So to die and be with Christ is, no doubt, the best thing (cf. Phil 1:21). Paul, however, desires first of all to serve the brethren, and this desire yet prevails over that of being with Jesus (cf. Phil 1:22f). From the anthropological point of view death, as indicated above, is defined again as separation of the soul and body. For Christians this separation is not the final word. We place ourselves before it with the hope of being with Christ and rising with him.

The enigma, or rather, the mystery of the human condition, reaches its apex in death. Christian faith presents us various approaches to death at the same time: on one hand, the death of man is natural (we see that other living beings die); on the other, in the biblical sources and those of Tradition, as the *CCC* has indicated earlier, death is placed in relation to sin. It proves impossible to clearly separate these two dimensions in our current experience of death, our own and that of others: even if we recognize its inevitability we do not resign ourselves to it; we consider it as a frustration and a rupture. But there is still a more definitive way to approach death, unique to the Christian faith: participation in the death of Christ, to be able to have a part in his resurrection. So, as for Jesus, entering into the glory of the Father took place through his death (and death upon a cross!), for us also, nearness to the Lord and being configured to his glorified body must pass through the sorrowful and mysterious moment of death. But no Christian dies alone. Jesus, who suffered the abandonment of death, accompanies us in this critical and decisive moment. Moreover, Christian death is participation in the death of Jesus, which has already been anticipated sacramentally in baptism. This is why the meaning of death has been transformed in Christ.

An inevitable consideration, on the subject of death, is the one introduced in n. 1007: death is the end of life, and inseparably, the end of the human journey, the end of our status as "underway." In other words, while we are able to change during the course of earthly life, we are able to sin and repent from sin, and so on, the situation in which we find ourselves before God in the moment of death becomes definitive for all eternity. In death, one "arrives": the journey of our life ends. Both our life's limitedness and the definitive character it acquires in the moment of death give our existence the character of "urgency." Each of the moments of our existence has an eschatological value of definitiveness. Hence the human responsibility to respond with faithfulness to the Lord and cooperate in his work and his plans for us in all the moments of our existence.

N. 1008 reminds us of what was stated earlier in nn. 374f and 400f, dealing with the condition of man in paradise and original sin. Death is a consequence of sin, according to Scripture and the Magisterium of the Church. God destined man to never die, even though his nature is mortal. This makes us pose the question, which we are unable to answer, of how the end of this life would have been brought about in the case that sin had not existed. Without speculating on unknown possibilities, we must say that the death we experience, which, as we have said, appears to us necessarily as a rupture and a frustration, cannot be explained without human sin: sin, breaking the relationship with God, profoundly altered the relations of man with himself and with the cosmos. Let us also note that the definitive immortality to which God calls us is participation in the life of the risen Lord. For this reason death is not the ultimate word about the human being. In Christ, we have just said, its meaning has changed. Jesus accepted it for our salvation, in obedience to the will of the Father. We too can offer ourselves entirely to God, associating ourselves with the mystery of the passion of Jesus. Our death in him can also have the meaning of salvation. After the general considerations about death, in which it was impossible to overlook explicit reference to the death of a Christian, this part returns to the topic with greater detail. Naturally many of the points that are addressed here have already been introduced and we have commented on them above.

Death unites us to Christ in the mystery of his death and resurrection, in which the Lord consummated his life of obedience to the Father. For us death is the consummation of our union with him in his redemptive act. What was already seen sacramentally in baptism is consummated in physical death. It is the moment of identifying ourselves with him in the deepest aspect of what was his life, his abandonment in love for the Father and for men, unto the end. Identification in death, identification in the glorified life: if we die with him, we shall live with him. The words of St. Ignatius of Antioch are most beautiful: in union with Jesus in death we are truly "human." Jesus is the model and the paradigm, the rule of the human being.

Death, called by God: in death God calls us to himself. In Christian language this terminology still lives: God calls us to his house. We have already referred to the desire, which Paul manifested and which the text mentions here, to be with Christ. For the Christian, to be with Christ is "better." Besides these references, we can also allude to another text of St. Teresa of Jesus in one of her poems: "I am dying because I am not dying."

The liturgy, privileged locus of the expression of faith *("lex orandi lex credendi")* constantly shows this hope for life with Jesus after death. The first preface of the dead in the *Roman Missal*, which is cited, is inspired by 2 Cor 5:1–10.

Death is the objective of the earthly pilgrimage. We have already spoken on this point. The time until death is time of grace and mercy, for realizing our existence according to the plan of the Lord. Quite fittingly the *CCC* alludes to the belief by some of our contemporaries in reincarnation. The Church cannot accept that, inasmuch as it means a devaluation of earthly existence, a loss of the eschatological sense in each of our acts. It makes us lose the sense of our definitive responsibility before God. The idea of reincarnation enormously impoverishes the vision of man. Indirectly it also means a devaluation of the earthly life of Jesus, who offered himself for us once for ever, who saved us in his whole human life, which culminated in his death and resurrection.

Given that the moment of death has this decisive significance for our eternal destiny, and in view of the uncertainty of the moment in which death will be able to reach us, the Church exhorts us to make preparation, to seek help for that moment, concretely to ask for the intercession of Mary and St. Joseph. The exhortation to live with our death in mind is not an appeal for sadness or pessimism, but for hope in the definitive encounter with the Lord, and for the right valuation of our present life.

Chapter Three, Article 12:
"I BELIEVE IN LIFE EVERLASTING"

Luis F. Ladaria

Death as the end of earthly life means the beginning of eternal life. The text of the *CCC* has already referred to this question which recurs here. The Church strengthens those who are in danger of death with absolution, with the sacrament of anointing of the sick, with Viaticum. The words of the commendation of the soul, which are cited here, show faith in the encounter with Jesus in the moment of death and entry into the paradise where Mary, the angels, and the saints await us.

I. The Particular Judgment

We have already said that death ends the time that God gives man to freely accept his love and his grace. In that moment the human being enters into definitive existence. Given that in his freedom man can have chosen for or against God during the time of his life, the definitiveness that awaits him can be one of salvation or of condemnation. Hence the necessity of judgment. Now, the idea of judgment, in the New Testament (we think, for example, of Mt 25:31, etc.) is joined above all to the Parousia of the Lord at the end of time (cf. further ahead, starting at n. 1038). But multiple passages are not lacking in the New Testament, cited by the *CCC* (n. 1021), which speak of a being with Jesus immediately after death, or of a differentiated situation for the good and the wicked starting at that moment (for example, Lk 16:22, the parable of Lazarus and the rich glutton). It is not easy to find in the New Testament itself an explicit harmonization among these passages which speak of the immediate situation of the person who dies and passages that refer to the final moment. But based on the conviction that man, after death, reaches a state of definitive salvation or condemnation, it is very easy to understand that the Church arrived at the idea of the particular judgment, that is, the judgment that happens at the death of each person and which means immediate recompense according to one's faith and works.

N. 1022 notes the principal magisterial tests that directly or indirectly speak of this judgment, which is, as we have said, a necessary prerequisite for that immediate recompense. Among them all, the constitution *Benedictus Deus* by Benedict XII, from the year 1336 (*DS* 1000–1002) deserves particular attention; it definitively resolved the issue of immediate recompense. Salvation and condemnation is the alternative before which each of us stands. These are the two possible "results" of the particular judgment. The text, however, mentions a third possibility, that of purification. A quick and superficial reading can give the impression that the three possibilities stand on the same level. In reality that is not the case: as will be explained clearly below, "Purgatory" is entirely part of the journey to salvation.

It is not a definitive result like the other two, nor an intermediate state between Heaven and Hell. It is the purification needed by the saved to enter into full communion with God, in the case when human imperfections do not allow them the joy of Heaven. The famous words of St. John of the Cross tell us that our love will be the object of God's judgment on us.

II. Heaven

The text now turns, after the discussion of the particular judgment, to deal with the various possibilities in which man can be found in the definitive life. Heaven is the first, because only Heaven truly merits the description of "eternal life"; the New Testament use of the word "life," sometimes associated with "eternal," leaves no room for doubt. The writings of John, which associate life with Christ, are particularly meaningful in this regard (cf., for example, Jn 3:36; 5:24; 6: 47,53–54; 11:25; 17:3; 1 Jn 3:14). Already in the New Testament the state of eternal life is associated with the vision of God (cf. the texts cited in the *CCC*). In the Magisterium the constitution *Benedictus Deus,* to which we have just referred, has special importance; it appears cited in its fundamental passages. One might also add a short passage which was not mentioned, and which comes just after the end of the text that is offered: "But the divine essence is shown to them bare, immediately, clearly and openly." The vision of God of which this speaks to us does not mean that God becomes understood, embraced; that there would no longer be any mystery for the blessed. Rather the contrary: the immediate vision of God immediately displays his incomprehensibility, into which the human being is more and more immersed.

While at some times theology has spoken of Heaven almost exclusively in terms of vision, now it is more conscious that in the New Testament and in Tradition other elements appear also. One of these is communion of life and love with God one and three. The "vision" is not merely intellectual, but embraces all the aspects and dimensions of human life. Along with communion with God, the fullness of the communion of the saints is mentioned, an important element in the tradition. In n. 1026 we shall return to this idea. If man has no other finality than God himself, reaching this full vision and communion is the full realization of the human being: the state of full happiness. It is worthwhile to mention a text of St. Thomas that takes up these and other elements of eternal life: "In eternal life the first thing is that man is united with God. So God himself is the reward and the end of all our efforts [...]. This union consists in perfect vision: 'Now we see in a mirror dimly, but then face to face' (1 Cor 13:12). It also consists in the highest praise [...]. And equally in the perfect satisfaction of desire [...]. In the happy communion of all the blessed; and this communion will be very peaceful because everyone will share all goods with all the blessed. So each one will love the other as himself, and therefore will rejoice in the good of the other as in his own" (*Opuscula Theologica,* 2).

N. 1025 indicates another fundamental point that should be brought out. Life eternal is "being with Jesus." The New Testament is clear about this. We ought, as soon as possible, to recover this idea of full communion with Christ, which is so decisive in the theology of the New Testament and the early years of the Church (cf., for example, Ignatius of Antioch, *Ad Romanos,* 5:3, for which martyrdom means 'reaching Christ'). But the text takes a step further, even one of great theological consequence. The chosen live "in Christ," in his risen body which embraces all of redeemed humanity. In Christ, in the vital space that is opened in his resurrection, the chosen are also in "God." St. Irenaeus formulated this in magisterial form in *Adversus haereses,* IV, 20:5: "As they who see light are in the light and share in his splendor, so they who see God are in God, sharing in his splendor." The triune God admits us to the inner life of the divinity, into the communion of love of the Father, the Son, and the Holy Spirit. But all this, says the text, does not mean that the saved person loses his personal identity. In union with Jesus this identity reaches its greatest realization. Relationship with God and the consistency proper to creaturely being grow at the same time; one is not opposed to the other. If the destiny of man is this union with God in Christ, whoever attains it is most fully himself.

N. 1026 takes up topics mentioned previously and to which we have made reference: particularly relationship with Christ, dead and arisen: it is he who, ascending to the Father, prepares a place for us (cf. Jn 14:2f). Jesus opens for us the way to heaven because he himself, as the locus in whom we enter into communion with God, is heaven. Because of this, there is no life in paradise except as an association with his glorification. We have also already referred to the communion of all the blessed as an essential dimension of "heaven." Each description that we try to make for the life hereafter will always seem inadequate. Thus the metaphorical and symbolic language which Jesus himself utilized, and which is used in general in Scripture and Tradition: the wedding banquet, the new wine, etc. The enumeration in n. 1027 is eloquent. What God has prepared for those who love him surpasses all our capacity to imagine because it is he himself. The infinite majesty of God is such that it can only be seen by those to whom God himself allows to know it. With our own powers we cannot reach God. The "beatific vision," so called because it makes one fully happy, fortunate, blessed, is a gift and is grace. Only God is he who can admit us into the joy of his Kingdom. The blessed continue to realize the plan of God in respect to other human beings and to creation. They intercede for those who are still on the way. The Second Vatican Council, in ch. 7 of *LG* (nn. 48–51), spoke of the eschatological character of the pilgrim Church and her communion with the heavenly Church. The blessed reign forever with Christ. They themselves are the Kingdom, inasmuch as the salvific lordship of Christ is totally realized in them, the lordship that eliminates every slavery and misery. In the blessed the Lord shows his loving and saving power. We can conclude this chapter dedicated to Heaven with the words with which St. Augustine ends his work *De Civitate Dei* (22:30): "There we shall rest and see, see and love, love and praise. This is what shall be in the end without end."

III. The Final Purification, or Purgatory

While considering n. 1022, we referred to the erroneous interpretation to which a hasty reading of the text could lend itself. An attentive reader of this section dedicated to purgatory will understand why. It makes no sense to speak of purgatory except in relation to salvation. He who dies in the grace and the friendship of God is not necessarily purified completely of sin; he may not have totally received the love of God in his life, he may not be free from every disordered inclination. On the contrary, we can suppose that such a situation is not at all abnormal. Purification after death is an event of grace. God wants us to be really worthy of him. For this reason he wants to purify us from every stain and renew us completely. The justification of a sinner, according to Catholic doctrine, means an interior transformation of the human being, his sanctification.

Analogously, definitive salvation must include our full transformation, total purification, and the full orientation of our entire being toward God. Purgatory is a truth of the faith that should open us to joy and hope. Our total purification, even if it involves some suffering, is a gift of God that calls for humble gratitude. The traditional formulations of the doctrine on purgatory insist on the character required in order to see God, which includes this purification. Some modern points of view, on which the *CCC* does not take any position, allude to the purifying character that meeting God must itself have, inasmuch as it frees us, not without some pain on our part, from everything that is not fully oriented toward him. The two lines have no reason to be incompatible. Even accepting this second interpretation, it remains clear that only "after" this purification, and as a consequence of it, when every obstacle opposed to communion with God is eliminated, the joy of meeting the Lord and the beatific vision can be perfect and full. The most important magisterial documents, like the biblical texts on which they are based, are mentioned in n. 1031. We need to draw attention to an important statement in this item. Purification is completely different from the punishment of the damned. Purgatory has nothing to do with a temporary hell. Hell is definitive separation from God, while purgatory is the journey toward the full possession of God. We have seen already that there can be no greater difference than this. Misunderstanding can arise due to the image of "fire" used in both cases. But in the case of Hell it is a punishment, and the in case of purgatory it is a purification. The meaning of fire, then, is very different in the one case and the other. It will be useful to note here what the Council of Trent recommended to pastors of the Church, that is, to see diligently that the doctrine on purgatory be presented and believed, while not catering to curiosity and superstitions (*DS* 1820). For the sake of that, sobriety is recommended for the presentation of these truths of the faith.

The doctrine of purgatory is intimately united with that of prayer for the dead. N. 1032 also mentions the basic texts of Scripture and the Magisterium on this topic. The soul who has to make account before God for his actions and suffer purification, in case it is necessary to be able to enjoy paradise, is not alone before God in this moment. The Church accompanies him with prayer, almsgiving and works of penance, intercedes for him; and above all offers the eucharistic sacrifice for him, in which Christ associates us all with his perfect oblation to the Father. In relation to Masses offered for the dead, which the Church warmly recommends, we can also recall another admonition of the Council of Trent contained in the same text we cited just before: that we avoid everything that can tend to "dishonorable gain" (cf. *DS* 1820).

IV. Hell

The doctrine of Hell causes difficulties for many of our contemporaries. It is essential, despite this, for a right understanding of the relationship between God and the human being and even for a right understanding of what Heaven is. In effect, the communion of love that God offers us and which he wants for all, is offered freely and therefore must be freely accepted. Love cannot be forced, lest it be destroyed. It is the mystery of human freedom and responsibility in all its greatness that obliges us to keep in the mind the possibility of rejecting God. Only if this possibility is real is our freedom real, the freedom that becomes full only in accepting the immense love God grants to us. The rejection of God's love is expressed in hatred toward him and toward our brother, in our closure to our neighbor and his needs. Anyone who is hardened in this attitude and, while remaining in it, is surprised by death remains separated from God. As the *CCC* indicates quite well, he excludes himself from communion with God and with the blessed. To be precise, God did not make Hell. His free creatures make it, inasmuch as they separate themselves from Him. Nor does God send anyone to Hell: it is the damned one who separates himself and does not want to enter into the Father's house. God, St. Irenaeus said, does not really look to punish the damned, but as they are deprived of all good things, it is the penalty that pursues them (*Adversus Haereses,* V. 27, 2; a similar idea in St. Augustine, *Enarrationes in Psalmos,* 5, 10: God abandons the sinner to his evil, he does not, properly speaking, give evil to anyone). Because of this, and despite what is said sometimes, we need to insist on the fact that Hell does not say anything against the infinite goodness of God. It only speaks in favor of the immense respect that God has for the freedom of human beings created in his image.

God does not want at any time to do away with this liberty, without which, as we have said, the acceptance of his love and grace would also not be possible.

The very words of Jesus in the Gospel clearly show the seriousness of the choice before which every man stands in life. It is irresponsible to minimize these hard expressions, while it remains that nothing in them can make us forget the love and mercy of God, who will that all men be saved (cf. 1 Tm 2:4) and that he sent his Son into the world, not in order to condemn the world, but that it be saved through him (cf. Jn 3:16f). Hell is no evidence against the universal salvific will of God.

In n. 1034 we find the fundamental statements of Jesus about Hell, conveyed by the Gospels. The image of unquenchable fire appears, and also the idea of distancing and separation: "Depart from me, you cursed" (Mt 25:41).

The teaching of the Church will follow this same line; we also find reference to the fundamental documents in n. 1035. References to fire are abundant in these texts also, but it is also indicated, very rightly, that the principal penalty of Hell must be seen in separation from God, since the happiness of man and the goods to which he aspires, and for which he was created, are found only in Him. Traditional theology has called this separation from God "the pain of loss," while it has reserved the name of "the pain of the senses" for the other torments of which it speaks: fire, etc. If, as we shall see shortly, the happiness of Heaven also corresponds to entering into a transformed and renewed world, we can also understand that separation from God also involves a separation from others and from the cosmos, a negative relationship with created reality, a perversion of the positive relation which we are called to have with the transformed world.

The responsibility before which man finds himself follows clearly from the biblical and magisterial statements. Man's eternal destiny depends on the use of his freedom. From this comes the need for a continual attitude of conversion and vigilance, in the face of our not knowing the day or the hour in which we will be called to render an account of our life to the Lord. The insistence on vigilance traces back to the teaching of Jesus himself (cf., for example, Mk 13:35; Mt 25:13; Lk 12:39); the text cited from Vatican II stands in the line of a continuous tradition. We have already said that God wills all men to be saved. The Church has rejected the idea of predestination to evil and to Hell. God is the first one interested, so to speak, in the salvation of man. The Father has sent his only Son into the world, not to condemn it, but that it be saved through him (cf. Jn 3:17). It is only the free decision of man, mortal sin and persistence in it (as we have already had occasion to see, cf. n. 1033), that provoke condemnation. The mystery of human freedom appears in all its seriousness before this tremendous possibility. Therefore we must unite ourselves to the prayer of the Church for the salvation of all. The question of how many will be saved or damned is common. It was already posed to Jesus, who did not answer it with direct information, but by exhorting his hearers about the personal responsibility to "enter by the narrow door" (cf. Lk 13:23f). The question of Hell cannot be asked in the third person, but in the first: each of us must be conscious of the fact that he can close himself to the grace of God and the fact that his eternal destiny is at play in his decisions. But he can and must at the same time trust in the grace of God and expect the gift of salvation from God's mercy, for himself and for other men.

V. The Last Judgment

The *CCC* has already spoken of the particular judgment after the death of every man.

Now it refers to the universal judgment at the end of time, of which the Gospel speaks, especially in the passages which the *CCC* cites. Man is, on one hand, a personal and unrepeatable being; on the other, he is found, placed in a human history in which all freedoms are interwoven. The particular judgment and the general therefore cannot be seen only in their separation from time (the moment of death, the end of history), but also in their intrinsic relationship: personal unrepeatability on one hand, humanity as a whole in which each of us finds himself placed, on the other. The final judgment stands in intrinsic relation with the final coming or Parousia of Christ, of which we have already spoken elsewhere in the *CCC*. It is an intrinsic dimension of this coming: "He will come to judge the living and the dead." It is equally in relation with the resurrection; already in the New Testament, the idea appears of the resurrection of all men before the universal judgment; a resurrection that for some is unto life and for some is unto damnation. We have already said previously that the New Testament also acknowledges a fuller concept of resurrection, which is participation in the glorious life of the risen Lord, which naturally is the resurrection of the saved. Jesus the Truth in person is also the "perfect man," as the Second Vatican Council says (cf. *GS* 22, 38, 41, 45). For this reason his appearing in glory, in the full manifestation of what He is, reveals the final truth about man, which consists in his relation to God. So the judgment is not an exterior addition to the Parousia. We can say that it itself is already the judgment, because Jesus, the judge to whom the Father has given all power to judge (cf. Jn 5:27), is at the same time the criterion of judgment. The final being of every man and of all history is measured in him. Thus the *CCC* rightly indicates that the Father, the one who knows and determines the day and the hour (cf. Mk 13:32; Acts 1:7) of the glorious return of Christ, will pronounce his definitive word on all of history through Jesus (n. 1040). The providence of God guides history to its end, consummation in Christ. In the definitive appearing of Jesus, the meaning of all things will appear, and the pathways, incomprehensible for us, by which God will have led all things to their final end, will be made plain. But God has willed to fulfill his plans with human cooperation. This is why the manifestation of His pathways has this dimension of discriminating judgment over men and their actions. A question, which can also be formulated in regard to the "particular" judgment, presents itself, of the harmonization of divine mercy and divine justice. But this justice is salvific: so it will represent, the text says, triumph over all the injustices committed by men. In the judgment God will appear as the defender of the weak and the poor. The hidden face of history, which we cannot know, and which many times we have contributed to hiding, will be made manifest. Jesus had put his disciples on guard against the pretense of anticipating the judgment, which he awaits only from God (cf. Mt 13:24–30,36–43, the parable of the wheat and weeds). In any case we need to underscore that the judgment will mean the victory of divine love, not of revenge or hatred. All of this does not do away, for our part, with the holy fear of God, who will give to each once according to his own works, whose the day we await, trusting in his merciful love. As was said already in regard to the lifetime that the Lord grants each of us, the message of final judgment means a call to conversion, to commitment for the kingdom of God and his justice. But the *CCC* very rightly indicates that at the same time it is a proclamation of hope. This attitude must prevail in the Christian who desires the final glorification of God, that is, the full realization of the end that God had in mind in creating the world.

VI. The Hope of the New Heaven and the New Earth

The title that closes the treatment of the last article of the Creed offers a summary of what has been said in the preceding sections. N. 1042, in turn, gives us a type of summary of what will be shown below: the eternal reign with Christ of the just, glorified in body and soul; this means, as the citation from Vatican II (*LG* 48) mentions, the consummation of the Church. Together with the human race the universe will also be transformed and will acquire its definitive perfection. The human being, according to what the Second Vatican Council teaches in *GS* 24, is the only creature of this world that God willed for himself. The others were willed by God for man. In reality, only inasmuch as man reaches his destiny in Christ can the universe also reach its own.

The whole of humanity and the transformed cosmos constitute the new heavens and the new earth, as the text states. At the same time it means the full dominion of the risen Christ over all. Nothing escapes his saving power. There will be full identity between the work of creation and that of salvation, which will be reached when everything is recapitulated in Christ (cf. Eph 1:10); with this recapitulation the divine plan before the creation of the world will be fulfilled (cf. Eph 1:4f).

The new heavens and the new earth, which are the heavenly Jerusalem, are characterized above all, according to chapter 21 of Revelation, by the presence of God. In the new Jerusalem God will have his dwelling among men. Heaven consists in this communion of man with God, as we indicated previously. And this includes the disappearance of every pain and every sorrow, because the Lord will wipe away every tear from our eyes.

Continuing, the text says what the heavenly Jerusalem will be for man and for the cosmos. For man, for whom the first place is awaiting, the heavenly Jerusalem means the unity of all the human race; the Church now is the sacrament, that is, the sign and the instrument, of this unity (*LG* 1), which will be perfect unity in the eschatological consummation. When we were speaking of the eternal life in heaven we already made reference to the perfect communion among men that will reign there. Then the Church will be the perfect bride of Christ without any blemish of sin. Perfect harmony among men will be the consequence of communion with God, the beatific vision, which, as the *CCC* says, is the source of happiness and peace and of communion among us. The relationship with God, perfectly attained, makes possible the perfect relationship of men among themselves and also with the cosmos, as is said further on.

As n. 1046 affirms, there is a communion of destiny between the material world and man. The classic text of Rom 8:19–23 is quoted, perhaps the most eloquent of the New Testament on the future cosmic transformation in relation to the glorification of humanity and the manifestation of the full freedom of the sons of God. Sin, changing man's relationship with God, also alters his relationship with the cosmos. The latter participates in its way in the slavery into which man is fallen. The transformation of the cosmos is ultimately a further element of the full dominion of the risen Christ over all creation, and of the salvation and perfect redemption of everything. As man is a being placed in the cosmos, and also called to perfection in his material and cosmic dimensions (resurrection), it is understood that this fullness cannot be reached without a transformed universe.

N. 1047, citing Irenaeus, sets forth the relationship between the fullness of the cosmos and the fullness of man: the restored universe stands at the service of the just. Resurrection, in its full sense of participation in the glorification of the Lord Jesus, does not mean that man is converted into an "acosmic" being: the contrary appears clearly. All of this revives man's sense of responsibility for the present world that God has entrusted to him.

Nn. 1048–1050 are composed, basically, of quotations from an important text of Vatican II, *GS* 39, which takes up precisely this biblical tradition of the transformation of the cosmos, perhaps a bit forgotten in later times. In first place there is mention of the uncertainty about the when and the how of the ending and the future world. Christian eschatology cannot "describe" the world that we await, because it surpasses our imagination and our capacities. But this does not diminish the certainty of faith in the new dwelling that the Lord prepares for us, the new heavens and the new earth. Now, the world that we await embraces all the dimensions of present reality: without doubt it is above all a gift of God, but at the same time, the fruit of the human response to the gift and to grace. This is why hope in the new earth does not reduce our interest in this earth, but on the contrary increases it, because in hope of the future transformation our efforts in this world are radically saved from vanity and from the transience that characterizes our present condition. What we do in this transitory world for the good of our brothers acquires dimensions of eternity. The Council spells out very well, on one hand, the "discontinuity" between our present condition and that of the future. We need to distinguish between earthly progress and the kingdom of God, among other things, because this progress is often ambiguous; it can represent an advancement in some aspects and a regress in others. On the other hand, however, "continuity" is also indicated: this progress, inasmuch as it contributes to an improvement of human society at all levels, is not indifferent for this Kingdom that we await. And this is why God does not want to destroy our effort or its fruits. He wants to transform it, because he wants to transform the world on which the work of man is engraved. For this reason we find, transformed and purified, everything that we shall have done in this world according to the command of God, in docility to the power of his Spirit. Everything in which we have been truly cooperators of God, in the fulfillment of his designs, will be part of the new heavens and the new earth. In some manner, therefore, the discriminating and purifying judgment of God to which we have made reference also relates to human work in the world, and must separate what man will have done according to God from the things in which man will be opposed to his saving plan. This purified and transformed world also forms part of the Kingdom that Jesus will present to the Father at the end of time, when everything will be submitted to him, and God will be all in all (cf. 1 Cor 15:28). Therefore the heavenly gifts that the Father gives us through the Son in the Holy Spirit, together with the universe of things he created and guides toward fullness, constitute the eternal life that we await.

"AMEN"

Rino Fisichella

It is meaningful that the conclusion of the first part of the *CCC* should end with a short, understanding explanation of the term "amen." As is well-attested, "amen" is a term that recurs often in the life of the Church. Our prayers end with the "amen" and so do the Creeds. As n. 1064 notes, the intention of the "amen" is to testify to the faith that has been professed.

The term "amen" is presented as the simplest word and at the same time as the word bearing the most commitment. It has been imprinted in all the modern languages in the same original Hebrew form, as if to witness to the sacrality of the term that cannot and should not be modified, due to the high value it possesses. In sacred Scripture the use of "amen" is differentiated. Somehow a biblical text can help us enter more directly into its profound meaning. We are at the time of King David and of his decision that Solomon, the son he had from Bathsheba, would succeed on his throne. "King David said, 'Call to me Zadok the priest, Nathan the prophet, and Benaiah the son of Jehoiada.' So they came before the king. And the king said to them, 'Take with you the servants of your lord, and cause Solomon my son to ride on my own mule, and bring him down to Gihon; and let Zadok the priest and Nathan the prophet there anoint him king over Israel; then blow the trumpet, and say, Long live King Solomon. You shall then come up after him, and he shall come and sit upon my throne; for he shall be king in my stead; and I have appointed him to be ruler over Israel and over Judah.' And Benaiah the son of Jehoiada answered the king, 'Amen! May the Lord, the God of my lord the king, say so. As the Lord has been with my lord the king, even so may he be with Solomon, and make his throne greater than the throne of my lord King David'" (1 Kgs 1:32–37).

The "amen" ("So be it") pronounced by the prophet Benaiah has a double meaning: on one hand, it indicates that the prophet has understood the will of King David; he approves it and joins in, even expressing the prediction that the Lord himself will be able to make the King's words happen. On the other hand, the "amen" indicates that the prophet is ready to fulfill everything that is required so that the order be executed. As we can see, a relationship exists between what the word of the king calls for, and what its realization involves. The "amen" pronounced by the prophet bears witness that inasmuch as it is the will of King David, it must be carried out. So a twofold relation is expressed: the "objective" relation that refers to the order expressed, which must find a response in its actualization; and the "subjective" relation that is created between the person who pronounces the "amen" and what he confirms with his concrete action. The prophet, then, pronouncing his "amen," indicates both his awareness of David's will and his assent to that will. This involves the submission of his person in conformity to the message, and his commitment to realize it.

At the end of the Creed, when the believer pronounces his "amen," he intends to express, above all, that he knows what he has professed, and that he desires to express it concretely in his daily life. The creed, therefore, is placed on two important columns that express the same unitary act from the beginning to the end. With the first "I believe," the believer testifies of accepting the truth of everything that will follow in his profession of faith, and of receiving it into himself, basing that acceptance on the testimony of God himself. With the last "amen; I believe," he confirms the faith expressed, and commits himself to give testimony of it.

Concluding this first part with the "amen," the *CCC* moves from the Creed to enter into the celebration of the Christian mystery with the liturgy. From there, passing through the commitment of living as disciples of Christ, it will enter into the fourth part with Christian prayer. The "amen" will be repeated also at that time as the certainty of having encountered God the Father, Son, and Holy Spirit, of trusting in him and of being heard in the necessities of every day.

PART TWO

THE CELEBRATION OF THE CHRISTIAN MYSTERY

Section One

THE SACRAMENTAL ECOMONY

Chapter One:

THE PASCHAL MYSTERY IN THE AGE OF THE CHURCH

Maria del Pilar Rio García

The contents of this brief innovative chapter concern liturgy and the sacraments in their appropriate theological context: the sacramental economy of salvation. The *CCC*'s framework of salvation history, in continuity with the doctrine of the Council constitution *SC* and the theological reflection of recent decades that is more rooted in Scripture, allows a "re-setting" of the sacraments within the liturgy and thus presents a very united vision. The *CCC*, unlike the manuals of sacramental theology, presents the sacraments as real and authentic liturgical celebrations, thus combining doctrine and liturgy, theology and celebration.

The presentation of this unity calls for integrating it with the material in the numbers that precede it and follow it: those relative to the liturgy in general (nn. 1066–1075) and to the celebration of the paschal mystery (nn. 1135–1209). Otherwise, the interpretation and explanation of the sacraments would be isolated from their liturgical-celebrative context and would not be faithful to the unified theological vision the *CCC* intends to convey. A catechesis on the sacraments that adheres to the text, then, should integrate the first chapter's doctrinal perspective with the second chapter's liturgical-celebrative perspective (see n. 1113). The explanation of the celebrative aspect, of course, assumes an understanding of sacramental economy (see n. 1135).

The *CCC* introduces the theological and pastoral content in the first section's two chapters with statements in n. 1076 that lay out the key categories leading to a theological understanding of liturgical and sacramental actions. These "master keys" are the biblical-patristic concepts of "mystery" and "economy" already presented at the beginning of the Second Part: "The Church confesses the mystery of the Holy Trinity and of the plan of God's 'good pleasure' [Eph 1:9] for all creation: the Father accomplishes the 'mystery of his will' by giving his beloved Son and his Holy Spirit for the salvation of the world and for the glory of his name. Such is the mystery of Christ [see Eph 3:4], revealed and fulfilled in history according to the wisely ordered plan that St. Paul calls the 'plan of the mystery' and the patristic tradition will call the 'economy of the Word incarnate' or the 'economy of salvation'" (n. 1066; see nn. 50, 236).

The historical fulfillment ("economy") of the divine plan of salvation ("mystery") goes through different phases of actualization. It moves from creation to the end of time and includes the Incarnation and the redemptive work of Christ that bring to fulfillment the plan in the Father's heart. Everything has its center in the paschal mystery through which Christ has released his Spirit and has united himself to his Church as one body (see n. 1067; *SC* 5), thereby opening a new phase in the dispensation of the mystery of salvation.

Number 1076 is directly connected to the biblical presentation of the "dispensation of the mystery" and expands on it, closely following its presentation in *SC*: "The Church was made manifest to the world on the day of Pentecost by the outpouring of the Holy Spirit [see *SC* 6; *LG* 2]. The gift of the Spirit ushers in a new era in the 'dispensation of the mystery'—the age of the Church" (n. 1076). This new phase of the "age of the Church" comes after the historical fulfillment in Christ through his Person and the mysteries of his life that culminates in his passion, death, and glorious resurrection. It is characterized by the fact that "Christ manifests, makes present, and communicates his work of salvation through the liturgy of his Church, 'until he comes' [1 Cor 11:26]" (n. 1076). This makes clear the "modality" by which the redemptive work of Christ is made present and is dispensed to people through the salvific "sacrament" (sign and instrument) that is his Church: "In this age of the Church Christ now lives and acts in and with his Church, in a new way appropriate to this new age" (n. 1076; see *LG* 1). This manner or modality is called "sacramental" because Christ "acts through the sacraments in what the common Tradition of the East and the West calls 'the sacramental economy'; this is the communication (or 'dispensation') of the fruits of Christ's Paschal mystery in the celebration of the Church's 'sacramental' liturgy" (n. 1076).

The "sacramental economy" corresponds to the current phase of the actualization of salvation in the Church and for the Church. Through the sacramental liturgy she announces and celebrates the mystery of Christ until the end of time "so that the faithful may live from it and bear witness to it in the world" (n. 1068; see *SC* 2). Mystery (paschal), action (liturgical-sacramental), and life are the three inseparable realities in the age of the Church.

In light of this theological framework, the title of this first chapter ("The Paschal Mystery in the Age of the Church") seems fully justified and clarified. The chapter deals with liturgy and the sacraments as "mystery," as the sacramental enactment of the paschal mystery. Since the liturgy is an event and a trinitarian work and the sacraments are its most sublime expression, the chapter focuses its two articles on the two topics of liturgy and sacraments. Their contents correspond, respectively, to discussions on the essence of liturgy and on general sacramental theology, and their excellent articulation opens up interesting perspectives, be they dogmatic, catechetical, or pastoral.

Article 1:
THE LITURGY—WORK OF THE HOLY TRINITY

The *CCC* begins by presenting the liturgical-sacramental dispensation of salvation in the light of the mystery of the Trinity, thus highlighting its essentially divine and salvific character. Everything in the history of salvation, and also in its liturgical "expression," occurs in a circular pattern that follows (*ad extra*) the intra-trinitarian dynamic (see n. 236). Everything flows from the Father as the initiator, and all returns to the Father as praise and adoration through Christ in the Holy Spirit (*a Patre per Christum in Spiritu Sancto ad Patrem*) through the Church's humble cooperation. Consequently, the principal protagonists of the liturgical celebration of the salvific event are neither the Church nor every Christian but rather the three Persons of the most Holy Trinity. We faithful are invited to actively participate in it, but it is above all an *opus Dei*, a work of God—or better yet, an *opus Trinitatis*, a work of the Trinity. With this important trinitarian perspective on the dynamic in liturgical and sacramental actions, the *CCC* fills out and enriches *SC*'s vision in which the liturgy and the sacraments appear primarily in relationship to Christ (see *SC* 7).

I. The Father—Source and Goal of the Liturgy

The *CCC* dedicates to the Father, the source and goal of the whole liturgical-sacramental economy, a brief but rich exposition that is based on a biblical matrix and is considered one of its most beautiful sections. Following the outline of the hymn of thanksgiving at the beginning of the Letter to the Ephesians (see Eph 1:3–6), the text connects the liturgy to the history of salvation and the marvels that God performs from the beginning to the end of time. It starts with the biblical category of "blessing": "Blessing is a divine and life-giving action, the source of which is the Father; his blessing is both word and gift (*bene-dictio*, εὐλογία)" (n. 1078). All the work by which God the Father brings his salvific plan to pass thus appears as "one vast divine blessing" (n. 1079). It is a blessing that unfolds over time and embraces the work of creation (see n. 1080), the history of Israel and the old covenant (see

n. 1081), and the work of salvation (see n. 1082). This immeasurable blessing is the history of the *magnalia Dei*, the great works of God, and of the mercies through which God has prepared his greatest blessing of all: the revelation of his Word and the total gift of himself in his beloved Son and, with him, the outpouring of the Holy Spirit offered to all human beings beginning at Pentecost. The liturgy, as we have said, is connected to the history of God's blessings as an "expression" of this very history, because in it this historical-salvific event is made manifest, is made present, and is communicated to human beings.

However, as the same Letter to the Ephesians indicates, the word "blessing" is also an action by human beings, and in this case it "means adoration and surrender to his Creator in thanksgiving" (n. 1078). It is the response that is born in the heart of every person for all of God's benefits, expressed in the worship of Israel for the marvels YHWH has done for his people, and that the Church addresses to the Father through its most sublime blessing. In liturgical action, therefore, God and the Church encounter and bless one another: "In the Church's liturgy the divine blessing is fully revealed and communicated. The Father is acknowledged and adored as the source and the end of all the blessings of creation and salvation. In his Word who became incarnate, died, and rose for us, he fills us with his blessings. Through his Word, he pours into our hearts the Gift that contains all gifts, the Holy Spirit" (n. 1082).

The liturgy is therefore "one vast divine blessing" that comes from its source, the Father, the principle of every good thing, and descends on human beings. At the same time it is a "blessing" full of faith and love that rises up to the Father. One can recognize here, then, a dual movement or dimension:

> On the one hand, the Church, united with her Lord and "in the Holy Spirit" [Lk 10:21], blesses the Father "for his inexpressible gift" [2 Cor 9:15] in her adoration, praise, and thanksgiving. On the other hand, until the consummation of God's plan, the Church never ceases to present to the Father the offering of his own gifts and to beg him to send the Holy Spirit upon that offering, upon herself, upon the faithful, and upon the whole world, so that through communion in the death and resurrection of Christ the Priest, and by the power of the Spirit, these divine blessings will bring forth the fruits of life "to the praise of his glorious grace" [Eph 1:6]. (n. 1083)

The priestly mediation of Christ, through the power of his Spirit, is the "bridge" for this dual movement of sanctification and worship that occurs and is effectively realized (see *SC* 7).

In this "encounter" or "dialogue" of the Father with his children through Christ in the Holy Spirit (see n. 1153), the Father always takes the initiative—he "loves us first"—and we his children, full of amazement, make remembrance of and acknowledge his gifts. Liturgy is therefore profoundly "paternal" and "filial." Consequently, liturgy is a wonderful school of prayer and life in which one learns to be grateful, to rely on our Father, to expect everything from him, and to know that we are part of his family to which all human beings are called (see *GS* 40).

II. Christ's Work in the Liturgy

Continuing with this trinitarian perspective, the *CCC* highlights the role of Christ in the liturgy. Following the sequence in *SC* (see nn. 5–8), it reiterates the Council doctrine on the presence and centrality of the salvific event of Christ in the worship of the Church, but it deepens it. It goes one step further and sets it forth more explicitly. The presentation, laid out in four sections according to the christological-liturgical principle of the Council, is preceded by four headings that together summarize the development of the theme.

Christ glorified…

The first part begins with an understanding of liturgy as the "place" in which Christ, our Redeemer and High Priest now glorified, continues his living and operative presence in his body, the Church, through the outpouring and power of his Spirit. He continues to act now with the Church and for her through the sacramental liturgy that he instituted to communicate his grace (see nn. 1084, 662, 1069). Through the sacraments, which the *CCC* defines for the first time in n. 1084, the glorified Christ manifests his priestly mediation until the end of time and assures his operative, active, and efficacious presence among human beings.

As the text explains next, "In the liturgy of the Church, it is principally his own Paschal mystery that Christ signifies and makes present" (n. 1085). The liturgy is essentially the presence of the historical-salvific event of Christ's paschal mystery that occurred "once for all." This important conviction is elaborated in n. 1085 and constitutes something new with respect to the doctrine set forth by *SC*. In fact, even though this Council document affirmed the presence and centrality of the redemptive mystery in the liturgy (see *SC* 7), it maintained that such a presence occurs only "in a certain way" (*quodammodo praesentia*) that is due to the power and merits of the Lord (*divitias virtutem atque meritorum Domini*) (see *SC* 102, 61). The *CCC* goes a step further and is more explicit about this:

> During his earthly life Jesus announced his Paschal mystery by his teaching and anticipated it by his actions. When his Hour comes [see Jn 13:1; 17:1], he lives out the unique event of history which

> does not pass away: Jesus dies, is buried, rises from the dead, and is seated at the right hand of the Father "once for all" [Rom 6:10; Heb 7:27; 9:12]. His Paschal mystery is a real event that occurred in our history, but it is unique: all other historical events happen once, and then they pass away, swallowed up in the past. The Paschal mystery of Christ, by contrast, cannot remain only in the past, because by his death he destroyed death, and all that Christ is—all that he did and suffered for all men—participates in the divine eternity, and so transcends all times while being made present in them all. The event of the Cross and Resurrection abides and draws everything toward life. (n. 1085)

This event, which recapitulates the life and salvific work of the God-man, is actually present in the liturgy through the veil of signs. The *CCC* reaffirms this sacramental reality when it says, "the liturgy is the *memorial* of the mystery of salvation" (n. 1099; see nn. 1363–1364).

...from the time of the Church of the Apostles...

The heading's ellipsis is intended to point out the continuity of the action that comes from the glorified Christ, which, ever since the outpouring of the Spirit at Pentecost, is made present in a new, sacramental way in the Church. Quoting from *SC* 6, n. 1086 situates the liturgy in continuity with the mission that Christ received from the Father and transmitted to the apostles in order to continue his redemptive and salvific work until the end of time. This occurs through his word and its actualization through the power of the Spirit, that is, the proclamation of the gospel of salvation in Christ who died and was raised, as well as the actualization of this proclamation "through the sacrifice and sacraments, around which the entire liturgical life revolves" (n. 1086). The Gospel, because it is a salvific reality (like the redemptive work of Christ), represents the content of the *traditio viva* (living tradition), that, starting with the apostles, is transmitted to their successors from generation to generation in the Church. Precisely in view of this transmission, the risen Christ has given his apostles the Holy Spirit and has entrusted to them the power of sanctifying (see Jn 20:21–23), which they in turn have transmitted to their successors through the laying on of hands in the sacrament of Holy Orders. This makes them "signs of Christ" who are not substitutes for him but represent him sacramentally (see n. 1087). Through the ministry of the apostles and their successors, Christ ensures the continuity of his presence and his action in the liturgy of the Church.

...is present in the earthly liturgy...

As *SC* 7 teaches, the presence and action of the glorified Christ is achieved primarily through liturgical actions (see *CCC*, n. 1088). However, as that document explains, this unique presence—which is always the living and life-giving presence of the paschal mystery of Christ—is actualized in different forms and degrees according to the diversity of sacramental signs. The liturgical presence of Christ in the Church is, therefore, multifaceted (see nn. 1181, 1373–1374). In order of "intensity," the first is Christ's presence in the Eucharistic species, which is linked to the ordained ministers. Following this is his presence in the other sacraments, in the preaching of the word, and in the prayer of the Church. Although he is present in an analogous but real way in all these liturgical actions, only in the Eucharist is his presence "substantial" because under the species of bread of and wine, he is totally present as God and man (see Paul VI, *Mysterium fidei* 39, Sept. 3, 1965; *CCC* 1374). In line with the development of this theme in *SC*, the *CCC* concludes by affirming that in these liturgical actions "Christ, indeed, always associates the Church with himself in this great work in which God is perfectly glorified and men are sanctified" (n. 1089). In the liturgy a true "synergy" actually takes place between Christ and his Church, making it a "common work" by both.

...which participates in the liturgy of heaven

This last heading recalls *SC* 8 in which liturgical celebration is presented as the privileged place of communion between the pilgrim Church and the heavenly Church. Through it, we have a foretaste of and participation in the eternal liturgy, which is the fullness of the feast and communion that surpasses the signs (see n. 1136). We join in the hymn of glory that the heavenly hosts sing to the Lord, we venerate the Virgin Mary and the saints, we hope to participate with them in heavenly glory and be with them, and we await the definitive coming of the Lord in glory (see nn. 1090, 1137–1139). In every liturgical celebration—particularly in the Eucharistic sacrifice in which communion between the Church in heaven and the Church on earth occurs in an especially profound way—we renew the hope of reaching our destiny and of uniting ourselves forever in the song of praise to the One and Triune God (see *LG* 50).

The entirety of this section recalls that in the liturgy, Christ himself, now risen and glorified, continues to be present and to act in an efficacious way in our midst. He takes the initiative to encounter us and draw close to us in the various liturgical actions—in a special way in the Eucharist and the other sacraments. He is present in each of them and makes us participate in his

Passover in order to transform our existence. Salvation is chiefly the work of Christ in his Church through the Holy Spirit.

III. The Holy Spirit and the Church in the Liturgy

This section lays out a full and innovative presentation regarding the Holy Spirit's action in the liturgy. It completes and expands the Latin theological and liturgical reflection as well as the tentative pneumatology of *SC*. The heading indicates the presentation's perspective, which is made explicit in the first number: "In the liturgy the Holy Spirit is teacher of the faith of the People of God and artisan of 'God's masterpieces,' the sacraments of the New Covenant.... When the Spirit encounters in us the response of faith which he has aroused in us, he brings about genuine cooperation" (n. 1091). The perspective here is that of "synergy," a true collaboration, so one can maintain that "the liturgy becomes the common work of the Holy Spirit and the Church" (n. 1091).

The activity of the Holy Spirit in this "common work" is multifaceted and, in light of his work in the economy of salvation prior to Christ and during the age of the Church (see n. 737), the text of n. 1092 presents it as four actions that are reflected in this section's headings.

The Holy Spirit Prepares for the Reception of Christ

In this phase of the sacramental dispensation of the mystery of Christ, the Church age, the Holy Spirit acts the same way he did in the earlier phases of the economy of salvation: "he prepares the Church to encounter her Lord" (n. 1092). He does so in the sacramental economy by fulfilling the figures of the Old Testament (see n. 1093) articulated in the "typological" catechesis based on the harmony of the two covenants (see nn. 1094–1095). This occurs in such a way that the liturgy of the new covenant—every liturgical action but especially the celebration of the Eucharist and the sacraments—leads to the encounter between Christ and the Church and brings about the union of both in one body (see n. 1097). "The assembly should prepare itself to encounter its Lord and to become 'a people well disposed.' The preparation of hearts is the joint work of the Holy Spirit and the assembly, especially of its ministers. The grace of the Holy Spirit seeks to awaken faith, conversion of heart, and adherence to the Father's will. These dispositions are the precondition both for the reception of other graces conferred in the celebration itself and the fruits of new life which the celebration is intended to produce afterward" (n. 1098).

The Holy Spirit Recalls the Mystery of Christ

The function of remembrance that the Spirit accomplishes as "the Church's living memory [see Jn 14:26]" is the key to every celebration because the liturgy is a "memorial" (n. 1099). Accordingly, the Holy Spirit "recalls and makes Christ manifest to the faith of the assembly" (n. 1092). The two "inducements" the Spirit uses to revive the memory of the Church are the word of God and anamnesis. The Holy Spirit, the inspirer of the Scripture, recalls "the meaning of the salvation event to the liturgical assembly by giving life to the Word of God, which is proclaimed so that it may be received and lived" (n. 1100). In addition, "the Holy Spirit gives a spiritual understanding of the Word of God to those who read or hear it, according to the dispositions of their hearts" (n. 1101), and he also "'recalls' to the assembly all that Christ has done for us" (n. 1103). In so doing, "the Spirit puts both the faithful and the ministers into a living relationship with Christ" (n. 1101). He elicits the response of faith that the proclamation of the word of God requires, making the assembly a communion in faith (see n. 1102). Every liturgical celebration "'makes a remembrance' of the marvelous works of God in an anamnesis which may be more or less developed" (n. 1103). That involves not mere remembrance but the objective presence and actualization of the salvific events (see nn. 1363–1364). Awakening the memory of the Church, the Holy Spirit stirs up in the assembly the action of grace (the Eucharist) and praise (the doxology) through the paschal mystery of Christ (see n. 1103).

The Holy Spirit Makes Present the Mystery of Christ

The Holy Spirit, "by his transforming power...makes the mystery of Christ present here and now" (n. 1092). With theological precision, the *CCC* explains that, thanks to his active intervention, the liturgy not only recalls or simply repeats salvific events—and the paschal mystery of Christ in a central way—but also re-presents them: it brings them into the present and commemorates them. In every liturgical celebration "there is an outpouring of the Holy Spirit that makes the unique mystery present" (n. 1104). However, it is the celebrations that are repeated, not the mystery of Christ that always remains unique and unrepeatable as a salvific event. This means that the invocation of the Holy Spirit, together with the anamnesis, constitutes the center of the sacramental celebration, above all in the Eucharist (see n. 1106). The invocation is the *epiclesis* or "the intercession in which the priest begs the Father to send the Holy Spirit, the Sanctifier, so that the offerings may become the body and blood of Christ and that the faithful by receiving them, may themselves become a living offering to God" (n. 1105). That same transformative power of the Spirit in the liturgy "hastens the coming of the kingdom and the consummation of the mystery of salvation" (n. 1107). Consequently, it guarantees the reality of the celebration as a memorial of the past and as a prophecy of the future

The Communion of the Holy Spirit

The Holy Spirit, invoked in the epiclesis of every liturgical celebration, causes the assembly to enter into communication with the mysteries of Christ (see nn. 1108, 1092). The assembly "derives its unity from the 'communion of the Holy Spirit' who gathers the children of God into the one Body of Christ" (n. 1097). The Holy Spirit in the liturgy is therefore the Spirit of communion: he acts and remains in the Church, making it a sign and an instrument (sacrament) of the mystery of salvific union (see *LG* 1). His action brings forth fruit not only in communion with the holy Trinity and in fraternal communion (see n. 1108) but also in the Church's unfolding missionary communion. Therefore, the Church "asks the Father to send the Holy Spirit to make the lives of the faithful a living sacrifice to God by their spiritual transformation into the image of Christ, by concern for the Church's unity, and by taking part in her mission through the witness and service of charity" (n. 1109).

The excellent pneumatological presentation in this section with its rich implications underscores that the artisan and principal animator of the liturgical celebration is the Spirit, the Lord and giver of life. His powerful action in salvation history now flows into the liturgy, the school in which we learn to cooperate with him and are guided by him to encounter the Lord, who then leads us to the Father to receive the graces given to us in the celebration and the fruits of the new life to which we are called.

At the end of this first article, it is clear that according to the *CCC* the liturgy is a trinitarian work in the Church. It is the "place" in which the three Divine Persons act to make the faithful become participants—each with his or her own role—in the mysteries of intra-trinitarian life and to elicit from them a response full of faith that applies to all the dimensions of our lives.

Article 2: THE PASCHAL MYSTERY IN THE CHURCH'S SACRAMENTS

In the context of discussing the liturgy, the presentation now focuses on its core: the sacraments. In fact, "the whole liturgical life of the Church revolves around the Eucharistic sacrifice and the sacraments" (n. 1113; see *SC* 6). In the age of the Church, the dispensation of the fruits of Christ's paschal mystery occurs chiefly through sacramental liturgy (see n. 1076). As indicated at the beginning, this article deals with what is common to the seven sacraments (their "common denominator") from the doctrinal point of view. What they have in common from the celebrative point of view will be explained later in Chapter Two, and the characteristics of each sacrament will be described in the second section of that chapter (see n. 1113). An integrated understanding of their shared aspects requires, as we have said, the articulation of both their doctrinal and liturgical aspects. In terms of its content, this brief presentation sets forth the classic themes of general sacramental theology in a new light and presents the sacraments from a "relational" point of view in regard to Christ, the Church, faith, salvation, and eternal life. Elsewhere, these themes are also considered in relation to the Trinity (nn. 1077–1112) and to different cultures (nn. 1200-1209).

I. The Sacraments of Christ

The *CCC* begins by presenting the sacraments in relation to Christ, recalling with the Council of Trent, that they were instituted by him (see Council of Trent: *DS* 1600–1601; *CCC*, n. 1114). The assertion of faith concerning their institution goes beyond something simply external or legal because the sacraments proceed from Christ and receive their efficaciousness from him; he is their source and their foundation (see nn. 1120, 1084–1090). Subsequent numbers reiterate a sacramental understanding of salvation history, and the text explains the origin of the sacraments in Christ in a beautiful way with patristic points of view that have been rediscovered and referred to in the documents of Vatican II. The topic remains grounded in the economy of salvation, where it emerges clearly that the ever-present work of Christ continues in the Church and in the sacraments (see nn. 1066–1068, 1076).

The Son sent into the world by the Father reveals and fulfills the divine plan by actually entering into history and taking on flesh: "His humanity appeared as 'sacrament,' that is, the sign and instrument, of his divinity and of the salvation he brings" (n. 515). Christ, the incarnate Word, is the primordial and essential "sacrament" of salvation: he is its author as God and its instrument as man. During his time on earth, everything in his life demonstrates and brings to pass the Father's salvific plan: "Jesus' words and actions during his hidden life and public ministry were already salvific, for they anticipated the power of his Paschal mystery. They announced and prepared what he was going to give the Church when all was accomplished" (n. 1115; see nn. 512–521). The salvation he visibly brought through his humanity during his earthly life, and particularly through his paschal mystery, is now accomplished through his sacraments. Therefore, "the mysteries of Christ's life are the foundations of what he would henceforth dispense in the sacraments, through the ministers of his Church, for 'what was visible in our Savior has passed over into his mysteries' [St. Leo the Great, "Sermon 74," 2]" (n. 1115).

In the sacramental dispensation of the mystery of Christ, the Church is also included as a sacrament (see *LG* 1). We continue to "touch" Christ like the woman with the hemorrhage in the Gospel account (see Mk 5:30) because the sacraments are "like 'powers that came forth' from the Body of Christ [see Lk 5:17; 6:19; 8:46] which is ever-living and life-giving. They are actions of the Holy Spirit at work in his Body, the Church"; as such, "they are 'the masterworks of God' in the new and everlasting covenant" (n. 1116). The sacraments are thus "of Christ" because he is their source and foundation. They come from his pneumatic body and are true actualizations, through their signs, of the mysteries of his life and his paschal mystery. In them we truly encounter Christ and are met by him.

II. The Sacraments of the Church

The *CCC* goes on to present the sacraments from an unusual but relevant perspective on a personal as well as ecclesial level: the sacraments are "of the Church." What does that "genitive" here mean? It points to a task, not to origin or ownership. The Church, united to Christ in one single body vivified by his Spirit, has received from her Head and Lord the task of sacramentally conveying his redemptive work to human beings. Her mission is serving, stewarding, and faithfully administering the mystery of Christ with the light and guidance of the Holy Spirit (see Jn 16:13). Christ has entrusted to the Church the task of discerning sacramental actions, specifying their number as seven, and determining their dispensation (see n. 1117). However, since the Church is a "servant" of the sacraments, her authority over them, although exclusive, is neither arbitrary nor unlimited (see nn. 1125, 1205).

"Of the Church" also means that the sacraments exist "by the Church" and "for the Church" (n. 1118). They are "by the Church" because not only her ministers but the whole Church is involved in sacramental actions insofar as the Church "is the sacrament of Christ's action at work in her through the mission of the Holy Spirit" (n. 1118). The whole ecclesial body "makes" the sacraments (see *LG* 10–11; *CCC*, n. 1121) insofar as it is "an organically structured priestly community" (n. 1119). It has dual participation in the unique priesthood of Christ—a participation that through the sacraments confers their "sacramental" character. Some in the body perform a structuring and dynamic function in the worshiping community (see n. 1121), but because of Baptism and Confirmation, the whole Church is constituted as a priestly people who is qualified by a "common priesthood" to celebrate the liturgy. Holy Orders, which allows some of the faithful to have ministerial priesthood, equips them to sacramentally represent Christ the Head in a hierarchically structured priestly community in which Christ continues to act (see nn. 1119–1120). According to her organic structure, priestly by nature and sacramental at her core, the Church, vivified by the Spirit, operates as a sign and instrument of the very action of Christ. One important aspect in catechesis consists in highlighting the "we" that constitutes the celebrating subject that is united to Christ according to each person's place and function, given his or her vocation.

"For the Church" means the sacraments "make the Church." According to tradition, they "'make the Church,' since they manifest and communicate to men, above all in the Eucharist, the mystery of communion with the God who is love, One in three persons" (n. 1118). The sacramental liturgy, then, is an authentic "epiphany" of the Church: it is the sphere in which the ecclesial mystery is made present and expressed in a privileged way as a trinitarian work (see *SC* 26, 41). However, the Church is not just the "subject," the mediator, but is also the "object" of sacramental actions.

III. The Sacraments of Faith

According to the deeply traditional approach reiterated in the Council doctrine (see *SC* 59), the *CCC* speaks of the "the sacraments of faith." Faith does not appear as an element external to sacramental action but as an element incorporated into its very essence and structure. The text focuses on and makes explicit the relationship between faith and sacraments in their different aspects and levels, beginning with contextualizing it in the mission of Christ handed down through his apostles (see Lk 24:47; Mt 28:19; *CCC* 1122). Proclamation, faith, and sacraments are inseparable in that mission, and the *CCC* articulates that in a dynamic way: "The mission to baptize, and so the sacramental mission, is implied in the mission to evangelize, because the sacrament is prepared for by *the word of God and by the faith* which is assent to this word" (n. 1122; see *PO* 4).

This "sacramental faith," which comes about from the proclamation of the word and is presupposed for the sacraments, has the following characteristics that involve many pastoral and catechetical consequences.

1. Faith prepares for the sacrament and is simultaneously instructed, strengthened, nourished, and expressed by its celebration (see *SC* 59; *CCC* 1123). However, the personal faith that the sacraments presuppose is a departure point, not its destination. Faith is called to grow and to develop into a life of faith. At the same time, sacramental words and actions are a wonderful way to instruct the faithful.

2. Faith is personal but at the same time ecclesial because the faithful are invited to hold to the faith received from the apostles. The Church confesses

and celebrates this faith in sacramental actions, so it precedes the faith of believers who participate in it (see n. 1124). The entire ecclesial celebration is a faith-filled event, a celebration of faith. This means that the liturgy is a constitutive element of the living Tradition of the Church (see *DV* 8).

3. Faith is required for three inseparable aspects of the sacramental event: faith "professed" in the celebrated "mystery"; faith "celebrated" in the liturgical actions; and faith that must be "lived" in one's personal life (see n. 1124). Although the ritual and the existential dimensions are distinct, there is no division between the two. There is continuity because the sacraments are celebrations of "operative" faith.

4. Faith is manifested in several common ritual forms that cannot be modified arbitrarily. No rite can be modified or manipulated at will by the ministers, by the community, or even by the Church's supreme authority. These ritual forms express and develop the communion of faith in the Church, and the celebration of sacraments by the assembly is a sign of the same faith being professed. The liturgy, then, is one of the important criteria in ecumenical dialogue (see nn. 1125–1126).

IV. The Sacraments of Salvation

The Catholic Church explains the efficacy of the sacraments by first recalling, with the Council of Trent, that "Celebrated worthily in faith, the sacraments confer the grace that they signify [see Council of Trent, *DS* 1605–1606]" (n. 1127). The perspective that illuminates the meaning of this affirmation, however, is very consistent with a trinitarian understanding and the "synergy" of liturgical actions presented in Article 1. The sacraments are efficacious because Christ himself acts in them with the collaboration of his Church. The epiclesis asks the Father to send the Holy Spirit who, like fire (see n. 696), "transforms into the divine life whatever is subjected to his power" (n. 1127; see nn. 1084, 1105). Sacraments are efficacious because Christ, their primary agent, is present and operative in them; the Spirit, in synergy with the Church, is their great artisan; and the Father is the principle from which all salvation proceeds. According to nn. 1115–1116, one could say that Christ is the "sacrament" from whom all sacramental efficacy emanates. The *CCC*, always starting with Christ, makes explicit in a new light the significance of the tridentine affirmation of the *ex opere operato* efficacy of the sacraments. It occurs "by virtue of the saving work of Christ, accomplished once for all" (n. 1128). The sacraments, then, are efficacious because the unique and unrepeatable redemptive mystery of Christ is manifested in them; it is made present in them in an objective way and is communicated through their signs in all their salvific power (see n. 1085). In the end, they are efficacious because they constitute the liturgical-celebrative actualization of the plan of salvation historically accomplished in the mystery of Christ. He comes to us through them, offers the gift of salvation to every human being, and provides salvation to whoever receives it by faith through the power of his Spirit. The classic distinction between the "efficacy" and the "fruits" of the sacraments is recalled in this context (see nn. 1127–1128). "Efficacy" does not depend on the merits of the minister: "From the moment that a sacrament is celebrated in accordance with the intention of the Church, the power of Christ and his Spirit acts in and through it" (n. 1128). On the other hand, "fruitfulness" depends on the disposition of those who receive the sacraments.

The text also affirms with Trent that "for believers the sacraments of the New Covenant are necessary for salvation [*DS* 1604]" (n. 1129; see n. 1257). This explanation is in line with the operation of "sacramental grace," which is not intended to be different from "sanctifying grace" but which is presented as a unique sacramental gift—as "the grace of the Holy Spirit, given by Christ and proper to each sacrament" (n. 1129; see n. 2003). This produces its salvific dynamic as a healing action and configures believers to Christ: "The Spirit heals and transforms those who receive him by conforming them to the Son of God.... The Spirit of adoption makes them faithful partakers in the divine nature [see 2 Pet 1:4] by uniting them in a living union with the only Son, the Savior" (n. 1129). However, since the same Spirit operates in various sacraments, his action is diversified with respect to the different sacramental signs. Just as light going through a prism breaks up into various colors, so too the grace of the Spirit releases its power of healing and configuration to the mystery of Christ in a different way in each sacrament.

V. The Sacraments of Eternal Life

In this section the *CCC* presents the eschatological dimension of the sacraments in their intimate relationship to the action of the Holy Spirit. He is the one who orients the liturgy toward the *parousia* and grants the Church, through the sacraments, participation on earth as a guarantee of her inheritance (see nn. 1130, 1107). That inheritance includes the kingdom to come (see nn. 2816–2821), the fullness of communion with the Trinity (see n. 1107), and the fullness of love with the saints (see nn. 946–948, 953). The sacraments, then, are prophetic signs during the age of the Church that announce and anticipate these future benefits (see nn. 1130, 1152). Sacramental action functions, therefore, simultaneously as a memorial of the past, as a salvific event in the present, and as a participation in future fullness.

The *CCC* ends this section with a wonderful text from Thomas Aquinas (see *Summa Theologiae*, III, 60, 3) that can serve as a synthesis of catechetical recapitulation: sacraments are commemorative signs of the Passion of Christ (paschal mystery) that demonstrate grace (salvation) and prefigure the glory to come (eternal life) (see n. 1130). They have been entrusted to the Church and are received by faith.

In this rich theological framework in which the sacraments appear as "masterworks of God," their two descriptions in the *CCC* as "perceptible signs" and "efficacious signs" (see nn. 1084, 1131) complement each other and convey a living tradition rich with new insight that is better contextualized and understood in catechesis.

Chapter Two:

THE SACRAMENTAL CELEBRATION OF THE PASCHAL MYSTERY

Goffredo Boselli

The second part of the *CCC*, "The celebration of the paschal mystery," represents—after over twenty-five years—the most advanced point in the teaching of Catholic doctrine on the liturgy. During the thirty years between the end of the Second Vatican Council and the promulgation of the *CCC*, the Church's reception of the Council's liturgical reform has been accompanied and supported by authoritative interpretations and expert commentary on *SC* whether in magisterial documents or in theological scholarship. The liturgical catechesis offered by the *CCC* represents an important increase in our understanding of the meaning of the mystery's celebration. This is especially the case in light of the evangelical quality and genuine Christian spirit expressed in the *CCC*'s liturgical instruction with the biblical and patristic insights that are included. It draws deeply from the vast treasure of liturgical traditions in the East, which simultaneously enhances the value of the Roman liturgy renewed by the Second Vatican Council. Basically, the *CCC* links the Church's faithfulness to the great Christian liturgical tradition with her ability to express the meaning and value of celebrating the mystery in today's Church and world.

The sections that the *CCC* dedicates to the liturgy signal a significant maturation of what Vatican II expressed in the words and the spirit of *SC*, which has left an indelible mark on the whole treatment of liturgy. At the same time, the *CCC* is a sign of the progress in the lengthy, providential path the Church began early in the twentieth century, thanks to the work of the Liturgical Movement. That path, undertaken entirely through the liturgical renewal called for by Vatican II, has been subsequently implemented in the ordinary life of local churches through the reception and application of the Council's liturgical reform. However, it reaches its full theological and spiritual maturity here in the pages of the *CCC*. The unique doctrinal authority of the *CCC*, in terms of being the official teaching of Catholic doctrine, makes all of its liturgical content—and not just what is expressed in the Second Part—a landmark in understanding the mystery of the liturgy. It presents a particularly authoritative reference for any discussions about the theological principles underlying the liturgical renewal accomplished by the Church beginning with Vatican II, and it is likewise a solid and indispensable departure point for any liturgical renewal in future years.

The *CCC* indicates that the Church has faith in her liturgy, so believing in the Church, as professed in the creed, necessarily means believing in the liturgy she celebrates.

The Sacramental Celebration of the Paschal Mystery

The first section of this Second Part of the *CCC* (the "sacramental economy") has two chapters: "The Paschal Mystery in the Age of the Church" and "The Sacramental Celebration of the Paschal Mystery." The two chapters form a diptych whose two panels are essentially like two circles that intersect and reflect each other. However, it is not possible to speak of the celebration of the paschal mystery without first presenting the paschal mystery itself. Affirming the centrality of the paschal mystery, the *CCC* engages and develops what is recognized as the greatest and most decisive gain in liturgical theology by *SC*.

While the constitution on the liturgy presents the paschal mystery from a preeminently Christological perspective, the *CCC* greatly increases its trinitarian meaning and presents the liturgy as "the work of the holy Trinity" (Chapter One, Article 1). After the Father is defined as the perennial source and ultimate goal of the liturgy and the Son as the one who makes present and communicates his work of salvation through the liturgy of the Church, the large role reserved for the Holy Spirit in the liturgy emerges with unique importance. Developing the central point that the liturgy is the place in which the synergy between the Holy Spirit and the Church occurs (see n. 1108), these pages are enlightening because of their theological depth and spiritual richness. They represent the most innovative and original part and the most advanced contribution the *CCC* brings to Catholic doctrine about the liturgy and, in particular, about the presence and action of the Holy Spirit in liturgical celebration. This rectifies the scant attention given to the role of the Holy Spirit in the liturgy by the Latin West for centuries.

The *CCC* expresses the synthesis of this teaching well when it affirms the following: "The Paschal mystery of Christ is celebrated, not repeated. It is the celebrations that are repeated, and in each celebration there is an outpouring of the Holy Spirit that makes the unique mystery present" (n. 1104). Considering this to be a trinitarian work, the *CCC* goes on to expound the doctrine of the sacraments through which the community of believers celebrates the paschal mystery. The sacraments of Christ and the Church are the sacraments of faith, salvation, and eternal life.

The Sacramentality of the Word of God

During the more than twenty-five years since the promulgation of the *CCC*, we can observe that the most recent insights about the relationship between the paschal mystery and its liturgical celebration have been increased by the notable contribution of the post-synodal exhortation *VD*. In it Pope Benedict XVI describes not only the relationship between the word of God and the sacraments but, in particular, "the sacramentality of the word" (*VD* 56). This is a new and particularly significant theme that emerged during the work of the Twelfth General Assembly of the Synod of Bishops (October 5–26, 2008). It thus became necessary to complete and expand the *CCC*'s articulation of the paschal mystery and the Church's sacraments by an understanding of the sacramental quality of the word of God referred to in the apostolic exhortation: "The sacramentality of the word can thus be understood by analogy with the real presence of Christ under the appearances of the consecrated bread and wine" (*VD* 56). At the end of this section Benedict XVI states, "A deeper understanding of the sacramentality of God's word can thus lead us to a more unified understanding of the mystery of revelation, which takes place through 'deeds and words intimately connected'; an appreciation of this can only benefit the spiritual life of the faithful and the Church's pastoral activity" (*VD* 56). *VD* demonstrates here a full acceptance of the seventh proposition expressed earlier by the 2008 synodal assembly: "The synod fathers hope that a theological reflection on the sacramentality of the Word of God can be promoted. Without the recognition of the real presence of the Lord in the Eucharist, the intelligibility of the Scriptures remains incomplete" (Proposition 7, "Unity between the Word of God and the Eucharist").

Article 1:
CELEBRATING THE CHURCH'S LITURGY

The first panel of the diptych, an understanding of the paschal mystery and its sacramental nature, sheds light on the second panel, the sacramental celebration of the paschal mystery, by highlighting "the innovation of its celebration" (n. 1135). However, as we shall see, it also highlights its rationale and its cause. The Christian Passover generated the rites that celebrate it, so a look at the celebration itself will reveal the mystery being celebrated. The *CCC* first sets forth its pedagogical style for its liturgical instruction:

This fundamental catechesis on the sacramental celebrations responds to the first questions posed by the faithful regarding this subject:

– Who celebrates the liturgy?
– How is the liturgy celebrated?
– When is the liturgy celebrated?
– Where is the liturgy celebrated?" (n. 1135)

The *CCC*'s choice to lay out its liturgical teaching in the form of answers to four simple, concrete questions asked by the faithful defines not only the precise choice of "mystagogy" as its catechetical method, but it also makes the *CCC* itself a genuine mystagogy. Consequently, it makes those who turn to it initiates in the holy mystery. This deliberate choice among various possible options demonstrates the intimate connection between liturgy and catechesis. That connection comes not just from the patristic tradition but is also found in Scripture in the very event whose memorial is the basis for all Jewish and Christian rituals: the Passover. A catechism is in fact generated by the simple question posed by the author of Exodus, given that the question was certainly part of the ritual then and is still part of the celebration of the Jewish Passover today: "And when you come to the land which the Lord will give you, as he has promised, you shall keep this service. And when your children say to you, 'What do you mean by this service?' you shall say, 'It is the sacrifice of the Lord's passover, for he passed over the houses of the people of Israel in Egypt, when he slew the Egyptians but spared our houses'" (Ex 12:25–27).

This question from the Passover *Haggadah* is not posed by an adult to a child but by a child to an adult. The question comes from the "discoverers" who are catechumens, those being catechized, whether children or adults. More precisely it begins with the paschal mystery (the first part of the diptych) because the whole catechesis will always consist in "recounting," as Exodus 10:2 says, the paschal mystery in detail, just as our liturgy will always consist in celebrating the Passover of Christ (see Mt 26:26). Consequently, it is the Passover itself that asks, that raises questions in such a way that this Passover question becomes a synthesis and the intersection point of all the other questions about faith and Christian life.

I. Who Celebrates?

The liturgy is not the action of just one person whom the Christian community has delegated to celebrate the holy mysteries, because "Liturgy is an 'action' of the *whole* Christ (*Christus totus*)" (n. 1136). It is the action of the entire Church in a profound communion of the heavenly and earthly saints who constitute one single celebrating assembly. It is very important to emphasize that the *CCC*, in its presentation of "those who celebrate the heavenly liturgy" (see nn. 1137–1139), refers only to the New Testament text of John's Revelation and, in particular, to the vision of the Lamb on the throne who was slain (see Rev 5:6, 22:1), the crucified and risen Christ (see n. 1137). This means that according to the *CCC*'s liturgical teaching, the heavenly liturgy is not to be understood as a preexisting Platonic-like form that would become a model for the earthly liturgy. If in the Old Testament, according to the priestly tradition, the heavenly liturgy was the prototype for temple worship, the New Testament attests that the Passover of Christ has reversed the relationship between the two liturgies. The very life of Christ, culminating in his passion, death, and resurrection, is the liturgy he celebrated on earth. The memorial of Christ's Passover is celebrated in heaven and on earth by adoring the Lamb that was slain.

The *CCC* teaches that it is pivotal, however, for a Christian understanding of the heavenly liturgy that Jesus—the crucified and Risen One, ascended into heaven—is seated at the right hand of God, and reigns in glory as the Christian creed professes. This is a radical reversal with respect to the Old Testament perspective: the heavenly liturgy is not the model for the earthly one since heaven celebrates according to the orchestration of the earthly liturgy. What unites the heavenly and earthly liturgies is thus their shared participation in the liturgy of Jesus Christ, "the minister in the sanctuary (*leitourgos ton hagion*)" (Heb 8:2). Christ is the true minister of the Church's liturgy as much as he is of the heavenly liturgy because he presides over it as the "High Priest of the true sanctuary" (see Heb 4:14–15).

In defining "the celebrants of the sacramental liturgy" (see nn. 1140–1144), the *CCC* reiterates the teaching of the constitution on the liturgy, affirming that it is "the whole *community*, the Body of Christ united with its head, that celebrates" (n. 1140) and that "the celebrating assembly is the community of the baptized" (n. 1141). This is done in the name of the "common priesthood" of Christ in which all the members participate. The *CCC* then makes clear that the essential and exclusive service rendered to the community is performed by ministers who are "consecrated by the sacrament of Holy Orders" and who "act in the person of Christ the head, for the service of all the members of the Church" (n. 1142). With this explanation the *CCC* concludes the answer to the first question, "Who celebrates?", formulating a bold new expression in saying that it is "the whole assembly that is *leitourgos*" (n. 1144). In the face of objections to using the expression "the celebrating assembly"—a usage that had been explicitly forbidden—the *CCC*, by affirming that "the whole assembly is liturgy," goes much further. First, it teaches that the Christian community "as a whole celebrates the liturgy"—a phrase found in the title of the famous article by Yves Congar ("The *Ecclesia* or Christian Community as a Whole Celebrates the Liturgy," in *At the Heart of Christian Worship*, trans. and ed. Paul Philibert [Collegeville, MN: Liturgical Press, 2010], 15–68).

Second, it also teaches that the assembled community is not only fully the acting subject of the liturgical celebration but is herself liturgy insofar as she is *Ecclesia congregata*.

II. How Is the Liturgy Celebrated?

Christians celebrate the liturgy through signs and symbols from creation and from culture that became signs in the old covenant; these signs are fulfilled by Christ himself and have become the Church's sacraments. In affirming that "As a being at once body and spirit, man expresses and perceives spiritual realities through physical signs and symbols" (n. 1146), the *CCC* simultaneously points to the physical and spiritual dimensions of human beings. It is in fact through their bodies that people enter into relationship with others, with the world, with material objects, and therefore also with God. This necessarily determines the mode of celebrating since the body is the nexus of the relationship between God and human beings. A human being at prayer celebrates his or her faith through posture, gestures, and the use of his or her voice and words—elements that constitute the signs and symbols of liturgy.

The *CCC* attests that "the liturgy of the Church presupposes, integrates and sanctifies elements from creation and human culture, conferring on them the dignity of signs of grace, of the new creation in Jesus Christ" (n. 1149). The *CCC* thereby highlights that elements in creation—like water, oil, and fire—not only enter into the liturgy but are themselves liturgy because they are elements essential to the liturgical action, the place of communion with God, and represent the universe sacramentally located in God. At the same time nothing that is authentically human or is an expression of culture is excluded. Liturgy is the primary place that definitively emphasizes that what is most spiritual is also most human and vice versa. The liturgy, in addition, is the clearest and most eloquent demonstration of the rejection by Christian faith of any possible dualistic division between spirit and matter and, likewise, of every form of pantheism, because celebrating liturgy means invoking the transfiguration and sanctification of all of creation.

In the liturgy believers proclaim the "Amen" of faith to everything that exists, acknowledging before the Lord, along with the author of the book of Wisdom,

> For you love all things that exist,
> and you loathe none of the things which you have made,
> for you would not have made anything if you had hated it. (Wis 11:24)

God's love toward all creatures calls for the celebration of all of creation by human beings.

Recalling the signs of the covenant underscores that Christian liturgy has taken up the liturgy of the people of Israel. However, it has re-signified feasts and signs of the old covenant in light of the paschal mystery, not so much in their material aspects but in the depths of their biblical meaning. The signs and symbols of Christian liturgy would be deprived of their vital lifeblood without the Bible. This led Louis Bouyer to assert that if people want to understand the liturgy, they need to understand the Bible (see "Liturgy and Spiritual Exegesis," *Blackfriars* 28, no. 325 (April 1947): 151–158).

The intimate connection between the Word of God and liturgy is explored in this section's numbers that deal with liturgical words and actions (nn. 1153–1155). Recalling that "the liturgical actions signify what the Word of God expresses" (n. 1153), the *CCC* teaches that liturgical rites as a whole, and the sacraments in particular, are the manifestations of the inner significance of the word of God that now becomes action and gesture. The sacraments are the body of the word of God. Unlike the Greek *logos*, the Hebrew *dabar* is inseparably word and action, or word-event. What else is a sacrament but the expansion of the substance of the word of God that is its fulfillment not in speech (logos) but in an historical act? The word of God, having become liturgical gesture and action, has the ultimate goal of becoming an embodied reality in the life of the believer. Every liturgical and sacramental action is verified in the sense of being made real in the life of the one who celebrates it. "The liturgical word and action are inseparable both insofar as they are signs and instruction and insofar as they accomplish what they signify" (n. 1155). This means that the place in which the liturgical word and action fully achieve their meaning is in the word and action of the Christian: what they signify becomes actualized in the life of the believer.

Singing, music, and holy images are also elements of the celebration. In the numbers that follow, the *CCC* presents an understanding of liturgy as a work of art, recognizing that art is a language capable of transmitting an experience of God in a unique and original way. A song is capable of corresponding to the symbolic language of the liturgy: "As a combination of sacred music and words,... [song] forms a necessary or integral part of solemn liturgy" (n. 1156). Recalling the biblical psalmody in which prayer, poetry, and song are united, the *CCC* notes that a song is neither an adornment nor an embellishment of a liturgical action but is essential to it insofar as it augments the meaning of the text and enriches its words. A song can be a vehicle of meaning just as much as a text. It is not, however, merely a complement, and the music is not merely an accompaniment. Instead both "are 'more closely connected...with the liturgical action,' according to three principal criteria: beauty expressive of prayer, the unanimous participation of the assembly at the designated moments, and the solemn character of the celebration" (n. 1157). The beauty of the liturgy is the highest expression and the most effective narration of the goodness of the proclamation of Christ and his gospel. In liturgical singing, one hears the voice of a given church because every celebrating community has its own unique and inimitable voice.

The great theological value of the sacramentality of art in the liturgy is mentioned for the last time in the section on holy images (nn. 1159–1162), and in particular liturgical icons. It is sufficient to note here that the *CCC* includes a long citation from the Second Council of Nicea, a council that was misunderstood in the Latin Middle Ages and by Western Christianity as whole until relatively recently. The *CCC*'s teaching on liturgical iconography is strongly marked by the contribution of the Eastern Church's tradition in that the significance of an image is viewed as an epiphany of the mystery of God. Asserting that "Christian iconography expresses in images the same Gospel message that Scripture communicates by word" (n. 1160), the *CCC* emphasizes not only that making the word of God visible in the liturgy is necessary, and a true sacramental reality, but also that the iconic image is an integral and necessary part of the theology of the word of God. Knowledge of the Christian mystery is a question of seeing and not just of hearing.

III. When is the Liturgy Celebrated?

The *CCC* describes how the Church celebrates time through the liturgy. In the liturgy the Christian, a priest to the world, envisions time above all as a created entity that God has given to human beings. Time is a gift because it is the place in which God acts and saves, the place in which Christ lived out his days when revealing the mystery of God: the history of salvation implies the salvation of history. That is the meaning of the word "today" in the Church's liturgy: "This 'today' of the living God which man is called to enter is 'the hour' of Jesus' Passover, which reaches across and underlies all history" (n. 1165). This means that Christians can freely choose, like Jesus Christ, a precise *ethos* of time, the *ethos* of living one's life with a Eucharistic mindset, namely, with a mindset not of possessing but of sharing, not of consumption but of communion, not of instantaneous satisfaction but of patient waiting.

The *CCC* reaffirms the basic cornerstones of the celebration of faith in time: the Lord's Day (nn. 116–1167) and the liturgical year (nn. 1168–1171), which includes the sanctoral cycle (nos. 1172–1173) and the prayers for each day that constitute the *Liturgy of the Hours* (nos. 1174–1178). At the basis of the liturgical catechesis in the *CCC*, what is particularly evident is the synergy between the weekly ritual and the annual ritual, namely, between Sundays and the annual celebration of Easter. The liturgical year finds its complete theological rationale in the annual feast of Easter: Easter is what made it possible, has given birth to it, and has developed it in time.

If Easter is the theological foundation of the liturgical year and in some measure made its existence possible, the goal of the liturgical year is to make the Church live only through Christ. The Church is the body of Christ because on the day of Pentecost the Risen One so fully transmitted his Spirit, his life-giving breath, to the Twelve that it formed a community of human beings into one body. He so united them to himself, to the mystery of his death and resurrection, that he shared his very life with them. Celebrating the memorial of the mysteries of Christ from Sunday to Sunday and from feast to feast throughout the liturgical year, the Church lives by the life of Christ and grows in communion with him. Celebrating Christ's mystery is in fact the most effective way the Church knows for understanding and living the mystery of God.

For the members of the Church, the body of Christ, the liturgical year has the function of forming Christ in all believers, of molding them and leading them, according to Paul's words, to "the knowledge of the Son of God, to mature manhood [*eis andra teleion*], to the measure of the stature of the fulness of Christ" (Eph 4:1). Tertullian said to the neophytes, "People are not born Christian, they become Christians" (*Apology* 18, 4). This means that although Baptism is received only once, becoming a Christian is a task that is never accomplished once and for all in terms of attaining the *plenitudo Christi* ("the fullness of Christ"), which of course remains only an eschatological reality. The liturgical year is an instrument that is not exclusive in accomplishing this progress, but it is certainly decisive. In a homily for the feast of Epiphany, Gregory Nazianzus goes through each of the episodes of Christ's life celebrated in the liturgical year and concludes, "What solemnities for each of Christ's mysteries! But they all have one goal: to lead me to perfection, to mold me and lead me back to the first Adam" (*Discourses*, 38, 16).

"In the liturgical year, the various aspects of the Paschal mystery unfold" (n. 1171). This teaching by the *CCC* highlights that the liturgical year is a privileged and effective means of union with Christ. Sunday after Sunday, week after week, year after year, feast after feast, the liturgical year forms Christ in a Christian. Paul addresses an ultimately decisive challenge to Christians: "Examine yourselves, to see whether or not you are holding to your faith. Test yourselves. Do you not realize that Jesus Christ is in you?" (2 Cor 13:5). As Christians celebrate the mysteries of Christ during the liturgical year and come to an understanding and deepening of the mystery of Christ in all its various facets, Christ dwells in them more and more.

IV. Where is the Liturgy Celebrated?

The numbers in the *CCC* that deal with the location of the celebration (nn. 1179–1186) are a true mystagogy about liturgical space. It recalls the Christian innovation that worship "in spirit and truth" (Jn 4:24) "is not tied exclusively to one place" (n. 1179). It reminds us that the assembled Christian community constitutes a genuine "spiritual building" and that every Christian is 'the temple of the living God" (2 Cor 6:16). The visible Church is thus comprised of Christians who "make visible the Church living in this place" (n. 1180). The *CCC* teaches, therefore, that from the theological and ecclesiastic point of view, there is an inseparable link between the Church's consciousness of herself and the image that she presents through her buildings. This means that building up the Church spiritually is not unrelated to the material planning and construction of churches.

In presenting the meaning of the important elements that characterize liturgical space—the altar, the pulpit, the baptistery, the tabernacle—the *CCC* describes how liturgical space, especially during the time of celebration, is the normative symbolic place for the formation of Christian identity. It allows for seeing "the lexicon and the grammar," so to speak, of Christian life as they have been transmitted by Tradition. The connection between liturgical space and Christian identity is attested in the Gradual for the annual celebration of the dedication of a church: "*Locus iste a Deo factus est, inaestimabile sacramentum*" ("This place was made by God, a priceless sacrament") Liturgical space is thus *sacramentum* in the Augustinian sense of the word, namely, it is *quasi visibile verbum*, it is "a kind of visible word." If, as this Gradual sings, the liturgical space is *sacramentum*, it is then a "living and effective" word that works and acts on whoever is present in it, on whoever visits it day after day, on whoever dwells in it; it cooperates with the formation of Christian identity and thus of the Church's identity. Dwelling in liturgical space means dwelling in the Church's faith, and for this reason the church building edifies the Church.

Liturgical space is the first space in which people are invited to enter and to take their place; here they let themselves apprehend faith through the physicality of the place—the stones, the wood, and the light. These elements, by their composition and transformation, speak the Christian language and thereby speak the word of God. As *Ecclesia mater*, the space of a church is a true spiritual and cultural matrix in which Christians are generated in faith. It is in fact within a liturgical space that one is born into Christian life and, liturgy after liturgy here, believers grow and mature as men and women of faith. Since this is the role of the liturgical space in the formation of a Christian's identity, inevitably the distortions and ugliness of a liturgical space may sooner or later become deformity and pathology in the spiritual life of whoever is present there. We cannot help observing with a certain regret that certain churches are real obstacles to prayer and to an experience of God. This shows the extreme tenuousness of Christian liturgical space. Because of this it constantly needs, like every other Christian reality, to be "converted," that is, assessed, renewed, and corrected according to what is specifically Christian.

Article 2:
LITURGICAL DIVERSITY AND THE UNITY OF THE MYSTERY

"The mystery celebrated in the liturgy is one, but the forms of its celebration are diverse" (n. 1200). This is the premise for the *CCC*'s teaching about liturgical traditions and the universality of the Church. It is a premise that right from the start removes any possible ambiguity about the preeminence or superiority of the Latin rite. In this section the *CCC* forcefully affirms the extraordinary richness of the diverse rites and their "remarkable complementarity," but at the same time it calls for acknowledging that the multiplicity of liturgical traditions is itself the result of the very nature of the mystery of God revealed in Christ: "The mystery of Christ is so unfathomably rich that it cannot be exhausted by its expression in any single liturgical tradition" (n. 1201). To assert that no liturgical tradition exhausts the richness of the mystery means asserting that none of them can think itself superior, much less claim that it can do without the others. It is sufficient to note that the presence of four different Gospels in the canon of Scripture attests that Christianity, ever since its apostolic origin, sprang up with plural narrations of the life of the Lord Jesus Christ and yet still achieved a unity of confession of faith in him. Since the liturgy is an essential form of the confession of one faith, the Church has also had plural liturgical traditions as well. For this reason, the *CCC* deserves credit for very clearly presenting the crucial issue of the intersection of different cultures and the liturgy. This issue has been acknowledged in the very history of Church and her liturgy, whose fruits are visible in the extraordinary riches of the liturgical traditions of the Eastern Church.

In fact, in an earlier number that deals with the relationship between catechesis and liturgy, we read, "This Catechism, which aims to serve the whole Church in all the diversity of her rites and cultures, will present what is fundamental and common to the whole Church in the liturgy as mystery and as celebration, and then the seven sacraments and the sacramentals" (n. 1075). Wanting to present "what is common," the *CCC* acknowledges the legitimacy and the richness of what is proprietary and exclusive to the particular traditions of local churches and ecclesiastical regions, especially the liturgical traditions that are expressions of their own life of faith, history, and culture. To the extent that liturgy reflects the community that celebrates it, its celebration is consequently one of its most eloquent expressions. Based on this, the *CCC* notes the need for the intersection between the gospel proclamation and the richness in various cultures.

It is necessary to point out that *SC* 40, in its approach to "liturgical adaptation," insists that a relationship between the liturgy of the Church and that of a local culture—although the word "culture" does not appear in the text—must remain essentially on an external level. It may consist in the selection of different elements in a people's culture that can be adapted to the liturgy. A culture is not actually the simple sum of the components that are distinguishable from each other but is rather an organic whole in which each separate element finds its meaning. For this reason, liturgical praxis can influence a culture to the extent that the culture becomes a fruit that matures through its intersection with the Gospel. Otherwise, there could always be an insurmountable gap between a church's liturgy and the culture of the people. This is not due, however, to the irreducibility of Christ's gospel to any given human culture but to the inability of the liturgy to take on certain essential and constitutive traits of a culture that would be contrary to the faith. The *CCC* affirms that to accomplish its mission, the liturgy "generates cultures and shapes them" (n. 1207). It should be capable of expressing and at the same time enriching the culture of the people who celebrate it. For this reason, the *CCC* states that the mystery of Christ "must be proclaimed, celebrated and lived in all cultures in such a way that they are not abolished by it, but redeemed and fulfilled" (n. 1204).

The promulgation of the *CCC* on October 11, 1992, thirty years after the Council, has been recognized as an event of particular importance for the life of the Church. And now, over twenty-five later, the *CCC* still remains an indispensable and decisive instrument for the transmission of the Church's faith, which includes an understanding of the true meaning of the liturgy.

SECTION TWO

THE SEVEN SACRAMENTS OF THE CHURCH

THE SEVEN SACRAMENTS OF THE CHURCH

Philip Goyret

The *CCC* already dealt with the institution of the sacraments by Jesus in nn. 1114–1116. Now it looks at an important implication: after Jesus departed for heaven, the number and typology of the sacraments have been established. There are seven, no more and no less (the "sacramental septenary"), as confirmed by the Council of Trent. They include three sacraments of Christian initiation (Baptism, Confirmation, and Eucharist), two for healing (Penance and the Anointing of the Sick) and two for communion (Holy Orders and Matrimony). The *CCC*, in line with scholastic theology, makes an analogy between the development of the natural life of a human being and supernatural life: birth, growth, and nutrition (initiation); cleansing and preparation for death (healing); and formation of the family and ministry in the Church (service for communion). This best highlights the organic structure of the sacramental life.

Chapter One, Article 1:

THE SACRAMENT OF BAPTISM

Juan Carlos Carvajal Blanco

"The flesh is the very hinge of salvation (*caro salutis cardo*)" (Tertullian, *On the Resurrection of the Flesh*, 8; *PL* 2, 806). This statement by Tertullian asserts that the Christian economy of salvation occurs through people's flesh because of their human condition. God drew near to his people Israel and guided the events of their history to bring to pass his salvific plan through them. In the fullness of time he sent his Son, born of a woman (see Gal 4:4), so that in his paschal mystery the Holy Spirit would fully reveal his love and accomplish salvation through the flesh that was assumed in Mary's womb. Since then, the salvific action of God continues through the flesh of the Church, which represents Christ in history and is at the service of the sanctifying action of the Spirit that Christ himself sent from the Father (see Jn 15:26).

If the humanity of Christ is the great sacrament of divinity that he shares with the Father in unity with the Holy Spirit, and if it is through his flesh that salvation comes to all human beings, then analogously, as Vatican II says, the same can be said about the Church: "As the assumed nature inseparably united to Him serves the divine Word as a living organ of salvation, so, in a similar way, does the visible social structure of the Church serve the Spirit of Christ, who vivifies it, in the building up of the body [see Eph 4:16]" (*LG* 8).

The Church is the body of Christ growing throughout the course of history: she mediates for all human beings—in whatever time and place—the presence of their Savior and Lord. Christ, through his Spirit, gives people life through sacramental signs in such a way that the Church can be a witness of his redemptive work and an instrument of salvation for all human beings.

There are several signs with which the Church actualizes the salvation that Christ accomplished in his own Person. The Council of Trent, after a process of discernment based on a long tradition, solemnly declared that there are seven sacraments: Baptism, Confirmation, Eucharist, Penance, the Anointing of the Sick, Holy Orders, and Matrimony. The Church used two criteria for defining the seven sacraments. First, they were instituted by Christ himself (and here the Church acknowledges she does not have any power over the signs of salvation but is merely their mediator). And second, they were instituted for the good of all humanity.

The *CCC* points out the correspondence between the seven sacraments and the stages of a human being's life. The event of grace actualized during Jesus' life accompanies and configures those who receive the sacraments that the Church celebrates during their lives: "The seven sacraments touch all the stages and all the important moments of Christian life: they give birth and increase, healing and mission to the Christian's life of faith" (n. 1210). The celebration of the sacraments establishes a genuine relationship between Jesus and his disciples so that they could replicate the mysteries of their Lord in their lives and accomplish in the world the mission received from him: "As the Father has sent me, so I send you" (Jn 20:21).

Chapter One: THE SACRAMENTS OF CHRISTIAN INITIATION

The *CCC* begins this first chapter by presenting the sacraments of initiation—Baptism, Confirmation, and Eucharist—and affirms that their celebration lays "the foundations of every Christian life" (n. 1212). In later numbers, the *CCC* furnishes some indications about what Christian initiation involves (see nn. 1229–1233). For optimum clarity, we will anticipate and refer to the commentary in that section at times to emphasize the nature of Christian initiation and the integration of the process of faith with the celebration of the sacraments of initiation.

In the twentieth century, since Vatican II, sacramental theology has emphasized the topic of Christian initiation (see *SC* 65; 71; *AG* 14; *PO* 2; *RCIA*; *RBC*). Ever since the current process of secularization and social decline in Christendom, the Church has returned to its conviction that "People are not born Christians, they become Christians (*fiunt, non nascuntur*)" (Tertullian, *Apology*, 18, 4; *CCL* 1, 118). Gregory Nazianzus asks how people become Christian, and he gives an answer that seems particularly enlightening: "Faith is the womb that conceives this new life, baptism the rebirth by which it is brought forth into the light of day. The Church is its nurse; her teachings are its milk, the bread from heaven is its food. Faith is brought to maturity by the practice of virtue; it is wedded to wisdom; it gives birth to hope. Its home is the kingdom; its rich inheritance the joys of paradise; its end, not death, but the blessed and everlasting life prepared for those who are worthy" ("Sermon on the Resurrection of Christ," *PG* 46, 603–606).

In fact, to become Christians, people have to follow steps for the process of conversion and faith through which believers are freed from sin and regenerated as sons and daughters of God. They become members of Christ and of his Church, and with the power of his Spirit they participate in his mission. The Church, the instrument of the Spirit, is the womb in which Christians are generated as sons and daughters of God, and it offers them catechesis and liturgical-sacramental celebrations as sustenance (see *AG* 14).

In Christian initiation the catechetical path and the liturgical-sacramental path have a uniform character. To bring the work of God to pass, both functions are necessary and complete each other. In fact, "Catechesis is intrinsically linked with the whole of liturgical and sacramental activity, for it is in the sacraments, especially in the Eucharist, that Christ Jesus works in fullness for the transformation of men" (*CT* 23; *CCC*, n. 1074). The liturgy, meanwhile, "must be preceded by evangelization, faith, and conversion. It can then produce its fruits in the lives of the faithful: new life in the Spirit, involvement in the mission of the Church, and service to her unity" (n. 1072).

The unity between catechesis and the sacraments cannot be broken under any circumstance. It is the prerequisite for Christians to experience the divine life that Christian initiation offers, a life that is mediated by the Church and requires faith. Since the Church is "both human and divine, visible but endowed with invisible realities, zealous in action and dedicated to contemplation, present in the world but as a pilgrim" (*SC* 2, *CCC*, n. 771), Christians must have the eyes of faith to proceed "from the visible to the invisible, from the sign to the thing signified, from the 'sacraments' to the 'mysteries'" (n. 1075).

The *CCC* presents a brief outline of the history of Christian initiation in the Church (see nn. 1230–1232). Currently, the post-conciliar liturgical reform has responded to the needs of the present time with the renewal of two rites: the *Rite of Christian Initiation for Adults (RCIA) and The Rite of Baptism for Children (RBC)*. In the Roman Church rite, Christian initiation for adults is distinct from that for children. For adults, the traditional order and customs have been retained. After a process of catechumenate, adults receive the three sacraments of initiation during the celebration of the Easter Vigil: Baptism, Confirmation, and Eucharist. As for children, even though in principle the rite recognizes the traditional order of the sacraments, in practice, those baptized during the first months of their lives must depend on the post-baptismal catechetical process that follows during childhood, adolescence, and youth. In every case sacramental unity must be preserved, and the catechumenate, whether pre-baptismal or post-baptismal, prepares a person to accept baptismal grace and, once received, facilitates its necessary acceptance and development.

Article 1:
THE SACRAMENT OF BAPTISM

Basing itself on two magisterial documents, Session 8 from the Council of Florence (1439) and *The Roman Catechism* of the Council of Trent (1566), the *CCC* begins by defining the sacrament of Baptism. As a complement to the text that might be of interest, we will quote statements from the *RBC* and the *RICA*. In practice, the rite for children roots their Baptism in the salvific will of Christ for the benefit of all human beings and reveals the relationship between the sacraments of faith and the proclamation of the gospel: "Baptism, the door to life and to the kingdom of God, is the first sacrament of the New Law, which Christ offered to all, that they might have eternal life. He later entrusted this sacrament and the Gospel to his Church, when he told his apostles: 'Go make disciples of all nations, and baptize them in the name of the Father, and of the Son, and of the Holy Spirit.' Baptism is therefore, above all, the sacrament of that faith by which, enlightened by the grace of the Holy Spirit, we respond to the Gospel of Christ" (*RBC*, "Introduction," 3). On the other hand, the rite for adults describes the transformation that Baptism accomplishes in those who, being born of water and the Spirit, participate in the paschal mystery of Christ and are enlightened on their path toward new life: "This first sacrament pardons all our sins, rescues us from the power of darkness, and brings us to the dignity of adopted children, a new creation through water and the Holy Spirit. Hence we are called and are indeed the children of God" (*RCIA*, "Introduction," 2).

I. What Is This Sacrament Called?

In a certain sense the names this sacrament has received throughout the Church's tradition reflect the elements that this rite incorporates. It was first called "baptism" (from the Greek word *baptizein*, "to immerse") because the primary essence of the rite is immersion in water, by which the believer is buried into Christ's death and raised with him (see Rom 6:4). It has been called a "washing of regeneration and renewal in the Holy Spirit" (Tit 3:5) because the Spirit, working through the means of water, brings about a true birth in which the baptized person is born to new life as a child of God (see Jn 3:3–8). Another name has been "enlightenment" because the baptized, as they remain united to catechetical teaching, are enlightened by the grace of the gospel and have been changed into "sons of light" (1 Thess 5:5) and are now meant to radiate salvation among human beings (see Mt 5:14–16; Eph 5:8).

In the second century, St. Justin Martyr, in giving a reason for the Christian faith and its practices, refers to all three of these characteristics: "Those who are convinced and believe what we teach and say is true and decide to live accordingly…are brought to water and are regenerated in the same way we were. In the name of God, the Father and Lord of the universe, and of our Savior Jesus Christ, and of the Holy Spirit, they then receive the washing with water.… And this washing is called enlightenment, because those who learn these things are enlightened in their understanding" (*First Apology*, 61).

II. Baptism in the Economy of Salvation

Baptism is not an isolated rite. It focuses on the events of salvation history in which God is the protagonist with his people Israel, events that Jesus Christ has brought to fulfillment in his Person. Every celebration of Baptism is a *kairos*, a moment in which the historical love that God had for his people is now made concretely present, actualized through the prayer of the Church and the grace of the Spirit, for the person who is baptized.

The baptismal liturgy highlights the blessing the celebrant pronounces over the baptismal font (see *RCIA* 215, 389; *RBC* 60–63; *Roman Missal*, Easter Vigil). The *CCC* focuses attention on the text of this prayer and describes how throughout the course of history water has been the instrument of God's intervention to establish a covenant of love with his people. The beginning of the blessing indicates just that: "Father, you give us grace through sacramental signs, which tell us of the wonders of your unseen power. In Baptism we use your gift of water, which you have made a rich symbol of the grace you give us in this sacrament [*Roman Missal*, Easter Vigil, 42]" (n. 1217). With this reference the *CCC* reminds us of the salvation events that God has performed through water. First of all, it mentions the events of the old covenant that prefigure baptism: the creation, the flood, the passage through the Red Sea. Next, it notes the actions of Jesus that constitute the culmination of what had been prefigured and are the foundation for the paschal gift of himself in the baptism of the new covenant. Finally, the *CCC* mentions the command to baptize and its celebration by the Church. It should be noted that in the blessing of the baptismal water, and in its presentation in the *CCC*, the whole narrative concludes by focusing on the "today" of the Church and on the invocation of the Spirit of the Only-Begotten Son of God so that the work of regeneration can occur through the water: "Look now, we pray, upon the face of your Church and graciously unseal for her the fountain of Baptism. May this water receive by the Holy Spirit the grace of your Only Begotten Son, so that human nature, created in your image and washed clean through the Sacrament of Baptism from all the squalor of the life of old, may be found worthy to rise to the life of newborn children through water and the Holy Spirit" (*Roman Missal*, Easter Vigil, 46).

The *CCC* does not deal explicitly with the moment of Baptism's institution, but it does highlight that the water baptism Jesus received from John the Baptist manifests the Trinity, anticipates the redemptive work Christ will accomplish in his paschal mystery, and attributes to water the capacity to convey that redemption by the Spirit who descends on it: "The Spirit who had hovered over the waters of the first creation descended then on the Christ as a prelude of the new creation, and the Father revealed Jesus as his 'beloved Son' [Mt 3:16–17]. In his Passover Christ opened to all men the fountain of Baptism.... From then on, it is possible 'to be born of water and the Spirit' in order to enter the Kingdom of God [Jn 3:5]" (nn. 1224–1225).

The Church does not celebrate John's baptism, a baptism of water and repentance. However, as part of the missionary mandate of the risen Lord—"Go therefore and make disciples of all nations, baptizing them in the name of the Father and of the Son and of the Holy Spirit" (Mt 28:19–20)—the Church offers Baptism for the justification of those who convert and believe the Gospel. Baptism is in fact the sacrament of faith. Faith and baptismal washing are inseparable. The fact that the profession of faith, which is a trinitarian profession, is part of the same rite indicates that what is being confessed is being actualized through the sacrament. In turn, the grace that comes from the sacrament confers authenticity and reality to what is being professed. St. Basil expresses this essential link in a unique way:

> Faith and Baptism are the two means necessary to obtain salvation. They are inseparably united to each other. If it is the case that faith reaches its perfection through the work of Baptism, then Baptism is in turn based on faith. Both faith and Baptism receive their perfection from the other in the same three Names: we have faith in the Father, the Son, and the Holy Spirit, and similarly, we are baptized in the name of the Father, the Son, and the Holy Spirit. It is true that it is our profession of faith that first brings us to salvation, but soon after that comes Baptism, which seals our belonging to God" (*On the Holy Spirit*, XII, 28).

III. How Is the Sacrament of Baptism Celebrated?

To introduce us to the celebration of Baptism, the *CCC* takes a holistic perspective of Christian initiation as we highlighted at the beginning of this section. Let us move on to comment directly on the mystagogical catechesis that the text offers about the rites of the sacramental celebration.

In conformity with the Council of Trent, the *CCC* asserts that "The sacraments are efficacious signs of grace.... The visible rites by which the sacraments are celebrated signify and make present the graces proper to each sacrament" (n. 1131; see n. 1127). Beginning with this premise and following the same approach by the Fathers, the text deals with enumerating and examining the significance of the rites to help us pass over from the visible to the invisible, from the sign to its signification. The *CCC*'s presentation follows the celebrative dynamic that the *RBC* (in nos. 15–19, 36–80) lays out in four parts: rites of reception, the liturgy of the word, the liturgy of the sacraments, and the rites of completion.

The rites of reception. These rites are performed so that the faithful who are assembled constitute a community and are disposed to listen to the word of God and celebrate the sacraments worthily. Obviously in the case of the baptism of children, the parents and godparents have an important role in asking for the sacrament and committing themselves to educate the children in the faith, with a profession of faith by the entire community. The reception of the child through the sign of the cross "marks with the imprint of Christ the one who is going to belong to him and signifies the grace of the redemption Christ won for us by his cross" (*CCC*, n. 1235).

The liturgy of the word. This is the moment in which the faith of the participants is renewed and they pray together for the fruit of the sacrament. It continues with a prayer of exorcism in which the faithful ask for freedom from evil. This is followed by the anointing with oil and the laying on of hands for the catechumens, which strengthens the candidates to follow Christ.

The celebration of the sacrament. This central moment includes a preparation that consecrates the water through a prayer of epiclesis "so that those who will be baptized in it may be 'born of water and the Spirit' [Jn 3:5]" (n. 1238). It is followed by renouncing Satan and the profession of faith on the part of the parents and godparents in the child's name. Next, the essential rite of Baptism is performed, in which the ablution with water "signifies and actually brings about death to sin and entry into the life of the Most Holy Trinity through configuration to the Paschal mystery of Christ" (n. 1239). Other complementary rites are added to this one: "the anointing with chrism, which signifies the royal priesthood of the baptized and enrollment into the company of the people of God… [and then] the ceremonies of the white garment, lighted candle, and *ephphetha* rite" (*RBC*, 18, n. 3).

The rites of completion. These rites have two elements. First, the Our Father is recited around the altar to indicate that the baptized person is already a child of God through adoption and to prefigure a future participation in the Church's Eucharist. Second, there is the blessing of the parents and those present so that through their words and actions they may be witnesses of Jesus Christ to the baptized.

IV. Who Can Receive Baptism?

The *CCC* answers this categorically: "Every person not yet baptized and only such a person is able to be baptized" (n. 1246; see *CIC*, can. 864; *CCEO*, can. 679). Apart from this there is no limit of age, so a person can be baptized from infancy through adulthood. With different emphases, the practices of baptizing adults and children have been maintained throughout the history of the Church. The basis of the practice of baptizing children is found in the universality of original sin: "Children also have a need for the new birth in Baptism to be freed from the power of darkness and brought into the realm of the freedom of the children of God, to which all men are called" (n. 1250). It is also based on the special favor that Jesus showed toward the smallest ones in our midst: "Let the little children come to me" (Lk 18:15).

In every case, we need to keep in mind that the reception of Baptism is tied to the profession of faith: "Everyone who is to be baptized is required to make a profession of faith. This is done personally in the case of an adult or by the parents" (*Compendium*, n. 259).

Nevertheless, as the *CCC* affirms, if faith is necessary for the reception of the sacraments, we need to keep in mind that faith can grow only through the reception of baptismal grace and vital participation in the Church. In fact, since Baptism is the sacrament of Christian initiation, it "leads only to the threshold of new life" (n. 1254), the faith and life in Christ received at the baptismal font. The believer, under the impulse of grace, is tasked with making faith grow throughout his or her life, sharing with brothers and sisters the gift received in the Church.

V. Who Can Baptize?

The ordinary ministers of Baptism are the bishop, the priest, and, in the Latin Church, the deacon as well. The Church is convinced that God "desires all men to be saved and to come to the knowledge of the truth" (1 Tim 2:4) and that baptism is necessary for salvation. Therefore, the *CCC* states that in cases of necessity, anyone, even an unbaptized person, can baptize on the condition that he or she has the intention of doing what the Church does and uses the trinitarian formula.

VI. The Necessity of Baptism

The Church does not impose the necessity of baptism for salvation as a matter of Church discipline; it is instead linked to the command of the Lord since its necessity was actually established by Jesus himself. First, he asserts that one must be born of water and the Spirit to enter the kingdom of God (see Jn 3:51); later when he is about to return to the Father, he sends forth his disciples with the promise that "he who believes and is baptized will be saved" (Mk 16:16; see Mt 28:19). Consequently, "The Church does not know of any means other than Baptism that assures entry into eternal beatitude" (n. 1257).

However, as the *CCC* asserts, the Church firmly believes that "God has bound salvation to the sacrament of Baptism, but he himself is not bound by his sacraments" (n. 1257). Christian tradition has always held that there are two additional ways of receiving Baptism: the baptism of blood, the fruit of martyrdom, and the baptism of desire. Vatican II describes the second one this way: "Since Christ died for all men, and since the ultimate vocation of man is in fact one, and divine, we ought to believe that the Holy Spirit in a manner known only to God offers to every man the possibility of being associated with this paschal mystery of Christ" (*GS* 22; see *LG* 16, *AG* 7).

This means that the efficacy of Baptism and the salvation it brings can also be extended to those who, through no fault of their own, have not physically received Baptism. Since its reception is inevitably conditioned by the need to hear the Gospel and its acceptance by faith, people who have not heard about the Gospel, or have heard it in a distorted way, can nevertheless have an attitude of openness to divine grace that unites them to the Paschal Mystery in a mysterious way. It is a reasonable assumption that these people of good will would desire Baptism if the proclamation of the Gospel reached them in all its clarity.

What happens to children who have died without Baptism? It is would be time-consuming to treat the history of this topic in the Church's tradition. Today, however, the concern over this issue has been defused since, in virtue of the universal salvific will of God and the special attention Jesus gave children, the Church believes that their Lord has united them to himself, and his divine mercy has opened a way for them to be freed from original sin and to be made participants in his salvation.

VII. The Grace of Baptism

The effects of Baptism are signified by the tangible elements of the baptismal rite, as we would expect. The *CCC* correlates the two principal effects of this sacrament: the purification from sin by washing and the new birth by the Holy Spirit. This echoes the long tradition of the Church. Two references—from St. Basil of Caesarea and from St. Cyril of Jerusalem—are sufficient to elaborate the text we are commenting on. According to Basil, "Baptism has two goals: the destruction of the body of sin, so that it does not bring the fruit of death, and the life of the Spirit, so that the fruits of sanctification may abound. The water represents death, like a tomb receiving a body, while the Spirit's life-giving power restores our souls, renewed from the deadness of sin, to original life" (*On the Holy Spirit*, 35; *PG* 32, 130).

Through Baptism all sins are forgiven. For regenerated people nothing remains to impede their entrance into the kingdom of God. It is true that the effects of the original fall persist: sickness, death, weaknesses, and the inclination to sin that is traditionally called concupiscence. Nevertheless, the Spirit accomplishes a genuine regeneration in those who come up out of the water as St. Cyril attests: "Baptized into Christ and clothed with Christ, you have been made conformable to the Son of God.... You have been made Christs by receiving the seal of the Holy Spirit. In fact, all of this has come to pass for you in the form of symbol and image. Ultimately, you are images of Christ" (*Catechetical lectures*, 21 ["On the Mysteries," III]; *PG* 33, 1087).

Through the action of the Holy Spirit, a new creation is operative in baptized people, allowing them to participate in supernatural life. They are actually created as other Christs and, thanks to the gift of the Spirit, the Trinity dwells in them. Through the grace of Baptism, Christians are clothed in sanctifying grace that makes them capable of living in faith, hope, and love. They are adorned with the gifts of the Spirit and are assisted in growing in goodness through the exercise of moral virtues.

We should not forget the ecclesial dimension of Baptism: the event takes place in the baptismal font inside the Church and contributes to her edification. In fact, Baptism incorporates people into the Church. The one People of God are born from it; transcending all natural and human limits, they constitute a chosen race, a royal priesthood, a holy nation, God's own people, to offer through Jesus Christ spiritual sacrifices and to proclaim the wonderful deeds of the Lord (see 1 Pet 2:9). Every baptized person, in the process of being configured to Christ, becomes a "living stone" in the building of this priestly people; he or she contributes as a member to the communion of the ecclesial body and participates in the evangelizing mission received from the Lord.

Baptism creates a bond of fraternal unity for all those who have been reborn through water and the Spirit. This is why Baptism is the foundation of communion among all Christians, including those who are not yet in full communion with the Catholic Church. The *CCC*, in line with Vatican II, states that those who believe in Christ and have received a valid Baptism, even if they are not in perfect communion with the Catholic Church, are acknowledged by the Church's sons and daughters as brothers and sisters in the Lord (see *UR* 22).

The *CCC* concludes its presentation on Baptism by asserting that the reception of this sacrament imprints an indelible spiritual seal of belonging to Christ and a bond to the Church as a guarantee for entrance into eternal life. This is the reason it cannot be repeated, and having been given once and for all, it is always waiting to be developed by faith by those baptized in such a way that preserving this "seal of the Lord" until the end becomes their safe conduct to enter the Father's house. In fact, this seal, a sign of faithfulness to the Lord, cannot be cancelled by any sin even if sin can prevent a baptized person from producing the fruits of salvation (*DS* 1609–1619). "The baptismal seal enables and commits Christians to serve God by a vital participation in the holy liturgy of the Church and to exercise their baptismal priesthood by the witness of holy lives and practical charity" (n. 1273; see *LG* 10).

Chapter One, Article 2:
THE SACRAMENT OF CONFIRMATION

Juan Carlos Carvajal Blanco

The presentation of the sacrament of Confirmation in the *CCC* begins with an assertion that frames and orients the discussion that follows: "Baptism, the Eucharist, and the sacrament of Confirmation together constitute the 'sacraments of Christian initiation,' whose unity must be safeguarded. It must be explained to the faithful that the reception of the sacrament of Confirmation is necessary for the completion of baptismal grace" (n. 1285; see *Order of Confirmation*, 1).

The *CCC*'s systematic presentation aims to explain three things: how Confirmation is a sacrament; why, despite the different practices of the Eastern and Western Churches, it is classified as part of Christian initiation in relation to Baptism and the Eucharist; and how the signs of its liturgical celebration define its specific effects. Given the process of secularization in society today, the celebration of Confirmation involves a special pastoral concern whose practice is not exempt from polemic and difficulty. There is no doubt that the *CCC*'s exposition offers a very relevant orientation for the pastoral and catechetical activity that is needed for this sacrament.

I. Confirmation in the Economy of Salvation

God acts in salvation history through his Spirit. In creation the Spirit hovered over the dark, formless void (see Gen 1:2). In the course of history, the same Spirit raised up judges, kings, and prophets and anointed them with his power. He conferred on them the ability to lead the people of Israel to be faithful to the covenant of love God had established with them. In addition, this messianic and prophetic action accomplished by the Spirit contains an eschatological promise that is also the promise of a gift for all of humanity.

This promise actually refers first of all to a messianic king, to the servant of YHWH on whom the Spirit of the Lord would rest (see Is 11:2). When the

Holy Spirit descended on Jesus at the Jordan, it was a sign indicating that he was the promised Messiah, the Son of God (see Mt 3:13–17; Jn 1:33–34). Jesus himself says that he is performing his mission with the power of the Spirit (see Lk 4:16–21). As the *Compendium* asserts, "The whole life and mission of Jesus were carried out in total communion with the Holy Spirit" (n. 265). This was the case for Jesus, right up to his paschal mystery and especially after his glorious return to the Father when he would become the one who bestows the Spirit (see Jn 16:13–15; 20:21–23).

The prophets had promised the outpouring of the Spirit on all the people of Israel (see Is 44:3; Ezek 39:29); in addition, they had promised a universal outpouring of the Spirit on all flesh (see Joel 3:1–3). God wants to form a messianic people to be his servant to all the nations (see Ezek 36:25–27). This is precisely what happened at Pentecost. On that day, not only was the promise of the old covenant fulfilled but also the promise of Jesus before he returned to the Father (see Acts 1:4–8). Peter declares that this outpouring of the Spirit is the sign of the messianic age (see Acts 2:17–18) and that faith in the apostolic preaching and baptism are the conditions of receiving it (see Acts 2:38). Therefore, just as the baptism of the disciples was completed at Pentecost with the outpouring of the Spirit, in the same way, to fulfill Christ's will and to complete the grace of baptism, the apostles communicated the gift of the Holy Spirit to the neophytes through the laying on of hands.

This laying on of hands has been righty recognized in Catholic tradition as the origin of the sacrament of Confirmation that in a certain sense perpetuates the grace of Pentecost in the Church (see Paul VI, *Divinae consortium naturae*, 659). As a clearer way to indicate the gift of the Holy Spirit, the anointing with perfumed oil (chrism) was very soon added to the laying on of hands. As the *CCC* states, this explains the name "Christian," which means "anointed" and has its origin in the name of Christ "whom God anointed...with the Holy Spirit" (Acts 10:38). Therefore, in the Church's understanding, the full gift of the Holy Spirit is given in Confirmation. However, this raises the question about its distinction from Baptism. This question becomes more complex if we take into consideration the diverse liturgical-sacramental practices that are currently followed in the East and the West.

Very early on, Confirmation was part of a single celebration with Baptism, forming a "double sacrament" with it (see St. Cyprian, "Epistle 73," 21). The distinction between them in the single liturgical celebration was made clear by the allocation of the celebrants' functions. While the priest performed the sacrament of Baptism and an initial anointing of the neophytes, the two liturgical rites that today constitute the core of the celebration of Confirmation—the laying on of hands and the anointing with oil for thanksgiving—were reserved for the bishop (see Hippolytus of Rome, *The Apostolic Tradition*, 21). As time went by, when parishes multiplied and the bishop could not always be present, the churches in the East and in the West established different practices. In the East, all of the rites, including Confirmation, are performed by the priest to emphasize their sacramental unity. In the West, the Church reserves Confirmation for the bishop to emphasize the apostolic origin of the sacraments and to affirm an ecclesial bond with those who received it.

II. The Signs and the Rite of Confirmation

What is the basic rite of Confirmation? The answer in the *Compendium* introduces us to the basic elements of this sacrament: "The essential rite of Confirmation is the anointing with Sacred Chrism (oil mixed with balsam and consecrated by the bishop), which is done by the laying on of the hand of the minister who pronounces the sacramental words proper to the rite. In the West this anointing is done on the forehead of the baptized with the words, 'Be sealed with the gift of the Holy Spirit.' In the Eastern Churches of the Byzantine rite this anointing is also done on other parts of the body with the words, 'The seal of the gift of the Holy Spirit'" (*Compendium* n. 267).

There is no doubt that the whole rite has strong biblical resonances. The "laying on of hands" is a gesture that habitually occurs in salvation history to indicate the transmission of power and authority. In this case, it is the entryway to the central moment of the rite. In fact, after the profession of faith by the candidates, which refers to the Baptism they just received, the rite begins by inviting the congregation to ask God to pour out his Holy Spirit on them. After a moment of silence, the bishop extends his hands over the whole group of candidates and asks God to send the Holy Spirit, the Paraclete, on them to consecrate them as living stones in the Church and to fill them with his seven gifts (the spirit of wisdom and understanding, the spirit of counsel and fortitude, and the spirit of knowledge and piety) so that they would be filled by the spirit of a holy fear of the Lord (see *Order of Confirmation*, 25).

The gesture of "anointing" has other resonances with multiple meanings throughout salvation history (a sign of abundance, joy, healing, power, etc.). The rite at this moment focuses its attention on the act of identification with Christ, who declared he was himself marked with his Father's seal (see Jn 6:27). In the rite of anointing, the bishop lays hands on each of the candidates and makes the sign of the glorious cross of Christ on their foreheads, marking them with sacred chrism. This gesture means they belong completely to Christ and are identified with him. "In the anointing with Chrism and the accompanying words, the effect of the giving of the Holy Spirit is clearly signified. Signed with the perfumed oil by the hand of the bishop, the baptized receive the indelible character, the seal of the Lord, together with the gift of the Spirit that conforms them more fully to Christ and gives them the grace of spreading among men and women 'the pleasing fragrance of Christ'" (*Order of Confirmation*, "Introduction," 9).

The bishop's accompanying words declare to the one who receives this gesture, "Be sealed with the gift of the Holy Spirit" (n. 1300). In fact only the seal of the Holy Spirit can constitute the mark of totally belonging to Christ, of our enrollment in his service forever, and of the promise of protection in the great trial to come (see Rev 7:2–3; 9:4; Ezek 9:4–6). The rite concludes with a kiss of peace to signify ecclesial communion with the bishop and full integration into the Church community.

III. The Effects of Confirmation

Although the title of this section speaks of "effects" in the plural, the outworking of this sacrament points to producing a single effect: "the special outpouring of the Holy Spirit" (n. 1302; *Compendium* 268) from which the other effects derive. They all relate to the growth and increase of baptismal grace. Confirmation roots us more deeply in divine sonship, it unites us more securely to Christ, it enhances the gifts of the Holy Spirit, it makes our bond with the Church more perfect, and it strengthens us to be genuine witnesses of Christ (see n. 1303).

Baptism had already conferred the gift of the Holy Spirit on those baptized, but now this is the gift of a new outpouring that evokes the day of Pentecost. The link the *CCC* affirms between Baptism and Confirmation demonstrates that God's action remains the same even when two occasions are involved: Christ's Passover, which is the origin of every Christian grace, and Pentecost, in which that grace reaches its fullness because of the complete reception of the divine gift par excellence, the Holy Spirit. Given the extraordinary goodness of the Spirit, who would not desire to receive it? Considering the Holy Spirit's divine nature and his proceeding from the Father and the Son, St. Basil the Great addresses that question this way: "Although he is called the Spirit of God, the Spirit of truth who proceeds from the Father, the righteous Spirit, and the guiding Spirit, his precise and specific name is 'Holy Spirit.'... All who feel the need for sanctification turn to him. All who desire to live a virtuous life rely on him, and his inspiration is a kind of watering for them that helps them attain their natural destiny" (*On the Holy Spirit*, 9, 22).

Confirmation also imprints on the soul an indelible mark, the character or sign with which Christ seals a person with his Spirit to be his witness to the world. Jesus in fact linked the evangelistic mission to the reception of his Spirit (see Jn 20:21–22; Acts 1:4–8). In receiving a new seal through the gift of the Spirit, those who are baptized are now able to participate in a more powerful way in the Church's mission and "to profess faith in Christ publicly and as it were officially (*quasi ex officio*)" (n. 1305).

This means a stronger ecclesial bond, a greater participation in the communion and mission of the Church. These fruits of the sacrament of Confirmation in the life of a Christian, with respect to their consolidation and development, point to the inevitable reception of the Eucharist. In fact the reception of the sacrament of Confirmation contributes to emphasizing the unity of the sacraments of Christian initiation since they find their ultimate fullness in the Eucharistic celebration.

IV. Who Can Receive This Sacrament?

The candidate for Confirmation is any baptized person who has not yet been confirmed. For a Christian to be initiated fully into the life of faith, the unity of the sacraments of Christian initiation requires that he or she must receive three sacraments: Baptism, Confirmation, and Eucharist. In no case can someone dispense with receiving the sacrament of the Spirit because Christian initiation would then remain incomplete.

As for the age at which a person can receive the sacraments, we need to note the distinction in the *CCC* between "adult faith" and the "adult age of natural growth" (n. 1308), which are not necessarily the same. This distinction is of great importance in a time of extraordinary secularization and requires a process of discernment by the Church that goes beyond automatically setting in advance a specific age for its reception and goes beyond the idea that access to this sacrament is voluntary and could seem to be the result of merit. Confirmation is always a gift of God, never something merited or achieved, because it is a sacrament to be received by faith. (The public confession of faith by the candidates is part of the rite.) It requires those who will receive the gift of the Spirit to have certain fundamental dispositions formed by an appropriate catechesis that builds on the gifts received earlier in Baptism. The goal of catechesis for Confirmation is described by the *CCC* this way: "Preparation for Confirmation should aim at leading the Christian toward a more intimate union with Christ and a more lively familiarity with the Holy Spirit—his actions, his gifts, and his biddings—in order to be more capable of assuming the apostolic responsibilities of Christian life. To this end catechesis for Confirmation should strive to awaken a sense of belonging to the Church of Jesus Christ, the universal Church as well as the parish community. The latter bears special responsibility for the preparation of confirmands" (n. 1309).

To receive the sacrament the confirmand must be in a state of grace. For this reason, the *CCC* considers it suitable to have recourse to the celebration of the sacrament of Penance. There should likewise be an intense period of prayer to facilitate docility and a disposition to receive the gift of the Spirit. The confirmand should not forget to take the opportunity of relying on a godfather or a godmother as a sponsor, if possible, to demonstrate the unity between the two sacraments.

V. The Minister of Confirmation

The apostles laid hands on the Samaritans who were baptized by the deacon Philip (see Acts 8:17). In the first three centuries, the bishop, as a successor to the apostles and the head of a particular church, was the one who laid hands on those who had been baptized and administered the second anointing. When the Church expanded and it was no longer possible to have the bishop present at all baptismal celebrations, the practice became diversified. The Eastern Church considered it appropriate, in making the sacramental unity visible after a person received Baptism, to have the same priest administer Confirmation with the sacred chrism consecrated by the patriarch or the bishop. The Latin Church, with the exception of Christian initiation for adults, retained the practice of having the bishop as the minister of Confirmation (see *LG* 26). This way, the Church "demonstrates clearly that its effect is to unite those who receive it more closely to the Church, to her apostolic origins, and to her mission of bearing witness to Christ" (n. 1313).

Nevertheless, as the *CCC* notes, Vatican II substituted the adjective "ordinary" with the adjective "original": "The *original minister* of Confirmation is the bishop" (n. 1312; see *LG* 26). This acknowledges the value of Eastern practices and opens the door for the Latin Church, when pastoral situations require it, to delegate priests to administer the sacrament of Confirmation.

Chapter One, Article 3:

THE SACRAMENT OF THE EUCHARIST

Juan Carlos Caravajal Blanco

Let us begin the discussion of the third sacrament of Christian initiation with a citation from the Post-Synodal Apostolic Exhortation *SaC* in which Pope Benedict XVI emphasizes the place of the Eucharist in the initiation process and its relationship to the other sacraments of initiation:

> If the Eucharist is truly the source and summit of the Church's life and mission, it follows that the process of Christian initiation must constantly be directed to the reception of this sacrament.… It must never be forgotten that our reception of Baptism and Confirmation is ordered to the Eucharist. Accordingly, our pastoral practice should reflect a more unitary understanding of the process of Christian initiation. The sacrament of Baptism, by which we were conformed to Christ, incorporated in the Church and made children of God, is the portal to all the sacraments. It makes us part of the one Body of Christ (cf. 1 Cor 12:13), a priestly people. Still, it is our participation in the Eucharistic sacrifice that perfects within us the gifts given to us at Baptism. The gifts of the Spirit are given for the building up of Christ's Body (1 Cor 12) and for ever greater witness to the Gospel in the world. The Holy Eucharist, then, brings Christian initiation to completion and represents the center and goal of all sacramental life. (*SaC* n. 17)

I. The Eucharist—Source and Summit of Ecclesial Life

The Eucharist, in addition to being the culmination of Christian initiation, is also the culmination of the other sacraments, of various ministries, and of the works of the apostolate. Everything in the life of the Church is bound up with it and is oriented toward it. The reason is very simple: the Church puts faith in the words of the Lord at the Last Supper (see Mt 26:26–29; Mk

14:22–25; Lk 22:14–20) and believes the Eucharist contains Christ himself in person (see *PO* 5).

The Eucharist does not confer additional fruit to the redemptive act of Christ but rather communicates and makes Christ himself, in the mystery of his redemption, present in a sacramental way. Therefore, the whole of ecclesial life finds its source in it because it is in sacramental communion with Christ that the Church truly is the body of Christ and can accomplish her sanctifying work in the world. In addition, the Church reaches her fullness in the Eucharist since, united to the Christ, she accomplishes an offering of her life and service to the Gospel in order to participate in the heavenly liturgy that gives God glory. Ultimately, the Eucharist is the source and summit of our faith because in it the communion of life with God and the unity of the people of God are signified and actualized.

II. What Is This Sacrament Called?

The *CCC* lists, whether from Scripture or from the whole tradition of the Church, the various names this sacrament has been called. The *Compendium* lists them this way: "The unfathomable richness of this sacrament is expressed in different names which evoke its various aspects. The most common names are: the Eucharist, Holy Mass, the Lord's Supper, the Breaking of the Bread, the Eucharistic Celebration, the Memorial of the passion, death and Resurrection of the Lord, the Holy Sacrifice, the Holy and Divine Liturgy, the Sacred Mysteries, the Most Holy Sacrament of the Altar, and Holy Communion" (n. 275).

St. Thomas, on the issue of this sacrament being called by many names, says it is due to this sacrament's triple significance (*Summa Theologiae* III, 73, 4). First of all, the Angelic Doctor says, it refers to a past event: the memory of the Lord's passion. Therefore, the name of sacrifice and all that this salvific fact evokes is a suitable one. Second, the Dominican saint says it also refers to a present reality: Christ is present and brings about ecclesial unity through participation in his flesh and his divinity. Therefore, it is called communion. Last, it refers to the future because participation in this sacrament prefigures the enjoyment of God that will occur in heaven. Therefore, it is called *viaticum* and is already an anticipation of the heavenly liturgy.

Apart from any of these explanations, the multiplicity of names demonstrates that the Eucharistic sacrament makes present a mystery that is incomprehensible to the human mind, i.e., the real presence of Christ before which people of faith can do nothing less than sing holy praise and prostrate themselves in adoration.

III. The Eucharist in the Economy of Salvation

Human beings, like all living creatures, need food to survive; however, they have made the necessity for nourishment a symbolic act. People establish relationships at a shared table; they celebrate the events of their lives with food; they give it significance and use it to express their relationship with divinity in an extraordinary way.

This anthropological foundation justifies the fact that food has been a fundamental element in salvation history to express the covenant that God established with his people and to recall the central events of their salvation. After a brief mention of this, the *CCC* focuses its attention on the species of bread and wine, the elements at the heart of the Eucharistic celebration that become the Lord's body and blood through the words of Christ and the invocation of the Holy Spirit. However, the Eucharist cannot be explained either by the events of the old covenant that these species have summarized (see n. 1334) or by the different miracles that Jesus performed in his public life (see n. 1335). Something new is happening in the Eucharist: Jesus himself is transformed into the bread of life. This is such an innovation that when Jesus announced it many of his disciples were scandalized and left him (see Jn 6:6).

The Eucharist is among the few sacraments whose institution has detailed testimony. During the Last Supper on the night before his condemnation to the cross, Jesus instituted the sign of the new covenant in his body that was about to be handed over and his blood that was about to be shed. Different texts in the New Testament testify to this (see Mt 26:26–29; Mk 14:22–25; Lk 22:14–20; 1 Cor 11:23–26). However, for us to enter into the significance of this institution, we need to connect this Last Supper with other meals that Jesus took part in and also to contemplate it in the light of his appearances as the Risen One. Jesus' meals actually constitute a distinctive sign of his apostolate. Through them he enters into communion with sinners (see Lk 5:29; 7:36–50; 15:1–2; 19:2–10, etc.). At the same time these meals function to anticipate the messianic banquet of the kingdom (see Mt 14:13–21; 15:32–38, etc.). In terms of Jesus' post-resurrection appearances, we should note that many take place in the context of a meal (see Lk 24:30, 41–42; Jn 21:9–10). The Risen One makes clear that after having conquered death, he is fulfilling the promise he made to his disciples of giving himself personally to those who receive his body and blood.

The Last Supper is the privileged moment in which Christ institutes the Eucharist. Here we find the Jewish celebration of the Passover, and it unfolds as a sharing with those who will deny him later and as a proclamation of the future kingdom. However, Jesus' gestures and words promise something new that he wanted to make permanent in the course of history: the memorial of his death and resurrection, of the sacrificial gift of himself for the forgiveness of sins. The Eucharist is the pledge that Jesus left of his love and of his intention never to leave his disciples and to have them participate in his glorious Passover (see n. 1337). To understand the value of this institution, let us recall some words from the Council: "At the Last Supper, on the night he was betrayed, our Savior instituted the Eucharistic sacrifice of his Body and Blood. This he did in order to perpetuate the sacrifice of the cross throughout the ages until he should come again, and so to entrust to his beloved Spouse, the Church, a memorial of his death and resurrection: a sacrament of love, a sign of unity, a bond of charity, a Paschal banquet 'in which Christ is consumed, the mind is filled with grace, and a pledge of future glory is given to us'" (*SC* 47; *CCC*, n. 1323). Since that time, in obedience to the Lord's command, the Church has perpetuated the memory of his salvific Passover in celebrating the Eucharist every day and has made it the center of her ecclesial life. It is given as nourishment for a pilgrim people who, through the path of the cross, are advancing toward the heavenly banquet in which all the elect will be seated at the table in the kingdom.

IV. The Liturgical Celebration of the Eucharist

Closely observing the evolution of the celebration of the Eucharist over the course of two thousand years, one can recognize that its essential elements have remained unchanged over time. In fact, the explanation of Scripture and the breaking of the bread that Jesus did with the disciples at Emmaus (see Lk 24:13–35) still constitute the two meals that nourish the people of God today. In this regard, Pope Benedict XVI highlights the structural relationship that connects these two meals:

> The liturgy of the word and the Eucharistic liturgy, with the rites of introduction and conclusion, "are so closely interconnected that they form but one single act of worship." There is an intrinsic bond between the word of God and the Eucharist. From listening to the word of God, faith is born or strengthened (cf. Rom 10:17); in the Eucharist the Word made flesh gives himself to us as our spiritual food. Thus, "from the two tables of the word of God and the Body of Christ, the Church receives and gives to the faithful the bread of life." Consequently it must constantly be kept in mind that the word of God, read and proclaimed by the Church in the liturgy, leads to the Eucharist as to its own connatural end. (*SaC* 44)

The Eucharistic celebration begins with the gathering of Christians that constitutes the liturgical assembly. This is a highly symbolic moment although, unfortunately, the people of God may not always be aware of it. Since "Liturgy is an 'action' of the *whole* Christ (*totus Christus*)" (n. 1136), the opening rite involves something constitutive: the baptized gather together, forming the "body of Christ," and welcome the ordained minister, the bishop or priest, who represents Christ the Head. Immediately after that, every baptized person makes the sign of the cross in the name of God: Father and Son and Holy Spirit. Constituted as a holy nation and priestly people, the assembly begins the liturgical celebration in which, united to their Lord, they participate in the heavenly liturgy to offer God the spiritual sacrifices of their lives that are dedicated to the service of his kingdom (see 1 Pet 2:9). The entrance procession, the opening song, the bowing toward the altar, the penitential rite, the Gloria and the Collect—all serve to constitute this holy assembly. Christians are participants not only because of their presence but also because they are placing their lives on the altar of their Lord.

The liturgy of the word also constitutes, as we have said, one of the meals that nourish God's people. God continues to address his word to his people, which reveals the mysteries of his love. The writers of the Old Testament, together with those of the New Testament, represent the starting point from which God enters into dialogue with the assembly. In the liturgical proclamation, the Holy Spirit actualizes the divine word while at the same time preparing the believers' hearts to receive the human words that reach their ears as what they truly are: the word of God. The homily has a fundamental role here: if, on the one hand, it must explain the relevance of the marvelous works communicated by the word (see *SaC* 46), on the other hand, it must also facilitate the conversation that God wants to have with each of his sons and daughters (see *EG* 143). The liturgy of the word concludes with two actions that echo this dialogue: the confession of faith, affirming that God has really brought to pass what the word has proclaimed, and the prayer of the faithful in which the assembly asks God to continue to perform his marvelous works.

After the liturgy of the word, it is time for the Eucharistic liturgy. The *Roman Missal* explains this part of the Mass:

> For Christ took the bread and the chalice, gave thanks, broke the bread and gave it to his disciples, saying: Take, eat and drink: this is my Body; this is the chalice of my Blood. Do this in memory of me. Hence, the Church has arranged the entire celebration of the Liturgy of the Eucharist in parts corresponding to precisely these words and actions of Christ, namely: a) At the Preparation of the Gifts, bread and wine with water are brought to the altar, the same elements, that is to say, which Christ took into his hands. b) In the Eucharistic Prayer, thanks is given to God for the whole work of salvation, and the offerings become the Body and Blood of Christ. c) Through the fraction and through Communion, the faithful, though many, receive from the one bread the Lord's Body and from the one chalice the Lord's Blood in the same way that the Apostles received them from the hands of Christ himself. (n. 72)

To be faithful to the memorial Christ commanded, it is carried out for the assembly by the priest who represents Christ in the power of the Holy Spirit: "In the *epiclesis* the Church asks the Father to send his Holy Spirit (or the power of his blessing [see Roman canon 90]) on the bread and wine so that by his power they may become the body and blood of Jesus Christ and so that those who take part in the Eucharist may become one body and one spirit" (n. 1353).

The memorial is actualized through the anaphora, a prayer in which supplication, thanksgiving, consecration, and intercession unite as an expression of the heavenly liturgy in which the faithful, united to their Lord and in the power of the Spirit, give glory to the Father, the origin and the end of all creation. In the Eucharistic Prayer the Church always offers to God anew the unique and definitive sacrifice of Christ, his Son, and in virtue of the power of the Spirit, the Church unites herself to this offering of Christ on the cross. Therefore, as the *CCC* says next, the Eucharist is the sacrifice of Christ and of the Church. This sacrificial dynamic in which everything returns to the Father through Christ is specifically expressed in the final doxology: "Through Him, with Him, and in Him, in the unity of the Holy Spirit, all glory and honor is yours almighty Father forever and ever."

The Rite of Communion constitutes the preparatory moment for sacramental communion. The Lord's Prayer, the rite of peace, and the breaking of the bread create in those who come for communion the dispositions to receive the Eucharist fruitfully. This is certainly necessary, since the moment calls for that. Although natural food becomes part of the sustenance for whoever consumes it, in sacramental communion the effect is the opposite. The Eucharistic bread and wine, far from being assimilated into those who receive them, instead transform them. The promise that St. Augustine heard in his heart from Christ comes to pass here: "I will not be transformed in you as food for your flesh; it is you who will be transformed into me" (*Confessions* VII, 10).

The Eucharistic celebration ends with the closing rites. In the initial rites the assembly gathers together, but now those who participated in the Lord's mysteries and were transformed by them are blessed and sent out to live their ordinary lives in a Eucharistic way, that is, to do good, to praise and bless God, and to be witnesses of Jesus Christ and servants in his kingdom.

V. The Sacramental Sacrifice: Thanksgiving, Memorial, Presence

The final numbers of the article the *CCC* devotes to the Eucharist offer a systematic theology of this sacrament. In line with the title of this section, the perspective is that of sacrifice. The Eucharist is the sacrament of the sacrificial gift of Christ on the cross. We need to realize that it is not at all easy for our contemporaries to understand the significance of the word "sacrifice," and they do not understand how this salvific event can be made present in every Eucharistic celebration—let alone how Christ can be present under the species of bread and wine. The text here deals with the Eucharistic mystery from a holistic perspective. Each of the words in the title of this section allows us to penetrate into this great mystery of faith. "The Eucharist, the sacrament of our salvation accomplished by Christ on the cross, is also a sacrifice of praise in thanksgiving for the work of creation. In the Eucharistic sacrifice the whole of creation loved by God is presented to the Father through the death and the Resurrection of Christ. Through Christ the Church can offer the sacrifice of praise in thanksgiving for all that God has made good, beautiful, and just in creation and in humanity" (n. 1359).

This number in the *CCC* connects the different elements that comprise the Eucharistic sacrament and allows us to identify the reason for each of them. The central event the Eucharist sacramentally actualizes is the death and resurrection of Christ. This paschal event is referred to simultaneously as "our salvation accomplished by Christ on the cross" and as "a sacrifice of praise in thanksgiving…for all that God has made good, beautiful, and just in creation and in humanity." The Passover is presented as a sacrificial event in which Christ makes a gift of himself and, with him, of humanity and the rest of creation that he assumed in his Incarnation. However, this sacrificial gift of himself is articulated as thanksgiving for all that God has made in creation and in humanity itself. The context of sonship is what allows a definitive understanding of this sacrifice of thanksgiving that Christ accomplishes in his Passover. This, at least, is what the Gospelwriter St. John highlights at the beginning of the part of his Gospel that is referred to as the Book of Glory (see Jn 13:1–20:31): "Now before the feast of the Passover, when Jesus knew that his hour had come to depart out of this world to the Father, having loved his own who were in the world, he loved them to the end.… Jesus [knew] that the Father had given all things into his hands, and that he had come from God and was going to God" (Jn 13:1, 3).

Jesus, in the hour in which he was to accomplish the salvation of humanity by his paschal sacrifice to his Father, kept back nothing that the Father had placed in his hands. On the contrary, in the gift of himself on the cross—which combined obedience to God's will and love toward his own to the end—everything is handed back to the one who is the source of all creation. Jesus' paschal gift of himself is correctly called sacrificial because he held back nothing for himself. Instead, it is a sacrifice of thanksgiving because what Jesus yields up on the cross are the gifts the Father had previously given him, so he is cognizant of divine goodness and offers thanksgiving and praise. In this context the *CCC* recalls, "Eucharist means first of all 'thanksgiving'" (n. 1360).

Jesus' sacrificial gift of himself to the Father, which the Letter to the Hebrews says occurred "once for all when he offered himself" (Heb 7:27), was fully accepted by the Father by virtue of the resurrection. This is why he will exist throughout eternity in his present glorified form in heaven. Jesus Christ, seated at the right hand of the Father, is actually simultaneously priest and victim. He offers himself to the Father for all eternity, but in this act of thanksgiving he incorporates the lives of human beings who live righteously according to the commandment of love.

It is clear why the Eucharist is simultaneously a memorial and a sacrifice. It is a memorial because this unique event in which Christ gave his life to the Father for the salvation of humanity is actualized in every Eucharist as a re-presentation (being made present again) of the paschal mystery that takes place in it. Now that Christ is in heaven, he can make himself present sacramentally in his Church as priest and offering. He is now with the Father but he can make the gift of himself, accomplished on the cross for the salvation of human beings, present in every time and in every place. The Eucharist is also a sacrifice because it actualizes the gift that Christ made of himself in the Passover. As the *CCC* reminds us, the sacrificial character of the Eucharist is evident in the very words of its institution—"my body which is given for you" and "the cup which is poured out for you" (n. 1365)—that refer to the gift of himself on the altar of the cross. "The sacrifice of Christ and the sacrifice of the Eucharist are *one single sacrifice*" (n. 1367). The Eucharist is the sacrament of Christ's sacrifice made present by the Spirit through the faith of the Church.

In addition, the *CCC* reminds us that the Eucharist "*is also the sacrifice of the Church*" because "the Body of Christ participates in the offering of her Head" (n. 1368). There is a minor rite that most often goes unnoticed that expresses this incorporation of the liturgical assembly into the Lord's sacrifice: the gesture of adding water to the wine in the chalice. St. Cyprian, in the third century, explains the meaning of this rite: "When the wine is mixed with water in the cup, it means that the people are being united to Christ.... If someone offers only wine, then the blood of Christ is dissociated from us; if someone offers only water, then the people are dissociated from Christ" ("Epistle to Caecilius" [Epistle 62], 13; *PL* 4, 384 A).

The Eucharist, as we have said, is the source and summit of Christian life. Through the gift received and by being sent forth at the end of every Mass, Christians have sought to live Eucharistically. When they gather around the altar, they give over their very lives in the name of the Lord: "The lives of the faithful, their praise, sufferings, prayer, and work, are united with those of Christ and with his total offering, and so acquire a new value. Christ's sacrifice present on the altar makes it possible for all generations of Christians to be united with his offering" (n. 1368). The Eucharist is the place in which the consecration of the baptized acquires its full significance. Their lives, lived as a sacrifice of thanksgiving, rise up together with Christ's life to God's throne as a holy, pure spiritual offering in the hope that "When Christ who is our life appears, then you also will appear with him in glory" (Col 3:4). This explains the Council's interest in the participation of the faithful at Mass and how it understands it:

> The Church, therefore, earnestly desires that Christ's faithful, when present at this mystery of faith, should not be there as strangers or silent spectators; on the contrary, through a good understanding of the rites and prayers they should take part in the sacred action conscious of what they are doing, with devotion and full collaboration. They should be instructed by God's word and be nourished at the table of the Lord's body; they should give thanks to God; by offering the Immaculate Victim, not only through the hands of the priest, but also with him, they should learn also to offer themselves; through Christ the Mediator, they should be drawn day by day into ever more perfect union with God and with each other, so that finally God may be all in all. (*SC* 48)

Finally, the Eucharistic mystery is sacramental presence: "In the Eucharist, therefore, there is present in a sacramental way, that is, under the Eucharistic species of bread and wine, Christ whole and entire, God and Man" (*Compendium* 282). There is no opposition between the real presence and the sacramental presence of Christ. Christ makes himself really present in the Eucharist, but his presence is sacramental because it is mediated by the species of bread and wine "through the efficacy of [his] word…and by the action of the Holy Spirit" (*Compendium* 283). Although retaining their external appearances, the species are substantially transformed into Christ's body that was handed over and his blood that was shed.

The Eucharistic species of bread and wine, now converted into the body and blood of Christ, represent the whole and complete Person of Christ in the act of giving himself over, through which he constitutes his Church and saves all of creation and humanity that the Father gave him as an inheritance. This explains the caveat by the *CCC* that even though the presence of Christ is in the Eucharist par excellence, his presence is not there exclusively (see n. 1374). We could say that Christ is present in the Church in multiple ways and in various degrees (see n. 1373). This presence overflows into the world in some way because, in the words of Pope Francis, "Christ's resurrection is not an event of the past; it contains a vital power which has permeated this world" (*EG* 276), and "the resurrection is already secretly woven into the fabric of this history, for Jesus did not rise in vain" (*EG* 278). Today when secularization seems to be increasing, Christians need to understand this connection. Those who participate in the Eucharist with the eyes of faith and contemplate the real presence of Christ in the Eucharistic species need to train themselves to recognize their Lord in the midst of the world as well, especially among the poor with whom he identified himself (see Mt 25:40–45).

VI. The Paschal Banquet

"The Holy Eucharist is the paschal banquet in as much as Christ sacramentally makes present his Passover and gives us his Body and Blood, offered as food and drink, uniting us to himself and to one another in his sacrifice" (*Compendium* 287).

This statement in the *Compendiun* highlights the fact that the Eucharistic celebration is the actualization of the paschal supper. This implies that from the time Christ offers himself as true food and true drink (see Jn 6:55–56), believers enter into full communion with him only when they eat his body and drink his blood. At that moment, they experience full union not only with him, but through him and in him they also experience union with the Father and among themselves.

Through Eucharistic communion, the wonderful exchange due to the Incarnation that the Church Fathers speak about occurs in an efficacious way: the Son of God became man to make us sons and daughters of God. In fact, the deification of human beings, which consists in becoming participants in the very life of God, occurs through communion. A text from St. Hilary underscores the paramount role of Eucharistic communion in this process of divinization: "The Word became flesh and we eat the Word made flesh at the Lord's supper. Are we not then bound to believe that his nature dwells in us since he assumed our human nature united it to his eternal nature in the sacrament that communicates his flesh? Through the Eucharist we all become one because the Father is in Christ and Christ is in us.... The Father in Christ and Christ in us make us one with them" (Hilary of Poitiers, *On the Trinity*, 8, 13; *PL* 10, 246).

As we can see, communion with Christ in the Eucharist fuels the process of divinization in the Christian that was initiated through Baptism. Expanding on this fact, the *CCC* looks at the fruits of Eucharistic communion from a triple perspective: our bond with Christ, the constitution of the Church, and participation in eternal life. First of all, communion increases our intimate union with Christ, which presupposes a separation from sin and a strengthening of charity in one's life—a life whereby a Christian becomes a witness of Christ in the midst of the world and a servant in his kingdom (see nn. 1391–1395).

Second, in uniting ourselves more closely to Christ, the Eucharist produces, as a subsequent effect, a unity that forms one single body, the Church, among all those who are in communion with the Lord. This is the sequence of that unity: before the Church "makes" the Eucharist (see *Ecclesia de Eucharistia*

26), that very same Eucharist makes the Church. The following words by Benedict XVI clarify this very point: "The Eucharist is Christ who gives himself to us and continually builds us up as his body. Hence, in the striking interplay between the Eucharist which builds up the Church, and the Church herself which 'makes' the Eucharist, the primary causality is expressed in the first formula: the Church is able to celebrate and adore the mystery of Christ present in the Eucharist precisely because Christ first gave himself to her in the sacrifice of the Cross. The Church's ability to 'make' the Eucharist is completely rooted in Christ's self-gift to her" (*SaC* 14).

The love of God is always prior: "he first loved us" (1 Jn 4:19). The causal precedence of the Eucharist to the Church brings us back to what has always been its ontological source: the love of God. It expresses the Church's essence and its mission of being living witnesses to this divine love in the world in order to summon human beings to give glory to God the Lord.

VII. The Eucharist—"Pledge of the Glory to Come"

Finally, the Eucharist is also an anticipation of celestial glory. It is an anticipation of the eschatological banquet that God promised to prepare on his holy mountain for all peoples (see Is 25:6–9). This is the banquet that Jesus announced he would share with his disciples in his Father's kingdom (see Mt 26:29), the very banquet that celebrates the marriage supper of the Lamb (see Rev 19:9) in which he will be united once and for all with his bride, the Church. "Having passed from this world to the Father, Christ gives us in the Eucharist the pledge of glory with him" (n. 1419).

One final observation. The *CCC* has treated the sacraments of Christian initiation from the point of view of their unity: only through the combination of Baptism, Confirmation, and the Eucharist is a Christian born. We need to remember, however, that in this process of initiation it is necessary to add catechesis to the sacramental dynamic, which enters in its own right into the process of "making Christians." Nevertheless—and this is the observation—the protagonist of Christian initiation is the Spirit that Christ sent from the Father. He is the one who incorporates the sons and daughters of God into the bosom of the Church. Both catechesis and liturgical and sacramental actions are ecclesial mediations that the Spirit activates through his grace to manifest and consummate the mysterious but real action that he himself carries out in those who are open to the Gospel through faith. Ecclesial activity, in order to be effective, must avoid being robotic in any way so that it can support the action of the Spirit and uphold the free response of those whom it serves and to whom it gives birth in the faith.

Chapter Two, Article 4:

THE SACRAMENTS OF PENANCE AND RECONCILIATION

Antonio Miralles

Penance is the sacrament of victory over sin for baptized people. The *CCC* starts off with the words of Vatican II that highlight the ecclesial dimension of Penance. Sin is an offense against God, and victory over sin consists first of all in remission of the offense. However, it also causes a wound to the Church (see n. 1422). The Council's language is very specific that an offense is not the same as a wound. Every sin offends God, but not every sin offends the Church. What offends the Church is only what constitutes an attack on her honor, her unity, or her external order.

Every sin, on the other hand, does wound the Church because it is contrary to charity and thus to communion. Whoever does not persevere in charity "remains indeed in the bosom of the Church, but, as it were, only in a 'bodily' manner and not 'in his heart'" (*LG* 14) like a withered member. Even venial sin wounds the Church, although to a less serious degree; it does not destroy the communion of charity but it slows its growth and impedes the full force of charity.

Once the offense to God is forgiven, the wound with the Church is also healed, and a person once again becomes a healthy member who is contributing to the building up of the body (see Eph 4:16). The Church does not leave the sinner alone on his or her path back to the Father or limit herself to selective intervention only at the moment of reconciliation; she accompanies the sinner all through the process before and after sacramental absolution.

I. What Is This Sacrament Called?

In the ordinary language of the faithful this sacrament is primarily called "Confession" because confessing sin is an essential part of the sacrament and is seen as its most significant feature. The name "sacrament of Penance" has predominated in theological language for centuries since that title best describes the rite as a whole. It is called the "sacrament of Reconciliation" to highlight its effect, just as Baptism can be called the "sacrament of regeneration" because of its effects (see nn. 1423–1424).

II. Why a Sacrament of Reconciliation after Baptism?

The struggle against sin by the faithful, and thus within the Christian community, is ongoing in the life of the Church (see nn. 1425–1429). New Testament writers do not present the Church as a community of people who do not sin.

The proof of this above all is found in the paradigm of Christian prayer, the Lord's Prayer: "And forgive us our debts, as we also have forgiven our debtors" (Mt 6:12). This echoes the admonition in 1 John 1:8–9: "If we say we have no sin, we deceive ourselves, and the truth is not in us. If we confess our sins, he is faithful and just, and will forgive our sins and cleanse us from all unrighteousness." There is also an exhortation from James 5:15: "Therefore confess your sins to one another, and pray for one another, that you may be healed." This applies not only to the inevitable sins of daily life but also to the much more serious and not uncommon sins that St. Paul decries: "Do not be deceived: 'Bad company ruins good morals.' Come to your right mind, and sin no more. For some have no knowledge of God. I say this to your shame" (1 Cor 15:33–34). He also warns, "I fear that perhaps I may come and find you not what I wish.... I may have to mourn over many of those who sinned before and have not repented of the impurity, immorality, and licentiousness which they have practiced" (2 Cor 12:20–21). Quotes could be multiplied here to show that repentance in the Church is not the result of a deterioration of virtue after a golden time of Christian fervor. From the beginning, the call to repentance has resounded not just outside the Church but within the Church to those who have already accepted the proclamation of the Gospel.

The Church has had to react more than once against those who wanted to reduce her to a community of the perfect and sinless. For example, we see St. Ambrose's reproof to the followers of Novation: "If you reject all the fruits of repentance, you are saying, 'Let no one who is wounded enter our group and let no one come to be healed in our Church; we do not care for the sick because we are whole and have no need of a physician'" (*On Penance*, 1, 6, 29; *BA* 17, 191). On the contrary, the faithful always find a remedy in the Church for sin, and although the struggle against sin is always personal—no one can replace the individual in that struggle—it is not a private matter. The sinner is not left alone, because he or she finds forgiveness in the Church and through the Church.

III. The Conversion of the Baptized

The path of conversion for the faithful in the Church has some very specific external signs motivated by interior repentance. Although repentance also has a role in the first conversion that leads to Baptism, it is quite different from the role it has in the sacrament of Penance. Baptism presupposes the inner conversion of a person who has reached the age of reason and is penitent. However, it cannot quite be called the "sacrament of the first Penance" because the repentance that accompanies Baptism takes on another form. Baptism is a participation in the death and resurrection of Christ through the rite of burial in water and resurrection from the water, and it includes a trinitarian invocation.

IV. Interior Penance

The sacrament of Reconciliation could, however, be described as the "sacrament of second repentance" because it is the repentance of baptized people according to the manner established by Christ and, therefore, according to the apostles and their successors. The Council of Trent teaches that repentance is necessary for the remission of sin, but before the coming of Christ there was no sacrament, and after his coming pre-baptismal repentance was not a sacrament (see *DS* 1670). Repentance for the baptized has now acquired a concrete form established by Christ that constitutes a sacrament. The elements that form a person's penitential disposition (the virtue of repentance) are found in sacramental Penance. The very first step that begins the works of repentance occurs in the human heart, interior repentance, and it is the motive for the external works of penance and guarantees their authenticity. It is in the human heart that the interweaving of divine grace and human cooperation first occurs.

V. The Many Forms of Penance in Christian Life

Interior repentance leads to many external works of penance that aim at destroying sin and its consequences (see nn.1434–1435). Among those works, the first are those that are part of the sacrament of Penance. Even the Eucharist becomes a work of penance in the sense that the faithful seek life-giving contact with Christ's sacrifice, the source of all reconciliation, and draw strength from it to overcome temptations (see n. 1436). In addition, the Eucharist prompts a Christian to have recourse to the sacrament of Penance. "The Christ who calls to the Eucharistic banquet is always the same Christ who exhorts us to penance and repeats his 'Repent' [Mk 1:15]. Without this constant ever renewed endeavour for conversion, partaking of the Eucharist would lack its full redeeming effectiveness and there would be a loss or at least a weakening of the special readiness to offer God the spiritual sacrifice [see 1 Pet 2:5] in which our sharing in the priesthood of Christ is expressed in an essential and universal manner" (*RH* 20).

VI. The Sacrament of Penance and Reconciliation

Reconciliation with God occurs through this sacrament. God forgives the offenses of his children, and they separate themselves from sin and submit to God's will to remedy their offenses.

All of this happens in Christ through the power of the Holy Spirit. Access to the Father occurs through Christ, through the encounter and union with him. Christ makes himself visible in the priest, his minister, who has been given the authority to remit sins by the apostles and their apostolic successors.

Christ desires the Church to participate with him in this work, so the action of the Church is especially focused on the minister who represents him. Nevertheless, all the members of the Church help the sinner—thus, they all help each other—on the path of reconciliation with God. They help by prayer, by example, and by works of penance, thereby creating a solidarity among the faithful in their satisfaction for offenses against God. As Thomas Aquinas explains, when charity unites two friends, one can offer satisfaction to God in the other's place, since shared love, perfected by charity, makes the works of the friend one's own, and even more so if the friend must suffer on his behalf (see *Summa contra Gentiles*, 3, 158, 7).

The most complete meaning of the words "bind and loose" is explained in n. 553. They include the authority to govern and to pronounce judgment in doctrinal matters. In terms of forgiveness of sins one must interpret that authority in conjunction with John 20:22–23: "'Receive the Holy Spirit. If you forgive the sins of any, they are forgiven; if you retain the sins of any, they are retained'" (see nn. 976, 1141). With these words the risen Christ conferred on the apostles the power to forgive sins in the sacrament of Penance (see *DS* 1703). This sacrament is not just meant to remedy a person's exclusion from communion with the Church because of serious sin; its primary goal is the forgiveness of sin. Venial sins, for example, do not break communion with the Church, but they are also the object of forgiveness.

The *CCC* does not treat the issue of sacramental Penance in the early centuries without mentioning the "order of penitents," which involved public penance for serious sin (see n. 1447). The topic has been debated by scholars, but the debate has not altered the conclusions about the basic structure of the sacrament of Penance. A comparison of the structure of ancient public Penance (and a person's admission to the "order of the penitents") with the present form of Penance shows that its modality was quite dissimilar; nevertheless, it is clear that the sacrament of Penance, in terms of its fundamental elements, has remained unchanged over the centuries.

The sacrament of Penance is constituted by the actions of the penitent—contrition, confession, and satisfaction—and by the priest who judges and absolves the sins (see n. 1491). These actions are external and visible, so they are fitting as the signs of this sacrament (see n. 1131), and they are in continuity with interior repentance and are animated by it. They signify externally the interior effect of the sacrament: separating oneself from sin, turning back to God, and receiving God's forgiveness. Unlike Baptism, in Penance the acts of the penitent are part of the sacrament. Something similar happens in natural life: at birth, at the beginning of life, a baby is completely passive; in healing, the adult must cooperate with the therapeutic process overseen by the doctor.

The assignment of the means of satisfaction by the Church's minister is a fundamental element of the sacrament. The sinner submits his sins to the judgment of God's minister and the Church—he submits them to the "power of the keys"—not so much for the priest to judge the authenticity of the repentance but rather for the assignment of penance according to the Church's judgment and, in the last analysis, according to God's judgment for the offense against him.

VII. The Acts of the Penitent

Contrition is an act of the will (see nn. 1451–1454). Just as sin is voluntary, accepting responsibility is also voluntary. Human beings exercise their dignity as free creatures precisely in repenting and addressing the issue of their conduct before God. The sorrow of the will can be accompanied by feelings such as sadness and regret, and this usually happens because of the integrated nature of the human being. However, such emotions do not determine the authenticity or the degree of repentance.

Contrition concerns the future just as much as the past. It looks to the past because repenting involves not simply giving up sin but implies hate for the sin committed. It looks to the future because it includes a resolution not to sin again. The sincerity and strength of that resolution guarantees the genuineness of the contrition. Without a resolution not to sin in the future, the will is not truly resisting sin.

The motives for repentance can vary, but since they give rise to true contrition, they should be supernatural in nature: because God who is offended by sin is infinitely good; because of fear of the eternal pains of hell; because of the moral repulsiveness of sin, etc. Merely natural motives do not lead to true contrition. A businessman who regrets committing fraud only because he has lost a client does not have true contrition. If repentance is motived by charity, namely, by a love for God who is loved above all else, then the contrition is perfect. It is a gift of God because no human being can succeed in repenting on his or her own in such a perfect way.

Contrition for sin after Baptism, if it is perfect, includes "the firm resolution to have recourse to sacramental confession as soon as possible" (n. 1452). Otherwise, it is not perfect. After Baptism there are not two paths for the remission of sins: a sacramental one and an extra-sacramental one. There is only one path, and the sacrament of Penance is just as necessary for salvation for those who have sinned after Baptism as Baptism is necessary for the unbaptized (see *DS* 1672).

The sacrament of Penance is not normally completed quickly; it is instead like a journey. Perfect contrition—an effect of charity and therefore of sanctifying grace—is often preceded by imperfect contrition called "attrition." A person who has only attrition for his or her sins has not yet obtained reconciliation with God, but it can lead to approaching sacramental confession. Then that person, in receiving the grace of the sacrament, can become perfectly contrite.

An examination of conscience is needed to identify the sins to repent of and confess. There is no fixed formula for this. It can be very brief, or it may require more time and diligence depending on what is being confessed and whether grave or minor sins are involved.

Confession to a priest is essential because without it sins are not submitted to the Church's judgment, to the "power of the keys" (see nn. 1455–1458). It is not enough to declare oneself a sinner in general; the confession needs to be detailed: "A member of the Christian faithful is obliged to confess in kind and in number all serious sins committed after baptism and not yet directly remitted through the keys of the Church nor acknowledged in individual confession of which one is conscious after diligent examination of conscience" (*CIC*, can. 988, 1). This means we also need to confess serious sins that are perhaps already forgiven but not acknowledged in an individual confession because of having been forgotten or because of some other circumstance.

Sacramental confession is necessary from the moment a person is capable of serious sin and has in fact sinned. Therefore, a Church precept requires confession of serious sins at least once a year, and this obligation begins at the age of reason.

We may add to this the tremendous usefulness of frequent confession for children as well since it is a great help for them in developing a correct attitude toward God as a father who always forgives. The joy of being forgiven is common for adults and for children, but children are especially sensitive to it.

The precept that a person should receive sacramental absolution for mortal sins before receiving Holy Communion is not simply an ecclesiastical law that is subject to change. It rests on the solid dogmatic basis found in St.

Paul's words in 1 Corinthians 11: 27–29 as interpreted by the living Tradition of the Church (see *DS* 1646–2647): "Whoever, therefore, eats the bread or drinks the cup of the Lord in an unworthy manner will be guilty of profaning the body and blood of the Lord. Let a man examine himself, and so eat of the bread and drink of the cup. For any one who eats and drinks without discerning the body eats and drinks judgment upon himself." St. John Paul II categorically affirmed that this norm pronounced by St. Paul and by the Council of Trent will always "remain in effect" in the Church (see *Ecclesia de Eucharistia* 36; see also *AS* 20).

The advantage of frequent confession for venial sins comes chiefly from the sacrament's effects: the grace of forgiveness brings strength to overcome sin in future struggles, and above all it configures us to Christ who defeated sin on the cross by his docile submission to the Father's will.

After sacramental absolution of sin, sin is not yet completely eliminated (see nn. 1459–1460). Sometimes the necessary tasks of reparation for the harm caused by sin still remain: restitution of stolen goods, repayment for damages, making amends for scandal, rectifying slander, etc. And then there are the works of penance imposed by the confessor. These always have the simultaneous purpose of healing and expiation. They are healing because the works of the penitent, even if they are minor, always involve a certain penalty, at least the penalty of the effort and exertion of overcoming our resistance to doing good works. Through these penances a human being practices doing good, strengthening good dispositions, and becoming more cautious about not yielding to temptations in the future.

The expiatory purpose of the works of penance comes from the fact that it is appropriate for sinners, who have indulged in certain pleasures despite displeasing God in a serious or minor way, to put themselves out now by distancing themselves from created things in some way to belong more decisively to God. In brief, through these works of penance one atones for the "temporal punishment" of sin (see nn. 1472–1473). If that is not atoned for in this life, it will then be atoned for in Purgatory.

In this life, then, we can do penance that allows us to grow in the love of God, to unite ourselves to Christ who suffered for us, and to progress in virtue. The value of the works of penance comes from union with Christ. The particular expiatory efficaciousness of sacramental satisfaction comes from this union because the salvific efficaciousness of the passion of Christ works through it, as it does in all the sacraments. In addition, union with Christ is measured by charity, and it is from charity that the works of penance should arise. Satisfaction for sin does not actually consist in submitting to God's vengeance but rather in offering him something that would please him to a greater degree than the degree to which he detests the sin (see *Summa Theologiae* III, 48, art. 2).

VIII. The Minister of This Sacrament

By its nature the sacrament of Penance requires that its ministers be priests who "are conformed to Christ the Priest in such a way that they can act in the person of Christ the Head [of the mystical body]" (*PO* 2). In addition he must have under his pastoral care the faithful for whom he exercises the ministry of reconciliation as well as the faculty to hear their sacramental confessions (see nn. 1461–1467).

Throughout history the assignment of this faculty has been regulated in various ways by the Church. It has always been the official position that the bishop is the moderator of penitential discipline. Other priests have that faculty by virtue of their office (a parish priest, a canon penitentiary, a superior of a religious institute or a society of apostolic life, etc.). However, it is by concession of the ordinary in that place. According to Church law, "Those who enjoy the faculty of hearing confessions habitually whether in virtue of office or by grant from the ordinary of the place of incardination or the place in which they have a domicile can exercise the same faculty everywhere unless the local ordinary denies it" (CIC, can. 967, 2; see *CCEO*, can. 722). In addition, "Cardinals by the law itself possess the faculty to hear the confessions of the Christian faithful anywhere" (CIC, can. 967, 1). If a penitent is in danger of death, the Church grants every priest the faculty to hear that confession (see CIC, can. 976; *CCEO*, can. 725).

The call to repentance is an indispensable part of the ministry of the word by priests. They have the task of teaching "the word of Christ..., and it is to conversion and holiness that they exhort all men" (PO 4). Concretely, "In the spirit of Christ the Shepherd, they must prompt their people to confess their sins with a contrite heart in the sacrament of Penance, so that, mindful of his words 'Repent for the kingdom of God is at hand' (Mt 4:17), they are drawn closer to the Lord more and more each day" (PO 5).

In line with his obligation to invite the faithful to conversion, the priest also has an obligation to make himself available for the ministry of the sacrament of Penance as a requirement of his priestly mission and not just as an administrative task. There is great pastoral value in the following canonical norm: "All to whom the care of souls is committed by reason of an office are obliged to provide that the confessions of the faithful entrusted to their care be heard when they reasonably ask to be heard and that the opportunity be given to them to come to individual confession on days and hours set for their convenience" (CIC, can. 986, 1).

Being a minster of Christ and of the Church, the priest must become an interpreter of Christ's heart and of the Church's will. Therefore, "In the administration of the sacraments, the confessor, as minister of the Church, is to adhere faithfully to the doctrine of the magisterium and the norms enacted by competent authority" (CIC, can. 978, 2). A priest would be committing a grave injustice against a penitent if he let his judgment and his counsel be guided by a personal point of view that is not in accord with the doctrine taught by the Church's Magisterium. The penitent lays bare his conscience to him because he sees God's minister in him, and if he finds severity rather than mercy, doubts and darkness rather than the light of truth, he would be the victim of a spiritual fraud.

IX. The Effects of This Sacrament

The grace of reconciliation with God is sanctifying and justifying grace, and when it is received through Penance it also includes sacramental grace (see nn. 1129, 2003). The faithful are strengthened through that grace to be victorious in their struggle against sin in the future. In fact, they are made participants in Christ's victory over sin, achieved by his obedient submission to the Father's will and in suffering expiatory pains for human beings' sins. That participation shapes the virtue of the faithful, giving it a penitential flavor and encouraging a spirit of repentance to be present in a Christian's whole life.

X. Indulgences

In order to understand fully what an indulgence is, we need to keep in mind the necessity of paying for the temporal punishment due to sin whose guilt is now forgiven. Sin, in fact, leaves sinners in the state of guilt before God whom they have offended and deserves punishment. If sinners do not obtain forgiveness for a serious offense against God, the punishment reserved to them will be the loss of eternal life and separation from God for all eternity, which is sin's eternal punishment (see n. 1035). In addition, sin deserves another punishment: reparation for an inordinate attachment to a creaturely good despite its being contrary to God's will. Even a light offense against God deserves a proportionate punishment:

> It is therefore necessary for the full remission and—as it is called—reparation of sins not only that friendship with God be reestablished by a sincere conversion of the mind and amends made for the offense against his wisdom and goodness, but also that all the personal as well as social values and those of the universal order itself, which have been diminished or destroyed by sin, be fully reintegrated whether through voluntary reparation which will involve punishment or through acceptance of the punishments established by the just and most holy wisdom of God, from which

> there will shine forth throughout the world the sanctity and the splendor of his glory. (ID 3)

This addresses the "temporal punishment" that needs to be dealt with either in this life or in the next in Purgatory.

According to its definition in the *CCC*, taken from ID, an indulgence effects a genuine "remission before God of the temporal punishment due to sins" (n. 1471). It is a remission granted outside of the sacrament of Penance that also remits the punishment sacramentally. Although it is outside of the sacrament, it is not independent from it because the remission of punishment presupposes the remission of the guilt. As long as the guilt persists, the human being remains as someone who has offended God and merits punishment. The forgiveness of serious sins and often also of venial sins, however, occurs only through the sacrament of Reconciliation. To receive an indulgence, the faithful must be "duly disposed" (n. 1471) because it is obtained when one is in a state of friendship with God, namely, in the state of grace. It is given "under certain prescribed conditions" (n. 1471) because certain defined actions need to be performed to obtain it. More precisely, "The aim pursued by ecclesiastical authority in granting indulgences is not only that of helping the faithful to expiate the punishment due sin but also that of urging them to perform works of piety, penitence and charity—particularly those which lead to growth in faith and which favor the common good" (ID 8).

The authoritative intervention by the Church to impart indulgences, which is referred to in the definition, and the nature of the "Church's treasury" are explained in nn. 1478 and 1475–1477, respectively.

A plenary indulgence frees a person from all the temporal punishment due to sin. "To acquire a plenary indulgence it is necessary to perform the work to which the indulgence is attached and to fulfill three conditions: sacramental confession, Eucharistic Communion and prayer for the intentions of the Supreme Pontiff. It is further required that all attachment to sin, even to venial sin, be absent" (ID, norm 7). It is precisely this third condition that makes a truly plenary indulgence difficult to obtain, but it is a vital condition because if some attachment to venial sin remains, the corresponding temporal punishment is not remitted.

To what extent is an indulgence partial? Obviously the remission of temporal punishment is not able to be calculated numerically and is known only to God. "The faithful who at least with a contrite heart perform an action to which a partial indulgence is attached obtain, in addition to the remission of temporal punishment acquired by the action itself, an equal remission of punishment through the intervention of the Church" (ID, norm 5). All good works in this life have a certain quality of suffering, even those that do not entail the deprivation or the removal of some created good—for example, acts of faith, hope, and love—because they must always overcome some resistance in us that is the consequence of original sin. Therefore, all our good works can have the value of satisfaction measured by charity, which is their source.

A partial indulgence guarantees us, so to speak, solidarity with the Church in our duty to conduct ourselves as genuine Christians as well as solidarity in the purification of sin, making our works of penance doubly efficacious.

The most common prayers and acts of piety among the faithful bring a partial indulgence. The Christian faithful "are encouraged to infuse with a Christian spirit all the actions that go to make up their daily lives and to strive in the ordering of their lives toward the perfection of charity" (*Manual of Indulgences*, p. 23). Three general concessions that encompass all the practices of Christian life are added that show the Church is continually present to assist the faithful in their expiation of sins. The first general concession: "A partial indulgence is granted to the Christian faithful who, while carrying out their duties and enduring the hardships of life, raise their minds in humble trust to God, and make, at least mentally, some pious invocation" (*Manual of Indulgences*, p. 25). Second: "A partial indulgence is granted to the faithful who, led by the spirit of faith, give compassionately of themselves or of their goods to serve their brothers in need" (*Manual of Indulgences*, p. 28). Third: "A partial indulgence is granted to the Christian faithful who, in a spirit of penance, voluntarily abstain from something that is licit for and pleasing to them" (*Manual of Indulgences*, p. 31).

The doctrine and practice of indulgences are clear expressions of faith in the communion of saints. There exists, in fact, a communion of spiritual goods among the members of the body of Christ, the Church. It includes the expiation offered to God for freedom from sin and is constituted by an accumulation of spiritual riches the faithful can draw on to satisfy the debt of their guilt since those who are united in charity can offer satisfaction to God for one another. Clement VI, in his *Bull Unigenitis* for the Jubilee Year in 1350, called that accumulation of spiritual riches the "treasury of the Church" (see *DS* 1025–1027). It is inexhaustible because it includes, first of all, the satisfaction and merits of Christ the redeemer, and added to that are those of the Blessed Mary Virgin and of all the saints. Although the expiation offered by Christ for all of humanity's sins is more than enough, he nevertheless wants to associate the members of his mystical body in the work of redemption with himself, according to what St. Paul says: "Now I rejoice in my sufferings for your sake, and in my flesh I complete what is lacking in Christ's afflictions for the sake of his body, that is, the church" (Col 1:24). This is why the victories of one believer over sin can flow out on behalf of other believers.

The intervention of the Church in the acquisition of indulgences is authoritative because its treasury is entrusted to it to be dispensed to the faithful for their salvation. As Thomas Aquinas explains, "The one who gains an indulgence is not thereby absolved from the punishment that is owed but is given the means by which that debt can be paid" (*Summa Theologiae*, Suppl. 25, art. 1–2).

According to ID, "The aim pursued by ecclesiastical authority in granting indulgences is not only that of helping the faithful to expiate the punishment due [to] sin but also that of urging them to perform works of piety, penitence and charity—particularly those which lead to growth in faith and which favor the common good" (n. 8). This is particularly evident in the granting of plenary indulgences. Any of them can be acquired by all the faithful on any day of the year if they perform the following works, together with the other general conditions for every plenary indulgence: adoration of the Blessed Sacrament for at least half an hour; devout reading of holy Scripture for at least half an hour; the pious practice of the *Via crucis* (Stations of the Cross); the recitation of the rosary in a church or public oratory, or in a family, a religious community, or a pious association (see *Manual of Indulgences*, p. 36ff).

The communion of saints unites not only the members of the pilgrim Church among themselves and with the saints in heaven but also includes the souls being purified in Purgatory. The faithful can offer God the indulgences they receive on behalf of these souls, asking God to accept them so that they are relieved of the punishment they are undergoing and may soon enter into eternal glory. This is why we say that indulgences "can always be applied to the dead by way of suffrage" (ID, norm 3).

XI. The Celebration of the Sacrament of Penance

The liturgy of the sacrament of Penance is very sober when it comes to its rites and ceremonies (see n. 1480). The initial greeting by the priest, the confession of sin, the counsel of the confessor, his exhortation to repentance, the imposition and acceptance of a penance—all these things have little, if anything, ritual about them. They are instead highly significant indications of God's activity in the penitent's heart.

The ecclesial dimension of Penance is adequately expressed in the actions of the penitent and of the confessor that make up this sacrament. However, one can also find that dimension better expressed in a communal celebration of preparation and thanksgiving that includes personal confession of sin and the individual absolution of penitents (see n. 1482).

If personal and full confession and individual absolution are impossible (physically or morally) and there exists a great need, the sacrament may be performed with a general confession and a general absolution given to all the penitents together (see nos. 1483–1484). In these cases, the *Rite of Penance* provides an appropriate mode of celebrating the sacrament. It is, however, "an extraordinary means to be used in wholly exceptional situations" (St. John Paul II, *Motu Proprio*, *Misericordia Dei*, May 2, 2002). This kind of communal celebration is less expressive of the ecclesial dimension of Penance in relation to its ordinary form of personal and individual absolution. Reconciliation with God through the personal encounter with Christ, which is the basis for reconciliation with the Church, becomes less clear in group absolution, just as the submission of sins to the keys of the Church is less clear.

In these exceptional cases, the faithful who make a general confession and are absolved collectively must "intend to confess individually the serious sins which at present cannot be so confessed" (CIC, can. 962, 1; *CCEO*, can. 721, 1). This is an essential duty because submitting all serious sins to the keys of the ministers of the Church is part of the essence of the sacrament. For this reason true contrition includes the intention mentioned above that when it is done only partially in a general way through necessity, it will be completed later since the penitent's sincerity will lead him or her to complete it.

Chapter Two, Article 5:

THE ANOINTING OF THE SICK

Antonio Miralles

The sacrament of the Anointing of the Sick is in continuity with the sacrament of Penance. The Council of Trent presents it as perfecting not only the sacrament of Penance (see *DS* 1694) but also all of Christian life. The whole of Christian life receives a penitential character from the sacrament of Penance; it has a particular value of purification from the vestiges of sin in accord with the priest's prayer after sacramental absolution: "May the Passion of our Lord Jesus Christ…, whatever good you do and suffering you endure, heal your sins, help you to grow in holiness, and reward you with eternal life."

In this context illness has a particular meaning and can contribute considerably to giving Christian life an ongoing sense of repentance. Therefore, the *CCC*, after explaining the doctrine concerning the Anointing of the Sick, takes time to discuss illness in the economy of salvation.

The first number, n. 1499, gives an introductory overview that allows us to understand, among other things, its presentation on illness from the perspective of the sacrament of Anointing of the Sick. In its brief synthesis, taken from Vatican II's *LG* 11, it refers to all the elements that constitute this sacrament: the essential rite, its minister, the people for whom it is intended, its effects, its ecclesial dimension, and the responsibility of the sick person after receiving the sacrament.

I. Its Foundations in the Economy of Salvation

"Grave illness" is the topic here, illness that leads to death because the sick person may not be able to survive it. Medical science is very advanced now and can effectively heal many serious diseases, but illness can still have a certain existential heaviness that weighs on the sick person. Illness is in fact linked to suffering (see nn. 1500–1501). Even when medicine succeeds in healing sick people, it does not always succeed in removing their suffering despite its effort to alleviate it. The sacrament of Anointing of the Sick is linked to "grave illness" because it has a specific place in the economy of salvation. Grave illnesses do not include ailments, indispositions, and the aches and pains that are inevitable in earthly life.

The Old Testament begins to give an answer to the human question about illness: it has a place in God's plan of salvation (see n. 1502). It is tied to evil and sin but also to salvation. The prophetic messages of God's future interventions of salvation are often full of promises of healing from sickness and disease. However, the most comprehensive answer about the meaning of illness is not revealed until the New Testament.

In Jesus' public life, illness constitutes an ongoing indicator of his messianic action (see nn. 1503–1504) since the majority of his miracles are healings that are simultaneously signs of messianic blessings. Jesus does not just restore health to a body: a physical healing is accompanied by a healing of the soul. The Gospel highlights Jesus' compassion; nothing human left him indifferent, and he was particularly moved at the sight of the sick people: "Jesus in pity touched their eyes, and immediately they received their sight and followed him" (Mt 20:34); "As he went ashore he saw a great throng; and he had compassion on them, and healed their sick" (Mt 14:14). The Gospel-writer discerns in these healings Jesus' assumption of our sicknesses, his compassion ("suffer together"), and sees in them the fulfillment of the prophecy about the Suffering Servant: "That evening they brought to him many who were possessed with demons; and he cast out the spirits with a word, and healed all who were sick. This was to fulfil what was spoken by the prophet Isaiah, 'He took our infirmities and bore our diseases'" (Mt 8:16–17). With his approach to the sick, Jesus demonstrated that they had a central place in the Church, not a marginalized one.

Jesus gives the definitive response regarding the meaning of sickness in God's plan through his passion and death on the cross, as he fully takes on suffering (see n. 1505). From that time until now, all human suffering has a positive value in the work of redemption. According to St. John Paul II,

> Gradually, *as the individual takes up his cross*, spiritually uniting himself to the Cross of Christ, the salvific meaning of suffering is revealed before him.... Faith in sharing in the suffering of Christ brings with it the interior certainty that the suffering person "completes what is lacking in Christ's afflictions" [see Col 1:24]; the certainty that in the spiritual dimension of the work of Redemption *he is serving*, like Christ, *the salvation of his brothers and sisters*. Therefore he is carrying out an irreplaceable service. And so the Church sees in all Christ's suffering brothers and sisters as it were a *multiple subject of his supernatural power*. (*SD* 26–27)

Jesus' reaction to his own suffering and to the suffering of others is a model for his disciples and for all Christians (see nn. 1506–1508). "Christ's revelation of the salvific meaning of suffering *is in no way identified with an attitude of passivity*. Completely the reverse is true. The Gospel is the negation of passivity in the face of suffering. Christ himself is especially active in this field.... He goes about 'doing good' [see Acts 10:38], and the good of his works became especially evident in the face of human suffering" (*SD* 30). A similar active attitude is expected of the Church, which is called to do all that she can through her sons and daughters for the sick. The Church has even been given the charism of the gift of healing, so throughout the centuries miraculous healings have not been lacking in the Church. For the whole Church to do all she can means that the sick have a role as well: they are active members of the Church and contribute in great measure to its good insofar as their suffering is a means of union with Christ.

According to *SD*, "And all those who suffer have been called once and for all to become sharers 'in Christ's sufferings' [see 1 Pet 4:13], just as all have been called to 'complete' with their own suffering 'what is lacking in Christ's affliction' [see Col 1:24]. At one and the same time Christ has taught man *to do good by his suffering* and *to do good to those who suffer*. In this double aspect he has completely revealed the meaning of suffering" (n. 30).

Christ not only left a model of behavior toward sickness and disease, but he is also still present in the Church which has been charged to continue his actions toward the sick (see n. 1509). He is present in the Church that cares for the sick and thereby exercises charity this way. In fact, "He is present in the Church as she performs her works of mercy, not just because whatever good we do to one of His least brethren we do to Christ Himself [see Mt 25:40], but also because Christ is the one who performs these works through the Church and who continually helps men with His divine love" (Blessed Paul VI, *Mysterium fidei*, 35). He is also present in the Church as she prays for the sick. His presence is heightened for the sick in the sacraments as well, especially in the Eucharist where his presence is particularly at work and substantial, and in the Anointing of the Sick.

The Anointing of the Sick is the sacrament specific to the sick (see nn. 1510–1512). James 5:14–15 refers to a normal practice that is a support for the sick, especially for their spiritual benefit. In fact, the reference to faith expressed in the prayer and to the forgiveness of sins in this passage indicates that the effects are primarily spiritual.

Among the testimonies in Tradition that acknowledge the Anointing of the Sick as a sacrament of the Church, the first explicit one is a letter by St. Innocent I to the bishop of Gubbio, in 416. In clarifying the issue, he declares that the anointing by priests of the sick, according to James 5:14–15, can *a fortiori* be done by bishops and that they are the ones who should bless the oil. He adds that this sacrament should not be given to those who are not yet reconciled to God and to the Church since the other sacraments are also denied to them (See *DS* 216). In addition this sacrament is listed as one of the seven sacraments of the Church by the Second Council of Lyon, the Council of Florence, and the Council of Trent (see *DS* 860, 1310, 1601).

The material element of this sacrament is the oil blessed by the bishop (see *DS* 1695). This oil for the sick [see n. 1513] is blessed, like other holy oils, during Mass on the morning of Holy Thursday. Unlike the case of the chrism for Confirmation, however, this particular oil does not need to be blessed by the bishop. In case of necessity any priest may bless it during the celebration of this sacrament. Blessed Paul VI determined that the oil need not necessarily be olive oil and that oil from any plant could be used, as long as it was similar to olive oil (see *On the Sacrament of Anointing of the Sick*). In addition, he simplified the rite so that there are only two anointings: of the forehead and of the hands.

According to the introduction to the text on the blessings of oils by the Italian Episcopal Conference, oil "is a therapeutic, aromatic and convivial substance. It heals wounds, it perfumes limbs, and it enlivens a table. This multifaceted nature of oil is reflected in biblical-liturgical symbolism and has the specific value of expressing the anointing of the Spirit who heals, enlightens, comforts, and consecrates the whole body of the Church, imbuing it with gifts and charisms." The anointing of the sick with oil signifies the grace of the Holy Spirit who heals and comforts them.

II. Who Receives and Who Administers This Sacrament?

This sacrament is for the gravely ill who are in danger of death (see n. 1514). They need the grace of the Anointing of the Sick precisely when they begin to be in danger of death. If the sacrament is deferred to the final moments before death, the sick person is deprived of precious supernatural help that he or she needs not just at the end of life but also during the whole course of that grave illness. If the underlying condition does not entail the danger of death but brings only great suffering, a person is not a candidate for receiving the Anointing of the Sick. However, they are not deprived of the other sacraments, so they can always have recourse to the Eucharist and to Penance. Old age, insofar as it does not carry a danger of death, does not constitute a serious illness per se. Age criteria is not relevant: this sacrament is particularly for the sick, not for those in old age or in retirement age when people can still be in good health.

To receive this sacrament, a person must still be alive. Once the soul is separated from the body, it can no longer receive anything for its mortal remains. Sacraments belong to the current pilgrim Church on earth, so people who have concluded their journey on earth cannot approach it. In addition, the sick person also needs to be baptized. A person who has not been configured to Christ through the seal of Baptism and has not been incorporated into his mystical body cannot take part in the Church's sacramental actions. Sacramental actions have no value or significance for that person.

The Anointing of the Sick is not repeated for the same illness (see n. 1515) because the spiritual effects of the sacraments are conferred to configure the sick person to Christ's redemptive passion and to assist him or her in overcoming the difficulty of a particular illness. If someone's illness subsequently gets worse, the sacrament can be repeated since the status of the illness is different. Similarly, it can be repeated if a person has a new illness that is serious.

The ministers of the Anointing of the Sick are the presbyters (see n. 1516), as indicated in James 5:14, namely, the same ministers for Penance, precisely because of the connection between these two sacraments. To the extent that the presence of the priest to comfort the sick is not limited to administering the Anointing of the Sick—he also hears their confession, brings them communion, visits and comforts them with his advice and encouragement—it will be easier for people to overcome their fears about calling for a priest to administer this sacrament when it is not always seen as a sign of imminent death.

Good dispositions on the part of the sick are very necessary since this sacrament calls for the person who receives it to be in a state of grace. This is the reason it is appropriate to have sacramental Confession normally precede the Anointing of the Sick.

III. How Is This Sacrament Celebrated?

The statements from *LG* 11 that begin the *CCC*'s presentation on this sacrament point to its ecclesial dimension (see n. 1517). Through the ministerial action of the priests, "The whole Church commends those who are ill to the suffering and glorified Lord" (n. 1499). Those who receive the spiritual fruit of this sacrament not only gain a personal advantage but also contribute to the good of the People of God. This ecclesial dimension is found in every celebration of the Anointing of the Sick, even when only the priest and the sick person participate in it. Nevertheless, the fact that the whole Church commends the sick to the Lord suggests a wider participation of the faithful as well as a celebration for sick people as a group, as long as that does not interfere with its spiritual benefit.

"The other sacraments…are tied together with the Eucharist and are directed toward it" (PO 5). The Anointing of the Sick is no exception. In fact, the configuration to Christ suffering in his redemptive passion that is specific to this sacrament disposes the sick to unite themselves more to Christ, our Passover who was slain (see 1 Cor 5:7), and to participate in his passage from this world to the Father (see Jn 13:1).

Among the different elements of the celebration, the essential part is the anointing with oil accompanied by the celebrant's words that constitute a prayer of the Church on behalf of the sick person (see n. 1531).

IV. The Effects of the Celebration of This Sacrament

The Anointing of the Sick, along with Penance, is a sacrament for the "healing of the soul" (n. 1520). The grace of the Holy Spirit that strengthens the sick against temptations also heals them of the residue of sin (see *DS* 1696), that is, it heals them of the sickness of sin from which they still need to recover through Penance. This connection to Penance means that the forgiveness of sins a sick person could not obtain through the sacrament of Reconciliation is now given through the Anointing of the Sick (see n. 1532). According to James, "if [the sick person] has committed sins, he will be forgiven" (5:15). The acts of the penitent (contrition, confession, and satisfaction) are part of the sacrament of Penance, but it can happen that the sick person, because of frailty (or even loss of consciousness), is not able to perform them. He or she can instead receive forgiveness as a fruit of the Anointing of the Sick, as long as grace is not blocked by a stubbornly hostile will but finds instead habitual repentance, even if it is imperfect contrition, called attrition (see n. 1453).

The sick are "in a certain way...consecrated" (n. 1521). We normally speak of a person's consecration in reference to the sacramental seal received from certain sacraments (see n. 1121), which constitutes a participation in Christ's consecration, depending on the essential modality of a given sacrament. Jesus Christ is the one "whom the Father consecrated and sent into the world" (Jn 10:36) with a mission that included his redemptive passion. Jesus who suffered and died on the cross is the Suffering Servant, the One anointed by the Father in the Holy Spirit. In this case, through this anointing, the sick are configured to the Christ who suffers so that they can unite themselves to his passion and death. Even though this anointing does not confer an indelible mark, it can easily be understood and described in terms of consecration at least, as the *CCC* says, "in a certain way."

V. Viaticum, The Last Sacrament of the Christian

Whether it be the three sacraments of Christian initiation or the sacrament that concludes the earthly journey, the sacraments have a proper sequence. Just as Confirmation perfects the initial action of Baptism and disposes a person to the Eucharist in which Christian initiation culminates, so too the Anointing of the Sick brings to completion the purification from sin through Penance and disposes the faithful to a perfect union with Christ in Eucharistic communion, the sacrament of passage from this world to the Father (see n. 1524).

Chapter Three, Article 6:

THE SACRAMENT OF HOLY ORDERS

Philip Goyret

The *CCC* briefly introduces the discussion of this third group of sacraments within the general context of the other sacraments (see nn. 1534–1535). Whereas the sacraments of initiation ground the vocation of a Christian in holiness and evangelization and confer the necessary grace, the sacraments of Holy Orders and of Matrimony "are directed towards the salvation of others" (n. 1534). All of the sacraments of course contribute either to personal salvation or to the salvation of others in some way, but each of these two sacraments has an essential principle and significance that reduces a person's choice to one or the other of these possibilities.

For these "sacraments of service," "*particular consecrations*" (n. 1535) are added to the general consecration conferred by Baptism and Confirmation. They are "particular" either because they are not meant for every one or because they confer an ability and an orientation for a particular mission. On this basis, we can say of spouses they are, "as it were, consecrated" (n. 1535). In this case, however, there is not an indelible sacramental character, also called consecration, but an indissoluble marital bond that constitutes a vocation to Christian life and to mission, particularly in regard to children, that is carried out by the spouses together.

The Sacrament of Holy Orders

In harmony with Vatican II (see *LG* 19–21), the discussion begins with noting that apostolic succession is the cardinal element of Holy Orders, and that is why it is called "the sacrament of apostolic ministry" (n. 1536).

I. Why Is This Sacrament Called "Orders"?

The etymology of the words "order" and "ordination" is not to be confused with the origin of the theological reality they indicate. Holy Orders, its structure, and the act by which someone is constituted a deacon, a priest, or a bishop are not modelled on the practices of imperial Rome (which had senatorial, military, etc., orders). They come from biblical revelation and, more specifically, from the constitution of the apostolic college and its succession. The foundational intention for the Church and her ministers in that succession includes not only the sacrament of Holy Orders in three degrees but also its exercise within a ministerial communion. Therefore, the generic name "order" was chosen, which "in Roman antiquity designated an established civil body" (n. 1537).

Through ordination a candidate is consecrated for his respective order. That could seem obvious, but we need to note, as the *CCC* does, that the ordination is by nature a sacramental reality distinct from election, delegation, or installation. The words "ordination" and "consecration" do not always imply sacramentality (as in the case for the minor orders of the Eastern rite and the consecration of virgins). Up until now there has not been any uniform terminology for distinguishing these situations. Vatican II uses the words "consecration" and "ordination" interchangeably for both bishops and priests. In the Latin Rite currently in effect, the word "ordination" is used exclusively for the conferment of the episcopate, the presbyterate, and the diaconate, while the words "blessing," "consecration," "institution," and "dedication" are applied to abbots/abbesses, consecrated virgins, readers, and acolytes and to churches and altars; there are also "blessings" for objects and places.

II. The Sacrament of Holy Orders in the Economy of Salvation

The Priesthood of the Old Covenant

The Levitical priest appears as an essential element in the history of the people of Israel. The configuration of the twelve tribes as a true people actually occurs in the reception of the Mosaic Law and the institution of the priesthood near Mt. Sinai. It is clear that this priesthood is merely a prefiguration of the new priesthood, and, therefore, it is not the first phase from which the priesthood of the New Covenant would evolve. The ancient priesthood, although instituted at God's initiative, involved a mediation that was incomplete. In a certain sense the relationship between the Israelites and YHWH, with Old Testament priests as intermediaries, was constituted essentially as an ascending movement of human beings to God, and so it did not involve real justification, although it was intrinsically connected to justification because of the people's faith in the Messiah who was to come.

Nevertheless, it was a true priesthood: through its sacrificial cult it offered YHWH the worship owed to him, and it proclaimed faith in the Messiah to come. As a prefiguration of the future priesthood, it is not, therefore, to be undervalued, and the current liturgy of ordination in the Latin Rite for all its three degrees refers to it in the context of salvation history.

The One Priesthood of Christ

In the Letter to the Hebrews we find mention of the prefigurative aspect of the Levitical priesthood, but Christ's priesthood is presented as a priesthood according to the order of Melchizedek, the priest of the Most High God, who was prior to the Levitical priesthood and was "without father or mother or genealogy" (Heb 7:3). The character of Christ as priest is described as unique (no priest exists outside of him), as perennial (he lives forever), as universal (he is the mediator not just for one people but for all human beings), and as sacrificial (he made one unique sacrifice for all of humanity). His sacrificial character signifies not only his function of offering sacrifice but of becoming a sacrifice: the offering and the one who offers it coincide in his Person.

The uniqueness of Christ's priesthood has been reaffirmed recently by the Church's Magisterium in the 2000 Declaration *Dominus Iesus* by the Congregation of the Doctrine of the Faith, although it does not explicitly use the word "priesthood." It affirms "the unicity and universality of the salvific mediation of Jesus Christ" (n. 16). This uniqueness, broadly understood, leads necessarily to understanding the priestly ministry as a participation in the priesthood of Christ because there is no other priesthood. We cannot then think of an autonomous priesthood that is independent of Christ's priesthood, and this significant uniqueness is emphasized in Catholic theology.

Two Participations in the One Priesthood of Christ

Similarly, the common priesthood shared by the faithful, which comes from Baptism and Confirmation, is a participation in the priesthood of Christ and is never independent from it. Although common priesthood and ministerial priesthood share in this unique priesthood of Christ, there exists an essential difference between them that cannot be considered as merely an incremental increase (see *LG* 10). Ministerial priesthood is not a development of the common priesthood as if it were its intensification, because each of the two priesthoods comes directly from Christ's priesthood. This doctrine has many implications in the spiritual and ministerial spheres: the ministry of priesthood is not to be thought of as the crowning of Christian life and even less as a right. It presupposes, of course, the common priesthood, but it is a completely free gift for the good of the community.

It can be said of these two forms of participatory priesthood, using the expression from *LG* 10, that they "are ordered one to another." Ordained ministry is in fact related to common priesthood since it exists to help form it through the preaching of the word of God and the celebration of sacraments in order to advance the mission of the Church. For the ordained minister, then, service is not simply a spiritual attitude suitable for his progress in holiness, it is also a theological reality and an ecclesiastical necessity. That is why it is called "ministerial." A priest who is not dedicated to service betrays his identity.

The structure of the ordained ministry itself—consisting in the three levels of diaconate, presbyterate, and episcopate (received in that order)—is modelled on this ministerial sequence and accounts for the fact that the sacramental diaconate does not cease with presbyteral ordination or episcopal ordination. One can expect that presbyteral and eventually episcopal functions are also exercised as services. This is demonstrated liturgically by having the bishop wear the diaconal dalmatic (usually of light material) under the chasuble when celebrating the pontifical rite.

At the same time, however, we need to take note that in the Church, which is an episcopal church, a hierarchical authority exists within the ordained ministry that is ascribed primarily to the bishops who are then assisted by priests and deacons. From this perspective, the common priesthood, which is not hierarchical, is in turn ordered toward ministerial priesthood. This reciprocal ordering constitutes the engine that drives the Church's mission.

In the Person of Christ the Head

In order to specify the characteristic trait of the ministerial priesthood better, the *CCC* does not hesitate to return to the phrase "*agire in persona Christi Capitis*" ("to act in the person of Christ the Head")—a legacy from the scholastic sacramentary but actually coined by the Church Fathers in their commentaries on the Psalms, especially concerning their inspired authors. It thus aims to emphasize the strong sense of instrumental causality in ministerial action. When the priest exercises his ministry, the true agent of those actions is Christ himself ("I absolve you..."; "This is my Body...") whereas the minister's role is exclusively that of instrumentality. The presence of Christ the Head is thus made visible to the faithful in a way that is free of any possible subjective interpretation.

We need to clarify, however, that the theological reality of acting "in the person of Christ" has an analogical dimension, so the *CCC* very accurately adds that "the power of the Holy Spirit does not guarantee all the acts of the minister in the same way" (n. 1550). Concretely, whereas the presence of Christ is guaranteed in sacramental ministry even in the case of unworthy ministers, the human condition of the minister can leave its traces in his preaching and pastoral guidance that could be obstacles to the grace being conferred. To clarify this distinction in the guarantee of Christ's presence in ministerial actions, the phrase *repraesentatio Christi* is used for the minister when he preaches and governs, and the phrase *in persona Christi* is reserved exclusively for his function in sacramental liturgy.

We also need to add that in the diaconate ministry there is no acting *in persona Christi* in the true sense, even though deacons act *auctoritate Christi*, "with the authority of Christ." Therefore, the *CCC*, in discussing the hierarchical constitution of the Church, takes this distinction into account: "Bishops and priests receive the mission and faculty ("the sacred power") to act *in persona Christi Capitis*; deacons receive the strength to serve the people of God in the *diaconia* of liturgy, word, and charity, in communion with the bishop and his presbyterate" (n. 875; see n. 1588).

"In the name of the whole Church"

Besides making Christ present to the Church, ministerial priesthood acts "in the name of the whole Church" because the minister presents the prayers and the worship of the Church to God (n. 1553). The *CCC* makes it a point to dismiss any possible perception that this ministry is the delegation of a power that originally belonged to the community and was only later entrusted to the minister. The ordained minister represents the Church, the Body of Christ, because he represents its Head, Christ. In the words of John Paul II, "The priest's relation to the Church is inscribed in the very relation which the priest has to Christ, such that the 'sacramental representation' to Christ serves as the basis and inspiration for the relation of the priest to the Church" (*PVD* 16). This refers to the fundamental aspect of priesthood, understood on the basis of biblical data, as a participation in the salvific mediation of Christ, a mediation that is both "ascending" and "descending." The "descending" aspect, in which God comes to human beings to offer them salvation, is decidedly the most important. Nevertheless, human beings who respond to and accept this offer through their worship and charity also present themselves to God through the priesthood of Christ made visible in his ministers. The *repraesentatio Ecclesiae* ("representative of the Church") makes possible the "ascending" priestly movement from human beings to God and is manifested in a particular way in the Eucharistic liturgy.

Because the priesthood exists "in the Church and on behalf of the Church" (*PDV* 15), it will always be exercised within a hierarchical and ministerial communion: in the episcopal college for bishops, and in the diocesan presbyterate for priests presided over by their bishop. At the same time being a minister "on behalf of the Church" is reflected in the universal dimension of the priesthood that corresponds to the inherited apostolic mission, which is also universal. The priest offers himself to the whole Church, to all human beings without discrimination, even if he is actually performing his mission within a given community.

III. The Three Degrees of the Sacrament of Holy Orders

Although there is an essential difference between common priesthood and ministerial priesthood that does not involve degrees, we do find degrees of participation in the priesthood of Christ within the ministerial priesthood. With episcopal ordination, "high priesthood" is conferred in its fullness, obviously not in a way that exhausts the whole reality of Christ's priesthood but because there is no possibility of any higher participation (see n. 1557). The priesthood also confers a participation in Christ's priesthood in the ministerial sphere, but it occurs "in a lesser degree" (*PO* 2), that is, in a partial and not a full way. The diaconate is not a third degree of priesthood in this sense, but it certainly belongs to Holy Orders and is at the service of the other ministers and of the whole Church, so it can certainly be correctly described as participation in Christ's priesthood in the line of ministry.

The text that introduces this section of the *CCC* states, "The divinely instituted ecclesiastical ministry is exercised in different degrees by those who even from ancient times have been called bishops, priests, and deacons" (n. 1554; see *LG* 28). This goes back to the *Decree on the Sacraments of Holy Orders* from the Council of Trent whose sixth canon states, "If anyone says, that, [sic] there is not a hierarchy by divine ordination, consisting of bishops, priests and ministers, let him be anathema." In the way this canon articulates it, not only the existence of Holy Orders but also its tripartite sacramental structure belongs to the faith. The Eastern rite additionally has minor orders and a subdiaconate, but they are not sacramental in nature.

In describing each of the degrees, the *CCC* follows Vatican II in which the episcopate is the original and foundational reality while the presbyterate and diaconate are derived from it. We need to keep in mind that the institution of Holy Orders by Christ occurred with the institution of the college of apostles, with bishops as their successors. We could say that Christ instituted the episcopate when he instituted the apostolate of the Twelve who, through the laying on of hands, then transmitted what could be transmitted of their office to the bishops. Next, the apostles as well as the bishops transmitted their function in a subordinate way to priests and deacons as seen in the New Testament. This apostolic practice goes back to the foundational will of Christ in the whole New Testament revelation. Therefore it is relevant to affirm the divine institution, although in diverse ways, of the episcopate, presbyterate, and diaconate.

Episcopal Ordination—Fullness of the Sacrament of Holy Orders

More concretely, in regard to the episcopate, the *CCC*, always following Vatican II, presents the origin of the episcopate within the framework of apostolic succession. The text refers to the central passage of *LG* that affirms that among the various offices in the early Church, "the chief place, according to the witness of tradition, is held by the function of those who, through their appointment to the dignity and responsibility of the bishop, and in virtue consequently of the unbroken succession going back to the beginning, are regarded as transmitters of the apostolic line" (n. 1555; see *LG* 20). These few words condense the whole biblical and historical testimony reported in the Council document (see Acts 20:20–21, 28; 1 Tim 5:17; 2 Tim 2:2, 4:5; Tit 1:5; Clement of Rome, Tertullian, Irenaeus of Lyon). We need to take note of these testimonies because while the institution of the apostolate of the Twelve is undeniable for those who believe the Gospels, their succession is not so evident. What causes hesitation is the absence in the New Testament of the phrase and even the concept of "apostolic succession." However, the "reality" of succession is instead very present and is precisely what the testimonies indicate.

If we want to understand the topic better, we also need to take note of the "rationale" for apostolic succession that *LG* speaks about: "That divine mission, entrusted by Christ to the apostles, will last until the end of the world [Mt 28:20], since the Gospel they are to teach is for all time the source of all life for the Church. And for this reason the apostles, appointed as rulers in this society, took care to appoint successors" (n. 20). The key to the argument is in the meaning of "Gospel." It is not simply a written document handed down without any need for bishops but is "for all time the source of all life for the Church." According to Paul, the Gospel is "the power of God for salvation to every one who has faith" (Rom 1:16). It is the living and life-giving word of God that is proclaimed (through preaching) and celebrated (in the liturgy) to dispense its whole salvific power. It is thus transmitted and incarnated in the personal testimony of the Church's ministers and above all the bishops. Episcopal succession carries on the apostolic tradition whose content is precisely "the Gospel they are to teach."

The content of the function carried out in episcopal succession is such that it necessarily requires a sacramental nature because the ordinary Christian condition does not have the capacity to transmit the Gospel in the modality just mentioned. Here too the *CCC* follows the thinking of the Council in indicating the significant relationship between succession and the sacramentality of the episcopate. In the words of *LG*, "the apostles were enriched by Christ with a special outpouring of the Holy Spirit coming upon them [see Acts 1:8, 2:4; Jn 20:22], and they passed on this spiritual gift to their helpers by the imposition of hands [see 1 Tim 4:14; 2 Tim 1:6–7], and it has been transmitted down to us in Episcopal consecration" (n. 21). This "imposition of hands" does not just involve the simple assignment of an office but the transmission of a spiritual gift in view of fulfilling the mission entrusted to them, and we call it "sacramental" precisely because it is a spiritual reality transmitted through a visible sign. The sacramental nature of the episcopate was defined in the Church's Magisterium for the first time by Vatican II (see *LG* 21).

Important details are added regarding the sacramentally transmitted episcopal function. On the one hand, together with the office of sanctifying (for example, the power to ordain), it includes the offices of teaching and governing, which make these offices much more substantial than being merely administrative functions. Concerning the offices of teaching and governing, we need to remember that by their very nature they "can be exercised only in hierarchical communion with the head and the members of the college" (*LG* 21). This is not the case with the office of sanctifying, which can occur among bishops who are not Catholic and whose episcopate is recognized as valid by the Catholic Church, just as their other ministerial functions (like Ordination, Confirmation, Eucharist, etc.) are also considered valid.

On the other hand, in episcopal ordination the sacramental character of bishops is "so impressed, that bishops in an eminent and visible way sustain the roles of Christ Himself as Teacher, Shepherd, and High Priest, and that they act in His person" (*LG* 21). There is an ontological-sacramental capacity that is characteristic of bishops, indicated by the phrase "in an eminent way," which goes beyond that of ordinary priests and largely explains reserving certain actions, like sacramental ordinations, for bishops. We should also remember that even if a priest may administer Confirmation in special circumstances (through a designated faculty and other cases) and in Eastern rites, he can do it validly only by using chrism consecrated by the bishop. That is why *LG* calls bishops "the original ministers" of Confirmation (n. 26).

Finally, the collegiate nature of the episcopate is affirmed not just as exclusively juridical but also as sacramental. With episcopal ordination, a priest becomes a bishop in the episcopal college. Becoming a bishop and a member of the college constitutes a unique effect of the sacrament. In other words, he is a bishop together with other bishops. Naturally the status of being a member of the college involves being in hierarchical communion with the head of the college and its members. In a case in which this communion does not exist, the sacramental status of a bishop would be detached from his collegial status and would constitute a serious anomaly, even if it does not affect the validity of his episcopal ordination.

Episcopal ordination is exclusively a task for bishops, and it was already prescribed in the ancient world that it be performed by at least three bishops. The collegiate nature of the episcopate is demonstrated liturgically this way so that the new candidate is received by a body represented by three ordaining bishops. It is even recommended that all the bishops present take part in the ordination. This practice involves two points that deserve to be noted. On the one hand, with at least three witnesses the validity of the conferred ordination is greatly ensured, and this is important in any church with an episcopal structure like the Catholic Church. On the other hand, the simultaneous presence of three ministers best guarantees the sacramental validity of the ordination in the potential case that one of the three consecrating bishops had not been validly ordained.

These considerations lead to a better understanding of apostolic succession. At times it is understood in the sense of successive ordinations analogous to links in a chain: it reaches from the apostles down to each of the current bishops. From a historical point of view, in fact, every bishop could trace his episcopate back to the original apostles, going back up the "chain." Nevertheless, theology and history show us that this topic is more nuanced. On the one hand, at least until recent times (before the retirement of older bishops established by Paul VI), it was not customary for a bishop to ordain his successor. In addition, the fact that ordinations were conferred in ancient times by at least three ordaining ministers means that episcopal succession is formed not as links that make up a chain but as a tight net. Even more important, when we look at the topic from an ecclesial perspective, the apostolic-episcopal succession does not occur from one bishop to another but from one college to another: the episcopal college succeeds the apostolic college.

Since becoming a bishop means becoming a member of the college, the legitimacy of episcopal ordination always requires the intervention of the bishop of Rome, who is the head of the episcopal college. In the Latin Rite, this intervention consists in the pontifical mandate to proceed with an ordination (see *CIC*, can. 1013). In the case of an ordination without this mandate, the ordaining bishop and the ordinand incur *latae sententiae* excommunication, automatic excommunication (see *CIC*, can. 1382). In addition it is necessary to have the nomination of the bishop by the pope prior to his ordination although there are particular cases of legitimate election in which the role of the Roman Pontiff is only that of confirming the election (see *CIC*, can. 377, 1). In Eastern rites a legitimate mandate from the Roman Pontiff, the Patriarch, or the Metropolitan is necessary (see *CCEO*, can. 745).

The primary function of the bishop is to be the head of a local church as its legitimate pastor. The *CCC* notes that this function must always be combined with a concern for the whole Church since his status as a member of the episcopal college involves that as well. Furthermore, the bishop governs his own church as a member of the college: he makes the universal Church present in his own particular church and governs it in harmony with the bishop of Rome and other bishops. This is a significant consequence of the bi-dimensional structure of both the episcopate and the Church. On the one hand, it is necessary to affirm with St. Cyprian that "the episcopate is one, each part of which is held by the bishop for the whole" (*On the Unity of the Church*, 5). On the other hand, there exists a rapport between each particular church and the universal Church of "mutual interiority" ("Some Aspects of the Church as Communion," n. 9, May 28, 1992): in every particular church "the one, holy, apostolic of Christ is truly present and operative" (*CD*, 11). The episcopate and the Church interpenetrate each other and extend reciprocally in both directions.

The Ordination of Priests—Co-workers of the Bishops

The *CCC*, always following Vatican II, proceeds with a discussion of the presbyterate by anchoring it to the consecration and mission of Christ, that is, to the aspects of his priesthood that the apostles and their successors the bishops participate in and that priests participate in as well, although in a subordinate degree. Priests do not participate in the priesthood of their bishop but in the priesthood of Christ even though they are meant to perform their duties as "co-workers of the episcopal order" (*PO* 2). The following summarizes the characteristics of the presbyteral function: it is a participation in the priesthood of Christ that is not full and is to be exercised subordinately to the bishops as their co-workers in view of the "proper fulfillment of the apostolic mission entrusted to priests" (*PO* 2). It is to be noted that priests are not successors of the apostles even though they participate in the apostolic mission. On the other hand, we can say that the mission that is moved forward through apostolic succession is carried out by bishops who are assisted by priests (and by deacons).

This explanation overcomes the troublesome problem about the distinction between the episcopate and the presbyterate that was present for many centuries. In the fifth century a theological tradition began with St. Jerome who denied the sacramentality of the episcopate. According to that famous biblical scholar, one could conclude, in analyzing some New Testament texts (see Tit 1:7; Phil 1:1; Acts 20:28; Heb 13:17; 1 Pet 5:1–2), that "presbyters are the same as bishops" ("Epistle 146," 1). With Jerome having dismissed the sacramental difference, the distinction between the two *orders* had to be found elsewhere: in the level of dignity, or in jurisdictional authority, or in the power to ordain and confirm. These criteria are deficient, however, or at least insufficient. While a difference is self-evident in the first criterion, in terms of jurisdictional power (which is theoretically present for the bishop and absent for the presbyter), the mission performed by bishops is far greater than its jurisdictional aspect. There are also actual cases of priests with more jurisdictional authority than that of many bishops. The *potestas confermandi* ("power to confirm") is also not a decisive criterion, as was already explained in the cases in which Confirmation may be conferred by a priest. The *potestas ordinandi* ("power to ordain") could possibly be considered a criterion for the distinction, but it is not exempt from drawbacks since it raises questions about some minor historical cases of ordination conferred simply by priests. Vatican II returns the episcopate to the sacramental sphere and marks its distinction from the presbyterate in three significant areas of their interrelationship: the episcopate is priestly fullness while the presbyterate is priesthood on a subordinate level; the bishops are successors of the apostles while the priests participate in the apostolic mission but are not successors of the apostles; and the primary function of the bishop is to be the head of a particular church while the function of the presbyterate is to cooperate with the episcopal function.

The priest's function is described more specifically by the *CCC* following *LG* 28: "they are consecrated in order to preach the Gospel and shepherd the faithful as well as to celebrate divine worship as *true priests of the New Testament*" (n. 1564). They act *in persona Christi Capitis* ("in the person of Christ the Head") and with his authority. Divine worship, and more concretely the celebration of the Eucharist, has an absolute centrality: we could say that someone becomes a priest in view of the Eucharistic celebration. This is not an issue that pertains only to spiritual life but is also key to the pastoral and missional dynamic of the Church. In fact, "The other sacraments, as well as with every ministry of the Church and every work of the apostolate, are tied together with the Eucharist and are directed toward it.... The Eucharist shows itself as the source and the apex of the whole work of preaching the Gospel" (*PO* 5). The centrality of the Eucharist exists not only on the institutional level but also and above all in the lives of the faithful. The entire lives of Christians are intended to be inserted into the Eucharist to become an offering acceptable to God. In the words of *LG* about lay people, let us recall that "All their works, prayers and apostolic endeavors, their ordinary married and family life, their daily occupations, their mental and physical relaxation, if carried out in the Spirit and even the hardships of life, if patiently borne—all these become 'spiritual sacrifices acceptable to God through Jesus Christ' [1 Pet 2:5]. Together with the offering of the Lord's body, they are most fittingly offered in the celebration of the Eucharist" (n. 34).

Concerning presbyteral life, the *CCC* describes two important characteristics. First, the priests in a particular church constitute one single presbyterate dependent on the bishop. This dependence, hierarchical in nature and with juridical implications, originates from the very office of priests who are "prudent cooperators with the episcopal order" (*LG* 28). As a consequence of this dogmatic fact in the ministerial sphere, this "dependence" is not only in the juridical sphere but first and foremost in the sacramental and ecclesial spheres. In a certain way, presbyters make their bishop present to the community of the faithful and accomplish the apostolic mission together with him.

Second, priests relate within the presbyterate according to "a sacramental brotherhood," a significant phrase the *CCC* takes from Vatican II (see *PO* 8). In addition to its liturgical manifestations (like the laying on of hands in presbyteral ordination or concelebration of the Eucharist), the brotherhood is lived out as a family. A priest's first responsibility is to his brother priests: visit the sick, support the weakest ones, pray for them, help each another, be in harmony in the discharge of pastoral duties, etc. In short, they need to live in communion, whether ministerial or existential, in such a way as to implement the Lord's command, "A new commandment I give to you, that you love one another; even as I have loved you, that you also love one another. By this all men will know that you are my disciples if you have love for one another" (Jn 13:34–35).

The Ordination of Deacons—"in order to serve"

As to the diaconate, the *CCC*, following the doctrine of Vatican II here as well, reaffirms that the diaconate is a reality in the hierarchical sphere that derives from the sacrament of Holy Orders. This is an important affirmation because sometimes it is not easy to detect the difference between the deacon's functions and the exercise of some of those functions by the non-ordained faithful. Therefore, a special effort is called for to return to the specific theological nature of the diaconate.

On this topic, the *CCC* references the famous phrase from *LG* 29 about the imposition of hands on the deacons "*non ad sacerdotium sed ad ministerium*": "not unto the priesthood, but unto the ministry" (n. 1569). This is taken from the *Constitutiones Ecclesiae Aegyptacae* (*Egyptian Church Order*), an ancient fourth-century document that was influenced by *On the Apostolic Tradition* at the beginning of the third century attributed to Hippolytus of Rome. If one reads the phrase literally, the diaconate would remain outside the ministerial priesthood and that could sound reasonable since the deacon cannot offer the Eucharistic sacrifice. However, the diaconate's absolute exclusion from priestly ministry would mean its ministry derives from the common priesthood since that is the only other possibility. That conclusion must absolutely be rejected since it has been well established that the diaconate does not flow from Baptism (and Confirmation) but from Holy Orders. Although the deacon is not a priest (because he does not consecrate), we can assert that the diaconate is a participation in the priesthood of Christ in the ministerial line. This is not just word play here. We need to remember that the priesthood of Christ, beyond its worship component, also includes a prophetic and royal aspect, and it is from this perspective (as well as some non-Eucharistic aspects like baptismal ministry) that we speak of diaconal participation in the priesthood of Christ.

The *CCC* reaffirms the sacramental character of Holy Orders for the deaconate as the effect of ordination. It does not involve, as it does for priests and bishops, the capacity to act *in persona Christi Capitis* (and that is why deacons cannot consecrate). However, it does allow the deacon to perform his ministry as a *repraesentatio Christi* ("representative of Christ") in such a way that the true agent of this function is Christ himself. Through him Christ makes himself a deacon for everyone. This is the case when deacons preach, when they practice charity toward the poor, when they assist bishops and priests in the liturgy, when they baptize or assist in marriage or preside over a funeral, and when they perform still other services.

The permanent diaconate was restored to the Church by Vatican II. Earlier during the first half of the first millennium, this order was held in great honor, culminating in the third and fourth centuries with great saints like St. Lawrence and St. Vincent Saragossa. During the second half of that millennium, however, it gradually disappeared and remained only as a step toward the presbyterate. At the Council of Trent there was a slight attempt to restore it—in the context of minor orders and subdeacons—but it was only after Vatican II that the diaconate succeeded in becoming an established reality in local churches and also became open to married men.

The complex and specific theological ordering of the diaconate requires a particularly careful formation for candidates to the permanent deaconate so that its exercise remains in the authentically ministerial sphere. The works of charity, highlighted in the account in Acts 6 when deacons were instituted to care for the widows' tables, must be at the center of their ministry without, however, becoming merely social services. Their preaching is carried out *auctoritate Christi* ("with the authority of Christ") and is more than just "a talk." Their liturgical duties are not the same as those of other assistants in a church service. Ultimately the diaconate ministry makes Christ present to the community of the faithful even if it is not through the typical characteristics of Eucharistic ministry.

IV. The Celebration of This Sacrament

The *CCC* describes the liturgy of ordination with a wonderful summary and complete overview, so not many comments are needed here. The *CCC* lists the essential elements of the diverse ritual traditions: the laying on of hands by the ordaining bishop on the head of the ordinand and the prayer of consecration specific to the degree conferred. It distinguishes these from the elements that do not constitute part of the sacramental sign but that can help us better understand the mystery celebrated. This distinction between the essential and the non-essential aspects was stipulated once and for all by Pope Pius XII in his Apostolic Constitution *Sacramentum ordinis* in 1947. Prior to its publication, people were uncertain whether or not the so-called *traditio strumentorum* ("handing over the objects of the office) was part of the essential core of the sacrament: the handing over of the Gospels to the deacon and the bishop, and the handing over of the paten and the chalice to the priest. Pope Pius XII clarified the issue without diminishing the appropriateness (and the obligation) of respecting the prescribed non-essential elements. According to him in that document, "What we have above declared and provided is by no means to be understood in the sense that it be permitted even in the slightest detail to neglect or omit the other rites which are prescribed in the *Roman Pontifical*" (n. 6).

V. Who Can Confer This Sacrament?

Solus episcopus: only the bishop (validly ordained) may validly confer Holy Orders in its three degrees of episcopate, presbyterate, and diaconate. According to the New Testament revelation and the life of the early Church, it was the apostles and their successor bishops who laid hands on candidates to continue their ministry on different levels. From the very beginning the Church understood herself to be bound to this practice and considered it always to be binding insofar as it went back to the foundational design of the Church. It is therefore consistent that "the sacrament of apostolic ministry" be conferred by the successors of the apostles in their ministry, namely, the bishops. Given the importance of guaranteeing the fitness of the ordinands and the validity of the ordination performed, Canon Law provides that the consecrating bishop be the bishop of the candidates to the diaconate or presbyterate or that he receive legitimate dimissorial letters (see *CIC*, can. 1015, 1) and that all three categories of ordination are duly registered in the curia of the place in which the ordination occurs (see *CIC*, can. 1053, 1). As we have said, a pontifical mandate is needed for the legitimacy of episcopal ordinations.

VI. Who Can Receive This Sacrament?

Solus vir baptizatus ("only a baptized male") may validly receive ordination (*CIC*, can. 1024). It is of course also necessary for the candidate to have the desire to be ordained, namely, that there is full understanding on his part and the absence of coercion. In fact the Church takes care to ascertain in advance that the ordination will be received on the part of the candidate "of his own accord and freely" (*CIC*, can. 1036).

The stipulation of being baptized is easily understandable, but it is also necessary to certify that fact with appropriate documentation to avoid the risk of possible cases of invalidity (see *CIC*, can. 1050, 3). As to the candidate being male, we need, on the one hand, to distinguish the "fundamental reasons" from the theological reasons and, on the other hand, to consider the degrees of episcopate and presbyterate as distinct from that of the diaconate.

As the recent post-conciliar Magisterium affirms, the "fundamental reasons" to reserve Holy Orders exclusively for men include "the example recorded in the Sacred Scriptures of Christ choosing his Apostles only from among men; the constant practice of the Church, which has imitated Christ in choosing only men; and her living teaching authority which has consistently held that the exclusion of women from the priesthood is in accordance with God's plan for his Church" (John Paul II, *OS*, 1). To understand these reasons we need to keep in mind that Jesus acted in full freedom without letting himself be influenced by the mindset and customs of time and place. This is evident in other aspects of his life, like in his attitude toward women and his relationship with publicans and sinners. The apostles understood themselves to be bound by Jesus' practice and chose only men as their successors, even though the early Christian community included many women who were more faithful than the men, not the least of which was Mary most holy. This position by the apostles remained unchanged even in geographical locations where the ordination of women would not have caused a problem because of the existence of priestesses in other religions there. The sub-apostolic and patristic traditions continued this practice, recognizing it as a permanent apostolic practice. When considering these arguments as a whole, John Paul II declared and established that "the Church has no authority whatsoever to confer priestly ordination on women and that this judgment is to be definitively held by all the Church's faithful" (*OS* 4).

The rationale for reserving ordination exclusively for men does not, therefore, come from any hypothetical misogyny but from a tradition that goes back to Jesus and is thus held to be binding. We can add to this that the characteristic *repraesentatio sacramentalis Christi* of ministerial priesthood, in terms of "signifying" or "representing" Christ, is correctly performed by a man and not by a woman because of the unambiguous fact that the Son of God was incarnated as a male: Christ was and remains a man. In addition, the spousal significance of priesthood is not to be underestimated: the salvation transmitted through it, in fact, is revealed under the privileged image of a marriage between Christ and the Church. The love of the Bridegroom is present to the Church, the Bride, through ministerial priesthood: it can be signified only by a minister who is male. Finally, we need to remember that women do not have access to priesthood for the same reason that men do not have this right either: the priesthood is an absolutely undeserved gift and is not configured as a development of baptismal priesthood and even less as its crowning.

The "fundamental reasons" mentioned above and John Paul II's declaration apply to "priestly ordination," that is, to the episcopate and presbyterate levels. Now we need to address the question of the admissibility or not of women to the sacramental diaconate. At first sight, the answer would seem to be positive, since Romans 16:1 speaks of "our sister Phoebe, a deaconess of the Church at Cenchreae" and the grammar of 1 Timothy 3:8–13 allows for hypothesizing the presence of women as candidates for the diaconate. We even find various documents from the ancient Eastern tradition that attest the presence of deaconesses (the third-century *Didascalia Apostolorum*; canon 19 of the Council of Nicea; the fourth-century *Apostolic Constitutions* of Syria; canon 15 of the Council of Chalcedon; and still others). This tradition continued until late into the eight century. Since history has ascertained their past existence, we could possibly think of this as something to restore.

It is necessary, however, to note that the "deaconesses" mentioned in these sources were not necessarily on an equal footing with deacons in the technical sense. From a study of these sources, particularly liturgical ones, there emerges a picture of a female diaconate that is different from the male diaconate. The deaconesses performed their functions especially in the area of administering baptismal immersion for women for reasons of preserving modesty; in the area of preparing female catechumens and their anointing; and in any area in which contact between a male minister and a woman could have been the occasion for scandal especially in a society where the separation of men and women was very pronounced. The sources also reveal that deaconesses were not allowed to distribute Eucharistic communion, to give blessings, to be in the presbytery, or to preach. The totality of these characteristics means we cannot equate ancient "deaconesses" with the deacons of our day. We need to add to this the theology of ordination, which affirms the importance of the oneness of ordained ministry and applies the same arguments to the inadmissibility of women to the diaconate that were given for the episcopate and presbyterate. The Church's Magisterium, however, has not wanted to decide the question in a definitive manner until the relevant study that has been undertaken is concluded. At this time, however, there is a canonical discipline in effect that prohibits the ordination of women to the diaconate (see Congregation for the Doctrine of the Faith, *Normae de gravioribus delictis*, art. 5, 1–2).

Only those who are called may enter ministerial priesthood; it is a "vocation" from God that cannot be reduced to a professional choice and even less to an existential accommodation. This vocation finds its authentic confirmation in the invitation to ordination by the hierarchical authority, which then waits to certify the candidate's suitability, the prerequisite qualifications, and their verification.

In the Latin Church, the law of celibacy applies to the three levels of ordination with the exception of the permanent diaconate. There are also some particular cases like married ministers in other Christian communions who are received into full communion with the Catholic Church and who then desire to exercise their ministry and are re-ordained (if their ordination is not held to have been valid) without the obligation of continence. To understand this topic adequately we need to note that the call to priesthood is addressed to those who previously received the charism of celibacy from God. The rule of celibacy, more than being a requirement to renounce marriage in favor of priesthood, means the Church selects for the ministry from among only those who have received that gift. The Church is proceeding here in line with a tradition that goes back to the first centuries with the awareness that Christ himself remained celibate, dedicating his life exclusively to the mission he received from the Father. The spousal character of priesthood calls for loving the Church with an undivided heart, which also leads to fruitfulness.

The Eastern Churches follow a different legitimate discipline that permits the priesthood within the context of married life. This does not contradict what has previously been said, since the episcopate in the East—the "high priesthood" already mentioned—is reserved exclusively to celibates, and celibate priesthood is also practiced and held in great honor. The pairing of ministerial priesthood with celibacy does not come from a theoretical devaluation of married life but from the universality of the mission entrusted to the Church. Whoever is married devoutly performs the Church's mission in loving his spouse and educating his children; whoever is celibate devoutly performs the Church's mission in a wider evangelistic sphere. The diverse practices of the East and the West correspond to the diverse deployment of the degrees of ordination in the missionary order of the Church.

Finally, we need to remember that in no case—neither in the East nor in the West for diaconal, presbyteral, or episcopal degrees—is marriage allowed after ordination except in approved cases of resignation from the clerical state. The *impedimentum ordinis* ("impediment of ordination") would render the marriage invalid.

VII. The Effects of the Sacrament of Holy Orders

The Indelible Character

The *CCC* rightly reminds us that through sacramental ordination the new minister is equipped to act as a representative of Christ the Head (see n. 1581). A representative in this case is not comparable to the typical "representative" we find in social and political life and even less to a "representation" in the visual arts. It is clear from the writings of the Church Fathers that it means the real presence of the One who is being represented. During sacramental ministry, this "representative" becomes able to act *in persona Christi,* as we have said. This is included in the concept of the sacramental "character" of Holy Orders, which indicates an ontological capacity that is sacramentally received to act in this way, and that capacity remains with the minister in a permanent and indelible way. Therefore, we say, "*semel sacerdos, sempre sacerdos*": once a priest, always a priest. This means it is impossible for there to be a priesthood *ad tempus* ("for a time"), whether as a part-time activity or one that has a time limit.

We need to clarify that in the case of an ordained minister who no longer exercises his ministry, whether for just cause or because of personal weaknesses, he does not thereby cease being a priest. The existence of a regulation for the dispensation of assumed obligations of ordination—which can in certain cases also prohibit the exercise of priestly functions—can in no way be considered as a termination of the sacramental reality previously conferred. It is a different case, however, if there is a declaration of nullity regarding the ordination when it is proven, for reasons that must be clearly demonstrated, that the ordination was not validly conferred.

The Grace of the Holy Spirit

There is also sacramental grace with ordination that is conferred for each degree in the liturgical formula for consecration that is meant to help each ordinand "to perform properly ecclesiastical functions" (Pius XII, *Sacramentum ordinis,* 1). For bishops it is the grace for the fullness of ministry; for priests, it is the grace to persevere in their office with great dignity; for deacons it the seven-fold gift of the Spirit to faithfully do the work of ministry (see n. 5).

Ultimately, the grace of ordination, together with the strength necessary for the efficacious carrying out of the priestly function, confers to the ordinand special assistance against temptations that can emerge during the course of his ministry. It prompts him to form the consciences of the faithful not according to his own personal opinion but according to God's will with the highest respect for people's personal freedom and responsibility. That grace provides him with pastoral prudence that gives each person what he may need at the right time. In sacramental ministry, while the indelible character of ordination guarantees the efficacy of the sacraments in themselves, the presence of grace is meant to prevent any kind of "automatic performance" of the ministry, minimizing the danger of the minister falling into a routine or of becoming a kind of "robotic dispenser" of sacraments.

Chapter Three, Article 7:
THE SACRAMENT OF MATRIMONY

Ina Siviglia

The Sacraments "at the service of communion"

The third chapter of the *CCC* correlates the sacrament of Matrimony to the sacrament of Holy Orders to avoid the ambiguity, which was quite frequent in the past, of attributing a superior significance to Holy Orders with respect to marriage. The chapter describes the points shared by the two sacraments that are both built on Christ as their cornerstone and constituted to develop communion in the Church and between the Church and the world. Both sacraments lead the faithful to holiness in diverse but equally worthy ways that converge with regard to their common goal of salvation.

Both sacraments "are directed toward the salvation of others; if they contribute as well to personal salvation, it is through service to others" (n. 1534). It is understood between the lines that this service of communion can be exercised through the equally legitimate choice of service primarily to God's people or primarily within the human family: priesthood and marriage.

Both sacraments exist for generous, freely given service to others. Obeying the call to an unconditional offer of self (see Rom 12:1) is the *conditio sine qua non* for personal salvation and, in the case of marriage, for the salvation of the couple. In both these vocations, the ecclesial subjects, on the basis of the sacraments of Christian initiation, freely prepare themselves to receive "particular *consecrations*" (n. 1535). Ordained ministers are consecrated "in Christ's name to feed the Church by the word and grace of God" (n. 1535). Christian spouses in turn are, "as it were, *consecrated* for the duties and dignity of their state by a special sacrament" (n. 1535). It is worth noting that oil, among the sacramental signs, is an unambiguous element in every consecration starting with the basic oil for Baptism. Although oil is present in ordination, it is not used in the celebration of marriage which is "like" a consecration in the sense that it calls for putting the relationship with God first as individuals and as a couple. Conjugal love, raised by Christ to the dignity of a sacrament, establishes an indissoluble nuptial union.

People who consciously live whichever of these two sacraments they receive will be able continually to call on the Christian community, since no one is saved on his or her own. In the gift of themselves, especially to someone who is more fragile, who is poorer, and who is marginalized, people can hope to present themselves together as "children of the one Father" who desires the salvation of each person so much that he sent his Son so that all might be saved.

The authors of the *CCC* have highlighted the uniqueness of the originality of marriage between a man and a woman and compared it to ordained ministry and, in nn. 1618–1620, to the special vocation of consecrated virginity that witnesses to the world the joyful awaiting of their spouse and his kingdom.

One thing is certain: whatever state of life a person chooses, each is called to convey the Gospel and proclaim it, deeply living out his or her relationship with the Lord in existential situations that are obviously diverse but always all-encompassing. Every *Christifidelis* ("faithful Christian") must choose to follow Christ, learning from friendship with him how to live in the world as a mature Christian in the faith according to the spirit of the beatitudes. Christian spouses know that the grace of this sacrament reinforces their willingness to serve others according to their ministry in the Church.

From the pastoral point of view spouses and consecrated ministers can greatly benefit from shared missionary activity: they can combine the gifts they have received and cooperate in diverse but harmonious ways in various initiatives by fully exercising their charisms, especially in the areas of evangelization and formation. Whether as priests or as Christian spouses, their ministries correspond to the charisms they received—one for the institution and one for family life—but both ministries are recognized in and by the Church. Such gifts need to be activated for the good of the community as well as for society.

Three Key Words

The experience of marriage between a man and a woman is so rich and so difficult to describe that it cannot be communicated in a single word. To build together "a partnership of the whole of life" (n. 1601) seems impossible to some and a beautiful undertaking to others, but it is hard to carry out. For those who believe in the power of the grace of this sacrament, a new horizon opens up that has something miraculous about it: everything is possible when the Lord is welcomed into the life of the couple as a companion on the journey, the way it happened for the two disciples at Emmaus.

The first three paragraphs of Article 7 adopt not one but three different words with multiple resonances to describe as fully as possible what marriage is: "covenant" (n. 1601); "mystery" (n. 1602); and "vocation" (n. 1603). These three words ultimately converge into one word that incorporates all of them and points toward that necessary and ineffable "ulterior perspective" of the infinite, of transcendence, and of eternity: the word "love" (n. 1604).

It is worthwhile to briefly review the three key words in their logical and theological order.

1. The word "vocation" immediately introduces the realm of faith. To be married "in the Lord" implies a consciousness that such a step involves a faith journey for two baptized people. They discover, in the light of shared spiritual discernment, that God is calling them to bring about a plan of love together—according to the Creator's intention "in the beginning"—that will make them more like the triune God who is Love.

The sacrament of Matrimony is considered by many to be an arrival point, but it is actually a new departure point for the journey of the life of two spouses. The ecclesial subject is no longer the individual baptized person but the couple who has become "one flesh" and who now manifests, in an analogous way, the dynamic of the Trinity, three Persons but one God.

2. The word "mystery" comes from the Greek *mysterion* (in Latin, *sacramentum*), and it has various semantic equivalents: a) it generally means something hidden and obscure; b) it deals with a visible reality that points to an invisible reality as in the case of a sacrament; c) in Pauline terminology it means the plan of God, the economy of salvation, that is hidden for centuries but revealed in history (see Eph 1:3–10). Paul's description is full of amazement: "This is a great mystery and I mean in reference to the Church" (Eph 5:32). Such an assertion gives the two spouses strength as they face a mystery that is greater than themselves. They are an integral part of that mystery, and they represent, not always consciously, its full meaning as their lives are given unconditionally to God and to others as prompted by the Holy Spirit who dwells in them and establishes them as a single reality.

From the linguistic context in n. 1062, the word "mystery" seems to mean that what is seen and experienced is partly veiled and partly unveiled for whoever has the eyes of faith. When we recognize the authenticity of a merely human love, we realize that the couple is not outside of the divine plan. However, spouses can either consider their marriage as a destination that is static and ends right where it began, or they can move beyond the encounter with the other and experience contact on a higher level with God-Love. For the person who prays with faith, especially if it a couple, true love is the window through which one glimpses and contemplates the love between the three divine Persons. The couple, attracted to that dynamic, is called to approach this mystery "with unshod feet," similar to Moses before the burning bush (see Ex 3:1–6), until they find themselves to be a reflection of that dynamic, even if it is a faint reflection, and are always able to call on the true Life, the life that does not end.

3. Finally, the "covenant" between the two spouses, on the one hand, goes back to the purely juridical dimension (something freely agreed on by two subjects). On the other hand, it strongly evokes the biblical category of the Old Testament covenant that involves the commitment between YHWH and the people of Israel who were asked to abide by the Torah, the Law, and the New Testament covenant between Christ and his Church.

The synthesis of the three key words occurs in n. 1604 where we read that "God who created man out of love also calls him to love," insofar as he "created [them] in the image and likeness of God." The human couple, in expressing reciprocal love according to God's will, manifests in an analogous way the very identity of God-Love. They approach the *agape* of the most holy Trinity to receive and in part to experience the *proprium*, the essential nature, of the tender love and *eros* between God and his people, between Christ and the Church.

The spouses are called to live the sacred bond of reciprocal love that, nourished by this sacrament, allows them to reach "an unbreakable union" (n. 1605), an inviolable fidelity and indissolubility for their whole lives. These are the essential characteristics of every genuine love (see n. 1614, Mt 19:6), and they are actualized in part or in whole depending on the weakness of individuals involved and taking into account "the first sin" (n. 1607).

The words of Genesis—"And they become one flesh" (Gen 2:24)—are written in the difference between the bodies that are made for one another. The theology of the body includes the profound significance of human sexuality that is based on the differences between the sexes and that, when seen in faith, leads to the threshold of the trinitarian mystery, the *unum* being in three hypostases. Man and woman, at the apex of God's creative work, together constitute an object of wonder for the Creator himself who, in contemplating them in their nakedness, now considered everything that he had made "very good" (Gen 1:31), unlike earlier creatures whom he had considered "good" (Gen 1:4, 10, 12, 18, 21, 25).

Therefore, relationship disorders in the couple—sharp conflicts, the desire to possess the partner as though he or she were an object to use for one's pleasure, the disordered feelings of jealousy and rancor, infidelity, blind passions—are all due to sin, which inspires wrongdoing and tends to spoil the harmony of created reality, sowing a spirit of chaos, division, non-communication, and domination of the other, at times even leading to homicidal violence.

The struggle is on-going. When they are not sustained by the sacrament, the couple is at risk of each finding themselves each more egotistical and more closed in on themselves because of sin. That has been evident in all times and places. To presume to overcome sin by oneself and to try to mitigate its adverse consequences can mean the couple at times may lose themselves in a maze of conflict, rancor, offenses, anger, and a desire for revenge.

Alternatively, the couple can overcome temptation and sin if they call on God with humility and hope for his plan to be fulfilled. The man and woman can allow themselves to be conformed to the Son in view of the kingdom. The sacrament is the source of healing and salvific power that God offers the Christian couple. He makes himself present in ways and through paths that only he knows (see nn. 1608–1615) to transform them and "make all things new" (Rev 21:5).

One theme that runs through all of Scripture, from Genesis to Revelation, is marital love that is lived out, even if imperfectly, in its uniqueness and originality. Nuptial love in Scripture functions as a type to manifest the love of God for his people by virtue of the new covenant between Christ, who died and was raised, and all of humanity (see n. 1612). Biographies of the saints have echoed this analogy: God has revealed himself as a fiancé, a spouse, a lover, a husband. Perhaps he chose the spousal relationship because there is no other experience that is so full and profound to express God's "erotic love" (*Deus caritas est*, 9, Dec. 25, 2005). There is nothing more expressive, nothing more joyful or gratifying in human experience, than the passionate love between a man and a woman.

Jesus' imperative—"What therefore God has joined together let no man put asunder" (Mt 19:6)—needs to be harmonized with the concession in the Mosaic Law of a "bill of divorce" in the case of divorce [see Dt 24:1]. There is no doubt that divorce is not according to God's will as expressed "in the beginning," which is the original norm for all human beings at all times.

In that case, Jesus explains, it was a concession intended to correct the failures due to "hardness of heart" (Mt 19:8) in the area of spousal relationships. In Moses' time it intended to protect the woman and shield her from her husband's contempt in his demand to be free.

"Adultery" in Jewish society was considered "the sin of sins" insofar as it involved, even if only analogously, the love between God and his people. In the New Testament the love of Christ the Bridegroom for the Church, his Bride, and for all of humanity implied an eschatological perspective in which the saved would eternally contemplate the fulfillment of that love in the "marriage supper of the Lamb" (see Rev 19:7–9). The union of the spouses, who are assisted by their reciprocal acceptance of the power of grace, can ultimately be established according to God's plan, and it will be characterized by unity, uniqueness, indefectibility, faithfulness, and indissolubility because of the bond that is reinforced more and more by this sacrament.

Without God the love of a man and a woman can remain incomplete, at times faceless or at least powerless, if the couple tries to reach the goal of authentic love that is written in them on their own. Authentic love makes them capable of the unconditional gift of self and of living with the other's limitations with a charity that expresses itself in forgiveness, in reconciliation, and in starting over each day with faith and hope in denying themselves and taking up their own cross to follow Christ.

Without taking anything away from the beauty of elevating human love to the dignity of a sacrament—which we see in Jesus' active presence at the wedding in Cana in Galilee (see Jn 2:1–11)—we must also consider the great value of virginity for the kingdom. It involves a free and all-encompassing choice, a whole-hearted willingness to follow Christ more closely, the Christ who is poor, chaste, and obedient. While approving marriage, Christ chose the path of virginity for himself in view of his freely chosen sacrifice for the salvation of all of humanity.

To accept living the mystery of the cross together, the mystery of the death and resurrection of the Son of God, through all the circumstances of life is an integral and indispensable part of Christian spouses building their house on a rock. This is what accounts for its difference from all the other ways of understanding and living the man-woman relationship.

Pope Francis with *AL* has given more momentum to this theme. He has wanted to advance the ideal of the wedding of Christ, the Bridegroom, and the Church, the Bride. Making use of the most suitable means at hand—"the imperfect analogy"—he has preserved the Pauline teaching on the one hand, and on the other hand he has exalted the beauty of human love. With pastoral sensitivity the pope affirms that "the Gospel of the family also nourishes seeds that are still needing to grow" (*AL* 76). On the other hand, he places unmarried partners among those who participate in the life of the Church "in an imperfect manner" (n. 78) although their situation is not irredeemable. The theological framework of his exhortation is in continuity with preceding biblical and magisterial dictates. With these foundational elements the text articulates a discussion that is concrete, related to daily life, direct, and helpful. In the spousal relationship, especially between two baptized people, its unitive value grows and there is a spiritual increase of the gift that each spouse gives to the other. Spousal love, elevated to the dignity of a sacrament, makes the couple open to grace for each other.

II. The Celebration of Marriage

The paschal mystery constitutes, as we have seen, the foundation for Christian marriage. For this reason, it has always been considered appropriate that the liturgical Rite of Matrimony should occur in the context of a Eucharistic celebration. Here the Christian spouses offer themselves together on the altar with Christ's offering of himself, giving his body and blood for his Bride, the Church, and with the gift of self by the priest who celebrates the holy mysteries. The Eucharistic table allows the highest level of reciprocal interpenetration and of oneness between the spouses and Christ and between

Christ and the whole people of God in one mystical body. People who are divorced and remarried can also partially participate in the Eucharistic celebration. Not having been excommunicated but finding themselves in an objective state of sin, they cannot approach the Eucharist, but they can participate in the communal prayer of the assembly and in parish life, even performing some important services.

According to the tradition of the Latin Church, the rite is a public celebration that culminates in the vows of the spouses while the assembly prays for the Holy Spirit to dwell in them and transform them. They themselves are the ministers of the sacrament in the presence of qualified witnesses and of the bishop, priest, or deacon who will bless them. In the Catholic Christian East, the rite uses different signs, among which the most significant is the "crowning." After the vows of the couple, the priest crowns the bride and groom to signify the covenant that God is establishing with this new Christian couple and is filling with blessings. The pneumatological element here is decidedly more present and powerful than in the Western rite.

The spouses commit to being open to procreation, cooperating with the action of the Creator himself; they promise to receive from God the children he might give them and commit to their Christian education. The same commitments are made in mixed marriages (see *CIC*, can. 1124–1129), but they can be more difficult to carry out.

III. Matrimonial Consent

Beginning with serious discernment based on an awareness of the commitments involved in marriage, the two spouses, with completely clear consciences, choose each other for the rest of their lives. Their publicly declared consent is the basis on which the whole "building" of the couple is constructed for their relationships with each other and with their children. This consent has various aspects. a)"Anthropological": The man and the woman, accepting the challenges unconditionally, fully exercise their freedom, their wills, their feelings of love in its wide-ranging spectrum (tenderness, *eros*, friendship, etc.), their minds, and their emotions in the reciprocal physical and spiritual gift of themselves in the conjugal act—in a word, all that they are. b) "Liturgical-sacramental": This relates to the couple now being an cecclesial subject." Normally the spouses exchange their vows during the course of a Eucharistic celebration in the presence of a priest who is the designated representative of the Church. Every word and every gesture of the rite has value and meaning. Spouses who are baptized accept living the paschal mystery not only in the liturgical-sacramental sphere but every day of their lives together. c)"Juridical-social": The society in which the spouses exchange their vows should be present and participate by showing their acceptance of the new couple that is beginning a new family. Society is dependent in large part on the health of this "new social cell." d) "Ecclesiastical": The community of believers praises the Lord with the spouses and acknowledges them fully as the legitimate "ministerial subject." The couple, by the mere fact of having freely exchanged vows and promises—not just with words but with whole-hearted intentions of mutual aid—fully live the passion of Christ for the Church through their bond of love and witness to the Church and to the world. Both spouses are jointly entrusted with the education of their children, especially education in the faith, and with skillfully training the children and the youth whom they will encounter in their lives, helping them open themselves to Love and to Christian marriage.

The heart of this teaching is and always will be that "Authentic married love is caught up into divine love and is governed and enriched by Christ's redeeming power and the saving activity of the Church" (*GS* 48).

There are many manifestations of concrete charity to which the members of the Christian family could be called, for example, engaging in foster care or permanently adopting disabled minors derived of emotional stability. These are not two irreconcilable loves—love for the members of one's own family and love for so many of the "poor" in need. They represent one great love that expands to embrace many other people who suffer. In contrast to a pharisaical approach, we read in Isaiah,

> Is this not the fast I choose…?
> Is it not to share your bread with the hungry,
> and bring the homeless poor into your house;
> When you see the naked, to cover him,
> and not to hide yourself from your own flesh? (Is 58:6–7).

IV. The Domestic Church

In the first centuries of the Church's life, especially during times of persecution, Christians, in addition to going to the Temple daily where they publicly demonstrated their faith, broke bread together in their homes, as Acts 2:46 tells us. The family home of newly baptized people would become a great center of attraction and gathering. Their homes provided an opportunity for people to grow in fraternal life and to learn the heritage of the truth of the Gospel and of the teaching of the apostolic community and the Fathers.

The factors that qualified a home to be a domestic church can be summarized in six points. 1) The communion of life and the love of Christian couples who welcomed others was the sacramental and ministerial base for a "domestic church." 2) Gathering in a home seemed more productive for their missionary goals than going outside to find people to evangelize. The affection and trust of non-believers was won every day through cordial hospitality, as we see in

Acts 2:47. 3.) The family, more than other ecclesial subjects, could be a school for humanity and Christian life in which the complete transmission of faith to young generations was ensured. 4) The domestic church was a training ground for human relations and moral life. 5) The "Eucharistic celebration" at the family table, namely, the "bread and wine" of everyday life, created a special atmosphere for prayer. 6) They shared their goods and had them in common (see Acts 4:32–34).

Their lifestyle was marked by the spirit of the beatitudes. It was admiration and esteem for such families that inspired the anonymous author of the "Epistle to Diognetus" at the end of the second century to say, "Christians display something wonderful and extraordinary in their way of life. They live in their countries as though they were foreigners.... Like everyone else they marry and have children, but they do not expose their newborns to die.... They live in the flesh but they are not governed by the desires of the flesh. They live on earth but they are citizens of heaven" (5, 4–10).

Chapter Four: OTHER LITURGICAL CELEBRATIONS

Edward McNamara

This chapter describes many rites and devotions that fall outside the scope of the seven sacraments. Under this heading the *CCC* includes sacramentals (blessings and exorcisms in Article 1) and Christian funerals (Article 2). The title, however, could cause a certain confusion because Article 1 includes popular devotions that are not considered liturgical celebrations as such, and the *Liturgy of the Hours* and the liturgical year, which *are* liturgical celebrations, are treated separately elsewhere (see nn. 1163–1178). It might have seemed more logical to treat popular piety in the section dedicated to prayer, but some of the forms of popular piety do contain liturgical elements, for example, blessings that are often closely connected to liturgy, so there is justification for including them in this section.

Article 1: SACRAMENTALS

The *CCC*, inspired by *SC* 60–61, points out the elements that define the nature of sacramentals and at the same time distinguishes them from sacraments (see no. 1667). Sacramentals can initially seem similar to sacraments, and in the past there has not always been a clear distinction between them. For example, canon 7 of the Third Lateran Council in 1179 comments, "it is utterly disgraceful that in certain churches…a charge is made for the enthroning of bishops, abbots or ecclesiastical persons, for the installment of priests in a church for burials and funerals, for the blessings of weddings and for other sacraments." The text is not clear if by "other sacraments" the Council is referring only to Matrimony as a sacrament or to all of the liturgical events listed here. In any case, just as the Church took centuries to develop a clear and definitive articulation of trinitarian and christological doctrine, it is not surprising that more reflection was needed later to distinguish its numerous rites and practices.

One primary distinction is that Jesus Christ instituted the sacraments while the Church instituted sacramentals. The concept of "institution" introduced by Hugh of St. Victor (1096–1141) is the crux of the matter to help us understand sacraments. Even though the word "sacrament" acquired a strong juridical significance after the Council of Trent (1545–1563), St. Thomas Aquinas (1225–1274) defined it better as a sign from God to give grace that make us participate in his divine life (*Summa Theologiae*, III, 64, art. 2 *sed contra*). Just as only God can give grace, so too only the rites essential to the birth, care, and strengthening of divine life have been instituted by him and are distinct from non-essential rites.

We can also expand the concept of institution to include the Church as sacrament and to say that the sacraments are those rites that God has established as essential for the birth, care, and strengthening of the Church as well. In other words, the Church and her members could not exist without the seven sacraments. All the other rites are contingent on the Church's existence even if they are useful to her well-being. Approaching the concept of institution as a form of a juridical decree originating from Christ rather than from the Church is not, however, enough to distinguish a sacrament from a sacramental. Some sacramentals, like exorcism, have their foundation in the actions of Christ himself, who then transmitted that authority to the apostles, but some of Jesus' actions and gestures have never been considered sacraments. On the other hand, the essential elements of the rites of certain sacraments, like Matrimony and Confirmation, have their origins in the Church. Only the Holy See can create new sacramentals.

A second distinguishing feature between sacraments and sacramentals has to do with their effects. The sacraments directly confer (*ex opere operato*) a participation in divine life to those who have the necessary interior dispositions. On the other hand, sacramentals "prepare us to receive grace and dispose us to cooperate with it" (n. 1670) through the prayer and intercession of the Church, so their efficacy is technically defined as *ex opera operantis ecclesiae* ("accomplished through the work of the Church") and *praesertim operante Ecclesia* (see CIC, can. 1166; CCEO, can. 867).

Sacramentals, then, are first and foremost prayers of intercession by the Church to God and secondarily prayers of intercession for the sanctification of a person or an object. Despite these differences, sacramentals share certain aspects of a sacrament's efficacy, for example, like not being dependent on the personal holiness of the minister to produce their spiritual effect. It is an effect that is always granted to the measure in which Christ unites himself to the prayer of his Church. The same obstacles that would prevent a fruitful reception of a sacrament would also make a sacramental ineffective, even if those sacramentals establish some form of permanent new status in a person or object that would remain valid. In any case, the spiritual benefits derived from sacramentals presuppose faith, in particular by whoever would benefit most directly from their celebration. Unlike the effects that depend only in part on the faith of those who receive them, sacramentals do not normally operate without this living faith, even though some blessings can be imparted to catechumens and to non-Catholics as well (see the *Book of Blessings*, General Introduction, 10, 31).

One further characteristic of sacramentals is their ability to sanctify the most diverse events in life. The sacraments mark the most significant moments in life: birth, marriage, sickness, and death. Sacramentals, instead, can mark any event of human life by offering it to God. Through sacramentals and the *Liturgy of the Hours*, the Church's intention is to honor the command to pray without ceasing and to give thanks in all circumstances (see 1 Thess 5:16–18).

Blessings

Almost all sacramentals are blessings. A blessing is above all a divine action through which the Father gives life. God manifests his blessings in creation and in the events of salvation history; a blessing by human beings signifies adoration and the gift of self to the Creator in thanksgiving. The greatest blessing from the Father, and at the same time the greatest response from a human being, is Christ himself (see *CCC*, n. 1083). All those who are baptized in Christ are thus simultaneously called "to be 'a blessing' and to bless" (n. 1669).

The General Introduction to the *Book of Blessings*, which many consider the mature fruit not only of *SC* but also of *LG* and *DV*, sets forth a theological summary for blessings. God who is blessed through the ages (see Rom 9:5) makes all things good (see Gen 1:4, 10, 12, 18, 21, 25, 31). Despite the fall he continues to pour out his blessings as a sign of his merciful love in creation and in his choice of Abraham and his descendants to be custodians of the covenant as they awaited the coming of his Son and as he prepared them to receive the Redeemer. Christ is the apex of these blessings through his redemption and in sending the Holy Spirit, so that those who would become sons of God by adoption would become capable in turn of offering blessings, praise, and genuine thanks to the Father. Christ himself glorified and blessed the Father and whoever he met, especially children (see Mt 24:19, 26:26; Mk 6:41, 8:6–7, 14:22; Lk 9:16, 24:30, 24:50; Jn 6:11). Christians, following Christ's example, have learned to integrate blessings into daily life. The blessings and doxologies in St Paul's letters show how he prayed in a specific way about the most significant moments of the divine mystery (see Rom 1:25, 9:5, 11:36).

The mystery of the Incarnation also elevates the innate goodness in all creatures to a new level of holiness in such a way as to be an even greater sign of God's blessings so that they might bless him. We could say that the sanctification of all material objects that are present in the sacraments and sacramentals in some way derive from the foundational blessings of the Incarnation. The culmination of blessings is contained in the Eucharistic celebration in which we bless the Father for the gifts of bread and wine as gifts coming from his goodness and also as "the work of human hands." Christ, with and through the Holy Spirit, transforms these very gifts into his holy and living sacrifice, "the bread of life" and "our spiritual drink," thanking the Father and blessing him.

A blessing, whether from God or from an intermediary, is always a promise of divine assistance and a proclamation of his favor and faithfulness. When human beings are the ones doing the blessing, they praise God for his goodness and invoke his divine assistance for individuals or for those gathered in an assembly. The General Introduction to the *Book of Blessings* ends by saying, "Blessings therefore refer first and foremost to God, whose majesty and goodness they extol, and, since they indicate the communication of God's favor they also involve human beings, whom he governs and in his providence protects. Further, blessings apply to other created things through which, in their abundance and variety, God blesses human beings" (n. 7).

Ministers and Structure of the Celebration

The *CCC* clarifies that since sacramentals "derive from the baptismal priesthood…lay people may preside at certain blessings" (n. 1669). The participation of lay people is reduced or eliminated when a sacramental is closer to being a sacrament. For the sacramentals presided over by lay people, the *Book of Blessings* sets forth certain restrictions and limitations to the use of words and gestures that are reserved for ordained ministers. For example, a lay minister never pronounces a greeting that normally solicits the response "and with your spirit." We find this salutation in the Book of Ruth when Boaz greets the gleaners with "The Lord be with you," to which the people answer, "The Lord bless you" (Ru 2:4). St. John Chrysostom (344–407) refers to the spirit of this greeting as the indwelling Spirit and as an allusion to the fact that the bishop performs the sacrifice of the Mass through the power of the Holy Spirit.

In the Roman liturgy, this greeting—"May the Lord be with you," "And with your spirit"—was considered sacred from the beginning and was intended to be used only once during Mass, at the beginning of the Eucharist Prayer. At that moment it represents a prayer between the priest and the assembly, so to speak, to the Holy Spirit to rekindle the gift given to everyone in Baptism and the gift given to the priest in Holy Orders so that what is about to take place may be accomplished and be fruitful. Similar reasons could be given to explain why certain gestures are reserved to the person who has received the sacrament of Holy Orders: lay ministers do not stretch forth their hands when praying but hold them together in the "praying hands" manner. They do not extend their hands to bless or to impart a blessing; they instead make the sign of the cross to prompt the assembly to do the same.

The structure of the rites of blessings is based on their category as liturgical acts. As such, the revised rites of blessings follow the fundamental structure underlying the other reformed rites. Their celebration begins with the proclamation of the word of God to ensure that the blessing is an effective sacred sign, and that is followed and accompanied by a prayer of praise of God with specific external signs comprised of ritual words, gestures, and songs. The words for the formulas of blessing are permeated by themes from salvation history and remind us of God's salvific acts and the works of Christ, focusing attention on the sacraments of the Church that originate in the paschal mystery. The principal elements of the blessing rite are so important that Article 23 of the *Book of Blessings* states, "These may never be omitted even when the shorter form of the rite is used." Article 27 is even more rigorous: "It is ordinarily not permissible to impart the blessing of any article or place merely through a sign of blessing and without either the word of God or any sort of prayer being spoken."

The signs, symbols, and gestures chosen by the Church to accompany the words of the prayer involve our senses and remind us of salvation history. Incense, when it is used, recalls the prayers of the saints that ascend to God with an odor of sweetness (see Rv 8:3; Ex 40:27). As is true for the majority of the reformed rites, the presence of an assembly that participates actively, rather than people being in a private or a one-on-one setting, is the preferred and richest way to celebrate a blessing (see *Book of Blessings*, General Introduction, nn. 16–17).

The Various Forms of Sacramentals

The General Introduction of the *Book of Blessings* emphasizes that blessings are for people at particular moments in their lives, for the objects they use, and for the places in which they work or live (see nn. 12–13). There are many blessings for all three categories, and in some cases such blessings can also apply to other situations. There exists, in any case, two kinds of blessings that are generally shared: constitutive blessings and invocative blessings. The constitutive blessing (which is actually both constitutive and invocative) modifies the juridical *status* of a person, object, or place by separating them from their normal use and making them sacred. A sacred place or object that has received such a blessing is treated with respect and should not be used for secular purposes even if it is privately owned. The invocative blessing asks for God's blessing on a person, object, or place, but it does not change their juridical *status* or separate them from their normal use.

The most important liturgical rites of the Church incorporate both invocative and constitutive blessings. For example the *Roman Missal* has invocative blessings like the blessing of a deacon before his proclamation of the Gospel and the blessing at the end of Mass. Other books for rites, like the *Rite of Baptism*, include invocative blessings like the blessing of the baptismal water. Some invocative blessings for people, places, and things involve stand-alone rites.

Constitutive Blessings for a Person

Constitutive blessings for people should not be confused with sacramental ordination.

– *The blessings of an abbot or an abbess for a monastery.* The abbot and the abbess have been considered venerable figures since ancient times, and they exercise a spiritual fatherhood or motherhood but with juridical authority. This dual aspect of their role has led to special rites of blessing from the sixth century on, although the first actual formulas for this blessing are found in the *Sacramentario Gregoriano*. Over time the rite became more complex and came to resemble an episcopal ordination. The new rite has been simplified and is now more conformed to the spiritual mission of the abbot. After the prayer of blessing, the book of the Rule for that religious order is consigned to the new abbot. He then receives the insignia of the mitre and the ring. The blessing of an abbess is similar, but she receives only the book of the Rule of her order. This rite is generally presided over by the local bishop.

– *The rite of religious profession.* The rite in which a person professes the evangelical counsels of poverty, chastity, and obedience has been a solemn occasion ever since the beginning of monasticism. The current rite offers an outline that every religious order may adapt to its own distinct traditions. It contains a description of the rite for the beginning of religious life and another for the first temporary profession for a pre-determined period. It can include investiture with the order's habit or the consignment of symbols and a very simple renewal of vows. The rites conclude with the solemn, perpetual profession celebrated during a Mass that includes the Litany of the Saints.

– *The consecration of virgins.* In the past, this rite, in which a young woman consecrates her life to God, combined elements drawn from Matrimony (because this woman is the Bride of Christ) and elements from funeral rites as a symbol of being dead to the world. This rite fell into disuse starting in the fifteenth century when the majority of these women became religious. The new rite promulgated in 1970, is addressed to religious, but it restores the order of virgins as lay women who are consecrated but remain active in the world. The new rite is presided over by the diocesan ordinary and is similar to a perpetual profession except that the secular virgin only professes the vow of chastity. After the solemn prayer of consecration, the insignia of consecration, like a ring, is given.

– *The institution of lay ministers of the Church as readers and acolytes.* Since ancient times there have been some official liturgical ministries that have not called for the laying on of hands. In 251 Pope Cornelius wrote that besides priests and deacons in Rome at that time, there were 7 subdeacons, 42 acolytes, and 52 exorcists, readers, and doorkeepers. As time went on these ministries disappeared as separate ministries and became steps on the path to priesthood with the subdiaconate as a major order and the others as minor orders. In 1972 Paul VI's reform abolished these minor orders and replaced them with the two lay ministries of reader and acolyte that were open to laymen and to seminarians. The reader proclaims the word of God in the assembly and in other instances like Occasional Celebrations. The acolyte serves the altar, purifies the sacred vessels if the deacon is absent, and can be delegated as an extraordinary minister of communion. The rites of institution for both ministers are similar. After an initial teaching that describes the similar duties of these ministers (and can also replace the homily), the bishop invokes the blessing of God and consigns that which is appropriate to each minister: sacred Scripture to the reader and the paten and chalice to the acolyte.

– *The institution of extraordinary ministers of communion.* This rite is similar to that of the institution of ministries, although it does not have any consignment. Unlike instituted ministers, the extraordinary minister of communion may serve only within the limits established by the bishop and loses that delegation beyond the boundaries of the diocese.

Constitutive Blessings of Places and Objects

– *The dedication or blessing of a church or an altar.* The oldest reference to a rite of dedication of a church goes back to St. Eusebius around 340 A.D. The rite continued to develop and to blend Roman and Eastern elements so that starting from the ninth century it included various aspersions with blessed water as well as oil for the church's altar, its walls, and its door, with inscriptions in Greek and Latin on the floor and many uses of incense and recitations of psalms and prayers. One important part of the rite was the placing of relics beneath the altar. The new rite, which is very simplified, has four parts: entrance into the church, the liturgy of the word, the prayer of dedication and anointing of the church and the altar, and the Eucharistic celebration. The prayer of dedication is proclaimed after the Litany of the Saints and after the deposition of the relics. The anointing of the altar with holy chrism makes it a symbol of Christ, the "Anointed One." The anointing of the four (or twelve) walls sets the building apart from secular use and dedicates it exclusively to Christian worship. The altar is incensed and then, whether the sign of this sacramental is the people of God or the church building itself, the building now becomes a house of prayer and a living temple of God (see Rom 12:1). At this point the altar is covered with a linen tablecloth and decorated with flowers. The candles are lit and the whole building is completely illuminated. Finally, the Eucharist, celebrated for the first time, represents the only rite that is truly essential for the dedication of a Church.

– *The blessings of holy oils, sacred vessels, sacred vestments, bells, etc.* These blessings are for all the objects used in Christian worship. The most important is the blessing of the oil for chrism and the blessing of oil for the sick because these oils are essential for the administration of the sacraments of Confirmation and the Anointing of the Sick. The blessing of oil for catechumens and the blessing of baptismal waters are also important for the sacrament of Baptism, but these are not essential for the rite itself. Other rites for liturgical objects emphasize their being set apart for specific use in Christian worship. A few liturgical blessings, like those for ashes and palms, have a limited celebrative context because those blessed objects are not for other uses.

– *The blessings of objects of popular devotion.* These blessings, like the blessings of rosaries, scapulars, medals, and sacred images, are both constitutive and vocative. Such objects are already sacred in themselves in some way, so the blessing reminds those who use them that they are not decorations but are meant to encourage prayer and devotion. In some cases, the granting of indulgences depends on the blessing of an object.

Invocative Blessings of People

The various types of blessings for which the Church invokes God's blessings for different categories of people indicate that no sector of human society is excluded. The *Book of Blessings*, for example, dedicates a whole section to the blessings of the family community, the sick, participants in catechesis and public prayer, students and teachers, participants in conferences for pastoral workers or in voluntary organizations for public need, pilgrims, and travelers.

The largest chapter concerns the family unit. Through these blessings, parents can renew their prerogative, rooted in the Bible, of imparting blessings on their children. Including the blessings of the parents in daily life emphasizes the importance and the responsibility of the parents to reflect the divine image in family life. In addition to the blessings of parents, there are other blessings that embrace the whole of family life, starting with mothers before and after childbirth, and even a blessing for the elderly.

Invocative Blessings of Places and Objects

The General Introduction to the *Book of Blessings* stipulates that in blessing places and objects one should take care that "such blessings are invoked always with a view to the people who use the objects to be blessed and frequent the places to be blessed" (n. 12). Therefore, the *Book of Blessings* reiterates continually that objects or places should not be blessed without the presence of the people who use them or live in them.

Under the heading "Blessings Related to Buildings and to Various Forms of Human Activity," we find blessings for new building sites, homes, factories, offices, boats, technical equipment, animals, fields and flocks, seeds and harvest, athletic events, and special meal events. Other sections of the *Book of Blessings* concern blessings linked to feasts and seasons, to inaugural speeches of thanks by public officials, and to other special circumstances. Almost all human activity can be the object of a blessing guided only by pastoral prudence; prudence would prohibit imparting a blessing whenever it might be inappropriate, for example, in the case of weapons.

Exorcisms

When the Church publicly asks, with authority in the name of Jesus Christ, that a person or object be protected from the influence of the Evil One and removed for his domain, this is called an exorcism. The practice of exorcism already existed in Judaism (see Tb 3:8, 17; Lk 11:15). Christ practiced exorcism, so the Church derives her power and her duty to exorcize from him (see Mt 8:16; Mk 1:25–26, 6:13, 16:17; Lk 8:2). The mission and preaching of Christ inaugurated his kingdom and the defeat of the Satan (see Mt 12:28; Jn 12:31). In the practice of exorcisms, Jesus clearly distinguishes between the healing of an illness and exorcism. In the first case he speaks directly to the sick person (see Mt 8:1–4; Lk 8:43–48; Jn 5:2–9). In the second case he speaks directly to the demon and prevents the evil spirit from speaking (see Mk 1:25, 34; Lk 4:35). Evil spirits testify of him (see Mk 3:11).

Christ grants the Church this power in order to free people from unclean spirits (see Mt 10:1; Mk 3:15, 6:7, 13). In fact this authority is one of the specific signs of being a disciple (see Mk 16:17). After Pentecost the disciples performed exorcisms, for example, Peter (see Acts 5:16), Philip (see Acts 8:7), and Paul (See Acts 19:11–16). Following the example of Christ and the apostles, the Church has always performed exorcisms, although after Pope Innocent I (401–417) exorcism was reserved to clerics with episcopal authorization ("Epistle 26" to Decentius, 6). This restriction is still in effect today: only a bishop, or a priest duly and specifically authorized by the local ordinary, can legitimately perform an exorcism on those who are possessed.

There are two kinds of exorcism: simple and solemn. Simple exorcism is performed during the celebration of Baptism and in some blessings that use the extraordinary form of the *Roman Ritual.* Solemn or "major" exorcism aims directly at expelling demons or at freeing a person under demonic influence through the spiritual authority that Jesus entrusted to his Church. The *CCC* calls for prudence on the part of the exorcist to avoid confusing the presence of an evil spirit with a psychological illness that sometimes has similar manifestations. Solemn exorcisms should never occur during Mass or other liturgical celebrations and need to be separate from any rites of healing.

From the theological point of view, exorcism is easily a sacramental because of its biblical foundation and institution. It is also a sign and thus analogous to a sacrament. In the case of exorcism the particular signs are ritual words pronounced by the exorcist in the form of invocative prayer or deprecatory prayer. Certain gestures are traditionally associated with this prayer, like the imposition of hands, sprinkling with holy water, the proclamation of the word of God, and the invocation of the saints. Exorcism is also an action of the Church that, in addition to the exorcist himself, participates on behalf of a soul through her intercession. Consequently, even if the exorcism occurs in a confidential way out of consideration for the subject involved, it remains a rite of the Church, and so it must follow an approved ritual and include an assembly united in prayer to assist the exorcist while he prays for the freedom of the possessed person.

It is not always clear how an exorcism prepares people to receive grace and disposes them to cooperate with it (see *CCC*, n. 1670). The possession does not necessarily imply the loss of grace or its increase. Nevertheless, it predisposes the soul to receive grace by removing an obstacle that causes abhorrence of the sacred, and this facilitates a fruitful reception of the sacraments and other sacramentals.

Popular Piety

The *CCC* states, "the religious sense of the Christian people has always found expression in various forms of piety surrounding the Church's sacramental life, such as the veneration of relics, visits to sanctuaries, pilgrimages, processions, the stations of the cross, religious dances, the rosary, medals, etc." (n. 1674). After Vatican II there was a period in which popular piety was disapproved of in some spheres as being outmoded and not adapted to the times and of being earmarked to be substituted exclusively by liturgical forms of adoration. Teachings by many popes like Blessed Paul VI in *Marialis cultus* (Feb. 2, 1974) and the publication of the *CCC* tried to address this situation and to propose a healthy balance between liturgical worship and popular piety.

In 2001 the Congregation for Divine Worship promulgated the Directory of Popular Piety and the Liturgy: Principles and Guidelines. This wide-ranging document summarizes previous teachings that furnish a solid theological base for popular piety and its relationship to the liturgy. Let us look at its essential points. It must first be acknowledged that popular piety

> is a living reality in and of the Church. Its source is the constant presence of the Spirit of God in the ecclesial community; the mystery of Our Savior is its reference point, the glory of God and the salvation of man its object, its historical moment "the joyous encounter of the word of evangelization and culture." On several occasions the Magisterium has expressed its esteem for popular piety and its various manifestations, admonishing those who ignore it, or overlook it, or even distain [sic] it, to adopt a more positive attitude toward it, taking due note of its many values. Indeed, the Magisterium sees popular piety as a "treasure of the People of God." (n. 61)

The subject of popular piety is "every Christian—clerics, religious and laity—both privately when moved by the Spirit of Christ, and when praying within community in groups of different origins and types" (n. 67).

Among the values of popular piety is "an innate sense of the sacred and the transcendent,...a genuine thirst for God and 'an acute sense of God's attributes—fatherhood, providence, constant and loving presence' and mercy" (n. 61). It also promotes some interior dispositions and virtues like "Christian resignation in the face of irremediable situations"; confident abandonment to God; the capacity to suffer and to perceive "the cross in everyday life"; a sincere desire to please the Lord and to do reparation and penance for offenses against him; detachment from material things; and openness to others with "a sense of friendliness, charity and family unity" (n. 61). In a similar way it gladly turns its attention to the mysteries of the Christian faith, like the mystery of the passion and death of Christ, communion with Mary, the angels, and saints, and suffrage for the souls of the dead (see n. 62).

Popular piety is also uniquely able to adapt the Christian message and give it expression in a particular culture. "In genuine forms of popular piety, the Gospel message assimilates expressive forms particular to a given culture while also permeating the consciousness of that culture with the content of the Gospel, and its idea of life and death, and of man's freedom, mission and destiny" (n. 63). It also has a very important role in transmitting and guarding the faith in those places where Christians are deprived of pastoral assistance (see n. 64).

Nevertheless, popular piety is not without dangers that can cause it to deviate, and as such it requires an ongoing prudent and patient evangelization. Among these dangers is the disproportion between an esteem for the veneration of the saints and an awareness of the absolute sovereignty of Jesus Christ; a lack of understanding of the role of the Holy Spirit; a lack of contact with Scripture and the Church's sacraments; at times the tendency to a dichotomy between worship and the duties of Christian life; and a utilitarian view that can lead to superstition, magic, fatalism, and oppression (see n. 65).

In terms of the liturgy the *CCC* reminds us that "These expressions of piety extend the liturgical life of the Church, but do not replace it" (n. 1675). The *Dictionary* clarifies this teaching, saying, "The Sacred Liturgy, in virtue of its very name, is by far superior to pious exercises, and hence pastoral praxis must always accord to Sacred Liturgy 'that preeminent position proper to it in relation to pious exercises.' Liturgy and pious exercises must co-exist in accordance with the hierarchy of values and the nature specific to both of these cultic expressions" (n. 73). Attention to these principles "should lead to a real effort to harmonize, in so far as possible, pious exercises with the rhythms and demands of the Liturgy, thereby avoiding any 'mixture or admixture of these two forms of piety'" (n. 74).

The first theological principle behind the renewal and evangelization of popular piety is that the life of Christian worship is fundamentally trinitarian and sacramental. It is thus lived in communion with the Father through Christ in the Holy Spirit through participation in sacramental life (see nos. 76–78). "From the principles already outlines [sic] above, popular piety should always be formed as a moment of the dialogue between God and man, through Christ in the Holy Spirit" (n. 79).

The second principle concerns the Church as a worship community. In this regard, besides the liturgy, other forms of popular piety are fruits of the Holy Spirit and expressions of the Church's piety, so the Church herself recommends many of them (see n. 83). However, the expression of popular piety needs to be illuminated by "the ecclesiological principle" (n. 84) of Christian worship so as to maintain a correct view of the relationship between a particular church and the universal Church and not to close itself off to universally valued activities. The veneration of the Blessed Virgin, the angels, saints, and the blessed, as well as suffrage for departed souls, should be set in the context of the relationship between the heavenly Church and the pilgrim Church. In addition the relationship between "ministry" and charism" should be understood in a fruitful way (see n. 84).

Other theological principles are linked to the common priesthood in popular piety and to the Word of God in Christian life (see nos. 85–86). "Since the Church is built on, and grows through, listening to the Word of God, the Christian faithful should acquire a familiarity with Sacred Scripture and be imbued with its spirit so as to be able to translate the meaning of popular piety into terms worthy of, and consonant with, the data of faith, and render a sense of that devotion that comes from God who saves, regenerates and sanctifies" (n. 87).

Popular piety is marked by historical and cultural factors, so its introduction and inclusion in daily life are clear signs of the grounding and inculturation of faith at the heart of a given people even if it must always be oriented, guided, and directed by the liturgy (see nn. 91–92). Some expressions of popular piety are local while others have become part of many different cultures, and the *CCC* mentions some that are universal (n. 1674). These include the veneration of the relics of saints who have distinguished themselves as members of the mystical Body of Christ and temples of the Holy Spirit because of their impressive sanctity and who now dwell in heaven. The veneration of relics reminds us that the physical body is also sanctified and participates in the process of sanctification. Visits to the Blessed Sacrament, pilgrimages, and processions can foster a healthy balance between liturgical life and popular piety. The "Via Crucis" is a meditative accompaniment of Christ during the last phases of his life on earth. The Rosary is chiefly related to Marian devotion and is a kind of summary of the Gospel; as such it is a profoundly Christian devotion that helps faith in contemplating the mysteries of the life of Jesus Christ through the eyes of the Virgin Mary (see St. John Paul II, *Rosarium Virginis Mariae*, Oct. 16, 2002).

Finally, the *CCC* highly recommends fostering a devotion to the Sacred Heart of Jesus: "Jesus knows and loves us each and all during his life, his agony, and his Passion and gave himself up for each one of us: 'The Son of God...loved me and gave himself for me' [Gal 2:20]. He has loved us all with a human heart. For this reason, the Sacred Heart of Jesus, pierced by our sins and for our salvation, 'is quite righty considered the chief sign and symbol of that...love with which the divine Redeemer continually loves the eternal Father and all human beings' without exception" (n. 478).

Article 2: CHRISTIAN FUNERALS

The *CCC*'s presentation of the rite of Christian funerals is quite thorough and conveys the spirit of the current rite. In a certain sense the current rite attempts to restore the spirit of ancient Christian funerals. These rites are characterized by the choice of local customs. Some customs, like ritual laments and food offerings to the dead, have been rejected while others have been welcomed and assigned a Christian significance. Christians introduced the recitation of psalms before a burial early on, and their burials were quite different in spirit from those of their pagan contemporaries. Above all, faith in the resurrection meant that they did not attribute absolute importance to following a prescribed ritual for the ultimate destination of a departed soul.

There are two testimonies of Eucharistic celebrations for funerals as early as the fourth century, but it did not become common practice for several centuries. The ancient rite was simple but rich with paschal signification. The body was prepared at home and accompanied to the church with the recitation of Psalm 97: "The LORD reigns; let the earth rejoice." At the church there was a brief prayer with Psalms 4 and 42, and then the body was taken to the cemetery as Psalms 15 and 52 were recited. During the burial itself, Psalm 118 was intoned with its antiphon, "Open to me the gates of righteousness."

During the Middle Ages, the rite became more elaborate. A Mass became common and the rite added incense and aspersion of the body with holy water in remembrance of Baptism. The tone was more measured with a marked emphasis on sorrow, sin, judgment, and the need to implore divine mercy. The body was accompanied to the church with Psalms 130 and 51. The Gloria and Alleluia were omitted, as were blessings and joyful responses. The end of the Mass included the prayer "*Non intres in iudicium*": "Enter not into judgment with your servant; / for no man living is righteous before you" (Ps 143:2). This rite remained in use until the *Roman Ritual* of 1614 simplified it and restored certain paschal elements to it, like the joyful antiphons "*In paradisum*" ("May the angels lead you into paradise…") and "*Chorus angelorum*" ("May choirs of angels receive you…"). The new rite introduced in 1969 fits with the teachings of the *CCC* and aims to enrich the contents of the rites. It also restores a complete vision of Christian doctrine about death, especially its paschal nature. In addition, the new rite includes prayers for the family of the deceased and for other living persons, which the previous rite lacked. The basic rites in the *Order of Christian Funerals* include the following:

The prayer vigil at the home of the deceased, or in another location according to the circumstances, during which the family, friends, and members of the Christian community gather to lift up a prayer to God for the deceased, comforting whoever is weeping. This expresses Christian solidarity in accordance with the words of the apostle, "weep with those who weep" (Rom 12:15).

The celebration of the Eucharist. The Christian community hears the word of God that proclaims the paschal mystery. It offers the hope of meeting again in the kingdom of God. It revitalizes our piety on behalf of the deceased and exhorts us to testify to a truly Christian life.

The rite of commital, funeral procession, and burial. In the committal (or final commendation), the deceased is commended to God with the Christian community's final farewell to one of its members before the body is brought to the grave. In the funeral procession Mother Church, who has sacramentally carried this Christian in her bosom during his or her earthly pilgrimage, accompanies the deceased with the psalm of the dead to the place of his or her repose, awaiting the day of resurrection (see 1 Cor 5:42–44).

The *Dictionary of Popular Piety and Liturgy* has some pertinent reflections on the rite for the deceased (see nn. 248–260) that elaborate what the *CCC* says. It affirms that for the Christian, "Death is the passage to the fullness of true life. The Church, subverting the logic of this world, calls the Christian's day of death his *dies natalis*, the day of his heavenly birth, where 'there will be no more death, and no more mourning or sadness [for] the world of the past has gone' (Rev 21:4). Death is the prolongation, in a new way, of life as the Liturgy says: 'For your faithful, O Lord, life has changed not ended; while our earthly dwelling is destroyed, a new and eternal dwelling is prepared for us in Heaven'" (n. 249). The death of a Christian is a grace-filled event having a positive value and significance in Christ and through Christ that is based on the teaching of Scripture: "To me to live is Christ, and to die is gain" (Phil 1:21), and "The saying is sure: If we have died with him, we shall also live with him" (1 Tm 2:11).

PART THREE

LIFE IN CHRIST

Section One

MAN'S VOCATION: LIFE IN THE SPIRIT

MAN'S VOCATION: LIFE IN THE SPIRIT

Renzo Gerardi

What is a Christian? Peter's frank answer consists of a tireless life plan: a Christian is someone who loves the Lord Jesus "though [he has] not seen him, and still without seeing him" (1 Pt 1:8), believes in him, and follows him.

Having become a "new person," the baptized person is called to live in Christ, in communion with his Spirit and his Body, following his words and his example. Christ is the perfect model and teacher. From him arise ethical principles and the possibility of living an authentic life. The third part of the *CCC*, which is titled "Life in Christ," covers all of this. It is subdivided into two sections: "Man's Vocation: Life in the Spirit" and "The Ten Commandments."

There is no doubt that the term "life" has a rather broad meaning which is so rich and complex that it can be described more easily than it can be defined. Here, we refer to "life in Christ." He is life. He had it originally (cf. Jn 1:4) and he has absolute ownership of it. He gives his life (cf. Jn 10, 11:17). He, "the prince of life," was killed. "God, however, raised him from the dead," (Acts 3:15), and he will be the judge of the living and the dead (cf. 1 Pt 4:5).

Man can participate in the life of God due to the Spirit of Christ, "who is God and gives life." The manifestation of God in flesh was intended to allow for our participation in divine life and the manifestation of the mystery of his incarnation in us.

One of the great merits of the Second Vatican Council was having recognized the community of mankind as a whole and using this as a cornerstone of the constitution *GS*. "Man himself, whole and entire, body and soul, heart and conscience, mind and will" (n. 3) was created "to the image of God" and is "capable of knowing and loving his Creator, and was appointed by Him as master of all earthly creatures that he might subdue them and use them to God's glory" (n. 12). For this reason, "Though made of body and soul, man is one. Through his bodily composition he gathers to himself the elements of the material world" (n. 14). "For by His incarnation the Son of God has united Himself in some fashion with every man" (n. 22), restoring his divine likeness, giving him the possibility of fully developing his talents and to realize his dignity. For this reason, human beings are called to collaborate with God, living their lives as a response to a personal vocation. In giving life, God orders men to honor it and to realize it to the best of their ability. However, the Lord of Life also provides rules and regulations so that life can be lived to the fullest.

Each man is called to be a faithful and wise guardian of his own life and of the lives of others. However, the service of life—a "fundamental" good, which is a prerequisite and condition for all the others—is only truly service of life when lived in accordance with moral law, which expresses its value and its duties. The best wish, full of hope, which is made in the Bible is that of a "long life" as a reward for those who observe God's commandments. But we know—because God revealed it and gave it to us—that there is an eternal life, an ultimate and definitive reality, a life "beyond death." And that is what truly counts: life "in God."

The section on "Life in Christ" in the *CCC* is introduced by nine numbers (1691–1698) on which we will now focus our attention. We will propose a few points of reflection and indicate opportunities for deeper study.

Number 1691 contains a quote by St. Leo the Great from a Christmas homily in which Christians are urged to "recognize [their] dignity" as "children in the Son." As "children of God" (Jn 3:1) and "partakers of the divine nature" (2 Pt 1:4), Christians are called to behave in a way that is worthy of the gospel of Christ—that is, to live "in Christ and in the Spirit."

Through baptism, liberation from the power of sin took place: the "old" person was submerged in water and left as a "new" person. Due to the glorious cross of Christ, the Christian is a new person in all his being. Therefore, his relationships with other human beings, with history, with nature, with the cosmos also cannot be anything other than "new." The "crucifixion" and "burial" of the old person have marked a rebirth, establishing a new principle: the future is new and is living with Christ, in Christ, and for Christ.

Christians exist under the rule of the Crucified and Risen Lord. The suppression of the power of sin was the goal and consequence of having been crucified with Christ during baptism. The power of sin can continue to prevail only if one obeys it, but Christians must not obey it. This would make no sense! Continuing to live in sin is absurdity because it means going against the new reality of baptized people and going against a new way of being. Paul's question from the beginning of chapter 6 in the Letter to the Romans comes to mind: "What should we say then? Should we remain in sin so that grace may be given the more fully?" (Rom 6:1). The answer is a decisive "Out of the question!" Never. Now that we have "died to sin" (Rom 6:2), we can no longer live in it.

Just like the Risen Christ now lives for God, the baptized, who have died to sin, must live for God under the rule of Christ while awaiting the definitive unfolding of eternal life.

In the following number, n. 1692, our vision expands to "all the sacraments" from a perspective of faith and of giving thanks for God's gifts.

The immersion of baptism is only a beginning and a guarantee. It is a beginning because the impetus comes from God—in other words, it is grace. It is a guarantee because God's gift comes without repentance. It is a characteristic, a reality that remains, and classifies and definitively consecrates us as "priests in the Church." But that is not all.

It is a beginning because it leads toward a participation in the Paschal Mystery that becomes steadily more complete (through confirmation and communion) and more differentiated and complementary (through the other sacraments of the Church). It is a guarantee because it is the gesture to which Christians must always refer and which they can always count on in order to collaborate in the realization of an answer to God's "calling." But that is still not all.

Christians need to grow and mature, and growth—becoming Christian—must occur by going through the steps of the Paschal mystery. The "new creature" has to become "the perfect Man, fully mature with the fullness of Christ himself" (Eph 4:13). This occurs in the same way that the physical life of a man progresses, from conception to birth. The entire future man is already present in the embryo. Vital energies, abilities, attitudes, propensities…these are all collected in that fragile person that looks toward life and comes into the world, and they need only to develop and mature over the entire arc of existence. It is rare that a human analogy is so pertinent for illustrating a fact about faith. Jesus made use of the same one when speaking to Nicodemus: "Do not be surprised when I say: You must be born from above" (Jn 3:7). Baptism summarizes the entire Christian life because it a fundamental cornerstone of life as a Christian. What follows is development, clarification, and fulfillment. All the virtualities are there, ready to be developed, and the fundamental laws for the progress that will lead the Lord's Passover to perfection in the Christian are already established.

For this reason, the project of a Christian life has to be coherent with the choice of faith made during baptism. It is a path of perfection (cf. Jas 1:4) in the Church, a community of salvation and grace in the Spirit, who was given to us.

The memory of the beginning, of baptism, can therefore be a savior and problem-solver for anyone at any time. Baptism is the "gate to spiritual life" and the "source of life," a decisive, objective, and ecclesial element of faith. The primacy of faith in life comes from baptism. Faith is like a force that pushes us to keep adhering to Jesus Christ, who we put on during baptism like a second skin. A Christian's spiritual life derives its constitutive Paschal dimension, which classifies it as existence in faith, in hope, and in charity, from baptism.

This baptismal conscience is a constitutive element of the face of the Church and of the believer. It must impregnate and direct theology and spiritual life. The life of a Christian is essentially *martyría*—baptismal witness, since faith has a baptismal identity. Only if the Christian makes this priority of faith a cornerstone of his spiritual life can he embark on a journey that also represents human and spiritual vivification of himself, of the community, and of society.

It is a faith that is capable of dialogue and communion, of witnessing and of service. As Pope Paul VI wrote, "The person who has been evangelized goes on to evangelize others. Here lies the test of truth, the touchstone of evangelization: it is unthinkable that a person should accept the Word and give himself to the kingdom without becoming a person who bears witness to it and proclaims it in his turn" (*EN* 24).

In this way, and only in this way, the will of God is done. His desire, which the Christian, a new creature in the Holy Spirit, is capable of discerning due to the illumination of the Holy Spirit, is fulfilled. It is God's will that each person fulfill his providential role in the growth of the one Body of Christ in accordance with his abilities so that his Kingdom comes.

This all occurs due to baptism "in the name of the Father and of the Son and of the Holy Spirit" (Mt 28:19). In this way, our existence receives a trinitary "orientation": toward the Father, through Christ, and in the Holy Spirit.

In n. 1693, baptized people are first of all invited to "look to the Father" in order to be able to live "in the light of his face." This means imitating Jesus, "the face of the Father," acting as he wants us to act, in communion with him, in order to become "perfect."

We were baptized into the death of Jesus. "So by our baptism into his death we were buried with him, so that as Christ was raised from the dead by the Father's glorious power, we too should begin living a new life" (Rom 6:4). According to this symbolism, the baptismal fountain is like the Paschal tomb, where the neophyte casts off his old skin and is reborn with Christ as a new man. By casting off his skin, he becomes a new creature, remodeled in God's image by the power of the Holy Spirit.

People who have been baptized can be called holy, and they truly are. We could easily say that this is one of the cases in which a relationship becomes so profound that it becomes an equation. There is a perfect equation to be found in baptism, Christian life, perfection, and holiness: people who are born through baptismal immersion are holy because those waters were fecundated by the Spirit. There, a holy people is born for the heavens. Evidently, in order for the equation to continue to hold firm, baptism must be "lived." It is lived baptism that makes a Christian, a perfect person, a holy person. Creating a true equation between baptism and holy life: this is the meaning and goal of Christian life.

For the Christian, baptism is what the source is to a river: the event from which his life in Christ flows. With it, man becomes a part of his people, who continually experience the Gift because they know that they are a saved people. And the population is saved because God, Love, gave himself.

Baptism incorporates the Christian in Christ and engages the believer in the Church (cf. 1 Cor 12:13), providing ecclesiastical structure for his existence. This is what is stated in n. 1694 through a tapestry of quotes from the New Testament (from the writings of Paul and John): incorporated into Christ by Baptism, Christians are "dead to sin and alive to God in Christ Jesus" and therefore participate in the life of the Risen Lord. Following Christ and united with him, Christians can strive to be "imitators of God as beloved children, and walk in love" by conforming their thoughts, words and actions to the "mind…which is yours in Christ Jesus," and by following his example.

The "new" beginning—which can be called a "conversion" [in Greek: *metánoia*]—indeed starts with thinking [in Greek: *noéin*], but it is not a simple product of our reflection. *Metánoia* is an act of obedience to That which proceeds us, so it does not originate within us. More precisely, what proceeds us is not a "thing" but a "him," a person. It is a "you": Christ, the Word made flesh. He is the new beginning, from which we "are designed" and "think." And what is attributable to him is an obedience that "remains," because he who comes before us, once we have met him, does not become a portion of our thoughts. On the contrary, each one of us becomes his. In becoming him, each person becomes part of an "us," his living body.

The principles of the Church and the spring of life, which washes all the world, are derived from the pain of Christ as he died on the cross. This spring is the first precious gift that the Spirit gave to the Church. While the Church performs a baptism, baptism in the Spirit forms and edifies the Church. Children who were born in the water thanks to the breath of the divine creator are born from the mother Church with virginal purity and are continuously called to grow in holiness in their lives.

In order to complete the description of the new reality of baptism, a gift from the triune God, n. 1695 specifically reminds readers of the "action of the Spirit." Another tapestry of Pauline texts is found here: healing the wounds of sin, the Holy Spirit renews us interiorly through a spiritual transformation. He enlightens and strengthens us to live as children of light through all that is good and right and true. Justified in the name of the Lord Jesus Christ and in the Spirit of our God, sanctified (and) called to be saints, Christians have become the temple of the Holy Spirit. This Spirit of the Son teaches them to pray to the Father and, having become their life, prompts them to act so as to bear the fruit of the Spirit by charity in action.

The Spirit is the Person-Love, the divine artist who is in an intimate and ever novel dialogue of love with the believer in order to make his life conform to the image of Christ (cf. 2 Cor 3:18). The progress of Christian life is mainly the work of the Spirit of God. He is the first great gift: the Spirit who is love itself through which God loves us. "Love is from God [...] This is the proof that we remain in him and he in us, that he has given us a share in his Spirit" (1 Jn 4:7, 13). The Spirit is the "heavenly gift of God Most High," as invoked in the ancient hymn *Veni Creator*. It is "the first gift to those who believe," according to Eucharistic Prayer IV—a gift bestowed by he who is the giver, the Father of mercies, absolutely freely, through Jesus Christ his Son.

Consequently, n. 1696 states that "the way of Christ leads to life" (cf. Mt 7:14). Christ is the path to take in order to have life, taking the cross "every day" (Lk 9:23). Jesus, in stating "I am the way" [in Greek: *odós*] (Jn 14:6), invited his disciples to convert, to believe in the Gospel (cf. Mk 1:15), and to follow him.

The "way" is not only Christ but also Christianity. Initially, before the word "Christians" was commonly used, the Christian religion was simply called "the way." In his speech to the Jews on the steps of the temple, the apostle Paul confesses that he persecuted "this Way" [in Greek: *odós*] to the death (Acts 22:4). The Christian faith is "a way." It is the way toward life, while the opposite way "leads to destruction" (Mt 7:13).

At the beginning of the Christian "way" (cf. Acts 9:2, 24:22)—and, precisely, of any walk of faith of a man—is the encounter with the Word. The Church's permanent task is to be a "community of the way," which shows the righteous way to live, the way toward life, in a concrete manner, always rendering the moral content of faith newly visible through the proclamation of the word of God. To man, who is tempted to illuminate the way with his own lantern, the Church offers the unchanged splendor which comes from the revelation. It is the light of the face of God, which shines in all its brilliance in the face of Christ, in whose mystery the mystery of man finds true light. And if every man's actions must be performed "in truth," this is even more true for the Christian, for the person who must be the "light for the world" (Mt 5:14). This can only occur if he lives in the light of life and of the example of Christ.

As a result, it is necessary to walk in the light (cf. 1 Jn 1:7). The Christian faith is a truth that must be lived, and Christians can be witnesses through a moral life. Walking the true way means allowing oneself to be guided by the Spirit, following the path that is Jesus, who is truth and life.

The Letter to the Hebrews sees Christian life as an exodus according to the life model posed by our "ancestors" (cf. Heb 11). Christ's sacrifice is characterized by exodus: he "suffered outside the gate" (Heb 12:12); the Christian community is urged to "go outside the camp" toward Jesus (cf.

Heb 13:13), who is a "new way which he has opened for us, a living opening" (Heb 10:20). Believers, who are "strangers and nomads" (Heb 11:13), accept that they will make their entire life into a "pilgrimage" by accepting God's promise. They do not know the length or the path, but since they are members of the faith, they know the goal.

The final objective is full communion with the Father. But a personal encounter with God, the God of Jesus Christ, is also the calling that starts the "way," the walk, following the God-Man Jesus, a "pilgrim on earth" who completed his exodus to Jerusalem (cf. Lk 9:31). Ours is a voyage that goes "beyond" and "after," directed toward the heavenly Jerusalem, location of the end of time and setting of the judgment, occupied with history but looking toward the Father, who only Jesus can make us know and love.

Traveling as pilgrims on this earth is the parable of faith and hope, of expectation and of the future, of standing against the temptations of remaining devoted to one's own "shell" and one's own things, of inertia, of possession, and of selfishness.

Next n. 1697 of the *CCC* states that it is important to make the joy and demands of the way of Christ, which is the way of life, extremely clear in catechesis. Catechesis is absolutely necessary so that the Christian can learn about the mystery of Christ more deeply in the light of the Word. In its various forms and phases, catechesis must always accompany the people of God. It is catechesis of the Spirit, of grace, of the beatitudes, of sin and forgiveness, of human and Christian virtues, and of the commandment of charity. And it is ecclesial catechesis.

First comes the apostolic *didaké*, or the "preaching" of the Word of God. From the Church emerges the voice of the herald, who proclaims the *kerygma*, or the primary and fundamental proclamation that Jesus himself made at the beginning of his ministry: "The time is fulfilled, and the kingdom of God is close at hand. Repent, and believe the gospel" (Mk 1:15). Without a proclamation of the Word, no one can listen, and "faith comes from hearing" (Rom 10:17).

The Kingdom of God was inaugurated because the Father rose the Son that he sent, Jesus, from the dead and gave us his Spirit. Jesus is the only God: "Only in him is there salvation; for of all the names in the world given to men, this is the only one by which we can be saved" (Acts 4:12). The Christian is called to bear witness to his hope "with courtesy and respect and with a clear conscience" (1 Pt 3:17), ready to withstand rejection and persecution, aware that "it is better to suffer for doing right than for doing wrong" (1 Pt 3:17). Preaching about the Christ event is part of the Church's mission.

Moreover, it is its reason for existing. It does this through proclamation, catechesis, and homily. These involve reading and comprehension, explanation and interpretation, and an involvement of the mind and heart.

The catechesis of the "new life in the Christian" must first of all be "pneumatological," or "of the Holy Spirit," which the Church invokes as the perfect Consoler, the sweet guest of the soul, the light of hearts, and the giver of gifts. Communion is the purview of the Spirit. He, the bond of love, binds us to Christ and brings us, through him, to the Father.

All of this is his gift, in the order of nature and in Christian life. With his divinizing power, he purifies and elevates through grace, supernatural virtues, and gifts. These make up the totality of our lives and our acts and provide the ultimate fulfillment of the acts of the virtues, teaching them the "deiform way." They do not only give the man a basis for his life but also a divine way of living. It is a marvelous spiritual web of divine influences that the Holy Spirit weaves along the entire arc of a Christian life. The entire existence of those who have been opened up to him through baptism and do not resist him but rather allow themselves to be formed by his actions and tamed by his teaching is supported and guided by this divine Guest.

He is the Spirit of wisdom and intellect, of advice and fortitude, of science and of mercy and of fear of God. The gifts of the Spirit are like a divine spring from which knowledge of the commandments of Christian life can be drawn. Through these, we can discover whether the Holy Spirit resides in us. They are "clothes" through which the soul perfects itself in order to readily obey the will of God. They produce what Paul calls "the fruit of the Spirit" (Gal 5:22) and the even more perfect works that correspond to the beatitudes.

The gifts are interventions through which the Spirit makes the believer, in the dimensions of the various virtues and the fundamental characteristics of his life choices, ever more submissive to his actions. For this reason, Christians must openly accept the gifts, cultivate them, facilitate them, and defend them from the enemies of the life of grace.

Consequently, the catechesis of the "new life of the Christian" cannot be "a catechesis of grace." The moral Christian life cannot be expressed as pure and simple ethical behavior. The reference point is conformity with Christ, fullness of moral life, and holiness. When Christian actions are supported by grace, the union with God's will is expressed, as specified by the Gospel.

Through the grace of baptism, man is configured to Christ in the Paschal mystery of death and resurrection. For this reason, following Christ is the fundamental, essential, and original element of Christian morality. Only in losing one's life for Jesus's sake can one find it again (cf. Mt 10:39). And it makes sense to lose one's life in Jesus because the first to give himself completely for us was the Father with his gift of Jesus and the Spirit.

The experience of identifying with Christ is expressed in strong terms by Paul when he says "I have been crucified with Christ and yet I am alive; yet it is no longer I, but Christ living in me" (Gal 2:19–20). He then reminds the baptized that "In him, in bodily form, lives divinity in all its fullness, and in him you too find your own fulfilment [...] You have been buried with him by your baptism; by which, too, you have been raised up with him through your belief in the power of God who raised him from the dead" (Col 2:9,12).

Baptism is the fundamental event of Christian existence. It is a decisive and irreversible act which leaves an invisible mark, a seal, on our existence. Everything that happens afterwards is founded and rooted in this grace, in this gift. Everything that is given only perfects what it already contains. In expressing, marking, and giving the faith of which it is a sign, baptism places us in the missionary dynamic of that faith.

Under the shelter of and with the cooperation of grace, the Christian is united with the Holy Spirit and starts to ardently desire what God wills. In this way, his will becomes love, because love is nothing other than an ardent desire for good.

The catechesis of the "new life of the Christian" must also and above all be "a catechesis of the beatitudes."

Blessed is he who allows himself to be guided by the wisdom of God by observing the law and who lives an honest life. The psalmist proclaims "How blessed are those whose way is blameless, who walk in the Law of Yahweh!" (Ps 119[118]:1). "Way" and "walk" refer to the proverbs and conventions that direct and orient man in moral life. And a man is called just when he works to translate God's will as expressed by the law into his practical life. Wishing to feed on the lifeblood contained in it, he continues to ponder. "How blessed is anyone who [...] delights in the law of Yahweh and murmurs his law day and night" (Ps 1:1–2). The behavior of a just man is blessed because from adherence to God comes happiness. "How blessed is anyone who fears Yahweh, who delights in his commandments!" (Ps 112[111]:1). The joy of the law is the happiness of personal communion with God.

Since we can freely choose whether to take our steps on either of the ways which open before us, the true disciple is he who chooses to travel the way of life: he who chooses to love the Lord his God and to observe his commandments, his laws, and his rules. In this way, he can find complete joy: learning from Christ and following him. Jesus is the pastor who guides the people who choose to move up the ladder of evangelical perfection through the steps of the beatitudes.

While the beatitudes proclaim these things, Jesus lives them. He is poor, gentle, merciful, pure in heart, a peacemaker, just, suffering, and persecuted... He is the prototype of the new man described in the beatitudes. After him comes the multitude of saints, with the Virgin Mary in the first row. Each Christian is called to travel the same road, which is the way of life, because the beatitudes express the calling of the faithful who are associated with the glory of Christ: they are to be poor, afflicted, gentle, hungry and thirsty for uprightness, merciful, pure in heart, peacemakers, and persecuted for the cause of uprightness (cf. Mt 5:3–11).

A life lived in accordance with the beatitudes prepares one for the blessing of an existence full of complete and definitive communion with God. Each beatitude is connected to a promise, and that promise expresses the work of God. In fact, they open our eyes to the completeness of his actions. The idea is to shift our attention beyond what we perceive the problem to be by telling us God's answer, that God's future is our future.

However, the catechesis of the "new life in Christ" must also be "a catechesis of sin and forgiveness." The New Testament states that the way "to be saved" (Acts 16:17) is the opposite of the way that leads to destruction. The latter is the way chosen by people who refuse God and his love through sin.

More than a lack of reason, truth, and conscience, sin is most of all an offense towards God. The psalmist recognizes that "Against you, you alone, I have sinned, I have done what you see to be wrong" (Ps 51[50]:6). Sinning is going against God's love for us. It distances our hearts from him. It is a transgression against true love toward God and toward our neighbors.

Man must always recognize that before God, he is like a poor beggar. His so-called "merits" are nothing compared to the overabundance of the gift freely given. Here, there must be radical poverty. There, there is the immensity of grace, which fills man's emptiness. The path of the faithful requires the awareness of what one is not and of the will of God, who envelops us in his mercy. Salvation only occurs through God. For this reason, Jesus must always be one's first priority and be placed above all other things. This is the substance of the call to conversion: "Return to the house of the Father: the kingdom of the heavens has come to you."

For this reason, after Christ's Passover, continuing to refuse the greatest love (that which God first offered men without receiving anything in return, sending his Son to his death for our redemption: cf. 1 Jn 4:10) is substantially, due to the monstrous ingratitude involved, the essence of sin itself. This is because it is a deliberate separation from he who is truth and life. It is the refusal of love which provokes affliction and sadness and leads to death.

The root of sin is found in the free will of man: "For from the heart come evil intentions: murder, adultery, fornication, theft, perjury, slander. These are the things that make a person unclean" (Mt 15:19–20).

The number of different sins is large, and the Bible provides various lists. Paul contrasts acts of self-indulgence with the fruits of the Spirit: "When self-indulgence is at work the results are obvious: sexual vice, impurity, and sensuality, the worship of false gods and sorcery; antagonisms and rivalry, jealousy, bad temper and quarrels, disagreements, factions and malice, drunkenness, orgies and all such things. And about these, I tell you now as I have told you in the past, that people who behave in these ways will not inherit the kingdom of God" (Gal 5:19–21).

Sins can be classified based on their content (as can be done for all human acts), based on the virtues of which they are opposites, or based on the commandments on which they infringe. They can also be subdivided into those which regard God, one's neighbor, or oneself. They can be divided into spiritual and carnal sins, or into sins of thought, word, action, or omission.

The distinction between mortal sin and venial sin, which is not clear in the Bible, was set up as part of the tradition of the Church. Mortal sin destroys the spirit of charity in a man's heart due to a serious violation of God's law. It involves turning away from God, who is man's ultimate purpose and his beatitude, in favor of a lesser good. As a consequence, the man is deprived of saving grace. Venial sin, on the other hand, does not break man's covenant with God and is "repairable" for humans through his grace. It is committed when one disobeys the rules prescribed by moral law with regards to a minor matter or when one disobeys moral law with regards to a grave matter but without full awareness or without total consent.

Next, the *CCC* states that the catechesis of "new life" is also "a catechesis of the human virtues."

There are few things that need to be in the "pilgrim's pouch." The pilgrim is poor compared to God. His skeleton and the substance of his being are provided by faith and hope. He must fill himself with love, living in prayer, fasting, and almsgiving. He has chosen to make every person his neighbor in order to already encounter God here. He is a virtuous man: a mixture of prudence and justice, temperance and fortitude.

The concept of virtue has been discussed since the morals of man became a subject of reflection in antiquity. According to the traditional language, virtue refers to the ability to orient oneself stably toward a certain thing that is right. Hence, it is a permanent internal strength, because men freely decide to work toward a determined good or value in various different situations

For Christians, virtuous life is essentially theological: a life of faith, hope, and charity. In addition to these three theological virtues, there are the four so-called cardinal virtues, and "nothing in life is more useful for human beings" (Wis 8:7). The four virtues—temperance, prudence, fortitude, and justice—are the weapons with which the "good fight" is fought. They are qualities that allow liberty to take the form of a gift in the various concrete choices of moral life. They are the strategies of love which open men up to a communal dynamic, with the objective of giving of themselves through charity.

Judgment is necessary for making choices in life. For this reason, the virtue of "prudence," without which the entire moral edifice cannot stand and would collapse, is essential. Prudence is based on the good of reason, which is the resource of men. Its purpose is to decipher the concrete reality of life in order to evaluate each operational aspect. It makes man know and practice what is right. But a prudent person is not satisfied simply because the objective is right. He wants the means and the way to be right, as well. For this reason, he makes a concrete decision about the time and place in which he should act, avoiding useless or incorrect steps. People who are prudent are stable, an unmistakable characteristic of spiritual maturity.

"Justice" is the moral virtue that pushes people to respond to the calling to "give each man his due." Given the individual and social nature of human beings, the other person to which justice refers can be considered in his individuality or in his social solidarity. For this reason, there is both specific and general justice (for the common good). It is evident that the virtue of justice is so rich in importance that it plays a decisive role in the consciences of men and of society. The novelty of Christian love does not exclude justice but rather applies and assumes it. The structures of justice should be animated, enlivened, and supported on the inside by love in order to avoid having them become structures that are only superficial and are not capable of creating lasting values. But a specific commitment toward doing justice, with all its demands, is necessary in each individual community and in relationships between communities.

It is true that many extol the virtues of physical force, even arriving at the point of approving of extreme manifestations of violence. In reality, man experiences his own weakness each day, especially spiritually and morally. He gives into the impulses of internal passions and the pressures that the surrounding environment puts on him. In order to resist the pull of these numerous factors, the virtue of "fortitude" is necessary. It works in two opposite but complementary directions. It is a tendency to resist and a tendency to attack, both a brake and an accelerator. Fortitude moderates audacity and overcomes fears. People who are audacious can commit the sin of imprudence. Fear can become cowardice. Fortitude moderates the impetuosity of audacity and reassures the fearful. It is not only necessary to endure things that are difficult but also to initiate things that are arduous.

Finally, the virtue of "temperance" guides life toward a harmonious balance and dictates proper measures. Fundamentally, it consists of moderation in all things. Temperance does not only mean repression of the desire for pleasure but also refers in its original meaning to the "mixture" of the proper proportions. For this reason, it must influence every aspect of life, moderating them with respect to a person's gradual, regular, total growth. The job of temperance is to keep our feelings in balance, not only by making each action conform to the objective order of values but also by directly supervising the powers of the soul and their activity through self-control and a conscious effort toward personal education. Temperance is the virtue of liberty, liberation from the dominance of sensitivity, and the affirmation of the primacy of the spirit.

However, the *CCC* adds, stopping at human virtues is not sufficient for a complete catechesis of the "new life in Christ." Most of all, "a catechesis of the Christian virtues" is necessary.

The fundamental choice to follow Christ is fundamentally expressed by living "faith, hope, and charity," which enable the Christian to participate in the triune life, which he has received as a gift, through his actions. By living the theological dimension, the Christian follows Christ, truly participating in his life experience.

Through faith, the Christian is rendered a participant in the knowledge that Christ has about the mystery of the Father's love. Through hope, he welcomes the salvation brought about by God through Christ with trust. Through charity, he shares the love of God and of his neighbor, the love that Christ felt to the point that he gave us his life. Faith, hope, and charity are fundamentally a single entity: faith which hopes and which loves. They represent a unique and complete relationship with the God of salvation.

The experience of a theological life, which has Christ at its center and which is powered by the Spirit, gives the life of the Christian specificity and unity. By accepting the gift of faith, hope, and charity, the Christian makes a fundamental choice that directs his every action and places each decision and action on a theological plane—that is, in the light of the triune God. From this perspective, the theological virtues are the basis for, power, and characterize the moral actions of the Christian. They inform and give life to all the moral virtues.

The attitudes of faith, hope, and charity feed off each other and expand man's capacity for knowing, desiring, and loving and his openness to the transcendent while working toward truth, joy, and love. Faith and hope work through charity, which is the heart of the Christian moral proposal. These three attitudes are closely connected to each other since faith and hope converge in the most important, charity: "As it is, these remain: faith, hope and love, the three of them; and the greatest of them is love" (1 Cor 13:13).

For this reason, the catechesis of the "new life" must be a "catechesis of the twofold commandment of charity set forth in the Decalogue."

Love of God and love of one's neighbor cannot be separated. What was already the core of the faith of Israel and the center of the faithful Israelite's existence, or the commandment to love God ("'Listen, Israel: Yahweh our God is the one, the only Yahweh. You must love Yahweh your God with all your heart, with all your soul, with all your strength" (Dt 6:4–5), was joined by Jesus to the commandment to love one's neighbor (which was already stated in Lv 19:18: "You will love your neighbor as yourself") to form a single commandment (cf. Mk 12:29–31).

The basis and reasoning behind this "new" commandment which Jesus gave us is that God loved us first and made himself our neighbor. For this reason, love is no longer a simple commandment. It is a response to the gift of love through which God comes to us. The commandment to love becomes possible because it is not simply a demand. Love can be commanded because first, it was given.

With this new commandment, Jesus associates his disciples with that which he has lived, giving them the ability to love as he loved. At the Last Supper, he prayed "that the love with which you loved me may be in them, and so that I may be in them" (Jn 17:26). He does not only give us words that we must follow. He gives himself. With the gift of the new commandment, Jesus turns his presence into a gift.

It is true that communion with God is created by observing the commandments: "Whoever keeps his commandments remains in God, and God in him" (1 Jn 3:24). But it is also true that the numerous commandments are summarized in the new single great commandment. This means that the individual commandments given by God cannot be considered to be separate entities. Each commandment is a partial and necessary realization of the love that envelops the world. Paul states this clearly: the commandments "are summed up in this single phrase: You must love your neighbor as yourself. Love can cause no harm to your neighbor, and so love is the fulfilment of the Law" (Rom 13:9–10).

Through the commandments, God shows us how to love Him and our neighbor. And with the gift of the Spirit, he gives us the strength and the opportunity to do what seems impossible for man: love like Jesus himself loved us.

While setting the course of the pilgrimage, Christ left the tracks of his blood for his people. He gave them a viaticum of life and grace, and he awarded them the same mission that he himself received from the Father. In this new covenant, Christ has made himself man's travel companion, becoming his viaticum through the signs that he has ratified it. The Eucharistic food is the viaticum that the Church obtains from the Father as it invokes the Spirit and awaits the coming of the Lord in the pull toward his *parusía*.

For this reason, the catechesis of the "new life" cannot be anything other than "ecclesiastical." Christian life can grow and be communicated only through the "communion of the saints." The path of followers of Jesus is not individual. Yes, the response to the calling is personal, but what then occurs is that the person joins a people, the *ekklesía*, the assembly. The Church is a population on a journey because the Church is moving "from the Trinity toward the Trinity." It comes from God, and it is moving toward God.

Christ's fullness, the Church is moving through history. The Church is a missionary, the herald of Christ. Christ, the Head, extends his kingdom to stretch across the entire universe through the church, his Body. As a sacrament of the unity of the human race, it places itself beside all the peoples and all the people on the journey and makes itself available to meet their every just need or expectation. It works for the good of them, expanding the boundaries of its charity in this way beyond every border.

Through its nature and grace, the Body looks toward its Head, and from the head come infinite riches and extraordinary gifts. This force is characterized in each member through his conformation to Christ and through his assumption of its ministries. It is renewal through the work of the Spirit of Christ, which is unique and identical in the Head and the members. He gives the whole Body life, unity, and movement.

Finally, in n. 1698, we are once again reminded that it is "Jesus Christ" who is "the way, the truth, and the life" (Jn 14:6), the initial and final point of reference for the catechesis of the "new life." Only in looking to him is there the real possibility of life and salvation. "The truth is that only in the mystery of the incarnate Word does the mystery of man take on light" (*GS* 22). Moral structure must be built in Christ, the New Man: each man is created in the image and in the likeness of God (cf. Gn 1:26) and is saved by Christ. The true image of the invisible God, Christ is the revealer of man's full significance.

For this reason, the centrality of the person of Jesus Christ and the concreteness of the existence of the human person must be placed at the center of catechesis. Fulfilling our calling occurs with Christ so that he can personally and fully realize the answer that man must give to God. The specific contents and the ultimate motivations for the moral proposal are found in Christ, man's contemporary for all of time, because he is the fulfilment and the perfection of all the laws.

In Christ, the way of truth and life, the Christian finds a cohesive force that gives meaning and unity to his entire existence because the divine image impressed on the world during creation and disfigured through sin is restored in Christ. In being "molded to his image" (cf. Rom 8:29), we are made to "share the divine nature" (cf. 2 Pt 1:4)—that is, the life of God, and we fully realize our humanity.

This anthropological vision can provide a reason for the fundamental human calling to act "for nature according to the law" since his words are "engraved on our hearts" (cf. Rom 2:14–16). Each man, created in Christ, has a power engraved in him in the deepest part of his very being to fulfill his purpose according to the image of the Son—that is, to act with sense and truth.

It is for this reason that Christian morality is fundamentally presented as the actualization of a new and eternal covenant that Jesus Christ creates through his death and resurrection. It is a calling to participate in the Paschal mystery of Christ, who is the supreme expression of love. In this way, the believer, who has been regenerated in Christ and pushed into constant action by the Spirit, can proclaim the Gospel of universal salvation through the Lord to the world through his own life.

"O Wonderful Exchange! [*O admirabile commercium* in Latin] The Creator of the human race took to himself a human body and was born of a virgin, and becoming man he granted us divinity," proclaims the Christmas liturgy.

And the *CCC,* in the conclusion to this introduction, quotes from a text by St. John Eudes (who lived in the 17th century), which invites, pleads, and begs us to "consider" Jesus in order to better consider ourselves and to know Jesus's desires in order to desire what he desires. As the apostle says, "For to me, to live is Christ" (Phil 1:21).

Chapter One:
THE DIGNITY OF THE HUMAN PERSON

Ángel Rodríguez Luño

The first chapter of the third part of the *CCC* is dedicated to the consideration of human dignity. Christian moral life is born from and expresses what a Christian "already is" and the calling that he has "already received" through the Christian's desires and actions. For this reason, it presumes that one's dignity as a son of God in Christ through the Holy Spirit is recognized. The exposition of human dignity, and all that this implies, is studied in eight articles. Their essential contents are briefly illustrated here.

Article 1:
MAN: THE IMAGE OF GOD

Christ revealed the mystery of the Father, and he also revealed that man possesses a supreme dignity because he was created in Christ in the image and likeness of God and is destined for eternal beatitude. "God created man in the image of himself, in the image of God he created him" (Gn 1:27). What does it mean "to be created in the image and likeness of God?" Is divine perfection reflected in a similar manner in creatures that are not human?

It is true that all things reflect the perfection and greatness of God in some way, but only human beings are the image of God. When we speak about images, we refer to the expression and imitation of the specifics of the model. Man was created in the image and likeness of God because God not only gave him being and life, like he gave to the animals and plants. He also infused them with a spiritual soul, and with this, he left an "imprint" on man which imitates—although in an imperfect manner—what is most specific about God, due to whom human beings are able to converse with him and can enter in communion with him, know him, and love him freely. In this image of God, which each man possesses, are the roots of his supreme dignity, which implies a vocation to participate in the eternal beatitude which is unique to God.

Some of the signs mentioned in the *CCC* which demonstrate the divine image present in man, from which human dignity comes, are intelligence and conscience, through which man distinguishes good from evil, and free will, through which he commands his own actions and is made capable of planning his life in a loving correspondence of God's love and in the service of his neighbor.

Free will is realized through love, in the free affirmation of good for the sake of good, but it brings with it the possibility of not recognizing what is good and adhering to what is evil. The revelation teaches us that man sinned at the beginning of history, damaging his dignity as the son of God. Through his passion, Christ freed us from the dominion of sin and earned a new life in the Holy Spirit for us. In union with Christ, man "attains the perfection of charity which is holiness. Having matured in grace, the moral life blossoms into eternal life in the glory of heaven" (n. 1709).

The consideration of human dignity at the beginning of the moral section of the *CCC* is intended to help us understand what will be stated further on about how good works are an expression of what man is: the image of God elevated to the dignity of a son, and not an external alien imposition of the human condition.

Article 2:
OUR VOCATION TO BEATITUDE

I. The Beatitudes

Created in the image of God, man is called to eternal beatitude. It is in the light of this calling that we must understand the beatitudes, which play the role of introducing the great Sermon on the Mount in the Gospel of Matthew. They become a type of "program" which summarizes the attitudes necessary to enter into and belong to the Kingdom of Heaven. Poverty of spirit, meekness, hunger and thirst for justice, poverty, purity of heart, etc. briefly define the spirit of the disciples of Christ and, at the same time, help us see the events and circumstances of life through his eyes. They join them to a promise that, although sometimes paradoxical, showers us with peace and hope.

II. The Desire for Happiness

Jesus's words regarding the beatitudes respond to the desire for happiness which burns deeply in the human heart. All men want to be happy, but few know how to achieve this, and many follow paths that empty the heart or fill it with bitterness. Jesus's brief and incisive phrases illuminate and orient the deepest desire of the human soul, which feels called to delight in goods which satiate without satiating, with consoling promises.

III. Christian Beatitude

The New Testament uses various expressions to characterize the beatitude to which man is called: the kingdom of God, the vision of God, entering into the joy of the Lord, and entering into God's rest. This is how the deepest dimension of human and Christian dignity is clarified: man is called to a true communion with God, to contemplate him face to face and to share his eternal and infinite beatitude. This eternal life in God is a condition that cannot be reached simply with a human being's natural strengths, and for this reason, the *CCC* says that it is a gratuitous and supernatural gift. It is given by merciful divine generosity to those who wish for it more than anything else in the world, distancing their hearts from the idols of each era that deceitfully promise something that they cannot give. As the text on which we comment suggests, the catechesis of Christian beatitude leads to purification of man's heart and desires. Christians are characterized not only by what they do but most of all by what they desire and by what they love.

Article 3:
MAN'S FREEDOM

I. Freedom and Responsibility

Freedom is a supreme mark of the dignity of man, who was created in the image of God. Men are free, like their Creator is free. Human freedom is a true freedom, although it is finite and fallible. It is initiative and dominion over one's actions. It is the power to act or not to act, or to do this or that. In general, it is being the true author who sets the direction of one's life. God respects freedom, which gives human beings a deep dignity, in a serious way and allows for all the consequences of free actions to unfold, regardless of how grave these may be. Human freedom is not a circus show that takes place above a safety net. If man slips, he truly falls, and he gets hurt. God never abandons us, but he always respects our freedom. People who know how to make good use of this freedom, binding themselves to what they recognize to be good, becomes ever more free. People who use it poorly become slaves to their vices.

God's respect demonstrates that freedom is inseparably joined to responsibility. Given that we have true freedom and we can all freely plan our own actions and our own lives, we can and must answer for our actions and their consequences. Naturally, the scope of our responsibility coincides with that of our freedom. Freedom that has atrophied due to ignorance, inadvertence, fear, violence, etc., corresponds to a similarly diminished responsibility. Moreover, only things that one wished would happen are imputable. This is the reason that certain negative collateral effects that are inseparable from necessary actions are not imputable. These are effects that we are obligated to tolerate but which we do not desire. "For a bad effect to be imputable it must be foreseeable and the agent must have the possibility of avoiding it, as in the case of manslaughter caused by a drunken driver" (n. 1737).

Human freedom, which is an essential part of human dignity, must be recognized by civil and ecclesiastical authorities. Its exercise can be legitimately limited only to the point required for the common good in order to render coexistence and collaboration between free citizens of the State or members of the Church possible. The convictions of the conscience in religious matters must be immune from civil coercion. "This right must be recognized and protected by civil authority within the limits of the common good and public order" (n. 1738).

II. Human Freedom in the Economy of Salvation

In numbers 1739 to 1742, human freedom is considered from the point of view of the history of salvation. Human freedom has its own history: it was given to us by the Creator and fortified by great gifts, it collapsed and became a slave to sin, and it was finally freed by Christ through his passion, death, and resurrection. It was then strengthened through the action of the Holy Spirit, which is the Spirit of freedom. The grace of Christ makes a new dimension of freedom possible: freedom-liberation from misery and sin.

Grace does not oppose freedom but rather expands it and provides reassurance in the face of tests and dangers. "By the working of grace the Holy Spirit educates us in spiritual freedom in order to make us free collaborators in his work in the Church and in the world" (n. 1742).

Article 4:
THE MORALITY OF HUMAN ACTS

Given that man is free and given the scope of his freedom, he is a moral subject. Actions that are deliberately planned and freely performed have a particular goodness or malice and are called good or evil. This is different for acts that originate from animal instinct or necessity, which are not governed by freedom. Events that are not free (an accident, an illness, etc.) can also be good or bad for human beings but do not imply moral good or evil.

I. The Sources of Morality

What determines whether a voluntary action is morally good or evil? It depends on three components of the action: "the object chosen; the end in view or the intention; [and] the circumstances of the action" (n. 1750).

The object chosen is the object desired or the good toward which the will deliberately directs itself. This can be good or evil based on whether our intelligence sees it as a virtue or a vice. The object chosen classifies the willful act morally. If a person gives someone a book, what the person "wants" to do is give a book to that person. "Give the person a book" is therefore the "object chosen." If that person steals a book, what he "wants" to do is steal a book. "Steal a book" is the "object chosen." The book is not the "object chosen" in either of these examples. If the object was the book, the two actions just mentioned would be identical—a statement which is obviously false.

The intention, and the goal that this intention is directed at, is the good or the reason for which the object is chosen. One can give someone a book as an act of friendship, as an act of vanity, or in order to obtain an illicit favor in exchange. There are intentions that explain why one or two actions are performed and actions that explain many actions or even one's entire life. For this reason, the *CCC* says that intention "is not limited to directing individual actions, but can guide several actions toward one and the same purpose; it can orient one's whole life toward its ultimate end" (n. 1752).

A good intention does not render an action with a bad "object chosen" good or just, just like the intention of giving someone a book that one has previously stolen as an act of friendship does not justify the robbery. The end does not justify the means. A bad intention, on the other hand, can make an action that could in and of itself be good evil, like how the intention of obtaining an illicit favor renders the action of giving someone a book malicious.

Circumstances—the place where an action is performed, the duration of the action, the way it is performed, the quality of the person who performs it, etc.—are secondary elements of actions. Depending on the specifics, the circumstances can aggravate or reduce the goodness or malice of an action or increase or reduce its imputability, but they cannot make an action with a bad "object chosen" good.

II. Good Acts and Evil Acts

When the object chosen, the end, and the circumstances are considered together, it is necessary to keep in mind that good behavior requires that the object chosen, the intention, and the circumstances all be good, and if the "object chosen" is bad, this always determines the evilness of the action. For this reason, the *CCC* presents a principle that is very important in practice: "There are some concrete acts—such as fornication—that it is always wrong to choose, because choosing them entails a disorder of the will, that is, a moral evil" (n. 1755). When free will deliberately turns to or approves an action that directly opposes a virtue (such as how stealing a book is in conflict with the virtue of justice, for example), it opposes the virtue itself and is therefore an evil desire although it has a subjectively good intention. Actions that are unjust cannot advance the cause of friendship or justice, just like the causes of love and chastity cannot be advanced through impure actions.

For this reason, it is wrong to judge the morality of human acts by considering only the intention that inspires them or the circumstances that frame them. Likewise, during pastoral work, one should never forget that evil actions are generally preceded by malicious intentions, so it is necessary to pay close attention to purifying people's hearts and desires and to training people's ability to find the just way to realize good intentions (prudence and discernment). Good intentions are necessary, but not sufficient.

Article 5:
THE MORALITY OF THE PASSIONS

I. Passions

In accordance with theological tradition, the *CCC* discusses the emotions or movements of the sensitive appetite of passions. The concept of passion alludes to the "passive" character of sentiments: while actions are active initiatives (one decides to study), passion is passive (one becomes sad) and reactive (a feeling of pessimism or distress arrives when one witnesses a negative event). Passions are part of normal human psychology and represent the reaction of sensitivity to something good or bad perceived by the external or internal senses (vision, memory, imagination, etc.). The fundamental passion is love, which is the attraction aroused by something good that is perceived, imagined, or remembered. Desire for good and satisfaction with the good possessed come from love. The perception of evil, on the other hand, causes hate, aversion, fear, and sadness.

II. Passions and Moral Life

In and of themselves, passions are not morally imputable. Only when they are planned by intelligence and enabled or supported by will can they constitute a merit or a fault. Despite this, they are of great importance because they are one of the most frequent stimuli for voluntary actions. They anticipate the judgment of reason (one tends to see things that cause pleasure as good and things that are unpleasant as bad) and suggest a course of action (go toward what is pleasant and run away from what is unpleasant). In this sense, passions that imply true judgement and lead people toward good and away from evil can be considered "good" and passions that are based on false judgment and lead toward evil can be considered "evil."

Due to the fact that they create predispositions and the influence that they have on the perception of good and evil, education of feelings and sentiments is fundamentally important. It is easier to behave correctly if feelings are helpful and do not constitute an obstacle to be overcome. Moral education should result in man being pushed toward good not only through reason and will but also by the heart and by his feelings. The action of the Holy Spirit heals the wounds of sensitivity, which originate from sin, and directs all the energies of the human soul toward good.

Article 6:
MORAL CONSCIENCE

What is stated in the *CCC* can be more easily understood if one considers that normally, we speak about moral conscience in two different ways: broadly, like for the presence of moral law in the deepest part of the human heart, and in a strict sense, like for judgments about the moral quality of concrete actions. In the first sense, a person could say that he cannot in good conscience agree with the decision that a certain government official made. In the second sense, a person can think that he acted poorly when he did not listen to someone who had previously asked him for help.

I. The Judgment of Conscience

In a strict sense, "Conscience is a judgment of reason whereby the human person recognizes the moral quality of a concrete act that he is going to perform, is in the process of performing, or has already completed" (n. 1781). In making this judgment, moral law and in the end the voice of God, which is written on the heart of man through natural law, make their presence known, as do the law of Christ and the motions that the Holy Spirit can instill in the soul in a concrete moment. When a person is honest with himself, his conscience represents the deepest center of his soul, in which the person, the calling to do good which comes from God, and the evaluation of the particular circumstances of each situation are found. An intimate and sincere conviction, conscience has the same dignity that the person has. For this reason, man should never be obligated to "to act contrary to his conscience. Nor must he be prevented from acting according to his conscience, especially in religious matters" (n. 1782).

II. The Formation of Conscience

With regard to the conscience, something similar to what happens with the natural human ability to speak occurs. Everyone has this capacity, but only people who have received a certain education are capable of expressing themselves properly, clearly, and with elegance. In order for the judgments of the conscience to be true—that is, for it to judge what is good to be good and what is truly evil to be evil—it is necessary to mold it. The formation of conscience is a complex task that lasts for one's entire life and requires loving virtues and good and knowing their concrete requirements on the one hand and eliminating obstacles such as pride, selfishness, lack of honesty with oneself, fear, doubts, and superficiality on the other. Reflection on the Word of God, prayer, and sincere and humble examination of one's conscience facilitate the formation of an upright and sensitive conscience, as do the advice of prudent people and an attitude of meekness before God and before the teachings of the Church. This certainly does not mean, however, renouncing trying to understand the reason behind things.

III. To Choose in Accord with Conscience

It is common knowledge that, when faced with a concrete decision, the conscience can make a right or true judgment—one that conforms with what is reasonable and conforms with divine law—or an erroneous judgment that deviates from moral law or good reason. Sometimes, we must confront difficult problems, and it becomes necessary to have a sincere attitude of searching for truth and justice while trying to understand what God wishes, knowing how to interpret past and present experiences, exercising prudence by consulting with expert persons, and invoking the help of the Holy Spirit.

The *CCC* reminds us of a few general rules that can help us in the case of doubt: we are never permitted to do evil because good results from it, the Golden Rule (we must treat others as we would like them to treat us), and we must always treat our neighbor and his conscience with respect. Others could be added, such as not judging others' intentions, considering others to be innocent until it is demonstrated that they are guilty, presuming that people who habitually behave well have acted properly and that people who generally make mistakes in these circumstances have made a mistake, and so on.

IV. Erroneous Judgement

One must always act in accordance with the judgment that one's moral conscience makes with subjective certainty—that is, without revealing any doubt about the matter. Otherwise, one would act against his conscience, performing actions that he had judged with certainty to be evil or not performing actions that he considered with certainty to be obligatory. Sometimes, however, a subjectively certain judgment can be erroneous. In this case, the *CCC* distinguishes between two types of errors: vincible or culpable errors and invincible or innocent errors.

"Vincible" errors are those where the person is personally responsible because they are the fruit, for example, of a habitual lack of dedication when searching for the truth, of negligence when informing oneself about a concrete problem that one is facing, or the repetition of sins that have made the conscience insensitive and almost blind. In these cases, "the person is culpable for the evil he commits" (n. 1791). Essentially, when an error is vincible, the judgment of the conscience is not fully certain because at one point or another the individual realizes that he has not worked hard enough to find the truth or that his judgment is conditioned by his vices. If someone observes even for an instant that it is possible that his judgment is erroneous, he is obligated to gather further information to correct his error. It is very difficult for a person that is conscious of the fact that his conscience's judgment goes against the teachings of the Church or the common sentiment among righteous persons who are experts in the matter not to feel guilt.

"Invincible" errors are those that completely dominate the conscience due to causes beyond the person's will in such a way that in a given place and at a given moment in time, the person has no possibility of recognizing and overcoming the errors. In this case, "the evil committed by the person cannot be imputed to him" (n. 1793), but it does not cease to be an evil or a disorder for this reason. In this case, man is always obligated to educate his conscience better and to work to recognize and overcome the errors.

Article 7:
THE VIRTUES

I. The Human Virtues

Human virtues are firm and stable dispositions that work to perfect human faculties (intelligence, will, appetites of the senses) so as to help the person more easily understand what is good and how to realize it. Although there are also intellectual virtues, such as wisdom and science, the *CCC* mainly refers to the moral virtues which allow for a stable refinement of freedom and one's capacity to choose. Justice, for example, is the virtue through which a man who possesses it is able to find the proper solution for every problem and put it into practice. The human moral virtues are "habits" that one acquires through the continued practice of good actions. People who act in a just way from time to time through their own personal strength acquire the virtue of justice, which allows them to act with justice in a steadily easier and more secure manner. The moral virtues are not an automatism or the simple habit of always doing the same thing but rather a true moral refinement of one's capacity to choose. A just man does not always do the same thing but rather always acts with justice, even if the decision that is just differs depending on the circumstances and the context.

The Cardinal Virtues

The four fundamental moral virtues, around which all the others are grouped, are called cardinal virtues. They are prudence, justice, fortitude, and temperance.

"Prudence" determines what is good to do in every concrete case. For this reason, it is the condition on which all the others are founded, since it is prudence that decides what conforms to justice, fortitude, and temperance at any given place and at any given moment. For this reason, we say that prudence is the rule and measure of virtuous actions, the *auriga virtutum*, which guides the other virtues. "Justice" is the constant and firm desire to give each man what he is owed and that to which he is entitled. The "virtue of religion" regards what God is owed. "Fortitude" helps man persevere in working toward good that is difficult to realize, overcoming the fear that is created by difficulties, temptations, persecutions, and dangers. The most exalted act of fortitude is martyrdom. "Temperance" overpowers the attraction of pleasures and the repulsion of pain so that a person is not drawn away from doing good due to these factors. It moderates man's inclination toward sexuality, eating, drinking, gambling, etc.

The Virtues and Grace

Moral virtues acquired through human dedication "are purified and elevated by divine grace" (n. 1810) so that the Christian can do good works in the light of the faith and move toward the eternal beatitude, not only toward what is good according to natural reason. The majority of theologians believe that the grace of God instills the infused moral virtues in the Christian (infused prudence, infused justice, etc.). Others believe that it is enough to think that grace purifies and elevates human moral virtues. This is a theological question that the *CCC* leaves open because grace is not defined by the Church. Regardless of whether it is explained in one way or the other, there is no doubt that grace and theological virtues modify the behavioral criteria of human virtues in some way. For example, human temperance leads man to eat what is necessary to maintain his health and his capacity to work. Christian temperance, on the other hand, sometimes calls man to eat somewhat less than what is necessary or even to fast for atonement and spiritual growth.

II. The Theological Virtues

While the moral virtues regulate a person's relationships with others, with himself, and with the use of the resources of creation, theological virtues relate directly to the One and Triune God. They are infused by God so that man can act as his son and therefore merit eternal life. The theological virtues are faith, hope, and charity. These three virtues animate and give life to the moral virtues and characterize Christian moral life.

Through "faith," we believe in God and all that he has revealed. It is the origin of human salvation and the basis for and the root of each justification. Through faith, human beings are introduced to God's plan of salvation in Christ. Through "hope," we aspire to eternal beatitude, trusting in Christ's promises and in the help of the Holy Spirit's grace. It is the virtue that responds to the desire for happiness rooted deep in the human heart, that purifies and elevates it. Through "charity," we love God above all things for his own sake and our neighbors as ourselves for love of God. It is the greatest of all the virtues. Saint Paul says "if I am without love, I am nothing" (1 Cor 13:3). It is considered to be the "form" of all of the virtues because it articulates and orders them amongst themselves, and as Saint Augustine says, the other virtues are in a certain sense forms of love.

III. The Gifts and Fruits of the Holy Spirit

The moral life of Christians is further enriched by the gifts of the Holy Spirit, which are permanent dispositions which make man docile in following his inspirations. Guided by the Spirit, the Christian acts in a way which is in a certain sense superhuman—for example, by arriving at conclusions or actions intuitively and immediately where rational reasoning, even when illuminated by faith, could not have led or to where we would have been led only after a long period of time. The Tradition of the Church recognizes seven gifts of the Holy Spirit (cf. n. 1831). These perfections—such as joy, peace, kindness, and others—which are the result of divine action on the human soul, are called fruits of the Holy Spirit.

Article 8:
SIN

I. Mercy and Sin

The central message of the Gospel is that God wanted to save humanity through Christ, freeing us from our sins. Salvation, however, presumes that sin has occurred and is recognized. Without sin, there would be no need for a Redeemer or a Savior. The doctrine of sin is an essential part of the proclamation of the Gospel. This is precisely because the Gospel is a proclamation of mercy and salvation.

II. The Definition of Sin

Saint Augustine defines sin as "an utterance, a deed, or a desire contrary to the eternal law" (n. 1849). Since human reason is a form of participation in divine Reason, sin is also contrary to proper reason and human good.

The essential element of sin is an offense toward God, refusing to accept his love, with a component of disobedience and sometimes of rebellion. Furthermore, man damages himself and others through sin and relates to creation in a disordered way. Christ, the Head of the sinner humanity, displays the considerable pain that comes with sin and which is necessary to heal it through his passion.

III. The Different Kinds of Sins

The catalogue of the sins contained in the Scriptures demonstrates that there are numerous kinds of sins. Sins can be classified based on their object (stealing, killing, etc.), based on the virtue which they oppose (sins against charity, against justice, etc.), or based on the commandments they violate (sins against the fourth commandment, against the fifth, etc.).

IV. The Gravity of Sin: Mortal and Venial Sin

There is a great difference between mortal and venial sin. Mortal sin results in a loss of charity, deprives man of saving grace, and turns man away from God and eternal beatitude. Liberation from mortal sin requires a new initiative of God's mercy and a conversion of heart which is normally accomplished within the setting of the sacrament of reconciliation. Venial sin, on the other hand, does not destroy charity, although it offends it and wounds it. It implies a disorder that inhibits spiritual progress and the practice of good. Deliberate venial sin which is left unpunished predisposes man to mortal sin. Venial sin merits temporal punishment, and it also differs from mortal sin, which brings with it eternal punishment, in this sense.

For a sin to be mortal, three conditions must be met: grave matter, full knowledge, and deliberate consent. Grave matter is specified by the ten commandments and occurs when the action which violates the commandment is gravely contrary to the requirements of a virtue (for example, a substantial robbery or a lie that leads to significant damage go against justice). Warning, or full awareness, means that the person realizes what he is doing and that what he is doing goes seriously against moral law. Deliberate consent is given when will deliberately chooses the sinful action. If man's awareness is not full, his consent cannot be fully deliberate.

A person commits a venial sin when he deliberately commits a disordered action in a less serious matter or even in a grave matter, but without full awareness or total consent.

V. The Proliferation of Sin

If sin is not followed by penitence, it triggers a greater proclivity toward sin until the sin becomes a vice that cloud's one's awareness and makes correct appreciation of good difficult. Sin tends to proliferate. Sins that generate other sins are called capital vices. These are pride, avarice, envy, wrath, lust, gluttony, and sloth or acedia. There are sins that are so grave that it is said that they "cry to heaven" (cf n. 1867).

In addition to a person's own actions, a man can sin by collaborating or becoming complicit in the sins of others—by participating directly and voluntarily in them; by ordering, advising, praising, or approving them; by not disclosing or not hindering them when we have an obligation to do so; or by protecting evil-doers. Through sin, man loses his dignity as the son of God, but divine mercy comes to meet the sinner to restore his dignity. "But however much sin increased, grace was always greater" (Rom 5:20).

Chapter Two:
THE HUMAN COMMUNITY

Gaetano De Simone

Article 1:
THE PERSON AND SOCIETY

I. The Communal Character of the Human Vocation

Man cannot give himself to a project that is solely human, an abstract idea, or false utopias. As a person, he can give himself to another person or persons and to God, who is the author of his being and the only one who can fully accept his gift. For this reason, people who refuse to transcend themselves and experience the giving of oneself and the formation of an authentic human community moving toward its final destiny, God, are alienated.

Societies that render the realization of this gift and the construction of this inter-human solidarity difficult through their social organization or organization of production and consumption are alienated. Human beings cannot and must not become instruments of social, economic, and political structures because each man is free to direct himself toward his final destiny. On the other hand, each cultural, social, economic, and political entity must always be considered in terms of their relative and provisional aspects since historically they have served as a vehicle for socialization and the transformative effect that this has on the universe. This is an eschatological relativity in the sense that man and the world move toward their objectives, the fulfillment of their destinies in God, and a theological relativity since God's gift, through which the final destiny of humanity and creation will be fulfilled, infinitely exceeds the possibilities and expectations of man. Any totalitarian vision of society and the State and any purely earthly ideology of progress run contrary to the full truth of the human person and to God's plan for history.

The Church places itself concretely at the service of the kingdom of God first and foremost by proclaiming and communicating the Gospel of salvation and by constructing new Christian communities. Moreover, this serves the kingdom of God by spreading evangelical values, which are the expression of the Kingdom and help men to accept God's plan, around the world. It is true, therefore, that the incipient reality of the Kingdom can also be found outside the confines of the Church in humanity as a whole, since it is humanity that lives evangelical values and opens itself to the action of the Spirit, who blows whenever and wherever he pleases (Jn 3:8). It is necessary to immediately add, however, that this temporal dimension of the Kingdom is incomplete if it is not coordinated with the kingdom of Christ present in the Church, striving toward eschatological fulfillment. In particular, it follows that the Church should not be confused with a political community and should not be connected to any political system. In fact, the political community and the Church in its proper role are independent and autonomous from each other. They both serve the personal and social vocation of the same human beings, although in different ways. Actually, it could be stated that the distinction between religion and politics and the principle of religious freedom constitute a specific acquisition of Christianity which is of great historic and cultural importance.

II. Conversion and Society

With its social doctrine, the Church takes responsibility for the proclamation that the Lord entrusted to it. It renders the message of liberation and redemption in Christ, the Gospel of the Kingdom—a Gospel that still echoes in the lives of men today through the Church—current regardless of the historical period. The complete realization of the human person, implemented through Christ due to the gift of the Spirit, which has matured over the course of history and is mediated through the person's relationships with other people—relationships that reach perfection through complete commitment to making the world better through justice and peace. Human action throughout history is significant and effective in and of itself for the definitive establishment of the Kingdom, although this is still a fully transcendent gift from God. These actions, when they respect the objective order of temporal reality and are illuminated by truth and charity, become instruments for a steadily more complete implementation of justice and peace and anticipate the promised Kingdom in the present. By conforming to Christ the redeemer, man perceives himself as a creature that is wanted and eternally chosen by God, called to grace and glory in all the fullness of the mystery of which he has become a participant through Jesus Christ. Conformation with Christ and the contemplation of his face infuse the Christian with an irrepressible yearning to anticipate what will one day be the definitive reality in human relationships in this world, working to give food, water, a house, medical care, hospitality, and company to the Lord who knocks on his door (cf. Mt 25:35–37).

Man is unique and unrepeatable. He is an "I," capable of understanding himself, being his own master, and determining his own destiny. Humans are intelligent and aware beings, capable of reflecting on themselves and therefore being aware of themselves and conscious of their own actions. However, it is not intelligence, consciousness, and freedom that define a person but rather the person who is the basis for acts of intelligence, consciousness, and freedom. A just society can only be created by respecting the transcendent dignity of human beings. This is the ultimate objective of society, and society is organized around this principle. For this reason, social order and progress must always help the good in people prevail because the order of things must be suited to the order of people, not vice versa. The solidity of the family unit is also a resource that determines the quality of life in a society. For this reason, civil communities cannot remain indifferent to tendencies toward disintegration that fundamentally threaten the key pillars of family life. The task of the Christian community and of everyone who cares about the good of society is to reaffirm that the family is more than a mere legal, social, and economic unit. It is a community of love and solidarity that is uniquely suitable for teaching and transmitting cultural, ethical, social, spiritual, and religious values which are essential for the development and for the well-being of its members and society.

Article 2: PARTICIPATION IN SOCIAL LIFE

I. Authority

Human beings are the basis for and objective of political cohabitation. Equipped with rationality, humans are responsible for their own choices and capable of pursuing projects that give meaning to their lives on an individual and societal level. Openness to Transcendence and to others is the trait which characterizes humans and makes them stand out. Only through their relationships with Transcendence and with others can human beings reach full and complete self-actualization. This means that for man, who is a naturally social and political creature, social life is not ancillary but rather an essential and ineradicable part of life. Political communities are born from the nature of people, whose consciences reveal the order that God has sculpted in all his creatures and peremptorily order them to follow it. This is an ethical and religious order which affects the directions and solutions with which problems of individual life, life within national communities, and relationships between national communities more than any other material value. This order must gradually be discovered and developed by humanity. Political communities, which are an innate part of human life, exist so that an objective that would otherwise be unreachable can be obtained: the more complete growth of each of its members, who are called to collaborate permanently for the common good, driven by their natural desire for the truth and for good. Jesus rejected the oppressive and despotic power of the heads of nations (Mk 10:42) and their presumption in calling themselves benefactors (Lk 22:25), but he never directly contested the authorities of his time. In his speech on the tribute that should be given to Caesar (Mk 12:13–17; Mt 22:15–22; Lk 20:20–26), he affirms that God should be given what is God's, implicitly condemning any attempt to divinify and absolutize temporal power. Only God can demand everything from man. At the same time, temporal power has the right to what it is owed—Jesus did not consider Caesar's tribute unjust. Submitting to power, not passively but for reasons of conscience (Rom 12:5) constitutes compliance with the order established by God. Saint Paul defined Christians' relationships with and responsibilities toward the authorities (Rom 13:1–7).

Humans are essentially social beings because this was the will of God, who created them. Human nature reveals itself, in fact, to be the nature of a being that satisfies its needs based on a relational subjectivity, or in the manner of a free and responsible actor who recognizes the need to integrate himself and to collaborate with his peers and is capable of living in a communion of knowledge and love with them. A society is a group of people connected in an organic way by a unifying principle that is bigger than any of them. A visible and spiritual assembly, a society endures over time. It inherits the past and prepares for the future.

It is therefore necessary to emphasize that community life is a natural characteristic that distinguishes man from the rest of the creatures of the Earth. Social behavior carries within itself a unique mark of man and humanity: that of a person who operates as part of a community of people. This mark determines the community's interior classification and in a certain sense constitutes its nature. This relational characteristic acquires a deeper and more stable meaning in the light of faith. Social life is not therefore extrinsic to man—he can neither grow nor realize his vocation if not through relationships with others. Human sociability does not automatically result in communion among people, in the giving of oneself. Each society can consider itself to be in the right when each member, due to his capacity to know what is good, works toward good for himself and for others. It is love for the good of oneself and others that unites us in stable groups that work toward the common good. Human sociability is not uniform but has numerous expressions. The "common good," in fact, depends on healthy societal pluralism. The multitude of societies are called to form part of a united and harmonious social fabric, inside of which it is possible for each one to conserve and develop its own face and autonomy. Some societies, like families, civil communities, and religious communities, respond more immediately to the intimate nature of man.

A consequence of this is the necessity of respect for the principle of "subsidiarity." According to this principle, societies of higher order should take the position of providing aid, or *subsidium,* to lower order communities—in other words, a position of support, promotion, and development. In this way, intermediate social bodies can adequately perform the functions as they should without having to unjustly cede them to other higher-level social groups, by which they would eventually be absorbed and substituted. This would result in refusing the bodies their proper dignity and vital space. When understood in the positive sense, as an economic, institutional, and legislative aid offered to smaller social entities, subsidiarity corresponds to a series of negative implications which require the State to refrain from infringing on the vital space of its minor bodies, which are essential to society. Their initiative, freedom, and responsibility should not be supplanted. The principle of subsidiarity protects people from the abuses of superior social entities and asks these groups to help individuals and intermediate bodies to develop their functions. This principle is essential so that each person, family, and intermediate body has something original to offer to the community. Experience has taught us that the denial of subsidiarity or its limitation in the name of so-called democratization or equality of all societies limits and sometimes even eliminates the spirit of freedom and initiative.

The principle of subsidiarity stands in contrast with forms of centralization, bureaucratization, welfarism, and unjust and excessive presence of the State and public administration. By intervening directly and taking responsibility away from society, the welfare State causes human energy to be lost and leads to a boundless increase in the size of the government, dominated more by bureaucratic logic than by concern about serving its citizens, and an enormous increase in public spending. Enacting the principle of subsidiarity corresponds with respect and effective promotion of the primacy of the individual and of the family, the valorization of intermediate associations and organizations, of their fundamental choices, and of all the choices that can be delegated or made by others, encouragement of private initiatives so that each social organism remains in the service of the public good with its own particularities, the pluralistic articulation of society and the representation of its vital forces, the safeguard of human rights and of the rights of minorities, bureaucratic and administrative decentralization, balance between the public and private sectors and the consequent recognition of the private sector's social function, and adequate empowerment of the citizen as part of the country's political and social structure.

II. The Common Good

From dignity, unity, and equality of all persons is derived, first of all, the principle of the common good, to which each aspect of social life must refer in order to be fully meaningful. The common good refers to the collective presence of the conditions in social life that allow the group and its individual members to reach perfection in the fullest and fastest way possible (cf. *GS* 26).

The common good does not consist of the simple sum of the individual good of each subject in the social body. Since it belongs to the society and to every individual, it is and will remain shared. This is because it is indivisible and because only by working together is it possible to arrive at, expand upon, and guard it while looking toward the future. Just like the moral action of the individual involves doing good works, social action reaches completeness by working toward the common good. In fact, the common good can be understood as a social and communal dimension of moral good. A society that wants to deliberately remain in the service of human beings at all levels is one that makes the common good its primary objective, since the common good represents the good of all persons and of the person as a whole. People cannot find fulfilment in themselves—that is, without being "with" and "for" others. This truth does not mandate simple coexistence at the various levels of social and relational life, but rather endless pursuit of good—that is, of the meaning and truth that can be traced back to the existing forms of social life—in a practical form and not only in an ideal one. No form of expression of sociability—not the family, the group, the association, the economic enterprise, the city, the region, the country, nor the community of peoples and of nations—can avoid the question of the true common good. The common good gives these organizations meaning and is their authentic *raison d'être*—the reason for their existence. The common good mobilizes every member of the society. No one is exempt from collaborating in its realization and development in accordance with his personal abilities. The common good needs to be served fully, not in accordance with reductive visions that are subordinate to the advantages that special interests can obtain from it but rather based on a logic that tends toward the broadest possible assumption of responsibility.

III. Responsibility and Participation

A characteristic consequence of subsidiarity is participation, which is essentially expressed in a series of activities through which the citizen, as an individual or in association with others, directly or through his representatives, contributes to the cultural, economic, social, and political life of the civil community to which he belongs. Participation is a duty that must be consciously performed by everyone in a responsible way and while looking toward the common good. This cannot be limited or restricted to a few particular parts of social life, given its importance for growth, especially human growth, in contexts such as the working world and the internal dynamics of businesses, information, and culture, and its utmost importance for social and political life even at the highest levels—the levels which depend on the collaboration of all the peoples of the world in order to create a cohesive international community. From this perspective, the need to promote participation, especially that of the most disadvantaged, and the alternation of political leaders in order to avoid establishing hidden privileges, becomes essential. Moreover, strong moral pressure is necessary so that public affairs may be conducted through the co-responsibility of each member of society toward the common good.

Participation can be obtained in all the possible relationships between the citizen and institutions. To accomplish this goal, particular attention must be paid to the historical and social contexts in which this should occur. Overcoming cultural, legal, and social obstacles, which are often true barriers to the "shared participation" of citizens in the affairs of their communities, requires working toward informing and educating members of the society.

Article 3:
SOCIAL JUSTICE

Justice is a value that accompanies the exercise of the corresponding cardinal moral virtue. In its most classic definition, it "consists in the constant and firm will to give their due to God and neighbor." From a subjective point of view, justice translates to an attitude that is determined by the desire to recognize one's neighbor as a person. From an objective point of view, on the other hand, it constitutes the determining criterion of morality in intersubjective and social situations. The social Magisterium requires respect for the classic forms of justice: commutative justice, distributive justice, and legal justice. Of these, "social justice," which represents a true expansion upon general justice and which regulates social relationships based on observance of the law, has steadily acquired more relevance. Social justice, a requirement that is connected to the social question that today takes on a global dimension, concerns the social, political, and economic aspects of justice and, moreover, the structural dimension of problems and their corresponding solutions. The full truth about man allows us to transcend the contractual view of justice, which is limited, and expand its horizon to include solidarity and love. "By itself, justice is not enough. Indeed, it can even betray itself, unless it is open to that deeper power which is love."

A deep bond exists among the virtues as a group, and in particular between virtues, social values, and charity, and this bond must be recognized ever more carefully. The values of truth, justice, and liberty are born from and develop through the inner spring of charity.

Human co-existence is ordered, results in good works, and responds to the dignity of man when it is based on truth. It is realized through justice, or through the true respect for rights and the loyal fulfillment of duties. It is realized through freedom fit for the dignity of men, who are encouraged by their rational nature to assume responsibility for their actions. It is given life through love, which makes us feel that the desires and needs of others are also our own and makes the communion of spiritual values and the concern for material necessities ever more intense. These values constitute the pillars from which the building of life and action gains its solidity and consistence. They are values that determine the quality of each action and social institution.

I. Respect for the Human Person

The human person should always be understood in his unique and ineradicable singularity. In fact, man exists first and foremost as a form of subjectivity, as a center of conscience and freedom, which has a unique story that cannot be compared to be any other and which expresses its irreducibility in the face of any attempt to squeeze it into patterns of thought and systems of power, whether they be ideological or not. First of all, this creates a need not only for simple respect from each individual, and especially from political and social institutions and their officers regarding each man on this earth, but also for each person's and especially each institution's primary commitment toward promoting the full development of each person.

In respecting human dignity, respect for the following principle absolutely cannot be overlooked: it is necessary to consider all of one's neighbors, with no exceptions, to be additional versions of oneself, taking their lives and the means necessary for them to live with dignity into account before anything else. In no scenario can the human person be used as an instrument for purposes other than his own development, which can only be fully and definitively realized through God and his project of salvation. In fact, man transcends the universe in his inner soul and is the only creature that God wanted for himself. For this reason, neither his life nor the development of his thoughts nor his good works nor the people who share in his personal and familiar story can be subjected to unjust restrictions regarding the exercise of his rights and his freedom. People cannot be used as tools for projects of an economic, social, or political character that have been imposed on them by any authority, regardless of whether it is in the name of advancement of the civil community as a whole or of other people in the present or in the future. For this reason, public authorities must be constantly vigilant to avoid restricting people's freedom, to avoid imposing any burden on people's personal actions that is detrimental to people's personal dignity, and to guarantee the effective practicability of human rights. Once again, all of this should be built on the foundation of the vision of man as a person—that is, as an active subject who is responsible for his own growing process together with the community of which he is a part.

II. Equality and Differences Among Men

The roots of human rights are found in the dignity that belongs to each human being. This dignity, which is innate to human life, is equal for all people regardless of the multitude of differences between them. This dignity can be embraced and understood primarily through reason. The natural basis for human rights appears to be even more solid if one considers human dignity in a supernatural light. After having been given to man by God and having been severely wounded by sin, it was assumed and redeemed by Jesus Christ through his incarnation, death, and resurrection. Only the recognition of human dignity can make communal and individual growth possible for everyone. In order to promote a similar growth, it is necessary in particular to support the least fortunate, effectively ensure that there is equal opportunity for men and women, and guarantee that there is objective equality among the different layers of society before the law. Conditions of equity and parity in the relationships between peoples and States are also a prerequisite for authentic progress in the international community. Equal recognition of the dignity of each person and of each people must also correspond to awareness that human dignity can be safeguarded and promoted only through communities and by the whole of humanity. Only when men and peoples that are sincerely interested in the good of everyone work together can an authentic universal brotherhood be created. On the other hand, conditions of grave disparity and inequality impoverish everyone.

III. Human Solidarity

The new interdependent relationships between men and peoples, which are in fact forms of solidarity, must be transformed into relationships that work toward true ethical-social solidarity, which is a moral requirement inherent in all human relationships. Solidarity, therefore, takes the form of two complementary aspects: the social principle and the moral virtue. Solidarity must be cultivated first and foremost as a social principle that brings order to institutions, based on which the "structures of sin," which dominate the relationships between people and peoples, must be overcome and transformed into structures of solidarity through the creation or appropriate modification of laws, market regulations, and legal systems. Solidarity is also a moral virtue, not a feeling of vague compassion or shallow distress at the misfortunes of so many people, both near and far. On the contrary, it is a firm and persevering determination to commit oneself to the common good. Solidarity rises to the rank of a fundamental "social virtue" because it is a dimension of justice, the highest virtue in terms of the common good and in the "to the good of one's neighbor with the readiness, in the gospel sense, to 'lose oneself' for the sake of the other instead of exploiting him, and to 'serve him' instead of oppressing him for one's own advantage (Mt 10:40–42; 20:25; Mk 10:42–45; Lk 22:25–27).

The principle of solidarity requires that the people of our time work harder to develop an awareness of the debt that they owe the societies that they are part of. Men are indebted to society because of the conditions that make human existence livable, such as the indivisible and indispensable patrimony of culture, scientific knowledge and technology, tangible and intangible resources, and everything that humans have produced throughout history. This kind of debt should be honored through various kinds of social actions so that the progress of man is not interrupted but keeps going for the present and future generations—generations that are called together to share in the same gift in solidarity.

Chapter Three: GOD'S SALVATION: LAW AND GRACE

Aristide Fumagalli

Life in Christ results from profession of faith and celebration of the sacraments. Rooted in man's personal and social vocation, life in Christ is animated by the Holy Spirit, which guides man through the law, supports him through grace, and makes him a participant in God's salvation.

In the parable of the true vine, which Jesus told to illustrate his bond with his disciples (cf. Jn 15:1–8), the Holy Spirit can be compared to the sap through which the vine (Christ) penetrates the branches (disciples) and the branches strengthen on the vine.

The spiritual allegory of the vine and the branches allows us to interpret law and grace, which are expressions of the Spirit, as the dissolution of Christ in man and the solidification of man in Christ respectively. The law shows the work that the Holy Spirit does to human freedom. Grace represents the work that the Holy Spirit does through human freedom. Law and grace tell us how the Spirit works and what the Spirit enacts through man, respectively, so that he can participate in God's salvation through Christ.

Article 1: THE MORAL LAW

We could look at the law as a kind of bond. In light of Christian revelation, this bond results from the covenant that God has established with men in Christ through the Spirit. The law expresses the strictly moral aspect of the covenant, which regards human action and exercising man's freedom through actions.

Moral law is not a human product but rather a divine gift, "the work of divine Wisdom" (*CCC* 1950) that is born from the covenant that God has freely offered man. Moral law is a gift because it shows man the roads that lead to good, allowing him to enjoy the love of God, and moves him away from the roads that lead to evil which instead deprive him of the enjoyment of divine love. God's gift of moral law commits man, for whom the moral law therefore takes the form of an obligation. Moral law binds man to God, just like a gift creates an obligation of the recipient to the donor. Moral law is not an extrinsic obligation that is imposed by divine authority but a gift offered so that by following it, man can intimately participate in God's providence toward him.

The covenant between God and man, which has a history that stretches from creation to redemption, turns moral law into a gradual dynamism that comes to completion in Christ: "Jesus Christ is in person the way of perfection" (n. 1953).

The gradual dynamism of moral law is understood in the theological tradition through the three consecutive and coordinated concepts of natural law, Old Law, and New Law. These three concepts are stipulations of eternal law, through which God provides for all of creation, that regard human beings.

I. The Natural Moral Law

The fundamental specification of moral law is found in "natural law," which is a part of and is exclusive to human nature. Unlike all other creatures, God created man by infusing law befitting him into his unique nature.

The creative act of God that infuses natural law, although it escapes human comprehension, can be understood through the metaphor of the artist who stamps the image of a ring into wax, the sculptor who carves a statue, or the writer who writes on a page. In terms of natural law, these metaphors reflect how it is derived from God on the one hand and how it is befitting of man on the other. The twin meanings of these metaphors cannot be separated because this would result in misunderstanding natural law as law that is imposed on man from the outside or, on the contrary, as law that is born from man himself. Neither heteronomous nor autonomous, natural law is instead participatory. It is the wisdom of God the Creator that is shared with human beings so that they may be responsible for their actions.

Due to its participation in divine wisdom, natural law is a form of knowing and can therefore be defined as intelligence and reason. Natural law is human intelligence illuminated by divine intelligence, human reason enabled by divine reason. Natural law is an expression of moral reason—of the reason, that is, that regards human action and prescribes good works that should be done and evil things that should be avoided.

Natural law forms part of the basis for human action. It is an original moral sense that indicates the principle norms for moral life and serves as the principle of discernment for particular actions. The fundamentalness of natural law translates into the protection and promotion of the two fundamental relationships of moral law, the relationship with God and the relationship with one's neighbor, and the fact that it can essentially be articulated through the commandments of the Decalogue. Its fundamental position puts natural law at the foundation of the moral rules which regulate personal and social life and also makes it the underpinning of the norms of civil law, which has been laid out by man.

Suited to man as a creature, natural law is a part of all men. This is true in both a synchronic and a diachronic sense—that is, it is true for people living in any geographical region at any point in history. Since it is part of human nature, natural law is universal and immutable.

The universalness of natural law gives each man the dignity of being responsible for his actions and at the same time makes him responsible for his relationship with God and with others. The immutability of natural law is due to the fundamentalness of its precepts, which are invariable and permanent and serve to safeguard and promote the good that makes up human beings. A part of human nature, natural law could be eliminated only by eliminating human nature—only if a man were to become no longer human. In this sense, natural law is indestructible.

The universalness and the immutability of natural law do not compromise but rather require particularities and differences in the customs and moral norms through which natural law is implemented in different cultures and in different historical periods. The difference between the universal and immutable precepts of natural law and its changing regulations, which are unique and variable, explains how natural law serves as an interpretative principle and an evaluative criterion for the evolution of customs and moral rules in addition to serving as their foundation. The promotion and the transgression of natural law are indicators of progress toward good or regression toward evil respectively.

In the dynamism of the story of salvation, which is aimed at the beatitude of men in full communion with God, natural law represents the first step. It corresponds to creation in Christ and provides instructions for fulfilment through him. In order for the story of salvation to reach its conclusion, a moral law that first and foremost remedies the difficulties and errors of the fragile and sinful human race through the clear and immediate knowledge of the natural law and especially that enables man to understand and do good at the same level of perfection as Christ's love is necessary.

The answer to these two necessities is found in revealed law in its two forms: Old Law and New Law.

II. The Old Law

The story of salvation, which has creation as its prologue, contemplates the self-revelation of God, who established a covenant with the whole of humanity first through the people of Israel and then fully through Christ. The first covenant with Israel concerns the gift of the "Old Law," which was revealed to Moses. This first form of revealed law is expressed in summary form through the Ten Commandments. For this reason, the moral precepts of the Old Law coincide with those of natural law. The revelation of the precepts of the Decalogue, which were already known to man since they are contained in natural law, is linked to the sinful fragility of human beings. Since man, who has been hardened by evil, is able to find the natural law that is infused in his heart only with great difficulty and tenacity, God reveals it to him so that he sees it more clearly and with more certainty. The Old Law is the written reminder of the natural law that men have difficulty reading in their hearts. The Decalogue revealed to Israel instructs moral reason, clarifying its murkiness and providing a guarantee of what constitutes good works that must be completed and evil that must be avoided.

As "the first stage of revealed law" (n. 1962) and "the first stage on the way to the kingdom" (n. 1963), the Old law is already "spiritual" (Rom 7:14) and "holy" (Rom 7:12). It is therefore already part of the work of the Holy Spirit because it teaches man how to love God and his neighbor. As the first step—although an imperfect one—toward love, the Old Law is undeniable and its ten words, pronounced by God, are a lesson that lasts for eternity, even in the face of the perfection of the New Law.

The imperfection of the Old Law with respect to the New Law is found in the fact that it obligates man to do good without, however, strengthening him so that he does good without giving in to the temptations of evil. Obligating without strengthening, the law reveals man's inability to carry it out and therefore shows his sin. On the other side, the notification that man has sinned allows his liberation through grace to be foretold. The Old Law is completed by the teachings of prophets and the sapiential books and sets the stage for the New Covenant realized through Christ.

Although chronologically the Old Law was revealed first, followed by the New Law, from the viewpoint of the history of salvation the two laws have always been in effect. For this reason, there were men in the times prior to the Old Covenant that followed the New Law and there were men who in the period following the New Covenant continued to follow the Old Law.

III. The New Law or the Law of the Gospel

With the "New Law," which corresponds to the new and eternal covenant realized through Christ, moral law reaches perfection. The New Law perfects the Old Law, fulfilling its hidden potential and surpassing it in its demands. The fulfillment of the New Law does not abolish the Old Law, and it does not add external precepts in surpassing it. The New Law fulfills the Old Law in the sense that it operates in the innermost part of man, at the root of human action. The New Law frees man's heart from sinful hardening and further shapes it, perfecting the infusion of moral law performed by God during creation.

Freely given to man when he was unable even to carry out natural and Old Law, the New Law is nothing other than the "grace of the Holy Spirit." Unlike natural law and Old Law, the New Law does not only instruct man about the good works that must be done but also sends him the strength to perform them, especially through the sacraments.

The fact that the New Law is freely given does not mean that it is imposed on man, since there is nothing that man must do to earn the grace of the Holy Spirit, and he is also not obligated to accept it. The acceptance of the Holy Spirit which graces human freedom, liberating man from the evil of sin and empowering him to do good through love, requires faith. Christian faith is "setting love free" (H.U. von Balthasar)—the love that the Holy Spirit pours into our hearts (cf. Rom 5:5).

The instruction of faith, which, in accepting the law, works through charity is especially reflected in the Sermon on the Mount (Mt 5–7). Faith that corresponds to the grace of the Holy Spirit is illustrated by the conditions of poverty, humility, grief, purity of heart, and persecution for the cause of Christ listed in the "beatitudes" of the Gospel (cf. Mt 5:3–12) and is realized through "acts of religion" such as prayer, especially the Our Father, fasting, and almsgiving. By setting the love that was freely given by the Holy Spirit free, faith works together with Christ's charity toward his neighbors to teach us the "Golden Rule" that asks us to treat others as we would like them to treat us (cf. Mt 7:12) and especially the "new commandment" of Jesus, to love others as he has loved us (cf. Jn 15:12).

Charity operated by faith animates the numerous virtues of Christian life and illuminates the judgment of our conscience through the inspiration of "moral catechesis of the apostolic teachings" (cf. Rom 12–15, 1 Cor 12–13, Col 3–4, and Eph 4–6, for example).

Charity that corresponds to the New Law does not only remove what goes against it but also anything that hinders the most speedy and perfect possible practice of it. This perfection of charity is reflected in the "evangelical counsels," which best put charity into practice as related to the state of life and individual vocation of each person.

The New Law, through the grace of the Holy Spirit, frees man's liberty from the incapacity to love and empowers him to practice the same love that God revealed in Jesus Christ. In this sense, the New Law can be classified in three ways: as the law of grace, as the law of freedom, and as the law of love.

Article 2:
GRACE AND JUSTIFICATION

The mystery of how divine love, which was freely given by the Holy Spirit and freely accepted by man, is translated into human love is not fully comprehensible. Man cannot surprise God while he sends him his vital love. Man discovers that he is loved by God when God gives him life and keeps him alive, just like how a child is loved by his parents even before he is aware of anything. God is at the origin of every human action and his action can never be fully understood by man, whose attempts are comparable to those of the hand that tries to grasp the wrist to which it is attached.

The communion of love within which the Spirit attracts freedom eludes any attempt to precisely determine the effect of either of the two. The blending of the loving embrace between the Spirit and freedom, however, does not prevent one from observing their inseparable relationship that is *ex parte Spiritus* and *ex parte libertatis*—considering, that is, the action of the Spirit on freedom and the action of freedom on the Spirit whenever possible. For this reason, after having prioritized the perspective of the Spirit under the title of moral law, one must assume the perspective of freedom under the title of grace. Consideration of the Spirit as the law for freedom must be replaced by consideration of the Spirit as grace for freedom. Since the Holy Spirit graces man through his justification and sanctification, the theological logic of the argument would be more linear and coherent if grace was discussed prior to justification, as the title of the article implies. However, in following the paragraphs of the text, we will immediately consider how the grace of the Holy Spirit justifies.

I. Justification

The Holy Spirit justifies man. Infusing himself at the heart of man's freedom, the Spirit renders him just, freeing him from the unjust practice of evil and giving him the abilities necessary for the just practice of good. The justification performed by God is the most excellent manifestation of his mercy—of the love that he freely offered man, who had fallen into the misery of sin. The merciful grace of God renders man just because it places him in a just relationship with God. By reestablishing the bond that sin had broken, God communicates his justice to man. He communicates the way that he is just, the way that Jesus revealed by loving men "to the end" (Jn 13:1), up to the point where he gave the ultimate and supreme gift of his life so that they could have life and have it to the full (cf. Jn 10:10). Justification is the action of God that makes man just by restoring his relationship with him. A just man is only just because he is in and remains in a relationship with God, who renders him just. Man cannot claim to be just in his own right regardless of God's permanent justifying action, and he also cannot claim to be truly just if he has not been permanently justified by God.

Justification is performed by the Holy Spirit, who attracts men through Christ and vitally joins them to him, assimilating them to him, the Father's only begotten son, as adopted sons of God. Justification, which is a fully divine process, does not justify man without considering him but rather by involving him through faith. The implementation of faith primarily occurs through baptism, which is first among the sacraments and is the historical event in which Christ's only Easter is made contemporary to men at all points in history.

The mystery of the cooperation of man's freedom with the justification of the grace of God cannot be understood through theological intelligence. Theological intelligence can, however, better study this mystery when guided by the faith of the Church, which excludes the two extremes of justification which does not fully derive from divine grace and justification in which human freedom is merely passive.

Justification is not an instantaneous action but rather a process of conversion that only begins with liberation from the injustice of sin and then continues with the acceptance of God's justice. God's justice infuses the virtues of faith, hope, and charity and places man in the just position of love with respect to God and his neighbor. Since justification is performed by the Holy Spirit, which dwells in human freedom, it coincides with the sanctification of man. Man becomes holy to the degree which he allows himself to be sanctified by the Spirit.

II. Grace

The grace of God, which justifies man, is not a simple gift given to man by God like a giver would give an object to a recipient but a gift from God of his own divine life. Divine grace is therefore a freely given pardon with which God establishes his relationship with man. Viewed in this light, the grace of the Holy Spirit is nothing other than the Holy Spirit dwelling in the human person. The Spirit makes man participate in the Trinitarian life of God, placing him in communion with Christ and making him the son of God the

Father through Christ. Grace cannot be confiscated. It is a personal bond that, since it binds man to God, transcends human nature and is therefore supernatural and divine.

Since grace is an action that God performed gratuitously for man, it is divine freedom that interacts with human freedom. Divine freedom begins the initiative and human freedom accepts it. The encounter between God's free initiative and man's free response is a mystery of love, which on the one hand cannot be directly experienced by man but on the other hand can be recognized by man through the effects that it generates. Like the sap that flows hidden through the branches and reveals its activity through the fruit that it ripens, the inexpressible grace of the Holy Spirit accepted through faith manifests itself in works of charity.

Cooperation with divine freedom is not limited to a single moment in the history of human freedom but is instead permanent. The acceptance of divine grace is not a simple act of human liberty but rather man's cooperation with God's initiative. The entire process of justification, from the root of conversion to the fulfilment of sanctification is relational. It proceeds due to divine initiative and human acceptance. The fact that divine action works in a different way—it involves taking initiative, unlike human action, which involves acceptance—explains not only why divine activity does not imply human passivity but also why, on the contrary, divine activity creates and requires human freedom.

The interaction between grace and liberty—which is in any case permanent—can be characterized in a different way by taking into account the different ways in which grace is transmitted to freedom and the different effects that it induces. This is what is brought to light by the different classifications of grace: "sanctifying or deifying," when grace establishes the justification process through baptism, "sacramental," when it is communicated through sacraments; "habitual," when it stably accompanies free human action; "actual," when it is provided by God in particular moments of one's life story; "special," when it consists of a charism for the sanctification of a person and the good of the Church; and the grace "of state," when it is especially given for the exercise of a responsibility or of a service in Christian and ecclesiastical life.

III. Merit

Because justification is a gratuitous action performed by God for men, freeing them from sin and sanctifying them in love, it is not merited by man as a just recompense for his autonomous capacity to do good works. Since man has received not only the law of God but also the ability to follow it from God, he has no right to claim anything as a just compensation for his actions, because if they are good, it is because they have been graced and are therefore the fruit of divine grace. For this reason, there is no space in the theology of grace for the conception of the autonomous merit of man before God.

However, merit can be understood from a relational point of view as the overabundant grace that God gives man when man accepts his grace. Acceptance of divine grace through faith allows the Holy Spirit to continue to pour it into the heart of man so that he becomes progressively sanctified. From this point of view, man's merit consists in cooperation with God's works and in not objecting to the grace of the Holy Spirit but rather allowing it to freely carry out the entire justification process.

IV. Christian Holiness

The sanctifying grace of the Holy Spirit, when accepted by man through faith, leads to Christian holiness. Holiness only requires accepting God's gratuitous initiative and is a vocation that is common to all believers, who the Holy Spirit conforms to Christ by empowering them to love as he loved so that they become perfect like him through love. Christian holiness is holiness because it is realized by the Holy Spirit, and it is Christian because it conforms man to Christ. The conformation of man to Christ in his way of living and loving does not occur through exterior imitation but through the intimate union that the Spirit creates between man and Christ, a communion whose intensity is expressed through the term incorporation in theology.

Christian holiness requires that freedom be subject to the work of divine grace and therefore contains an ascetic and also mortifying dimension. The way of Christian holiness is a cruciform path that the Holy Spirit supports by powering hope through the grace of final perseverance and blessed recompense—that is, the hope of corresponding to divine grace until the end of earthly life so that one is graced with an eternally blessed life in definitive communion with God and everyone that he has blessed.

Article 3: THE CHURCH, MOTHER AND TEACHER

The vocation to Christian holiness is a personal vocation. All Christians are, however, called to holiness in the Church, the communion of those who have been called to union with Christ by the Spirit. The Spirit, although he acts mysteriously in the world and in history, operates certainly and fully in the Church, which Christ entrusted with the proclamation of his Word, the celebration of his sacraments, the Magisterium of his Gospels, and the witness of his saints.

The working presence of the Spirit in the Church makes it a mother, involving it in the generation of growth of the faithful so that they live what they believe. The moral life of the faithful, inasmuch as it is acceptance that corresponds to the grace of the Holy Spirit, is spiritual worship: worship because it is an offering of oneself to God in obedience to his love and spiritual because it is supported and strengthened by the same Spirit of God that empowers man to love, in communion with Christ, like he loves. For this reason, the source and culmination of Christian moral life is the Eucharist, the sacrament of the extreme and supreme love of Christ.

I. Moral Life and the Magisterium of the Church

The working presence of the Spirit in the Church makes it a teacher in addition to a mother, involving it in the education of the faithful so that they are able to know "the love of Christ, which is beyond all knowledge" (Eph 3:19). In the Church, the people of God who walk the path of the Kingdom of heaven, moral teaching is not exclusive to any one person but belongs to all the individual believers to the extent that they, in living in Christ, communicate their knowledge of him and witness his love.

In the Church, the Spirit gives each person the gift of moral teaching, supporting ministries and charisms for the common good. Of these, the Magisterium of the pastors of the Church is of particular importance.

Aided by the *sensus fidelium*, the knowledge that spiritual authors gain from the study of theologians, the Magisterium of the pope and the bishops guarantees that the *depositum fidei*, which consists of the deposit of Christian morality, is transmitted. The *depositum moris* is comprised of the commandments and the virtues that instruct and form Christian life and extends to the precepts of natural moral law. By participating in the authority of Christ, the Magisterium of the pope and the bishops who are in communion with him are ordinarily considered to be authentic teachers, to the point that in terms of truths that are essential to revelation or necessary for it to be faithfully safeguarded and transmitted, they are insured by the charism of infallibility.

The moral authority exercised by the Magisterium of the Church is aimed at instructing men about faith and Christian morality. In the general contemporary framework of crisis in the relationship between authority and freedom, the relationship between the hierarchic Magisterium and personal conscience may appear adversarial. Aside from any prejudicial contradictions, it is necessary first of all to recognize that the Magisterium and conscience are not alternatives or rivals. The authoritative service of the Magisterium helps peoples' consciences make personal decisions, and vice versa—Christians' personal discernment provides the Magisterium with stimuli and suggestions for their authoritative discernment in the tradition of the *depositum fidei*. The *sensus fidelium*, or more precisely the *consensus fidelium*, although difficult to accept, is an integral part of the affirmation of moral truth. The Magisterium and the conscience are not two moral authorities that are in conflict and can at best hope for a reasonable compromise. They both depend on the single authority of the Spirit, who helps human freedom adhere to Christian truth in both cases.

The necessary and opportune cooperation between conscience and Magisterium on the one hand implies that the faithful have a right to be taught by the Magisterium and on the other hand requires them to accept its teaching with a filial spirit. The authority that the Magisterium has due to the particular assistance that the Holy Spirit provides means that individual consciences are invited to conform to the Magisterial indications when they are not certain of their judgment. However, it may also be that what the properly formed conscience dictates does not coincide with what the Magisterium dictates in a particular situation. In this case, the conscience had the final word on that particular situation. This does not mean that this particular judgment can be made to be hold for the general case. According to the Catholic conception, the authenticity and potentially the infallibility of moral teaching is the exclusive prerogative of the Magisterium. The Magisterium, however, cannot replace the conscience, since conscience "is the most secret core and sanctuary of a man. There he is alone with God, Whose voice echoes in his depths" (*GS* 16).

II. The Precepts of the Church

The authoritative interpretation of moral law by the Magisterium is expressed at the most basic level through the five precepts of the Church, which reference the indispensable conditions necessary for the most minimal nourishment of Christian life. They recall three pillars that are common to various religious traditions: prayer, fasting, and almsgiving. In terms of prayer, the first three precepts require Sunday rest, participation in Sunday and holiday Mass, confession at least once a year, and Holy Communion at least during the Easter season. The fourth precept addresses fasting and recommends that it occur on pre-established days. The fifth precept addresses almsgiving, reminding Christians to respond to the needs of the Church.

III. Moral Life and Missionary Witness

The moral life of Christians, who have been justified and sanctified through the grace of the Holy Spirit, bears witness in the world to the authenticity of the salvation that God gave to men through Christ. There is no solution of continuity between the vocation to holiness and missionary witness. As sap gives life to the branch and at the same time renders it fruitful, the Holy Spirit that is accepted through faith sanctifies the life of believers and renders them fruitful through charity.

The sanctification of believers through Christ makes them capable of loving each other as he loved them. For this reason, the holiness of the individuals leads to the communion of believers, who in this way construct the Church. The first fruit of Christian holiness is ecclesiastical communion. But the ecclesiastical communion of believers through the love of Christ already serves as a missionary to the world in accordance with what Christ taught his disciples: "It is by your love for one another, that everyone will recognize you as my disciples" (Jn 13:35).

Christian witness is essential for the credibility of the Gospel because it expresses divine love in human form and therefore makes it comprehensible to man. The witness of the life of Christians, who make up the body of Christ through the Church, extends the mystery of the incarnation of the Son of God through the entire history of men.

Like a wheat grain that falls into the earth and yields a rich harvest (cf. Jn 12:24), Jesus Christ planted the seed of the kingdom of God in human history. To the extent to which the faithful allow it to operate in their lives by accepting the Spirit of Christ through faith, they contribute to the definitive advent of the kingdom of God and accelerate the movement of the story of salvation toward its full completion.

Section Two

THE TEN COMMANDMENTS

THE TEN COMMANDMENTS

Stefano Zamboni

The third part of the *CCC* has "Life in Christ" as its theme. Before describing the concrete demands asked of Christians, the *CCC* correctly emphasizes the human vocation in order to reiterate that before ethical imperatives comes divine instruction, the gift of salvation. The ten commandments are examined in this light. The *CCC* could have used a different perspective—the one adopted, for example, by Thomas Aquinas in *Summa Theologiaie*, who after reflecting on the vocation of man (beatitude) and the acts that lead toward it, conducts a systematic analysis of the individual virtues that teach man true freedom in accordance with divine law. The *CCC* instead opts for an exposition based on the commandments. This is probably out of respect for the cathetical tradition, which was consecrated by the *Roman Catechism*, the third part of which is dedicated to the "Precepts of the Decalogue." As we can see, this choice, however, is in consonance with the biblical tradition, where the Decalogue does not only obviously have an essential importance for Old Testament law but is also explicitly evoked in Jesus's teaching, as the *CCC* immediately points out in the introduction to the commentary on the subject.

I. "Teacher, What Must I Do…?"

The reflection on the commandments begins with a reference to the famous Gospel story of the rich young man. "And now a man came to him and asked, 'Master, what good deed must I do to possess eternal life?' Jesus said to him, 'Why do you ask me about what is good? There is one alone who is good. But if you wish to enter into life, keep the commandments'" (Mt 19:16–17). The text of the *CCC* uses this Gospel story to highlight a few relevant aspects. The encyclical *VS*, written not long after the *CCC*, also uses this example: "In the young man, whom Matthew's Gospel does not name, we can recognize every person who, consciously or not, *approaches Christ the Redeemer of man and questions him about morality*. For the young man, the *question* is not so much about rules to be followed, but *about the full meaning of life*. This is in fact the aspiration at the heart of every human decision and action, the quiet searching and interior prompting which sets freedom in motion. This question is ultimately an appeal to the absolute Good which attracts us and beckons us; it is the echo of a call from God who is the origin and goal of man's life" (n. 7).

The four numbers of the *CCC* which introduce this section (nn. 2052–2055) allow for a brief explanation of the meaning of this call to good, of this "moral question," by relating it to the great questions of God, of the law, of love, and of following Christ. Now we will see how.

First of all, it is stated that only God can provide an authentic answer to the entirety of the desire for life shown by the rich young man: "There is one alone who is good," Jesus answers. He appears to avoid the young man's question, but in reality he orients it and shows the real sense behind it. Only God can answer the question about good since he is "the supreme Good and the source of all good" (n. 2052). When examined carefully, every question about good is of a religious nature, since God is the fullness of goodness: he is at its origin, even if he is not always explicitly recognized, of every question and every aspiration toward good (cf. *VS* 9).

Jesus then explains to the rich young man that to enter into "life," the commandments are necessary. They show the way of life and lead man toward it. Jesus lists the commandments of the Decalogue that regard one's neighbor (the so-called "second tablet" of the Decalogue) and can be summarized as a call to "love your neighbor as yourself." The commandments therefore represent the basic condition for loving one's neighbor and constitute "the *first necessary step on the journey toward freedom*, its starting-point" (*VS* 13). In other words, after noting that there is only one that is good—God, that is—and that therefore good life is ultimately derived from him alone, Jesus clarifies that one cannot arrive at God and his goodness if not through love of neighbor, as is guaranteed by the commandments of the second tablet of the Decalogue. In this way, love—the "twofold yet single commandment" of love of God and of one's neighbor—is the correct hermeneutic of the commandments, as the quote from Rom 13:10 which concludes this section of the *CCC* reminds us: "Love (*agápe*) is the fulfilling (*pléroma*) of the law" (n. 2055).

Third, it must be noted that Jesus fulfills God's commandments, particularly the commandment of love for one's neighbor, by interiorizing and radicalizing its demands—remember the famous verse "For I tell you" (cf. Mt 5:20ss.). For this reason, "the Law has not been abolished, but rather man is invited to rediscover it in the person of his Master who is its perfect fulfillment" (n. 2053). The *VS* states, "*Jesus brings God's commandments to fulfilment*, particularly the commandment of love of neighbor, *by interiorizing their demands and by bringing out their fullest meaning.* Love of neighbor springs from a loving heart which, precisely because it loves, is ready to live out *the loftiest challenges.* Jesus shows that the commandments must not be understood as a minimum limit not to be gone beyond, but rather as a path involving a moral and spiritual journey toward perfection, at the heart of which is love (cf. Col 3:14)" (n. 15).

We are all aware that the rich young man is not content to simply observe the commandments, which he has always observed. He notes that something is missing and the feeling of "nostalgia." Jesus leverages this nostalgia when he offers him the way toward perfection: "Jesus said, 'If you wish to be perfect, go and sell your possessions and give the money to the poor, and you will have treasure in heaven; then come, follow me'" (Mt 19:21). It should be noted that this call to perfection applies to everyone, and for this reason in the wake of Vatican II, which speaks about the "universal call to holiness" (cf. *LG*, chapter V), the traditional distinction between the normal way—the way of the "commandments," which is necessary for salvation, and the way of "perfection," which is professed by the "evangelical counsels"—should be rejected. As the *VS* once again reminds us, "The way and at the same time the content of this perfection consist in the following of Jesus, *sequela Christi.*" For this reason, "following Christ is thus the essential and primordial foundation of Christian morality." This does not involve simply "disposing oneself to hear a teaching and obediently accepting a commandment. More radically, it involves *holding fast to the very person of Jesus*, partaking of his life and his destiny, sharing in his free and loving obedience to the will of the Father" (n. 19).

II. The Decalogue in Sacred Scripture

After introducing the general meaning of the commandments within the moral dynamic and Jesus's proposal, the *CCC* analyzes the Decalogue's place within Biblical revelation. The Decalogue (from the Greek word *dekálogos*, which means "ten words"), which is found in two versions in the Bible (Ex 20:1–17, Dt 5:6–22), "must first be understood in the context of the Exodus, God's great liberating event at the center of the Old Covenant" (n. 2057).

Exodus alludes to the gratuitous liberating intervention of God, the covenant at the meeting point between two freedoms, and a bond that has been established through a free decision that at the same time preserves the quality of the reciprocal relationships. For this reason, the Lord speaks to his people and urges them, reminds them, of the urgency of obedience: "So now, if you are really prepared to obey me and keep my covenant, you, out of all peoples, shall be my personal possession, for the whole world is mine"

(Ex 19:5). Through the words "If you are really prepared to obey me…" God calls on the freedom of Israel. Its people can finally exercise what they saw appear with the liberating intervention of the Lord. God asks for an answer. Only in answering can Israel truly converse with God as a free people that stands before their liberator.

It seems, however, that God wishes to restrict the people's freedom. The external imposition of a series of rules like those contained in the Decalogue appears to be in irreconcilable opposition to the requirements of freedom. In reality, the Decalogue does place a limit, but it is not a limit "on" freedom but rather a limit "for" freedom. It shows under which conditions man is free, what the prerequisite for his freedom is. In this sense, it "defines" human liberty by showing what the conditions are that allow it to emerge and develop. "Whether formulated as negative commandments, prohibitions, or as positive precepts […] the 'ten words' point out the conditions of a life freed from the slavery of sin. The Decalogue is a path of life" (*CCC* 2057).

The fact that the Decalogue takes on meaning within the covenant is restated multiple times in this section (cf. nn. 2060–2061). But what does God's covenant with his people involve? The document *The Bible and Morality: Biblical Roots of Christian Conduct* (05/11/2008), written by the Pontifical Biblical Commission, reveals that the meaning of the covenant can be explained through four verbs: the God of Israel "accompanies" because he shows man the path in the desert, he "delivers" from the yoke of oppression and death, he "gives" a double gift: he donates himself as the God of the people and grants the "way" (*derek*) to enter and remain in a relationship with him to this people, and he "gathers" his emerging people around a common project, the assignment to "live together" (cf. n. 16). For this reason, we could say that the Decalogue could be interpreted as a sign of this accompaniment, a memory of this liberation, an instrument for remaining in this gift, and the foundation of this divine convocation.

The *CCC* correctly insists that divine action be prioritized and that God comes before any human action. In effect, the Decalogue opens with God's introduction of himself and his initiative of salvation: "I am Yahweh your God who brought you out of Egypt, where you lived as slaves" (Ex 20:2, Dt 5:6, cf. *CCC* 2061). This means that the "ten words" "belong to God's revelation of himself and his glory. The gift of the Commandments is the gift of God himself and his holy will" (*CCC* 2059). We could remark that the meaning of the commandments is "theological" more than it is ethical because it shows God's identity, how he takes care of his chosen people, and his desire to "reveal Himself and to make known to us the hidden purpose of His will" (*DV* 2).

In affirming that God's gratuitous initiative comes first, the *CCC* recognizes that "The Commandments properly so-called come in the second place: they express the implications of belonging to God through the establishment of the covenant. Moral existence is a response to the Lord's loving initiative" (n. 2062). The document *The Bible and Morality* expresses the same concept when it notes that "Logically, morality is secondary to God's founding initiative" (n. 4). God's initiative is a gift freely offered to men, and the commandments are man's response to the calling inscribed in this gift. The indicative of salvation is the basis for the moral imperative. The fact that the Hebrew word *Tôrah*, which is usually translated as law, actually refers to teaching or instruction is not insignificant. The commandments are a practical lesson given to us by God so that we can adequately respond to God's gift and therefore remain deserving of the freedom offered by his salvation initiative.

In the conclusion for this section, the *CCC* duly notes that in the commandments, "all the obligations are stated in the first person ('I am the Lord.') and addressed by God to another personal subject ('you')" (n. 2063). This expresses what could be defined as the "personalist and dialogic connotation" of the Decalogue, which is founded on a covenant between two freedoms and between two subjects who are capable of responsibility and ultimately love.

III. The Decalogue in the Church's Tradition

These numbers reiterate that the Church has acknowledged that the Decalogue is of particular importance (cf. n. 2064) and briefly outlines the history of its ecclesiastical reception from Augustine to today, highlighting the differences in the division and numbering of the commandments (cf. nn. 2065–2066). Next, the *CCC* states that the commandments can be subdivided into two parts: the first three primarily refer to love of God and the other seven state the requirements for love of neighbor (n. 2067). Finally, we are reminded of a proclamation by the Council of Trent about the obligation of the justified man to observe the commandments (in spite of every anti-social temptation) and one from Vatican II (*LG* 24) about the obligation of the bishops to proclaim the Gospel to every creature so that all men—through faith, baptism, and "observance of the commandments"—can obtain salvation (cf. n. 2068).

With regard to the numbering of the commandments, it should be observed that in the Bible, the number ten refers to a complete set, such as in the ten plagues of Egypt, and makes for easy memorization (you can count to ten on two hands). In terms of the subdivision of the commandments, we must also remember that the precept of not creating likenesses (cf. Ex 20:4) is treated differently in the Catholic and Orthodox Churches. In the Tradition of the Catholic Church, this is not considered to be a commandment in and of itself, and for this reason, the commandment about desire is divided in two ("You shall not set your heart on your neighbor's spouse" and "You shall not set your heart on your neighbor's possessions") in order to arrive at ten. In the Orthodox Church and in Calvinism, the ban on creating likenesses is considered to be the second commandment and the commandment about desire is considered to be a single commandment. There are also differences in the division of the two tablets. As the *CCC* notes, the Catholic Tradition follows Augustine's example in discussing three commandments that regard God and seven that regard one's neighbor, but the Jewish Tradition, which is based on a different subdivision of the commandments, speaks about two tablets with five commandments each.

It would be very interesting to discuss these differences in detail and trace the history of how these different ecclesiastical traditions collected and transmitted the teaching of the Decalogue throughout history in more detail. It would be neither possible nor opportune to do so here, but it is important to emphasize that the Tradition of the Church is not something that simply exists in the past but rather is a living process through which the Church of every age is called to reappropriate the faith that it has received. For this reason, each Christian generation is asked to dig deeper into the intelligence of the "ten words." An interesting is discussion found in the aforementioned document *The Bible and Morality*, which at a certain point (n. 30) discusses an "axiological" understanding of the Decalogue. What does this mean?

This involves reading the contents of the Decalogue in terms of a "morality of values." The prohibitions and precepts, the document explains, in and of themselves concentrate only on behaviors that must be avoided or observed and in this way encourage a morality of minimal actions. "Commitment to values, however, represents an open-ended project, whose demands are unlimited." For this reason, "translated into a terminology of values the precepts of the Decalogue point to the following values: the Absolute, religious homage, time, the family, life, the stability of the male and female couple, freedom [...] good reputation, the household, the house and its material belongings." In this way, we have a program for life that touches on all the elements of existence and requires moral attention and commitment that never ends. In this way, the document affirms, the Decalogue "opens up a broad way toward a liberating morality, giving first place to God's sovereignty over the world (values nn. 1 and 2), offering every individual the possibility of dedicating time to God and of managing time in a constructive manner (n. 3), broadening the opportunities of family life (n. 4), defending life, even an apparently unproductive life of suffering, against arbitrary decisions of the system and subtle manipulations of public opinion (n. 5), neutralizing the seeds of division that render married life so fragile, especially in our days

(n. 6), preventing all forms of exploitation of the body, of the heart and of ideas (n. 7), protecting personal reputations from attack (n. 8) and from all kinds of deception, of exploitation, abuse and coercion (nn. 9 and 10)" (n. 30).

IV. The Unity of the Decalogue

Only one number is dedicated to the subject of the unity of the Decalogue (*CCC* 2069). The unity of the Decalogue refers to the fact that it "forms a coherent whole. Each "word" refers to each of the others and to all of them; they reciprocally condition one another." This consideration is a consequence of what was stated previously regarding the nature of the gift of the commandments: since they come from the God's concern for man's salvation, they are all directed toward the full humanity of man.

The axiological reading that I have just illustrated helps us better understand the "organic unity" formed by the commandments. Human beings should be considered in all of their dimensions—as a whole, as the Magisterium loves to say—with their economic needs and political relationships, in family life and in their constitutive opening to the Absolute. If this is true in the positive sense, it is also valid in the negative sense—that is, with regard to transgression of the commandments. "To transgress one commandment is to infringe all the others." This is because sin represents a break in the relationships that make up the person; it is an infraction that damages the integrity of the relationships that make a person fully free and complete. Naturally, this statement should not be interpreted in a fundamentalist manner. Not all infringements of the Decalogue are on the same level with no differences between them (cf. n. 2073). It must instead be taken as an indication of the anti-relational nature of sin, which threatens the deep unity of human moral life.

The *CCC* previously noted that "The Decalogue must be interpreted in light of this twofold yet single commandment of love, the fullness of the Law" (n. 2055). It is love (*agápe*), through which the law is fulfilled and on which it is based, that is the meaning behind this deep unity of the commandments. Love of God and love of neighbor cannot be separated because they feed off of each other in such a way that love for God is inseparable from love for one's brother, and authentic love for neighbor is ultimately rooted in love for God. "The Decalogue brings man's religious and social life into unity." This refers both to relations with God (faith, hope, and charity) and with one's neighbor (family, society, and so on).

V. The Decalogue and the Natural Law

In numbers 2070–2071, the *CCC* addresses a theological problem that was frequently discussed in the past, the relationship between the Decalogue and natural law, which the *CCC* defined in these terms: "The natural law expresses the original moral sense which enables man to discern by reason the good and the evil, the truth and the lie" (n. 1954).

The question is addressed in two ways. First of all, it is emphasized that "The Ten Commandments belong to God's revelation," and are therefore given, as we have seen, in the context of the covenant that God freely offered to his people. At the same time, they "teach us the true humanity of man" because they bring to light fundamental aspects (duties and rights) of human beings that transcend the particularities of a given population and are universally valid for all people in all eras. In this way, "the Decalogue contains a privileged expression of the natural law" (n. 2070).

If this is true, we could ask why a specific revelation was required for something that could be discerned through human reason. The answer to this objection is contained in the words of Saint Bonaventure (*In libros sententiarum*, 4, 37, 1, 3), who is quoted in the second number of this section: "A full explanation of the commandments of the Decalogue became necessary in the state of sin because the light of reason was obscured and the will had gone astray." What would not have been necessary in an abstract sense was in fact necessary due to the condition of sin in which the human race found itself. "To attain a complete and certain understanding of the requirements of the natural law, sinful humanity needed this revelation" (*CCC* 2071).

Although the *CCC* makes use of all of his theses, Thomas Aquinas is not cited here. In his treaty on law, Aquinas delves deeply into these questions and states that all the moral precepts of the Old Law (including the Ten Commandments) belong to natural law, but are learned in a different way. Some are absolutely evident, but others require a deep and direct analysis of divine teaching to be discovered (cf. *Summa Theologiae*, I–II, 1000). For Thomas, therefore, divine revelation provides a remedy for the insufficiency of evidence for natural law in the face of the fallen nature of human beings. Although they still maintained their indelible orientation toward good, humans needed the light of the revelation to recognize the good to which they were called with certainty.

VI. The Obligation of the Decalogue

In what way is the Decalogue an obligation? The *CCC* previously noted (cf. n. 2053) that the Christian is also obligated to follow the precepts of the Decalogue since Jesus came not to abolish but rather to fulfil the old law (cf. Mt 5:17). The question that the *CCC* answers in these numbers is of a moral nature and regards the obligation that the law places on the human conscience. These obligations, as stated in n. 2072, are "grave" (due to their nature), "fundamentally immutable," and "oblige always and everywhere" (*semper et ubique*). This statement is based on the fact that the Decalogue sets out essential obligations toward God and toward others, obligations that are "engraved by God in the human heart." Infringing upon one of these fundamental requirements means not being faithful to one's humanity. As the *VS* affirms, "The Church has always taught that one may never choose kinds of behavior prohibited by the moral commandments expressed in negative form in the Old and New Testaments" (n. 52).

The *CCC* recognizes, however, that in accordance with the Church tradition, "Obedience to the Commandments also implies obligations in matter which is, in itself, light" (n. 2073). This recalls the distinction between mortal and venial sin, which the *CCC* discussed in n. 1854–1864. We should note that John Paul II provided the following definition in *Reconciliatio et paenitentia*: "Mortal sin is sin whose object is grave matter and which is also committed with full knowledge and deliberate consent" (cf. *CCC* 1857). If one of these conditions is not met, the sin is not considered mortal.

VII. "Apart from Me You Can Do Nothing"

After these statements of an exquisitely moral nature, we return almost by inclusion to what we can define as the "Christological foundation" of the Decalogue (*CCC* 2074). In the Gospel of John, Jesus states that while without him we can do nothing (cf. Jn 15:5), in him and with him we can bear fruit, and this fruit "is the holiness of a life made fruitful by union with Christ." In fact, the *CCC* continues, "When we believe in Jesus Christ, partake of his mysteries, and keep his commandments, the Savior himself comes to love, in us, his Father and his brethren, our Father and our brethren" (*ibid.*). It is a statement that recalls what Jesus himself stated in another passage in the Gospel of John: "Anyone who loves me will keep my word, and my Father will love him, and we shall come to him and make a home in him" (Jn 14:23). The indwelling of God in the life of believers is made possible by the acceptance of the initiative of love of the unitrine God through faith and moral life. The commandments are then no longer seen as external obligations but rather are lived as a requirement of our love for God, the Master of our life.

"His person becomes, through the Spirit, the living and interior rule of our activity." It was von Balthasar who proposed the idea of considering Christ as a concrete and universal rule. Christ is a concrete person, but since he fulfilled the will of his father, he is offered to us as a model for how to behave. In this sense, *VS* reiterates that Christ is "a living and personal Law"

(n. 15). Von Balthasar then adds that Christ does not only tell us what we must do but also gives us the capacity to do the will of his father so that "the actions of Christians in their capacity as sons of God are completed because we can do them, not because we must" (*Nine Theses in Christian Ethics*: first thesis, in J. Ratzinger—H. Schürmann—H.U. von Balthasar, *Principles of Christian Morality*, Città Nuova, Rome 1986). For Christians, duties are not the foundation of ethics, like they are for Kant. First comes grace, through which God makes good possible. "What God commands he makes possible by his grace" (*CCC* 2082).

Chapter One, Article 1:
"YOU SHALL LOVE YOUR GOD WITH ALL YOUR HEART, AND WITH ALL YOUR SOUL, AND WITH ALL YOUR MIND"

Cataldo Zuccaro

Article 1:
THE FIRST COMMANDMENT

I. "You Shall Worship the Lord Your God and Him Only Shall You Serve"

When viewed superficially, it would appear that this number which introduces the first commandment does not directly deal with the material of the Decalogue. In some of the many discussions at the time of the Second Vatican Council, the fear was even expressed that assuming love as a criterion for morality might distract the faithful from the observance of the commandments themselves. It was as if St. Augustine's adage "love and do what you will" represented the danger of a relativistic and non-binding interpretation of the Decalogue (cf *De Ordine Morali*, 15, in *Acta et Documenta Concilio Oecumenico Vatica- no II Apparando. Series II* [*Praeparatoria*]. Volumen II: *Acta Pontificiae Commissionis Centralis Praeparatoriae Concilii Oecumenici Vaticani II*. Pars II: Sessio tertia 1/15/1962). The *sensus fidei* had already led the Council Fathers to reaffirm the centrality of love in Christian moral life with confidence, emphasizing how love is the distinctive commandment of Christianity.

In reality, the *CCC* also highlights another important aspect: the commandment of love is not an external obligation imposed on the believer but rather a need that is born from the awareness of the nature of God, who is love. There is an intrinsic connection between the indicative and the imperative in the sense that God's revelation, where he presents himself as a liberator and provider of good—"I am Yahweh your God, who brought you out of Egypt, where you lived as slaves"—incites a feeling of love and recognition in people that accept it. This is the approach of the Decalogue:

it expresses the operative interpretation of the love that God offers to man and that of man, who responds to God's gift. "For the Bible, morality is the consequence of the experience of God, more precisely the God-given human experience of an entirely unmerited gift" (Pontifical Bible Commission, *The Bible and Morality: Biblical Roots of Christian Conduct* [05/11/2008], 4).

For this reason, it is God's gift that precedes humanity's response and renders it possible. The necessity of assuming a perspective that surpasses the judicial conception of moral law, starting from the Decalogue, and of insisting on love as a commandment that Jesus requires of his disciples, emerges here. It is not that this last aspect does not reflect the truth, but it should not be emphasized to the point that what is more important, God's love for us, is left hidden or considered to be of secondary importance. Without this awareness, Christian moral life is left without its specific foundation and risks being presented as the external imposition of a series of rules. Man's recognition of God's identity generates and provides the foundation for the awareness of man's own identity as a creature. Anthropologically, this shows the great dignity man has from the moment he is created "in the image and likeness of God." In terms of action, on the other hand, it provides a basis for the need for man to recognize and accept God's presence, acting in conformance with his being. For this reason, the *CCC* cites the *Catechism of the Council of Trent* in order to demonstrate how the requirements of faith, hope, and charity are in some way contained in the recognition of the identity and nature of God. Because of this, man cannot accept God without living his life coherently: "The first commandment embraces faith, hope, and charity [...] Hence the formula God employs in the Scripture at the beginning and end of his commandments: 'I am the LORD.'"

Another important aspect, however, comes from this interplay between God's revelation and human life. Man is only able to arrive at and grasp the heart of his identity by accepting divine revelation. It is easy to see the lesson of the Second Vatican Council here, when Jesus is presented as the full revelation of God and of man: "The truth is that only in the mystery of the incarnate Word does the mystery of man take on light. For Adam, the first man, was a figure of Him Who was to come, namely Christ the Lord. Christ, the final Adam, by the revelation of the mystery of the Father and His love, fully reveals man to man himself and makes his supreme calling clear" (*GS* 22).

Faith

The perspective that opens up the horizon of the moral life of the believer now becomes clear: "Our moral life has its source in faith in God who reveals his love to us" (*CCC* 2087). Here, we are brought back to the genesis of our moral life, where the adhesion of faith to God's offer of love has already become our first and fundamental moral decision and the source of the moral decisions that follow it. In this sense, faith, which is God's free gift that stays with us forever, enters the moral dimension because it is the object of a decision made by the conscience of the believer. At the same time, it becomes a principle that animates and inspires the believer and determines his subsequent actions. In this sense, we should note that adhesion to faith while "bypassing" the dynamism of the moral conscience is not possible.

It is not the anthropological reduction of faith but rather its authentically human acceptance that makes it possible to nourish and protect it "with prudence and vigilance, and to reject everything that is opposed to it" (n. 2088). For this reason, the first commandment also makes it necessary to avoid any attitude or action that runs contrary to faith, such as voluntary or involuntary doubt (n. 2088), incredulity, heresy, apostasy, and schism (n. 2089). Faith is put to the test in every era through particular temptations; cases of heresy, apostasy, and various schisms are documented throughout history. Perhaps we could ask what tests faith most today, but there would be no single correct answer because cultural and geographic differences mean that different believers live under different conditions.

For the Western world, there is a common element behind the various sins against faith listed: indifference. We could believe that people do not in reality decide against faith in the sense that they fight or act voluntarily against it. In reality, it is exactly this attitude of indifference that forms the basis for the death of faith, which begins to starve. What could represent a challenge for growth instead becomes an opportunity for moral weakening and exhaustion. This is true for doubt, for example, which is not necessarily bad for faith but rather serves as an opportunity for growth and deepening of faith if the person works to overcome it. Visually, we could imagine that the collapse occurred up top because the foundation had already ceased to be stable.

Hope

The revelation of the goodness of God generates not only faith for man but also opens his heart to hope—that is, to the trust that "God will give him the capacity to love Him in return and to act in conformity with the commandments of charity" (n. 2090). The attitude of hope, which is a gift that gives rise to confidence that one can correspond to God's love, offers an alternative to two attitudes that are opposite but equally opposed to hope: presumption and despair.

Both of these attitudes can come from God being eclipsed in the world, from disregard for his presence and his mercy. In fact, God's death created the myth of the superhuman that believes that he has the ability to save himself, but the delirium of omnipotence before the tragedies of history and the limit of death unveils the metaphysical abyss of nothingness and throws man into despair. When this general climate is freely and consciously adopted by man, who lives and acts while removing his life from God, despair becomes sin. The same could be said for presumption, from the moment when, in both cases, man no longer believes in mercy or divine providence (nn. 2091–2092). The sinner, in this sense, remains an "autistic person," or a *homo incurvatus in se* according to Luther's famous interpretation.

In reality, our profoundly fragmented cultural climate, although it may facilitate contact, makes having a relationship in terms of being able to meet the needs of and participate in the life of another person difficult. This other person is almost never viewed as a neighbor. Much more often, this person is viewed as a threat or as an object of indifference. In the face of the phenomenon of mass migration, which is by now irreversible and global, we feel it necessary to combine security and welcoming, but feelings of closedness toward others are also increasing. This closedness can also become a sin against hope. Whether this occurs is based on the extent to which one refuses to believe in the possibility that it is possible to recognize and collect the signs of hope connected to the love of good in everything that happens throughout history. In this case as well, the result of refusing to recognize and accept God's action in history, resorting to irreparable apocalyptic scenarios or institutionalized violent reactions, is despair and presumption.

Charity

Faith's answer to the revelation of the identity of God is effectively verified through the response of human charity to divine love. The perspective of the commandment of love is not based on human force but rather on God's gift. For this reason, as Saint Thomas writes in a frank and effective manner, it is God who makes us capable of loving him by loving us. In this context, citing Proverbs 8:17 ("I love those who love me"), he explains that this should not be understood in the sense that God is waiting for love from men as a necessary condition in order to be able to reciprocate. On the contrary, it is God who loves man first and it is through this love that he empowers them and makes them able to love him ("*Deus enim nos amando, facit suos dilectores; Prv 8,17: ego diligentes me diligo: non quasi prius fuerint diligentes, sed quia ipse eos diligentes facit diligendo*," Thomas, *Super Johannem*, ch. 15, lectio 3).

As explained in the *CCC*, the commandment does not only imply man's love for God but also orders us to love "all creatures for him and because of him." Once again, we find the echo of a preoccupation of the Second Vatican Council, which immediately abandons the individualistic conception of Christianity and takes up a point of view that is more open to relationships and to society: "For by his innermost nature man is a social being, and unless he relates himself to others he can neither live nor develop his potential" (*GS* 12; this is addressed explicitly in *CCC* 1878–1896). But it is also necessary to take another step and take the *CCC* text that discusses "all creatures" into account. All of creation is included in this commandment.

For this reason, the commandment of love for God is not only inseparably connected to the commandment of love for one's neighbor but also to all the other living things that are a sign of God's love for man but are also a reflection of divine goodness: "Saint Francis, faithful to Scripture, invites us to see nature as a magnificent book in which God speaks to us and grants us a glimpse of his infinite beauty and goodness" (Pope Francis, *LS* 12). Therefore, it is for love of God that the believer is called to love creation and the other beings that live in it. The Christian must find the proper balance between a predatory attitude with respect to the rest of nature and exaggerated environmentalism that eliminates every distinction between man and the rest of nature. Pope Francis notes that it is not possible to separate a person's attitude toward creation from his attitude toward his neighbor. Both love and contempt for one affect a person's attitude toward the other. "The creation accounts in the book of Genesis [...] suggest that human life is grounded in three fundamental and closely intertwined relationships: with God, with our neighbor and with the earth itself" (*LS* 66). This provides the perfect context for understanding what the *CCC* teaches us: "Faith in God's love encompasses the call and the obligation to respond with sincere love to divine charity. The first commandment enjoins us to love God above everything and all creatures for him and because of him" (*CCC* 2093).

After introducing how love is necessary for the response of authentic faith to God, the *CCC* lists the possible ways that this love can be betrayed. They are identified as indifference, ingratitude, lukewarmness, acedia, and hatred, and a brief but meaningful profile is provided for each one. If we had to arrange these attitudes in order of severity, we would probably have to begin with the last of the list, hate, which is the most immediate, direct, and explicit form of opposition to God's love. In reality, it is perhaps necessary to place more emphasis on the other attitudes for pedagogical reasons; they are common, although better hidden, and creeping, but they are no less poisonous for the life of the believer. In fact, these attitudes do not often lead to explicit and formal affirmations of hate toward God, but it is easier to fall into the trap of acedia or indifference or laziness by believing that small failures or betrayals are not enough to completely deprive us of God's love. In traditional terms, this is the relationship between venial and mortal sin and the different natures of the two. Only mortal sin deprives the believer of grace. But the importance of "venial sins" lies in the fact that they represent a slow and continuous erosion of love which reaches a point in which the believer can no longer withstand the impact of evil and falls into grave sin. Now, we must not be misled by the single act of mortal sin; it is true that it rises to the surface only in the moment when it has been completed, but this was only made possible following a gestational period in the shadow of acedia, indifference, and spiritual laziness. On the horizon is the necessity of reading the biography of mortal sin in light of man's fundamental choice.

II. "Him Only You Shall Serve"

God's revelation, especially in the Old Testament, implies the affirmation of his unique, absolute, and universal dominion. This affirmation already emerges in the creation story in Genesis, where the Jewish faith recognizes that what had been perceived as gods by the neighboring peoples (light, darkness, chaos, etc.) were none other than creatures of God. This same awareness continues through the salvation story and gets its final confirmation through Jesus's preaching, at the center of which the kingdom of God, or the universal, unique, and absolute dominion that God expresses through his merciful action, is proclaimed. Jesus's proclamation, which is centered on this Kingdom of mercy, is not self-referential, although he does demonstrate the awareness that the Kingdom is already come and in operation through him. God's final judgment over humanity is performed in the face of the acceptance or rejection of Jesus. By now, no one can remain neutral and no escape is possible. People must take a side: with Jesus or against him. The final judgment is already anticipated in a way by the decision that people make in their lives before Christ: whether to accept or refuse their brothers and sisters, especially the least fortunate.

Before determining the concrete actions needed to put the choice of making God an exclusive priority in Christian life into practice, it is necessary to adequately understand what this means. In particular, it should not be thought that the affirmation that God must have absolute priority in the life of a Christian means that all other human values should be disregarded. God does not impede or compete with love for one's children, health, friendship, frugality, or any other human value. This is because he places himself on a plane that does not belong to any other created value. The opposite, however, is true, in general terms. The affirmation of God's absolute dominion guarantees a correct relationship between human values. God does not place himself in the web of human values by tangling himself up in them. He is not the primary or the greatest human value, he is a presence that in some way guarantees theirs, as if he were the condition that makes them possible.

The necessity of moving beyond a fundamentalist view of the dominion of God, as if this could be expressed without any mediation or analogies, but rather in a random form, is born here. The famous adage "Without my grace, not even a leaf can move" cannot be naively understood to mean that God blows directly on the leaf in order to move it. This interpretation would erroneously lead one also to connect the circumstances of death, which are often tragic and painful, to direct action by the hand of God, or to believe that the aberrant circumstances of an act of violence or a rape that leads to pregnancy occurred through God's initiative. The Christian's attitude should not be one of renouncing what is authentically human in order to affirm God's dominion but rather one of affirming God's dominion in order to fully appreciate what is authentically human. Naturally, the authentic human should not be taken for granted. He is constructed within a complex web of relationships, and it is here that we can find situations that are incompatible with the affirmation of God's absolute dominion. It is not health that places God's dominion in doubt, but exaggerated worship of health that tends to overpower every other good thing.

Adoration

The theological virtues of faith, hope, and charity are expanded and put to work through the moral virtues. In terms of the first commandment, these are specified through the virtue of religion. At the center of this virtue is the attitude of a creature who places himself in worship of the Creator and therefore recognizes his Creator's absolute dominion and his absolute dependence on him. The aforementioned characterization of the sinner as a *homo incurvatus in se* is contrasted with that of the man who "bows before God" in order to recognize his absolutely unavailable and transcendent otherness. As the *CCC* notes, this attitude of adoration "sets man free from turning in on himself, from the slavery of sin and the idolatry of the world" (n. 2097). In reality, bending one's knee to the Lord Jesus is the strongest guarantee that allows us to experience freedom, both by standing up to pretensions or false forms of authority and by bowing down to others in an attitude of service.

Prayer

Here, prayer is presented not in its broadest meaning, as in the fourth part of the *CCC*, but in relation to the adoration of the one Lord. Consequently, the obediential character of prayer, both when it takes the form of praise or thanks and when it takes the form of intercession or questioning, is emphasized. Prayer expresses the recognition of one's dependence on the Creator and one's willingness to obey his commandments in all its forms.

Sacrifice

Sacrifice, "a sign of adoration and gratitude, supplication and communion" is presented along the same lines of recognition of one's dependence on God and affirmation of his dominion. In this context, sacrifice is expressed in three directions: internally, by overcoming the danger of self-righteousness; mercy toward one's neighbor, overcoming the danger of sterile ritualism; and the liturgy of love, overcoming the risk of fragmentation because by uniting ourselves to Christ's sacrifice, "we can make our lives a sacrifice to God" (n. 2100).

Promises and Vows

These actions, which are related to each other but are not identical, are presented by the *CCC* in a way that avoids evoking misleading images connected to bizarre fantasies of a religion that consists of practices that have little meaning for Christian life. In fact, although it recognizes individual believers' freedom to "promise to God this action, that prayer, this alms-giving, that pilgrimage, and so forth," it places the fact that forms of promises connected to sacraments such as baptism, confirmation, marriage, and ordination already exist in the foreground (n. 2101). In the same way, in terms of vows we are reminded that "the Church recognizes an exemplary value in the vows to practice the evangelical counsels" (n. 2103). The logic of promises and vows encompasses the paradigm of recognition of God's dominion, and especially in the case of vows, of conforming more fully to Christ, as *LG* 42 suggests.

The Social Duty of Religion and the Right to Religious Freedom

The final title of this second paragraph concludes with the subject of religious liberty, which is in fact given much more space than the other titles. This documents the importance that the *CCC* attributes to this subject. Moreover, the choice of including it within a discussion of man's duties of recognizing and worshiping the absolute dominion of God is logical. This duty, in fact, since it must be expressed in a humanly authentic and meaningful form, requires the freedom to pursue different forms of worship and different religious actions. The Second Vatican Council certainly took a few steps forward in terms of the concept of the right to religious freedom and the necessity for this to be able to be expressed publicly. For example, we could note that Gregory XVI referred to "that absurd and erroneous proposition which claims that liberty of conscience must be maintained for everyone," (Encyclical letter *Mirari Vos* [10/15/1832]) and more recently, Leo XIII spoke of "liberty in individuals which is so opposed to the virtue of religion, namely, the *liberty of worship*" (Encyclical letter *Libertas* [06/20/1888]). It is doubtless that we should welcome the courageous doctrinal evolution that the Second Vatican Council established, which is expressed in the declaration on religious liberty *DH*, which is frequently cited in these numbers.

The *CCC* draws on the problems that emerged and that were often resolved during the Second Vatican Council's approval process for the declaration. First of all, the *CCC* states that it is the duty of each person to search for the truth and to adhere to it once he has discovered it. It specifies that this duty derives from the nature of man himself (n. 2104). Adhering to the truth about God means that "the duty of offering God genuine worship concerns man both individually and socially" (n. 2105). Likewise, this duty corresponds to the fact that "the right of all citizens and religious communities to religious freedom must be recognized and respected as well" (n. 2107).

Moreover, the text seems to respond to the concerns that arose during the Council's discussion about the equalization of religious freedom and indifference, as if they were the same phenomenon. The *CCC* reminds us that the basis for religious freedom is not related to the truth of one's choice. Religious freedom is based directly on human dignity. Naturally, this does not mean that every choice man makes regarding religion is insignificant. In fact, while recognizing that different religions "frequently reflect a ray of that truth which enlightens all men" (n. 2104), the text emphasizes that Christians must "make known the worship of the one true religion which subsists in the Catholic and apostolic Church" (n. 2105). Moreover, the *CCC* clarifies that "the right to religious liberty is neither a moral license to adhere to error, nor a supposed right to error" (n. 2108).

Freedom of conscience is the larger context in which religious freedom is contained. The former is a subtype of the latter. For this reason, "nobody may be forced to act against his convictions, nor is anyone to be restrained from acting in accordance with his conscience in religious matters in private or in public, alone or in association with others, within due limits" (n. 2106). Naturally, the reference to moral conscience is based on the Council's doctrine from *GS* 16. In light of this, dignity should be interpreted in a way that mandates respect and the obligation to not force anyone to act against his conscience. The declaration does not enter into a discussion of individual theological problems, such as in this case the debate on invincible erroneous conscience. What is important is the reaffirmation of the dignity of moral conscience, "the most secret core and sanctuary of a man, [where] he is alone with God, Whose voice echoes in his depths."

The *CCC*'s point of view cannot be understood without making note of the vein of realism reflected in the placement of limits on the exercise of religious freedom and freedom of worship. The reason behind the limits, which are mentioned multiple times (cf. nn. 2106, 2108–2109), is the respect and promotion of the common good: "The 'due limits' [...] must be determined for each social situation by political prudence, according to the requirements of the common good, and ratified by the civil authority in accordance with 'legal principles which are in conformity with the objective moral order'" (n. 2109). The logic that emerges is that attention must be paid in order to avoid having on the one hand every claim of conscience related to religion automatically become an authentic exercise of religious freedom and on the other hand every intervention seeking to limit the expression of freedom of conscience automatically finding justification and legitimacy. In other words, both religious freedom and interventions to limit it can become compromised and turn into ideology, thus betraying their very nature. This is why the *CCC* is so cautious in describing the conditions for the exercise of religious freedom and its limits in the clearest way possible.

III. "You Shall Have No Other Gods Before Me"

This prohibition is based on the recognition of God's unique dominion, which is absolute, universal, and exclusive. For this reason, no person or reality in the life of a Christian can pretend total obedience, which only God can request. The heart of the believer therefore cannot become like a condominium, divided into spaces to which various more or less important entities are allocated, all of which are comparable to God. The cultural context of today in which the Christian is called to observe this commandment does not help but sometimes acts as an obstacle. It makes it difficult to conceive of a unifying principle for one's life, especially when this principle specifically refers to a single person who gives unity and significance to the multitude of experiences had over a lifetime. In fact, at each level, what is mandated is the absolutization of the fragment that has been detached from the web and the exaltation of individual experience as a benchmark and subjective guide for action. The just conquest of freedom emphasizes autonomy and often sacrifices it on the altar of responsibility and relationships. In this universe of fragments and suspicion of anything that makes autonomy opaque, the affirmation of a unique and absolute personal reference such as the sense of existence becomes difficult.

In particular, in terms of religion this culture seems to invite syncretism, choosing elements from profoundly different religious traditions and having them coexist in the life of a person outside of their original contexts. Each person tends to construct his own religion like a mosaic with tiles borrowed from different religions. Perhaps an analogy would be that we are watching the transition between a dictatorship of religion and a dictatorship of subjective religious desire. But the general climate of indifference toward faith and religion, sometimes justified through the scientific veneer of agnosticism, is perhaps more common than syncretism.

The commandment pushes us to ask ourselves if there are other presumed gods that usurp God's place in our lives and what these may be. In this sense, we cannot ignore that God's main competitor is man himself. This idea already appears in the story of the temptations in Genesis. However, man lives within a network of relationships that form who he is and that he himself contributes to building. The interaction between people and the community is structured through institutions. These, once created, condition the relationship from which they are born. For this reason, it is these structures that sometimes become so invasive that they take the place of God in the life of the believer. Think, for example, of the economy, and particularly of the pretense of the market that requires people to sacrifice themselves in order to live and prosper. Or think of dictatorial powers, or the various forms of hidden power that work in the undergrowth of illegality. Every time someone or something presumes to take God's place, it always produces a result, albeit in various ways, that is not the exaltation of man but rather his ruin.

Superstition—Idolatry

Superstition is the presumption of obtaining God's favor by forcing him to be present in religious practices or signs that may even be of a sacramental nature without corresponding to a coherent interior disposition. In this sense, the truth of religion is distorted because its transcendent dimension is eliminated, and the true identity of God is betrayed. He becomes domesticated, placed at the disposition of a creature. Fundamentally, superstition is related to idolatry in the sense that the true God is replaced with gestures or objects of a material nature that are used as a substitute for him. In reality, "The first commandment condemns polytheism. It requires man neither to believe in, nor to venerate, other divinities than the one true God" (n. 2112). Many of the gods that were recognized while the Old Testament was being written disappeared with the downfall of the cultures that produced them. The *CCC* appropriately notes, however, that "not only refers to false pagan worship. It remains a constant temptation to faith. Idolatry consists in divinizing what is not God. Man commits idolatry whenever he honors and reveres a creature in place of God, whether this be gods or demons (for example, satanism), power, pleasure, race, ancestors, the state, money, etc." (n. 2113). The fundamental reason why idolatry "is a perversion of man's innate religious sense" is the fact that it crushes the transcendence of the Christian religion onto the anthropological plane.

Divination and Magic

It is natural for each person to worry about his life and his future and to try to adequately provide for them. The *CCC* explicitly recognizes that "improvidence, however, can constitute a lack of responsibility" (n. 2115). The current anthropological climate, which is full of uncertainties for the future, creates a heightened sense of insecurity and paves the way for answers that give the illusion of being able to take control of and direct a person's life in accordance with his desires. For this reason, we are inclined to place our faith in self-styled wizards and soothsayers that predict a future that has been carefully designed to respond to the anxieties of the people who come to them. Theologically, the error here consists in presuming that a person can determine the course of his life based on a perspective that systematically disregards divine Providence. The word of the wizard is not, in fact, the word of a prophet who speaks God's name ("God can reveal the future to his prophets or to other saints": n. 2115), but rather an alternative to divine providence. For this reason, placing our faith in that word means lacking faith in God. In a balanced fashion, the *CCC* helps understand how both a life based on magic (n. 2117) and on divination in its various forms (n. 2116) and a life lived "randomly" without any foresight become attitudes that run contrary to the first commandment, and, in particular, to faith in divine Providence. In the case of magic, this occurs because the person does not believe in Providence. In the case of improvidence, on the other hand, it occurs because the person erroneously lives with a faith in Providence that works magically, as if man's cooperation were not required. It is necessary to remember that the relationship between God and man is not like the relationship between servant and master or a relationship based on competition but rather a relationship based on the model of the family. In fact, as the son of God, man is called to interpret the Father's providential plan and put it into action as a son would, not in a magical way but with freedom, responsibility, and the awareness that this is how his life is constructed.

Irreligion

First of all, it should be noted that the term irreligion does not refer to the attitude of someone who absolutely does not believe in God and therefore performs no acts of worship. Irreligion in instead the attitude of a person who, although he believes in God and may perform acts of worship, nevertheless misrepresents God's identity in various ways, and therefore performs acts of worship that distort, obfuscate, and offend the true divine image. The temptation to misrepresent the true face of God is already present in the serpent's deceit of Adam, as told in the book of Genesis. The serpent wants to convince Adam that fundamentally God is not so loving. On the contrary, he is jealous, to the point that he does not wish to give man the gift of immortality. The meaning of the temptation is not to convince man not to believe in God, but rather not to believe in God as he truly is—in other words, to change and mutate the deepest part of his nature, love. The other acts that the *CCC* places under the heading of irreligion, sacrilege (n. 2120) and simony (n. 2121), also involve this misrepresentation. In the case of sacrilege, in fact, the sacraments and other liturgical actions are used in a way that does not respect their objectives or the spiritual goods. Through simony, on the other hand, spiritual goods lose their worth as free gifts and become opportunities for trading, as if they were human property and not dependent on God, who freely bestows them on all people.

Atheism—Agnosticism

Atheism, which the *CCC* describes as a rejection of man's intimate and vital bond to God (n. 2123) and identifies in its various forms of practical materialism, atheistic humanism, and economic liberation, represents the rejection of God himself. Atheism has always been present in human history and has varied in the extent to which it is common and visible during the various eras and in different geographical locations. According to the *CCC*, atheism is based on "a false conception of human autonomy, exaggerated to the point of refusing any dependence on God" (n. 2126). In fact, autonomy is a conquest of modernity, which has delivered man from a type of "dependent subjectivity," which is from time to time defined in reference to sex, to social status, to religion, and so on. The result of this liberation of the subject has unfortunately not infrequently sacrificed the relationship of the person, who is conceived of in an absolute and self-referential manner. As we touched upon previously, it is man's creatural dependence on God that allows for both autonomy and relationships without sacrificing either dimension on the altar of the other. Agnosticism, which "is all too often equivalent to practical atheism" (n. 2128), is closely related to atheism. All too often, it is cloaked in a veil of scientism and is justified through the impossibility of proving that God exists.

IV. "You Shall Not Make For Yourself a Graven Image…"

This divine commandment is born from the recognition of God's identity, which is absolutely transcendent. As the *CCC* explains through the words of Dt 4:15–16, "Since you saw no form on the day that the Lord spoke to you at Horeb out of the midst of the fire, beware lest you act corruptly by making a graven image for yourselves, in the form of any figure…" In the history of the Church, the problem of the veneration of images was posed and resolved right from the beginning: "Basing itself on the mystery of the incarnate Word, the seventh ecumenical council at Nicaea (787) justified against the iconoclasts the veneration of icons—of Christ, but also of the Mother of God, the angels, and all the saints. By becoming incarnate, the Son of God introduced a new 'economy' of images" (*CCC* 2131). It became clear that the veneration of images has nothing to do with idolatry but rather involves having a respectful attitude toward sacred images. "Religious worship is not directed to images in themselves, considered as mere things, but under their distinctive aspect as images leading us on to God incarnate" (n. 2132).

Perhaps our cultural sensitivity, which is so attentive to the world of icons, can help us here with the authentic understanding of the divine commandment. An icon does not replace the person that it represents but is an attempt to express one of his personality traits in a visual manner. The *CCC* correctly speaks of a new economy of images based on the incarnation of Jesus. Making use of an analogy, this is like a type of sacramental economy where the sign makes the entity depicted present in a different way. Icons and sacraments are not the same, but this is true in an analogical sense, and we must keep in mind that analogies are often the most suitable language for expressing the truth of faith: "Now we see only reflections in a mirror, mere riddles, but then we shall be seeing face to face. Now I can know only imperfectly; but then I shall know just as fully as I am myself known" (1 Cor 13:12).

Chapter One, Article 2:
THE SECOND COMMANDMENT

José M. Galván

The second commandment is expressed as a negative: "You shall not misuse the name of Yahweh your God" (Ex 20:7, Dt 5:11). This formulation, in addition to emphasizing that not every human word is immediately directed at God, indicates a minimum below which one cannot go because any use of human beings' symbolic capacity (thoughts, words, external signs) that is directly or indirectly disrespectful to the holy name of God is prohibited. Starting from this minimum, the commandment shows us the path toward trying to convert every human action into an opportunity to freely show our adoration and recognition of God. In fact, free human action must at least implicitly be an expression of the fact that we have been created in the image and likeness of God.

The religious nature of man means that the duty of praising God's name is not under discussion because it is a demonstration of our recognition of the personal nature of divinity and of its attributes. Turning toward God is a necessary expression of the religiosity that is just as obligatory as worship and is based on the capacity to recognize God in all of creation. This duty, which is based on our condition as creatures of God, is elevated to a demonstration of our condition as children of God through grace. Prayer, therefore, is a demonstration of piety and filial love.

The *CCC* expands upon the contents of this commandment in three paragraphs. The first regards the holiness of God's name and the obligation to glorify it, including the most obvious sin against this commandment, blasphemy. The second mainly addresses the moral value of a promise made in God's name. The final paragraph refers to the name of each Christian, both the one that we receive during baptism and the name that God has given to each human being, personally identifying us in all of eternity and for all of eternity.

I. The Name of the Lord Is Holy

As we know, for the people of Israel, a person's name was much more than a mere identifier or a convention that allowed him to be unequivocally called and distinguished from others. Without abandoning this fundamentally social meaning, the name was most of all a symbolic manifestation of one's being, a way of saying who its bearer was. For this reason, being able to call someone by name also means having access to the true being of the person being called, knowing the essence of his person, and in a sense being able to make use of him. Therefore, the gods of the religions of the peoples near Israel had a name with which they were indistinctly identified when named or during liturgy. This name was not simply the generic title that referred to their divine nature ("god" or "goddess") but a true name that was personal and nontransferable and unequivocally defined who was the recipient of a prayer or sacrifice and especially who was religiously revered and feared. Israel generally shared this attitude, to the point that they were expressly and absolutely prohibited to "name" the other gods because in a certain sense this would have meant recognizing them as real: "do not mention the name of any other god: let none ever be heard from your lips" (Ex 23:13).

The people of Israel, did not immediately receive the name of God. In the beginning, he was only referred to generically (*'el*) or using an expression that summarized all possible divine attributes through an irregular plural (*'elohîm*). There is no lack of requests for God to unveil his name so that the people might have immediate access to him: "Please tell me your name" (Jn 32:30). This petition will finally be answered through the revelation to Moses at Horeb (cf. Ex 3:13–14): the people can have full trust in God because they know his name, YHWH: "This is my name for all time, and thus I am to be invoked for all generations to come" (Ex 3:15). The sacred telegram therefore becomes not only the transcendent container of the faith of Israel but also the final foundation for hope because by knowing God's name, the people could have an unshakeable trust in his unwavering loyalty to the promises made to the Ancestors. In fact, before giving his name, he introduced himself as "the God of Abraham, the God of Isaac and the God of Jacob" (Ex 3:6).

As n. 2143 of the *CCC* notes, everything that God wanted to reveal to believers in the Old Testament, showing himself to them as a mystery of confidence and intimacy, is summarized in this single word. For Israel, the highest divine attribute is "sanctity," which more than any other divine characteristic expresses the absolute transcendence of God and his unattainable nature, despite his closeness and the role that he freely assumed as Lord of history. Due to his sanctity, he is not trapped in the era in which he works, and he does not suffer the negative effects. Rather, his sanctity becomes God's unifying force since his presence in history attracts everything to him. Men, eras, and places become holy in the extent to which they are included in the power of holiness which is manifested as "glory." "You have been sanctified and have become holy because I am holy" (Lv 11:44, 45).

YHWH is the name of he who is Holy. It seems logical, therefore, that the name, which is so closely connected to God's very being cannot be taken in vain and that saying his name is connected to especially significant moments in worship and praise. The people can experience their religion by invoking the name of YHWH (Gn 4:26; 12:8; 21:33; 1 Kgs 1:24; 2 Kgs 5:11; Ps 105:1; Is 64:6…).

Now let us return to the negative formulation of the precept. The first commandment was also negative in its original form ("You shall have no other gods to rival me": Ex 20:3; Dt 5:7). However, Jesus later pronounced it in the positive form, which is the form usually used: "You must love the Lord your God with all your heart, with all your soul, and with all your mind" (Mt 22:37; cf. *CCC* 2083). In the Tradition of the Church, this did not occur for the formulation of the second precept, which has remained negative. This is probably due to the importance of setting an insuperable lower limit. The context clearly indicates, however, that there is no upper limit on how much one can praise God's name. Above the lower bound exists a whole world of possibilities leading to the maximum possible exaltation of God and of his works.

The word, in all of its possible configurations (internal, external, corporal, gestural, etc.) reflects the consciously religious nature of human beings, who must praise God not only ontologically, like the other creatures, but also in their capacity for free and intentional actions in an especially meaningful way. The word is the primary instrument of the natural virtue of religion and the most "logical" way to be in a "dialogue" with the Creator. For this reason, we could say that this commandment directly reminds us of humans' most basic moral obligation. As the Second Vatican Council notes, "From the very circumstance of his origin man is already invited to converse with God. For man would not exist were he not created by God's love and constantly preserved by it; and he cannot live fully according to truth unless he freely acknowledges that love and devotes himself to His Creator" (*GS* 19).

Although, as stated previously, the precept has traditionally remained in the negative form, we can find its positive expression in the contents of the first petition of the Lord's Prayer: "May your name be held holy" (Mt 6:9; cf. *CCC* 2807–2815). The fact that the positive manifestation of this obligation is found in the Lord's Prayer in the New Testament is especially meaningful. The Old Testament seems to favor the formulations in which the true glory of the Name is entrusted directly to YHWH: it is he, the Holy One, who sanctifies his name, which has been profaned among the nations (cf. Ez 36:23). Man cannot sanctify his name except through his assumption in the world of divine holiness. In fact, the holy name (Ps 33:21, 103:1,

105:3; Is 57:15; Wis 10:20; etc.) is not directly sanctified if not through people who have been flooded with holiness in sacred times and in sacred places. Only under these conditions can the name YHWH be used. The name is used by the Levites for the liturgical blessing (Dt 10:8) and by the Kings (2 Sam 6:18). This may be another reason why the Old Testament precept is expressed in the negative form.

But once Jesus revealed the existence of the Trinity, which is the true content of holiness, all of humanity, which has been mysteriously and truly united to his holiness, was able to glorify the name of God through him. He is given the "name which is above all other names" (Phil 2:9), and "of all the names in the world given to men, this is the only one by which we can be saved" (Acts 4:12). We are joined to Jesus, the Word made flesh, through the action of the Holy Spirit, and thanks to the third Person we can say that Jesus is the Lord and address the Father, *Abbà* (cf. Rom 8:15; Gal 4:6). The "true names" of divine holiness become the primary intellectual expression of our faith, which is received "in the name of the Father and of the Son and of the Holy Spirit" (Mt 28:19). Confessing our Faith in God the Father, the Son, and the Holy Spirit becomes our primary act of religious worship, which is present in abundance in the New Testament (cf. Rom 15:19; Heb 13:15; Rev 15:4). And our actions are adapted to this confession and therefore become a manifestation of the glorification of God in history and in the world so that "Yahweh will become king of the whole world, [and] when that Day comes, Yahweh will be the one and only and his name the one name" (Zec 14:9).

Man praises God's name with every dimension of his being. Every one of his actions affirms or conceals God's presence: "My heart and my body cry out for joy to the living God" (Ps 83:3; cf. *CCC* 2153). This occurs primarily through his intelligence, which is strengthened by all his other cognitive powers. Man knows how to discover the hand of he who supports everything—and in which he places his trust through the voluntary actions which direct all of his tendencies—behind everyday events. Then, like in any interpersonal relationship, emotions also become involved, and man can elevate and "humanize" this human-divine dialogue through direct invocation. Finally, corporality, song, clothing, place, time, and many other factors can help "incarnate" this spiritual encounter. Every one of our symbolic actions must be in praise of God.

"Blasphemy" is the opposite of all of this. Man's thoughts, the feelings in his heart, his external words, and his bodily gestures can freely be directed against God, contradicting their originally religious nature at the most basic level. For this reason, these are grave violations of the virtue of religion, for which man is called to freely demonstrate his ontological debt to his Creator.

In the context of the grace of Christ, the gravity of blasphemy means that it acts as a deep offense toward the loving Father committed by one of his sons. For this reason, due to its deliberately offensive or harmful content, blasphemy is a very grave sin of hate toward God and the theological virtue of charity. Many classical authors, in fact, call direct and intentional affronts to divine Persons "diabolical blasphemy." Note that many times, the difficult circumstances that may lead to indirect blasphemy are also an opportunity for supplication and for asking God if we can rely on him or asking him for help. In some sense, this increases the gravity of the sin due to the deliberate omission of filial supplication. Since outward blasphemy is scandalous, it can easily be included in the list of sins against theological charity directed at one's neighbor.

Only imperfection of the action due to inadvertence or lack of consent can render blasphemy venial. This is only the case if the action was not voluntary "in causa" due to a habit that was not corrected. In the latter case, not only does the gravity of the sin remain, but it can also be increased due to the neglectful contempt of the offense and the possible scandal. On the other hand, no sin is committed when thoughts or expressions that are offensive toward the Lord or sacred things arise in one's heart. These can be temptations or manifestations of an altered psychological state. In these cases, the necessity of overcoming the temptation and the sincere displeasure that it produces can serve as opportunities to experience internal and external actions of love toward God more intensely.

In the end of n. 2148, the *CCC* expands the concept of blasphemy to include the "use of God's name to cover up criminal practices, to reduce peoples to servitude, to torture persons or put them to death." Here, the offense does not come from offensive gestures or words but rather actions that are performed in the name of God and gravely damage his honor. Depending on the gravity and the public meaningfulness of the action performed, these sins also have a strong scandalous dimension and can provide a reason for others to repudiate faith.

II. Taking the Name of the Lord in Vain

In the previous paragraph, the *CCC* indicated that "Promises made to others in God's name engage the divine honor, fidelity, truthfulness, and authority. They must be respected in justice. To be unfaithful to them is to misuse God's name and in some way to make God out to be a liar" (n. 2147, cf. 1 Jn 1:10). This text seems to already indicate what the *CCC* will note further on: vows, since they involve the invocation of the name of God in order to testify to the truth, are an act of the virtue of religion. Invocation refers to a true act of praise and supplication before God, with the corresponding expressions or ritual forms for the particular circumstance, through which God is asked to reinforce the truth of the human words said in his name with his omnipotent wisdom.

Another similar action, which also explicitly involves witness of God, should be performed "truthfully, justly, uprightly" (Jer 4:2; *CIC,* can. 1199 § 1: "An oath, that is, the invocation of the divine name in witness to the truth, cannot be taken unless in truth, in judgment, and in justice").

The first condition for oaths is therefore truthfulness. In the case of an "assertory" oath (the assertion of a past or present truth), the person making the oath must be completely convinced of the truth of the words he utters. One cannot swear to an uncertain truth without explicitly stating so. In the case of "promissory" oaths, which refer to future events, one must have a firm and sincere intention of performing what is being promised. The sin of perjury occurs when the truth of the oath is violated. In an assertory oath, this means swearing that a false affirmation is true, regardless of the objective gravity of the lie (an irrelevant lie, if sworn to, becomes a grave sin). In the case of a promissory oath, a person who does not intend to perform the action promised or does not perform it without being impeded has committed perjury. "A person who freely swears to do something is bound by a special obligation of religion to fulfill what he or she affirmed by oath" (*CIC,* can. 1200, § 1).

The second condition is prudence. In order to "invoke the divine truthfulness as a pledge of one's own truthfulness," (*CCC* 2150), there must be a proportionally important reason. In fact, the *CCC* seems to stress Jesus's apparent prohibition in the Sermon on the Mount (Mt 5:34; cf. *CCC* 2153: "I say to you, do not swear at all") more than the permission given by Paul (cf. 2 Cor 1:23; Gal 1:20; *CCC* 2154) or in the Old Testament (cf. Dt 6:13; Is 65:16; Jer 12:16). This seems to indicate that there is a fundamental restrictive criterion: "the holiness of the divine name demands that we neither use it for trivial matters" (*CCC* 2155). Christians must be aware of the holiness of oaths, such as in the case of the use of God's name without serious reasons. For this reason, as a matter of principle, they must follow God's instructions, to which we referred previously, and swear oaths only in cases of true necessity and very rarely. In general, except for these special cases, we could say that Christians should only swear oaths when required by a legitimate ecclesiastical or civil authority. The common moral doctrine considers futile oaths to be venial sins, and if it becomes a useless habit, one can easily fall into the trap of a serious sin by improperly using God's name and through the increased possibility of swearing to falsehoods.

The third condition for oaths comes into play here. Oaths should also be made justly. In fact, an illegitimate or unjust authority or one that request oaths for reasons that run contrary to the dignity of the human person and of society loses the right to require oaths: "When an oath is required by illegitimate civil authorities, it may be refused" (*CCC* 2155). Part of this condition is not swearing oaths about things which, although true, are sinful in and of themselves. For example, it would be doubly grave (against charity and against religion) to swear an oath that slanders another person or to promise to perform a dishonest action in the name of God. Ultimately, the contents of the oath must always be morally permissible.

III. The Christian Name

"Thus he chose us in Christ before the world was made to be holy and faultless before him in love, marking us out for himself beforehand, to be adopted sons, through Jesus Christ. Such was his purpose and good pleasure" (Eph 1:4–6). Baptism, through its indelibility, creates a configuration to Christ ("in him") for the members of the Church, which Paul highlights in this text. Chosen for all of eternity, each human being is "named" by the Trinity with a name that indicates our interpersonal relationship with the Father, with the Son, and with the Holy Spirit. We are not given the chance to learn this name in this life; it will be unveiled in the *parusía*: "to those who prove victorious I will give some hidden manna and a white stone, with a new name written on it, known only to the person who receives it" (Rev 2:17, cf. *CCC* 2159).

The *CCC* wishes to remind us that these names—those of the Trinity, on the one hand, and ours, on the other—are the basis for the development of a perennial dialogue to which we are called from the moment of our creation. The Triune God calls us "by name," just like we nominally respond to each of the Persons. In fact, the sign of the cross—"In the name of the Father and of the Son and of the Holy Spirit"—is not only a liturgical sign that is central to worship and praise. Perhaps it is also one of the most common and immediate ways to address God when asking for help or protection. What is naturally present in the faith of Christians corresponds to a profound theological truth: the God that supports us and consoles us along the path of history is the One and Triune God that calls each of us by name. Many sociocultural elements and lots of instinctual automatisms, not to mention authentic pathologies of faith, can certainly be present in the sign of the cross, which many Christians repeat mechanically in moments of real or apparent need. However, the fact that this is the sign of the three Persons and not any other form of addressing divinity means that the trinitary faith has deep roots in personal piety through true interpersonal dialogue. The task of Christians is to consciously experience every "sign of the cross" with ever-increasing devotion with the help of the Church.

Although it is not the name with which the Trinity calls us for all of eternity, the name that we receive from our parents during baptism somehow represents the role of parents as God's collaborators in the genealogy of the person. The person is identified by the name that they give him in the moment when he sacramentally becomes a child of God: "When they transmit *life to the child, a new human 'thou' becomes a part of the horizon of the 'we' of the spouses*, a person whom they will call by a new name: 'our son…; our daughter…'" (Saint John Paul II, Letter to Families *Gratissimam sane* [02/02/1994], 11). For this reason, it is important that the name given to the person being baptized reminds us of his insertion into the family of the sons of God. This mainly occurs through the use of names of saints, who can be viewed as models and intercessors. In any case, and contrary to common contemporary habits, the *CCC* reminds us of the *CIC*'s strong plea: "Parents, sponsors, and the pastor are to take care that a name foreign to Christian sensibility is not given" (can. 855). The name received during baptism represents the true name that God has given us in a mysterious but real sense because it is an icon of filial dignity. It would be quite appropriate for Christian parents to keep in mind that the choice of a suitable name is a great gift for the child that lasts his entire life and a permanent reminder of his vocation to holiness.

Chapter One, Article 3:

THE THIRD COMMANDMENT

Cettina Militello

I. The Sabbath Day

"Remember the Sabbath day and keep it holy. For six days you shall labor and do all your work, but the seventh day is a Sabbath for Yahweh your God. You shall do no work that day, neither you nor your son nor your daughter nor your servants, men or women, nor your animals nor the alien living with you. For in six days Yahweh made the heavens, earth and sea and all that these contain, but on the seventh day he rested; that is why Yahweh has blessed the Sabbath day and made it sacred" (Ex 20:8–11). "Observe the Sabbath day and keep it holy, as Yahweh your God has commanded you. Labor for six days, doing all your work, but the seventh day is a Sabbath for Yahweh your God. You must not do any work that day, neither you, nor your son, nor your daughter, nor your servants—male or female—nor your ox, nor your donkey, nor any of your animals, nor the foreigner who has made his home with you; so that your servants, male and female, may rest, as you do. Remember that you were once a slave in Egypt, and that Yahweh your God brought you out of there with mighty hand and outstretched arm; this is why Yahweh your God has commanded you to keep the Sabbath day" (Dt 5:12–15).

Although the two versions of the commandment have many words in common, it seems evident that the two contain different "theological" requests. We are faced with a precise commandment from God, and both fall within the sphere that addresses our relationship with him through the "ten words." In one case, there is an appeal to "remember," and in the other, an invitation to "observe." The text from Exodus, which is older, evokes the creation and recounts God's abstention from the work of creating. In six days, God made the "cosmos" from the "chaos," and therefore organized what was originally nebulous into beauty. The first creation story tells us of how he separated the heavens, the earth, and the waters; how he established the celestial indicators of day (sun) and night (moon); how he populated the waters and the earth with all different types of living things; and how he created (in his own image) human beings, man and woman. On the seventh day, God stepped back from his work, marking the end of his creative extroversion. As some Jewish writing states, he put an end to his contraction, to the act of making space for what he placed outside of himself. In the division of time into weeks, sacerdotal sources document that the community justified rest on the "Sabbath" through its resemblance of God's rest. Analogously, people who follow God and honor and sanctify his name must pause all work (*CCC* 2168–2169). This is another reason for the commandment found in Dt 5:12–14. The basis for this was essentially not the liturgical succession of Hexaemeron (think of the acclamation "and God saw that it was good"). The attention of the community in the book of Deuteronomy is shifted toward Passover and therefore emphasizes the strong act that God performed for his people in freeing them from the toil and suffering of slavery in Egypt (*CCC* 2170–2171).

We will start by highlighting how, in both Exodus and Deuteronomy, we are offered a precise list of the people who must stop working on the Sabbath: heads of the families (and their wives, although not explicitly named), sons and daughters, male and female slaves, and foreigners living with them in Israel. Moreover, even the animals must take a break from work. In Deuteronomy, these are represented through the oxen and the donkey—the animals most commonly used and abused for farming and for transporting what was produced. In other words, there were no inherent exceptions related to social condition, gender, or species when it came to who should rest on the Sabbath. The Sabbath is a global requirement regardless of one's socioeconomic situation. It is an opportunity for every male and female being, regardless of whether human or animal, to replenish their strength and to heal from the stress that was part of and imposed by their daily work (n. 2172). But all of this does not form the basis for this precept and its doubtless socioeconomic requirements, which were quite consequential. On the Sabbath, Israel acts like its God acted. In marking the end of his work as a "creator," he rendered the "Sabbath" a blessed and holy day. The "Sabbath," the seventh day, is therefore in honor of God (n. 2170).

The post-exile community—the one that produced the second version of the Decalogue—carried with it the scars of the recent exile. For this reason, it colors the Sabbath rest with a humanistic character and leaves space for those not part of Israel—the foreigners who are staying within its gates, the male and female slaves—projecting the victimization that they had endured onto these people and making them a reminder of their life as slaves. The "Sabbath" must be holy for everyone. For all men and women, the "Sabbath" is for the Lord the God of Israel. This alludes to its festive aspect, to rest, and to the space that is given to the memory of God's action. It also alludes to the injustice that was endured and the rest that was denied. For this reason, Israel is obligated to guarantee this both for its own citizens and the people staying within it who are marginalized or enslaved (n. 2172).

As previously mentioned, the version found in Exodus focuses on "remembrance" and the one in Deuteronomy emphasizes "observance." In moving from one to another, our perspective shifts toward a more perceptual and legal view of the "Sabbath." Observing it means obeying a precise order given by God. In the long term, this formulation helps with formal comprehension but risks erasing the part of the "Sabbath" that is a "gift" because it is time that is given back to the kingdom of God. This latter aspect frequently pertains to the actions of Jesus, who is often accused of not observing the Sabbath. He returns the law to its original meaning, stating that the Sabbath was made for man, not man for the Sabbath (cf. Mk 2:27; *CCC* 2173).

II. The Lord's Day

For us Christians, the Sabbath of celebration and rest hast become "Sunday," the day which memorializes the resurrection of the Lord. The Christian weekly celebration is the *dies Domini* or *dominicum* (*CCC* 2174). These expressions are similar but different. They are expressions in which time and space intertwine and in which the ecclesial event and the gathering of the congregation, including its sharing in the body of the Lord, are evoked.

If Sunday—along the lines of the Sabbath—is a day of rest, restoration, *vacatio*, joy, giving, blessing bestowed by God, and blessing of God, celebrating it as the *dies Domini* means recognizing it as "the first day of the week" (Jn 21:1), the day in which Mary Magdalene first encountered the Risen Christ in the garden of new creation. It means experiencing it as "the first day of the week" (Lk 24:1; Mk 16:9) or the day "after the Sabbath" (Mk 16:2; Mt 28:1). Sunday is the first day *par excellence*, the day when Eden was re-opened, the day in which creation was restored to its original beauty through Christ's victory over death. The memory of the beginning, *kairós*, or time which has become opportune and benign, the *dies Domini* represents Christ's triumph and also the expectation of his glorious return. In other words, Sunday anticipates the *dominicus dies velut octavus* sung by Augustine in the *De civitate Dei* (XXII, 30). In fact, the week prior to Easter is a time of expectation/tension/awaiting the glorious return of the Lord.

All of these things are concepts that have been ingrained in the minds of Christian communities since ancient times. It is no coincidence that in n. 2174, the *CCC* references a well-known passage from Saint Justin Martyr's *First Apology* which provides a reason why Christians gather on the "day of the sun," the first day of the week and the day in which the darkness was definitively vanquished by the glorious light of the Risen Christ.

Sunday—Fulfillment of the Sabbath

Temporally sanctifying the celebration means first of all celebrating the Lord's Easter week after week. This does not mean only instituting a memorial pause that interrupts the *contiunuum* of time. It means situating the fundamental and founding event within time itself, week after week, celebrating the *acta et verba Christi* and his act of salvation. These actions and words are collected in the interpretive key for the liturgical year (n. 2173). Here, Advent, Christmas, Lent, and Easter follow one after another and characterize their respective Sundays. The remaining spaces in the calendar are filled *per annum* by reviewing words and actions that have already been celebrated in a different way. The liturgical reform completed by the Second Vatican Council further characterizes the mystical aspect of time. We are told to read the most important passages from the sacred Scripture over a three-year period and to listen to one of the Synoptic Gospels each year. In this way, Matthew, Mark, and Luke each offer us their own particular theological perspective. In other words, Sundays are presented to us in all of the richness of the proclaimed word and of the salvation which is effectively evoked and offered to us. All of this is embedded in and interpreted by this *euchology*, or set of prayers, which often offers us the true interpretative key for the celebration and the true and fruitful mystagogical paradigm of liturgical time.

This centrality of time joins seamlessly with the centrality of space. Both in the past and in the present, the gathering of communities occurs not only in the immediacy of "time" but also in the concreteness of "place." In particular, the local dimension characterizes the communities which are structured around gatherings in homes—the *ekklesía kat'ôikon* referred to in the New Testament—in order to celebrate the memory of the Lord's death and resurrection until his return. The day of the Lord is temporally the day in which people gather and experience the space that makes the gathering possible.

This belongs to the oldest Tradition. It characterizes communities and renders them communities. In fact, we gather on the day of the Lord in order to remember him while living in what is at the same time his house and our house.

The Sunday Eucharist

We celebrate Sundays, and they are sanctified through living in and visiting the house of God, which is the house of the Church. We celebrate Sundays by converging upon the concrete place that the people of God has built for itself and for God himself in order to be near to him and to be near to those who believe in him. The *dominicum*, or Sunday, is marked by the Risen Christ making himself present. He once again calls us to the table of his Word and of his Body, and this occurs in the meeting place, in the house of the people of God. The house of the people of God remains although the image of the Church, which has always expressed the mystery that the Church represents in its own way, changes over time.

It is no coincidence, in fact, that the building where worship takes place, the church, has the same name as the Church, the salvific meeting. The metaphor of construction which is used many times in the New Testament to explain its mystery can be used here. In Eph 2:18–22 or *1 Pt* 2:4–5, construction powered by the Spirit uses living stones, who are the people who believe in Christ, although they may have different functions. The church building, the spatial icon of the mystery, must therefore suggest what it represents. This is especially true for the parish church—the word parish comes from the verb *paroikéo*, "live nearby." Here, a local community gathers—a local community that is not coincidentally called the "Church of God" (cf. *LG* 28). N. 2179 in the *CCC* expressly refers to the parish churches, or the smallest communities which together form a diocese, in this way. Through these communities, the presbyter exercises his ministry, represents the bishop of the diocese, and presides over the Eucharist in his name. Through these communities, Christians usually participate in Sunday worship. Through these communities, everyone benefits from the sacraments, starting with Christian initiation. Through these communities, God is worshipped publicly. This does not render calling on him and blessing him all the time and in every place superfluous. On the contrary, it renders the Church a community gathered by him. In fact, God did not choose to save us individually but rather as a people gathered in his name (cf. *LG* 9). This gathering of salvation was fulfilled through the mystery of giving us his Son and through the gift of his Spirit.

We gather, therefore, in the spatial context of a building which is itself the concretion and the image of the congregation, the *ekklesía*, convened in Christ and in the Spirit. The mysterious nature of the congregation is expressed in the multitude of charisms and of ministries that mark and diversify the gathered people. The "unison of minds" (cf. *CCC* 2179—this is a quote by John Chrysostom) or "the symphony of the *agápe*" (as Ignatius of Antioch calls it—*Ad Ephesinos*, 4, 2) is born from the harmonious fusion of each individual's tasks. The Sunday congregation, in fact, has a multitude of ministries and ministers, who work in synergy, each according to his own abilities, in royal priesthood and in service to the people of God so that this people bring his royal, priestly, prophetic statue to fulfillment. These tasks do not stop at simply participating in liturgy but also inform the lives of all of the members of the community. The parish has a role in this, both in terms of proclamation and catechesis and in terms of charity and its exercise. These are certainly given space in the congregational celebration and increase its efficacy, indicating that the community's job is not to close in on itself but to witness and be missionaries.

The Sunday Obligation

The *CCC* reminds us of the Sunday obligation (nn. 2180–2183), the obligation to participate in the Sunday Eucharist either on Sunday or the evening of the day prior. This is not a purely formal obligation. Not participating in the Eucharist on the day of the Lord—as is the case for all the other solemnly festive days—means in a way abdicating from one's identity as a Christian and renouncing the testimonial strength that participation brings with it. Moreover, it means refusing to nourish oneself on the Word and the Body of the Lord, as if one could survive without either. In fact, this is affirmed in n. 2182: "Participation in the communal celebration of the Sunday Eucharist is a testimony of belonging and of being faithful to Christ and to his Church. The faithful give witness by this to their communion in faith and charity. Together they testify to God's holiness and their hope of salvation. They strengthen one another under the guidance of the Holy Spirit." In fact, the *dominicum* is not only a time (*kyriakê eméra*), not only a place (the church-home), and not only a convening/gathering (*ekklesía*) but also communion/communication (*koinonía*) with the Body and Blood of the Lord. In nourishing themselves on it, the faithful can witness the fact that they belong to Christ and their loyalty to his Church. Only through the Church can the faithful draw on the reciprocal communion and the reciprocal charity which emerges from the holiness of God in the Eucharist in which they participate and which is increased through them due to the incessant and transformative presence of the Spirit. In other words, the obligation is in fact an obligation but is not born from a simple rule that is to be respected. One cannot be a living member of the Body of Christ, who is the Church, without drawing on the nourishment that he does not cease to offer us by giving us his body.

The ecclesiastical situation in which we live, with a shrinking number of priests and therefore a chronic scarcity, often makes it difficult if not impossible to celebrate the Eucharist on Sundays. In n. 2183, the *CCC* recommends responding to this emergency by taking part in a liturgy of the Word celebrated in one's parish church or elsewhere where possible. By now, there are many Sunday congregations that gather without a presbyter. In these congregations, what counts is the testimonial value of the gathering and the nourishment that is still offered both through the proclamation of the Word of God and through the participation in the Body and Blood of the Lord. This occurs through the work of a deacon or a prepared and capable Christian through the methods established by the diocesan ordinary. If even this is not possible, the faithful still have a duty to pray on their own, with their families, or in groups of families. In the latter case, the awareness that the group is the "Church" regardless of any impediments, any objective impossibility, and any barriers toward gathering as a congregation provides Sundays with a strong direction.

A Day of Grace and Rest From Work

This awareness of Sunday and the necessity of living it to the fullest, which remains alive, constitutes the last observation that the *CCC* makes on the subject in nn. 2184–2188. In these numbers, Sunday is presented as a day of grace and rest from work. Now, returning to the previously stated theme from Genesis of God's pause from work, the necessity of alternating work and rest in human life is emphasized. The latter is not optional. Deciding whether or not to rest is not a painless choice. This goes to the heart of the quality of life itself, which cannot be absorbed only through moments of work or of profit. The paradigm from Genesis becomes an indicator of an authentically human type of planning which allows us to achieve complete fulfillment, growing socially and culturally while making space for our families and for the web of relationships that characterizes and enhances each person's life. Nor is it a pure and simple form of evasion. The time of *vacatio* from work refers to being open to joy, to being open to one's community which gathers to praise God, and to alacrity to carry the burdens of others. And if, as sometimes occurs, we are forced to work on Sundays, the text asks us that this does not become a habit that prejudices one's view of resting on Sundays.

N. 2186 further examines this concept by listing the work one can do for others on the day of rest: works of charity, visits to the ill and elderly, visits to family, study, and reflection. First of all, however, it asks Christians to remember those who cannot take advantage of the day of rest for reasons of poverty or misery. Everyone has a right to rest, not only some people. In the following number, this becomes a call to do what one can so that everyone can take advantage of Sunday as a day of rest and at a minimum to work to guarantee that people who are unable to rest on Sundays due to social reasons have other times that are dedicated to rest. In truth, this touches a nerve for the author due to the tendency to make Sunday a working day just like the others, and not only in the fields of essential services but also in retail, industry, and so on. As Christians, we should work to have civil legislation recognize Sunday and holidays as a day of rest for reasons of religious freedom and the common good. Moreover, it is our duty as Christians to make the joy of Sunday, the joy of shared prayer, and the joy of gathering together tangible. Additionally, in the case of impediments, the duty to witness the strong meaning of Sunday, a day of celebratory gathering of the firstborn sons inscribed in the heavens, remains.

The summary found in nn. 2189–2195 restates the essential contents of the third commandment. We believe that we need to call readers' attention to a few aspects.

First of all is the anthropological aspect, which is connected to each human being's necessity to mix work and rest. The first is not more important than the second; the second is a *condition sine qua non* for efficiency in the first. Work provides human beings with fulfillment to the extent to which it does not alienate them but rather leaves them open to a relationship with God, with their brothers, and with the entire community.

The Sabbath is the paradigm of this in the tradition of Israel. God's rest sanctions the rest of human beings, whose need for rest should be put into law as much as possible. The Sabbath is a gift that man gives to God by making what God has done into a rule. And if the rule seems more a duty than a form of praise, it is Jesus himself who returned the Sabbath to its free and interior meaning and gave it back its value.

Sunday replaces the Sabbath, giving it the new conclusive element of Easter. Here, the "day of the Lord" becomes a combined evocation of time, place, community, and communion. The theological value of the *dominicum* obligates the Christian community to gather to celebrate the memory of how the Lord gave himself for us in the completeness of a place and in the fullness of an intertwined relationship with God himself and with our brothers. Pause, rest, and *vacation*, Sunday is most of all an attestation of the gratuitousness of the gift—an attestation of a God who comes to meet us, lives with us, and gives us a history that therefore sanctifies and transforms us.

The Christian community cannot ignore the call to gather, nor can it ignore the nourishment of the Word and of the Eucharist, nor can it ignore the cause of brotherhood, nor can it forego the expression and meaning of the joy which characterizes all of this.

The Church is born from the joy of Easter, and this joy must bear witness in the world until the second coming of the Lord. For this reason, we gather every Sunday to give meaning to the faith and hope of the Church in the ardent exercise of the charity which the Spirit bestows upon us and nurtures.

Chapter Two, Article 4:

"YOU SHALL LOVE YOUR NEIGHBOR AS YOURSELF"

Carmelo Dotolo

Article 4: THE FOURTH COMMANDMENT

The fourth commandment must be understood within the fundamental perspective of the Decalogue: at the origin of human existence is the constitutive action of God's liberation and salvation. Recognizing this God means allowing for a change in perspective, through which we acquire a decisive principle: our identity and existence is marked by a "gift," which is a sign of a relationship with the loving God of life and of the love that is the logic behind "being in the relationship." This gift first comes to us through our parents, who express the relationship with the source of life and also show us how the deepest and most immediate bond between men is the relationship of filiation. The path toward the development of one's individual personality is inscribed in this relationship (cf. *CCC* 2215). This implies awareness that no one can live without relying on ideals, values, and people. Arriving at a complete identity means knowing how to choose values based on which we create a plan and which we translate into our very existence. This is the reason why ignoring the meaning behind and the breadth of the relationship means placing our existence at risk, compromising the path of maturation of one's independence, and creating instability in interpersonal relationships up to the point where the human condition itself is lost (cf. n. 2200). For this reason, the perspective in which the fourth commandment has meaning places the love event at the center. Love implies the inversion of the connatural movement of I versus myself and shatters the illusion of self-sufficiency while orienting the person toward spaces of recognition and acceptance. The verb "honor" should be understood in this context: it implies giving one's mother and father their proper weight and considering these people who summarize and represent the entire complex of human relationships to be important (cf.

n. 2212). Honoring them means recognizing the debt that each person owes to God and to others (cf. n. 2199), without which the person would not be who he is. Essentially, the fourth commandment is a model of what it means to be a person called to accept, develop, and share the gifts received. The opposite is the image of the *self-made man*, whose individualistic retreat ruins the intentionality of creation. The fundamental law of creation is found in the relationship with otherness as a form of authentic development: "It is not right that the man should be alone" (Gn 2:18).

I. The Family in God's Plan

It would appear to be coherent, then, that in the structure of the fourth commandment, the family emerges as a privileged place for human identity, and that thinking of the family and of marriage in terms of God's plan (cf. *CCC* 2202–2203) means interpreting the symbolic architecture of human existence in the difficult art of love and of its teaching. We must recognize that the "marriage event" is a long process with many shades of meaning and within which we never stop learning. This, however, does not authorize us to simplify its scope or to feel that we are excused from the effort of discerning and reflecting on its meaning. This is because loving in the style of the family requires a commitment that involves more than the logic behind the market of feelings and because it is not so difficult to render the experience of love similar to that of making a deal, with asking prices and bids, while forgetting that what is in play is not merchandise but rather the endless encounter of two beings. For this reason, one of the characteristics of the family is in the differential quality of the relationships (cf. n. 2206), in which the balance between the emotional sphere and the value of the bond is very important.

The reevaluation of the importance of the emotional sphere represents an important step in the reaffirmation of relationships that are less bureaucratic or less functional. It is important for the family to teach its members to overcome the risk of emotional illiteracy, demonstrating how reciprocal understanding, tenderness, compassion, and sincere dialogue can guide and give shape to our existence (cf. n. 2206). However, it seems that the affirmation of pure relationships and of love that travels on the train of desire is more practical. The thesis behind the contemporaneity is that love is enough and does not need stabile bonds or the recognition of institutions. This favors lightness and speed, not to mention variety and novelty. In other words, the presumption of omnipotence of emotions and love's capacity to overcome every obstacle and to turn situations that seem impossible on their heads prevails. This preliminary judgment implies that the art of loving is a natural talent and that learning to love is not necessary.

In this context, it appears necessary to reemphasize how the "Christian form" of the family (cf. nn. 2204–2205) is in the image of the trinitary relationships, through which love, gathering, and reciprocal solidarity are fed by communion and the capacity of giving, which is elevated from the plane of having to the plane of being. In the view of the "domestic church," the family becomes a place where the need to love and be loved is joined to personal liberty, just like the choice of stability, expressed through marriage, frees the person from egocentric infiltrations which do not allow him to transmit an authentic life. This choice, however, must be freed from the purely judicial and economic idea of the family, whose institutional form gives the impression of cohabitation that disregards the people with their assets and their fragility. From this perspective, fidelity becomes the paradigm for a qualitatively different relationship which needs time because it is always directed toward the event that is the other. In other words, this means accepting one another like the promised land of one's transformation. To walk this path, a bond based on the model of a contract with a fixed period of validity is inconceivable. "Authority, stability, and a life of relationships within the family constitute the foundations for freedom, security, and fraternity within society" (n. 2207). Fidelity calms the uncertainties that can arise during the call to love as a gift, feeding one's trust that despite of any failures and any hurt, the project is possible. This is also due to the love that the Spirit weaves in this adventure of reciprocity. "It is not your love that sustains the marriage, but from now on, the marriage that sustains your love" (D. Bonhoeffer, *Resistance and Submission: Letters and Papers from Prison*, San Paolo, Cinisello B. 1988, 103).

In this sense, training "familial spirituality" is more indispensable than ever because it means assuming the responsibility for constructing a community that goes beyond a simple social convention because it supports the unconditional value of generosity, of giving, and of service. Generosity is the mark of the action of the Spirit, which allows one to unselfishly give of oneself within the family, working toward justices, which fosters togetherness through a network of rights and duties.

II. The Family and Society

There is no doubt that the principle of the community is infused within the entity of the family. Consequently, the "social dimension" is part of understanding the vocation to conjugal love. First of all, this is because the family plays an irreplaceable role in teaching its members how to be people. It is the school of humanity where the social values of justice, freedom, and solidarity are learned. It constitutes a microcosm of society, where its members experience the preciousness and delicacy of interpersonal relationships, respect for authority, the sense of the common good, and the shared responsibility to protect the environment as a whole. Second, this is because the family institution can represent a cultural model for elaborating on and practicing the relationship between emotional and educational bonds and social bonds, which is how a common *éthos* is built. "The family is the community in which, from childhood, one can learn moral values, begin to honor God, and make good use of freedom. Family life is an initiation into life in society" (*CCC* 2207). This is especially true with regard to those who need concrete and collaborative help. The importance of the family for life and for the well-being of the society is therefore proportional to the degree to which the culture encourages conviviality, in which differences help join political realism to human and religious hope. The family therefore becomes a "pedagogical itinerary" of comparison, listening, and commitment to others in order to create a common home in which openness, attention, care, and one's capacity to understand and also to transform oneself in relation to what is new and different constitute the main elements of a fruitful organization of existence. If the fourth commandment "illuminates other relationships in society" (n. 2212), it is because it expands the concept of family to include intergenerational, social, and community elements. The family includes relatives, a word which refers to people bonded through alliances or filiation, through which the family tree grows and creates a broader web of relationships. Brothers, sisters, grandparents, aunts, uncles, cousins, grandchildren, in-laws, and so on all make the family feel like a social body, help us feel connected to others, and help us feel that we are participating in a more expanded life. As Pope Francis writes, "The individualism so prevalent today can lead to creating small nests of security, where others are perceived as bothersome or a threat. Such isolation, however, cannot offer greater peace or happiness; rather, it straitens the heart of a family and makes its life all the more narrow" (*AL* 187). This experience allows us to better interpret the effort required to be ourselves because it defeats the danger of an anonymity that slowly destroys the experiences of solidarity and free belonging. In this context, the social dimension of the family goes both ways. On the one hand, being part of a marriage (in which becoming a spouse also means becoming a son-in-law or daughter-in-law and sister-in-law or brother-in-law) promotes the possibility of cultivating and consolidating the conjugal bond, including in the case of spousal conflicts. On the other hand, adding the family to the vital tapestry of the larger community dynamizes the members' familiar identity by demonstrating the usefulness of a solidarity that goes beyond the boundaries of blood and of region.

Due to this institutional dimension, the family is involved in a distributive process: it gives life and distributes affection, care, and education while implementing the exercise of the responsibility that its members take on.

Its distributive role, however, is performed in contact with other families and social institutions, such as through volunteer work, participation in civil life, and instruction toward living a dignified economic lifestyle (cf. *CCC* 2213). This is the reason why the "social mission" of the family must be supported (cf. nn. 2210–2211), promoting the establishment of networks of reciprocal help and solidarity in order to share new lifestyles and establish intergenerational bonds. It makes reconciliation between our family and professional lives practical and provides the opportunity to make space for a morality of friendship, shared responsibility for the quality of life, solidarity with people who live in unfortunate situations and who are marginalized, and the growth of a sense of hospitality toward our neighbors (cf. n. 2212), especially if these people are different from us, and toward foreigners. In this context, the value of education about the "common good" as a priority for the maturation and growth of humanity appears crucial. In civil society, authority figures are in fact responsible for this service, which implies the choice of a hierarchy of values that allows for the promotion of the principle of the common good and allows us to guide those who are learning. Through this, the political and social community must exercise its responsibility in accordance with the principle of subsidiarity (cf. n. 2209) and serve as an aid to people through all the intermediate entities between the family and global society. Subsidiarity must, however, be articulated through the "principle of solidarity," which prevents us from making the error of becoming a dependency culture or of isolationism in situations of economic and work crisis.

In fact, the current state of poverty in which millions of people are living and the weakening of welfare structures require a new model of economic and financial policy that has the "human family" as its objective, moving past the logic of the market, which places the interests of the few above those of the many. The model of the family (cf. n. 2224) can help build a society if human rights policies come before export policies, if the duty of the culture to stand in solidarity and for a just economic order inspires the right to live well, and if reciprocal respect is more important than the ideology of competition or consumerism.

III. The Duties of Family Members

Despite the succession of models of reference and identity crises, history shows that the family is one of the places most suited to the transmission of experiential knowledge. This is mainly because in taking care of others, we care for the humanity of parents and children in the concreteness of everyday life and in the difficulty of making choices. Through this, we can experience what "initiating a human being into solidarity and communal responsibilities" (n. 2224) entails through elaborating meanings, identifying sets of practices, and stating the criteria for discernment and the fundamental values through which we can learn about the authentic conditions of freedom. In this sense, the "educational question" should be reconsidered within the context of planning and of responsibility to work toward the blossoming of life. We could say that this constitutes the main characteristic of the family: it is the primary and most basic "school of vocation" where the educational function of parents is directed toward the maturation of their children. Children are invited to grow in independence and shared responsibility through a collection of coherent choices that range from how to spend their free time to their choice of profession (cf. n. 2230), from their studies and attitude toward research to how they care for their bodies and from their relationships with civil society to the commitment to the idea of a culture that is more attentive to human dignity. For children, learning the difficult profession of being men and women depends on the "testimonial capacity" of the parents. This is defined in terms of their courage in knowing how to discuss themselves, the logic of listening, the humility of knowing how to compare themselves with others, and the sharing of their experiences with faith. This kind of development is possible if the children experience the feeling that they are called, that they are requested—an event that demolishes their ideas of function and role. Only in this way is it possible to think of life as a project and together become, regardless of their different roles in their educational relationship, the builders of a vision of existence that can be based on the strength of personal relationships, that can be fed by openness toward transformation through love, and that can cooperate in personal and intersubjective maturation. In other words, educational passion must accompany the act of moving past an infantile reading of reality where temperamental factors and momentary conditions disguise the path toward a state of stability and independence. This can only occur if family life is able to attest (cf. n. 2223) that although the journey may be long, it is possible. This requires the gradual rejection of self-centeredness in search of readily available satisfactions with a view toward the elaboration of criteria for independent judgment. It invites and provides the opportunity for children to develop critical thinking skills and arrive steadily closer to the truth, through which they can create harmony in their lives by constructing them based on good, happiness, and the realization of their personal ideals. "The home is well suited for education in the virtues. This requires an apprenticeship in self-denial, sound judgment, and self-mastery—the preconditions of all true freedom" (n. 2223). Within the educational space of the family, therefore, the child-parent and parent-child relationships are fed on reciprocal respect and acceptance. These give form to open identities in which each person can delineate his or her own personality within the context of an encounter and of comparison. This does not, however, provide an excuse for avoiding the requirement for change. Reciprocal respect and docility imply awareness of boundaries, fragility, and the imperfections which are not flaws in one's identity but rather conditions for the modification of one's viewpoint toward oneself and others regardless of the pervasiveness of errors and defects.

IV. The Family and the Kingdom

In this context, the parent's task of "education about faith" and of being willing to show that the Gospel is the custodian of the Word which disrupts our habits through interpretation of ourselves, the world, and others is valuable. It is not difficult to imagine how in the Christian perspective, the quality of life and the maturity of the human person occur through the choice of an "evangelical spirituality." This is fed on the formative processes that are part of liturgy, especially the Eucharist, and through which we experience the ethics of the everyday through the signs of the bread and the wine but also through parish life—the life of a community where the values of the Kingdom are learned (cf. n. 2226). Moments of sharing, of joy, of prayer, and of reflection feed the continual discovery of the Good News that the God of Jesus Christ brings fulfillment to our lives (cf. n. 2232). This is also true for the choice to pursue consecrated life or priesthood. But paying attention to the Kingdom invites the family to live a kind of life where it is possible to bet on the construction of a civilization of love. This involves, therefore, following Christ in accordance the model of the missionary, which evokes the need to free oneself from the conditions of one's culture which impede the perception of the presence of the Spirit and the paths of the Gospel in history and society.

V. The Authorities in Civil Society

If the common good (cf. nn. 2234; 2240) is the interpretative scenario and the constitutive objective of the institutions which form part of the public sphere, the people who are responsible for exercising authority must know how to take inspiration from the communal principle to which humans are called (cf. n. 2236). It is the community that has this maieutic function with regard to the person because human dignity can be fully recognized in the quality of cohabitation for the whole of society through the community. For this reason, the emphasis of the rights and duties of both civil authorities and citizens appears to be important with respect to the logic of the right to have rights. The "political authorities" have the task of "respecting the fundamental rights of the human person," by trying to "dispense justice humanely by respecting the rights of everyone, especially of families and the disadvantaged" (n. 2237), but their responsibility for creating the conditions for a civil community that creates a good that supports sharing, eating together, hospitality, and finally ecological responsibility is no less important. The principle of the common good, therefore, can promote the configuration of new lifestyles and an economy of communion that places a culture that knows how to create opportunities for cooperation, work, and development for everyone, especially foreigners and immigrants, at the center (cf. n. 2241; cf. *La famiglia tra sfide e prospettive*, Qiqajon, Magnano 2015). At the same time, the citizens' duty toward "the good of society in a spirit of truth, justice, solidarity, and freedom" (n. 2239) through an open and critical participation must also involve the knowledge of how to pay more attention to the need-right relationship than to the relationship with rights as capacities. This is the paradoxical Christian proposal which, based on the priority of men over things (cf. n. 2244), suggests how this duty becomes an interpersonal, community, and social right. This duty ranges from not infringing on the rights of the weakest to the care and recognition of others to the resistance to oppression and proposing ways to modify structures that are unjust and that alienate the human person. The mission of the Church falls on this level (cf. nn. 2245–2246): the search for the common good requires institutional change and a political attitude that recognizes the communal principle, respects fundamental rights, and pays attention to them.

Chapter Two, Article 5:
THE FIFTH COMMANDMENT

Stefano Zamboni

In a very meaningful way, while analyzing what the fifth commandment implies, the *CCC* uses as a premise not only its formulation within the Decalogue ("You shall not kill": Ex 20:13) but also Jesus's interpretation in the context of the so-called "antitheses" of Matthew: "You have heard how it was said to our ancestors, you shall not kill; and if anyone does kill he must answer for it before the court. But I say this to you, anyone who is angry with a brother will answer for it before the court" (Mt 5:21–22). In this way, the contents of the commandment are amplified and expanded to the point where they refer not only to the act of suppressing the life of another but also everything that gravely threatens someone else's dignity. Jesus's disciple, in the logic of overabundant justice (cf. Mt 5:20), does not stop at simply not killing other humans but also shuns any behavior that is harmful to his humanity. For this reason, the *CCC*, after the section dedicated to the "respect for human life" (I), addresses "respect for the dignity of persons" (II) and concludes with "safeguarding peace" (III). At the beginning of the discussion, the premise on which the basic argument of the *CCC* is built is established: "Human life is sacred [...] from its beginning until its end" (n. 2258). This statement could be conveniently completed through the Christological root of man's personal dignity: "By becoming one of us, the Son makes it possible for us to become 'sons of God' (Jn 1:12), 'sharers in the divine nature' (2 Pt 1:4). This new dimension does not conflict with the dignity of the creature which everyone can recognize by the use of reason, but elevates it into a wider horizon of life which is proper to God, giving us the ability to reflect more profoundly on human life and on the acts by which it is brought into existence" (*DP* 7).

I. Respect for Human Life

The reflection on human dignity begins with a brief biblical survey (nn. 2259–2262). The ideas which it emphasizes could be summarized in the following manner: hate of others is rooted in the condition of sin in which man finds himself (the story of the first murder, the murder of Abel by his brother Cain: Gn 4:1–16, is emblematic; cf. *CCC* 2259); the Scripture unequivocally condemns murder (*CCC* 2260–2261); and Jesus adds the prohibition against anger, hated, and revenge and the commandment to love one's enemy (n. 2262). We should note that the subject of the commandment is formally expressed as "deliberate murder of an innocent person" and the law that prohibits it "is universally valid: it obliges each and everyone, always and everywhere" (n. 2261). This means that this is a rule that prohibits a behavior that is intrinsically immoral and is valid, as we say in moral theology, *semper et pro semper*—in every possible case with no exceptions.

If, however, this is true, how do we interpret "legitimate defense"? Is this not perhaps an exception to the peremptoriness of "You shall not kill"? The *CCC*, in introducing the numbers dedicated to this subject (nn. 2263–2267), clearly states that "The legitimate defense of persons and societies is not an exception to the prohibition against the murder of the innocent" (n. 2263). As Thomas, who is cited in support of this text, explains (*Summa Theologiae*, II–II, 64, 7), two effects can occur as a result of the same action, one which is intentional (defense of one's life) and another that is preterintentional (*praeter intentionem*, and not "involuntary," as the translation in the first edition of the *CCC* stated), or the killing of the aggressor. In this way, legitimate defense does not represent an exception to the commandment not to kill (in this case, the killing is preterintentional, and moreover, it is inflicted on an unjust aggressor and therefore not on an innocent) but rather should be traced back to the fact that "it is legitimate to insist on respect for one's own right to life" (n. 2264). Thomas is also cited here. He makes note of the criterion of proportionality (defense is legitimate when it is proportional to the aggression suffered) and recognizes that the motivation behind legitimate defense is love for oneself and the need to see to one's own life before those of others. At this point, we must ask ourselves whether placing love for oneself above love for others is in line with Jesus's ethical proposal, which is explicitly expressed in the Sermon on the Mount. We could also ask ourselves whether insistence, which is partially legitimate, on the guilt of the aggressor risks denying the dignity of each human being, since the aggressor is also human. Regardless of the answer, the *CCC* continues by stating that aside from being a right, legitimate defense can be a "grave duty" for those who exercise authority and therefore have the responsibility of defending those who have put their trust in them, including through the use of weapons, if necessary (n. 2265).

In this context, the *CCC* pauses to examine the meaning of "punishment." Here, we find a formulation for n. 2266–2267 that is different than that of the first edition. In the first edition, it was stated that the traditional teaching of the Church has recognized the right/duty of authority to inflict proportional punishment on the offender "not excluding, in cases of extreme gravity, the death penalty" (n. 2266, first edition). This statement gave rise to numerous controversies, especially given the strong commitment professed by the Magisterium during recent papacies toward the promotion of the abolition of the death penalty worldwide. How, then, can this assertion in the *CCC* be explained? The statement was limited to restating the "traditional teaching of the Church," which did in fact allow for the possibility of the death penalty in order to protect the common good (think of Saint Thomas: *Summa Theologiae*, II–II, 64, 2). In the new edition of the *CCC*, the authors wished to spend more time on the question and explain it more clearly. After reaffirming the right/duty of authority to inflict punishments that are proportional to the offenses committed and reminding us of the functions of punishment—redressing the disorder introduced by the offense, expiation, preserving the public order, and correcting the offender (n. 2266)—the *CCC* explains, "The traditional teaching of the Church does not exclude, presupposing full ascertainment of the identity and responsibility of the offender, recourse to the death penalty, when this is the only practicable way to defend the lives of human beings effectively against the aggressor." As we can see, this statement returns to the judgment pronounced about the death penalty in the traditional teaching of the Church. The *CCC* then adds that in fact, today, given the means that the State has to "repress crime by rendering inoffensive the one who has committed it, without depriving him definitively of the possibility of redeeming himself, cases of absolute necessity for suppression of the offender "today…are very rare, if not practically non-existent'" (n. 2267). Here, the *CCC* quotes n. 56 from *EVi*, where John Paul II reemphasized the possibility of resorting to capital punishment "in cases of absolute necessity: in other words, when it would not be possible otherwise to defend society." He then states, however, that these cases are practically non-existent. As we can see, the explanation offered in the second edition of the *CCC* does not negate what was stated in the first edition but rather further clarifies its scope, excluding the possibility of resorting to such a punishment, which would in principle not always be illegitimate, today. Numerous moral theologians and a not insignificant number of members of the episcopal Magisterium have expressed that they favor ceasing to use this interpretation, demonstrating the difficulty of placing the death penalty within the context of legitimate defense on the one hand and emphasizing the fact that "not even a murderer loses his personal dignity, and God himself pledges to guarantee this" (*EVi* 9) on the other hand. It would therefore be auspicious if the universal Magisterium were to be more courageous and refute even the theoretic legitimacy of capital punishment.

The following two paragraphs are dedicated to "intentional homicide" (*CCC* 2268–2269). In addition to stating that "the fifth commandment forbids direct and intentional killing as gravely sinful" (n. 2268), it notes that an action that has the intention of "indirectly" provoking the death of a person is equally forbidden. This would be the case when someone is placed in mortal danger without a serious reason or when a person refuses to help another person who is in danger. In this sense, the grave conditions of misery in which entire societies live and the usurious and mercantile practices that lead to hunger and therefore death are also included in this category (n. 2269).

The *CCC* then confronts the subject of "abortion" (nn. 2270–2275). Here, we are reminded of the Church's teaching with regard to the evil of directly procured abortion, "that is to say, abortion willed either as an end or a means" (n. 2271). The Second Vatican Council spoke about this proposition as an "unspeakable crime" (GS 51). What is the reason for taking such a severe and harsh position? The *CCC*, which follows and extensively quotes the Congregation for the Doctrine of Faith's *Donum vitae* from 1987 (in the mean time, we will use a more updated instruction from the same dicastery, *DP*), notes that "from the first moment of his existence, a human being must be recognized as having the rights of a person—among which is the inviolable right of every innocent being to life" (*CCC* 2270). In fact, the embryo "must be treated from conception as a person" (n. 2274). We should note that the *CCC*, in accordance with the instruction *Donum vitae*, does not use a philosophical type of definition and state that the embryo "is" a person because it does not attempt to resolve the perennial question of animation, which was frequently debated in the past. Although it does not provide any kind of ontological indication (which is, however, presumed), this does not make the ethical injunction any less binding. Consequently, the embryo should be protected, including judicially, because "the inalienable right to life of every innocent human individual is a constitutive element of a civil society and its legislation" (*CCC* 2273). One particular form of protection is represented in canon law by the *latae sententiae* excommunication (which means that it is incurred due to the fact that one has committed the offense) incurred by people who procure abortions (n. 2272). The reason for this provision is that the Church wishes to emphasize the gravity of abortion in opposition to the tendency of contemporary legislation to legalize it and even consider it a human "right." The criterion for judging whether medical interventions on an embryo are licit (nn. 2274–2275) is derived from the ethical principal of treating the embryo "as a person." The "no's" pronounced here by the Magisterium are related to the "yes" given toward the life that

God has willed and loved, as these words from *EVi* remind us: "Human life is sacred and inviolable at every moment of existence, including the initial phase which precedes birth. All human beings, from their mothers' womb, belong to God who searches them and knows them, who forms them and knits them together with his own hands, who gazes on them when they are tiny shapeless embryos and already sees in them the adults of tomorrow whose days are numbered and whose vocation is even now written in the 'book of life' (cf. Ps 139: 1, 13–16). There too, when they are still in their mothers' womb [...] they are the personal objects of God's loving and fatherly providence" (n. 61).

After covering the beginning of life, the *CCC* moves on to the question of its end in the numbers dedicated to "euthanasia" (nn. 2276–2279). Euthanasia is a term which comes from Greek and literally refers to a "good death" (*eu* = good, well; *thánatos* = death). It is used to refer to a death that is supposedly "merciful," which is given to those who live in unbearable suffering which is said to be incompatible with the dignity of the person. After noting that particular respect should be given to the ill and differently abled (n. 2276), it declares that "direct euthanasia" is ethically inadmissible, "whatever its motives and means." It talks about a "murderous act" and defines it in these terms: "an act or omission which, of itself or by intention, causes death in order to eliminate suffering" (n. 2277). In order to avoid terminological confusion, we should note that direct euthanasia does not refer to the means by which it is committed. Rather, euthanasia is direct when it—"of itself or by intention"—determines the death of the sick person. It can consist of an action (such as administrating a fatal medicine) or an omission (not providing the necessary cure to keep someone alive). Regardless of the way in which it occurs, it always constitutes "a murder gravely contrary to the dignity of the human person and to the respect due to the living God, his Creator." This verdict is confirmed and even reinforced by John Paul II's exercise of his Petrine authority: "In harmony with the Magisterium of my Predecessors 81 and in communion with the Bishops of the Catholic Church, I confirm that euthanasia is a grave violation of the law of God, since it is the deliberate and morally unacceptable killing of a human person. This doctrine is based upon the natural law and upon the written word of God, is transmitted by the Church's Tradition and taught by the ordinary and universal Magisterium" (*EVi* 65). Euthanasia should be distinguished from the refusal of "over-zealous treatment." The decision to discontinue "medical procedures that are burdensome, dangerous, extraordinary, or disproportionate to the expected outcome" can be perfectly legitimate. In fact, "Here one does not will to cause death; one's inability to impede it is merely accepted" (*CCC* 2278). With respect to the treatments offered to the sick, n. 2279 specifies that ordinary treatments should always be guaranteed, painkillers used to alleviate the suffering of the patient are licit even if there is the risk of shortening life (principle of double effect), and palliative care, which "is a special form of disinterested charity," should be encouraged. The final question which is addressed is that of "suicide." The moral judgment that this is not acceptable is based on the fact that "we are stewards, not owners, of the life God has entrusted to us" (n. 2280) and is essentially articulated by the arguments already posed by Thomas (cf. *Summa Theologiaie*, II–II, 64, 5), who recognizes that suicide involves a grave lack of just love for oneself, for one's neighbor, and for the living God (n. 2281). The consideration of the moral malice of suicide does not mean, however, lack of mercy for people who commit it, both because their responsibility can be limited by a few factors (n. 2282) and because the Church does not stop praying for those who have taken their lives (n. 2283), as demonstrated by the fact that not all who commit suicide are denied burial rites.

II. Respect for the Dignity of Persons

This second paragraph analyzing the fifth commandment contains a number of elements regarding the "dignity of persons" that are expanded upon and brought back together, perhaps not always altogether persuasively. Here, we will provide a brief summary, especially because the synthesis included at the end of article five of the *CCC* dedicates only a single number to the questions considered here (cf. n. 2326).

First of all, the question of "scandal," which is viewed as a lack of "respect for the souls of others" (nn. 2284–2287). This is defined as "an attitude or behavior which leads another to do evil" (n. 2284) and is particularly grave if it is committed by authority figures (legislators, teachers, heads of companies, etc.) and if the weak and the little ones (cf. Mt 18:6) are the ones to suffer through it. Then, respect for "health" is examined (nn. 2288–2291). One's health must be cared for because it is a gift from God and requires conditions that society must guarantee for everyone (food and clothing, housing, medical care, basic education, work, and social security). This does not mean that respect for corporeal life is an absolute value, as a certain conception that the *CCC* defines as "neo-pagan" tends to do. This conception leads to the formation of a true "cult of the body." Respect for the body also implies the virtue of temperance, which works toward the avoidance of any kind of excess (food, alcohol, tobacco, etc.), and is obviously negated through the use of drugs. Third, there is a reflection on the respect for the person during "scientific research" (nn. 2292–2296). The *CCC* recognizes that this constitutes "a significant expression of man's dominion over creation" and that therefore it should be encouraged when it is conducted in the service of man and his complete development. However, the *CCC* notes, it is illusory to claim a presumed "moral neutrality in scientific research and its applications."

The research must be directed toward the good of the person without giving in to dominant ideologies or criteria determined exclusively based on its technical efficacy or social usefulness. In terms of concrete cases, the themes of experimentation on human beings, which is morally licit if conducted in a way that respects human dignity and does not place people at disproportionate risk, and organ transplant and donation are touched upon. Fourth, respect for "bodily integrity" (nn. 2297–2298) is examined. Here, behaviors that are rather different from one another (kidnapping and taking hostages, terrorism, torture, amputation, mutilation, and sterilization) converge. In today's world, the brief reference to terrorism absolutely merits more in-depth treatment in another context. We should note that in n. 2298, the *CCC* recognizes the responsibility, including that of pastors in the church, that people bear for not protesting against and having tolerated "cruel practices [used] to maintain law and order." Today, we must work resolutely toward their abolition. The final aspect addressed is "respect for the dead" (nn. 2299–2301). In particular, we are reminded of the care and attention that should be given to the dying and of the respect owed to the corpses of the dead (the burial of the dead is a work of corporeal mercy). The legitimacy of cremation (according to the new rules in the 1983 *CIC*) when this choice does not call one's faith in the resurrection of bodies into question is also mentioned.

III. Safeguarding Peace

As noted previously, the *CCC* places Jesus's words about anger toward one's brother (Mt 5:21–22) on the same plane as the injunction contained in the Decalogue ("do not kill"). In this way, the discussion of peace and of war, the subject of this third paragraph, is brought back to the "heart"—in other words, according to the vision of the Bible, back to the seat of thoughts, emotions, and man's decisions. In this way, the *CCC* first focuses on "anger" (*CCC* 2302) and "hatred" of one's neighbor (n. 2303).

We should note that the *CCC* helpfully covers the subject of "peace" (nn. 2302–2306) before that of war. Although it is true that people often tend to define peace as the absence of war based on the empirical fact that unfortunately there have been very few periods of peace during the history of humanity, the *CCC* first reflects on the nature of peace. It follows in the tradition of Vatican II, which stated that peace "is not merely the absence of war" but rather "results from that order structured into human society by its divine Founder." In fact, it "symbolizes and results from the peace of Christ which radiates from God." It "is never attained once and for all" because "insofar as men are sinful, the threat of war hangs over them." This peace needs to be built on a foundation of "justice" and "love," and in "the studied practice of brotherhood," which is not at all unfamiliar to Christians, who are called as they are to "join with all true peacemakers in pleading for peace and bringing it about" (*GS* 78). For this reason, the *CCC* states that peace is not merely the absence of war, but rather, according to the Augustinian definition (cf. *The City of God*, XIX, 13, 1), "the tranquility of order," the fruit of justice and charity (*CCC* 2304). We will be reminded that the encyclical *Pacem in terris*—the great prophetic encyclical of John XXIII (1963)—began by noting that "peace on Earth—which man throughout the ages has so longed for and sought after—can never be established, never guaranteed, except by the diligent observance of the divinely established order" (n. 1). This order is supported by respect for the human person, for human freedom, for justice, and for the truth. From a biblical point of view, peace is God's definitive promise to his people: it is fulfillment and blessing (*shalôm*) and is given to us completely through Christ, who is peace itself. "For he is the peace between us, and has made the two into one entity and broken down the barrier which used to keep them apart, by destroying in his own person the hostility, that is, the Law of commandments with its decrees" (Eph 2:14). In reminding us of this, the *CCC*—which once again cites *GS*—states that "earthly peace is the image and fruit of the peace of Christ" (*CCC* 2305). In this context, those who "renounce violence and bloodshed" in order to safeguard human rights are finally mentioned (n. 2306). These people bear witness to "evangelical charity" and without a doubt are a prophetic sign of great value.

After addressing peace, the *CCC* reflects on "avoiding war" (n. 2307–2317). There is no doubt that we have to work and pray until the world is free from "the ancient bondage of war" (n. 2307), but where there is no possibility of effective intervention by international authorities in order to end conflicts, governments' right to self-defense cannot be denied, as *GS* (n. 79) teaches us (*CCC* 2308). The social doctrine of the Church has insisted and continues to insist that a community of peoples and nations that works toward the universal common good and provides a guarantee of peace be formed. In this sense, the Second Vatican Council called for the institution of "universal public authority acknowledged as such by all and endowed with the power to safeguard on the behalf of all, security, regard for justice, and respect for rights" (*GS* 81). However, when appealing to that authority is not effective and every possibility of a peaceful resolution of the conflict has been exhausted, a "legitimate defense by military force" can be justified (*CCC* 2309). Such a defense is morally legitimate only if it meets "rigorous conditions." "At one and the same time, the damage inflicted by the aggressor on the nation or community of nations must be lasting, grave, and certain; all other means of putting an end to it must have been shown to be impractical or ineffective; there must be serious prospects of success; [and] the use of arms must not produce evils and disorders graver than the evil to be eliminated."

The *CCC* specifies that the evaluation of these conditions "belongs to the prudential judgment of those who have responsibility for the common good" because the conditions depend on the historic and political contingencies, which are impossible to determine *a priori*. It then adds that "these are the traditional elements enumerated in what is called the 'just war' doctrine." The so-called just war theory, however, which originated in the fourth century and is still used to day, has been called into question by numerous theologians, who call for it to be abandoned based on the contradictory connection between the adjective "just" and the noun "war." Effectively, although the *CCC*'s statement is watertight from a historical perspective, it does lead to confusion when in n. 2309, the *CCC* correctly discusses the legitimacy not of war but of armed defense, which is analogous to the legitimacy of using police forces to maintain public order in individual States. I would like to make one final comment on this number, which is without a doubt one of the most important in this section. With respect to the last condition ("the use of arms must not produce evils and disorders graver than the evil to be eliminated"), the *CCC* adds that "the power of modern means of destruction weighs very heavily in evaluating this condition." The *CCC* is aware of the peculiarity of modern war in terms of its destructiveness (cf. n. 2314). For this reason, it would without a doubt be opportune to reference the famous and authoritative statement made in *Pacem in terris* about the absurdity of resorting to war in modern times here: "In this age which boasts of its atomic power, it no longer makes sense to maintain that war is a fit instrument with which to repair the violation of justice" (n. 127). The other numbers in this section are dedicated to national defense, including the definition of soldiers as "servants of the security and freedom of nations" (*CCC* 2310) and to conscientious objection to the use of weapons (n. 2311). It is then noted that during the course of armed conflicts, not everything is licit: moral law and the so-called "law of nations" (*jus gentium*), with its universal principles, always remain valid. In particular, the horrible crime of genocide, which unfortunately we have witnessed even in modern times, is condemned (nn. 2312–2313). Particular mention is given to the question of weapons (nn. 2315–2316) and specifically what is stated about the "accumulation of arms." Although the so-called Cold War is considered to have legitimized the use of balance between arms in order to dissuade one's adversary from using their power ("deterrence"), this logic, which is still in use today, must be the subject of "strong moral reservations." In fact, the *CCC* continues, "The arms race does not ensure peace. Far from eliminating the causes of war, it risks aggravating them" (n. 2315).

This third section concludes with a great text from Vatican II (*GS* 78) that reminds us realistically how humans, as sinners, are always under the threat of war until the second coming of Christ. They can, however, overcome the roots of sin and violence through love (cf. *CCC* 2317). The Church must therefore continually pronounce that God is the God of peace: fully, definitively, and irrevocably. This is what should be emphasized during critical comparison with the places where contemporary philosophy and its practices are taught while denying the presumed "naturality" or "originality" of conflict, which are its ultimate justification. Of course, war and violence are evidently real. But a desire for peace that is even more original dwells within man. If the "reality" of the human race is represented by war, its "truth" is that humans are peaceful beings.

Chapter Two, Article 6:

THE SIXTH COMMANDMENT

Artistide Fumagalli

Life in Christ, which is guided and animated by the Spirit, corresponds to the new commandment that Jesus left his disciples: "Love one another, as I have loved you" (Jn 15:12).

The new commandment, which expresses the perfection of moral life, brings to completion the old teaching of the Decalogue, whose ten words were already summarized in the double commandment of love, which was also formulated by Jesus: "You must love the Lord your God with all your heart, with all your soul, and with all your mind. This is the greatest and the first commandment. The second resembles it: You must love your neighbor as yourself" (Mt 22:37–39).

The double commandment of love for God and for one's neighbor essentially recalls the distinction which can be found in the Decalogue between the first three commandments of the so-called first tablet, which relate to God, and the other seven from the so-called second tablet, which relate to one's neighbor. The ten words of the Decalogue, which all shed light on one another, are the components of a single declaration of love—the love of the Lord God who, in freeing his people from the slavery of sin, teaches them how to remain free in order to enjoy the benefits of the covenant. The Decalogue configures moral life as an answer to God's loving initiative.

What is true for the Ten Commandments in general is especially true for the sixth, which in the formulation of the Scripture that addresses the loving relationship *par excellence*, that between man and woman, in prohibiting adultery. Through the ninth commandment, the Decalogue has already taught us how to avoid adultery at its root, which is desire for someone else's wife. Jesus, who references the sixth commandment, radicalizes this teaching by stating that "if a man looks at a woman lustfully, he has already committed adultery with her in his heart" (Mt 5:28).

In contrast with the other commandments, whose catechetical formulations are based on the formulations of the Scripture, although expressed in abbreviated form, the sixth commandment changes more obviously, reformulating "do not commit adultery" to "do not commit impure acts." This change, which expands the scope of the commandment to include all parts of sexuality, signals the intimate resonance and the strong effect that sexual actions have on human and Christian experience. However, the catechetical formulation of the commandment should be adequately explained in order to avoid misunderstandings and concerns about human sexuality, which have not failed to undermine its value in the past. The pastoral principal put forward by the *CCC* is especially valid for the interpretation of the sixth commandment. The principal states that the introduction of "doctrine and its teaching must be directed to the love that never ends. Whether something is proposed for belief, for hope or for action, the love of our Lord must always be made accessible, so that anyone can see that all the works of perfect Christian virtue spring from love and have no other objective than to arrive at love" (n. 25).

In a negative conception of human sexuality, which while exalting the spiritual and rational dimension of man disregards his corporeal and passionate dimension, the set of impure acts would coincide *sic et simpliciter* with the set of sexual acts. In effect, the negative prejudice toward human sexuality, which has been generated by various forms of Gnosticism throughout history, has long contaminated the teaching of the Church in a premature way. In the authentically Christian view of sexuality, on the other hand, the impure acts prohibited by the sixth commandment are not all sexual acts but rather sexual acts which instead of manifesting Christ's love, contradict it. And because Christ's love can essentially be expressed as giving one's life for others (cf. Jn 15:13; 10:10), impure acts are sexual acts which, instead of vitalizing a life of love, demean it. Sexual acts which express the giving of oneself for someone else are pure; acts which selfishly close the subject in on himself or herself are impure. If "spiritual worship" consists in offering our "bodies as a living sacrifice, dedicated and acceptable to God" (Rom 12:1), then offering one's body during sexual acts, if experienced through the love of Christ, is also a spiritual form of human love, or a form of love in accordance with the Holy Spirit.

I. "Male and Female He Created Them…"

The sixth commandments instructs men and women on how to experience sexuality in correspondence with the love of God, which is revealed and infused in the hearts of the faithful by the Holy Spirit.

The connection between human sexuality and divine love has its roots in the creation of man in the image and likeness of God (cf. Gn 1:26–27). The mystery of the love of God is reflected in man, who was created male and female. The trinitary God, the communion of Father and Son in the unity of the Spirit, corresponds to the union of man, the fruit of the loving relationship between man and woman, which is expressed symbolically through sexual acts and through procreation.

Human sexuality is a differential and relational condition that also distinguishes humans from the numerous other species of living things. It is a differential condition because it divides human beings into males and females. It is a relational condition because the differences between them are expressed relative to each other. The differential relationship which distinguishes human beings is a condition for the possibility of an authentic loving communion which avoids both the incommunicability of people who are different without being in a relationship and the confusion of those who are in a relationship without being different.

Sexuality is an anthropological condition that is pervasive in the sense that it affects man as a whole. It is not limited to only the corporeal dimension, but given the indissoluble union between body and spirit, also characterizes the spiritual dimension of the person. The corporeal complementarity between male and female expresses the personal reciprocity between men and women, whose union symbolically reflects the communion and fecundity of God. The sexual reciprocity of men and women, both of whom were created by God, assigns them the same personal dignity which expresses the power and tenderness of divine love in different ways.

Because sexuality is a spiritual and corporeal condition, the sexual identity of a person cannot be resolved simply through the fact that he/she has a male or female body. Rather, it has to do with recognizing a person's corporeal nature as male or female based on a part of him or her. Given the relational nature of sexuality, this recognition can only satisfactorily occur through the relationship between man and woman. This relationship, however, is always mediated by social culture, which can give value to their sexual difference in view of their personal communion or devalue it through its removal.

In presenting a relational kind of anthropology, the Christian revelation contests the possibility of arriving at one's sexual identity individually and maintains that instead this can only be acquired through the interpersonal relationship between man and woman. The sexual gender of a person cannot be defined based on the individual, as demonstrated by how it becomes confused in theories which claim to define it based on gendered relationships.

The Christian perspective does not only unveil the essential relationship between man and woman but also reveals what practices within this relationship can allow human beings to discover their specific identities, avoiding the double danger of undermining the dignity of the person in the name of sexual difference or nullifying sexual difference in the name of the equal dignity of human beings. This practice is illustrated through the "how" of Christ's love, to which men and women are called to conform their relationships in order to give value to their specific difference within their equal dignity.

II. The Vocation to Chastity

Sexual love involves the entire person in an interpersonal relationship. The virtue of chastity, which manifests personal love in gendered bodies, making them expressions of the gift of oneself for another, allows for this integration.

The Integrity of the Person

Love involves the human person as a whole, his or her entire spiritual-corporeal being. The unity of spirit and body is not a pre-established fact with respect to the person's actions but rather the result of an action that the body brings about and the spirit employs. The unification performed by the spirit is aimed at having the body, which is valued in its objectivity and organicity, become a symbol that expresses personal love. Appreciation for the gendered body as an expression of personal love excludes the idea that the body could be a slave to the spirit in accordance with a spiritualistic understanding of love that disregards or demonizes the body. On the other hand, appreciation of the body cannot mean worshiping the body to the point where it rules over the spirit in accordance with a materialistic understanding of love which undervalues or denies the existence of the spirit.

Adequate appreciation of the body by the spirit takes its most suitable form in responsibility and ability—in other words, in interacting with the psychophysical dynamisms which represent it in order to give personal love a human form. Responsibility for gendered bodies, both our own and those of others, implies that the dynamisms and sexual potentialities are recognized and used as the grammar for interpersonal love. Men and women are responsible for realizing the spousal meaning of their own and others' gendered bodies so that their loving gestures express their reciprocal gifts of themselves in the fecund communion of love. The responsible employment of one's gendered body as an expression of personal love assimilates sexual love to language, whose truth requires the unification of what the person wishes to say with what is said, avoiding the deceitfulness that masks the person's true intentions instead of revealing them.

The responsibility for the gendered body to embody personal love is what corresponds to "chastity" in the moral tradition. Chastity is a Christian virtue which is considered to be rather anachronistic and is often misunderstood. In its most authentic definition, chastity is the spiritual art of responsibly assuming the psychophysical dynamisms of the gendered body without censoring them and without suffering from them. In order for personal love to be expressed through the acts of the gendered body, it is necessary that sensual emotions and psychological feelings—the so-called passions—do not drag the spirit into behaviors that are more endured than enacted. If this were to occur, personal love would be distorted because it would be deprived of the personal spirit.

In contrast with the debasement of love, chastity is the disposition that allows the person to be the master of his sexual acts so that they reveal his personal love within the sensual and emotional dynamisms of loving gestures. Chastity is the spiritual energy which draws from the psycho-physical passions and embeds personal love in the person's sexual behaviors.

The Christian tradition, which latches on to the cardinal virtue of temperance, continues chastity to be at the same time a moral virtue and a fruit of the Spirit. It is an ability, therefore, that is born from the collaboration of human freedom with divine grace. Human freedom is asked to participate in a long learning period and continuously practice so that chastity does not become a momentary decision but rather a stable disposition: this is the virtue of chastity. Like every virtue, chastity grows gradually over time, following steps that involve different commitments at the various stages of life, which are marked by imperfection and frequently by sin. Personal commitment toward virtuous growth in chastity always occurs within a social culture that can promote it or work against it, especially through information and education. Attainment of the virtue of chastity does not simply occur through an autonomous effort by the subject within society but rather relies on the grace of the Holy Spirit, which is accepted and cultivated within a life of faith. By infusing himself in the dynamisms of human sexuality, the Spirit empowers the subject to make it an expression of Christ's way of loving.

Chastity also considers the pleasure connected to sexual acts. In and of itself, sexual pleasure is a criterion for the morality of sexual actions, which should depend on the Christian love that they express or infringe upon. If anything, sexual pleasure provides information about the quality of the interpersonal love and the extent to which it is complete and reciprocal: complete in the sense that it involves the entire person and does not simply involve physical enjoyment but also psychological well-being and spiritual joy and reciprocal in the sense that it is not sought out in an individualistic manner for personal satisfaction but rather experienced from an interpersonal perspective as a sensitive manifestation of communion.

The Integrality of the Gift of Self

The Christian concept of virtues, which are fruits of the Holy Spirit accepted through faith by human freedom, views them as expressions of God's love which, when poured into the heart of man, enlivens and animates his numerous different activities. From this viewpoint, chastity is the expansion of Christ's charity into the gendered actions of men and women and their sexual behaviors.

The inevitable sexuality of the human person—inevitable because the person's love is always expressed in a gendered form even if it is not specifically sexual—renders chastity a vocation for everyone which pertains to every interpersonal relationship, starting with friendship between people of the same or of different genders. When experienced in the context of chastity, friendship becomes a profound spiritual communion with one's neighbor.

The Different Forms of Chastity

A vocation for all Christians, who are called in their gendered state to love as Christ loved them, chastity assumes different forms in relation to the person's particular stage of life. The principal difference is found between marriage, the only stage of life in which a sexual union can be contemplated in accordance with Catholic morality, and the other stages of life, where it must be excluded.

The virtue of chastity is in the service of charity within the boundaries of human sexuality, and its most complete fulfillment is found in marriage, where the actions of man and woman, which remain gendered, assume a truly sexual dimension. Within the marital covenant, the virtue of chastity renders the sexual union expressive of interpersonal love, involving the man and woman in their entirety in the reciprocal gift of oneself for another. Conjugal chastity sets the couple up to join together and reproduce while expressing the personal and fecund communion of sexual love through their gendered bodies.

Outside of marriage, the virtue of chastity calls for continence, or abstention from sexual relationships. Containing sexual expression does not mean censoring personal love but rather verifying its consistency and allowing it to mature in a suitable manner. In this sense, sexual continence does not represent castration but rather the growth of love. "Chastity in continence" is called for in the various stages of life which precede, follow, or do not involve marriage. Juvenile chastity regards men and women who do not yet entertain amorous bonds and involves mastery of one's gendered body in order to responsibly experience one's sexual instinct and drive. Premarital chastity regards men and women who are close to marriage—those who are "engaged," in traditional terms—and involves corporeal expression suited to the degree of interpersonal love experienced. The chastity of widows and widowers is that of men and women who have survived the death of their spouse and involves living in continence in order to testify to a spousal love that is "[as] strong as Death" (*Cant* 8:6). Unmarried chastity regards single men and women and involves renouncing the sexual expression of love and recognizing and crediting the marital covenant as the proper place for sexual love. Virginal chastity, which regards men and women who have been consecrated for the Kingdom, consists in the definitive choice of continence as a radical form of witness to the primacy of the love of Christ with respect to its sexual expression.

Offenses Against Chastity

By orienting the person as a whole toward the gift of himself/herself, chastity renders human sexuality an expression of Christian charity. Offenses against chastity are therefore sexual behaviors which inhibit or go against wholly personal love.

Love becomes depersonalized when sexual acts are not aimed at interpersonal communion but rather only at venereal pleasure. In this sense, "lust" is morally disordered not because it involves seeking pleasure but rather because it involves seeking pleasure without interpersonal love.

Depersonalized seeking of venereal pleasure is what characterizes "masturbation," which does not involve a sexual relationship with another person and provokes a kind of hedonistic autism. "Fornication" is instead characterized by a sexual relationship that nevertheless violates interpersonal love because it occurs between people who are not in a conjugal union and is not for reproductive purposes. "Pornography" is depersonalizing because it removes human sexuality from the context of interpersonal intimacy and flaunts it obscenely in public. Pornography that is displayed and looked at is morally reprehensible not because it involves seeing sexual nudity but because it does not involve personal profundity.

The depersonalization of sexual love is realized through "prostitution," in which the sexual relationship involves the commodification of people, especially women and children, who are reduced to objects of pleasure, often violently. During "rape," the reduction of the person to an object is obtained through violence, whose grave and permanent consequences for the victim are amplified if the victim is a relative or a subordinate of the perpetrator.

This summary, which is only indicative of the sexual behaviors that damage interpersonal love, refers to actions which can be judged objectively regardless of the level of responsibility of the perpetrator. For this reason, they are defined as gravely disordered or intrinsically evil acts.

Subjective responsibility can be influenced by psycho-physical and socio-cultural factors, such as moral limits and fragility, which can minimize the personal imputability of an action. In any case, sexual behaviors which violate interpersonal love gravely offend the dignity of the person, both because the person is deprived of his or her dignity and because other people are deprived of the possibility of answering the vocation to interpersonal love. Moreover, these behaviors also have scandalous implications for society because they serve as an obstacle that inhibits education about authentic sexual love and instead incentivizes the culture to dissociate sex from love.

Chastity and Homosexuality

The fact that the genesis of homosexuality is still quite unexplainable prevents us from defining it as a psychological illness, a deliberate choice, or a moral vice. The variability of its cultural and historic forms would, moreover, invite us to consider not homosexuality but rather homosexualities. This conception appreciates the uniqueness of people in terms of homosexual orientation and behaviors. Just like all people, homosexual people have a dignity that prohibits any unjust discrimination against them, and like all Christians, homosexual people are called to follow God's will by practicing chastity.

Homosexual chastity, like every other type of non-marital chastity, does not allow for sexual relations, which for homosexual people do not involve a difference in sexes or reproductive potential. The absence of sexual complementarity and the possibility for life is the reason for which homosexual acts, when objectively considered, are said to be intrinsically disordered with respect to conjugal acts between men and women according to the moral Tradition of the Church.

For a non-negligible number of people, homosexual acts are induced by a deeply rooted homosexual tendency that puts their practice of chastity to the test. The possibility of growing gradually and decisively in the virtue of chastity in order to follow Christ's commandment to love as he loved in the unique condition of homosexuality cannot exclude the grace that the Holy Spirit communicates through prayer and sacraments, not to mention through the unselfish friendship of those who also follow Christ and live in obedience to his love.

III. The Love of Husband and Wife

The reciprocity of man and woman, which are similar in their humanity and different in their sexuality, orients them toward the loving intimacy and union for life that constitutes the essence of marriage. Marital communion involves the spouses, who give meaning to and empower their interpersonal love through the sexual union of their gendered bodies, in their totality.

The Christian marriage of two baptized persons, moreover, given their union with Christ, is a sacrament—a royal sign of their nuptial love for the Church. Christ's nuptial relationship consists in the giving of his life so that human beings, which are vitally joined to him through faith, can have life in abundance and love each other as he loves. Supported by the grace of sacramental marriage, the spouses mutually give each other their entire lives. The conjugal love of the spouses renders them fecund while it unites them—their bond is a fecund union and a unitive fecundity. Conjugal love is already fecund when it unites the spouses because it gives life to a new personal subject, the couple, so that "they are no longer two, therefore, but one flesh" (Mt 10:6). The fecundity of conjugal love, moreover, is embodied in the child to whom life is transmitted.

Conjugal Fidelity

The reciprocal and total gift of one's life, which the spouses promise to give in their marital vows, assigns matrimonial love the properties of unity and indissolubility. The unity of marriage is the fruit of loving fidelity, which in participating Christ's faithful love for the Church, keeps the marital promise to give oneself completely to one's spouse. The unity and indissolubility of Christian marriage are not two extrinsic impositions on the love of the couple but rather two intrinsic requirements that correspond to a love that is experienced by man and woman as a complete communion of life.

The Fecundity of Marriage

The fecundity of marital love finds its most unique, although not its only, expression in reproduction. A child is the love of the spouses which becomes a single flesh, realizing their desire to be within each other which is experienced through sexual union. The intimate connection that the sexual union allows for through the transmission of life motivates the teaching of the Church to avoid dividing the two meanings, unitive and procreative, of the sexual act—in other words, of the personal communion of the spouses and their attitude toward reproduction (cf. *HV* 12).

This division occurs in the case of "artificial contraception," which eliminates the attitude of promoting reproduction and destroys the procreative meaning of the sexual act. Not all sexual acts have a procreative meaning, however, because the cyclic nature of female fertility involves the alternation of fertile and infertile periods. During the infertile periods, sexual acts express only their unitive meaning. Their procreative meaning, although absent, cannot be positively excluded like it can in the case of artificial contraception. For this reason, the moral teaching of the Church legitimizes and promotes the use of infertile periods to regulate births. These are known as "natural methods."

The regulation of births, on the other hand, regards "procreative responsibility." Since this is a type of responsibility, it involves the duly formed personal consciences of the spouses, and since it is procreative, it is conceived of as cooperation with God's creative work in obedience to his will and his commandments. Responsible procreation is supported by the fact that the human life transmitted by the parents, after leaving earth, is destined for eternal life.

The Gift of a Child

The life of the child is not created by the parents but rather received and transmitted by them. In this sense, the child is already a gift granted to the parents by the mystery of a life that is much greater than theirs. In terms of faith, a child is a gift that parents accept from God through cooperating with his creative action. The parents do not have a right to the child, nor is he an object that belongs to them. Instead, the child has the right to be raised and taught by the same parents that gave him life and to be respected as a person created by God from the moment of conception.

We can understand the moral gravity of "heterologous artificial insemination and fertilization" through these two rights that the child possesses. By involving third parties in conception (sperm donors) and/or in gestation (surrogate mothers), these forms of assisted procreation dissolve the connection between fatherhood and motherhood. The two spouses do not become a mother and a father through each other. Heterologous artificial insemination and fertilization, moreover, multiplies and fragments the group of parental figures (biological, gestational, emotional, legal, etc.), complicating the child's acquisition of a personal identity.

Less morally grave but nonetheless contrary to the properly human quality of procreation is "homologous artificial insemination and fertilization," which substitutes the conjugal act with a technical procedure. Since a child is not a biological product but rather the fruit of the personal love of the spouses, his dignity as a person requires that he originate from a personal act performed by his parents.

Since children are gifts, not duties, being granted numerous children is a divine blessing, although sterility is not a curse. The opportunities for clinical tests and potential medical treatments are not the only way to confront physical sterility, which could otherwise lead the spouses to make use of forms of conjugal fecundity that are no less noble, such as the adoption of children without parents or providing family hospitality to a needy neighbor.

IV. Offenses Against the Dignity of Marriage

The dignity of marriage is the goodness and beauty of the love in which man and woman give each other their lives. Marital love is mortally damaged when, in the case of "adultery," one of the partners is mortified by betrayal instead of being vitalized by love. Adultery occurs even prior to the extra-conjugal sexual union with the intention of and with the desire to commit it. But matrimonial love begins to be adulterated from the moment when it is no longer cultivated. This is also true for the love of the children, which can no longer enjoy the loving communion of their parents.

Divorce

The sacrament of marriage is celebrated so that man and woman can love each other as Christ loved "to the end" (Jn 13:1). The indissoluble love, which is given to Christian spouses through divine grace, is negated through "divorce," which the Canonical Order of the Catholic Church does not allow. The Canonical Order also consequently excludes new sacramental marriages for those who have already been married through the sacrament of marriage.

Aside from the religious significance of marriage, divorce contradicts family unity and causes grave damage to the spouse who is abandoned and especially to the children. Divorce also damages society to the extent to which it loosens social cohesion, which is based on the stability of the family. Although the sacramental bond cannot be dissolved if it is established in a valid manner, conjugal separation and possibly civil divorce, which only regards the civil effects of religious marriage, can be legitimate in some cases for reasons relating to the dignity or rights of the person or to the safeguarding and care of children.

The different personal responsibility of the partners in the case of separation or civil divorce makes it difficult to necessarily determine the moral culpability of the people who find themselves involved in a situation that is objectively not in accordance with the Gospel. Separation and even civil divorce can be provoked by one partner and endured by the other. The different moral responsibility and personal imputability in matrimonial situations that do not correspond to the teaching of the Church are relevant conditions that influence the pastoral determination of the paths of Christian life along which to accompany the interested persons.

Other Offenses Against the Dignity of Marriage

The totality of the gift of oneself to one's partner, which is a part of marriage, excludes "polygamy," which contradicts the personal dignity of the woman, who would be doubly hurt if she were abandoned by a husband who becomes Christian without respecting his obligations to her.

The loving communion of marriage is undermined by "incest," which causes grave damage to one's personal dignity. Incest does not safeguard the essential difference between sexual union and reproductive bonds. Incest is comparable to "sexual abuse" of minors by adults, especially when these adults have the responsibility of educating them.

The integrity of marital love is inhibited by the numerous forms of "free unions," where sexual intimacy is experienced outside of the definitive communion of marital life and the public commitment that this involves. Premarital sexual relations also fall into this category, even when they are justified as trial marriages. Sexual union is not a means for determining whether to commit through love but rather the expression of committed life of love.

Chapter Two, Article 7:

THE SEVENTH COMMANDMENT

Sabatino Majorano

The detailed study of the seventh commandment proposed by the *CCC* is held together by the imploration to work harder to overcome individualistic visions of Christian morality, something that was given particular emphasis in the Second Vatican Council: "Profound and rapid changes make it more necessary that no one ignoring the trend of events or drugged by laziness, content himself with a merely individualistic morality" (*GS* 30). Christian maturity, toward which catechesis must pull Christians, requires that each baptized person be "led individually in the Holy Spirit to a development of their own vocation according to the Gospel, to a sincere and practical charity, and to that freedom with which Christ has made us free" so that they are able to determine "what is required and what is God's will in the important and unimportant events of life" (*PO* 6).

This is what the apostle Paul asked of the Philippians: "It is my prayer that your love for one another may grow more and more with the knowledge and complete understanding that will help you to come to true discernment, so that you will be innocent and free of any trace of guilt when the Day of Christ comes" (Phil 1:9–10). An indispensable characteristic of this discernment is openness toward the requirements of the common good while freeing oneself from selfish closed-mindedness: "'Everything is permissible'; maybe so, but not everything does good. True, everything is permissible, but not everything builds people up. Nobody should be looking for selfish advantage, but everybody for someone else's" (1 Cor 10:23–24).

These are the implorations that Pope Francis has made forcefully since the beginning of his magisterium. In *EG* he dedicated the entire fourth chapter to the social dimension of evangelization: "The *kerygma* has a clear social content: at the very heart of the Gospel is life in community and engagement with others. The content of the first proclamation has an immediate moral implication centered on charity" (n. 177). However, we must never forget that "if this dimension is not properly brought out, there is a constant risk of distorting the authentic and integral meaning of the mission of evangelization" (n. 176).

In the following encyclical, *LS*, we are invited to take a broader and more responsible look, inspired by respect and solidarity, at our relationship with our resources. We must free ourselves from the slavery of selfish possession, accumulation, and consumption, and experience the joy of caring for our shared home, where "the bond between concern for nature, justice for the poor, commitment to society, and interior peace [is inseparable]" (n. 10).

The commandment "You shall not steal" from Ex 20:15 and Dt 5:19, which is restated in Mt 19:18, is therefore studied in the *CCC* in a manner that clearly appears to be an elaboration of the "twofold commandment of charity" which is referred to in the introduction to the third part dedicated to "Life in Christ" for programmatic reasons (n. 1697). We are invited to participate in a catechesis that is first of all concerned with helping us grow in our awareness of the evangelical meaning of our resources and which leads us to a proper relationship with them. Gifts of the Creator given for the happiness of all, they are entrusted to the responsible freedom of each person and each community. The fruits of work and of the ingenuity of each individual, in interdependence with others, they are an expression of and work to promote gathering and solidarity. Indispensable for the quality of life, they however are always at risk of being transformed into idols and losing their meaning as means to be shared. For this reason, the relationship cannot be one of simple consumption, and definitely not one of intense selfish consumption, but rather one of sharing, care, and responsible use.

The social doctrine of the Church attempts to make these implorations concrete through an evangelical discernment of the socio-economic reality in order to "offer, through the purification of reason and through ethical formation, her own specific contribution toward understanding the requirements of justice and achieving them politically" (*DCE* 28). This is not, however, a case in which certain "recipes" can simply be applied. Instead, it involves using the criteria and instruments available so that the choices of people and communities can constructively embody evangelical values.

These considerations allow us to understand the elaboration and the articulation of the discussion of the seventh commandment. The first two sections focus on the two fundamental perspectives that render one's relationship with our resources evangelical: the interdependency between universal destination and private ownership (section I) and the one between respect for persons and respect for their goods (section II). This is followed by a call for the use of the social doctrine of the Church as an instrument for discernment (section III). The *CCC* then addresses the principal problems of social justice in economic activity (section IV) and of solidarity between nations (section V). The last section emphasizes that love for the poor is a fundamental evangelical criterion of socio-economic life (section VI).

I. The Universal Destination and the Private Ownership of Goods

Before all goods, both those that are natural and those that are the fruit of human work, the fundamental attitude of the believer is reverent thanksgiving: "The heavens declare the glory of God, the vault of heaven proclaims his handiwork" (Ps 19:1). It is a thanksgiving that becomes praise: "Though made of body and soul, man is one. Through his bodily composition he gathers to himself the elements of the material world; thus they reach their crown through him, and through him raise their voice in free praise of the Creator" (*GS* 14). It is a thanksgiving that generates responsibility through the discovery that everything is in God's hands: "Yahweh our Lord, how majestic is your name throughout the world! Whoever keeps singing of your majesty higher than the heavens...what are human beings that you spare a thought for them, or the child of Adam that you care for him? Yet you have made him little less than a god, you have crowned him with glory and beauty, made him lord of the works of your hands, put all things under his feet" (Ps 8:1, 4–6). It is an "ability" in the image of that of God himself. It is love that works to bring his creation to fulfilment, that takes care of them and respects them while they are used so that they remain instruments that can be used for the happiness of everyone. For this reason, the *CCC* emphasizes that "the ownership of any property makes its holder a steward of Providence, with the task of making it fruitful and communicating its benefits to others, first of all his family" (n. 2404).

This vision of "private property" does not deny its importance as a condition which allows people to affirm their dignity and for the efficacy of economic processes. Instead, it denies every form of absolutization, which always leads to conflict, which is sometimes violent; disagreements; and fear toward others and to a "throw away culture" which excludes the poor, considering them to be the "outcast, the 'leftovers'" (*EG* 53). This selfish absolutization is the richness about which Christ does not hesitate to bitterly state that "In truth I tell you, it is hard for someone rich to enter the kingdom of Heaven. Yes, I tell you again, it is easier for a camel to pass through the eye of a needle than for someone rich to enter the kingdom of Heaven" (Mt 19:23–24).

It is the "right and duty" of political authorities to "regulate the legitimate exercise of the right to ownership for the sake of the common good" (*CCC* 2406). This should occur while taking into the account the details of the goods over which this right is exercised, the concreteness and the differences of the socio-economic contexts, and the differences in cultural traditions. For the Christian community, this involves frankly bearing witness to the fact that "solidarity is a spontaneous reaction by those who recognize that the social function of property and the universal destination of goods are realities which come before private property. The private ownership of goods is justified by the need to protect and increase them, so that they can better serve the common good; for this reason, solidarity must be lived as the decision to restore to the poor what belongs to them" (*EG* 189).

II. Respect for Persons and their Goods

The respect owed to the person also extends to the goods that legitimately belong to them, since these are a condition and an instrument for his dignity. For this reason, we must not only avoid taking goods from others but also avoid unjustly damaging them. However, it is not theft when the circumstances lead us to assume that the owner gives his consent and especially when private ownership comes into conflict with the universal destination of goods: "The seventh commandment forbids theft, that is, usurping another's property against the reasonable will of the owner. There is no theft if consent can be presumed or if refusal is contrary to reason and the universal destination of goods. This is the case in obvious and urgent necessity when the only way to provide for immediate, essential needs (food, shelter, clothing…) is to put at one's disposal and use the property of others" (*CCC* 2048).

In a context in which we tend to absolutize the right of ownership, it is important that catechesis clearly put forth the idea that each person's right to life be given priority in the case of a lack of essential resources. However, this does not legitimize disengagement or the shirking of responsibility, as the apostle Paul warns: "We urged you when we were with you not to let anyone eat who refused to work" (2 Thess 3:10).

The ways in which one can steal are numerous and are based on the development of economic dynamics. In the *CCC*, the most common ways in which both personal and social goods are stolen are listed. In catechesis, these should be made more concrete in order to allow Christians to recognize the risks present in new financial instruments and e-commerce innovations.

We should emphasize the urgency of overcoming every form of corruption, which is one of the strongest expressions of the "new idolatry of money" in today's world. Corruption can distort all social dynamics. By denying "the primacy of the human person," it results in a situation where "while the earnings of a minority are growing exponentially, so too is the gap separating the majority from the prosperity enjoyed by those happy few" (*EG* 55–56). In catechesis, we must be careful not to limit ourselves to denouncing and condemning the most scandalous cases but learn how to free ourselves from the "but everybody does it" mentality and propose practices and lifestyles that are centered around respect for and promotion of the common good.

It is also important to emphasize the moral meaning of fiscal regulations as an expression of solidarity for the common good. Their just creation is one of the fundamental responsibilities of political authority. We must also recognize that the distribution of fiscal resources is not always just. This is sometimes caused by the speed of social-economic change. Due to this, constant verification and reformulation of fiscal regulations is necessary. However, all of this should not make us forget the imploration for solidarity which is at its root. In this way, it is possible to confront any situations or limits which are inadequate or unjust in a morally valid way.

In contrast with fashions, which are also common among youth and adolescents, we must promote styles and behaviors that respect public goods—the environment; work, school, and entertainment buildings and public transportation; and works of art and public parks and green spaces. These are not things and places that should be taken advantaged of or even selfishly consumed. They are goods that belong to everyone and it is everyone's responsibility to protect them.

It is becoming increasingly more common to play "games of chance" in our society. These can lead to forms of addiction that are difficult to overcome and can become a social illness. It is true that some use these games to try and solve particularly grave economic problems, but this is illusory, and the games are a source of other problems. It is the responsibility of the entire community to prevent the weakest members from being infected by the charm of the various forms of betting, which are too often well publicized.

The just formation and respect for "contracts," starting from those which concern work, is a decisive factor in peaceful social living. The Christian community must bear witness to the fact that when stipulating the terms of contracts, defending the rights of the weakest members of society must be our first concern. This is because without concern for this concept, the big fish's right to eat the little fish will always prevail. For this reason, political authorities are responsible for oversight and for encouraging this attitude, especially when the contracts involve multinational corporations. On the other hand, we must always encourage respect for the commitments made in contracts, starting from the simplest ones regarding everyday life.

The "restitution of goods" which one has obtained in an unjust manner is a moral duty. This is also true for theft or damage of public property, although it is not always easy to quantify the damage done or the way in which it can be repaired. In any case, conversion is evangelical only if we recognize that we are responsible for what we have done and we work sincerely to remedy the damage caused where possible.

A special implication of the seventh commandment is the requirement for a sincere commitment toward eradicating everything that can lead to "the enslavement of human beings, to their being bought, sold and exchanged like merchandise, in disregard for their personal dignity" (*CCC* 2414). Pope Francis denounced these exploitative dynamics while making references to many forms of connivance that the public is not always aware of: "I have always been distressed at the lot of those who are victims of various kinds of human trafficking. How I wish that all of us would hear God's cry: 'Where is your brother?' (Gn 4:9). Where is your brother or sister who is enslaved? Where is the brother and sister whom you are killing each day in clandestine warehouses, in rings of prostitution, in children used for begging, in exploiting undocumented labor? Let us not look the other way. There is greater complicity than we think. The issue involves everyone! This infamous network of crime is now well established in our cities, and many people have blood on their hands as a result of their comfortable and silent complicity" (*EG* 211).

The second paragraph of the seventh chapter concludes by reminding readers of the necessity of respecting and taking care of all of creation. In reality, today there are numerous hopeful signs of increased awareness of the urgency of a shared commitment to creating effective solutions to ecological problems. However, the questions and risks for the future of our planet and quality of life are also increasing. The *CCC*'s statements should be examined and elaborated on in accordance with the judgments of the following Magisterium. They should be made concrete by the challenges of the context in which we live today.

In *CV*, Benedict XVI emphasized the interdependence between environmental ecology and human ecology. After reiterating that "the Church has a responsibility toward creation and she must assert this responsibility in the public sphere," he adds that this refers not only to the protection of the earth, water, and air "as gifts of creation that belong to everyone," but also especially to the protection of mankind "from self-destruction." In fact, the deterioration of nature is "closely connected to the culture that shapes human coexistence: when 'human ecology' is respected within society, environmental ecology also benefits. Just as human virtues are interrelated, such that the weakening of one places others at risk, so the ecological system is based on respect for a plan that affects both the health of society and its good relationship with nature" (n. 51).

In *LS*, Pope Francis makes an urgent appeal "for a new dialogue about how we are shaping the future of our planet. We need a conversation which includes everyone, since the environmental challenge we are undergoing, and its human roots, concern and affect us all" (n. 14). Some themes are particularly important for the Christian community, including "the intimate relationship between the poor and the fragility of the planet, the conviction that everything in the world is connected, the critique of new paradigms and forms of power derived from technology, the call to seek other ways of understanding the economy and progress, the value proper to each creature, the human meaning of ecology, the need for forthright and honest debate, the serious responsibility of international and local policy, the throwaway culture and the proposal of a new lifestyle" (n. 16).

It is the responsibility of catechesis to project the light of hope onto ecological problems. Through catechesis, it will be possible to guide consciences so that they feel responsible for these problems in accordance with each person's effective possibilities and without ever losing sight of the global perspective. Constructive criticism of the "'myths' of a modernity grounded in a utilitarian mindset (individualism, unlimited progress, competition, consumerism, the unregulated market)" is certainly necessary. It is especially necessary to dedicate oneself to "restor[ing] the various levels of ecological equilibrium [and] establishing harmony within ourselves, with others, with nature and other living creatures, and with God. Environmental education should facilitate making the leap toward the transcendent which gives ecological ethics its deepest meaning" (*LS* 210).

In this context, we can understand the *CCC*'s call to respect and care for animals: "Animals are God's creatures. He surrounds them with his providential care" (n. 2416). For this reason, it is "contrary to human dignity to cause animals to suffer or die needlessly." At the same time, however, we should consider it "unworthy to spend money on them that should as a priority go to the relief of human misery." Love for and care of animals must not mean that they become recipients of "the affection due only to persons" (n. 2418).

III. The Social Doctrine of the Church

The positive proposal about the requirements of the seventh commandment leads the *CCC* to reiterate the importance of the social doctrine of the Church in all kinds of catechesis. In *SRS*, John Paul II emphasizes that "the teaching and spreading of her social doctrine are part of the Church's evangelizing mission" (n. 41), and adds the following in *ChL*: "This is especially true for the lay faithful who have responsibilities in various fields of society and public life. Above all, it is indispensable that they have a more exact knowledge...of the Church's social doctrine" (n. 60).

The *CCC* does not present all of the detail and complexity of the social doctrine but simply reiterates its fundamental affirmations. In this regard, Pope Francis observes that "we have a most suitable tool in the Compendium of the Social Doctrine of the Church, whose use and study I heartily recommend" (*EG* 184). The social doctrine should not be considered to be a set of recipes but rather a tool for the maturation of consciences in view of the evangelical discernment of social problems. *GS* reminds lay persons that "it is generally the function of their well-formed Christian conscience to see that the divine law is inscribed in the life of the earthly city; from priests they may look for spiritual light and nourishment. Let the layman not imagine that his pastors are always such experts, that to every problem which arises, however complicated, they can readily give him a concrete solution, or even that such is their mission. Rather, enlightened by Christian wisdom and giving close attention to the teaching authority of the Church, let the layman take on his own distinctive role" (n. 43).

Personal judgment is supported by community judgment. *EG* emphasizes this by reminding us of what Paul VI stated in *Octogesima adviens*: "In the face of such widely varying situations, it is difficult for us to utter a unified message and to put forward a solution which has universal validity. This is not our ambition, nor is it our mission. It is up to the Christian communities to analyze with objectivity the situation which is proper to their own country" (n. 184).

The continuity of the social teaching of the Church should not be understood as repetition but rather as the creativity of faith in responding to the new signs of the times. The *CCC* notes that it is "a body of doctrine, which is articulated as the Church interprets events in the course of history, with the assistance of the Holy Spirit, in the light of the whole of what has been revealed by Jesus Christ" (n. 2422). In order to facilitate comprehension of this dynamic faith, catechesis should help Christians understand the three different levels of the statements it makes: "The Church's social teaching proposes principles for reflection; it provides criteria for judgment; it gives guidelines for action" (n. 2423). It is obvious that these guidelines are highly affected by the concrete elements of the situations to which they attempt to respond.

Social teaching aspires to the dialogue and collaboration of the Christian community with everyone who cares about the future of humanity and the Earth, especially in terms of the developments that occur closest to us. Serving as a witness without retreating from a particularly difficult situation is obligatory so that Christianity can be understood as a tool in the service of everyone. Christ's warning to his disciples also applies here: "It is not anyone who says to me, 'Lord, Lord,' who will enter the kingdom of Heaven, but the person who does the will of my Father in heaven" (Mt 7:21).

The close relationship between the promotion of the dignity of the person and the construction of the common good will always be at the center of the work of the Christian community. As the *CCC* reminds us, separating these two objectives or radicalizing one or the other leads to the negation of both:

"Regulating the economy solely by centralized planning perverts the basis of social bonds; regulating it solely by the law of the marketplace fails social justice, for 'there are many human needs which cannot be satisfied by the market'" (n. 2425).

IV. Economic Activity and Social Justice

The profound changes in the economy which are caused by the development of technology, starting with manufacturing, require careful judgment on the part of the Christian community. The community recognizes and is grateful for the many elements that lead to a better quality of life in many fields, especially sanitation and communication, which are being created. However, it does not accept the capitalization of development for the benefit of the few which leads to marginalization and the creation of waste. Likewise, the Christian community respects "the autonomy of earthly affairs" because we know that "created things and societies themselves enjoy their own laws and values which must be gradually deciphered, put to use, and regulated by men." However, it maintains that this cannot mean that "created things do not depend on God, and that man can use them without any reference to their Creator" (*GS* 36). For this reason, it cannot accept that "the idea that technology is self-sufficient when too much attention is given to the 'how' questions, and not enough to the many 'why' questions underlying human activity… Produced through human creativity as a tool of personal freedom, technology can be understood as a manifestation of absolute freedom, the freedom that seeks to prescind from the limits inherent in things" (*CV* 70).

The political crisis of these last few decades has led to economic processes being left to the mercy of the strongest so that they can profit. For this reason, it is urgent that the political community return to its role in guiding society toward the common good, bringing the interests and preoccupations of groups and individuals to the table. These concerns are legitimate only when they are open to those of others.

The inevitable disagreements that occur due to the complexity and diversity of the interests involved must not become true conflicts. Instead, people should trust in one another and search for shared points of view. As Pope Francis observes, "When conflict arises, some people simply look at it and go their way as if nothing happened; they wash their hands of it and get on with their lives. Others embrace it in such a way that they become its prisoners; they lose their bearings, project onto institutions their own confusion and dissatisfaction and thus make unity impossible. But there is also a third way, and it is the best way to deal with conflict. It is the willingness to face conflict head on, to resolve it and to make it a link in the chain of a new process. 'Blessed are the peacemakers!' (Mt 5:9)" (*EG* 227).

The *CCC* correctly invites us to always start from the dignity of work, which is an expression of how "persons [are] created in the image of God and called to prolong the work of creation by subduing the earth, both with and for one another" (n. 2427). For this reason, we must never lose sight of the fact that "work is for man, not man for work" (n. 2428). Of course, this does not mean forgetting the needs of the processes of production but rather asking for a sincere effort toward respecting the dignity of the person during their planning and realization on the part of all those involved.

In today's world, even work is at risk of becoming a privilege of the few. The result of the way in which the processes of globalization and the reorganization required by new technologies have been carried out is the following: "Today everything comes under the laws of competition and the survival of the fittest, where the powerful feed upon the powerless. As a consequence, masses of people find themselves excluded and marginalized: without work, without possibilities, without any means of escape. Human beings are themselves considered consumer goods to be used and then discarded" (*EG* 53). For this reason, we cannot "trust in the unseen forces and the invisible hand of the market." We must enact "decisions, programmes, mechanisms and processes specifically geared to a better distribution of income, the creation of sources of employment and an integral promotion of the poor which goes beyond a simple welfare mentality" (*EG* 204).

For the Christian community, claiming and promoting a universal right to work and respect for the dignity of the person for each worker are duties born from justice and charity that are paramount. At the same time, we must work to make each person feel more responsible for themselves. In the context of the common good, every activity is in the service of others. We are less responsive to the requirements of justice and charity when we reduce jobs to simple locations and tools for earning money and for selfish profit. This is particularly true for those who work in public service. The spirituality of work, which makes us capable of experiencing the joy of the inevitable effort that is always present, although in different ways, in various activities allows us to give these activities a more human character.

The speed at which the economy is evolving means that more creativity is required today in order to be ready to address new possibilities. We should expand upon "the right to economic initiative" from this perspective. This right has always been defended by the Christian community, and the *CCC* notes that due to this right, "everyone should make legitimate use of his talents to contribute to the abundance that will benefit all and to harvest the just fruits of his labor" (n. 2429). Statements of principle should always be made concrete through policies that work to promote them, especially among youth. The simplification of bureaucratic processes appears to be indispensable, but we should not do away with the monitoring and oversight suggested by the common good. Likewise, the Christian community is asked to clearly denounce all forms of usury, from blatant forms of loan-sharking to those disguised as more or less legitimate loans.

Increased sensitivity toward the responsibilities that enterprises have toward society is a wonderful development in today's world. "Those responsible for business enterprises are responsible to society for the economic and ecological effects of their operations" (n. 2432). In *EG*, Pope Francis adds, "Business is a vocation, and a noble vocation, provided that those engaged in it see themselves challenged by a greater meaning in life; this will enable them truly to serve the common good by striving to increase the goods of this world and to make them more accessible to all" (n. 203). These are perspectives that the Christian community is called to promote coherently while always emphasizing that not only must factories respect the environment but part of their profits should also be reinvested to protect the environment. This is the case for the numerous initiatives of the so-called "third sector" and the new forms of the "'civil economy' and the 'economy of communion'...a broad new composite reality embracing the private and public spheres, one which does not exclude profit, but instead considers it a means for achieving human and social ends" (*CV* 46).

V. Justice and Solidarity Among Nations

The intensification of the processes of globalization is turning our world into more and more of a "global village." For this reason, as Benedict XVI reminds us in *CV*, "the common good and the effort to obtain it cannot fail to assume the dimensions of the whole human family, that is to say, the community of peoples and nations, in such a way as to shape the earthly city in unity and peace, rendering it to some degree an anticipation and a prefiguration of the undivided city of God" (n. 6). Due to its wealth of experience with universality, the Christian community can make a precious contribution to society by emphasizing that being citizens of the world does not mean losing one's roots and connection to one's own culture but rather turning it into a treasure that can be shared in reciprocal respect and in dialogue with others. Likewise, the community should frankly note the risk of "de facto interdependence of people and nations [that] is not matched by ethical interaction of consciences and minds that would give rise to truly human development. Only in charity, illumined by the light of reason and faith, is it possible to pursue development goals that possess a more humane and humanizing value" (n. 9).

The *CCC* places a special emphasis on the "grave moral responsibility" of more developed nations toward those that "are unable to ensure the means of their development by themselves or have been prevented from doing so by tragic historical events." This is a duty that goes beyond "solidarity and charity" and also involves "justice if the prosperity of the rich nations has come from resources that have not been paid for fairly" (n. 2439). The search for effective solutions to the problems posed by migration from the poorest countries should be framed through this perspective, overcoming all kinds of fear and exploitation.

In this way, it is possible to promote an integral and sustainable vision of development with the knowledge of how to take responsibility not only for the respect for and affirmation of the dignity of persons and peoples but also for the care of creation. As Pope Francis notes, "Authentic human development has a moral character. It presumes full respect for the human person, but it must also be concerned for the world around us and 'take into account the nature of each being and of its mutual connection in an ordered system' Accordingly, our human ability to transform reality must proceed in line with God's original gift of all that is" (*LS* 5).

Most of all, we must be convinced that without development that is shared among peoples, true peace will be impossible because "a peace which is not the result of integral development will be doomed; it will always spawn new conflicts and various forms of violence" (*EG* 219). Listening to "cry of entire peoples, the poorest peoples of the earth" with the knowledge that "even human rights can be used as a justification for an inordinate defense of individual rights or the rights of the richer peoples" will be decisive for its formation. We must not tire of stating that "the planet belongs to all mankind and is meant for all mankind; the mere fact that some people are born in places with fewer resources or less development does not justify the fact that they are living with less dignity" (*EG* 190).

VI. Love for the Poor

In keeping with the fundamental choice of understanding the Decalogue as an elaboration of the two-fold commandment of love, the *CCC* concludes the article dedicated to the seventh commandment by reminding us of the centrality of love for the poor throughout Christian life. This is an active kind of love that allows itself to interact with their needs and attempts to provide an adequate response to each one, like the Samaritan in the parable in Luke (10:29–37). For this reason, it is a love that promotes justice in order to effectively remove the many factors behind discrimination, exploitation, and marginalization present in society.

Saint John Paul II connects active solidarity toward the poor to the credibility of evangelization itself. In *Novo millennio ineunte*, after referring to the Gospel story where Christ identifies with the needy man (Mt 25:31–46), he adds, "By these words, no less than by the orthodoxy of her doctrine, the Church measures her fidelity as the Bride of Christ." This is because "as the unequivocal words of the Gospel remind us, there is a special presence of Christ in the poor, and this requires the Church to make a preferential option for them" (n. 49).

The call for acceptance and an active commitment toward those in need is a constant refrain in the teaching of Pope Francis. In *Misericordia et misera*, he notes, "Our communities can remain alive and active in the work of the new evangelization in the measure that the 'pastoral conversion' to which we are called will be shaped daily by the renewing force of mercy" (n. 5). For this reason, "a culture of mercy based on the rediscovery of encounter with others, a culture in which no one looks at another with indifference or turns away from the suffering of our brothers and sisters" (n. 20) should be promoted at all levels of society.

The *CCC* stresses that all of this "is incompatible with immoderate love of riches or their selfish use" (n. 2445). This echoes James's condemnation: "Well now, you rich! Lament, weep for the miseries that are coming to you [...] Can you hear crying out against you the wages which you kept back from the laborers mowing your fields? The cries of the reapers have reached the ears of the Lord Sabaoth" (5:1–6). This also connects back to the patristic tradition (John Chrysostom, Gregory the Great), according to which "when we attend to the needs of those in want, we give them what is theirs, not ours. More than performing works of mercy, we are paying a debt of justice" (n. 2446).

Chapter Two, Article 8:
THE EIGHTH COMMANDMENT

Réal Tremblay

"There is no room in my house for anyone who practices deceit" (Ps 101:7).

"I am the way, I am the truth, I am the life. Remaining with the Father, the truth and life; putting on flesh, He became the way" (Saint Augustine).

"Truth [...] What is that?" (Jn 18:38). This question is Pilate's reaction to Jesus's testimony: "It is you who say that I am a king. I was born for this, I came into the world for this, to bear witness to the truth; and all who are on the side of truth listen to my voice" (Jn 18:37). The Roman procurator's skepticism is apparently left unanswered. But in reality, Jesus's testimony about the truth will be realized. His testimony will be the cross.

Without trying to force things, we could say that nn. 2464–2513 of the *CCC*, which clarify and elaborate on the eighth commandment of the Decalogue (cf. Ex 20:16) and its echo in the "Sermon on the Mount" (cf. Mt 5:33), could take the form of the cross. In what way?

A. Its large vertical arm that reaches toward the sky is a symbol of the truth which originates and gains its consistency from on high, from God, who is the truth. Effectively, the truth comes from the Father because he is the source and reason for all things (cf. 1 Cor 8:6). It is he who sends his Son-"Truth" into the world (cf. Jn 4:16; 14:6). The "Spirit of truth" comes from him so that we can understand the truth that his Son has taught us (cf. Jn 14:16–17:26; cf. *CCC* 2465–2466).

I. Living in the Truth

The large vertical arm of the cross is planted in in the ground and crosses all the different types of terrain of the human heart. First comes well-formed terrain, because man is fundamentally led toward truth because he has the moral duty to search for it, to honor it, and to conform his life to it. The truth as "uprightness in human action and speech" is called "sincerity" or "candor." Christ's disciples agree to "live in the truth," or to live in "the simplicity of a life in conformity with the Lord's example" and abide in it (cf. *CCC* 2467–2470).

II. To Bear Witness to the Truth

This is also permeable terrain, tamed by the energies that come from on high in order to seed it, take root, and produce the fruit of bearing witness. With this pneumatic "virtue," the baptized are hit with the dynamism of "exodus," of leaving themselves in order to proclaim and spread the truth of the Gospel that they have received with their lives and their words, paying the price of their lives if necessary. The *CCC* claims that bearing witness is a duty (n. 2471–2472) that is derived from a life lived in the Church of the Spirit of Christ. It comes from "justice," which is understood as the spreading of truth. We know that bearing witness by giving the gift of one's life was given great consideration in the early days of the Church. This consideration is documented by the "Acts of the Martyrs," which are carefully preserved and which the church views as "the archives of truth written in letters of blood" (n. 2473–2474).

III. Offenses Against Truth

Finally comes the hard and rocky, soft and sandy, stratified and torturous, and sterile and polluted terrain. The *CCC* looks deep into the recesses of men's hearts in order to identify the words and actions that run contrary to the truth, such as "false witness" and "perjury" (n. 2476); "rash judgement," "detraction," and "calumny" (n. 2477); and "flattery," "adulation" (n. 2480), "boasting," and "irony" (n. 2481). Each of these offenses against truth is accurately defined with particular emphasis, according to the specific cases, on the social or brotherly impact of their malice, which is also perceived as an attack on one's neighbor's reputation or honor.

In this section, the lion's share of the text is naturally dedicated to "lying." The *CCC* underlines that the malice behind lying comes from its relationship with the devil, the "father of lies" (*Jn* 8:44, *CCC* 2482), right from the beginning. After defining it as "the most direct offense against the truth," in the sense that it is told in order to lead someone who has the right to the truth into error (n. 2483), the *CCC* works to measure the malice of the lie according to its objective (the nature of the deformed truth), the circumstances and intentions of the person who tells it, and the harm suffered by its victims (nn. 2484–2486). Lying is in and of itself venial, but it can become mortal when it does grave damage to justice or charity. For this reason, the duty to make moral and material reparations for the wrong is obligatory "in conscience" (n. 2487).

B. In addition to its large vertical arm, the cross also has a horizontal arm that gathers the community of the baptized, who are called to "communicate the truth." For this category of actions, there are instructions and rules to consider.

IV. Respect for the Truth

For practical purposes, the right to the communication of the truth, which is much appreciated today, is not unconditional. It must always be weighed in relation to brotherly love, and more precisely in relation to whether it is appropriate to reveal the truth to someone who asks for it in a given set of circumstances. The *CCC* illustrates what this category involves with the help of a few cases that help us to clearly understand the positive character of what may appear to be unjustified reservations in the eyes of the people of today. The good and safety of others, respect for privacy, the common good, and especially the duty to avoid scandal suggest that we use discretion and that no one feels that he has a duty to tell the truth to a person who has no right to know it (n. 2489).

Other situations require complete and inviolable silence, such as in the case of the "secret of the sacrament of reconciliation." There is no pretext that authorizes the confessor to reveal anything about the confession of the penitent. Here, the prohibition is absolute (n. 2490). Other secrets include "professional secrets" in the world of politics, defense, medicine, law, and other important sectors in community life. These secrets must be kept. This is also the case for those revealed under a seal of secrecy, which can only be revealed under exceptional circumstances, such as where keeping the secret would cause grave harm "to the one who confided it, to the one who received it or to a third party" and this damage could be avoided only by divulging the truth. Finally, the *CCC* notes that even when private information that is harmful to another is not confided under the seal of secrecy, it cannot be divulged "without a grave and proportionate reason" (n. 2491).

Everyone should be appropriately discrete when it comes to people's private lives. This is especially true for people who work in communication. A proper balance should be struck between the requirements of the common good and the respect for particular rights. Here, the *CCC* emphasizes that "interference by the media" in the private lives of politicians or public figures is not justified "to the extent that it infringes upon their privacy and freedom" (n. 2492).

As can be seen, the *CCC* is particularly sensitive to the relationship between the truth and the good of persons, a pair of concepts that is often defiled by a world that is constantly in search of something new, sometimes paying the price of serious offenses against the *humanum*. This pair of concepts, which is symbolized by the horizontal arm of the Cross, Jesus's response to Pilate about the truth, is given support and efficacy that expands to the infinite scope of divine charity that the *CCC* examines further by reflecting on the use of social communications media.

V. The Use of Social Communications Media

In modern society, "information, cultural promotion, and formation" are supported by social communications media. Far from shrinking, this role is becoming more significant every day due to technological refinement and progress, and the quantity of the news transmitted and "influence exercised on public opinion" are increasing (n. 2493).

The media must transmit information for the public good to society, which has a right to information that is "based on truth, freedom, justice, and solidarity." This means that the subject of this communication must be "true" and the communication must occur "within the limits set by justice and charity." It must also be "complete." The means through which the information is acquired and distributed must also conform to moral law, human rights, and human dignity (n. 2494). While working together for the "diffusion of sound public opinion," users of mass media can fall into a certain kind of "passivity" that leads them to have less vigilant attitudes as consumers. In order to resist "unwholesome influences," moderation, discipline, and formation of the conscience are necessary (nn. 2495–2496). Due to the nature of their profession, "journalists have an obligation to serve the truth and not offend against charity in disseminating information." They should therefore try to respect "the nature of the facts and the limits of critical judgment concerning individuals." They should avoid defamation (cf. n. 2497).

Civil authorities have "particular responsibilities" due to their duty to protect the common good. To this end, they should ensure compliance with and promulgate laws that work toward a "true and just freedom of information." They should see that "public morality and social progress are not gravely endangered" through abuse of the media. They should punish "any violation of the rights of individuals to their reputation and privacy." They should inform populations about the "general good" in a "timely" and "reliable" manner and should avoid manipulating public opinion by providing biased information, as occurs in the totalitarian states, which are a true "plague" that must be condemned (cf. nn. 2498–2499).

C. Jesus's body, the body of "the most handsome" of all men (cf. Ps 45:3), is suspended on the large arms of the cross/testimony of the truth. Why do we speak of the "most handsome" body, when the corpse of a crucified man was considered to be the worst kind of aberration in ancient times? Saint Paul echoes this observation when he speaks of the cross as something that is "to the Jews an obstacle they cannot get over, to the gentiles foolishness" (1 Cor 1:23), along the lines of the "fourth song of the suffering servant" found in the book of Isaiah (52:2).

Jesus is "the most handsome" of all men in the ugliness of crucifixion. What is the reason behind this *sub contrario*? The cross is the expression of God's love for sinful humanity. Now, as Saint Leo the Great stated, "If God is love, charity should know no limit, for God cannot be confined" (*Sermone sul digiuno quaresimale* 10, 3, in *I sermoni quaresimali e sulle collette*, EDB, Bologna 1999, 223). That means that in order to express himself through sinful *humanum*, the love of God had to join itself to the emptiest human form, even more naked than any other human (cf. Phil 2:5), to flesh without any appearance, to a naked body covered in holes, including a heart which was the object of scorn and denial by humanity—in other words, to the man humiliated at Calvary.

VI. Truth, Beauty, and Sacred Art

The *CCC* does not seem to refer to this *sub contrario* beauty when it recalls the most meaningful Biblical passages that refer to Christ's splendor (cf. end of n. 2500) in order to support its idea of beauty. But be careful! Before returning to this point to make some further clarifications, let us review the principal elements of the *CCC*'s idea of beauty and its role.

Just like how the practice of good is accompanied by a spiritual pleasure and moral beauty, the truth involves joy and spiritual splendor. "Truth is beautiful in itself." In addition to the truth of the Gospel, which is an expression of the knowledge of the created and uncreated reality, there are also other complementary forms of truth. This is because before revealing himself to the human race through the words of truth, God also revealed himself "through the universal language of creation." "Through the grandeur and beauty of the creatures we may, by analogy, contemplate their Author" (Wis 13:5), who is the source of beauty itself (cf. Wis 13:3; 7:25–27, 29–30; *CCC* 2500).

[illegible] image of God, man also expresses the truth of his relationship with [illegible]r "by the beauty of his artistic works." Art is born from talent given to man by the Creator and requires man's effort, since it is a form of practical wisdom that unites knowledge and skill "to give form to the truth of reality in a language accessible to sight or hearing." Humans take inspiration from the truth and love for human beings, and so their activity is similar to that of their Creator. Like other human activities, art is not "an absolute end in itself" but rather works toward man's ultimate end (n. 2501).

Sacred art is true and beautiful when it translates the mystery of God, "the surpassing invisible beauty of truth and love" which is visible in Christ. The *CCC* cites Heb 1:3 in support of its Christological affirmation: Christ "reflects the glory of God and bears the very stamp of his nature," and "the whole fullness of deity dwells bodily" in Christ (Col 2:9). This beauty is "reflected" in the Virgin Mary, in the angels, and in the saints. In this way, authentic sacred art leads man toward adoration and prayer toward God, the "Creator and Savior, the Holy One and Sanctifier" (*CCC* 2502). For this reason, bishops and their delegates are invited to see to the authenticity of sacred art and remove everything that disfigures it (n. 2503).

Previously, I alluded to the idea that the *CCC* does not base its idea of beauty on the *sub contrario* beauty of the crucified Christ. At the same time, I advised readers to proceed with caution and wait to closely examine the numbers that are more directly dedicated to beauty. After this examination, we can see that this observation is confirmed. In this regard, it is interesting to note that the quote from Heb 1:3 is only part of the verse. Heb 1:3c is omitted: "and now that he has purged sins away…" This clearly alludes to the crucifixion of Christ. Two expressions used at the end of n. 2502, however, seem to open the door to my approach. The expressions are "Savior" and especially "Sanctifier," which refer to Heb 2:10–11, "It was fitting that God, for whom and through whom everything exists, should, in bringing many sons to glory, make perfect through suffering the leader of their salvation. For consecrator and consecrated are all of the same stock; that is why he is not ashamed to call them brothers," and Heb 10:10, 14, "And this 'will' was for us to be made holy by the offering of the body of Jesus Christ made once and for all […] By virtue of that one single offering, he has achieved the eternal perfection of all who are sanctified." The allusion to the cross is subtle, but it is there. If the text were to be revised, it would be desirable to include more substantial elaborations on the idea of the cross understood as a priestly consecration "in truth" (cf. Jn 17:19).

It is undeniable that based on the cross understood as Jesus's answer to Pilate's question about the truth, the catechetic content of the eighth commandment and its reprise on the "Mountain of the Beatitudes" is especially important today. In fact, the greater the possibility to spread the truth on an individual and societal level, the greater the possibility of its substance changing. In this light, the doctrinal clarifications found in the *CCC* are more than welcome.

They offer a series of criteria that allow us to not lose our sense of direction in a sector that is so significant for human and Christian fulfillment.

One particularly relevant aspect in this field is the question of knowing how to respect the truth whether "welcome or unwelcome" (cf. 2 Tm 4:2). Pilate was not able to do so because he never searched for the truth. His life as an opportunist politician rendered him deaf to the "voice" (cf. Jn 18:37) of Truth that stood before him. The behavior of the Roman procurator serves as a warning: one can serve the truth always and everywhere only by being of the truth. This was the strength of those who wrote the "archives of truth" conserved by the Church in their blood (cf. *CCC* 2474). This will be the strength of the new martyrs in our world. Think, for example, of the Christian doctors who are under strong social pressure in favor of what is known as "assisted suicide," to the point where they are threatened with losing their right to practice their profession if they do not enter into the parameters of the dominant ideology or of "political correctness" and who do not want to fold to the desires of their patients and of the State which supports them. The *CCC* confirms that "human life is sacred" and only God can give it or take it away (cf. n. 2258).

It follows that the service of the truth cannot be improvised. One must prepare for it, and the way to do so is by constantly synchronizing oneself with the *mens Christi* of which Saint Paul speaks, attributing it to the "spiritual person" who judges everything (cf. 1 Cor 2:15–16).

Chapter Two, Article 9:

THE NINTH COMMANDMENT

Martín Carbajo Núñez

While the sixth commandment focuses on lustful acts, the ninth warns against concupiscence of the flesh, which manifests itself in impure thoughts and desires. In this way, it asks us to correctly channel our psycho-physical drives, especially those of a sexual nature. "Every one who looks at a woman lustfully has already committed adultery with her in his heart" (Mt 5:28). The tenth commandment also asks us to overcome concupiscence, but it concentrates on our eyes—that is, avarice, envy, and the disordered desire to possess the goods of others. In the Old Testament, both types of concupiscence are included in a single commandment (Ex 20:17; Dt 5:21). The current division was originally proposed by Saint Augustine.

Concupiscence refers to any intense, anxious, and possessive form of human desire, which "unsettles man's moral faculties" and "inclines man to commit sins" (*CCC* 2515). People who allow themselves to be guided by their desires become slaves to their drives and unable to channel them in a controlled and rational manner. In order to be free and "enter into life," human beings must control concupiscence, purifying their hearts and practicing the virtue of temperance.

By concentrating on intention and desire, the ninth commandment indicates that exterior actions acquire their full human specificity when they are the result of a choice made freely and responsibly. Only in this case can we speak of "human actions." Physiological actions that are generated by reflexes or instincts and do not depend on free will even if performed consciously are called "acts of man." Along the same lines, animal sexuality, which responds to biological and hormonal dynamics, is different from human sexuality, where these dynamics are subordinate to its interior dimensions, which express the subject's free will. The gravity of feeding impure thoughts and desires comes from this concept.

Called to Freedom

Through the Decalogue (the "ten words"), our loving God shows us the path to liberation in order to "enter" into eternal life and accept the gift that He offers us. These "words" express a personalist morality that seeks a free and loving encounter with God, with others, with oneself, and with nature. In reality, the Decalogue was part of the prayer that the Israelite faithful recited every morning. The New Testament frames it in the law of Christ, which is free and gratuitous love. We are not looking for legal purity as an end in itself but rather for the freedom of being children of God, which is the gift of himself for love. This gift requires us to control concupiscence and "prevail over the seductions of pleasure and power" (n. 2549).

Concupiscence Prevents Us From Being Free

In order to be authentically human, sexuality must free itself from the principle of pleasure. Instead of placing everything at the service of his sensations and experiences, man must open himself to others with serenity, affectionately loving everything that surrounds him without trying to dominate, trick, or subjugate. We are immersed in a world that is hyper-connected and full of pretenses, and we need to overcome concupiscence of the flesh, which pushes us to view others in terms of our own needs. Concupiscence does not search for a serene and affectionate relationship but rather the satisfaction of our drives.

Accepting the Mystery of the Person

The fight against concupiscence means stopping looking at others in an unhealthy manner and trying to familiarize oneself with concupiscence in order to control it. By controlling these drives, the subject purifies his heart and is able to recognize the mystery of each person, seeing the living face of God in others and also viewing himself as a temple of the Spirit. In fact, a person is much more than the awareness he has of himself and can only perceive his inner self indirectly or through reflection. He is never able to know himself well enough to objectively write his own biography. This is because in order for judgments to be objective, the judge ("I) and the judged ("me") must be distinct. As Saint Augustine stated, "What I do know of myself, I know by Thy shining upon me; and what I know not of myself, so long know I not it, until my darkness be made as the noon-day in Thy countenance" (*Confessions*, X, 5, 7).

I. Purification of the Heart

The ninth commandment invites us to purify our hearts and minds in order to experience sexuality as a gift of oneself given through freedom. "Blessed are the pure in heart: they shall see God" (Mt 5:8). This purification cannot be reduced to a pure legal, exterior purity which leads to Pharisaic hypocrisy, to considering oneself to be superior to others, and to becoming "like whitewashed tombs" (Mt 23:27). A pure heart frees the gaze, opens man to beauty, and allows him to discover that all of reality is theophanic. Saint John of the Cross arrived at this purified perspective, which allowed him to think of his Beloved in nature in a real and immediate way and in turn to perceive "the mountain and the hill, where the pure water flows" in the beauty of the Beloved (*Spiritual Canticle*, 26). God allows himself to be glimpsed in the beauty and harmony of the cosmos, and through the manifestations of his divine beauty, he helps us to perceive the true importance of everything that exists.

The Battle for Purity

When his heart has not been purified, the subject is not able to accept the mystery of the person and frequently reduces the body to a product, the object of diseased observation, and therefore falls into exhibitionism or voyeurism. Impure eyes cannot perceive the religious dimension of the body —both one's own and those of others—which is "a temple of the Holy Spirit, a manifestation of divine beauty" (n. 2519). In order to arrive at the virtue of chastity and purity of heart, which is a gift and a task, human beings must open themselves to the action of the Holy Spirit in order to overcome the tendencies of flesh (cf. Rom 8:5–8), which belong to the old man. This means that man must prepare, constantly ask for divine grace, and try to discipline his feelings and imagination, desires and passions, and intentions and internal and exterior gaze.

Modesty

The information society is putting a lot of stress on the traditional social consensus regarding modesty and decency. Communication is centered around one's inner self and one's emotions, and brazen displays of one's innermost dimension and morbid curiosity that leads to no feelings of guilt or punishment are becoming ever more common. Social media unabashedly exploits every vein of intimacy and abuses the body—especially the female body—in advertising in an unhealthy manner. Today, people boast of personal details that used to be jealously guarded secrets. Infractions against modesty no longer seem to break that deep order that was considered to be indispensable for the individual and for society itself. These infractions are often seen as an expression of originality and the critical spirit that must animate the individual within society. The transgressor is presented as a sort of hero that helps free us from ancient repressions. Modesty is viewed as a social imposition that suffocates natural human expressivity. Modesty in dress and in personal expression is viewed as the result of complexes and obsessions that must be overcome.

Purity Requires Modesty

Purity requires modesty, which frees man from eroticism and morbid curiosity, governs people's gazes, and preserves personal intimacy. Modesty is therefore positive because it protects the mystery of the person (cf. *CCC* 2521–2522). It is not a way to close oneself off but rather to be able to have authentic interactions with others while avoiding possessive desires.

Through psychological and corporeal (interior and exterior) modesty, human beings attempt to not be reduced to observable and manipulable objects. While psychological modesty defends the most intimate parts of our personality, corporeal modesty prevents the body from losing its mystery and becoming an object that can be possessed and therefore something that is marginal. During profound personal communication, modesty ceases to serve as a barrier to the delivery of one's intimate self. This guarantees the authenticity of the relationship. It is no coincidence that the Nazis used attacks on modesty to denigrate and destroy their prisoners' sense of dignity.

Modesty Protects Intimacy and Facilitates Communication

Modesty protects intimacy. In other words, it facilitates one's ability to organize his life and freely manage his inner thoughts, experiences, and life. Cultivating this internal world is more important than hiding certain information. In fact, intimacy is much more than intimate information or defensive barriers. It belongs to the world of being more than that of having. The worst offense against intimacy is not revealing a personal secret but rather attacking internal freedom. We should not concentrate on hiding "something" but rather on protecting our personal richness and not ceding control of our lives.

Although exhibitionism and morbid curiosity (voyeurism) alter one's experience of intimacy, their opposites, closing in on oneself and not knowing others sufficiently well, produce similar effects. Intimacy always implies a certain impenetrability, but it is also unimaginable without a certain degree of transparency. No one can claim the right to know another person's inner self, but a balanced experience with one's own also involves transcending it and sharing one's personal richness freely and trustingly. Closing oneself off completely serves as an obstacle to shared living and authentically human relationships because dialogue is impossible without sharing something about oneself, and loving another is impossible without recognizing him as "someone."

The Virtue of Temperance

Modesty is an integral part of temperance and requires chastity. In fact, dominion over oneself ("temperance") requires the giving of oneself ("charity"; cf. n. 2346). Temperance does not exist to repress sexuality but rather to instruct it and make it mature. Being in command is very different from being a subordinate. In antiquity, people discussed subordinating the body, subjugating it through mortification in order to free the person's spiritual and rational dimension which are trapped within it—in other words, to be able to think without being impeded by passions. In Christian thought, however, the body is not the enemy of the soul but rather its necessary and harmonious complement. The body as an entity has an ontological meaning in and of itself because everything that we are and have was willed by God. It is a question of coordination, not of subordination. Instead of repressing, ignoring, or denying the drives of the flesh, human beings must make them their own and coordinate them so that nothing prevents them from loving God, their neighbors, and all creatures with all of their being.

The virtue of temperance leads us to do penance, to embrace our internal poverty, and even to renounce legitimate goods. All of this is experienced as a path of freedom, growth, and participation in the Paschal mystery: "If anyone wants to be a follower of mine, let him renounce himself and take up his cross and follow me" (Mt 16:24).

When faced with recurring dualistic anthropologies, the Second Vatican Council emphasized the unity of human beings. In order to state this, the Latin ablative was used instead of the genitive (*GS* 14), therefore reinforcing this sense of unity. In effect, perfection is not reached by moving away from the material and from our own bodies in order to obtain purity of thought and an imperturbable spirit but rather by assuming and coordinating everything that we are. The Word incarnate does not redeem us from the material but rather with the material and with the body. Mortification makes us free to be able to love.

Emotional Maturation

In today's liquid society (cf. Bauman), many people lack a personal project to which they can sacrifice time and energy. Instead, they are governed by desires, drives, and emotions which last for short periods of time and must be immediately satisfied. In this context, formation and accompaniment in order to mature emotionally are needed. Freedom is not possible without a certain discipline that allows a person to watch over his heart and vision and monitor his emotions and sentiments. It means experience yearning within certain limits and integrating it with human weakness and the potential for failure (*VC* 63), dominating one's drives and overcoming addiction to immediate gratification.

"Chastity has laws of growth." The chaste man "day by day builds himself up through his many free decisions" (*CCC* 2343). Specific voluntary actions are not sufficient. Nor does this involve repressing one's sexual drives along with the thoughts and desires they provoke. Rather, it involves gradual growth in knowledge, communication, and maturity. In other words, it means integrating all the dimensions of one's being, accepting "others as 'neighbors'" (n. 2519). Education is especially necessary for young people (cf. n. 2526). Without this psychological, sexual, and emotional maturity, continence can easily be transformed into depersonalizing frustration and love into a mere illusion that disappears as soon as the first difficulty is encountered.

II. The Battle for Purity

"Christian purity requires a purification of the social climate" (n. 2525). In fact, today's media-focused and permissive society promotes "widespread eroticism" and presents lots of "entertainment inclined to voyeurism and illusion" (n. 2525). Technology, which facilitates interpersonal communication, can also be used to exploit one's neighbor as a simple object of diseased observation (voyeurism, reality show). In this social context, the Church's teachings on sexuality are often contested or ignored.

Strengthening the Ideal of Authenticity

The progressive privatization of society and the process of individualization which have been ongoing in the West starting from the Renaissance have caused a turn to the self and an increased valorization of the emotional dimension. The old morality of self-denial has been replaced by the morality of self-fulfillment. While the first promoted social virtues and rigorous values—sincerity, loyalty, sacrifice, responsibility, fidelity to the social group—the new morality is centered around psychological values. Instead of addressing one's drives with self-control and discipline, now pleasure is proposed as a criterion for morality.

Some authors speak of a narcissistic culture, while others maintain that the ideal of authenticity prevails in our society. This ideal, according to Charles Taylor, is not an invitation to moral anomie and atomistic self-indulgence. Rather, if interpreted properly, it generates interiorizing moral imperatives and makes the individual a more autonomous, social, and responsible being. We need to bring the values that are cherished in our society, such as the notions of freedom and individuality, and purify them by removing dangerous additives that transform people's identities and make them fragmentary, superficial, and egocentric.

Integrating Experience into a Project for Life

In terms of sexuality, the turn to the self has led to increased permissiveness in social customs and to the prioritization of emotions, sentiments, and one's own experience above other social considerations. We want our romantic relationships is to be authentic, the fruit of love, and positive, but often we do not put in the effort necessary for the relationship to grow and mature. Many marriages break because the spouses do not have enough emotional maturity and do not work to overcome their differences and strengthen their love day after day. When one source of excitement is missing, we immediately look for another. M. Lacroix maintains that many people today get lost in a succession of disconnected emotions and experiences that are "strong" but insignificant and not fully developed. People consume emotional shocks but are not able to contemplate them, transcend them, and cultivate true feelings. They become excited, but they do not feel. When one's experience is not adequately interiorized, it is difficult to harmonize the various dimensions of one's being and integrate past experience into the present through projects and future plans. One's identity is experienced in a fragmentary way and it becomes impossible to articulate one's story in a coherent manner. Unity, continuity, and an itinerary of meaning are lacking.

Openness to Others on Social Networks

Social networks are one kind of marvelous new technology that facilitates relationships and global communication in today's world, but they can also be used as showcases for one's life. Often, people try to be the center of attention but do not allow others the same privilege. This type of narcissism leads people to confuse themselves with the public profiles that they have made for themselves. In this way, self-esteem and one's very identity are subject the emotional reactions that these idealized images provoke in others. When people are obsessed with their reflections in others' mirrors, they are not able to discover their own identity or those of others.

"The speed with which information is communicated exceeds our capacity for reflection and judgment, and this does not make for more balanced and proper forms of self-expression" (Francis, Message for the XLVIII World Communications Day, [01/24/2014]). On social networks, each user speaks about himself and his own experiences in an emotional manner, skipping from one event to another without ever articulating a true narrative. It all seems like an emotional bazaar, a mosaic of experiences without a clear logical sequence with no meaning or direction. "Learning how to live wisely, to think deeply and to love generously" becomes very difficult (*LS* 47). For this reason, today "we sense the challenge of finding and sharing a 'mystique' of living together" (*EG* 87).

We must overcome this disjointedness in order to rehabilitate our ability to tell our own stories and therefore give meaning to our experiences, to the succession of events, and to our growth as people. In this way, we create a polyphonic narrative instead of a fragmented set of information about ourselves. In this way, we can properly channel the ideal of authenticity which forms the basis for contemporary culture.

The ninth commandment warns against concupiscence of the flesh, which does not permit us to be authentic in order to freely give ourselves to others. We must purify our hearts and our social environment in order to be able to construct gratuitous, selfless, and free relationships both with our neighbors and with all other creatures. Only in this way is an eco-spirituality that both heals the roots of consumerism in our disposable culture and the narcissism of those who exploit others without feeling that they are brothers and at the same time makes us able to hear the cry of the earth and the cry of the poor possible. The information technology available today can nourish our carnal concupiscence and lead us to establish narcissistic relationships, but "if used wisely, they can contribute to the satisfaction of the desire for meaning, truth and unity which remain the most profound aspirations of each human being" (Benedict XVI, *Message for the XLV World Communications Day*, [01/24/2011]).

Chapter Two, Article 10:

THE TENTH COMMANDMENT

Mauro Cozzoli

Man's freedom is undermined by concupiscence, or by the desire for pleasure and its fulfillment. In addition to "lust of the flesh," there is also "lust of the eyes" (cf. 1 Jn 16). The first is related to desires created by psycho-physical drives, especially sexual ones. The second is related to desires created by goods and objects that can be possessed. The cardinal virtue of "temperance" frees man from both the first and the second, establishing the primacy of freedom from instincts and passions. Through temperance, it is the person who determines his life, assuming, shaping, and directing drives, attractions, and desires. These desires do not determine his life. Determining our lives and not letting them be determined for us is a mark of humanity. "The animal lives to the limit; it must. But man must not" (R. Guardini, *Learning the Virtues that Lead You to God*, Sophia Institute Press, Manchester, New Hampshire, 2013, 86).

Like the ninth commandment "forbids carnal concupiscence," (*CCC* 2514) and shapes temperance with regards to psychophysical drives and passions, the tenth "forbids coveting another's goods" (n. 2514) and shapes temperance with regard to the instinct and desire for possession.

Here, we will highlight the theological and moral aspects of the tenth commandment, which are introduced by a reflection on temperance with regard to possession, which provides an ethical and regulatory framework for the commandment.

The Temperance of Possession

People live among the goods of this world and benefit from them, so they must assume and cultivate the proper relationship with them. Justice, which is required by the seventh commandment and regulates their rights of use and possession, is not enough. At the same time as—and even before—justice, man needs temperance, the virtue that moderates the "sensitive appetite," or human passions, each of which pushes us to satisfy a need through the pleasure that accompanies its satisfaction.

Now freedom, which is intelligence and will, does not fall under the "principle of pleasure." In order to be human and humanizing in its practice, it cannot use pleasure as a guiding standard for decisions. This would mean negating freedom. The person would allow himself to be dragged along and commanded by his desires. The spirit, which is liberty, would not come first. Rather, the psyche, which is sentiment, would. But sentiments are passive and do not instruct freedom. Feeling is a way of experiencing. Freedom therefore ends up conditioned by drives and instincts, attractions and desires. These are the things that determine liberty and its quality.

A characteristic of man's growth and development is moving from childhood, which is dominated by the "principle of pleasure," to adulthood, which is governed by the "principle of moral good," which must be personally recognized and accepted as a guiding standard for options and decisions. "Temperance" is a virtue that qualifies adult freedom, which is capable of assuming desires, channeling them, and directing them to a project of complete human growth. Intemperate freedom, which is at the mercy of seduction and greed, is an immature freedom. It has regressed to or is stuck in a childlike state and is not able to control and direct instincts and drives. As the Apostle tells us, it is the freedom of "children, or tossed one way and another, and carried hither and thither by every new gust of teaching" (Eph 4:14), unable to assert what is true and good in the face of the "wind" of opinions and passions.

The way of temperance is not that of repression or removal of passions. Passions are not disowned or depreciated but rather recognized and valued as a psycho-physical potential for action which is required for and directed toward the person's project for life.

Temperance is the virtue of "freedom from" domination by the psycho-physical "for the" primacy of the spirit. It is a freedom that assumes and subjects the impulsive energy of drives to the person's intelligent will and planning, directing it toward the person's full realization. As R. Guardini writes, "The spirit gives a new meaning to the urge. It works into the urge and gives it depth, character, and beauty. It brings it into relation with the world of values, and also with that which bears these values—the person—and so lifts it to the sphere of freedom. In the animal, the drives constitute 'nature'; the spirit makes of them what we call 'culture,' taking this word as an expression of responsibility and self-conquest [...] The spirit elevates man above the urge, not thereby destroying it [...] By the spirit, man acquires the possibility of ordering and forming the urge and so leading it to greater heights, to its own perfection, even as an urge" (R. Guardini, *Learning the Virtues that Lead You to God*, op. cit., 86).

One of man's particular passions is the one generated by the instinct to have and possess and the attraction exercised by these. The desire to have is rooted in human sensitivity: "The sensitive appetite leads us to desire pleasant things we do not have" (*CCC* 2535). The main manifestations of this desire arise from vital needs such as satisfying hunger and defending oneself from the cold (cf. n. 2535). This desire then extends to all the goods that we desire, that satisfy us, and that give us pleasure. In and of itself, desire/the need to have things is "good" (cf. n. 2535) because it pushes man to procure goods that are necessary to satisfy real needs. Its goodness comes from the goodness of the good, which is the object of the person's desire: it is good to desire good things or at least things that are morally indifferent.

The desire for possession, however, can become "concupiscence": "covetousness" (n. 2514) of goods. Their need becomes "avarice" (n. 2534): yearning and covetous longing. In this way, freedom is overcome by desire. Freedom submits to desire and does not dominate it but rather is dominated by it. The "lust of the eyes" extends to all goods which attract and please the eyes and lead to the desire to arrive at them and possess them. And when the good achieved is always only a fraction, with a part outside of our reach, that we do not yet possess, the "lust of the eyes" becomes limitless and insatiable. It takes away the person's freedom to "be satisfied" with the goods that he has justly obtained. It deprives him of the joy that their assistance provides and of his gratitude toward God, the provider of all that is good. It only offers him the pleasure of an ephemeral conquest as he his sucked into a perverse and exhausting spiral of insatiable greed.

The individual depends on the goods that he possesses and ends up "possessed" by them. He becomes steadily less free to arrange his goods and steadily more "arranged" by them. The object takes over the subject, having taken over being, necessity, freedom, and the person—who has an identity as a subject (not an object) who has value for what he is (and not for what he has), and who is freedom (and not necessity)—loses his identity and his vocation. This is case for the "man of great wealth" from the Gospel who cannot enter God's Kingdom (cf. Mt 19:23–26). He is a man dominated by "lust of the eyes." His eyes are weighed down and distorted by the greed of having and are incapable of elevating, opening up to, and trusting in God's love.

The "temperance of possession" frees man from this concupiscence. It is the virtue of "new eyes" because it frees man from yearning for possession. It moderates the desire to have things and empowers us to discern and distinguish what is necessary and important from what is superfluous and secondary. It is the virtue of a proper relationship with the goods of this world. Its fruit is "sobriety," which is the capacity and attitude of dominating the instinct for using and having, containing it within the boundaries necessary for a dignified and respectable life. "Freeing us from" the exhaustion of yearning and "from" the subjugating possession of wealth, the temperance of possession "frees us for" love, or gratuitousness toward one neighbor and gratitude toward divine Providence as well as respect for and proper use of the world's goods and resources, which takes the form of ecological responsibility.

Another result of temperance of possession is "penitence," or the attitude of agreeing to or forcing oneself to renounce goods which may be legitimate, useful, and necessary as a way to access freedom, and ethical and spiritual growth and participate in the cross of Christ. This takes a unique form in the denial of oneself that the Gospel requires as a condition for following Christ and achieve salvation: "If anyone wants to be a follower of mine, let him renounce himself and take up his cross and follow me. Anyone who wants to save his life will lose it; but anyone who loses his life for my sake will find it. What, then, will anyone gain by winning the whole world and forfeiting his life?" (Mt 16:24–26). This is not a stoic, ascetic sacrifice of one's life but is rather directed toward what is better, "earning" one's life.

Particular expressions of penitence are "fasting" (cf. *CCC* 1434–1438), which is the decision not to satisfy one's need for nourishment at certain times and under certain circumstances, and "abstinence" from particular foods.

Theological and Moral Requirements

We will now analyze the theological and moral requirements that the *CCC* lists as the reasons behind and the requirements of the tenth commandment.

I. The Disorder of Covetous Desires

"Lust of the eyes" is desire that has become "avarice": an encaptivating and incontinent view of desirable goods. "Encaptivating" because every good that is pleasing to the eye leads to the desire to possess it. A glimpse of the object attracts the person's freedom to look in a possessive way. Objects of pleasure and objects of possession become one and the same. It is "incontinent" because the desire and the pleasure of possession know no limits—not in terms of scope, leading to cravings for property, exploitation, salary, enjoyment, success, advantage, career, or power. In other words, it takes over the whole range of "having," which does not only refer to the possession of objects. Nor does it have limits in terms of intensity. The yearning consumes the whole person, affecting his drives, emotions, intelligence, intentions, energies, will, ideas, plans, and projects.

Avarice is therefore accompanied by greed. Greed refers to the unrestrained desire for goods and pleasure and is an inherent part of avarice. Avarice is an insatiable greed. And from the moment when the yearning to have renders us insensitive to others and unwilling to give, greed leads to "avarice": the act of keeping everything for oneself in an uncontainable and obsessive spiral of accumulation. Due to the desire for possession that it inspires and nourishes, greed is at the root of every sin of injustice (cf. n. 2536).

Avarice and greed are moral evils that sink in to the person and take shape within the person's operational faculties: intelligence, will, feelings, and drives. The moral evils are not only actions (*actus*) that are sinful and that are repeated and accumulate. They are habits (*habitus*), or permanent dispositions of the person that the acts generate and nourish. These are called vices: inclinations of freedom toward evil, which lead to "states of sin"—in this case gluttony and covetousness. The gravity of these states is proportionate to how deeply they are rooted in the subject and to the degree of disregard for the virtue of temperance. A state of sin disposes and leads man to commit sinful acts in a spiral that feeds and is fed by *actus* and *habitus*.

It is not merely desiring others' things that is the sin. The commandment "do not covet" is not an indifferent condemnation of desire. The sin is found in unrestrained and insatiable desire and in wishing ill on others in order to obtain an advantage (cf. n. 2537).

Lust of the eyes is found at the origin of "envy," one of the seven "capital vices" that destabilize the person's moral freedom. Envy is the unpleasant feeling of "sadness" that is created by others' goods, qualities, and merits that the person wishes to have for himself which is accompanied by hostility, rancor, and resentment toward the person who has them (cf. n. 2539). When it becomes an acquired *habitus*—a vice, in other words—envy predisposes freedom toward that sentiment. The person loses the joy of pleasing his neighbor, who is perceived as a rival. The yearning to have things, which forms the basis for envy, fuses with "pride," which does not tolerate others having goods or results that are better or equal to the person's own (cf. n. 2540).

When not improved by conscience or moral responsibility, which are minimized, rationalized, or removed, and not challenged by temperance and humility, "envy can lead to the worst crimes" (n. 2538). Any way you look at it, envy involves wishing ill for one's neighbor. As Saint John Chyrsotom notes, "From envy are born hatred, detraction, calumny, joy caused by the misfortune of a neighbor, and displeasure caused by his prosperity" (*Moralia in Job*, 31, 45: *PL* 76, 621). Temperance and humility free us from envy so that we can experience benevolence and satisfaction and admiration for our neighbor (cf. n. 2539).

II. The Desires of the Spirit

For Christians, temperance is more than a human virtue which is acquired through moderation and control over one's instincts and passions. It is a virtue generated by the grace of the Holy Spirit, who performs man's conversion from "natural person[s] (*sárkikos/psychikòs ánthropos*)" to "spiritual person (*pneumatikós ánthropos*)"; from his "old self" (Eph 4:22; Col 3:9), which falls under the dominion of the flesh, with its passions and concupiscence—which is "corrupted by following illusory desires" (Eph 4:22) and "enslaved by different passions and dissipations" (Ti 3:3)—to the "new man" (Eph 4:24; Col 3:9), who is free with the freedom of those "who belong to Christ Jesus" who have "crucified self with all its passions and its desires" (Gal 5:24; cf. Rom 8:5–13; Gal 5:16–25).

The result of this conversion is life "in the Spirit": a life of freedom from the "things human nature desires" lived for "spiritual things" (cf. Rom 8:5–8). Now, the behavior of he who lives "by the Spirit" (Gal 5:25) is "guided by the Spirit" (Gal 5:25) in the sense that he adheres to the Spirit's desires and works: "Instead, I tell you, be guided by the Spirit, and you will no longer yield to self-indulgence. The desires of self-indulgence are always in opposition to the Spirit, and the desires of the Spirit are in opposition to self-indulgence: they are opposites, one against the other" (Gal 5:16–17).

Christians experience temperance not as a law but rather as a gift and assignment of grace. Not as a law, which tells us what sin is through the commandment "do not covet." This knowledge fosters "concupiscence": "all kinds of covetousness" and "sinful passions" which lead to spiritual death. Saint Paul calls it the "law of sin and death" (cf. Rom 7:5, 7–13; 8:2). Nor is it "that law of sin which lives inside my body" which is opposed by "the law in my mind," which is an expression of "God's law." It is a law whose result, according to Paul, is that "I do not act as I mean to, but I do things that I hate" (cf. Rom 7:14–25; cf. *CCC* 2542–2513).

A new man, the Christian is "dead to the Law so that [he] can be alive to God" (Gal 2:19; cf. Rom 7:4–6). This is an expression of the "desire for the Sovereign Good" (*CCC* 2541), through which all that is good is good and desirable. Christians live for the freedom that life by the Spirit gives them (cf. 2 Cor 3:17): "Brothers, you were called to be free" (Gal 5:13). Not free will, which is "an opening for self-indulgence," but freedom which is innervated by charity and supported and nourished by the grace of the Holy Spirit (cf. Gal 5:13–14; 2 Cor 3:17; Rom 5:5).

III. Poverty of Heart

"For wherever your treasure is, there will your heart be too" (Mt 6:21). The heart is the wellspring of love. It is loving itself, which finds its "treasure" in its beloved. It is important to love, but the object of that love is decisive. This determines the quality of the love. Each man answers the fundamental questions: "Who or what do you love?"; "In who or in what do you place your trust?"; and "What is the good or value that is the center of attraction and consistency in your life?"

Merely human wealth, power, and pleasure are ephemeral and deceitful "treasures." Making them the gravitational center of our love, chasing them as the primary and decisive goods and values of our lives, the objects in which we place our fundamental trust, is illusory and delusory. A person cannot be satisfied by anything that is worth less than his heart. Only God and his Kingdom—which came and was disclosed to us with the arrival of Jesus, the Lord—are the "treasures" that measure up to the human heart and satisfy its desires.

Whence the requirement found in the Gospel to "set your hearts on his kingdom first, and on God's saving justice" (Mt 6:33). This is the "treasure" and the "pearl" which, when found, leads the person to "[go] off in his joy, [sell] everything he owns and [buy it]" (cf. Mt 13:44–45). It is therefore the "treasure in heaven" (Mt 19:21). What is important is not "having" essential goods and having them in abundance. The disciple of the Gospel does not accumulate "treasures for [himself] on earth, where moth and woodworm destroy them and thieves can break in and steal" (cf. Mt 6:19–20). It is not a question of devaluing earthly goods but rather "relativizing" them: taking them for what they are, as means for living well and practicing justice and love for one's neighbor and not as "ends" which seduce and pervert our hearts. When they are sought after as goals, the heart surrenders to the idolatry of wealth and money. They are idols that the Gospel calls "mammon" or "money": the "master" that takes the place of God and directs the worship owed to God to it (cf. Mt 6:24; Lk 16:13).

"Poverty of heart" frees us from this idolatrous perversion. It is a virtue that has its roots in and takes its energy from the heart. A person can lack possessions and power and not be poor because he is dominated by desire or envy which are provoked by their scarcity. Poverty is primarily internal. It is an attitude of the heart. Jesus proclaims, "How blessed are the poor in spirit," which is expressed by the heart. He adds, "The kingdom of Heaven is theirs" (Mt 5:3). The virtue which makes us blessed and determines whether the Kingdom belongs to us is not a lack of goods and resources. It is poverty of the inner spirit, where our intentions, desires, and attitudes are formed. In the spirit, freedom is removed from the dominion of possession. It is detached from the things we possess, and our desire is purified. The virtue of poverty is a disposition of the spirit which overflows with profundity. It takes shape in the person's actions and lifestyle.

On the contrary, "Alas for you who are rich: you are having your consolation now. Alas for you who have plenty to eat now: you shall go hungry" (Lk 6:24–25). By making earthly wealth and satisfactions his "treasure," the rich man remains outside the economy of the Kingdom and of salvation (cf. Mt 19:23–26). There is no place in his heart for the liberating grace that comes from God. Like the heart of the Pharisee is stuck in the pleasure of his works, the heart of the rich man is stuck in the enjoyment of his possessions. Both have received their recompense (cf. Mt 6:1–6): they have excluded themselves from God and from his Kingdom. He who does not place his trust in the security of his own abilities and accumulated possessions is instead poor. He has a heart that is confident and docile to grace. He accepts its solicitations, converting himself toward justice and gratuitousness. He makes himself poor in spirit." This theological meaning of poverty and wealth tells us that both are more than conditions and human ways of living. They are ways of directing oneself toward God that are decisive in the way that they relate to goods and people. Only a heart that has been converted and is open to God can work toward poverty in the way that it relates to the goods of this world and uses them to benefit itself and others.

We can understand, therefore, why an agnostic and worldly conception and way of experiencing life do not promote the virtues of temperance and poverty but rather favor greed for possessions, pleasure, and power. The heart of the man who is far from God is stuck in these things. His happiness depends on them and his freedom is subject to them. Trust in God and temperance of possession work together.

IV. "I Want to See God"

The search for God's face is the invocation of the person who prays and the aspiration of the wise man in the Bible. "I want to see God" is the deep and supreme desire of the man who knows that he cannot place his hope in ephemeral and relative goods. "Seeing God" is the happiness of man (cf. *CCC* 2548). This is not the sensorial and intellectual way of seeing and knowing. It is the heart's way of seeing and knowing—that is, the way of love. The "loving vision" of God is man's greatest good: "beatitude." This is no ordinary happiness but rather a complete and perfect happiness that only the love of the Sovereign Good can ensure. As Saint Gregory of Nyssa notes, "He who has seen God has received all the good of which one can possibly conceive" (*Orationes de beatitudinibus*, 6: PG 44, 1265A).

The hope of seeing God, which is ensured by faith full of charity, is the hierarchical and harmonic principal of goods and of the liberation and fulfilment of desire. Goods acquire value and priority in relation to the Sovereign Good. Desire in turn establishes the proper relationship with each good without making what is primary secondary or allowing itself to be influenced or misled.

The desire to see God frees us from lust of the eyes. By directing our gaze toward God, it is made pure because the greed for possessions is removed. It is therefore made free to seek and desire everything that should be sought and desired without possessively fixating on some goods but rather using each to love and directing everything toward God and toward its full and definitive fulfilment in him through love. This gives us the freedom to mortify emotions and desires which may even be honest and licit in order to access the blessed divine vision. The desire to see God absolutely does not alienate man, it lets him find himself again: it "frees man from his immoderate attachment to the goods of this world so that he can find his fulfillment in the vision and beatitude of God" (*CCC* 2548). "In order to possess and contemplate God, Christ's faithful mortify their cravings and, with the grace of God, prevail over the seductions of pleasure and power" (n. 2549).

PART FOUR

CHRISTIAN PRAYER

Section One

PRAYER IN THE CHRISTIAN LIFE

Chapter One:
THE REVELATION OF PRAYER

Enzo Bianchi

Introduction

"For Thou madest us for Thyself, and our heart is restless, until it repose in Thee" (*Confessions*, I, 1,1). This famous affirmation by Augustine clearly specifies the foundation for Christian prayer, which was established during the time of the great Fathers of the Church and has made it all the way to the present day. The desire of human beings for the supreme *bonum* is expressed primarily through prayer, which is the movement of the human heart toward what is infinite, eternal, and absolute.

The definition which follows has essentially been accepted, although with slight differences, by all spiritual authors in the East and in the West. St. John Damascene, who collected and established the Eastern tradition, defines prayer similarly as "the raising of one's mind and heart to God or the requesting of good things from God" (*Defide orth.* III, 24). These words were taken up in the West by Thomas Aquinas (*Summa Theologiae*, II–II, 83, 1). This presentation of prayer in terms of human beings' search for God today seems, if not proven wrong, at least insufficient, especially because new generations are allergic to the ascendant and vertical conceptions found in all of Christian spirituality.

In this way, we are brought back *per aliam viam* to a fundamental fact of Biblical theology: the presence of the living God is given to man, not molded or achieved by him, and man is expected to welcome his epiphanic coming. The God of Biblical revelation is the subject, and the living God, who is not a result of reasoning on our part, is not found in the logic of our concepts but rather in his acts and his interventions, which show that he is a God who searches for man right from the start: "Where are you?" (Gn 3:9). It is God who wants a dialogue and establishes one, entering into communion and into a covenant with us. It is God who, from creation to the apocalypse, comes to, looks for, calls, and interrogates human beings throughout history.

The God who "first loved us" (1 Jn 4:19) speaks and starts a dialogue in history, and men and women react to God's self-revelation in faith through benediction, praise, works of grace, worship, questioning, intercession, and confession of their sins. Through prayer, in other words, which always seeks to be obedient to he who spoke and expressed himself as faith, hope, and charity. Essentially, people respond to the benediction with which God offers his gifts to humanity with their own benedictions and even by trying to make their entire lives into benedictions.

While taking this Biblical perspective, which is clearly illustrated in nn. 2566–2649 of the *CCC* (which we will not cite explicitly because they are the foundation that underlies this reflection), into consideration, we would like to list a few fundamental elements of the revelation of Christian prayer. It is a perspective that makes the reason why, even when prayer takes the form of a search for God, prayer is at its most basic level a response stimulated by grace and is always and essentially a gift from God that clearly emerges. In this way, the "I" that reaches up to God is not at the center of prayer. God remains the protagonist and the subject—God, who searched for us first, who came to us while we were enemies, rebelling against him (cf. Rom 5:6–10).

Prayer in the Old Testament

The Pentateuch presents two great figures of prayer: Abraham and Moses. Their prayer occurs within the bounds of "friendship": Abraham is a "friend of God" (Jas 2:23), and Moses was a man with whom "Yahweh would talk [...] face to face, as a man talks to his friend" (Ex 33:11; cf. Nm 12:6–8; Dt 34:10). This familiarity explains the insistence and boldness of Abraham's (cf. Gn 18:16–33) and Moses's (cf. Ex 8:8,26; 9:33; 10:18; 17:8–16; 32:11–14, 30–32; 34:5–9; Nm 11:1–2, 10–30; 12:13–14; 14:10–19; 16:20–22; 17:6–13; 21:7–9) intercessions. In Ex 32:31–32, in particular, Moses's intercession becomes a vicarious offer to give his life for his people. Although intercession is the most commonly found form of prayer, there is no lack of supplications (Gn 15:2–3; 24:12–14; 32:10–13). These are mainly the result of the sterility of women in the patriarchal stories (Gn 25:21), and God hears their prayers (Gn 30:6,17,22). The song in Ex 15, which is both narration and prayer at the same time, is the prayer of the people in response to the salvific action with which God brought the sons of Israel out of Egypt.

A bitter lamentation is found in the book of Joshua (cf. Jos 7:7–9), while the book of Judges shows God answering the pleas of the sons of Israel in periods of political and military difficulty (cf. Jgs 3:9,15; 4:3; 6:6; 10:10) or those of particular persons, such as Manoah (cf. Jgs 13:8), the Gideon judges (cf. Jgs 6:36–40), and Samson (cf. Jgs 15:18; 16:28). In the books of Samuel and

Kings, Hannah's prayer in Shiloh (cf. 1 Sm 2:1–10)—which had an influence on Luke's version of the *Magnificat* (cf. Lk 1:46–55)—David's humble act of grace after God's revelation to Nathan (cf. 2 Sm 7:18–29), his confession of his sins after the census (cf. 2 Sm 24:10, 17), Solomon's prayer in Gibeon (cf. 1 Kgs 3:4–14), his supplication during the inauguration of the Temple (cf. 1 Kgs 8:22–53), and Hezekiah's prayer for the liberation of besieged Jerusalem (cf. 2 Kgs 19:14–19) stand out. Samuel (cf. 1 Sm 1:1–25:1) has become the symbol of the great intercessor of God (cf. Ps 99:6) in the Biblical tradition.

As for the prophetic experience, the "Elijah-Elisha cycle" (cf. 1 Kgs 17–2 Kgs 13) places Elijah's experience at the forefront. After living through anguish and sadness, he arrives at an encounter with the presence of the Lord—before whom he has lived his entire life (cf. 1 Kgs 17:1)—which is unveiled to him with an unrepeatable intensity in the "light, murmuring sound" (1 Kgs 19:12). The texts of the writing prophets present the prophet as a man who shares the "*páthos* of God" (A. J. Heschel), the person to whom God reveals his will (cf. Am 3:7). The prophets' closeness to YHWH makes them audacious intercessors that advocate for the people but also passionate defenders of God's law and demanding facilitators of divine justice for the people's sins. The prophets frequently criticize hypocritical worship and community prayer that is separated from the practice inspired by justice and law (cf. Is 1:15; Am 5:21–27; Mi 3:4, 6:6–7; etc.). But most of all, it is Jeremiah who emerges as the model for prayer, starting with the dialogue that marks the beginning of his vocation (cf. Jer 1:4–19). According to 2 Mc 15:14, he is the one who "prays much for the people and the holy city." His so-called "confessions" (cf. Jer 12:1–6; 15:10–21; 17:14–18; 18:18–23; 20:7–18), which are composed with unforgettable lyrical accents, are dramatic personal prayers that take the form of a "struggle" between the prophet and the one who sent him.

But the book of the Bible *par excellence* when it comes to prayer is the Book of Psalms, the book where the Word of God becomes the prayer of man, which the Jewish tradition attributes to the king and poet David. The prayers are made with intelligence and awareness, and the psalms are a true school of prayer, a whole within the fragment, a microcosm of the relationship between God and the person who believes in him. They remind the person praying that prayer is first and foremost the act of listening. The words that come out of God's mouth, in fact, form a dialogue due to their acceptance in the hearts of individuals or in the soul of a community and due to the response that is sent up to God as a result. The loving grace of God (*chesed*) precedes and forms the foundation for the prayers of man, which always consist of listening to and answering the Word of God and therefore his interventions in history and the love that originates from him. "You have only to open your mouth for me to fill it" (Ps 81:11), God says. The psalms are the words that God places in the mouths of human beings in order to teach them how to talk to him, like a father does with his son.

In particular, the psalms teach us the unity between prayer and life, which is masterfully expressed in the following stunned observation: "My very bones will all exclaim, Yahweh, who can compare with you?" (Ps 35:10). The psalms are life and history in the form of prayer, placed before God. To say that the psalms teach us how to pray means saying that they teach us how to live before God in all the facets of our everyday lives. In fact, this implies the unity of the human person. Far from divisions between the spiritual and material, between the intellectual and practical planes, the true subject of psalmic prayer is the body. Not only in the sense that the body takes on different positions during prayer (kneeling, prostrating oneself with one's face to the ground, raising one's eyes to the sky, dancing, etc.), but also in the sense that the entire human being is involved in prayer. The unity between prayer and life also includes the intrinsic relationship between what is personal and what is of the community. The psalmist does not say "I" without also saying "we"—in other words, without knowing that his ability to give thanks for what he has received is due to the fact that he belongs to the people of the covenant and that the sin that he has committed and for which he pleads to God for forgiveness has repercussions for the entire community of which he is part (cf. Ps 51:20–21).

The historical and existential significance of the psalms is expressed through a prayer that develops within a fundamental dynamism consisting of the bipolarity of praise and supplication. Not only are praise and supplication the two fundamental lungs of prayer, but the entire Book of Psalms is also structured in such a way as to present a path from supplication to praise, from the darkness to the light, a Paschal path from death to life, through the way that it is organized. The psalms teach us that in prayer, praise is always the context for supplication because supplication always requires a confession of faith in the name of God. Additionally, supplication must always tend toward praise—that is, toward the reestablishment of a full relationship with God. The expression "I will praise him still!" pronounced by the Levite in exile (Ps 42:6,12; 43:5) can be extended to all of prayer, which is a path toward full communion with God.

The registers of thanksgiving (which is more punctual than praise, refers to a precise event, and implies a clear discernment of God's action in history) and protest are situated within this bipolarity. Protest is particularly instructive and can revitalize our prayer, which is often too sterile. The psalms describe people who know how to express their pain and know how to say that they are suffering during illness or suffering. They allow themselves to yell, lament, and ask the piercing question "Why?" The infinite range of languages that the psalms present (silence, tears, sobs, yells, whispers, internal dialogues, laughter, wonder, confidence, etc.) reminds us that prayer is a relationship with God—a concrete, everyday, existential, historic relationship. They remind us that prayer is life before God.

Prayer in the New Testament

Jesus prayed. He belonged to a people that knew how to pray, the people that created the psalms and found the rule that informed their faith within Israel's practice of prayer. Liturgical prayer was modeled on the Jewish methods and forms of prayer at the time, as occurred during worship in the synagogue and at the temple of Jerusalem on holidays: psalms, recitations from the *Shema' Yisra'el* (cf. Dt 6:4–9; 11:13–21; Nm 15:37–41), *Tefillah* (or the "Eighteen Benedictions," the main prayer which was recited at the end of each service), readings from the *Tôrah* and the Prophets, etc. The inspiration for Jesus's creativity came from this source. The Lord's Prayer, for example, has some obvious similarities with the *Tefillah* and the *Qaddish* (the old doxology often used during the prayer service). In particular, the words "Hallowed be thy name, thy kingdom come" seem to follow a rule that is expressed in the *Talmud* in the following manner: "Any blessing that does not contain the mention of God's name is no blessing, any blessing that does not contain a mention of the divine kingship is no blessing" (Babylonian Talmud, *Berakhot* 40b). Each time that Jesus ate a meal with his disciples, he presided over the table and said a blessing. It is no coincidence that during the Last Supper, which the Synoptic Gospels place in the context of Passover, the *Hallel* (Ps 113–118, which concluded the Passover feast) was recited as a community by Jesus and his disciples (cf. Mt 26:30; Mk 14:26).

Jesus's personal prayer is also given great emphasis. His public ministry was regularly interrupted by frequent "retreats," especially at night or early in the morning, going to pray in a "deserted place," in "a lonely place," "alone," and "up the mountain" (Mt 14:23; Mk 1:35; 6:46; Lk 5:16; 9:18,28), and in particular making his way "as usual to the Mount of Olives" (Lk 22:39). Luke is the apostle who insists the most on Jesus's prayers, connecting them to the salient moments of his life and his mission: Jesus prays when he is baptized by John (cf. Lk 3:21–22); he prays before choosing the Twelve (cf. Lk 6:12–13); he prays at the transfiguration (cf. Lk 9:28–29); prayer is the context for Peter's confession of faith (cf. Lk 9:18); his teaching on prayer for his disciples is born from his own prayer (cf. Lk 11:1–4); before the passion, he declares that he has prayed for Peter so that his faith may not fail (cf. Lk 22:32); in Gethsemane, his prayer is especially intense (cf. Lk 22:39–46); and finally, Jesus prays on the cross, calling for the Father to pardon his executioners (cf. Lk 23:34), and then trustingly placing his very breath in his Father's hands (cf. Lk 23:46; cf. Ps 31:6).

Jesus's prayer is highly personal. He addresses God, calling him "Dad," with the particular intimacy and confidence inherent in the Aramaic word *Abbà*: this is the gateway to the mystery of his personality and a mark of his identity as the son of his beloved Father. And the Father responds to Jesus, who prays with insistence and perseverance, by entering into dialogue with him: "You are my son, today have I fathered you" (Ps 2:7; Heb 1:5; cf. Mk 1:11), words that are fulfilled on the day of resurrection (cf. Acts 13:32–33). The majestic "prayer of the hour" (often called the "high priestly prayer": Jn 17:1–26) deserves separate consideration. Situated between the farewell discourse (Jn 13:31–16:33) and Jesus's arrest (Jn 18:1–11), the prayer already encompasses the age of the Church and is the intercession that the glorified Son makes for those that the Father has given him. Finally, we must not forget the prayers that Jesus says in public during his teaching: the confession of praise for the Father, who reveals his Kingdom to the little children and the poor and not to the intellectuals who are conceited in their knowledge (cf. Mt 11:25–27; Lk 10:21–22), and the full invocation of confidence in the Father himself before Lazarus's resurrection (cf. Jn 11:41–42).

Jesus taught his disciples to pray based on his experience with prayer, and he did it through an authoritative interpretation of the teaching on prayer contained in the holy Scriptures and in the tradition that he received. For this reason, it is essential that authentic prayer take the advice about prayer that Jesus gave his disciples, who listened to it, preserved it, and delivered it to Christian communities and which was therefore put into practice by the faithful until it was deposited in the Gospels as Scripture. These indications are still the essential spiritual and pastoral elements for Christian prayer today. Before examining them in short (cf. E Bianchi, *Why Pray: How to Pray*, Saint Pauls Publishing, United Kingdom 2015, chapter II section 1), I would like to remind readers that Jesus summarized his teaching on prayer through the Lord's Prayer—which is addressed in another section of the *CCC*—which has correctly been defined as "an abridgement of the entire Gospel" (Tertullian, *Prayer* I, 6).

First of all, Jesus warned us how not to pray. Not like the hypocrites, to show off, to be seen and praised, but rather "in secret," or confiding in the Lord who sees our hearts and recognizes the uprightness of our intentions (cf. Mt 6:5–6; Mk 12:40; Lk 20:47). Not with a large number of words like pagans or going to great length without purpose (Mt 6:7; Mk 12:40; Lk 20:47). In fact, Jesus said, "Your Father knows what you need before you ask him" (Mt 6:8). We must pray with insistence, without relenting, and with perseverance (cf. Lk 11:5–13; 18:1; 21:36), with great faith and trust in the goodness of the Father who we are addressing (cf. Mt 7:11; Lk 11:13). This faith must become trust that our prayers will be answered (cf. Mt 21:21–22; Mk 11:22–24; Mt 17:20; Lk 17:6; Mt 7:7–8; Lk 11:9–10). The prayer of petition contains a hierarchy of requests. The sanctification of the Name, the coming of the Kingdom, and the fulfillment of God's will come before every other petition: "Set your hearts on his kingdom first, and on God's saving justice, and all these other things will be given you as well" (Mt 6;33; cf. Lk 12:31). We must ask "in Jesus's name" (cf. Jn 14:13–14; 15:16; 16:24,26)—in other words, we must convert our will into the will of the Father manifested in Jesus. Jesus's prayer at Gethsemane, which makes fulfilment of his request subordinate to the fulfillment of the will of the Father, shows the two poles within which the prayer of petition as Jesus taught it is situated: the freedom of the son who audaciously asks the Father, submitting the person praying to the will of God (cf. Mt 26:39; Mk 14:35–36).

The authenticity of the invocation lies in one's willingness to fulfill the will of the Father (cf. Mt 7:21; Lk 6:46). Prayers which occur in a communion of intentions in the name of the Lord will be answered (cf. Mt 18:19). Asking that one's sins be forgiven requires being ready to forgive others (cf. Mt 6:14–15; Mk 11:25). Reconciliation with one's brother is essential for the truth of prayer and liturgical actions (cf. Mt 5:23–24). We must pray with humility and with sincerity, recognizing our sins (cf. Lk 18:9–13). We must pray and be ready for the second coming of the Lord (cf. Lk 21:36) and to be kept from temptation (cf. Mt 26:41; Mk 14:38; Lk 22:45). We must pray for our enemies (cf. Mt 5:43–48; Lk 6:27–38) and to be able to cast away certain demons (cf. Mk 9:29). Most of all, we must ask for the gift of the Spirit before any other requests. As Jesus decisively states, "If you then, evil as you are, know how to give your children what is good, how much more will the heavenly Father give the Holy Spirit," or what is the most good (given the parallel with Mt 77:11), "to those who ask him!" (Lk 11:13).

Finally, remaining with the Gospels, I would like to remind readers of Mary's prayer, which is expressed through the *Magnificat* (cf. Lk 1:46–55) and the two other canticles that the Church repeats daily in the Liturgy of the Hours: the *Benedictus* (cf. Lk 1:68–79) and the *Nunc dimittis* (cf. Lk 2:29–32).

Prayer in the Age of the Church

The Acts of the Apostles, the second part of Luke's work, first present the reality of the prayer of the Church, or community and liturgical prayer. One of the cornerstones of the Church is found in perseverance in prayer (cf. Acts 2:42) and in the *fractio panis*, or the Eucharist (*ibid.*). The first Christians still followed the rhythms of Jewish prayers by going to the Temple (cf. Acts 2:46; cf. also 3:1; 21:26; and 22:17). They probably made the Portico of Solomon (cf. Acts 3:11; 5:12) the meeting point where they met as a group characterized in their faith in Jesus as the Christ (cf. Acts 3:11–4:31; 5:12–42). The Christians also prayed in private homes, where they praised God and practiced the *fractio panis*, especially on the first day of the week (cf. Acts 20:7–11; see also 2:1,46; 4:23–31; 12:5,12). Prayer has a constitutive ecclesiastical dimension: it is the Church's first gesture following the Ascension (cf. Acts 1:13–14) and the watercourse that prepares the way for the Spirit to come down on Pentecost (cf. Acts 2:1–11). The method of praying is essential in Acts. Praying must be done with perseverance, in harmony, and in unity. All important community decisions are preceded and accompanied by prayer, such as when the replacement for Judas was chosen (cf. Acts 1:15–26) and when the seven are appointed (cf. Acts 6:6).

More generally, it was the entirety of everyday life in the Church that was accompanied by prayer: persecution (cf. Acts 4:23–31; 12:1–5), missions (cf. Acts 13:2–3; 14:23), and apostolic ministry (Peter and Paul are frequently shown in the act of prayer: cf. Acts 0:40; 10:9; 20:36; 28:8). This is a way of affirming that there can be no ecclesiastical or Christian life without prayer. The very name for the disciples of Christ, before they were called "Christians," is "those who invoke the name of the Lord" (cf. Acts 9:14,21). The ministry of Paul is characterized by his participation in the liturgy in the synagogues in the various cities in which he finds himself, during which he preaches that "Jesus is the Christ" (Acts 9:22; cf. 9:20–22; 13:5,14ss.; 14:1; 16:13; 17:1ss.; 18:4; 19:8). But the Acts also emphasize the personal dimension of prayer: Stephen at the moment when he is to be martyred (cf. Acts 7:55–60), Paul after the event that occurred on the road to Damascus (cf. Acts 9:11), Peter on a housetop at noon (cf. Acts 10:9). Prayer also occurs in jail (cf. *Acts* 16:25) and on the riverbank (cf. Acts 21:5). It is expressed through hymns (cf. Acts 16:25) or intercessions (cf. Acts 12:5), through praise (cf. Acts 2:47) or acts of grace (cf. Acts 28:15). It molds the life of the Church as a whole.

We could also examine in detail how prayer is presented in the other books of the New Testament (particularly in the *corpus* of the Pauline letters), but in following nn. 2623–2642 of the *CCC*, we will briefly analyze the various forms of prayer (cf. E. Bianchi, *Lessico della vita interiore*, BUR, Milano 2004, 131–152). The most well-documented form of prayer in Scripture and Jesus's most commonly requested prayer is that of questioning. This is also the form that has posed the most problems in the Christian tradition, which has often affirmed that prayers of praise (or gratitude that is translated into an awed and "poetic" answer to God's love, which we recognize in the greatness of his gifts to us) and of thanksgiving ["The main form of prayer is thanksgiving" (Clement of Alexandria, *Stromata* VII, 79, 2)] are superior and purer. Today, we are instead witnessing its reemergence in forms that are not authentically evangelical and which reduce it to a magical attitude, a kind of injunction directed at a God who is thought to be immediately "available" and that almost has a duty to satisfy our every need.

By turning to God and questioning in various existential situations, the believer, without renouncing his responsibility and his commitment, states that he wants to obtain the meaning behind his life and his identity from his relationship with God and confesses that he cannot "organize" his own existence. In this sense, prayers of questioning are certainly scandalous because they go against man's pretense of self-sufficiency. On a deeper level, behind every truly Christian prayer of petition lies a radical question about meaning that technological progress can never overcome and that directly involves not only the believer ("Who am I?") but also God, in whom "we live, and move, and exist" (Acts 17:28).

Moreover, with prayers of questioning, the believer establishes a waiting period between a need and its satisfaction and distances himself from his concrete situation. He rises up out of his need and transfigures it into a desire. Through prayers of questioning, we can learn to desire and, in other words, to know and discipline our desires, distinguishing them from our needs and attempting to conform them to God's desire. Put in another way, we ask for gifts that fulfill our needs and the Holy Spirit leads us to invoke the presence of the Giver—to ask for love, the desire of desire.

This is why prayers of questioning really regard the presence of the God who is being addressed even before the attainment of a specific good. They can only be made within a filial relationship with God which is experienced through the teaching of faith. It is within this relationship and within its limits that the Christian prayer of petition is situated. This prayer must not be confused with the prayer of petition common to all forms of religion but rather has its *norma normans* in the hierarchy of requests found in the Lord's Prayer and an inescapable criterion in the prayer of the Son Jesus Christ to his Father. Faith and the filial relationship as experienced by Jesus, which is the way he addressed the Father, in this way become models for the faithful.

In this sense, Jesus's aforementioned experience at Gethsemane, the decisive hour of his life, is extremely meaningful. As his passion looms imminent, he confesses that God is "Abbà, Father" (Mk 14:36), and asks with insistence that "that hour" (Mk 14:35), "that cup" (cf. Mt 26:39) might pass him by. At the same time, however, Jesus subjects his request to a precise criterion: "let it be as you, not I, would have it" (Mk 14:36, Mt 26:39). This is the authentic Christian prayer of petition, the prayer of a disciple of Jesus Christ!

A particular form of the prayer of petition is intercession. Etymologically, inter-cession means "taking a step between" or "inserting oneself" between two sides. In this way, it refers to an active way of compromising, a way of taking our relationship with God as seriously as our relationships with our human brothers and sisters. Intercession does not lead us to remind God of the needs of others but rather pushes us to open ourselves to their needs, reminding ourselves of them before God and receiving others from God once again, illuminated by the light of his will. Intercession teaches us to enter into every human situation in full solidarity with the God who made himself a man "for us men," as we recite in the Symbol of faith. Through this, we recognize how incredibly limited we are in our ability to do good for others and we position ourselves to take on the responsibility even when it is beyond our capabilities. Intercession is the most evident sign and the most mature fruit of our responsibility to our brothers and sisters because it is the act with which we accept this responsibility even when not in public—when it is not required by social conventions and does not produce any personal gratification.

The pinnacle of intercession does not consist in words pronounced before God but in living before him in the position of the Cross, faithful to God and in solidarity with all human beings until the end of time. The intercession *par excellence*, in which Christian intercession participates, is in fact that of Christ, who extends his arms on the cross, asking that his executioners be pardoned. In this way, he opens his arms to embrace all of humanity, turning the extreme weakness of death into an act of love through which the powerful mercy of God is manifested in him. In this act, the believer recognizes and confesses fully effective, limitless intercession which brings salvation to all of humanity.

In order to examine the other side of prayer, thanksgiving, we can look to the Gospel story of the ten lepers healed by Jesus (cf. Lk 17:11–19), where the words of God, "Your faith has saved you" (Lk 17:19), are only directed at one. They are directed to the one who returned to thank Jesus after being cured. Only people who give thanks experience salvation—the work of God in their lives. And because faith is a personal relationship with God, we do not give thanks simply externally with a few prayers. Rather, our whole beings must give thanks. This is what Paul asks us: "Always be thankful!" (Col 3:15; cf. 1 Thess 5:18). Christian faith is elementally Eucharistic, and the entire life of the Christian must be lived "with thanksgiving" (*metà eucharistías:* 1 Tm 4:4).

Even though it is so fundamental, thanksgiving is not at all spontaneous, especially from an anthropological point of view. It implies the sense of otherness and the capacity to enter into a relationship with a "you," because one can only say "thank you" to another entity that we recognize as a person. Entering into gratitude also means fighting against the temptations of consumerism in order to create the conditions necessary for a communion, for a relationship which forbids the exploitation of another for ourselves.

Even at this first level, therefore, prayer of thanksgiving is prayer which involves thinking of others, time, and space before God who is the one Lord of all of them. In this way, the prerequisites for a vision of Creation and our co-creatures that is not consumeristic.

In a personal relationship with the Lord, our capacity to give thanks shows the maturity of our faith. The believer recognizes that the love of the Lord precedes, accompanies, and follows his life. The action of grace is born from the central event of Christian faith: the gift of the Son Jesus Christ which the Father gave to humanity due to his immense love for us (cf. Jn 3:16). It is the saving gift that inspires man to give thanks and makes the Eucharist the ecclesiastical action *par excellence*. "It is truly right and just, our duty and our salvation, always and everywhere to give you thanks, Lord, holy Father, almighty and eternal God, through Christ our Lord." These words introduce the Prefaces of the *Roman Missal* and clearly indicate the continuousness of Christian thanksgiving. And because the Eucharist, and the Eucharistic Prayer within it, is the model for Christian prayer, the Christian is called to make his entire existence an opportunity for thanksgiving. The gratuitousness of God's action for man is answered by recognition of the gift, and this recognition is answered by gratitude. Christians are those who "always and everywhere giving thanks to God who is our Father in the name of our Lord Jesus Christ" (cf. Eph 5:20; Col 3:17).

The central role of the Eucharist—the prayer of prayers—in Christianity also reminds us that Christian worship essentially consists of a life that is capable of answering the inestimable gift that comes from God with gratitude. The Christian responds to God's gift by making his entire life an act of thanksgiving, a living Eucharist. In fact, he knows—or should know—the deep meaning of the Eucharistic gesture that Jesus made during the Last Supper (cf. Mk 14:17–25 and parallel versions). Jesus performed that action in order to avoid having the disciples see his death as an event that occurred randomly or that occurred due to an inevitable destiny that was the will of God. For this reason, he concluded his existence as he had always lived it: in freedom and for love of God and of humanity. And so that this was clear, Jesus prophetically forewarned his disciples about his passion and death, explaining to them with a gesture that could narrate the essence of his story: bread that was broken, like his life would be soon, and wine that was poured into a glass, like his blood that would soon be poured out of him during a violent death. In following him, Christians are called to *loghikè latréia*, to "worship according to the *Lógos*," and as stated in the Epistle, "to offer [our] bodies as a living sacrifice, dedicated and acceptable to God" (cf. Rom 12:1) through a life spent loving.

When understood in this light, the prayer of thanksgiving is not simply a punctual response to events in which we discern the presence and the work of God in our lives. It is the radical attitude of those who open the daily drama of their existence to the action of God, ready to place everything in God's hands so that he can transfigure their death into the birth of a new life. It is for this reason that the last words of Cyprian of Carthage during his martyrdom were "*Deo gratias*" and that before breathing her last breath, Clare of Assisi prayed "Blessed be You, O God, for having created me."

If on the one hand, the prayer of thanksgiving regards the past, what God has done for us, on the other hand, it opens toward the future, to hope. And all of this occurs while we configure the present as a peculiar dimension in which we can live our lives as Christians. Christ, in his wisdom, condensed all of this into the prayer that he delivered to Christians for the beginning of the day: "I adore You, my God, and I thank You for having created me, for having made me a Christian and preserved me this day." This is the goal of prayer: *agápe*, love that pushes us to live and to confess with all of our being that every day, until the day we die, is for us a gift of love from God.

Chapter Two:
THE TRADITION OF PRAYER

Anna Maria Cànopi

Article 1:
AT THE WELLSPRINGS OF PRAYER

It was a wise choice to dedicate the entire fourth part—the conclusion—of the *CCC* to prayer in the Christian life, therefore emphasizing that the Christian "doctrine" which was laid out and explained in the previous parts is not a rigorous code of rights and prohibitions but rather a guide for knowing the Lord in a deeper way in order to arrive at a dialogue of love: communion with God.

But what is prayer? And how do we pray? Before answering these questions, the *CCC* cites a beautiful quote by Saint Therese of Lisieux, according to whom prayer is "a surge of the heart; it is a simple look turned toward heaven, it is a cry of recognition and of love, embracing both trial and joy." These are words that are echoed and confirmed in many other texts by ancient and modern authors: prayer is the desire of the heart, the breath of the soul, and light in the darkness.

Prayer is essential for human life, as necessary as daily bread or air. Due to its very nature, it is first and foremost a gift from God to man. The great prayerful figures of the old and new covenant demonstrate this in an eloquent manner, from Moses to Jesus's disciples, who humbly ask their Master, "Lord, teach us how to pray…" (Lk 11:1).

After this overview of prayer, the second chapter—dedicated to the "Tradition of Prayer"—begins with two strong negative statements that counterbalance the positive statements that get to the heart of the experience of prayer.

Although prayer is "a surge of the heart," this surge is not a spontaneous emotion, which is connected to contingent factors that turn on in one moment and off in another. It is not sentimentalism or a search for esoteric experiences, but rather the result of a deliberate action: "In order to pray, one must have the will to pray" (*CCC* 2650). What does it mean to have the will to pray? Having the will to pray is certainly not a voluntary action, as if prayer depended on the strength of our will. Rather, it is an education of our will which leaves space for the Holy Spirit, stopping to listen to its "groans that cannot be put into words" (cf. Rom 8). Prayer, therefore, becomes a requirement of the heart, which wishes to enter into dialogue with God, who is sought out and loved above all things.

For this reason—here comes the second negative statement—prayer cannot be a technique learned from books or a mechanical repetition of words that have already been written: "Nor is it enough to know what the Scriptures reveal about prayer" (*CCC* 2650).

Between these two opposite risks—that of emotional sentimentalism and that of rigid intellectualism—authentic prayer travels the path of humble, active learning. "One must learn how to pray," like children learn to call their mothers and fathers, learn how to ask them for what they need, to thank them for what they receive, and express the simple joy of spending time with them.

"Through a living transmission (Sacred Tradition) within 'the believing and praying Church' (*DV* 8), The Holy Spirit teaches the children of God how to pray" (n. 2650). This is the Tradition!

There is an alphabet, a language of prayer that—if one is lucky enough to be born into a Christian family—one absorbs right from childhood and learns in a familiar environment, almost breathing an atmosphere of prayer consisting of words and gestures. These early experiences with prayer then grow in the arms of the Mother Church through participation in the sacred functions and the solemn celebrations that mark the liturgical year. Think of how many people could testify to this! St. Augustine can speak for everyone. He cried a river of tears—tears of purification—while he listened to the liturgical hymns sung in the church in Milan, which was filled to the brim with Christians who had gathered around their pastor, Saint Ambrose! (cf. *Confessions*, IX, 7, 16).

In praying with "the praying and believing Church," each Christian in turn learns to pray and believe, to deepen his knowledge of the Lord, and to view the events in his personal life and in the history of the universe in light of the Word of God. Like the Virgin Mary, he does not allow himself to be distracted by the many things that surround him but lives collecting and safeguarding the joy and suffering, anguish and hope of the entire world in his heart in order to present them to God in prayer (cf. *CCC* 2651). After receiving grace after grace, he becomes a living testimony of faith, a gushing "fountain" that restores the hearts of other poor men who painstakingly cross the arid deserts of doubt and the arduous paths of history.

Arriving at this level of maturity of faith, to the point where one can support others, is not a task that is reserved for a select few "prayer specialists" but the duty of all Christians because it simply coincides with the universal call to holiness. For this reason, the *CCC* lays out a simple and reliable itinerary which is suitable for everyone and has been carefully consolidated by generations and generations of believers who have walked on the paths of God, attentive to the "suggestions of the Spirit," since the origins of Christianity. In fact, the Holy Spirit is "the living water 'welling up to eternal life' (Jn 4:14) in the heart that prays. It is he who teaches us to accept it at its source: Christ" (n. 2652).

Now Jesus, a pilgrim that travels along the roads of history together with humanity, has particular locations where he likes to stop in order to meet with us in a more forceful manner, almost as if he were repeating the invitation that he gave his disciples: "Come away [...] and rest for a while" (Mk 6:31). These places are like oases in the desert and like fountains where we can restore ourselves before resuming the holy journey of life (cf. n. 2652).

Lectio Divina

The first preferred meeting place is the Word of God. One stops here not with the competence of an exegetic researcher—who is also a necessary figure—but with the simplicity of a heart that is hungry and thirsty for truth and love. This reading, which is profoundly different from the everyday way of reading books and newspapers, is called *lectio divina*, reading which is "divine" in two ways: first because the book which is read, contemplated, and experienced—the holy Scripture—is the Word of God but also because in *lectio divina*, it is God himself who speaks to the heart of the reader, and the reader, opening himself up to prayer and contemplation, speaks to God and encounters God himself.

It is certainly no coincidence that this way of reading—which must then become a way of living—was born in monasteries, where silence and prayer create an environment that is more favorable for listening to the Word. Each person, however, can create an "internal cell" and live, in a certain way, like a monk, putting God and his Word before all else (cf. nn. 2653–2654). In fact, this kind of concentration is necessary for an authentic life of prayer. On the one hand, *lectio divina* requires it. On the other hand, it promotes it and expands it, filling our souls with peace.

Given that *lectio divina* is a profound spiritual experience, how can it be learned, and how can it be taught? One cannot presume to have a profound experience with God through *lectio divina* without the necessary prerequisites.

The long practice of *lectio divina* in monastic life is characterized by four steps, in accordance to the famous and still valid teaching of Guigo I (twelfth century). The first step is true, proper, attentive "reading" which is done slowly so that the Word can penetrate the person's heart. The second step is "meditation" in order to search for the hidden truths in the word (here, it is recommended that we illuminate one Bible story using other similar Bible stories, or to read the Bible with the Bible). Next comes "prayer," which expresses both penitence for one's inadequacy before the part of the Bible but also the desire to experience it and the humble request for help from God, asking that he give us his grace. Then, almost spontaneously, prayer opens up into "contemplation" because God himself is found in the section read, and he comes to meet the person praying and shows him his face.

Put simply, "reading" involves looking for the sweetness of life blessed by God, "meditation" figures out what it is, "prayer" asks for it, and "contemplation" tastes it.

It is obvious that in practice, this does not happen through four even steps but rather more freely, directed by the unpredictable stimulus of the Holy Spirit, who is the true Teacher of *lectio divina*. Because the Word was written with the inspiration of the Spirit, we must read it, listen to it, and absorb it through the action of the Holy Spirit and in full communion with the Church, where the Spirit is present. Then, while we search, we find, we taste, and we are pushed to search more and to desire more. Because the search never ends. But in searching, we always find an invitation to live the Word and to enter into its "mystery."

Sacred Liturgy and Sanctified Time

The second preferred meeting place for encounters with the Lord is "sacred liturgy," especially Holy Mass and the Liturgy of the Hours. Here, the "mysteries of Christ" are realized, the history of salvation becomes extant, and time changes from a pure flow of hours, days, and years to something sacred with the rhythm of the life of Christ. For the believer, participating in sacred liturgy means becoming steadily more aware that he is one entity with Christ and with his brothers, that he forms one single body, and cooperating in the complete fulfilment of the universal plan of salvation. The Eucharist makes us all "one" in the strongest sense of the word: we become of the same blood and of the same body.

In this way, sacred liturgy is a great school of communion and, moreover, a great laboratory where we are transformed from individuals who pray into people in communion who "live Christ" and make him present "today." For this reason, "time" is very important in liturgy. In a certain sense, we could speak about the "time of liturgy." The more liturgically we live, the more we become aware that "time" flows differently: the hours of the day, the days of the week, and the months of the year take on a color. They take on their own characters, unique and unmistakable, each with a specific spirituality and richness.

The goal of the Liturgy of the Hours is not just remembering God and giving him generic praise or a generic supplication. Rather, it is a realization in time of the work of God that Jesus Christ came to fulfill and continues to fulfill through the Church—his mystic body—until the end of history, until every man can enter into the economy of salvation. The Liturgy of the Hours is truly the "new clock" of the Christian, just like his Paschal life is new.

The "Matins" is characterized by meditative and contemplative listening to the Word that lasts a long time. For this reason, it is particularly effective when it can be celebrated—as is done in monasteries—in the great silence of the night. The night is revealed as the mother's womb from which all the other Hours are born. It prepares the heart to accept the new day in grace.

The "Lauds"—which take place at dawn—remind us of the resurrection of Christ. They also express God's gifts of time, thoughts, and the emotions of the human heart. The "Vespers"—which take place at dusk—commemorate the Last Supper and the Lord's death and burial. Through the Vespers, what we have lived during the day is presented to God as a *sacrificium vespertinum* and we ask for forgiveness for our sins, which are due to human fragility. The Hours of "Terce, Sext, and None"—or more generally, the Daytime Prayer—are short restorative pauses during the course of our everyday journey. When they are celebrated individually, they also recall the life of Christ and of the Church: the descent of the Spirit, the agony of Jesus on the cross, and his death. "Compline" concludes the day and introduces the silence of the night, pacifying our hearts—with an examination of our conscience—and orients us toward serene rest under the maternal protection of the holy Virgin, who is tenderly invoked in the final antiphon of the Hour and of the day.

In this way, the voice of *Christus totus*, of Christ and his Church, after pronouncing the hours of light through song, is concentrated in our hearts and pronounces the hours of the night, as well, with the rhythm of silence, keeping the lamp burning while awaiting the dawn of the new day. This internal dimension, however, is not and must not be extraneous to any moment of the day. Liturgical prayer and *lectio divina* forge an attentive, concentrated man who is able to listen and contemplate. A man whose actions begin in the deepest part of his heart, which is like "an altar" (n. 2655).

Like the day, the "week" has a specific structure when lived according to the rhythm of the Liturgy of the Hours, and each day is like a note in a musical scale. "Sunday"—"the day of the Lord," the "first" day of the week—renews the grace of the day of the resurrection. What makes Sunday joyous and holy is gathering together to separate the "Passover of the Lord," making the reality of being a Church, a community of redeemed people, a community of friends in the Lord, visible. The secularization of our time makes it difficult to acquire and protect the feeling of the "day of the Lord." In this regard, all of the most recent popes have emphasized Sunday's importance as a Christian holiday that should be spent together multiple times and in various ways. "The disciples of Christ, however, are asked to avoid any confusion between the celebration of Sunday, which should truly be a way of keeping the Lord's Day holy, and the 'weekend,' understood as a time of simple rest and relaxation. This will require a genuine spiritual maturity, which will enable Christians to 'be what they are,' in full accordance with the gift of faith, always ready to give an account of the hope which is in them (cf. 1 Pt 3:15)" (St. John Paul II, *Dies Domini*, n. 4).

This requires paying attention to the formation of a more correct conception regarding the use of time. We must remember that "sanctifying holidays" means remembering that we belong to the Lord and must give our time first to him in gratitude. In life, we need holidays in order to also experience workdays properly.

The other days of the week are born from Sunday. In the first days, we could say that we relive the time of Christ's public mission. In letting ourselves be guided by the wise choice of psalms—the heart of the Liturgy of the hours, where we listen to the voice of Christ himself—it is not difficult to determine that "Monday" is characterized by looking at God's creative work, "Tuesday" has a markedly wise nature, and "Wednesday" is a song about faith in God, who patiently guides man along the paths of the history of salvation. The later days of the week, then, are a "Paschal triduum" in miniature, which should be experienced in full participation in the passion and death of Christ and while looking toward Sunday. In this way, all of time becomes a continuous immersion in Christ, and we grow with him until the end of time.

Days and weeks are precious fragments of the "liturgical year," which, like the calendar year, has its seasons and its "times." In the time of Advent and Christmas, we relive the mystery of waiting for the Messiah and for the incarnation of the Word until the moment when his mission of announcing the kingdom of God, of the Gospel of salvation, arrives. The pinnacle of the year occurs during the intense periods of Lent and Easter, when we relive the passion, death, and resurrection of Christ, the full manifestation of God's love for man. By looking to the one who is selfless Love personified, the believer enters into the dynamism of the Spirit, who pushes him toward the gift of himself. This is the meaning and the value of the long succession of weeks that is called "ordinary time": the time of the Spirit, the time for "living Christ" in everyday life, bearing witness to the Gospel "today."

"Today"

The *CCC* devotes considerable attention to "today" because it is the "lever of Archimedes" for living a holy life (cf. nn. 2659–2660). For the Christian, in fact, time has been freed from its fleeting and tragic nature because he who is the Lord of time—the Christ of yesterday, today, and forever (cf. Heb 13:8)—has entered into it and remained there. He has come to direct the entire history of man toward the kingdom of God.

Living means setting out toward our heavenly homeland, and life is a "path" that must be traveled, or rather, a person that must be followed: Jesus, who personally invites us to follow him, saying "If anyone wants to be a follower of mine, let him renounce himself and take up his cross every day and follow me" (Lk 9:23). Each day brings the possibility of new salvation for everyone.

The sacred Scripture is full of references to this "today" of salvation, which involves us and helps us discover the value of our lives.

It is no coincidence that the Liturgy of the Hours opens with the invitatory Psalm, Psalm 95 (94), which has the following verse at its center: "*Hodie, si vocem eius audieritis, nolite obdurare corda vestra*—If only you would listen to him today! Do not harden your hearts." Actually, it is not enough not to harden our hearts. We must open them, like little Samuel, who did not let a single word of the Lord go unnoticed, or moreover like Mary, who listened to the point where she allowed the Word to be made flesh. This listening in the "today" occurs by living the Lord's Prayer in a concrete manner, confidently abandoning ourselves to Providence, molding "humble, everyday situations" through prayer. "All forms of prayer can be the leaven to which the Lord compares the kingdom" (*CCC* 2660).

This attention given to "today," which the *CCC* correctly emphasizes, reminds us of another very important aspect of the Liturgy of the Hours: its personal value. Although, as we have already stated, this is a school of communion, this does not mean that the person as an individual is erased. Quite the contrary! True communion, in fact, is harmony of individuals. Each person, as a member of Christ, relives the mystery of redemption in him from birth to death. During the vicissitudes of life, each person is able to recognize the characteristics of one mystery or another that becomes flesh through him in a unique way "today." Birth is a Christmas event, suffering is a part of the Passion, reconciliation or the overcoming of a temptation is a new Easter. Each task, each service, each act of charity is a form of conformation to Christ the Sower of Seeds, Christ the Good Samaritan, and Christ the Celestial Doctor. In this sense, all of life is a great Advent, a vigil and laborious wait for Christ's final coming.

Purification of Our Hearts

By pausing in these "places" where we encounter the Lord in faith, the Christian finds himself near a very rich wellspring of grace that can not only quench his thirst but can also render him a channel of grace for other thirsty people. Only, however, if he draws upon it and drinks! In fact, one can die of thirst even when near a source of water. Abandoning this metaphor, it is necessary to listen to the Word and participate in liturgical celebration with the proper disposition of the heart.

The *CCC* touches upon this aspect (nn. 2656–2658) and offers valuable instructions in this regard. Returning to the image of the wellspring, we could summarize the three major steps proposed in the following manner: the Christian sees the spring if he has "faith," he drinks from the spring if he has "hope," and he leaves the spring running if he allows himself to be inspired by "charity." The three theological virtues—"faith, hope, and charity"—are a single but indispensable piece of luggage for the journey of life, which is a journey of prayer because we are all beggars in this world.

The originality of the *CCC* lies in the emphasis placed on the theological virtues, not on ascetic effort. At the root of prayer, and of Christian life, lies the gift of God, which is followed by the answer—positive or negative—of man. Through faith, questions, doubts, and needs do not remain closed in the hearts but become a shout directed at a you, whose willingness to listen and whose goodness is never in doubt. Through hope, the harshness and the darkness of the path and the silence of God do not become insurmountable obstacles but rather are a stimulus because hope moves forward as though it could see the invisible. Through the strength of the "charity" poured into our hearts (cf. Rom 5:5), prayer knocks down every dividing wall and builds bridges, and makes itself everything for everyone.

At this point, it is once again faith that gives us eyes that see the face of Christ in that of our neighbor. It is once again hope that bets on salvation for everyone because it knows that Christ makes himself present even in the deepest depths of the underworld. It is once again charity that pushes the Christian to intercede on behalf of everyone by offering himself. This journey of purification must be made every day without ever tiring because, as St. Benedict says, in fraternal relationships the "thorns of scandal" are apt to spring up (cf. *Regula benedicti*, XIII, 12). These make prayer infecund: "Whatever you do to avenge yourself against a brother who has done you a wrong will prove a stumbling-block to you during prayer.... If you desire to pray as you ought, do not grieve anyone; otherwise you run in vain" (Evagrius Ponticus, *On Prayer*, 13, 20). Humble love, on the other hand, inflames the heart for the good of all. As Symeon the New Theologian confesses, "I saw a man that wanted his brothers to be saved with such fervency that often, from the deepest part of his soul, with tears, he prayed to God either to save them as well or to condemn him along with them. Oh soul full of God that has arrived at supreme perfection in love of God and of neighbor" (*The Catechetical Discourses*, 8, 57–67).

We can hear the echo of Jesus's prayer: "Father, I want those you have given me to be with me where I am… I have made your name known to them and will continue to make it known, so that the love with which you loved me may be in them" (Jn 17:24,26). This is the highest form of prayer that coincides with love.

Article 2:
THE WAY OF PRAYER

"In the living tradition of prayer, each Church proposes to its faithful, according to its historic, social, and cultural context, a language for prayer: words, melodies, gestures, iconography" (*CCC* 2663). In this way, everything becomes part of life, and through active and conscious participation, the individual believers truly experience what is being celebrated, learning to know the Lord through their own inner experience and entering into his love, which forms communion. In this way, liturgy becomes admirable for its ever renewed youthfulness, which allows it to speak to the heart of all people, even as people age and as generations pass. The elements of which it is composed mainly come from the sacred Scripture—psalms, canticles, readings—which are integrated with Patristic, hagiographic, euchological, and poetic texts (hymns, troparions, etc.) which are also inspired by the Bible but at the same time are also expressions of the various cultures that created them.

By entering into liturgy with our whole hearts, open to the gift of the Spirit, Christians find everything that is truly necessary not only for learning how to pray well but also for "becoming prayer"—for praying continuously, without ever tiring, drawing life from prayer. The author of "incessant prayer" is the Holy Spirit. It is he who incessantly invokes "Abbá, Father" in man and gives us the sweetness of feeling that we are God's children. He is our internal Teacher who fills our hearts with the light of Christ. It is he who, if one tries to live in Christ, "awakens" prayer within us as a true experience of "falling in love" with Jesus Christ. Prayer, therefore, is no longer "words stated." It is a name, a face: the name and face of Jesus. It is the appeal of standing before him internally, of looking at him, of listening to him, wherever we find ourselves, whatever we are doing. And being with him means walking with the Father, with a desire for him that grows with every turn: "There is living water in me, which speaks and says inside me, 'Come to the Father'" (Ignatius of Antioch, *Letter to the Romans*, 7, 2).

In this way, prayer becomes an itinerary without breaks, that is never satisfied, that leads us to discover the gratuitousness of the Love that saves us more and more every day. This requires humility, abandon, and asking for forgiveness, as expressed in a sublime manner in the so-called "Jesus prayer": "Lord Jesus Christ, Son of God, have mercy on us sinners" (cf. *CCC* 2666–2667).

When it arrives at this essentiality, prayer also becomes an exceptional ecumenical gathering place. As the Patriarch of Antioch Ignatius IV states, "I think that the name of God can teach us the essence of prayer. The name of God, which is his presence, must cover our entire life. Our prayer is standing in his presence, mentioning his holy name" (*Un amore senza finzioni*, Qiqajon, Magnano 2006, 179–180).

Joy and pain, despair and hope, tears and song: all of these naturally enter into the shout of prayer which becomes steadily simpler: an invocation of the Father, an invocation of Jesus, and an invocation of the Spirit. As Isaac the Syrian says, "When you present yourself before God in prayer, you become like a stammering child" (*Mystic Treatises*, 19). In the most extreme case, even a simple, short prayer is too much. Often, it is silence that summarizes prayer. Sometimes, it is a tear, a "yes," or a "thank you," always said with an attitude of listening and of waiting for our restlessness to be transformed into a patient, trusting willingness. Once again, Patriarch Ignatius IV—who certainly speaks from experience—states, "When the face of God is illuminated within us, we do not say words that we have learned about God, but rather our entire being is born again. We are children of God" (*Un amore senza finzioni*, 181).

This was Jesus's prayer on Earth during the nights he spent in dialogue with the Father. This was also Mary's prayer. She is the human creature in which prayer became life in every aspect of its being. She was the perfect Daughter, Wife, Sister, Mother, humble Servant of the Lord, and then Queen in prayer.

For this reason, it is very important to pray to her, place ourselves under her protection in order to enter into communion with her (cf. *CCC* 2673–2679), and participate, in some way, in her mystery, which is the same mystery of the virgin, wife, and mother Church: "When we pray to her, we are adhering with her to the plan of the Father… The prayer of the Church is sustained by the prayer of Mary and united with it in hope" (n. 2679).

The question posed by the country priest in the famous novel by Bernanos is famous: "And the Blessed Virgin: Do you pray to the Blessed Virgin?… Do you pray to her as you ought? Do you pray well to her?" He then adds, "Do you realize what we are for her, we of the human race? […] The eyes of Our Lady are the only real child-eyes that have ever been raised to our shame and sorrow. Yes, lad, to pray to her as you should you must feel those eyes of hers upon you […] the eyes of gentle pity." Perhaps the secret for rediscovering the value of the presence of the holy Virgin in the Church and in our personal lives lies in realizing not so much "what she is for us" but rather "what we are for her."

The deep and certain intuition of that benevolent love has made antiphons and prayers that are genuine and moving expressions of piety, trust, abandon, and supplication well up from the hearts of believers right from the first generations. The main ones then found their proper place in ecclesiastical worship. Others continue to enhance personal prayer generation after generation. This feeling of trusting abandon certainly reaches its pinnacle in the Ave Maria, which was strictly inspired by the Scripture. Calmly repeated while reciting the holy Rosary, it becomes a sure guide for the contemplation of the mysteries of Christ with the Mother's heart, filling man with peace: "The Rosary has accompanied me in moments of joy and in moments of difficulty. To it I have entrusted any number of concerns; in it I have always found comfort" (St. John Paul II).

Article 3:
GUIDES FOR PRAYER

With this reference to the holy Rosary, we have arrived at the third and final article of this chapter of the *CCC*, which is dedicated to "The Tradition of Prayer." Right from the start, it covers a broad horizon. The reference to the "witnesses in a great cloud" (Heb 12:1) which support us along the path makes our hearts swell. We are pilgrims in this world, but we are not alone. The "communion of the saints" is the ever so sweet mystery of our faith. The communion of the saints is the Church itself, or all of us believers in Christ, gathered by the Holy Spirit—who is Love—to form a single mystic body, a single heart, and a single soul. The Church lives in two dimensions: the terrestrial one and the celestial one. It is a pilgrim on Earth, in time, and progressively enters into the heavens, into eternity, or into the breast of the holy Trinity, which is the mystery of communion. There is no separation between Heaven and Earth because Jesus Christ, through his passion, death, and resurrection, has rejoined humanity to God.

The saints who have already entered eternal life and we who are still traveling toward it form a single Church, a single family of children of God living in loving communion. They intercede for us with God in order to support us along our tiring journey. In this way, they express their charity (*CCC* 2683). By invoking them and following their examples, we can feel our friendship with them grow. And what fruit this friendship bears! It is a preview of blessed life in this world. The blessed Paul VI said, with mystic emphasis, "Oh the communion of saints: that marvelous world! The concept that we try to create for ourselves is like a dream, but the reality goes beyond the pictures of the imagination: it is better, more beautiful, and truer. The kingdom of sainthood is a paradise which is reflected down here but is fully realized up there in the heavens. It is the invigorating splendor of God." He then advised, "A desire invades our souls. It is a very pious desire that should be encouraged, and, where possible, satisfied. It is the love for hagiographic science which should be promoted and cultivated more than it is not now, as once occurred during the spiritual education of the faithful. The book of 'Martyrology' should come back into fashion in the Church" (*Homily* from 10/6/1968).

Our intercessors in the heavens, the saints have left broad and certain footsteps on earth which facilitate our journey. Their witness has given life to various complementary spiritualities and to a rich flowering of religious families and ecclesiastical movements, all of which share in various ways in the "living tradition of prayer and are essential guides for the faithful" (*CCC* 2684). In this way, the form of *sequela Christi* that is "consecrated life," a life given entirely to God for one's brothers, was born and developed in the Church. Its numerous concretizations are like different hues of a single selfless love. The gift of oneself is now expressed as concern for the material needs of the poorest and most abandoned children, as care toward their education, growth, and spiritual formation, as the capacity to listen and advise, or as simple and silent welcoming, woven together with prayer and shared participation. The "service of prayer" is certainly the very heart of consecrated life. Consecrated life is born from prayer and finds its true fecundity in prayer, since it is as much a contemplative life as an active life. As the *CCC* clarifies, consecrated life is "one of the living sources of contemplation and the spiritual life of the Church" (n. 2687).

Familiarity with prayer, with living heart to heart with the Lord, gives souls a deeper capacity for listening to the Spirit. This is why a very valuable service—which is requested increasingly often today—offered by clergy to the people of God is "spiritual guidance," or more accurately, spiritual "fatherhood and motherhood" (n. 2690). This is not a service that only clergy can render, but every spiritual guide must certainly be first and foremost a man or woman of prayer, because souls must first be accompanied by knees (cf. Eph 3:14–19). The secret to spiritual fecundity lies in prayer: life is transmitted not thorough discourses made of words but through a transfusion of the Holy Spirit from heart to heart, consummating itself in the silence of love.

Another valuable service provided by those living in consecrated life, and in particular by those who are monks, regarding the life of prayer of the people of God is the simple "welcoming and hospitable presence": the act of being a restorative oasis for people who wish to pause to pray. The environment of the monastery, with its prayerful silence, in fact favors listening to the Word of God, liturgical and personal prayer, and reflection and contemplation. In this environment, many can also find a consoling and peaceful resting place for their anguished souls, a place where they can lay down their anxieties and uncertainties. And not only a momentary resting place but a constant one, because welcoming always occurs in the heart.

Then again, "family life" can take inspiration and receive support for being what it was called to be, a domestic church and "the first place of education in prayer" (n. 2685), from monastic life. Today, families that wish to remain Christian must resist strong temptations that come from the world around them. For this reason, "prayer" is a necessity. Prayers made in the very heart of the family and prayers made by the entire Christian community for the family. The experience of praying together as a family, in addition to being healthy, is very beautiful. Praying together, in fact, means inviting the Lord into our house, and the Lord, with his presence, nourishes our love for one another and reinforces the bonds between us. God's collaborators, parents are entrusted with the highly delicate mission of the human and spiritual education of their children, from their first cries until they are grown up and even after they have grown up, because the task of being a father or mother is never complete. Even during pregnancy, a mother who prays often has already started to educate her child as a Christian.

We will conclude with an excerpt from a wonderful letter written by a Christian mother to her daughter in a moment of mental turmoil. "My dear Enrichetta," the blessed Maria Beltrame Quattrocchi writes, "make your life perennial praise of God. Make Jesus known through your soul. Be a monstrance, a particle of the Eucharist that gives itself like Jesus gave himself to us, without reservations. Be a Host of praise and love" (April 1924). How did Enrichetta answer the letter? Her answer was a life woven with prayer and zeal in charity until she died with an odor of sanctity.

Chapter Three:

THE LIFE OF PRAYER

Michael Schneider

The grace of the Christian vocation depends on prayer: "Prayer is the life of the new heart" (*CCC* 2697). Without prayer, there is no life with God, nor can there be service of humanity (n. 2744), "for cut off from me you can do nothing" (Jn 15:5). Even though it can be the most difficult thing to practice in life with God, it is as necessary as the air we breathe. For this reason, we are advised to "pray constantly; and for all things give thanks; this is the will of God for you in Christ Jesus" (1 Thess 5:17). Praying is not an art that the Christian grabs onto, it is "only" the act of answering He who has already prayed in him and worked through him for a long time.

The difficulty of prayer cannot be eliminated. It remains for our entire lives. For this reason, prayer cannot be left to chance, and we cannot pray from time to time (*CCC* 2743). Prayer requires order (n. 2742), especially the order of silence and isolation, because it is not possible or equally feasible under all conditions. This is especially true for people who, since they must live in this world, ask themselves how they can find the way of prayer and practice it while immersed in everyday life in faith (nn. 2697–2699).

Article 1:
EXPRESSIONS OF PRAYER

Because life and prayer are one and the same, we do not learn to pray simply by acquiring prayer methods and devotional books but rather by being willing to join, to "convert" our entire lives to God. Prayer is not an imposition on the course of a day or a spiritual technique but rather an expression of our lives, which are dedicated to God. In this way, prayer and life feed off each other and deepen each other: the desire to do God's will pushes us toward prayer and prayer deepens our understanding of God's will (*CCC* 2700). As

Saint Augustine notes, "For the desire of your heart is itself your prayer. And if the desire is constant, so is your prayer." (*En. in ps.* 37, 14).

Prayer becomes deeper as man orients himself ever more in accordance with God in all aspects and actions in his life. In order to progress in prayer and to be able to experience closeness with God, therefore, the Christian must bring his entire life into exterior and interior order, day by day (this is the reason why monks live their lives according to a "rule"). The way that man lives with his neighbors—whether he falls into envy, ire, or avarice; whether he says everything that comes to mind—is not unrelated to prayer. The way that he sleeps, the way that he eats, and the way that he rests are not unrelated to prayer. First and foremost, sin is the main impediment to prayer because it separates man from God and makes him blind.

The order of prayer obtains the criteria that determine how to pray and what to pray for from everyday life. According to Origen, this is because "small prayer," which is represented by individual prayers, should be an expression of the "great prayer," our entire lives, and it is important to choose prayers that are proper and suitable for our own lives. We must not "release" every prayer that comes to us but rather pronounce the prayers that are expressions of existence and of the momentary situation. All prayers in which the person praying wishes to "gain understanding" fall into this category: these are "prayers of request." If the person praying tells God, "Do what you wish with me!" he may not yet have achieved an attitude of complete self-denial, but he can still make the "request" to understand himself better. Growth in prayer consists of encountering God in the simplest, most natural, and therefore more profound way possible. In this way, prayer is a "means," not an end. The ultimate and decisive measure of vocal prayer is whether it is able to open the person's life to God and bring him closer to him.

Some important aids for configuring prayer in one's everyday life are derived from the internal unity between prayer and life and between "small" and "great" prayer. In terms of how one prays, the proper method to choose is the one that helps the person experience the presence of God more intensely. This is the purpose behind the spiritual practices that Ignatius of Loyola describes in the following way in the book *Spiritual Exercises*: "For as strolling, walking and running are bodily exercises, so every way of preparing and disposing the soul to rid itself of all the disordered tendencies, and, after it is rid, to seek and find the Divine Will as to the management of one's life for the salvation of the soul, is called a Spiritual Exercise" (*Spiritual Exercises*, n. 1).

Spiritual exercises are more than the simple execution of a spiritual plan. The exercise of prayer is not explained as an obligation that must be fulfilled but based on the premise that a given spiritual exercise leads to good experiences: joy, freedom, consolation, and new life. Spiritual exercise, therefore, is an act of the hope that similar, new, and positive experiences can be repeated and experienced more deeply. On the other hand, we must not insist on exercises that are performed under pressure from authority or due to a feeling of obligation (cf. *CCC* 2707).

Prayer is useful to the extent to which the person is willing to serve others and does not look toward his own "interests" (1 Cor 13:5: "Love…never seeks its own advantage") but sees that everything that God gives him must be for others, where he intends to find God, knowing that behind others is Christ, who gave his life for others. By discovering the face of God in his neighbors, the supplicant recognizes this as the result of his prayer and his prayer is in turn nourished by it. The experiential path of spiritual exercise is built on experiences (one's own and the ones passed down through the tradition of the Church) which have already been had and recalls the desire for experiential growth. The fundamental rule of not overdoing things but rather of making use of all the means and opportunities that push us to take additional steps on the way of joy in faith holds for this path. In this regard, the *CCC* (nn. 2700–2724) distinguishes between three forms of prayer: "vocal" prayer, "meditation," and "contemplative" prayer.

I. Vocal Prayer

The words of prayer are an "anchor of salvation," a fixed point in the often impetuous current of life (cf. *CCC* 2700). This especially true for prayers of the heart, which are said internally while following the rhythm of our breath: "Lord Jesus Christ, son of the living God, have mercy on me!" Because Christian prayer comes from the ardent desire of our hearts, prayer that first and foremost makes us desire God and express our feelings becomes healthy. There is no need for over the top sentimental affection or long and exhausting prayers. A short prayer, an exclamation, repeated throughout the day, is enough. These vocal formulas help us resist temptations, bring the spirit back to the quiet and away from all distractions, and to keep it in the presence of God.

The following example, taken from everyday life, demonstrates the strength of these exclamations. If the wife of a man who lives in a family and has an exhausting job that results in him coming home very tired sometimes asks him "Do you love me?" the answer that she would be given is, "Yes, of course!" If his wife continues to press, asking "But do you truly love me, even in this very moment?" the man would have to honestly admit, "No, right now I do not feel anything except from the pain in my back and my very tired body." But the man is right when he says that he loves her because he knows that despite his exhaustion, his love for her remains alive. It is in this sense that vocal prayers are irreplaceable, even for people who have already progressed in prayer (n. 2704: "Even interior prayer, however, cannot neglect vocal prayer").

Jesus himself teaches us vocal prayer. He, the beloved Son of the Father, in teaching us the Lord's Prayer prays both as God and as a man. Here, vocal prayer is no longer only a matter between man and God but rather a prayer of God directed at God. In intra-triune "prayer," in fact, each divine person prays to the other for the realization of their common will. Christ also made his disciples participants in this reciprocal adoration of the three divine persons: "I have given them the glory you gave to me, that they may be one as we are one. With me in them and you in me, may they be so perfected in unity that the world will recognise that it was you who sent me and that you have loved them as you have loved me" (Jn 17:22–23).

No man has ever prayed like Jesus. In him, prayer reaches its most perfect form and its meaning is fulfilled. In prayer, the supplicant takes part in what is God himself, precisely due to the Holy Spirit that the Risen Christ promised to those who believe in him. This Spirit leads the supplicant to a more intimate union with the Risen Christ. Christian prayer, therefore, is characterized by its triune fulfillment.

II. Meditation

The *CCC* refers to various methods and means of meditation: "We are usually helped by books, and Christians do not want for them: the Sacred Scriptures, particularly the Gospels, holy icons, liturgical texts of the day or season, writings of the spiritual fathers, works of spirituality, the great book of creation, and that of history the page on which the 'today' of God is written" (n. 2705).

In fact, everything in this world, since it has been designed and created in God, can become an object of prayer. Christian prayer does not therefore occur in an abstract manner, separated from the Earthly realities of human life, which only reach fulfillment in Christ.

In the spiritual tradition of the Church, a practice of prayer which is very useful for one's spiritual journey is recommended primarily: spiritual reading, or *lectio divina*. The Latin word *lectio* is not an unambiguous concept: it can mean the act of reading or the text read. The term *lectio divina* should be understood in the second sense: the text inspired by God, the sacred Scripture.

For the Fathers, the study of the Bible (*vacare lectioni* = dedicating oneself to the lesson) and encounters with God (*vacare Deo* = dedicating oneself to God) are two parts of the same whole. He who is free from Earthly preoccupations and is open to the Word of the sacred Scripture is internally free and open to God, because he who opens the Bible finds God in the words of the sacred Scripture. The supplicant, in fact, does not seek solitude as a goal in and of itself. Isolation and silence are not only moments of emptiness and of nirvana but rather prepare the supplicant for an encounter with God. Instead of looking to himself, the believer searches for openness to the call of God in solitude, and he achieves it through reading the sacred Scripture. Gregory the Great advises the supplicant to "bare (scoperchia) your heart to the Word of God" (Eph 4, 31).

Many spiritual writers have recognized the value of *lectio divina* as everyday nourishment for spiritual life. As mentioned previously, the expression *lectio divina* did not originally refer to the act of reading but rather the thing that was read, or the text itself. It was a synonym for "sacred scripture" ("sacred page"). The adjective *divina* referred to something that "comes from God." Until Medieval times, *lectio divina* was none other than study of the sacred Scripture, which was a part of everyday life and oriented toward the "experience of God." By meditating on a sacred text, the reader is touched by God in such a strong manner that his thoughts and words turn off and are directed to a profound silence by God because no one can appropriate God.

But the principle that the supplicant should not be passive, as though he were simply waiting for something, remaining an extraneous observer, also holds for the other forms of meditation which the *CCC* adopts. Rather, there should be a reciprocal permeation between the Word of God and man's answer that must make both God and the supplicant interact equally and make each move toward the other. In feeling and contemplating the Lord, the silent supplicant protects and meditates on the Word of God in his heart (cf. Lk 2:19) so that his life will participate in the mystery of the Lord (*CCC* 2724).

III. Contemplative Prayer

Contemplative prayer leads to joy and to the gift of steadfast hope through the Lord, who "is near" (Phil 4:5). In this way, prayer with the psalmist becomes praise of God: "My heart and my body cry out for joy to the living God" (Ps 84:3). To the extent to which the supplicant joints himself intimately to the prayer of Jesus Christ, contemplative prayer makes him participate in life with God: "The mystery of Christ is celebrated by the Church in the Eucharist, and the Holy Spirit makes it come alive in contemplative prayer so that our charity will manifest it in our acts" (*CCC* 2718). Participation in the prayer of Jesus is the prerequisite for knowing and understanding the person of Jesus, but each piece of knowledge also requires conformity (*adaequatio*) between the person who knows and the person who is known. Therefore, he who participates in the prayer of Jesus Christ is in communion with him, just like the Church and the Eucharist are born from the prayer of Jesus.

The Christian does not work alongside or outside of Christ but rather always works as a member of his body which is moved by its head. In this way, the affirmation of the Apostle—"it is no longer I, but Christ living in me" (Gal 2:20)—is transformed through contemplative experience: "I no longer work, but Christ works through me." Here, the Christian recognizes the greatness and dignity before God to which he has been called through the gift of baptismal grace.

But our hearts do not always rejoice in the closeness of God. When we feel God's absence and our separation from Him, all attempts to revive our joy fail. The living and intimate God can no longer be seen. He appears dead. Even while rereading the sacred Scripture, to the person praying, he seems mute. He no longer tells him anything. Moreover, the moment of silence and gathering becomes irritating and unproductive. Even the celebration of the Eucharist leaves him indifferent, and the words of God seem to be flavorless or bitter and do not communicate anything about the goodness and the love of God (*CCC* 2710; 2717–2718).

This period of darkness can last a long time (it accompanied Therese of Lisieux until her death) and can be of varying intensity depending on the spiritual state of the person. The life of the saints demonstrates that the closer someone is to God, the more he is blinded by the divine super-light. In this situation of darkness, the Christian feels that the impulse to pray does not come from him, but rather from the prayer of another that he himself cannot understand. However, this prayer contains a glimpse of him because the other has lived and prayed through him for a long time.

In the ninth rule of "knowing…the movements which are caused in the soul," Ignatius of Loyola recognizes three major reasons why Christians undergo times of darkness and "desolation." "The first is, because of our being tepid, lazy or negligent in our spiritual exercises; and so through our faults, spiritual consolation withdraws from us. The second, to try us and see how much we are and how much we let ourselves out in His service and praise without such great pay of consolation and great graces. The third, to give us true acquaintance and knowledge, that we may interiorly feel that it is not ours to get or keep great devotion, intense love, tears, or any other spiritual consolation, but that all is the gift and grace of God our Lord…" (*Spiritual Exercises*, n. 322; cf. also *CCC* 2710–2715; 2756–2733).

In times of trial for the supplicant, if he resists and keeps his gaze fixed on Jesus, he gains a "pure heart." The goal of prayer is not so much that God understands what the supplicant asks him but rather that the supplicant understands what God wants from him. Prayer, in this sense, also always requires a radical conversation, just like how "Christ did not indulge his own feelings, either" (Rom 15:3), behaving as though he "[had] nothing, and yet [owned] everything" (cf. 2 Cor 6:6–10).

Article 2: THE BATTLE OF PRAYER

Sometimes, someone is able to pray because he has found the proper place for prayer. This means that one should avoid frequently changing where he prays due to the positive influence that the place can have. Praying alone in my room or in a church and praying in the first pew or "some distance away" (cf. Lk 18:13) are different experiences.

There are various configurations for internal silence, which is a fundamental prerequisite for prayer: remaining in silence or reciting the Rosary, Jesus's prayer, or the Liturgy of the Hours. What is important is that we regularly "enter" into practice of the exercise, starting from whether we feel fervor in any given moment (*CCC* 2742). The repetition of prayers favors "continuous prayer": "Some [rhythms] are daily, such as morning and evening prayer, grace before and after meals, the Liturgy of the Hours. Sundays, centered on the Eucharist, are kept holy primarily by prayer. The cycle of the liturgical year and its great feasts are also basic rhythms of the Christian's life of prayer" (n. 2698).

The person who leads an unsettled and disordered everyday life will find the same feeling of being unsettled during prayer. Therefore, people who are frequently distracted and not concentrated during prayer should try to be more collected during everyday tasks, as well: order in everyday life leads to collected prayer (n. 2709). If thoughts and passions serve as obstacles to prayer, the only thing to do is to stop prayer momentarily in order to tend to the distractions first.

A great challenge in people's spiritual journeys are periods of crisis of faith, especially if they are also marked by "boredom" or "nausea." Each believer must go through the experience of *akedía* (*lethargy*), as the tradition calls it. This does not only lead to neglecting spiritual practice but rather represents a global crisis that makes it almost impossible to believe, pray, and put up with life. Desolation and despair, which can last for long periods of time, add to this and may push the believer to an existential decision that calls everything into question (*CCC* 2732–2733).

However, the person who prays and contemplates the Lord "incessantly" frees himself from himself and experiences a transformation that is the work of God: "And all of us, with our unveiled faces like mirrors reflecting the glory of the Lord, are being transformed into the image that we reflect in brighter and brighter glory; this is the working of the Lord who is the Spirit" (*2 Cor* 3:18). A profound transformation takes place in the supplicant, who is so fixated on the Lord, that he would not be able to achieve through his own (ascetic) strength (*CCC* 2739).

The *CCC*'s expositions (nn. 2746–2751) on prayer conclude with a reference to "sacerdotal prayer" (an expression coined by the Lutheran theologian David Chytraeus). "Our high priest who prays for us is also the one who prays in us and the God who hears our prayer" (n. 2749). Jesus Christ presents himself as a true high priest, who on the day of his expiatory crucifixion, brings true expiation and reconciliation to the whole world for all of time. This is because he prepares his body for the only true temple: "And that is why he said, on coming into the world: You wanted no sacrifice or cereal offering, but you gave me a body" (Heb 10:5). In his "hour" (cf. Jn 17:3, 6–10, 25) before his saving death, Jesus Christ consecrates himself for his apostles and gives his own sanctification to his people and to the entire world: "Finally, in this prayer Jesus reveals and gives to us the 'knowledge,' inseparably one, of the Father and of the Son, which is the very mystery of the life of prayer" (*CCC* 2751).

The Christian must dedicate himself first and foremost to the school of liturgy, where he can recognize the presence of the true mediator of God, the eternal high priest who intercedes incessantly for his people before the throne of grace of his Father, in an unsurpassable manner. In the Eucharistic celebration, the supplicant finds the strength to resist apparent alienations and distancing from God with ardent prayer, in profound silence and perhaps in great solitude. In prayer, what man is waiting for is realized. Liturgical prayers also end with the words "in Christ our Lord," since he is the origin of the faith on which each hope is founded. Through the Lord's Prayer, which he taught us, he guides us in the concrete practice of Christian hope. He who instead loses hope is no longer able to pray precisely because he no longer hopes. Only people who are convinced that there is something "above everything" can "enter" into prayer. People who pray learn to hope…and to live. During his life, the Christian tries to dedicate himself ever more completely to prayer so that in the hour of his death, he can "lose" his life for eternity in the person who has always been the most intimate being for him, even more intimate than himself. At this point, he will be transformed for eternity in the prayer in which was started and whose praise will never end. We do not need to have or recite a prayer, but rather become and be prayer incarnate. At that point, our whole lives will be an incessant liturgy: "I shall sing to Yahweh all my life, make music for my God as long as I live" (Ps 104:33).

Section Two

THE LORD'S PRAYER: "OUR FATHER"

THE LORD'S PRAYER

Ugo Vanni

I. Introduction

The *CCC*'s comments on the Lord's Prayer (nn. 2759–2865) present a large amount of material that, on the first reading, can even leave the reader perplexed. There are numerous Biblical references that extend throughout the entire New Testament, and many Old Testament antecedents are revisited. Most of all, the Lord's Prayer is reconsidered with references to the liturgy of the early Church, the patristic tradition, and to today's modernizations.

How can we orient ourselves within this lush abundance of material?

Since the Lord's Prayer was born from and formed by the experience of the early church, it may be illuminating to revisit its origin and its initial development. This is what we propose here, but allow us to further clarify what we mean.

At the beginning of the second century, we find that the "Lord's Prayer" was already in use in a formula that corresponds to the current one in the liturgy of the early Church (cf. *Didaché*, 8, 3), when the "quadriform" Gospel was also beginning to be read—that is, the Gospel according to Mark, Matthew, Luke, and John. The simultaneity of the use of the Lord's Prayer and the reading of the four Gospels is telling. It constitutes the arrival point of the development of a multifaceted Tradition that was developed within the context of various histories and tensions—just think of the tensions within the churches of Paul and John—and which culminates over the course of the second century in what was known as the "Great Church."

What was the path that the Lord's Prayer took in the merged tradition of the Great Chruch? More specifically, since the Lord's Prayer was seen as the synthesis of all of the Gospel (Tertullian), what is its specific relationship with the "quadriform Gospel"?

An answer to this question will allow us to, on the one hand, gradually identify the theological-biblical backbone of the Lord's Prayer and also to situate it within the living environment of the early Church.

We will establish a frame of reference in which we can situate and organize the material provided by the *CCC*. We will then examine, consequently, with regard to the Lord's Prayer, first all the antecedents of Mark, then Matthew's systematic presentation, Paul's push forward, Luke's accentuation, and finally, the mature synthesis found in John.

II. The Antecedents of Mark

We will start with the Gospel of Mark, which is also called the "Gospel of the Catechumen" because it is particularly suitable for Christian initiation. The "Twelve" go through a journey of faith whose main steps coincide with the steps developed in the text of the Gospel (cf C.M. Martini, *L'itinerario spirituale dei dodici nel Vangelo di Marco*, Borla, Rome 1976). This propaedeutic dimension of the Gospel of Mark that we have extrapolated from an internal analysis is confirmed by the Gospel's position within the context of the synoptic tradition. Mark is normally considered to be the first Gospel, and the material provided is included practically in its entirety in the other two synoptic Gospels. Therefore, there is a certain precedence that is also chronological, and this, together with the echo of the Petrine catechesis that can be identified in the Gospel of Mark, confirms the initiatory character of the text.

What information can we find in the Gospel of Mark regarding the Lord's Prayer? As we know, liturgical formulas can only be found in Matthew and Luke. In Mark, however, a few hints can be identified that manifestly pave the way for it and are telling.

The disciples are gradually introduced to prayer. They are pushed to address God with as much trust and confidence as possible (cf. Mk 11:22–24). They are advised to expect everything from God, as if when they asked they had already obtained it (cf. Mk 11:24). Living with Jesus and the act of "being with him" that is typical of the Gospel of Mark (cf. K. Stock, *Boten aus dem Mit-Ihm-Sein. Das Verhältnis zwischen Jesus und die Zwölf nach Markus*, Biblical Institute Press, Rome 1975) gradually lead the disciples toward the need for the Father and, we could say, prepares the space to welcome him.

First of all, this space is composed of forgiveness, which disciples must give others before praying: "And when you stand in prayer, forgive whatever you have against anybody, so your Father in heaven may forgive your failings too" (Mk 11:25). This is the only time that the Gospel of Mark explicitly talks about God as the Father of the disciples. This constitutes an arrival point in a journey in which the disciples, in direct contact with Jesus, have learned to have a deeper relationship with God, and only at the end of the journey is God understood as the Father. God's paternity is an element that is never taken for granted.

We can also observe a gradual manifestation of Jesus's relationship with his Father in the Gospel of Mark. Two explicit references are made, but they are made in the third person. Jesus, while discussing the "Son of man" and using the expression to refer to himself, mentions the "glory of his Father" (Mk 8:38). In terms of the day and the time when the story will conclude, no one knows anything "but the Father" (Mk 13:32).

The disciples must have been particularly struck when Jesus, at the apex of his interior passion at Gethsemane, asked God that his will be done as the most supreme gift, therefore fulfilling the truth of prayer for all of time. During this particularly dramatic predicament, the disciples are surprised to notice that Jesus addresses God by calling him Father and using words of familiar affection. They were struck by the use of the Aramaic word *'abbâ*: it is the invocation, made in confidence and with understanding, that children use to address their fathers within family life. And it is the only time that we encounter the term in the Gospels.

While living with Jesus and listening to him speak, the disciples gradually learn that God has made an offer that has to do with them: the offer is made concrete through a Jesus who is full of surprises and who seems to be the bearer of a kingdom that, upon final analysis, corresponds to him. It is the "Kingdom of God."

In their interactions with Jesus, the disciples are repeatedly invited to entrust their earthly concerns to him and to God. These concerns are concentrated in the bread, the symbol of what is necessary for living life. In Mark, there is a section which is marked by bread (cf. Mk 6:30–8:29) where the disciples, when confronted with Jesus's multiplication of the bread, are invited to look deeper and to understand: "Do you still not understand, still not realise? [...] Do you still not realise?" (Mk 8:17,21). What the disciples are urged to understand is full willingness and trusting reliance on the Father who, through Jesus, gives his time and, in great abundance, the bread which is necessary for life. What must be gradually understood is that Jesus is indispensable not only for life in terms of religion but also simply for life itself. Jesus cannot be fully understood if not in relationship to life, and life appears deficient, risky, and even uncertain without the nourishing presence of Jesus.

The familiarity with Jesus that the disciples gradually acquire also puts them into a unique kind of contact with each other. They have to understand each other, love each other, and forgive each other like Jesus knows how to do for them (cf. Mk 11:25).

Finally, right from the beginning of Jesus's ministry in Capernaum, the disciples come into contact with evil (cf. Mk 1:23–26,34,39, etc.). The roots of evil are in a certain sense transcendent, demoniac, and they are manifested in all the forms of suffering that damage the integrity of physical life. They add up to a presence, which is particularly disconcerting, of the devil in the human world. Jesus bitterly reprimands the filthy spirits that reveal his identity: it is up to Jesus himself to gradually declare and make people understand his true reality. But the reaction of evil—here, we could also say of "wickedness"—before Jesus is typical. It cannot coexist with Jesus. Evil and wickedness cannot withstand his presence. By trusting in Jesus completely, the disciples learn to overcome these mysterious forces that undermine human life.

These observations that we are making are distributed throughout the entire Gospel of Mark. When the disciples have absorbed all of these values, their prayer will spontaneously express them. At that point, they will learn to address God as their Father, to wish for the fulfillment of his kingdom, to trust in his will like Jesus did, to love each other, and to overcome the negativity of wickedness. In this way, a complete framework of the essential elements for Christian life that emerge from the Gospel of Mark is formed. These elements correspond precisely to the formula of the Lord's Prayer. For this reason, we can say that they pave the way for it and help us understand its meaning and function.

III. Matthew's Complete Formula

The liturgical text used in the Lord's Prayer uses the formula found in the Gospel of Matthew (Mt 6:9–13) which forms part of the great Sermon on the Mount (Mt 5–7). In order to fully understand the formula, one must first and foremost pay attention to the context, then to the text that expresses it, and finally to the implications that it contains and that are then expanded upon elsewhere in the Gospel of Matthew.

III/1. The context of the Lord's Prayer is the Sermon on the Mount. And this fact is in and of itself telling. The sermon represents a relatively complete program for Christian practice based on the initial beatitudes (Mt 5:3–11).

These represent the value judgments that Jesus makes about man's fundamental choices and about aspects of his life that are more or less valid. For three entire chapters, these basic choices are expanded upon, placed in greater detail, and applied to various situations. One of the concrete situations to which they are applied most precisely is typical Christian prayer. This does not have the extroverted, horizontal attitude that was sometimes a flaw in Judaic—and not only Judaic—prayer at the time. Jesus insists that prayer is directed at the "Father who sees all that is done in secret" (Mt 6:1, particularly 6:5–6). Christian prayer appears to be like a dialogue characterized by an intense filial intimacy that occurs between the Christian and God. Because this is an intersubjective dialogue, the Christian and God understand each other immediately. It is not necessary to use lots of words, like, as is explicitly noted, "the gentiles do" (Mt 6:7). Probably, in the ecclesiastical community in Matthew, there was a tendency to be verbose, and this must also have been reflected in prayer. Instead, the relationship between a Christian and the Father is bare, essential, like deep sea fishing.

The Lord's Prayer is situated in this specific context.

Its context characterizes it as an exquisitely Christian prayer that emerges from the heart of man and tends to arrive at, so to speak, the heart of God. With this essentialness, this profundity, and this openness that cannot always be conceptualized that characterize a mature relationship with the Father.

III/2. We can see how characteristic Christian prayer is articulated when we look more closely. Presentations of what has been called the Lord's Prayer can be found in Matthew (6:9–13) and Luke (11:2–4). The differences cannot be traced back to distinct models. The two versions are based on the so called "Q source" (cf. F. Neyring, *Q-Synopsis*, Peeters, Leuven 1988, 30–31), which was then reinterpreted and elaborated upon based on the requirements of the respective communities.

Let us begin our analysis of Matthew. We must premise this with an observation: the Lord's Prayer is not taught as a fixed formula. Even though, in the liturgical use of the community of Matthew and, later, in the early Christian community, it will become such, the Lord's Prayer constitutes a stimulating frame of reference that illuminates and guides the development of prayer and life. Reducing it to a formula would mean reducing and perhaps distorting its value.

Christian prayer inspired by the Lord's Prayer addresses God by calling him Father. The resonance that this term had in Jesus's environment and for the first disciples is first and foremost of a social character. The father is the person who, with a sense of responsibility and consideration, organizes the life of the family and provides the individuals with what they need (cf. Mt 13:52). In this way, the whole family revolves around the father—around his hard work, his capability, his skill, and his wisdom. Therefore, the Christian addresses God feeling that he is part of a family, part of a group, and with the awareness that God as the Father cares about us and takes care of us in a suitable manner.

From this perspective, the father is also the person who organizes the life of the family. The family obeys him, the person whose will must be done.

Alongside this phenomenology, in which the father is positioned within the collective environment of the family, the strictly intersubjective relationship should be emphasized. The father, in this new perspective that does not oppose the first one but rather further specifies one aspect of it, is the person who understands, who teaches us how to be people, who understands his children and in whom his children have full confidence.

The figure of the father as understood in this twofold dimension suggested by the environment Jesus lived in and the early Judeo-Christian community was used to refer to God. In this way, when the Christian called God Father, he felt united to him through the same kind of family bond, and, moreover, he felt loved and understood on the deepest level. God is truly the "Father who sees all that is done in secret" (*Mt* 6:6).

These two aspects emphasize the collective one: Christians say "Our Father," referring to the socio-familiar dimension that they are assuming. Perhaps this recalls the centrifugal tendencies of the community of Matthew. In any case, the fact that the Christians find themselves living together, not only as a social group but also due to the thread that unites them through their most intimate and personal values, is emphasized. The Father that "sees all that is done in secret" is also the Father that sees everyone unitedly.

The God who is thought of and experienced in the categories of the Father that one experiences on earth remains at his transcendental level. His transcendence does not diminish his paternity. On the contrary, we could even say that God multiplies his divinity through his paternity and his paternity through his divinity. In this way, we have a God that is infinitely a Father and a Father who is such on an infinite scale. All of this is reflected in the expression "who art in heaven." "Heaven" refers to the level that belongs to God, emphasizing his unreachable reality. It is also reminds us to avoid any banalization of God. Approaching God as the Father led to the risk not so much the feeling that he was too close—this never happens—but rather of thinking of him, so to say, in a reduced form, projecting the categories of experience—which are inevitably limited—of Earthly paternity onto God. Matthew sees this risk and warns us of it when he contrasts the level of man with the level of the "heavenly Father," an expression typical of Matthew.

The first request that is made of the heavenly Father regards his name: that it be hallowed. We can immediately clarify the meaning of this request by making one thing precise. In the cultural environment of the Bible, the name stands for the person, and it appears that it can never be reduced to a pure denomination or a title given by an outsider. The imposition and the changing of a name indicate a change of subject, a qualification in terms of the mission that must be completed, a new ability that is conferred. The name demonstrates and expresses what the person is and can only be understood if thought of within the sphere of the person himself. By asking the Father that his name be held holy, we are consequently asking him that he himself be held holy.

At this point, we should ask ourselves what "hallow" means. The semantic family to which the term belongs refers only to divinity. It refers to what belongs to or is typical of God. We should then ask ourselves how we could think that God could be "hallowed." The risk of talking in circles or of a meaningless discussion leads us to the alternative of interpreting holding God holy not in the sense of an ontological characterization that can be attributed to God but in the sense of a recognition. In this case, we could say that we are asking "your name" and you yourself be recognized as holy. This is a common interpretation. But in the Bible, the verb "hallow" is never used in terms of a relationship that is only cognitive that leads to recognition. It refers to an action. When used in its active form, "hallow" means making something holy, making it divine, or making it like God. When used in its passive form, it emphasizes the effect of this homogenization with respect to God that has been produced and realized. The same problem, therefore, comes up again, and there does not seem to be any way out: how is it possible to hallow what is Holy, to make God divine? A famous text by Ezekiel provides us with a solid basis for an answer: "*And I will sanctify my great name*, which was profaned among the nations, which you profaned in their midst, and the nations shall know that I am the Lord, *when I am hallowed among you* before their eyes" (Ez 36:23 according to the Septuagint; see also 28:22; 28:25; 38:16; 38:23; etc.). Ezekiel's text, especially given the close contact between Matthew and the entire Old Testament, is illuminating. The sanctification which is discussed is real and refers in parallel first to God's name, which then refers to God himself as the subject. It occurs not through an unthinkable addition to God's holiness but through a steadily more diffuse participation in that holiness which is shared by the people. According to this interpretation—which has already been proposed by Saint Cyprian—we are asking God the Father that his holiness be realized and spread through the great Christian family.

The next request has to do with God's kingdom, the kingdom of the Father who is in heaven. In order to understand this expression, we must retrace the theological and Biblical line regarding the kingdom, which is already found in the Old Testament and merges with that of the New Testament.

The "kingdom of God" is not limited to God's dominion over all of creation but rather implies a series of initiatives that pertain to God and man that we can summarize as follows.

First of all, there is the act of descending. In a certain sense, God steps outside his inaccessibility and comes to man with a proposal. It is the understanding between God and man, the "covenant," as it is called specifically, that is a bilateral agreement: God will work for the good of man, but in exchange he asks man to observe his commandments. Here, an act of ascending occurs: man steps out of his profanity and ventures toward God with an attitude of willing reciprocity. After taking note of the offer that God is making him, man says yes. The intersection between the two descending and ascending lines establishes a new situation which involves a close and secure sharing between God and man, almost a kind of symbiosis. This new reality is called the kingdom and is already put into practice in the Old Testament, starting at least from the covenant with Sinai. In terms of the New Testament, in the descending line God, who has revealed himself to be the Father, offers man the wealth of Christ. In the ascending line, man, taking note of this new and increased offer, opens himself to it completely through the yes of faith. The new situation, which is established in this way, is the kingdom of God in its typical meaning in the New Testament.

As we can see, there is an elaboration made, a step taken between the Old Testament and the New. Even once we have arrived at the level of the New Testament, there is an additional impetus: the "Kingdom" will involve a presence of Christ that becomes steadily more intermeshed in all of creation, in human beings and in things, and, through Christ, a presence of God that becomes steadily closer. The arrival point for all of this movement is the eschatological goal, where, as Paul reminds us, God will be "all in all" (1 Cor 15:28). As viewed in this conclusive phase, the kingdom belongs to the future. It is strictly eschatological.

We will now return to our text. When the Christian asks that the kingdom of the Father "come," he places himself within this onward development. What he is asking for is a greater presence of the wealth of Christ among men, in their lives, in their buildings, and in the world in which they live. The request regards both God and man, precisely because God wanted to involve himself with man through the offer that he makes him.

Another request presented to the Father regards the realization of his will.

The will of the Father is understood objectively: it is everything that God devised for man: first the commandments, and then all the directions that are given to man by the Word of God incarnate in Christ and interpreted by the Spirit.

Moreover, given that God, the creator of everything, also arranges the progress of history, and does all of this for man, we can say that a message expressing his will can also be found within the stories of individuals. Doing God's will means full executive docility with respect to this broad range of actions that manifest it.

Asking the Father that his will be done is not passive resignation. It is cordial sharing: the Christian becomes aware that what is best for him is what God proposes to him. The desire to do God's will—there is no true prayer without desire—is derived from this.

This conception involves, on the one hand, God himself, since he loves man, designs him, and ardently desires that it be fully realized. On the other hand, it involves man, who recognizes with trepidation and joy that God the Father follows him minute by minute, that he takes care of him, and that he manifests his will in the strength of the love that he has for him.

What follows for the Christian is the ideal of a proper execution, of an execution that starts from the level of man, arrives at the level of God himself, and brings the totality of heaven, which is the area of God, to Earth, the area of man.

In this sense, we should specify that the execution of the will of God occurs on Earth, but an optimal level of transcendent perfection, something of God, a relationship with heaven, is brought to it.

The request for bread—as R. Meynet observed—is at the center of the seven requests in Matthew's formula. It is also the one that seems to be the most characteristic of the Christian who addresses God as Father: it is the father who gives bread to his children. In effect, the request for bread brings us back to the framework of the family in which the figure of the father is situated. In the cultural environment of the Bible, bread is both concrete and symbolic at the same time. In realistic language, bread represents the basic form of nourishment for life. God the Father, who concerns himself with the life of man in the concrete context of his story, therefore also takes care of the nourishment that makes it possible. This consideration is reinterpreted through the lens of family life here. The nourishment which is asked of God is no longer grass, as we find in Genesis (cf. 1:29), but rather bread, the form of nourishment that man makes for man and which is shared within the family by the individuals that make it up. By addressing God specifically as Father, the Christian wholeheartedly asks him for the nourishment that he needs to live by emphasizing God's familial paternity.

But bread is also symbolic. As a symbol, it evokes everything else that is necessary for living life within space and time, everything that tends to make family life not only possible but also pleasurable. This includes clothing and a home—in other words, everything else that surrounds us that, although secondary with respect to nourishment, contributes to a life that can be lived with serenity and dignity.

The bread is asked for today and for today. The idea of "every day" is insisted on twice. And this is telling: in fact, we assume—and are highly aware—that God as the Father follows the lives of his children, lives that unfold within space and time, with an attention that is worthy for him and his children. Therefore, the Father will follow his children with care always and everywhere, without even the smallest break in continuity. It is this living relationship, which is constantly simultaneous, with the Father that pushes his children to ask for what is necessary and useful for their existence moment by moment, occasion by occasion, and in place by place. They do not try to collect all the Earth's treasures, or even to obtain provisions for the following days by closing themselves within human calculations about the unforeseeable circumstances of the future. The Christian knows how to live day by day because he knows that day after day he is cared for, loved, guided, and protected by the Father without any advances or delays.

Finally, the familial framework in which the request is made involves the completeness of the family. The bread requested is "ours," not "mine": it is bread for everyone, that arrives for everyone. We each ask for it for our neighbors.

The family spirit which is suggested by the Biblical figure of paternity, as we have repeatedly emphasized, also involves a horizontal reciprocity between Christian brothers. They must feel that they are all sons of the Father together. This awareness will then allow them to have an attitude that reflects the vertical attitude that the Father has toward them in their reciprocity.

Christians are aware that they have "debts" that they owe God the Father. This is a symbolic image that expresses a sad reality: the emptiness, the incomplete insufficiency that Christians can also create in their own existences through the incorrect choices they make, "sins."

Man owes what God gives him. An emptiness within the reality-values context created by God therefore becomes a debt—according to the symbolic image of a contract that man makes first with himself. But since God is the Father and is the Father on an infinite scale, through loving appropriation, he considers the harm that man does to himself to be done to him personally. This process of loving appreciation is given more precise boundaries when, for example, we talk about the covenant, the commandments, and other laws that comes from God and the expression of his loving will. God the Father takes man seriously and wants to be taken seriously by man.

If, therefore, what God asks of man—although it is for man's good—is not done, an emptiness that touches God himself is created, and a crack in the inter-subjectivity forms.

God the Father cares for man with an uninterrupted flow of goodness. His encounter overcomes the cracks, and he fills the emptiness. Continuing with the same metaphor, God forgives our debts. He wants man to ask him for this so that he gains awareness of the stakes.

We have seen how the relationship with God the Father is realized within the concrete context of the family. The Christian has other children of God, who are his brothers, next to him. And since God's attitude toward individuals is the paradigm, the Christian must bring what he receives from the vertical relationship to the horizontal relationship. Consequently, the "holes" that are opened in reciprocal relationships, the cracks, everything that constitutes lack of respect for a commitment, that is an omission, a lack of good, of attention, of help, or of love toward others, constitute a list of horizontal "debts" that must be eliminated just like we wish to eliminate our "debt" toward God. Otherwise, the flow of goodness that comes from God and that should pass through men in order to return to God would be blocked.

In terms of the horizontal plane, man moves around his own field. Unable to fill the gaps that separate him from God, to "pay his debts" with him, the Christian man can do this for the other men that are on the same level as him. And he must do so. There is a "family" requirement that God the Father, who wishes to be imitated in his extreme constructive good, places on man. Consequently, in order to be able to invoke God as the Father, the Christian must first help his brothers. We could say that God refuses to be invoked outside of this collective family environment and turns back men who hope to reach him on their own while excluding others.

Positively, doing to others what one would wish for oneself, and, in terms of the "debts" owed, forgiving, remediating, and tenaciously reconstructing the malformations that are created in horizontal relationships, the Christian can be certain that he will be welcomed by the Father.

The final two requests in the Lord's Prayer in Matthew once again have to do with the mystery of sin as seen in terms of the elements that easily influence it: temptation and evil.

The Biblical concept of temptation is unique and, more than one concept in a strict sense of the word, it is a conglomerate of concepts. One is tempted when certain values that were previously fulfilled, either individually or collectively, are placed under pressure. This may be an individual pressure or a collective pressure, a momentary or protracted pressure.

The clearest example is the walk through the desert that separates the exit from Egypt and the entrance into the promised land. They are the forty years of "the time of Massah in the desert" (Ps 94:8). The values of the covenant, proposed to and accepted by the people, are placed under multiple pressures: everyday existence, the lack of dramatic events, especially the subterranean maturation of the group of the people of God that gradually mixes together and learns to be free, and, finally, the pressure of the uncomfortable circumstances. Temptation can have a positive result. It can lead to a consolidation of the previous values as a result of the trial that one has undergone. In this way, for example, the First Book of the Maccabees emphasizes that Abraham was "tested and found faithful" during his temptation (1 Mac 2:52; cf. Sir 27:5,7). Given man's weakness, however, temptation can lead to a negative result. If the pressure of the trial exceeds man's capacity to hold strong, temptation becomes an irreversible opportunity to make a wrong choice (cf. Mt 26:41; Mk 14:38; Lk 22:40,46). The temptation and trial add up to the mystery of the malice with which man is always in contact. And the mystery of malice also means the mystery of his incoherent weakness. For this reason, we ask God the Father to defend us. We ask him that he prevents us from entering into the shifting sands of temptations which could have a negative result.

The experience of the people of God in the desert suggests another possible interpretation, which is more closely related to the terminology used: "temptation," which has an active meaning in Greek, more than temptation that is experienced, could refer to temptation in which man is the protagonist. Often, during their experience in the desert, the people are lead to "tempt" God, to put him to the test (cf. Ex 17:27; Dt 6:16; 9:22; Ps 94:8; for "temptation" in the sense of tempting God, see C. Spicq, *Notes de Lexicographie Néo-testamentaire*, Cerf, Paris 1978–1982, III, 548–559). This is a negative attitude because it is opposed to the trusting abandon and lack of reservations that the way that God cares for his children would merit. But most of all, this represents a lack of filiality: it means not trusting, it means presuming to expect a guarantee that calms man within man's own world.

If temptation already puts us into contact with the mystery of malice, this becomes larger and more explicit when malice itself is personified in evil: evil is demonic, satanic. The experience that the Christian has been able to have both through his personal observations and by listening to the Old Testament tells him that there is a complex network of hidden dangers and negativity which, when they are concrete parts of his story, tend to envelop him. The Christian knows that he has weak points on which evil could take hold, and it is even difficult for him to be aware of all of them. This situation—which could result in dramatic tension—does not affect the basic serenity of the children of God. God the Father has overpowered evil throughout history, right from the start, and has weakened it through the death of Christ. For this reason, he can properly defend his children, not only by putting them on alert but also by factually almost tearing them out of the hands of "evil."

This final request essentially serves as a reference to the realism of the precarious situation of the Christian. A person cannot believe, even as a true child of God, that he has already reached a level of security at which there is no risk. He is on a journey. And therefore, he asks the Father to protect him on his journey, to free him even from himself, from the areas in which the "evil" that he feels and that he brings with him attacks.

Finally, we can note that—both in terms of "temptation" as a trial and limitation and in the active sense of the word—man also entrusts his fears, the risk of doing wrong, and even of not trusting in him, to God during prayer. Man does not insist on a kind of voluntarism that stimulates him but rather asks God even for what should come from man himself. Aware, because he has been trained by the mystery of malice, that he is weak and fragile and that he could even fail to meet his basic commitments, the Christian also entrusts these negative eventualities to God. He does not close himself within his own short circuit but rather courageously throws himself into the arms of the Father.

III/3. After having analytically retraced the formula of the Lord's Prayer in Matthew, we now ask if any repercussions of the themes that have emerged in the individual requests can be observed within the world of Matthew. And the answer is surprisingly positive: there are numerous repercussions and elaborations. Here are a few examples.

The first one regards the expression "Our Father who art in heaven," which recalls the other expression "heavenly Father."

As we have already mentioned, use of the term "heavenly" to refer to God and explicitly to refer to God the Father is typical of Matthew: it occurs seven times in the Gospel. We encounter only two other instances of the word "heavenly" in the New Testament, and they refer to angels (Lk 2:13) and a vision (Acts 26:19).

Of the seven instances of the word "heavenly" in reference to the Father, two relate to Jesus—"my heavenly Father" (Mt 15:13; 18:45)—and five are spoken by Jesus and directed at Christians—"your heavenly Father" (5:48; 6:14; 6:26,32; 23:9).

A passage from Jesus to the Christians exists when the Christians accept Jesus's message and to the extent to which they accept it.

When "my heavenly Father" becomes "your heavenly Father," we become capable of saying "'Our Father' who art in heaven."

We will find that—even more implicitly—the concept of participation in God's holiness, which is expressed through the request that his "name" be hallowed, is elaborated upon. When Jesus insists that men have the same attitudes as the heavenly Father, and therefore that they know how to love as he does, forgive as he does, and act as he acts in conformity with what he is, an appeal to the transcendent reality characteristic of God and to his holiness is made. It is possible, for example, to use the goodness that the heavenly Father uses because, like children who are similar to him on the inside, we share the root of his holiness (cf. Mt 5:48).

The request that his Kingdom come is more broadly developed in Matthew than in Mark. The kingdom of God—which Matthew calls the "kingdom of heaven" thirty-three times and the "kingdom of my Father" twice (13:43; 26:26)—takes form through the Church, which is the situation that emerges when the Father's offer of Christ is accepted by mankind.

Reality, the development of time, and the eschatological horizon are outlined by this situation. The "parables of the kingdom" (cf. Mt 13:1–51; see 13:11) where the "kingdom of heaven," the kingdom of the Father, is seen as it unfolds with the typical elaboration noted above are characteristic.

The reference to God's will, which must be fulfilled optimally, is suggested first and foremost by the context which we have examined in which the formulation of the Lord's Prayer is situated, the Sermon on the Mount. It contains broad and detailed documentation about what God's will is and what God's ambitions are—we could say—for mankind, his children. The petition for full realization of the will of God fully coincides with the imploration, which is perfectly clear even though it is implicit, that what is stated in the Sermon on the Mount, from the beatitudes which introduce it to the factual acceptance of the Word of God with which it concludes, be understood and put into practice.

Confirmation and further elaboration of all of this can be found in the insistence, which is also typical of Matthew, on the will of the Father: it is an attentive will, one where he wishes that none of the little ones be lost (Mt 18:14), where he requires concrete realization in addition to verbiage (Mt 7:21), and where he produces a very close bond with Jesus (Mt 12:50). It is Jesus—Matthew follows in the tradition of Mark, which we examined above—that brings the will of the Father for himself and for men to maximal fulfillment when, at Gethsemane, he tells him, "Your will be done!" (Mt 26:42).

The request for daily bread—in the broad sense that we illustrated previously—is given continuity and an explanation in Matthew when the requirement to place our full trust in God in terms of our food and clothing, which is provided day after day, as a part of everyday life: "Each day has enough trouble of its own" (Mt 6:34).

The request that our "debts" be forgiven in a way that is directly proportional to how Christians treat their own "debtors" is mirrored in the requirement to welcome, to forgive, and to use mercy and is particularly emphasized by Matthew. The most engaging text is the parable of the two debtors (Mt 18:21–35). The goodness of the master who "felt so sorry" (Mt 18:27) and forgave an immense debt, if correctly understood and evaluated by the servant who was in debt to him, should obviously lead him to in turn use his goodness and mercy on a horizontal level where the debts are much weaker. The words of Jesus are cutting: "And that is how my heavenly Father will deal with you unless you each forgive your brother from your heart" (Mt 18:35). Jesus asks for unconditional openness to the goodness of the Father, but not passive openness and acceptance. The infinite goodness of the Father must be personalized, reinterpreted, and made his own by the man who wishes to truly be a child of God.

The request to not enter into temptation in Matthew and Luke is framed by a comparison of the critical points on which the pressure activated by the devil can be activated: the story of Jesus's temptations (Mt 4:1–11; Lk 4:1–13; here we will follow Matthew's version). Jesus is "tempted" to use his ability to perform miracles for his own advantage. It is a question of bread, of the bread which is necessary for life. Jesus, after fasting, feels the need for this bread, for this nourishment, but he places all of his trust in God. He is truly the Son of God, but he will use this qualification to serve others (cf. Mt 4:2–4). Many temptations hit upon the need or daily bread, circling around man's need for nourishment, for elements that are indispensable—or elements he believes to be indispensable—for his life. He will have to work and give himself something to do, but first and foremost he must remember the primary need to look for the "kingdom first, and on God's saving justice" (Mt 6:33).

The "rest," including bread, will be provided in abundance. All the Christian needs to do is ask.

A second area that temptation hits upon is trust in God. The suggestion of malice made to Jesus is characteristic: there is a binding statement by God that Jesus could twist and use in his favor (Mt 4:5–6). This type of temptation occurs through the pastiche of reasons with which man tends to enclose what belongs to God—his existence, his word, his interventions, and his providence—within the short circuit of his reasoning. If God exists, he cannot allow this. It is an insidious temptation from which man emerges only by renewing his unconditional trust in God, whose means are not those of man. Man must avoid "[putting] the Lord [his] God to the test" (Mt 4:7).

This is what is requested in the Lord's Prayer, according to one of the two interpretations of temptation proposed.

The third area is more evident: Jesus is offered a terrestrial kingdom. It is the temptation of absolute valorization, of a closed circuit of things that are temporary, perceivable, and material.

In general, temptation is inevitable, and it can even be useful. The Christian, who keeps himself—like Jesus—in a situation of dialogue with the heavenly Father and also speaks to him about his temptations, avoids the risk of isolation, of the kinds of interrupted contacts which the disciples fell into at Gethsemane despite Jesus's warning.

Liberation from "evil"—the last detailed petition which is made to the Father—is particularly relevant within the Gospel of Matthew, which uses the term with a characteristic frequency (twenty-six occurrences in Matthew, two in Mark, thirteen in Luke, and three in John). The rather broad range of attributions provides a unified articulation: the root of evil which is established by the devil (Mt 5:37; 13:19) tends to germinate in the hearts of the men who bow to pressure and are therefore called "subjects of the Evil One" (Mt 13:38). By becoming active protagonists of evil (Mt 9:4), men who belong to the devil make up an "evil and unfaithful generation" (Mt 12:39) and know how to speak "all kinds of calumny" (Mt 5:11). The cloudy wave of evil tends to reach even Christians, who must defend against it decisively (cf. Mt 6:23; 13:19). In other words, there is an entire organized context of "evil" that is the opposite of the goodness of God: cf. Mt 20:15. This originates with the devil and tends to trap men. Only contact with the Father, which makes the Christian his child and like him, can keep man from being trapped.

The examples of how the Lord's Prayer resonates within the Gospel go on and on. The ones that we have seen are sufficient to introduce us to an important fact. The Lord's Prayer branches off and bores into the entire text of Matthew.

In addition to being summarized in an outline that may have already been recited during liturgy at the time, the "formula" was also widespread throughout the polyvalent experience of the community of Matthew.

IV. Paul's Push Forward

We do not find a formulation of the Lord's Prayer that corresponds to Matthew's version in its entirety in Paul. But a few corresponding elements, which are clearly apparent, are telling. One element in particular merits close study: not once, but twice, Paul insists that we, as Christians guided by the Spirit, address God and "cry out, 'Abba, Father!'" (Rom 8:15; Gal 4:5–6).

This is an invocation that takes place in the context of liturgy, as the characteristic verb "cry out" indicates.

The assembly feels the need to express an invocation that connects them directly to the Father out loud. According to certain researchers (Lietzmann, Grundmann, Cullmann, Jeremias: cf. for documentation U. Wilckens, *Der Brief an die Römer*, 2, Benziger—Neukirchener Verlag, Zürich-Neukirchen-Vluyn 1979, 137), this refers to a recitation of the Lord's Prayer out loud. This would provide a close connection between the synoptic traditions, especially with that of Luke. Starting from the Lord's Prayer, even an approximate version—which would be improbable during the 50s—a bold surge toward God the Father is created collectively—"we cry out"—within the liturgical assembly. Even though we do not yet have the formula, we have at least found a starting place.

In this surge toward the Father, we should note the use of the Aramaic word "*Abbà*," or "dad," that we observed in the Gospel of Mark and which was used only by Jesus. According to this testimony by Paul, Christians dare to address God with familiar intimacy—as indicated by the word *Abbà*—which Jesus, according to the documentation we have, reserved for his own use.

A persuasive explanation for this audacity, proposed by Marchel (cf. W. Marchel, *«Abba, Père». La prière de Jésus et des chrétiens*, Biblical Institute Press, Rome 1971), brings us into a deeper study of the choice. The ecclesiastical community gradually comes aware of the support of the Spirit that animates them, announces the truth of Jesus, and formulates the law for them while also giving them the energy to enact them. The Spirit of God and of Jesus, which, "poured" into the heart of the Christian (Rom 5:5), organizes his entire life. Since the Spirit serves as a vehicle for the content of Christ, an affinity with Christ himself is produced. As it slowly enters into the entire life of the Christian, it also penetrates his conscience. In the context of the new awareness that is created in this way, the Spirit witnesses his reality and his filiation to the Christian (cf. Rom 8:16).

In this way, we can understand how the community can dare to address the Father with the same familiarity as Christ does.

Although this is the aspect that we can find in the world of Paul that is closest to the Lord's Prayer, there is no lack of other connections of particular interest. We will limit ourselves to a few examples. Paul demonstrates a particular sensitivity toward the paternity of God. God is normally called "God our Father and the Lord Jesus Christ" (Rom 1:7; 1 Cor 1:23; 2 Cor 1:2,3; Gal 1:3; etc.). Paul regularly relates God's paternity of Jesus Christ to God's paternity of us. Our filiation is not only placed beside that of the Son, but also depends on "eldest of many brothers" (Rom 8:29). In relation to Christ and by remaining in contact with him, the Christian perceives that he has a clear path and even a push toward the Father (cf. Rom 5:1; 1 Cor 8:6). We constantly circle around "*Abbà*-Father." We should note that Paul never uses the term "heavenly" to refer to God the Father and never explicitly relates him to "heaven."

Participation in God's holiness within the Christian community occurs, according to Paul, through the determining influence of the Spirit, which is explicitly called "the Spirit...of holiness" (Rom 1:4). This starts with baptism, based on which Christians are called "holy" and "sanctified."

Because it is derived from baptism, the holiness of the Christian is in relation to Christ and is always activated by the Spirit. One of the weightiest statements in this regard is found in 1 Cor 1:30: "Christ Jesus [...] for us was made wisdom from God, and saving justice and holiness and redemption." It is clear that the sanctification which Christ brings us comes "from God" is none other than participation in God's holiness, a participation that occurs and that spreads within the context of "us," of the community.

In Paul, the Kingdom of God is the future with an eschatological meaning. This is different from the synoptic Gospels. Consequently, the kingdom which is said to "come" will be built on the participation of everyone and everything in the resurrection of Christ, as will occur when the Son "will hand over the kingdom to God the Father" (1 Cor 15:24) and God will be "all in all" (1 Cor 15:28).

Paul elaborates on the theme of the will of God in a unique manner.

As a recent study brought to light (cf. J. Palliparambil, *The Will of God. A Commitment to Man*, Università Gregoriana, Rome 1986), the will of God in Paul is always treated in a bipolar manner.

On the one hand, always present and in the forefront, there is "God who wills." We can understand the will of God if, before looking at the objective content that it expresses, we establish a warm contact with God as the Father: his is "the will of our God and Father" (Gal 1:4), as he reveals himself to be over the course of the history of salvation from the Old to the New Testament. God's will involves people personally and in parallel with his "good pleasure" (cf. Eph 1:9). The other "pole" of God's will in Paul is its objective content. In summary, we could say that the objective content of God's will is condensed in Christ. We can find what God wants expressed in Christ, in his teaching, in his behavior, and in his person. The Sspirit takes this "raw material" which is concentrated in Christ and takes responsibility for "proclaiming it" moment by moment, situation by situation.

Paul does not insist on the request for bread. But various references show that he is also aware of this aspect.

Of the seven references to "bread," seven refer to Eucharistic bread and three refer to bread in its normal meaning, with an emphasis on the need to work (2 Thess 3:8,12), and, especially, on the need to trust in God, who provides "food to eat" (2 Cor 9:10). This circles around the filial request for bread that we found in Matthew.

Most of all, Paul tries to frame nourishment in the great context of the liturgy of life, based on which everything done is for God: "Whatever you eat, then, or drink, and whatever else you do, do it all for the glory of God" (1 Cor 10:31).

In terms of the overcoming of malice that Matthew expresses through the metaphor of the forgiving of debts, Paul digs deeper. He shows that he has fully grasped the meaning behind the Sermon on the Mount (cf. Mt 5:38–48) and elaborates upon it through his characteristic ability to concentrate and find the essence of a concept. Using a direct reference to the Sermon on the Mount, Paul states that the Christian must have a constructive attitude before people who hurt him, to the point of giving food and drink to his enemy (cf. Rom 12:20). "Do not be mastered by evil," Paul says, "but master evil with good" (Rom 12:21). This is already a big step, but Paul is not satisfied. By elaborating on the metaphor of the debt in an original manner and with a positive perspective, Paul decisively states that the Christian always and only owes others love: "The only thing you should owe to anyone is love for one another" (Rom 13:8). The level of elaboration with respect to that of Matthew is truly noteworthy. The discussion no longer involves overcoming hostilities from others by simply allowing them to fall off our shoulders, not considering them, and forgiving "the debt." This involves a counterattack. If the only true debt is love, the Christian is obligated to have this attitude toward his brothers and, more generally, to all people. No form of malice will catch him unprepared, in a state of blissful ignorance, and he will also not simply be willing to systematically ignore the hurt that is done to him. The Christian has a constructive attitude. He will not allow himself to be defeated by malice, not only in the sense that he will not use the same weapons, but especially in the sense that he will not be blackmailed by his pessimism. Malice can and will be overcome, but only through an inundation of good.

In terms of temptation, we can find a complex and well-developed list of cases in Paul. Paul personally experienced the pain of being tested. He felt himself "battered" by Satan (2 Cor 12:7–10). For this reason, he speaks with the personal involvement that is his typical attitude: Paul presents what he has personally experienced as a paradigm for others. He insists on two aspects that he feels are fundamental. The temptation or test must be accepted by the Christian, who must adequately equip himself with the means to defend himself. The test is a true battle, and it should be confronted as such (cf. Eph 6:10–17). God allows it as a consolidation and protects Christians so that they are not tempted beyond their capacities to resist (cf. 1 Cor 10:13).

But good will, even when translated into the realistic commitment to self-defense, is not sufficient: recourse to God through prayer in order to avoid having the temptations resolve in accordance with the insidious willfulness of the tempter Satan (cf. 2 Cor 2:11; 11:14; 2 Thess 2:9). Within the context of temptation, the mystery of malice and of evil on the one hand and the unknowns of the human heart, with its capacity for endurance and its sudden concessions, merge. The strength of God and of Christ is needed so that the Christian can "come out of" temptation without remaining prisoner to it (cf. 1 Cor 10:13). A parallel discussion could be had regarding "evil." Paul establishes its presence in history an arrogant and insidious power. Satan can sneak into all aspects of man's life. He can wait for the Christian at any point along his path and act by becoming temptation.

The Christian, however, should not live in fear of the devil. The seriousness of what is at stake remains, but by joining oneself to Christ through the power of prayer, he can overcome the devil and experience his filiation with joy.

In summary, the elements of the Lord's Prayer can be found in Paul. They are found in a fluid state, but one that we could call incandescent. Although the formula for the Lord's Prayer cannot necessarily be found here, the unequivocally liturgical dimension in which the invocation "*Abbà*-Father" is situated brings us a fragment of an equivalent prayer which is notable for its intensity and for the pressure of the Spirit. But the "fluid state" is determined by the multitude of life experiences in which the elements that correspond to the formula appear to be inserted. We could say that there is a type of commutation present here, from the liturgical formulation to Christian life and from Christian life to the formulation. In this way, a mechanism of elaboration is activated, and this also leads to an essentialization. This is what we find in Luke's presentation.

V. The Consequent Accentuation of Luke

V/1. As we observed initially, a formula for the Lord's Prayer is also found in Luke. It is worth examining closely.

In order to understand it, we must keep one general fact in mind: the close contact between Luke and Paul—as it appears from the Book of Acts, written by Luke himself—also left an impression on the Gospel of Luke. We can expect to find what we have observed in Paul in Luke, as well.

But now we arrive at the Lord's Prayer.

While Matthew includes it within the Sermon on the Mount and explicitly within the context of a prayer that avoids pagan verbosity, Luke gives us a few more concrete references which relate to Jesus's attitude. Jesus prays. In order to do so, he often goes to isolated places, away from even the disciples. The disciples realize this. They appreciate their Teacher's behavior and are inspired to imitate it. They ask him, therefore: "Lord, teach us to pray" (Lk 11:1).

Jesus's answer is fascinating. He tells them: "When you pray, this is what to say" (Lk 11:2). We can assume that the disciples had a decisive, serious, committed desire to pray. The formula that Jesus suggests is therefore the perceivable expression of a prayer that first comes from inside the Christian.

Luke's typical formula then follows. The prayer is addressed to "Father." Matthew's clarification "who art in heaven" is not added. The reason why has been considered. After throwing out the fantastical hypothesis of two formulas taught by Jesus, the basic idea that emerged was that this apparent simplification by Luke is in reality an elaboration. This is what W. Marchel advocates. And the elaboration is the following: "Father" closely recalls the Aramaic term "*Abbà*" and is the most immediate and spontaneous translation of the word. We can say, therefore, that in Luke, we find what appeared to be a form of crying out to the Father in Paul, which is expressed with the familial intimacy used by Jesus during his terrestrial life and is suggested to Christians by the Spirit.

The result is the elaboration of Paul's point of view into a formula.

This elaborated view of a prayer that knows and feels that it is animated by the Spirit of Jesus and that therefore leads the Christian to address God by simply calling him Father makes the addition of "who art in heaven" in a way superfluous because it is already incorporated.

Let us clarify. As we have already seen, this is not a kind of compromise in Matthew, either. He is not telling the Christians not to forget, while they invoke God as their Father, that this Father is in heaven, not immediately available on Earth. As we saw previously, the meaning is deeper because it involves the transcendence of God. It is the action of the Spirit that brings, in a certain way, this transcendence into direct contact with man. If it is truly the Spirit who animates the prayer of Christians and pushes them to address the Father, there is a pressure of transcendence that unfolds within them. Without emphasizing, we could state that "heaven" is found within the heart of man, in the sense that it is within the heart of man that the Spirit, which has been "poured" (Rom 5:5) into it, acts.

The sanctification of the name of God and the coming of his kingdom acquire a unique neatness when we illuminate Luke through Paul. The sanctification of the name is the diffusion of the personal holiness of God within the Christian community here as well. The kingdom, whose closer presence is desired, is the one we saw in Matthew, perhaps with an emphasis on its movement toward the eschatological conclusion. Consequently, the coming of the Kingdom always refers to the reality that is born when the descending and ascending lines meet. The fact that these two requests are taken verbatim and the variation of the basic invocation makes us think that there must have been a common point of contact between the tradition of Luke and that of Matthew with the Q source. However, this resulted in an original elaboration.

The uniqueness of Luke first appears in the omissions. We do not find the request, which is so explicitly emphasized in Matthew, that God's will be done. Here as well, this is an elaboration more than an omission. In Paul—and Luke, as we observed, is probably based on it—we saw how the will of God, which is condensed in Christ, is delivered and proposed to man in concrete form through the action of the Spirit. So the problem has shifted. God is not asked that his will be done with a perfection that implies transcendence, because all of this is already in motion: the illumination and the push of the Spirit leads man to identify and fulfill the will of God moment by moment. The will of the Father is fulfilled in this way in real time with an organicity that penetrates every aspect of life, with no gaps to bridge.

We do, however, find a particular insistence within the request for bread: Luke emphasizes the daily aspect. While Matthew emphasizes that the bread is requested "today" (Mt 6:11), Luke makes the request more explicit, adding "give us each day our daily bread." This slight difference is meaningful. The request, in other words, is that the bread—in the broader sense that we already saw in Matthew—be given by God in accordance with the plan that he established regarding the continuity of life, which occurs day by day. It is clear that the bread that is needed for today is requested today, with the attitude of simultaneity toward the Father that we noted previously. However, it is just as clear—and this is the meaning behind Luke's slightly different version—that an infinite reserve is not requested, nor is a reserve that lasts more than one day requested. Like the manna given by God day by day in the desert (cf. Ex 16:1–20; Wis 16:20–21), bread is requested daily in accordance with God's plan. With this request, we ask with insistence on one hand by trusting God completely on the other.

Next, we ask that God "forgive our sins, for we ourselves forgive each one who is in debt to us" (Lk 11:4).

With respect to the formulation in Matthew, we should note that there are two variations, which serve as clarifications. What Matthew calls "debts" are called "sins" here. This is an interpretation that tends to elaborate, interpreting the meaning behind the metaphorical "debts" as though Luke wished to tell us not to think only of the "debts" that we owe God due to our formal shortcomings, which, in the practice of the Old Testament, could be overcome through a ritual offering that was clearly specified and proportional to the magnitude of the transgression. The debts are sins. In other words, every time that man errs, stepping outside what is his context as designed by God, a sin has occurred. A sin always regards God, and not only when the incorrect action is directed directly at him—as is the case for blasphemy—but also when the sinful decision only affects man. God loves man like a Father, and he does not tolerate—given the irresistible force of his love—men, his children, doing themselves harm. Once, however, the sinful decision is made and the harm is done, only God can remediate through his new creation which is his way of forgiving. In asking God to forgive our sins, we ask him for total restoration, even a creative action with respect to the emptiness, the "nothing," that is created in our system through sin.

The restoring repair of the hole of sin is asked of God in direct proportion to our constructive attitude toward others. Luke exchanges the term "debts" for the term "sins" with regard to God, but he keeps the metaphor of the "debts" that must be forgiven with respect to the Christian's attitude toward his brothers. This is also telling. The chasm opened by sin is wider than the "debts" that we contract with each other our everyday lives. Their forgiveness means that we are required to constantly reestablish a balance that has been upset, not to reconstruct a hole.

One final element that is emphasized regarding the continued forgiveness of the "debts" that others owe us is its universality. Obviously, no exception to this willingness to forgive would be admissible in Matthew, either. Luke, however, makes this explicit. We ask that our sins be forgiven, adding "for we ourselves forgive each one who is in debt to us" (Lk 11:4). It is like a challenge: there may always be brothers or men in general that have a negative effect on the Christian, doing harm to his rights and becoming "debtors." When faced with any action of this type, especially when faced with any person who behaves in this way, the Christian will always have the same response: to forgive the debt with the joy of imitating the goodness of the Father—"we ourselves" also forgive—and the goodness of Jesus, who, according to Luke and in accordance with Sinaitic law, said "Father, forgive them…" (Lk 23:34) while on the cross.

Finally, in Luke we find a simplification of the final request that regards temptation and evil. The phrase "deliver us from evil" is left off, and only the request "do not put us to the test" remains. The reason for this omission—in all likelihood—relates to the elaboration that tends to simplify the concept. We have seen how the devil, according to Paul's reconsideration—which is shared by the other authors of the New Testament—does not act alone but rather infiltrates human structures and pressures man through these. Pressure to make the wrong choice of sin is temptation, which does not remain isolated: if there is temptation, there is also a tempter that activates it. Keeping this fact in mind, delivery from evil is already contained in the request that God not put us in temptation. It is as if to say that temptation will be present and if one escapes it, it can have a positive effect. But a particular kind of support from God, which is obtained through prayer, is necessary so that this temptation, which is in fact inevitable, does not become a mortal trap. Overcoming temptation involves neutralizing the effect of the devil and therefore full liberation from his negative influence. It is difficult for temptation that comes only from man to have such a strong and worrying impact that we would need the Father to escape unharmed.

V/2. As it is situated within the living context of Jesus's prayer—Luke is particularly sensitive to this aspect, which leaves an impression on his entire Gospel—the Lord's Prayer branches off and has numerous points of contact, just like we observed in Matthew.

The emphasis—for example—on God's paternity recalls the parable of divine goodness that Luke presents us—and he is the only evangelist to do so—in chapter fifteen. It is especially in the third (Lk 15:11–32), which S. Kierkegaard called the parable of the Father, and which is commonly called the parable of the prodigal son, that the figure of the father emerges—and the father is clearly God—as the Gospel of Luke sees him. The father, who is obstinately constructive, wants only what is best for everyone and for his children. No form of malice, not the macroscopic malice of the younger son who takes his possessions and squanders them nor the more sophisticated malice of the older son who, although he follows all the rules and lives at home continuously, has not yet understood his father and tries to prevent him from doing good. The father truly knows how to overcome every form of malice through creative good, which is suited for and pertains to their situation. This suggestive figure is the one that comes to the mind of the Christian when he addresses God by calling him with the name of Father.

The sharing of God's holiness within the community through the gift of the Spirit is of notable interest to Luke. This is realized, in continuity with the Gospel, in the first part of Acts, when the Christian community, which truly begins to participate in some way in the sanctity of God, becomes "united, heart and soul" (Acts 4:32). The imminence of the kingdom of God is particularly emphasized by Luke, who also insists on the idea of an engaging presence which digs deep and involves man in his interiority in the Kingdom: "the kingdom of God is among you" (Lk 17:21).

This extremely positive evaluation of the presence of the Kingdom is in perfect synergy with the request that "your kingdom come," but the kingdom of God is also seen here as the best of man.

The insistence on daily trust in God's providence, which we observed in Matthew and which is derived from the Q source, has a close correspondence in Luke (cf. Lk 12:22–34; with regard to the Q source, cf. F. Neyring, *Q-Synopsis*, 42–43).

The same could be said for the dynamic of temptations which Luke, in parallel with Matthew, works to illustrate in the presentation that Jesus makes at the beginning of his public life (cf. Lk 4:1–13).

In other words, the Lord's Prayer is neither isolated nor can it be isolated from the whole of the Gospel of Luke and of the Acts of the Apostles. On the contrary, it is an illuminating point of reference, a source of light that allows us to better understand—or, more basically, in a unitary manner—the dynamism of the story of salvation which begins with the Father and leads to the coming of the Father's kingdom.

VI. The Mature Elaboration of the Johannine Circle

VI/1. The Johannine movement in the New Testament represents a particularly advanced ecclesiastical experience. We can situate it, in terms of its most mature expression, between the years 80 and 120 in the area of Ephesus. Its typical representations are of course the Fourth Gospel, the Letters of John, and likely also Revelation. We should then ask ourselves whether and in what way the Lord's Prayer is reflected as a formula or especially as part of the contents of this part of the early Church.

One initial approach risks provoking disappointment: no formula for prayer that directly reminds us of the Lord's Prayer appears to be documented within the writings of John. It is doubtless that prayer is discussed, John insists that we should address the Father in the name of Jesus during prayer (cf. Jn 15:16; 16:23–24), and prayer that is directed at Jesus himself and made in his name is also emphasized, but no prayer that is directed to the Father directly by Christians and that can be identified through any kind of formula or schematization can be found.

Instead, we find a prayer that is addressed to the Father himself and expressed directly by Jesus. It is found in chapter seventeen of the Fourth Gospel.

Is there a relationship of some kind between this prayer, which is emphatically shown to be important by the evangelist, and the Lord's Prayer, which is presented to us in the Synoptic Gospels and which Paul probably alludes to in the fragmentary manner we examined previously? In order to answer this question, we must carefully contextualize it. In other words, we must clarify what the relationship between Jesus and the Father is. This relationship is emphasized in a completely unique manner in this prayer, but it begins earlier on and is documented throughout the Fourth Gospel.

In the Gospel, Jesus is presented right from the beginning as the "only Son of the Father, full of grace and truth" (1:14). As the only Son, he has a relationship with the Father that is his alone, and the Fourth Gospel works to clarify it. Only a few references are necessary, since it is a well-known aspect.

Jesus's entire life is regulated by the Father. It unfolds, we could say, in the light of the Father moment by moment, hour by hour (cf. 11:9–10), in a continual dialogic situation.

And this means that Jesus is always working, just like the Father is working (cf. Jn 5:17). What the Father does serves as a paradigm for Jesus in the most absolute sense possible: all the Father has to do is do something for Jesus to want to do it and almost be obligated to do it as well. Between Jesus and the Father, there is perfect working synergy (cf. 5:19).

However, this is not a mechanical parallelism. This perfect reciprocity is the result of the dizzying love that exists between the two. Jesus recognizes this and expresses it, almost with awe and certainly with joy: "For the Father loves the Son and shows him everything he himself does" (Jn 5:20). And this love pushes the Father to show the Son what he does and pushes the Son to accept it as the Father's will (cf. Jn 5:30).

The Son demonstrates passionate enthusiasm for the Father's will: the Father's will constitutes "[his] food" (cf. Jn 4:34), and his ideal is to "always do what pleases" the Father (Jn 8:29). This extreme reciprocity leads Jesus to give himself for mankind. When the "hour" grows closer—the hour of his death and resurrection—Jesus feels a shiver. This is the normal human reaction when confronted with suffering and death (Jn 12:27). But after having asked the Father to free him from that hour, he recovers immediately and, repeating to himself that he came into the world precisely to live that hour, expresses his most ardent desire to the Father: "Father, glorify your name" (Jn 12:28). This glorification—it is the answer that comes from the Father—has already been realized through the concrete existence of Jesus before the hour and will find its final expression in that hour itself (cf. Jn 12:28b): "And when I am lifted up from the earth, I shall draw all people to myself" (Jn 12:32). This is an unequivocal reference to the death on the cross that represents the highest point of Jesus's work and of his relationship with the Father.

When starting the "hour" with his passion, Jesus solemnly declares to the disciples, "The world must recognise that I love the Father and that I act just as the Father commanded" (Jn 14:31).

This relationship of maximal reciprocal openness, together with the implications that we have seen between Jesus and the Father, puts the finishing touch on the "prayer of the hour" from which we started and that we could call Jesus's Lord's Prayer. Jesus addresses the Father by raising "his eyes to heaven" (17:1). But the transcendence, which is evoked by the word "heaven," is found in Jesus himself: "I am in the Father and the Father is in me" (Jn 14:10). "The Father and I are one" (Jn 10:30).

The prayer of the hour unfolds—as we know—in three concentric circles. In the first, Jesus speaks to the Father about himself and asks for his glorification so that he can in turn glorify the Father and in this way giving men what the Father has given him: eternal life (cf. Jn 15:1–5). In the second concentric circle, Jesus speaks to the Father about his disciples (Jn 17:6–19). They have received the manifestation of the "man"—in the sense of the person—from the Father. Jesus asks the Father to take care of them always by keeping them "true to your name" (cf. Jn 17:11) so that in sharing the reality of the Father and Jesus, they may be "one like us" (Jn 17:11). This stunning situation must be defended, and Jesus prays that the Father keep them far away from "the Evil one" (Jn 17:15).

In the third circle (17:2–20), Jesus's prayer to the Father reaches everyone that will believe in him. Jesus transfers his "glory" (Jn 17:22), his truth and value, to these people. Consequently, they will be, no less than the disciples, "one, just as, Father, you are in me and I am in you" (Jn 17:21). And all of this is pushed along on an eschatological level in accordance with the category of eschatology created by John: "Father, I want those you have given me to be with me where I am, so that they may always see my glory which you have given me because you loved me before the foundation of the world" (17:24).

The points of contact between the prayer of the hour and the Lord's Prayer are numerous and suggestive.

The invocation of God as the Father, placed in Jesus's mouth, takes up and overtakes the intimacy witnessed by the Father and repeated by Luke. The reference to heaven is reinterpreted.

The "name" of the Father, which refers to the person, is discussed repeatedly. The holiness that is created through the sharing by the Christian community in John 17 is the glory, in the sense of the truth and value that passes from the Father to Jesus and from Jesus to his people, starting from his disciples, that we saw previously, whose final result is a transcendent unity between the Father, Jesus and them which is created in this way.

When viewed in this perspective—as "one," both reciprocally and with respect to the Father and Jesus—the ecclesiastical community constitutes a particularly stimulating interpretation of the Kingdom in the sense indicated above: it is the situation that is determined by the meeting of the descending line—the Father who so loved the world that he offered and gave the Son (cf. Jn 3:16)—and the ascending line, which is constituted by man's acceptance of faith.

If the disciples and Christians are then truly one vertically and horizontally, they will fully realize the Father's will and will love each other to the fullest extent.

Their presence in the world will expose them to temptations. Jesus did not want to remove them but rather prays that the Father "deliver them from evil," as we find in Matthew's version.

In summary, the Lord's Prayer only appears to be missing.

In reality, we can find a greater reformulation of what constitutes it basic requests: this is Jesus's Lord's Prayer.

VI/2. This prayer by Jesus shines a light on the attitude of the person praying by suggesting specific contents. Luke makes note of this attitude, and it is the context in which the Lord's Prayer is taught.

The disciples pray by learning from Jesus in John, as well. Therefore, is it possible to confirm, like we did for the Lord's Prayer, the points of interest on which the prayer of the Johannine community had to hit in a particular manner? How did the Johannine Church learn to pray, in continuity with the first disciples?

We will start from a consideration that on first glance seems to be a given: Jesus's prayer with which the Christian addresses the Father assumes that he is a child of God. Within the Johannine movement, filiation with respect to God was keenly felt. Right from the beginning, John states that people who believe in Jesus are given the "power" to "become children of God" (Jn 1:12). The disciples are certainly among those who, having believed, have this power. But while the Fourth Gospel often speaks about the filial relationship between Father and Jesus over the course its text, the filiation of the disciples is not emphasized. It is only discussed as a fact that occurred within the context of the "hour" when the risen Jesus, while speaking to them, explicitly characterizes them as his "brothers" and states, "I am ascending to my Father and your Father, to my God and your God" (Jn 20:17). The ability to become children of God appears to have been created at this point. Its creation constituted a journey that unfolded within the context of the "book of signs" (Jn 1:19–12:50): the disciples, who were in direct contact with Jesus, gradually increased and consolidated their ability to accept him. They nourished themselves on his words, on his truth, expressing their appreciation for it even in moments of crisis (cf., for example, Peter's profession, "You have the message of eternal life," after the Eucharistic discourse, Jn 6:68).

Having matured in this progressive acceptance of Jesus, the disciples make a qualitative step forward in their filiation in the book of the "hour": Jesus, whose truth, value, and "glory" they admired—"We saw his glory, the glory that he has from the Father as only Son of the Father" (Jn 1:14)—communicates this qualification of his to them. He states this in the prayer of the hour, which we already examined: "I have given them the glory you gave to me, that they may be one as we are one" (Jn 17:22). It is participation in the "glory," in the truth and value of the Son, that activates the "power" to become children of God, in a very close union with Jesus, with the Father (cf. Jn 17:23), and with each other, in the disciples and in everyone who believes through their words.

Joy (cf. 17:3), peace, and holiness (cf. 17:19) follow as consequences of this extreme realization of filiation. All of these relate directly to an infusion by Jesus and to a participation that he makes through himself.

And the most characteristic consequence is prayer. Jesus, starting from the "book of signs," practices a continuous dialogic prayer with the Father, who, every so often, is made explicit in its contents (cf. Jn 6:11: "gave thanks"; especially Jn 11:41). But a prayer by the disciples directed at the Father is never discussed. Now, however, that in participating in the "glory" of Jesus, they have also become children of God, they are expressly encouraged by Jesus to pray in his name: "…Anything you ask from the Father he will grant in my name. *Until now you have not asked anything in my name.* Ask and you will receive, and so your joy will be complete" (Jn 17:24).

In conclusion, we could say that the disciples, who have gradually arrived at the full extent of their filiation, are now able to express their prayer to the Father in perfect synergy with Jesus. Jesus involves them in his relationship with the Father.

Consequently, the disciples' prayer—and the prayer of all Christians—will always be a prayer that is fulfilled on Jesus's level, in synergy with whom the disciples address the Father, and will tend to assume the traits that are typical of his truth and elaborate upon them.

Here are a few clarifications, following the formula of the Lord's Prayer. We can make these clarifications legitimately because it is highly probable that, at the end of the first century, Matthew and Luke's formula for the Lord's Prayer was already known and used in liturgy in the Church of John around Ephesus. This likelihood is suggested by the close relationship that Paul and Luke had with Ephesus. Matthew, who is explicitly mentioned by Papias of Hierapolis—who also was in the area of Ephesus—a few decades later, must have been read and known. The "quadriform Gospel" was being formed.

The disciples—and, more generally, the Christians of the Johannian school, as we find them in the First Letter of John—will work for the glorification of the name of the Father like Jesus did.

We find this very aspect, which corresponds to the first request in the Lord's Prayer, made explicit. The disciples hear Jesus say, "Whatever you ask in my name I will do, so that the Father may be glorified in the Son" (Jn 14:13). The glorification and sanctification of the Father—in the sense of the participation of the ecclesiastical community indicated above—occurs as a consequence of the disciples' prayers.

As we have already seen, the glorification and sanctification of the glory of the Father occurs "through the Son" and, notably, the through the "exaltation" of Jesus. This is his crucifixion, which is seen as his universal kingship (Jn 19:19–22) and as an indivisible unity (Jn 19:23–24) in a new relationship that is established between Mary and Jesus's new brothers (Jn 19:25–27) through Jesus's death, which represents the last spasm of love for the Father and for mankind and which leads Jesus to his supreme perfection (Jn 19:28–30) and finally leads to that profusion of gifts, including the Spirit, which then leads to the sacramentality of the Church—symbolized by the water and by the blood that flows out of Jesus's side, which is particularly evocative (Jn 19:31–37). This context of sanctification and glorification shows the Christian the broad horizon along which he moves when he asks the Father that "his name be held holy," using Matthew's formula, which was probably already widespread in the Johannian community, as well.

While thinking of the kingdom of God, the disciples see that it is connected to Jesus, "the Son of God, [...] the king of Israel" (cf. Jn 1:49). By realizing his kingdom that is not "of this world" (cf. Jn 18:36) through his crucifixion (cf. Jn 19:19–22), Jesus renders Christians a "kingdom" (Rev 1:5) by engaging them in the realization of the "kingdom of the world" and the "kingdom of our Lord and his Christ" (Rev 11:15; for more in-depth analysis and documentation, cf. U. Vanni, *Regno «non da questo mondo» ma «regno del mondo». Il regno di Cristo dal quarto Vangelo all'Apocalisse; La promozione del regno come responsabilità sacerdotale del cristiano: Ap 1,5; 5,10; 20,6*, in *L'Apocalisse. Ermeneutica, esegesi, teologia*, EDB, Bologna 1991, 279–304; 349–368) through their practice of sacerdotal mediation.

For this reason, the Christian who asks the Father that his Kingdom come is really asking for a particular presence of Jesus and for the power of his crucifixion, with his ability to attract everything and everyone to him, first within the Christian community and then in the whole world.

By looking at how Jesus loves passionately and fulfills the entire will of the Father, the Johannian Church sensed what it means to ask that the Father's will be done "on earth, as it is in heaven": the Father's will, fulfilled by Jesus, expresses the transcendence—"as it is in heaven"—of the fulfilment of the Father's will on a terrestrial level. The will that the Christian finds in the truth and value of Jesus, which is fulfilled under the continual influence of the Spirit, who interprets it (cf. Jn 16:13). The request that the Father's will be done is therefore in perfect synergy with Jesus's attitude and is directed toward the "doing" of the truth in a concrete manner (cf. Jn 3:21; 1 Jn 1:6).

The request for daily bread from the Father is given particular emphasis in John. All of chapter six is dedicated to an in-depth study of what bread represents for Christians.

Here, we discover that Jesus, who puts his divinity in the service of mankind, gives men food (cf. Jn 6:1–13). The following day in the synagogue of Capernaum, he himself explains the meaning of this "sign," which involves various levels according to which Jesus is realized as bread. Bread in a realistic sense, which was eaten the first day together with the fish, is in continuity with bread in the symbolic sense, and the group is invited to understand this on a deep level: Jn 6:26–27—which coincides with Jesus, "the living bread which has come down from heaven" (Jn 6:51) and which is given by the Father (Jn 6:32). The nourishment that we should search for and that we should ask the Father for is therefore Jesus himself, "the bread of life" (6:48), with the various forms of nourishment that he provides: he nourishes us with his word, with his example, and with the spirit. He especially nourishes us with the Eucharist (Jn 6:52–59), which is insisted on to the point where it gives listeners a discomfort that can only be overcome through the dizzying faith that Jesus asks for (Jn 6:60–69).

In this way, we can glimpse the flood of implications contained in the request for bread that the texts of both Matthew and Luke allowed us to see.

In summary, in John's elaboration, the Father gives Jesus as bread, and Jesus performs this task of his both by taking care of the physical requirements for existence on this earth and by giving himself fully.

In this way, Jesus is understood and felt by the Church of John to be the one who is able to fully power our lives as children of God, which allows

Christians to create a particularly close relationship with the heavenly Father that is both alarming and joyful at the same time: "You must see what great love the Father has lavished on us by letting us be called God's children—which is what we are!" (1 Jn 3:1).

The request for forgiveness should be reinterpreted and analyzed more deeply. Forgiveness comes through Jesus, through which the Christian passes from death to life and is freed completely from sin.

This passage which has occurred sets the tone for all of ecclesiastical life: the Christian, in part, as a child of God who remains in him, does not sin (cf. 1 Jn 3:6). This goes beyond the risk of that basic negative choice, sin understood as the refusal of the law of the Spirit which by now guides him (cf. 1 Jn 3:4). There may be, in any case, partial insufficiencies, risks, and fears, but appealing to Jesus, who maintains his permanent function as a liberator from sin (1 Jn 2:1) and an unconditional faith in God, who is "greater than all our feelings" (1 Jn 3:20) allows Christians to live properly as children of God.

Children of God and brothers. John places a lot of emphasis on this dimension. He does not explicitly discuss the forgiving of offenses but clearly includes it in a broader and more engaging vision.

Love for one's brothers, when practiced properly, constitutes a diagnostic criterion for overcoming the death of sin: "We are well aware that we have passed over from death to life because we love our brothers. Whoever does not love, remains in death" (1 Jn 3:14). The filial relationship that is established with God—and in the Johannian vocabulary, God is always the Father—is positively and immediately poured out toward one's brothers: "My dear friends, let us love one another, since love is from God and everyone who loves is a child of God and knows God. Whoever fails to love does not know God, because God is love" (1 Jn 4:7–8). While Matthew and Luke emphasize imitating the Father in forgiving "debts" and "sins," John courageously expands this emulation of the Father through a constructive and unlimited perspective. We have already made the commitment to love as he loved—to love with the same intensity and the same style: "My dear friends, if God loved us so much, we too should love one another" (1 Jn 4:11). This type of love which is created within the Church will make the Father's characteristics observable (cf. 1 Jn 4:12).

The last petition in the Lord's Prayer, for defense against temptation and evil, is also given a new Christological emphasis. As we have seen, Jesus explicitly asks the Father to defend the disciples from evil and the "Evil One" (Jn 17:15). After having conquered the world (cf. Jn 16:33) and given that he is above the "prince of this world" (Jn 16:11), he can guarantee the Christian that all demonic threats will be vanquished. These threats will be felt—the book of Revelation, which shows how the devil acts by infiltrating himself in the structures of history, particularly emphasizes this. Christians will always be able to vanquish them because they participate in the "blood of the Lamb" (Rev 12:11)—in the vitality symbolized by the blood of Christ, the "lamb" (cf. Rev 5:6) that Christ obtained for his people and continuously gives them by activating the resources of his death and resurrection.

We certainly do not find an evanescent optimism that ignores the existence of evil in John. Rather, the emphasis placed on the strength of darkness (cf. Jn 1:5; 8:12; 12:35; etc.), which is typical of the Fourth Gospel, is surprising. But the Christian, who is joined to Christ and "remains in" him, feels it even more strongly. His prayer can and must be addressed to the Father in order to overcome the threats of evil, but his main preoccupation should be maintaining contact with Christ and to be and remain a "branch" joined to the vine Jn 15:2)—in other words, to always be full of the vitality of Christ. In this situation, the Christian can overcome evil in all its forms, even the most threatening ones.

In John, we find a suggestive elaboration of the basic nucleus of the Lord's Prayer that is expressed in detail. No aspect is missing. However, in addition to the presence of the details that can be observed, the synthesis of what the Christian community has developed and continues to develop, moving forward, maturing, and steadily realizing the great values which it brings to humanity more and in a better way, emerges. And the values that the Christian community realizes have only one name: Christ. It is Christ, with his truth and his life, that is given continuously to the community through the mediation of the Spirit. And in this way, the Father sanctifies and glorifies his name, he involves the community in his kingdom which is realized day by day, and he establishes reciprocal love that leads to a passionate desire to fulfill his will. By giving us Christ as nourishment, the Father gives man what is best for him, for his present and for his future, explaining how to love with his type of love and defending him from all threats. By traveling in the orbit of Christ, the Christian becomes a child of the Father in full.

VII. Conclusion

The summary examination that we have conducted of the main texts of the New Testament that regard the Lord's Prayer—although there are still more ramifications, such as the fulfillment of the Father's will in the Letter to the Hebrews—shows that the prayer is in motion. It starts with Mark, where the elements that constitute it are not yet connected in a formula for prayer. The formula is presented in Matthew and Luke, but the values that it expresses, far from being easy to identify within the context of these two Gospels, are reinterpreted and elaborated upon. Paul, through his emphasis on the law of the Spirit, pushes us toward a deeper analysis. He made the community reflect on what God's paternity means and the implications involved.

Finally, John offered a mature re-elaboration of the basic elements of the Lord's Prayer centered around Christ.

Now, we will see that the Lord's Prayer is not a stereotype but rather the tip of the iceberg and one conclusion that this implies. The prayer travels within the Church and has vast and deep repercussions. It pushes the Church to mature and, at the same time, allows it to condense and re-express the maturation that has occurred.

If we take a look at the *CCC*'s presentation of the Lord's Prayer and we measure it against the Biblical parameters that we have obtained, we can observe a close correspondence.

The general outline of the elaboration which we have observed—from Jesus to Mark to Matthew's and Luke's formulas, from the formula of Jesus, who acts within the Church through the Spirit which is found in John—corresponds to that of the *Catechism's* introduction and illuminates it and gives it more depth. The "summary of the whole Gospel," the Lord's Prayer is concentrated in Jesus, who is "at the center of the Scriptures," is made explicit in the formula of "the Lord's Prayer," and becomes the "prayer of the Church" (nn. 2759–2722).

The Lord's Prayer is a formula. The *Catechism* gives special importance to Matthew's formula, which is the most articulate and which was put into liturgical use. This formula is instilled, analyzed, and summarized in its seven petitions, and these are constantly referenced.

In this way, the *CCC* wishes to fully recall the Christian prayer of petition: all seven petitions are essential, although it is not necessary to present them all simultaneously.

But the formula is a condensed version of life. The basic values of the experience that the Church has accrued and developed during its history merge together, as we find in the Pauline communities and in the ones behind the Gospels.

The numerous elements that are reported or mentioned by the *CCC* are situated within the framework that we identified through direct examination of the "quadriform Gospel" and of Paul, and in this way they acquire solidity and perspective.

A few examples illustrate what we have discussed.

The confidence with which the Christians move toward the Father, daring to address him with the familiarity of the term "*Abbà*" (cf. nn. 2777–2782) acquires its full meaning when examined through the experience of the Spirit in the Pauline community, in which the Christians appropriate what was, in Mark, an attitude exclusive to Jesus.

The interpretation of the expression "who art in heaven" (nn. 2794–2796) correctly the excludes the idea that God is far away. More than his majesty, however, as we have seen with Matthew's use of "heavenly Father," it gives his paternity an infinite dimension. The passage from the heavens, which are a symbol of transcendence, to the "hearts of the just" (n. 2794, quoting St. Augustine) is clarified through the Biblical perspective illustrated by reminding readers that the Spirit that leads Christians to invoke the Father with the word "*Abbà*" acts on their hearts, which therefore become a location where transcendent action takes place.

The explanation of the first petition correctly insists on the Father's own holiness which is fulfilled through the community of Christians (nn. 2807–2815), which is equivalent to glory (n. 2809). The Biblical perspective, from Matthew to John, makes the "estimative" aspect (n. 2811) conditional by making it a corollary of royal participation in the Father's holiness.

The Father's will, which is done on Earth "as it is in heaven" can be clearly understood form the perspective of an execution that touches on the perfection of transcendence. We observe this in Jesus as described by John and in the Letter to the Hebrews. Otherwise, there is the risk that the parallel with God's salvific will, which is assumed to have already been fulfilled in the transcendence of heaven, remains vague (nn. 2822–2827).

The petition for bread from the Father acquires a true Eucharistic significance. But more than the debatable interpretation in this sense of *epiúsios* (nn. 2842–2844), the reinterpretation of the "bread of life" that we find in John appears to be determinative.

Finally, the overcoming of all of the gaps, the "debts," in the reciprocal relationship that enters into the "outpouring of mercy" (nn. 2838–2841) that is characteristic of God is properly developed through the experience with the God of love in the Johannian community.

The examples go on and on. However, it is essential to remember a fundamental fact: the Lord's Prayer continues to evolve in today's Church, just like it developed in the early Church.

The numerous comments—which are frequently cited in the *CCC*—which have been made throughout the history of the Church reflect the problems of various historical situations and summarize and interpret them.

One stop on Lord's Prayer's journey in the life of the Church was the publication of the *CCC*. This step is not the last, however: the Lord's Prayer will continue to serve as a summary and as inspiration—almost like a kind of systole and diastole—with respect to the Gospel until the end of time.

REFERENCE INDEX

SACRED SCRIPTURE

Old Testament

Proverbs

Acts of the Apostles

Romans

1 Corinthians

2 Corinthians

Professions of Faith

(Cited by DS numbers)

Ecumenical Councils

(Cited by DS numbers, except for Vatican II)

Nicaea I(325)

Constantinople I (381)

Ephesus (431)

Chalcedon (451)

Constantinople II (553)

Constantinople III (680–681)

Nicaea II (787)

Constantinople IV (869–870)

Lateran IV (1215)

Lyons II (1274)

Vienne (1311–1312)

Constance (1414–1418)

Florence (1439–1445)

Lateran V (1512–1517)

Trent (1545–1563)

Particular Councils and Synods

(cited by DS number)

Rome (382)

Decretum Damasi

Carthage (418)

Statutes of the Early Church

Orange II (418)

Synod of Constantinople (543)

Braga I (561)

Toledo IV (633)

Toledo VI (638)

Lateran (649)

Toledo XI (675)

Pontifical Documents

Ecclesiastical Documents

Roman Catechism

Congregations

Congregation for the Doctrine of the Faith

Congregation of the Clergy

Congregation of Rites

Congregation of Studies

Synod of Bishops

Episcopal Assemblies

Canon Law

Canon of the Apostles

Codex Iuris Canonici

Liturgy
LATIN RITE

19, 19: CSEL 40/2, 407
(PL 41, 647) 2185
22, 17: CSEL 40/2, 625
(PL 41, 779) 1118
22, 30: CSEL 40/2, 665–666
(PL 41, 801–802) 1720, 2550

De diversis quaestionibus octoginta tribus
64, 4: CCL 44A, 140
(PL 40, 56) 2560

De disciplina christiana
7, 7: CCL 46, 214
(PL 40, 673) 2539

De fide et Symbolo
10, 25: CSEL 25, 32
(PL 40, 196) 2518

De Genesi contra Manichaeos
1, 2, 4: PL 36, 175 338

De gratia et libero arbitrio
17, 33: PL 44, 901 2001

De libero arbitrio
1, 1, 1: CCL 29, 211
(PL 32, 1221–1223) 311

De mendacio
4, 5: CSEL 41, 419
(PL 40, 491) 2482

De moribus Ecclesiae catholicae
3, 4: CSEL 90, 6
(PL 32, 1312) 1718
1, 25, 46: CSEL 90, 51
(PL 32, 1330–1331) 1809

De natura et gratia
31, 35: CSEL 49, 258–259
(PL 44, 264) 2001

De sancta virginitate
3, 3: CSEL 41, 237
(PL 40, 398) 506
6, 6: CSEL 41, 240
(PL 40, 399) 963

De sermone Domini in monte
1, 1, 1: CCL 35, 1–2
(PL 34, 1229–1231) 1966
1, 1, 3: CCL 35, 4
(PL 34, 1232) 2547
2, 4, 16: CCL 35, 106
(PL 34, 1276) 2785
2, 5, 18: CCL 35, 108 109
(PL 34, 1277) 2794
2, 5, 19: CCL 35, 109
(PL 34, 1278) 2149
2, 6, 24: CCL 35, 113
(PL 34, 1279) 2827

De Trinitate
8, 3, 4: CCL 50, 271–272
(PL 42, 949) 1766*
14, 15, 21: CCL 50A, 451
(PL 42, 1052) 1955
15, 26, 47: CCL 50A, 529
(PL 42, 1095) 264

Enarrationes in Psalmos
57, 1: CCL 39, 708
(PL 36, 673) 1962
62, 16: CCL 39, 804
(PL 36, 758) 2628
72, 1: CCL 39, 986
(PL 36, 914) 1156*
74, 4: CCL 39, 1027
(PL 37, 948–949) 796
85, 1: CCL 39, 1176
(PL 36, 1081) 2616
88, 2, 5: CCL 39, 1237
(PL 37, 1134) 996
102, 7: CCL 40, 1457
(PL 37, 1321) 2005
103, 1, 15: CCL 40, 1488
(PL 37, 1348–1349) 329
103, 4, 1: CCL 40, 1521
(PL 37, 1378) 102

Enchiridion de fide, spe et caritate
3, 11: CCL 46, 53
(PL 40, 236) 311

Epistulae
98, 5: CSEL 34, 527
(PL 33, 362) 1274
108, 3, 8: CSEL 34, 620
(PL 33, 410) 2539
130, 8, 17: CSEL 44, 59
(PL 33, 500) 2737
130, 12, 22: CSEL 44, 66
(PL 33, 502) 2762
187, 11, 34: CSEL 57, 113
(PL 33, 845) 774

In epistulam Johannis ad Parthos tractatus
1, 6: PL 35, 1982 1863
8, 9: PL 35, 2041 1779
10, 4: PL 35, 2056–2057 1829

In evangelium Johannis tractatus
5, 15: CCL 36, 50
(PL 35, 1422) 1584
12, 13: CCL 36, 128
(PL 35, 1491) 1458

ANALYTICAL INDEX

A

B

F

Good

H

I

J

M

N

P

Q

R

S

Y

Z